melius enim erat ipsum
pulverem non esse natum
ut non sensus inde fieret,
nunc autem nobiscum cres-
cit sensus et propter hoc
torquemur. quoniam scientes
perimus. lugeat hominum
genus. et agrestes bestiae
laetentur; lugeant omnes
qui nati sunt. quadrupedia
vero et pecora iocundan-
tur; multum enim meli-
us est illis quam nobis,
Non enim sperant iudi-
cium. nec enim sciunt
cruciamenta nec salutem
post mortem repromis-
sam sibi, Nobis autem
quid prodest quoniam salvati
salvabimur. sed tamen
tormento tormentabimur?
Omnes enim qui nati sunt.
commixti sunt iniquita-
tibus; et pleni sunt peccatis.
et gravati delictis; et si
non essemus post mor-
tem in iudicium venientes.
melius fortassis nobis
venisset, Et respondit
ad me. et dixit, et quan-
do altissimus faciens
faciebat saeculum
Adam et omnes qui cum eo
venerunt primum prae-
paravit iudicium et quae
sunt iudicii, et nunc de
sermonibus tuis intelle-
ge quoniam dixisti. quia
nobiscum crescit, qui
ergo commorantes sunt
in terra. hinc crucia-
buntur quoniam sensum
habentes. iniquitatem
fecerunt. et mandata ac-
cipientes. non servave-
runt ea. et legem con-
secuti. fraudaver-
unt eam quam acceperunt,
et quid habebunt dicere
in iudicio. vel quomo-
do respondebunt in
novissimis temporibus;
quantum enim tempus ex
quo longanimitatem
habuit altissimus.
his qui in- habi-
tant sae- culum.
et non propter eos sed propter
ea quae providit tempora,
et respondi. et dixi.
si inveni gratiam coram
te domine. demonstra et hoc
servo tuo. si post mor-
tem. vel nunc. quando
reddimus unusquis-
que animam suam.
si conservati conserva-
bimur in requie. donec
veniant tempora illa:
in quibus incipies creatu-
ram renovare. aut amo-
do cruciamur. et res-
pondit ad me et dixit,
ostendam tibi et hoc, tu
autem noli commisceri.
cum eis qui spreverunt.
neque connumeres te
cum his qui cruciantur,
etenim est tibi thesaurus
operum repositus a-
pud altissimum. sed non
tibi demonstrabitur.
usque in novissimis tem-
poribus, Nam de morte
sermo; quando profectus
fuerit terminus sententiae
ab altissimo. ut ho-
mo moriatur. recedente
inspiratione de
cor- pore. ut dimit-
tatur iterum ad eum qui
dedit adorare gloriam al-
tissimi. primum; et si
quidem esset eorum qui
spreverunt. et non ser-
vaverunt viam altissimi.
et eorum qui contempser-
unt legem eius. et eorum qui
oderunt eos qui timent deum.
haec inspirationes in ha-
bitationes non ingredien-
tur. sed vagantes erunt
amodo in cruciamentis.
dolentes semper et tristes,
via prima. quia spreverunt
legem altissimi. secun-
da via. quoniam non possunt
reversionem bonam facere
ut vivant, tertia via
vident repositam mercedem
his qui testamentis altissimi crediderunt, quarta
via considerabunt sibi
in novissimis repositum
cruciamentum. quinta via
videntes aliorum habita-
cula ab angelis conservari
cum silentio magno, sexta
via videntes quemadmodum
de eis pertransient in cruciamentum

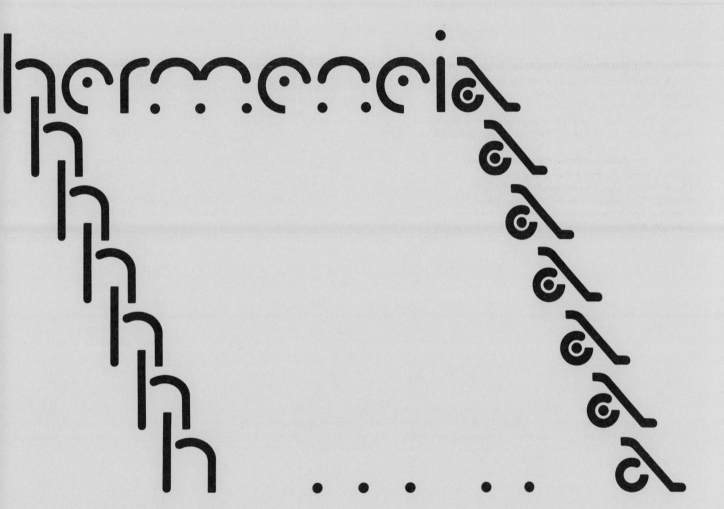

**Hermeneia
—A Critical
and Historical
Commentary
on the Bible**

Fourth Ezra

A Commentary on the
Book of Fourth Ezra

by Michael Edward Stone

Edited by
Frank Moore Cross

**Fortress
Press**   Minneapolis

Fourth Ezra

A commentary on the Book of Fourth Ezra

© 1990 Augsburg Fortress

Scripture quotations are adapted from the RSV.

Cover and interior design by Kenneth Hiebert
Production management by Publishers' WorkGroup
Typesetting on an Ibycus System at Polebridge Press

Library of Congress Cataloging-in-Publication Data

Stone, Michael E., 1938–
    Fourth Ezra : a commentary on the book of
Fourth Ezra / by Michael Edward Stone ; edited by
Frank Moore Cross.
      p. cm. — (Hermeneia—a critical and
historical commentary on the Bible)
    Includes bibliographical references and index.
    ISBN 0–8006–6026–9
    1. Bible. O.T. Apocrypha. Esdras, 2nd–
Commentaries.
I. Cross, Frank Moore. II. Title. III. Series.
BS1715.3.S76   1990
229′.1–dc20   90–44627
                            CIP

The paper used in this publication meets the minimum requirements of American National Standard for Information Sciences—Permanence of Paper for Printed Library Materials, ANSI Z329.48–1984.

Manufactured in the U.S.A.   AF 1–6026

94 93 92 91 90 1 2 3 4 5 6 7 8 9 10

**Contents
Fourth Ezra**

The name *Hermeneia*, Greek ἑρμηνεία, has been chosen as the title of the commentary series to which this volume belongs. The word *Hermeneia* has a rich background in the history of biblical interpretation as a term used in the ancient Greek-speaking world for the detailed, systematic exposition of a scriptural work. It is hoped that the series, like its name, will carry forward this old and venerable tradition. A second, entirely practical reason for selecting the name lies in the desire to avoid a long descriptive title and its inevitable acronym, or worse, an unpronounceable abbreviation.

The series is designed to be a critical and historical commentary to the Bible without arbitrary limits in size or scope. It will utilize the full range of philological and historical tools, including textual criticism (often slighted in modern commentaries), the methods of the history of tradition (including genre and prosodic analysis), and the history of religion.

Hermeneia is designed for the serious student of the Bible. It will make full use of ancient Semitic and classical languages; at the same time, English translations of all comparative materials—Greek, Latin, Canaanite, or Akkadian—will be supplied alongside the citation of the source in its original language. Insofar as possible, the aim is to provide the student or scholar with full critical discussion of each problem of interpretation and with the primary data upon which the discussion is based.

Hermeneia is designed to be international and interconfessional in the selection of authors; its editorial boards were formed with this end in view. Occasionally the series will offer translations of distinguished commentaries which originally appeared in languages other than English. Published volumes of the series will be revised continually, and eventually, new commentaries will replace older works in order to preserve the currency of the series. Commentaries are also being assigned for important literary works in the categories of apocryphal and pseudepigraphical works relating to the Old and New Testaments, including some of Essene or Gnostic authorship.

The editors of *Hermeneia* impose no systematic-theological perspective upon the series (directly, or indirectly by selection of authors). It is expected that authors will struggle to lay bare the ancient meaning of a biblical work or pericope. In this way the text's human relevance should become transparent, as is always the case in competent historical discourse. However, the series eschews for itself homiletical translation of the Bible.

The editors are heavily indebted to Augsburg Fortress for its energy and courage in taking up an expensive, long-term project, the rewards of which will accrue chiefly to the field of biblical scholarship.

Frank Moore Cross
For the Old Testament
Editorial Board

Helmut Koester
For the New Testament
Editorial Board

I offer this study to the public in the hope that it will throw some light on a single document of Jewish antiquity and through it provide some insights into a remarkable religious figure, its author, and the world in which he lived. This book is the fruit of eleven years' writing and as many years' prior preparation. I am conscious of its weaknesses and hope that whatever insights I have been granted will compensate for the many more things that I know I might have said.

It may be of help to the reader for me to indicate certain of the principles that have guided my work, knowing that other scholars might have chosen different, perhaps better, paths. The primary sources that are thought to be relevant to 4 Ezra, and the scholarly books and articles that touch on one or another aspect of it, are numerous. I consulted all works of whose existence I knew, though there are undoubtedly not a few that escaped my eye. However, throughout the commentary I tried to keep a single aim before me, that of elucidating the meaning of 4 Ezra. To this end I avoided burdening my commentary with citation of primary sources or discussion of secondary sources that I judged not to contribute directly to the understanding of 4 Ezra's text and meaning. Finally, the work of composition was completed in February 1988. I have made no attempt to incorporate into this book writings that were published after that time.

The study of Jewish literature of the Greco-Roman period has seen remarkable advances in the past two decades. I have benefited greatly from the stimulation of fellow workers in the field as my study has advanced and have surely included ideas generated in fruitful joint learning. Tributes are too many to give, twenty years is time enough to incur many debts. Yet some cannot be passed over in silence.

It was the late Professor Yehoshua Gutman of the Hebrew University under whose tutelage I first read 4 Ezra, in 1960–61. My doctoral thesis, also on 4 Ezra, was directed by Professor Frank Moore Cross, Jr., to whom I owe more than can adequately be expressed here. It was he who asked me to undertake this commentary, in 1965, and it was he who encouraged me to continue in times of deep despair, when the task seemed endless. Without him, I think, I would never have finished it at all.

The Netherlands Institute of Advanced Study in Wassenaar has on many occasions willingly embraced me with its particular environment of tranquil creativity, in which the heart of this book was fashioned. That debt I can only repay by its acknowledgment.

I have learned much from my students at the Hebrew University. Kerstin Ipta served as my research assistant in 1985–86, and her keen perceptions were matched by her devoted help. The assistance of Adolfo Roitman is also gratefully acknowledged. The references were checked a second time by Anna Hetzel, Leslie Kobayashi, and Nira Stone. They saved me from many errors.

I have been privileged to dwell in a living Jerusalem and there to study another human's pain at its ancient destruction and the transmutation of that pain into faith and insight. The Hebrew University has been my academic home for many years, and its Institute of Jewish Studies provided some research support, which I gladly acknowledge here. I have enjoyed the hospitality of other universities too, while this work progressed: the University of Pennsylvania, Ormond College of the University of Melbourne, and Harvard University. The colleagues and friends at each have enriched this book in their way.

My children, Aurit and Dan, have lived with "Ezra" since their birth. They have borne with it forgivingly on the whole, sharing me with it. It is fitting, therefore, that I dedicate this book to them. It is a *topos* of prefaces such as these to thank one's wife, yet for all that it is true that to Nira I am indebted above all others. Words cannot express it all, or even part of it. To her too I dedicate this work, a gift of mind and heart.

Michael Edward Stone
Cambridge, Mass.

1. Sources and Abbreviations

When a work is cited for the first time in this commentary, it is given in full. Subsequent citations use only the author's surname and a short form of the title. All works cited are listed in the Bibliography at the end of this book.

Exceptions to the above rule are a number of standard commentaries, and a few other works, which are cited throughout by abbreviation. All such abbreviations are included in this list of Bibliographic Abbreviations. The list also includes forms of reference to primary sources, excluding the biblical books and the most common of the apocryphal and pseudepigraphic writings. For the latter, the standard *JBL* reference system has been employed.

Often different printings and editions of rabbinic sources employ varying chapter and subsection divisions and numbering. To enhance accuracy in citation of rabbinic sources, the standard edition of the source and its page numbers are indicated in parentheses following the section and subsection reference. This is done, of course, only for those writings for which standard editions exist. All works other than primary sources that are included in this list of Bibliographic Abbreviations are also listed in full in the Bibliography.

The list of Bibliographic Abbreviations also contains certain abbreviations peculiar to the textual criticism of 4 Ezra. These are used in the textual notes but are avoided in the other parts of the commentary.

1QH	Thanksgiving Scroll from Qumran Cave 1
1QM	War Scroll from Qumran Cave 1
1QS	Manual of Discipline from Qumran Cave 1
1QpHab	Commentary on Habakkuk from Qumran Cave 1
1QpMic 17–19	Commentary on Micah 17–19 from Qumran Cave 1
4QDibHam	The Words of the Luminaries from Qumran Cave 4
4QEn^c	Ms c of Enoch from Qumran Cave 4
11QMelch	Melchizedek Text from Qumran Cave 11
11QPs^a	Ms a of Psalms from Qumran Cave 11
2 Apoc Bar	*2 Apocalypse of Baruch*
3 Apoc Bar	*3 Apocalypse of Baruch*
2 Clem	*2 Epistle of Clement*
1 Enoch	*1 (Ethiopic) Enoch*
2 Enoch	*2 (Slavonic) Enoch*
Act Thom	*Acts of Thomas*

Ambrose, *De exec. sat.*	Ambrose, *De execessu fratris sui satyri*
ANRW	*Aufstieg und Niedergang der römischen Welt*
Ap John	*Apocryphon of John*
Apoc Abr	*Apocalypse of Abraham*
Apoc Mos	*Apocalypse of Moses*
Apoc Elijah	*Apocalypse of Elijah*
Apoc. NT	M. R. James, *Apocryphal New Testament*
Apoc Paul	*Apocalypse of Paul*
Apoc Peter	*Apocalypse of Peter*
Apoc Sedrach	*Apocalypse of Sedrach*
Apost. Const.	*Apostolic Constitutions*
Ar1	Arabic1 version
Ar2	Arabic2 version
Aramaic Levi	*Aramaic Testament of Levi*
Arm	Armenian version
ARN	*Abot de R. Natan*
Asc Isa	*Ascension of Isaiah*
b. Abod. Zar.	Treatise *Abodah Zarah*, Babylonian Talmud
b. Baba Batra	Treatise *Baba Batra*, Babylonian Talmud
b. Ber.	Treatise *Berakot*, Babylonian Talmud
b. Erub.	Treatise *Erubin*, Babylonian Talmud
b. Hag.	Treatise *Ḥaggigah*, Babylonian Talmud
b. Kidd.	Treatise *Kiddushin*, Babylonian Talmud
b. Ned.	Treatise *Nedarim*, Babylonian Talmud
b. Pesah.	Treatise *Pesaḥim*, Babylonian Talmud
b. Rosh Hashanah	Treatise *Rosh Hashanah*, Babylonian Talmud
b. Sanh.	Treatise *Sanhedrin*, Babylonian Talmud
b. Shabb.	Treatise *Shabbat*, Babylonian Talmud
b. Soṭa	Treatise *Soṭa*, Babylonian Talmud
b. Sukka	Treatise *Sukka*, Babylonian Talmud
b. Ta'an.	Treatise *Ta'anit*, Babylonian Talmud
b. Yeb.	Treatise *Yebamot*, Babylonian Talmud
b. Yoma	Treatise *Yoma*, Babylonian Talmud
Baldensperger	W. Baldensperger, *Das Selbstbewusstein Jesu . . .*
Barn.	*Epistle of Barnabas*
Bensly	R. L. Bensly, *The Fourth Book of Ezra*
Bensly, *MF*	R. L. Bensly, *The Missing Fragment*
Ber.	*Bereshit (Zohar)*
Bib Ant	*Biblical Antiquities of Pseudo-Philo*

BM	*Bet Hamidrasch* (A. Jellinek)
Box	G. W. Box, *The Ezra-Apocalypse*
BZ	*Biblische Zeitschrift*
BZNW	Beihefte zur *Zeitschrift für die neutestamentliche Wissenschaft*
CCAG	Corpus Codicum Astrologorum Graecorum
CD	Damascus Document
cents.	centuries
CG	Cairo Gnostic (codices)
chap.	chapter
Clem. Recog.	Pseudo-Clement, *Recognitiones*
Coptic Apoc Elijah	*Coptic Apocalypse of Elijah*
Coptic Apoc Zephaniah	*Coptic Apocalypse of Zephaniah*
CSCO	Corpus Scriptorum Christianorum Orientalium
De cher.	*De cherubim* (Philo)
De ebr.	*De ebrietate* (Philo)
De execrat.	*De execratione* (Philo)
De migr. abr.	*De migratione abrahami* (Philo)
De opif.	*De opificio mundi* (Philo)
De praem.	*De praemiis et poenis* (Philo)
De somn.	*De somniis* (Philo)
DER	*Derek Ereṣ Rabba*
DEZ	*Derek Ereṣ Zuta*
DJD	*Discoveries in the Judean Desert*
Echa Rabbati	*Midrash Echa Rabbati*
Ep Jer	Epistle of Jeremiah
Ep. 1 ad Cor.	*First Epistle to the Corinthians* (noncanonical)
Exod. R.	*Midrash Exodus Rabba*
Gen. R.	*Midrash Genesis Rabba*
Geoltrain	P. Geoltrain, in Dupont-Sommer and Philonenko, *La Bible: Ecrits intertestamentaires*
Ginzberg, *Legends*	L. Ginzberg, *The Legends of the Jews*
Gosp. Egypt.	*Gospel of the Egyptians*
Greek Apoc Esd	*Greek Apocalypse of Esdras (Ezra)*
Gry	L. Gry, *Les dires prophétiques d'Esdras*
Gunkel	H. Gunkel, in Kautzsch, *Die Apokryphen und Pseudepigraphen des Alten Testaments*
Ḥag.	Tractate *Ḥaggigah*
Harnisch	W. Harnisch, *Verhängnis und Verheißung der Geschichte*
Hermas Mand.	*Hermas, Mandates*
Hermas Sim.	*Hermas, Similitudes*
Hermas Vis.	*Hermas, Visions*
Hilgenfeld	A. Hilgenfeld, *Messias Judaeorum*
Hist. eccl.	*History of the Church* (Eusebius)
IDB	*Interpreter's Dictionary of the Bible*
IOS	*Israel Oriental Studies*
j. Ber.	Treatise *Berakot*, Palestinian Talmud
j. Demai	Treatise *Demai*, Palestinian Talmud
j. Ḥag.	Treatise *Ḥaggigah*, Palestinian Talmud
j. Meg.	Treatise *Megillah*, Palestinian Talmud
j. Sanh.	Treatise *Sanhedrin*, Palestinian Talmud
j. Shek.	Treatise *Shekalim*, Palestinian Talmud
Jahr. f. deut. Theol.	*Jahrbuch für deutsche Theologie*
Jas	Epistle of James
Josephus, *Ant.*	*Jewish Antiquities* (Josephus)
Josephus, *War*	*The Jewish War* (Josephus)
Jub	*Book of Jubilees*
Kabisch	R. Kabisch, *Das 4. Buch Esra auf seine Quellen untersucht*
Kahana	A. Kahana, *HaSefarim HaḤiṣonim*
Kaminka	A. Kaminka, *Sefer Ḥazonot 'Assir She'alti'el*
Keulers	J. Keulers, "Die eschatologische Lehre . . ."
Knibb	M. A. Knibb and R. J. Coggins, *The First and Second Books of Esdras*
Lampe	P. Lampe, *A Patristic Greek Lexicon*
Leg. all.	*Legum allegoria* (Philo)
Lev. R.	*Midrash Leviticus Rabba*
Licht	J. Licht, *Sefer Ḥazon 'Ezra*
LSJ	Liddel-Scott-Jones, *Greek-English Lexicon*
Lücke	F. Lücke, *Versuch einer vollständigen Einleitung . . .*
LXX	Septuagint
m. Abot	Tractate *Abot*, Mishnah
m. Ber.	Tractate *Berakot*, Mishnah
m. Gittin	Tractate *Gittin*, Mishnah
m. Kidd.	Tractate *Kiddushin*, Mishnah
m. Sanh.	Tractate *Sanhedrin*, Mishnah
m. Soṭa	Tractate *Soṭa*, Mishnah
m. Taʿan.	Tractate *Taʿanit*, Mishnah
Mart Isa	*Martyrdom of Isaiah*
Meg.	Tractate *Megillah*
Mek.	*Midrash Mekilta* (cited by name of parashah)
MGWJ	*Monatsschrift für Geschichte und Wissenschaft des Judentums*
Midr. Haggadol	*Midrash Haggadol*
Midr. Konnen	*Midrash Konnen* (BM)
Midr. Mishle	*Midrash Mishle*
Midr. Song	*Midrash Song of Songs*
Midr. Tann.	*Midrash Tannaim*
Midr. Teh.	*Midrash Tehillim*
Molitor, *Gloss. Iber.*	J. Molitor, *Glossarium Ibericum*
MT	Masoretic Text
Myers	J. M. Myers, *1 and 2 Esdras*
NEB	New English Bible

NHL	*The Nag Hammadi Library* (ed. J. M. Robinson)	*Test Patr Jud*	*Testament of Judah*, Testaments of 12 Patriarchs
Num. R.	*Midrash Numbers Rabba*	*Test Patr Levi*	*Testament of Levi*, Testaments of 12 Patriarchs
Od Sol	*Odes of Solomon*		
Oesterley	W. O. E. Oesterly, *2 Esdras*	*Test Patr Naphth*	*Testament of Naphthali*, Testaments of 12 Patriarchs
OTP	*The Old Testament Pseudepigrapha* (ed. J. H. Charlesworth)	*Test Patr Reub*	*Testament of Reuben*, Testaments of 12 Patriarchs
Paen Adam	*Penitence of Adam*		
Para Jer	*The Paralipomena of Jeremiah*, or *4 Baruch*	*Test Patr Sim*	*Testament of Simeon*, Testaments of 12 Patriarchs
Pauly-Wissowa	Pauly-Wissowa, *Real-Encyclopädie der classischen Altertumswissenschaft*	*Test Patr Zeb*	*Testament of Zebulun*, Testaments of 12 Patriarchs
Pes. R. K.	*Midrash Pesiqta de Rab Kahana*	Theod	Theodotion
Pes. Rab.	*Midrash Pesiqta Rabbati*	*ThLB*	*Theologische Literaturblatt*
PG	*Patrologia Graeca*	Thunder	Treatise Thunder (in *NHL*)
PL	*Patrologia Latina*	TU	Texte und Untersuchungen zur Geschichte der altchristlichen Literatur
Pr Man	*Prayer of Manasseh*		
Praep. ev.	*Praeparatio evangelica* (Eusebius)		
PRE	*Pirqe de R. Eliezer*	*TWNT*	*Theologisches Wörterbuch zum Neuen Testament* (ed. Kittel)
Ps Sol	*Psalms of Solomon*		
q.v.	see this one	Vagany	L. Vagany, *Le problème eschatologique* . . .
Qoh	Qohelet (Ecclesiastes)	Violet 1	B. Violet, *Die Esra-Apokalypse*
Qoh. R.	*Midrash Qohelet Rabba*	Violet 2	B. Violet, *Die Apokalypsen des Esra und des Baruch* . . .
Refut.	Hippolytus, *Refutation of All Heresies*		
RSV	Revised Standard Version	*Vit Ad*	*Life of Adam and Eve*
Schatzhöhle	*The Cave of Treasures*	*Vit Mos*	*Vita Mosis*
Schieffer	F. W. Schieffer, *Die religösen und ethischen Anschauungen des IV. Ezrabuches*	Volkmar	G. Volkmar, *Handbuch der Einleitung in die Apokryphen*
		Volz	P. Volz, *Die Eschatologie der jüdischen Gemeinde*
sec.	section		
Sed. El. Rab.	*Seder Eliyyahu Rabba*	Vulg	Vulgate Wellhausen,
Sefer Eliyyahu	Medieval Hebrew Elijah Apocalypse	*Skizzen*	J. Wellhausen, *Skizzen und Vorarbeiten*
Sib Or	*Sibylline Oracles*		
Sifre Deut.	*Midrash Sifre on Deuteronomy*	*Yalq.*	*Yalqut Shimoni*
Sifre Num.	*Midrash Sifre on Numbers*	*ZWT*	*Zeitschrift für wissenschaftliche Theologie*
Song R.	*Midrash Song of Songs Rabba*		
SOR	*Seder Olam Rabba*		
Syr Ps	Syriac Psalms		
t. Ḥag.	Tractate *Ḥaggigah*, Tosefta		
t. Sanh.	Tractate *Sanhedrin*, Tosefta		
t. Soṭa	Tractate *Soṭa*, Tosefta		
t. Sukka	Tractate *Sukka*, Tosefta		
Tanḥ.	*Midrash Tanḥuma*		
Tanḥ. (Buber)	*Midrash Tanḥuma* (ed. S. Buber)		
Tanna debe El.	*Tanna debe Eliyyahu*		
TDNT	*Theological Dictionary of the New Testament* (ed. Kittel; ET)		
Test Abr	*Testament of Abraham*		
Test Dom	*Testament of the Lord*		
Test Job	*Testament of Job*		
Test Mos	*Testament of Moses* (Assumption of Moses)		
Test Patr Benj	*Testament of Benjamin*, Testaments of 12 Patriarchs		
Test Patr Dan	*Testament of Dan*, Testaments of 12 Patriarchs		
Test Patr Jos	*Testament of Joseph*, Testaments of 12 Patriarchs		

2. Short Titles of Commentaries, Studies, and Articles Often Cited

Adler and Davis, *Day of Atonement*
Adler, N. and Davis, J., eds., *The Service of the Synagogue: Day of Atonement*, part 2 (14th ed.; London: Routledge & Kegan Paul, 1949).

Agourides, "Sedrach"
Agourides, S., "Apocalypse of Sedrach," *OTP*, 1:605–613.

ANET
Pritchard, J., *Ancient Near Eastern Texts* (Princeton: Princeton University, 1954).

Baldensperger
Baldensperger, W., *Das Selbstbewusstein Jesu im Licht der messianischen Hoffnungen seiner Zeit. I. Die Messianisch-apokalyptischen Hoffnungen des Judentums*, (3d ed. rev.; Strassburg: Heitz & Mündle, 1903).

Bensly
Bensly, R. L., *The Fourth Book of Ezra* with Introduction by M. R. James (Texts and Studies 3.2; Cambridge: Cambridge University, 1895).

Bensly, *MF*
Bensly, R. L., *The Missing Fragment of the Latin Translation of the Fourth Book of Ezra*, (Cambridge: Cambridge University, 1875).

Blake, "Georgian Version"
Blake, R. P., "The Georgian Version of Fourth Esdras from the Jerusalem Manuscript," *HTR* 19 (1926) 299–375.

Bloch, "Greek Version?"
Bloch, J., "Was There a Greek Version of the Apocalypse of Ezra?" *JQR* NS 46 (1956) 309–20.

Bogaert, *Baruch*
Bogaert, P. M., *L'Apocalypse syriaque de Baruch* (Sources chrétiennes 144–45; 2 vols.; Paris: Cerf, 1969).

Bornkamm, "Sohnschaft und Leiden"
Bornkamm, G., "Sohnschaft und Lieden" *Judentum, Urchristentum, Kirche: J. Jeremias FS* (ed. W. Eltester; BZNW 26; Berlin: Töpelmann, 1960) 188–98.

Bousset, *Antichrist*
Bousset, W., *The Antichrist Legend* (trans. A.H. Keane; London: Hutchinson, 1896).

Bousset-Gressmann
Bousset, W., *Die Religion des Judentums im späthellenistischen Zeitalter* (Handbuch zum NT 21; 3d ed. rev. H. Gressmann; Tübingen: Mohr, 1926).

Box
Box, G. H., *The Ezra-Apocalypse* (London: Pitman, 1912).

Box, *APOT*
Box, G. H., "4 Ezra," *Apocrypha and Pseudepigrapha of the Old Testament* (ed. R.H. Charles; Oxford: Clarendon, 1913) 2:542–624.

Brandenburger, *Adam und Christus*
Brandenburger, E., *Adam und Christus: Exegetisch-Religionsgeschichtliche Untersuchung zu Röm 5:12–21 (1 Kor. 15)* (WMANT 7; Neukirchen: Neukirchener, 1962).

Brandenburger, *Verborgenheit*
Brandenburger, E., *Die Verborgenheit Gottes im Weltgeschehen* (ATANT 68; Zurich: Theologischer Verlag, 1981).

Breech, "These Fragments"
Breech, E., "These Fragments I Have Shored Against My Ruins: The Form and Function of 4 Ezra," *JBL* 92 (1973) 267–74.

Casey, *Son of Man*
Casey, M., *Son of Man: The Interpretation and Influence of Daniel 7* (London: SPCK, 1979).

Charlesworth, *OTP*
Charlesworth, J. H., ed., *The Old Testament Pseudepigrapha* (2 vols.; New York: Doubleday, 1983, 1985).

Charlesworth, *Pseudepigrapha and Modern Research*
Charlesworth, J. H., *The Pseudepigrapha and Modern Research with a Supplement* (2d ed. SBLSCS 7S; Chico, Calif.: Scholars, 1981).

Clemen, "Die Zusammensetzung"
Clemen, C., "Die Zusammensetzung des Buches Henoch, der Apokalypse des Baruch und des vierten Buches Esra," *TSK* 71 (1898) 211–46.

Cohen, S.D. "The Destruction"
Cohen, S.D., "The Destruction: From Scripture to Midrash," *Prooftexts* 2 (1982) 18–39.

Collins, *Genre*
Collins, J. J., *Apocalypse: The Morphology of a Genre* (Semeia 14; Missoula, Mont.: Scholars, 1979).

Collins, *Imagination*
Collins, J. J., *The Apocalyptic Imagination* (New York: Crossroad, 1984).

Collins, *Daniel*
Collins, J. J., *The Apocalyptic Vision of the Book of Daniel* (HSM 16; Missoula, Mont.; Scholars, 1977).

Denis, *Fragmenta*
Denis, A.-M., ed., *Fragmenta pseudepigraphorum quae supersunt graeca una cum Historicarum et auctorum Judaeorum Hellenistarum Fragmenta* (PVTG 3; Leiden: Brill, 1970).

Denis, *Introduction*
Denis, A.-M., *Introduction aux pseudépigraphes grecs d'Ancien Testament* (SVTP 1; Leiden: Brill, 1970).

Dimant, "Qumran Sectarian Writings"
Dimant, D., "Qumran and Sectarian Literature," *Jewish Writings of the Second Temple Period* (CRINT 2.2; Assen and Philadelphia: van Gorcum and Fortress, 1984) 483–550.

Dillmann, "Adlergesicht"
Dillmann, A., "Über das Adlergesicht in der Apokalypse des Esra," *Sitzungsberichte der Berliner Akademie* 8 (1888) 215–37.

Dillmann, "Pseudepigrapha"
Dillmann, A., "Pseudepigrapha," *Real-Encyklopädie für protestantische Theologie und Kirche* (ed. J. J. Herzog; vol. 12, 1st ed.; Gotha: Besser, 1860) 312.

Dinzelbacher, "Die Vision Albrichs"
  Dinzelbacher, P., "Die Vision Albrichs und die
  Esdras-Apokryphe," *Studien und Mitteilungen zur
  Geschichte des Benediktiner-Ordens* 87 (1976) 435–42.

Drummond, *The Jewish Messiah*
  Drummond, J., *The Jewish Messiah* (London:
  Longmans Green, 1877).

Even-Shmuel
  Even-Shmuel, Y., *Midrešei Ge'ula* (Tel Aviv: Mosad
  Bialik, 1943).

de Faye
  Faye, E. de, *Les apocalypses juives* (Paris: Fischbacher, 1892).

Festugière, "Expérience religieuse"
  Festugière, A.-J., "L'expérience religieuse du
  médecin Thessalos," *RB* 48 (1939) 45–54.

Finkelstein, *Introduction*
  Finkelstein, L., *Introduction to the Treatises Abot and
  Abot de R. Nathan* (New York: Jewish Theological
  Seminary, 1950). In Hebrew.

Geoltrain
  Geoltrain, P., "Quatrième Livre d'Esdras," *La
  Bible: Ecrits Intertestamentaires* (ed. A. Dupont-
  Sommer and M. Philonenko; Paris: Gallimard,
  1987) 1400–1470.

Gfrörer, "Jahrhundert"
  Gfrörer, A., "Das Jahrhundert des Heils" *Geschichte
  des Urchristentums*, vol. 1 (Stuttgart: Schweitzerbart,1838).

Gildemeister
  Gildemeister, I., *Esdrae liber quartus Arabice e codice
  Vaticano* (Bonn: Adolphus Marcus,1877).

Ginzberg, *Kirchenvätern*
  Ginzberg, L., *Die Haggada bei den Kirchenvätern und
  in der apokryphischen Literatur* (Berlin:1900).

Ginzberg, *Legends*
  Ginzberg, L., *The Legends of the Jews* (6 vols.;
  Philadelphia: JPS, 1928).

Gry
  Gry, L., *Les dires prophétiques d'Esdras* (2 vols.;
  Paris: Geuthner, 1930).

Gunkel, *Der Prophet Esra*
  Gunkel, H., *Der Prophet Esra* (Tübingen: Mohr,
  1900).

Gunkel, *Schöpfung*
  Gunkel, H., *Schöpfung und Chaos in Urzeit und
  Endzeit* (Göttingen: Vandenhoeck & Ruprecht,
  1895).

Gunkel, *TLZ*
  Gunkel, H., Review of Kabisch (q.v.), *Theologische
  Literaturzeitung* 16, no. 1 (1891) 5–11.

Gunkel
  Gunkel, H., "Das vierte Buch Esra," *Die Apokryphen
  und Pseudepigraphen des alten Testaments* (ed. E.
  Kautzsch, Tübingen: Mohr, 1900) 2:331–402.

Gutschmid, "Apokalypse des Esra"
  Gutschmid, A. von, "Die Apokalypse des Esra und
  ihre spätern Bearbeitungen," *ZfWT* 3 (1860) 1–81.

Harnisch
  Harnisch, W., *Verhängnis und Verheißung der
  Geschichte: Untersuchungen zum Zeit- und Geschichts-
  verständnis im 4.Buch Esra und in der syr. Baruch-
  apokalypse* (FRLANT 97; Göttingen: Vandenhoeck
  & Ruprecht, 1969).

Harnisch, "Prophet"
  Harnisch, W., "Der Prophet als Widerpart und
  Zeuge der Offenbarung: Erwägungen zur Inter-
  dependenz von Form und Sache im 4.Buch Esra,"
  *Apocalypticism in the Mediterranean World and the
  Near East* (ed. D. Hellholm; Tübingen: Mohr,
  1983) 461–93.

Hartman, *Prophecy Interpreted*
  Hartman, L., *Prophecy Interpreted* (Coniectanea
  Biblica, N.T. Series 1; Lund: Gleerup, 1966).

Hartom
  Hartom, A. S., *Hasefarim Haḥiṣonim: Ḥezyonot*, part
  2 (Tel Aviv: Yavneh, 1969).

Hayman, "Problem"
  Hayman, A.P., "Rabbinic Judaism and the
  Problem of Evil," *Scottish Journal of Theology* 29
  (1976) 461–76.

Hayman "Pseudonymity"
  Hayman, A.P., "The Problem of Pseudonymity in
  the Ezra Apocalypse," *JSJ* 6 (1975) 47–56.

Heinemann, "A Homily"
  Heinemann, J., "A Homily on Jeremiah and the
  Fall of Jerusalem," *The Biblical Mosaic: Changing
  Perspectives* (ed. R. Polzin and E. Rothman; SBLSS;
  Philadelphia: Fortress and Scholars, 1982) 27–41.

Hengel, *Judaism and Hellenism*
  Hengel, M., *Judaism and Hellenism: Studies in Their
  Encounter in Palestine During the Early Hellenistic
  Period* (trans. J. Bowden; Philadelphia: Fortress,
  1974).

Hertz, *Authorized Daily Prayer Book*
  Hertz, J. H., *The Authorized Daily Prayer Book*
  (London: Shapiro & Valentine, 1947).

Hilgenfeld, *Apokalyptik*
  Hilgenfeld, A., *Die jüdische Apokalyptik in ihrer
  geschichtlichen Entwickelung* (Jenna: Mauke, 1857).

Hilgenfeld, *Esra und Daniel*
  Hilgenfeld, A., *Die Propheten Esra und Daniel und
  ihrer neusten Bearbeitungen* (Halle: Pfeffer, 1863).

Hilgenfeld, *Messias Judaeorum*
  Hilgenfeld, A., *Messias Judaeorum* (Leipzig:
  Reisland,1869).

Himmelfarb, *Tours of Hell*
  Himmelfarb, M., *Tours of Hell: An Apocalyptic Form
  in Jewish and Christian Literature* (Philadelphia:
  University of Pennsylvania, 1983).

Hollander and de Jonge, *Commentary*
  Hollander, H. W., and Jonge, M. de, *The
  Testaments of the Twelve Patriarchs: A Commentary*
  (SPVT 8; Leiden: Brill, 1985).

Issaverdens, *Uncanonical Writings*
  Issaverdens, J., trans., *The Uncanonical Writings of
  the Old Testament Found in the Armenian Mss. of the*

Library of St. Lazarus (Venice: Monastery of St. Lazarus, 1901; 2d ed., 1934).

James, *Apoc. N.T.*

James, M. R., *The Apocryphal New Testament* (Oxford: Clarendon, 1963).

James, *Apocrypha Anecdota*

James, M. R., *Apocrypha Anecdota* (Texts and Studies 2,3; Cambridge: Cambridge University, 1893).

James, *Biblical Antiquities*

James, M. R., *The Biblical Antiquities of Philo* (London: SPCK, 1917; repr. with Prolegomenon by L.H. Feldman, New York: Ktav, 1971).

Jellinek, *BM*

Jellinek, A., *Bet ha-Midrasch* (repr. Jerusalem: Bamberger and Wahrmann, 1938; 6 vols. in 2).

Jervell, *Imago Dei*

Jervell, J., *Imago Dei* (Göttingen: Vandenhoeck & Ruprecht, 1960).

Kabisch

Kabisch, R., *Das vierte Buch Esra auf seine Quellen untersucht* (Göttingen: Vandenhoeck & Ruprecht, 1889).

Kahana

Kahana, A., *HaSefarim HaHitsonim* (Tel Aviv: Masada, 1959). In Hebrew.

Kaminka

Kaminka, A., *Sefer Hazonot 'Assir She'alti'el* (Tel Aviv: Dvir, 1936). In Hebrew.

Keulers

Keulers, J., "Die eschatologische Lehre des vierten Esrabuches," *Biblische Studien* 20, nos. 2–3 (1922) 1–240. Also *separatim* Freiburg i. Br.: Herder, 1922.

Klijn, *Lateinische Text*

Klijn, A. F. J., ed., *Der lateinische Text der Apokalypse des Esra* (TU 131; Berlin: Akademie, 1983).

Kneucker, *Das Buch Baruch*

Kneucker, J. J., *Das Buch Baruch* (Leipzig: Brockhaus, 1879).

Knibb

Knibb, M. A., and Coggins, R. J., *The First and Second Books of Esdras* (Cambridge Bible Commentary; Cambridge: Cambridge University, 1979).

Knibb, "Apocalyptic and Wisdom"

Knibb, M. A., "Apocalyptic and Wisdom in 4 Ezra," *JSJ* 13 (1982) 56–74.

Koch, "Ezras erste Vision"

Koch, K., "Esras erste Vision: Weltzeiten und Weg des Höchsten," *BZ* NF 22 (1978) 46–75.

Kraft, "'Ezra' Materials"

Kraft, R.A., "'Ezra' Materials in Judaism and Christianity," *Aufstieg und Niedergang der römischen Welt* (Band 19.1; ed. H. Temporini and W. Haase; Berlin: de Gruyter, 1979) 119–36.

Kuhn, "Zur *Assumptio Mosis*"

Kuhn, G. von, "Zur *Assumptio Mosis*," *ZAW* 43 (1925) 124–29.

K'urc'ikidze, *Dzveli*

K'urc'ikidze, C'., ed., *Dzveli Ag't'k'mis Apok'rip'ebis Versiebi* (2 vols.; Tbilisi: Mec'niereba, 1970, 1973).

Laurence, *Versio Aethiopica*

Laurence, R., *Primi Ezrae Libri Versio Aethiopica* (Oxford: Oxford University, 1820).

Lewy, *Chaldean Oracles*

Lewy, H., *The Chaldean Oracles and Theurgy* (Recherches d'archéologie, de philologie et d'histoire 13; Cairo: Inst. Franc. d'arch. orien., 1956).

Lewy, *Sobria Ebrietas*

Lewy, H., *Sobria Ebrietas: Untersuchungen zur Geschichte der Antiken Mystik* (BZNW 9; Gießen: Töpelmann, 1923).

Licht

Licht, J. S., *Sefer Hazon 'Ezra,* (Sifriyat Dorot 6; Jerusalem: Bialik Institute, 1968). In Hebrew.

Licht, *Serakim*

Licht, J. S., *The Rule Scroll* (Jerusalem: Bialik Institute, 1965). In Hebrew.

Licht, "Taxo"

Licht, J. S., "Taxo or the Apocalyptic Doctrine of Vengeance," *JJS* 12 (1961) 95–103.

Loewenstamm, "Death of Moses"

Loewenstamm, S., "The Death of Moses," *Studies on the Testament of Abraham* (ed. G. W. E. Nickelsburg; SCS 6; Missoula, Mont.: Scholars, 1976) 198–201.

Luck, "Weltverständnis"

Luck, U., "Das Weltverständnis in der jüdischen Apokalyptik dargestellt am äthiopischen Henoch und am 4.Esra," *ZfTK* 73 (1976) 283–305.

Lücke

Lücke, F., *Versuch einer vollständingen Einleitung in die Offenbarung des Johannes und in die apokalyptische Literatur überhaupt* (2d ed., Bonn: Weber, 1852).

Meade, *Pseudonymity and Canon*

Meade, D. G., *Pseudonymity and Canon* (Grand Rapids: Wm. B. Eerdmans, 1986).

Mercati, *Note*

Mercati, G., *Note di Litteratura Biblica e Cristiana Antica* (Studi e Testi 5; Rome: Vatican, 1901).

Merkur, "Visionary Practice"

Merkur, D., "The Visionary Practice of Jewish Apocalyptists." Forthcoming.

Metzger, "'Lost' Section"

Metzger, B.M., "The 'Lost' Section of II Esdras (= IV Ezra)," *JBL* 76 (1957) 153–65.

Momigliano, "Universal History"

Momigliano, A., "The Origins of Universal History," *Annali della Scuola Normale Superiore di Pisa*, ser. 3, 12.2 (1982) 533–60.

Moore, *Judaism*

Moore, G. F., *Judaism in the First Centuries of the Christian Era* (3 vols., Cambridge: Harvard University, 1962).

Mueller and Robbins, "Vision of Ezra"
Mueller, J. R and Robbins, G. A., "Vision of Ezra," *OTP*, 1:581–90.

Müller, *Messias*
Müller, U. B., *Messias und Menschensohn in jüdischen Apokalypsen und in der Offenbarung Johannes* (SZNT 6; Gütersloh: Mohn, 1972).

Mundle, "Religiöse Problem"
Mundle, W., "Das religiöse Problem des IV. Esrabuches," *ZAW* NF 6 (1929) 222–49.

Mussies, "Graecisms"
Mussies, G., "When Do Graecisms Prove that a Latin Text Is a Translation?" *Vruchten van de Uithof: H.A. Brongers FS* (Utrecht: Theologisch Institut, 1984) 100–119.

Myers
Myers, J. M., *1 and 2 Esdras* (AB 42; Garden City, N.Y.: Doubleday, 1974).

Nau, "Deux opuscules"
Nau, F., "Analyse de deux opuscules astrologiques attribués au prophète Esdras," *ROC* 12 (1907) 14–15.

Nickelsburg, *Jewish Literature*
Nickelsburg, G. W. E., *Jewish Literature Between the Bible and the Mishnah* (Philadelphia: Fortress, 1981).

Nickelsburg and Stone, *Faith and Piety*
Nickelsburg, G. W. E., and Stone, M. E., *Faith and Piety in Early Judaism* (Philadelphia: Fortress, 1983).

Oesterley
Oesterley, W. O. E., *2 Esdras (The Ezra Apocalypse)* (Westminster Commentaries; London: Methuen, 1933).

Oesterley and Box, *Religion of the Synagogue*
Oesterley, W. O. E., and Box, G. H., *The Religion and Worship of the Synagogue* (London: Pitman, 1907).

Philonenko, "L'âme à l'étroit"
Philonenko, M., "L'âme à l'étroit," *Hommages à André Dupont-Sommer* (ed. A. Caquot and M. Philonenko; Paris: Adrien-Maisonneuve, 1971) 421–28.

Philonenko, "Remarques"
Philonenko, M., "Remarques sur un hymne essénien de charactère gnostique," *Semitica* 11 (1961) 43–54.

Porter
Porter, F. C., *The Messages of the Apocalyptical Writers* (New York: Scribner's, 1905).

Porter, "Yeçer Hara"
Porter, F. C., "The Yeçer Hara," *Biblical and Semitic Studies: Yale Bicentennial Publications* (New York: Scribner's, 1902) 146–52.

Riessler, *Schrifttum*
Riessler, P., *Altjüdisches Schrifttum ausserhalb der Bibel* (Heidelberg: Kerle, 1928).

Rigaux, *Antéchrist*
Rigaux, P. B., *L'antéchrist et l'opposition au royaume messianique dans l'ancien et le nouveau Testament* (Paris: Gabalda, 1932).

Rosenstiehl, *Elie*
Rosenstiehl, J. M., *L'Apocalypse d'Elie* (Textes et Etudes pour servir à l'histoire du Judaism intertestamentaire 1; Paris: Geuthner, 1972).

Rosenthal, *Vier apokryphische Bücher*
Rosenthal, F., *Vier apokryphische Bücher aus der Zeit und Schule R. Akiba's* (Leipzig: Schulze, 1885).

Rowland, *Open Heaven*
Rowland, C., *The Open Heaven* (New York: Crossroad, 1982).

Russell, *Method and Message*
Russell, D. S., *The Method and Message of Jewish Apocalyptic* (OTL; Philadelphia: Westminster, 1964).

Sargant, *Battle for the Mind*
Sargant, W. W., *Battle for the Mind: A Physiology of Conversion and Brainwashing* (New York: Doubleday, 1957).

Schechter, *Aspects*
Schechter, S., *Some Aspects of Rabbinic Theology* (London: Black, 1909).

Schieffer
Schieffer, F. W., *Die religiösen und ethischen Anschauungen des 4.Ezrabuches* (Leipzig: Dörffling & Franke, 1901).

Scholem, *Gnosticism*
Scholem, G. G., *Jewish Gnosticism, Merkabah Mysticism and Talmudic Tradition* (New York: Jewish Theological Seminary, 1960).

Scholem, *Major Trends*
Scholem, G. G., *Major Trends in Jewish Mysticism* (New York: Schocken, 1941).

Schrader, *Keilinschriften*
Schrader, E., *Die Keilinschriften und das Alte Testament* (Berlin: Reuther & Reichard, 1902).

Schreiner
Schreiner, J., *Das 4.Buch Esra* (ed. W.G. Kümmel et al.; JSHRZ 5,4; Gütersloh: Mohn, 1981).

Schürer
Schürer, E., *Geschichte des jüdischen Volkes im Zeitalter Jesu Christi* (3 vols.; 4th ed.; Leipzig: Hinrichs, 1909).

Singer, *Authorized Daily Prayerbook*
Singer, S., trans., *The Authorized Daily Prayer Book* (London: Eyre & Spottiswoode, 1900).

Sjöberg, *Menschensohn*
Sjöberg, E., *Der Menschensohn im äthiopischen Henochbuch* (Lund: Gleerup, 1940).

Sjöberg, *Der verborgene Menschensohn*
Sjöberg, E., *Der verborgene Menschensohn in den Evangelien* (Acta reg. soc. humanorum litt. Lundensis 51; Lund: Gleerup, 1955).

Sparks, *Apocryphal Old Testament*
Sparks, H. D. F., *The Apocryphal Old Testament* (Oxford: Oxford University, 1984).

Steck, "Aufnahme"
Steck, O.H., "Die Aufnahme von Genesis 1 in Jubiläen 2 und 4.Esra 6," *JSJ* 8 (1977) 154–82.

Stone, "Apocalyptic Literature"
Stone, M. E., "Apocalyptic Literature," *Jewish Writings of the Second Temple Period* (ed. M. E. Stone; CRINT 2.2; Assen and Philadelphia: van Gorcum and Fortress, 1984) 383–441.

Stone, "Apocryphal Notes"
Stone, M. E., "Apocryphal Notes and Readings. 7. Saeculum as 'Heaven' in 4 Ezra," *IOS* 1 (1971) 129–31.

Stone, *Armenian Version*
Stone, M. E., ed., *The Armenian Version of IV Ezra* (University of Pennsylvania Armenian Texts and Studies 1; Missoula, Mont.: Scholars, 1979).

Stone, "Coherence and Inconsistency"
Stone, M. E., "Coherence and Inconsistency in the Apocalypses: The Case of 'the End' in 4 Ezra," *JBL* 102 (1983) 229–43.

Stone, *Features*
Stone, M. E., *Features of the Eschatology of 4 Ezra* (diss., Harvard University, 1965; HSM; Atlanta: Scholars, 1989).

Stone, "Greek Apocalypse of Ezra"
Stone, M. E., "Greek Apocalypse of Ezra," *OTP*, 1:561–79.

Stone, "Lists"
Stone, M. E., "Lists of Revealed Things in the Apocalyptic Literature," *Magnalia Dei (G.E. Wright Memorial)* (ed. F.M. Cross, W.E. Lemke, and P.D. Miller; Garden City, N.Y.: Doubleday, 1976) 414–54.

Stone, "Manuscripts and Readings"
Stone, M. E., "Manuscripts and Readings of Armenian 4 Ezra," *Textus* 6 (1968) 48–61.

Stone, "Messiah"
Stone, M. E., "The Concept of the Messiah in 4 Ezra," *Religions in Antiquity: E. R. Goodenough Memorial* (ed. J. Neusner; SHR 14; Leiden: Brill, 1968) 295–312.

Stone, "Metamorphosis"
Stone, M. E., "The Metamorphosis of Ezra: Jewish Apocalypse and Medieval Vision," *JTS* NS 33 (1982) 1–18.

Stone, "Natural Order"
Stone, M. E., "The Parabolic Use of Natural Order in Judaism of the Second Temple Age," *Gilgul: Werblowsky FS* (ed. S. Shaked, D. Shulman, and G. Stroumsa; Numen Supplement 50; Leiden, Copenhagen, and New York: Brill, 1987) 298–308.

Stone, "Paradise"
Stone, M. E., "Paradise in 4 Ezra iv.8 and vii.36, viii.52," *JJS* 17 (1966) 85–88.

Stone, *Patriarchs and Prophets*
Stone, M. E., *Armenian Apocrypha Relating to the Patriarchs and Prophets* (Jerusalem: Israel Academy of Sciences and Humanities,1982).

Stone, *Penitence of Adam*
Stone, M. E., *The Penitence of Adam* (CSCO 429–430; Scriptores Armeniaci 13–14; Louvain: Peeters, 1981).

Stone, "Question of the Messiah"
Stone, M. E., "The Question of the Messiah in 4 Ezra," *Judaisms and Their Messiahs at the Turn of the Christian Era* (ed. J. Neusner, W. S. Green, and E. S. Frerichs; New York: Cambridge University, 1987) 209–24.

Stone, "Reactions"
Stone, M. E., "Reactions to Destructions of the Second Temple," *JSJ* 12 (1982) 195–204.

Stone, *Signs of the Judgement*
Stone, M. E., *Signs of the Judgement, Onomastica Sacra and The Generations from Adam* (University of Pennsylvania Armenian Texts and Studies 3; Chico, Calif.: Scholars, 1981).

Stone, "Some Features"
Stone, M. E., "Some Features of the Armenian Version of 4 Ezra," *Le Muséon* 79 (1966) 387–400.

Stone, "Some Remarks"
Stone, M. E., "Some Remarks on the Textual Criticism of 4 Ezra," *HTR* 60 (1967) 107–15.

Stone, "Three Transformations"
Stone, M. E., "Three Transformations in Judaism: Scripture, History, and Redemption," *Numen* 32 (1985) 218–35.

Stone, "Two New Discoveries"
Stone, M. E., "Two New Discoveries Touching on the Non-canonical Ezra Books," *Sion* 52 (1978) 45–50. In Armenian.

Stone, "Vision or Hallucination?"
Stone, M. E., "Apocalyptic: Vision or Hallucination?" *Milla wa-Milla* 14 (1974) 47–56.

Stone, "Way of the Most High"
Stone, M. E., "The Way of the Most High and the Injustice of God," *Knowledge of God Between Alexander and Constantine* (ed. R. van den Broek, T. Baarda, and J. Mansfeld; Leiden: Brill, 1989) 132–42.

Stone-Strugnell, *Elijah*
Stone, M. E., and Strugnell, J., *The Books of Elijah: Parts 1–2* (SBLTT 18, PS 8; Missoula, Mont.: Scholars, 1979).

Strack-Billerbeck
Billerbeck, P., with Strack, H. L., *Kommentar zum Neuen Testament aus Talmud und Midrasch* (Munich: Beck, 1922–61).

Thompson, *Responsibility*
Thompson, A. L., *Responsibility for Evil in the Theodicy of IV Ezra* (SBLDS 29; Missoula, Mont.: Scholars, 1977).

Tischendorf, *Apocalypses Apocryphae*
Tischendorf, C. von, *Apocalypses Apocryphae Mosis, Esdrae, Pauli, Iohannis* (Leipzig: Mendelssohn, 1866).

Urbach, *Sages*
  Urbach, E. E., *The Sages: Their Concepts and Beliefs* (Cambridge: Harvard University, 1987).
Vagany
  Vagany, L., *Le problème eschatologique dans le IVe livre d'Esdras* (Paris: Picard, 1906).
de Villiers, "Way"
  Villiers, P.G.R. de, "Understanding the Way of God: Form, Function and Message of the Historical Review in 4 Ezra 3:4–27," *SBL 1981 Seminar Papers* (ed. K.H. Richards; Chico, Calif.: Scholars, 1981) 357–78.
Violet 1
  Violet, B., *Die Esra-Apokalypse (IV Esra), Band 1: Die Überlieferung*, (GCS 18; Leipzig: Hinrichs, 1910).
Violet 2
  Violet, B., *Die Apokalypsen des Esra und des Baruch in deutscher Gestalt* (GCS 32; Leipzig: Hinrichs, 1924).
van der Vlis, *Disputatio Critica*
  Vlis, C. J. van der, *Disputatio Critica de Ezrae Libro Apocrypho Vulgo Quarto Dicto* (Amsterdam: Müller, 1839).
Volkmar
  Volkmar, G., *Das vierte Buch Esrae ("Esdra Propheta") Handbuch der Einleitung in die Apokryphen*, vol. 2 (Tübingen: Fues, 1863).
Volz
  Volz, P., *Die Eschatologie der jüdischen Gemeinde* (2d ed.; Tübingen: Mohr, 1934).
Wahl, *Apocalypsis Esdrae*
  Wahl, O., *Apocalypsis Esdrae, Apocalypsis Sedrach, Visio Beati Esdrae* (PVTG 4; Leiden: Brill, 1977).
Wellhausen, *Skizzen*
  Wellhausen, J., "Zur apokalyptischen Literatur," *Skizzen und Vorarbeiten* (Berlin: Reimer, 1899) 6:215–49.
Westermann, "Klage"
  Westermann, C., "Struktur und Geschichte der Klage im Alten Testament," *ZAW* 66 (1954) 44–80.
Wieseler, "Das vierte Buch Esra"
  Wieseler, K., "Das vierte Buch Esra nach Inhalt und Alter untersucht," *TSK* 43 (1870) 263–304.
Wilder, *Early Christian Rhetoric*
  Wilder, A. N., *Early Christian Rhetoric: The Language of the Gospel* (London: SCM, 1964).
Wright, "Rîb"
  Wright, G.E., "The Lawsuit of God: A Form-Critical Study of Deuteronomy 32," *Israel's Prophetic Heritage: Essays in Honour of James Muilenberg* (ed. B. W. Anderson and W. Harrelson; London: SCM, 1962) 26–67.
Yadin, *War*
  Yadin, Y., *The Scroll of the War of the Sons of Light Against the Sons of Darkness* (Oxford: Oxford University, 1962).

Yovsēpʻian', *Ankanon Girkʻ Hin Ktakaranacʻ* (Venice: Monastery of St. Lazarus, 1896). In Armenian.
Zimmermann, "Underlying Documents"
  Zimmermann, F., "Underlying Documents of 4 Ezra," *JQR* 51 (1960/61) 107–34.

Michael Stone's *Fourth Ezra* is the first of a series of
volumes commissioned to provide major commentaries
on Jewish literary works of Hellenistic and Early
Roman times, most of them belonging to what are
frequently labeled Old Testament Apocrypha and
Pseudepigrapha. The New Testament Board of
Hermeneia similarly has expanded its coverage of
Christian literature with the publication of William R.
Shoedel's commentary on Ignatius of Antioch. Such
commentaries were already promised in the editor's
foreword to the *Hermeneia* series, and the modern
student of the Bible, whose interests may range from
historical to literary to theological, will find that
serious commentaries on such non-canonical or
deutero-canonical works are necessary tools for
scholarship.

In the Latin language tradition that prevailed in
Europe and the Western world, a large section of 4
Ezra (7:36–106a) was unknown from the Middle Ages
through the nineteenth century because it was missing
in all the known manuscripts. Around 1870, Robert
Bensly discovered a Latin manuscript in the Bibliothèque Municipale in Amiens, France, that contained
the "missing section." The front endpaper of this
volume reproduces two pages from the middle of the
missing section in the Amiens manuscript (folios 63
verso to 64 recto, containing 4 Ezra 7:63–86). The
back endpaper shows two pages from the end of the
missing section (folios 64 verso to 65 recto, containing
4 Ezra 7:86–109).

Photographs are courtesy of the Bibliothèque
Municipale, Amiens, France.

—Frank Moore Cross
Harvard University

1.0. Section 1:
Text and Transmission

1.1. Hebrew and Greek

As will be demonstrated in section 2.3 below, it is most reasonable to assume that 4 Ezra was originally composed in Hebrew. No fragments of the Hebrew text of 4 Ezra have survived, however, and there is no evidence of its use in ancient Jewish literature.

The Hebrew text was translated into Greek in antiquity, but the Greek text in its entirety has not survived. There are, however, some quotations from the book in Greek writers and some allusions to it. In addition, 4 Ezra seems to have inspired the document upon which two Byzantine Greek apocalypses were based as well as some other works. These Byzantine Greek works are the *Greek Apocalypse of Ezra (Esdras)* and the *Apocalypse of Sedrach*.[1]

Unambiguous Greek quotations are rather few:[2]

a. Apost. Const. 2.14.9 is close to 4 Ezra 7:103.

b. Apost. Const. 8.7.6 quotes 4 Ezra 8:23.

c. Clement of Alexandria, *Stromateis* 3:16, quotes 4 Ezra 5:35.

d. Barn. 12:1[3] is sometimes claimed to quote 4 Ezra 5:5a.[4]

e. Clement of Alexandria, *Stromateis* 1:22, is claimed to be an allusion to 4 Ezra 14:21–22 and 14:37–47.

f. Bensly, *MF*, 68 would see a reminiscence of 7:94 in *Hermas Vis.* 1.3.[5]

It is possible to restore further Greek readings from the extant versions in three ways. First, the Latin and Coptic versions contain a number of transliterated words. Second, in some instances the variants between the various versions enable the restoration of the Greek from which they must have derived. Third, those versions which have been studied carefully have yielded a crop of instances in which it is possible to ascertain the Greek text behind them from internal evidence. In any event, the sum of all of these is a scattering of words, and we are still far from a coherent Greek text.[6]

As an example of one type of evidence, we list words transliterated from Greek found in the Latin version of 4 Ezra: 5:5, *gressus* (from corrupt uncial Greek ΓΡΕΣ⟨ΑΕΡΕΣ⟩); 5:8, *chaus*; 5:25, 5:52, et al., *abyssis*; 6:5, *thesaurizaverunt*; 6:21, *scirtiabuntur*; 6:35, *ebdomadas*; 6:40 et al., *thesauris*; 7:36, *clibanus*; 7:36, *lacus*; 7:43, *ebdomada*; 8:21, *thronus*; 8:38, *plamsa*; 9:21 et al., *botru*; 10:1 et al., *thalamo*; 10:22, *psalterium*; 10:22, *hymnus*; 10:38, *mysteria*; 13:43, *Euphraten*; 13:58, *gubernare*; 14:24, *buxus*; 14:39, *calix*.

It is, of course, not certain that all of these words were drawn from the Greek text of 4 Ezra, and some of them

---

1. The Greek citations of 4 Ezra were recently assembled by A.-M. Denis, ed., *Fragmenta pseudepigraphorum quae supersunt graeca una cum Historicorum et Auctorum Judaeorum Hellenistarum Fragmentis* (PVTG 3; Leiden: Brill, 1970) 130–32. A detailed discussion of the Greek fragments is to be found in A.-M. Denis, *Introduction aux Pseudépigraphs grecs d'Ancien Testament* (SVTP 1; Leiden: Brill, 1970) 194–200. The Byzantine Ezra apocalypses were most recently edited by O. Wahl, *Apocalypsis Esdrae, Apocalypsis Sedrach, Visio Beati Esdrae* (PVTG 4; Leiden: Brill, 1977). New English translations have been published in *OTP*, 1:561–90 (*Apocalypse of Esdras*) and 1:605–13 (*Apocalypse of Sedrach*). These and other works belonging to the corpus of later Ezra literature will be discussed in sec. 6.2 below.

2. "Introduction" to Bensly, pp. xxviii–xxx.

3. The margin of the Constantinople manuscript of *Barnabas* attributes *Barn.* 4:4 to Δανιὴλ καὶ Ἔσδρας ἀπόκρυφος, which M. R. James considers a reference to 4 Ezra 12:10 sqq. (see Bensly, p. xxviii). Some further data relating to the Greek of 4 Ezra are the

following: an apocalypse of Ezra is mentioned in the List of Sixty Books, though this might be the *Greek Apocalypse of Esdras*. An Oxyrhyncus papyrus of the fourth century contains a fragment of the Greek text of 6 Ezra, i.e., 15:57–59 of the Latin version (A. S. Hunt, ed., *The Oxyrhynchus Papyri* [London: Egyptian Exploration Fund, 1910], 7:1–15). This is not part of 4 Ezra.

4. This citation, together with a number of others, is rated doubtful by James, *apud* Bensly, pp. xxviii–xxx. Violet 1, pp. xiii–xiv, rejects it. This is discussed in detail by P. Prigent, *L'Epître de Barnabé i–xvi et ses sources* (Etudes Bibliques; Paris: Lecoffre, 1961) 116–18. He rejects this hypothesis as well as other suggested borrowings; see also ibid., 157.

5. A relationship between Hermas and 4 Ezra was argued in detail by Volkmar, pp. 291–92. He cites F. Lee, *An Epistolary Discourse Concerning the Books of Ezra, Genuine and Spurious* (London: "by a Friend," 1722) 91–95.

6. Hilgenfeld, *Messias Judaeorum*, attempted to reconstruct the whole Greek text of the book.

were clearly domiciled in the Latin of the period.[7]

Next, it should be taken into account that the *Greek Apocalypse of Esdras* and the *Apocalypse of Sedrach* may well preserve phrases drawn from the Greek of 4 Ezra. A list of such parallels was prepared by B. Violet.[8] However, this evidence is not secure, since, in some instances, where both later apocalypses utilize the same part of 4 Ezra, their Greek wording differs. Any residual doubt about the existence of a Greek version of 4 Ezra has been removed by G. Mussies in a most careful study of Graecisms in the Latin version of 4 Ezra. The cumulative evidence assembled by him there is absolutely convincing.[9]

1.2. The Versions Secondary to the Greek

From the above it follows that the chief evidence available for the text of 4 Ezra is drawn from the versions secondary to the Greek.[10] 4 Ezra survives in Latin, Syriac, Ethiopic, Georgian, two independent Arabic translations, Armenian, and in a fragment of a Coptic version. In addition, an Arabic fragment, a fragmentary Modern Greek version, a second Armenian translation, a second Georgian translation, a Slavonic translation, and a Hebrew translation exist which were made from the Latin. There is also a third Arabic version which was made from the Syriac. It is the assured conclusion of scholarship[11] that, with the exception of the tertiary versions last mentioned, all of the translations were made from the Greek text.[12]

Violet published, in 1910, a synoptic edition, printing in parallel columns Latin, Syriac, Ethiopic, Arabic1, Arabic2, Armenian, Coptic (where extant), and the Syro-Arabic fragment known to him. The Latin column was a new edition of the Latin text, and the other columns were translations into German of the relevant versions.[13] A second synoptic edition was produced by L. Gry, but it is of limited scope and in a far less convenient format.[14] At present, A. F. J. Klijn is preparing a new synoptic edition to replace that of Violet in the same series.

1.2.1. Relations Between the Versions

The clearest statement to date of the relationship between the versions was formulated by R. Blake.[15] He showed quite convincingly that the Latin and Syriac versions form one branch of the tradition and that the Georgian, Ethiopic, and Coptic form a second branch.

---

7   Instances in which a Greek reading can be reconstructed from the variants between the versions or from the readings of the individual versions may be found throughout the textual notes. Some examples are 3:18; 3:26; 4:2; 4:4; 4:7; 4:12; 4:24; 4:35; 4:43; 4:44; 4:51; 5:1; 5:5; 5:8; 5:24; 5:28; 5:32; 5:35; 5:37; 5:41; 5:48; 6:18; 6:19. Most recently, A. F. J. Klijn, ed., *Der lateinische Text der Apokalypse des Esra* (TU 131; Berlin: Akademie, 1983) 11, gives a list of instances in which, in his view, the formulation of the Latin enables the reconstruction of the Greek phraseology behind it. Such lists were made in earlier generations; see, e.g., Volkmar, pp. 313–17. Were the knowledge of the style and characteristics of the other versions comparable to the knowledge of Latin it would be possible to make similar lists from them.

8   Violet 1, pp. li–lix.

9   "When Do Graecisms Prove that a Latin Text Is a Translation?" *Vruchten van de Uithof: H. A. Brongers FS* (Utrecht: Theologisch Institut, 1984) 100–119. Mussies's work is methodologically meticulous and a paradigm of careful scholarship in this difficult matter. The theory of J. Bloch that no Greek versions existed may thus be regarded and finally refuted ("Was There a Greek Version of the Apocalypse of Ezra?" *JQR* NS 46 [1956] 309–20; cf. idem, "The Ezra-Apocalypse: Was It Written in Hebrew, Greek or Aramaic?" *JQR* NS 48 [1957–58] 279–94).

10   In general, throughout the work we refer to these as "versions."

11   See, e.g., proofs adduced by Box, p. xi; Violet 2, pp. xxix–xxxi; Gry, pp. xviii–xxi; and Klijn, p. 12. We do not give lists of examples, but many may be found in the textual notes.

12   A dissenting opinion is that of Bloch, "Greek Version?" 309–20. He argues that both the Latin and the Syriac versions were translated directly from a Semitic text. See on this M. E. Stone, "Some Remarks on the Textual Criticism of 4 Ezra," *HTR* 60 (1967) 107–15. See sec. 2.3 below.

13   Violet 1. Petermann's Latin translation of the Armenian was printed as Violet 1's last column.

14   Gry.

15   R. P. Blake, "The Georgian Version of Fourth Esdras from the Jerusalem Manuscript," *HTR* 19 (1926) 308–14.

On the basis of lists of examples that he published, he reached the following stemma, illustrating the relationship between these five versions:

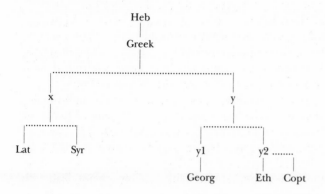

(The hyparchetypes x and y were, presumably, Greek.) In our work we have seen nothing to contradict this basic position.

The particular importance of the publication of the Georgian, therefore, was that it made possible the reconstruction of this bifurcate stemma which facilitates the evaluation of instances of variation between the versions.

The characterization of the affinities of the other versions is a more complex task. It has long been recognized that Arabic1 is close to Latin and Syriac and is somewhat reworked, while Arabic2 and Armenian are extensively reworked texts. Arabic2 has not been studied sufficiently, and its character has not yet been elucidated. Not so the Armenian.[16] It has been shown that the Armenian is based on a reworked form of the Greek text and that, since the Armenian translation was made in the fifth century, the reworking of the Greek text had taken place before that time.[17] The text underlying the reworking, moreover, where it can be recovered, does not show the special readings that characterize the Ethiopic and the Georgian.[18]

1.3. Group 1—The Latin and Syriac Versions

This group of witnesses has been the most influential on Western scholarship on the book, both because of the ready availability of the Latin version through the Vulgate and because Syriac is the best known of the Oriental languages in which 4 Ezra has been preserved. Indeed, in the RSV, for example, readings of the Latin have repeatedly been given inordinate weight, as is pointed out in the textual notes. Nonetheless, it remains true that this is probably the most important group of witnesses to the text of 4 Ezra.[19]

1.3.1. The Latin Version

The Latin version has been most recently edited by Klijn, in 1983.[20] His work is based on that of Violet, which was published in 1910.[21] Violet's edition was in turn deeply indebted to the crucial work of the English scholar R. Bensly. In the Latin text of 4 Ezra as it was included in the manuscripts of the Vulgate, a lacuna was to be found in chapter 7, from verse 35 to verse 106 of the present verse numbering. This passage is present in the other versions and first became known in the West with the publication of S. Ockely's translation of the Arabic1 version in 1711 which included it.[22] Moreover, Ambrose of Milan quoted a Latin form of certain of these missing verses in *De bono mortis*.[23] In 1865, J. Gildemeister discovered that the Latin Codex Sangermanensis of the year 822 C.E. contained the stub of a leaf that had been cut out. The preceding and following pages end and commence with the words preserved in the Vulgate. Gildemeister inferred therefore that the

---

16   M. E. Stone, ed., *The Armenian Version of IV Ezra* (University of Pennsylvania Armenian Texts and Studies 1; Missoula, Mont.: Scholars, 1979).

17   Ibid., ix.

18   Such statements as this are subject, always, to the complexity of the textual information. This is the predominant picture.

19   In our translation it is the "default" text, that to which we have recourse when a determination on the basis of the other versions is impossible.

20   Klijn, *Lateinische Text*.

21   Violet 1.

22   "Appendix," in W. Whiston, *Primitive Christianity Reviv'd: Vol. IV An Account of the Faith of the Two First Centuries* (London: The Author, 1711); separately paginated appendix. Here an English translation of the Arabic is given and in a parallel column an English translation of the Latin text. The Missing Fragment is translated on pp. 51–62, while chaps. 1–2 and 15–16 precede and follow the whole work.

23   See Bensly, *MF*, 74–76, where they are quoted in full.

missing leaf had contained the lost material (the "Missing Fragment").[24] It follows from this fact, as he pointed out, that all Latin manuscripts that lack this passage are dependent on Codex Sangermanensis. Bensly undertook the search for manuscripts that preserved the text of the Missing Fragment and eventually discovered one in Amiens. This he published with an exceptionally fine commentary in 1875.[25]

Bensly set about preparing a critical edition of the Latin text but died while his manuscript was in semifinal form. It was brought to press with an erudite introduction by M. R. James in 1895.[26] Bensly based his text on four manuscripts that by that time had been discovered to contain the Missing Fragment. He knew of two more. It was James, apparently, who divided these manuscripts into two families, one French and the other Spanish,[27] a basic division that has never been challenged.

To this material, one further manuscript was added in a discovery of D. de Bruyne in 1907[28] and included in the text published by Violet in 1910. Violet's text was based on full collations of all the known manuscripts. He published some further new information on the Latin version in the introduction to the second volume of his work, in 1924.[29] There he reported on discoveries relating to this text since 1910. These had also been made by de Bruyne and included yet another complete manuscript and three fragments. Most notable was a fragment from the seventh century.[30]

Since that time, there have been three editions of the Latin text: one by Gry, the second in the Stuttgart edition of the Vulgate, and the third by Klijn.[31] In addition to the manuscripts cited by Violet 1, Klijn includes one new manuscript and a full collation of the last manuscript discovered by de Bruyne. The Prayer of Ezra (8:20–36) is contained in numerous liturgical manuscripts that were collated in the various editions.[32]

The Latin version of 4 Ezra includes two additional chapters at the beginning (chaps. 1–2, called 5 Ezra) and two at the end (chaps. 15–16, called 6 Ezra).[33] These are not found in any other version[34] and are not original to 4 Ezra, though they are interesting works of early Christian or Jewish-Christian writing. They are not dealt with in the present commentary.

The Latin text was widely known and cited by Latin fathers from Tertullian on. The most extensive quotations are to be found in Ambrose of Milan.[35]

In our study we have utilized the Latin column of Violet, together with the edition of Klijn.

1.3.1.1. The Arabic Latin Fragment

An Arabic fragment extant as a marginal note in a Madrid Latin Bible Codex was published by Violet 1 (p. 443) and translated (ibid., pp. 88–95). It was translated from Latin.

---

24 Gildemeister's letter to Bensly is quoted in ibid., 5. In fact, John Palmer, professor of Arabic at the University of Cambridge, had discovered and transcribed the Missing Fragment from a manuscript in Alcala in Spain in November 1826. His transcription was only published after his death, by J. S. Wood, "The Missing Fragment of the Fourth Book of Esdras," *Journal of Philology* 7 (1877) 264–78. Wood's publication, though two years after Bensly's, does not mention the latter.

25 The whole story is related in some detail in the first forty pages of Bensly, *MF*. There are further details of this matter, and particularly about German translation of the Arabic text, in B. M. Metzger, "The 'Lost' Section of II Esdras (= IV Ezra)," *JBL* 76 (1957) 153–56.

26 Bensly.

27 Ibid., xxi.

28 D. de Bruyne, "Un manuscrit complet du IVe livre d'Esdras," *Revue Bénédictine* 24 (1907) 254–57.

29 Violet 2, pp. xiii–xxvii.

30 Ibid., xviii–xix; D. de Bruyne, "Quelques nouveaux documents pour la critique textuelle de l'Apocalypse d'Esdras," *Revue Bénédictine* 32 (1920) 43–47.

31 Gry; R. Weber, ed., *Biblia Sacra Iuxta Vulgatam Versionem* (3d ed.; Stuttgart: Deutsche Bibelgesellschaft, 1969), 2:1931–74; and Klijn, *Lateinische Text.*

32 See the useful overview and listing in Klijn, *Lateinische Text,* 13–17.

33 In the "Spanish" manuscripts, the majority, 5 Ezra is in fact found at the very end of the book, following 6 Ezra.

34 As noted in n. 3 above, one papyrus fragment of the Greek text of 6 Ezra does exist.

35 See the list, arranged chronologically, in Violet 1, p. xlv. The genuineness of the earliest citations by Tertullian and Cyprian has been challenged. The Latin citations were identified by James (Bensly, pp. xxx–xxxvii) and have not been increased in number since his day. They are printed in an appendix by Violet 1, pp. 433–38.

1.3.1.2. The New Greek Fragment

A New Greek fragment, containing the eagle vision, was published by R. Rubinkiewicz in 1976. This too was made from the Latin.[36]

1.3.1.3. The Second Armenian Version

This translation was made from the Vulgate and was included in the first printed Armenian Bible, edited by Oskan Erevancʿi in 1666.[37] It does not contain the Missing Fragment, includes chapters 1–2 and 15–16, and is entitled "Fourth Book of Ezra." All of these are clear signs of its origin from the Vulgate. Samples of its text from a manuscript of 1686 have also been published, and it has been shown that the manuscript was not directly derived from Oskan's printing but that the two come from a common source.[38]

1.3.1.4. The Slavonic Version

A Slavonic version of 4 Ezra exists. It was translated from the Vulgate for the Gennadian Bible, published about 1496. This translation was revised again according to the Latin version for inclusion in the Ostrog revised version of the Slavonic Bible, published in 1581.[39]

1.3.1.4.1. The Second Georgian Version

The second Georgian version was reprinted in the edition of the Georgian apocrypha in 1973.[40] It was translated from the Slavonic version by King Arcril, according to the edition of 1663.[41] It starts on p. 320 with chapter 1 = 5 Ezra. It does not contain the Missing Fragment but includes 6 Ezra.

1.3.1.5. The Hebrew Version

The fact of the existence in manuscript of a translation of the book into Hebrew was published by Y. L. Bialer. The manuscript is preserved in the Sir Isaac Wolfson collection of manuscripts belonging to the Chief Rabbinate of Israel. It is written in an Italian hand dating from the sixteenth century.[42] The manuscript is annotated with technical comments in Latin. Of the manuscript text in general, Bialer comments: "The translation was made from the ancient versions in Greek, Syriac, and Latin."[43] The manuscript contains chapters 1–2 and 15–16 (i.e., 5 Ezra and 6 Ezra). Bialer quotes several variants of the manuscript:

3:1	tricesimo	]	hundredth Ms
	ego Salathiel, qui et Ezras	]	omit Ms
3:14	et demonstrasti—noctu	]	omit Ms
4:11	vas	]	body Ms
5:4	turbatam	]	trumpet Ms
	tubam is the reading of Ms A.		
5:16	Phalthiel	]	Salathiel Ms

The manuscript does not contain the Missing Fragment.[44] It is obvious, therefore, that in fact it was translated from the Vulgate, though only one of the quoted variants corresponds to any reading quoted by Klijn.

---

36 R. Rubinkiewicz, "Un fragment grec du IVe livre d'Esdras (Chapitres XI et XII)," *Le Muséon* 89 (1976) 75–87.

37 Oskan Erevancʿi, ed., *The Bible* (Amsterdam, 1666) 719–44 (in Armenian).

38 M. E. Stone, "Two New Discoveries Touching on the Non-Canonical Ezra Books," *Sion* (Armenian Patriarchate of Jerusalem) 52 (1978) 54–58 (in Armenian). Metzger, "'Lost' Section," 156, does not distinguish between this Armenian version, based upon the Latin, and the old Armenian version (sec. 1.6 below).

39 I owe this information to Dr. Francis Thomson of Antwerp. Some details about these editions may be found in G. Freidhof, *Vergleichende sprachliche Studien zur Gennadius-Bibel (1499) und Ostroger-Bibel (1580/81)* (Frankfurter Abhandlungen zur Slavistik 21; Frankfurt-am-Main: Athenäum, 1972) 11–28.

40 Cʿ. Kʿurcʿikidze, ed., *Dzveli Agʿtʿkʿmis Apokʿripʿebis Kʿartʿuli Versiebi* (Tbilisi: Mecʿniereba, 1970), 1:326–405.

41 Information kindly communicated by B. Outtier.

42 Y. L. Bialer, *Min Hagenazim: Description of Manuscripts and Historical Documents* (Jerusalem: Hechal Shlomo, 1969) (in Hebrew), describes the manuscript on p. 36.

43 Ibid., 38 (my translation—M.E.S.).

44 The examples have been rendered from Bialer's Hebrew (pp. 52–53). The Latin is drawn from the edition of Klijn.

1.3.2. The Syriac Version

The Syriac text was first edited by A. M. Ceriani in 1868. It is to be found in full in a single manuscript, the famous Ambrosian codex of the Peshiṭta.[45] The manuscript is of the sixth or seventh century. The most recent edition, by R. J. Bidawid, also includes collation of portions of 4 Ezra used in Jacobite lectionaries.[46] The Syriac version was translated into German in Violet 1's second column, into French by Gry, and into English by G. H. Box.[47]

1.3.2.1. The Syro-Arabic Version

This name, taken over from Violet, denotes an Arabic version translated from Syriac. A fragment of it, from a Berlin manuscript, was published by Gildemeister in 1877.[48] This fragment was translated into German by Violet 1 and into French by Gry. A full manuscript of this version has since been discovered, no. 589 of Atiya's list of the Arabic manuscripts in St. Catherine's Monastery.[49] A preliminary evaluation made on the basis of sample collations shows that its importance is chiefly as a second witness to the Syriac text, attested as the latter is only in the single Ambrosian codex.

1.3.3. The Arabic1 Version

This version, which is known from two manuscripts, was published by H. Ewald.[50] It had already been translated into English in 1711 by S. Ockley,[51] and a German translation is included in Violet 1's fourth column. Violet rejects views that it was translated from Coptic or from Syriac and concludes that it was translated directly from Greek.[52] The Arabic1 version is reworked to some extent but seems to show an overall affinity with Group 1 of the versions.

1.4. Group 2—The Ethiopic, Georgian, and Coptic Versions

This group is composed of a complete Ethiopic version, a Georgian version that includes about two-thirds of the book, and a small Coptic fragment. The Ethiopic has been known since the early eighteenth century, while the Georgian version was not published until the 1920s. The textual importance of this family was only fully recognized with the publication of the Georgian. At that point, readings that had seemed idiosyncratic in the Ethiopic were corroborated by a second version, which permitted the inference that they had existed in Greek. The new perception enabled Blake to establish the stemma given above (sec. 1.2.1). That stemma must now form the basis of textual work on 4 Ezra.

1.4.1. The Ethiopic Version

The first edition of the Ethiopic version was published by R. Laurence in 1820.[53] The best edition, however, is that of A. Dillmann, published in 1894 on the basis of ten manuscripts.[54] Dillmann knew of other manuscripts, and still further copies have been discovered since, so that a new edition is desirable.[55] Latin translations of the version were made by Laurence in his edition and by Praetorius in A. Hilgenfeld's *Messias Judaeorum*.[56] French translations of the Ethiopic version were made by R. Basset and by Gry,[57] and it is translated into German in Violet 1's third column.

45 A. M. Ceriani, *Monumenta Sacra et Profana e codicibus praesertim Bibliothecae Ambrosianae* (Milan: Ambrosian Library, 1861), 1:99–124; photolithographic reproduction in idem, *Translatio Syra Pescitto Veteris Testamenti ex codice Ambrosiano sec. fere VI photolithographice edita* (Milan: Pogliani, 1876–79). 4 Ezra is on fols. 267r–276v.

46 R. J. Bidawid, ed., "4 Esdras," *The Old Testament in Syriac According to the Peshiṭta Version*, part 4, fasc. 3 (Leiden: Brill, 1973). A preliminary edition of this text was published by Bidawid in *The Old Testament in Syriac According to the Peshiṭta Version. Sample Edition* (Leiden: Brill, 1966).

47 G. H. Box, *The Apocalypse of Ezra* (London: SPCK, 1917).

48 Gildemeister, pp. 40–41; introductory comments on p. 3.

49 M. E. Stone, "A New Manuscript of the Syro-Arabic Version of the Fourth Book of Ezra," *JSJ* 8 (1977) 183–84.

50 H. G. A. Ewald, *Das vierte Ezrabuch: Nach seinem Zeitalter, seinen arabischen Übersetzungen und einer neuen Wiederherstellung* (AKGWG 11; Göttingen: Dieterichs, 1863).

51 See n. 22 above.

52 Violet 1, pp. xxxv–xxxvi.

53 R. Laurence, *Primi Ezrae Libri Versio Aethiopica* (Oxford: Oxford University, 1820). Many remarks on Laurence's edition may be found in C. J. van der Vlis, *Disputatio Critica de Ezrae Libro Apocrypho Vulgo Quarto Dicto* (Amsterdam: Müller, 1839).

54 A. Dillmann, ed., *Biblia Veteris Testamenti Aethiopica*, vol. 5: *Libri Apocryphi* (Berlin: Asher, 1894) 154–92; details of the manuscripts employed on pp. 192–93.

1.4.2. The Georgian Version

The Georgian version was published by Blake in two articles, in 1926 and 1929.[58] It survives in two manuscripts: the Jerusalem codex of the prophets copied in the mid-eleventh century and the Iviron (Mt. Athos) codex copied in 978 C.E. Blake published an excellent study of it, showing the affinity of its *Vorlage* with that of the Ethiopic, its place of origin, linguistic character, and so forth. He ventured the view, earlier advocated by N. Marr, that it was translated from an Armenian that went back to Greek. The comment has been made, however, that if that is the case, the Armenian text underlying the Georgian was quite different from the extant Armenian version and has left no discernible trace in the Armenian tradition.[59] This text was reprinted in Tbilisi in 1970.[60] That edition presents the text of 4 Ezra in two columns. In one column is the text that Blake published, while in the second column another Georgian version, translated from the Vulgate, is given (see sec. 1.3.1.4.1 above).[61] A study of the Georgian version of 4 Ezra is given in the second volume of the same work.[62] There, K'urc'ikidze suggests that the Georgian was translated from a Semitic *Vorlage*, shared with the Ethiopic, a view with which B. Outtier concurs. If so, it must be remarked that this view probably reflects the fact that 4 Ezra was originally written in Hebrew. Since Georgian and Ethiopic share a hyparchetype, it would still seem most reasonable to assume that this was a Greek text form. Blake's determination of the textual relationships is unassailable and is confirmed by our own studies.[63] Blake's Latin translation was reprinted by Gry.

1.4.3. The Coptic Version

A papyrus fragment, containing parts of 13:29–46 in Sahidic Coptic, was published in 1904.[64] This papyrus was apparently written in Egypt in the sixth to the eighth century C.E. and was translated into Coptic from Greek. Its affiliation with the Group 2 versions was established by Blake on the basis of another document. This is a Coptic ostrakon preserving the names of extracanonical books, including 4 Ezra. In the title the name Salathiel appears as "Southiel," a form related to the spelling of this name in Ethiopic (Sutā'ēl) and Georgian (Sut'iel or Syt'iel).[65] A German translation is given in Violet 1.

1.5. The Arabic2 Version

Another full Arabic version is represented by one complete manuscript, an extract, and a single fragment. The complete manuscript and the extract were published by Gildemeister in 1877,[66] while Violet discovered and utilized the fragment.[67] Violet is of the opinion, which we find no reason to contradict, that this translation was made from Greek. It had been assumed by H. Gunkel that it was based on a Greek translation from Hebrew independent of the Greek translation upon which all the other versions had been made. The reason for this was that Gunkel observed three readings in which he thought that Arabic2 represented a different translation of Hebrew from the other versions, in 5:34, in 8:23, and in 14:3.[68] He assumed that this second translation into

---

55 E. Isaac has communicated a copy to me of a manuscript in the Princeton University library.

56 Hilgenfeld, pp. 262–322.

57 R. Basset, *Les apocryphes éthiopiens,* no. 9 (Paris: Bibliothèque de la haute science, 1899) 1–111; Gry, in his third column.

58 R. P. Blake, "Georgian Version"; and idem, "The Georgian Text of Fourth Esdras from the Athos Manuscript," *HTR* 22 (1929) 57–105.

59 See Stone, *Armenian Version,* 41.

60 K'urc'ikidze, *Dzveli,* 1:326–405.

61 See sec. 1.3.1.4.1 above. In the course of 4 Ezra, where the Old Georgian had a lacuna, the version deriving from the Vulgate is printed alone. The Missing Fragment is included in the Old Georgian (pp. 363–67).

62 C'. K'urc'ikidze, ed., *Dzveli Ag't'k'mis Apok'rip'ebis*

K'art'uli Versiebi (Tbilisi: Mec'niereba, 1973), 2:270–308. See also Outtier's review of this book in *Bedi Kartlisa* 33 (1975) 380–83.

63 We are greatly indebted to Outtier, who provided us with much helpful information about the Georgian version.

64 J. Leipoldt, "Ein säidisches Bruchstück des vierten Esrabuches," *ZfÄS* 41 (1904) 138–40.

65 Blake, "Georgian Version," 310. The ostrakon, numbered BP 1069, was discussed by W. E. Crum, "The Literary Material," *The Metropolitan Museum of Art Egyptian Expedition: The Monastery of Epiphanius at Thebes* (by H. E. Winlock; New York, 1923; repr., Milan: Ristampe Anastatica, 1977), 1:197.

66 Gildemeister, published in 1877.

67 Violet 1, p. xxxvi.

68 Gunkel, p. 333.

Greek was conflated with the first one, on which the other versions were based, and that this conflated Greek version formed the *Vorlage* of Arabic2. We concur with Violet's view that these readings are not adequate to support this hypothesis.[69] The Arabic2 version was translated into Latin by Gildemeister and into German by Violet 1.

1.6. The Armenian Version

The Armenian version was first published in the Armenian Bible of J. Zohrabian in 1805.[70] This text was reprinted by S. Yovsēpʻiancʻ in 1896 and translated into English in 1900.[71] Some German extracts had been published by H. Ewald in 1865, and a Latin translation was made by J. Petermann and published by Hilgenfeld in *Messias Judaeorum*.[72] This Latin translation was checked by F. Conybeare and printed by Violet 1 in his sixth column. A critical edition with a new English translation was published in 1979 by M. E. Stone on the basis of twenty-two manuscripts.[73] Six further manuscripts have recently become known, and preliminary collations of them show that they are unlikely to upset the stemma or to affect the edited text in a major way. The Armenian version is typified by extensive reworking and particularly by some long additions. It seems likely that the reworkings existed for the most part in its Greek *Vorlage* and that the additions, while not preserving parts of 4 Ezra proper, most likely preserve some fragments of ancient Ezra literature.[74] It is not very probable, however, that the special readings of Armenian preserve original Greek readings of 4 Ezra.

1.7. Assessment of the Textual Situation

It is clear, then, that the textual character of 4 Ezra is rather complex. First, the fact that all of the surviving versions are either secondary or tertiary to the Greek means that it is almost impossible in most instances to reconstruct the Hebrew text. Second, the Greek text is also often lost beyond recovery, even as to its sense, let alone its exact wording. This is particularly so in instances in which there is considerable diversity among the versions.

In the present work the following principles have been applied in the establishment of the translation and in the preparation of the textual notes:

a. The translation follows the RSV except in instances in which the editor's judgment is that another reading is preferable. Such judgments are made on textual grounds alone, not on those of style, prosody, word choice, or the like. The editor has not been conservative in departing from the RSV and, particularly, has given greater weight to the readings of Ethiopic and Georgian than did the translators of the RSV.

b. The textual notes remark on all instances in which one of the following conditions is fulfilled: first, that a reading or readings of the Greek or the Hebrew can be reconstructed from the surviving textual evidence; second, that the readings exhibited by the versions witness to possible relationships between them; third, that the reading of a particular version is of some intrinsic interest. Other idiosyncratic readings of the individual versions are not mentioned. The textual notes are therefore only positive and not negative witness.

69   Violet 1, p. xxxvii.
70   J. Zohrabian, *The Scriptures of the Old and New Testaments* (Venice: Monastery of St. Lazarus, 1805); separately numbered appendix following the New Testament (in Armenian).
71   S. Yovsēpʻiancʻ, *Ankanon Girkʻ Hin Ktakaranacʻ* (Venice: Monastery of St. Lazarus, 1896) 251–99 (in Armenian); and J. Issaverdens, trans., *The Uncanonical Writings of the Old Testament Found in the Armenian Mss. of the Library of St. Lazarus* (1901; 2d ed. 1934; Venice: Monastery of St. Lazarus) 364–501.
72   H. G. A. Ewald, *Nachrichten von der Gesellschaft der Wissenschaften zu Göttingen* (1865) 504–16, cited by B. Sarghissian, *Studies on the Apocryphal Books of the Old Testament* (Venice: St. Lazarus, 1898) 325 n. 5 (in Armenian); Hilgenfeld, pp. 378–433. For the further history of the version, see Stone, *Armenian Version*, 32.

73   Stone, *Armenian Version*.
74   Ibid., ix. M. E. Stone, "Some Features of the Armenian Version of 4 Ezra," *Le Muséon* 79 (1966) 387–400, deals with some of the techniques of this version and, on pp. 395–400, analyzes one of these expansionary passages in detail. Other hypotheses, such as that of Preuschen, can be regarded as superseded in this matter; see already Violet 2, pp. xxv–xxvii.

c. We have excluded from the textual notes all of the very many speculations of earlier scholars about reconstructions of the Greek or the Hebrew texts unless such reconstructions are based on clear textual grounds such as graphic error or mistranslation. We have also excluded quotations from the versions given in various ancient writings, such as Ambrose's quotations from the Latin.

In a book with as complicated a textual history as 4 Ezra there will always be latitude for difference of opinion and judgment in matters of text. In our view, it is essential to bear in mind that, given the situation of the versions, this latitude is broader here than it is in the case of other, more directly attested works.

2.0. Section 2: Date, Place, and Original Language

2.1. Date

The only external evidence for the date of 4 Ezra is provided by the citations from the book. Some scholars have considered the oldest citation to be in the *Epistle of Barnabas.* If this were certain, it would prove that 4 Ezra was in existence at the very beginning of the second century C.E. or even in the last years of the first century. That citation has been queried, however, and the oldest indubitable citation is that by Clement of Alexandria. Clement is thought to have written his *Stromateis* toward the very end of the second century C.E., and 4 Ezra is definitely cited in that composition (see sec. 1.1 above). Consequently, we can definitely assume that 4 Ezra existed and had been translated into Greek by about the year 190 C.E. The early citations by Tertullian and Cyprian in Latin have also been questioned, and the oldest universally accepted citations in Latin are by

Ambrose of Milan in the fourth century C.E..

There is no other external evidence for the date of the book;[75] consequently, internal evidence must be used for the dating. The use of internal evidence is burdened by the pseudepigraphic framework of the book and by its apocalyptic literary characteristics.

Attempts were made in the past to date the book internally, using as indications of date the various "signs" of the end foretold in the angelic oracles. This was done by identifying certain of them with known historical events. Thus, the unexpected ruler (5:6) was identified with a historical ruler.[76] Similarly, the splits of the earth mentioned in 5:8 have been thought to be inspired by the earthquake of 31 B.C.E. or the eruption of Mt. Vesuvius in 79 C.E.[77] Now, admittedly, in 9:1–2, the angel tells Ezra: "Measure carefully in your mind, and when you will see that a certain part of the predicted signs are past, then you will know that it is the very time when the Most High is about to visit the world which he has made." However, the actual signs listed in 9:3 are very general, and the specific events predicted in the other lists earlier in the book were part of the traditional repertoire of happenings that formed the "messianic woes," so it is difficult to interpret them as referring to particular historical events.[78]

Another piece of evidence that is sometimes considered is the date given in the opening verse. The book is dated to "the thirtieth year after the destruction of our city" (3:1). Yet an analysis of the possible exegeses of this

---

75 The absence of the book from among the Dead Sea Scrolls does not prove that it is later than the destruction of Qumran.

76 Most frequently Herod (A. von Gutschmid, "Die Apokalypse des Esra und ihre spätern Bearbeitungen," *ZfWT* 3 [1860] 78) or Octavian (Kabisch, p. 154; and A. Hilgenfeld, *Die jüdische Apokalyptik in ihrer geschichtlichen Entwickelung* [Jenna: Mauke, 1857] 237).

77 E. de Faye, *Les apocalypses juives* (Paris: Fischbacher, 1892) 44–45 (earthquake); J. Wellhausen, "Zur apokalyptischen Literatur," *Skizzen und Vorarbeiten*

(Berlin: Reimer, 1899) 6:247 (Vesuvius); and Box, p. xxxi. J. J. Kneucker, *Das Buch Baruch* (Leipzig: Brockhaus, 1879) 53, considers 6:29 to refer to an earthquake in Rome.

78 The Esau-Jacob passage (6:7–10) has also been used in this way by identifying Esau as various historical individuals; see M. E. Stone, *Features of the Eschatology of IV Ezra* (diss., Harvard University, 1965; HSM 35; Atlanta: Scholars, 1989) 6–7. This seems to be unjustified, and Esau is very clearly the kingdom of Rome, which will be followed by the kingdom of Israel; see Commentary.

date shows that it is best taken as derived typologically from Ezek 1:1. At most, it can be said that in general terms it fits the date arrived at by other considerations.[79]

The soundest evidence for dating the book is garnered from two different arguments. The first, a general one, is that it seems inconceivable that the book was written before the destruction of Jerusalem by Titus in the year 70 C.E. This event is absolutely central to the author's thought.[80] This bespeaks a date after the year 70 C.E. When combined with the quotation by Clement of Alexandria, it enables us to say that the book was written between 70 C.E. and the end of the second century.

One passage, however, enables us to narrow this down to a rather precise dating for the book.[81] This is Vision 5 (chaps. 11–12). This dream of the eagle that rose from the sea, of its heads, of its wings and little wings and their doings, and of the destruction of the eagle by a lion, is a detailed historical forecast. In it, history is presented as a total, schematic process, and the author's interest is not academic but to know exactly where he stands in the historical process. For scholars, moreover, such historical recitals, which are common in apocalypses of the Second Temple period, are particularly important for dating the works. Although, in his pseudepigraphic *persona,* the author can relate events actually past as if they were future, there is a point at which he is forced to abandon the "prediction" of the actual course of past events and really to foretell future happenings. That is the point of time at which he lived. Thus the identification of it will yield an indication of the actual date of the author.

This technique has been used extensively in study of 4 Ezra and in particular of the eagle vision. The central point in any unraveling of the symbolism is the identification of the three heads, for the end of history is expected during the days of the third head. The wings and little wings are identified with various emperors, and the second wing, which ruled longest, is Augustus. The most persuasive theory takes the heads as Vespasian, Titus, and Domitian, for the details given admirably suit contemporary knowledge of these emperors. The book was thus composed in the time of Domitian (81–96 C.E.), probably in the latter part of his reign, when his cruelty and oppression reached unprecedented heights.[82]

A date such as this would fit with the other considerations mentioned above. It is within the broad range of the "thirtieth year," on the one hand, and close enough to the destruction of the Second Temple, on the other.

2.2. Place of Composition

There is no external evidence relating to the place of composition of the book. The only passages that provide any internal evidence are 3:1 and 3:29; cf. 12:40 and 12:50. The first refers to Ezra's being in Babylon and the second to his arrival there. Some scholars have maintained that from these passages we may infer that the author was in Rome, since Babylon corresponded to Rome, just as Ezra corresponded to the author. It may be questioned, however, whether the intent of this pseudepigraphic framework is to provide a cryptic one-for-one key to the author's actual situation.[83] If not, then the book's intimate connection with *2 Apocalypse of Baruch,* as well as its clearly Hebrew *Vorlage,* would favor an origin from the land of Israel. This remains speculative nonetheless.

2.3. Original Language

The opinion of Klijn is that 4 Ezra was written in Hebrew with some Aramaic influence, and he adduces a number of examples to prove the point.[84] Not all of his examples are convincing, thus the supposed reading of

79 See 3:1 Commentary for a detailed analysis of the possible ways of reading this verse.

80 This point was already made by E. Schürer, *Geschichte des jüdischen Volkes im Zeitalter Jesu Christi* (4th ed.; Leipzig: Hinrichs, 1909), 3:323. It seems self-evident, but as can be seen from the opinions cited above, other views were predominant particularly in the nineteenth century.

81 Some of the sentences in this paragraph and the next are drawn from M. E. Stone's essay on 4 Ezra in *The Books of the Bible* (ed. B. W. Anderson; New York: Scribner's, 1989) 2:29.

82 The various views and their proponents are set forth in detail in 12:10–36 Function and Content. They will not be repeated here. Possible linguistic criteria touching on the date of composition are discussed in Stone, *Features,* 10–11. Although not in themselves conclusive, they are not incompatible with the date proposed here.

83 See 3:1 Commentary for a detailed discussion.

84 Klijn, *Lateinische Text,* 9–10.

gzr dyn, which he has taken over from Violet and Gunkel. Violet, in his commentary, following on many occasions the suggestions of Box, proposed numerous Hebrew retroversions, most of which should be regarded with some suspicion. In the introduction to his translation, however, he does discuss the question of the Semitic original in some detail.[85] The only issue at stake in scholarship today is whether the original was in Hebrew or Aramaic. The latter position was defended valiantly by Gry throughout his Commentary.[86] Critiques of Gry, however, have shown this view to be without real basis and that all of the decisive examples that are not misconstructions are more easily explained by the theory of a Hebrew original.[87]

The Hebrew theory was persuasively urged by J. Wellhausen and Gunkel and has been supported by numerous other scholars.[88] Violet has presented an extensive list of the Hebraistic syntactic, semantic, lexical, and idiomatic usages in the book. He drew this list from the work of Wellhausen and added some further examples to it.[89] To this he adjoins a list of instances in which he detects corruptions or mistranslations that took place at the Hebrew level.[90] Doubtlessly, some of these examples can be disputed, and others may be added, but the preponderance of evidence in favor of the Hebrew original is clear.[91]

Our growing familiarity with the Hebrew language of this period, which is due to the investigation of the Dead Sea Scrolls, shows that Hebrew was used as a literary language and that it was under considerable Aramaic influence.[92]

3.0. Section 3: Chief Critical Issues

3.1. The Chief Critical Issues

The chief critical issues that have been raised in connection with the book can be divided into two. The first issue is that of literary unity: Is the book substantially a literary unity, the work of one author, who may have utilized diverse sources but whose individual hand may be discerned throughout? Alternatively, did a redactor weave together sources that were clearly independent in origin and can easily be unraveled? This issue dominated scholarship in the latter part of the nineteenth century and well into the twentieth. The second central issue, raised in recent decades, is the question of the overall purpose and meaning of the book and the relationship between its various parts. This problem could be raised only because the question of literary unity had been resolved in favor of unity. Once the book became treated as a work written by a single author, the questions of purpose, overall role, and function could be asked.

In this section we shall discuss the ideas of representative proponents of the various views in order to gain insight into these differing positions and their implications for the study of 4 Ezra.

3.1.1. The Source Theory

In the latter part of the nineteenth century, the literary-critical or source-critical school in biblical studies, associated particularly with the names of Graf and Well-

---

85 Violet 2, pp. xxxi–xxxix.

86 Gry, passim.

87 See Stone, "Some Remarks," 109–11, for detailed criticism.

88 Wellhausen, *Skizzen,* 234–41; and Gunkel, p. 333. It was first urged in 1633 by J. Morinus, *Exerc. bibl.,* 225 *(non vidi).* For the history of this view, see Violet 2, p. xxxi.

89 Violet 2, pp. xxxiv–xxxvii.

90 Violet 2, p. xxxviii.

91 In Stone, "Some Remarks," 111–12, we assessed the claims made by Gunkel and some others that evidence can be isolated of more than one translation from Hebrew into Greek and concluded that at most one could talk of glosses. Today our position would be even more reserved. We would no longer claim the two additional examples we then suggested (6:20;

7:28) and consider that all the instances adduced are most easily explained in other ways. The only example with any weight is a variant of *la'ed* and *le'ad* in 8:23, where one of the readings is supported by the citation in *Apost. Const.;* see further, textual notes there.

92 We would be reserved about some of Klijn's examples of Aramaisms; see Klijn, *Lateinische Text,* 9–11.

hausen, dominated the field. In 1889, R. Kabisch published a small book in which he made the first thoroughgoing attempt to apply such methods to the study of 4 Ezra.[93] He was followed by a number of scholars, of whom the most influential was the Englishman G. H. Box in his major commentary on 4 Ezra written in 1912. Box also published his views in the section on 4 Ezra in R. H. Charles's authoritative *The Apocrypha and Pseudepigrapha of the Old Testament*.[94]

Box's investigations led him to conclude that 4 Ezra was put together by a redactor who used various sources:

S: *A Salathiel apocalypse* in 3:1–31; 4:1–51; 5:13b–6:10; 6:30—7:25; 7:45—8:62; 9:15—10:57.

E: *An Ezra apocalypse* in 4:52—5:13a; 6:13–29; 7:26–44; 8:63—9:12.

A: *The eagle vision*, chaps. 11–12, with revisions by the redactor.

M: *The son of man vision* in chap. 13, with much revision by the redactor (see below).

E2: *Another Ezra piece* included in 14:1–17a; 14:18–27; 14:36–47.

The redactor himself (R) composed 4:52; 6:11–12; 6:29; 10:58–59; 12:49–51; and 14:49–50, which are links tying the aforesaid sources together. In addition, R was responsible for numerous adjustments within the text of the sources. First, some parts of the S source have been moved to different places: 5:14–15; 12:40–48; 13:57–58; and 14:28–35. Second, R has made long insertions: 3:32–36; 7:26–44; 8:63—9:12; and 13:13b–24. Third, R executed small revisions in Visions 4–7, including those in 10:45; 10:46; 11:12; 11:20; 12:8; 12:9; 12:14; 12:15; 12:26b-28; 12:32; 12:34; 12:39; 13:26b; 13:29–32; 13:36; 13:48; and 13:52. Finally, R is responsible for a number of further minor adjustments in the book in 3:1; 4:1; 6:20; 6:24; 14:8b; 14:17b; and 14:28.[95]

This obviously very complex theory clearly reflected scholars' confidence that they could draw very fine distinctions within the book. Box was so sure of his results that, in printing the translation of 4 Ezra in *The Ezra-Apocalypse*, he utilized different typefaces for the various sources. What were the means by which these delicate distinctions were drawn?

One criterion was literary. The argument commenced from "I, Salathiel, who am also Ezra" in 3:1, an identification that is strange historically and that was taken to be the way the redactor incorporated the Salathiel material (S) into the Ezra framework.[96] Having thus "established" the existence of S, Box pronounced on its extent: it included Visions 1–4, although some other sources and some redactional touches were incorporated into those Visions. He then proceeded to inquire whether Visions 5–7 were also "embodied" in the work by R. For Vision 5 he argued, first, that it has the appearance of an independent work and, second, that its eschatological conceptions differ radically from those of S. Consequently it was incorporated by R, who attempted to harmonize the differing views. The same argument is applied to Vision 6, while Vision 7, tied to Ezra in Babylon, cannot be thought to be the work of the author of a Salathiel apocalypse which must have had a different historical setting.[97] Box's final step was to argue that the four predictions of messianic woes and eschatological wonders, 4:52—5:13a; 6:11–29; 7:26–44; and 8:63—9:12, being of traditional character, bear clear signs of insertion into their present contexts and so were later additions by R rather than having been set in the Salathiel document originally by S. Having drawn all of these distinctions, he proceeded to assume that all points at which the sources other than S appeared to bear a resemblance to the ideas of S, or vice versa, were redactional glosses or adjustments.

This analysis produced the results described above and reduced the book to a mosaic of five sources. The work of the redactor was understood as completely secondary and technical. This analysis by Box was based on that

---

93 Kabisch.
94 (Oxford: Oxford University, 1913), 2:549–53. Similar in most details is the solution proposed by de Faye, *Les apocalypses juives*, 155–65. A like methodology was employed by C. C. Torrey, *The Apocryphal Literature: A Brief Introduction* (New Haven: Yale University, 1945) 116–21, but his results differ in many details.
95 Box, pp. xxvi–xxvii; *APOT*, 2:551.
96 Box, p. xxii.
97 Ibid., xxiii–xxv.

performed by Kabisch and agreed with it in almost every detail.

It will be observed that literary criteria play a very minor role in the drawing of the distinctions by Box. His argument turns chiefly on the question of the compatibility of the eschatological conceptions in the different parts of the book. Claiming that the conceptions of one type are contradictory to those of another type, Box drew distinctions between various source documents. Moreover, he then proceeded to excise, as editorial reworkings, passages and phrases in which the text of the newly distinguished sources did not seem to maintain those distinctions or to exhibit that consistency which he saw so clearly.[98]

The critique of this theory proceeded along a number of clear lines. W. Sanday stated the chief of them succinctly: "I believe that there is a danger of looking for too much logical symmetry and consistency, which is more to be expected in the literature of Greece and the West than in that of the East, and especially in subject matter of this kind, where many heterogeneous details were handed down by tradition and not fitted into a coherent scheme. . . . I doubt if he [i.e., Box—M.E.S.] would have had recourse to the hypothesis of interpolation if he had not been put on the track of a 'Salathiel-Apocalypse' at the outset."[99]

Sanday acutely put his finger on two chief weaknesses of Box's argument. The only literary criterion that Box employs is the phrase in 3:1. That is obscure and open to many explanations.[100] To extract a whole source from it is far from necessary. Even more, the "consistency" of the eschatological thinking served Box as a criterion for the drawing of distinctions, as Sanday aptly remarked. Yet this criterion has been found wanting, both on such general grounds as Sanday has adduced and in particulars.[101] It may be remarked in conclusion that the very complexity but consistency of the sources "discovered" stand in stark contrast to the unintelligent and quite inconsistent work of the redactor.

As so often happens, however, there are important things to be learned from the literary-critical analysis. In particular, it highlighted real differences in the book: the contrast between the first four visions and the fifth, sixth, and seventh ones. This is an inevitable fact of the book and one that all theories in the future had to take into consideration.[102]

In recent years, this consideration led W. Harnisch to propose the view that Visions 5 and 6 were introduced into the book at a later time. The motive for this lay in the results of his analysis of the nature of the dialogue and of its dynamic, into which Visions 5 and 6 did not fit.[103] His arguments have been cogently refuted.[104]

---

98 A detailed analysis of this procedure, as applied in the eagle vision (Vision 5), may be found in M. E. Stone, "The Concept of the Messiah in 4 Ezra," *Religions in Antiquity: E. R. Goodenough Memorial* (ed. J. Neusner; SHR 14; Leiden: Brill, 1968) 298–300.

99 "Prefatory Note," in Box, p. 6*.

100 On the Ezra-Salathiel question, see 3:1 Commentary.

101 See the extensive discussion in Stone, *Features*, 12–21. The chief aspects of this view are also refuted in detail by Keulers, pp. 46–55. Further criticisms are expressed by A. P. Hayman, "The Problem of Pseudonymity in the Ezra Apocalypse," *JSJ* 6 (1975) 48. In 7:26–44 Function and Content and in Excursus on Natural Order, pp. 102–5, alternative ways of viewing such "inconsistencies" are proposed. See for analysis of a single, supposedly inconsistent concept, M. E. Stone, "Coherence and Inconsistency in the Apocalypses: The Case of 'the End' in 4 Ezra," *JBL* 102 (1983) 229–43.

102 Vagany, pp. 10–11, suggests that, although Visions 5–6 are not demanded strictly by the contents of the book, since they form a repetition of ideas presented earlier in it, the very contemplation of messianic grandeur was a comfort for the seer's soul.

103 See W. Harnisch, "Der Prophet als Widerpart und Zeuge der Offenbarung: Erwägungen zur Interdependenz von Form und Sache im 4.Buch Esra," *Apocalypticism in the Mediterranean World and the Near East* (ed. D. Hellholm; Tübingen: Mohr, 1983), esp. 468–70. E. P. Sanders, *Paul and Palestinian Judaism* (London: SCM, 1977) 409–18, presents a similar argument, even less rigorously. Noting that the sixth and seventh visions do not fit his analysis of the purpose of the book, he regards these as a "saving" appendix to make 4 Ezra more palatable in Jewish circles. Yet his basic analysis is quite one-sided. Virtually ignoring Visions 1 and 2, he concentrates on Vision 3, to argue that the whole purpose of the book is the proclamation of an extreme, rigorous divine demand for obedience. Our difference from his views is profound: it chiefly stems from our overall attitude to the book in which we assess the views both of Ezra and of the angel as forming part of its purpose. This purpose is expressed in the

3.2. Theories of Literary Unity

There are a number of theories that maintain the literary unity of the book. In the wake of such theories, the issues arising from that unity come to the fore. The first of these is the relationship between Visions 1–4 and the last three visions. Although rejecting the "mosaic" theory of composition, scholars who regard the book as a literary unity have to face the question of the relationship between these different parts of the book. Again, the character of the dialogues in the first three visions with their complicated train of thought and their apparent repetitions and circularity must be understood. In recent decades attempts have been made to explain these difficulties in the light of specific concepts of the overall structure and purpose of the book. Criteria of structure and purpose have been added to those of coherence and consistency previously employed.

3.2.1. Gunkel

The attack on Kabisch's source-critical theory was opened within two years of the publication of his book. A review of Kabisch's study[105] was published by H. Gunkel, who was to translate and comment on 4 Ezra in E. Kautzsch's *Die Apokryphen und Pseudepigraphen des alten Testaments*.[106] He developed and refined his ideas in the introduction to his German translation and commentary.[107] Already in his review of Kabisch, Gunkel recognized the distinctions drawn between the major parts of the book. However, he was not of the view that the differences were to be explained by their stemming from different authors or source documents. Instead,

Gunkel, like others after him, argued that these obvious differences were not such as to impose a source theory. Indeed, he observed, the incompatibilities perceived by Kabisch between the thought of the different parts of the book were engendered largely by misinterpretations by Kabisch.[108] Gunkel also introduced a new criterion into the analysis of the book, a psychological approach to the author. The author's deep and complex nature, he claimed, engendered thought that was not always consistent. Therefore, for "contradictions" in ideas to be accepted as crucial for distinguishing documents they must be not only formal but such as the sensitive critic feels to be truly incompatible.[109] "According to Gunkel, the splitting of the author's being into the man and the angel . . . corresponds with his inner life."[110] In addition, Gunkel greatly stressed the role of oral traditions in the composition of the book and the author's use of such source traditions. This he thought to be particularly the case in the area of eschatology.[111] Moreover, he points to the anomaly inherent in the concept of a redactor, subtle enough to touch up small details in extensive passages, yet so inept as to leave in the book those blatant contradictions so readily seen by Kabisch.[112]

By means of this complex of three arguments, Gunkel succeeded in casting considerable doubt on the source analysis of Kabisch and those who followed him. The attack, to recapitulate, proceeded at three levels, providing alternative evaluations of the "contradictions" within the author's thought, perceived to be so compelling by Kabisch. First, many of the contrasts and contradictions were held to be based upon misinterpre-

---

dynamic of the book's development rather than in its supposed proclamation of theological ideas. Our views are set forth in detail in the next section of this Introduction.

104 E. Brandenburger, *Die Verborgenheit Gottes im Weltgeschehen* (ATANT 68; Zurich: Theologischer Verlag, 1981) 92–104.

105 In *TLZ* 16.1 (1891) 5–11.

106 Gunkel, 2:331–401.

107 See n. 106 above.

108 *TLZ* 16.1, 7–9. Cf. his discussions of 3:7 and 7:32 on p. 10 for particularly striking instances.

109 Ibid., 7, 10–11; see in greater detail in Gunkel, pp. 335–48.

110 Hayman, "Pseudonymity," 49. L. Hartman, *Prophecy Interpreted* (Coniectanea Biblica, NT Series, 1; Lund: Gleerup, 1966) 33, holds the same view as Gunkel on

this point.

111 Gunkel, p. 343 and particularly p. 348. Cf. also C. Clemen, "Die Zusammensetzung des Buches Henoch, der Apokalypse des Baruch und des vierten Buches Esra," *TSK* 71 (1898) 211–12. Much of his treatment of 4 Ezra is devoted to a critique of the theories of Kabisch and de Faye.

112 Gunkel's commentary on 4 Ezra was also published in a more popular form as *Der Prophet Esra* (Tübingen: Mohr, 1900).

tation of the text and the application to it of inappropriate categories. Second, the author used traditional sources, the incorporation of which has engendered some unevennesses. Third, the author's own psychological makeup is complex, leading to a complex and at times repetitive or contradictory composition.

3.2.2. Some Subsequent Views

Most subsequent scholars have followed Gunkel's views on the issue of literary unity. Different explanations or analyses have attempted to reinforce or refine Gunkel's arguments, but the methodological basis of his analysis has not been refuted.[113] In particular, the problem of inconsistencies has been attacked in various ways. Gunkel's idea of the utilization of "oral" and "traditional" sources was developed by J. Keulers, who employed his own "two eschatology" formulation to explain many of the eschatological incompatibilities (Keulers, pp. 47–51).[114] This theory is laid out in 7:26–44 Function and Content and is evaluated there. A view of "associational complexes" was developed by M. E. Stone, the idea that although there were not two opposed, separate eschatologies, one national and the other universal, as Keulers had proposed, there were two major complexes of eschatological ideas, one associated with the messianic kingdom and the other with the day of judgment. When context or argument required parts of one idea, then other aspects of it tended to be introduced by association.[115] In a different but associated argument, Stone showed how one specific term, "the end," which seemed to denote different events in various places in the book, in fact meant "the crucial event of the eschatological process" and that which event this was depended on context and association. Such arguments provide a way of understanding the thought of this author, thought that is neither consistent nor incoherent.[116]

3.3. Brandenburger

In an article published in 1929, W. Mundle asserted that previous scholars had ignored the position held by the angel. Mundle was perhaps overzealous in redressing the balance, but his observation pioneered the path followed recently by E. Brandenburger and W. Harnisch.[117]

These two German scholars have made the most consistent attempt to reach an overall understanding of the thought and purpose of the book. We have noted above that Harnisch was led by his analysis of the book to the view that Visions 5 and 6 were a later addition, a view strongly opposed by Brandenburger.[118] In spite of these differences, however, the basic orientation of these two scholars is very similar. Their analyses, most recently epitomized in Brandenburger's *Die Verborgenheit Gottes im Weltgeschehen*, have proved very controversial.[119]

---

113 Gunkel, *TLZ* 16.1, 11. See, however, the comments of Harnisch, "Prophet," 461–63. Brandenburger, in particular, has rejected energetically Gunkel's psychological approach to the tensions within the book; see Brandenburger, *Verborgenheit*, 33–36. His view of the theological confrontation and the firm, unmoving ideas of the author leads him to resist any development within Ezra's personality or any tensions (cf. pp. 85–87). All the tensions within the book he describes repeatedly as "literary." His view is criticized below.

114 J. Keulers held a modified Gunkel position. He argued against Box on Box's own grounds (Keulers, pp. 45–55).

115 Stone, *Features*, 21–33.

116 Stone, "Coherence and Inconsistency."

117 W. Mundle, "Das religiöse Problem des IV. Esrabuches," *ZAW* NF 6 (1929) 222–49. The observations that formed such a powerful starting point for Brandenburger and Harnisch are almost incidental in his article; see pp. 235–36.

118 Brandenburger, *Verborgenheit*, 92–104.

119 The basic position was formulated by Brandenburger in *Adam und Christus: Exegetisch-religionsgeschichtliche Untersuchung zu Röm. 5:12–21 (1. Kor. 15)* (WMANT 7; Neukirchen: Neukirchener, 1962). His analysis there was focused on the twin issues of the origins of sin and the origins of death, as relevant to the passage in Romans. The points about the roles of Ezra and the angel that later became so influential in his and Harnisch's thought are set forth as an exegetical principle briefly on pp. 29–30. In this treatment, Brandenburger paid no attention at all to the last three visions or to overall structural issues; indeed, Visions 4–7 are not discussed at all. His work stressed theological issues: original sin or inherited evil inclination, death as decreed punishment, physical death and eternal death, and so forth (pp. 15–67). His views were taken up and developed by W. Harnisch in *Verhängnis und Verheißung der Geschichte*. (The very title of Harnisch's book is dependent on Brandenburger's formulation in *Adam und Christus*. The word *Verhängnis* occurs there throughout the relevant pages, while the *Verheißung*

As their point of departure both Brandenburger and Harnisch take the idea that the book is the work of one author, though both readily admit the possibility that he used preexisting sources. (Harnisch, of course, considers the work to be Visions 1–4 together with Vision 7.) What is more important, however, are the criteria by which attempts to interpret the book as a whole are evaluated. In the first place, any intepretation offered must account for the book as a literary whole and expressing the author's intent and ideas.[120] Moreover, Brandenburger and Harnisch are much concerned to account for the disputatious dialogue in Visions 1–3. They rightly observe that the views forwarded by the angel in the first three visions, which Ezra resists there, are the very ideas that Ezra embodies in his *Abschiedsrede* in 14:28–36. Consequently, they question how the author understood the role of Ezra in the first three visions, both the arguments forwarded by him and his rejection of the angelic predictions. Moreover, observing the breaking off of the dialogue between Ezra and the angel in Vision 4, Brandenburger demands that any theory presented explain this as well as the relevance of the two dream visions to the *Problematik* presented by Visions 1–3 together with Vision 7.[121]

It was the realization of the continuity between the views proposed by the angel in Visions 1–3 and those preached by Ezra in Vision 7 that provided the central key for the development of this approach. Brandenburger annd Harnisch concluded that the author was eager to promote the angel's point of view: he set his opinions in the angel's mouth and not in that of Ezra. In other words, as Brandenburger put it, the problem is one of the "myself" of the book.[122]

What then, we may be led to ask, are the views that Ezra urges in Visions 1–3 in opposition to those of the angel? Where did they originate? There is some difference of emphasis between Brandenburger and Harnisch in answering this question. Harnisch goes so far as to regard these as views actively propagated by particular sects or groups within Jewish society of the day, groups perhaps of a gnosticizing character.[123]

Brandenburger is more ambiguous on this point. While avoiding the term "polemical," he speaks of these views as "skeptical" and reflecting streams in Judaism of the day.[124] His conception of the social matrix in which these views were born is unclear.[125] At one point he says

---

is particularly formulated on *Adam und Christus,* 30.) Harnisch has also published three further studies related to this matter: "Das Geschichtsverständnis der Apokalyptik," *Bibel und Kirche* 29 (1974) 121–25; "Die Metapher als heuristisches Prinzip: Neuerscheinungen zur Hermeneutik der Gleichnisreden Jesu," *Verkündigung und Forschung* 24 (1979) 53–89; and "Prophet." In his more recent book, cited in the text, Brandenburger takes issue with Harnisch's development of his ideas and with other recent writing (particularly in German). He also addresses the chief literary and structural issues of the book, as he perceives them. Consequently, our presentation in this section will take account chiefly of this most recent expression of his views.

120 These criteria are set forth systematically by Brandenburger, *Verborgenheit,* particularly pp. 50–52. Indeed, his comments there are rooted in more specific issues, but they clearly reflect this basic understanding.

121 See Brandenburger, *Verborgenheit.* We disagree with this formulation of the problem in rather basic ways, which will be expounded in the next section of this Introduction.

122 Brandenburger, *Verborgenheit,* 32, 148–53. This attitude is reinforced, e.g., in Harnisch's critique of the work of E. Breech ("These Fragments I Have

Shored Against My Ruins: The Form and Function of 4 Ezra," *JBL* 92 [1973] 267–74), Hayman ("Pseudonymity"), and A. L. Thompson (*Responsibility for Evil in the Theodicy of IV Ezra* [SBLDS 29; Missoula, Mont.: Scholars, 1977]), whom he finds to have undervalued radically the importance of the angel's speeches ("Prophet," 461–64).

123 See the presentation of the issues so perceived and the evaluation of past scholarship in the light of them: Brandenburger, *Verborgenheit,* 7–57. See also Harnisch, "Prophet," 477.

124 Harnisch, pp. 87, 142–43, cf. 146, and passim; cf. also idem, "Prophet," 477 and n. 38; see the comments of Brandenburger, *Verborgenheit,* 47.

125 See Brandenburger, *Verborgenheit,* who is unclear on precisely this point. On the one hand, he talks of *Auseinandersetzung* with *Denkströmungen* and, on the other, raises the possibility of its being a reflection of the author's *Realitätsbewusstsein.*

that the views forwarded by Ezra are the setting into literary form of the chief problems of the group to which the author belonged.[126] On other occasions, however, he speaks of "streams of thought" that these views represent, while denying that these are separate groups.[127] In spite of this denial, he talks of well-developed arsenals of skeptical arguments, of skeptical views as well defined, of there being a long, drawn-out conflict between such views and apocalyptic theology.[128] These latter observations clearly support by implication the more definite view of Harnisch.

It is difficult to regard this collocation of contradictory statements as meaning simply that the dispute is directed only against the chief problems of the author's group.[129] This is the more so when the author is described as holding clear, defined, and faithful views which are represented by the angel before Ezra's turning and by Ezra after it.[130]

In their analysis of the disputes, Harnisch and Brandenburger stress that Ezra is posing questions on a number of interrelated issues that fall within the realm of theodicy. Their analysis is clearly expressed in the titles of their books. On the one hand, there is the complex of problems raised by God's promises to Israel and the fact that these promises appear not to have been kept (Harnisch, *Verhängnis und Verheißung der Geschichte*). This issue, which clearly arises out of the destruction of the Temple, is worked out in very great detail by Harnisch in particular. The second chief, interrelated issue, according to this analysis, is the attitude toward Torah. Brandenburger stresses that by this concept is intended the idea of the *lebenspendenden Gesetz im eschatologisch-apokalyptischen Sinne*.[131] This Torah was given in order to produce life, yet God did not grant mankind the capability of preserving it. A third connected issue is that of

the few and the many, the few created and the many damned. All of these issues touch on the underpinnings of divine governance of the world.[132]

It is a central aspect of Brandenburger's views that the plaints of Ezra in which these ideas are forwarded, and the dialogues in which Ezra disputes the answers given to him by the angel, reach no conclusion. At this point his opinion differs from that of Harnisch, who, like many other scholars before him, pictured Ezra as being overcome by the angel's argument by the end of the third vision and therefore changing his views.[133] At the end of the third vision, Brandenburger stresses, just as at the start of the first, Ezra remains in the same aporia.[134] Therefore the shift in the fourth vision is very dramatic. Through the stress on the continuity between the ideas propagated by the angel in Visions 1–3 and by Ezra in Vision 7 (in the *Abschiedsrede*), the particularly important role of Vision 4 and the change in Ezra's views that result from it come to take a central position. Furthermore, the question of the relation of Visions 5–6 to Visions 1–3 +7 becomes more acute. Brandenburger addresses these issues in his most recent book.

He correctly views Vision 4 as a central turning point in the book.[135] Brandenburger, however, founds his analysis of that relationship on the following bases. First, the plaint in Vision 4 contrasts the *Heilsgeschichte* to present suffering and in the course of this denies the power of the Torah. Yet the vision that follows cannot be a response to this, because Ezra, who, according to Brandenburger's view, has not changed from the start of Vision 1 to the end of Vision 3, remains as an opponent of God's view and therefore cannot be a recipient of revelations.[136] Therefore, he argues, Ezra undergoes a sudden and unexplained change, in the course of which

---

126 See Brandenburger, *Verborgenheit*, 87.

127 Brandenburger, *Verborgenheit*, 47.

128 Brandenburger, *Verborgenheit*, 50, 66–67.

129 See Brandenburger, *Verborgenheit*, 154–55. The book, according to this view, is a confrontation of the author, the present sage, with Israel of his time (p. 159).

130 Brandenburger, *Verborgenheit*, 44–45, 152.

131 Ibid., 44. One wonders where such a phenomenon might be found. Its existence should be demonstrated in the context of the idea of Torah existing at that time.

132 These ideas are so central to both books that there is no point in citing page numbers. See in summary, Brandenburger, *Verborgenheit*, 44–45.

133 Brandenburger, *Verborgenheit*, 46–48.

134 Cf. the comments in Brandenburger, *Verborgenheit*, 30 and particularly p. 66.

135 See sec. 4 below. Brandenburger is indebted in his analysis at this point to Harnisch, "Prophet," 478–80.

136 In fact, this is patently not accurate, since Ezra receives a series of revelations throughout the first three visions. Brandenburger is conscious of this, and elsewhere in the book he talks of Ezra receiving

he becomes no longer opponent but accepts the angel's (i.e., God's) position. This change Brandenburger calls *das Mysterium der Verwandlung*,[137] and he repeatedly speaks of the mysterious character of its happening.[138]

The turning of Ezra is, according to this view, a turning from foolishness to wisdom and an opening of self to the hidden wisdom that was revealed but not accepted in the first three visions.[139] Brandenburger particularly uses the terminology of wisdom to describe this change, something that is not justified by Vision 4, in which this terminology does not occur.[140] Ezra's wisdom, then, is presented as the end of his skepsis and leads to his change or comfort. In an important supporting analysis of the transformation of Zion, Brandenburger has outlined part of the role reversal which takes place and during which Ezra takes over the task of comforting and consequently changes.[141] In summary, then, Brandenburger argues that 4 Ezra is not the deposit of an inner struggle, that it is dominated by a single, clear theological formulation, and that the change presented in Vision 4 is basically a literary event and provides coherence to the presentation of the author's ideas, including the possibility of the introduction of Visions 5–7.

In fact, of course, there is a major difficulty here. If, as Brandenburger claims, the book is a sophisticated and carefully crafted theological treatise, then why are the theological problems it poses never answered on theological grounds? Significantly, they are not answered on any other grounds either in the two dreams that follow. The questions put by the "foolish" Ezra are never answered at all. Brandenburger's (just) perception of the pivotal role of Vision 4 does not change this fact. This basic weakness of Brandenburger's overall argument must be observed in spite of his numerous, exact specific observations.

Brandenburger's understanding of Vision 7, the second crux of the book, is that it is basically testamentary in character and that the true revelation ends with Vision 6.[142] It was written by the author of the whole book and has a very deliberate literary structure.[143] He regards the *Abschiedsrede*, Ezra's parting address to the people, as bearing the central weight of this vision. In this passage Ezra reasserts the views espoused by the angel in Visions 1–3, thus, for Brandenburger, tying the structure together.[144] What is striking in his treatment of Vision 7, and indeed of the whole of 4

---

proleptic revelations of future comfort even during the first three visions; see Brandenburger, *Verborgenheit*, 119, 125–28. His extreme formulation is forced upon him by the rigid opposition he draws between Ezra and the angel, on the one hand, and by his refusal to see any development or change in the Ezra figure, on the other. The first point was cogently taken by Hayman, "Pseudonymity," 50–51; see below. The second point is challenged in a basic way in the next section of this Introduction.

137 Brandenburger, *Verborgenheit*, 87.

138 It will be explained in the next section where our view differs from that of Brandenburger on this issue. *Brevo*, we are in complete agreement with the suddenness of the change in Vision 4, but since we consider the book to reflect profound psychological developments and not just theological conflicts, we offer a quite different analysis and explanation of the change, and indeed of all that leads up to it; see further, secs. 4.4.2–4.4.4. Incidentally, Harnisch, "Prophet," is even more unclear and elusive than Brandenburger as to the nature of this change (pp. 478–80).

139 See Brandenburger, *Verborgenheit*, 69–70, 80–81.

140 See Brandenburger, *Verborgenheit*, 81. In n. 52 he attempts to account for this. Later, in his discussion of 4 Ezra's theory of revelation (which is done

perfunctorily in the last pages of the book) he also adduces certain aspects of the revelation of Vision 4 (pp. 200–201).

141 See Brandenburger, *Verborgenheit*, 74–84. Brandenburger stresses the literary character of this event (pp. 75–76) and explains nothing of how Ezra changes.

142 See Brandenburger, *Verborgenheit*, 41, 134; cf. 104.

143 See Brandenburger, *Verborgenheit*, 134. We are in complete agreement with the idea of the unity and deliberateness of composition. In general, Brandenburger also takes the various narrative passages rather seriously and uses them as an important key in the exegesis of the book; see, e.g., pp. 91–97, 100–102. Again we accord with this approach, though our analysis of these passages differs from his at many points.

144 See Brandenburger, *Verborgenheit*, 69–70. On pp. 50–52 and again on p. 72 he stresses the centrality of the turn or change in Ezra, which provides him with the link to hold the three parts of the book together. His theory is most telling, however, when seen in the light of his view of the polemical character of the dialogue, of the unified view of the author, and of the manipulation of the Ezra figure (cf. pp. 44, 59, 87, 152). The moment we cease to regard "Ezra" in Visions 1–3 as a straw man, the point of this theory is

Ezra, is the minor role given to the idea of revelation and special knowledge, which only in the last pages of his book is discussed in any detail (e.g., pp. 187, 198–99). The same understandings are to be found in the work of Harnisch, with some variations.[145]

3.4. Breech

In a stimulating essay published in 1973, E. Breech attempted an overall analysis of 4 Ezra that drew together criteria both of form and of content.[146] Arguing that structure and meaning are mutually determinative ("Previous views see 4 Ezra as a container for ideas"), Breech determines that the formal principle of the book is consolation and the subject of the book is Ezra's (not the nation's) move from distress to consolation. Ezra is a prophet and is equivalent to the community which he represents.[147] He presents the community's problems to God. Breech observes the shift in Vision 4 and describes this as the turn of Ezra's sincere grief into consolation, while Visions 5–6 affirm God as the source for life and death for the community. Vision 7 is a conclusion and a reaffirmation.[148]

This analysis was most important. In the first place, Breech offered an early response to the work of Harnisch, questioning some of Harnisch's basic hypotheses.[149] Beyond that, however, Breech tried to look at the dynamic of the book as a whole, taking account of its structure as well as of its conceptual content. His stress on structure has been particularly important. The difficulties that his analysis encountered arise first and foremost out of the attempt to use the pattern of the communal lament too rigidly. Breech assumed far too easily the equivalation of Ezra, prophet, and community when there is no real evidence that this presentation of Ezra is the dominant part of his role. Second, Breech has no real sense of the major events related in Vision 4.[150] Third, it is not really evident how Visions 5 and 6 "reaffirm that the Most High is the true source of life and death for the community" (p. 274). To say that they function within a pattern of consolation does not make this more persuasive. Finally, he offers no explanation of Vision 7 and particularly not of the revelatory material in it.[151]

3.5. Hayman

Another critique of Brandenburger's *Adam und Christus* and Harnisch's *Verhängnis und Verheißung der Geschichte* was published in 1975 by A. P. Hayman.[152] In discussing Harnisch's work in particular, he makes the following points:

a. If the author did want to present a heretical viewpoint in order to contradict it, the choice of Ezra as a mouthpiece is most problematic.[153]

---

removed.

145 See Harnisch, "Prophet," 484–85, where the importance of the narrative elements and the revelatory aspect of Vision 7 are completely ignored.

146 Breech, "These Fragments," 267–74.

147 See ibid., 269–72. His analysis of the book into "tryptichs" is overly simple and takes too little account of internal development within the tryptichs.

148 Breech bolsters his analysis by comparing the overall structures of the book to the *Volksklagelied* which had been recently discussed by C. Westermann, "Struktur und Geschichte der Klage im Alten Testament," *ZAW* 66 (1954) 44–80. This part of his analysis is not convincing; see the critique of it in 3:4–36 Form and Function, n. 12. It is not essential to his analysis.

149 See Breech, "These Fragments," 270–71. He notes that Harnisch's solution does not resolve the issues of the structure of the whole, and indeed, as we have remarked, it forced Harnisch into a theory of interpolation of Visions 5–6; see sec. 3.1 above. Moreover, Harnisch ignores the community aspects of the problems in Visions 1–3. Harnisch responded

to Breech briefly in "Prophet," 461. He did not come to grips with Breech's central claims. The influence of Breech's work may, perhaps, be discerned in that article of Harnisch's, for he presents it as an attempt to investigate the relationship of form and content, thus carrying on Breech's agenda.

150 See secs. 4.4.2–4.4.4 for our analysis of this.

151 Brandenburger, *Verborgenheit*, 52–54, gives a critique of Breech from his perspective.

152 Hayman, "Pseudonymity."

153 Ibid., 50–51. Brandenburger has responded to part of Hayman's critique in *Verborgenheit*, 48. He claims that both Hayman and Breech attack Harnisch's view of a distinct, clear opposition group in an unfair fashion, oddly stating: "Die Kritik bei Breech und Hayman hat sich einseitig nur auf die extremen Äusserungen Harnischs gestürzt" and that "Die Äusserungen Harnischs zu dem hier verhandelten Problem sind ambivalent" (p. 48). Yet Brandenburger's attempts to soften this issue are not convincing (to speak of the opposition point of view being not that of a social group but that of *Denk-*

b. In fact, though there is real tension between the views of the angel and those of Ezra, they also overlap.[154]
c. The "heretical" views set in Ezra's mouth are, Hayman claims, "perfectly acceptable in the mouth of an orthodox Jew. They are neither heretical nor gnostic" (p. 52).
d. At no point does Ezra break down and change his views, in sharp contrast to opponents of Christianity as presented, for example, in other polemical dialogues.[155] Hayman himself attempts to ease the tension between the first three visions and the last three by supposing that they are addressing different problems, the origins of sin on the one hand and the delay of the end combined with dominance of Rome on the other. To respond to these, Hayman suggests, the author uses different eschatological patterns.

3.6. Knibb

In an important article, M. A. Knibb suggests that 4 Ezra is to be seen as a work of learned character directed toward esoteric, learned circles.[156] He supports this claim by the following considerations. First, 4 Ezra is deeply influenced by sapiential ideas and terminology.[157] Indeed, it is directed toward a self-conscious, distinct social group of the wise.[158] Second, he claims that this learned character is also evident in the conscious and deliberate use of biblical texts and allusions. This too is, in his view, a characteristic of learned literature.[159] As a result of this analysis, he is led to characterize 4 Ezra as "a kind of interpretative writing." He would even consider extending this characterization to other apocalypses.

3.7. Thompson

In his book *Responsibility for Evil in the Theodicy of IV Ezra,* A. L. Thompson pursues a very specific line of exegesis. His general views are that 4 Ezra is to be appreciated as a whole. Moreover, the dialogue format is to be taken seriously as reflecting real tensions in the author's personality. The final three visions are a not very convincing and a rather limited consolation for the turmoil of the first three visions.[160]

In particular, Thompson discerned in 4 Ezra an interplay between national and universal concerns ("one/many" and "few/many"). This is clearly reflected in the title of his extensive chapter 4: "From Lament Over Israel, to Lament Over All Mankind, to Conso-

---

strömungen does not illuminate anything). Brandenburger does not come to grips with Hayman's telling points about (a) the overlap between the views of Ezra and the angel and (b) the assessment that the supposedly heretical, opposition views are in fact well within the range of contemporary Jewish "orthodoxy."

154 Hayman points particularly to the angel's words in 4:30–31 and those in Ezra's mouth in 9:27–37. He points out that Harnisch is pressed to account for these instances ("Pseudonymity," 51–52). Other examples of such inconsistencies may be found on p. 52.

155 See Hayman, "Pseudonymity," 53. Harnisch responds briefly to these criticisms in "Prophet," 461–62.

156 M. A. Knibb, "Apocalyptic and Wisdom in 4 Ezra," *JSJ* 13 (1983) 56–74.

157 Cf. our analysis in 14:23–26 Function and Content, pp. 428–31. U. Luck, "Das Weltverständnis in der jüdischen Apokalyptik dargestellt am äthiopischen Henoch und am 4.Esra," *ZftK* 73 (1976) 283–305, also presents a view much occupied with wisdom. He claims that the heart of Ezra's revelation, typified by chap. 14, is of "wisdom" divorced from its natural and redemptive correlative "Law." In 4 Ezra, humans have no symbiosis with law, he maintains, and the

point of the book is an esoteric revelation encouraging them to observe the law even when it seems pointless. In our view, however, the term "wisdom" by the time of 4 Ezra has become an "empty vessel" into which a variety of contents might be poured. Moreover, chap. 14 must be seen in relation to the overall understanding of revelation in 4 Ezra, for it is the revelation of more than *Gesetz,* it is the revelation of eschatological secrets. Furthermore, Luck fails to take account of the difference between the revelation to the people and the revelation to the wise.

158 Knibb, "Apocalyptic and Wisdom," 72–73.

159 Ibid., 73. Our critique of this view is found within the commentary, chiefly at 14:23–26 Function and Content, p. 431.

160 These views are summarized by Thompson, *Responsibility,* 107.

lation for Israel." He is most concerned to lay out in detail the dynamic of the interplay of these elements.[161]

In the first part of the book, Uriel presents a narrower, more unyielding, and less "attractive" point of view than Ezra (Thompson, pp. 137–48), and Ezra's concern for "few/many" (i.e., his universal concern) is quite absent from the angel's responses.[162] While in Visions 1 and 2 the author is concerned to establish Ezra's position as spokesman for Israel, in Vision 3 Ezra becomes the spokesman for all mankind.[163] The author is, of course, responsible for the views both of Ezra and of the angel. Moreover, in the final analysis, Uriel's views triumph, yet Ezra's questions are not answered.[164]

Thompson views this as a subtle technique, abetted by the choice of the orthodox Ezra as spokesman for his doubts, to preserve "the appearance of orthodoxy while raising a powerful voice of dissent" (p. 217). Yet, we may remark, this analysis does not clarify the issues much. Thompson terms Vision 4 "transitional" (p. 220) and "diagrammatic" of the author's own experience (p. 222). It represents the shift from "one/many" to "many/few" and back to "one/many" (pp. 222–23). Thompson ignores Ezra's transformation altogether and finds the relationship between the dynamic he discerns and eschatology "enigmatic" (p. 235).[165]

The latter part of Thompson's book deals with the implications of the above approaches for the issue of theodicy. It will be amply evident from section 4 and from the arguments demonstrated in the course of the Commentary that our assessment of 4 Ezra differs radically from that of Thompson.[166] This difference does not affect so much the particular distinctions that he draws as it does the overall assessment of 4 Ezra. To analyze 4 Ezra under categories such as "moral" and "physical," while ignoring the organic and developmental features of its thought, is to miss much of the point of the work.

4.0. Section 4: The Present Commentary

4.1. Our View of Literary Unity

The position taken here on the issue of literary unity is that 4 Ezra is the work of a single individual. Above, in section 3.1, previous criticisms of the source theory of Kabisch and Box were discussed. These we judge to be telling. To them should be added the consideration that a great deal of skill and sophistication is exhibited by the structure and the framework of the book. For example, in the course of the Commentary the careful and purposeful application of elements such as Ezra's physical position on receiving a vision, the place in which he is found after receiving it, his response to it, and the number of days between each vision, will be explained.[167] Very much of 4 Ezra is deliberately structured so that meaning is conveyed by changes in context and framework as well as by explicit statement. Such clearly explicit elements combine with the very seven-vision structure of the book to convince us that one skilled and sophisticated hand has directed the composition of the whole book.[168]

4.1.1. Use of Preexistent Sources

It does not follow from the above strong statement that the author was responsible for the composition *de novo* of every word and for the creation of each idea in the book. This is patently absurd. Not only does the book contain quotations from and allusions to the Bible (7:17 Commentary; 7:21 Commentary; 7:106–110 Commentary; et al.) but it also contains certain blocks of material that have been drawn from preexistent sources, either oral or

---

161 Ibid., 157–256.

162 At many points Thompson's detailed arguments are not convincing on exegetical, textual, or philological grounds. This is pointed out in a number of instances in the course of the Commentary below.

163 This is the import of the argument in Thompson, *Responsibility*, 157–256.

164 See ibid., 216–17.

165 See also ibid., 240–41.

166 Thompson's particular arguments are addressed at various points throughout the Commentary.

167 See secs. 4.3.3–4.3.5 below.

168 There are numerous further elements that attest to the same fact, and these are repeatedly noted throughout the Commentary. On seven-vision structure and literary unity, see Brandenburger, *Verborgenheit*, 143–44. He deals at some length with the role of the narrative sections of which the book is composed, particularly as they convey meaning (ibid., 42, 93–102, etc.).

written, and embedded in their present position. Many years ago we established that in Vision 6 (the vision of the man), the author drew the section that describes the content of the dream from an existing source.[169] A similar preexistent source may be utilized in the mourning woman's tale in the fourth vision (9:43–10:3).[170] Three particular short passages also seem to be based on very specific preexisting material. The first is the passage about the souls of the righteous (4:35–37).[171] The second is the description of Behemoth and Leviathan (6:49–52),[172] while the third such individual tradition deals with the ten tribes (13:40–47).[173]

These three passages are marked out both by their crystallized and distinct character and traditions and by the fact that they expatiate on their subject far beyond the requirements of context. Certainly some of the author's building blocks can be discerned here.

It should be remarked at once, both with respect to all of these passages which we have just mentioned and with respect to those which will be discussed below, that they are integrated well into their context. This is so much so that it is often difficult to decide whether a written or an oral source is here being adapted. In this we may discern once again clear evidence of the skilled hand of the author.

There are further passages that bear a distinctly individual literary character. The description of the post-mortem state of the souls in chapter 7 is unique in Jewish literature of the Second Temple period.[174] Moreover, not only is the content unique but this passage is marked off by a clear introduction and conclusion. It opens,

"Now, concerning death, the teaching is: . . ." (7:78) and concludes, "This is the order of the souls of the righteous, as henceforth is announced" (7:99). Furthermore, the second subdivision of this passage is also marked by a heading: "But this is the order of those who have kept the ways of the Most High" (7:88). Thus the passage is clearly a distinct literary unit. One can even argue, on the basis of its heading and conclusion, that it was drawn from a preexisting literary source, perhaps of a didactic character.[175] Nonetheless, the natural place of this passage in the structure of the third vision is unmistakable, just as is true of each of the short sections mentioned above in its own context. Consequently, we must reckon with the use by the author of preexisting sources, both written and oral, in the composition of 4 Ezra. However, these sources are made integral parts of the book and serve the overall literary and conceptual goals of the author.

A number of further passages can be analyzed in the same way. One is the creation poem in 6:38–54 (in which the Behemoth and Leviathan passage [6:49–52] is included).[176] Another such source is formed by the two eschatological Prediction 2 passages[177] (5:1–13 and 6:18–28) which are probably two parts of an original single document.[178]

4.1.2. Reuse of Existent *Gattungen*

Striking are the reuses of commonly known *Gattungen*. The *rîb* which is used in the plaint in 3:4–26 is one such, and the riddle questions in 4:5–8 and 5:36–37 are another.[179] In both of these instances the author has

---

169 Stone, *Features*, 122–25; idem, "Messiah," 303–10. We still hold that position; see 13:20b–55 Function and Content, pp. 399–400.

170 This possibility was first vetted by Gunkel, p. 344; see for further considerations 9:38–10:4 Form and Structure, p. 311; cf. Brandenburger, *Verborgenheit*, 91–92.

171 This is discussed, and the arguments are adduced, in the Commentary on those verses.

172 See 6:38–59 Function and Content, pp. 182–83.

173 See 13:20b–55 Form and Function, p. 399, and Commentary on these verses. Another such passage may be 6:1–6; see 5:41—6:10 Form and Structure, p. 145.

174 See 7:75–99 Function and Content, pp. 238–39.

175 See discussion in detail in 7:75–99 Form and Structure, p. 238.

176 This is discussed in full in 6:38–59 Function and Content, pp. 182–83.

177 On this terminology, see General Structure of the Book below.

178 See 5:1–13 Form and Structure. These passages are analyzed into tiny, complex units by Harnisch, "Prophet," 469 n. 20, while Gry puts forward a highly speculative reconstruction of an eschatological "document" based on these three passages: L. Gry, "Essai sur le plus ancien teneur et la fortune du catalogue des signes de la fin: IV Esdras V 1–14, VI 18–29, VII 26–31," *RSPT* 29 (1940) 264–77.

179 See 4:5 Commentary; the matter is discussed in great detail in M. E. Stone, "Lists of Revealed Things in the Apocalyptic Literature," *Magnalia Dei: G. E. Wright Memorial* (ed. F. M. Cross, W. E. Lemke, and P. D. Miller; Garden City, N.Y.: Doubleday, 1976)

taken a *Gattung* well known in earlier literature and, in making it serve his purpose, has inverted its original intent and role. The proem to the *rîb* is no longer God's recital of his gracious deeds toward Israel in order to form the basis of an indictment of Israel for sinning against him; it is Ezra's recital of God's deeds toward Israel with the purpose of indicting God. The riddle questions, originally praise of God as creator of nature and its wonders, and later lists of revealed apocalyptic secrets, become in our author's skilled hands unanswerable and foolish riddles serving to demonstrate human inability to gain knowledge.[180]

The common feature of all of these examples is the following. The author has clearly used preexisting sources and literary forms. He has, however, skillfully worked them into his book, making them serve the overall literary purposes, conceptual structure, and religious dynamic of his composition. Therefore the book is a literary unity, the product of an accomplished, sensitive, and purposeful author, and not a rather unthinking patchwork of preexisting sources.[181]

4.1.3. Summary of View on Literary Unity
The book is therefore a literary unity incorporating certain preexistent materials, both oral and written. In some instances, as has been pointed out in the previous section, the exact limits of this material may clearly be isolated.[182] Moreover, the analysis of a number of such cases has shown that the author exercises his craft proficiently, deftly subordinating the preexistent material to his particular literary and conceptual purposes. He even takes over *Gattungen* that have clearly defined functions and roles in previous literature and molds them to his particular needs, reversing or changing their original meaning and function. Consequently,

in the work of such a deliberate writer, the structure and the framework of the book, as well as the details of the discourse itself, should be examined carefully and assessed for their significance.[183]

4.2. The Overall Meaning

4.2.1. The Overall Meaning in Previous Scholarship
The approach to the book according to source-critical scholarship, typified by the conclusions of Kabisch and Box,[184] did not take the question of the overall unity of the book seriously. Typically, such critics referred to a "redactor" rather than to an author of the whole; moreover, they regarded the "redactor's" work as secondary and even rather slipshod when compared to that of the "authors" of the constitutive documents. These very assumptions obviated any serious attempt to understand the book as a whole.

4.2.2. Gunkel
Gunkel's approach was rather different. He did take the book to be a whole, the work of a single author, who also used some sources. Moreover, he used psychological considerations as a means of understanding critical issues in the book. Brandenburger wrongly rejects this approach, but his observation that Gunkel's psychological analysis does not resolve chief literary issues in a satisfactory fashion is just.[185] For example, Gunkel did not account for the fact that the views maintained by the angel throughout the first three visions become those forwarded by Ezra in the latter part of the book, particularly in Visions 4 and 7. Likewise, Gunkel's view of Vision 7, as a pleasing conclusion to the book, is surely inadequate.[186]

414–52.

180 See ibid., 419–21.

181 It should be pointed out that the literary "building blocks" are even more in number and greater in complexity than we have indicated. This is made evident at numerous places throughout the ensuing Commentary. Only some, most prominent instances have been adduced here.

182 See secs. 4.1.1–4.1.2.

183 Breech laid special emphasis on structure as conveying meaning in 4 Ezra; see "These Fragments," 269. This was also stressed at length from a different

perspective by Brandenburger, *Verborgenheit*, esp. 94–124.

184 See sec. 3.2 above.

185 See Brandenburger, *Verborgenheit*, 36–37.

186 Gunkel, p. 348; cf. Brandenburger, *Verborgenheit*, 34. Breech does not advance far beyond Gunkel in understanding Vision 7; see "These Fragments," 274.

4.2.3. Brandenburger and Harnisch

The most serious attempt so far to account for the over-all meaning of the book has been made by the German scholars E. Brandenburger and W. Harnisch. Their views have been presented in section 3 but should be discussed here in greater detail as they bear upon the central issues of the meaning of 4 Ezra. The observation that the fourth vision is pivotal, the attempt to relate the seventh vision to the rest of the book, and the search for understanding the fifth and sixth visions are very important emphases.[187]

It is central to their understanding of 4 Ezra that there is no advance or development in the course of the first three visions. Essentially the problems outlined by Ezra in his plaints receive, they maintain, no resolution. This view is typified by Brandenburger's stress on the words in 9:15: "I said before, and I say now, and will say it again."[188] The dialogic discussion as well as the revel-atory discourses of the angel have been basically pointless, and the turning point does not come until the fourth vision, when the exchange of roles takes place. Now, on this central issue in the interpretation of the book, the results of our study differ completely from those of Brandenburger and Harnisch.

4.2.4. Structural Aspects of Development in Visions 1–3

The analysis of the first three visions shows a very distinct and very sophisticated development of ideas.[189] Our arguments are given in detail in the pericope com-mentary of the various sections of those visions. In brief, however, it is quite clear that Ezra's position moves from the stress of doubt with which chapter 3 is so marked to an acceptance of some of the ideas set forth by the angel, a process already under way in the first vision and sus-tained throughout Visions 2 and 3. This analysis is aided

by the distinction that must be drawn between two different types of dialogue between Ezra and the angel. The first we have named disputatious dialogue (dispute), and the second is revelatory dialogue, which we have called Prediction 1.[190] Visions 1 and 2 open with Ezra's address; it is followed by dispute; then, most significantly, Ezra abandons argument and also abandons the position of dominating interlocutor and proceeds to pose short questions designed to elicit information from the angel on specific eschatological matters (Prediction 1). In a final response to his questioning, the angel moves into predictive monologue which we have called Prediction 2.[191]

The third vision is more complex, being divided into three subdivisions, but each subdivision itself is charac-terized by movement between disputatious and predic-tive sections, chiefly of a dialogic character.[192]

This structure implies a development on Ezra's part, for each instance of shift from dispute to dialogic predic-tion implies that he accepts in some measure the argu-ments that the angel has presented. The seer's requests for further clarification of specific points in the Predic-tion 1 dialogue are based upon his acceptance of the matters he wants explained. Thus our case is not made simply on the basis of formal structure but also on the basis of the very arguments the author uses.

4.2.5. "The Way of the Most High" and Ezra's Development

One example of this development may be traced by examining the theme of "the knowledge of the way of the Most High" in the first part of the book.[193] The aporia about divine justice that is the motive for the indictment of God in chapter 3 makes Ezra's request for knowledge of the way of the Most High, first raised in 3:31 and

---

187 See sec. 3.3 above. As noted there, Harnisch, "Prophet," actually claims that Visions 5 and 6 are a later addition to the original book. See the discussion in sec. 3.2 above.

188 Brandenburger, *Verborgenheit*, 31, 47. Thus he also compares 7:116 and argues against Gunkel's view that Ezra is "half comforted" in the first three visions (pp. 38–39).

189 These views were first developed in our paper "The Way of the Most High and the Injustice of God," *Knowledge of God Between Alexander and Constantine* (ed. R. van den Broek, T. Baarda, and J. Mansfeld;

Leiden: Brill, 1989) 132–42.

190 See General Structure of the Book, pp. 50–51.

191 See ibid., where the formal characteristics and the actual structures of the visions are set forth.

192 On the structure, see ibid.

193 "Way of God" in this sense occurs elsewhere, e.g., 1QH 7:31–32; Rom 11:33; *2 Apoc Bar* 14:8; 20:4. In 4 Ezra 5:34 and *2 Apoc Bar* 44:6, "way" stands parallel to "judgment," cf. Isa 40:14 and *2 Apoc Bar* 15:4. The problem of understanding God's way in the destruction of the Temple is also to the fore in *b. Ber.* 3a. Naturally, more detail is to be found in our

taken up in 4:2–3; 4:11; 4:23; 5:34; et al., urgent. The "way" is, it seems, God's way of conducting the world; knowledge of it may explain God's injustice toward mankind.[194] However, the angel answers Ezra's request by asserting strongly that "the way of the Most High" cannot be understood by human beings.[195]

This idea, which is one aspect of the concepts of revelation and understanding central to the book, holds 4:1–25 together. Treating the seer's plaint in chapter 3 as a question, the angel picks up Ezra's expression from 3:31: "(thou) hast not shown to anyone how thy way is to be comprehended," and chides him for presuming that he can understand the way of God, the working of divine providence. In 4:5–8 (and in 5:36–37) the angel uses lists of riddle questions to demonstrate that human beings cannot know such things.

These riddle questions originate in catalogues of revealed things in the apocalypses, going back to earlier biblical sources.[196] In 4 Ezra 4:5–8 and 5:36–37 a list of revealed things has been deliberately combined with the interrogative type of list which stresses human inability to know certain things, found in Job 37–39; Sir 1:2–3; and other sources. The writer thus emphasized the limits

of human knowledge not just by having the angel ask the seer some insoluble riddles but by choosing as riddles a catalogue of those very subjects which in the "normal" run of events were considered central to apocalyptic revelations. He thus daringly denies the availability of certain types of special knowledge and therefore of a specific part of apocalyptic tradition. In their inversion of the original purpose of the literary form, then, these riddle questions strikingly make their point that Ezra cannot even understand the wonders of nature, how much less divine providence. The parable that follows repeats the point that "those who dwell upon the earth can understand only what is on the earth, and he who is above the heavens can understand what is above the height of the heavens" (4:21).[197] Ezra, who is corruptible (and therefore a fragile vessel), is incapable of grasping the way of him who is incorruptible (4:11).[198]

Commentary on the various verses below, particularly 3:31 and 4:2–4. Here we wish only to sketch the chief lines of thought.

194 The inaccessibility of knowledge of God's action is already highlighted by texts like Isa 40:13 and Job 9:10; cf. in general *Od Sol* 7:8: "He who created wisdom is wiser than his works." The language of understanding connects with wisdom terminology, which, although present in Vision 1, is much more prominent in Vision 2; cf. 5:22; 5:32; and language used in 5:34; 5:37; and 5:40.

195 Brandenburger describes the problem as the conflict of faith and reality (*Verborgenheit,* 169). On "ways" in 4:3, clearly denoting the "riddles" with which it is parallel, see Commentary and the literature cited there. It is particularly intriguing since in 4:2; 4:4; 4:11; et al., the word is used with a specific and clear sense which is central to the whole vision. The polyvalency of the word "way" is at play in the discussion; see 4:23 and cf. 4:8: compare with 4:2 and 4:4. From 4:22–25 it is clear that the meaning of the "way" is not exhausted by something like "the reason for the existence of the evil heart."

196 For a full analysis of the form with numerous examples and extensive discussion, see Stone, "Lists"; see also M. E. Stone, "Paradise in 4 Ezra iv.8 and vii.36, viii.52," *JJS* 17 (1966) 85–88. Some chief

instances of these lists are *2 Bar* 59:5–11; *1 Enoch* 41:1–7; 43:1–2; 60:11–13; 60:14–22; and *2 Enoch* 23:1–4. Furthermore, some of the apocalypses actually describe how these actions, such as the weighing of the winds, took place; see, e.g., *2 Enoch* 40:2–3. It seems evident that *Bib Ant* 19:10 also belongs with the lists of revealed things. Even though that work is not an apocalypse, the context in which the list occurs is clearly analogous. In Wisd 7:17–21, however, the rather different range of revealed information derives from Solomon's well-known role as magician.

197 The gap between earthly and heavenly knowledge is a common theme; cf. Wisd 9:16–17. Divergent attitudes toward this question may provide one key for differentiating theories of knowledge and revelation; see Stone, "Lists," 438–39; cf. also Isa 55:8–9 and John 1:12–13. Note the acute related observations of S. Loewenstamm, "The Death of Moses," *Studies on the Testament of Abraham* (ed. G. W. E. Nickelsburg; SCS 6; Missoula, Mont.: Scholars, 1976) 198–201.

198 The terms "corruptible" and "incorruptible" occur throughout the book. See 4:11 Commentary.

Ezra, however, rejects the angel's response. He did not ask about heavenly matters but about the earthly suffering of Israel. He will not accept the view that Israel's fate cannot be understood, and he buttresses his refusal by pointing out God's special relation to Israel and the Torah. Israel is called by God's name (4:23–25).

The emphasis on understanding is the more telling because of the limits 4 Ezra has placed on the role and range of revealed knowledge. The rejection of cosmographical and uranographical speculations in 4:5–9 makes the cry of despair in 4:12 with its implicit questions the more piercing and the questions in 4:22–25 the more acute. Ezra's understanding, the angel asserts, is human, limited, and corruptible (4:11; 4:20) and he cannot comprehend the heavenly realm. Ezra does not deny this, but he claims that what he wishes to know is within the human range. The search for understanding the way of the Most High lies for him at the heart of purposeful human existence. It is better, he claims, to die than to suffer and not understand why (4:12). Else why, he asks, were we given the "power of understanding"?[199] The seer and the angel both reject knowledge of heavenly secrets. Ezra has not sought it, nor has he been granted it. The proper concern for the mind, then, is the fate of Israel.

The seer's pain over his lack of understanding bursts forth in striking laments over the mind. The first is in chapter 4 with two cries of woe, one following each angelic demonstration of Ezra's innate inability to comprehend the way of the Most High (4:12 and 4:22). In 7:63–75 there is another extensive lament over the mind bewailing its very creation, which distinguishes humans from beasts and thus makes them liable to judgment.[200]

The angel replies that God created all that pertains to judgment when he created Adam: "For this reason . . . those who dwell on earth shall be tormented, because though they had understanding they committed iniquity, and though they received the commandments they did not keep them" (7:72). They will have nothing to say in judgment, which is delayed only because God foreordained the times (7:73–74). Consequently, mind, being consciousness so it seems, is that part of humans which makes them liable for judgment at all.[201]

At this juncture in chapter 4, a cryptic statement by the angel ensues about sowing and harvest, about the future—Ezra must await future vindication of the righteous in order to see the resolution of his problems (4:26–32). This forms the transition to the second part of the dialogue, for, following it, dispute is abandoned for a series of requests for eschatological information which the angel answers.[202] In each answer he stresses the predetermination of the times (4:36–37; 4:40; 4:44–46). Yet this emphasis is paralleled by and in tension with a growing sense of urgency and haste.[203] This tension is

---

199 In this passage: (1) heart = mind = power of understanding (3:30); (2) it is human and limited; (3) its satisfaction is central to purposeful human existence. This accords with the use of the term in 3:1; 5:21; 9:27; and 14:40.

200 Ezra has been informed that in the final judgment there will be no mercy for the sinners. He then addresses the earth, reproaching it with having produced a mind from the dust, "for it would have been better if the dust itself had not been born, so that the mind might not have been made from it" (7:63). The mind grows with humans who are tortured by the very knowledge that they will perish in final judgment (7:65). The beasts, who have neither torment nor salvation, are much happier (7:65–69). The "heart" that has received the law will perish along with human beings who have not

observed it (9:36–37).

201 Although this seemingly contradicts the point of chap. 4, that humans cannot understand the way of the Most High, the anomaly is readily resolved if the contexts of the two passages are borne in mind. Chapter 4 discusses the incomprehensibility of the working of divine justice when the fate of Israel is compared with the abundance of Babylon (i.e., Rome). On the other hand, 7:62–72 concerns the actions of humans in general; in that context it is precisely thought or consciousness that distinguishes humans from beasts and makes them liable to be judged.

202 On the distinction of the two types of dialogue, see General Structure of the Book, pp. 50–51.

203 This is clear from 4:26, from the image of 4:42, and from the parable of the third question.

inherent in the author's thought. Ezra's questions in this section proceed on the assumption that indeed the order of events is predetermined. His acceptance of that idea is a major step forward, and it explains differences between the first and the second vision. It is precisely here that growth and development may be observed, and it is this process that is not recognized by the analysis of Brandenburger and Harnisch. The search to understand the way of the Most High has issued in Ezra's acceptance of a central concept promoted by the angel.

The second vision opens with a speech that sets the tone and introduces the themes that characterize the first part of the ensuing dialogue. The issues it raises resemble those highlighted in the address and dispute sections of Vision 1, but it reproves God less pressingly and differs in its focus.

In the address in Vision 1, Ezra had summoned God to court to answer the questions arising from Israel's suffering. In the course of the predictions in the latter part of that vision, however, Ezra's views modify, and by its end he accepts the idea that history's process is predetermined. Although this acceptance does not diminish his distress or alleviate his pain, it does lead him to pose his questions about the destruction of Zion from a quite different perspective. No longer is the reason for the actual punishment of Israel central, but the question, "Why is Israel, the faithful and elect people, punished *by the Gentiles,* the hated Romans?" This minor theme of Vision 1 now becomes dominant. "If thou dost really hate thy people," he cries out, "they should have been punished at thy own hands" (5:30).[204] How anomalous is Israel's fate when viewed in the light of Israel's election and God's love! So God's punishment of Israel is called "hate" (5:30).[205]

Since the address focuses on election and love, the angel's opening question in the dispute that follows is not, Why does Ezra search to understand the ways of providence? (contrast 4:2), but whether Ezra loves Israel more than God does (5:33). The changed emphasis is

clear, and it is well illustrated by contrasting the following verses:

I also will show you *the way* you desire to see,
    and will teach you *why the heart is evil.* (4:4)

So Vision 1, while in Vision 2 we read:

    and then I will explain to you *the travail you seek to understand.* (5:37)

Of course, at the root of Ezra's concern is the fate of Israel: here he poses the question to God in terms of God's love of Israel, while in Vision 1 it was formulated in terms of divine providence and God's conduct of the world. The changed formulation raises a less acute theological issue, although emotionally a no less distressing one. Ezra has moved from his doubt about the justice lying at the basis of God's conduct of the world to bewilderment at divine actions. Ezra has, in spite of it all, advanced in "knowledge of the way of the Most High."

A disputatious passage corresponding to that in the first vision (5:33–40) ensues. First the angel reproaches Ezra with his distress (5:33), to which Ezra responds that he is deeply upset all the time as he seeks to comprehend the way of the Most High (the only instance of the expression in this passage; contrast Vision 1). The angel again poses riddle questions to which Ezra responds that only the superhuman can know these things but that he is "without wisdom." The angel assents, saying that Ezra cannot know God's judgment.

After the discussion with the angel in Vision 1, Ezra had asserted that his mind, his ability to know, is properly to be applied to the subject matter of his questions, that is, the way of the Most High (4:22–25). The dynamic of the book is evident when at the end of the dispute in the second vision (5:31–40) Ezra no longer repeats this demand for understanding. Instead, he seems to accept the limitations of his wisdom and

---

204 It is foreshadowed in 4:23 in a passage that presages many of the themes of Vision 2.

205 Interestingly, God's punishment of Israel is not described in legal terms by the seer in his speech (5:28–30), even though in 5:34 and 5:40 "the way of the Most High" (also absent from the speech) is described as "judgment." *2 Apoc Bar* 44:6 speaks of the making known of God's "judgment" and "ways."

A most striking parallel is *2 Apoc Bar* 20:4, which says that in the events of the eschaton:

  I will show the *judgment* of my might,
    And my *ways* which are unsearchable.

abilities.[206] So he simply proceeds with his questioning.

Here the basic axiom of divine righteousness is no longer questioned, and indeed this is another indication of the change from Vision 1. God is not indicted here, he is simply not understood; he is admonished only in the last verse of the address (5:30). The angel responds that Ezra cannot love Israel as God does or understand God's judgment or the end of his love, implying both God's justice and his mercy.

This implication opens the way into dialogic revelation which is in fact paradoxical, for Ezra's admission that he *cannot know* the way of God's love leads into his further revelatory questions. The seer has understood the first part of the dialogue to lead to the conclusion that God loves Israel and that his love, contrary to appearances (5:30), has a goal, an end (5:40). God's ways are unknowable by Ezra (5:38), but the angel/God has (in 5:40) made a response pregnant with promise.

From this example alone, it is clear that the idea that there is no development in the first three visions is mistaken. The line traced above is only one of a variety of paths of development that are spelled out in more detail in the Commentary.

Brandenburger and Harnisch, in their studies, lay much emphasis on the roles of Ezra and the angel.[207] Moreover, Brandenburger rightly stressed that any explanation of the book must take account of the change of Ezra's role in the fourth vision. Yet he rejected any psychological approach to the figure of Ezra, such as Gunkel had suggested.[208] However, we maintain that it is precisely such an approach that, together with the perception of the developments of the Ezra figure in the first three visions, provides a key for understanding the dramatic change in Ezra's role that took place by the end of the third vision.[209]

Ezra's development, unlike that in a Platonic dialogue, does not start at a certain point and progress regularly step by step from beginning to end. It starts, advances, regresses, advances some more, returns to earlier issues, and so forth. The dynamic by which this takes place is laid out in the Commentary. What is deeply significant is that there is a very distinct overall progressive development in Ezra's position which implies a far more complex underlying structure in the book than Brandenburger and Harnisch have assumed.

4.3. Our Approach

4.3.1. Our Analysis of the Significance of the Framework
Any new approach to 4 Ezra must take account of all the problems that have been raised by Brandenburger and Harnisch. What will be proposed below is an overall understanding of the book. For most of the detailed exegeses and analyses upon which it is based, reference should be made to the Commentary.

The first element in our overall analysis is a sensitivity to the meaning of the framework and structure of the book. The apocalypse is presented as seven visions.[210] In an obvious way they divide into three visions of dialogue (Visions 1–3), one vision that is part dialogue and part waking experience (Vision 4), two symbolic dreams and their interpretations (Visions 5 and 6), and a final narrative about the receipt of a revelation (Visions 7).

4.3.2. Developments Inherent in Formal Structures
This structure is paralleled by the details of Ezra's regimen. The first three visions are preceded by fasts and lamentations.[211] They take place in Ezra's room in Babylon, privately, on his bed at night. Each of them is opened by an address by Ezra, an address described as

---

206 Yet in spite of this, in 12:4 Ezra speaks of the search for understanding as the motive of his receiving visions. See Commentary there.

207 See sec. 3.3 above.

208 See Brandenburger, *Verborgenheit*, 36, and n. 113 above.

209 D. Merkur has written a fascinating study of 4 Ezra from a psychoanalytic perspective. He would strongly support an analysis that views both Ezra and the angel as parts of the author's personality, allowing "no serious doubt that the doctrinal dispute between Ezra and Uriel in these verses [4:48–49—M.E.S.]

represents a conflict between the author's ego and superego ['Visionary Practice,' manuscript p. 63]."

210 On the term "Visions," see General Structure of the Book, p. 50.

211 See 3:1 Commentary on the missing fast before Vision 1.

ecstatic.[212] Furthermore, the first two visions, and in a much more complex way the third vision, are composed of the seer's address, disputatious dialogue, predictive dialogue, and angelic prediction.[213] This very division of the types of discourse implies a dynamic of change in the relationship between Ezra and the angel within these visions. First, Ezra speaks his plaint alone ("address"); then, he expresses it in dialogic dispute ("dispute"); next, Ezra moves to predictive dialogue in which he is eliciting information from the angel by brief questions ("Prediction 1"); finally, the angel alone delivers his prediction while Ezra is completely passive ("Prediction 2"). This structure does not accord with a simple, skeptical polemic; its repetition throughout the first three visions confirms this point.

Furthermore, this repetition raises meaningful and problematic issues of composition that form a basic position for understanding this part of the book. In these visions Ezra repeatedly moves from his initial quandary to receipt of some revealed answers. Yet the repetition of the pattern makes evident that each set of answers received is not satisfactory. To advance beyond this basic perception, which is reached on the basis of structure, demands an analysis of the content of each of these repetitions. Does Ezra's position and do Ezra's views change in the substance of the matter? Is, therefore, the cycle not merely repetitive but also progressive?[214] This issue has already been broached. Before we return to it in sections 4.4.3–4.4.4, we need to consider further dimensions of the structure of the book.

4.3.3. Structural Indications of Pivotal Position of Vision 4

In the injunctions preceding the fourth vision, the pattern of seven days' separation and prayer is maintained, but with some highly significant differences. First, the locale changes. Ezra is no longer in his bedroom in Babylon at night. Now he is in a field, and instead of fasting he is to eat flowers.[215] It is not certain, by any means, that the fourth vision was experienced at night.

Moreover, the fourth vision, like the three preceding ones, opens with a passage that describes Ezra's distress and the inspiration that comes upon him. With the inspiration, speech bursts forth, as it did in the three previous visions. Indeed, all of these introductory elements resemble the corresponding features of the three preceding visions, except for the place and the food, which have changed. After the address, however, the unexpected happens, and a quite different sort of experience is recounted, the waking experience of the mourning woman in the field. This has features in common with the following dreams, but it is far from identical with them.[216] The fourth vision thus shares structural elements with those visions which precede it and with those which follow it.

4.3.4. Structural Elements of the Dream Visions

The significance of these structural elements is confirmed by the next two visions. They are of a new type, dreams, symbolic in nature. They also share a common structure: the dream itself, the seer's response to the dream; the angelophany, the intepretation, and the concluding injunctions. The injunctions at the end of the fourth vision, which form the transition to the fifth vision, the first dream, are equally notable, for they signal the change that has now taken place. Ezra is to remain in the field, but he is to observe no special regimen, and after a further two nights he will see another vision. No prayer is mentioned, and no special food, though it becomes clear from 12:51 (in the transition between Vision 5 and Vision 6) that he has maintained the vegetarian diet. Thus, though the location and the food patterns continue those which preceded in Vision 4, further elements of the pattern evident there have now been abandoned. No agitation, no distress, and no inspired address or plaint occur here.

The two days' period seems odd initially, particularly in view of the seven days' periods that have occurred consistently throughout the book to date. The periods of

---

212 See Excursus on Inspiration, p. 121.

213 See General Structure of the Book, pp. 50–51, for the pericope division and the characterization of these various parts. The third vision, which is extremely long, is divided into a number of "sub-visions" structured chiefly of the same elements as Visions 1 and 2.

214 Above, one example of the progression of Ezra's

thought was expounded, in connection with "understanding the way of the Most High."

215 This has been noted before, of course, and the various opinions about it are discussed in 9:26–28 Form and Function, pp. 304–5. Breech's view that it symbolizes the shift from mourning to consolation is not atypical (see ibid.).

216 See General Structure of the Book, Table 2.

time between the visions are irregular in the rest of the book, but there is a reason for this, as will be explained below.[217]

The transition between Vision 5 and Vision 6 resembles this one, both as to location and regimen, but the period of time is there seven days. It is most significant that the elements of agitation, distress, and inspired address are quite absent. The fourth vision displayed these elements which occurred regularly in the first three visions and, on the other hand, was set in the field and involved the consumption of vegetable food, typical features of the fifth and sixth visions. This highlights the pivotal position of Vision 4. Something has happened by the end of Vision 3 which is indicated by the partial shift, and something much more radical happened in Vision 4 itself which made the fixed elements of the framework of Visions 1 to 3 no longer appropriate.

4.3.5. Structural Indications in Vision 7

An even greater change is marked at the end of the sixth vision. Ezra is told to wait in the field for three more days (13:56). He arose, walked in the field, and praised God for his wonders. This description forms a remarkable contrast to the beginning of the first vision. Ezra commences his vision experience lying on his bed, in Babylon, weeping in the dark of his room over the destruction of Zion. By the start of the seventh vision he is outside in the field, where no human building has stood (cf. 10:53), and he is walking around praising God the Creator.[218] Furthermore, as has been pointed out, each of the three parts of Vision 7 takes place in a different location or position (14:1–26; 14:27–36; and 14:37–48).[219]

4.3.6. Conclusions from Structure

Thus it is evident that the framework forms an important initial key to the understanding of the book, and here we have noted only the most salient aspect of its interlocking structures. In the course of the Commentary, repeatedly, it will be made evident that the devel-opment of the ideas in the book and its inner dynamic are very intimately related to and indeed are reflected in the changes in the literary structure. Our approach to this issue is profoundly anchored in the view that, whatever sources the author may have used, the book is a very deliberate composition of his. Indeed, the considered structure bespeaks a very conscious author and a very skilled one.

This consideration combines with the example given above of the development of a single concept within the first three visions. Together they lead to the conclusion that there is a deliberate development not only through-out the whole book but also within the first three visions.

4.4. Ezra

4.4.1. Ezra and the Angel—Brandenburger and Harnisch

This calls us to reassess the position of Brandenburger and of Harnisch on the absolutely central issue of the *personae* of the angel and of Ezra as they are reflected in 4 Ezra. Their analysis, which is set forth above,[220] has been most important, for they highlighted the difficulties of the role of the angel which had been little considered by prior scholars. It seems to be quite correct that the positions taken by the angel or by God, and the angel often speaks as if he were God,[221] cannot and should not be ignored. They must be an essential part of the author's teaching. It seems to us that, having discovered this important truth, these scholars then proceed to the other extreme, for the role of Ezra cannot be ignored either.

Their analysis would make the book predominantly a polemical work,[222] propagating the views of the angel in Visions 1–3, views that are accepted by Ezra by the time of Vision 7 (see 14:28–36). That these views are rather conventional does not in itself invalidate Branden-burger's and Harnisch's position, but certain literary facts do call for a reassessment of their estimation of the position of Ezra in the first three visions.

---

217 On the days in the book and their significance, see 12:37–39 Function and Content, pp. 373–74.

218 The contrast with the beginning of Vision 1 is deliberate and is expressed not just in the form and structure of the two introduction-transition passages but also in the content of the words ascribed to Ezra. This is set forth in detail in 13:56–58 Function and Content, p. 409.

219 See Brandenburger, *Verborgenheit*, 134; cf. 115.

220 See sec. 3.3, p. 16.

221 See 7:17 Commentary.

222 Brandenburger's disclaimers do not change this position; see sec. 3.3, pp. 16–17.

4.4.2. What Happened to Ezra?

After all, the book is in the first person, the hero is clearly Ezra. This literary phenomenon is so obvious that, until the work of Brandenburger, the role of the angel was not perceived in its complexity. Something has obviously happened to "Ezra" by the end of the third vision, and something more happens in the fourth vision, as is evident from the analysis of the formal and structural elements we have pursued above. In the most basic way, the book reflects what happened to "Ezra." What was it?

The results of what happened to Ezra are very clearly to be seen in the fourth vision. In response to his address there, no angel appears, but he sees a woman weeping in the field, he comforts her and she is transformed into a glorious city. The tale of the woman may have been drawn from folklore. For our analysis, however, the parallels between the mourning woman and the Ezra of the first three visions are deeply significant.[223] Both are promised or receive redemption after thirty years (3:1; 9:43); both fast, mourn, and weep. When Ezra comforts the woman in the latter part of this experience, the complementary reversal of roles takes place and Ezra acts toward the woman as the angel had acted toward him.

His role as comforter is skillfully highlighted by a series of close literary parallels between his discourse and activities and those of the angel earlier.[224] This reversal of roles is very striking and is possible only because Ezra has accepted fully what the angel has said to him in the course of the previous visions. Part of this process may be traced in the course of those visions, as we have shown above, but even at the very end of Vision 3, Ezra had difficulty in assenting unquestioningly to the clear implications of the angel's teachings about the few and the many.[225] In 10:10, however, he states as part of the words of comfort he offered to the woman that "all go to perdition, and a multitude of them are destined for destruction." This idea is precisely that view at which Ezra has rebelled at the end of the previous vision, that

there are few saved and many damned.

Ezra's acceptance of the consolation the angel had earlier offered him is even more amazing. He declares, "For if you acknowledge the decree of God to be just, you will receive your son back in due time" (10:16). In the address at the start of Vision 1, Ezra cast deep doubt on the justice of God's action; here he holds out God's very justice as a comfort to the woman. He offers wholeheartedly that comfort which he was unable to accept when it was extended to him.

Once he accepted all that he was taught, the issue of the few and the many withdrew to the background and the mourning for Zion reasserted itself poignantly. Vision 1 had opened with pain over the destruction of Zion and the abundance of Babylon (3:2), and the same theme completely dominates this fourth vision. It is the meaning of the woman's tale, it is the mainspring of Ezra's subsequent comfort. Ezra's deep emotions about the destruction of Zion were channeled by the access of the woman's grief and the human need to console her. The act of reaching out in comfort catalyzed the internalization of Ezra's newly integrated worldview.

4.4.3. Ezra's Conversion

At this very point (10:25–27), Ezra undergoes a powerful religious experience. The woman is transformed into a glorious city and Ezra's powers of vision and hearing, and his very physical orientation, are disturbed; he is badly frightened, he loses consciousness and calls for his angelic guide. The experience described is unique not just in 4 Ezra but in the whole of Jewish apocalyptic literature. Its intensity complements the pressure of unrelieved stress evident in the first part of the vision, and it resembles the major reorientation of personality usually connected with religious conversion.[226]

It is quite clear therefore that the change in Ezra involves at least two elements, a gradual acceptance of some of the angel's teachings during the course of the first three visions and then, in the fourth vision, a power-

---

223 Parts of this and the following four paragraphs are drawn from Stone, "Apocalypse of Ezra."

224 See 10:5–24 Function and Content, pp. 318–21.

225 See, e.g., 8:4–36. This is discussed in detail in 8:62—9:22 Function and Content, p. 293.

226 See M. E. Stone, "Reactions to Destructions of the Second Temple," *JSJ* 12 (1982) 203–4, where this theory was first raised. The literature on religious

conversion is very extensive and the structures and categories employed to describe it vary greatly. A broad survey of the literature is L. R. Rambo, "Current Research on Religious Conversion," *RSR* 8.2 (1982) 146–59. Rambo has also written a summary article in *Encyclopedia of Religions.* Two passages there are particularly appropriate to the description of Ezra's experience: "Some kind of crisis

ful religious experience during which these teachings are internalized. At a deeper level, one might say that in the first three visions the author externalizes his convictions in the figure of the angel, while in the fourth, by a conversion experience, he internalizes those convictions and externalizes his grief and hope in the form of the woman-city. Once this basic dynamic is grasped, the functioning both of the Ezra figure and of the angel becomes quite clear. For this reason the angel, after the conversion experience, returns to the traditional role of *angelus interpres.* For this reason too, Ezra takes on, gradually, the role of a prophet, and that role is fully recognized by him and by the people in the narrative following the fifth vision (12:40–49).[227]

4.4.4. The Odyssey of Ezra's Soul

Our claim therefore is that the thread that holds the book together is the Odyssey of Ezra's soul. Brandenburger rejects Gunkel's psychological approach, preferring to regard the whole book as a theological *Auseinandersetzung.*[228] We hold that Gunkel's basic insight must be followed, though the book must be analyzed in quite different ways from those followed by Gunkel.

Ezra is truly the hero, the dominant *persona* of the book. At the same time, throughout the first three visions this Ezra is in dialogue, nay in dispute, with the angel. The dispute that commenced because of the destruction of the Temple pushed Ezra beyond the basic assumption of the justice of God. Ezra does not accept his own doubts, however, but struggles with them by means of the angel, who represents that part of himself which wishes to accept but is forced to doubt by the impact of events of the history of Israel and the world. Thus it is in the first three visions. Ezra and the angel are both the author but are Janus faces of the author's self.[229]

The weeping woman whom he sees in the fourth vision is also an aspect of his own experience—she is his pain and distress over Zion. In comforting her, the seer undergoes a dramatic change, a shift, a conversion. That which had been outside him, as "God" or "the angel," suddenly became dominant; instead, he sees his pain and distress as externalized.[230] The key to the understanding of the fourth vision is that it is a description of a major religious experience, a conversion. This perception makes the sudden shift in Ezra's expressed positions comprehensible.[231] The significance of that sudden shift

precedes conversion. . . . During this crisis, myths, rituals, symbols, goals and standards cease to function well . . . creating great disturbance in the individual's life" (4:75). Moreover, Rambo presents the idea of "identification," a type of conversion that is "a revitalized commitment to a faith with which converts have had previous affiliation." This occurs when the faith of such persons becomes central to their lives or when they "intensify involvement through profound religious experience and/or explosive new insights" (4:74–75). A great range of views and approaches to conversion is presented by W. E. Conn, *Conversion: Perspectives on Personal and Social Transformation* (New York: Alba House, 1978). In a chapter included in that book, R. Thouless describes the same phenomenon of second or mature conversion that profoundly affected and reorientated the lives of the individuals concerned. One view is that Ezra's conversion described here is of this type. An analysis of the psychological mechanics involved from an essentially behaviorist perspective is by W. W. Sargant, *Battle for the Mind: A Physiology of Conversion and Brainwashing* (New York: Doubleday, 1957). Cf. also 10:25–28 Form and Function.

227 Other themes exhibit the same process of development, and these are traced in detail in the course of the Commentary. One is the theme of Ezra's right-

eousness, attitudes toward it, and Ezra's own eventual acceptance of it. This is discussed particularly in 6:32 Commentary and in 8:62 Commentary. Cf. also 12:36. The incident with the people is analyzed in detail by Brandenburger, *Verborgenheit,* 111–13.

228 See Brandenburger, *Verborgenheit,* 36. Brandenburger, in fact, has been sensitive to aspects of this, even though that runs against his own view of the book; see ibid., 89 n. 68; cf. p. 156.

229 See n. 209 above.

230 For one description of possible psychological mechanisms underlying this reorientation of the author's personality, see Sargant, *Battle for the Mind.* A rather different psychological dynamic is assumed by D. Merkur, "The Visionary Practice of Jewish Apocalyptists," who sees the fear and collapse described in his manuscript on pp. 41–43 as a crucial element in this reorientation.

231 Brandenburger, in his analysis, quite correctly stresses and restresses the shift in Ezra's personality in the fourth vision. This is the dominant subject of his third chapter (*Verborgenheit,* 58–90). Because of his chariness of psychological explanations, however, he ends up talking only of *das Mysterium der Verwandlung Ezras* (p. 87), with no further explanation.

can be appreciated only when it is perceived not as the result of deliberate "authorial" policy, designed to advance certain views to the disadvantage of others, but as the result of profound religious experience.

In making this statement, we imply that the religious experiences described in 4 Ezra were real religious experiences, and it is our view that they were the actual experiences of the author.[232] We do not maintain that in every detail the experiences are exact reports of alternate states experienced by the author, but this is so of major parts of them. This opinion is confirmed by the fact that certain central types of the religious experiences related in 4 Ezra are quite unparalleled in the other apocalypses.[233] Now, the fact that a vision is of a unique type strengthens the argument for its not being mere "stage dressing." However, once the probability is admitted that the author's actual religious experience lies behind that of "Ezra" in certain central instances, it becomes distinctly possible that even where the vision forms described are of a quite conventional type, they nonetheless reflect the author's actual experiences.[234] Here lies one major key to the understanding of the book.

Addressing the problem of whether the texts "fictionalized self-reports or were thorough fictions by skillful authors," D. Merkur comments:

Where we can detect evidence of unconscious pro-

cesses in documents written prior to Freud's discoveries, even the most remote possibility of literary artifice is excluded. Ancient authors cannot have counterfeited what they did not know to exist. A second criterion must also be applied. . . . It is when unconscious materials . . . erupt massively into consciousness, dominating thought, that the psyche has entered an alternate state.[235]

Merkur concludes that the vision experience of 4 Ezra and of certain other apocalypses rings true, and he makes suggestions about the psychological dynamic involved.[236]

4.5. Ezra and Revelation

4.5.1. Accounting for Vision 7

One further line of thought must be followed in order to complete an elementary outline of our perception of 4 Ezra and its meaning. This will center around the seventh vision. Rightly, again, Brandenburger has urged the central importance of this vision and demands that any basic understanding of the book account for it.[237] His own thesis does not satisfactorily deal with the whole latter part of the book, trying to explain it as apocalyptic wisdom = Torah, related to Ezra's new prophetic role in Vision 4.[238]

---

232 See already M. E. Stone, "Apocalyptic: Vision or Hallucination?" *Milla wa-Milla* 14 (1974) 47–56. The possibilities were explored further in M. E. Stone, "Apocalyptic Literature," *Jewish Writings of the Second Temple Period* (ed. M. E. Stone; CRINT 2.2; Assen and Philadelphia: van Gorcum and Fortress, 1984) 429–31. See also the discussion by C. Rowland, *The Open Heaven* (New York: Crossroad, 1982), particularly p. 243. The whole problem is reassessed in Excursus on Inspiration below. There are, of course, no "hard and fast" proofs of this, but the detail, uniqueness, and ring of psychological truth in the descriptions of the book mean that what is described is either the reflection of real experience or deeply insightful writing based on a sensitive knowledge of real experience. The exegetical implications of both of these positions are much the same.

233 Note the description of the access of inspired speech, found both in the narratives with which Visions 1–3 open and in Vision 7 where Ezra receives sacred scripture; this is discussed in Excursus on Inspiration, pp. 119–21. Also very important in this context is

the "conversion" experience which is analyzed in 10:25–28 Function and Content, pp. 647–50.

234 The most conventional of the visions in the book are the symbolic dreams in Visions 5 and 6. Such dreams are common in the Jewish apocalypses. Hartman, *Prophecy Interpreted*, 105, holds that the apocalypses may present real visionary experience in conventional form.

235 Merkur, "Visionary Practices," 2.

236 Ibid.

237 See Brandenburger, *Verborgenheit*, 132–39, on this vision.

238 See ibid., 29–30. See sec. 3.3, above pp. 17–18.

4.5.2. Ezra as Prophet and "the End of the Times"

After the experience of Vision 5—the dream of the eagle, which was interpreted as a prophecy of the end of the Roman Empire—two new elements are introduced into the narrative structure. One is a confrontation between Ezra and the people.[239] In 12:44 the people cry, "Better that we die," a cry that had been Ezra's in 4:12. In chapter 4 the angel had answered Ezra in God's name and here Ezra answers the people in God's name (12:47). This makes far more explicit the role reversal that was observed above to take place in Vision 4, and a further, new element is introduced here. The people cry, "For of all the prophets you alone are left to us" (12:42). For the first time Ezra is referred to as a prophet. In accordance with this role he comforts the people in God's name.[240] Ezra does not deny this role but apparently accepts it.

Earlier in this vision, Ezra had responded to the dream by saying: "For thou hast judged me worthy to be shown the end of the times and the last events of the times" (12:9). The subject of Ezra's worthiness is a sustained one throughout the book, and here it reaches a particularly important stage, for it is now Ezra who asserts it, not the angel.[241] But it is the term "end of the times" that catches our attention. This occurred previously in 3:14, where it is the content of the secret revelation to Abraham.[242] Equally, the revelation to Moses is said to have been about "the end of the times" (14:5). So Ezra's assertion here is, in the first place, a reflection of how deeply his self-consciousness is changed, of his new role as prophet.

4.5.3. "The End of the Times" and Esoteric Revelations

However, this has further ramifications, since "the end of the times" is the subject of the *esoteric* revelations to the greatest of past figures. Here, in 12:37, Ezra is instructed to write the secrets revealed to him in a book, to hide it and to instruct the wise in this esoteric teaching. This is an element found at the end of other apocalyptic visions,[243] but it is the first occasion on which such a command is given in 4 Ezra. This again marks the completion of the change in Ezra's position that took place in Vision 4. The change from challenger to comforter signals his acceptance of the way the world is conducted, and consequently he can function like other apocalyptic seers. Now he can receive esoteric revelations, and he is commanded to write them and transmit them.

Moreover, this is completely in line with the author's views of special and revealed knowledge. What was rejected in 4:5–9 and 5:36–37 was not all types of revealed information, for there, immediately after the rejection of special knowledge, Ezra proceeds to inquire about eschatological secrets. Instead, it is speculative cosmology and uranography that are rejected, while eschatological secrets are part of the inner revelation to Abraham, to Moses, and to Ezra himself.

4.5.4. Vision 7 and Revealed Knowledge

These attitudes provide an essential key to the understanding not just of the relationship of the fifth and sixth visions to the first four but also of the function of the seventh vision. This vision is of a quite different type from any of the preceding, being a narrative about the receipt of a revelation rather than a narrative of the revelation. It is complex, and only certain themes will be taken up here.[244] The address with which it opens is by God to Ezra, the reverse of Ezra's speeches to God with which Visions 1–4 commenced. God alone is Ezra's interlocutor in this vision. We regard these contrasts as deliberate and flowing from Ezra's changed role. The

---

239 This is perhaps comparable to the meeting between Ezra and Paltiel following Vision 1 (5:15–18). Both of these incidents take place following the first vision of a new part of the book.

240 See further 12:40–51 Function and Content, p. 376.

241 Contrast, e.g., 10:38–39 and 10:55–57, where the angel does so.

242 The fifth vision itself refers to "the end of the times" as coming (11:39; 11:44) and revealed to Ezra (12:9).

243 See further 12:37–39 Function and Content, p. 372.

244 As was true above, here too the detailed argumentation to support our assertions is to be found in the Commentary on this vision. The kernel of the matter is set forth here, in order to give an overview of our understanding of the central thrust of the book's conceptual, structural, and literary development. Gunkel had characterized Vision 7 as an "aesthetically pleasing conclusion to the book" (Gunkel, p. 348; cf. idem, *Der Prophet Esra*, xxix).

address is a historical recital of the *magnalia Dei,* culminating in the revelation of the Torah and the eschatological secrets to Moses on Sinai.[245] Following the historical recital, God proceeds to injunctions and prediction. The end is close, Ezra will be assumed so as not to experience the horrible events of the last generation (14:7–18). In particular, he is told to keep secret the chief preceding eschatological revelations, called "signs, visions and interpretations."[246]

Immediately preceding the verse in which Ezra is commanded to keep these revelations secret (14:8), reference is made to God's command about the double revelation to Moses: "These words you shall publish openly, and these [i.e., "the secrets of the times" and "the end of the times"—M.E.S.] you shall keep secret." The conjunction is highly significant. Already in 12:37, as we have noted, Ezra was instructed to write down the eschatological secrets and teach them. His assumption is close.

4.5.5. Vision 7 as Revelation of Exoteric Knowledge
It is in the light of this conjunction of circumstances that Ezra's petition in 14:19–22 may be understood. Indeed, he has achieved prophetic status and has been granted esoteric, eschatological revelation. That revelation was completed by the end of the sixth vision. As pointed out above,[247] the framework at the end of that vision is the positive complement to the framework at the beginning of the first vision. Ezra is truly comforted for the destruction of Zion by the esoteric revelation. Now he asks for a renewal of the exoteric, the open revelation, and that is what is granted to him in Vision 7 (14:37–48). At the end of this revelation he is given the same command that Moses had received, to make the twenty-four open books public and to transmit the esoteric ones secretly. There-

fore the revelation in the final vision makes Ezra truly a new Moses: it moves him from being a prophet to being equal to the greatest of the prophets. Then he is taken to heaven alive to be with the Messiah and the elect.

This relationship between Ezra and Moses is also expressed in an important structural element. Ezra is commanded at various points to remain in the field and to fast or to abstain from certain foods. When all the days of fasting or abstention are totted up, from Vision 1 to the end of Vision 6, they make a total of 40. To the three weeks of 6:35[248] we add seven days between Visions 3 and 4, two days between Visions 4 and 5, the week between Visions 5 and 6, and the three days between Visions 6 and 7—40 in all. In Vision 7, Ezra fasts for 40 days while receiving the revelation of Scriptures, as Moses did. This revelation is parallel to the revelation of eschatological secrets in the first six visions. Both are associated with 40 days' fasting.[249] A crucial key to the double revelation of the book is thus provided.[250]

Consequently, not just Ezra's speech to the people ties the seventh vision to the fourth[251] but the central message of the seventh vision is the completion and complement of the first six. The requirement set up by Brandenburger that the seventh vision be shown to be an integral part of the whole book and to cohere within its structure is amply fulfilled, and great insight is gained thereby into the central dynamic of the work.

4.6. The Central Theme of 4 Ezra

4.6.1. The "Message" of the Book
The description of the inner dynamic and development of the book that has been given here does not deal in detail with the development of ideas within it. The author's point of departure in the address of Vision 1 is a

---

245 Note that not only did Ezra relate the history and use it as a sort of *"Unheilsgeschichte"* in Vision 1 but there Moses' role is not mentioned. Here it is central.

246 The "signs" are the messianic woes (5:1; 6:12), while "dreams" and interpretations refer to Visions 5 and 6.

247 See sec. 4.3.5 above.

248 This total is reached by taking the "three weeks" referred to in 6:35 as indicating not just the two seven-day periods mentioned between Visions 1 and 2 and Visions 2 and 3 but also a third seven-day period, not mentioned explicitly in the text there, preceding Vision 1. See further 6:35 Commentary.

249 This is the reason why the number of days is not seven consistently throughout but is reduced to two on one occasion and three on another. Otherwise, the total of 40 would be passed. Observe that the short periods precede the dream visions on the one hand and the revelation of the Torah on the other.

250 See further 12:37–39 Function and Content.

251 Thus Brandenburger, *Verborgenheit,* 50–51, who lays quite undue stress on this speech.

questioning of the very justice of God as expressed in divine action in history and in particular in the destruction of the Temple. This initial problem is answered during the first vision but leads to a series of further basic problems about theodicy—the tension between Israel's fate and Israel's election; the tension between purposeful creation, on the one hand, and the few saved and the many damned, on the other; and the tension between God's mercy and justice, to mention the central ones. All of these, however, are issues flowing from that of the destruction of Zion.

Conceptually speaking, these problems are extremely interesting, since the author is no mean thinker and his formulations are sharp and perceptive. The answers given by the angel, however, are rather conventional. God's workings are a mystery and beyond human comprehension; God loves Israel and will vindicate Israel in the end; God rejoices over the few saved and is not concerned over the many damned; God's mercy works in this world, while his justice is fully active only in the world to come.

In an essential way, the response to the underlying issues is given in the vision of the heavenly Jerusalem which comforts Ezra for Jerusalem's present destruction and by the two dream visions which promise the destruction of Rome and the redemption and vindication of Israel. Of course, modern men and women would say that the issues enumerated are, in the final analysis, intractable if approached as problems of systematic theological reflection. It is certainly true that 4 Ezra's questions are much more interesting than the answers given by the angel. In the course of the Commentary, we have tried to spell out these conceptual developments in detail and to trace the parallels to them in contemporary thought. These are of significance for the history of Judaism and of Christianity and are often paradigmatic of the impact of the events of history on Jewish thought.

What has particularly fascinated us, however, has been understanding how these commonplace answers served the author as adequate responses to the profound questions that he posed. By adequate we do not mean theologically adequate but religiously satisfying. How, we may ask, did they provide the author's worldview with a coherence that had been lost or profoundly threatened by the destruction? Why does Ezra, initially the skeptic, accept, nay embrace, these commonplaces and praise God for them? It may be that in the course of the introduction we have overly stressed this aspect of the development of 4 Ezra, not dealing in adequate detail with its theological and conceptual structures and development. These are discussed exhaustively in the Commentary, however, and our understanding of them is basically conditioned by the understanding here proposed of the religious dynamic of the book.

5.0. Section 5: 4 Ezra in Jewish Literature

From the section on text and transmission (sec. 1), it is evident that 4 Ezra was not preserved within the Jewish tradition. As far as is known, the book was transmitted only by various Christian churches. In this respect, 4 Ezra is not unique, and most of the Jewish literature of the Second Temple period survived only outside Jewish tradition.

5.1. An Apocalypse

We have frequently referred to 4 Ezra as an apocalypse. Without entering into a long, complicated debate in modern scholarship about the definition of apocalypse and the distinction between apocalypse and apocalypticism, we may quote J. J. Collins's definition of this literary genre:

> "Apocalypse" is a genre of revelatory literature with a narrative framework, in which a revelation is mediated by an otherworldly being to a human recipient, disclosing a transcendent reality which is both temporal, insofar as it envisages eschatological salvation, and spatial, insofar as it involves another, supernatural world.[252]

It is quite clear that 4 Ezra falls within the boundaries of Collins's definition.[253] In the following, therefore, we use "apocalypse" to designate a distinct literary genre, and, in our view, Collins's definition has not yet been surpassed.[254] Other chief apocalypses from the Second Temple period are *1 Enoch, 2 Enoch, 2 Apocalypse of*

---

252 J. J. Collins, ed., *Apocalypse: The Morphology of a Genre* (*Semeia* 14; Missoula, Mont.: Scholars, 1979) 9. The matter is dealt with succinctly by Stone, "Apocalyptic Literature," 392–94. References to prior bibliography may be found there.

253 We would distinguish the genre from the complex of

Baruch, 3 Apocalypse of Baruch, and *Apocalypse of Abraham,* as well as the biblical books of Daniel and Revelation.

The author places himself solidly within apocalyptic tradition. The eagle in Vision 5 is explicitly identified with the fourth of the beasts revealed "to your brother Daniel."[255] This sets the eagle vision, and by implication the whole book, within a continuing tradition of apocalyptic writing of which Daniel too was part. The author not only views himself as standing within such a tradition (cf. also 3:14 and 14:5) but has contemplated on and expands earlier writings belonging to it. The expression "your brother Daniel" is an important indication of his self-consciousness.[256]

5.1.1. The Figure of Ezra

In 3:1 Commentary the identification of Ezra, the pseudepigraphic author of the book, is discussed, and it seems to be beyond any doubt that he is Ezra the Scribe. No other apocalypse from the Second Temple period is attributed to him, however, and the later works associated with his name in Christian tradition all derived in the final analysis from 4 Ezra.[257] It is clear from chapter 14, the vision of the giving of the Torah, that Ezra was revered as a figure of great status, equal to that of Moses. Our interpretation of that vision makes that absolutely clear.[258]

In rabbinic sources too, though the references to Ezra are not numerous, he is given attributes similar to those of Moses. His particular role in the renewal of scriptures is stressed in all of these sources.[259]

The absence of Ezra apocalypses or even of many references to Ezra from earlier literature contrasts with the situation of figures such as Daniel and Enoch, who have a long history and a broad range of attestations.[260] This might be the result of the pure historical chance that earlier Ezra books have not survived. Ezra was a figure associated with exile and return, and this factor may also have played a role in the choice of him as pseudepigraphic author. In addition, various new or developing factors in the author's world may have made the selection of the Ezra figure particularly attractive.

It is deeply significant that part of Ezra's activities in the apocalypse, indeed, from one perspective their capstone, is the giving anew of scriptures that accompanied and perfected the revelation of eschatological secrets. Nothing of this sort is to be found in any earlier apocalypse.[261] Deep changes had taken place in Judaism in the Second Temple period when the sacred tradition of ancient Israel became written.[262] The process of writing down led in turn to the crystallization of a corpus of books and the gradual development in the direction of a Bible. The attitude toward scripture was thus profoundly transformed.[263] 4 Ezra is an apocalypse that bases part of its revelatory claims upon the results of that process. Its author felt the need to relate the apocalyptic revelation, for which very high claims were made (cf. 14:45–47), also to the revelation of scripture. It was not enough that Ezra received and transmitted the esoteric books, "the spring of understanding, the fountain of wisdom, and the river of knowledge." He also had to transmit or renew the central revelation of the twenty-four books of the Bible. This claim is comprehensible

---

ideas that scholars often call "apocalyptic" or apocalypticism. In this we follow the older discussion by K. Koch, *The Rediscovery of Apocalyptic* (Naperville, Ill.: Allenson, 1972) 28–33; see already our "Postscript" to "Lists," 439–44.

254 There were, presumably, other apocalypses which have been lost. Many such texts are listed by M. R. James, *The Lost Apocrypha of the Old Testament* (London: SPCK, 1920). Fragments are collected and discussed by Denis in his two complementary works: *Fragmenta* and *Introduction.*

255 See 12:11 Commentary and 12:10–36 Function and Content, p. 361.

256 See 12:11 Commentary.

257 See sec. 6 below.

258 See Commentary on chap. 14.

259 See sources cited in 14:1–2 Form and Function.

260 See M. E. Stone, *Scriptures, Sects and Visions: A Profile of Judaism from Ezra to the Jewish Revolts* (Philadelphia: Fortress, 1980) 39–41; and idem, "Apocalyptic Literature," 395–96.

261 Naturally, many apocalypses deal with the preservation of the revealed secrets as books. This was also a common theme of the Hellenistic world in general; see W. Speyer, *Bücherfunde in der Glaubenswerbung der Antike* (Göttingen: Vandenhoeck & Ruprecht, c. 1970). That does not diminish in any way the uniqueness of the claim of 4 Ezra to have received, like Moses, the revelation of Torah.

262 See M. E. Stone, "Three Transformations in Judaism: Scripture, History, and Redemption," *Numen* 32 (1985) 219–23 and previous bibliography there.

263 It should be remembered that 4 Ezra is almost

only in the light of the new role that the Bible must have come to play in the Judaism of that age.

Pseudepigraphy provided one way in which Judaism handled the confrontation with the deposit of past tradition. Traditions such as that associated with Enoch contrasted and competed with the legal-exegetical traditions that bore Moses' name. Their claims to antiquity, to reliability, and to present redeeming knowledge gave them a role as an alternate channel of authority.[264] From another perspective, "pseudepigraphy provided a way of handling the authoritative written tradition, in this respect parallel to the legal/exegetical tradition in function, though differing from it in content."[265] After all, the authors of the pseudepigraphic apocalypses claim to have a divinely inspired tradition that did not derive its authority from the revelation to Moses on Sinai. Yet that Mosaic revelation had enormous influence, even in the early stages of the development of apocalyptic. Thus, in spite of their sense of having an equally authoritative (even a rival) way of understanding the central truths of religion, the authors of the apocalypses felt impelled to set their way into the context of the received, age-old tradition. This is one function of the attribution of writings to figures from the past.[266]

In 4 Ezra, however, this process of confrontation with the written ancient tradition has gone one step farther. The pseudepigraphic device, which derives part of its authority from the Bible, did not suffice him. The role of the Bible as the source of authority had become so dominant that the author had to confront the actual written books. He did this in two different ways. One was to make the apocalyptic tradition anterior to the Sinai event and independent of it, yet at the same time to include it in the revelation at Sinai. This is done in 14:5,

where the same apocalyptic tradition that had been revealed to Abraham and was to be revealed to Ezra is said to have been revealed to Moses at Sinai. Moreover, not only was the apocalyptic lore revealed to Moses on Sinai as a tradition, *it was written down in books at Sinai.* This unique claim indicates the enhanced impact of the Bible on the way authoritative traditions were conceived. They must be written in books.[267]

The other means that the author used in order to handle the enormously enhanced authoritative role of the Bible in confrontation with his apocalyptic tradition was that of attributing the revelation of the Bible itself to his apocalyptic hero. This gives the final stamp of deepest authority to Ezra as a revealer. Again the extraordinary importance of Vision 7 in the book is absolutely clear. It provides a key insight into particular developments of the author's contemporary Judaism and is a clear example of how a conscious and sophisticated apocalyptic author handled them.

5.1.2. 4 Ezra and Known Jewish Groups or Sects

Extremely little can be said about the relationship between 4 Ezra and the groupings within Judaism toward the end of the first century c.e. As is clear from the Commentary, frequently 4 Ezra conforms to the exegetical or theological ideas preserved in the rabbinic tradition. It bears no signs of any special relationship to the Qumran sect.[268] An attempt has been made to discover something about the nature of its social matrix by examining its eschatological expectations.[269] The results of this examination were meager and threw only dim light on one aspect of the worldview of the group from which the author came. They contributed nothing directly to an identification of any group or trend within Judaism of that age which might have been the matrix

---

contemporary with R. Aqiba. In that generation, in rabbinic circles, the process of the integration of traditional learning into the exegesis of scripture was accelerated. Scripture becomes a dominant factor.

264 This matter is analyzed in detail in a forthcoming paper: M. E. Stone, "Pseudepigraphy and Reflexivity." See also 3:1–3 Form and Function, pp. 54–55. Rowland, *Open Heaven,* 69, suggests that pseudepigraphy was the means by which the authors guaranteed that their works would be treated reverently.

265 Stone, "Pseudepigraphy and Reflexivity."

266 These ideas are worked out in fuller detail in Stone, ibid.

267 Yet, for 4 Ezra, the independence of apocalyptic authority remained significant. Consequently, he can talk about the revelation of a *written* apocalyptic corpus at Sinai, in contrast to rabbinic ideas about the revelation of an *oral* Torah there.

268 See Stone, "Apocalyptic Literature," 414. M. Philonenko, "Introduction générale," *La Bible: Ecrits intertestamentaires* (Paris: Gallimard, 1987) cxvi, argues energetically but not convincingly for "multiples rapprochements avec la littérature

within which 4 Ezra was molded. The same is true of the work of Brandenburger and Harnisch, discussed in section 3 above, which attempted to isolate different, opposed groups or trends of thought by analysis of the dialogues in 4 Ezra. Nothing emerged from their work that enabled any direct or indirect identification of the book with known groups or sects.

5.1.3. 4 Ezra, *2 Apocalypse of Baruch,* and *Biblical Antiquities*

An examination of the relationships between 4 Ezra, *2 Apocalypse of Baruch,* and *Biblical Antiquities* also produces limited results. On the one hand, it is indubitable that there is an intimate relationship between *2 Apocalypse Baruch* and 4 Ezra. The difficulty is in isolating exactly what this relationship is. Even a cursory perusal of the Commentary will show that the body of parallels and similarities existing between these two works far outnumber those existing between 4 Ezra and any other

book. The similarities extend beyond specifics of phraseology and concepts to the seven-fold structure and the general historical setting. Violet in his study of the two works reached the conclusion that 4 Ezra served as a source for *2 Apocalypse of Baruch.*[270] The opposite conclusion was reached by P. Bogaert in his commentary on *2 Apocalypse of Baruch.*[271]

In fact, the existence of an intimate relationship is quite obvious, but the direction of dependence is very difficult to determine. If there were decisive arguments in one or the other direction, of course, the matter would not still be the subject of difference of opinion.[272] We have not discovered any arguments in the course of our work that seem to be decisive in the one or the other direction.

The situation with respect to *Biblical Antiquities* is even more uncertain. Striking parallels in formulation and turn of phrase have been listed by M. R. James and by Violet. Scholars who have examined the issue have

---

qoûmranienne." F. Rosenthal, *Vier apokryphische Bücher aus der Zeit und Schule R. Akiba's* (Leipzig: Schulze, 1885), attempted to relate 4 Ezra to particular streams in rabbinic thought of the period of Yabneh, and similar attempts have been made by other scholars. Such views have not met with acceptance, though affinities of many ideas in the book with those found in rabbinic thought are undeniable. An assessment of 4 Ezra's relationship with Jewish groups was made in an unpublished thesis by M. L. Gray, "Towards the Reconstruction of 4 Esdras and the Establishment of Its Contemporary Context" (B. Litt. thesis, Oxford University, 1976). Unfortunately I have been unable to examine his work in full, but his conclusion is much like ours, that 4 Ezra shows clear connections with rabbinic circles, yet is not rabbinic, while on the other hand 4 Ezra has no particular relationship with the Qumran sect. His grounds of argument differ from ours in a number of respects.

269 M. E. Stone, "The Question of the Messiah in 4 Ezra," *Judaisms and Their Messiahs at the Turn of the Christian Era* (ed. J. Neusner, W. S. Green, and E. S. Frerichs; New York: Cambridge University, 1987) 215–20.

270 Violet 2, p. lv, who quotes with approval the views of Charles, Box, and Zahn. He says, "Ich bin im Verlaufe der Arbeit seit 1910 nur umso sicherer geworden, daß Esra das Original, Baruch aber der Benutzer ist." Farther on, on pp. lxxxi-xc, he adduces a series of detailed arguments to demonstrate this hypothesis.

271 See P. Bogaert, *L'Apocalypse syriaque de Baruch* (Sources chrétiennes 144–145; Paris: Cerf, 1969). In vol. 1, pp. 26–27, he presents various views of the matter, choosing to follow that of Schürer, who came down for the anteriority of *2 Apocalypse of Baruch.* In that volume, on pp. 113–14, Bogaert discusses rabbinic traditions that set Baruch and Ezra in the relationship of master and disciple. This being chronologically impossible, Bogaert sees these traditions as in fact reflecting the relationship between the two apocalypses.

272 A sampling of recent opinion follows: G. W. E. Nickelsburg, *Jewish Literature Between the Bible and the Mishnah* (Philadelphia: Fortress, 1981) 287, regards the relationship as uncertain. This is also true of H. D. F. Sparks, *The Apocryphal Old Testament* (Oxford: Oxford University, 1984) 838, who talks of 4 Ezra, *2 Apocalypse of Baruch,* and *Biblical Antiquities* as reflecting the same background and period, which would account for the similarities between. Yet the relationships between 4 Ezra and *2 Apocalypse of Baruch* in particular are so striking as to force us beyond this cautious hypothesis. B. Metzger, on the other hand, in Charlesworth, *OTP,* 1:522, thinks that *2 Apocalypse of Baruch* "appears to have been written as an answer to the perplexities mentioned by the seer" (i.e., of 4 Ezra). Klijn in the same volume (p. 620) talks of a common source.

generally been of the opinion that *Biblical Antiquities* is definitely a source used by *2 Apocalypse of Baruch* and was most probably a source used by *4 Ezra*.[273]

Consequently, all that can be said about the place of the work in contemporary Judaism is that it shows a proximity to rabbinic teaching at a significant number of points and that it is intimately connected with *2 Apocalypse of Baruch* and somewhat less with *Biblical Antiquities*. These points are important for determining certain general things about *4 Ezra*, but they are of singularly little help if we pose a question about *4 Ezra*'s place within a securely known historical context of the late first century.

5.2. Social Matrix and Function

This aporia is rendered more acute by certain conditions resulting from the pseudepigraphic form. No source external to *4 Ezra* provides information about the author (or authors) or about his (their) way of life or habits. Whatever can be learned is by inference from the writing itself. Yet pseudepigraphy makes the latter process perilous. In a basic way, the book is motivated by the destruction of the Temple, and that provides a primary

context. Yet we do not know how the book functioned and to whom it was directed.[274] In Brandenburger's and Harnisch's view of the book as polemical, something is implied about the polemical opponents. Yet their type of analysis has been found to be far from satisfactory.[275] Nonetheless, the examination of *4 Ezra*'s discourse to seek for possible clues to views being opposed, and so to their social matrix, is not thereby disqualified in principle. Such approaches have been utilized successfully in other fields of learning. Yet in the case of *4 Ezra*, it is far from certain that it is a distinct polemical opponent that is being attacked. Many scholars have suggested that much of the conflict is within the author's personality.[276]

The issue of the sociological matrix of the apocalypses remains largely intractable. No source external to *4 Ezra* provides any information about its authors, and little can be learned within the book itself. Despite this, it has been argued that the apocalypses reflect, either directly or indirectly, some genuine religious experience.[277] Furthermore, the esotericism of the apocalypses does not seem to be the reflection of a conventicle with secret teachings.[278] These two features, together with a consid-

---

273 M. R. James, *The Biblical Antiquities of Philo* (London: SPCK, 1917) 46–53, sets out the parallels between this work and *2 Apocalypse of Baruch*, while on pp. 53–58 he lists those shared with *4 Ezra*. He concludes that *Biblical Antiquities* "is a product of the circle from which both *Baruch* and *4 Esdras* emanated: and it seems to me clear that the writer of *Baruch* at least was acquainted with *Philo*." James, moreover, observes that the Latin of *4 Ezra* is so similar to that of *Biblical Antiquities* that "one is tempted to say that they are by the same hand" (p. 54). That is quite a separate issue. In his prolegomenon to the reissue of James's work (New York: Ktav, 1971), L. H. Feldman provides a conspectus of recent views but reaches no conclusion. Violet 2 also set forth a list of some parallels between *4 Ezra* and *Biblical Antiquities*, but notes that the similarity of the Latin may lead to an illusion of greater resemblance than actually exists (pp. liv–lv). Nonetheless, he holds that *4 Ezra* used *Biblical Antiquities*. In his comments on the relationship between *Biblical Antiquities* and *2 Apocalypse of Baruch*, he says that the former is "eine der wichtigsten Quellen für die Ap. Baruch" (p. lxxxi). The matter is also discussed, with a marshaling of evidence but no clear conclusion, by Bogaert, *Baruch*, 1:244–58.

274 L. Hartman's view that the apocalypses may have

been read portion by portion at conventicles of apocalypticists remains sheer speculation (Hartman, *Prophecy Interpreted*, 51–52). Other such attempts are dealt with in Stone, "Apocalyptic Literature," 433–35. They all remain fanciful.

275 See sec. 3.3 above. Brandenburger's disclaimers in *Verborgenheit*, 47, make no difference to the question of whether the skeptical views that the author of *4 Ezra* is supposedly attacking have a social matrix and whether, therefore, by implication, the opponents of such views may also be assumed to work within such a distinct social context.

276 See secs. 4.4.1–4.4.4. This was, of course, the view of Gunkel, pp. 339–42.

277 See D. S. Russell, *The Method and Message of Jewish Apocalyptic* (OTL; Philadelphia: Westminster, 1964) 158–77; Stone, "Apocalyptic Literature," 429–31; and idem, "Vision or Hallucination?"

278 Stone, "Apocalyptic Literature," 431–32; see further n. 281 below.

eration of its eschatological hope, shed some light on the author's (or authors') context.

5.2.1. Evidence from Messianism

4 Ezra seems to have been written in the land of Israel, in Hebrew, about 100 C.E.[279] It was composed in response to the destruction of the Second Temple and in clear yearning for the end of the Roman Empire and the vindication of Israel. Consequently, for the author, the idea of redemption is pivotal, and the examination of his eschatological aspirations might serve as a key to evaluation of his present quandary. The Messiah played a significant role in that vindication and in the progress of the eschatological events.[280] He was described primarily as acting in legal terms rather than in military ones; his coming as king was not expected. Yet, in the context of the book's concern for theodicy and redemption, it is notable that, although central in the latter visions, which are most dependent on preexisting traditions and sources, the Messiah plays no role in the first four visions, except for his brief appearance in 7:28–29. So, although part of the author's repertoire of eschatology, he is not so essential as to have to be mentioned anytime it might have been possible to do so.

The author very much underplayed the Messiah's role as king and to a somewhat lesser extent as warrior. In the book, the messianic kingdom is expected to be but a stage on the way to final judgment. At its end the Messiah will die (7:29). Consequently, it seems clear that the restoration of the ideal situation of the Davidic monarchy did not play a major role in the author's expectations for his ideal future polity. The destruction of the Roman Empire was very important, and it is the point of Visions 5 and 6. However, the destruction of Rome was expected to take place through the Messiah's

exercise of judgmental functions rather than military. This again seems to reinforce the author's nonmonarchical view of the future state. It is impossible, at least at present, to determine what may be inferred about the actual situation of the author (or authors) from this. The vindication of divine justice through the final day of judgment stands at the peak of the author's expectations (7:30–44), and the restoration of David's empire was not central for him. These views hint, so it may be maintained, at the sorts of ideals the author fostered and perhaps at the actual situation that evoked these ideals.

5.2.2. Esotericism and Sectarianism

A good deal may be inferred from the "pseudo-esotericism" of the apocalypses. While generally presenting themselves as esoterically transmitted information (cf. 4 Ezra 3:14 and 14:5–6; 14:45–48), these works, it has been argued, were in fact not esoteric in character, that is, they were not the actual secret teaching of apocalyptic conventicles.[281] This does not mean that some of the apocalypses may not have originated in discrete social contexts. Indeed, scholars have claimed that certain groups of apocalypses, such as some Enoch writings, stem from very self-conscious sectarian contexts which have even been identified as historically known groups. This sort of conclusion about the Enochic writings was made possible by various pieces of information in the books, both details that can be interpreted historically and also elements of terminology.[282] Yet 4 Ezra is not so kind to the scholar, and such details are lacking.[283]

5.2.3. Cognate Writings and Cognate Groups

For the present discussion, the relationship between 4 Ezra and *2 Apocalypse of Baruch* is a significant matter.

---

279 See sec. 2 above.
280 See Excursus on the Redeemer Figure, where the Messiah and Redeemer figures are discussed in detail.
281 See Stone, "Apocalyptic Literature," 431–32. On the "conventicle" theory of apocalyptic origins, see J. J. Collins, *The Apocalyptic Imagination* (New York: Crossroad, 1984) 29.
282 So Collins, *Imagination*, 58–63, basically operating with all of *1 Enoch* except the *Similitudes* and identifying the Enochic works as originating in Hasidean circles. The argument is made primarily on the basis of the actual texts of the works themselves. Ideas and

terminology of self-designation were isolated that reflected sectarian self-consciousness. Historical connections were sought, in this case with some success. The commonality of certain of the Enoch writings and the differences between various of them are well-known facts; see recently J. C. Greenfield and M. E. Stone, "The Enochic Pentateuch and the Date of the Similitudes," *HTR* 70 (1977), esp. 55–56.
283 Thus, in his parallel treatment of this work, Collins, whose conclusions about the Enoch books are so far-reaching, finds himself nonplussed and can say nothing definite at all about its circles of origin or

The two books also exhibit affinities with the *Apocalypse of Abraham,* which is, however, rather different, and to a lesser extent with *Biblical Antiquities.* 4 Ezra, *2 Apocalypse of Baruch,* and *Apocalypse of Abraham* are three apocalypses that date from the period after the destruction of the Temple and all reflect a deep concern for the questions of theodicy raised thereby.[284] If *2 Apocalypse of Baruch* is in some way responding to 4 Ezra or to concerns very similar indeed to those raised by 4 Ezra (or, indifferently from the point of view of our argument, if the reverse is true), this provides some hint about the creation and transmission of the works. Not only are they consciously in a tradition of apocalyptic teaching but they are related to one another.[285] This must imply that those who composed them were socially coherent enough to cultivate a common tradition and one that was clearly at home in the Judaism of the period following the destruction.

5.2.4. The Seer in Society

In the light of this, then, the "esotericism" of 4 Ezra, and the claim for divine authority made through the last vision (chap. 14; note particularly vv 44–48), imply a deliberate social function and role. The book was not esoteric, or else it became common property very early on. It does locate the transmission of the apocalyptic tradition in an esoteric group within the people of Israel. It is not farfetched to see in this a reflection in broad terms of an element of the social context of the author.[286]

A brief insight into the dynamics of the role of the apocalyptic seer in that group may be provided by the analysis given in the course of the Commentary on the narrative of revelation found in Vision 7.[287] The three protagonists of that revelation are the people, the group of five scribes, and the seer himself. The first opposition is between Ezra together with the scribes and the people. The people are summoned by Ezra according to the divine command and are part of the drama of revelation. There are elements of staging: an exact time and place are specified. Then Ezra withdraws with his coterie of scribes, and the revelation takes place in their presence, so they serve as witnesses and confirmation. A similar threefold presentation of the protagonists is to be observed in *2 Apoc Bar* 5:5. This picture combines with the socially grounded attribution of prophetic office to Ezra in 12:42 to suggest something of the author's own entry into the role of apocalyptic author. This role too must have been created in the dynamic between the author and his social context, however limited the latter may have been. It was confirmed by the society's recognition of his role and by the staged context in which he functioned.

5.2.5. Concluding Remarks

The combination of these elements, while not enabling any identification of the social matrix of 4 Ezra with any known group or stream in Judaism of the latter decades of the first century, does permit us to say something about it. In spite of the individual character of 4 Ezra, the author seems clearly to have been rooted in a social context and tradition of apocalyptic teaching. His role was recognized and confirmed by that social context. At the heart of the aspirations of that social group were the destruction of Rome and the vindication of Israel, but their hope was centered chiefly on the day of judgment and less stressedly on the Messiah or a royal restoration. The absence of any royal characteristics of the Messiah is significant in this context.

Appendix: 4Q Pseudo-Ezekiel

In a lecture at a conference held in Haifa in April 1988, D. Dimant presented some details of a document entitled "Pseudo-Ezekiel," preserved in five of six manuscripts from Cave 4 at Qumran (4Q 385–390). The manuscripts are from the Hasmonean and Herodian periods.

In certain matters, this work apparently shows a similarity to 4 Ezra, although antedating it by a couple of

---

social function. Collins, *Imagination,* 168–71.

284 See sec. 5.1.5 above. See Collins, *Imagination,* 178–80, who discusses the relationship between these works and gives further bibliography in his notes there.

285 4 Ezra 12:11 refers to Daniel explicitly; moreover, the eagle vision as a whole is dependent on the beasts in Daniel 7, a chapter that has also influenced 4 Ezra

13.

286 This formulation does not foreclose the question whether 4 Ezra is the record of the inner struggle of the author. It does mean that in his overall view and understanding the author was not an isolated individual.

287 See 14:23–26 Form and Function.

centuries. The following remarks, based on an oral report, must remain tentative until the text is definitively published:

a. In parts, the text is a dialogue between the seer and God.

b. Certain of the questions posed by the seer, such as "When will these things happen?" resemble 4 Ezra.

c. Some questions are pervaded by a sense of eschatological urgency.

d. Specifically, there is a reference to the measuring of times and days (cf. 4 Ezra 4:36–37).

6.0. Section 6:
4 Ezra in Christian Tradition

6.1. 4 Ezra in the Early Church

Above, in section 1.1, references were noted to the certain and less certain allusions to and quotations from 4 Ezra in early Greek Patristic writing. Furthermore, a number of indirect allusions to the work, as well as the influence of its contents, have been chronicled in detail.[288] These are an obvious witness to the influence of 4 Ezra in those circles. Moreover, the large number of versions in the languages used by the ancient churches is extremely striking.[289] The spread and influence of 4 Ezra is thereby eloquently demonstrated.[290]

The reason for the disappearance of the Greek version of the book remains unclear. The multiplication of instances of the disappearance of the Greek versions of pseudepigraphic books in itself provides no explanation of this phenomenon, yet it is notable that the same

situation is to be observed with respect to *1 Enoch* and *Jubilees,* to mention only two of the most significant of the Pseudepigrapha.

The particular history of 4 Ezra in the Latin church, where it had a major impact over the centuries, is to be noted. 4 Ezra, together with the additional chapters conventionally called 5 Ezra (chaps. 1–2) and 6 Ezra (chaps. 15–16), was habitually included in manuscripts of the Latin Bible and, although its extracanonical status was confirmed by the Council of Trent, it is still printed in an appendix to the Latin Bible.[291] In the Church of England, it entered into the Apocrypha, where it is commonly found, together with 5 Ezra and 6 Ezra, under the title "II Esdras."

6.2. Other Writings of Ezra

It is rather interesting that a number of ancient works have been preserved that relate to Ezra. Most significant is a group of four apocalyptic works that seem to be dependent on 4 Ezra, or else on a lost composition in Greek which, in turn, was dependent on 4 Ezra.

6.2.1. *Greek Apocalypse of Ezra*

This work is preserved only in Greek, and the two manuscripts known to date have both been utilized in the most recent edition.[292] The *Greek Apocalypse of Ezra* was composed originally in Greek and seems to have utilized the Greek version of 4 Ezra which was in existence by the

---

288 See R. A. Kraft, "'Ezra' Materials in Judaism and Christianity," *ANRW*, 19.1:119–36. An extensive list of citations and allusions in Greek and Latin fathers is to be found in James's "Introduction" to Bensly (pp. xxvii–xliii). See also the rich material assembled by Violet 1, pp. xliv–l, and Violet 2, pp. l–lv.

289 Its status in the various churches differed. In the Armenian tradition, e.g., it was closely associated with the biblical corpus and often included in manuscript copies of the Bible. Twenty-seven Armenian manuscripts are known to date. In the Georgian church, on the other hand, it was not widely known, being preserved only in two, old manuscripts, both containing imperfect copies. The existence of three versions in Arabic is notable.

290 See sec. 1.1 above and nn. 1, 2, and 3 to that section. The history of 4 Ezra in the Armenian church is set

forth in Stone, *Armenian Version*, 35–41.

291 See sec. 6.4 below for a particular example of the importance of the book in European culture. Observe the number of tertiary versions made on the basis of the Latin. These include translations into Armenian, Georgian, Church Slavonic, modern Greek, and Hebrew.

292 The text was first published by C. von Tischendorf, *Apocalypses Apocryphae Mosis, Esdrae, Pauli, Iohannis* (Leipzig: Mendelssohn, 1866), and most recently by Wahl, *Apocalypsis Esdrae.* The most recent English translations are by M. E. Stone, "Greek Apocalypse of Ezra," *OTP*, 1:561–79, and by R. J. H. Shutt, "The Greek Apocalypse of Esdras," *The Apocryphal Old Testament* (ed. H. D. F. Sparks; Oxford: Oxford University, 1984) 927–41. In German see U. B. Müller, *Die griechische Ezra-Apokalypse* (JSHRZ 5;

second century.[293] It most likely originated sometime during the first millennium. The *Greek Apocalypse of Ezra* is clearly composite, and a number of sources have been distinguished within it.[294]

The book relates how Ezra fasted and prayed for revelation of the mysteries of God and is assumed to heaven, where he intercedes for the sinners. Ezra prays again, questioning the righteousness of the world, asking mercy for mankind (chaps. 1–2). Sin is due to Adam's sin, he is told. He is shown the signs, the messianic woes (2:26—3:6). Then he is taken down to the depths of Tartarus, where he sees various sinners being punished and receives a revelation of the signs of the antichrist (4:9—5:7).

A new subject is introduced, the development of the human infant (5:12–14), intensifying the seer's doubts about the creation of human beings (5:14–16). In the final part of the book the seer's struggle with the angel for his own soul and his death and burial are related (chaps. 6–7).

The relationship between this work and 4 Ezra is quite unmistakable. In addition to the list of parallels noted above, the very argumentative character of the seer in his discussion with God and the dialogic character of the book both derive from 4 Ezra.[295] By comparing it with 4 Ezra, we can see something of its possible sources and discern which aspects of 4 Ezra were of concern to the writers of later apocalypses.

6.2.2. *Vision of Ezra*

In most manuscripts this work is entitled *Visio Beati Esdrae*, "Vision of the Blessed Ezra."[296] It opens with a petition by Ezra that he should not fear when seeing the judgment of the sinners (v 1). He is taken to hell, where he sees the just passing the fiery gates, which the sinners cannot transverse (vv 4–10). He asks for mercy on them (v 11; this theme is prominent in *Greek Apoc Esd* 1:15; 5:6). Ezra passes the gates and enters Tartarus, which is described in far greater detail (vv 12–55) than the corresponding passage in *Greek Apocalypse of Ezra*. Then he enters paradise and intercedes with God for the sinners (vv 56–66). Material on the antichrist (vv 71–80) and on Ezra's argument with the angel over the taking of his soul ensues (vv 97–110).

The work survives only in Latin manuscripts chiefly from the eleventh to the fourteenth century,[297] and the

---

Gütersloh: Mohn, 1976).

293 Violet 1, pp. l–lix.

294 These are the following: First, a Descent to Tartarus (4:4–21), which is shared with the *Vision of Ezra* and formed a common theme of many Byzantine apocalypses (see M. E. Stone, "The Metamorphosis of Ezra: Jewish Apocalypse and Medieval Vision," *JTS* NS 33 [1982] 6–8; and M. Himmelfarb, *Tours of Hell: An Apocalyptic Form in Jewish and Christian Literature* [Philadelphia: University of Pennsylvania, 1983]). Second, a list of "hanging punishments" (4:22–25; 5:2–4 [?5–7], 8–11, 24), which has been broken up and interwoven with the Descent to Tartarus. It is also to be found in the *Vision of Ezra* (Stone, "Metamorphosis," 9–10). Third, a description of the physiognomy of the antichrist (4:25–43) identical with that in *Apocalypsis Ioannou* (Tischendorf, *Apocalypses Apocryphae*, 74–75). Many similar passages are known from later apocalypses (M. E. Stone and J. Strugnell, *The Books of Elijah, Parts 1–2* [SBLTT 18, PS 8; Missoula, Mont.: Scholars, 1979], 27–39). Finally, a Description of Paradise (5:20–23).

295 Stone, "Greek Apocalypse of Ezra," 569; and Himmelfarb, *Tours of Hell*, 26.

296 The text was published from the Vatican manuscript by G. Mercati, *Note di Litteratura Biblica e Cristiana Antica* (Studi e Testi 5; Rome: Vatican, 1901) 61–79.

It has been pointed out that another form of it circulated in Austria (P. Dinzelbacher, "Die Vision Albrichs und die Esdras-Apokryphe," *Studien und Mitteilungen zur Geschichte des Benediktiner-Ordens* 87 [1976] 435–42), a form first made known by A. Mussafia, "Sulla Visione di Tundalo," *Sitzungsber. d. Kaiserl. Ak. Phil.-Hist. Klasse* (Vienna, 1871) 157–206 *(non vidi)*. The most recent edition is by Wahl in *Apocalypsis Esdrae*. It was translated into German by P. Riessler, *Altjüdisches Schrifttum ausserhalb der Bibel* (Heidelberg: Kerle, 1928) 350–54, and into English by J. R. Mueller and G. A. Robbins, "Vision of Ezra," *OTP*, 1:581–90, and by Shutt in Sparks, *Apocryphal Old Testament*, 943–51.

297 Four forms of the text survive. The shortest is Vatican lat. 3838. Mercati, who first published it, regarded it very highly (*Note*, 64), a view followed by others (e.g., Mueller and Robbins, "Vision of Ezra," 582). The oldest manuscript, from Linz, Austria (tenth–eleventh cent.), is longer than this. A third form is found in the *Magnum Legendarium Austriacum* (twelfth cent.) and in other Austrian sources (Dinzelbacher, "Die Vision Albrichs"; and Wahl, *Apocalypsis Esdrae*, 22–23). Dinzelbacher compared these three text forms, and argued for the priority of the Vatican manuscript ("Die Vision Albrichs," 437). The fourth form is that of the Barberini manuscript

fullest text, recently made available by the publication of the text of Vat. Barberini Lat. 2318 (fourteenth–fifteenth cent.) by Bogaert, has additional material parallel to *Greek Apocalypse of Ezra* and *Apocalypse of Sedrach*.[298] In Bogaert's view, the Barberini manuscript preserves a somewhat corrupted copy of the oldest form of the *Vision of Ezra,* from which all the other texts devolve.[299]

In view of its close relationship with *Greek Apocalypse of Ezra* and *Apocalypse of Sedrach,* as well as on linguistic grounds, it seems that *Vision of Ezra* was apparently originally written in Greek. The date of the work is uncertain, but it antedates its oldest manuscript, which is of the tenth/eleventh century.

It is clearly related to *Greek Apocalypse of Ezra* and *Apocalypse of Sedrach* and to 4 Ezra, though the exact nature of that relationship will have to be reassessed in the light of the new manuscript. The same is clearly true of the relationship between *Vision of Ezra* and 4 Ezra.[300]

6.2.3. Apocalypse of Sedrach

It is not certain who the pseudonymous author of this writing was intended to be, but the most reasonable suggestion is that the name is corrupted from "Ezra."[301] This work tells of Ezra's translation to heaven, where he disputes with God about the purpose of creation. The sin of Adam, its results, and God's responsibility for it are

the chief subjects of discussion. Then, in chapter 8, God poses to Ezra a series of riddle questions to demonstrate his inability to know such matters (cf. 4 Ezra 4:5–9; 5:35–38). Then the struggle over the taking of the seer's soul ensues, marked by a remarkable dirge over the body. Next, issues of sin and repentance arise and, finally, the problems of proper memorial services for the dead, an interest shared with the *Questions of Ezra.*

The *Apocalypse of Sedrach* is known from a single Greek manuscript of the fifteenth century. M. R. James published the narrative portions of it, described above, but omitted the homiletic introduction and conclusion.[302] The work was composed in Greek, and it shows many linguistically late features.[303] It dates from the first millennium, presumably after the translation into Greek of 4 Ezra. The homiletic materials seem to have been later combined with the basic text.[304] Although S. Agourides has argued for a Jewish origin of the work, his arguments seem rather to show that it is atypical for Byzantine Christianity than that it is Jewish. That remains to be demonstrated.[305]

It is closely related to the *Greek Apocalypse of Esdras* and

---

discussed below.

298 P. M. Bogaert, "Une version longue inédite de la 'Visio Beati Esdrae,' dans le Légendier de Teano (Barberini Lat. 2318)," *Revue Bénédictine* 94 (1984) 50–70. This is the material present in vv 71–110.

299 The chief publications are noted in n. 296 above. Until the publication of the Barberini manuscript, it was generally accepted that the short form of the Vatican manuscript, preferred by Mercati, was indeed the oldest. This position must now be reassessed.

300 E.g., Mercati regarded the *Vision of Ezra* at one pole of a chain of development, followed by the *Apocalypse of Sedrach* and the *Greek Apocalypse of Ezra* (Mercati, *Note,* 67–68). Himmelfarb regarded it as later than those works (Himmelfarb, *Tours of Hell,* 165).

301 Daniel's companion was named "Sedrach" but does not seem plausible as the pseudonymous author. The corruption of "Esdras" was first suggested by M. R. James, *Apocrypha Anecdota* (Texts and Studies 2.3; Cambridge: Cambridge University, 1893) 130. It was James who first published the work, see ibid., 130–

37. A new edition was prepared by Wahl in *Apocalypsis Esdrae.* A German translation was published by Riessler, *Schrifttum,* 156–67. English versions have recently been published by S. Agourides in *OTP,* 1:605–13, and by Shutt in Sparks, *Apocryphal Old Testament,* 953–66. For some further details, see Denis, *Introduction,* 97–99; and J. H. Charlesworth, *The Pseudepigrapha and Modern Research with a Supplement* (2d ed.; SCS 7S; Chico, Calif.: Scholars, 1981) 178–79.

302 The manuscript is Bodl. Cod. Gr. Misc. 56, fols. 92–110. English translations are by A. Rutherford in *The Ante-Nicene Fathers,* 10:175–80, and by Agourides in *OTP,* 1:605–13. G. S. Mercati, "The Apocalypse of Sedrach," *JTS* 11 (1910) 572–73, first pointed out that the homily is perhaps to be attributed to Ephraem Syrus.

303 See Agourides, "Sedrach," 606.

304 Ibid., 606.

305 See most recently on this Sparks, *Apocryphal Old Testament,* 955.

Visio Beati Esdrae,[306] with which it shares distinctive themes and *topoi.*[307]

6.2.4. *Questions of Ezra*

The fourth of the writings associated with 4 Ezra is the *Questions of Ezra* which survives in two recensions in Armenian.[308]

Recension B is much shorter than Recension A, but where it contains material corresponding to A, it often preserves details not in A. There are two physical lacunae in the single manuscript of Recension A, following v 10 and following v 40. Conversely, it contains nothing corresponding to vv 11–30 of Recension A.

Like the two works discussed above, the *Questions of Ezra* is much concerned with the fate of the righteous and the sinners. It opens with this issue. Next, in Recension B, ensues a discussion of the purpose of creation and of the intermediate residences of the wicked. This is followed, in Recension A, by an intriguing passage concerning the seven steps up to the Divinity. The role of expiatory prayer in liberating souls from Satan is discussed, and finally, in Recension B alone, the resurrection and judgment are foretold.

The comparison of Recensions A and B indicates that there may have been two source documents. One was a dialogue between the prophet and an angel about the fate of souls (A, vv 1–10; B, v 4 or its original; A, vv 11–15; B, v 6 or its original; A, vv 31–40; and B, v 10–14 or its original). The second dealt with the ascent of the souls and comprised A, vv 16–30. This section has rather distinctive views and is a pastiche of older sources.

4 Ezra clearly influenced, indeed inspired, *Questions of Ezra.* The concern for the fate of the souls after death, the question-and-answer form, and the seven levels of the ascent to the Divinity are all features betraying its connection with 4 Ezra.[309]

6.3. Astrological Works of Ezra

In a variety of languages of the Christian Orient and of Europe the name of Ezra is to be found associated with calendrical prognostications. Why such works were connected with Ezra remains unclear, but his prophetic status, certified for the Middle Ages by 4 Ezra, must have been of influence.[310]

The best-known work of this type is the *Revelatio Esdrae,* which survives in several Latin manuscripts of the ninth century and later.[311] It prognosticates the weather of the seasons, the fertility of the flocks, and the abundance of the crops according to the day of the week upon which the calends of January fall.

The same text exists in Old French, Provençal, medieval Italian, German, and Czech.[312] In English, Ezra's name was later transformed into "Erra Pater," and under this title a calendaric work saw many printings

---

306 See Stone, "Metamorphosis," 6–7.

307 Set forth clearly by Sparks, *Apocryphal Old Testament,* 954. Sparks's assessment of the relationship between *Apocalypse of Sedrach* and *Vision of Ezra* must be reexamined in the light of the new manuscript of the latter work discussed in this section.

308 The first recension (A) was published in 1896 by Yovsēpʿiancʿ and translated into English by Issaverdens: see Yovsēpʿiancʿ, *Ankanon Girkʿ Hin Ktakaranacʿ,* 300–303 (in Armenian); and Issaverdens, *Uncanonical Writings,* 505–9. The text is drawn from a *Ritual,* Ms. 570 of the Mechitarist Library in Venice (1208 C.E.). No other copy is know. The second recension (B) occurs in the fourth recension Armenian *Menologium.* The text was published from the printed edition of 1730 by M. E. Stone with readings from a single further manuscript (Oxford Ms. Marsh 438 of the seventeenth cent.): "Two New Discoveries Relating to the Apocryphal Ezra Books," *Sion* 42 (1977) 58–60 (in Armenian). Another copy of it had been printed by Dashian, but its relationship to *Questions of Ezra* had not been

noted: J. Dashian, *Katalog der armenischen Handschriften in der Mechitaristen Bibliothek zu Wien* (Vienna: Mechitarists, 1895) 79–80. English translations of both recensions exist: M. E. Stone, "Questions of Ezra," *OTP,* 1:591–99.

309 Connections have been made between *Questions of Ezra* and other Armenian dialogic works that deal with the fate of the soul after death: Sarghissian, *Studies on the Apocryphal Books of the Old Testament,* 452–84 (in Armenian). It is impossible, however, to know whether *Questions of Ezra* was written in Armenian originally or in another language, such as Greek. Other even later Ezra apocalypses survive. One was published in Syriac text with a German translation by F. Baethgen, "Beschreibung der syrischen Handschrift 'Sachau 131' auf der königlichen Bibliothek zu Berlin," *ZAW* 6 (1886) 193–211. This is a post-Islamic work.

310 Stone, "Metamorphosis," 14–16. In general, on the *Revelatio Esdrae,* see Charlesworth, *Pseudepigrapha and Modern Research,* 118–19; and Denis, *Introduction,* 94–95.

both in Britain and in North America.[313]

In Greek, three such writings are known. The first deals with propitious and unpropitious days of the month.[314] The second resembles the Latin *Revelatio Esdrae*. A Georgian version of this exists in a tenth-century manuscript.[315] The third Greek document lists the thirty days of the lunar month and the birth or death of a biblical personality on it.[316]

6.4. Postscript

It is perhaps a curious footnote that, at the time of the discovery of the New World, 4 Ezra entered the debate that raged between scholars, both Catholic and Protestant, as to the origins of native American peoples. It was the passage in 4 Ezra 13:39–46, relating the withdrawal of the ten tribes, that was at the center of the debate by prominent authors. One party claimed, on this basis, that the American Indians were of Jewish descent, having originated from the ten tribes, while others denied this vigorously.[317] Positions held in this debate were related, as F. Schmidt has shown, to opposed attitudes to the authority of the Apocrypha in general and of 4 Ezra in particular.

6.4.1. Islamic Developments

In a recent article, H. Lazarus-Yaffe has studied the development of the Islamic understanding of the figure of Ezra.[318] Ezra is identified as El-ʿUseir mentioned in Sura 9:30 of the Quran, an identification also made by the Arabic Christian scribes of the Arabic1 and Arabic2 versions of 4 Ezra. The Quranic traditions are bizarre, and the figure of Ezra is viewed negatively. However, she shows that a different, positive picture of Ezra as restorer of the Torah and mourner for Zion was known to the ninth-century historian al-Tabari (ed. de Goeje, series 2, pp. 669–70). In this text even the detail of the wondrous, inspiring drink administered by the angel is to be found (cf. 4 Ezra 14:39–40), and a similar and even more detailed narrative is found in Arabic *Tales of the Prophets* (eleventh cent.) and other writings.[319] Moreover, the story of the mourning woman is also known in these sources.[320] Lazarus-Yaffe is of the view that this material entered the Islamic tradition through the Arabic translations of 4 Ezra and is consequently led to date the latter rather early.

311 Mercati, *Note*, 61–79, studied and published three Latin versions. More exist. An English translation is by D. A. Fiensy, "The Revelation of Ezra," *OTP*, 1:601–3.

312 E. A. Matter, "The 'Revelatio Esdrae' in Latin and English Traditions," *Revue Bénédictine* 92 (1982) 376–92, is replete with information about this work. She discusses the various versions on pp. 380–81.

313 Ibid., 384–86.

314 F. Nau, "Analyse de deux opuscules astrologiques attribués au prophète Esdras," *ROC* 12 (1907) 14–15; and Tischendorf, *Apocalypses Apocryphae*, xiii-xiv.

315 Nau, "Deux opuscules," 16–17. The Georgian version is discussed by M. Tarchnisvili, *Geschichte der kirchlichen georgischen Literatur* (Studi e Testi 185; Rome: Vatican, 1955) 355.

316 This work is also attributed to Aristotle, or said to have been found in a temple in Egypt (Nau, "Deux opuscules," 17–21).

317 The matter is laid out in F. Schmidt, "L'autorité du 'Quatrième livre d'Esdras' dans la discussion sur la parenté des juifs et des indiens d'Amérique (1540–

1661)," *La littérature inter-testamentaire, Colloque de Strasbourg (17–19 Octobre, 1983)* (ed. A. Caquot; Paris: Presses Universitaires de France, 1985) 203–20. A more extensive study by Schmidt will appear as "Azareth en Amérique: L'autorité du Quatrième Livre d'Esdras dans la discussion sur la parenté des Juifs et des Indiens d'Amérique (1530–1720)," *Moïse géographe: Recherches sur les représentations juives et chrétiennes de l'espace* (ed. F. Desreumaux and F. Schmidt; Paris: Vrin, 1988) 155–201.

318 H. Lazarus-Yaffe, "Ezra-ʿUseir: History of a Pre-Islamic Polemical Motif Through Islam to the Beginning of Biblical Criticism," *Tarbiz* 55 (1986) 359–79 (in Hebrew).

319 Ibid., 364.

320 Ibid., 365.

Fourth Ezra

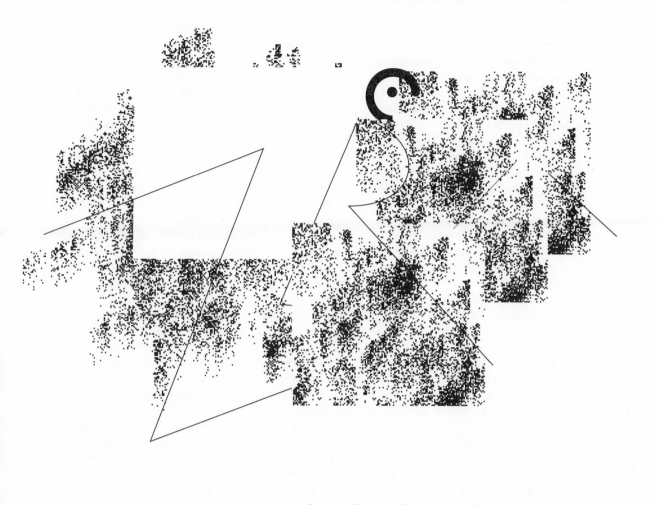

General Structure of the Book

The book is divided, very clearly, into seven sections which are usually called "Visions." The first three visions share a common overall structure.[1] The structure of Visions 1–2 is exactly the same, while the exceptionally long Vision 3 is more complex.[2]

Each of these three visions opens with an introduction that provides the setting in which the vision takes place. An address of Ezra to God follows in which certain issues are raised. The rest of the vision is the response to this address, a response that may, on grounds both of form and of content, be divided into three parts. These are the dispute and two types of prediction. The first predictive type (hereafter Prediction 1) is the transmission of information to the seer in the course of dialogue. The second (hereafter Prediction 2) is a revelation of signs by the angel, in the course of which the seer is silent: "Pay attention to me, and I will tell you more." This simple structure is elaborated in Vision 3. In that long vision is a series of dispute-prediction passages, repeating the same basic pattern with variations.

Vision 3, then, has three major subdivisions, structurally forming three "sub-visions":
1. Chapter 6:38—7:44, which starts with the idea of election and concludes with the prediction of the eschaton. It includes address, dispute, and Prediction 2.
2. Chapter 7:45—8:3, which starts and concludes with the issue of the few and the many and contains the prediction of the intermediate state of the soul. It includes dispute, Prediction 2, and dispute.
3. Chapter 8:4–62, which takes up the theme of creation initiated in sub-vision 1 and that of the few and the many highlighted in sub-vision 2. It contains the prediction of Ezra's eschatological bliss. It opens with a monologue and a prayer (corresponding to the address), followed by a dispute passage. Chapter 9:1–22 is a passage of the Prediction 2 type which concludes the whole.[3]

Each of the first three visions concludes with remarks on the reaction of the seer to the experience related, with injunctions transmitted to him, and with similar matters.

A basic issue to which no clear answer has been given is created by the exceptional length of Vision 3. Merkur, who interprets the visions in terms of the author's growing facility and experience of ecstatic practice, regards the third vision as a failed or only partly successful experience, which the seer repeatedly attempts to remedy.[4]

The dispute and the Prediction 1 segments are both formulated as dialogues. The distinction between them is in the character of the interchange and in the predominance of one or the other partner. In the dispute, the seer argues with the angel, and very often there is tension between the questions and the answers, which do not seem to follow from one another. Questions and answers both can be quite long. In the Prediction 1 passages, however, the questions and answers are predominantly short and responsive. The seer, having accepted certain of the teachings of the angel, proceeds to detailed inquiry in order to elicit further information about them. This is then really revelatory dialogue, questions asked about cosmic secrets and answers given revealing part of them. In this respect it somewhat resembles the sort of questions posed by seers who are on otherworldly trips or undergoing visionary experiences.[5] As in those instances, Ezra is eliciting information about something that he accepts as already existing or determined. This fundamental feature exhibits the deep, apocalyptic character of these predictive dialogues.[6] In short, it may be

---

1   The ambiguities of the term "vision," which does not necessarily imply only a visual experience but often an auditory one, are dealt with by K. Koch, "Esras erste Vision: Weltzeiten und Weg des Höchsten," *BZ* NF 22 (1978) 47–48.

2   Harnisch (p. 270), quoting Kabisch (pp. 21 and 41), points out that the structures of Visions 1 and 2 are almost identical. The analysis by which these scholars reach their conclusions is based more on content than on form.

3   See 7:45–74 Form and Structure, pp. 226–27, and 8:4–19 Form and Structure.

4   Merkur, "Visionary Practice," 26–29. We suspend judgment on this view which is, however, rather intriguing.

5   Cf. in biblical literature, e.g., Zech 4:4; 4:11; 4:12; etc. Such series of questions are to be found in the later apocalypses; see, e.g., *1 Enoch* 21; 25; 27; etc.; *2 Apoc Bar* passim; et al. They are also a variation on the series of explanatory introductory formulations to which there are no questions in the text in such sources as Daniel 2 and Daniel 8. The occurrence in a text like Daniel 2 suggests that this listing of elements and interpretations may originate in dream books. This seems to be borne out by the listing of dream features in Joseph's interpretation in Gen 41:26–32. A similar series of explanations of specific elements of a dream may be observed here in Vision 5 (12:10–35). In the context of such dreams, the actual occurrence or absence of the questions is surely merely a literary convention. In relation to our passage, however, it is not, but is essential, since the question form has taken on significance in its own right; see Introduction, sec. 4.1.2.

Table 1

	1	2	3
Introduction	3:1–3	5:21–22	6:35–37
Address	3:4–36	5:23–30	6:38–59
Dispute	4:1–25	5:31–40	7:1–25
Prediction	4:26–52	5:41–6:10	7:26–44
	.	.	(Pred. 2)
Dispute	.	.	7:45–74
Prediction	.	.	7:75–115
Dispute	.	.	7:116—8:3
Monologue	.	.	8:4–19
Prayer	.	.	8:20–36
Dispute	.	.	8:37–62
Prediction 2/Revelation	5:1–13	6:11–29	9:1–22
Conclusion/Injunctions	5:14–20	6:30–34	9:23–25

Table 2

	4	5	6	7
Introduction	9:26–28	11:1A	13:1	14:1–2
Address	9:29–37	.	.	14:3–18
Vision	9:38—10:4	11:1B—12:3	13:2—13A	.
Response	10:5–24*	12:3–9	13:13B–20A	14:19–22
Injunctions	.	.	.	14:23–26
Ezra's Speech	.	.	.	14:27–36
Revelation	.	.	.	14:37–48
Transformation	10:25–28	.	.	.
Angelophany	10:29–37	.	.	.
Interpretation	10:38–54	12:10–36	13:20B–55	.
Conclusion	10:58–	12:37–	13:56	14:49
Injunctions	59	39	58	.
Narrative	.	12:40–50	.	.
Conclusion 2	.	12:51	.	.

*cf. 10:31–37

said that the contrast of dispute and Prediction 1 is the contrast of "why" questions and "when" questions.

The boundary between the dispute and the prediction is usually signaled by a remark of enigmatic character touching on eschatological matters, made by the angel (so 4:26–32; 5:40; 7:25; 7:74; 8:3).

What is more, in the first two visions there is a movement from Ezra's speech → disputatious dialogue → questions eliciting predictive responses → the angel's speech of revelation. This shift is paralleled by a shift in speakers: first Ezra, then Ezra disputes with the angel in tension and at length, next the angel makes the chief pronouncements, while Ezra's questions are about details.[7] Finally comes the angel's concluding speech which, notably in the first two visions, balances the seer's opening address.[8]

The structure of Visions 4–7 differs, and there is great variation between them. Their structure has been set forth in Table 2, but it will be fully discussed in the commentary on them. In broader terms, the brief revelations with which Visions 1–3 conclude, are supplemented and complemented by the extensive revelations of Visions 5–6. These revelations reflect the shift of the author from questions to receipt of revelation, from questioning to acceptance.[9]

---

6 Collins properly remarked that it is the transmission of information about realities that have already been determined that distinguished apocalyptic revelations. See J. J. Collins, *The Apocalyptic Vision of the Book of Daniel* (HSM 16; Missoula, Mont.: Scholars, 1977) 76.

7 Naturally, other divisions of this material have been suggested by scholars. For example, a division into seven parts on formal grounds is suggested by Koch, but it does not take full account of the shift between "Dispute" and "Prediction 1" passages; see Koch, "Ezras erste Vision," 50–51. On the other hand, Breech discerned three major divisions—complaint, dialogue, and revelation of signs ("These Fragments," 270). Brandenburger (*Verborgenheit*), like Harnisch, does not really evaluate the implications of the differences of Prediction 1 and Prediction 2

material, differences that he barely recognizes (see esp. pp. 144–46). Knibb briefly observes the differences in dialogue types but does not explore their significance; see Knibb, "Apocalyptic and Wisdom," 66. Yet another analysis is that of Thompson, *Responsibility*, 122–23.

8 See Koch, "Esras erste Vision," 52.

9 Harnisch, p. 270 n. 1. Naturally, for Brandenburger (*Verborgenheit*) the nature of the dialogue as dispute is central (see, e.g., p. 42), but, as noted in the Introduction, secs. 4.2.3–4.2.4, he denies all movement within the dialogues. He correctly distinguishes the disputatious dialogue of Visions 1–3 from the dialogues in Visions 4–6 (*contra* Harnisch: see p. 104).

3

1

In the thirtieth [a] year after the destruction of our city, [b] I, Salathiel, [c] who am also called Ezra, was in Babylon. I was troubled as I lay on my bed, and [d] my thoughts welled up in my heart, 2/ because I saw the desolation of Zion and the wealth of those who lived in Babylon. [e] 3/ My spirit was greatly agitated, and I began to speak anxious words to the Most High, and said,

Notes

3:1   a "Third" Georg, graphic error inner-Georg or Greek; cf. 3:29.

b "City of Jerusalem" Ar1; "Jerusalem and Judea" Lat Ms L; "of Jerusalem and the exile of Judea" Arm, probably independent expansions; cf. 3:24 note j, 3:29 note n.

c "Suta'el" Eth; "Syt'iel" Georg.

d Georg and Eth seem to reflect a corrupt phrase at this point, presumably deriving from a common Greek text.

2   e "Wealth . . . Babylon" Ar2 omits; this version also omits mention of the city in 12:40 and 12:50 but preserves it in 3:30.

Form and Structure

This passage serves both as a general introduction to the book and as the introduction to Vision 1. It gives the dating formula as customary at the start of many biblical and apocryphal books (3:1; cf. Isa 1:1; Jer 1:1–2; Bar 1:2; etc.). The actual formula here is probably modeled on Ezek 1:1: "In the thirtieth year, in the fourth month."

Next, the situation of the seer is set forth and the protagonist identified. The phrases used for this are drawn from Daniel and in particular from Dan 7:1, where we have a date, the name of the seer, and his lying on his bed; his Babylonian locale is not mentioned there, but see Dan 8:2. The description of Ezra's state of mind is close to Dan 2:1. In 3:3 the actual introduction to Ezra's address is given, parallel to the introductions to Vision 2 in 5:21–22; Vision 3 in 6:36–37; and Vision 4 in 9:27–28.

Function and Content

The combination of grief over the fate of Israel or of mankind and a vision experience may be observed elsewhere, such as in *2 Apoc Bar* 21:1–3; 21:11–18; *3 Apoc Bar* 1:1–2; and *Test Patr Levi* 2:4–5. In 4 Ezra this combination also occurs at the beginning of Visions 2, 3, and 4. Although this probably reflects a real situation, notably in 4 Ezra it is spoken of in language drawn from Daniel. In the introductions to the first three visions, the ele-

ments of psychological disturbance and inspired speech are to be found. This latter point is explicit in 3:3 both in the way the seer speaks of his thoughts (3:1) and in his agitation of spirit (3:3).[1] These three verses set the stage for the whole book. Ezra, in Babylon a generation after the destruction of the Temple, is distressed to see "the desolation of Zion and the wealth of those who lived in Babylon." The destruction of Zion and the implications of that destruction form one of the predominant motifs of the book. Here the author's point of departure is twofold—Zion's suffering and the contrast between this and Babylon's wealth. The closest contemporary parallel is *2 Apoc Bar* 11:1–2:

Now this I, Baruch, say to you, O Babylon:

If you had lived in happiness and Zion in its glory, it would have been a great sorrow to us that you had been equal to Zion. But now, behold, the grief is infinite and the lamentation is unmeasurable, because, behold, you are happy and Zion has been destroyed.

Here in *2 Apoc Bar* 11:2b the same antithetical form serves to express the same idea as in 4 Ezra 3:2.[2]

Kaminka points out the similarity to the piyyuṭ composed by R. Ammitai (ninth cent.):

Lord, I remember and am sore amazed,
to see each city standing in her state,

---

1   See Excursus on Inspiration, p. 50, for a full discussion of this aspect of the pericope. Cf. also 5:20–22 Form and Function, p. 118.

2   A similar antithetical formulation of this idea may also be observed in a midrash in *Exod. R.* 29:9 and parallels (*j Ber.* 9:3), but there the point is somewhat

and God's own city to the low grave razed:
yet in all time we look and wait.[3]

This is, on the whole, a fairly obvious point. Nonetheless, it is one of profound concern, the more so in a generation close to the destruction itself.

The setting of the book in the period of the Babylonian exile corresponded in general to the context of the author, who lived after the destruction of the Second Temple. There are, however, certain anomalies inherent in the presentation of Ezra as the pseudepigraphic author. The first is that the date in 3:1 implies a shortening of the period between the exile and the actual age of Ezra, so that Ezra could be said to live in Babylon in the thirtieth year after the destruction. Perhaps the traditional figure of seventy years for the duration of the exile was applied implicitly to the time between the destruction of the Temple and Ezra's return. This would have involved dating Ezra's Babylonian activity sometime before the putative seventy years had passed. If this were so, it might explain the chronological difficulties that were of such concern to critics like Kabisch, for then Salathiel, son of Jehoiachin, would (anachronistically, of course) be of the same generation as Ezra.[4]

A second anomaly arising from the attribution to Ezra is the following. In the Prediction 1 passages (as also in 14:15–18 and particularly in 14:18) the angelic or divine predictions of the future are not made in symbolic form but in direct dialogue with Ezra. This means that predictions of the closeness of the end, which graphically express a consciousness of the impending eschaton, stand in potential contradiction to the fact that Ezra lived and died half a millennium before such predictions were actually composed or read. This tension is implicit, of course, in all pseudepigraphy, but it is rendered particularly acute in 4 Ezra by the dialogue form. The author is conscious of it, and for this reason he is careful to avoid giving information about Ezra's own life (4:52) and Ezra is eventually assumed to heaven (14:9; 14:50).[5] Repeatedly Ezra is assured of his own place among the righteous (7:76–77; 8:51–52; 8:62).[6] By these means the literary tensions are moderated, but they cannot truly be resolved, for they are part of the ambiguity of the role-playing of pseudepigraphy.[7]

Harnisch suggests that by 4:26–32 the fictitious situation of 3:1–3 is abandoned.[8] To say this is to ignore the implicit paradox noted above and the author's evident consciousness of it. In fact, 4:26–32 does express an acute sense of the imminent end, but with 4:52 the writer withdraws from the danger of stretching that tension beyond the breaking point and so of fracturing the pseudepigraphic structure. Moreover, the image of Ezra is consistently preserved throughout the book.

Two issues seem to be implied by this: (1) How seriously did the writer and his contemporary or later readers take this pseudepigraphic form? (2) How genuine was the visionary experience?[9] A case will be urged below for real experience being at the heart of "Ezra's" visions. As for pseudepigraphy, it was undoubtedly taken seriously, but to say this does not imply that ancient readers examined their texts microscopically to see whether they ever transgressed the canons of true historical chronology. "Problems" similar to those in 4 Ezra

---

different.

3 N. Adler and J. Davis, eds., *The Service of the Synagogue: Day of Atonement,* part 2 (14th ed.; London: Routledge & Kegan Paul, 1949) 263.

4 Kabisch, pp. 6–8. The expectation of the end, discussed in the next paragraph, is no less disconcerting if applied to the lifetime of Salathiel than to that of Ezra.

5 This issue is analyzed further in 14:3–18 Function and Content, p. 417.

6 See 8:37–62 Function and Content, p. 280.

7 See 4:26 Commentary on these problems.

8 Harnisch, pp. 270–71.

9 Pseudepigraphy was widespread in the ancient world. For the Jewish sources, see the indicative remarks of M. Hengel, *Judaism and Hellenism: Studies in Their Encounter in Palestine During the Early Hellenistic Period*

(trans. J. Bowden; Philadelphia: Fortress, 1974) 1:205–6, and notes in vol. 2; cf. also M. Smith, "Pseudepigraphy in the Israelite Literary Tradition," *Pseudepigrapha* I (Entretiens sur l'antiquité classique 18; Vandoeuvres-Geneva: Fondation Hardt, 1972) 191–227, and other articles in that volume. On pagan and Christian literature, see W. Speyer, *Die literarische Fälschung im heidnischen und christlichen Altertum* (HAW 1,2; Munich: Beek, 1971), though many of his criteria could be questioned. See also 14:23–26 Function and Content, pp. 429–31, where further discussion of the issue is to be found. On this, see Stone, "Apocalyptic Literature," 427–30. The question of inspiration is discussed in Excursus on Inspiration. See also Hengel, *Judaism,* 1:205–6; and Russell, *Method and Message,* 164–66. Cf. also Stone, "Vision or Hallucination?" 52–56.

also arise in *2 Apocalypse of Baruch,* where in chapter 25 the seer is told that which Ezra is never told, that he will be preserved alive for the end time! In passages like these the distance between the period of the pseudepigraphic author and that of the writer (or reader) is bridged or even negated.

Commentary

■ 1 There seems to be no reason in the text itself here to lead us to assume, with Kabisch and Box, that a preceding introduction was lost. The reference in 6:35 to "three weeks" of fasting which Ezra was enjoined to observe, however, clearly implies that a fast was considered to have existed before Vision 1. The author most carefully uses the fasts and other preparatory activities to indicate the dynamic of development inherent in the book. However, since there is no sign in the text here of the loss of a phase or phases, the difficulty of 6:35 remains unresolved (see further 6:35 Commentary on this).[10] The chief views on the date, "the thirtieth year after the destruction of our city," are: *(a)* that it is a veiled reference to the real date of composition, in the year 100 C.E., which is thirty years after the destruction of Jerusalem by the Romans;[11] *(b)* that it provides a general, not a precise, indication of the date of composition;[12] and *(c)* that it is part of the author's pseudepigraphic "stage setting" and of no particular significance.[13]

There are no other examples in the apocalypses of the use of dates with the intent of indicating the precise year of composition by exact correspondence. It cannot be doubted, however, that the book was written after the destruction of the Second Temple. So the selection of the date, "thirtieth year," which is a borrowing from Ezek 1:1, may be due to its approximate equivalation to the author's time, for the book can be dated, on quite other grounds, to the last decade of the first century C.E. (see Introduction, sec. 2.1). Dating by the destruction of the Temple is found in *m. Gittin* 8:5, cf. *Mek. BaḤodeš* 1 (Horovitz-Rabin, p. 203). Arabic2, probably motivated by the chronological difficulty, reads "building," not "destruction." Perhaps the same sort of "historicism" led this version to make Salathiel the seer's father.

The formula "Salathiel, who am also called Ezra" may best be compared with Dan 4:5: "Daniel . . . he who was named Belteshazzar." The second name is used throughout Daniel 4, just as only Ezra is used elsewhere in 4 Ezra.[14] If Salathiel (the Greek form of Hebrew Shealtiel) is Zerubbabel's father, then both figures, Ezra and Salathiel, lived in the exilic age. Two explanations have been offered for this identification: (1) that the name Salathiel is a frozen remnant of one of the sources of 4 Ezra, a putative "Salathiel Apocalypse";[15] and (2) that the figure Ezra-Salathiel is to be distinguished from Ezra the Scribe. This view is to be found in a number of ancient sources in Latin, Greek, and Armenian.[16] The name "Ezra-Salathiel" is then taken to be a misreading of the admittedly difficult Hebrew אסיר שאלתיאל בנו, "the

---

10   This is discussed in the Introduction, secs. 4.3.1–4.3.6. See also Breech, "These Fragments," 270, and 5:20b–22 Form and Structure, p. 118.

11   Kabisch, pp. 85, 132; Baldensperger, p. 52 n. 2; Box, pp. xxviii-xxxiii; Kahana, p. 609; Keulers, p. 119; Gry, pp. xcviii-xcix; Licht, ad loc.; and Bogaert, *Baruch,* 284–86, who cites Gry's view with approval.

12   Gunkel, p. 352; and Porter, p. 334.

13   Lücke, pp. 194–95; Hilgenfeld, *Apokalyptik,* 190; idem, *Die Propheten Esra und Daniel in ihre neusten Bearbeitungen* (Halle: Pfeffer, 1863) 10–11; R. C. Dentan, "The Second Book of Esdras," *The Interpreter's One-Volume Commentary on the Bible* (ed. C. M. Laymon; London and Glasgow: Collins, 1971) 521; and Vagany, p. 15. Volkmar, p. 360, sees 30 as a number portending the rebuilding of the Temple. Kaminka regards it as indicating 556 B.C.E., the

14   actual date of composition in his view (pp. xix-xxviii). The same date recurs in *Greek Apoc Esd* 1:1. Our view on dating is set forth in Introduction, sec. 2.1.

14   Note also Acts 13:9: "Saul who is also Paul" (Clemen, "Die Zusammensetzung," 238). Gry points out that Targ Mal 1:1 speaks of "Malachi whose name was called Ezra the Scribe." This identification is already to be found, however, in *b. Meg.* 15a. See also n. 21 below.

15   So first Kabisch, pp. 6–10, followed by Box, p. xxii; N. Turner, "Esdras, Books of," *IDB* 2:142; and others.

16   So already Nestle reviewing Violet 1 in *ThLB* (1910) 507–8; M. R. James, "Ego Salathiel qui et Esdras," *JTS* 18 (1917) 167–69; idem, "Salathiel qui et Esdras," *JTS* 19(1918) 347–49; M. E. Stone, "The Apocryphal Literature in the Armenian Tradition,"

captive [Heb: *'asir*—misread as Ezra] Shealtiel his son" in 1 Chron 3:17.[17]

The source analysis is unacceptable on independent grounds (see Introduction, sec. 3.2), nor is there any evidence that an Apocalypse of Salathiel ever existed.[18] The suggested misreading of 1 Chron 3:17 certainly is the explanation of those ancient sources which distinguish two Ezras. Yet it remains incontrovertible that our apocalypse was really attributed to Ezra the Scribe, as is particularly evident from chapter 14. Ezra the Scribe was of priestly descent, as is quite clear from Ezra 7:1–5 and 1 Esdr 8:1–2, while Salathiel was a Davidid.[19] Hence they could not have been the same person. It is, of course, not certain from the text of 4 Ezra that the Salathiel mentioned is the son of Jehoiachin. This seems likely, however, since otherwise the identification is completely pointless.[20]

The historically imprecise identification may depend on traditions that have not survived elsewhere. The

shortening of the Persian period in rabbinic sources (see *SOR* 29; *Lev. R.* 29:2) does not help here. Moreover, it could be that the identification was suggested by a possible etymology of Salathiel's name. Understood as *š'lty 'l*, "I asked God," it would be a singularly appropriate cognomen for the Ezra who is such an insistent questioner throughout the first part of the book.[21]

Ezra's Babylonian locale is also clear in 3:27–29. Babylon is also, presumably, the city referred to in 12:40 and 12:50. It is quite appropriate for Ezra the Scribe to be pictured in Babylon whence he came according to Ezra 7:6. Babylon is the type of Rome in various first-century sources and later. Doubtless the words spoken against Babylon are really directed against Rome.[22] It is questionable, however, whether statements that Ezra was in Babylon or that he had spent thirty years in Babylon (3:29) hint at the author's actually living in Rome.[23] This is just another part of the "scenery"; Ezra, supposedly an exile writing in the thirtieth year after the destruction,

Proceedings of the Israel Academy of Sciences and Humanities 4 (1971) 67; and Stone, "Metamorphosis," 1–3. Details of the sources may be found in these writings. Much information is also given, together with an interesting analysis, by Kraft, "'Ezra' Materials," 119–36. A Falasha prayer in W. Leslau, *Falasha Anthology: The Black Jews of Ethiopia* (1951; repr., New York: Schocken, 1969), reads: "Ezra and Sutā'ēl saw a vision and when the city of Israel fell and the children of Zion were taken prisoners they mourned and cried" (p. 139). In a note on p. 165, Leslau refers to Sutā'ēl as an angel and prophet. "Sutā'ēl" is the form found for Salathiel in the Ethiopic version of 4 Ezra which is clearly behind the reference here. Ezra and Sutā'ēl seem to be regarded as two separate persons.

17 Kaminka maintains, implausibly, that the book is not a pseudepigraphon but was really composed by 'Asir Shealtiel at the time of the Babylonian exile (see n. 13 above).

18 Such is scarcely supplied by the later Hebrew apocalypse attributed to Salathiel's son, Zerubbabel; see Y. Even-Shmuel, *Midrĕšei Ge'ula* (Tel Aviv: Mosad Bialik, 1943) 71–88. A new, annotated English translation of this text is to be published by M. Himmelfarb in M. Mirsky and D. Stern, *Rabbinic Fantasies: Imaginative Narratives from Classical and Mediaeval Hebrew Literature* (Philadelphia: Jewish Publication Society, 1989). For this family relationship, see Hag 1:12; Ezra 3:8; etc. Contrast 1 Chron. 3:19.

19 In the *Revelatio Beati Esdrae* and the Syriac *Apocalypse*

of Ezra, as well as in some of the magical Ezra texts, he is dubbed "high priest"; see Stone, "Metamorphosis," 1–3. Some rabbinic traditions set Ezra in Babylon, delaying his return so that he could study at the feet of Baruch b. Neriah; see *b. Meg.* 16b and *Song R.* 5:4.

20 Kahana surmises that Salathiel was the author's own name (p. xxviii).

21 See 5:16 Commentary, where other similarly significant names in the book are discussed. An analogy may be the story of Susanna in which Daniel's legal role is probably related to an etymology of his name from the Hebrew דו׳ן, "to judge." Ginzberg, *Legends*, 6:446, suggests that the name is a corruption of Hebrew שליח אל, "I Ezra, messenger of God." This he relates to the identification of Ezra with Malachi, which name means "my messenger"; see n. 14 above.

22 For Babylon = Rome, see Rev 14:8; 16:19; 17:3–5; 8:2; *Sib Or* 5:143; 5:159; *2 Apoc Bar* 11:1; Eusebius, *Hist. eccl.* 2.15.2. Further sources are cited by Kneucker, *Das Buch Baruch*, 62, but his view about Baruch seems unjustified. See also the extensive material assembled by H. Fuchs, *Der geistige Widerstand gegen Rom* (Berlin: de Gruyter, 1964) 20–22, 60–62, 67–74, 78–79.

23 This is claimed by Volkmar, p. 329, and Violet 2, p. 33.

was seen to have spent the interim in Babylon. It no more indicates his exact location than do the thirty years his exact date. It is equally impossible to learn of his travels from 3:33. Nowhere else in the apocalypses is the pseudepigraphic author placed in a chronological or geographical situation typologically corresponding precisely to that of the actual author, and nothing else indicates that this is so in 4 Ezra.

The first three visions are apparently experienced at night and in a prostrate posture (3:1; 6:17; cf. 6:30; 6:36; 9:27),[24] as are the fifth and sixth visions (10:59; 11:1; 13:1). Unlike these, however, the first four visions are presented as waking experiences, like that described in chapter 14.[25] Contrast with this the situations described in Dan 2:29; 4:2; and 7:1, all of which are dreams. This is not contradicted by the dependence of 4 Ezra upon the language of Daniel, noted above. Numerous dream visions are described elsewhere in the apocalypses, for example, *1 Enoch* 14:2; 85:1; *Test Patr Levi* 2:5; 8:1,18;

and *Aramaic Levi* 7–8. 4 Ezra clearly distinguished the experience described here and in Visions 2–4 from the dreams described in Visions 5 and 6. Here the onset of the experience is signaled by excitement and the inspiration of the seer; there it is simply recorded as coming in a dream at night. Here the psychological excitement precedes the experience; there it follows upon the symbolic dream. In the waking vision the seer is disturbed, his thoughts well up, an involuntary happening regarded as originating outside the seer's consciousness.[26]

The Hebrew of this expression was most probably עלה על לבי; see Isa 65:17 and Ezek 38:10; cf. *2 Apoc Bar* 83:4.
■ **2** This verse is compared by Violet 2 with 6:65. There, however, the problem is not the abundance of the nations but their lording it over Zion.
■ **3** The divine title "Most High" is by far the most frequent designation of God in 4 Ezra, occurring in every chapter, sixty-eight times in all.[27]

---

24 It is not certain that Vision 4 was given at night; see 9:27 Commentary. On Ezra's position, see also 6:13.
25 See 5:14 Commentary.
26 See further Excursus on Inspiration, p. 121, on the nature of this experience.
27 The figure is given for the Latin text by Bensly, Index, s.v. *altissimus*.

3

4

"O sovereign Lord, didst thou not speak at the beginning when thou didst form the earth [a] —and that without help—and didst command the dust [b] 5/ and it gave [c] thee Adam, a lifeless body? Yet he was the workmanship of thy hands, and thou didst breathe into him the breath of life and he was made alive [d] in thy presence. 6/ And thou didst lead him into the garden [e] which thy right hand had planted [f] before the earth appeared. [f] 7/ And thou didst lay upon him one commandment; [g] but he transgressed it, [h] and immediately thou didst appoint death for him and for his descendants. From him there sprang nations and tribes, peoples and clans, without number. 8/ And [i] every nation walked after its own will [j] and did ungodly things before thee and scorned thee, and thou didst not hinder them. 9/ But again, [k]in its time [k] thou didst bring the flood upon the earth and [l]the inhabitants of the world [l] and destroy them. 10/ And the same fate befell them: as death came upon Adam, so the flood upon them. [m] 11/ But thou didst leave one of them, Noah with his household, and all the righteous who have descended from him. [n]

12

"When those who dwelt on earth [o]began to multiply, they produced [o] children and peoples and many nations, and [p] again they began to be more ungodly than were their ancestors. 13/ [q]And when they were committing iniquity before thee, [q] thou didst choose for thyself one of them, whose name was Abraham; 14/ and thou didst love him, and to him only didst thou reveal the end of the times, [r] secretly [s] by night. 15/ Thou

Notes

4   a "Heaven and earth and all that is in them" Arm, cf. Arm 6:38; see Stone, "Manuscripts and Readings," 53.

b Lat corrupt; Bensly emends to *pulveri*, "dust," like Syr, Eth, Georg; so already did Volkmar.

5   c Lat corrupt; Bensly emends to *dedit tibi*, "it gave you," like Syr, and cf. Eth; "you made man with your incorruptible hands" Arm, cf. Ar2; see Violet 2 on "man" for "Adam" in Arm; cf. also *Greek Apoc Esd* 2:10–11, τὸν πρωτόπλαστον Ἀδὰμ τὸν πρῶτον τίς ἐποίησεν; . . . αἱ χεῖρές μου αἱ ἄχρανται; *Apoc Sedrach* 4:3, διὰ τί ἐκοπίασας τὰς ἀχράντους σοῦ χεῖρας καὶ ἔπλασας τὸν ἄνθρωπον;: cf. also 7:116.

d Arm omits.

6   e + "of delight" = "garden of Eden" Arm, Lat Ms L; cf. 7:36; see Stone, "Manuscripts and Readings," 53.

f–f Arm omits; for "earth," Ar2 reads "man"; Violet 1 suggests אדם ⟨ אדמה; Hilgenfeld suggests πρίν τινα for πρὶν τὴν γήν.

7   g "One commandment" Ar1; "one righteous commandment" Eth; "a commandment" Syr, Arm; "one commandment of these" Lat; perhaps *tuam* of Lat is dittography from the end of *diligentiam* in Lat ψ text; Ar2 is expanded; Arm H adds "that he should know the Lord"; Arm ψ adds "that he should know that he is your work."

h Arm H adds "and was overcome"; Arm ψ adds "and was deceived"; inner-Arm variant; cf. 3:21.

8   i Arm is quite different, merely recording the sins.

j So Lat, Georg, Ar1; "works" Syr, cf. *2 Apoc Bar* 43:38; "fashion" Eth, Ar2.

9   k–k Arm omits.

l–l So Syr, Eth, this must have existed in Greek; *habitantes saeculum* Lat; "people of that age" Ar1; "them" Ar2, Arm.

10   m Arm omits verse; translation based on Lat, Syr, Eth; for "flood," Syr reads "the death of the flood"; Ar1 and Ar2 are periphrastic.

11   n Textual remarks are incorporated in commentary on this verse.

12   o–o "The earth caused mankind to increase from his seed" Arm H; "you caused mankind to increase from his seed" Arm ψ.

p "They acted impiously before you" Arm, where "before you" probably comes from 3:13.

13   q–q "They constantly acted wickedly" Arm H.

14   r "The time of rest" Ar1; "rest" is a term for eschatological reward, cf. 7:85 etc.

s For "secretly," Syr has "between you and him," cf. Eth, Ar2; "by himself" Arm.

didst make with him an everlasting cove-
nant, ^t and promise him ^u that thou wouldst
never forsake his descendants, ^v and thou
gavest to him Isaac, and to Isaac thou
gavest Jacob and Esau. ^w 16/ And thou
didst set apart Jacob for thyself, but Esau
thou didst reject; ^x and Jacob ^y became a
great multitude. 17/ And when thou didst
lead his descendants out of Egypt, ^z thou
didst bring them to Mount ^a Sinai.

18   Thou didst bend down the heavens
        and shake ^b the earth,
    and move the world,
        and make the depths to tremble,
        and trouble the universe. ^c

19/ And thy glory passed through the four
gates of fire and earthquake and wind and
ice, to give ^d the Torah to the seed of Jacob,
and thy commandment ^e to the posterity of
Israel.

20   "Yet thou didst not take away from them their
evil heart, so that thy Torah might bring
forth fruit in them. 21/ For the first Adam,
burdened with an evil heart, transgressed
and was overcome, as were also ^f all who
were descended from him. 22/ Thus the
disease became permanent; ^g the Torah was
in ^h the people's heart along with the evil
root, but what was good departed, and the
evil remained. 23/ So the times passed and
the years were completed, and thou didst
raise up for thyself a servant, named David.
24/ And thou didst command him to build a
city for thy name, ⁱ and in it to offer thee
oblations from what is thine. ^j 25/ This was
done for many years; but the inhabitants of
the city transgressed, ^k 26/ in everything
doing as Adam and all his descendants had
done, for they also were burdened with ^l the
evil heart. 27/ So thou didst deliver the city
into the hands of thy enemies.

    28/ "Then I said in my heart, Are the
deeds of those who inhabit Babylon any
better? Is that why she has gained domin-
ion ^m over Zion? 29/ For when I came here I
saw ungodly deeds without number, and my
soul has seen many sinners during these
thirty years. ⁿ And my heart failed me, 30/
for I have seen,
    how thou dost endure those who sin,
        and hast spared ^o those who act
           wickedly,
    and hast destroyed thy people,
        and hast preserved thy enemies,
31/ and hast not shown to anyone how thy
way may be comprehended. ^p
    Are the deeds of Babylon better than
        those of Zion?

---

15   t–v Arm omits, replaced by biblical phrases.
    u–v Ar1 omits, replaced by biblical phrases.
    v Eth, Georg omit from here to "descendants" in
3:17 by homoeoteleuton (Violet 1).
    w "And Esau" omitted by Arm, which has sub-
stitute text to end of 3:21.

16   x Syr, Ar1, Ar2: Lat "set apart"; alternatively a
text like Lat has been revised according to Mal 1:3.
    y Syr adds "as an inheritance."

17   z Syr adds "and made an eternal covenant with
him": dittography of 3:15; Licht includes in text!
    a Ar1 "desert of."

18   b Syr, Eth, Georg; *statuisti* Lat; ἔστησας for
ἐσεί(η)σας through itacism seems likely (Volkmar),
and Hebrew reconstructions are superfluous.
    c Lat, cf. Georg, Eth (as emended); plural in Syr,
Ar1; see Commentary.

19   d Literally, "that you might give."
    e Singular Lat, Eth; plural Syr, Ar1; "truth"
Georg. Ar1 varies in first phrase of verse; Ar2
periphrastic in last phrase.

21   f Following Lat, Syr; Eth, Ar1, Georg each vary,
since the text seems slightly short.

22   g Syr, Ar1, Arm add "in them"; *eorum* Georg.
    h Lat *cum corde* corrupt; Arm omits phrase; see
Excursus on Adam's Sin.

24   i Arm ψ omits.
    j Additional passages follow in Lat Ms L and Arm;
see Commentary.

25   k Syr, Ar1, Georg add "before you."

26   l Lat has *utebantur*, which is strange. Hilgenfeld
emends to *induebantur*. Box conjectures φορέω in the
sense of "clothed self" here and in 3:21. The Greek
seems likely and was understood in the sense of
"bore" by most versions and "put on" by Georg
here, in 3:21 (same verb) and perhaps by (corrupt)
Ar1 here. Sense is better taken as "bore" or "was
burdened with"; see Commentary.

28   m I.e., *dominavit*: so Bensly emends Lat, without
support of versions. Syr "you abandoned Z."; "Z. is
abandoned" Eth; or "delivered over" Georg; or
"spurned" Arm; Eth, Ar2 vary. Gunkel emends Lat
to *abominavit*; Violet 2's reconstruction is not
plausible, cf. Gressmann's note there. Text uncertain.

29   n Eth, Ar1, Arm; "in this thirtieth year" Lat, Syr;
"this is three years" Georg, cf. 3:1; "behold" precedes Lat Ms L, Arm H, cf. Eth; see Stone, "Manuscripts and Readings," 51.

30   o Perles, "Notes," 184, suggests mistranslation of
original Hebrew נושא, "bear," instead of "forgive."

31   p So Syr; *dereliqui* Lat perhaps ⟨ καταλειφθῆναι
(Clemen, "Zusammensetzung" [1898]); "how this
[their, Georg] way will turn out" Eth, Georg; Ar2
varies; Arm omits verse.

32/   or has another nation known ^q thee
        besides Israel?
      or what tribe has ^r so believed thy
        covenants as Jacob? ^s
33/   Yet their reward has not appeared
      and their labor has borne no fruit.
For I have traveled widely among the
nations and have seen that they abound in
wealth, though they are unmindful of thy
commandments. 34/ Now, therefore, weigh
in a balance our iniquities and those of the
inhabitants of the world; and so it will be
found which way the turn of the scale will
incline. 35/ When have the inhabitants of
the earth not sinned in thy sight? Or what
nation has kept thy commandments so
well? 36/ ^tThou mayest indeed find individual men ^uwho have kept thy commandments, ^v but nations thou wilt not find."

32   q "Have you known" Syr.
    r "Tribes . . . have known" Lat.
    s So Syr, Eth, Ar2, Arm, Georg; "these [scil.
tribes] of Jacob" Lat; "the house of Jacob" Ar1.
    t–u Eth omits by homoeoteleuton.
    v *Per nomina* Lat; "with names" Syr; "few" Arm;
"by name" Georg.

Form and Structure

By its position, this speech directed toward God opens the first vision. It follows upon the description of the seer's psychological state and his inspiration. The speeches preceding the second, third, and fourth visions (5:23–30; 6:38–59; and 9:29–37) are in the exactly corresponding positions. These four addresses are argumentative in character and thus are to be distinguished from the prayer in 8:19b–36, which is first and foremost a petition for divine mercy.

In structure, 3:4–36 falls into two chief sections: (1) a historical narrative from the creation of Adam down to the destruction of the Temple (3:4–27); and (2) Ezra's queries that arise from this (3:28–36). Section 1 is built of four parts, each of which tells a story of sin and punishment.

3:4–7a   *a.* Adam is created, sins, and is punished by death.

3:7b–10   *b.* The generations after him sinned and were punished by the Flood, which is the same as death.

3:11–22   *c.* The following generations are Noah, whose descendants sinned but were not punished; the Patriarchs; the exodus, with which is associated the Torah—then Israel sinned.

3:23–27   *d.* Election of David, sin, and exile.

This quadripartite structure is unbalanced, since the third section is much longer than the first two and more complex in construction.

The four sections are marked off by the punishments which each ends.[1] Adam sinned and "immediately you appointed death for him and his descendants" (3:7); the generations down to Noah sinned and God brought the Flood, and here the relationship to Adam is stressed: "as death came upon Adam, so the flood came upon them" (3:10); after the giving of the Torah, Israel sinned, "for the first Adam transgressed" (3:21).[2] Again, leading up to the exile Israel sinned, "in everything doing as Adam . . . , for they also had the evil heart, so thou didst deliver the city into the hands of thy enemies" (3:26–27). Thus, the first part of the address is tied together by the references to Adam's sin and its consequences.

Addresses to God of an argumentative character are not particularly common in the apocalypses, especially when they function, as here, to present the seer's inspired plaint against God. This is not prayer or petition to God awaiting fulfillment but is a challenge to God's justice. Somewhat similar are *2 Apoc Bar* 14:4–7; 21:12–26; and *3 Apoc Bar* 1:2. It is likely, however, that *2 Apocalypse of Baruch* is dependent on 4 Ezra.[3]

A similar casting back of the responsibility upon God is to be found in the prayer of the oppressed souls in *1 Enoch* 9:4–11. That prayer is definitely in a legal context and provokes divine action. A similar demand upon

1   Koch, "Esras erste Vision," 63, divides the recital somewhat differently (vv 4–8, 9–12, 13–22, 23–27). He observes that each section except his third has a clear reference to time (vv 4, 9, and 23). In our division, such a reference might also be seen in the repeated "and when" in the third section.

2   The idea expressed in 3:21 recurs in 3:26, just preceding the exile.

3   Perhaps *3 Apocalypse of Baruch* also depends on the same tradition.

divine justice is implied by Taxo's words in *Test Mos* 9:7.[4] Neither of these resembles 4 Ezra 3:4-36 in function.

At the basis of 3:3-27 lies a historical recital of the mighty acts of God, and, of course, it relates many such acts. What makes it special, however, are those elements which do not usually occur in *heilsgeschichtliche* recitals. These have to do with the nature of God's punitive action and the formulations touching on divine responsibility for human action and its consequences. Such recitals of the *magnalia Dei* serve in various places in the Hebrew Bible and stem originally, it seems, from covenant contexts.[5] Two chief elements relevant to 4 Ezra should be noted. First, the recital of God's mighty acts in the earlier sources may be part of the proem to an indictment of Israel, supporting the charge made against Israel by God or his representative.[6] Second, the indictment of God by an individual may be found in Job. Unique to 4 Ezra, however, is the use of the recital of the mighty acts of God as a part of a calling of God before the bar of his own justice. Setting forth the specific charges follows this recital in 3:28-36.[7]

In this final section of the address, 3:27—which is the climax of the first part of the speech—is taken up and its point reinforced. This second part of the address, 3:28-36, is also composed of three parts, divided by repetitions of the question "Is Babylon better than Zion?" and a stressing of the consequent incomprehensibility of

Israel's fate. These occur in 3:28; 3:31; and 3:34; the last is phrased in the language of balance and weight.

Function and Content

Ezra's challenge to God in 3:4-36 is the opening of the first vision. This passage sets forth the issue that focuses the central concerns of the whole book, viz., the fate of Israel and the destruction of Zion, and the book may be regarded as a series of responses to it.[8] It should be stressed that the problem of concern to the seer is the sufferings of Zion, while the more general issue of Adam's sin and its results is actually part of the seer's argument and is adduced as a way of heightening this central point. The particular dimension of this theme stressed in the present passage is the questioning of the destruction of Zion in terms of providence and divine justice. Issues such as the sacrosanctity of the Temple and its cosmic role are not raised by 4 Ezra, even though they clearly concerned other writers of his age.[9]

The sophistication of the writer of 4 Ezra is evident in his use of a historical recital to open the book. The formulation of this recital as an address to God enables the writer particularly to stress God's role in creation. God alone created the world, formed and vivified Adam, planted the garden and placed Adam in it. God commanded Adam and punished him for transgression. And so the repeated emphasis continues all the way through

---

4   See J. S. Licht, "Taxo or the Apocalyptic Doctrine of Vengeance," *JJS* 12 (1961) 95-103.

5   Cf. also 14:27-35, and see 14:27-36 Form and Structure, p. 433. It has been stressed by the commentators that this narrative, starting as it does from creation, witnesses the universal views of the apocalyptic writer. Observe, however, that the Pentateuch itself also starts from creation. Kaminka points out the resemblance between this narrative and that which, in poetic form, is the first part of the *Seder ʿAboda* ("The Recital of the High Priest's Liturgy") of the Additional Service of the Day of Atonement. Purpose and function differ, however, as well as form; the common material probably goes back to the biblical sources of both.

6   See, e.g., Ezekiel 20. An element of this is also present in Joshua 24 and Nehemiah 9. It is particularly part of the *rîb* form; see G. E. Wright, "The Lawsuit of God: A Form-Critical Study of Deuteronomy 32," *Israel's Prophetic Heritage: Essays in Honour of James Muilenburg* (ed. B. W. Anderson and W. Harrelson; London: SCM, 1962) 26-67; see also J.

Harvey, "Le 'Rîb-Pattern,' réquisitoire prophétique sur la rupture de l'alliance," *Biblica* 43 (1962) 172-96.

7   Abraham's reproach of God in Gen 18:25 is similar in some respects.

8   See the observations of G. Bornkamm, "Sohnschaft und Lieden," *Judentum, Urchristentum, Kirche: J. Jeremias FS* (ed. W. Eltester; BZNW 26; Berlin: Töpelmann, 1960) 188-98.

9   See *2 Apocalypse of Baruch* 3-4 and particularly chap. 4, which carefully distinguishes the heavenly and the earthly city of Jerusalem, as a way of minimizing problems arising from the destruction of the earthly. Cf. Stone, "Reactions," 199-200. For different solutions, see also *2 Apocalypse of Baruch* 6; 2 Macc 1:19; 2:1-5; *Para Jer* 1:1-3:11. See further Stone, "Reactions," passim.

the history of Israel, down to the destruction so as to accentuate the injustice of God. Thus a recital, of a type used elsewhere to praise God or to accentuate Israel's faithlessness, serves here to highlight the problem arising from Zion's destruction.[10] The repeated "thou" and "thou alone" is a powerful literary instrument serving together with the striking reapplication of the form of the recital of God's deeds to exhibit the author's theological daring. This is not the story of God's deeds seen as gracious acts to Israel; instead, it is the story of God's deeds viewed as responsible for the fearful fate of Zion.

With the conclusion of this section in 3:27, a change in style and structure may be detected. An almost reflective tone enters: "Then I said in my heart." The first person thought of the seer appears as he considers the result of the historical process he has described in 3:4–27. In this section of the speech, reproaches that were only incidental in the preceding verses become more explicit and stronger (3:28, 30–33, 34–36). The author's sense of

justice is here to the fore as he shakes his fist at the Almighty in righteous wrath. The first part of the speech, 3:4–27, relates God's actions; the second part sets forth the implications that are drawn from the consideration of these actions. It is significant for the overall understanding of the book that those questions relate exclusively to the fate of Zion and its meaning.[11]

Moreover, this passage clearly formulates and sets forth in quasi-legal form charges laid against God. A case is argued using the same techniques and forms that elsewhere are part of the indictment of Israel before the divine court.[12] This passage is therefore better called an address or a speech or a plaint than a prayer.[13]

Some scholars—notably Westermann, followed by Myers, Harnisch, and others—have related the three speeches at the start of the first three visions to the Psalms of National Lament (*Volksklagelied*). The speeches do share with these psalms a recital of certain of God's acts, but in Visions 2 and 3 the acts are not his acts in

---

10 On the author's powerful reapplication of older *Gattungen* (genres) here and elsewhere in the book, see Introduction, sec. 4.1.2. Thompson conceives of this passage as a prayer (see n. 15 below). Consequently he sees it as describing "God's saving acts of election and the massive outbreaks of sin" and therefore as an appeal for God's salvation in present crisis. He does not account for those features which have led us to a different, more radical interpretation of this address (Thompson, *Responsibility,* 161–63).

11 It follows from this that Breech's characterization of 3:4–36 as "the seer's complaint to the Most High" should be modified (Breech, "These Fragments," 270). Cf. also Brandenburger, *Verborgenheit,* 56.

12 Wright, "Rîb" passim. The legal dimension of this address was already noted by Brandenburger, *Verborgenheit,* 29 and n. 141. Westermann, "Klage," 77–79, wishes to analyze this and certain other prayers in terms of the "communal lament" form found in Psalms and Lamentations. This is not particularly helpful here, for the recital of the *magnalia dei* is not at home in that form. Some influence of it on the questions in 3:27–36 may be isolated, but even this is far from certain. Westermann's view has been widely accepted and has had extensive influence, particularly on German scholarship. Thus, e.g., Koch, "Esras erste Vision," 48–49.

13 The formal description of this *Gattung* is to be found in H. Gunkel and J. Begrich, *Einleitung in die Psalmen* (Göttinger Handkommentar zum AT; Göttingen: Vandenhoeck & Ruprecht, 1933) 117–39. Myers (pp. 199–200) suggests that 5:23–30 has the formal

characteristics of such a lament. He lists: (1) vocative address; (2) political aspect; (3) implicit prayer to take note of and resolve the misfortune; (4) groping for understanding; and (5) recognition that the misfortune is due to alienation from God. Harnisch (pp. 20–23) points to the same formal context, particularly that the actual lament is preceded by a review of God's redemptive acts. This pattern, he points out following Gunkel and Westermann, is clear in Psalm 44 and is also to be less distinctly discerned in Psalms 85 and 89, as well as other psalms. In 4 Ezra, Harnisch argues, the role of the recital of God's historical acts is played by the first part of the speeches, i.e., 3:4–27; 5:23–27; and 6:38–54. Westermann, building on earlier analyses and his own investigations, claims that the Psalms of Communal Lament have, in 4 Ezra, ceased to function as prayers but are instead doubt-instilling challenges to God; see Westermann, "Klage," 52–56. Brandenburger sees the whole of 3:4–36 as a deliberate reversal of the deuteronomic scheme leading to a questioning of the power both of the Torah and of the Creator (*Verborgenheit,* 170–75).

Jewish history but very different from them. In Vision 2 the election of Israel is hymned, while the recital in Vision 3 is a sort of hexaemeron. The analysis we have given of chapter 3, which is the closest of the three addresses in 4 Ezra to the Psalms of Communal Lament, showed it best to be understood in terms of the covenant lawsuit.[14]

The author's reproach in 3:4–27 is based upon the views that (1) God created human beings and punished them (3:4–10); (2) God let Noah survive, elected Abraham, gave the Torah, raised up David, who built the city and offered oblations, and punished Israel (3:11–27); and (3) there was an evil heart in Adam from the beginning and even the gift of the Torah could not prevail against it (note particularly 3:20 and the Excursus on Adam's Sin). From this it follows that God is doubly responsible. First, it was God who created human beings with a weakness which led to sins. Second, having created human beings in this fashion, he then punished them for sinning.[15] Human free will, Ezra claims, is meaningless, if the ultimate result of human action is, in any case, inevitable punishment because of the very way the world is constituted by its divine creator.[16]

Excursus on Adam's Sin

Questions of the evil heart and human sin, and their results, figure prominently in chapter 3; moreover, they are central to the understanding of the book.[17]

The Origin of the Evil Heart
4 Ezra says that Adam "bore" or "was burdened" with the evil heart (3:21) and it became permanent in his offspring (3:22, 25–26; cf. 7:63–72), but he carefully avoids directly attributing the creation of this evil inclination to God.[18] He does not restrict himself to the language of the heart, and in 4:30 a different image, not of the heart but of seed and sowing, is to be found: "For a grain of evil seed was sown in Adam's heart from the beginning." Neither in 3:21 nor in 4:30, however, does the writer make the origin of the evil heart clear. Indeed, the riddles in 4:3–4 are designed to show Ezra's unfitness to know "the origin of the evil heart" which there is described as knowledge of "the way of the Most High." Yet another term for this is apparently "the evil thought which was formed with them" (7:92). If so, then 7:92 comes closest to implying that God created it. Nonetheless, it should be stressed that 4 Ezra is not explicit on this point, even in chapter 3, where it could so well serve

---

14 So Harnisch himself calls it a radical *Anklage Gottes* (p. 22) but still locates it in the *Volksklagelied* context rather than in that of the covenant lawsuit. On the address in Vision 2, see 5:23–30 Form and Structure.

15 Thompson, *Responsibility,* treats the three addresses of Visions 1–3 and the passages 10:27b–28, 12:3b–9, 13:13b–10, and 14:99–22 under the rubric "Prayers for Enlightenment." This misses the stark differences between the texts.

16 D. Winston has pointed out that such critiques of divine action are also to be found in rabbinic sources and even in some classical texts. They are not presented as sectarian, though sometimes, but not always, set into the mouths of sinners. See D. Winston, "Freedom and Determinism in Greek Philosophy and Jewish Hellenistic Wisdom," *Studia Philonica* 2 (1974) 40–41 In that article Winston deals with tensions present in Jewish thought of the Hellenistic period and later, arising from different attitudes toward free will.

17 A sober and sensitive analysis is that of F. C. Porter, "The Yeçer Hara: A Study in the Jewish Doctrine of Sin," *Biblical and Semitic Studies Yale Bicentennial Publications* (New York: Scribner's, 1902) 146–52. A good overall survey of the views of the Rabbis is A. P. Hayman, "Rabbinic Judaism and the Problem of Evil," *Scottish Journal of Theology* 29 (1976) 461–76.

18 The technical term "evil heart" is probably derived from Gen 6:5 and occurs chiefly in 4 Ezra (see 4:30; 7:92). In the Bible, see also Gen 8:21; Jer 3:17; 7:24; 11:8; 16:12; and 18:12. Cf. also 1QS 1:6 בשרירות לב אשמה, but the view put forward by that text is different. The term יצר הרע, "evil inclination," is probably also derived from the same verses of Genesis; see Porter, "Yeçer Hara," 108–9; L. Ginzberg, *Die Haggada bei den Kirchenvätern und in der apokryphischen Litteratur* (Berlin, 1900) 153 note; and Hayman, "Problem," 462. "Heart" and "inclination" were often identified in rabbinic thought; cf. *m. Ber.* 9:5 and *Sifre Deut.* on 6:5 (Finkelstein, p. 55). On older uses of the term "(evil) inclination," see Porter, "Yeçer Hara," 136–46. See also 11QPs[a] 19:15–16; CD 2:16 מחשבת יצר אשמה. The terminology is discussed in some detail by Thompson, *Responsibility,* 332–39. Thompson also concurs with our observation that God is nowhere said to be responsible for creating the evil inclination (ibid., 336). Koch energetically rejects the identification of 4 Ezra's "evil heart" with the Rabbis' "evil inclination" ("Esras erste Vision," 60–61). The distinction between the terms that he presses so strongly seems forced. Our exegesis of the three central passages argued by Koch (4:30; 3:22; and 7:92) speaks for itself.

the purpose of his argument.[19]

Developing the image of sowing and harvest used in 4:30, the author says that the eschatological rectification of the situation will be the "sowing of heads of grain without number" (4:32).[20] The same terminology recurs in 8:6 relating to the eschaton, while a changing of the heart at the end is spoken of in 6:26. The removal of the evil heart by God is prayed for and desired, and indeed predicted, but still its origins are not made clear.[21]

In contrast, the rabbinic sources are quite specific about the origin of the evil heart. God created the evil inclination, but, the Sages add, he gave humans the ability to overcome it.[22] 4 Ezra also strongly argues for free will, and in one series of passages mankind is described as struggling to overcome the evil inclination and achieve righteousness.[23] It is illuminating also to compare Abraham's question addressed to God

according to the *Apocalypse of Abraham*:

> O Eternal, Mighty One! Wherefore hast Thou willed to effect that evil should be desired in the hearts of men, since Thou indeed art angered over that which was willed by Thee, at him who is doing what is unprofitable in Thy counsel?[24]

Yet the author of 4 Ezra seems deliberately to avoid the bald statement that it was God who created the evil inclination in mankind. Perhaps this is because of the large role that free will plays in his thought.[25]

The evil heart caused Adam's sin which brought death as its punishment

Adam, "burdened with an evil heart, transgressed" (3:21) and "immediately thou didst appoint death for him and for his descendants" (3:7; cf. also 7:116–126). The idea that death was the chief result of Adam's sin is derived from Gen 3:19. It is widespread in Jewish

---

19 Harnisch, deriving from Brandenburger, *Adam und Christus,* 32–33, whose views came in turn from Box, would distinguish the "evil inclination" from the "evil heart," the latter being the result of the working of the former; see Harnisch, 48 note. This is not justified; see 3:26 Commentary. See also the refutation of Harnisch's position by Thompson, *Responsibility,* 334–35. The terms are substantially equivalent.

20 On this image, see 4:28 Commentary and 4:30 Commentary.

21 Old prayers for the removal of the evil inclination are in 11QPs ᵃ 155:13–14 (19:15–16); cf. the prayer of Rabbi *b. Ber.* 16b. *B. Sukka* says that God helps humans overcome their evil inclination which would otherwise cause their death (52b). Its power is overcome by the study of Torah, *Sifre Deut.* 45 (Finkelstein, pp. 103–4) and *b. Kidd.* 30b. It will be removed at the end of days. For this, see already Ezek 11:19 and *Apoc Mos* 13:5; and see also *Song R.* 1:2.4; *Tanh. Ki Tissa* 13 (Buber, 2:114); or after death, see *Bib Ant* 33:3. Hayman sensitively analyzes the interrelation in rabbinic thought between the concept of the evil inclination, the hypostasis of God's quality of judgment, and the idea of Satan. He traces a process of withdrawal from the concept of Satan in some streams of rabbinic thinking ("Problem," 470–71). It is worth remarking that in 4 Ezra the figure of Satan plays no role.

22 E. E. Urbach, *The Sages: Their Concepts and Beliefs* (Cambridge: Harvard University, 1987) 472, and bibliography there; and G. F. Moore, *Judaism in the First Centuries of the Christian Era* (Cambridge: Harvard University, 1962), 1:453, 480. See also *b. Ber.* 61a; Targ J Gen 2:7; and *b. Kidd.* 30b. On God's "regret" for having created the evil inclination, see *b.*

Sukka 52b; *Gen. R.* 26:4 on Gen 6:4 (Theodor-Albeck, p. 258); Moore, *Judaism,* 1:480–81; and Urbach, *Sages,* 480. A discussion in *b. Sanh.* 91b between "Antoninus" and Rabbi deals with the question of whether the evil inclination rules over humans from the moment of conception or only from birth. A more ambiguous attitude toward it is *Gen. R.* 9:7 (Theodor-Albeck, pp. 71–72).

23 See 7:18; 7:92 Commentary; 7:127 Commentary; and 8:56. This may be compared with the struggle between the two spirits in 1QS 4:23. Harnisch, p. 166 note, following earlier writers and in view of the correspondence between the external world and the human heart in 1QS, would stress that this view is an internalization of a dualistic worldview. J. S. Licht, however (*The Rule Scroll* [Jerusalem: Bialik Institute, 1965] 91 [in Hebrew]), sets the phrase break after עול, so making the struggle external to the heart, as is also implied by 1QS 3:18–19. This undermines the supposed similarity between 1QS and 7:125. It is still possible, of course, that the conflict between the two inclinations in the human heart is the result of the "psychologization of a dualistic world-view," but that case must be made on other grounds. Certainly, in 4 Ezra it has left no clear traces. On free will, see *2 Apoc Bar* 15:5–6 and 54:15; cf. Sir 15:17 and *1 Enoch* 98:4.

24 *Apoc Abr* 23:14; chap. 24 in one respect corresponds to the narrative part of 4 Ezra 3. It is the story of the working out of evil in the world.

25 The Armenian version is particularly sensitive to this issue and it omits all passages that mention the evil heart; see *Armenian Text Commentary.* On free will in 4 Ezra, see 7:6 Commentary.

---

sources,[26] and is also Paul's view; see Rom 5:12–14 and 1 Cor 15:21–22.[27]

A second result of Adam's sin is that life on earth became toilsome and difficult. This view is also derived from the biblical text (Gen 3:17–19) and is clearly expressed in 4 Ezra 7:12, cf. also *Vita Adam* 34.[28] A third result was the disruption of the order of creation. This world was not long pristine.[29]

The evil inclination is inherited by Adam's descendants
Strongly prominent in 4 Ezra is the view that the evil inclination is an inherited weakness that took root as a result of Adam's sin (3:21–22, 25–26; 4:30; 7:118 and Commentary there). This view stands, of course, in tension with the idea of free will, which issue is discussed below; see 7:48. The idea of free will arises frequently in the book. It is most pointedly expressed in 7:19–24; 7:72; 8:56–62; and 14:34; cf. *2 Apoc Bar* 15:6; 54:21; 84; and 85:7. A strong statement on this is also made in *Ps Sol* 9:7.[30] Some scholars would maintain that in 7:116–126 the idea of an inevitable sinfulness of mankind, inherited from Adam, is to be found.[31] Others would, rightly, deny this, highlighting

the inherited nature of the evil inclination, of death but not of sin.

Thompson justly observes that the author has not integrated his understanding of Adam's fall with his view about the evil inclination. This means that the idea of Adam's fall loses (or perhaps does not gain) any major importance as a way of understanding the origins of evil.[32]

The Concept of Death
The concept of death in 4 Ezra is worthy of special attention. After all, death is the primary result of Adam's sin. 4 Ezra uses the language of death in two major fashions. The first is of physical death. As noted above, this is the result of the sin of Adam (3:7), and there are those who are excepted from it, "who were taken, who did not taste death from their birth" (6:26). Indeed, Ezra himself in 14:9 is told to prepare for such a fate. He is instructed:

Renounce now the corruptible life,
Remove from yourself mortal thoughts,
Cast away from yourself human burdens,
Put off the infirm nature,

---

26 It occurs in Sir 15:14; 15:17; and particularly 25:24; *2 Apoc Bar* 23:4; 54:15; *2 Enoch* 30:16; cf. also *Mek. BaḤodeš* 9 (Horovitz-Rabin, p. 237); *Exod. R.* 32:1; *b. Abod. Zar.* 5a; *b. Shabb.* 55b; *Gen. R.* on 2:17 (Theodor-Albeck, p. 151); *Tanh.* (Buber, p. 29); *Tanh.* on Gen 3:22; *Lev. R.* 27:4; *Sifre Deut.* 339 (Finkelstein, p. 388); and Ginzberg, "Kirchenvätern," 153. See also Brandenburger, *Adam und Christus,* 45–58, for a conspectus of views on this.

27 Brandenburger, *Adam und Christus,* 45–47, argues that, indeed, this is the view of Genesis 3. Adam lost other things as a result of sin, e.g., "glory" (*Apoc Mos* 21:2); "angelic food" (*Vit Ad* 4:2); paradise and spiritual joy (ibid., 10:4); there are other views in addition.

28 Naturally, also his expulsion from Eden followed on his sin in Gen 3:23; so *Jub* 3:26 and *Test Patr Levi* 18:10–11. Other views attributed not death but a shortening of days to Adam's sin; see, e.g., *Jub* 4:30.

29 See 7:11, also *2 Apoc Bar* 56:5; cf. Rom 8:18–22. One sign of this is the beasts' disobedience; see *Apoc Moses* 11, 24; *Vit Ad* 27; and *Test Patr Naph* 8:6. At a more general level, the order of creation is said to have been corrupted by human action; see 9:19–20; cf. 8:50.

30 See note on this in H. E. Ryle and M. R. James, *Psalms of the Pharisees commonly called The Psalms of Solomon* (Cambridge: Cambridge University, 1891) 91. See 7:116—8:3 Form and Function and 7:128 Commentary. The tension of predeterminism and free will is expressed in paradoxical terms in *m. Abot* 3:15: "All is foreseen and choice is granted." A

tannaitic view was that the giving of the Torah at Sinai negated the results of Eve's pollution by the serpent; see *b. Shabb.* 146a. See also Brandenburger, *Adam und Christus,* 25–26, who is also sensitive to these tensions. See further 3:21 Commentary on inherited evil. Moreover, the difficult expression in 1QS 11:9 might also express the idea of the inherent wickedness of humans. Compare in different terms the idea that Adam's exit from Eden was also determined, *Pes. R. K.* 12 (Buber, p. 102b). In *2 Apoc Bar* 48:42–43 the implication is that Adam and Eve's actions brought their descendants to sin and consequently to Gehenna; cf. also Rom 5:12. This point of view is (seemingly polemically) opposed in *2 Apoc Bar* 54:15, 19, and see Moore, *Judaism,* 1:478.

31 So particularly Harnisch, pp. 54–56. This extreme formulation serves him in the presentation of the problematic which he claims to be central to the book—the conflict between the divine promises to Israel and the inevitable nature of sin (pp. 55–56). Cf. the comments of Porter cited in 7:67 Commentary and discussion there. Harnisch seems to go beyond the position of Brandenburger, *Adam und Christus,* 35–36. See also Introduction, sec. 3.3.

32 Thompson, *Responsibility,* 335–36.

And place on one side the thoughts which distress you,
And hurry to move from these times. (14:13–14)
In this interesting passage it appears that the corruptible, mortal element in human life, from which he is to remove himself, is the end of life through death. This supposition is further strengthened when, in 7:15–16, in a context having nothing whatsoever to do with Ezra's assumption, the angel asks him why he is disturbed by his corruptible and mortal nature and admonishes him to think of what is to come, not of what is present. Again the parallelism of mortal and corruptible and the general sense of the passage support the view that mortal and corruptible are virtually synonymous.[33] A similar consciousness of human mortality may be discovered in 4:11. In 8:53–54 the text tells how, in the world to come, death and Sheol will be hidden away and immortality made manifest; cf. 7:13.

A somewhat different context illustrating the use of the word "death" for "ordinary" physical death is found in 7:78. The passage, discussing the intermediate state of the soul immediately after death and before resurrection, described death as the separation of the soul from the body in accordance with the divine decree; cf. also 7:88 and 7:100. God's direct responsibility for death is also mentioned in 8:13. The fact that judgment and punishment or reward follow after death is discussed in 8:38; 9:12; and 14:35, while in 7:29 the messianic kingdom is said to conclude with the death of the Messiah and of all humans. Thus it may be observed that in one series of passages, physical death is considered highly undesirable. It is the same as corruptibility (cf. also 2 Apoc Bar 42:7). It will be, above all, that which will be removed in the future world.[34]

This view of death is not connected with a negative evaluation of the body, although it is clear (e.g. in 7:78) that the body is the part of human beings that dies.[35] The fact that the body is, evidently, not considered evil is significant, for such an outlook could easily have arisen. In other series of passages, however, death is seen simply as a stage in the total life of human beings and after it, punishment and reward will come. In these passages there appears to be no evaluation of death as either good or evil, desirable or undesirable.

The second major use of this notion is more general, less precisely defined. In it death appears as the equivalent of perdition or damnation and in opposition not just to life but to eternal life.[36] Thus 7:48 tells us that the "evil heart" has made known "ways of death . . . and removed us far from life," and 7:92 expresses the same idea. In 7:119 death opposes the *immortale tempus*, in 7:131 destruction opposes life, and in 8:31 death is simply the equivalent of eternal punishment. Clearly, too, in 7:137–138 life means salvation, and 8:6 says that it was prepared by God for human beings. Various of the versions of 4 Ezra translated "live" as "be saved."[37] In 8:38–39 death, judgment, and destruction contrast with "pilgrimage," salvation, and reward.[38]

It appears that this usage is a natural development from the negative evaluation of physical death observed above. It most clearly stems from cases like 7:48–49. In this passage, too, the connection with the evil heart is of great interest. The evil heart is directly linked to Adam as the cause of his transgression (3:21–22) and is said in 7:92 to bring human beings to death. From context and sense it is proper to understand 7:48–49 as representing an example of the second usage of death with the meaning "damnation" or the like, although it is the same evil heart which brought physical death to Adam and through him to his descendants which here is the cause of damnation, eternal death. This once again illustrates the complex

---

33 Cf. the versions of 8:31, where "mortal" and "corruptible" appear to be interchangeable. See further 2 Apoc Bar 42:7, where "corruption" is parallel and opposite to "life." See further 4:11 Commentary and 7:31 Commentary. Note that healing is a feature of the eschatological state: 2 Apoc Bar 73:2.

34 Cf. 8:53 and Isa. 25:8; Rev. 21:4; 2 Apoc Bar 21:22–23; see 4:11 Commentary.

35 Cf. 14:14; 2 Apoc Bar 49:3.

36 Cf. 10:10; b. Ber. 28b: "eternal death." On the term *perire*, see Harnisch, p. 149 note.

37 See textual note k on 8:3; see also 9:15.

38 So also the use of "life" in 7:21 (and Commentary); 7:66; 7:82; 7:92; 7:129; 8:6; 9:13; 14:30; 14:35; see Violet 2 on 7:60 and Harnisch, pp. 140, 142, and 149 note, who cites yet further references. Cf. the LXX of Ezek 33:12 ("saved") and Hebrew ("live"—so

Box), and note *Bib Ant* 16:3: "And then [i.e., at the time of renewal of the earth] shall they die and not live"; *Ps Sol* 14:3; 15:13; *1 Enoch* 96:6; et al. The terminology is discussed in general in Volz, pp. 341–42 and in considerable detail by N. Messel, *Die Einheitlichkeit der jüdischen Eschatologie* (BZAW 30; Giessen: Töpelmann, 1915) 120–29. He maintains that the term "live," "life" denotes more generally "reward" rather than specifically "eternal life" (pp. 120–28). In 10:10 Commentary we have discussed the term "perdition," perhaps reflecting Greek ἀπωλεία and Hebrew אבדון.

implications of this term and the interrelatedness of its various uses.[39]

Commentary

■ **4** The dual title "sovereign, Lord" appears in Visions 1–3 at the start of the addresses (cf. 5:23 and 6:38) as well as elsewhere in 4 Ezra: 4:38; 5:38; 6:11; 7:17, 75(?); 12:7; and 13:51; cf. 6:38. Compare the double appellations found in the Hebrew Bible such as ה׳ אדני or ה׳ ה׳. The particular combination of Latin words found here, *dominator domine,* is unusual.[40] The dual address sometimes refers to God, as it does here and in 5:23 and 6:38, and sometimes to the angel (e.g., 4:38; 5:38; 6:11; 7:58; 7:75).[41]

The idea that God created the world by speech is notable and is also emphasized in 6:38 (and see Commentary there) and 6:43, while 7:116, which also refers to the creation of Adam, does not necessarily contradict this view. This is nicely stated already in Ps 33:6:

By the word of the Lord the heavens were made, and all their host by the breath of his mouth.

Compare also Ps 33:9 and 148:5. It occurs in other ancient sources, so, for example, Sir 42:15; Wisd 9:1; Heb 11:3; and *2 Apoc Bar* 14:17:

When in the beginning the world did not exist with its inhabitants, you devised and spoke by means of your word and at the same time the works of creation stood

before you.[42]

Compare the Jewish Daily Morning Service: "Blessed be he who spake and the world existed."[43]

The emphasis on God's creating alone serves the author's point admirably. It may also be directed against the view that other beings played a role in creation. This was particularly said to be so in the creation of human beings, often as an exegesis of Gen 1:26.[44]

Many commentators have connected the phrase "at the beginning" with an exegesis of the Hebrew מקדם in Gen 2:8 (rendered "in the east" by RSV; see further 3:6 Commentary). It seems likely, however, that the present verse derives from a combination of Gen 1:1 and 2:7. If so, most probably the expression "at the beginning" is drawn from Gen 1:1. Genesis 2:8 refers to paradise and was utilized by 4 Ezra in 3:6.

■ **5** This verse is based on Gen 2:7, which it expands somewhat. Mankind is said to have been created by the dust at God's command; cf. 7:116; 7:139; 10:14; and *2 Apoc Bar* 48:46. Humans are also said to be the "workmanship of (God's) hands." The idea that human beings were created by God's hands also occurs in 4 Ezra 8:7; 8:44; and elsewhere in the Pseudepigrapha.[45] A later expression of views resembling those here is in *Alfa-Beta de R. Aqiba* (Jellinek, *BM*, 3:59): "*alef-taw-alef* is Adam; *taw* is that he is the beginning of His creation (Hebrew wordplay); the whole world was created through the speech of

---

39 See further Harnisch, p. 149, on eschatological death.

40 See further Box on 4:38; see 4:38 Commentary and 5:23 Commentary; see also Harnisch, p. 23 note.

41 See 7:17 Commentary on confusions and shifts between God and angel.

42 Cf. also *2 Apoc Bar* 21:4; *Apoc Abr* 9:9; 22:2; and Heb 11:3. 2 Pet 3:5, which is sometimes quoted in this context, is not precise. In the cosmogony in *2 Enoch* 24–30, creation is through a series of commands without any particular stress being laid on the idea that it is through the divine word. Many rabbinic sources speak of creation through speech; see, e.g., *Mek.* on Exod 15:17 (Horovitz-Rabin, p. 150). In *b. Hag.* 12a, a saying of Rab is reported in which he says the world was created through ten things, including wisdom but not including speech, דבור, though other words indicating speech-acts are found.

43 *The Authorized Daily Prayer Book* (trans. S. Singer; London: Eyre & Spottiswoode, 1917) 16. An interesting contrast is Isa 45:12, "It was my hands that stretched out the heavens, and I commanded all their host"; see also *Od Sol* 16:19. In Wisd 18:15 we

have the broader idea of the immediate effectiveness of divine speech. In *b. Rosh Hashanah* 32a reference is made to the ten pronouncements by which the world was created. See also Ginzberg, *Legends* 5:63, who cites many sources. The related idea of the active divine word is discussed in 8:22 Commentary and 13:10 Commentary.

44 See *2 Enoch* 30:8 (A); *PRE* 11; et al. Cf. also the comments of R. McL. Wilson, "The Early History of the Exegesis of Gen 1,26," *Studia Patristica,* vol. 1.1 (TU 63; Berlin: Akademie, 1957), 420–22.

45 So *2 Enoch* 44:1 (A); *Apoc Mos* 37:2; *Apoc Sedrach* 3:8; on the latter, cf. 4Q 381, frag. 1, line 3, published in E. M. Schuller, *Non-Canonical Psalms from Qumran: A Pseudepigraphic Collection* (HSS 28; Missoula, Mont.: Scholars, 1986) 71, and cf. her note on p. 79. See also C. Bezold, *Die Schatzhöhle* (Leipzig: Hinrichs, 1883) 1:3. J. Jervell, *Imago Dei* (Göttingen: Vandenhoeck & Ruprecht, 1960), thinks this may have had a polemical point (p. 48). The image is already present in the Bible; cf. Isa 45:11; 60:21; and many other places.

the Holy One and man was created by his hands" (cf. *PRE* 9; contrast Philo, *De somn.* 210). An apparent contradiction exists between these two formulations. Yet the expression about "God's hand" is presumably not intended literally, and it serves to emphasize humanity's special position in creation and God's particular involvement in creation of mankind. The description of the vivification of Adam here should be compared with *Gen. R.* 14:8 (Theodor-Albeck, p. 132); *PRE* 11; and others. Compare also 4Q 381, frag. 1, line 7 (Schuller, *Non-Canonical Psalms from Qumran*, 71). It derives, of course, directly from Gen 2:7.

■ **6** No clear parallel has been found to the statement that the Garden of Eden was planted by God's right hand. Indeed, the idea that he planted the garden is, of course, already present in Gen 2:8, and the expression "which your right hand planted" is probably taken from Ps 80:16. The present verse is the oldest attestation of the idea that paradise was created before the creation of the world. The idea comes from an exegesis of מקדם in Gen 2:8 as "of old." In Ps 74:12, the LXX renders this Hebrew wordplay by Greek πρὸ αἰῶνος.

The Garden of Eden is one of a list of seven (or six) objects that existed before the creation of the world, according to a number of rabbinic sources. This list includes the Torah, repentance, Gehenna, the throne of glory, the Temple, and the Messiah's name.[46] This idea was opposed by R. Samuel b. Naḥmani in *Gen. R.* 15:3 (Theodor-Albeck, p. 137), who commented on the word מקדם: "You might have thought that this means before the creation of the world. This is not so! It means before

Adam, for Adam was created on the sixth day, but the garden of Eden on the third."[47]

The idea that paradise or recompense was prepared in advance for human beings, and thus for Adam himself, is explicit in 7:70; cf. also 7:36. This also lies behind the view of R. Samuel b. Naḥmani cited above, and it is a view that is admirably suited to 4 Ezra's contention here. More generally, the things pertaining to judgment were readied in advance; see 4:29; 6:6; 7:26; 7:31; 7:70; 7:83–84; 7:121; 8:52; 13:26; and 13:36.

The term "Garden of Eden" or "paradise" seems to occur in various senses in 4 Ezra. First, here in 3:6 it means Adam's garden which was created before the creation of the world. This view is also to the fore in 6:2, where "before the foundations of the garden were laid" indicates a time of remote antiquity (see 6:2 Commentary). The other chief use of the term is in the context of reward for the righteous. In 7:36 paradise, the place of rest, is opposed to Gehenna, the fiery furnace. It is also a term for eschatological reward in 7:123 and 8:52. Perhaps also 4:7–8 reflects a view of an existing, heavenly paradise and those verses show some striking parallels with the technical use of the term "paradise" or *pardes* in somewhat later Jewish mystical texts.[48] Notable is the Armenian text of 7:36 and 8:52 which refers to "true paradise" *tšmarit draxtn*.[49] All of these senses are well attested in the literature of the age of 4 Ezra.[50]

Keulers maintains quite strongly that all of these terms are spiritualized and serve in 4 Ezra simply as ways of referring to eschatological reward. The term "spiritualization" does not seem appropriate and is not sup-

---

46 See *b. Ned.* 39b; *b. Pesah.* 54a; *PRE* 3; *Midr. Teh.* on 72:16 and 90:13; *Sed. El. Rab.* 31 (Friedmann, p. 160); and elsewhere. *Gen. R.* 1:1 (Theodor-Albeck, p. 6) has a somewhat different version. For the same view, see also Targ O and Targ J on Gen 2:8; cf. also Targ J on Gen 3:24. See further Excursus on Judgment; 6:6 Commentary; 7:14 Commentary; and 7:33 Commentary. The special role of the Temple is stressed by J. H. Charlesworth, ed. and trans., *The Odes of Solomon* (Oxford: Oxford University, 1977) 23 n. 3 (on 4:2), and the issue of precreation is also discussed in *Sifre Deut.* 11:10 (Finkelstein, p. 70).

47 See also *Yalq. Gen.* 20. Paradise is said to have been created on the third day, on which vegetation came into being (Gen 1:11–12), by older sources, notably *Jub* 2:7; see also *2 Enoch* 30:1 (A). This is also so in 4 Ezra 6:44 if, as Gunkel suggests, the creation of

paradise has influenced the description of the creation of vegetation at that point. *Tanh. Exod.* 17 speaks in a different vein of the precreation or predestination of many elements and events.

48 See Stone, "Paradise," 85–88; G. G. Scholem, *Jewish Gnosticism, Merkabah Mysticism and Talmudic Tradition* (New York: Jewish Theological Seminary, 1960) 14–19. In the translation it has been given as "the garden" when referring to the primordial paradise and "paradise" in other contexts. See also Keulers, pp. 181–88.

49 Scholem, *Gnosticism*, 14–19, distinguishes between פרדס, "garden" or "orchard," a technical term of Jewish theosophy, and גן עדן, "the garden of Eden" or "of delight," as it is traditionally interpreted (cf. for a possible original sense W. Andrae, "Der kultische Garten," *Die Welt des Orients* [Wupperthal:

ported by the text. The close association of different terms for eschatological reward may indicate, however, a lack of systematic eschatology in the book; see, for example, 8:52.[51]

Little information is offered in 4 Ezra about the nature of paradise. In 7:123 its incorruptible fruit is spoken of, while 8:52 says that it contains the tree of life. Presumably also the flowers mentioned by 6:3 and its divine cultivator (3:6; cf. Gen 2:8) are elements of this picture too. Paradise, whether primordial or eschatological, is viewed as a garden.[52] The "materialism" of such a description, which refers to paradisiacal fruit or flowers, has disturbed some scholars. In general, however, when the author speaks of the tree of life or the flowers or fruit of the garden, he should be taken to mean what he says.[53] Our author does not see an opposition of material and spiritual, and so we should assume that he attributed at least the same physical reality to the heavenly realm as to the earthly. So, even though many details are not given, paradise is to be regarded as one element of the joyous future state. Views of paradise in other sources are quite explicit, and 4 Ezra's views are in general congruent with them.[54]

It is worth observing that although the author refers to paradise on a number of occasions, he gives only the most meager details about it.[55] This is a feature of many of his eschatological descriptions. Moreover, although the typology of $\tau \grave{\alpha}$ $\check{\epsilon} \sigma \chi \alpha \tau \alpha$ $\dot{\omega} s$ $\tau \grave{\alpha}$ $\pi \rho \hat{\omega} \tau \alpha$ "the last things (are) like the first" is clearly at work in the passage, the question of the relationship of the primordial paradise and the eschatological one remains untouched.

In 6:2 Commentary; 7:6 Commentary; and 7:26 Commentary, further aspects of the descriptions of paradise are discussed, particularly its wondrous fruit and its likeness to a walled city.

■ 7 "One commandment": Jervell points out that in a series of later sources, the commandment is thought to be the Torah or righteousness.[56] This is perhaps implied in 4 Ezra 7:11 and is discussed in detail in connection with that verse; see also 7:1–25 Function and Content, pp. 194–95.

Adam's sin and its consequences are discussed in the Excursus on Adam's Sin. Observe that his expulsion from the garden and related themes are not mentioned here. The biblical source is Gen 2:16—3:21. An expression similar to this verse is 2 Apoc Bar 23:4: "when Adam sinned and death was decreed on those who were to be born." By the conjunction of phrases, the verse implies that the begetting of children is a corollary of death.

■ 8 God is taken to task for not preventing the sins of Adam's descendants. In 3:20 this idea is further developed, and compare also the similar hyperbolic reproof of the earth in 7:116. The phrase is also found in Ps Sol 2:1, there of God's not preventing the desecration of the Temple.[57]

■ 9 The expression "in its time" is closely paralleled in 8:41; 8:43; 10:16; 11:20; and 14:32. It implies the predestinarian view of fixed times also reflected in 4:27; 4:33–34; 4:37; 5:49; 6:5–6; 7:74; 11:44; 13:58; and 14:9; cf. 3:14; 14:5; and 2 Apoc Bar 21:8.[58] It could have been maintained that if the Flood is predetermined, then humanity's sin and its punishment were also predeter-

---

Putty, 1947] 1:487). This distinction is difficult to maintain in Greek or in translations made from Greek. Note that "truth" and "righteousness" both fall within the semantic field of קושטא.

50 In 8:52 paradise may be identified with the heavenly Jerusalem; see Schieffer, pp. 30–31; Keulers, pp. 181–88; etc. See further 8:52–53 Commentary.

51 Keulers, pp. 181–88, following Box, p. 196, and others; see Stone, *Features*, 197–204, on this issue.

52 This indeed is the meaning of the word; see *IDB* s.v.

53 Both Box and Keulers have stressed the "transcendental" or "heavenly" nature of the idea of paradise. Together with associated concepts, it is merely a symbol of the future, transcendental state of the righteous. This implies that Ezra *hat . . . mit dem himmlischen Paradies nicht mehr die plastische Vorstellung eines wirklichen, wenn auch wunderbaren, Gartens*

verbunden, "had no longer tied to the heavenly paradise, the idea of a real, even if wondrous, garden" (Keulers, p. 186).

54 See Keulers, pp. 186–87; Schieffer, pp. 30–31; etc

55 Contrast, e.g., *2 Apoc Bar* 51:11–12.

56 Jervell, *Imago Dei,* 43.

57 For an earlier foreshadowing of this view, see *1 Enoch* 9:10–11; see G. W. E. Nickelsburg, "Apocalyptic and Myth in 1 Enoch 6–11," *JBL* 96 (1977) 387. It is presented in a rather colorful way in *Apoc Sedrach* 7:13–8:1.

58 See 4:37 Commentary; 6:5 Commentary. Cf., somewhat differently, 10:16. The matter is discussed further in Excursus on Natural Order, p. 102. The idea was widespread in the Second Temple period; see, e.g., the references and discussion in Volz, 138.

mined—in other words, that God created human beings knowing in advance that he would destroy the world through the Flood. It is notable that the author of 4 Ezra does not use this argument, even though it would have supported his contentions. For him the idea of free will is so deeply rooted that he does not work out the ramifications of his predestinarian assumptions. See 7:127 Commentary.

■ 10 Nowhere else is the correspondence between the punishments of Adam and that of the generation of the Flood made as explicit as here. It serves, of course, to mark the end of a block of text; compare the mention of Adam in 3:21 and 3:26. Somewhat similar, however, is *2 Apoc Bar* 56:8–16.[59]

■ 11 This verse is preserved in two forms, one in Latin and associated versions and the other in Armenian. Violet 2 thinks that preserved in Armenian to be preferable. What is clear is that the text of the other versions raises certain difficulties not present in the Armenian; nonetheless, on the whole, it appears to be acceptable.

The Latin, as it stands, seems to mean "Noah with his house, all the righteous (who issued) from him." The text of Latin has support from Arabic1, and one suspects that this is what lies behind the Armenian as well. It implies that "his house" is the same as "all the righteous." This text is difficult to construe in Latin, however, or in a Greek retroversion of it. Another possibility is raised by some Latin manuscripts that introduce *et* ("and") before "all the righteous." That text might then be interpreted to mean that with Noah were saved both his house and all his righteous descendants. This seems tautological, but perhaps his descendants are regarded as saved while they are still "in the loins of their ancestor" Noah (cf. Heb 7:10). Yet a further possible interpretation along these lines (not consonant with the grammar of the Latin version) is that of the Syriac, "and from him sprang all the righteous"; cf. also Ethiopic. Since all human beings sprang from Noah, this statement seems pointless,

although it might be compared with *1 Enoch* 65:12, a prophecy addressed to Noah: "From thy seed shall proceed a fountain of the righteous and holy without number forever."[60]

The other form of text occurs in Armenian and is rather different. It reads, "You had mercy upon your servant Noah, and on his account upon his sons; and together with all his house he found favor before you because he was pleasing to you." As remarked above, Violet 2 considers this form of the verse, except for the phrase "and on his account upon his sons," to be original. The idea expressed here, that Noah's sons were saved from the Flood for his sake, may also be found in *Jub* 5:19. Nonetheless, on textual grounds it is unwise to accept unsupported readings of the Armenian against the other versions.[61] The name "Noah" is omitted by Syriac and Ethiopic.

■ 12 This verse is structurally parallel to 3:7b–8, as is emphasized by the word "again." Nothing here corresponds to 3:9, because no punishment is recorded at this point. The author stresses the persistence of human sin. The expressions in the first part of the verse are probably drawn from Gen 6:1, which fact again highlights the parallels that the writer sees between the two situations. With the last phrase, compare *Ps Sol* 1:8.

■ 13 Abraham is here said to be chosen by God, as were Noah (3:11) and Jacob (3:16). Farther on in the book, Israel's election is a prominent theme; see, for example, 4:25; 5:23–27; and 6:58. Abraham's discovery of God is not mentioned, only his election by him. This easily serves the author's purpose. Abraham is also called "loved of God" in the next verse (q.v.). Structurally similar to 3:13–15 is *Bib Ant* 8:2–4, while *Bib Ant* 23:5 resembles 3:13 in general import, although it does not include the term "elect" or "choose." The expression "one of them," already found in 3:11, recurs here.

■ 14 Abraham is not termed "beloved of God" in the Pentateuch. This appellation occurs in Isa 41:8 and 2 Chr 20:7. It is frequent in later Jewish and Christian

---

59   The parallel of 2 Pet 2:4–5 cited by Box is not close, except as a list of divine punishments.

60   Berossus, quoted by Josephus, *Contra Apionem* 1.130, stresses Noah's role as the ancestor of Israel. See further Ginzberg, *Legends*, 5:179, for discussion of the idea of the righteous as dependent on Noah. *Apocryphon of John*, CG 2:1, 29:6–12, has a form of the tradition associating the salvation of many of the

righteous with Noah (*NHL*, 114).

61   See Introduction, sec. 1.2.1.

sources.[62] Gry suggests emending to "You called Abraham my beloved one," but this seems superfluous.

The occasion of the revelation to Abraham was doubtlessly the Covenant Between the Pieces (Genesis 15), which took place at night (Gen 15:17). The biblical text itself records a revelation of the future to Abraham at that juncture (Gen 15:13–16), and this provided occasion for later writers to expand the nature or scope of the event. *Bib Ant* 23:6–7 attributes the revelation of Gehenna (not named) and "torches of fire whereby the righteous will be enlightened," as well as a series of historical prophecies, to this time. The *Apocalypse of Abraham* presents its major revelation as occurring at this juncture. According to *2 Apoc Bar* 4:3–4, the heavenly temple was made known to Abraham in the course of that event.

A series of targumic and rabbinic sources put a revelation of the whole future course of history and the four empires at this time. See *Gen. R.* 15:10 (Theodor-Albeck, p. 437; cf. *PRE* 28); *Gen. R.* 15:12 (Theodor-Albeck, pp. 439–40); and *Mek. Yitro* 9 (Horovitz-Rabin, p. 236). Both of the latter sources reckon the fourth kingdom as Rome. For Targ J Gen 15:12 the last kingdom is Sasanian Persia. Other rabbinic sources mention various things revealed to Abraham on that occasion: Gehenna, the giving of the Torah, and the parting of the Red Sea (R. Nathan in *Mek.* ibid.); and the Temple and the order of sacrifices (ibid.; cf. also *Gen. R.* 15:10 [Theodor-Albeck, p. 437]). The same source records a dispute between R. Yoḥanan b. Zakkai and R. Aqiba as to whether the world to come was revealed to Abraham as

well as this world, or only the latter.[63] Targ J2 Gen 15:17 has judgment, Gehenna, and reward of the righteous. The mention of Gehenna in these sources implies the same exegesis as in *Bib Ant* 23:6–7, cited above.

It is difficult to decide what the Hebrew original corresponding to "end of times" might have been. In 4 Ezra, Latin *tempus* is generally equivalent to Syriac *zbn',* Armenian *žamanak,* and Ethiopic *mawaʿel* (e.g., 6:34; 7:73; 13:46). The usage in the Bible is of no help in trying to determine what the original of this might have been.[64]

The existence of a tradition of secret knowledge transmitted from ancient times lies, of course, at the basis of much of apocalyptic literature. In 4 Ezra it is attested here and in chapter 14. There, in 14:5–6, the revelation to Moses is seen as composed of an open revelation and an esoteric one. A similar double revelation is asserted to have been received by Ezra in 14:26 and 14:45–47. There it is typologically identified with the revelation to Moses (see 14:1–2). The contents of the two revelations, the Abrahamic and the Mosaic, are the same, cf. 3:14 and 14:5.[65] The end of times is also part of what is revealed in the visions of 4 Ezra (see 11:39; 11:44; and 12:9). We also find "end of world" or "end of age" or the like (see 6:7; 6:9; 6:25; 7:112; 7:113; and 12:34).[66]

■ **15** The latter part of this verse, as Gunkel observed, is adapted from Josh 24:3–4. In structure the verse resembles *Bib Ant* 8:3–4. God's eternal covenant with Abraham was, of course, related in Gen 15:8–21, the same chapter that 4 Ezra used in the preceding verses.

---

62 So *Jub* 17:8; Dan LXX and *Theod* 3:35; Jas 2:23; Clement of Rome, *Ep. 1 ad Cor.* 10:1 (φίλος); *Mek. Yitro* on Exod 20:6 (Horovitz-Rabin, p. 227); *b. Soṭa* 31a; *t. Soṭa* 6:1; and many other sources.

63 Kaminka quotes the Passover *Haggada:*
   Blessed be he who keeps his promise to Israel, blessed be He. For the Holy One calculated the end so that he might do as he promised Abraham in the covenant between the Portions, as it says (quotation of Gen 15:13–14).
   See further Ginzberg, *Legends,* 5:229.

64 There is some variation in the usage of the versions of 4 Ezra. On this, as well as on possible patterns of use in the Hebrew Bible, see Stone, *Features,* 53–54. LXX Dan 9:27 has καὶ κατὰ συντέλειαν καιρῶν, but these words have no equivalent in the Massoretic text. See further 7:26 Commentary n. 45 on the terminology.

65 On traditions of secret revelations, see Russell, *Method and Message,* 107–18. See also Stone, "Lists," 444–45, for further lists of Mosaic material. The matter is discussed in detail in 14:3–18 Function and Content.

66 The exact meaning of the term "end" is the subject of a long discussion in Excursus on Natural Order, pp. 103–5; see 12:9.

■ **16** The formulation of the last part of the verse is indebted to Mal 1:2–3; see the textual comments. Compare also Josh 24:3–4, which is, however, not the direct source. Gunkel suggests that "Esau" here signifies Rome. This is certainly the case in 6:7–10, and it may be that, here too, Esau was singled out for hostile treatment because of his association with Rome. Jacob as the father of Israel figures here and in 3:19.

■ **17** Compare 14:4. Moses is not mentioned here, presumably to highlight God's direct responsibility for Israel's situation.

■ **18** This verse and the next describe God's descent onto Sinai, related in Exod 19:18. There God's descent and the accompanying earthquake are mentioned; cf. also Ps 18:9 and Judg 5:4–5. The bowing down of the heavens features in the descriptions of the theophany in Ps 18:10 and 144:5; cf. Isa 63:19. See *Mek.* on Exod 20:22 (Horovitz-Rabin, p. 238). Here the descent is traced through the cosmos: heavens, earth, inhabited world, and deep, concluding with the whole universe.

The meaning "heaven" proposed for *saeculum* at the end of the list (Box, Gunkel) cannot be accepted.[67] "Times" (RSV) and "the age" (Myers) are possible translations, but the descent pattern and the geographical connotations of the preceding four terms incline one in the direction of "universe" or "world." Perhaps a word has been lost, such as "foundation of"; cf. Sir 16:18–19 and 1QH 7:8–9. God's descent with a plethora of natural phenomena is described in *Bib Ant* 23:10, based on an exegesis of Ps 18:9. The activity of a series of natural phenomena—the flame of fire, the springs of the deep, the course of the stars, the sound of thunder, the fullness of the wind, the motions of the clouds, the storm of the hosts—is then said to cease. This bears a certain resemblance to the meteorological phenomena mentioned in

the next verse.

■ **19** "Glory" here denotes God. This usage is already to be found in the Bible: Exod 24:16 (of Sinai); 33:18; Ezek 1:28. It occurs in various apocryphal and pseudepigraphic compositions, such as *1 Enoch* 14:20; 102:3; and *Test Patr Levi* 3:4. This also seems to be the usage at 4 Ezra 8:30. Often, however, in 4 Ezra it appears as an attribute of God rather than as a surrogate for his name, for example 8:21, and frequently it is said to be viewed by the righteous as their reward or by the wicked as their punishment (7:42; 7:78; 7:87; 7:91). Probably 7:122, which says that the divine glory will protect the righteous in judgment, is connected with this idea.[68] Doubtless this language is used here to avoid excessive anthropomorphism in describing the descent of God onto Sinai and is influenced by Exod 33:18.[69]

Most scholars have maintained that the "gates" are those leading from one heaven to another (e.g., Box, Gunkel, Myers). There is no evidence, however, for the location of these four elements in four descending heavens. *Test Patr Levi* 3:2 does put fire, snow, and ice "above the first heaven." Meteorological phenomena are set in the first heaven by *2 Enoch* 3:3–6; 5:1–2; and 6:1; they are found in a similar place to the luminaries in *1 Enoch* 76 (cf. *1 Enoch* 75), and this seems to be implied by *1 Enoch* 36:1 (Aramaic תרעין, 4QEn^c). It is clear that gates were seen as leading from one heaven to another. This is quite explicit in *3 Apoc Bar* 2:2; 3:1; etc.[70] The view that these are the gates mentioned by 4 Ezra, however, would imply a quite unparalleled uranography, four heavens characterized by meteorological phenomena.

More likely is the view that the "gates" here in 4 Ezra are the portals associated with the phenomena of weather. Such are to be found in *1 Enoch* 36:1, 76; cf. Ps

67 See M. E. Stone, "Apocryphal Notes and Readings. 7. Saeculum as 'Heaven' in 4 Ezra," *IOS* 1 (1971) 129–30. Violet 2 suggests that the verse originally had a poetic structure, 2 x 2, and that an extra hemistich has been added to the first line. This remains speculative.

68 Scholem points out that כבוד is a theosophic term for Him who is enthroned on the Merkabah. It is to the fore in the second century c.e. but is gradually replaced by other terms. So in *t. Hag.* 2:1 לדרוש בכבוד אבינו, which becomes לדרוש במעשה מרכבה in *j. Hag.* 2:1. See G. G. Scholem, *Major Trends in Jewish*

Mysticism (New York: Schocken, 1941) 46, 358 n. 16; and idem, *Gnosticism*, 37. Note also 4 Ezra 8:21. Different aspects of this concept are discussed in 7:42 Commentary, 7:97 Commentary (eschatological glory of the righteous), and 10:50 Commentary (glory of Zion). Note the expression "the glory of my name" in *Apoc Abr* 29:17.

69 On more general questions of "buffer language," see the remarks of G. F. Moore, "Intermediaries in Jewish Theology—Memra, Shekinah, Metatron," *HTR* 15 (1922) 41–85. See also Urbach, *Sages*, 40–41.

78:23. The list of four such phenomena is based on those which appeared to Elijah in 1 Kgs 19:11–12; viz., wind, earthquake, and fire. These have been taken as heavenly phenomena, and ice has been added to them.[71] Thus what is described here is the awesome descent of God onto Sinai from the heavens for the purpose of giving the Torah; for the expression "to give the law," compare Deut 33:4; Sir 23:13; et al.[72]

■ **20** On the "evil heart," see the Excursus on Adam's Sin. Here God is taxed with not removing it at the time of the giving of the Torah, so that the Torah was not effective in ensuring the righteousness of Israel. This repeats and strengthens the accusation already explicit in 3:8b.[73]

The expression "to bring forth fruit" serves in various senses in 4 Ezra. Here it denotes "reward." Close to the present context are 3:33; 4:30; 6:28; and 8:6. Particularly similar is 9:31: "I sow my law in you, and it shall bring forth fruit in you, and you shall be glorified through it forever." The fruit of the Torah is therefore eternal reward.[74]

It is possible that the idea of the fruit of the tree of life is involved in this concept; see Gen 3:22 and see 4 Ezra 7:13; 7:123; and 8:52. Its fruit gives eternal life; see also *Test Patr Levi* 18:11, which says of the eschaton: "He will give the saints to eat from the tree of life."[75] The connection is particularly notable in the light of the fact that from quite ancient times biblical verses about wisdom

were interpreted as being about the Torah.[76] Thus Proverbs says of wisdom, in a verse famous in its application to Torah: "She is a tree of life to those that lay hold of her" (Prov 3:18; cf. Prov 11:30). So Torah is the tree of life whose fruit is immortality and Torah is planted in human hearts.

■ **21** It is possible that the expression "first Adam" is the same as rabbinic אדם הראשון. It denotes Adam's position as the first human.[77] For "was burdened with," see 3:26. The turn of phrase "was overcome" evokes the image of humanity's struggle with the evil inclination as a war or an athletic contest. This is also clearly at play in 7:127 (see Commentary there) and in Armenian 4 Ezra 3:7 (Ms H).[78] A view opposed to that expressed here is to be found in *2 Apocalypse of Baruch* 54:

> 15 For although Adam sinned first and has brought death upon all who were not in his own time, yet each of them who has been born from him has prepared for himself the coming torment. And further each of them has chosen for himself the coming glory. . . . 19 Adam is therefore not the cause, except only for himself, but each of us has become our own Adam.[79]

The mention of Adam marks the conclusion of the third part of the historical recital; see 3:10 Commentary.

■ **22** The term "root" or "evil root" is also found in 8:53; cf. Deut 29:17, which is cited in *Bib Ant* 25:5. The term is first attested in 11QPs[a] 155:13–14 = Syr Ps 3, where

70   See also *3 Apoc Bar* 11:2; cf. *1 Enoch* 104:2; Rev 4:1; et al. The general term "gate of heaven" is to be found already in Gen 28:17; cf. *Test Patr Levi* 5:1.

71   The place of these meteorological phenomena in heaven is assumed also in the list in *b. Hag.* 12b.

72   On the expression "seed of Jacob," see also 9:29–37 Function and Content, p. 307.

73   In *Song R.* 1:2 the idea is that it was removed at Sinai but returned with the sin of the Golden Calf. Cf. also *Sifre Deut.* 45 on Deut 11:18 (Finkelstein, pp. 103–4).

74   Cf. also Rom 7:4–5 and, in a different sense, *2 Apoc Bar* 32:1; "fruit of righteousness" is found in *Lev. R.* 27:1. *Od Sol* 8:2 speaks of a holy life which brings forth fruit to the Lord. The associated ideas of sowing and harvest are discussed in 4:28 Commentary. In 8:6 Commentary, a striking parallel to 3:20–21 is discussed.

75   See H. W. Holander and M. de Jonge, *The Testaments of the Twelve Patriarchs: A Commentary* (SPVT 8; Leiden: Brill, 1985), ad loc., for many additional references. See further *1 Enoch* 24:4 and *2 Enoch* 8:3. Cf. *Ps Sol* 14:3–4, where the righteous are called

trees of life.

76   See G. W. E. Nickelsburg and M. E. Stone, *Faith and Piety in Early Judaism* (Philadelphia: Fortress, 1983) 203–31.

77   It is not the same as ὁ πρῶτος ᾿Αδαμ of 1 Cor 15:45 which stands in contrast to ὁ ἔσχατος ᾿Αδαμ. Nor should it be connected with *Urmensch* speculations or the like, as Gunkel would.

78   See also 6:28.

79   Cf. *Tanh.* (Buber) Gen 29: "Adam said (i.e., to God): 'Do not write of me that I brought death into the world.'" An interesting contrast with 4 Ezra here; see also 7:46 Commentary.

the roots of evil are referred to:

Purify me, O Lord, from (the) evil scourge,

and let it not turn upon me.

Dry up its roots from me

and let its leaves not flourish within me. (*DJD*, 4:71)

Lewy points out that the expression ῥίζα τῆς κακίας occurs in the Chaldean Oracles, deriving from Euripides.[80] The same image of the plant of evil striking root is explicit in Sir 3:28: "A plant of wickedness has taken root in him [the proud]," and cf. 1QH 4:14. A similar usage to the present is *1 Enoch* 91:5, 8.[81]

The general import of this verse reflects a view that with Adam's sin the evil root became a permanent weakness of humanity. This evil root is in human beings together with the Torah and leads, according to the argument put forward here, to human sin and disobedience (cf. Paul's view in Romans 7). It is the universality of the latter conclusion that is debated and modified later in the book (see 3:32–36; 7:116–131). It may be that it was put forth initially in a deliberately broad fashion in order to strengthen the central thesis of this address. So it is not the same as 1QS 4:23–24: "To here the spirits of Truth and Perversity shall struggle; they shall go in man's heart in wisdom and foolishness." In 1QS it is not a conflict between the two spirits in a single human heart but the existence of the two spirits, in one of which a human being finds himself. It is to be noted that Moses in not mentioned by name in the recital of the Sinai events and that the narrative moves directly from exodus to David. This contrasts strikingly with the situation in chapter 14, where Moses' role in Sinai is central.

■ **23** No Commentary.

■ **24** In 10:46, Solomon is named as builder of the city; see Commentary there. Jerusalem is called "city of David";

so, for example, 2 Sam 5:9 and 1 Chr 11:7. Perhaps for this reason David is here said to have been commanded to offer to God oblations. This statement runs directly against 2 Sam 7:5 and 7:12–13 but cf. 2 Sam 6:17–18. Here the Syriac version reads: "and a house in which, . . ." while Armenian has an extensive passage not found in the other versions: "After him, you raised up his son Solomon, whom you commanded to build the Temple, in a night vision. And (you commanded) all the people to say prayers and offer sacrifices in it." This does not obviate all the difficulties noted above, but Violet 2 considers it to be the original. The detail of the night vision is surely drawn from 1 Kgs 3:5 and 1 Kgs 9:2 // 2 Chr 7:12. It might have been lost from an original by a homoeoteleuton of "sacrifices." The form of text in Armenian still has David offering sacrifices in Jerusalem. Lat Ms L has, "And Solomon, his son, built a house for your name and set up a sacrificial altar in it on which the priests would bring you offerings as you commanded Moses your servant." Although it is similar to Armenian, the special reading of this text cannot be regarded as sharing a common source with the Armenian.[82]

If a text of the general character of the versions other than Armenian and Latin L is accepted, then it is appropriate to comment that for this text the only purpose for the building of Jerusalem is that sacrifices be offered in it.[83] Jerusalem is known in the Bible as the city called by God's name; see Jer 25:29; compare "city of God" in Ps 46:5; 48:2; 48:8; and 87:3; see also Rev 3:12. On the other hand, the idea is found that God's name dwelt in the sanctuary, and here the city is clearly the sanctuary.[84]

■ **25** No commentary.

■ **26** This verse would resemble Hos 6:7a if "Adam" there is taken as a person and not as a place, as was done by some Midrashic teachers. In *Gen. R.* 19:9 on Gen 3:9

80   H. Lewy, *The Chaldean Oracles and Theurgy* (Recherches d'archéologie, de philologie et d'histoire 13; Cairo: Inst. Franc. d'arch. orien., 1956) 277.

81   Cf. *Thunder* 19:16–17, "the root of sin" (CG VI.2). The use in Sir 40:15 is somewhat different. In 1 Macc 1:10 Antiochus Epiphanes is called a "sinful root." In 1 Tim 6:10 the expression occurs in a rather different sense (cf. Heb 12:15), while in *1 Enoch* 91:5, 8 the talk is of "cutting off at roots" of unrighteousness, meaning its extirpation. Note the similar expression "root of wisdom" in Sir 1:6; 1:20; 24:12; Wisd 3:15; *2 Apoc Bar* 51:3; and 59:7.

82   See also M. E. Stone, "Manuscripts and Readings of Armenian 4 Ezra," *Textus* 6 (1968) 51–52. See our observations on Armenian as an unsupported witness in 3:11 Commentary.

83   See already Gunkel's comment.

84   K. Baltzer, "The Meaning of the Temple in the Lukan Writings," *HTR* 58 (1965) 265–68.

(Theodor-Albeck, pp. 178–79), R. Abahu comments in the name of R. Jose b. Ḥanina:

they like Adam (Hos 6:7): like Adam the first man. Just as I introduced Adam into the Garden of Eden and enjoined him and he transgressed my injunction and I condemned him to expulsion and I lamented him by singing *Lamentations* . . . so I introduced his children into the Land of Israel and enjoined them and they transgressed my injunction and I condemned them to expulsion and I lamented them by singing *Lamentations.*

The Midrash has drawn exactly the same parallel between Adam's lot and that of his descendants as does 4 Ezra. See also *Echa Rabbati,* Petiḥta 4.

This latter part of the address is tied to the first part, both conceptually and thematically by 3:26. Compare in particular 3:7; 3:10; and 3:20–22 and observe how, in these verses, Adam's sin plays a central conceptual and structural role. The translation "were burdened with" (3:21) is more precise than Box's "clothing himself with." Box comments, "Adam 'clothed himself' with the *cor malignum* by yielding to the suggestions of the 'evil impulse'" (on 3:20); but the sense of the verb is "burdened." Yet the term "evil impulse" does not occur in 4 Ezra, and "evil heart" is his term for it.[85] Thus the implication that a distinction should be drawn between the two should be resisted.[86] Moreover, to attribute the "evil heart" to humanity's voluntary action, as is implied by this rendering, would run against the argument of the chapter.[87]

■ **27** Compare 10:23. The verse implies the biblical understanding of exile as the punishment for Israel's sins. Yet the succeeding verses question this very theory. Certain scholars have identified this destruction with one or another of the destructions or desecrations of the Temple in the Hellenistic or Roman periods. If any, the destruction by Titus is implied, for it is this which gives the following verses their point.

■ **28** Violet starts a new section with 3:29, including 3:28 together with 3:23–27. Yet the historical recital ends with 3:27; and 3:28, opening with the words "I said in my heart [i.e., to myself]," is the beginning of the seer's ensuing questioning of the significance of the course of history (3:28–36).

The moral quality of those who destroyed Zion had already concerned the prophets (e.g., Isa 10:5–8; cf. Jer 25:8–14; 50:17–18, 33–34). The prophets did not question the justice of the punishment of Zion; instead, they pronounced doom upon the nations who destroyed Zion. The nations' fault was that of arrogance; they did not recognize that they were instruments of God. For 4 Ezra, however, the moral faults of Babylon raised questions about the justice of the punishment itself. This, of course, is far beyond the position implied by 3:27.[88]

Babylon here means Rome; see 3:1 Commentary.

■ **29** Ezra is located in Babylon. This, however, does not mean that the author was in Rome; see 3:1 Commentary. For the expression "during these thirty years," compare Gen 31:38. See textual note n.

■ **30** This verse contains four hemistichs of poetry. They are in parallelism, the first two synonymous and the second two contrasting. This leads to a certain lack of

85 See P. G. R. de Villiers, "Understanding the Way of God: Form, Function and Message of the Historical Review in 4 Ezra 3:4–27," *SBL 1981 Seminar Papers* (ed. K. H. Richards; Chico, Calif.: Scholars, 1981) 357–78, esp. 359–60; Koch, "Esras erste Vision," 60–61 n. 11.

86 See Excursus on Adam's Sin, n. 19.

87 See Excursus on Adam's Sin, pp. 63–64, on these terms.

88 Contrast the views of suffering discussed by Bornkamm, "Sohnschaft und Lieden," 189–90. His discussion of 3:28–36 (pp. 191–92) does not exhaust the implications of the passage. The analogous problem in *Test Mos* 9:2–4 is defined by Licht, "Taxo," 98: "The general tendency . . . is a plea of relative innocence. [The] punishment . . . is not entirely undeserved [but] . . . cannot be termed absolutely just; it is excessive." The problem in 4 Ezra here differs from the oppression of the righteous by the wicked, as in Hab 1:13 and Jer 12:1 (*pace* Myers). The complexity of some rabbinic explanations of the destruction of the Second Temple has been analyzed sensitively by R. Goldenberg, "Early Rabbinic Explanations of the Destruction of Jerusalem," *JJS* 33 (1982) 517–25. The issues he finds to be stressed differ greatly from those in 4 Ezra.

balance in the whole, for three hemistichs deal with the nations and only one with Israel.[89] The problem is here formulated in terms of the contrast between the fate of Israel and that of the nations. Zion has suffered and the wicked nations flourish. God has brought suffering upon Israel, yet he is prepared to endure the wickedness of the Babylonian destroyers of Zion. The same problem is formulated in rabbinic thought, in discussions of the destruction of the Temple.[90]

■ **31** The request for knowledge of the way of the Most High is taken up in 4:2–3; 4:11; 4:23; 5:34; etc. The "way" is God's way in conducting the world.[91] The "way of God" in this sense occurs elsewhere, for example, in 1QH 7:31–32; Rom 11:33; *2 Apoc Bar* 14:8; and 20:4. In 4 Ezra 4:2; 4:11; 5:34; 12:4; and *2 Apoc Bar* 44:6, "way" stands parallel to "judgment."[92] Contrast the sense in, for example, CD 1:11 and 1QS 3:10. The inaccessibility of knowledge of God's action is already highlighted by texts like Isa 40:13 and Job 9:11–12. The latter part of the verse is substantially a repetition of 3:28, serving to stress the author's point.[93]

■ **32** "Covenants" as a general term is plural in Latin and Syriac and varies in the other versions in, for example,

3:32; 5:29; 7:24; 7:83; and 8:27.[94] It is singular referring to specific covenants in 3:15 and 10:22.[95] Some exegetes have suggested that the present verse contradicts the idea of Israel's sin stressed above (3:20–26), but see 3:29 and 3:31. The author does not claim that Israel is perfect but that others are not as good even as Israel.[96]

■ **33** The rendering "labor" is preferred here. Box and Violet, following a suggestion of Wellhausen, would reconstruct Hebrew פעולה in the sense of "recompense"; see Isa 40:10; 62:11; etc.[97] This is exegetically unnecessary. Gunkel, Oesterley, and Myers see this phrase as an indication of the "burden" of the law, doubtless under the influence of Matt 23:4 // Luke 11:46; Gal 3:4; et al. There is no indication of such an attitude elsewhere in 4 Ezra, and the imagery of labor and its reward applied to the service of God is widespread; see, for example, *m. Abot* 2:14–16.[98]

The second part of the verse is parallel in function and type to 3:29 above. Both give the author's own eyewitness evidence for the wickedness of the Gentiles. The theme of the wealth of the nations was already raised in 3:2 and here it is contrasted with the situation of Israel.

89   Myers calls this "a little psalm of complaint." He points to a series of parallels, most of which do not seem immediately illuminating. Closest to our text is Ps 106:40–41. The term *Psalm of complaint* might better be rephrased as "poetic plaint," and it probably derived from Gunkel's term as employed by Westermann, "Klage," passim. Myers also suggests that a response to the problem is offered in *2 Apoc Bar* 78:5. In that passage the view is urged of the expiational value of suffering of Israel. This is not to be found in 4 Ezra, either here or elsewhere.

90   See S. D. Cohen, "The Destruction: From Scripture to Midrash," *Prooftexts* 2 (1982) 30–33.

91   Described by Harnisch, p. 35, as *"Verfahren" Gottes;* cf. also ibid., 147 note.

92   Ezek 18:25, 18:29 is a striking parallel to the present passage, though there are some differences in stress and a clear contrast in meaning. "Yet the house of Israel says, 'The way of the Lord is not just.' O house of Israel, are my ways not just? Is it not your ways that are not just?" Compare also Isa 55:8. God's incomprehensible ways, in a quite different sense, are stressed in Job 26:14. On the term, see 4:1–4 and Commentary.

93   On the sense of such repetitions, see 3:4–36 Form and Structure, p. 61.

94   Cf. Rom 9:4 and Gal 4:22; we have preferred the reading "injunctions" in 7:83.

95   On the Syriac usage, see Violet 2, p. 257. On the use of terminology for covenant, see Harnisch, p. 30 note.

96   This is the point of the statement about "covenants." The Sages relate that the Torah was offered to various nations who refused it, before being offered to Israel; see *Mek. BaḤodeš* 5 on Exod 20:2 (Horovitz-Rabin, p. 221); *Sifre Deut.* 343 (Finkelstein, pp. 395–97); and *Pes. R. K.* 29.2 (Friedmann, pp. 185b–86a). They claim also that the nations did not even observe the Noachid covenant, and Urbach points out that, according to the above Midrash they rejected the Torah because of certain Noachid commandments in it. See Urbach, *Sages,* 531–32, and *Sifre Deut.,* ibid.; *b. Abod. Zar.* 2b. These statements should be understood as part of the polemic surrounding the idea of the election of Israel. See 7:45; 7:1–25 Form and Function, pp. 194–95 and n. 18.

97   Violet 2, ad loc.

98   On the terminology of reward, see M. Smith, *Tannaitic Parallels to the Gospels* (JBLMS 6; Philadelphia: SBL, 1961) 161–84.

The English "I have traveled widely" renders what are, in the various languages, expressions corresponding to Hebrew infinitive absolute with a finite verb.[99] It should not be concluded from this verse that the author was widely traveled, see 3:1 Commentary.

■ **34** The image of the scales for weighing the deeds of human beings has biblical roots. It may be observed in Ps 62:10; Prov 16:2; 16:11; 21:2; 24:12; Job 31:6; Dan 5:27; and a similar use in *Ps Sol* 5:4. The image is used in extrabiblical sources of God's eschatological weighing of human deeds; see *1 Enoch* 41:1; 61:8; *2 Enoch* 44:5; 49:2; 52:15; and *2 Apoc Bar* 41:6, as well as in Greek and ancient Near Eastern literature. The scales have materialized to become the central feature of the judgment scene in *Testament of Abraham* A 12.[100] The closest of the earlier texts to ours in language is *2 Apoc Bar* 41:6: "Or perhaps the time of these will assuredly be weighed, and as the beam inclines will they be judged accordingly?" In 4 Ezra here the image serves to stress the righteousness of the deeds of Israel when compared with those of the Gentiles, but it derives doubtlessly from the more specific idea of God's weighing righteous and wicked deeds.[101]

■ **35** Previously Babylon had been noted to be sinful and

Israel to be less sinful than Babylon (3:28). Here there is an extension of the observation upon which the author embarked in 3:32, that Israel is less sinful than the nations. Indeed, as he observes, there is no nation that is as free of sin as Israel.[102] So Israel's virtue is superior, not just when compared with that of Babylon, but when compared with that of any other nation.

■ **36** This verse draws a further logical step from 3:35. There may be individual persons who have kept God's commandments, but there are no whole nations. The translation "individual men" interprets the difficult text to mean "men few enough to be enumerated by name." The chief alternative is "famous men," that is, going back to Hebrew אנשי שם (Gen 6:4; etc.) or other variants of this expression. This is possible. Kaminka reconstructs a dittographic corruption of אנשים to אנשי שם. A most interesting parallel is Ezra 10:16: וכולם בשמות.[103]

---

99 See 5:29 Commentary on the general subject of this verse.

100 See M. R. James, *The Testament of Abraham* (Texts and Studies 2.2; Cambridge: Cambridge University, 1892) 70–72; he argues for an Egyptian origin of the scene. See also F. Schmidt, *"Le Testament d'Abraham"* diss., Strassbourg, 1971) 1:74–76, cited in idem, "The Two Recensions of the Testament of Abraham," *Studies on the Testament of Abraham* (ed. G. W. E. Nickelsburg; SCS 6; Missoula, Mont.: Scholars, 1976), n. 18, and his remarks there on pp. 78–79; and Harnisch, p. 37 n. 1. More recent bibliography is to be found in Harnisch, pp. 31–34. The heart's feelings are weighed in *Bib Ant* 40:1. See also K. Koch, "Der Schatz im Himmel," *Leben angesichts des Todes: H. Thieleke FS* (Tübingen: Mohr, 1969) 54–55. An interesting parallel is to be found in *Pes. Rab.* 45 (Friedmann, pp. 185b–86a):

On the Day of Atonement Satan comes to indict Israel. He details Israel's sins and says, "Lord of the world! There are adulterers among the nations and equally in Israel; there are thieves among the nations and equally in Israel." The Holy One details Israel's merits. What does he do? He takes the beam of a scale [and weighs] the sins over against the merits and the sins and merits are weighed over against one another. The pans of the

scales are found to be level and Satan goes to bring sins to put into the pan of the sins and weigh it down. What does the Holy One do? While Satan looks for additional sins, the Holy One takes the sins from the pan and hides them under his purple (i.e., royal garment).

This text may be compared with a similar midrashim in *b. Sanh.* 35a, in *Pes. R. K.* 26:2 (Buber, p. 167a), and in *Midr. Teh.* 30:4. See also Harnisch, p. 37 n. 1. E. Böklen, *Die Verwandtschaft der jüdisch-christlichen mit der parsischen Eschatologie* (Göttingen: Vandenhoeck & Ruprecht, 1902) 54–56, points to some possible Iranian sources.

101 See 5:1 Commentary for a discussion of the term "inhabitants."

102 See de Villiers, "Way," 360–61 n. 21. Thompson, *Responsibility*, 171–76, puts a very forced interpretation on this passage involving both an emendation and a meaning of a Hebrew word otherwise uncorroborated.

103 On observance of all of God's commandments, see *b. Shabb.* 55a; contrast *b. Abod. Zar.* 3a.

4

1 Then the angel that had been sent to me, whose name was Uriel, answered 2/ and said to me, "Your understanding is quite confounded ^a regarding this world, ^b and do you wish to ^c comprehend the way ^d of the Most High?" 3/ Then I said, "Yes, my lord." And he replied to me, "I have been sent to show you three ways and to put before you three problems. 4/ If you can solve one of them for me, I also will show you the way you desire to see, ^e and will teach ^f you why the heart is evil." ^g

5/ I said, "Speak on, my lord." And he said to me,

"Go, weigh for me ^hthe weight of ^h fire,
or measure for me a measure ⁱ of wind,
or call back for me the day that is past."

6/ I answered and said, "Who of those that have been born can do this, that you ask me concerning these things?"

7/ And he said to me, "If I had asked you,

'How many dwellings are in the heart of the sea,
or how many springs ^j are at the source of the deep,
or how many ways ^k are above the firmament,
or which are the exits ^lof hell,
or which are the entrances ^m of Paradise?'

8/ perhaps you would have said to me,

'I never went down into the deep,
nor as yet did I descend ⁿ into hell,
nor did I ever ascend into heaven,
^onor did I enter Paradise.' ^o

9/ But now I have asked you only about fire and wind and the day, things through which you have passed ^p and without which you cannot exist, and you have given me no answer about them!" 10/ And he said to me, "You cannot understand the things ^q with which you have grown up; 11/ how then can your vessel comprehend the way of the Most High? ^rFor the way of the Most High is created immeasurable. ^r And how can one who is corrupt in the corrupt world ^s understand the way of the incorruptible?" ^t When I heard this, I fell on my face ^u 12/ and said to him, "It would be better for us not to be ^v

Notes

2 a Lat, Syr, Eth, Georg show reflex of Hebrew infinitive absolute and finite verb.

a–b Eth, Georg, Ar2 omit.

c "Wish to": Lat has *cogitas;* perhaps ἐνθυμεῖ for ἐπιθυμεῖς (Violet 2).

d "Plan of glory" Eth; "glory" Georg.

4 e "To see": Eth, Arm have "to know"; perhaps εἰδέναι for ἰδεῖν; see 4:43 note u.

e–g Arm omits; see Excursus on Adam's Sin.

f Lat has *doceam,* for which form see Bensly, *MF,* 16.

5 h–h "On one balance" Eth, Georg.

i Lat *flatum,* "blast," perhaps corrupt for *satum,* "measure" (Hilgenfeld); on versions, see Violet 1.

7 j So most versions; Lat has *venae,* "streams"; on Arm, see *Armenian Text Commentary.*

k So most versions; Lat has *venae,* "streams"; perhaps corrupt for *viae,* "ways," under influence of preceding.

l–m Lat omits perhaps by hmt.

m So Arm, Georg; cf. Ar2; Lat omits; Syr, Eth, Ar1 "paths"; probably from Hebrew מבוא and reckon a Greek corruption, perhaps εἰσίν ⟨εἰς⟩όδοι, cf. 4:8; see 7:4 Commentary.

8 n The verb is omitted by Lat; see Box for further cases.

o–o So Lat Ms L, 2 Eth Mss, Arm; Ar2 and Georg read "nor did I see Paradise"; the other witnesses omit. The phrase could be regarded as secondary under the influence of the preceding verse, but is most probably original; see Commentary.

9 p So Lat, Syr, Georg, cf. Arm; "the day which is past" Eth, Ar1, and Georg (this version has both readings); cf. 4:5. Read with Gressmann in Violet 2, and for possible Greek reconstructions, see most fully Violet 2.

10 q Lat adds "which are yours."

11 r–r Lat omits; Ar1 paraphrases; Ar2 shortens.

s For "corrupt in," Lat as emended reads "already worn out by" (RSV); the other versions except Ar2 support the text we give. The phrase "in a corrupt world" was omitted by Eth, Georg; Ar1 cannot be determined.

t "Way of " Syr, Eth; "ways of " Ar1, Arm, Georg; Lat omits and reads "incorruption."

t–u So Syr, Eth, Ar1, Georg; Lat corrupt; Ar2 omits; Arm paraphrases.

12 v Perhaps the original was a form of γεννάω and not of γίνομαι; γεννάω is used in *Greek Apoc Esd* 1:6; 1:21; 5:14; and in *Apoc Sedr* 4:2 the Ms reads

here than to come here and live in ungodliness, and to suffer and not understand why we suffer." [w]

13 He answered me and said, [x]"Once upon a time the forests of trees of the plain set forth [x] and they made a plan 14/ and said, 'Come, let us go and make war against the sea, that it may recede before us, and that we may make for ourselves more forests.' [y] 15/ And in like manner the waves of the sea also made a plan and said, 'Come, let us go up and make war against [z] the forest of the plain so that there also we may gain more territory for ourselves.' 16/ But the plan of the forest was in vain, for the fire came and consumed it; 17/ likewise also the plan of the waves of the sea, for the sand stood firm and stopped them. 18/ If now you were a judge between them, which would you justify, and which condemn?"

19 I answered and said, "Each has made a foolish plan, for the land is assigned to the forest, and to the sea is assigned [a] a place [b] to carry its waves."

20 He answered me and said, "You have judged rightly, but why have you not judged so in your own case? 21/ For as the land is assigned to the forest and the sea to its waves, so also those who dwell upon the earth can understand only what is on the earth, and he who is [c] above the heavens can understand what is above the height of the heavens."

22 Then I answered and said, "I beseech you, my lord, why [d] have I been endowed with the power of understanding? 23/ For I did not wish to inquire about the ways above, but about those things which we daily experience:

> why Israel has been given over to the Gentiles as a reproach;
> why the people whom you loved has been given over to godless tribes,
> and the Torah of our fathers has been made of no effect,
> and the written covenants no longer exist;
> 24/ and why we pass from the world like locusts,
> and our life is like a mist, [e]
> and we are not worthy to obtain mercy?

25/ But what will he do for his name, by which we are called? [f] It is about these things that I have asked." [g]

$\dot{\epsilon}\gamma\epsilon\nu\dot{\eta}\theta\eta\nu$. The two verbs are often confused in the LXX, particularly in the aorist passive; see Gen 24:4; 24:7; Exod 19:16; etc. See 5:35 note p; 10:9 note h–h.

w Lat omits; Ar2 omits the whole verse.

13 x–x So Syr, Eth, Georg, cf. Arm; Lat reads (corruptly), "I went into a forest of trees of the plain."

14 y Singular in Eth, Arm (most Mss), Georg, Syr(?).

15 z Lat "subdue"; Georg "rule over."

19 a "Is assigned": these words are implied by context but have actually been introduced only by Georg.

b The better Latin Mss and Syr read "a place of the sea"; "place" is omitted by Eth, Ar2; with Ar1, cf. Jer 5:22.

21 c "They who are" Ar2, Arm, Georg; Lat is ambiguous; see Commentary.

22 d Thus Syr, Eth, Arm, Georg; Lat is corrupt.

24 e Lat Mss, Syr, Ar1; "smoke" Eth, Georg, perhaps $\dot{\alpha}\tau\mu\dot{o}s \langle \dot{\alpha}\tau\mu\dot{i}s$; Arm expanded; most Lat Mss *pavor*, "fear," for *vapor*, "breath."

25 f–g Ar1, Ar2, Arm omit.

g Lat Ms L, Eth, Georg add "you."

Form and Structure

This section opens with the appearance of an angel—a feature that recurs in Visions 2 and 3 following the opening address (5:31; 7:1) and in Vision 4 following the vision and preceding the interpretation (10:29). In Visions 5–6 no angel features at this juncture, but as noted above, Visions 5 and 6 are dream visions and structurally different from Visions 1–4 (see 3:1 Commentary).[1] An angel is present in the latter part of Vision 5 to pronounce the interpretation; see 12:39 and 12:51. This is less clear in Vision 6, but compare 13:56. In neither of these visions is the actual angelophany described. No angel is mentioned in Vision 7.

The language of 4:1 is close to that of 5:31–32 and 7:1–2. The form of the first three visions differs from most apocalyptic revelations. Usually, angels appear either at the onset of the inspiration to serve as guides or after the receipt of the visions to serve as interpreters.[2] Here, the angel appears in response to the seer's inspired prayer and engages upon a dialogue with the seer. This dialogue is not paralleled in its scope or character in any other apocalypse. Other apocalypses do contain occasional passages of question and answer, particularly relating to the interpretation of visionary symbols,[3] but there is little to resemble what is found here. Closest to the dialogues of 4 Ezra are passages like *2 Apocalypse of Baruch* 22–30, but even this passage resembles not the disputations of 4 Ezra but the dialogic predictions, for it is a revelation made by the angel in response to questioning by the seer.[4]

The biblical Book of Job is, of course, structured as dialogues between Job and God and Job and his three friends. 4 Ezra shows a number of connections with Job, but the poetic dialogues of the latter differ from the inspired conversations of 4 Ezra.[5]

The questions are generally fairly short, especially in the predictive parts of the dialogue where they are formulaic and rather obvious. This is not completely so in the disputatious sections, where the questions tend to be somewhat longer and are often argumentative in tone (e.g., 4:22–25).

A second feature of the dialogic visions in 4 Ezra is the extensive use of parables and questions bearing the character of riddles. In the present section there is one series of riddle questions (4:5–12) and one parable (4:13–21). Both of these types of literary figures recur in the other dialogic portions of the book.

Riddle questions are used on one additional occasion in 4 Ezra to prove that human beings cannot achieve knowledge (5:36–37). The immediate sources of such questions are to be sought in the wisdom literature, particularly in Job 37:14—39:30. There, a long list of questions proves human inability alongside God's power and knowledge. Below in 4:7 Commentary, some of the differences between the presuppositions of the Jobian questions and those in 4 Ezra are noted.[6] Certain of the questions in Job and in the passage at the start of Sirach (1:2–3) are related to the two passages here (see Commentary).

Series of questions designed to show human inability to know the wonders of nature, and a fortiori of the heavenly realm, recur in apocalyptic texts like *1 Enoch*

---

1 For an analysis of the angelophanies, see 5:31–40 Form and Structure, p. 134.

2 For the former, see Ezek 40:4; *1 Enoch* 10:3, etc.; 72:1; *2 Enoch* 1:4; and *3 Apoc Bar* 1:3; for the latter, see Dan 8:16; and *2 Apoc Bar* 55:3. In this respect, Dan 7:16 and Zech 1:9, etc., are unclear, although Zech 2:2–4 seems to imply that the angel is with the prophet all along; see also Zech 3:1; 4:1.

3 Such are *1 Enoch* 24:5—25:6.

4 The question of the literary relationship between 4 Ezra and *2 Apoc Bar* was discussed in Introduction, sec. 5.1.5.

5 Koch, "Esras erste Vision," 56–58, discusses possible origins of this dialogue form and asserts an origin in biblical prophetic forms.

6 There are, moreover, other lists of questions about nature designed to show God's presence in all of the cosmos or associated with the sapiential themes of the search for wisdom or her presence in creation. See, e.g., Ps 139:7–11; Prov 30:4; Job 28; Sirach 24; and Bar 3:29–34. With the latter, cf. Deut 30:11–14. See also Nickelsburg and Stone, *Faith and Piety*, 205–10. Cf. the lists of natural phenomena discussed by G. von Rad, "Hiob xxxviii und die altägyptische Weisheit," *Gesammelte Studien zum Alten Testament* (Munich: Theologische Bücherei, 1958), 262–72. John 3:12–13 is not the same, despite some similarities of wording.

93:11–14. Moreover, the structure of the list of questions in *2 Apoc Bar* 22:2—23:2 is similar in some ways to that in 4 Ezra, but the questions there are analogous not to the cosmological lists but to the parables that will be noted below.

Equally intriguing is the fact that many of these same seemingly nonsense questions, such as those about the weight of the wind or the number of the drops of rain, recur in lists of things revealed as part of apocalyptic secret knowledge. Exceptionally close to our text is *2 Apoc Bar* 59:5–11, which enumerates subjects of revelation many of which also occur in the two interrogative lists in 4 Ezra. There are many other such lists, all summary statements of revelations made to apocalyptic seers.[7]

Furthermore, not only do such lists of revealed secrets exist but certain of the apocalypses actually describe how these actions, such as the weighing of the winds, took place in heaven (e.g., *2 Enoch* 13:22).[8]

From the above it follows that a distinct form, the list of revealed things, may be discerned.[9] In 4 Ezra 4:5–8 a list of the objects of secret knowledge has been combined with the interrogative lists of the type found in Job 37–39; Sir 1:2–3; etc. The result is a pointed rejection of the very sort of apocalyptic speculation that greatly interests other apocalypses. This is done deliberately; 4 Ezra rejects an apocalyptic view of revealed knowledge. Indeed, the book seems deliberately to avoid all intimations of revealed, speculative knowledge and to limit itself to discussion of eschatological matters.[10]

Function and Content

The theme that holds this section together is understanding. The angel regards the whole of chapter 3 as a question. Picking up the theme in 3:31, "(Thou) hast not shown to anyone how thy way is to be comprehended," the angel chides Ezra for presuming that he can understand the way of God, the working of divine providence. Twice he demonstrates to Ezra that he cannot understand God's way. First, by the riddle questions (4:5) which show Ezra that he cannot even understand the wonders of nature, how much less divine providence. Second, by the double parable of the trees and the sand which teaches that "those who dwell upon the earth can understand only what is on the earth, and he who is above the heavens can understand what is above the height of the heavens" (4:21); on doubled parables, see 4:48 Commentary. In neither case does the angel specifically take up the question of the fate of Israel, which is dealt with only by implication.[11]

In 4:23–25, Ezra told the angel that, in fact, his answer was not to the point. First, he observes that human beings have been given the power of understanding and this ability leads them to want to understand. Moreover, he notes, responding to 4:20–21, he did not ask about heavenly matters but about the earthly suffering of Israel.[12] The outcome of Ezra's response in 4:22–25, therefore, is to tell the angel that he has given unsatisfactory answers. Ezra cannot accept the premise that the fate of Israel is incomprehensible, and he strengthens this refusal by recalling God's special relation to Israel and the Torah. Israel is called by God's name.

By rejecting the angel's answer, Ezra seems to return the discussion back to the point at which it stood at the end of chapter 3. He questions God's attitude toward Israel and has raised the issue of election.

At this juncture a cryptic statement by the angel ensues about sowing and harvest, that is, about the future. Ezra must await future vindication of the righteous in order to see the resolution of his problems (4:26–

---

7   The whole of the issue of these riddle questions is discussed in Stone, "Lists," where the *Gattung* was first described.

8   A special case is the list of information revealed to Solomon in Wisd 7:17–21, where the range of revealed information is a function of Solomon's well-known role as a magician. Cf. Stone, "Lists," 436–37.

9   For a full analysis of the form with numerous examples and extensive discussion, see Stone, "Lists"; see also Stone, "Paradise," 85–88.

10   On the role of speculative materials in the apocalypses, see Stone, "Lists," and idem, "Apocalyptic Literature," 391–92. On the relationship of speculative to eschatological knowledge, see 12:37–39 Function and Content, p. 373.

11   On "understanding the way of the Most High," see M. E. Stone, "Way of the Most High," 132–42.

12   The theme of understanding recurs a number of times and has been discussed further elsewhere. It is dealt with in some detail in Excursus on Inspiration and see also Introduction, sec. 4.2.5. See Stone, "Way of the Most High," 137–38, and cf. 4:12 (Armenian) and 7:62–71.

32). This forms the transition to the second part of the dialogue, for following it the line of argument is abandoned and a series of requests for eschatological information occurs. A similar transitional passage occurs following the dispute in Vision 2 (6:8–10).

It is important to observe that Ezra ceases his dispute here and proceeds to inquire about details of the prediction the angel has made. This happens in both the first visions at the corresponding point and is a highly significant indicator of the development that is taking place in Ezra.[13] It implies his acceptance of certain of the angel's ideas; see further Introduction, sec. 4.2.4.

The emphasis on understanding is the stronger because of the limits that 4 Ezra has placed on the role of knowledge and what can be revealed to the seer. This theme will recur throughout the book. For the present, note that the rejection of cosmographical and uranographical speculations in 4:5–9 makes the cry of despair with its implicit questions in 4:12 the more piercing and the questions in 4:22–25 the more poignant. The seer and the angel both agree that humans cannot know heavenly secrets. Ezra has neither sought such knowledge nor been granted it. The proper concern for the mind, then, is the fate of Israel.

Commentary

■ 1 In this verse the angel Uriel is introduced by a relative clause, as if already known. Uriel is the angel who regularly appears to Ezra as revealer of secrets or interpreter of visions thus in 5:20 and 10:28. The abruptness of his appearance has led some scholars to assume that a previous appearance of Uriel, perhaps preceding 3:1, has been lost.[14] Others, however, point out that 4 Ezra is not as interested in the supernatural trappings as in the substance of the visionary discourse experience. Thus,

like biblical sources such as Zech 1:9; 3:1; 3:3; and Dan 7:16, 4 Ezra is abrupt, indeed excessively so, in introducing the angel.[15] Even more persuasively, the supernatural element may be deliberately underplayed here, since Ezra is not yet in a fit state for its full measure. This verse then contrasts with the experience described in 10:25–28; see Form and Function there. However, the angelophany in that vision is also very low-keyed, and that forms an interesting contrast with the description of the direct divine address to Ezra in 14:1–2.

Uriel is one of the four archangels, the highest class of angelic beings. He occurs in lists of the four archangels in various sources, for example, *1 Enoch* 9:1; *Apoc Mos* 40:2; *ARN* 12; *Num. R.* 2:10; *Pes. Rab.* 188a; and *Midr. Konnen* (Jellinek, *BM*, 2:39). He also occurs in a list of seven archangels in *1 Enoch* 20 and in Targ J Deut 34:6, and of three angels in *Apoc Mos* 40:2. In 1QM 13:14–15 he is replaced in a list of four by Sariel, in *1 Enoch* 40:9 and 71:8 in a similar list by Phanuel (both texts from the *Similitudes*), and in *Seder Gan Eden Recension 2* (Jellinek, *BM,* 3:138) by Nuriel.[16]

This uncertainty about Uriel's place in the lists may be explained by the negative attributes attaching to him in certain sources. In *1 Enoch* 20:2, Uriel is said to be set "over the world and over Tartarus" (so in the Greek); in *Num. R.* 2:10 he is said to be "at His left hand, corresponding to Dan who is in the north," while in *Midrash Konnen,* loc.cit., he is said to be "in the north, corresponding to Dan who is darkness." He who is in charge of this world is, in many sources, Satan; Satan is the prince of Dan (*Test Patr Dan* 5:6) from which tribe, according to later belief, the antichrist will spring. The left hand is the sinister one; evil will issue from the north (cf. Jer 1:14; etc.).

This group of sources, then, suggests negative aspects

---

13   See Introduction, sec. 4.2.5.

14   So Kabisch, pp. 11–12, following de Faye, and see 3:1 Commentary. Kabisch combines another inconsistency with this one. In 6:35 three weeks' fasting are mentioned, while only two week-long fasts have been recorded, in 5:19 and 6:31: see on this 6:35 Commentary.

15   Thus, cf. with Dan 8:15–16, 9:21. Notably in this latter case the angelophany follows a prayer. This view is urged by Gunkel, Clemen, "Die Zusammensetzung," 238, and others.

16   He seems to be replaced by Suriel in the Gnostic list

quoted by Origen, *Contra Celsum* 6.30. The angel is named Suriel by Ms V of Arabic2 here. On Suriel, see H. J. Polotsky, "Suriel der Trompeter," *Le Muséon* 49 (1937), 231–243; on the lists of four, see the excellent comments by Y. Yadin, *The Scroll of the War of the Sons of Light Against the Sons of Darkness* (Oxford: Oxford University, 1962) 237–40.

of Uriel. These also seem to be implied by the conflict between Uriel and Jacob-Israel in The *Prayer of Joseph*.[17] Perhaps for this reason there is uncertainty about him in various sources.

His function here as revealer of secrets is in keeping with his role as guide and interpreting angel in *1 Enoch* 19:1; 21:5, 9–10; 27:1–2; and the *Book of the Luminaries*. His connection with Torah in *Num. R.* 2:10, *Midrash Konnen*, loc. cit., is clear, and in Targ J Deut 34:6 the angels mentioned are "mighty in wisdom." These characteristics may be involved in Uriel's role as Ezra's guide and mentor.

■ **2** Instead of "is quite confounded," Box has "has utterly failed," and in his footsteps Myers renders the whole "since your thinking is so completely wrong." Behind the Syriac, Ethiopic, Arabic1, Armenian, and Georgian versions stands a verb expressing astonishment; the idea is "You are at a loss"; cf. 5:33. The term "the way of the Most High" was discussed above (see 3:31 Commentary). The particular content of the way is first formulated here in 4:4 but importantly restated at the end of this section in 4:22–25. Even though the angel informs Ezra that he cannot understand the way of the Most High, Ezra returns to the problem repeatedly; see also 5:34, where the angelic response is far less sarcastic.[18]

■ **3** On the nature of these three riddles, see Form and Structure, pp. 80–81. The word "ways," clearly denoting the "riddles" with which it is parallel, is difficult, particularly so since in 4:2; 4:4; 4:11; etc., the word is used with a specific and clear (and different) sense; cf. 3:31 Commentary and 5:50 Commentary.[19] The word that

the versions render "similitude" or the like probably reflects Heb משל, a common term of wisdom writing which may mean "riddle," "conundrum." Greek τρόπον is rendered by Armenian *aṙag*, "proverb," in *Paen Adam* 36(9); see Stone, *The Penitence of Adam* (CSCO, vol. 430), 9.

■ **4** The "way" is the way of the Most High, referred to in 4:2 above. The polyvalency of the word "way" is at play in the following discussion see 4:23 and cf. 4:8. The reason for the existence of the evil heart should not be viewed as exhausting the meaning of the way, as is abundantly clear from 4:22–25. Indeed, it is a problem to which the author refers again only rarely in these terms.

■ **5** The material in 4:5; 4:7; and 5:36–37 forms a list of questions that are, in their context in 4 Ezra, to be regarded as unanswerable. As is set out in the commentary to each phrase, these very "unanswerable" questions have many parallels.[20] The chief parallels are either in lists of things revealed to apocalyptic seers or in contexts designed to glorify wisdom or to praise God. In all of these types of usages the subjects of the list are far from self-evidently unknowable. Indeed, they are revealed or catalogued or shouted out in praise.

Closest overall to our passage is *2 Apoc Bar* 59:5–11, an extensive list of the things revealed to Moses on Sinai. This list includes many of the elements contained in the 4 Ezra verses.[21]

Consequently it may be concluded here that the author of 4 Ezra has taken a list of revealed things and

---

17   Accepting the exegesis of J. Z. Smith, "The Prayer of Joseph," *Religions in Antiquity: E. R. Goodenough Memorial* (ed. J. Neusner; SHR 14; Leiden: Brill, 1968) 274–81.

18   See Stone, "Way of the Most High," on the issue. The problem of understanding God's way in the destruction of the Temple is also to the fore in *b. Ber.* 3a; cf., in general, *Od Sol* 7:8: "He who created wisdom is wiser than his works."

19   Wellhausen, *Skizzen*, 6:240, suggested a Hebrew word, probably דרך, meaning "fashion." This is difficult to accept without a determining context. Koch evades this exegetical issue in his discussion of the term ("Esras erste Vision," 64): *Erkenntnis dieser Wege, wir würden sagen, der Natur- und Zeitgesetze— wäre ein erster Schritt zur Einsicht in den allumfassenden einen göttlichen Weg und zur Orientierung des men-*

schlichen Verhaltens an dieser Grösse. ("Recognition of these ways we might say, of the laws of nature and time, was a first step forward into the all-comprehensive, one, divine way and toward the orientation of the human relation to these values.")

20   Stone, "Paradise," 85–88; a detailed treatment is in Stone, "Lists"; see also Function and Content above.

21   Set forth schematically in Stone, "Lists," 419ff. Other significant parallel passages are *2 Enoch* 23:1; 40:1–13; *1 Enoch* 41:1–7; 60:11–22; and *Bib Ant* 19:10. Cf. with these Job 28 and 38; Sirach 43; Psalm 148; and Song of the Three Children. The wisdom type may be found in Sir 18:4–5 and Wisd 9:13–17, with which cf. *2 Apoc Bar* 14:8–9 and *1 Enoch* 93:11–14.

broken it up and reused it in a radical way. "The writer wishes to emphasize the limits of human knowledge, to deny the possibility of such revelations. To do this he does not simply have the angel ask the seer some riddles, to show him how limited his knowledge is. He chooses those riddles and adduces other elements of knowledge from a complex of ideas, a catalogue of those very subjects which in the 'normal' run of events apocalypticists considered as central to their revelatory experiences. When seen in this light, the passage receives its full dramatic dimension. It is a denial, daring, perhaps even polemical, of the availability of certain types of special knowledge, a denial therefore of a specific part of apocalyptic tradition."[22]

The "weight of fire" may be observed in *2 Apoc Bar* 59:5; see 48:4. The "measure of the wind" features in various ways, in the same verse from *2 Apocalypse of Baruch* 59 and in Job 28:25, while "the day which has passed" may be compared with 4 Ezra 5:36; *2 Enoch* 23:1; and Sir 1:2. The features of counting and measuring are common to many of these lists.[23]

The introduction of this angelic injunction by the command "go" is also to be observed in 4:40.

■ 6 The verse is parallel in role to 5:38. The expression "those who are born" sets human beings in contrast with the unborn, heavenly, or angelic beings; see 4:21. The line of the angelic argument is quite clear here, and the list material continues in the next verse.

■ 7 These questions are clearly patterned on Job 38:16–17. In 4:5, preexisting material was utilized in order to make a point quite different from its original intent. Here too, behind the questions is not just a sense of wonder at God's greatness in creation. The questions here are formulated in the literary tradition in which books like *1 Enoch* or *2 Enoch* or *3 Apocalypse of Baruch*

have related revelations of just those cosmological features which the author of 4 Ezra is apparently rejecting.[24]

Nonetheless, the verses from Job mentioned above are very close indeed to our passage on literary grounds as well, and phrases substantially common to the two sources are italicized:

38:16 Have you entered into the *springs of the sea*, or walked in the *recesses of the deep*?

38:17 Have *the gates of death* been revealed to you, or have you seen the gates of deep darkness?

It is open to question whether the word "dwellings" should not be rendered as "chambers," as in certain versions; cf. Ps 33:7. The gates of death (cf. Armenian 4:8) or exits of hell (Latin *infernum;* Syriac, Ethiopic *Sheol*) are well compared with Ps 9:14; 107:18; and Isa 38:10. The springs or streams of the deep are well known from Ugaritic texts on; see Gen 7:11; 8:2; 1QH 3:15; etc.[25]

The "ways above the firmament" are surely the orbits of the heavenly bodies (cf. Judg 5:20 and 1QH 1:13), while in *1 Enoch* 14:11 and 14:17 the "paths" of the stars are seen in the ceiling of the heavenly palace.[26] With the expression "entrances of paradise," compare *Bib Ant* 13:9 and 19:10.

■ 8 While 4:7 has five questions, 4:8 has only four responses. If the last phrase were not original, as some have suggested, then it would have only three. The last phrase should probably be accepted, therefore, and it should be observed that the first two questions in 4:7 are identical in content to the responses here. Paradise is, however, to be distinguished from heaven. The latter is apparently the starry sphere; cf. 4:7 Commentary. "Paradise," however, may mean the heavenly object of theosophical knowledge, as Scholem pointed out.[27] It is difficult to

---

22 Stone, "Lists," 420. For special knowledge of measures of time, see *b. Ber.* 7a, which, though different in form, is notable from the perspective of content.

23 The "weight of the wind" is also to be found in *Gen. R.* 24:4 (Theodor-Albeck, p. 232) and in *Qoh. R.* 1:6, which stress the element of danger in the blasts of wind which so require moderation. See also *1 Enoch* 41:3–4; 60:12; and *2 Enoch* 40:11, where the mechanics of weighing out the wind are described.

24 See further 4:5 Commentary; and Stone, "Lists," 419–26.

25 For another possible exegesis, see 5:25 Commentary; their unknowability is mentioned in a different context in 13:52.

26 See further Stone, "Lists," 428–29.

27 See *b. Hag.* 14b on "four who entered Paradise"; see also Scholem, *Major Trends,* 52–53; idem, *Gnosticism,* 14–19; and Stone, "Paradise," 85. This interpretation has been controversial; see the reevaluation with reference to the scholarly literature in Rowland, *Open Heaven,* 315–16.

decide between "entered" of most versions and "seen" of Arabic2 and Georgian.[28]

These things are among those shown to Moses on Mount Sinai; see *2 Apoc Bar* 59:5–11.[29] The expression "nor *as yet* did I descend into hell" may have provided the *point d'appui* for the attribution of visions of Tartarus to Ezra in later Ezra writings, such as *Greek Apocalypse of Esdras*.[30]

■ **9** The point that the angel is making is like that made by God in Job 37:14—39:30. This is a reuse of a list of objects of apocalyptic knowledge. Therefore the angelic riddle is only unanswerable on the face of it, but in fact is answered in many apocalypses; see further 4:5 Commentary.

■ **10** The phrase "and he said to me" has raised difficulties, since it usually serves to signal a change of speaker, while here the angel is already the speaker (cf. 4:7). It has been omitted by the Arabic2 and Armenian versions, while the Georgian introduces before it, "I answered and said, 'I cannot understand that.'"

It does not seem appropriate to see in the elements mentioned (fire, wind, the day that has passed) a reference to four or any other number of elements from which humans were created.[31] These are features of physical nature in which human beings live; even these, the angel says, Ezra cannot understand.

■ **11** The word "vessel" has raised difficulties. It occurs in Latin, Syriac, and Arabic1 and may lie behind Ethiopic (see Violet 2). Theories have been postulated to explain it, ranging from a corruption (Violet) to a mistranslation of a Greek word (Gressmann). In 7:88 the "corruptible

vessel," that is, the body, is mentioned and the simplest explanation of the present text is that "your vessel" means "you" or "your body." This was also the interpretation of Arabic2, Armenian, and Georgian. In view of 7:88 and of 4:11, where corruptibility is the weakness singled out, it seems most probable that the body is the specific referent. This is also the meaning of σκεῦος in contemporary and later Greek texts. Another example of the same usage is in *Apoc Mos* 31:4.[32]

The balance of the verse raises a number of technical difficulties; see the textual notes. The sense, however, is quite clear: Ezra who is corruptible (and therefore a fragile vessel) is incapable of grasping or comprehending the way of Him who is incorruptible.[33]

The terms "corruptible" and "incorruptible" occur throughout the book. They do not have any obvious biblical parallels. "Corruptible" or "corruptibility" is a typical quality of this world (e.g., 7:15; 7:96; 7:111; 8:34; 14:13). It signifies death and is brought about by the evil heart (7:48). It is said to be overcome at the end or in the eschatological state (6:28; 7:31; 7:96 [after death]; 7:113; 8:53).[34] Equally, the world is said to be corruptible (4:11; cf. 7:31) and the world to come or the heavenly world is incorruptible (4:11; cf. 7:31).[35] Thus the incorruptible is typical of the heavenly (4:11) or of the

28 The biblical and apocryphal parallels to the material in this verse are given above in Form and Function, pp. 80–81, and in 4:7 Commentary.

29 See Stone, "Lists," 414–16. A discussion of a different sense of the entries of paradise and Gehenna may be found in *b. Erub.* 19a.

30 Stone, "Metamorphosis," 5–10.

31 Contrast 8:8, *pace* Gunkel, Oesterly, Myers; so also Ginzberg, *Legends,* 5:65, 388.

32 See Lampe, s.v. Cf. also the Gizeh papyrus reading in *1 Enoch* 2:2. See further on this matter Lewy, *Chaldean Oracles,* 265. M. Philonenko, "L'âme à l'étroit," *Hommages à André Dupont-Sommer* (ed. A. Caquot and M. Philonenko; Paris: Adrien-Maisonneuve, 1971) 424–25, adduces from pagan writing a number of examples of "vessel" with the sense of body. Philonenko would relate the idea of "vessel"

here and in 7:88 with the idea of "narrow," "straight" as typifying this world; cf. 7:12, etc. The narrowness, according to his view, is the prison-like aspect of the body, a concept he finds, obviously, widespread in Greek philosophy. We submit that his suggestive comment perhaps lays too great a burden on the admittedly intriguing texts of 4 Ezra. Geoltrain observes that "le vase est aussi l'oeuvrage du potier et l'image renvoi aux rapports de la créature avec son créateur."

33 An apparently similar use of language may be observed in *2 Apoc Bar* 21:18; 28:5; 43:2; *2 Enoch* A 65:10.

34 See also *2 Apoc Bar* 44:9 and Excursus on Adam's Sin, p. 66.

35 So the earth will be changed with the new age: 6:16; 7:31; 7:113.

eschatological (7:13).[36]

The Greek was probably φθαρτός, and so forth, but the Hebrew remains enigmatic.[37] Licht suggests כלה which occurs in this sense in the Dead Sea Scrolls.

Although the term "corruptible" refers to the body or bodily life (cf. 14:13–14), it is by no means certain that a dualism of soul and body is the primary feature of the present passage, which rather seems to stress the contrast between the heavenly and the earthly.[38]

The idea that the secrets of God are unknowable is, of course, not limited to this passage in 4 Ezra.[39] This theme, which is further developed by the angel below, is also present, for example, in 1QH 10:2–5:

> and it will be, against your will, nor will all contemplate your statutes (3), nor will all consider your secrets; and what indeed is man who is earth, (4) he was made from [dust] and to dust is his return; will you enlighten him with such wonders (5) and make known to him the secret of your truth?[40]

Ezra falls on his face and prostrates himself in order to ask the next question. This is not the same as the fainting or weakness which follows the climactic revelatory experiences, for example, in 5:14 and 10:30.

■ 12 The general sentiment that it were better to be dead than alive or not to have been born may be found in Jonah 4:3; cf. 1 Kgs 19:4; Jer 15:10; 20:14; 20:17–18; Job 3:11; 10:18; and Qoh 4:2–3. In the context of the sinner, see also Mark 14:21 and parallels; *1 Enoch* 38:2; and *2 Apoc Bar* 28:3. Compare also the general view expressed in *2 Apoc Bar* 10:6; and see further 5:35 Commentary. An allied sentiment, that human beings were better not born or at least not sinning, may be found in 4 Ezra 7:116, cf. 7:69, *2 Enoch* 41:2; the apparent reverse is found in 4 Ezra 7:45, but compare 7:46. Close to 4:12 in language are the four repetitions of this sentiment in *Greek Apoc Esd* 1:6; 1:21; 5:9; and 5:14; and in *Apoc Sedrach* 4:2.[41]

The only text that formulates this sentiment in terms of the understanding is *2 Apoc Bar* 15:5–6. As in many other cases, however, *2 Apocalypse of Baruch* seems designed to deflect the point of Ezra's plaint:

> 15:5 It is true that man would not have understood my judgment if he had not received the Law and if he were not instructed with understanding. 15:6 But now, because he trespassed, having understanding, he will be punished.

Here clearly, understanding is of the Torah and of God's judgment of humanity, presumably for transgressing it. Human beings are culpable because they knew or had understanding. This differs profoundly from Ezra's view.

Students have been exercised by the expression "come here" or "be here" and have compared it with Hebrew "come into the world" or phrases like John 1:9. It should be observed that Ethiopic and Armenian have "be born."

---

36 See further 7:13 Commentary, and cf. *2 Apoc Bar* 74:2 and 85:5. In *2 Apoc Bar* 44:12 it is parallel to "perdition."

37 Cf. Dan 10:8 משחית = διαφθοράν (Theod.) φθοράν (OG), and also *Ps Sol* 4:6 φθορά.

38 See, however, 7:88. Note τὰ ἄφθαρτα in *Test Patr Benj* 6:2. On pagan Greek usage of ἀφθαρσία and its influence on Wisdom of Solomon, see J. M. Reese, *Hellenistic Influence on the Book of Wisdom and Its Consequences* (Rome: Biblical Institute, 1970) 65–69. Observe, however, that the term φθαρτός, etc., is not found in Wisdom of Solomon. Note the usage in 1 Cor 15:53–54.

39 A similar structure and phrasing may be observed in Jud 8:14.

40 Cf. also Wisd. 9:14–16:
> 14 For the reasoning of mortals is worthless, and our designs are likely to fail,
> 15 for a perishable body weighs down the soul, and this earthly tent burdens the thoughtful mind.
> 16 We can hardly guess at what is on earth,

and what is at hand we find with labor. Wisdom of Solomon adds, however, that God reveals these secrets to human beings (9:17–18); see also Stone, "Lists," 438; cf. John 3:12; G. von Rad explored the limits of knowledge in *Wisdom in Israel* (trans. J. D. Martin; Nashville and New York: Abingdon, 1978) 97–110.

41 For adaptations of this *topos*, see 7:62 Commentary and 13:13b–20a Function and Content, pp. 389–90. It is typical of the four laments in 4 Ezra, which are discussed in 7:116–8:3 Form and Structure, pp. 255–56. Urbach has recently urged that the famous dispute between the houses of Hillel and Shammai as to whether it were better for humans not to have been born refers to the sinner and in any case may not be authentic (*b. Erub.* 13b); see Urbach, *Sages*, 252. He also adduces some pagan parallels to this view. James, *Biblical Antiquities*, 55–58, refers to numerous parallels in that work.

The possibility exists of confusion of forms of the Greek γεννάω, "to bear," and γίνομαι, "to become," which would be very similar, for example, in the aorist passive. Indeed, they alternate in the similar phrases from *Greek Apocalypse of Esdras* and *Apocalypse of Sedrach* which were quoted above (see Violet 1, p. lvi).[42]

■ **13** The Hebrew infinitive absolute and finite verb, which is reflected in various versions, served in Judg 9:8, for example, to open a parable. Box's "once upon a time" is a felicitous English rendering of this, gladly accepted here.

A symbolic vision in which a conflict between the forest and the waters figures is also found in *2 Apocalypse of Baruch* 36. Note particularly the very similar phrase "forest of trees planted in a plain" (ibid., 36:2); cf. also a similar expression in 5:23.

■ **14** No commentary.

■ **15** If the battle of the sea with the dry land mentioned here reflects an old mythical theme, then the conflict between the trees and the sea in 4:14–15 is perhaps a balancing structure developed by the author. The view that a mythical theme is in the background of this parable is urged by Gunkel and others. It is certainly beyond doubt that this mythical subject was well known in biblical and postbiblical literature alike. In any case, the mythical elements are very much in the background of this nature parable which partakes of the character of popular gnomic lore, comparable with Jotham's parable (Judg 9:8) and also 2 Kgs 14:9.[43]

■ **16** The image must have been commonplace in wooded land; cf., e.g., Ps 83:15.[44]

■ **17** The idea of sand as the impassable barrier may be drawn from Jer 5:22. It also occurs in a conflict context in *1 Enoch* 69:18.[45]

■ **18** Elsewhere in 4 Ezra, parables also conclude with questions or statements drawing their inferences; so 7:3–16 and 7:57–60; cf. 4:50 and 8:41. The same technique also occurs in the New Testament (e.g., Mark 4:13–20; Luke 7:41–43; 10:30–37), while rabbinic parables, too, often end with the drawing of explicit inferences. Whether the inferences are drawn by means of questions and answers or by means of pronouncements depends chiefly on the broader literary context in which the parable is used.[46]

The chief textual difficulty here is Latin *incipies indicare* which Volkmar suggested derives from ἠρχόω; so Box (note) "would you have undertaken." If it reflects μέλλειν, however, as seems likely (see 4:33 below), the translation given here is preferable. Nothing corresponds to it in the other versions, so its textual status is doutful.

■ **19, 20** No commentary.

■ **21** This verse concludes the whole first section of this dialogue. The riddles and the parable were both intended to show Ezra that "the way of the Most High," which he so desired to see, is beyond human ken. The expression "he who is above the heavens" is plural in a number of textual witnesses. Even where it is singular, it could be a general statement about various heavenly beings, although it may well refer exclusively to God. The gap between earthly and heavenly knowledge is a

---

42 See also 7:45 Commentary n. 16 for this terminology. If the reading "born" is accepted, then the verse provides a less secure basis for a doctrine of preexistence of the soul.

43 *B. Baba Batra* 74b preserves a late form of the legend of the conflict between God and the Prince of the Sea over creation, which ends with God kicking the Prince of the Sea and killing him. This is also the background of *Midrash Konnen* (Jellinek, *BM*, 2:25). See the discussion of this by I. Jacobs, "Elements of Near Eastern Mythology in Rabbinic Aggadah," *JJS* 38 (1977) 1–3. The text in 4 Ezra is far less explicit than those cited by Jacobs. For other mythological reflexes, see 8:23 Commentary.

44 See also *Book of Giants*, where there is a dream about trees, water, and fire; cf. G. W. E. Nickelsburg, "The Bible Rewritten and Expanded," *Jewish Writings of the*

Second Temple Period (ed. M. E. Stone; CRINT 2.2; Assen and Philadelphia: van Gorcum and Fortress, 1984) 96; cf. also the very similar symbolism in *2 Apoc Bar* 36:4.

45 The idea that God set up a barrier for the sea, without sand being specifically mentioned, may be found elsewhere, e.g., Ps 104:9; Job 26:10; 38:11; Prov 8:29; etc. See also 6:42 Commentary.

46 A. Jülicher, *Die Gleichnisreden Jesu* (Tübingen: Mohr, 1899), 1:93, deals with some of the literary forms with which Jesus' parables conclude.

common theme. Compare Wisd 9:16–17 for a different solution:

> 16c but who has traced out what is in the heavens?
> 17 Who has learned thy counsel,
>   unless thou hast given wisdom
>   and sent thy holy spirit from on high?[47]

■ **22** In this and the following verse the question that was raised above is reformulated once again, in terms of understanding—why were human beings given the power of understanding? But, Ezra adds in response to the angel's words preceding, by understanding God's way I did not mean understanding heavenly matters but ordinary earthly ones. The central such earthly matter is the fate of Israel. To these questions the angel gives no response at this point; they are taken up once more at the start of the dispute section of Vision 2 (5:33). The dialogic prediction that follows here is tied to 4:25 which provides the basis for the shift from dispute to Prediction 1.

Ezra repeatedly asks not only why God made the world the way it is but also why God granted human beings a mind or understanding by means of which they perceive the state of the world.[48] Some quite similar sentiments may be observed in *Testament of Job* 38.

On the address "Lord" referring to the angel, see Box; cf. also 3:4 Commentary.

■ **23** In this verse Ezra responds to the angelic refutation. "I did not wish to inquire," he says, "about the ways above." This response grants the angel his point: a human cannot know the heavenly. However, through the expression "ways above" the seer is playing on "the ways of the Most High" (4:2) and "the way above the firmament" (4:7). The ways of which I ask, he implies, are "of the Most High" but are not "above the firmament." For this reason, he claims, the strictures of 4:21 do not apply. In *Test Job* 38:6 a similar formulation and dynamic may be observed. The question to which he returns is the suffering of Israel. This is a common question in the Bible. The formulation here is close to 4

Ezra 5:28–29, 6:57–58; *Para Jer* 1:6; and particularly to *2 Apoc Bar* 5:1:

> So then I shall be guilty in Zion,
> that your haters will come to this place and pollute your sanctuary,
> . . .
> and rule over them whom you love.
> . . .
> And what have you done to your great name? (Cf. 4:25)

The presentation of the question here should also be compared with the end of chapter 3. Here it is not Israel's relative righteousness that forms the basis of the claim but God's love for Israel; cf. 4:25 below. In Exod 32:11–13 and Num 14:13–16, similar, if less sophisticated, arguments are presented: compare further Wisd 12:22 and 2 Macc 8:15. The argument here from God's love of Israel contrasts with the theodicy of *Ps Sol* 9:1–2 and *Mek. BaHodeš* 1 (Horovitz-Rabin, pp. 203–4), while yet other arguments for divine mercy are urged by *2 Apoc Bar* 3:5.

Israel is frequently referred to as God's beloved (so Isa 43:21; Jer 31:2–3; Hos 11:1; *Ps Sol* 9:8; and *Para Jer* 4:7; cf. also Rom 11:28). Particularly striking is the parallel in *2 Apoc Bar* 21:21, "because on account of Thy name Thou hast called us a beloved people," and cf. 4:25 below. The theme of love is picked up again in Vision 2; for an expression like that here, see 5:27 and Commentary.

Kaminka has pointed out that the Torah here presumably includes all of sacred scripture. This view finds support also in 14:21, and Kaminka adduces many later occurrences of the same extension of meaning of this term. The expression "Torah of our fathers" is not particularly frequent; analogous expressions occur in 1 Macc 2:21; 2:50; 2 Macc 6:1; and 7:37. The expression "written covenants" is even rarer, no exact parallels being known.

■ **24** The first two of the three questions in this verse

---

47 Different attitudes to this question may provide one key for differentiating different theories of knowledge and revelation. See Stone, "Lists," 419–26; cf. also Isa 55:8–9. See the observations of Loewenstamm, "Death of Moses," 198–99.

48 See Stone, "Way of the Most High," where this issue is explored.

emphasize the transitory nature of human life. It is not certain whether the "we" is Israel or mankind in general. In the overall context, the former seems more likely, especially in the light of the third question. A similar shift from apparent reference to mankind to reference to Israel in particular may be seen in the prayer from the Jewish Daily Morning Service:

What are we? What is our life? What is our piety? What our righteousness? What our helpfulness? What our strength? What our might? What shall we say before thee, O Lord our God and God of our fathers? Are not all the mighty men as nought before thee, the men of renown as though they had not been, the wise as if without knowledge, and the men of understanding as if without discernment? For most of their works are void, and the days of their lives are vanity before thee, and the pre-eminence of man over the beast is nought, for all is vanity.

Nevertheless, we are thy people, the children of thy covenant, the children of Abraham thy friend, to whom thou didst swear on Mount Moriah; the seed of Isaac his only son, who was bound upon the altar; the congregation of Jacob, thy first-born son, whose name thou didst call Israel and Jeshurun by reason of the love wherewith thou didst love him, and the joy wherewith thou didst rejoice in him.[49]

The two images in the first part of the verse are designed to show the impermanence of human life, and both are already found in the Bible.[50]

Some scholars would discern in this verse a reaction to opinions like *Ps Sol* 9:8: "Behold and show pity, O God of Israel, for we are thine. And remove not thy mercy from us lest they assail us." In the next verse, *Psalms of Solomon* refers to the election of Abraham and the calling of Israel by God's name. In 4 Ezra 4:23–24 the same ideas

are presented, but while *Psalms of Solomon* 9 regards God's visitation as righteous and nonetheless is sure of God's ultimate mercy, 4 Ezra is uncertain of the justice of the punishment and appeals for mercy. Both base their attitude on God's election of Israel, not on Israel's righteousness. The combination of a statement of the nothingness of humans and a consequent call for mercy to be granted by God's goodness and not deserved by Israel is also striking in the following extract from the High Holydays Liturgy:

As for man, he is from dust, and unto dust will he return: for he getteth his bread with the peril of his life; he is like a fragile potsherd, as the grass that withereth, as the flower that fadeth, as a fleeting shadow, as a passing cloud, as the wind that bloweth, as the floating dust, yea, and as a dream that flieth away.

But thou art the King, the living and everlasting God![51]

Compare also 8:34.

■ **25** The idea that Israel is called by God's name is well known in the Bible. Compare the texts cited to 4:23 above and see also 4 Ezra 10:22; Isa 63:19; 2 Chron 7:14; *Ps Sol* 9:9; and *Mek.* on Exod 23:17 (Horovitz-Rabin, p. 334); cf. also Isa 43:7; and Sir 36:17.[52] Similarly the prayer to God to act for his name's sake is widespread, and here the appeal continues that line of thought outlined in the preceding verses. The present verse probably draws directly from Josh 7:9 and see also Jer 14:7; Ezek 36:22; 2 Macc 8:15; *2 Apoc Bar* 5:1 and 21:21. Analogous is the idea that God's name has been honored by the activity of the righteous (7:60).

---

49 Singer, *Authorized Daily Prayer Book,* 7–8. A movement in the reverse direction, from Israel to humanity in general, may be observed in 7:10–11. See in detail 7:1–25 Form and Function, pp. 192–95.

50 Locusts: Nah 3:17; Ps 109:23; breath or mist: Ps 39:7; 144:4; Qoh 6:12; Job 7:16; cf. Hos 13:3. See also 4 Ezra 7:61; 13:20; *2 Apoc Bar* 14:10; and 82:3.

51 Adler and Davis, *Day of Atonement,* part 2, 150.

52 See also S. Schechter, *Some Aspects of Rabbinic Theology* (London: Black, 1909) 63.

26 He answered me and said, "If you are alive, you will see, and if you live you will often marvel, [a]because the [b] world is hastening swiftly to its end. 27/ For it will not be able to bring the things that have been promised to the righteous [c]in their appointed times, [c] because this world is full of sadness and infirmities. 28/ For the evil [d] about which you ask me has been sown, but the harvest of it has not yet come. 29/ If therefore that which has been sown is not reaped, and if the place where the evil has been sown does not pass away, the field where the good has been sown will not come. 30/ For a grain of evil seed was sown in Adam's heart from the beginning, and how much fruit of [e] ungodliness it has produced until now, and will produce until the time of threshing comes! 31/ Consider now for yourself how much fruit of ungodliness one [f] grain of evil seed [g] has produced. 32/ When heads of good [h] grain without number are sown, how great a threshing floor they will fill!"

33 Then I answered and said, "How long [i] and when will these things be? For [j] our years are few and evil." 34/ He answered me and said, "You do not hasten faster than the Most High, for your haste is for [k]yourself, [k] but the Highest [l]hastens on behalf of many. 35/ Did not the souls of the righteous in their treasuries [m] ask about these matters, saying, 'How long are we to remain [n] here? and when will come the harvest of our reward?'

36/ And Jeremiel the archangel answered them and said, 'When the number of those like [o] yourselves is completed;'

for he has weighed the age in the balance,

37/ and measured the times by measure, [p]and numbered the times by number; [p] and he will not move or arouse until that measure is fulfilled."

38 Then I answered and said, "But, O sovereign Lord, behold! [q] all of us are full of ungodliness. 39/ Is it also perhaps on account of us that the time of threshing is delayed for the righteous—on account of the sins of those who dwell on earth?"

40 He answered me and said, "Go and ask a woman who is with child if, when her nine months have been completed, her womb can keep the child within her any longer."

41 And [r] I said, "No, lord, it cannot."

And he said to me, [s] "The underworld and the treasuries of the souls are like the womb. 42/ For just as a woman who is in

Notes

26   a–d Georg omits.

     b "This" Ar1, Ar2, Arm.

27   c–c So Lat, Arm; Syr, Eth, Ar1, Ar2 omit.

28   d Ar1 "the evil seed"; Ar2 "unbelief"; Arm is reworked, cf. next note.

30   e "Fruit of" omitted by Lat; "seed of" Ar2; Arm reworked to avoid mention of evil heart, see Excursus on Adam's Sin, and it omits this word.

31   f "One": so Syr, Eth, Georg, Ar1, Ar2; Lat omits perhaps by hmt.

     g Syr adds "which has been sown," cf. Ar1; probably secondary expansion perhaps at Greek level.

32   h Literally, "ears of good"; Lat, Ar2 omit "good": Thompson, *Responsibility*, regards this as an exegetical issue (pp. 164–67).

33   i Lat difficult here; Bensly emends to *usquequo*.

     j "Why are?" Lat alone; see Commentary.

34   k–k Lat corrupt; Arm of first part of verse is periphrastic.

     l Ar1 lacuna to 4:42 due to loss of leaf in the Bodleian Ms.

35   m "In their treasuries" Ar2, Arm omit.

     n *Spero sic* Lat, perhaps μένω μέν for μενῶμεν or μενόμεν (Violet 1).

36   o Lat corrupt.

37   p–p Eth, Georg omit phrase; Syr infinitive absolute is Semitizing, cf. Job 6:2; perhaps different words lie behind *tempora*, but they cannot be recovered; the versional variation is secondary.

38   q Lat *et;* "behold" is supported by Syr, Eth, Georg; Arm interprets 4:38–39 differently. Ar2, Arm omit "Lord"; see 7:75 note a.

41   r Arm rephrases 4:41–42.

     s "And" Lat omits; *in inferno* Bensly; *infernum et* Violet 1 and Klijn.

travail makes haste to escape the pangs of birth, so also do these (places) [t] hasten to give back those things that were committed to them from the beginning. 43/ Then the things that you desire to see [u] will be disclosed [v] to you."

44 I answered and said, "If I have found favor in your sight, [w]and if it is possible, and if I am worthy, [w] 45/ show me this also: whether more time is to come than has passed, or whether for us the greater part has gone by. 46/ For I know what has gone by, but I do not know what is to come."

47/ And he said to me, "Stand at my right side, and I will show you the interpretation of a parable."

48 So I stood and looked, and behold, a flaming furnace passed by before me, [x]and it came to pass, [x] when the flame had gone by I looked, and behold, the smoke remained. 49/ And after this a cloud full of water passed before me and poured down a heavy and violent rain, and when the rainstorm had passed, drops [y] remained in the cloud. [z]

50 And he said to me, "Consider it for yourself; for as the rain is more than the drops, and the fire is greater than the smoke, so the quantity [a] that passed was far greater; but drops and smoke remained."

51 Then I prayed and said, "Do you think that I shall live until those days? or what will take place [b] in those days?"

52 He answered me and said, "Concerning the signs [c] about which you ask me, I can tell you in part; but I was not sent to tell you concerning your life, for I do not [d] know."

42 t "The earth" Eth, Georg; "the chambers of the earth" Arm, which is reworked.

43 u "To know" Eth, Arm εἰδέναι for ἰδεῖν (Hilgenfeld); see next note and 4:4 note e.

v "I will show" some Eth Mss and Georg; "you will see" Ar2; "you will see and know" Arm.

44 w–w Lat, Syr with support of Ar2, Arm; Eth "if you reckon it, that it is possible for me" and Georg *si fas tibi videtur (si) possum* (Ms O) go back to a common variant Greek text; there is reversal of the last two clauses and confusion of ἄξιος and ἀξιόω: which was original cannot be determined.

48 x–x So Lat, Syr, Georg, Arm; Eth, Ar1, Ar2 omit.

49 y "Dew" Arm, Georg: perhaps independent.

z Literally, "in it"; Eth, Arm omit.

50 a "Times" Georg; "part of time" Arm; "time" Ar2; probably independent exegetical variants, cf. particularly Arm.

51 b Eth, Georg, Ar1, Ar2; "who will be" Lat, Syr; doublet Arm; ΤΙ/ΤΙΣ ΕΣΤΑΙ uncial Greek variant: see Commentary here.

52 c Singular in Eth, Georg.

d Syr, Eth, Georg add "even"; so also Lat Ms A.

Form and Structure

This long section has been isolated as marking a new part of the vision by most students from Kabisch on. It is formed of two chief parts. First are the transitional verses 26–32 which stand between the questionings of the preceding pericope and the predictive discourse which follows. These verses contain a prediction formulated in somewhat cryptic terms, and although they are dominated by the metaphor of sowing and reaping, they do not exhibit formal features of a parable.

Similar, somewhat cryptic prophecies occur elsewhere in the book at points of transition from dialogic dispute to (usually dialogic) prediction (5:41–2; 6:8–10; 7:25; 8:3). They have something of the oracular style to them and serve to change the pace and mood of the section.

The main body of the predictive discourse then follows. It can be differentiated from the preceding dispute discourse by content and emphasis, not by overall form. The subject is the telling of the future. The questions posed by the seer are modest and request information. The angelic response transmits that information in a more or less clear fashion. The discourse employs small similes and parables, just as the preceding dispute did, and it concludes with a transition into the second part of the prediction. A most significant structural feature, however, is the difference in the amount and character of discourse attributed to Ezra and to the angel. In this predictive discourse, Ezra's portion steadily reduces. He asks shorter, innocuous questions which the angel answers at great length.

Function and Content

The transitional section opens with a prediction that "the world is hastening to its end." The removal of evil is then foretold, and the flourishing growth of good. The detailed exegesis of these verses will be presented below;

they imply both a renewal of human hearts and a renewal of the world or age (4:26–32). Having received this overall prophecy, the seer proceeds to ask a series of questions designed to increase the precision of it: first, When will this take place? (4:33); second, Is man's evil delaying it? (4:38); and third, Is more time past than is to come? (4:45–46). To the first the angel replies that the times are predetermined (4:34–37); to the second, that the times are predetermined and will not delay (4:41–43); and to the third, that most of the time is past (4:50). Finally the prophet asks whether "those days" are imminent (4:51), to which the angel replies by Prediction 2.

It should be observed, however, that each of these questions has a tension implicit in it. The angel in each response emphasizes the idea of predetermination of the times (4:36–37; 4:40–42; 4:50). Yet this emphasis is parallel to and set over against a sense of urgency and haste which is cumulative (4:26; the image of 4:43; the parable of the third question). This tension is inherent in the author's thought.

The question central to the preceding dispute section (4:1–25) had been the fate of Israel and human beings' understanding of their situation in the world. The angel initially denied Ezra's request for knowledge and understanding of the way of God, and the section concluded with the redefinition of the issue in a series of questions posed in 4:23–25.

In Prediction 1, the present passage, an oblique response was made to this, but the questions were not answered in the terms in which they were posed. It is as if the angel, taking up only the last of Ezra's questions in 4:25 ("What will he do for his name?") answers it alone. It is evident from the continuation of the discussion in Vision 2 that the seer is not satisfied with this response, for there he returns to his redefined questions.

The same obliqueness of response was observed above in the angel's answers to some of the questions in the dispute. It is, of course, difficult to decide whether this is merely a literary technique employed by the author or whether it in fact corresponds to something in his experience.

Excursus on the Two Ages

Designations
In this section the idea is introduced that the present age is going to come to an end.[1] This refers to the conception, widespread in 4 Ezra,[2] that there are to be two ages and that the present age is destined to be succeeded by a future one. This is stated most explicitly in 7:50 but is also obvious from many other places: thus most clearly 7:50 and see also 6:7–10; 6:34; 7:12–13; 7:29–31; 7:47; 7:75; 7:112–113; 8:1; and 8:46. These two ages are referred to as "times" (6:7–10; 6:34; 8:52 [Lat]), "the time of renewal of creation" (7:75), or "ages" (*saecula*—6:7–10; 7:30–31; 7:50; 7:112–113; 8:1; etc.). This world and the world to come are often contrasted and the word *saeculum* and equivalents are the terms used.[3]

This age, referred to alone, is called "times (of the world)" in 14:9[4] or *saeculum* and equivalents (4:26–27; 6:20a; 6:25). It is not referred to as "this world/age" except in contrast with "the world to come."

Characteristics of the Ages
The world or age to come is described in various ways in 4 Ezra. It will be complete; its ways are broad and safe (7:13); in it glory will be fully revealed and judgment, by implication, perfect (7:113). It is for the few righteous alone (7:47; 8:1), and its benefits will be for those who will inherit eternal life (8:46).[5] The future age is to bring reward and punishment (7:47; 7:75); life, joy, and so forth, for the righteous (7:119; 8:52); immortality (7:13; 7:31); and freedom from corruption, death, and infirmity (8:53). In it the evil

---

1   See 7:26–44 Form and Function, pp. 204–6, where the idea of the two eschatologies is discussed. Terminological aspects of this subject are dealt with in Excursus on the Term "Age."

2   It occurs, of course, in many other sources; see, e.g., those cited by Volz, p. 36. Cf. *2 Apoc Bar* 48:50; 51:16; *2 Enoch* 50:2; *Bib Ant* 34:3; etc., and see also Keulers, pp. 18, 38.

3   This term is dealt with in Excursus on the Term "Age." "Two worlds" also occurs in rabbinic literature, e.g., see *Gen. R.* 53:12 (Theodor-Albeck, p. 659).

4   The exact denotation of "times" is discussed in 4:37 Commentary. Many discussions deal with this terminology of "two worlds"; see Box, pp. 190–91, and Harnisch, p. 94. On p. 105, Harnisch points out that in 7:50 and 8:1 the verb *facere* is used of both worlds.

5   Concerning 8:46, see Commentary.

heart will be removed (4:28–30).

It is notable that all of these statements imply, basically, a difference of world order in the new age. By contrast, these blessings are reversed in description of the present age. The evil heart is present in it (4:28–30), it is "full of sorrow and weakness" (4:27); it is full of corruption, death, evil, and illness; the justice of God and his righteous judgment are obscured: see further 7:12 (and Commentary) and 7:113–114; cf. 7:111 and 8:53.[6]

The different parts of the eschatological scheme are not integrated fully in 4 Ezra, but the general weight of his two ages outlook is quite evident. Such views are often termed "dualistic." Certainly, the author sees a clear separation of two ages, of two states of world order. He considers the end of this age to be imminent, even though there is some uncertainty about exactly which point on the eschatological timetable is called "the end."[7] In chapter 14, moreover, there is a passage that refers to a calculation of the exact periods of history.

This concept, more highly developed elsewhere, is present in 4 Ezra and is clearly based upon deterministic suppositions.[8] The times are determined, weighed and divided, fixed in advance. These ideas are expressed tellingly in the present section. Even the number of righteous souls is fixed in advance. For the Qumran sectaries, dualistic determinism is carried down to the individual man. His lot is fixed before his birth, in that of God or that of Belial.[9]

4 Ezra has already been noted to hold firmly to the view of individual free will (see 3:9 Commentary). This clearly stands in tension with the deterministic ideas he propounds elsewhere. Such conflicts or tensions are not surprising in authors like those of the apocalypses.[10]

Commentary

■ **26** This verse opens the predictive discussion which continues until 4:52, with the words, "If you are alive, you will see. . . ." This formulation seems to imply the immediate imminence of the end: it might even come in the seer's lifetime! Similar is 5:4: "But if the Most High grants that you live. . . ." If the text had stated outright that the end is expected in the lifetime of the seer, it would have abandoned its pseudepigraphic convention (see 3:1–3 Function and Content). In fact, both here and in 5:4 it carefully avoids doing this by using the conditional "if." Indeed, in 4:51–52, by which the present discussion is concluded, the author seems to recoil from the danger of shattering the literary framework.

Formally, then, the structure is preserved; yet the language of 4:26 heightens the sense of immediacy which characterizes the author's expectations. It strains the formal situation to its limits. After all, Ezra had been dead and gone for centuries by the time these words were written. The tension is generated by a narrowing of the gap between the seer's actual self-consciousness and the pseudepigraphic *persona* of the author of the vision. In the literary formulation this is offset by the constraints of pseudepigraphy.[11]

The term "marvel," "wonder," or "to see marvels," or "wonders," is used almost exclusively of eschatological events. So the occurrences here and in 7:27; 13:14; 13:50; 13:56; and 14:5; cf. 13:57.[12]

---

6 See also 14:14 Commentary. Similar views may be observed in *2 Apoc Bar* 16; 21:13–14; 44:9; and 85:5. L. Finkelstein, *Introduction to the Treatises Abot and Abot de R. Nathan* (New York: Jewish Theological Seminary, 1950 [in Hebrew]), suggests that in rabbinic texts the term העולם הבא may refer either to the state of souls after death, when they are immediately judged to paradise or hell, or to the eschatological world which is to follow the present one. In the latter case, the souls were thought to be in a treasury between death and resurrection, ibid., Appendix I, 213–23. He has assembled much interesting material there on these conceptions. The terms "the world to come" and "days of the Messiah" are confused in *Tanna debe El.* 3 (Friedmann, pp. 14–15).

7 See Excursus on Natural Order, pp. 103–5.

8 Licht, "Taxo."

9 See 1QS 3:13–16; see the excellent statement by J. S. Licht, *Serakim*, ad loc. (Hebrew).

10 The passage 7:79–99 deals with the intermediate state of the souls. This tends to bridge the temporal opposition of two successive ages, though it is certainly not incompatible with them. In Excursus on Natural Order some distinctions, arising from the idea of "the end," are drawn that supplement the material on the present Excursus. See also Harnisch, pp. 117–18.

11 See on this 14:23–26 Function and Content, pp. 428–31, in further detail.

12 On "seeing," see 6:25 Commentary; on "wonders," see 9:6 Commentary. Chapters 6:48 and 13:44 refer to other wondrous acts of God; cf. Sir 18:6. Cf. with this *2 Apoc Bar* 51:7; 55:7; 55:8; 54:9, cf. 29:6: in

The idea that the world is hastening away is a chief theme of the present section.[13] It recurs in 6:20; see also 14:11–12; 14:18; cf. also 4:42. Close to the formulation of the idea here are *2 Apoc Bar* 20:1 and 1 Cor 7:31.[14]

The first two phrases of this verse are written in a balanced, poetic form. Violet 2 terms it *mašal*, but his basis for this categorization is unclear.[15] 4 Ezra sometimes uses such balanced, rhythmic pronouncements, frequently of somewhat mysterious character, by way of response to questions posed. Other examples include 4:36b–37; 5:42, "Just as for those who are last there is no slowness, so for those who are first there is no haste"; 6:10, "For the beginning of a man is his hand, and the end of a man is his heel; between the heel and the hand seek for nothing else, Ezra!"; 7:25, "Therefore, Ezra, empty things for the empty and full things for the full"; and 8:46, "Things that are present for those who live now, and things that are future for those that will live hereafter"; cf. also 6:34. Each of these occurs in a transitional point in the structure of the book, either at the start or at the conclusion of a section. The sayings are angelic pronouncements about the future delivered in somewhat oracular style. They have no obvious parallels in other sources. They are reminiscent of certain sorts of sayings in rabbinic literature, such as those attributed to Hillel in *m. Abot* 1:13; 2:7; and *Lev. R.* 1.5.

■ **27** The term "appointed times" carries with it the predestinarian view that the cosmic timetable has been established in advance. Such a view is also present in *2 Apoc Bar* 20:1, frequently in the Qumran literature (such as 1QS 1:14–15), and in other sources. The word

translated "bring" might be given as "bear" or "sustain." Here the evil state of this world is offered as the reason for its inability to bear the reward of the righteous. This assumes a dualism of the two worlds according to which the present world is imperfect. When the expression "will not be able to bring" is taken together with 4:26, we may perceive the idea that aging of this world brings about a progressive weakening of it[16] and that it is this weakening which prevents the appearance of the reward. But this idea is not made explicit.

A further ambiguity arises when the verse is put into relationship with 4:29–30. Verse 29 speaks of the fact that the place where evil is sown must pass away before the place where good is sown can appear. In v 30 the text continues: "For a grain of evil seed was sown in Adam's heart from the beginning." Here a second application of meaning for the passage becomes explicit: there will be not only a new world but also a new heart. (See further 4:30 Commentary.)

"The things that have been promised [or: predicted]" means the eschatological recompense; see also 8:59.[17]

■ **28** The imagery of sowing and harvest, like that of planting and producing fruit,[18] occurs in various places in 4 Ezra. In the book the imagery of sowing expresses productivity in a number of contexts. First, in the parable of 8:41 the imagery of sowing describes humans, who are like seed sown: some take root, while others do not.[19] Chapter 5:48 describes humans being produced by the earth as sowing, and this metaphorical use is found in its fullest development in 8:41, which states that many are sown but that few are saved.[20]

54:11 the reference is to creation.

13   On the term "world" *(saeculum)*, see Excursus on the Term "Age"; see Harnisch, p. 98, on the ambiguity of αἰών in 4:26–27.

14   Biblical roots are, e.g., Isa 65:17 and 66:22. Cf. *Jub* 1:29 and Stone, "Apocryphal Notes," 125–26, and also *1 Enoch* 45:4–5. In addition, see *Apoc Elijah* 43:6; 4 Ezra 9:20; *2 Apoc Bar* 3:7; and 85:10. On the sense of the imminence of the end, see 14:18 Commentary.

15   He is also followed by Harnisch, p. 271.

16   This idea is explicit in 5:55 (cf. *2 Apoc Bar* 85:10) and is discussed further in 5:50 Commentary. 4 Ezra 14:16–17 has the quite distinctive idea that the weaker the world becomes through old age, the more sins increase (see further 14:16–17 Commentary). The idea of progressive deterioration is already in *Jubilees* 23. *On the Origin of the World* (CG 2.126.33)

speaks of the sinful cosmos which could not sustain the archons.

17   Cf. *Ps Sol* 11:8; 12:6; *2 Apoc Bar* 21:25; 83:4; cf. Wisd 12:21.

18   On the imagery of bringing forth fruit, see 3:20 Commentary.

19   4 Ezra 9:34 makes an analogous point to 4:28–31.

20   The simile is widespread, of course; see, e.g., Isa 61:11 and *2 Apoc Bar* 22:5–6.

A second use of this language is to be found in 8:6. There Ezra prays for "seed of our heart and cultivation of our understanding whence fruit may be produced." This is perhaps analogous to 9:31, which speaks of sowing the Torah in the hearts of mankind which sometimes gives fruit and sometimes is barren; cf. also 9:34.[21]

In the third place, in 9:17 a gnomic utterance is found: "As is the ground, so is the sowing; . . . as is the husbandman, so is the threshing floor." "Threshing floor" signifies "reward"; see further 4:30 Commentary, and see 4:39.[22] There is a particular connection between the idea of harvesting and judgment, and this imagery is already found in the Bible; see Jer 51:33; Hos 6:11; and Joel 4:13; cf. Rev 14:15–20. *2 Apoc Bar* 70:2 speaks of what will happen "when the time of the world has ripened and the harvest of the seed of the evil one and good ones has come." The imagery in *2 Apocalypse of Baruch* is strikingly like 4 Ezra here; cf. also 4:35.

The usage here may perhaps be compared with the parable in Matt 13:3–9, 18–23, 24–30, and 39 and parallels. The predestinarian idea is to the fore; the evil about which Ezra has asked is the evil heart, see 4:4 and 4:30. That evil must run its course before the good can come.[23]

■ **29** The terms "place" and "field" have double meaning. They are usually held to refer to this world or age and the future one, and this interpretation is supported by 4:26–27.[24] The terms also have a second meaning, the human heart. This is clear from 4:30, which identifies the place where evil was first sown as Adam's heart. The idea that the human heart will be changed at the end

occurs elsewhere in 4 Ezra; see the Excursus on Adam's Sin, p. 66; cf. already Ezek 11:19; 36:26.

■ **30** On the view of evil, see the Excursus on Adam's Sin. The term "evil seed" is perhaps parallel to Philo, *Leg. all.* 3:242, σπέρμα κακίας; for the image of seed and sowing in the heart in general, cf. 8:6 and 9:31 ("in you"). An interestingly different use of this imagery and that of the threshing floor may be observed in 9:17, and see 4:28 Commentary on this. This latter term seems to mean "harvest"; cf. 4:32 and 4:39. The term used in Latin, Syriac, and so forth, refers to the threshing floor itself, although it has been translated "time of threshing." Syriac at *2 Apoc Bar* 70:2 is corrupt, but similar language to that here is found: "Behold! the days are coming and it will happen when the time of the world has ripened and the harvest of the seed . . ." (see 4:28 Commentary).

The use of the image of sowing seed in the heart here, as well as in 8:6, where God is besought to give seed which will enable people to gain (eternal) life, implies that Adam was not responsible for the formation of this seed but that it was set in him by some outside agency. The heart is the place where evil and good are said to be sown also in *2 Apoc Bar* 32:1 etc. Earlier, Ps 40:9 speaks of the Torah "in my inner parts," a use of language that, like "in my heart," is commonplace in the Bible,[25] while Jer 31:32 speaks of the setting of the Torah in the human heart which is very similar.[26] 4 Ezra is reserved about the bald attribution of Adam's evil inclination to God; see the Excursus on Adam's Sin, p. 63.[27]

■ **31, 32** No commentary.

---

21 Here Harnisch, following Brandenburger, would systematize: the human heart is a place in which there may be sown either the Torah or the evil inclination, and which of them will produce fruit is the result of human free choice (p. 172). Clearly the language of sowing—heart—giving fruit is used in both these ways, although it is far from certain that the author would have combined these ideas into a system as Harnisch does; see further in 4:30 Commentary on the heart. A combination of somewhat similar terms is Sir 24:11–12, where the Torah is said to take root in Israel.

22 See Stone, *Features*, 66–67. In general, for this image in another context, see *Greek Apoc Esd* 5:12.

23 The text here does not necessarily imply the idea that evil must reach a peak before the end, just that it must come to its harvest. An analogous idea is

suggested by Zimmerli to lie behind Gen 15:12–15; see W. Zimmerli, *Die Weltlichkeit des Alten Testaments* (Göttingen: Vandenhoeck & Ruprecht, 1971) 75. There, as he presents it, divine justice is the surety of fulfillment of the promise.

24 So C. J. Ball, *The Ecclesiastical or Deuterocanonical Books of the Old Testament* (London: Eyre & Spottiswoode, 1892), ad loc.; and Box, Licht, etc.

25 Its meaning is complex there; see *IDB* s.v. and the long study in *TDNT*, 3:605–13. See also 4:28 Commentary.

26 Cf. also 1QH 4:11.

27 A midrash attributed to R. Jose states: "The latter [Adam] transgressed but one divine command, and see with how many deaths this transgression has been punished again and again in him and the following generations"; translation after W. O. E. Oesterley

■ **33** Ezra proceeds to inquire in detail as to the time of the promised end; see also 8:62b–9:22 Form and Function. Such questions occur elsewhere following predictions or preceding them (so 8:63; *2 Apoc Bar* 16:1; 21:19; 24:4; Mark 13:4).[28]

The inquiry in 4:33a is first answered by 4:34–37, that is, that the times are predetermined. The latter part of the verse is a question only in Latin, and its reading "Why are our years . . . ?" is probably corrupt on text-critical grounds. Moreover, the question so posed receives no answer. The text of the other versions, reflected in the translation here, suits the context admirably. It expresses Ezra's sense of urgency.[29] The seer's same interest in his own life span and its relation to the eschatological events is also expressed in 4:51–52.[30]

■ **34** A related idea recurs in 5:44, while similar reproaches to Ezra occur in 5:33 and 8:47, formulated in like language.[31] Gunkel remarks that the sense of urgency by which Ezra is beset is typical of apocalyptic eschatology. The term "many" may simply denote "numerous" as opposed to Ezra, a single individual. On the other hand, it may be compared with the "many" of Dan 12:3: "those who turn [the—M.E.S.] many to righteousness," which would point toward the contemporary use of the word as a technical term for the community of the Qumran sectaries.

■ **35** Treasuries of souls are mentioned here and in 4:41; 7:32; 7:80; and 7:95, while analogous uses of the term occur in 5:9; 5:37(?); and 6:22. "Treasuries" translates Latin *promptuarium* and Syriac *'wṣr*. The term in the daughter versions probably reflects Greek ταμεῖον.[32] The rendering "treasuries" has been selected because of the great likelihood that the Hebrew original was אוצר. This was a technical term for the place of the repose of the souls after death, and it is found in a number of rabbinic sources. A term such as "room" or "chamber" does not serve in such contexts in Hebrew sources.[33] The treasuries are repositories of the souls of the righteous after death (7:32; 7:80 [and Commentary]; 7:95; 7:101; *Sifre Deut.* on 33:3 [Finkelstein, p. 401]; *2 Apoc Bar* 21:23) and in certain contexts, of all souls after death (see 7:32 Commentary; 7:80 Commentary).

The angel's response is that not just Ezra, whose years are few and evil, is inquiring about the duration of this present state but even the souls of the righteous in their heavenly repositories ask the same questions. Ezra's "how long and when" (4:33) resound in the souls' "how long and when" (4:35). This passage implies some sort of intermediate state of the souls in which they remain between death and resurrection; see 7:75–99 Function and Content, p. 238. On the imagery of harvest, see 4:30 Commentary.[34]

■ **35–36a** This passage may be drawn from a source document. This is indicated by the actual form of the

---

and G. H. Box, *The Religion and Worship of the Synagogue* (London: Pitman, 1907) 93, from R. Martini, *Pugio Fidei adversus Mauros et Judaeos cum observationibus* (ed. J. de Voisin; repr., Farnborough: Gregg, 1967).

28 A similar sentiment, not eschatological in character, is Ps 13; for similar expressions in a different context, see 6:59, *2 Apoc Bar* 13:7 and 16:1. The time of the end, according to other views, is a divine secret, see, e.g., Acts 1:6–7. This is, of course, a difference in the view of what can be known.

29 The expression probably draws on Gen 47:9; for a similar formulation, see also *2 Apocalypse of Baruch* 16.

30 The tension this raises with the pseudepigraphic framework is discussed in 4:26 Commentary.

31 See 5:33 Commentary. See also *2 Apoc Bar* 20:2: "that I may more speedily visit the world in its season." The point of 2 Pet 3:8, often cited as a parallel to this verse, is actually quite different.

32 *Habitaculum* = Syriac *'wṣr* (7:80; 7:85; 7:101; 7:121) also most likely goes back to the same. With 7:121, cf. *Bib Ant* 19:12: *habitationem immortalem. Promp-*

tuarium translates ταμεῖον in Old Latin Ezek 28:16 (Box). It occurs in Vulgate Ps 143 (144):13, where the LXX has ταμεῖον. In neither case does the Massoretic text have אוצר. Ταμεῖον means also "room"; indeed, the LXX uses it predominantly for Hebrew חדר (33 times). It seems to be suggested as the *Vorlage* of the versions by the fact that some of them sometimes use words for "treasury" and other times words for "room"; cf., e.g., Lat 7:80 and Arm 5:37.

33 The term "treasury" seems also to be found in *Bib Ant* 32:13; *2 Apoc Bar* 21:23; 30:2; et al. That the term is אוצר seems confirmed by rabbinic usage; so *Sifre Num Pinḥas* 139 (Horovitz, p. 185); *Qoh. R.* on 3:21; and *PRE* 43. Cf. Aramaic גניז. For the concept, not the term, see *1 Enoch* 39:4–5. Souls of the righteous are under the divine throne according to R. Eliezer b. Hyrcanus; *b. Shab.* 152b; *ARN* 12 (Schechter, p. 50); and *2 Apoc Bar* 59:3; on the general concept, see Harnisch, p. 125 n. 2.

34 With the question, cf. Rev 6:10.

question, "Did not the souls . . . ?" as well as by the
assumption that the reader knows what is being discussed, even though these matters occur in this form
nowhere else in 4 Ezra. Moreover, the unique appearance of an angelic name other than Uriel, Ezra's revealing angel, might indicate the author's dependence on a
preexisting source.[35] The same is also implied by the
term "archangel," found nowhere else in the book.

It is well, however, to recall the structural relation
between 4:33 and 4:35 (see 4:35 Commentary). If the
author is quoting a source in 4:35, then he structured
4:33 on the pattern of 4:35. If, however, he is merely
alluding to a source, this is not necessarily so. As shown
above, the questions in Prediction 1 (4:26–52) are
carefully structured, which means either that the source
document contained an extraordinarily apt quotation or
that the author adapted the source document to his
needs. It seems to us that the unit of quoted material,
whether direct or indirect quotation, probably comes to
an end with the words "is completed" in 4:36. The
speech of the angel Jeremiel concludes there, and 4:36b–
37 is Uriel's direct speech to Ezra.[36]

Similar subordination of preexisting sources to the
needs of the author's discourse is to be observed elsewhere in the book. See 4:5 Commentary; 6:11–29
Function and Content, pp. 165–66; and 6:38–59 Form
and Structure, n. 5.

■ 36 The name of the angel is Jeremiel, apparently
ירחמיאל (cf. Jer 36:26): cf. Latin, Georgian (variant
reading); he is not the same as Remiel or Ramiel of, for
example, 1 Enoch 20:8 (ʿΡεμειηλ—contra Geoltrain—not
extant in Aramaic); 2 Apoc Bar 55:3; etc.[37] He is referred
to as Eremiel in Coptic Apocalypse of Zephaniah, where he is
in charge of the souls from the Flood on and in charge of
the dead.[38] He is also apparently known to the Zohar,

Ber. 41a, as Jeraḥmiel "who is appointed over the souls of
the proselytes." The old name and the function of this
angel have thus been preserved in later sources.[39]

The expression "those who are like you" recurs as a
term for the righteous in 2 Apoc Bar 21:24 as well as in 4
Ezra 8:51 and 8:62. It serves to emphasize Ezra's righteousness, which he deprecates.

The idea that the number of those destined to be
created is predetermined occurs graphically in 2 Apoc Bar
23:4–5; cf. 48:46. So also 1 Enoch 47:4, which also
mentions the prayer of the righteous. It is also found in
rabbinic literature, most strikingly in Gen. R. 24:4
(Theodor-Albeck, p. 233): "The son of David will not
come until all those souls which are destined to be born
will be born."[40] In context here the deterministic implication of the concept is to the fore. See 4:27; 5:36
Commentary; and 7:132.

Uriel's speech resumes in a rhythmic, semipoetic style
and concludes this unit of discourse (4:36b–37). The
somewhat mysterious, oracular discourse resembles 4:26
and fulfills a similar function; see Commentary there.
Therefore the object "them" supplied by RSV is superfluous.

■ 37 The first two phrases of this verse belong together
with the last phrase of 4:36. The three are parallel in
structure. The terms "measure," "number," and "weight"
are found in this order in Wisd 11:20, and some commentators would see that verse as the origin of the verse
in 4 Ezra (Violet, Gry). Note, however, that this type of
language is common in 4 Ezra (4:5; 6:5), and striking
parallels to the language here are to be seen in 2 Apoc Bar
59:5, which refers to measures, depths, weights, and
number.[41] Moreover, creation by measures is referred to

---

35 So already Kabisch, pp. 31, 33, quoting Spitta.

36 The question of literary composition of the book and
its incorporation of sources is dealt with in Introduction, sec. 4.1.1.

37 In 1 Chr 2:33 the name ירחמיאל has equivalents of
ʿΡαμεήλ in B and ʾΙεραμεήλ in Lucian.

38 Himmelfarb, Tours of Hell, 151–52. He is also
mentioned in the Coptic Jeremiah Apocryphon 34; see
Kraft, "'Ezra' Materials," 128.

39 2 Apoc Bar 23:4: "the dead are guarded." In 2 Apoc
Bar 48:6, God is said to take care of the souls of the
righteous dead.

40 For parallels, see Theodor's commentary there. Most
notable are b. Yeb. 62a, 63b; Lev. R. 15:1 on Lev
13:2; b. Abod. Zar. 5a; and Qoh. R. 1 on 1:6, which
adds to the dictum "these are the souls which are
mentioned in the Book of Adam, as it says, 'This is
the book of the generations of Adam' (Gen 5:1)."
The idea also occurs in early Christian and Gnostic
sources; see C. J. van Unnik, "Die 'Zahl der vollkom-
menden Seelen' in der Pistis Sophia," Abraham unser
Vater: O. Michel FS (ed. O. Betz, M. Hengel, and P.
Schmidt; Leiden: Brill, 1963) 467–77.

41 Weighing and measuring are typical activities in

in *Test Patr Naphth* 2:3, where a similar series of terms is used. The usage is much older, of course; so already Isa 40:12; Job 28:25; and Dan 5:25–27.

In addition to the poetic language and the possible dependence on Wisdom of Solomon, and more significant than they are, is the idea that the times are fixed by God. The idea is well expressed in 7:74, in terms close to this verse, viz., the end delays until the appointed time arrives. Consequently, in 11:44 God is said to examine the times and see that they are ended. The deterministic idea does not just apply to the end. All things happen in due time (3:9, see Commentary) and those times are fixed by God (7:74; 13:58; *2 Apoc Bar* 21:8; 48:2–5; 56:2). It follows, therefore, that the times can be the subject of revelation, for example, to Abraham (3:14), Moses (14:5), or Ezra (12:9); and equally they can be typical of things beyond ordinary human attainment.[42]

The view that the times are foreordained by God meant that events past and future were fixed, and the end could not be brought about except in its due time.[43] The idea of the fixed times is to be found in many apocalypses and in other contexts in Judaism of the age. Thus one can point to all the predictive visions that divide history into a given number of segments, such as Daniel 7; *1 Enoch* 85–90; *2 Apocalypse of Baruch* 53–66; etc.[44] This idea too makes possible the revelation of the end, which, when it became combined with intense eschatological expectation, had great implications for apocalyptic revelatory understanding.

The last phrase of the verse refers to the resurrection of the dead. The same sort of language is used in 7:32

(see Commentary) and 7:35. What is intriguing is that the two very similar verbs, perhaps the identical ones that were in the original of 4 Ezra, occur together in Song 2:7; 3:5; and 8:4. The triple repetition there shows that the phrase was fixed in more ancient times. The continuation of the verse in Song of Songs is also suggestive from our perspective. Perhaps a Midrashic exegesis of it lies behind the structure of the verse here.[45] If so, this would be a very early Midrash on Song of Songs.

■ **38** This verse forms a response to the angel's words that have preceded it. We are wicked; perhaps in contrast to the souls of the righteous.

The title "sovereign Lord," strictly a title of God, is here applied to the angel; see 3:4 Commentary. This is typical of 4 Ezra, however, who does not always distinguish between the angel and God.

■ **39** In this verse the "time of threshing" is mentioned again; cf. 4:28 above. As there, it refers to the eschatological recompense. It is clear that "those who dwell on the earth" contrast with "the souls of the righteous in their treasuries." "Us" means "we who dwell on earth" and we are wicked. So, all the inhabitants of the earth are sinful according to this statement.[46]

■ **40** A comparison forms the response to the question that Ezra asked. It is introduced by the angel, who addresses Ezra, "Go, . . ." a form also to be observed in 4:5. The question is to be put to the earth, see 7:45–74 Form and Structure, p. 227.

The simile of the pregnant woman is here applied to the treasuries of the souls. Elsewhere it is used where the earth is seen as the mother (so 5:46; 5:48 Commentary;

---

many texts; e.g., *2 Enoch* 40. See further Stone, "Lists," passim.

42 These matters are dealt with in 14:3–18 Function and Content, pp. 416–17, and 14:5 Commentary. See Stone, "Lists," 420, and also *2 Apoc Bar* 56:2. Time is weighed or measured but in a different context in *2 Apoc Bar* 41:6. On the term "times," difficult to reconstruct confidently in Hebrew, see Stone, *Features*, 53–54. On times, see also 7:26 Commentary and 12:9.

43 This may be contrasted with the ideology of *Testament of Moses* where Taxo and his sons, by their death, attempt to bring about the end immediately. See Licht, "Taxo," 95–103. 4 Ezra was written long after the *Testament of Moses* and not from the perspective of a martyred community but of one that, a generation after the tragedy, is still trying to

comprehend it.

44 So Licht, ad loc. Charles sees an indication of sources in this but is well refuted by Violet 2.

45 No similar midrashim on these phrases were found. In *Pes. R. K.* 5:7–9 may be found eschatological interpretations of adjacent verses from the Song of Songs. See also J. Heinemann, *Agadot veToldotehen: Iyyunim beHishtalshelutan shel Masorot* (Jerusalem: Keter, 1974) 72–73 and 220–21. Other exegeses of Song of Songs in 4 Ezra are discussed in 5:26 Commentary.

46 This perhaps, if we demand complete consistency, stands in conflict with the end of chap. 3. The tension between proclamation of universal sin and the view that there are a few who are righteous is discussed in 7:45 Commentary. See 7:17 Commentary on confusions between God and the angel.

5:51; 10:9–11; and 10:14: cf. 7:62 Commentary).[47] The inevitability of birth after a full term of pregnancy is the comparison for the inevitability of the end after the treasuries of the souls are full to their maximum measure (so also *2 Apoc Bar* 22:7). The image is obvious and commonplace.[48]

■ **41** Bensley emends the text "the underworld and the treasuries" to "treasuries in the underworld" (so also RSV, Licht, Myers, Keulers implicitly on p. 158). There is no textual basis for this emendation; such certainly cannot be found in Arm 4:42. Two possible explanations of the difficult expression arise. The first is that it is a hendiadys simply meaning the place of the souls. The other is that there is a distinction between the underworld, which is the place of the wicked souls, and the treasuries of the righteous souls (so basically Box).

4 Ezra applies "treasuries" in general to the place of the souls of the dead where no distinction is made between the righteous and the wicked; so 7:32 (and Commentary) and 7:101 (and see 7:80 Commentary). He also uses the term for the place of the righteous souls in passages contrasting them with the wicked (so 4:35; 7:85; and 7:95, and the term is discussed in 4:35 Commentary). In such contrastive passages no further detail is given about the place of the wicked. This is exactly the situation in *2 Apoc Bar* 30:2–4,[49] and it is a sort of use of terminology that may be observed elsewhere in 4 Ezra. In any case, the repositories of the souls are intended.

Since there is no evidence for treasuries being in the underworld, and indeed the souls of the righteous are usually thought of as being in heaven, either the verse is using language loosely or else it is actually referring to two different places.[50] The passage 7:78–99 expounds in detail the very different fates of the souls of the righteous and the wicked after death, which take place in different locations.

■ **42** The imagery of the verse is a little obscure. The point is, of course, that just as when a woman reaches her term she enters labor and gives birth and cannot delay, so once the number of souls decreed upon have entered the treasuries, they will bring them forth immediately in the resurrection.[51]

The expression "those things that were committed to them" also occurs in the same context in 7:32 and in a very similar one in *1 Enoch* 51:1, which is probably somewhat older than 4 Ezra. The expression is very similar to or identical with that used in 1 Tim 6:20; 2 Tim 1:12; and 1:14 of that committed to someone, perhaps the soul but perhaps teachings. See also *Hermas Mand.* 3.2 and *Greek Apoc Esd* 6:3; 6:17; and 6:21 of the soul.[52] Notably, *Bib Ant* 3:10 reads *et reddet infernus debitum eum*, "and the underworld will pay back its debt"; and compare also *Test Job* 19:4, cf. Job 1:21. 4 Ezra might go back to a Hebrew like פקדון, used of the soul in a rabbinic source that stems, apparently, from the early second century; see *TDNT*, 8:162–64, and compare *Midr. Mishle* 31:10 (Buber, pp. 54b–55a).[53] 4 Ezra thus enables us to date this terminology back by quite some decades.

All of these texts speak of the soul as something entrusted that must be returned to God. It is intriguing that the pseudepigraphic sources speak of the soul as

47 The earth is said to bring forth many things: Adam (7:116), the mind (7:62), humans (6:54), and cattle (6:53); see 5:48 Commentary and 7:116 Commentary. A quite different view of pregnancy may be observed in 8:8–11. These ideas have clear and obvious biblical antecedents, from Genesis 1 on. See also 1 Cor 15:47–48.

48 The idea of a fixed period of pregnancy being nine months may be seen in a saying of Rab in *b. Yoma* 10a and *b. Sanh.* 98b.

49 In *2 Apoc Bar* 21:23, "Sheol" and "treasuries" of the souls occur in two parallel stichs. It is difficult to tell, however, whether this indicates that they are identical or rather that they have separate functions as repositories of different classes of souls. The passage in *2 Apocalypse of Baruch* bears a considerable resemblance to the list of eschatological elements in

8:53, where "underworld" occurs again. In *2 Apocalypse of Baruch* an unclarity surrounds Sheol, like that observed in 4 Ezra with the treasuries; see 23:4–5; 48:16; and 52:2. See also Stone, *Features*, 144–45.

50 Gunkel's view that the "treasuries" are those of unborn souls, while the underworld is the place of the dead, is difficult to sustain, as Box already remarked. Keulers's views on the location of the dwellings of the righteous and the wicked souls seem too literalistic; see Keulers, p. 158.

51 The image of the "mother" is discussed in Vision 4, and see 4:40 Commentary.

52 See also Lampe, s.v.

53 Cf. also a similar concept with different terminology in Josephus, *War* 3.374. In ARN A 29 (Schechter, p. 30a), the body seems to be called פקדון; the term, together with אוצר, "treasury," occurs in *Qoh. R.* 3:21

something entrusted to the earth or, after death, to the treasury, while the Christian texts and also *Midrash Mishle* speak of the soul as entrusted to human beings. This may indicate a shift in emphasis from the idea of the soul as really belonging to human beings to the idea that it really belonged to God. "From the beginning" is well rendered by NEB as "since time began."

■ **43** This verse takes up the theme of knowledge, which was the chief subject of the dispute (4:1–25). As had already been said in 4:26, Ezra will learn what he wants to know at the time of the end. The theme of knowledge, significantly, arises again in 4:52, at the end of the third question, where it forms the transition to Prediction 2 (see 4:52 Commentary).

■ **44** The expression, "If I have found favor" is frequent in 4 Ezra.[54] It serves to open up a new section, question, or matter. The difficulties of the versions here are discussed by Violet 2, but the expression is also common in the Bible. See the textual notes. The heaping up of three "if"s, as here, occurs in 4 Ezra again only in 12:7, in Ezra's prayer for interpretation of the vision. "If it is possible" means, presumably, "If I am capable of knowing this"; cf. *Bib Ant* 53:7 *si possibilis sum*.

■ **45** This question refines the inquiry in 4:26, and the answer given there; cf. also 5:50. The repetition of the question witnesses, as Gunkel correctly observed, to its importance for the author.[55] On each occasion the angel responds by a simile and the actual reckoning of the times is reserved for chapter 14.[56] Yet, for our author the secret of the times is at the center of the esoteric revealed tradition; see 3:14 and 14:5. Consequently, the

particularly elaborate introduction to his request may be understood; he is requesting for himself a revelation like that to Abraham and that to Moses.[57]

A very close parallel in phrasing and content is Moses' request of God before his death (*Bib Ant* 19:14). Note also the elaborate introduction:

> And Moses said: If I may ask yet one thing of thee, O Lord, according to the multitude of thy mercy, be not wroth with me. And shew me what measure of time hath passed by and what remaineth.

In *Bib Ant*, however, a fairly precise calculation follows.

It should be remarked, of course, that although the idea of the fixed times lies behind this question, Ezra does not use an actual reckoning until 14:11–12.[58] The absence of actual calculation suits the view that this is a great secret.

■ **46** Compare *2 Apoc Bar* 24:3–4. Ezra is asking for revelation of the future.

■ **47** According to 3:1, Ezra is lying on his bed. Here he is told to stand at the angel's right, a position fitting for the revelation of secrets. The right-hand side was fortunate or particularly honorable; cf., e.g., 9:38; 1 Kgs 2:19; Ps 110:1; Luke 1:11; Mark 16:5; Matt 25:34; John 21:6; and *Hermas Vis.* 3.1.9.[59] The command to rise or stand up in order to receive a divine prophecy is found in the Bible, for example, Ezek 2:1, and see Num 23:18; Judg 3:20; and Dan 10:11. This does occur in Vision 2, but at the very end, before the Prediction 2 revelation of the eschatological recompense. It also occurs in Vision 3 (7:1) and in Vision 4, after the vision itself, where he is commanded in 10:33, "Stand up like a man and I will

(end); cf. also *Sifre Num Pinḥas* 139 (Horovitz, p. 185).

54 See also 5:56; 6:11; 7:75; 7:102; 12:7 ("in thy sight"); contrast 8:42; 14:22 ("before thee"), and cf. 7:104.

55 There are other repetitions in the book. Box suggests that the question is a traditional one and thus explains its repetition. He compares this with the repetition of the prophecies of the signs (e.g., 4:51—5:12; 6:11–28; and 9:3–4). Yet the only two parallels to this "traditional" question that have been adduced outside 4 Ezra are the close one in *Bib Ant* 19:14 and the somewhat more remote one in *2 Apoc Bar* 85:10, both works that have particularly close relationships with 4 Ezra. Moreover, the formulation in the three places in 4 Ezra is different from that in those sources.

56 Knibb suggests that 4 Ezra does not reckon the times because of the place that extreme expectations played in national disaster; he contrasts Dan 7:25b;

8:13–14; 12:7; and 12:11–12. He does not mention 4 Ezra 14:11–12, and see 14:11 Commentary. A similar search for precise knowledge may be observed in *b. Sanh.* 97b.

57 See further the discussion of revealed eschatological knowledge in 12:37–39 Function and Content, p. 373.

58 Harnisch, pp. 293–94, suggests that this is because of his lack of eschatological intensity.

59 Zech 3:1 does not contradict this; Satan there holds pride of place as prosecutor; cf. *IDB* s.v. In general, see "Left and Right" in *Encyclopedia of Religions*, 8:495–97. An interesting example from the Hellenistic world is Plutarch, *De iside et osiride* 361, who quotes Plato, *Laws* 771A–771B. In these texts the positive aspect of the right hand is highlighted.

instruct you." Then he received the angelic explanation of his vision. He is recumbent throughout two dream visions (Visions 5 and 6) but rises at the end of the second to give praise to God (13:57). In 14:2, God addresses him directly and he rises when he hears the divine call.

"My" is not in the textual witnesses but seems to be a most likely interpretation; of course, the phrase could simply mean "to the right." The last words of the verse are unclear. In fact, the angel shows Ezra both the parable and its interpretation.[60] But the text of the versions, except for the Armenian, reads "interpretation of a similitude." Armenian reads "form of a similitude," which, although it makes better sense, may in fact be due to the difficulty here noted.

■ **48** In 4:48–49 the author makes use of a parable, but it is not left as a rhetorical device but turned into a vision. The double, repetitive character of the visionary parable resembles 4:13–18 and 7:3–9, but in both those instances the parable remains rhetorical. Note, however, the rather similar double vision in Jer 1:11–14. In 4 Ezra these figures of speech are used with a didactic purpose. The parable may have become a vision here because of the increase of tension as the eschatological revelation of Prediction 2 approaches. On the imagery, see 7:61 with Commentary and 13:11.[61]

■ **49** No commentary.

■ **50** The image of the storm and the drops is very much like 9:16. The word "quantity" taken strictly here refers to the rain and fire, but it refers directly of course to the times, which is an exegetical conclusion that Arabic2, Armenian, and Georgian have made explicit in their texts. In fact, there is no need for the author to draw any more explicit conclusions here; the repetition of the verb "passed," taken up from 4:45, serves to make his intention clear.

■ **51** This verse contains two questions: "Will I be alive at that time?" and "What will happen then?" These are directly derived from 4:26, which says, "If you are *alive* at that time, you will *see wonders.*" In the interchanges following on 4:26, Ezra has determined that the age is close to its end. He then returns to the matters raised by 4:26. Furthermore, 4:52 is readily seen as a response to 4:51.

Box, following Kabisch, and in greater detail, claimed that the text of the verse should follow that of the Latin and Syriac versions, which read the second question as "Or who will be alive in those days?" This question he then saw as inappropriate to the response in 4:52 which talks of signs. Box regarded the roughness thus isolated as a mark of the interpolation of the "signs" passage (5:1–13) from a second source. On textual grounds the reading of Ethiopic and Georgian, with the support of Arabic1 and Arabic2, is at least as strong as that of Latin and Syriac. Both readings occur in Armenian. The corruption can be explained either as a haplography or as a dittography in Greek (see the textual notes). Therefore the decision between the two readings must be made on exegetical grounds. These have been set forth in the first paragraph.[62]

Violet 2 would base his decision between the two readings on *2 Apoc Bar* 41:1. Although that verse is somewhat similar to the present one, it cannot be used to support one or another reading in 4 Ezra. *In nuce* then, the reading accepted here fits the context, structure, and meaning of the passage and there is consequently no reason to doubt its originality. The problematic reading of Latin and Syriac seems to originate in a Greek corruption. For the general sentiment, compare 5:41 as well as Ps 39:5. The idea of a fixed time relating to specific humans may be observed in Job 14:5 and 14:13.

---

60 So the translations of Licht and NEB, with no textual basis. Equally unfounded is Myers's "the meaning by similitude."

61 The fiery furnace in a visionary context may be compared with Gen 15:17. Smoke and drops occur together in *2 Apoc Bar* 82:4 and 82:6 but in a very different context. Contrast the use of the imagery of smoke in 1Q27 1:6 (*DJD*, 1:103) and the "mist" in 4 Ezra 4:24. For a flying oven, cf. also W. von Soden, "Zum akkadischen Wörterbuch. 88–96," *Orientalia* 26 (1957) 127–28.

62 The only problem, and it is peripheral, is that the term "signs" does not occur in the question. It is not to be excluded that the "signs" passage does draw upon an oral or a written source (see below); see already Keulers, p. 50. The term "signs" might have come with that material.

Excursus on Natural Order

The Parabolic Use of the Natural Order
The order of nature or the natural world serves the author as a basis for comparison. It occurs repeatedly in this way in the dialogic parts of the book, where the use of this sort of didactic device would be most appropriate. The chief such instances of nature in parables are the following: 4:13–18—the forest and the sea; 4:48–49—the furnace and the clouds; 4:41–42; 5:41–53; 10:9–13—the womb and the mother; 7:3–9—the sea and the city; 7:52–56; 8:2—base matter and precious stones; and 8:41–43, cf. 9:17—seed and sowing. What is striking is that nearly all of these instances use the comparison with the natural order to show the fixed order of the world, or of nature, or of creation. This attitude is very much like that found in *1 Enoch* 2–5, where the order of nature serves (admittedly in a different way) as a paradigm for regularity and faithfulness.[63] Chapter 6:6 uses the order exhibited by the acts of creation as an overall demonstration of God's control of the eschaton.

Hortatory Use of the Natural Order
In a few places we find the use of the wonder of creation as an argument in the mouth of the seer. This contrasts with the cases mentioned in the previous section which were set in the mouth of the angel. Thus, in 6:38–54 there is an extended praise of God as creator which shows clear similarities with 6:1–5. Differing, however, from the angel's use in this last-mentioned passage, in 6:38–54 Ezra does not draw a clear conclusion about world order from the recital of the work of creation. Nonetheless, 6:38–54 is important for us, since it clearly reflects the author's sense of awe and wonder at the magnificence of the divinely created natural order.

The same sense of wonder comes to the fore in 8:8–11, the extraordinary passage on the creation of human beings. Again, as in 6:38–54, here also the seer draws conclusions about the working of divine providence. There is, of course, a theoretical contradiction implicit in the use as a comparison of the order of nature or the magnificence of the creative act of the growth of an infant in its mother's womb. The contradiction is with the view, also put forward in the book, that human life is but a fleeting thing and that the order of creation is hastening to its end. Consequently, one might argue, the order of nature is not a convincing paradigm for human action or divine providence since it is transient. Yet our author seems to be as innocent of this contradiction as he is innocent of a dualism of matter and spirit.

Order of Times and the Eschaton
The idea is also present in the book that the times and their order and length have been fixed by God in advance. This idea is most explicit, in a way, in 14:11–12, which speaks of the division of the time of this world into a fixed number of parts, most of which have passed. See also 4:36–37; 5:49; 6:5; 7:74; 11:44; and 13:57.[64] The end of the times is also a secret revealed to Abraham (3:14) and Moses (14:5). This implies that it is foreordained and can consequently be made known. Similarly explicit are a number of passages that speak of the times, the age, or the world reaching their end; note particularly 4:26–28, and see further 4:37 Commentary; 11:44; and 13:19.

In response to the seer's questions and urgings for a hastening of the end and speedy vindication, the foreordained character of this order of the times of creation is emphasized. Naturally, this is particularly clear in the first chapters: 4:36–37 and 5:48–49 are prime passages in this connection. In more general terms, 13:58 asserts the divine control of time and whatever things come to pass in their seasons. There is, of course, a strongly deterministic strain to these ideas, but it is held in tension with the idea of human free will.[65]

It should probably be taken to indicate the general cast of Ezra's religiosity that he does not get involved in extensive quasi-mathematical calculations. He also draws back, on the whole, from too great a specificity

---

63   L. Hartman, *Asking for a Meaning* (Coniectanea Biblica, NT Series, 12; Uppsala: Almqvist & Wiksell, 1979), has devoted a monograph to these chapters of *1 Enoch*. The matter of this excursus is discussed further in M. E. Stone, "The Parabolic Use of Natural Order in Judaism of the Second Temple Age," *Gilgul: Werblowsky FS* (ed. S. Shaked, D. Shulman, and G. Stroumsa; Numen Supplement 50; Leiden, Copenhagen, and New York: Brill, 1987) 298–308.

64   See 14:11 Commentary and particularly 4:37 Commentary.

65   In 3:6 Commentary, we dealt with those things which were prepared before creation. They include eschatological reward; see also 7:70, and cf. 7:26–27. Rowland, *Open Heaven*, 144–45, sensitively points to the ambiguity of predestinarian views of history in the apocalypses. Cf. also the tension between the ideas of evil heart and free will discussed in Excursus on Adam's Sin, pp. 64–65.

concerning the details of reward, heavenly matters, and so forth.[66]

The Term "End"

The very use of the term "end" can be construed to reflect part of Ezra's attitudes to the course of history. Naturally, the idea of an end that can be known in advance, that can be determined or predicted, is the function of a concept of the historical process that is totally fixed in advance.

There are a number of specific issues concerned with the term "end" in 4 Ezra that should be considered here.[67] Given the systematic eschatological scheme available to the author, in which the present age is followed by the messianic kingdom, and then by a new creation, the day of judgment, and the future age, it could be expected that the term "end," used in an eschatological context, denotes some specific point on the timetable of events. At this particular point and no other, one might assume that the present world or age will come to its consummation or the new world will commence. However, this is not simply so, and the matter is worthy of more extensive consideration.

In 4 Ezra "the end" is used technically, as is evident from the fact that it is sometimes employed without any attributive. Examples of this usage are 5:41 and 6:15.[68] What is odd is that in 4 Ezra "the end" in the technical sense refers to different events in the eschatological series. In two cases, there are outright statements that the end is the day of judgment: "This present world is not the end; the full glory does not abide in it; therefore those who were strong prayed for the weak. But the day of judgment will be the end of this age and the beginning of the age to come" (7:112–113). In 12:34 we read: "But he [i.e., the Messiah] will deliver in mercy the remnant of my people, those who have been saved throughout my borders, and he will make them joyful until the end comes, the day of judgment, of which I spoke to you at the beginning."

A number of other passages set "the end" earlier on in the cosmic timetable. In 11:39–45, "the end" is said to come with the destruction of the fourth kingdom (11:39, 44). In 6:26 "the end" is mentioned at the end of the Prediction 2 passage.[69] A similar setting of "the end" may also be seen in 5:41.[70] In 14:9, Ezra is told, "For you shall be taken up from among men, and henceforth you shall live with my servant and with

those like you until the times are ended." The context connects "the end" clearly with the peaking of evil in the messianic woes and the subsequent messianic kingdom.[71] Similar also is 12:9.

In a number of passages the end is an indeterminate future event. This is true of 3:14 and 14:5, both referring to the revelation of the end of times to elect individuals in the past. Two further passages seem to belong in this category, 4:26 (a difficult passage) and 6:15. These are discussed in detail in the Commentary on them.

The issue then arises that "the end," an indubitably technical term, is used to refer to two different things, or to both of them at once or unclearly to either of them. In spite of the attempts by Keulers and Kabisch,[72] these different meanings cannot be associated with two different eschatologies, one national and the other universal. A careful analysis of "the end" in context may help to resolve the problem. What eventuates when the twelve instances that have been cited are evaluated in context is that the supposed relationship between "the end" as the day of judgment and the universal eschatology, and that between "the end" as the onset of the messianic kingdom and the national eschatology, breaks down. In fact, the contextual analysis yields three other categories: *(a)* Three of the passages use the term "the end" to designate a central subject of revelation (3:14; 14:5; and 12:9). *(b)* Four occur in the eagle vision: 11:39; 11:44; 12:9; and 12:34. Of these, 12:34 identifies "the end" as the day of judgment, while for the other verses it is the end of the fourth wicked kingdom and the onset of the messianic age. *(c)* Three occurrences are in predictions of the signs of the end. Of these, 4:26 and 6:15 are bivalent, while 6:25 (occurring in the same pericope as 6:15) identifies the end as the messianic kingdom. In addition, 5:41 and 14:9 both identify "the end" as the messianic kingdom, and both have the mode and/or time of consummation as their context and the suffering of Israel as their central concern; only 7:112–113 fits the pattern of "universal eschatology" in referring both to the day of judgment and in concern with the general human condition.

Since, therefore, the term "the end" has different referents in the book and since this phenomenon is not explained by the "two eschatologies" theory, another explanation may be offered—"the end" is less a specific

66   See in detail, Stone, "Lists," 420.
67   See in greater detail in Stone, "Coherence and Inconsistency." The following paragraphs are based on that study.
68   In addition, "end" is quite often used in a nontechnical sense in the book. Thus, e.g., 6:11 is a nontechnical use in an eschatological context.
69   See Commentary there; see Stone, "Coherence and Inconsistency," 232–33.
70   The verse is difficult, and see 5:41 Commentary.
71   See Stone, "Coherence and Inconsistency." 233.
72   Keulers, p. 143; and Kabisch, pp. 67–70, 75 and passim.

point in the eschatological process than it is something like "the decisive point in the eschatological scheme." The careful examination of the instances of the use of "the end" bears this out.

Chapter 7:112–113 is the first explicit statement that "the end" is the day of judgment. In 7:106–111, Ezra responds to the angel's statement that there is no intercession in final judgment and argues that if there is intercession in this imperfect world, then it should exist in the world to come which is perfect. In 7:112–113 the angel points out to him that it is precisely because this world is imperfect that there is intercession in it,[73] but the day of judgment is the end of this imperfect world. Thus "the end" serves to emphasize the difference of this world order from the future, especially in the area of judgment. In the light of this, it is clear why "the decisive point of history" should be said to be the day of judgment.

A similar analysis shows that the two different meanings of "the end" in 12:30–34 are determined by the context and the specific traditions used. While 12:30 refers to the situation before the end of the fourth kingdom and is concerned with why the two little wings are reserved, and in 12:32 there is a specific tradition of the preservation of the Messiah for the end, presented in a verse describing the Messiah and his coming, 12:33–34 tells of the actions of the Messiah and his kingdom, and from the perspective of the messianic kingdom the decisive point, yet to come, is judgment.[74] Similar analyses of 6:7–10; 6:25; 11:39–46; and 14:9 also show that the event called "the end" in these verses is determined by context and associa-

tion of ideas.[75] Thus, although "the end" does not always refer to the same event, it is used consistently. It means primarily "the decisive turning point in history," and just what point this is in any given instance is determined by context, purpose, and association.

This being the case, it is clear that the idea of the end is deeply rooted in the concepts of predetermination of the historical process. That process, like the natural order, is fixed by God. The description of it in the terms implied here is important for understanding the author's attitudes toward the temporal and the spatial dimensions of the world surrounding him. It is God's creation, it moves to a fixed terminus, an "end," a decisive turning point, will change natural and temporal order. God built judgment and the things associated with judgment into the very fabric of creation.

Terminological Aspects of "End"
In 4 Ezra the term "end" is usually indicated by Latin *finis*, Syriac *šwlm'*, and their set parallels in the other versions.

The Latin *novissimus*, a common word in Latin 4 Ezra for "last," "last times," and so forth, is regularly paralleled by *'ḥr'*, *'ḥryt'* in Syriac, forms of *dxr* in Ethiopic, and *vaxčan* in Armenian.[76] In the Hebrew Bible this complex of language usually represents אחרון/אחרית.[77]

On the term "times," sometimes found in eschatological contexts, see the discussion in 7:26 Commentary. In 4 Ezra the expressions reflecting אחרית הימים seem to have fallen into the background, as is

---

73   In Stone, "Coherence and Inconsistency" this statement reads by typographical error: "that there is no intercession in it."

74   The charge of circularity is avoided here when we bear in mind that the author did not have to chose the term "the end" to describe these events. If he did so, it is because the term was related in his mind with the events described.

75   See Stone, "Coherence and Inconsistency," 240–41. Aspects of our position on this matter, the essence of which is set forth again in the preceding paragraphs, were challenged by P. Schäfer, "Die Lehre von den zwei Welten im 4.Buch Esra und in der tannaitischen Literatur," *Studien zur Geschichte und Theologie des rabbinischen Judentums* (AGAJU 15; Leiden: Brill, 1978) 256–63. In particular, Schäfer denies the idea that "end" means "the decisive point in the eschatological sequence." He claims that, especially in the cruxes in 12:31–34 and 6:7–10, our position carries logic too far and leads to false results (p. 262). He would resolve the exegetical and conceptual difficulties that we pointed out by giving "end" a

rather general sense, denying a focus on a particular point in the eschatological scheme. Yet his solution does not convince us, since it fails to account for the overall evidence of the book or the close exegesis of the texts. It is difficult, e.g., to regard 6:7–10 as anything but a rather specific question "when?" to which a specific answer is given, albeit in allegorical form. Consequently, this passage goes beyond an assertion of the "eschatologische Wendpunkt." The rabbinic usage, which Schäfer has presented in convincing detail, may have provided a false analogy at this point.

76   7:73; 7:77; 7:84; 11:9; 12:23; 12:25; 12:28; 13:20 (Syr *šwlmhwn dzbn'*); cf. 12:9 (Armenian *katarac*); cf. 10:59 (Ethiopic varies); Armenian alone omits 5:42; 6:34; 7:87; 8:50; 8:63; 13:18; 13:46; 14:22; Ethiopic and Armenian omit 7:95.

77   Thus, e.g., Syriac, Greek, Hebrew, Latin, Armenian in Gen 49:1; Deut 4:30; and Jer 30:24. Armenian uses synonymous *yetins* with all other versions parallel in Isa 2:2; Jer 23:20; Ezek 38:16; Mic 4:1; Prov 31:25; and Dan 2:28. A third word appears in a

particularly clear from the examination of *tempus* and parallels. In the Dead Sea Scrolls the expression קץ אחרון is coming into usage.[78] This is an expression which almost never occurs in Mishnaic Hebrew, where, in any case, קץ is rather rare. Perhaps it lies behind 4 Ezra's terminology here.

■ **52** "Signs" is the technical term used in 4 Ezra to designate those events called "the messianic woes" in other works. Thus it is also used in 5:1; 5:13; 6:11; 6:20; 7:26; 8:63; 9:1; and 13:32, all of these in the context of predictions of woes. The term is also found in other books with the same meaning.[79] The actual events constituting the woes are listed in 4 Ezra 5:1–12; 6:20–24; 9:3; and 13:30–31. They are also mentioned or referred to on a number of other occasions.[80] The chief parallel texts will be cited as appropriate in the Commentary on the relevant verses. Not only are the signs the events preceding the messianic kingdom (so 6:25; 9:7–8; and 12:34)[81] but they contribute also to the description of

the last, wicked kingdom in chapters 11–12. In general, they reflect the breakdown of the natural and social order which is the outcome of human wickedness.

The revelation of the signs is said to be "in part" because the description is continued in 6:11–28. Gunkel observes that the author has a dual concern. First, to know the signs of the end, but second, that too precise a knowledge would reflect on the character of God's rule. The limitation of such revelation to that which is permitted may also be observed in *Hermas Vis.* 3.3.4.[82]

Observe that here the angel asserts his lack of knowledge. Ezra's inability to know certain things was the main theme of 4:1–25. Knowledge also figured in 4:43. Ezra will learn what he desires at the eschaton. Even angels have limited knowledge, the present verse asserts and provides thereby a transition to the revelation of that which is permitted and known.

---

78   See, e.g., 1QS 4:16–17 and 1QpHab 7:7, 12.
79   *2 Apoc Bar* 25:1–2; 72:2; *Sib Or* 3:796; *b. Sanh.* 98a (bottom); *Otot HaMashiah* (Jellinek, *BM,* 2:58–63); *Sefer Zerubbabel* (ibid., 55); *Signs of the Judgment* (M. E. Stone, *Signs of the Judgement, Onomastica sacra and The Generations from Adam* [University of Pennsylvania

further series of instances. See further Stone, *Features,* 243 n. 37.

Armenian Texts and Studies 3; Chico, Calif.: Scholars, 1981] 22–23, 30–31, 42–43); Antichrist text in James, *Apocrypha Anecdota;* cf. *Sib Or* 2:154.
80   8:50; 8:63; 10:59; 13:16; 13:19; 14:16–17. See, in further detail, 5:2 Commentary.
81   8:50ff. is unclear on this point.
82   For similar ignorance, see Mark 13:32.

5

1 "Now concerning the signs: [a] behold, the days
  are coming when those who dwell on earth
  shall be seized with great terror, [b]
     and the portion [c] of truth shall be hidden,
     and the land shall be barren of faith. [d]
  2/ And unrighteousness shall be increased
        beyond what you yourself see, [e]
     and beyond what you heard of for-
        merly.
  3/ And the region [f] which you now see
        ruling
     shall be waste and untrodden, [g]
     and men shall see the land [h] desolate.
  4/ But if the Most High grants that you live,
  you shall see the earth [i] thrown into confusion after the third . . . [j];
     and the sun shall suddenly shine forth at
        night,
     and the moon during the day.
  5/ Blood shall drip from wood,
        and the stone shall utter its voice;
     the peoples shall be troubled,
        and the atmospheres shall be
           changed [k].
  6/ And one shall reign whom those who
        dwell [l] on earth do not expect,
     and the birds shall fly away, [m]
  7/ and the sea of Sodom shall cast up fish;
  and one whom [n] the many do not know shall
  make his voice heard by night, and all shall
  hear his voice.
8
     There shall be chasms [o] also in many
        places,
        and fire shall often break out,
     and the wild beasts shall roam beyond
        their haunts,
        and women shall bring forth mon-
           sters. [p]
  9/ And salt waters shall be found in [q] the
        sweet,
     and all friends shall fight [r] one an-
        other;
     then wisdom shall hide itself,
        and understanding shall withdraw
           into its treasury,
  10/ and it shall be sought by many but shall
        not be found,
     and unrighteousness and unrestraint
        shall increase on earth.
  11/ And one country shall ask its neighbor,
  'Has righteousness, or anyone who does
  right, [s] passed through you?' And it will
  answer, 'No.'
  12/ And at that time men shall hope but not
        obtain, [t]
     they shall labor but their ways shall
        not prosper.

Notes

1   a *Mercede* Georg; cf. Arm ψ and *Armenian Text
Commentary.*
     b Syr, Georg, cf. Eth; Lat corrupt; Arm "wonder"
(ἐκπλήξις Hilgenfeld).
     c Or "lot" Syr, Eth, Georg; "way" Lat, Ar1;
perhaps ὅρος/ὁδός; re Arm, see *Armenian Text
Commentary.*
     d *Sterelis a fide* Lat; Lat and other versions perhaps
come from Greek γὴ πίστεως ἄκαρπος.
2   e Syr, Ar1 add "now"; Arm is quite different and
tendentious, see *Armenian Text Commentary.*
3   f *Regio* Lat, so Eth; plural Georg, cf. Ar1.
     g Lat, Eth are obscure; Greek is uncertain but
perhaps ἄβατος (Box, etc.); for the translation given
here, see Syr, Georg, cf. Ar1 Arm.
     h So Syr, Eth, Georg; "earth" Ar1.
4   i Eth, Georg, Ar1, Arm omit; implied by Lat; "it"
Syr.
     j Text uncertain; *tertiam turbatam* Lat; "the third"
Syr; "three months" Eth; "third day" Georg; "three
signs" Ar1; "third vision" Arm.
5   k So Syr, Georg, Ar1, Ar2, Arm (5:6B); *gressus*
Lat; "stars" Eth ⟨ ἀστέρες for ἀέρες (Violet 1).
6   l So Lat, Ar1, Ar2; "many" Syr, *Eth, *Georg;
Eth, Georg omit to "many" 5:7, but Georg has "and
many," where "and" is probably secondary; Arm is
reworked.
     m *Commigratio* Lat.
7   n Following Syr, Ar1, Ar2; Lat *quam,* perhaps for
quem; cf. Vulgate.
8   o There is some uncertainty in the versions here,
but "chasm" or "abyss" seems to be supported by
Lat, Syr, Ar2, Arm (5:6B), and less directly by Ar1,
Eth, Georg; see Violet 2.
     p The versions offer "monsters," "signs," and
"wonders"; Violet 2 plausibly posits Greek τέρας,
which means "sign," "wonder," or "monster" and
particularly "monstrous birth"; see LSJ s.v.
9   q Eth, Georg, Ar2 omit.
     r "Conquer" Lat; Syr, Eth add "suddenly."
11   s Arm is much expanded in this and the next
verse; "righteousness that does right" Lat.
12   t The text is uncertain. Syr has a second clause,
"they shall toil and not find," cf. Arm; Eth, Georg
read "they shall marry and not be happy"; Lat, Ar1,
Ar2 have no middle clause. The readings of Syr and
Ar2 and of Eth and Georg both doubtlessly existed
in Greek. It is impossible to decide whether either
or both should be reflected in our translation. Arm
has a considerable Christian addition to this verse.

13/ These are the signs which I am permitted to tell you, and if you pray again, and
weep as you do now, and fast for seven
days, you shall hear yet greater things than
these."

Form and Structure

This passage is made up of predictions of the various
signs and woes that will come upon the earth. Taking up
Ezra's double question in 4:51 about the signs and his
life, and his own double response (4:52), Uriel now
proceeds to set forth the signs. In 5:1 he states that *the
signs* are the following: "days are coming when . . ." (5:1–
3), but he adds in 5:4 "*if you live*, you shall see . . . ," and
what Ezra will see is set forth from 5:4 to the end of 5:12.
Then, in 5:13 he concludes: "*These are the signs* which I
am permitted to tell you." Thus, just as he has said he
would, he has revealed signs but nothing about the seer's
life, although there is a reference to it in the middle. The
passage stands, therefore, within an *inclusio* marked by
the reference to signs at its opening and at its conclusion.

With 5:4b there is a shift from prose prediction to
parallelistic, oracular style. The oracular material itself
falls into four chief parts, each marked by a thematic
inclusio (not by a *Stichwort*):

    a. Cosmic signs (5:4b–5)
    b. Eschatological ruler (5:6–7)
    c. Chaos (5:8b–9b "another")
    d. Loss of wisdom (5:9c–11)

These are followed by two oracular stichs in contrasting
parallelism which conclude the signs (5:12).

While 5:1–3 is in prose, of the oracular material only
5:9c–11 interrupts the rhythmic, poetic style of discourse. It is notable, furthermore, that the prose verses
9c–11 use a very powerful literary figure to make their
point.

In Vision 2, Prediction 2 we find a structure very
similar to that here (6:18–28). There are preliminary
statements, "when" conditions (6:18–20c), and two
verses of concluding oracular stichs (6:27–28). In broad
terms the same structure is to be found in 7:26–44. First,
a series of statements occur dependent on "For, behold
the time will come" (7:26); next, there is a transition
(7:27) and then the actual prediction. The conclusion,
however, differs.[1]

Two more comments should be made on this passage.
In it, the author abandons the dialogic form that he has
been using. The vision opened with his prayer; it concludes with the prediction by the angel. Between these is
the dialogue between the seer and the angel, moving
from dialogic dispute to dialogic prediction. The present
passage, however, like a number of others in the book
(6:18–29; 7:26–44; 8:52–54; and 9:3–12), is direct
prediction by the angel. As such, it has an oracular style
that is examined in closer detail in the Commentary on
the several verses but that delights in poetic parallelism,
in somewhat mysterious predictions, and in the use of
evocative words like "suddenly."

The shift in style and character from dialogue to direct
prediction has led a number of scholars to assume that
the passage was inserted here from another document.
This thesis is dealt with in 4:51 Commentary. It is superfluous in its simplistic form, but it is based on the true
observation that a very distinct change in style and form
can be detected. This is purposeful, however, and part of
the structure of the book. The actual list of signs is highly
traditional in character and might be known from a
preexisting source (see Function and Content).

Function and Content

This prediction forms the conclusion to the first vision.
Its general role parallels that of Prediction 2 of Vision 2
and the various predictive passages in the third vision.
Moreover, it responds to the prayer and the dispute that
precede it, just as Visions 5 and 6 respond to Visions 1–
3. Prediction 1 moves from dialogue to prediction, just
as Vision 4 moves from the three dialogue visions to the
dream Visions 5 and 6.

The prediction chiefly concerns the terrible events
that will precede the eschatological redemption. The
parallels to the specific details are presented in the
Commentary to the various verses, but certain general
observations are appropriate.

---

1   See 6:11–29 Form and Structure, p. 164, and 7:26–
    44 Form and Structure, p. 204. The structure of
    9:1–13 is different, as is its context.

First, the idea that evil will peak before the end is found in many sources. This process will be marked by a disruption of social, familial, and natural order. This disruption will be the result of the wickedness of humans which, from the time of the covenant curses on, was seen as leading to a disruption of order and the influx of chaos (see further 5:2 Commentary).

Second, the chief biblical contexts in which the signs originated are the covenant curses in Leviticus and Deuteronomy and the various descriptions of the reaction of nature to the awesome epiphany of God, particularly in his wrath. To material issuing from these contexts of origin are added certain specific traditions, the most striking of which in our passage being that of the eschatological wicked ruler (5:6–7).

As was stated in the preceding section, this prediction falls into two parts. The transition from the prose introductory sentences to the poetic oracular text clearly takes place in the first part of 5:4, which commences the actual list of signs, while 5:1b, 2, and 3 are all dependent on "Behold, the days are coming when" in 5:1. These introductory verses are simple prediction; when the great events happen, the angel says, then if you are alive, you will see the signs. These are first described in 5:4a as confusion and then set forth in detail in 5:4b–12. Moreover, although the angel has already said that he cannot know about Ezra's life, before he starts to enumerate the signs he repeats that he does not know about this subject.[2]

Each of the divisions of the prediction that were listed above (Form and Structure, p. 107) contains a mixture of elements. The one named in the list, however, seems to be predominant and forms the *inclusio*. The same structural/stylistic mixtures occur in the other predictive passages in the book. The events described here, like those in 6:18–24, do not seem to be presented in chronological order.[3]

The literary-critical questions that bear on this passage are most important for its understanding. Above, it was observed that the passage differs in style and atmosphere from the preceding dialogic dispute and prediction. In the discussion of 4:35–36 the possibility was raised that the author had taken over that passage from preexistent literature but that he had admirably integrated it into the context. The same is true, so it seems, of 4:5–8. The prediction of signs here resembles the latter passage in that it too seems to be of a piece with other passages in the book.

The list lying behind 4:5–8 continues in 5:36–37; similarly, the eschatological predictions continue in 6:11–29; 7:26–44; 8:52–54; and 9:3–12. All of these are angelic prediction and not dialogical in character. They are all in a style that is widespread in the apocalypses,[4] and similar predictions occur in many texts: for example, *2 Apoc Bar* 48:32–41. Consequently, it is difficult to determine on this basis that they are parts of a separate literary document that have been mechanically inserted in their present context.[5]

So, even if we admit with Keulers and others that the author is using received traditions or even literary units, the precedent of his practice elsewhere in the book leads us to assume that he has integrated them thoroughly into his own discourse. If this is so, then the predictions of 5:2–3 surely refer back to the end of chapter 3 and to chapter 4. So Ezra refers in 3:29 and 3:33 to the evil of Rome which he himself has seen, while in 5:2 he is told that that evil will be increased far beyond what he saw. Equally, 5:3 can be seen as referring to the same events and providing, in consequence, the beginning of Ezra's consolation. That nation which now rules Israel will be made desolate; compare 3:28 and 4:23, which put the heart of Ezra's plaint.[6]

Commentary

■ 1 "Behold, days are coming": a common expression in predictive or prophetic contexts. See Isa 39:6; Jer 7:32; Amos 8:11; 4 Ezra 6:18; 7:26; 13:29; *2 Apoc Bar* 20:1; 24:1; 39:3; 70:2; et al. It may introduce prophecies of

---

2   Despite the observations of Harnisch, the exact time of the end is not under discussion here (p. 271 n. 2).

3   Thus, e.g., if 5:3 refers to the destruction of Rome, that should immediately precede the messianic kingdom; see Vision 5.

4   See, e.g., the texts quoted in 5:1 Commentary.

5   The other basis for this assertion disappears with our exegesis of 4:51–52.

6   It seems forced to interpret 5:2 of Israel, although this is attractive on structural grounds. "Portion of truth" and "land of faith" could, in Hebrew, also mean "true portion" and "faithful land."

weal or of woe.

For "terror," see 6:23. Closest is *2 Apoc Bar* 25:3, "A stupor shall seize the inhabitants of the earth"; *2 Apoc Bar* 70:2 relates that at the end God will bring "perturbation of spirit and stupor of heart" upon the inhabitants of the earth. The idea of panic cast upon men by divine or external force is also to be found in the Bible. It is one of the covenant curses in Lev 26:16; cf. 26:36 and Deut 28:20. It is brought by God upon enemies of Israel, for example, in Judg 7:22; see also Job 12:24.[7]

The expression "the inhabitants of the earth" occurs in 4 Ezra predominantly in eschatological contexts.[8] It is difficult, however, to discern any particular significance in this. Box suggests that it has a negative connotation in 4:39; 5:6; 6:24; 7:72; 10:59; and 13:30.[9]

The reading "portion of truth" or "lot of truth" should be accepted. This was a Greek reading, as is evident from the distribution of the witnesses, and seems original to 4 Ezra. Observe that it suits the literary context admirably, forming a good parallel to "the land of faith."[10] The image is, of course, that truth or faithfulness is a barren land, perhaps related to the biblical verse "Truth shall spring from the earth" (Ps 85:12). The hiding or barrenness of this land of truth here and in 5:9–11 should be compared with rabbinic statements that, as part of the messianic woes the Torah will be forgotten or obscured. This occurs *inter alia* in *m. Soṭa* 9:15; *b. Sanh.* 97a; and

Tosefta Derek Ereṣ 1 (Higger, pp. 243–45) and is much developed in *Midr. Haggadol* on Gen 41:1 (Margalioth, pp. 683–85). Intriguing in this connection is the expression found in all three sources: "and the truth will be removed." This must derive from Isa 59:15, and in *b. Sanhedrin* and *Midr. Haggadol* it is connected with it. This might be the "hiding" of truth in 4 Ezra 5:1, a supposition strengthened by the fact that the removal of judgment and righteousness is the subject of the preceding verse in Isaiah.[11]

This terminology is closely connected with that of the eschatological poems discussed in 6:11–29 Form and Content, pp. 165–66. It is striking that the closest biblical parallel to these poems is Isa 59:14–15, which contains the phrase discussed in the previous paragraph. Moreover, the closest parallel to our passage is in one of the eschatological poems, for in 4 Ezra 7:34, in connection with the judgment that will follow the messianic woes, the text reads, "Truth shall stand, and faithfulness shall grow strong."[12] The standing and strengthening of truth and faithfulness are, therefore, the exact reversal of their removal. This reversal will take place at the end of days, in the process of judgment.[13] Consequently, the hiding of the region of truth is part of the breakdown of cosmic order which will typify the events before the end.[14]

---

7 It is perhaps noteworthy that the terror cast upon enemies is one of the features isolated by von Rad as typical of Holy War. See G. von Rad, *Der heilige Krieg im alten Israel* (Zurich: Zwingli, 1951) 65; in addition to material cited in the text, cf. 4 Ezra 13:30 and *1 Enoch* 1:5. It should also be observed that the idea that violent emotions derive from an external force is common in ancient Israel as well as in Greek thought. See, in a different context, 4 Ezra 12:3 and Commentary there.

8 Harnisch, p. 104; quoting 3:12; 3:35; 4:21; 4:39; 5:1; 5:6; 6:18; 6:24; 6:26; 7:72; 10:59; 11:5; 11:32; 11:34; 12:23–24; 13:29–30; and 13:52. Note also "inhabitants of the world": 3:9; 3:34; 7:74; and 8:50.

9 See Box's commentary to 3:34. More probably, what is significant is that these events will affect all of humanity rather than any inherent connotation of the expression "inhabitants of the earth" itself.

10 Expressions analogous to "way of truth" (the variant reading here) may be observed in Ps 119:30. The hiding or revealing of "way" or "judgment" figures in Isa 40:10 and 40:28. Is the verse here an allusion to

the land of Israel? cf. 5:3.

11 See also Luke 18:8; the hiding of faith and wisdom features in *2 Apoc Bar* 48:36; cf. also *2 Apoc Bar* 39:6 and 70:5.

12 See also 7:114 and 14:17; *2 Apoc Bar* 59:10 includes "the place of faith and the region of hope" among the eschatological secrets revealed to Moses.

13 Judgment is sealed with truth (7:104) and the seal of God is truth (*b. Yoma* 69b). On truth in judgment, see Excursus on the Term "Judgment," p. 150.

14 The "land now hidden" which will be revealed before the messianic kingdom (7:26) is suggestive alongside the present verse, but the relationship between the two expressions remains unclear.

Box suggests that 5:1–12 is not part of his S source. In this he follows Kabisch. His arguments arise from the supposed problem with "signs" in 4:52 (see Commentary there) and from their incompatibility in "style and tone" with the wider context (see Function and Content, p. 107).

■ **2** The idea that evil will reach a peak in the period immediately preceding the coming of the Messiah is common. In many sources of the period of the Second Temple, as well as in rabbinic and Christian thought, this idea is combined with descriptions of the breakdown of social and cosmic order.[15] The various specific ideas associated with this view will be discussed as they arise in 4 Ezra. Its origins are complex and it comprises many originally disparate elements.[16] The messianic woes, from which the righteous will be delivered in the last generation, are often made up of these events. Specific phrases about the "increase of unrighteousness" are part of the prediction of woes in Matt 24:12; similar expressions occur in differing contexts elsewhere.[17] The idea is clearly expressed in many of the sources cited in notes 15 and 16 above.[18] The most striking biblical parallels are Gen 6:5; Joel 4:13; and Dan 12:1.

The evil "which you now see" may refer to Ezra's experience described in 3:29 and 3:33.

■ **3** If the exegetical line proposed in Function and Content, p. 108, is followed, this verse refers to the destruction of the Roman Empire. This is also the chief point of Vision 5. Moreover, the wealth of Rome which is so offensive to the seer (3:33), is turned to desolation. The seeing of the end of Roman rule is again emphasized, complementing Ezra's seeing in chapter 3.

■ **4** With "if . . . you live" cf. 4:26. The expression stresses the proximity of the end; it may be compared with 4:51, where Ezra asks about his own life span. That inquiry is rejected as unanswerable in 4:52. In several places, those who live at the end are called "survivors"; see 6:25 Commentary.

"The third" is problematic. The versions are uncertain (see the textual notes), and all that can be concluded is that here the Greek text apparently had the feminine, ordinal numeral. Divergent interpretations have been suggested, none of which is compelling.[19]

The reversal of the sun and the moon is part of the confusion of natural order which typifies the messianic woes. Exactly the same portent is found in *Asc Isa* 4:5 and a very similar one in *1 Enoch* 80:4–5. Biblical sources associated disturbances of the luminaries with the day of the Lord or with God's fearsome theophany. Particularly typical of these biblical contexts is the darkening of the sun, moon, and stars.[20] This is also said to happen as part of the messianic woes in a number of the writings of the Second Temple period[21] as well as in the New Testament.[22]

---

15 See, e.g., *Test Patr Levi* 4:1; *Test Patr Jud* 21:7—22:1; *Jub* 23:11–25; *1 Enoch* 80:2–4; 91:6–7; 99:4–9; 100:1–3; *Sib Or* 3:796–807; 5:74; *2 Apoc Bar* 25–27; 48:31–43; Matt 24:6–29 and parallels; Revelation 8–9 et al.; *m. Soṭa* 9:15; *Tosefta Derek Ereṣ* (Higger, pp. 243–45); *b. Sanh.* 97a–b; *Midr. Haggadol* on Gen 41:1 (pp. 683–86); *Test Dom* 1:3 et al. Other descriptions of the woes are to be found in *2 Apocalypse of Baruch* 70; *Apocalypse of Abraham* 30; cf. Dan 12:1. Related to the woes material is the long description of the curses in Philo, *De praem.* 127–152.

16 The chief texts in 4 Ezra relevant to this idea are the present passage; 6:13–25; 7:27; 8:50; 9:1–8; 11:40–43; 12:23–30; 13:16; 13:19; 13:23; 13:30–32; and 14:16. See also 4:52 Commentary on the term "signs." On origins of this complex idea, see 5:1 Commentary.

17 1 Macc 1:40; 2:30; Sir 47:24; *1 Enoch* 80:8; et al.

18 Cf. also 4 Ezra 5:10, etc.; *2 Apoc Bar* 48:31.

19 Gunkel, followed most recently by Myers, relates the number to Babylonian mythology (see H. Gunkel, *Schöpfung und Chaos in Urzeit und Endzeit* [Göttingen:

Vandenhoeck & Ruprecht, 1895] 268 n. 1 and 269 n. 1); Box and others relate it to Daniel's 3½; this is in turn connected by some with the 9½ + 2½ parts of the world age in 14:11, but just how remains a bit unclear (see Box). One might remark further that according to the *Apocalypse of Weeks*, seven weeks of history are followed by three weeks of eschatological events and also that three earthquakes precede the end, according to *Sefer Eliyyahu* (Even-Shmuel, *Midrĕšel Ge'ula*, 42), which could be connected with Latin read as "third confusion." One might even wish to relate the text here to the confusion that will follow the rule of the third of the eagle's heads (4 Ezra 12:30) or to the three hours during which the springs cease flowing, mentioned among the signs of 6:24, or to the passing of the four kingdoms (Y. Guttmann, oral). These all remain speculations, and see further 14:11 Commentary.

20 Isa 13:10; Joel 2:10; and 3:15; cf. Ezek 32:7; Isa 24:23; Amos 8:9; and Zech 14:7. Contrast the use of luminaries in Jer 31:34–35, where their unchangeability is stressed.

The use of "suddenly" is typical of apocalyptic revelations of this sort; cf. 6:23.

■ **5** "Blood . . . wood" is very close to *Barn.* 12:1, but it is not certain that *Barnabas* was quoting 4 Ezra (see Introduction, sec. 1.1). It recurs in *Signs of the Judgment* Latin 5/6, Armenian 4; compare *Ladder of Jacob* 7:5. It is clearly well suited to christological application, as is found in *Barnabas* and *Ladder of Jacob*.[23]

"Stone . . . voice" was apparently a proverbial expression perhaps deriving from Hab 2:11 (Box); see Luke 19:40. In 4 Ezra it is used as one of the signs of the end, a solemn and fearful omen.[24]

The idea that peoples shall be troubled is a common one; see, for example, *Test Patr Jud* 22:1; *1 Enoch* 99:4; *b. Sanh.* 97a; and *2 Apoc Bar* 48:37. It may be related to the idea of internecine strife which, at the end, will signal the breakdown of social order. This is introduced into the Armenian text of 5:5, and some phrases relating to it occur in 5:9.[25]

"Atmospheres": considering the textual evidence, it is difficult to understand the number of scholars and translators who prefer the unsupported reading of Latin ("stars shall fall") against the almost unanimous witness of the other versions. Various suggestions have been brought forth to resolve the reading of Latin or that of the other versions, none of which seems compelling. The sign can be seen as one of a number of portents conveyed by strange happenings in the natural elements, such as the first two in this verse; cf. also Arm 6:20C.

■ **6** The "unexpected king" is one of the traditional elements of the terrible events that are to precede the eschaton, and Baldensperger pointed out that the evil king's place in this pattern was assured from the time of Daniel on.[26] The relation of this figure to the "antichrist" complex of ideas, particularly in its political aspect, is well established,[27] and many scholars agree that the figure of the wicked king plays a part in the formation of the antichrist type.[28] Thus the idea of the eschatological wicked ruler is also to be found in *2 Apoc Bar* 40:1; *Test Mos* 7:2; and *Asc Isa* 4:2, and in many other sources in many of which it developed in the direction of antichrist or Armilus.[29]

By older scholarship this ruler is identified with some historical monarch, most frequently with Herod[30] or Octavian.[31] This view does not ignore the relation of this figure to the complex of the woes but maintains that it has also a specific historical reference. Contemporary events could be, and from time to time clearly were, interpreted as falling into the scheme of the messianic woes; some of the elements of the scheme of woes could be glossed over to facilitate this interpretation; others could be emphasized. Yet the very lack of detail in this passage,[32] a brief reference to an evidently well known tradition, makes it an inadequate basis for dating. The

21   *Sib Or* 3:801–803; 4:56–57; *Test Mos* 10:5; *Test Patr Levi* 4:1.

22   Matt 24:29; cf. Luke 21:25. In *Bib Ant* 34:1–4 it is part of a magician's acts.

23   Rivers flow with blood, *Sib Or* 3:684, and stones drip blood, ibid., 804.

24   Perhaps compare the talking tree, *Test Abr* A 3:3.

25   See *Armenian Text Commentary* for a full treatment of these and the other expansions of lists of signs in the Armenian version.

26   Baldensburger, pp. 180–82. A phrase similar to the text here may be observed in Sir 11:5.

27   So already E. Böhmer, "Zur Lehre von Antichrist, nach Schnackenburger," *Jahrbücher für deutsche Theologie* 4 (1859) 405–67, esp. 413–15; W. Bousset, *The Antichrist Legend* (trans. A. H. Keane; London: Hutchinson, 1896) 191–95; P. B. Rigaux, *L'antéchrist et l'opposition au royaume messianique dans l'ancien et le nouveau Testament* (Paris: Gabalda, 1932) 184.

28   Box, p. xxxi, and ad loc., Violet 2. Like Box, Keulers, who sees it thus, suggests that it draws on the idea of *Nero redivivus*, who will return to be the fearful king ·

         of the end (Keulers, p. 64). He compares with *Sib Or* 4:138f.; 5:33–34; 5:214–227; Violet 2 sees the passage as based on a Sibylline Oracle, but see Rigaux, *Antéchrist*, 184.

29   So, e.g., *Test Patr Dan* 5:6; 5:10; 1 John 2:18; 2:22; 2 Thess 2:4; and in many later sources. See for a sampling of the sources Stone and Strugnell, *Elijah*, 38–39.

30   E.g., von Gutschmid, "Apokalypse des Esras," 78.

31   E.g., Kabisch, p. 154; and Hilgenfeld, *Apokalyptik*, 237. See, in general, the comments in Introduction, sec. 2.1.

32   Cf. the brief treatment here, e.g., with Dan 7:7–14. The detail in 11:40–43 and 12:23–24 is greater than here.

lack of detail is a clear indication that the author had no particular ruler in mind. It is perhaps noteworthy that the antichrist figure plays a prominent role in the later Ezra writings in Greek and other languages.[33]

As for the birds that fly away, Jer 4:25 is similar to the context here. Birds were frequently regarded as bearers of omens.[34] In general, it is possible that certain of the omens here are structured on Ezek 38:19–20, which speaks of earthquake shaking the fish (see 5:7), the birds (see 5:6), and the beasts of the field (5:8). This passage of Ezekiel has surely been picked up in *Sib Or* 3:675–679.

■ **7** The exact nature of the sign involving the Sea of Sodom has been greatly debated. The reading "sea of Sodom" should be sustained, as it is witnessed by all texts.[35] Consequently, the sign is the presence of fish in the Dead Sea, and what remains in doubt is only whether they are in the sea (cf. Ezek 47:8–9) or are cast forth from it (cf. Isa 50:2).[36]

As for the second part of the verse, it has been even more troublesome for the exegetes. The reading of Latin, which implies that it is the sea that gives voice, is difficult to accept on text-critical grounds. Admittedly, this only reflects the Greek stage of the transmission, for if the Hebrew relative pronoun אשר stood behind the Greek, it would be impossible to determine the exact antecedent by means of the syntax.[37] Some scholars have viewed the voice as a simple portent, comparing, for example, Josephus, *War* 6.299, or *b. Sanh.* 97a.[38] This is certainly a possible interpretation, although no very clear parallels have been found.

It is also possible to interpret this half-verse in the light of the first sign in verse 6. We have observed above that the list of signs is formed of a series of smaller units of material, each of which is delimited by an *inclusio*, opening and closing with a variant on the same theme (Form and Structure, p. 107). The half-verse we are now discussing concludes one of these small units, which opened with verse 6. Here and in 5:6 an "unexpected" or "unknown" figure is described. Perhaps "make his voice heard" is related to the "speaking of great things" that characterizes the wicked ruler, the little horn, in Dan 7:8; 7:20; and 7:25. In any case, the wicked king of the end is not described in great detail in 4 Ezra, and no clear parallels to his "making his voice heard" have been uncovered.

■ **8** The chasms can be compared to the cleaving of the Mount of Olives (Zech 14:4) and the opening of chasms as a portent in *Sib Or* 3:341.[39] The idea of the fire breaking forth in many places might, when combined with the chasms that open up, originate in volcanic or seismic realities. These happenings are, of course, not presented thus by the text but simply as part of the signs that precede the end. No exact parallels are found.[40] When wild beasts wander far from their haunts, they come into settled areas and attack humans. This is one of the curses already in Lev 26:22. The monstrous births are another of these signs; cf. Codex Trev. 36, *Antichrist Text* (James, *Apocrypha Anecdota*, 1:154). For one aspect of these, see 6:21 and *Jub* 23:25; cf. Matt 24:19, which may perhaps be interpreted in this light.[41]

■ **9** The phrase relating to the salt water and the sweet is repeated almost verbatim in *Para Jer* 9:18. The sign is

---

33 See Stone, "Metamorphosis," 5–9.

34 See Qoh 10:20 and Job 35:11. For classical sources, see Pauly-Wissowa, s.v. *augures* (2.2, esp. cols. 2331–34).

35 *Contra* Wellhausen, *Skizzen*, Box, *APOT*, and Box. Kaminka's "sea of blood" is equally unacceptable.

36 See textual notes. According to *t. Sukka* 3:9 the waters of the Sea of Sodom are destined to be "cured"; see also Ginzberg, *Legends*, 5:242.

37 Thus, Gunkel's explanation that this is the voice of the sea would be impossible at the Greek level, although it might be acceptable at the Hebrew. See his commentary here, and for his and other views, see Box; Keulers, pp. 68–69.

38 See also *Tosefta Derek Ereṣ* 1 (Higger, pp. 243–45); cf. also the text of the "Book of Clement" quoted by Bousset, *Antichrist*, 268.

39 *1 Enoch* 18:11–12 and 21:7 also mention fiery chasms but in a somewhat different context. Cf. also *Od Sol* 24:5, and see differently Mic 1:3–4.

40 Keulers has set the fire in the context of cosmic conflagration, an idea found in a number of other sources which he thinks may be in the background of 4 Ezra, see pp. 66, 148; cf. also Stone, *Signs of the Judgement* 7 and commentary there. Volz would put the sign in the context of a view that fire lies under the earth (p. 324). Fiery rain or fire from heaven is mentioned by Luke 17:29 and *2 Apoc Bar* 27:10, and fiery signs in *2 Apoc Bar* 70:8. In spite of Box's suggestion, we have retained the word "often."

41 They were regarded as omens also in ancient Mesopotamia and in the classical world; see 11:1 Commentary. Some critics, e.g., Box, would introduce 6:21–22 into the text here, but that seems

the opposite of that in 5:7, where the salt water of the Dead Sea will be full of fish and thus sweet.

The conflict between friends forms the second sign in this verse. This is one element drawn from a larger complex statement of internecine strife that is the reversal of social order, just as the events of nature that are described are a reversal of its order. Other elements of this complex of ideas can be found in 6:24 and 13:31.[42] The lists of persons involved in conflicts have been expanded in the Armenian version of 4 Ezra, which reads, for example, in 5:9:

> And men shall fight with one another, sons with fathers and fathers with sons, mothers and daughters opposed to one another, brothers with brothers, friends with acquaintances, nations with nations, peoples with peoples, priests with priests, and minis- trants with ministrants.

The Armenian also expands 6:24 and 13:31. The same sort of conflict material may also be found in *Greek Apoc Esd* 3:12.[43]

These lists draw on biblical sources such as Isa 19:2 (MT and LXX); Mic 7:6; and 2 Chron 15:6, while similar material may be found in apocryphal,[44] New Testament, and rabbinic sources; see, for example, *1 Enoch* 56:7; *Jub* 23:19; Matt 24:7 // Mark 13:8; *m. Soṭa* 9:15; *b. Sanh.* 97a; and *Tosefta Derek Ereṣ* 1 (Higger, pp. 244–45).[45] They are further expanded in later sources. What is more, they occur beyond the purely Jewish and Christian spheres, and may be found in strikingly similar form in Mesopotamian texts as well as in Hesiod. One Mesopo- tamian text reads:

> City (will turn against) city, family will turn against family, brother will slay brother, friend will slay friend.[46]

So the text here seems a natural utilization of widespread ideas and formulation of the breakdown of human society at times of stress.

Here the conflict tradition functioned within the author's eschatological worldview. The conflicts will bring about widespread death, as the term and concept of "the survivors" shows (see 6:25 Commentary). Conse- quently, they form part of the process of separation between the righteous and the wicked that will take place at the end of days. This aspect of the conflicts will be discussed further below,[47] but the cumulative effects of the woes is well described in *2 Apoc Bar* 70:8:

> And it will happen that everyone who saves himself from the war will die in an earthquake, and he who saves himself from the earthquake will be burned by fire, and he who saves himself from the fire will perish by the famine.[48]

The final element of woes in this verse also continues into the first phrase of the next verse, that is, the hiding of wisdom. This typifies the generations before the end and will be reversed at the time of judgment; here the author repeats an idea that he has already raised in 5:1.[49] A striking parallel to 5:9–10 is *2 Apoc Bar* 48:36:

> And many shall say to many in that time, "Where did the multitude of intelligence hide itself, and where did the multitude of wisdom depart?"[50]

---

superfluous (cf. Violet 2).

42 See also 9:3. Different dimensions of the reversal of order may be observed in *2 Apoc Bar* 48:35 and 70:3– 5. A somewhat similar list of relatives, but used in a quite different context, may be seen in 7:103–104; see 7:100–115 Form and Structure, p. 248.

43 On the lists of conflicts, see *Armenian Text Com- mentary*, Excursus on 5:9; with the conflict of faith featured in the Armenian, cf. *Sib Or* 2:168–170.

44 A close linguistic parallel is Sir 37:2.

45 Cf. material in *Armenian Text Commentary* Excursus; see, in general, *Test Patr Jud* 22:1; *2 Apoc Bar* 70:3–4; 70:6–7; and *Sib Or* 3:635–636.

46 R. Biggs, "More Babylonian 'Prophecies,'" *Iraq* 29 (1967) 121; for further parallels, see *Armenian Text Commentary*, Excursus on 5:9; see A. H. Gardiner, "New Literary Works from Ancient Egypt," *Journal*

of Egyptian Archaeology 1 (1914) 104, quoting an Egyptian oracle text. There are numerous examples from Egypt and Mesopotamia.

47 So also Keulers, p. 85; see Excursus on the Term "Judgment," p. 151.

48 From a literary viewpoint, this verse is well compared with Isa 24:18. There too the cosmic earthquake features.

49 For parallels, see Commentary there; see also Keulers, p. 48.

50 See also Isa 59:14–15 and *2 Apoc Bar* 48:33. This verse is supposedly that cited by Cyprian, *Test. libri III ad Quirinium* 3:29. There it is embedded in a rather long passage attributed to "Baruch" which bears only general resemblance to *2 Apocalypse of Baruch* 48. See also 5:1 Commentary. Cf. the text with *Apoc Elijah* 3:85: "Les chemins se diront entre eux: 'Avez-vous

Another element that may be at play here is the idea of the search for wisdom. A series of texts from Job on contain passages describing a search for personified wisdom which is hidden. As has been pointed out, this may go back ultimately to a myth about wisdom that is lost and found. In the present passage this myth provided only one of the building blocks of a sentence which, by use of dramatization, stresses the degeneration of life that will be the central feature of the messianic woes.[51] The "treasury" or "storehouse" of wisdom is mentioned in 1 Bar 3:15.

■ 10 The first phrases of the verse are in an antithetical style, while the last phrase reflects a concept antithetical to that of the preceding verse. In the short wisdom poem in *1 Enoch* 42 it is also the withdrawal of wisdom that permits the flourishing of wickedness. The phraseology of the last part of the verse is comparable with 7:111.

■ 11 This verse concludes the literary figure that involves the personification of wisdom and an unsuccessful search for her that commenced in 5:9b. Questions are addressed to natural phenomena in a similar context in Job 28:14–22.[52]

■ 12 This verse is a reversal of blessings of the hands or works of mankind. No exactly similar passage was located, but statements in *m. Soṭa* 9:9 and parallels somewhat resemble it. Its roots lie, without doubt, in the covenant curse context, and it bears some resemblance to

Lev 26:20; 26:26; and Deut 28:29–31.[53] These two poetic stichs conclude the revelation of the signs themselves.

■ 13 Here the first vision experience comes to an end. Next follows a description of Ezra's reaction to the vision and then the narrative transition to Vision 2. The mention of the signs serves to seal the angelic prediction, just as it opened it. Fasts separate the visions of 4 Ezra in 5:20 and 6:35, while food is limited to plants in 9:26–27 and 12:51. Unfortunately it is very difficult to learn anything about any way of life or discipline followed by the apocalyptic seers designed to induce visions.[54] Moreover, the parallels lead to the conclusion that this fasting is not part of apocalyptic visionary discipline but rather related to repentance which, by common Jewish practice, was signaled by prayer, lamentation, and fasting. Naturally, fasting and repentance are appropriate activities in the purification and preparation of self. On the seven days' fast, see 6:35 Commentary. In Armenian 4 Ezra 5:20, Ezra is said to confess his sins; this is probably not original but is in line with the interpretation of the fast being offered here. Contrast the view of Myers (p. 199), who calls these "seven days of flagella-

entendu aujourd'hui la voix d'un homme marchant, qui n'est pas venu au jugement du Fils de Dieu?'" ("The ways say to one another, 'Have you heard today the sound of a man walking who has not come to the judgment of the Son of God?'") French translation by J. M. Rosenstiehl, *L'Apocalypse d'Elie* [Textes et Etudes pour servir à l'histoire du Judaism intertestamentaire 1; Paris: Geuthner, 1972] and see his commentary on this verse).

51   Chief sources are Job 28:12–28; 1 Bar 3:15–37; *1 Enoch* 42; et al. They are discussed in Nickelsburg and Stone, *Faith and Piety*, chap. 6.

52   Other parallels to the figure of speech have been mentioned in the Commentary on the preceding two verses. Amos 6:10, often quoted as a parallel, has similar phrases but differs greatly in context and content.

53   The reverse construction is found in Isa 40:31. Similar in language but different in context is James 4:2–3. Hartman, *Prophecy Interpreted*, 31, relates this passage to *Jub* 23:18; Philo, *De execrat.*, 141f.; and 1QpMic 17—19:2ff., united by the theme "man's labor is in vain."

54   See Stone, "Vision or Hallucination?"; and idem, "Apocalyptic Literature," 430. The structural function of the fasts and their nature is discussed fully in 5:20–22 Function and Content, pp. 118–19.

55   Keulers, p. 14, considers this to be weeping over the fate of Zion. See also 5:32 Commentary. On asceticism, see also 6:32 Commentary.

5

14 **Then I awoke, and my body shuddered violently, and my soul was so troubled that it fainted. ª 15/ But the angel who had come and talked with me held me and strengthened me and set me on my feet. ᵇ**

Notes

14   a Addition of Arm here; see Armenian Text Commentary.

15   b Addition of Arm here; see Armenian Text Commentary.

Form and Structure

This small narrative unit describes the physical and mental state of the seer after receipt of the vision. Similar sections are found in 4 Ezra following the visionary experiences but preceding the interpretations in Visions 4–6. Here the seer is frightened and faints and is strengthened by an angel. His state of mind and physical condition are similarly described in 10:27; 10:30; and 13:13b. At the end of Vision 6 he is apparently seized by exultation and joy and so walks in the field blessing God.[1]

It is difficult to determine to what extent these reactions are a traditional element and to what extent they may reflect actual visionary experience of the author. It is certain that they are formulated in traditional language, and the same basic reactions are described repeatedly in Daniel (so 7:15; 7:28; 8:17–18; 8:27; 10:9; 10:11). In Daniel they are described both at the end of the symbolic visions and as a conclusion to whole vision experiences. By way of contrast, such reactions are scarcely mentioned in *2 Apocalypse of Baruch.*

Our view is that behind the experiences that the book attributes, often in a fairly conventional manner, to Ezra lie real religious experiences of the author.[2]

Commentary

■ **14** Charles and others have regarded the word "awoke"

as an indication that this is a dream vision. It was pointed out in the 3:1 Commentary that it is distinctly not one, in contrast to Visions 5 and 6. Instead, the "I awoke" can be taken in the same sense as "he awakened me as one who is awakened from my sleep," which is how Zechariah describes his reaction to the vision he saw and the angel's approach to him (Zech 4:1). A similar use of the verb "awaken" where a visionary state and not sleep is involved may be found in the Gizeh papyrus to *1 Enoch* 14:25, which seems to be original. Thus the term "awaken" sometimes referred to the end of a visionary or trance state and not just sleep.

The physical syndromes of shuddering and fainting occur elsewhere, always in response to visions or numinous experiences, such as Dan 7:15 and 10:17b. Even if these descriptions are conventional in some places, they mostly go back to some original experiential event, since similar reactions are common to visionary experiences described in other contexts.[3]

■ **15** The expression "the angel who had . . . talked with me" is very close to Zech 2:2 and 4:1. The *angelus interpres* sets Daniel on his feet after his visions in 8:18 and 10:10–11 and strengthens him (10:18); cf. Rev 1:17. A similar psychological state and similar angelic action are graphically described in *Apoc Abr* 10:2–5.[4]

---

1   It may also be that the movement of the earth that follows Prediction 2 of Vision 2 belongs to this type of phenomenon.

2   On the experiential aspect of the apocalypses, see Stone, "Vision or Hallucination?" 47–56. See Excursus on Inspiration, where this issue is discussed in detail, and Introduction, sec. 4.

3   This matter is discussed in detail in Excursus on

Inspiration.

4   The reflection of genuine ecstatic states in this book was demonstrated by Scholem, *Major Trends,* 52.

5

16   Now on the second night Paltiel, a chief of the people, came to me and said, "Where have you been? And why is your face sad? 17/ Or do you not know that Israel has been entrusted to you ᵃ in the land of their exile? 18/ Rise therefore and eat some bread, so that you may not forsake us, like a shepherd who leaves his flock in the power of cruel wolves."
19   Then I said to him, "Depart from me and do not come near me for seven days, and then you may come to me and I will tell you the matter." ᵇ
20a   He heard what I said and left me. ᶜ

Notes

17   a "You have been entrusted with Israel" Syr, Ar1, cf. Ar2.
19   b Lat omits; Arm omits "and then . . . matter."
20a   c This phrase varies in the versions.

Form and Function

This section provides the transition from Vision 1 to Vision 2. The author has similarly separated the other visions by a small section of text, although they are not all involved with a narrative concerning the exiled community. Such divisions can be found in 6:30–34 (between Vision 2 and Vision 3), in 9:23–25 (between Vision 3 and Vision 4), in 10:55–59 (between Vision 4 and Vision 5), in 12:40–51 (between Vision 5 and Vision 6), and in 13:56b–58 (between Vision 6 and Vision 7). The only one of these which, resembling 5:16–19, contains the people's plaint and the seer's response is 12:40–51.[1] The variety of styles used in these transitions is another indication of the author's literary skill.

It is significant that this narrative section involving Paltiel follows the first dialogic vision, just as the other narrative section, also involving Ezra and the people, occurs after the first dream vision, that is, 12:40–51.

Commentary

■ **16** The name Paltiel is doubtlessly Hebrew פלטיאל which occurs in Num 34:26 and 2 Sam 3:15. Violet 1 suggests that the figure is based on Pelatia "of the heads of the people" in Neh 10:23; cf. 1 Chr 3:21.[2] It does not seem to us that Violet's suggestion can be proved.

It is significant that nearly all proper names in the book, with the exception of names of biblical characters, are "el" formations: Salathiel (3:1), Paltiel (5:16), and the two angelic names Jeraḥmeel (4:36) and Uriel (4:1). Salathiel and Paltiel, at least, might be names hinting at the role of their bearers: Salathiel, which could be (mis)translated "I asked God," a cognomen for Ezra the tireless questioner, while Paltiel could be taken as "God's refuge" (?"God has spared"), the leader of those who were not "consumed in Zion" (12:44).[3] Ezra's sad countenance was probably thought to be the result of the rigors, perhaps a fast, that he had undergone; cf. Matt 6:16 and also Armenian here.

■ **17** No commentary.

■ **18** As Knibb aptly comments, this verse serves to emphasize Ezra's role as leader of the exiled remnant of Israel. The image of the shepherd and his flock is often used in both biblical and postbiblical literature for the leaders of the people and their subjects.[4] Particularly striking from our viewpoint is *1 Enoch* 89, where, as part of an extensive animal apocalypse, Israel is spoken of as sheep and its

1   See 12:40–51 Form and Function for a discussion of this correlation which is an important key to the understanding of the book. Most significantly, here Ezra is greeted by the leader of the people and not by the people as a whole.
2   The name Paltiel occurs in postexilic sources. The names *Plty* and *Plṭyh* occur in the Elephantine papyri, together with a woman's name *Plṭh*. The former two are quite common; see A. E. Cowley, *Aramaic Papyri of the Fifth Century B.C.* (Oxford: Clarendon, 1923), s.v.; Josephus, *Ant.* 6:309 and 7:26 records the form φέλτιος for the biblical figure, but he mentions no one else of that name. The form here resembles

φαλτιηλ found in the LXX.
3   See 3:1 Commentary on Salathiel. Perhaps Jerahmeel ("God is merciful") also fits the angel appointed over the souls of the righteous dead. J. Heineman, "A Homily on Jeremiah and the Fall of Jerusalem," *The Biblical Mosaic: Changing Perspectives* (ed. R. Polzin and E. Rothman; SBLSS; Philadelphia and Chico, Calif.: Fortress and Scholars, 1982), following L. Prijs, points to the deliberateness of the theophoric names in the famous homily in *Pes. Rab.* 26 (p. 34).
4   Ezekiel 34; Zech 11:4–17, etc.; *Bib Ant* 19:3 and elsewhere.

angelic rulers in the postexilic period as shepherds. Naturally, shepherds who abandon their flock expose the hapless sheep to fierce wolves; see Acts 20:29, cf. Matt 10:16 and parallels, from which derived *2 Clem.* 5:1–4. A quite remarkable parallel is quoted by Ginzberg, *Legends,* 6:383, from Targ 2 of Esther 1:2 (end) "where it is said that Pelatiah the son of Benaiah . . . remonstrated with Nebuchadnezzar on account of his cruelty to the Jews. He said to him: 'When one delivers his flock to a shepherd and a bear comes and snatches away a sheep, of whom will it be required?' The king answered: 'From the shepherd will it be required.'" Whereupon Pelatiah rejoined: 'Let thine ears hear what thy mouth has uttered.' . . . The similarity between the words of Pelatiah in Targum and those of Paltiel, 'the

prince of the people,' (comp. Ezek. 11:1), in 4 Ezra 5:16–18 is obvious, though in this pseudepigraphic writing it is Ezra who is the shepherd and not Nebuchadnezzar, as in the Targum."

The same concern of the people at being left by Ezra also comes to the fore in 12:40–50 and, somewhat differently, in 14:23–36. See also *2 Apoc Bar* 32:9 and *Test Mos* 11:9.

■ **19** "The matter" is perhaps the answer to the questions at the end of 5:16.

■ **20a** On the purpose of the fast and lamentation, see 5:13 Commentary. The seven-day fast is dealt with there and also in 6:35 Commentary. *Greek Apoc Esd* also opens with a fast, though it is a much longer one (see 1:3; 1:5).

5

20b	So I fasted seven days, mourning and weeping, as Uriel the angel had commanded me.
21	And ᵃit came to pass,ᵃ after seven days the thoughts of my heart were very grievous to me again. 22/ Then my soul received ᵇ the spirit of understanding, and I began once more to speak words ᶜ in the presence of the Most High.

Notes

21   a–a So Lat, Syr, Georg, Arm; other versions omit.

22   b So Syr, Eth (emended), Georg, Arm; *resumpsit* Lat.

c So Lat, Arm, cf. Syr; Eth, Georg, Ar1, Ar2 omit; both readings probably existed in Greek; cf. 3:13, where Ar1 and Ar2 also omit, and contrast 6:36.

Form and Function

These few lines continue and complete the narrative transition from Vision 1. They refer back to the angelic commandment in 5:13 (the fasting) and also to the introduction to Vision 1. Each of the main features of that introduction is reproduced, with a good deal of verbal identity as well. A similar pattern may be found in the introduction to Vision 3, except for a reversal of the order of the last two elements. Vision 4 is very similar as well, but Visions 5 and 6, as has already been observed, break this pattern, since they are true dreams. Consequently, there was no need to describe the context of the onset of inspiration in them. Vision 7 is different from all of the preceding Visions 1–4:

	Vis 1	Vis 2	Vis 3	Vis 4
1. Setting and time	3:1a	5:21a	6:35	9:26–27
2. Seer's distress	3:1b	5:21b	6:36a	9:27b
3. Inspiration	3:3a	5:22a	6:37	9:28a
4. Onset of speech	3:3b	5:22b	6:36b	9:28b

Visions 1–3 are set in Ezra's room in Babylon, Visions 4–6 are set in the field called Ardat, while Vision 7 is under an oak in the field. The pivotal role of Vision 4 is thus clear.[1] On the one hand, it is described as taking place in the same way as Visions 1–3; on the other, it is in a new physical setting which it shares with Visions 5–7. As in Vision 1, here the introduction is followed by Ezra's plaint.

Function and Content

This passage is the introduction to Vision 2. It uses the description of Ezra's inspiration to set the stage for the address that follows. The autobiographical, first person narrative is preserved. The passage not only sets the stage for the following prayer, it also indicates the continuity of Vision 2 with Vision 1 by relating the execution of the commands given at the end of Vision 1 by Uriel (5:13). Furthermore, by its similarity in structure and wording with the introductions to Visions 3 and 4 it serves to integrate Vision 2 firmly into the ongoing pattern of the book. This end is also served by the emphasis both in 5:13 and in 5:20–22 on the fact that the content of Vision 2 complements that of Vision 1. In 5:13, Ezra is told to "pray *again*"; that he shall hear "yet *greater* things than these"; in 5:21 his thoughts are said to be grievous *again*; then his soul "receives the spirit of understanding" (5:21) and he begins "*once more* to speak" before the Most High (5:22).

This series of stressed repetitions impressively and obviously anchors Vision 2 very firmly in the progress of the book. It indicates that Vision 2 will go through and beyond the positions reached in Vision 1.

The nature of the fast undertaken by Ezra has been discussed. It is related more to mourning and repentance than to an ascetic practice or discipline (see 5:13 Commentary). It may be that fasting and prayer are regular before apocalyptic visions, as some have maintained.[2] Nonetheless, the mourning brought up here is not mentioned in Uriel's injunctions in 5:13; but compare also 3:1–2. A number of scholars sought the significance of the fasts of the first three visions in contrast with the eating of flowers of the fourth.[3] This matter is most

---

1   See Introduction, sec. 4.3.3, on this. On the structure of these introductions, see also 3:1–3 Form and Structure, pp. 53–54, and in particular Excursus on Inspiration, p. 121. The significance of the change in regimen before Vision 4 was also discussed by Brandenburger, *Verborgenheit,* 58. His analysis of the Injunctions and Narratives is designed of course, to support his views of the development of the book,

but he has been most sensitive to many of the points made here.

2   Knibb; yet his examples are taken from Daniel 9 and *2 Apoc Bar* 21 of which the former serves as a prototype for 4 Ezra (see 5:13 Commentary) and the latter stands in a literary relationship with 4 Ezra (see Introduction, sec. 5.1.5).

3   See 9:26–28 Form and Structure on possible

complex, and the eating of the flowers or the grass in 9:24; 9:26; etc. is discussed below.[4]

Periods of prayer and fasting or other special food intervene between the visions of the book:
Between—

Vision 1 and 2	7 days' fast [5:13; 5:19–21]
Vision 2 and 3	7 days' fast [6:31; 6:35]
Vision 3 and 4	7 days' eating of flowers [9:23; 9:27]
Vision 4 and 5	2 days [10:59; 11:1]
Vision 5 and 6	7 days' eating of flowers [12:51; 13:1]
Vision 6 and 7	3 days [13:56; 13:58; 14:1]

In *2 Apocalypse of Baruch* four of the visions are also separated by 7 days' fasts, viz.:
Between—

Vision 1 and 2	7 days' fast [9:2; 10:1]
Vision 2 and 3	7 days' fast [12:5]
Vision 3 and 4	7 days' fast [21:1]
Vision 5 and 6	7 days' fast [47:2]

2 Apocalypse of Baruch also has seven visions, as does 4 Ezra.[5]

Breech made much of the point that the shift from fasting to the eating of flowers symbolizes and marks Ezra's shift in the book from distress to consolation.[6] And indeed this point is well taken, although we would prefer to modify his formulation (see Introduction, sec. 3.4). Others have compared the seven days' fast here to the seven years' abstinence in *Test Patr Reub* 1:9–10 and

Test Patr Jos 3:4. The chief comparison, however, has been made with Dan 10:2–3. Yet, although a three weeks' period is mentioned there (see below), what is described, as Kaminka notes, is not a complete fast but an abstinence from certain foods and actions, such as is normal Jewish mourning custom.[7] 4 Ezra 14:43 mentions specifically Ezra's forty days' abstinence from eating and drinking when he received the revelation of scripture. That is not described as fasting.[8] Thus the question of just what type of abstinence is being described here must be regarded as an open one and is discussed further in 9:24 Commentary and in 9:26–28 Form and Function.

Excursus on Inspiration

Inspiration in 14:37–38

The concepts of mind and understanding play a great role in 4 Ezra. This terminology derives from the wisdom tradition, although it is used very differently in various contexts in the book. The first passage to be considered is 14:37–48. It describes the giving of the Torah, indeed of the whole of the Bible and the esoteric books through Ezra. They had been destroyed or lost, we are told, in the destruction of Jerusalem.[9] In 14:22, Ezra has prayed to God to send his "holy spirit" into him so that he may write the Bible again and, as a result, humans who wish to live at the end can find the path. God responds by promising (v 25) to "light the lamp of understanding" in Ezra's heart which shall not be put out until he has written the whole Bible.

The process of Ezra's inspiration is then described in the most graphic terms; he is given a cup to drink "full of something like water, but its color was like fire"

---

4   See 9:26–28 Form and Function, p. 304.

5   *Test Patr Naphth* 6:1 also has a seven days' interval between visions. The literary structure of *2 Apocalypse of Baruch* has recently been studied by G. B. Sayler, *Have the Promises Failed: A Literary Analysis of 2 Baruch* (SBLDS 72; Chico, Calif.: Scholars, 1984). See particularly pp. 11–39. Although differing from

interpretations of this. A fast preceding Vision 1 is not mentioned in the text but seems to be assumed; see 6:35 Commentary. Our interpretation both of the fast and of Ezra's ecstatic experience (5:20–22) is radically different from that of Myers, who says: "The seven days of flagellation only served to intensify the concern of Ezra. His thoughts became even more perplexed, but he composed himself enough to resume his discourses with the Lord" (p. 199).

the outline here in some respects, she maintains the sevenfold division of the book.

6   Breech, "These Fragments," 272.

7   Kaminka also raises the question of whether the fasts included the Sabbaths, upon which day fasting is not permissible. He also compares *Jub* 50:12 and Judith 8:6, both of which mention the cessation of fasts on the Sabbath (and Judith on Friday and certain other days as well).

8   If fasting means complete abstinence from food and drink, this cannot have lasted seven days, except under miraculous conditions.

9   See 14:19–21, cf. 4:23, and in detail 14:1–2 Function and Content, pp. 411–12.

(14:39). When he had drunk it, he says,

> 40 My heart poured forth understanding,
> and wisdom increased in my breast,
> and my spirit retained its memory,
> 41 and my mouth was opened, and was no longer closed.

This passage is most significant and the following chief points should be noted: (1) God's holy spirit lights the "lamp of understanding" in Ezra's heart (14:25). (2) Ezra's receipt of the spirit is described in terms of drinking. This is reminiscent of: *(a)* Ezekiel's consumption of a scroll (Ezek 2:8—3:3; Rev 10:9–10); *(b)* the Hellenistic theme of "divine drunkenness" as a way of describing inspiration, which is particularly striking in Philo's *De ebr.*:

> Now when grace fills the soul, that soul thereby rejoices and smiles and dances, for it is possessed and inspired, so that to many of the unenlightened it may seem to be drunken, crazy and beside itself. . . . For with the God-possessed not only is the soul wont to be stirred and goaded as it were into ecstasy but the body is also flushed and fiery, warmed by the overflowing joy within, which passes on the sensation to the outer man, and thus many of the foolish are deceived and suppose that the sober are drunk. Though, indeed, it is true that these sober ones are drunk in a sense . . . and they receive the loving-cup from perfect virtue. (146–148)[10]

and *(c)* the various "cups of poison" and the like which are mentioned in biblical prophecy. God gives them to his enemies to drink.[11] (3) As a result of this, his "heart poured forth understanding and wisdom increased in [my] breast." (4) Verses 40c and 41 are parallel; they describe that aspect of Ezra's mental state which fitted him for dictation of sacred scripture, viz., that his *spirit* retained its *memory*, that is, his mind, as we would say, kept clearly the "wisdom" and "understanding" which resulted from drinking the holy spirit, while his tongue was able to articulate what he remembered. Thus these verses describe (1) the onset of inspiration; (2) the feeling of enlightenment that followed ("heart," "breast"); (3) the retention of the content of this in his spirit; and, finally, (4) his inspired ability to articulate this and dictate it *(os).*[12]

Interestingly, the secret revelation given in this vision is also described in wisdom language that intersects with the psychological terminology here under consideration.

> For in them is the spring of understanding,
> the fountain of wisdom,
> and the river of knowledge. (14:47)[13]

This remarkable passage, then, is an unusually full description of what must have been seen as the very summit of revelatory experience. Ezra—a new Moses—receives the Bible, overt and covert books alike, and this is described as a pneumatic experience.

---

10 Cited from F. A. Colson and G. H. Whitaker, *Philo* (Cambridge, Mass., and London: Harvard University and Heineman, 1954), 8:395. See in further detail the excellent study by H. Lewy, *Sobria Ebrietas: Untersuchungen zur Geschichte der antiken Mystik* (BZNW 9; Giessen: Töpelmann, 1929), which deals in detail with this metaphor. Lewy points out that this is also the interpretation given the incident by Clement of Alexandria, *Stromateis* 1.22, 149.3. A.-J. Festugière, *L'hermétisme et la gnostique païenne* (Paris: Aubier-Montaigne, 1967) 100–112, deals specifically with baptism in a *krater* (*Corpus Hermeticum* 4:3–4) and adduces much interesting material. The same image recurs in *Od Sol* 11:6–8.

11 See, e.g., Isa 51:17; 51:22. Cf. also "cup of salvation" in Ps 116:13.

12 This interpretation, in part, follows Box's comments. Lewy contrasts the passage with *Asc Isa* 6:10–16. There, however, although the visionary was in a trance, he did retain the vision's content and recount it later (cf. 10:16). The same theme recurs in Lydus, *De mens* 4.47 (ed. Wünsch); see Lewy, *Sobria Ebrietas,* 95 n. 2, for references. This text refers both to the scribes not being swift enough to record the flow of oracular speech and also to the fact that the Sibyl's memory did not retain the content of the revelation. The combination of two distinctive elements of

Ezra's seventh vision in this pagan text suggests a common *topos.* Lewy adduces a number of further parallels, among the most notable of which is the Prologue of the *Sibylline Oracles,* lines 85–90. There the fault of the secretaries is cited, who cannot keep pace with the flow of speech or even were ignorant, and not any fault of the prophetess. The same tradition of the Sibyl's lack of memory and the scribe's inaccurate record because of the speed of the Sibyl's speech is found in the scholion to Plato, *Phaedrus* 224B. There the absence of meter in some Sibylline verses is attributed to this cause. Somewhat different is pseudo-Justin *Cohortatio ad graecos* (*PG* 6:309), where the erroneous meter is attributed to the ignorance of the scribes. For the Sibyl's memory of what had been said ceased when the inspiration stopped. Note Ezra's deliberate reversal of this! Further developments of the theme may be found in Lewy, ibid. He points out that Jewish and Greek views of prophecy differ over the point of whether the prophet understands what he is saying. See discussion in 14:23–26 Function and Content, p. 429.

13 On the double meaning of "understanding," see p. 122 below.

Inspiration in the Framework of Visions 1–4
Elsewhere in the book as well, Ezra talks of inspiration.
The most explicit passages that describe his psychological state occur in the framework of the seven
visions. In each of the first four visions three different
stages of inspiration are recounted.[14] a. First is the
seer's feeling of distress at the problem that is agitating
him. The language that is used to describe this is
uniform:

> *I was troubled* as I lay on my bed, and my *thoughts*
> welled up in my heart. (3:1)
> The *thoughts* of *my heart* were very *grievous* to me.
> (5:21)
> *My heart* was *troubled* within me. (6:36)
> *My heart* was *troubled* again as it was before. (9:27)[15]

Here the place of *thoughts* that are *troubled* is the *heart*.
It has even been proposed that this mourning was a
technique for the induction of ecstasy.[16] b. The onset
of inspiration is then described: an arousal of the spirit,
a distress of the soul, or an opening of the mouth:

> My spirit was greatly agitated. (3:3)
> Then my soul recovered the spirit of understanding.
> (5:22)
> My spirit was greatly aroused and my soul was in
> distress. (6:37)
> My mouth was opened. (9:28)

The descriptions of this stage vary somewhat. In 3:3
and 6:37, Ezra's agitation and arousal of spirit are
mentioned. This is apparently the subjective aspect of
the event described in 5:22 and 9:28, the actual onset
of inspiration. It is noteworthy that, in contrast with
stage a, the language of *spirit* is prominent. The arousal
of Ezra's spirit is the same as his receipt of revelation.
Both expressions refer, it seems, to the one event, and
its result is Ezra's mouth being opened. The passive
expression "was opened" (9:28) clearly indicates the
inspirational aspect of this experience.[17] c. After the
onset of inspiration, Ezra begins to speak:

> And I began to speak fearsome[18] words to the Most
> High. (3:3)
> And I began once more to speak words in the
> presence of the Most High. (5:22)

> And I began to speak in the presence of the Most
> High. (6:36)
> And I began to speak before the Most High.
> (9:28).[19]

Visions 1–4 and Vision 7 Compared
It is noteworthy that the same three stages of inspiration connected to the same anthropological elements
occur in Vision 7 (14:40–41). There is a significant
difference, however, in the situation in Visions 1–4
and that in Vision 7. In Visions 1–4 the inspiration
comes upon the seer following upon his distress and
agonizing, while in Vision 7 it follows upon his
drinking of the goblet of inspiration. This difference is
correlated with the contrast in content—Visions 1–4
are worry, concern, and subsequent arousal; Vision 7 is
all exultation and rejoicing:

> And when I had drunk it
> My *heart* poured forth *understanding,*
> and *wisdom* increased in my *breast.*

(Contrast the "troubled thoughts" of Visions 1–4.)
> For *my spirit* increased its memory. (14:40)
(The onset of inspiration, related to the spirit in
Visions 1–4, has here been described as the drinking of
the goblet.)
> And *my mouth was opened,* and was no longer closed.
> (14:41)
(This element has already been introduced into the
descriptions of the inspiration in Vision 4, which once
more in this matter is intermediary between 1–3 and
5–7.)

Here again heart and breast denote the intellectual
capacities—thought—while the spirit and the tongue
are the inspiration and the power of articulation. This
is exactly the same series as in Visions 1–4. Moreover,
there Ezra speaks his prayer; here he dictates the
sacred books—again a functional equivalent.[20]

Somewhat like these passages of 4 Ezra is the
introduction to *2 Enoch* (1:3–5). He is lying on his bed

14 See also 5:20–22 Form and Structure, p. 118.
15 Visions 5 and 6 are different—they are dreams and
the onset of the dream is described simply, "I had a
dream" (11:1) and "I dreamed a dream in the night"
(13:1). Vision 7, which is different from all the
preceding ones, has been described above.
16 See Merkur, "Visionary Practice," 9–19.
17 Since Visions 5 and 6 are dreams, this stage of the
inspirational experience is not relevant to them. On
Vision 7, see below.
18 Latin *(verba) timorata*, Syriac *dḥylt'*, etc. The Greek
was likely φοβερός and the Hebrew נורא. Arm *ahagin*,

etc. Bousset-Gressmann point out the parallel
expressions in 5:22 and in *2 Apoc Bar* 10:1: "the word
of God came upon me" (p. 396).
19 Anxiety or fear occurs only in the first vision at this
point (Merkur, "Visionary Practice," 20). Note the
somewhat similar terms in Ezra's address to his soul
in 8:4. The three stages of inspiration describe also a
movement from passivity toward activity on the part
of the seer.
20 Passive expressions involving the mouth are quite
common to describe the onset of inspired speech. Cf.
Deut 18:18; Isa 51:16; 59:21; Jer 1:9; and Ezek 33:1;

sleeping; he is distressed and dreams that he is weeping. Then he dreams of two huge men who summon him and awakes and sees them. The elements of bed, distress, and inspiration are shared with 4 Ezra. The actual ecstatic experience is different. Somewhat similar to 4 Ezra are also the passages in *2 Apocalypse of Baruch* that establish a relationship between weeping and the onset of vision; note particularly, however, 6:2–3 and compare 36:1. Compare also *3 Apoc Bar* 1:1–3, where the combination of weeping, prayer, and vision also occurs. See also *Test Patr Levi* 2:3–6.[21]

The Seer's Response

In the dream Visions 5 and 6, as well as in the waking Vision 4, the seer's response to the visionary experience is described. In these descriptions the same psychological and anthropological language is used as in the descriptions of inspiration in Visions 1–4. The seer's response is described in 10:28 as "overwhelming bewilderment";[22] he faints and is said to be deprived of his understanding (10:30). The angel encourages him, asking, "Why are your understanding and the thoughts of your mind troubled?" (10:31). Ezra's response to the vision is bewilderment described in terms like those used for stage a above.

A similar passage, 12:3–9, follows the eagle vision (Vision 5). Ezra awakes "in great perplexity of mind and great fear" (12:3). He reproaches his own spirit for searching to understand the ways of the Most High and bringing this spiritual exhaustion upon him (12:4–5).[23]

"Understanding the Way of the Most High"

In 3:29, Ezra, having seen the fate of Israel and the wealth of Babylon, cries out that his heart has failed him, for God has not shown how God's way may be comprehended. The search for this comprehension is the leitmotif of the dispute that follows, being set out in 4:2 and concluded in 4:22.

The angel's two riddle questions, 4:5–9 and 4:13–19, are designed to show Ezra that he cannot understand the way. The "heart" of 3:30 is the site of understanding, the faculty of thought. This accords with the use of the term in 3:1; 5:21; 9:27; and 14:40. This understanding, the angel claims, is human, limited, and corruptible (4:11; 4:21). Ezra does not deny this but claims that what he wishes to know is within the human range. Ezra sees the search for

understanding the way of the Most High to be at the heart of purposeful human existence. It is better, he claims, to die than to suffer and not understand why (4:12). Why, he asks, were we given the "power of understanding"? In this passage, (1) heart = mind = power of understanding; (2) it is human and limited; and (3) its satisfaction is central to purposeful human existence.

At the start of the second vision, in 5:33–40, a passage like the one above recurs. In it the terminology differs from that in chapter 4, and the stress on comprehension of the way of the Most High is markedly less.

In 5:33 the angel reproaches Ezra with his distress,[24] to which Ezra responds that his reins distress him all the time when he seeks to comprehend the way of the Most High (the only time the expression occurs in the passage; contrast chapter 4). To the angel's riddles Ezra responds that only the superhuman can know these things but that he is "without wisdom." The angel assents, saying that Ezra cannot know God's judgment.

Notable here are the following points: (1) In Latin, *mens* serves here where "heart" served in chapters 3–4; (2) "reins" also plays the same role; (3) understanding the way of the Most High is described as "discovering his judgment"; and (4) understanding is referred to as knowledge and wisdom.

In both of these passages, and particularly in the first one, not the problematic of the situation itself but that of the comprehension of the situation is set at the peak of Ezra's aspirations. The instrument of understanding is "heart, mind, reins." At the end of 5:31–40, Ezra does not repeat his demand to understand the way of the Most High. Instead, he seems to accept the limitations of his wisdom and insight. Yet in 12:4 he can still speak of the search for understanding as the motive for his receiving of visions.

Ezra's Plaints over Mind

Two passages embody Ezra's plaints over the mind. The first is in chapter 4 with two cries of woe of Ezra, one following each angelic demonstration of Ezra's innate inability to comprehend the way of the Most High.

> It would be better for us not to be here than to come here and live in ungodliness, and to suffer and not understand why we suffer. (4:12)

---

cf. Exod 4:11–15; 1QH 10:7; 12:33 (Myers). This is a standard way of talking of inspired speech in different cultures.

21   Some analysis of these experiences was given by Bousset-Gressmann, p. 396. While seeing some underlying religious experience, they regard it as having been modified in a quite imaginary fashion by the author and do not follow up the implications of

their initial insight.

22   For the expression, see 4:2.

23   On this search, see also 13:54–55 and p. 123 below.

24   Lat "of mind." For a similar expression, see 10:28 and 12:3. Both of these describe Ezra's confusion of mind in response to visions.

And again:

> I beseech you, my lord, why have I been endowed with the power of understanding? (4:22)

In the passage 7:63–77 there is a second extensive lament over the mind. Ezra has been informed that in the final judgment there will be no mercy for the sinners. He then addresses the earth, reproaching it with having produced a mind from the dust, "for it would have been better if the dust itself had not been born, so that the mind might not have been made from it" (7:63). The mind grows with humans who are punished because they perish and know it (7:64). The beasts, who have neither torment nor salvation, are much happier (7:65–69). The "heart" that has received the Law will perish along with humans who have not observed it (9:36–37).[25]

In 7:72 the angel replies that God created all that pertains to judgment when he created Adam, "for this reason . . . those who dwell on earth shall be tormented, because though they had understanding they committed iniquity, and though they received the commandments they did not keep them." They will have nothing to say in judgment, which is only delayed because God foreordained the times (7:72–73).

Consequently, mind is an innate part of human beings; they have it, while they do not understand why they suffer. Chapter 7:64 says that humans are tortured by the very knowledge that they will perish in final judgment. Indeed, mind, being consciousness so it seems, is that part of humans which makes them liable for judgment at all.[26] The seeming contradiction between the concept of mind in the two laments is readily resolved when the contexts of the two passages are borne in mind. In chapter 4 the discussion turns on the incomprehensibility of the working of divine justice when the fate of Israel is compared with the abundance of Rome. It is this which human beings do not understand. On the other hand, 7:62–74 discusses the actions of humans in general; in that context it is precisely the power of thought that distinguishes humans from beasts and makes humans liable to be judged.

The Grant of Wisdom: Ideal and Eschatological
It follows from the above that there should be an eschatological aspect of this idea. In this context, 8:3–6 must be considered. Chapter 8:3 concludes the third

dispute of Vision 3. This dispute revolves around the question, Why are so many created but so few saved? This is embodied in the parable of the base and precious metals; its message is, in the final analysis, that the ways of providence are unknowable. Ezra's monologue (8:4–19a) follows Dispute 3. In it he calls on his soul and heart to drink their fill of wisdom and understanding. They are not willingly born and die equally loath (8:4–5). Then he turns to God and asks him for "seed of heart" and "cultivation of understanding" which give life, that is, eternal life.

Thus this passage presents the idea that the soul or heart receives wisdom, cultivation, fruit, and life. The term "understanding" is ambiguous. In 8:4 it stands parallel to wisdom, while in 8:6 it corresponds to "heart." Consequently, it is both that which is given and the faculty that receives. This cognitive faculty is related to birth and death, so connecting with 7:62–64 which speaks of the mind that grows up with humans. It is also related to the imagery of agricultural produce. In a number of passages there is reference to the Torah producing fruit of life (see 3:20–21 Commentary). Moreover, the notion that the understanding or heart can be cultivated connects with 4:26–30. In 4:30 evil is said first to have been sown in Adam's heart and "if the place where the evil has been sown does not pass away, the field where the good has been sown will not come" (4:29).[27] Here it receives a clearly eschatological dimension.

In 8:12, in the continuation of the passage, God is said to have brought children up in righteousness and instructed them in wisdom. This is part of Ezra's argument that God has created with so much trouble, so why should he destroy. Similar in its view of wisdom and understanding as central human virtues is 13:54–55. The angel compares the unknowability of the servant with that of the depths of the sea (13:52; cf. 4:7 and above). Ezra alone is granted the interpretation because "you . . . have searched out my law, for you have devoted your life to wisdom, and called understanding your mother" (13:54–55). It is difficult to know whether this is just a general sentiment relating to Ezra's virtues or a specific reference to his search to understand the way of the Most High (see above, p.

---

25 Analogous is the apostrophe and reproach he directs to his spirit in 12:4: "Behold you have brought this upon me because you search out the way of the Most High."

26 On the nature of the mind, see 7:62 Commentary and also the observations of Myers on 7:63 (p. 236).

27 In 10:30 "understanding" seems to mean something like "consciousness."

122). A similar implication, that rule over the intellectual faculties helps salvation, is to be found in 14:34.

This idea is expressed elsewhere in the book. So in 6:26 we read as part of the story of redemption:

And the heart of the earth's inhabitants shall be changed and converted to a different spirit.

This is surely related to the prophetic saying at Ezek 11:19:

I will give them one heart and put a new spirit in them. I will remove the heart of stone from their bodies and give them a heart of flesh.

And Ezek 36:26:

A new heart I will give you, and a new spirit I will put within you; and I will take out of your flesh the heart of stone and give you a heart of flesh.[28]

Another aspect of eschatological wisdom is reflected in 8:52 which refers to "wisdom perfected beforehand" as part of a list of eschatological gifts.

What is apparently yet a further aspect of the eschatological role of the mind or wisdom is 5:9, which predicts their concealment as part of the signs to precede the eschaton (see 5:1 and 5:9 Commentary). The passage here, like those mentioned in the footnote above, refers to the hiding (or eventual granting) of wisdom or understanding. Predominantly in 4 Ezra, however, it is the heart, mind, or understanding that is to be changed.

Commentary
■ **20b, 21** No commentary.

■ **22** Most English versions have translated "recovered" in accordance with the Latin, where we have "received." The reading "recovered" is not supported by the other versions. The sense is not inappropriate, in general terms, as is clear from the end of the verse ("once more"), although the hypercritical might ask where the first receipt of the spirit is mentioned. This is irrelevant, and the translation was selected on textual, not exegetical, grounds.

Of the introductions to Visions 1–4 this is the only one that describes Ezra's inspiration as the receiving of "a spirit of understanding." Yet these introductions all emphasize the fact that Ezra's discourse is initiated by the onset of inspiration (see the Excursus on Inspiration). The situation in chapter 14, however, is close to 5:22, and that is not one of the introductions. There Ezra prays to receive God's holy spirit (14:22); God's spirit lights "the lamp of understanding" in Ezra's heart (14:25); then he drinks of the goblet of the spirit (14:39) as a result of which his "heart poured forth understanding" (14:40).[29]

In chapter 14 the particular relationship between the receipt of the spirit and the idea of "understanding" is abundantly clear. This is also evident in 5:22, which describes the receipt of *"the spirit of understanding."*[30] It is this "spirit of understanding" which enables Ezra to speak words before the Most High.

---

28   The idea that special wisdom would be granted to the righteous at the eschaton is found in other apocalypses; see, e.g., *1 Enoch* 5:8; 9:10. Cf. *1 Enoch* 48:1, and see Stone, "Lists," 425.

29   For a fuller analysis, see Excursus on Inspiration, pp. 119–20, and the Commentary on chap. 14.

30   There are various speculations about possible biblical origins of this term; see, e.g., Violet 2 and Myers, who refer to Exod 31:3; 35:31; and Isa 11:2. Gunkel regards this as a modified form of an originally divine or demonic spirit of possession. The givenness of inspiration is quite unmistakable in 4 Ezra. On the use of "wisdom" terminology, i.e., "understanding," see Excursus on Inspiration, pp. 122–23.

5

23
> And I said, "O sovereign Lord,
>> from all the forests [a] of the earth and
>>> from [b] its trees
>>> thou hast chosen for thyself [c] one
>>> vine,
24/ >> and from all the lands of the world,
>>> thou hast chosen for thyself one
>>> region, [d]
>> and from all the flowers of the world,
>>> thou hast chosen for thyself one lily, [e]
25/ >> and from all the depths of the sea,
>>> thou hast filled [f] for thyself one river,
>> and from all the cities that have been
>> built,
>>> thou hast consecrated Zion for thyself,
26/ >> and from all the birds that have been
>> created,
>>> thou hast named for thyself one dove,
>> and from all the flocks that have been
>> made,
>>> thou hast accepted [g] for thyself one
>>> sheep,
27/ >> and from all the multitude of peoples,
>>> thou hast gotten [h] for thyself one
>>> people; [i]
>> and to this people whom thou hast
>> loved,
>>> thou hast given the Torah which is
>>> approved by all. [j]
28/ > And now, O Lord,
>> why hast thou given over the one to the
>> many,
>> and dishonored the one root beyond the
>> others, [k]
>> and scattered thine only one among the
>> many?
29/ And those who opposed thy Torah [l]
have trodden down those who believed in
thy covenant. [m] 30/ If thou dost really hate
thy people, they should be punished at thy
own hands."

Notes

23   a Singular in some Lat Mss and Eth; Violet 1
suggests that Eth is "collective singular."

b Lat adds "all"; Ar2, Arm different formulation;
see Commentary.

c "For thyself" Lat Mss except C omit; present in
all other versions.

24   d Thus Syr, cf. Eth, Ar1, Ar2, Arm; this is within
the semantic range of χώρα/ χωρίον/ τόπος (cf. Deut
12:5 etc.). Some such reading is required on literary
and exegetical grounds. Lat *fovea* and Georg *iatʿakʿa*
("floor," "basis") may derive from βοθρος and βαθρον
respectively. If so, either this is original (on stem-
matic grounds) and the other versions are interpretative or at least two Greek readings are witnessed,
viz., βο/αθρον and that from which the other
versions derive. In that case, the other Greek
reading was probably none of those proposed in this
note, since they bear no particular relationship to
βο/αθρον. The question of meaning, moreover,
would remain acute. Another approach would be to
abandon the proposal βο/αθρον and to search for a
Greek term within whose semantic range all the
versions could fall. If this option is chosen, then
τόπος has the best claim. See 7:26 and note o.

d–e This follows 5:25a Syr; Eth, Ar2 omit.

e "Lily" Lat, Arm, Georg; "flower" Syr, Ar1; "lily
flower" Arm doublet.

25   f So Lat, Eth, cf. Ar1; Ar2 omits the phrase;
glorificasti Georg, cf. Syr; perhaps from πληθύνω.

26   g So Syr, Ar1, Georg; "chosen" Eth, Ar2; *providisti*
Lat.

27   h "Chosen" Eth, Ar1; probably secondary, cf.
preceding note.

i Ar2 adds sentence here: "und du leitest die
Dinge durch deine Kraft und führst sie aus mit
deiner Weisheit." This strikingly resembles the
addition of Arm in 5:23 at the start of this pericope:
"O Lord! You are he who, by the will of the Most
High, made and prepared everything, and by your
wisdom you conduct everything and you requite
each according to his ways." This fragment of text
does not occur in the other versions.

j The text of this stich is uncertain.

28   k "Other roots" Eth, Georg. For "dishonored, Lat
has *proepurasti* ⟨ ἡτοίμασας for ἡτίμασας (Mussies, p.
105).

29   l "Torah" Eth, Georg, Ar2; "commandments" Syr;
"promises" Lat; either the reading of Syr or that of
Eth, etc., seems to be original; cf. 7:24 and Box's
note there, as well as 7:46.

m Plural in Lat; "law" Georg.

Form and Structure

The passage is a direct address by Ezra to God. It falls into two parts, 5:23–27 and 5:28–30. The first part, 5:23–27, is a series of statements "of all . . . you have chosen" or "named" or "gotten for yourself." This culminates in the election of Israel (5:27a–b) and the giving of the Torah "approved by all" to Israel (5:27c–d). There are seven of these comparisons, and Israel is the eighth. The second half of 5:27 then serves to mark the transition to the second part of the speech.

The second part of the address is composed of three questions that take up the theme of the one and the many; these are brief, each being a single hemistich (5:28). Then follow two further parallel stichs that introduce the categories of obedient and disobedient, which are not mentioned in the rest of the address (5:29). This is concluded by the question, Why is Israel punished by the nations and not by God himself (5:30)?

This address is parallel in structure and form to the speech with which the first vision opens (3:3–36), but it is much shorter. In structure, both addresses fall into two parts. The first is a sustained discourse (3:3–27 and 5:23–27) and the second a series of questions consequent to the discourse (3:28–36 and 5:28–30). As has been shown above, the address in 3:3–27 is a reversed *rib* in form, but the statements about election in the discourse in 5:23–27 are quite different from that (see below).

However, the second parts of the two addresses are rather similar in structure, in form, and in content. In both, three questions are posed in which the fate of Israel is contrasted with that of the nations (3:31b–32 and 5:28). Moreover, both in content and in form, 5:29 is particularly close to 3:30 and 5:30 to 3:28.

The first part of the address (5:23–27) is notable for the regular and repetitive formulation of the sentences that culminate in the statement of the election of Israel. Some similar passages exist. The latter part of the first dispute in this vision, that is, 6:1–6, is also a piece of rhythmic, climactic prose, while a remarkable passage in

Tanh. Bamidbar 20 has a very similar structure. To illustrate the verse פקוד את בני לוי (number the sons of Levi; Num 3:15), the Midrash cites a series of things that God chose, opening and closing with Levi. Each is said to be "selected" or "chosen" by God "for himself": the Sabbath of the (days); the Sabbatical year of the years; the Jubilee year of the weeks of years; the land of Israel of the lands; Arabot of the heavens; and Israel of the nations.[1]

A similar passage occurs in *PRE* 18, partly pareleled by *Num. R.* 3:8, according to which God created seven of various things and chose one of them: *maqom* of the heavens; Israel of lands; Kinneret of seas; Kadesh of wildernesses; the seventh, eschatological world of all worlds; the Sabbath of the days; and the Sabbatical year of the years.[2]

As to the view that the form of the *Volksklagelied* is here reflected, note that this address is much less like the examples that have been adduced from the biblical psalms and their developments than is the address in chapter 3 (*pace* Westermann).[3] There is no recital of historical events, and there is no prayer. So we should be more reserved than are many scholars in seeing it as a development of the *Volksklagelied*. It should also be observed that the almost ritualistically formulaic character of 5:23–27 has no parallel in the *Volksklagelied*.[4] Is every speech directed to God that mentions some of his deeds and asks questions or expresses dissatisfaction dependent on this particular *Gattung*?

Function and Content

The address is the outcome of the inspiration that has come upon Ezra. It sets the tone and introduces the themes that characterize the first part of the ensuing dialogue. The issues it raises resemble those stressed in the address in Vision 1, but it is less pressing in its reproof of God and differs in its emphasis.

The focus of the address in Vision 1 had been the fact of Israel's punishment by the nations. Ezra summoned

---

1   Each item in the Midrash's list is supported by a biblical verse or biblical verses. The passage was adduced by Box (with incorrect reference); there are parallels in S. Buber's edition of *Midrash Tanḥuma*. The parallels between *Midrash Tanḥuma* and 4 Ezra 5:23–27 are not only formal and stylistic but also in content, i.e., the lands and the peoples.

2   See also *Mek. Bešallaḥ* to Exod 15:16, and see 6:59

Commentary n. 55.

3   For full discussion, see 3:4–36 Form and Function, pp. 62–63.

4   On 6:38–59, see pp. 179–81 below.

God to the bar of his own justice to answer the questions arising from Israel's suffering and exacerbated by Ezra's pain at seeing it. In the course of Vision 1, Ezra's views were modified, and by its latter part he came to accept the idea that history's process is predetermined. His acceptance of this idea, however, did not diminish his distress or alleviate his pain, but it did bring him to pose his questions about the destruction of the Temple from a different perspective. No longer is the reason for the actual punishment of Israel central, but the question, "Why is Israel, the faithful and elect people, punished *by the Gentiles,* the hated Romans?" This was a minor theme of Vision 1; now it becomes dominant. "If thou dost really hate thy people," he cries out, "they should have been punished at thy own hands!" (5:30).

The chief exegetical problem of the speech is this: the seven statements of 5:23–27 speak each of one chosen thing of its kind: the vine of the trees (5:23), one region of the lands (5:24), the lily of the flowers (5:24), one river of the waters (5:25), Zion of the cities (5:25), the dove of the birds (5:26), and the sheep of the flocks (5:26). Now certain of these elect objects are clearly identifiable— "one region" is surely the land of Israel, "one river" is the Jordan, and Zion is explicitly stated to be the city. The other elect items have biblical sources and rabbinic parallels; each of them can simply be regarded as the premier exemplar of its class. At one level, this is surely the case, and the purpose of the passage is to say that Israel was elected by God as a climax of his selection of a choice and special member of each class of creation.[5]

Yet there is another possible level of exegesis. Each of these items—the vine, the lily, the dove, and the sheep— can also serve as a symbol for Israel. They are used as such in biblical discourse, and their identification with Israel is explicit at many points in rabbinic exegesis. The selection of these particular four elements, therefore, is not mere chance. They operate on two levels—both as premier representatives of their kind and as indications of the election of Israel. This creates the climax of the passage.

Election is described as "love"; God loved Israel (5:27), and the theme of love recurs elsewhere in the dispute (5:31–40).[6] Interestingly, God's punishment of Israel is not described in legal terms by the seer in the address (5:28–30), even though in 5:34 and 5:40 "the way of the Most High" (also absent from the address) is described as "judgment."[7] In the address, however, the emphasis is on election and love, and so on the anomaly of the fate of Israel when it is seen in the light of Israel's election and God's love. Consequently, the term "hate" describes God's punishment of Israel (5:30). Moreover, throughout the first part of the speech, God is said to elect whatever it is *for himself.* This repeated stress is readily comprehensible in view of the theme of election and love of Israel which lies at its heart.

Of course, at the root of Ezra's concern is Israel's fate: here he questions God about it, formulating the question in terms of God's love of Israel. This is different from Vision 1, where it was set out in terms of divine providence and God's conduct of the world. The formulation in 5:23–30 raises a less acute theological issue, although emotionally a no less distressing one. Ezra seems to have moved from his doubt about the justice of God's conduct of the world to bewilderment at his actions. The reasons for this were indicated in the first part of the present section.

Commentary

■ **23** Observe that the title "sovereign Lord" occurs at the start of each of the three addresses (3:4, here, and 6:38 in most versions) as well as elsewhere.[8]

The Armenian has an addition at the start of this verse that greatly resembles the addition of Arabic2 to 5:27.[9] Since these two versions share part of this additional text, it must have been at home somewhere in the Greek version of 4 Ezra. The addition of the Armenian reads:

O Lord, You are he who, by the will of the Most High, made and prepared everything, and by your wisdom

---

5   The order of the elements follows no particular logic. Only the Armenian version has ranged them more "sensibly": trees, flowers, birds, animals, rivers, city, and land. This nicely leads up to Israel as a climax but is secondary, since the other order is witnessed by the other versions with only slight variation. See textual notes. A variant form of the list occurs in *Apoc Sedrach* 8:2. The order there is

humans, sheep, olive, vine, bee, Jordan, Jerusalem. Four of these elements overlap with the list in 4 Ezra.

6   It is foreshadowed in 4:23 in a passage that presages many of the themes of Vision 2.

7   Koch ("Esras erste Vision," 71) makes much of this equivalation; see our discussion on p. 137 below.

8   See 3:4 Commentary and also Harnisch, p. 23.

9   See textual note i on 5:27.

you conduct everything and you requite each according to his ways. You, O Lord. . . .

This addition enhances the parallel between this speech and Visions 1 and 3 by introducing a reference to creation, which they also share. Moreover, its added emphasis on divine purposiveness highlights the anomaly of God's punishment of Israel. Thus the special Armenian material skillfully uses common themes to achieve a literary effect.[10]

Violet 2 suggested that this whole section (5:23–27) was originally composed of ten phrases, and consequently he proposed various emendations. The supposed "illogicality" of the order of the elements in these verses, however, which was pointed out above, does not seem to be so acute as to demand Violet's emendations.[11]

There is a somewhat similar passage in *Apoc Sedrach* 8:2. The elements listed there as loved by God are the following: humans of all creatures; sheep of quadrupeds; olive of trees; vine of fruit; bee of winged things; Jordan of rivers; and Jerusalem of cities. This differs from 4 Ezra in many details, although it clearly draws its structure and general sentiment from it. This is typical of the relationship between the later Ezra literature and 4 Ezra.[12] Consequently, 4 Ezra cannot be emended on the basis of *Apoc Sedrach* 8:2 (3). Another list of three things more beloved than others of their class occurs in *Sifre Deut.* on 10:10 (Finkelstein, p. 18). They are Torah, the Temple, and the land of Israel.

The expression "from every forest of the earth and from all its trees" seems pleonastic, but a very similar formulation occurs in 4:13.[13] The use of the vine for

Israel recurs in 4 Ezra 9:21—"One grape out of a cluster and one plant out of a great forest."[14] A remarkable parallel is Ps 80:9–17, which speaks at length of Israel as the vine that God planted.[15] The same image occurs elsewhere in biblical literature, thus Isa 5:7; Jer 2:21; Ezek 17:6; Hos 10:1; 14:7; and Joel 1:7.[16] It is also to be found in the Apocrypha and the Pseudepigrapha, notably in *2 Apocalypse of Baruch* in the vision of the forest and the vine (chaps. 35–40). There the vine is the symbol of the messianic age.[17] The most striking parallels, however, are *Bib Ant* 23:12 and 28:4, where Israel is the plantation elected by God from his vineyard, named with his name (cf. v 26).

■ 24 The idea of the election of the land of Israel has clear biblical roots. Already described in Gen 12:1 as "the land which I will show you," its particular and pleasing character as the land elected by God is a sustained theme of biblical literature.[18] The land of Israel is "the place that I have chosen" (*2 Apoc Bar* 40:2), "thy country" (ibid., 3:5). It is praised for its many qualities and particularly is "first known" by God (*Sib Or* 5:328–333).[19]

The Holy One, blessed be he, said, "The land of Israel is more beloved by me than all (lands), because I surveyed it, as Scripture says: 'A land I had searched out for them etc.' (Ezek 20:6). And it is beauteous more than all the lands, as Scripture says: 'And I gave you a pleasant land, a heritage most beauteous of all nations (Jer 3:19).'"[20]

A *baraitha* in *b. Taʿan.* 10a sings lengthy praises of the land of Israel which is God's own care in all respects, while the particularly pleasant nature and special role of

---

10 See further *Armenian Text Commentary*, ad loc.

11 *Function and Content*, n. 5. It is possible, of course, that some lines are lost, corrupted, or displaced; such a view remains speculative and not a necessary conclusion from the present situation of the text.

12 See, e.g., the comments in Stone, "Metamorphosis," 4, and idem, "Greek Apocalypse of Ezra," 569. See also 5:23–30 *Function and Content*, n. 5.

13 On the formulation in Armenian, see *Armenian Text Commentary*.

14 The use of "plant" and "forest" in 9:21 removes the supposed difficulties discovered by Violet 2 in 5:23.

15 A strange contrast is *3 Apoc Bar* 4:8, which identifies the vine as the tree of knowledge that was planted by the angel Samael. The passage continues with what is apparently a Christian interpolation relating to wine in 4:15–16.

16 Israel as a vineyard also occurs in Isa 27:2–3 and 27:6; cf. also Latin 4 Ezra 5:23, which reads *vineam*. Jerusalem is God's vineyard, *3 Apoc Bar* (Slavonic) 1:2.

17 Compare Ryssel's emendation there (*apud* Kautzsch); it is also listed by W. Baars in *Peshiṭta* 4.3, p. [47]. The same image is used of wisdom in Sir 24:17.

18 Note the terms used by Jeremiah of the land; it is "my vineyard," "my portion," and "my pleasant portion" (12:10), the word "portion" clearly implying election. Perhaps "vineyard" refers to the land (or the city) in *3 Apoc Bar* 1:2. Compare also Joel 2:3 and Ps 78:54; references could be multiplied manyfold.

19 It is called "blessed" in *1 Enoch* 27:1.

20 The Midrash continues there with a long passage in praise of the land of Israel.

the land are discussed in *Sifre Deut.* on 11:10, referred to above (on 5:23).[21]

The lily is premier among the flowers, noted for its blooms (Isa 35:1). It is an appropriate comparison for a beloved woman (Song 2:1–2). Israel is already in the Bible likened to a lily (Hos 14:6) and, in later Jewish sources, is often referred to as a "lily." This is the result of an allegorical interpretation of Song 2:1–2. Thus a piyyuṭ of the Kalir (sixth to seventh cents.) simply calls Israel "lily," as do many later liturgical poets.[22] This exegesis of Song 2:1–2 is already found in rabbinic Midrashic sources, such as *Song R.* on that verse,[23] and may well be in the background of the use here.

■ **25** There have been various suggestions as to possible Hebrew originals of the expression "depths of the sea"; see Violet 2, Myers, Kaminka, and others. Possible parallel expressions are numerous; see, for example, Mic 7:19; Ps 69:3; and Isa 51:10.

The river referred to seems to be the Jordan. The parallel stichs dealing with Zion (5:25) and apparently the land of Israel (5:24) make this most probable. This is also the interpretation of the Armenian version of 4 Ezra and *Apoc Sedrach* 8:2 (3).[24] It is a commonplace that the Jordan is the most prominent river in the land of Israel.

The verb "filling" has attracted attention, but there seems no reason to change it.[25] There are a number of ancient sources that reflect the sense of wonder felt at a river which, arising as a small stream or tiny spring, becomes a mighty torrent.[26] This idea can only be in the background of our text which reflects the cosmological view that rivers arise out of the deep—perhaps the subterranean deep. This idea might also be referred to by the phrase "springs at the source of the deep" in 4:7, although those are most probably the sources of the deep itself.[27]

The expression "city that has been built" recurs in the book. It is found in the parable of 7:6 but much more significantly in the description of the heavenly Jerusalem in 10:27; 10:42; 10:44; and 13:36; cf. 9:24. There the heavenly Jerusalem is said to be a "built city" with "great foundations." David is said to have built the city (3:24). A rather similar description of Jerusalem is found in Ps 122:3: "Jerusalem, built as a city which is bound firmly together."[28] Our verse, in contrast with the above, singles out Jerusalem from among all the built cities. This seems to suggest that "built city" is a particular sort of city,[29] perhaps a substantial or well-constructed one. This character of Jerusalem was already stressed by the psalmist. It is the building of the city walls that signified its status; compare the struggle between the Jews and the

---

21 (Ed. Finkelstein, pp. 69–70). On the role of the land in rabbinic thought, see Finkelstein's comments there and also Ginzberg, *Legends,* 5:14. A detailed analysis of attitudes toward the land of Israel may be found in W. D. Davies, *The Gospel and the Land: Early Christianity and Jewish Territorial Doctrine* (Berkeley and Los Angeles: University of California, 1974). See also Volz, p. 100, par. 5, for further references.

22 Adler and Davis, *Day of Atonement,* part 2, 134. Another well-known example is the final (fifth) stanza of the Hannuka hymn *Maʿoz Ṣur;* there are many other instances.

23 See also *Midr. Teh.* 1.20. On the flower itself, see *IDB,* s.v. "lily" and references there.

24 Gry has suggested that the reference is to the stream of Siloam, and similarly also Knibb, who cites Isa 8:6 in support of this view. One might also consider the association of a wondrous and vivifying stream with the temple in Ezekiel's ideal picture (47:1–12). A similar description is found in the apocalyptic vision in Zech 14:8. Note, however, that the stream described in *Od Sol* 6:18 flows into the temple, but

even its description draws on the same symbolism, adapting it to the author's point of view.

25 Hilgenfeld suggested that it is really a corruption of ἐπλήρωσας ⟨ *ἐκλήρωσας, "allot" or "assign." Note that the previous phrases all have a verb of election, while from the next phrase on the verbs vary. Context thus does not impose an emendation, nor does it make sense. See further the textual notes.

26 See, e.g., Isa 8:6–7; Song 4:15; Sir 24:30–31; *Od Sol* 6:8; and Add Esth 11:10; cf. *2 Apoc Bar* 36:3–4. The image recurs in these sources in varied contexts.

27 In *2 Apoc Bar* 53:11, twelve rivers arise from the sea in the vision; contrast Qoh 1:7.

28 The expression from Psalms served in many midrashim to indicate the heavenly Jerusalem; see V. Aptowitzer, "Heavenly Temple According to the Aggadah," *Tarbiz* 2 (1931) 267–68 (Hebrew). He has assembled numerous texts there on pp. 266–69.

29 This line of interpretation was already put forward by Violet 2. He suggests that, just as the Jordan, a minor river, was nonetheless the elected one, so Jerusalem which was relatively small among the

Samaritans in the Persian period over this point.[30] Similarly, the Romans capped their destruction of the city by razing nearly all of its walls.[31] So "all the built cities" seems clearly to be a particular sort of city, the fully built one, and of these Jerusalem was selected.

In the Bible, Zion is "elected" by God as his dwelling (Ps 132:13; cf. 78:68). He is said to have founded Zion (Isa 14:32) or built it (Ps 102:16; cf. Isa 18:7).[32] Here the author employs the language of "consecration" rather than that of election or building, which clearly indicates the cultic and sacral aspect of Zion, the site of the Temple. This view is very prominent in 4 Ezra; see 3:24–25. There the purpose of the building is to offer sacrifices, an idea that is even more prominent in 10:46–47 and other parts of Vision 4.[33]

■ 26 The chief biblical source that is used here by our author is an allegorical interpretation of Song 2:14 and 5:2. This type of interpretation of Song of Songs was already observed in the case of the lily in 5:24 (see Commentary there). In Ps 74:19 the righteous community is referred to as "turtle-dove."[34] Nonetheless it is the allegorical interpretation of Song of Songs that is serving our author. This type of approach is well exemplified in *Midr. Song* on 1:15 and on 4:1, both on the same verse and presenting the same extended working out of the simile of Israel and the dove. Another interpretation of Song of Songs was observed in 4:37. Thus an allegory of

Song of Songs was part of the author's stock in trade. This particular interpretation is also found explicitly in *Bib Ant* 39:5, which is most likely older than 4 Ezra, and in *b. Ber.* 53b.[35]

The verb "named" is a little odd. Some scholars have supposed a misapprehension of קראת and ἐκάλεσας (e.g., Violet 2) and that the original sense was "you summoned." Another possible approach would be to compare with *Bib Ant* 28:4, which states of the vine (= Israel) *nominabo eam nomine meo* (I will call it by my name). This is a calling by divine name, however, which is not found in 4 Ezra.[36]

The terminology of sheep and shepherd for God and his people must have been very ancient in a society that still preserved active, if somewhat nostalgic, memories of its nomadic origins. "Shepherd" also designated the king in many contexts. Of the numerous biblical instances, some of the most striking are Ps 74:1; 79:13; 80:2; 95:7; Hos 4:16; Mic 7:14; and all of Psalm 23. The sheep/shepherd symbolism also plays a major role in the *Animal Apocalypse* in *1 Enoch* 85–90. In nearly all of the sources cited, the sheep is Israel. The election of the sheep from among all the animals in 4 Ezra is easily to be understood on this basis.[37]

■ 27 The idea of God's election of Israel is basic to biblical and postbiblical Jewish thought. We will not document it here in full, but Isa 43:21 and Exod 15:16 (perhaps

---

πόλεις ᾠκοδομημέναι was nonetheless the consecrated one. This is particularly so, he says, from the point of view of an author living in Rome, but contrast our view on this expressed in 3:1 Commentary.

30   See Ezra 4:13; 4:21; Neh 1:3; 2:8; et al.

31   Schürer-Vermès-Millar, 1:508. Violet 2, commenting on 9:4, points to Xenophon, *Anabasis*, in which often a πόλις ᾠκοδομημένη is contrasted with a ruined city.

32   Zion's special role needs no demonstration. One of the oldest texts is perhaps Exod 15:17, and there are many other biblical sources reflecting this idea.

33   See Stone, "Reactions," 198–200; see further on God's role in relation to the Temple *Sifre Deut.* on 11:10 (Finkelstein, pp. 79–80).

34   In Isa 59:11 Israel's call in distress is said to be like the dove's; cf. Nah 2:8. 4 Ezra 2:15 celebrates the dove's joy in raising its young. A detailed survey of styles of interpretation of Song of Songs is to be found in M. Pope, *Song of Songs* (AB; Garden City, N.Y.: Doubleday, 1964) 89–229.

35   See further Ginzberg, *Legends*, 6:286. On the

esoteric interpretation of Song of Songs, see S. Liebermann, Appendix D, in Scholem, *Gnosticism*, 118–26. Admittedly, Liebermann's learned exposition refers basically to the esoteric interpretation of Song of Songs, not just the allegorical. Of the esoteric interpretation there seems to be no hint in 4 Ezra.

36   *TDNT*, 5:253–61, s.v. ὄνομα, on calling by name and name theology.

37   Observe that it is probably the reference to Israel that has determined the selection of the sheep. When the chief of the ruminants is given in Ezekiel's beasts, it is the ox who appears with the man, the lion, and the eagle; see Ezek 1:10.

supporting here the retroversion ἐκτήσω suggested by Gunkel, going back to קנית) are particularly close to our verse. Numerous other passages could be cited.[38]

Much more problematic is the description of the Torah "which is approved by all." The text is not quite certain, but this translation is supported by Latin, Syriac, and Georgian. Box, following Ethiopic, as do Gunkel and Keulers (p. 30), renders, "the law which thou didst approve of all (laws)." This certainly fits the present series of verses better structurally, but its textual basis is not at all convincing.

As it stands, the phrase "which is approved by all" seems to imply that the Torah is regarded with approval by all human beings but was given to Israel. Kabisch (pp. 42–43) stresses the tension between this statement and others in the first part of the book, which indicated that the Gentiles transgressed or did not know the Torah, and would attribute the former to the redactor. Myers stresses the identification of Torah and wisdom in Second Temple Judaism and would thus account for both the universality and the particularity of the Torah. In some ways our phrase is comparable with Deut 4:8, "And what great nation is there, that has statutes and ordinances so righteous as all this law which I set before you this day?" Another parallel is *2 Apoc Bar* 77:3, "For to you and your fathers the Lord gave a law more excellent than to all peoples." Neither of these passages, however, stresses the general recognition of the excellence of the Torah implied by our verse.[39]

One might remark further that the preceding seven comparisons (5:23–26) have all led up to, indeed foreshadowed, 5:27a. Verse 5:27b marks the end of this series. It abandons the comparisons (*pace* Box and others), which in any case nearly all refer to Israel, and again reverts to prose and introduces a new subject,

Israel's possession of the Torah. The formulaic, semipoetic style is replaced by plain prose. This half-verse introduces themes that are central to the following part of the vision: God's love of Israel recurs in 5:33 and again in 5:40, while Israel's attitude toward the Torah and that of the Gentiles is taken up by the next verse. Both of these themes are already foreshadowed in 4:23, which also refers to Israel as "the people whom you loved." This half-verse is transitional in the address, marking the shift from the first part (5:23–27a) to the second part (5:28–30). Its distinct literary character indicates this change both in literary style and in thought.[40]

■ **28** It has already been observed (Form and Structure, p. 126) that this verse is parallel to 3:28–36 in form, in function, and in general meaning. The expression "and now, Lord" occurs at a very similar point in the opening address in 6:57, and it functions as does "Then I said in my heart" in 3:28 to change the direction of the discourse.[41]

The language of "one" and "many" that follows is the natural consequence of the stress on election in the first part of the address. The term "one root" is well compared with *1 Enoch* 93:8, "And the whole race of the chosen root shall be dispersed." This verse in *1 Enoch* interestingly draws together themes also found in our passage: the election, the root, and the dispersion; compare also Isa 60:21. Here, then, "root" is a term for Israel.[42]

Kahana and Knibb have suggested that the scattering of Israel is drawn from the reality of the diaspora in the author's days. This is not necessarily the case, however, and he could be using biblical terminology or referring to the aftermath of Nebuchadnezzar's destruction. There are, of course, numerous references to the dispersion of the Jews in the Roman world.[43]

---

38 Cf. also *2 Apoc Bar* 48:20.

39 See 7:1–25 Function and Content, p. 194, for slight differences.

40 See above, Form and Structure, p. 126. The change in style must have contributed to Kabisch's attribution of the material to the redactor. It is possible, of course, that the series of 7 + 1 comparisons is drawn from another source and used by the author of 4 Ezra for his own purposes. This is by no means definite, however, and is not required by anything in the content of the passage. The author of 4 Ezra was master enough of his pen to

produce this passage himself, using traditional themes.

41 See also Harnisch, p. 25, who stresses the adversative character of this term as highlighting tension between God's assurances and the historical reality.

42 Note also "the root of Jesse" in Isa 11:10; cf. 53:2, and see also Ps 80:16. The image of planting is quite widespread, being taken up particularly in Qumran and associated documents; see, e.g., 1QH 6:14–16; 8:4–10; et al. Cf. also Ps 80:15–16 (14–15), which refers to Israel as a vine (5:23 above) and as "the son whom thou hast reared for thyself."

The expression "only one" probably reflects the Hebrew יחיד. In 6:58 the author asks why "we thy people, whom thou hast called thy first-born, only-begotten . . . have been given into their hands."[44] Here the verse refers to election, while 6:57–58 refer to Israel's role in creation.

■ **29** With the support of the versions and of most translators, we regard this verse as a declarative statement and not as a continuation of the series of questions posed in 5:28. This also accords with its function in the address. Its overall point is that Israel, who has observed God's commandments, has been oppressed and destroyed by the Babylonians (Romans) who "opposed his promises." Attention has been directed by some commentators to the fact that here the Gentiles are accused of rejection of the Torah, a sentiment that also occurs elsewhere in the book. So 3:33 refers to the nations that prosper though they are "unmindful of thy commandments."[45] This theological problem arises very acutely in 7:20–24.[46]

Quite clearly, 4 Ezra employs this sort of language to characterize the wicked. Harnisch has suggested that the primary motive for it is 4 Ezra's preoccupation with God's promises to Israel.[47] This may well be the case,

and the use of this language should be accepted flexibly.[48]

■ **30** This verse concludes the questions of the preceding two verses. Why is Israel's punishment administered not by God himself but by the Gentiles? Within the address the contrasts are double: God has elected, chosen, and loved Israel. If he now *hates* Israel, nonetheless he himself should have punished them, not the Gentiles.

The *topos* of preferring that ordained punishment should come from God and not from human beings is an old one. It occurs, for example, in 2 Sam 24:14 and Sir 2:18. In both of these cases, the reason for preferring God's punishment is that he is more likely to be merciful than is a human being. This point recurs in *Ps Sol* 7:1–4.[49] All of the passages cited bear a certain verbal similarity to 4 Ezra 5:30. In 4 Ezra the emphasis is very different, of course, from that of the other passages cited, but they are all based on an acceptance of the inevitability of God's punishment of Israel. The question, very clearly, is, Why in this fashion? How is the form of Israel's fate congruent with Israel's election?[50] The use of the language "love" and "hate" serves to highlight this issue.

---

43   Cf. the different attitude toward the scattering of Israel in *2 Apoc Bar* 1:4.

44   See also *Ps Sol* 18:4. See Box on 6:58 for possible relations between this terminology and the New Testament. The term μονογενής is discussed in detail in *TDNT*, 4:737–41. Psalm 25:16 is not really parallel to our verse.

45   Note also 3:32. Much of the language of 4:23 is related to that of 5:29, although the idea expressed is not the same. This provides a literary and thematic connection between them.

46   See 7:1–25, Function and Content, pp. 194–95, and further 7:72 and 8:56–57, where the difficulty is again prominent.

47   Harnisch, pp. 150–51. It is surely an anachronism to set 4 Ezra into a Procustean bed of systematic theology or to impose on him a series of questions arising out of the development of Christianity. See in general Stone, "Coherence and Inconsistency."

48   It seems unlikely that the reference is, e.g., to the Gentiles not observing something like the Noachid commandments. Nor does it seem that we should distinguish an "apocalyptic" view of the Law from a "rabbinic" one (see Harnisch, p. 152, quoting Rössler). The use of "Torah," "commandments," is very nonspecific in many apocryphal and pseudepigraphic writings. Indeed, some rabbinic texts that

stress the election of Israel or Israel's peculiar role contrast Israel's observance of various commandments with the transgression of the Gentiles; see, e.g., *Pes. Rab.* (ed. Friedmann) 200a, cf. 43a. On the term "covenant," see 3:32 Commentary. For the expression "trodden down," see 8:57; *2 Apoc Bar* 72:4; and 1QH 6:32, et al.

49   Further developments of this view are to be observed in Jer 10:24 and again in 1QpHab 5:3. Particularly noteworthy in our context are *2 Apoc Bar* 5:3; 7:1; and 80:1–4. All of these emphasize that God and his angels will destroy Zion but not human enemies, lest the Gentiles regard Zion's fall as God's weakness. The same idea recurs, probably drawn from *2 Apoc Bar*, in *Para Jer* 1:6.

50   Harnisch, pp. 42–43, contrasting 3:28–36 with 5:30, suggests that the problem turns basically for 4 Ezra not on Israel's sin but on Israel's fate in contrast with divine promises.

5

31   When [a] I had spoken these words, the angel
         who had come to me on a previous night
         was sent to me, 32/ and he said to me,
              "Listen to me, and I will instruct [b] you;
                 pay attention to me, and I will [c]tell
                 you more." [c]
                   33/ And I said, [d] "Speak, my [e] lord."
                 And he said to me,
              "Are you greatly disturbed [f] over Israel?
                 Or do you love him more than his
                 Maker does?"

34   And I said, "No, my lord, [g] but because of my
         grief [h] I have spoken; for every hour I suffer
         agonies of heart, [i] while I strive to under-
         stand the way [j] of the Most High and to
         search out part of his judgment." [k]

35   And he said to me, "You cannot." [l]
         And I said, [m]
              "Why not, [n] my [o] lord? Why then was I
                 born? [p]
              Or why did not my mother's womb
                 become my grave,
              that I might not see the travail of Jacob,
                 and the exhaustion of the people of
                 Israel?" [q]
         36/ He said to me,
              "Count up for me those [r] who have not
                 yet come, [s]
              and gather for me the scattered
                 raindrops,
              and make the withered flowers bloom
                 again for me;
         37/ open for me the closed treasuries,
              and bring forth for me the winds [t] shut
                 up in them,

Notes

31   a "And it came to pass when" Lat ψ, Arm, Georg.

32   b "Speak" Eth, Georg; Ar2 has reversed the order
of the verbs; Ar2 and Arm have dissolved the
parallelism.

c–c In Latin the verb "tell" occurs only in Ms L. It
is also found in Eth and Arm. There is some
variation connected with this verb and two versions
at least read "word" instead of "more," viz., Syr and
Georg. Syr for the verb might be a corruption of
*w'syp to w'sym. Alternatively it might derive from
προθήσω/προσθήσω in Greek.

33   d Lat, Ar1, Ar2, Georg; the other versions
expand in various ways.

e "My" Lat, Syr, Arm; the other versions omit.
Included in translation for stylistic reasons, see note
o below.

f Or "astounded"; Lat adds "in mind"; Arm adds
"your heart"; cf. 4:2, where most versions read
"heart." See Excursus on Inspiration.

34   g "My lord" Syr, Ar1, Ar2, and Lat Ms L; others
omit; in translation for stylistic reasons, see note o
below.

h Eth, Georg seem to have two additional words
which might have been "about him/it."

i Literally, "reins" or "kidneys."

j Plural Ar, Arm, Georg; cf. 4:3 (chiefly singular)
and 4:23 (chiefly plural).

k On this expression, see Commentary.

35   l Arm adds text based on ben Sira 3:21–22 and 4
Ezra 4:2; see Gry contra Violet 2, and see Armenian
Text Commentary.

m Syr, Eth, Ar1 add "to him"; this might be
original, but it is formulaic.

n "Can I not" Syr as emended and Georg.

o Stylistic addition in translation not supported by
most versions.

p "Become" Ar1; confusion of forms of γεννάω
and γίνομαι. See 4:12 note v.

q Greek quoted by Clement of Alexandria,
Stromateis 3:16:
     διὰ τί γὰρ οὐκ ἐγένετο ἡ μήτρα τῆς μητρός μου
     τάφος; ἵνα μὴ ἴδω τὸν μόχθον τοῦ Ἰακώβ, καὶ τὸν
     κόπον τοῦ γένους Ἰσραήλ, Ἐσδρας ὁ προφήτης λέγει.

36   r "The days" Eth; "the hours" Georg; perhaps
from common exegesis at the Greek level, cf. 4:5.
Restoration uncertain.

s Extensive expansion of Arm here.

37   t Presumably πνεύματα; Syr is ambiguous; Eth,
Arm give both "spirits" (as do Ar1, Georg) and
"winds."

or show me the appearance of him
  whom [u] you have never seen, [v]
or show me the picture of a voice;
and then I will explain to you the travail that
  you seek to understand." [w]

38 And I said, "O sovereign Lord, who is able to know these things except he whose dwelling is not with men? 39/ As for me, I am without wisdom and miserable, [x] and how can I speak concerning [y] the things which thou hast asked me?"

40 He said to me, "Just as you cannot do one of the things that were mentioned, so you cannot discover my judgment or the goal [z] of the love that I have promised my people."

u "Which" Georg; perhaps ου/ο, the next word probably started with ου.

v The whole phrase is omitted by Lat (and? by the *Vorlage* of Ar2) through hmt, either at Greek or Latin level. This and the next phrase seem only to be fully preserved in Syr, Eth, and Georg; cf. Ar1.

w Georg and Eth perhaps reflect the same Greek δεῖ taken as impersonal, instead of second person singular middle present. Arm is variant and based on 5:34 and its parallels above.

39 x "And miserable" Lat omits; Arm omits whole verse.

y So Lat, Syr, cf. Ar2; Eth, Georg omit "concerning."

40 z Or "end"; Arm has an addition here.

Form and Structure

This dispute opens with an angelophany (5:31) which is composed of two elements: the description of the appearance of the angel and his promise to give further instruction (cf. 5:13). Similar appearances of angels are related at identical positions in Vision 1 (4:1) and Vision 3 (7:1–2). However, the apparition of the mourning woman plays a different role in the structure of Vision 4, where it corresponds to disputes in Visions 1, 2, and 3. Following it, the seer's meeting with his angelic interlocutor is related (10:29–31). There is no explicit angelophany in Visions 5 and 6. In Vision 7 the author develops a typology of Moses. As in the case of Moses, the Most High himself appears to Ezra in the burning bush and addresses him (14:1–3).

Thus Visions 1–4 present an angelophany, Visions 5 and 6 have dialogue with God himself or with an angel addressed as God (cf. 12:51) following on a dream vision, while in Vision 7 the deliberately evocative theophany opens a major revelatory climax of the book.[1]

The second structural element of this pericope is the dialogic dispute between the seer and the angel. In 5:32 the angel calls for attention and promises instruction. A dialogue ensues (5:33–35); in 5:36–37 riddles are posed and a promise is given, while in 5:40 the angel draws conclusions from the riddles. In general, this disputatious dialogue is parallel to that of Vision 1.

Literary elements strengthen the pericope's structural coherence. Two *inclusio*s can be observed: one, in 5:33 and 5:40, involves the language of *love* and relates back to 5:27 and even farther back to 4:23. The other, in 5:34

and 5:40, is the language of *judgment,* and it points ahead into the next pericope (5:42 and 5:43).

Finally, there is a conclusion, still in the form of dialogue, which is made up of two elements. First the angel draws his conclusions from the dialogue (5:40 // 4:20) and second the seer poses his questions which form a transition to the oracle following (5:41 // 4:21–5). This last verse stands between this pericope and the next and is dealt with fully there.

Function and Content

As was already observed in the preceding section, the angelophany occurs at different places in the various visions. This seems to be deliberate and to indicate the progressive elevation of the type of vision and of the seer's interlocutor as the book progresses. The first three visions are dialogic revelations with the angel. In the fourth, there is the vision of the weeping woman, different from the dialogues, although the angelic partner remains. The next two visions are dream visions in which the *angelus interpres* plays a receding role, while the seventh vision is a great theophany and direct, divine revelation of sacred scripture.

The second part of this pericope is the dialogic dispute. In some ways this repeats the dispute dialogue of Vision 1 (4:1–25) but does so refocusing from the perspective of this vision which has shifted, as we noted above.[2] Consequently, the opening question does not relate to Ezra's distress at not understanding the ways of providence. It is whether he loves Israel more than God does (5:33). Already in this the different emphasis is

1   On the general function of angelic appearances, see 4:1–25 Form and Structure, p. 86.

2   See also Harnisch, p. 38.

clear, and it is well illustrated by contrasting the following verses:

Vision 1   I also will show you *the way* you desire to see, and will teach you *why the heart is evil*. (4:4)

and

Vision 2   Then I will explain to you *the travail you seek to understand*. (5:37)

Thus the literary *inclusio* of love (pointed to in Form and Structure, p. 134) and its connection with 5:27 function in this vision in the same way as the language of "way" and "understanding" did in Vision 1.

A second chief theme of the dispute is God's judgment. In 4 Ezra, judgment is often eschatological in character. However, sometimes the term denotes God's historical actions in general (e.g., 7:19) or toward Israel (e.g., 5:34, 40; 7:11; cf. 7:37).[3] In this section judgment is the object of Ezra's search (5:34), that which the angel says he cannot discover (5:40) and, in fact, the chief point of the oracle in 5:42–44. Thus it also forms an *inclusio* for the dispute and ties it in to the following. Thus, from both a literary and a conceptual perspective, it complements the theme of love. Judgment, because of its double reference, both present and eschatological, serves as a sort of key. Ezra seeks to understand (this-worldly) judgment and is answered about (eschatological) judgment in 5:42–44.

In 5:34, parallel to judgment as the object of understanding are "the ways of the Most High." The term is isolated here in this vision, but it is used frequently in the parallel section of Vision 1.[4] The language of understanding connects with wisdom terminology which, although already present in Vision 1, is much more prominent here. Observe the following: "spirit of understanding" (5:22); the form of address (5:32); language of learning such as "strive to understand" and "search out" (5:34 and 5:37); "I am without wisdom" (5:39); and "discover" (5:40). Moreover, the riddle questions that follow are to be explained in sapiential terms.

The author has a very specific view of the limitations laid upon knowledge available to human beings. This is evident both from his explicit statements (see 5:38 Commentary and 14:1–2 Function and Content, pp. 410–12) and from the deliberately polemical way he uses the literary form. Both implicitly and explicitly he asserts the limitations of human knowledge and its applicability (see 5:36 Commentary). At the end of the discussion with the angel in Vision 1, Ezra claimed that his mind, his ability to know, is properly to be applied to the subject matter of his questions (4:22–25). Here he no longer makes this assertion but simply proceeds with his questioning. This flows from the development of the author's thought and the different focus of the present vision.[5]

The actual content of the passage carries us on from the seer's question: How does God's conduct toward Israel jibe with his election and love of Israel? This question is repeated in 5:34; Ezra's ability to discover "divine judgment" is denied in 5:40. Yet in 5:43, Ezra takes up the theme of judgment and asks his questions in a specific way about the eschaton. It is worth observing that in this vision, in striking contrast to Vision 1, Ezra does not question the basic axiom of divine righteousness. Indeed, this is an indication of the change from Vision 1. God is not charged here, he is simply not understood; he is admonished only in the last verse of the address (5:30). The angel responds that Ezra cannot love Israel as God does or understand God's judgment or the end of his love. This reply implies both the justice and the mercy of God.[6]

It is this implication which opens the way for the continuation into dialogic revelation, which is in fact paradoxical. Strangely, Ezra's admission that he cannot know the way of God's love seems to lead into his further revelatory questions. Some scholars have regarded 5:40 as a pessimistic end of the passage.[7] Yet if the formal parallel with Vision 1 is pursued, then 5:41 should stand at the end of the dispute and it is followed by the oracles. So 5:40 does not deny, but by implication asserts.

3   See Excursus on the Term "Judgment." See also Stone, *Features*, 188; and Keulers, p. 160.

4   See 3:31 and 4:2 and Commentary. See full discussion of this theme in Stone, "Way of the Most High," 138–40; cf. Koch, "Esras erste Vision," 71–72, but he overstresses the point.

5   For further developments, see 10:38–54 Function and Content.

6   There may lie behind this a reference to the idea of God's two qualities of mercy and judgment. This idea occurs elsewhere in 4 Ezra and is well known in rabbinic literature.

7   E.g., Myers, p. 200.

Above, it was noted that "judgment," because it faces toward the future as well as toward the past, serves to take the discussion on to the next pericope which is oracular and predictive. It has been observed aptly by Myers that the same dynamic is implicit in the term "goal (end) of love" in 5:40. These two dimensions of 5:40 serve to refocus the meaning of ideas that occur in the address and in the dispute. Ezra responds to them with the question of 5:41 which summons forth Prediction 1 (5:41—6:10).

Commentary

■ **31** The verse forms the start of the angelophany and resembles 4:1; 7:1; and 10:28. The expression "on a previous night" is a little difficult; cf. 6:12. The reference is not to *the* preceding night, since Ezra has been instructed in 5:13 to wait for seven days.[8]

■ **32** Similar parallel expressions are to be found in the Bible, particularly in wisdom literature or literature influenced by wisdom terminology,[9] and indeed Knibb remarks on the sapiential character of this verse.[10] The first stich is repeated more or less verbatim in 7:49. It seems, therefore, to have been something of a cliché for our author.

The angelic promise to reveal "yet greater things" or the like is found elsewhere in the book, notably in the injunctions at the end of Vision 2 (6:31), Vision 4 (10:55—60), Vision 5 (12:39), and Vision 6 (13:56).[11] Here the angel takes up and fulfills the promise made in 5:13.

A question arises as to whether this promise is fulfilled in the present pericope, the purpose of which seems to be to deny Ezra's ability to know; see commentary on the next verse.

■ **33** In his response, Ezra addresses the angel as "lord" or "my lord"; see also 5:35. In 5:38, however, there seems to be a transfer from the angel to God, and an unmistakable divine title is used.[12]

The first part of the angel's question to Ezra, relating to the seer's state of mind after his speech, is parallel to 4:2. A similar response in a like context is described in *2 Apoc Bar* 13:3; 22:2; and 23:2.[13] The second part of the question has raised various interpretations. Some stress that this very assertion is a word of hope for Ezra, "However much you love Israel, and your distress over Israel's fate stems from your love of Israel, God loves Israel even more."[14] Others would subordinate this verse and the following to the author's concern to stress Ezra's inability to know the ways of God, and therefore parallel it in meaning as well as in function to 4:1–11 and 4:13–21: "You can no more love Israel as God does than you can understand God's ways with the world."[15]

This second interpretation, of course, sets the verse in tension with the angel's initial assertion in the preceding verse that he will make a revelation and instruct Ezra. In fact, on the face of it, 5:40, which is also an assertion of Ezra's inability to know God's ways with Israel, really leads him on to the next series of revelations. So Gunkel's point should here be restated. The question, demanding an answer "no" given by the seer (5:34) and driven home by 5:36–39, in fact implies a message of hope, just as the denial of 5:40 forms an assertion. Ezra

---

8   It follows that the translation "the previous night" of Box (see also A. S. (H)artom, *Hasefarim HaHiṣonim, Ḥezyonot,* 2 [Tel Aviv: Yavneh, 1969]) is excluded on contextual grounds.

9   E.g., Job 33:1; 34:16; Prov 4:1, 20; 19:20; et al. The parallelism of two verbs of hearing in an invocation is, of course, to be found frequently; examples are Deut 32:1; Judg 5:3; Isa 1:2; and Ps 39:13. In these cases and many others we have the parallel pair שמע and האזין; cf. also Ps 5:2–3 and 17:1.

10 See also Function and Content, p. 135.

11 On the expression and its possible Greek and Hebrew *Vorlagern,* see the summary of views in Violet 2. On the concept, see 10:55–60 Function and Content, p. 340.

12 See textual notes here and on 5:35. On shifts between the angel and God, see 7:17 Commentary.

13 Cf. also *2 Apoc Bar* 15:1. On the psychological terminology, see Excursus on Inspiration, pp. 121–23. The Latin expression *excessus mentis* has been compared with Deut 28:28 (Box), a comparison opposed by Violet 2, who prefers to cite 10:28; 12:3; and 13:30, where the same Latin recurs. On the reading itself, see textual notes.

14 So Gunkel, Box.

15 Harnisch, p. 143.

cannot discover judgment or the end of God's love (or his own?). This very negation is a proclamation that both exist and is so accepted by the indefatigable seer who consequently subjects the angel to a severe cross-examination on both matters. This paradoxical dynamic of course explains the revelation that is promised in 5:32.

In the address and the dispute that form the opening of this vision, a number of questions are posed. Unlike the questions asked in the first part of Vision 1, these questions focus not on axiomatic ideas but on the relationship between God's election of Israel and Israel's fate. Here Ezra immediately asserts his actual pain (5:34–35) over Israel which moves him in the whole discussion. Thus, while the tension between the angel's "theoretical" answers and Ezra's "existential" pain is very explicit in Vision 1, in Vision 2 this tension lies in the background of the discussion but could scarcely be inferred from it without a knowledge of Vision 1.[16]

The formulation of the verse is well compared with 4:34, "You do not hasten more than the Most High" (and see Commentary there) and 5:47. Is there, in both instances, at least the hint of an accusation of *hybris*?

■ **34** Ezra's mourning for Israel is poignantly expressed elsewhere in the book; see, for example, 8:16. The word rendered "heart" is actually "kidneys." The kidneys serve in the Bible as a seat of personality, of moral conduct, and of emotions.[17] Closest to our context is Ps 73:21. "Judgment" is parallel here to "way(s) of the Most High" (on the number of "way," see the textual commentary). This relates back to Vision 1, where "the way of the Most High" is the chief object of knowledge to which Ezra

aspires (see 3:31; 4:2; and 4:11). This term generally describes God's way in conducting the world (see 3:31 Commentary). *2 Apoc Bar* 44:6 speaks of the making known of God's "judgment" and "ways," and a most striking parallel to our passage is *2 Apoc Bar* 20:4, which says that in the events of the eschaton,

> I will show the judgment of my might,
> And my ways which are unsearchable.[18]

Gunkel, followed by others, suggested that "part of his judgment" reflects Hebrew גזר דין, which might be rendered "judicial decision."[19] This is quite possible; cf. 5:40. It is also possible to maintain that "judgment" here, inasmuch as it is parallel to "way," has a more general reference, in which case גזר דין would be inappropriate. Consequently, we have kept the translation of RSV here.[20]

■ **35** The sentiment "Woe that I was born" is by no means original to 4 Ezra. It is expressed in contexts not dissimilar to the present one in 1 Macc 2:7; *2 Apoc Bar* 3:1–2; and particularly in *2 Apoc Bar* 10:6–7:

> 6 Blessed is he who was not born,
> Or he, who having been born, has died.
>
> 7 But as for us who live, woe unto us,
> Because we see the afflictions of Zion,
> And what has befallen Jerusalem.

---

16 Harnisch, pp. 38–39, sets up a general opposition between Ezra's "existential" questions and the angel's "theoretical" answers. Elsewhere he speaks of the subordination of the problem of theodicy to that of the fate of Israel (p. 157). Certainly here the fate of Israel is to the fore, but it is an aspect of theodicy. This is evidenced by the use of "ways of the Most High" in 5:34 (q.v.) and "judgment" in 5:34 and 5:40. The latter term indeed refers to God's action in history, but just as certainly the very use of the term "judgment" implies a legal/ethical view of divine action. Consequently the anomaly seen in Israel's fate leads back to the problem of divine righteousness. In chaps. 3 and 4, too, these issues are intertwined. Ezra's motive, the goad that drives him, is surely the fate of Israel. But the anomaly of that fate leads directly or circuitously to the problem of the

righteousness of God. God's future judgment, the vindication of Israel, comes to the fore as a resolution in the next section (Prediction 1). Consequently, Harnisch's opposition of "theoretical" and "existential" or of "theodicy" and "the fate of Israel" seems to us not adequately to express the situation.

17 See *IDB*, 3:9–10.

18 Cf. also *2 Apoc Bar* 15:3–6. The expression "way of your judgment" occurs in a different sense in Isa 26:8. See Harnisch, p. 35 note.

19 This suggestion is taken up by Box. Violet 2 offers many other supposed cases of this expression in 4 Ezra, but they are not identical with the present instance and do not seem convincing on the whole.

20 The meaning of the term is discussed in Excursus on the Term "Judgment," p. 149, and cf. Function and Content, p. 134.

This theme is common in the Bible and is discussed further in the 4:12 Commentary.[21] Contrast the reason for Ezra's despair here, "the travail of Jacob," with the reason in 4:22–25, viz., that he cannot understand why the fate of Israel is what it is. Again the different focuses of Vision 1 and Vision 2 are clearly explicit.

■ **36** This verse opens a series of seven riddles which complements the series in 4:5–8 and most probably is drawn from the same preexisting list.[22] Violet 2 makes much of the role of seven-stich poems in the book, comparing 7:119–125; 7:132–139; etc. Not all of his examples are certain, but they may be supplemented by the material adduced by Keulers (p. 21 note).

This list is much expanded by the Armenian version. Its text reads:

5:36A And he said, "Tell me the number of those who are going to be born and going to die, and of those who are and of those who are going to be and who are going to die! Relate to me the breadth of the sea and the multitude of the fish, or the heights of the heavens, or the hosts of stars, or the circuits of the sun, or the orbits of the stars, or the forms of the firmament, or the breadth of the earth, or the weight of dust! 5:36B Reckon for me the number of the hairs of your body, or the blinking of your eye, or the power of hearing, or the multitude of sight, or the preparation of smell, or the touches of hands, or the running of veins! 5:36C Or will you find the imprints of feet, or the appearance and measure of breath, or its form, or its color, or the nest of wisdom, or the wisdom of birds, 5:36D or the variety of creeping things which are on dry land and which are in the waters, which are hostile to one another, the runnings without feet; or the blowing of the winds? And gather for me the dispersed and scattered drops of rain, and make green

the flowers which have withered."

Another parallel to it is *Apocalypse of Sedrach* 8, and the expansions of Armenian and *Apocalypse of Sedrach* share certain elements. This indicates that the Armenian version is not simply inventing its expansions but that they are, at least partly, at home in the later Ezra traditions.[23] This is a typical example of the way the later Ezra works took up and expanded literary types drawn from 4 Ezra.[24]

The general function of the paradoxical riddles is to stress the limits of Ezra's knowledge. The fact that nearly all of the elements listed in the riddles are in fact things revealed to the seers in other apocalypses serves to highlight the "antirevelatory" tendency of 4 Ezra.

The text of the first colon formed a problem for Ethiopic and Georgian, yet since they read respectively "the days" and "the hours that have not yet come," it is difficult to posit more than a common exegesis somehow embedded in their *Vorlage*. This exegesis may have been influenced by 4:5, "Call back for me the day that is past," and designed to complement it. The other versions seem clearly to refer to the fixed number of people yet to be born.[25]

Inasmuch as it is a paradox, this expression resembles the third colon of 5:37, referring to unseen people. The idea behind the enigma is the notion that the number of those who are destined to be born is foreordained. This idea, which is also present in the question in 5:43, is discussed in 4:36 Commentary. In the Armenian expansion of 5:36A, it is even more explicit. This is well compared with *Apoc Sedrach* 8:6: "How many people have been born, and how many have died and how many shall die and how many hairs do they have?"[26] Compare also "the ⟨number⟩ of all generations," *Bib Ant* 21:2.[27] The expansions of Armenian 4 Ezra and *Apocalypse of Sedrach*

---

21 Westermann claims that this sentiment is typical of the *Klagelied* ("Klage," 76). See, however, our observations above on the doubtful relevance of this *Gattung* to the present pericope (3:4–36 Function and Content, n. 12).

22 See, in general, 4:5 Commentary.

23 See *Armenian Text Commentary* here.

24 On this, see Stone, "Greek Apocalypse of Ezra," Introduction, 569; and idem, "Metamorphosis," 4–14.

25 Gunkel and Box attribute this reading to Arabic, but cf. Violet 2.

26 Neither Armenian nor *Apocalypse of Sedrach* seems to preserve a perfect text, and both show some doublets. There are other parallels between the unique material of Armenian and *Apocalypse of Sedrach*.

27 On this text, see Commentary on the next verse.

are independent and based on 5:43.

The collection of the scattered raindrops is presumably a variation on the numbering of the drops of rain. In Sir 1:2 the number of drops of rain is said to be beyond human ken. This is also stated by *2 Enoch* 47:5, which, moreover, clearly implies that it is the glorious Lord who knows it. Complementary is a hymnic passage in *2 Apoc Bar* 21:8 in which God is said to cause the raindrops to fall by number upon the earth.[28] Most strikingly, *2 Apocalypse of Baruch* speaks of the revelation of the number of drops of rain to Moses on Sinai, while in *Apoc Sedrach* 8:9 we read, "How many drops have fallen upon the world and how many shall fall?"

The closest parallel to "make the withered flowers bloom again" is Ezek 17:24, even though that passage is in an allegory. A secondary development of our passage is doubtlessly *Greek Apoc Esdr* 4:2–3: "Count the flowers of the earth."

■ **37** It has been debated whether the word rendered "wind" should be translated thus or whether, depending on Greek or Hebrew ambiguities, it should be rendered "spirits." The term "treasuries" as well as the idea of treasuries of the souls may be found elsewhere in 4 Ezra as well as in other works (see 4:35 Commentary). However, winds are also said to be in treasuries (see, e.g., Jer 10:13; 51:16; Ps 135:7; *1 Enoch* 41:4; 60:12; *2 Enoch* 40:11)[29] or in chambers (חדר) (Job 37:9; 11QPs^a 26:14–15).[30] There thus appears to be no clear way on the basis of parallels to determine whether the presumed πνεύματα or רוחות were "winds" or "spirits." Exegesis is not decisive either, and respected critics have taken both

positions.[31] The colon dealing with "the appearance of him whom you have never seen" is original. This is to be compared with "seeing a soul or spirit" in *1 Enoch* 93:12 and the unemended *sensum omnium generationum* of *Bib Ant* 21:2 if that reading is not to be emended.[32]

Ginzberg notes in connection with the "vision of a voice" rabbinic exegesis of Exod 20:18 and compares it with speculations about visible voices and similar ideas in Philo.[33] If these verses and ideas have influenced our colon, then the possibility arises that it and the preceding colon are a reuse of language and ideas originally applied to God. Such language must have been radically toned down by our author.

"Travail" has raised problems for the critics.[34] It seems to be adequately explained by the latter part of 5:35.

■ **38** Here Ezra responds that the sort of knowledge that the angel has asked is beyond human ken. This he states also in the parallel verse in Vision 1 (4:6): "Who of those that have been born can do this?" In Vision 1, Ezra does not draw explicitly one possible implication of this, viz., that if mortals cannot do it, nonetheless the superhuman can. This is in fact the point of the parable in 4:13–19 and is stated explicitly in 4:21: "He who is above the heavens can understand what is in the height of the heavens." In Vision 2, however, this conclusion is set in Ezra's mouth as a clear and obvious fact. This is related to the prominent role of language of wisdom and knowledge in this section, yet the limits the author lays upon it. He does not deny the existence of such types of knowledge, he denies their availability to ordinary men and women.[35]

---

28 In *2 Enoch* 40:8, Enoch says that he has been shown how the clouds drop rain; cf. in general Job 36:27.

29 For "treasuries" of light, cf. 4 Ezra 6:40; of snow and hail, cf. Job 38:22; of clouds, Sir 43:14; "of darkness," 1QS 10:2; "of glory," 1QM 10:12 (partly reconstructed), etc.; similarly of many other natural phenomena elsewhere in contemporary literature.

30 This text as reconstituted seems to refer to the "treasuries of the winds," but observe that the reconstruction is based on Jer 10:13 and Ps 135:7; see J. A. Sanders, *The Psalms Scroll of Qumrân Cave 11* (Discoveries in the Judean Desert of Jordan 4; Oxford: Oxford University, 1965) 90–91.

31 Such are Gunkel "winds"; Box, Violet, and Wellhausen "spirits." Most ancient versions too did not seem to know which option to select; see textual commentary here. Myers favors "winds" apparently

on the basis of Volz's opinion that "chambers" contained only righteous souls. But cf. here 7:32, which contradicts this view, and see Commentary there.

32 But *sensum* is most probably to be emended to *censum* (J. Strugnell); see Stone, "Lists," nn. 9 and 41, and 5:36 Commentary.

33 R. Akiba in *Mek. BaHodeš* 9 (Horovitz-Rabin, p. 235): "they saw and heard that which was seen." Philo also knows these ideas; see, e.g., *De Decal.* 46–47: "for it is the case that the voice of men is audible but the voice of God is truly visible." See Ginzberg, *Legends*, 6:43, for further references and discussion. Myers apparently independently adduced Exod 20:19 and Deut 4:12.

34 See, e.g., Gunkel and Box with different speculations.

35 See Function and Content, p. 135, and 5:36

"Except he whose dwelling is not with men" has been taken by various interpreters, from the ancient versions on, to refer variously to Christ, God, or angels.[36] The expression is very much like Dan 2:11: "the gods, whose dwelling is not with flesh." It seems superfluous to argue for one or another specific referent, and the sense is clearly that only the superhuman can understand such mysteries.

The form of address "O sovereign Lord" is properly used of God. It is a stylized formula in prayers in 4 Ezra.[37]

■ 39 For similar self-deprecatory remarks, see Ps 73:22 and Prov 30:2. This verse relates to the theme of Ezra's worthiness, on which see 10:38–54 Form and Content, pp. 335–36.

■ 40 Although Gunkel argued that the angel spoke in 5:36, here in 5:38 he observes that the author has slipped from angelic speech to divine speech. Certainly the angel speaks for God, but this situation is not at all uncommon with divine messengers. The "goal" of God's love means the end toward which it is moving. It is this sense of the word "end" which is relevant, and this is combined with the term "judgment" to provide the stimulus and the bridge to the questions that the seer now proceeds to pose.[38] The term "promise" in the phrase "I have promised my people" of 5:40 takes up "the things promised" of 4:27.

Commentary.

36   See Arabic1, Arabic2, and Violet 1, p. 75. Box and Violet interpret of God; Gunkel and Keulers (p. 26) of angels.

37   See 3:4 Commentary. Commentators (e.g., Box) have made much of the author's tendency to address the angel as if he were God; see further 7:17 Commentary. We capitalize "Lord" hesitantly in the translation.

38   The addition of Armenian serves to emphasize both the limits of human knowledge and the eschatological reward.

5

41 And I said,

"Yet [a] behold, O Lord, thou dost promise [b]
those who are alive [c]at the end, [c] but what
will those do who were before us, or we, or
those who come after us?" [d]

42 He said to me, "I shall liken [e] my judgment to a
crown; [f]

just as for those who are last there is no
slowness,
so for those who are first there is no
haste." [g]

43 Then I answered and said, "Couldst thou [h]not
have created [h] at one time those who have
been and those who are and those who will
be, that thou mightest show thy judgment [i]
the sooner?"

44 He replied to me and said, "The creation
cannot make more haste [j] than the Creator,
neither can the world hold at one time those
who have been created in it."

45 And I said, [k] "How hast thou said to thy servant that thou wilt certainly give life to thy
creation at one time? [l]If therefore they (will)
live at one time [l] and the creation will sustain
them, could it even now support (all of)
them, [m] present at one time?"

46 He said to me "Ask a woman's womb, and say
to it, [n] 'If you bear ten children, [o] why one
after another?' Request it therefore to
produce ten at one time."

47 I said, [p] "Of course it cannot, but only each in
its own time."

48 He [q] said to me, "Even so have I made the
earth a womb [r] for those who from time to

Notes

41 a Syr, Lat; others omit.

b The verb seems to be the same as in 5:40. Latin
is corrupt and we accept the emendation of Violet to
promittis. "Promise" is then the reading of Lat, Syr,
Arm; Eth, Georg have verbs meaning "keep,"
"preserve" both here and in 5:40. Clearly, either two
Greek readings are involved or one ambiguous one.
No simple conjecture comes to mind. For speculation on the Greek, see Violet 2. RSV is dependent
on a different emendation of Lat which has no
support in any other version. In this verse in general
we follow Syr, Lat, largely supported by their
secondary witnesses, Ar1, Ar2, Arm. This procedure is supported by comparison with all versions
of 5:40.

c–c Eth, Georg omit; Arm perhaps derives from
τέλειος for τέλος.

d Arm is varied and expanded; see *Armenian Text
Commentary*.

42 e Past tense Syr, Eth; future tense Lat, Georg.
Ar2 has a different and expanded form of this verse.

f "Circle": Eth reading preferred by Box, Violet,
Myers, RSV, Harnisch (p. 292) for text-critically
unclear reasons. Violet 2 suggests γύρος on the basis
of a Hebrew wordplay. Note Georg, however, which
reads "crown" as do Lat, Syr, Ar1, Arm. This seems
to imply στέφανος in Greek. The supposed support
for Eth sought in Ar2 is not strong, and it would be
difficult to assume that five of six extant versions
produced independently an unusual but identical
exegesis of γύρος to κύκλος (on which see LSJ s.vv.).
So, even if enticed by Violet 2's restored Hebrew
wordplay, we cannot accept his readings.

g Cited by Ambrose, *De bono mortis* 10.

43 h–h Georg omits.

i "What has been prepared" Arm; cf. Arm 5:40.

44 j So Lat, Arm, Georg; "does not hasten" Syr, Eth;
Ar1, Ar2 vary.

45 k Lat; "I answered and said" Syr, Georg; "I said to
him" Eth, Ar1, Ar2; "I answered" Arm.

l–l Lat omits by hmt.

m I.e., the resurrected and those now alive. We
follow Box and others and add "all of " in the
translation.

46 n Syr omits "and say to it"; Georg omits "to it."

o The word "children" is not explicit in most
versions.

47 p Eth, Georg, Ar1 omit.

48 q Eth omits the verse; Georg omits "he said to
me"; cf. preceding note.

r Syr, Georg; Lat varies. The verb is literally

time come forth on it. [s] 49/ For as an infant does not bring forth, and a woman who has become old does not bring forth any longer, so I have organized [t] the world which I created."

50   Then I asked him [u] and said, "Since thou hast [v] given me the way, [w] let me speak [x] before thee. Is our mother, [y] of whom thou hast told me, still young? Or is she now approaching old age?" [z]

51   He replied to me, "Ask a woman who bears children, [a] and she will tell you. [b] 52/ Say to her, 'Why are those whom you have borne recently not like those whom you bore before, but are smaller in stature?' 53/ And she herself will answer you, [c]'Those born in the strength of youth are different from those born in [d] old age, when the womb is failing.' [e] 54/ Therefore [f] you also should consider that [g]you and your contemporaries are [g] smaller in stature than those who were before you, 55/ and those who come after you [h]will be smaller [h] than you, [i]as if born of a creation which already is aging and passing the strength of youth." [j]

56   And I said, "O Lord, I beseech thee, if I have found favor in thy sight, show thy servant through whom [k] thou dost visit [l] thy creation." [m]

6

1   And he said to me, [n]"The beginning is through [o] man [p] and the end is through [q] myself. [r]

For before [s] the circle of the earth existed, [t]
and before the assembled winds blew, [u]
2/ And before the rumblings of thunder sounded,
and before the flashes of lightning [v] shone,

"give" (Lat, Syr, Georg)—a Hebraism: see Box.

s Syr, Georg; "are sown upon it" Lat, cf. Ar1. Violet 2 suggests ἐπ᾽ αὐτῆς παρόντων and ἐπ᾽ αὐτῇ σπάρεντων as possible Greek originals.

49   t Eth adds "according to its time"; Georg adds "my people." Box accepts the reading of Eth on unstated grounds.

50   u Lat omits; Georg omits and reads "Lord" in the next clause.

v Lat adds iam.

w Apparently meaning "given me the opportunity" (RSV) or "opened the way" (NEB) or the like. Myers translates "revealed to me."

x "Enquire" Arm; Lat Ms L adds et interrogo te domine mi.

y Syr adds "Zion"; cf. Vision 4.

z Ar1 expanded this verse and Ar2 abbreviated.

51   a–b Georg, Arm omit by hmt or editorial; Violet 2 considers it a doublet and the short text original.

53   c–e Lat, Syr; Eth varies; Ar1 expands the whole verse; Ar2 omits; Arm, Georg have almost identical abbreviations.

d "In the time of" Lat.

54   f Lat; "also" Syr, Arm; "however" Eth; "thus" Ar1; Ar2 omits.

g–g Literally, "you [plural] are."

55   h–h Lat omits.

i–j Box, following Willamowitz, observes that Lat preserves literally a Greek genitive absolute.

j Lat, Syr; cf. Eth, Arm.

56   k Ar1, Ar2 had διὰ τίνα in their Vorlage; see note o below on 6:1.

l Present tense Lat, Syr; future Eth, Georg, Ar.

m Arm has extensive expansion here.

6:1   n–r Lat omits; present in some form in Syr, Eth, Georg, Ar1, Ar2, Arm (6:1G and 1I). There is no reason to consider it secondary. See note e below on 6:6. It is included in our translation, contra Box, RSV, NEB, Myers, Licht, etc.

o Georg and Ar read "for the sake of" here and also in 5:56c. Perhaps διά, which with a genitive may mean "throughout" and with an accusative "on account of" (LSJ s.v., BIII.1). See Georg 6:6 for the same variant. Box considers it to be doctrinal, which we doubt; see also Volkmar's suggestion cited in note k above on 5:56.

p "Son of man" Eth; cf. Arm 6:1G.

q See note o above.

s Lat omits "before" and the following "existed," perhaps as part of the same process that caused the loss of n–r.

t "Was created" Eth, Georg, Ar2; this may reflect a Greek reading or ambiguity.

u Syr reflects ῥόπαι for ῥίπαι of the other versions (Violet 2).

2   v "Stars" Georg, Ar1, Arm; Violet suggests a

and before the foundations ^w of the garden were laid,

3/   and before the beautiful flowers were seen,

and before the powers ^x of movement were established,

and before the innumerable hosts of angels were gathered together,

4/ and before the heights of the air were lifted up,

and before the measures of the firmaments were named,

and before the footstool ^y of Zion was established,

5/   and before the present years were reckoned, ^z

and before the imaginations of those who now sin were estranged, ^a

and before those who stored up treasures of faith were sealed— ^b

6/ then I planned these things, ^cand they came into being ^c through ^d me and not through another." ^e

7 And I answered and said, "What will be the dividing ^f of the times? Or when will be the end of the first age ^g and the beginning of the age that follows?" ^g

8 He said to me, "From Abraham ^h to Abraham, ⁱ because from him were born Jacob and Esau, ^jfor Jacob's hand held Esau's heel from the beginning. ^k 9/ ^lFor Esau is the end

corruption of ἄστρων/ἀστραπῶν. Would this be a coincidental corruption in these versions?

w Ar2 omits the colon; "land" Syr, Eth.

3   x Singular in Syr, Eth, Ar2, Arm.

4   y *Fundamentum* Georg, Ar1; colon omitted by Eth, Arm.

5   z So Lat, Syr, Georg; Eth varies somewhat and omits the next colon.

a The text of this colon is uncertain; for "imaginations" (Lat), Syr has "foolishness," Ar1 "works," Georg "ways"; for "estranged" (Lat), Syr has "conceived," "described," Ar1 "differentiated," Georg "created." Ar2 is reformulated, while Eth and Arm omit. See further discussion in Box.

b Arm omits from here to the end of 6:10.

6   c–c Syr (which adds "all"), Ar1, Ar2, cf. Lat *facta sunt;* Eth omits; *in corde occurrit mihi* Georg.

d *Propter* Georg; see note o above on 6:1.

e Lat here adds "just as the end shall come through me and not through another." This might have been original and omitted by all the other versions by hmt of ἕτερου—ἕτερου or the like. However, this seems unlikely. Box suggests that this clause is omitted by the "Oriental versions" for dogmatic reasons. A remarkable coincidence of dogma! Violet 2 suggests more cogently that it is a form of the part of 6:2 above that was lost by Latin. The last phrase of the Arabic gloss is secondary.

7   f So Lat, Syr, Ar; "sign" Eth, Georg; both readings existed at the Greek stage, but no Greek original suggests itself.

g Literally, "first . . . following" Lat; "first age/world . . . second" Syr; "first . . . second age/world" Eth, Georg; Ar is periphrastic.

8   h "Adam" Georg.

i So Lat, most Mss. The other witnesses show the marks of trying to soften this difficult text. Thus Lat Mss ψ, Eth, Ar2 Ms B read "Isaac"; Syriac reads like the majority of Latin Mss but adds a phrase: "Isaac was born of Abraham and from Isaac were . . ."; Ar1 treats the text similarly. The reading of Georg "Adam to Abraham," adapting the first rather than the second occurrence of "Abraham," clinches, in our view, the secondary nature of all of these developments. Had the versions been presented with the straightforward text of Lat Mss ψ, Eth, and Ar2 Ms B, it is hard to see what would have precipitated the complex adaptations outlined here. For the meaning of the phrase, see Commentary. Zimmermann's suggestion of *wa'ed* for *wa'ad* is not acceptable (*JQR* 51 [1960–61]).

j–k This next clause is omitted by Eth, Georg, and so apparently by their *Vorlage.*

k Syr, Ar2 omit.

9   l–l "For Jacob is the beginning of the coming age" Eth, Georg. Kabisch (p. 149), Box, and Violet 2

of this age, and Jacob is the beginning of the age that follows. ˡ 10/ For the end of a man is his heel, ᵐ and the beginning of a man is his hand; ⁿ between the heel and the hand ° seek for nothing else, Ezra!" ᵖ

10

read (partly with Syr) "the heel" instead of "the end" and "the hand" instead of "the beginning," but Syr is isolated in this respect.

m–n Lat omits nearly all of this verse. Syr has the order "hand . . . heel"; Georg, Eth have "heel . . . hand" and so apparently does Ar1. Compare also the next colon, which has "heel" first; so also Violet 2.

n–o Eth omits by hmt.

o Ar1 and Ar2 are somewhat periphrastic.

p "Israel" Georg.

Form and Structure

This series of predictive questions and responses may be divided into a number of sections:

1. Question and oracular response (5:41–42)—who?
2. Three ensuing questions:

5:43 question	5:44 response—when? how soon?
5:45 question	5:46–49 response
5:50 question	5:51–55 response

3. Major question with introduction—through whom? (5:56)

   oracular style response 6:1

   creation poem 6:1b–6

4. Concluding question—when will be division? 6:7

   concluding oracular-exegetical response—6:8–10

Preceding this section is the denial of the seer's ability to know in Vision 2, 5:40 (corresponding to Vision 1, 4:21), left with the future pointers "goal" and "judgment."

A. Question and Oracular Response (5:41–42)

In both Vision 1 and Vision 2, a question by the seer occurs at this point. In Vision 1 the question is one of basic principle: "What will he do for his name?" (4:25). In Vision 2 the question is based upon the promise of future reward implied by 5:40. In both cases the question is followed by an "oracular" statement (4:26 and 5:42).

Our division of the pericopes is thus somewhat inconsistent, for the question is included in the dispute of Vision 1 but in the prediction of Vision 2. This difference stems from the requirements of context and sense. In Vision 1 the prediction is of judgment itself; in Vision 2 it is about the details of judgment. Therefore this

difference indicates the distance the seer has come in his understanding. A further variation, demanded by literary context, can be observed in Vision 3 (7:25), where the oracular statement must be regarded as the end of the dispute.[1]

The oracular pronouncement in 5:42 has already been compared with functionally and stylistically similar statements in Visions 1 and 3 (see 4:26 Commentary). Here the balanced, poetical statement is preceded by an image—the likening of the judgment to a crown. The same combination, an image followed by a cryptic statement, is to be found in 4:26.

B. The Three Questions "When?" (5:43–55)

1. The question in 5:43 is followed by the response in 5:44 which has no particular literary character.
2. The question in 5:45 is answered by an extended presentation of the earth as a womb. The writer has used this figure earlier in the book (4:42) and it has clear biblical roots.[2]

In presenting this image, the author uses techniques like those of the "literary parable" in 4:13–19. He has the angel introduce the image, set the rules, instruct the seer to pose questions (5:46), and himself draw out conclusions from the seer's reply.[3]

3. In 5:50–55 the author uses a somewhat different literary technique; here the seer takes up the literary figure in a question to the angel (5:50), while in the angelic response the same techniques noted above are employed.

---

1 It should further be remarked that the "pericopae" here are often not recognizable *Gattungen* but that we have regarded the overall sense of the passage as the primary criterion for our pericope divisions. These questions and "oracular" responses could be isolated as separate units, but that seems superfluous.

2 See 4:40 Commentary. Zion as mother is, of course, the dominant image in Vision 4 and it is discussed in

that connection in 10:7 Commentary.

3 Box, who accepts the reading "sown," is obliged to talk of mixed images here. See also 10:12–14, where the same image is used.

C. Major New Question "Through Whom?" (5:56—6:6)
This question has a major introduction, of the sort that often opens new aspects of the dialogic development.[4] In Vision 1 the corresponding question (4:44) is answered by a visionary parable (see 4:48 Commentary); here too a distinctive literary form breaks the repetitiveness of question and answer. It encompasses a rhythmic, semi-poetical passage made up of fourteen phrases in a sort of climactic style (6:1–6).[5]

This passage is in many ways reminiscent of Prov 8:22–29.[6] It probably has its roots in some poetic creation recital which has been reused here and is carefully tied into its context by the first phrases and the last phrase.[7]

D. Concluding Question and Oracular-Exegetical Response (6:7–10)
The end of this pericope (6:8–10) is a metaphor in which the comparison is at two levels. The first is tied to biblical text and exegesis (Abraham—Abraham), while the second is the human body. The biblical text is used in a complex way, and although a unit of "Midrashic" exegesis lies behind the present text, it is not in itself a Midrash.[8]

Function and Content
In the preceding section the seer's questions were disputatious in character, arising from his address and challenging the existential situation and the explanations offered of it. Here he has accepted certain conclusions that emerge from the dispute in the preceding section and proceeds to elicit further details about them.[9]

The seer has understood the first part of the dialogue to lead to the conclusion that God loves Israel and that his love, contrary to expectation and appearances (5:30),

has a goal, an end (5:40). God's ways are unknowable by Ezra (5:38), but the angel/God has, in 5:40, made a response pregnant with promise.[10]

The first question (5:41) is whether the redemption will include all generations or only that actually alive at the moment of the end. The problem is analogous to that raised in other contexts, such as 1 Thess 4:13–17.[11] From the point of view of the argument here, it is not evident why what was said in 5:40 led the seer to think that the "goal of love" refers only to the last generation. Consequently, we are forced to assume that this element comes from elsewhere, most likely from the predictions in Vision 1. There Ezra had been concerned whether the end was close and whether he would live at that time (4:44–51). To this the angel had replied in an evasive fashion (4:52). This reply was followed by a prophecy, "Behold, the days are coming when those who dwell on the earth . . ." (5:1). This is, admittedly, a list of signs and not a prophecy of judgment, yet two comments are relevant.

a. First, that there is no necessary conflict between the two.
b. Second, that there are various modes of differentiation between the righteous and the wicked in 4 Ezra. One of them is clearly the events of the "messianic woes," the signs, which only the righteous will survive.[12] A prophecy of woes, therefore, is a sort of judgment.

It follows, therefore, that the question that the seer poses here in 5:41 is based on the overall development of the book. It introduces the revelation of the first vision into the revelation of the second.

The image of the crown used in the angelic response (5:42) is an intriguing one which is analyzed below (5:42 Commentary). The second part of the verse clearly states

---

4   For this stylistic feature, cf. 4:44 and Commentary there.

5   For a similar group of 14 phrases, see 8:52–54, while *2 Apoc Bar* 59:5–12 has 28 phrases. See Violet 2 on 8:52–54; cf. Keulers, p. 21 note in detail.

6   Both sources share a series of "before" clauses and a list of the works of creation *before* which a specific event took place. The actual lists differ quite a lot, however, reflecting different cosmological perceptions.

7   On the apparent displacement of the first part of 6:1 to the end of 6:6 in Latin, see textual notes on 6:6.

8   See 6:8–10 Commentary.

9   This revelatory dialogue is described in detail in General Structure of the Book, pp. 50–51.

10 See 5:31–40 Function and Content on the shift from dispute to prediction here.

11 Much has been written on the interpretation of this verse; see 5:41 Commentary. Its place in the development of eschatology is discussed there.

12 See Excursus on the Term "Judgment," p. 151, and 5:41 Commentary.

that the meaning of the image is that judgment will take place in an equal fashion for all. The implication of 5:45 seems to be that there will be a general resurrection.

The series of three questions that follows returns to a theme that Ezra had raised pointedly in Vision 1: his impatient desire to see the judgment as soon as possible (4:33–51). A secondary theme of that section of Vision 1 was Ezra's concern whether he would be alive at that time (4:33; 4:51). Here in Vision 2 (5:42) he has been assured that all will equally see judgment, and his impatience grows. If all the allotted number of human beings must be born before the end comes, then why were they not born simultaneously (5:43)?

This question was not answered in Prediction 1 of Vision 1 (4:26–32). There Ezra was told that the end cannot come until the appointed number of righteous souls have died and entered the treasuries. So far in the present vision he has been informed that judgment will be equal for all. Now, moved by his sense of urgency, he asks whether God (?the angel) could not have created all humans at once, so fulfilling both conditions known to him.[13]

The first part of the answer (5:44a) is that God has created and he has set the rhythm and pace of events. The phraseology and the idea are reminiscent of 4:34: "You do not hasten faster than the Most High." The second part of the response is that the world cannot support all of those who have been created at one time (5:44b). This argument reinforces the first part of the angel's response and raises Ezra's next, somewhat argumentative, question (5:45). This is, "You have said that in

the future all will be raised to life at once. In that case, the world will be able to sustain them all, so why not now?" That is to say, the seer taxes the angel with the fact that the response of 5:44 apparently contradicts what the angel said in 5:42.[14]

The angel answers once more using the image of the womb (5:46–49). In Vision 1 that image served to express the fixed order of creation, and here it serves the same function.[15] In 5:46 it works clearly enough: a womb cannot produce ten children at once, that would run against its innate capabilities. Similarly, the earth cannot produce all destined human beings at once, for that would contradict its natural properties. The image is sustained in 5:47 and 5:48. The fixed sequence of events is what these verses emphasize.[16]

In 5:49, however, another aspect of the analogy is taken up, though not completely clearly. The organization of the world is compared to a womb. The child cannot yet conceive and the old woman is no longer fertile. Birth can take place only at determined periods in a woman's life. As it stands, this statement serves to strengthen the observation that the process of birth is organized equally in the world and in the body of a woman and that order and organization cannot be changed.[17]

The author's artistry is evident in the use of this image in 5:49, however, since it also serves as a point of departure for the next question that is posed (5:50). Ezra picks up the image of the young and old woman to rephrase a question he has already asked (in 4:33 and 4:44–45): Is the end close (5:50)? In his reply the angel sustains the

---

13 Again unclarity may be discerned here between the angel and God as Ezra's partner in dialogue. See 7:17 Commentary. Harnisch analyzes these verses at length (pp. 296–98). He presents the questions of 5:43 and 5:45 as implausible and therefore is led to isolate the worldview they are designed to present, which is contradicted by the angel (who is the author, according to Harnisch). He takes it to be a view negating the historical process (p. 298) and even perhaps a gnosticizing one (ibid., note). His argument is interesting, but we must confess that, as we have explained, we do not find the questions as problematic as he does. And, it should be added, the negation of the historical process, if this is "Ezra's" position, is stated obscurely, to say the least. See further the critique of Harnisch's position in Introduction, sec. 3.3.3.

14 So also Box; cf. Myers.

15 On images expressing the fixed order of creation, see Excursus on Natural Order, p. 102.

16 Cf. Harnisch, p. 229. Licht regards this answer as basically evasive and Ezra's question as, in the final analysis, remaining unanswered.

17 It would be difficult to apply this analogy more directly. After all, Ezra does not deny that human beings were created close to the very generation of the world, nor that there will be humans born in its last generation. Consequently the point of the analogy must lie in the very order and organization of the processes. Box here does take the image to apply literally: "The earth, in its earliest stage (as a child) brought forth no human inhabitants, neither will it do so in extreme old age" (p. 61). This view is not supported by other passages in the book.

image. The children of the present and future ages are smaller than their predecessors—and this indicates that the end of the age is approaching (5:51–55).[18] This formulation of course relates to Ezra's overall view that this world or age is degenerating, passing away and moving toward its end.[19] The three questions of this series, then, work toward an increasing precision. They also underline the tension between the predetermination of the events and the seer's sense of urgency. The same tension was observed in the questions in Vision 1 in the same context.[20]

The next question is a new departure and is marked by an elaborate introduction (5:56; see Form and Structure above). Ezra, having accepted the idea that there is to be a judgment, that the judgment is universal, and that its time is fixed and cannot be changed, abruptly abandons the problem of timetable. Who will carry out the visitation? he wishes to know (5:56).[21] The answer given in 6:1 is that "the beginning is through man" (perhaps the Messiah, or other human agency), but the end and consummation of the visitation will be by agency of God.[22] God's being the sole agent of the end of the visitation (6:6) is strongly supported by the series of state-

ments in 6:1–5—he alone made the whole of creation, and before that he planned the events of the end and he alone will execute them.

This question and answer may have a "polemical" point. They certainly serve to stress God's exclusive role in final judgment, which point is also made elsewhere in the book.[23] This view has been characterized as "orthodox" or "rabbinic," as opposed to early Christian.[24] Certainly, in a variety of types of literature and social groups, figures other than God were involved in the actual process of judgment. Such figures were Melchizedek, the Son of man, Abel, and others.[25] It is singularly difficult to be more specific about the object of the "polemic," if this is such, or even the background against which the question is being asked.[26]

The final question introduces the transition between Prediction 1 and Prediction 2. This is in a mysterious oracular form. The question posed in 6:7 is double-barreled, but the double question is actually a single one: What and when will be the dividing of the times? The answer embraces paradox ("from Abraham to Abraham"), biblical interpretation (see Commentary), and symbolism. Its import is that nothing will separate the

Harnisch would argue that the passage once again stresses the sequentiality of events (p. 300). Neither explanation, however, leads to complete clarity.

18   On the idea of the degeneration of the generations, see 5:54 Commentary and particularly 14:10 Commentary. Contrast with 7:12, where not just the necessary succession of the generations but also the toilsomeness of this world is stressed. Cf. Harnisch, p. 305.

19   Cf. also Harnisch, p. 129.

20   It is in these terms that we choose to understand the interplay between the seer and the angel/God. The writer's actual conflicts are there being reflected; this view follows Gunkel in a basic way, telling against Harnisch's general approach. On this, see also Introduction, sec. 4.4.4. See 5:41 Commentary on the tension between eschatological urgency and predetermination.

21   Stone, "Coherence and Inconsistency," 231; Kabisch points out (p. 48) that here a new type of question, unrelated to theodicy, is raised.

22   There are exegetical problems as to the meaning of the first phrase; see 6:1 Commentary. These problems were already perceived by the versions, as is clear in the textual notes.

23   Cf. 7:33, and also the reinterpretation of the Son of man figure in chap. 13. See Stone, "Messiah," 307–

10.

24   So, e.g., Box; cf. also Knibb. According to Gunkel, this is opposed to Christian views, particularly to the role of Christ in final judgment.

25   See 11QMelchizedek, lines 9, 13; *Similitudes of Enoch; Testament of Abraham* 13; see Nickelsburg and Stone, *Faith and Piety,* 177–86; J. Theisohn, *Der auserwählte Richter* (Göttingen: Vandenhoeck & Ruprecht, 1975). This is in addition to figures celebrated in Christian and Gnostic texts. Kabisch, in line with his own analysis of the book, suggests that this is a summary rejection of the role of the Messiah in the events of the eschaton (p. 48).

26   Myers (p. 201) observes that the use of the creation langauge in 6:1–5 serves to join the preexistent with the end time, resulting in a devaluation of intervening history. Cf. the position of Harnisch noted above (n. 17). Yet it is to be questioned whether this is the case. Although sometimes the author's "end" is patterned after the "beginning" (e.g., 7:31), they are not made identical and he writes from the perspective of one living in the senescence of the world. The chief point of the passage seems to be the precreation and foreordination of the eschaton. Myers's interpretation of 6:7–10 (pp. 201–2), while supporting his point, does not seem to us based in the text.

beginning of the coming age from the end of this one (6:8–10).[27]

Commentary

■ **41** The view that those who are alive at the end, in the last generation, will be particularly fortunate is nicely explicit in *Ps Sol* 18:5–6:

> May God cleanse Israel against the day of mercy and blessing,
>
> Against the day of choice when he bringeth back his anointed.
>
> Blessed shall they be that shall be in those days,
>
> In that they shall see the goodness of the Lord which he shall perform for the generation that is to come.[28]

The same idea is clearly behind Dan 12:12.

The notion of the last generation and the righteous who will survive in it is encountered often in 4 Ezra. Observe various uses of this idea as follows:

a. The term that is usually but not always (cf., e.g., 7:67) employed is "the survivors" or "those who survive" (so 6:25; 7:27; 9:7–8; 13:16; 13:19). These all refer to those who will survive the messianic woes; so also does the next category.

b. More particularly, in 12:34; 13:26; and 13:48–49 it means those who survive the great eschatological battle waged by the Redeemer.[29]

c. In 4:26 it seems to be a reference to Ezra's own life, although it is not certain whether it means that he will live long enough or will survive the woes.[30]

d. A number of passages speak of the small number who will survive final judgment; such are 7:47–48; 7:60; 8:1–3; and 9:21–22.[31] These always contrast the few and the many and generally relate to judgment in general.

The concept, not the term, is encountered in 4 Ezra 13:13; *2 Apoc Bar* 29:1–2; 32:1; and 71:1, where survival is limited to those dwelling in the land; cf. 4 Ezra 12:34 and 13:48. Note also the use in a similar context in *1 Enoch* 10:17 (Gizeh and 4QEn). In Mark 13:13 the term occurs in precisely the same sort of context as here, while in 1 Thess 4:15 it is found related to a different eschatological view.

Box points out that this expression is paralleled by the rabbinic use of נצ״ל. Thus *b. Sanh.* 98b: מה יעשה אדם וינצל מחבלו של משיח יעסוק בתורה ובגמ״ח. ('What should a man do to be preserved from the messianic woes? Occupy himself with the Torah and with charity.')[32] Analogous to the use in 4 Ezra is CD 7:21 אלה ימלטו בקץ הפקודה ('These will escape at the time of the visitation.'), which refers to the sect in the future after the time of visitation.[33] Other examples of the use in Second Temple period literature are *1 Enoch* 83:8; 99:10; and *Sib Or* 5:384; cf. 4 Ezra 2:30.

In context here, the question implies that the divine promise will apply to those alive at the end, and exactly the exclusion of the seer, his predecessors, and his successors from this group is the subject of the question. In all the cases listed in categories a and b, those who survive are said to see the delights of the messianic age.[34] In virtually all of these instances the concept relates to those surviving the messianic woes. Compare also 6:25 and Commentary.

---

27 Box sees this as a denial of the temporary messianic kingdom parallel to the denial of the messianic judge in the preceding. It is not clear, however, why this should be thought to be the meaning of "end"; nor is it clear why he has capitalized "End." On this term and its polyvalency, see Stone, "Coherence and Inconsistency," and Excursus on Natural Order, pp. 103–4.

28 Cf. also *Ps Sol* 17:44. This latter verse is perhaps to be compared with the words of Simeon at Luke 2:29–32, which proclaim that, upon the presentation of Christ in the Temple, he realizes that he belongs to the blessed generation.

29 Another application in a special context is 7:67 and 7:140. Cf. also 13:16; 13:19; *2 Apoc Bar* 29:2; and 40:2. In some texts it is even implied that only those within the borders of the Holy Land will be saved at that time. So 4 Ezra 12:34; *2 Apoc Bar* 29:1–2; 32:1; and 71:1. See Harnisch, p. 140 note, 231 note, for further uses of this term; see also 1 Thess 4:15 and particularly *Sib Or* 5:384–385.

30 See 4:51 Commentary; cf. 7:45 and 7:47. Cf. also *Ps Sol* 17:44 (50).

31 See Harnisch, p. 231 n. 5; and *2 Apoc Bar* 44:13 and 44:15.

32 See further discussion in Stone, *Features*, 104.

33 The Qumran sect evidently applied to themselves the idea of the righteous remnant eschatologically conceived; thus, e.g., CD 1:4–5; 1QM 13:8; and 1QH 6:8. 1QM 14:8 is closely related to Isa 11:11; see Yadin, *War*, commentary ad loc. This sort of application of eschatological concepts is completely lacking in 4 Ezra.

34 See also n. 29 above.

The question and the answer, therefore, are taken by many critics as a rejection of a specific "this-worldly" eschatology in favor of a more universal line—that is, they are taken polemically.[35] Elsewhere we have argued against the "two eschatologies" theory as a model for analysis of the thought of 4 Ezra. This theory, assuming originally independent "this-worldly" and "universal" eschatologies, regards them as (clumsily) combined by the redactor of 4 Ezra.[36]

Box (p. 59) comments on this verse: "The old view, which is reflected in the older literature of the Bible, that the *community* as a whole was to be the subject of salvation would naturally give rise to questions such as this." He and others have compared the verse with 1 Thess 4:13–14. There the issue is clearly the question of Christians who have died before the eschaton and their situation at the end. Notable, moreover, is 1 Thess 4:15–17:

15 . . . We who are alive, who are left until the coming of the Lord, shall not precede those who have fallen asleep. 16 For the Lord himself will descend from heaven. . . . And the dead in Christ will rise first; 17 then we who are alive, who are left, shall be caught up together with them in the clouds to meet the Lord in the air; and so we shall always be with the Lord.

Here we may observe a stress on simultaneity, resurrection, and a different process of salvation for the resurrected and those who are alive. The passage in 1 Thessalonians also shows, however, the complexity of ideas that could be embedded in a single text. It is much more explicit than 4 Ezra, and 4 Ezra 5:41 must be exegeted in a nonharmonizing fashion.

Note, consequently, that 5:42 responds on the issue of simultaneity. Moreover, 5:45 appears to speak of resurrection of the dead and to understand 5:42 as a promise of resurrection made in terms of judgment. This could be formalized as a fairly deliberate shift from one associational complex to another, but that is not certain. The case of 1 Thess 4:13–17 remains as a powerful warning against overschematization in terms of "older" and "younger" views. After all, how much "older" is 1 Thessalonians than 4 Ezra, if at all?[37]

Excursus on the Term "Judgment"

Meaning of the Term

As was observed above, "judgment" is a central theme in this second vision. The simile of 5:42 refers to judgment, and the whole series of questions in 5:40–43 touches on Ezra's urgent desire to see judgment consummated. A change in the emphasis of the term may be observed. In 5:34, "part of his [God's] judgment" is parallel to "the way of the Most High," and so "judgment" means something like "God's way with the world" (see 3:31 Commentary). In the continuation of this passage, however, judgment takes on a distinctly eschatological aspect. So in 5:40 it is parallel to "the goal of my love," while in 5:42–45 it clearly refers to God's eschatological judgment.[38] Indeed, in the book this is the chief meaning of the term and, in eschatological contexts, of its virtual synonym "day of judgment." It occurs thus with no further qualifiers, for example, in 7:60, "judgment which I have promised."

In 7:66, in the course of the plaint over the mind, Ezra exclaims that the beasts are blessed, for "they do not look for judgment after death." This expression recurs in 7:69 but does not seem to refer to a post-mortem rather than an eschatological judgment, for, in the same passage, in 7:73 the angel responds, referring to the wicked, "What, then, will they have to say in judgment, or how will they answer in the last times?" The same conclusion emerges from 14:35: "For after death judgment will come, when we shall live again." As is explicit in 7:17–25 and 7:127–131, humans are judged for their own deeds (7:105), their obedience or disobedience to the Torah; see also 7:70–73.

Description of Eschatological Judgment

The most detailed description of judgment in the book is in 7:33–43. God is seated upon the throne of judgment.[39] This indicates (what is in any case clear

---

35 See, e.g., Kabisch, pp. 45–46; Box; and Harnisch, p. 293.

36 See 7:26–44 Function and Content, p. 205; and Stone, "Coherence and Inconsistency," 235–38.

37 In Stone, *Features*, 86–87 (cf. idem, "Coherence and Inconsistency," 233), the case was made for 5:41 referring to messianic kingdom ideas, for 5:42 shifting the ground to final judgment, and for 5:43–44 continuing the discussion in terms of the latter. Cf. also 14:20 and Form and Function there.

38 Cf. Keulers, pp. 160–71, and Stone, *Features*, 188ff., for general treatments.

39 1 Kgs 7:7; Isa 16:5; Dan 7:9; Ps 9:5; 122:5; Prov 20:8; Luke 22:30; Rev 20:11; *b. Pesah.* 54a; *b. Ned.* 39b; *b. Abod. Zar.* 3b; *1 Enoch* 25:3; 45:3; 55:4; 62:3; 62:5; etc. See further 7:33 Commentary.

from the book) that judgment is legal in character.[40] Thus the legal form of the rebukes in 7:37; 7:73; and 7:115 may be noted. All humans will be judged, those still alive and those resurrected (4:35–36; 5:41–42). Compassion will be withdrawn and only truth will stand forth (7:33; 7:82; and 7:104 Commentary); consequently, there will be no intercession on the day of judgment (7:105–115) or even repentance after death (7:82; 9:11–12);[41] see further 7:33 and 7:34 Commentary.

Indeed, the relationship between judgment and truth is very clear and much emphasized. This is the reason that compassion and intercession will be removed.[42] The same idea seems to be expressed by the term "to see the glory of God." On the day of judgment the natural phenomena will disappear (7:39–41) and only the glory of the Most High will illuminate the world. By it that which has been determined will be revealed (7:42). To see the glory is actually reward and punishment (7:87; 7:91; 7:112), and to receive glory is to receive reward (7:95; 8:49).[43] This world is imperfect and so glory is only imperfectly revealed in it; the future world, however, will see full glory (= judgment 7:112).[44]

Chapter 7:33 implies that judgment is equal for all,[45] while according to 7:66 it is only for humans. The withdrawal of mercy is a chief feature; consequently, intercession cannot take place on that day (7:102–105; 113–115). Another aspect of the same idea is expressed by the intimate connection between truth and judgment, which is discussed in 5:1 Commentary.

Characteristics of Judgment

The judgment and the things that appertain to it, like many other eschatological things, were created before the creation of Adam.[46] The day of judgment is identified as "the end of this age and the beginning of the age to come" (7:113) or as the "end" (12:34).[47] According to 7:43, it will last a week of years; this number probably reflects *Urzeit-Endzeit* patterning.[48]

Judgment will be carried out by God (7:33), and that the end will come through God alone is the point of 6:1–9. The eagle vision says that after the destruction of the fourth wicked empire the world will await the judgment and mercy of the Creator (11:46). In 12:33–34, in the interpretation of the eagle vision, not God but the Messiah is said to dispense these. Yet it is clear that in 12:34 this activity precedes the end, the day of judgment (cf. also 7:26–44). The ambiguity here, perhaps caused by a flowing together of different traditions, is in some ways parallel to the ambiguities engendered by the passage on the ascent of the soul (7:75–99).[49] Although it is aboundingly clear that what is being described there are intermediate states of the souls, nonetheless the language used of reward and punishment in this intermediate state is very much like that used of the final judgment.[50]

Judgment is designated "judgment of God" (5:42; 7:34; 7:44; 8:61), "judgment" (7:66; 7:69; 7:70; 7:73), "day of judgment" (7:38; 7:102; 7:104; 7:113; 12:34), and "judgment to come" (8:18). Only rarely is "judgment" used to refer to God's action in history, either toward human beings in general (7:11; 7:19) or toward Israel (5:34).[51]

---

40 Volz, p. 261. Observe that, in the passages dealing with judgment, the characteristics of the divine Warrior do not appear.

41 See further 7:33; 7:34; and 7:74 Commentary. The idea is clearly present in *1 Enoch* 38:6; 60:5–6; *2 Enoch* 53:1; cf. *2 Apoc Bar* 44:12; 48:27; and 85:12. Note in a different perspective *Hermas Vis.* 2.2.5 and *Sib Or* 8:350–351. Cf. Ginzberg, *Legends,* 5:160–61.

42 The day of judgment is decisive ("swift" Latin 8:18) and displays the seal of truth (7:104; cf. *b. Yoma* 69b); see further 7:42 and cf. *Mek.* on Exod 14:29 (Horovitz-Rabin, p. 112). The connections of truth with God are common already in the Bible; see Ps 85:8; 89:15; et al. Chapter 7:33–36 is a poetic passage expressing these ideas. It has a number of parallels in the book, and the whole is discussed in the 6:11–29 Form and Structure, pp. 165–66. The withdrawal of mercy on the day of judgment is also to be observed in *2 Apoc Bar* 44:12. Contrast the saying of R. Isaac in *b. Rosh Hashanah* 16a: "Charity (צדקה/צעקה) is appropriate for humans either before or after the giving of judgment."

43 Cf. also CD 20:26, which seems to reflect an analogous conception. See also *2 Apoc Bar* 55:8 and the crown of glory in *2 Apoc Bar* 15:8; cf. 48:49 and 66:7–8. Cf. also 1QS 4:7.

44 See further 7:42 Commentary, 7:97 Commentary, and 14:35 Commentary.

45 Cf. *2 Apoc Bar* 13:8–9.

46 7:70. Cf. 6:1; 6:6, and see 3:6 Commentary.

47 The ambiguities of this terminology are dealt with in Stone, "Coherence and Inconsistency," and in Excursus on Natural Order, pp. 103–4.

48 Contrast 7:39–42 with 6:1–5.

49 On the intermediate state of the souls, see 4:35–36.

50 Other terms seem to denote similar notions— "threshing" (4:40; 4:39); "visitation" (5:56—and see Commentary; 6:6; 9:2); and "see witness" (7:94). Judgment is sometimes equivalent to "punishment" (8:38; cf. 7:21) or "require" (6:19).

51 His action in such contexts is often judicial in character; see 3:7; 3:9; 3:27; and 5:30. Cf. 14:32, where God is said to be judge in the same context.

Final Judgment and the Separation of Righteous and Wicked
In Vision 5, as has been pointed out in the preceding
section, the activity of the Messiah is referred to as
"judgment" even though it precedes the eschaton and
is clearly distinct from final judgment.[52] A similar issue
of the exact referent of "judgment" also arose in the
preceding section in regard to the postmortem fate of
the souls. In more general terms, then, the question
may be raised of the relationship of eschatological
judgment to other events that also involve the
separation of the righteous from the wicked. In Vision
5 this is done for the last generation by the Messiah (cf.
2 Apoc Bar 72:4–6). In 7:27–28 it is effected by the
woes (cf. also 5:41 Commentary)—the concept of the
survivors presupposes this.

The most explicit passage that deals with the
separation of the souls of the righteous and the wicked
after death is 7:75–99, but it is also implied by 4:33–
37. In both of these cases there is explicit differentiation of the fate of the righteous and wicked souls,
yet it is abundantly clear in both instances that a final
judgment and recompense will follow. The relationship between the prefiguration of judgment in the idea
of the survivors and final judgment itself is one of the
factors at work in 5:41–45. Although the starting point
of the discussion in 5:41 concerns the inequality of
reward for the survivors and those to be resurrected,
the solution to that problem is clearly to be found in
the nature of the day of judgment. At issue is reward,
not inequality (see 5:42). It is precisely the decisiveness
and the permanency of the day of judgment that
characterize it in contrast to other divisions between
the righteous and the wicked.

So it is quite clear that 4 Ezra uses the language of
judgment in multiple senses. The eschatological day of
judgment is not the first point of division between the
righteous and the wicked; others indeed exist. Yet it is
also clear that in a description like ours, the different
matters should not be systematized. The author is
obviously utilizing a variety of conceptions and perhaps
a variety of written traditions. Yet he has no more urge
to systematize as relates to judgment than he has as
relates to other terms and concepts in the book.[53]

■ **42** The general point of this verse resembles 1 Thess
4:15 (see 5:41 Commentary). It has been compared to
Barn. 6:13: λέγει δὲ κύριος. ἰδού, ποιῶ τὰ ἔσχατα ὡς τὰ
πρῶτα (The Lord says, 'Behold, I make the last things
like the first.') (Hilgenfeld) and *2 Apoc Bar* 51:13. In
language, but not in content, it resembles Matt 20:16.[54]

As indicated in the textual notes, we prefer the
reading "crown" to that of "circle." The operative part of
the image is usually taken to be the circularity of the
crown, implying that there is no difference between first
and last.[55]

■ **43** No commentary.

■ **44** The ambiguity of the term here rendered "world"
has already been noted (see the Excursus on the Term
"Age"). Here it is parallel to "creation," which does not
help define it. It cannot hold all created beings

---

52   See Stone, "Messiah," 299; on the associated problem
     of "the end," see Stone, "Coherence and Inconsis-
     tency," and see Excursus on Natural Order, pp. 103–
     4.

53   In Ethiopic the terms "judgment" and "punishment"
     interchange (7:36; 7:47; 7:75; cf. Arm 7:70).
     Ethiopic has "judgment" where the other versions
     have "torture"—7:47; 7:66; 7:75; 7:83 (on which
     latter see Harnisch, p. 292 note). Ethiopic has
     "delight and torture" where the other versions have
     "judgment," see 7:70. On this, see Stone, *Features*,
     251 n. 151. See also Armenian 7:75, where "day of
     judgment" replaces "until those times come when
     thou wilt renew the creation." In 10:15, Ethiopic and
     Arabic1 add "judgment." S. Lieberman, "Roman
     Legal Institutions in Early Rabbinics and in the *Acta
     Martyrum*," *JQR* 35 (1944–45) 15 n. 99, points out
     that Hebrew *dyn* often means "torture."

54   Strikingly similar in formulation is the observation of
     opus imperfectum in matthaeum 34 (*PG*, 56:822),
     commenting on Matt 20:16:
       sicut enim in corona, cum sit rotunda, nihil

     invenies quod videatur esse initium aut finis: sic
     inter sanctos, quantum ad tempus in illo saeculo,
     nemo novissimus dicitur, nemo primus.
     In the course of its exegesis of Hab 2:4, 1QpHab
     7:6–14 deals with a problem analogous to that of 1
     Thess 4:13–14, i.e., the delay of the end. Similarity
     in language but not in content may be observed also
     in *Tanh.* Noah 1:2. The contrast "first/last" is
     obvious and is already to be noted in the Bible, e.g.,
     Isa 41:4 and Qoh 1:11.

55   Kabisch suggested it to be a crown of victory (pp. 45–
     46). In *2 Apoc Bar* 15:8 the world to come is said to be
     a "crown with great glory." Yet it is unclear how the
     two parts of the verse would cohere, according to this
     interpretation. The simultaneity of resurrection,
     Kabisch claims, has emerged already from 4:26ff. (p.
     46). We may remark that this does not obviate its
     specific repetition here.

simultaneously. Harnisch points out that this verse is parallel to 4:26–27, also a denial of this world's capability of holding all created beings.[56]

In form the verse is well compared with 4:34; 5:33; and 7:14. The first of these is particularly close in both formulation and meaning to our verse. The urgency and the inability of the created being is set over against the deliberateness and capability of the Creator. The same thought is expressed by the term "haste" in 6:34. This idea is well compared with rabbinic dicta opposed to those who would try to force or hasten the eschaton.[57] Yet haste is also attributed to the treasuries of the souls which desire to give back the souls entrusted to them (4:42).

■ **45** Ezra's question is argumentative to some extent, building on the apparent contradiction between 5:42 and 5:44. "How hast thou said?": the angel has not said this in the immediately preceding verses. The idea of a general resurrection is implied by 4:42–43 and rather indirectly by 5:42.[58] The idea of resurrection is to be found elsewhere in 4 Ezra (see 7:32 Commentary and 14:35). "Creatures" here refers to human beings. We take the phrase "could it now" as an interrogative; cf. Violet 2.

■ **46, 47** No commentary.

■ **48** The earth is said to be a mother and a womb also elsewhere in the book.[59] The earth is said to bring forth many things, including humans.[60] The application of the image of the earth as a womb or a mother in these verses is complex and has been discussed above (Function and Content, pp. 146–47).

■ **49** In Function and Content, pp. 146–47, the question of the exact meaning of the image in this verse was raised. This difficulty has motivated Arabic2 and Armenian to make additions that clarify the regularity that is implied by the image but not explicit.[61]

■ **50** The term "way" is problematic, and various translations have been suggested. Licht proposed that it means "way to ask," that is, Ezra's question is invited by the angel's previous responses.[62]

At its most general the question of whether the end is soon to come is a continuing concern of Ezra's. It is asserted to be close (e.g., in 4:26; 8:61; and elsewhere).[63] Ezra asks about this twice in Vision 1, in 4:33 and 4:45. In neither case does he receive an unambiguous answer, but a response is given by means of a symbol or image. As noted in Function and Content, pp. 146–47, here the author cunningly employs the image of the womb, developed in the previous verses, but gives it a special twist. Is the earth, mother of humankind, young or old? She is old, he is assured in the following verses. The image of the senescence of the earth recurs elsewhere in the book, in 5:55 and 14:10, which latter reads, "The age has lost its youth"; cf. 14:16. It is also strikingly to be found in 2 Apoc Bar 85:10, "For the youth of this world has passed away, and the power of creation is already exhausted."[64]

The image of senescence, based on a biological metaphor, was analyzed by Momigliano. While he finds that Greek pagan historians speak of older and younger races, he finds "no evidence to show that any pagan historian took the step of presenting world history in terms of the aging of an individual."[65] This metaphor, then, seems to

---

56 Harnisch highlights the obscurity of the definition in temporal/spatial terms (p. 98) and on p. 105 pushes rather hard for a temporal meaning. See Excursus on the Two Ages.

57 See b. Sanh. 97b: "Blasted be the bones of those who calculate the end" (R. Samuel b. Naḥmani), and particularly the adjuration in b. Ketubot 111a (with the variant ידחקן).

58 See Kabisch, pp. 46–47; cf. 2 Apoc Bar 30:2. Kaminka suggests that this refers to some biblical verse such as Neh 9:6 or Job 12:10.

59 See 4:40 Commentary and Excursus on Natural Order, p. 102. In 4:41 the underworld and the treasuries of the souls are also said to be a womb. Zion as mother is discussed in 10:7 Commentary.

60 See 4:40 Commentary n. 47.

61 Motivated by the same concern, Violet 2 tends to

62 See 4:1–4 and Commentary.

63 See Keulers, p. 59.

64 See further 9:20 Commentary, 14:10 Commentary. Keulers cites Lucretius, De rerum natura 2.1150–53:

Iamque adeo fracta est aetas, effetaque tellus
Vix animalia parva creat, quae cuncta creavit
Saecla, deditque ferarum ingentia corpora partu.
(Even now indeed the power of life is broken, and the earth exhausted scarce produces tiny creatures, she who once produced all kinds and gave birth to the huge bodies of wild beasts.)

(W. H. D. Rouse, trans., Lucretius, De rerum natura, rev. by M. F. Smith [LCL; Cambridge, Mass., and London: Harvard University and Heinemann, 1982] 185). Cf. also b. Sanh. 98a, the lessening of the gener-

have originated in Jewish (perhaps Jewish apocalyptic) thinking.[66] It is significant that this metaphor is a means of presenting an overall scheme of history. It thus resembles the use of the four empires pattern in Vision 5 and the use of the divisions of the ages in 14:11–12. The view must be rejected that it is the material aspect of the earth that in itself is the cause of the degeneration or of the evils. The terminology of "world" and "age" used indifferently shows that. Instead, the idea should be related to views of predetermination of the course of the times.[67]

Attention has been drawn, however, to the apparent contradiction between the seer's stressed urging of the end and the very clearly deterministic view of the progress of creation which is asserted in response to it (see, e.g., 6:1–6). These are precisely the sort of elements that create the inner tensions of the work.[68] What is true is that, with the exception of the rather vague timetable in 14:11–12, the author studiously avoids any specifics as to the "when?" of the eschaton.[69]

■ **51** "A woman who bears": this is literally "she who bears," which could be the womb or the woman. A similar turn of phrase is to be found in 4:40, but using a different aspect of the image.[70] In 4:40 the womb is the underworld with the souls dwelling in it (4:42). Here the womb or the woman is at the least the simile for the earth, a widespread sort of image.

■ **52** This verse contains a number of points of interest. The versions vary between "stature" (Latin, Syriac, Arabic1, and Georgian) and "strength" (Ethiopic and Arabic2); Armenian offers both, and no ready Greek retroversion comes to mind.

Of greater moment, however, are a number of aspects of the content of the verse. It is taken as given that the children of a woman's advanced years are more puny than those of her youth. This view is not supported by medical fact.[71]

On the basis of this view, the analogy is adduced between the degeneration of a woman's offspring and the degeneration of the generations. Myers aptly drew attention to Gen 6:4; Num 13:33; and Amos 2:9. These verses refer to the view that in ancient times there were giants.[72] Consequently, a diminution of the present generation may be assumed. To these verses may be added Gen 6:3, which, while not referring to a diminution of stature, seeks to explain the shorter lives of

---

ations is a sign of the imminence of the coming of the Messiah. Chapter 4:27 is sometimes cited in this connection, but the idea of progressive deterioration is not found there; see 4:27 Commentary.

65   See A. Momigliano, "The Origins of Universal History," *Annali della Scuola Normale Superiore di Pisa*, ser. 3, 12.2 (1982) 533–60. The quotation is from p. 538.

66   See Stone, "Three Transformations," on the changes in outlook this implies.

67   See 4:37 Commentary, and see Stone, *Features*, 188, on the whole issue.

68   This point is made much of by Harnisch, pp. 301–2 note. He would see a deliberate and polemical response to specific views in this, a cooling down of future expectations. Yet this seems to us to run against much of the passion of the book. The stress on urgency is of the essence here.

69   The view expressed here nicely contrasts with the comment by *Qoh. R.* on Qoh 1:1: "The earth, because it fulfills the instructions of the Holy One, does not wear out."

70   In 7:54, in a quite different context, the call to ask the earth a question is repeated. See 7:45–74 Form and Structure, p. 227.

71   Contrast the *Babylonian Theodicy* 24.260–263 (W. G. Lambert, *Babylonian Wisdom Literature* [Oxford:

Oxford University, 1960] 87), where the puniness of the elder son is regarded as being the natural order: "The first-born is physically inferior" (Lambert, ibid., 65). Lambert adds, intriguingly from the perspective of our text: "There is no need to seek statistics on the physiological truth or otherwise of this proposition. The writer had none. However common observation is adequate to show that there is some empirical proof of this idea, and this would be more apparent in the ancient Near East where women commenced childbirth at the earliest possible age, and so before they were fully grown." These assumptions are the exact opposite of those in 4 Ezra. Dr. M. Rayman of Jerusalem informs me that in the case of certain diseases, women giving birth in their forties may have smaller babies than usual but that this is not commonly the case.

72   To them may be added the relevant material from *1 Enoch* and *Book of Giants* from Qumran, although both of these writings draw on a very specific legend about the offspring of the daughters of men and the fallen angels. On aboriginal people as giants, see the material adduced by T. H. Gaster, *Myth, Legend and Custom in the Old Testament* (New York and Evanston: Harper & Row, 1969) 311.

people in the postdiluvian ages, and the idea of degeneration of the ages is implicit in it. This idea of the degeneration of the generations is also expressed by Philo, *De opif.* 141–142, and inherited from him by later Greek and Latin works.[73] The same idea is also to be found in rabbinic literature; see, for example, *j. Demai* 3:1 // *Gen. R.* 60:8 (Theodor-Albeck, p. 648) and *j. Shek.* 5:1; *b. Shabb.* 112b.[74]

That view is also a commonplace of Greek thought from Hesiod on at least. The same idea also functions, at another level of discourse, in the retrospective view of religious authority which took such a prominent role in some aspects of rabbinic presentation of the Jewish past.[75] The views presented by our text take for granted that Ezra will readily admit that his generation is less in stature (?worth) than previous ones. This in turn relates to the view of the "running down" of nature, reaching a point of absurdity in the prophecies of 4 Ezra 6:21 and *Jub* 23:26–28. All of this material serves our author's purpose of stressing the imminence of the end.[76]

■ **53, 54** No commentary.

■ **55** The ideas of the aging of the earth and the degeneration of humans were discussed in 5:50 Commentary. In the intervening verses the notion has been introduced that the degeneration of humans can serve as a way of telling the age of the earth. The same idea is expressed from a different perspective by Philo, *De opif.* 140:

> For as that which is in bloom is always better than that whose bloom is past, be it animal or plant or fruit or aught else in nature, so the man first fashioned was clearly the bloom of our entire race, and never have his descendants attained the like bloom, forms and faculties ever feebler have been bestowed on each succeeding generation.[77]

This verse, therefore, in broad terms sums up the answer to Ezra's question. The creation is aging and close to its end.[78]

■ **56** The introductory phrase, which is more elaborate than in the preceding verses, indicates a new question which is answered in a different literary form.[79] Ezra has accepted that there is to be a judgment and that it is near, and now he inquires about the agent of this judgment.[80]

Bensly pointed out that the word "Lord" often stands in immediate contrast to the word "servant."[81] This is true of many instances of "servant" in the book; see 6:1;

---

73 Momigliano, "Universal History," 534–35.
74 This matter is set forth also by Volz, pp. 159–60.
75 There are numerous instances of rabbinic dicta expressing this idea.
76 Harnisch, 300–301n raises the possibility that two polemically opposed stances are here reflected, the one emphasizing the fixedness of the processes of history and the other the author's stress and urgency. It seems to us that these do not necessarily come from different social contexts, but are instead differing tendencies within the author's thought.
77 Keulers cites a similar idea from Lucretius 2.1150–3. These verses clearly roused interest, since they are quoted or paraphrased in various patristic sources: Ambrose, *de bono mortis,* 10:
> Comparavit enim utero mulieris partus huius saeculi, quoniam "fortiores sunt qui in iuventute virtutis nati sunt, infirmiores qui in tempore senectutis." Defecit enim multitudine generantis hoc saeculum, tanquam vulva generantis et tanquam senescens creatura robur iuventutis suae velut marcenti iam virium suarum vigore deponit.
> (For Scripture compared the births of this world to a woman's womb, since "those who are born in the power of youth are stronger, while those in the time of old age, weaker." For this world has been weakened by the multitude of births, just like the

womb of a woman who gives birth, and just like a creature which grows old, it has laid aside the strength of its youth, as if its powers had degenerated from vigor.)
Cyprian, *ad Demetrianum* (ed. Hartel, vol. 1, 352):
> Illud primo in loco scire debes senuisse iam saeculum, non illis viribus stare, quibus prius steterat, nec vigore et robore ipso valere, quod antea praevalebat.
> (Here in the first place you should know that the world has now become old and does not remain in those powers in which it previously did, neither is it strong in that strength or vigor, in which it formerly prevailed.)
78 F. Zimmermann, "Underlying Documents of 4 Ezra," *JQR* 51 (1960/1961), 109 suggests that this verse may reflect a Hebrew wordplay עַל'ם/עוֹלם "world/youth." That might be so, but it is a literary decoration and not determinative of the conceptual structure of the passage.
79 See Form and Structure above and 4:44 Commentary.
80 See Function and Content above.
81 Bensly, *MF,* on 7:75.

7:75; 8:6; 8:24; 10:34–37; and 12:7–8.[82]

The term "visit" is taken to mean punitive visitation. This is one of the possible meanings of Hebrew פקד and is the only meaning of Latin *visitare* and parallels in 4 Ezra. See 6:18 and 9:2.[83]

■ **6:1** This verse raises a considerable number of problems and issues. In the textual notes the loss of the first phrase by the Latin version was discussed, and, as it stands in the other versions, the verse offers the answer to the question of 5:56: "Through whom will you visit your creation?" The answer is that although the beginning of the visitation is by human agency, its end will be through God.[84] It should be noted that "end" in 6:6 is not a technical term for the eschatological turning point but means "end of visitation" in opposition to its beginning.[85] So the answer is that the process of punishment will start through human agency (perhaps events of the messianic woes are indicated), but the end will be through God himself.

The next point, strengthening the one already made, is that God determined the process of judgment before the creation of the world. Just as he alone created, so he alone will judge, a point also made explicitly in 7:70.

This argument is concluded in 6:6, while the intervening verses of 6:1b–5 are a poetic creation passage of great interest.

In form, the verses of 6:1b–5 are all statements starting with "before." In this they resemble Ps 90:2:

Before the mountains were brought forth,

or ever thou hadst formed the earth and the world.

Like our passage, Ps 90:2 uses the "before" statements to predicate something about God. Another similar passage, more extended than Ps 90:2, also gives a list of created elements with "before" or "when" statements. This is the creation poem in Prov 8:22–26 (cf. 8:27–29). That passage is a cosmogony, and the predicates refer to wisdom, not to God.[86] Nonetheless, in the light of these examples, it seems very likely that our passage too is related to hymnic creation compositions.[87]

This having been said, however, it must be noted that the orientation of the poem in 6:1b–5 is heavily meteorological, although it has some cosmological features. It is also parallel in many details to *2 Apoc Bar* 59:5–11, a passage of great importance in other respects for 4 Ezra.[88]

---

82 "Servant" occurs without "Lord" in 3:23; 5:45; 7:102; and 13:14 (but see textual note b there); 7:104 is different.

83 See Stone, "Coherence and Inconsistency," 231 note. Harnisch, p. 308 note, argues for its being a technical term for God's eschatological coming; see, e.g., in *Bib Ant* 19:12; 26:13; *2 Apoc Bar* 20:2; 83:2. We would add that, in 4 Ezra at least, this verb indicates a punitive coming and so often in the Bible: so also Knibb. Similar are *2 Apoc Bar* 24:4 and 54:17. So also, e.g., *Test Patr Levi* 4:1. This probably reflects Hebrew *pqd;* cf. also 1QS 3:14; 4:11; 4:18–19; CD 7:9; and see Stone, *Features,* 253 n. 180.

84 Violet 2 suggests that the word "not" has been lost, perhaps because of doctrinal motives. This view is contradicted by Gressmann, who proposes that the "beginning," i.e., of judgment, was through such human agency as the Assyrians and Babylonians.

85 See Stone, "Coherence and Inconsistency," 231.

86 The elements involved are "earth" (Prov 8:23), "depths" and "springs" (v 24), "mountains" and "hills" (v 25), "earth" and "dust" (v 26), "heavens" and "the deep" (v 27), "skies" and "fountains of the deep" (v 28), "sea's limit" and "earth's foundation" (v. 29). Notably the form and context, but not the elements themselves, are what is shared. This form is taken up much later in a piyyuṭ by Kalonymus for the last day

of Passover: N. Adler and J. Davis, *The Service of the Synagogue: Passover* (14th ed.; London: Routledge & Kegan Paul, 1949), 259. Keulers (p. 21) and Violet 2 (although this latter by emendation) discern 14 cola in this poem, i.e., 2 x 7. Cf. the *Babylonian Creation Epic* 1:1: "when on high the heaven had not been named, / firm ground below had not been called by name" (Pritchard, *ANET,* 60–61).

87 See, e.g., Gunkel, *Schöpfung,* 401–2; and *ANET,* 60–61.

88 In 4 Ezra 7:39–42 the point is made that at the time of eschatological judgment, meteorological elements will be canceled. Moreover, now these "before" lists must be added to the interrogative lists and revelatory lists discussed in detail in Stone, "Lists." They are clearly a variation again on the enumeration of the elements of creation which has been found repeatedly in different modalities throughout the literature. The piyyuṭ of Kalonymus for the Seventh Day of Passover, referred to in n. 86 above, is similar.

Parallel elements in the two passages may be set forth as follows, and from this list the affinity of the two passages is evident.

A. Meteorological
gates of world
wind $\}$ —*2 Apoc Bar* 59:5; *1 Enoch* 41:3
thunder
lightning $\}$ —*2 Apoc Bar* 59:11; *1 Enoch* 41:3
B. Paradisical
paradise   *2 Apoc Bar* 59:7
flowers
C. Angelological
motive powers
angelic armies   *2 Apoc Bar* 59:11
D. Cosmological
heights of air   *2 Apoc Bar* 59:7
measures of the
firmaments
E. This world and age
footstool of Zion
years of the present
F. Paradoxical
imaginations of the
senses   ?*2 Apoc Bar* 59:10
treasures of faith   ?*2 Apoc Bar* 59:10.[89]

For "portals of the world," Box would translate "heavenly portals." These are clearly the passages from heaven to earth through which the winds blow (cf. *1 Enoch* 34; 35–36; 41:3). Zimmermann suggests a mistranslation of מוצא.[90]

Syriac reads "weight of winds." This is probably influenced by 4:5 (see Commentary there), and the phrase should be compared with *2 Apoc Bar* 59:5.[91]

■ **2** The thunder and the lightning are clearly parallel, as are the foundations of paradise and the "beautiful flowers" of 6:3a. These two groups of things, like the preceding, belong to the primordial stage of the world, before which, our author assures us, God created the eschatological events.

It may be that the thunder and the lightning are mentioned not merely because they are part of what precedes the creation (why these elements and not snow, hail, or rain?) but also because they are often said in scripture to precede or accompany theophanies. Such examples may be observed in Exod 19:16; Ps 104:7 (thunder); and Rev 4:5.

The concept of the Garden of Eden or paradise has many implications and meanings in the book. One of these is as Adam's garden, and when it is taken in this sense, there are views that set its creation before that of the world.[92] That is implied here. Its wondrous fruit is referred to in 7:123,[93] and long ago Gunkel suggested that the description of the wondrous flowers and fruit in 6:44, although presented by 4 Ezra as a description of the earth which was made on the third day, is in fact derived from the creation of paradise which, in certain texts, is said to have been created on the third day (so, e.g., *Jub* 2:7).[94] Be all this as it may, the verse clearly implies the antiquity of the creation of paradise, before mankind or indeed the whole world. God planned judgment even before that.[95]

■ **3** The flowers of paradise were discussed in the com-

---

89 The details of the parallels to and exegesis of each of these elements will be given in the Commentary on the several verses.

90 Zimmermann, "Underlying Documents," 116. Box suggests, following Gunkel, the *saeculum* here may mean "heaven." See the refutation of this in Stone, "Apocryphal Notes," 130. The phrase should be compared with Ps 24:7, פתחי עולם, although there the meaning is surely different, and שערי עולם in 1QH 6:31. Violet 2 suggests that the phrase is secondary, since it destroys the structure of 14 (2 x 7) cola which he discerns in the poem.

91 See Stone, "Lists," 416–20.

92 So already 3:6 and see Commentary there; cf. *b. Pesaḥ.* 54a; *b Ned.* 39b; and Targums to Gen 2:8. Indeed, the rabbinic dicta on this appear to derive from an exegesis of Gen 2:8. See 7:36 Commentary

and 8:52 Commentary on paradise as eschatological reward, as well as Stone, *Features*, 198.

93 This line of description is carried to a baroque extreme in *Seder Gan Eden* (Jellinek, *BM*, 2:53); cf. also Rev 22:2.

94 The description of paradise is discussed fully in 3:6 Commentary; see also Keulers, p. 186. Oesterley suggests that the term "foundations" of paradise indicates that it was thought of as a building. There is no doubt that in literature such as the *Life of Adam and Eve* it is conceived of as being walled (see 7:6 Commentary). That is also confirmed by the relationship of paradise and city discussed in 7:26 Commentary. This admirably fits in with later representations in Christian art.

95 Gunkel speculates, not completely convincingly, that the flowers are originally the stars. This finds some

mentary on the previous verse. The expression "powers of movement" has given rise to a number of exegetical problems. The Syriac version views this as earthquakes, an idea supported by Licht.[96] Most interpreters, however, following the sense of the parallelism, regard this as a term for angelic beings. Box compares it with αἱ δυνάμεις τῶν οὐρανῶν (the powers of the heavens) in Matt 24:29. Reference seems to be made to heavenly beings, perhaps the motive powers of the luminaries, personifications of the luminaries or the moveable stars, seen as a class of angels.[97]

The angelic host referred to in the last part of the verse is commonplace; cf. 8:21. Language strikingly similar to that in the present verse is 2 Apoc Bar 21:6, in a praise to God the Creator:

> You who reign with great thoughts over the powers which stand before you, and who rules [sic] with indignation the countless holy beings, who are flame and fire, whom you created from the beginning, those who stand around your throne.

■ **4** The first two phrases of this verse are parallel. In 6:41 the elevation of the firmament is described, and the height below it is presumably the "height of the air." This is one of the cosmological secrets revealed to Moses in 2 Apoc Bar 59:8. These heights are described in 2 Enoch J 3:1–2.[98] The establishment of the height of the air is an early part of the process of creation.

From the height of the air, the author proceeds to the measures of the firmament. His wording is "before the measures of the firmaments were named." Box regards these as the divisions of the heavens and consequently translates "spaces of the firmament." In fact, the measure of the firmament or of the height of the heavens is commonly found as a subject of apocalyptic revelation; compare 1 Enoch 93:14; Armenian 4 Ezra 5:36A; Sir 1:3, "the height of heaven . . . who can investigate?"[99] The apparently anomalous expression "naming the measures" has many parallels, cases in which naming is equivalent to measuring and *vice versa*.[100] What is described, therefore, is God's creative disposition of the heavens.[101]

The "footstool of Zion" must be taken to mean "the footstool which is Zion." It is a commonplace in the Bible that Zion or the Temple on Mount Zion, or even the Ark of the Covenant is God's footstool. See clearly Ps 99:5; 132:7; Lam 2:1; and 1 Chr 28:2. Thus the verse in 1 Chronicles reads:

> Then King David rose to his feet and said: "Hear me, my brethren and my people. I had it in my heart to build a house of rest for the ark of the covenant of the Lord, and for the footstool of our God."[102]

In the context of our verse, Zion is the city or the Temple and it has been discussed whether it is the earthly one or the heavenly one. The Rabbis list the heavenly temple among the things created before the

---

oblique support in the expression of Sir 43:9: κάλλος οὐρανοῦ δόξα ἄστρων.

96 On the variant reading, see textual notes. Note also that earthquake is one of the gates of heaven according to 3:19, although there 1 Kgs 19:11 is at play. See 3:19 Commentary.

97 These are most probably demythologized pagan deities, although that is far in the background in our text. Such personifications of luminaries or references to the angels controlling them are widespread in the literature of the period. Cf., e.g., Bar 3:34–35; 1 Enoch 69:21; 80:6; and 2 Enoch 14. Ephesians 2:2, sometimes cited in relationship with the present verse, is surely irrelevant. Kahana, following a different line of thought, suggests that an original גדודי כח was corrupted into נדודי כח.

98 A Greek corruption has been proposed, viz., ἀστέρες/ἀήρες; see textual notes. This does not seem likely on exegetical grounds either, for the parallelism is clear. In 2 Enoch the firmament not only serves to separate the sublunar sphere from the upper waters but in other texts firmaments serve as

demarcations between the various heavens.

99 On this, see Stone, "Lists," 422–24.

100 See 2 Enoch 40:2–3: "I have measured the number of the stars, the great countless number of them. . . . For not even the angels see their number while I have written their names." See also Isa 40:26 and Ps 147:4–5. Admittedly these cases relate to the naming or numbering of stars, but the same use of language seems to be regnant in the present context.

101 In certain developed speculations about the heavenly spheres, names are assigned to various of them; such are 2 Enoch J 21:6—22:1 and b. Hag. 12b. It is by no means certain that this is what is being described here.

102 This clearly has older background in the religion of ancient Israel, which is only incidentally relevant here. This same view is the background against which the prophet makes his polemical pronouncement in Isa 66:1: "Thus says the Lord: 'Heaven is my throne and the earth is my footstool, what is the House which you would build for me, and where is the place of my rest?'" See IDB s.v.

world.[103] A similar view of the primordial character of the Temple is expressed in *2 Apocalypse of Baruch* 4 where the heavenly Jerusalem is said to have existed before God decided to create paradise and man. So the three elements of this verse are things belonging to the very first stage of the process of creation.

■ **5** The three elements of this verse also appertain to the primordial age before which God formed the things relating to judgment. Gunkel comments on the extraordinary measure of predetermination thus implied: God fixed the visitation before he had even fixed the times of the world or the number of righteous and wicked. In 4:36–37 we also find the number of the times and the number of the righteous mentioned together. These two elements are intimately connected, and both are determined in advance by God.[104]

The meaning of "estranged" is not very clear. It obviously must be taken in contrastive parallelism with the "sealing of the faithful." Perhaps just as sealing expresses ownership, so the wicked are estranged from the same divine owner.[105] "Sealing," moreover, has a variety of connotations in the literature of ancient Israel. Here we will be concerned with only one: it is a mark or

guarantee of ownership.[106] Those belonging to God are sealed in Ezek 9:4–5, as are those belonging to God or Christ in the New Testament.[107] Certain scholars are bothered by the fact that the virtues of the righteous are described as "treasures of faith" in this Jewish book. This is, however, unexceptionable.[108]

The term "treasures" is applied to the virtues of the righteous also in 7:77 (see Commentary there) and 8:36.

■ **6** This verse concludes the argument started in 6:1. There it states that the beginning of visitation is through human agency but the end through God himself. To emphasize God's role as sole consummator of the visitation, the text stresses that he was also the sole creator and that he planned the eschatological events before he created the world.[109] God's primordial plan of judgment, with such an emphasis on predestination, is stressed in 4 Ezra 7:30 and 9:4.[110] What is correctly observed by Keulers is that the stress on God as creator enables his role as judge (p. 147). Compare 4 Ezra 8:7 on God as creator, as well as other places in the book.[111]

The last phrase of the verse is expanded in the Latin version and highlights God's sole role in the end events.[112] It is clearly a Jewish view that God alone will

---

103 See 3:4 Commentary.

104 See 4:37 Commentary.

105 Box's note with textual restorations has no basis.

106 See in general *TDNT*, 7:939–53; art. σφραγίζω; Keulers, p. 180: see 6:20 and Commentary there for a different sense. This is different from the sealing or closing of Sheol in *2 Apoc Bar* 21:23 or of the root of evil in 4 Ezra 8:53.

107 Cf. also Isa 44:5 as well as Deut 6:8 and 11:18. The Ezekiel and Isaiah texts are combined in *Apoc Elijah* 1:9, and see Rosenstiehl, *Elie*, there. Similar are *Od Sol* 8:13 and 8:19. In the New Testament, see 2 Cor 1:22; Eph 1:13; 4:30; Rev 7:2–3; and 9:4. In Christian sources, baptism is often viewed as sealing; see, e.g., *Hermas Sim.* 9:16 and *Od Sol* 4:6–7. In Jewish sources from an early time circumcision is regarded as a sealing. Thus already *Aramaic Levi* 2; cf. J. C. Greenfield and M. E. Stone, "Remarks on the Aramaic Testament of Levi," *RB* 86 (1979) 218, and, e.g., *Palaea Historica* (A. Vassiliev, *Anecdota Graeco-Byzantina* [Moscow: Imperial University, 1893], 1:212, line 6). On sealing, see further 6:20.

108 See particularly the comments of Box and Oesterley. Note that "faith" is a primary virtue of the righteous elsewhere, so 7:34 and by implication 5:1; cf. esp. 9:7 and 13:23. See also *2 Apoc Bar* 54:21.

109 Things pertaining to judgment were readied before

creation. This is often asserted in 4 Ezra; see 3:6 Commentary, 9:18 Commentary, and Keulers, p. 18.

110 Gunkel and Box see in the phrase "then I planned these things" a reference to creation through thought (cf. also Myers). This raises associations with Philo, yet most likely no metaphysical statement is being made. It is well to recall such statements as "[God] prepared [things] in the knowledge of his heart" (*Jub* 2:2), "before any person existed, a place of judgment was prepared for him" (*2 Enoch* A 49:2), and even *Genesis Rabba* relating to things that עלו במחשבה להבראות "occurred to the divine thought to be created" (on 1:1, Theodor-Albeck, pp. 46–47) or the creation of "the name of the Messiah," which serve as ways of speaking about the divine planning activity. Similar also is 1QS 3:15–16, referring to God's מחשבה: to the terms, see F. Nötscher, *Zur theologischen Terminologie der Qumran-Texte* (BBB 10; Bonn: Hanstein, 1956) 53–54. Cf. further *ARN* 12 (Schechter, p. 50). See also 12:32 Commentary; 13:26. 4 Ezra, like *2 Apoc Bar* 14:17, stresses creation through divine speech; see 3:4 Commentary. Elements of judgment are included by the Rabbis in lists of things created before the world; see 3:6 Commentary.

111 Note also the stress on this in 1QS 3:15–17, in striking contrast to what follows there.

be judge at the end.[113] It has been pointed out that the vision in chapter 13 that attributes many cosmic and judgmental functions to the redeemer is drawn from a preexisting source. In the interpretation of that vision, surely the work of the author of 4 Ezra, those functions are systematically removed from the redeemer and exclusively attributed to God.[114] What is clear, and should be stressed, is the author's opposition to the idea that the consummation of judgment will come through any agent but God. There were other views on this in the Judaism of the time; the Son of man, Melchizedek, and others vied for this role.[115]

■ **7** In the discussion of Vision 2, as far as 5:55, the seer has determined that the world is close to old age. In 6:1–6 he had turned aside from his preoccupation with timetable to discover that there will be a vindication that will be consummated by God himself.

With this clear in his mind he returns, at the conclusion of the dialogic prediction, once more to the question of timetable. He raises two questions: What will be the dividing of the times and when will be the end of the first age and the start of the second? These two questions seem to be of identical import. In the angel's response to them we find a prediction of signs that shift from woes to the wondrous divine action, first for punishment and then for renewal of the world (6:25–28).[116] The first answer to the seer's dual question comes in the following verses.

If we are correct and the "dividing of the times" is the same as the separation of the ages, then this provides some indication of the meaning of the difficult word עולם and equivalents.[117]

■ **8–10** This small pericope will be exegeted as a whole. It may be divided into eight statements, which may be enumerated as follows:

Paradox and Explanation
  1. From Abraham to Abraham (6:8)
  2. For from him Jacob and Esau
Citation of Biblical Verse
  3. Jacob's hand held Esau's heel
Exegesis of Biblical Verse
  4. Esau is the end of this age (6:9)
  5. Jacob is the start of the age to come
Proverbial Statement
  6. The beginning of a man is his hand (6:10)
  7. The end of a man is his heel
Injunction
  8. Between hand and heel seek nothing else
In the following discussion we shall refer to these statement numbers.

The passage is an answer to the double question of 6:7. Box suggested that statements 1 and 2 are the answer to the first question of 6:7: "What will be the dividing of the times?" Statements 3 to 7, however,

---

112 Latin here stresses the idea that τὰ ἔσχατα ὡς τὰ πρῶτα ("The last things like the first") (Barn. 6:13) which is implicit in the whole pericope in any case. In this general sense, see also 7:30. The view is widespread in "history of religions" scholarship. One famous exposition is by Gunkel, *Schöpfung;* see, e.g., 366–67. Cf. also Volz, pp. 359–60. For further references in Jewish and Christian thought, see Harnisch, p. 136 note. See also the apt comments by N. A. Dahl, "Christ, Creation and the Church," *The Background of the New Testament and Its Eschatology* (ed. W. D. Davies and D. Daube; Cambridge: Cambridge University, 1956) 422–31. Harnisch thinks that this view in 4 Ezra is anti-Christian. This is not necessarily the case. In the next sentence we mention the reinterpretation of chap. 13 in which there is nothing anti-Christian, yet which denies an effective role in creation to anyone but God. In the present pericope the argument does not turn on the question of the Latin addition, for the same point is already made in 6:1. The decisive text-critical arguments must be considered (see textual notes), and the critic may well ask us how a Christian copyist could have made this addition. Yet the conceptual pattern of the addition is present, say, in Barnabas as quoted, in the extensive *Urzeit-Endzeit* speculations, and elsewhere. The text-critical arguments remain compelling in any case.

113 See in Christian form in 1 Pet 1:20.

114 See Excursus on the Redeemer Figure, and Stone, "Messiah," 305–10. Keulers points out that the view expressed in 6:1–6 seems to contradict Vision 6 where the "end" is said to come through the Man. Yet, as has been pointed out, "end" in our pericope means "end of visitation"; that will come through God. Its beginning, indeed, is clearly stated to come through human agency. See Keulers, p. 135.

115 See Nickelsburg and Stone, *Faith and Piety,* 177–87.

116 The question here may be compared in general with Matt 24:3.

117 See Excursus on the Two Ages; Harnisch, p. 96. Does the term "the age that follows" actually reflect Hebrew העולם הבא and its Greek equivalents?

respond to the second question: "When will be the end of the first age and the beginning of the second?"

Statement 1 is unclear, and that caused variants in the versions as discussed in the textual notes. Its obscure style was designed to set an oracular tone which was taken up again in statements 6 to 8.[118] It answers the question by a deliberate paradox: the division will be between Abraham and Abraham, but since these are the same person, it appears that there will be no division. Yet there must be a division, or a change; this has been the point of the whole preceding discussion. The tension so generated is released by the second statement which offers egress from the dilemma. "Abraham" means Abraham, but it also implies his children.[119]

The introduction in statement 2 of Jacob and Esau is not self-explanatory. After all (in spite of certain of the versions), Isaac is missing.[120] Jacob and Esau, however, are required so as to introduce the exegesis of Gen 25:26: "Afterward his brother came forth, and his hand had taken hold of Esau's heel; so his name was called Jacob."

In rabbinic literature this verse is interpreted in an eschatological fashion. Box and Violet noticed a tradition in *Gen. R.* 63:9 (Theodor-Albeck, pp. 699–700; parallel to *Yalqut Shimoni* 110) quoted in the name of an unknown חד מן אלין דבית סילנא, or according to *Yalqut,* R. Gamaliel, and two other passages may also be men-

tioned.[121] The most explicit is in the late *Midrash Haggadol:*

"And his hand seized on Esau's heel," for there is no further kingdom in the world after Esau's kingdom except Israel's alone. Therefore it says "on the heel" (בעקב) i.e. immediately adjacent to it, and thus it says: "And it will be after this that I will pour out my spirit on all flesh (Joel 3:1)."[122]

Thus, at a period subsequent to 4 Ezra the eschatological exegesis of Gen 25:26 is well attested by rabbinic sources. The passage from *Midrash Haggadol* is strikingly like 4 Ezra in its interpretation. Our text is the oldest surviving witness to this exegetical tradition but probably not its originator.

With one or two exceptions, modern interpreters of 4 Ezra have interpreted the names Esau and Jacob to refer to specific kingdoms or eras. They have this in common with the rabbinic view cited above.[123] One interpretation, espoused by Kabisch and Box among others, is that Esau symbolizes this corruptible age and Jacob the incorruptible age to come.[124] Their view, as Keulers pointed out, is conditioned by the supposed peculiarities of the so-called S document's universal eschatology.[125] Keulers' own view, which many others before and after him have held, is that the passage refers to the eschatological kingdom of Israel which will follow that of Rome.[126] This understanding is strongly supported by

---

118 Licht simply regards it as incomprehensible. It has been speculated that the Greek might have been ἀπὸ τοῦ ʼΑβρααμ ἕως τῶν τοῦ ʼΑβρααμ. This would, at first glance, alleviate the exegetical problem, yet it is hard to conceive what Hebrew such a Greek might have represented, and why it is not found in the versions. Mussies supports the latter part of this reconstruction ("Graecisms," 111). A completely alternative exegesis is that of Kaminka, who says that the statement contrasts the period of idolatry before Abraham with the period of belief in God after him. This is difficult to integrate with the rest of the passage.

119 Cf. the argument in Heb 7:4, 9–10:
4 Abraham the patriarch gave him a tithe of the spoils. . . . 9 One might even say that Levi himself, who receives tithes, paid tithes through Abraham, 10 for he was still in the loins of his ancestor Abraham when Melchizedek met him.

120 Cf. 3:15–16.

121 Rosenthal, *Vier apokryphische Bücher,* 59 note, considers 6:8–9 to be a genuine quotation of R.

Gamaliel. This is not the case, as this spread of the traditions indicates.

122 The citation of Joel is striking in view of 6:26. The citation is from *Midr. Haggadol* on Gen 25:26; cf. *Pes. R. K.* 23b. An additional passage, also giving an eschatological exegesis of this passage, is *PRE* 32 (tr. Friedlander, p. 235): "Hence thou mayest learn that the descendants of Esau will not fall until a remnant from Jacob will come and cut off the feet of the children of Esau, as it is said: 'Forasmuch as thou sawest that a stone was cut out of the mountain without hands'" (Dan 2:45). See Ginzberg, *Legends,* 5:271.

123 Oesterley would stress that the intent of the passage is not the identification of Esau and Jacob but the fact of the immediate sequence. Older views identified Esau directly with the Herodian dynasty or even with Agrippa the younger. So Hilgenfeld, *Apokalyptik,* 195, 237; idem, *Esra und Daniel,* 22–23; and Volkmar, p. 361.

124 Kabisch, pp. 50–51; Box, pp. 67–70. Myers, Licht, and Hartom also follow this view without accepting

the identification of Esau with Rome.[127]

Thus the eschatological interpretation of Gen 25:26 serves to answer the questions of 6:7. Esau, the kingdom of Rome, is the end of this age and it will be followed by the kingdom of Jacob or Israel which will be the beginning of the next age. It will be followed immediately, just as heel ("the end of man") is followed by hand, his beginning.[128]

A final observation should be made about this piece of exegesis. It is not an allegory using the closeness of the grasping of the hand on the heel as a *symbol* of the succession of the two ages. It is an eschatological interpretation of the biblical text based, like the Qumran *pesharim*, on the idea that the biblical text has a veiled eschatological meaning.[129] Note the rather similar formulation in *2 Apoc Bar* 74:2. It differs from the Midrash on the same verse in the degree of specificity of its eschatological urgency, although the logic of exegesis is much the same.

The exegesis is followed by the general or proverbial statements 6 and 7. These answer the question that might be raised, particularly about the hand, as to whether it is indeed the beginning of man.[130] They serve to emphasize that the beginning of the "following world" will come immediately on the end of "this world."

Finally there is an injunction to Ezra, once more in the oracular form hinted at in statement 1: "Between the heel and the hand seek for nothing else, Ezra!" This could be taken to mean simply that there is nothing else between heel and hand. On the other hand, it might be set in the context of such statements as 8:55 and 9:13 in which Ezra is told to avoid asking certain questions.[131] It is also similar to the corresponding verse in Vision 1 in which Ezra, just before the revelation of signs in Prediction 2, is told that certain matters lie outside the permitted realm (4:52).

the literary source theories upon which Kabisch and Box found their opinions or, perhaps, even the exclusive character of the concept "coming age."

125 Consequently, Box, e.g., stresses that the exegesis deliberately excludes a messianic kingdom of Israel.

126 Keulers, pp. 41, 47–48, 107. So also Schürer, 3:326; Gunkel; Vagany, p. 41; et al. Knibb also subscribes to this view, while pointing out that it implies a contradiction to 7:28–33, which arose because the author had not completely integrated his world view (p. 147 n. 9). On the terminology "this world" and "the world to come," see 7:12 Commentary.

127 Esau = Amalek = Rome: Schechter, *Aspects*, 99–100, 108. Ginzberg, *Legends*, 5:272, adduces a considerable range of authorities. This matter is dealt with in detail by Schürer, 3:320 n. 78, and G. Cohen has devoted a study to it. In that study he claims that, though the identification of Esau as Rome has been made here in 4 Ezra, "it is only from the middle of the second century that we can discern the conversion of what may have been but one midrash among many . . . into a popular and explicit symbolism" ("Esau as a Symbol in Early Medieval Thought," *Jewish Medieval and Renaissance Studies* [ed. A. Altmann; Lown Institute Studies and Texts 4; Cambridge: Harvard University, 1967] 19–20). The eagle of 4 Ezra 12:11, the last wicked kingdom, is

clearly Rome. Babylon is identified as Rome in many sources of the period; see 3:1 Commentary.

128 Harnisch, p. 302 note, quotes Ströbel's view that the very use of heel (עקב) hints at an attitude that would restrain the eschaton by a Hebrew wordplay. A. Ströbel, "Die Allegorie von der Ferse Esaus," *Untersuchungen zur eschatologischen Verzögerungsproblem* (Leiden and Cologne: Brill, 1961), 37–40, deals with 4 Ezra 6:7–10. He suggests that the wordplay invokes rabbinic preoccupation with the word מעכב. Yet he does not explain quite how this fits with the overall interpretation of the chapter, or even of the passage.

129 D. Dimant, "Qumran and Sectarian Literature," *Jewish Writings of the Second Temple Period* (ed. M. E. Stone; CRINT 2.2; Assen and Philadelphia: van Gorcum and Fortress, 1984) 505–8.

130 Stone, *Features*, 51, even suggested that in 6:9 a wordplay of ראש/ראשית may be at work. This seems to be so in Arabic2 in 6:10.

131 Cf. also *1 Enoch* 60:10 and other places. On oracular form, see 4:26 Commentary.

11 I [a] answered and said, "O sovereign Lord, [b] if I have found favor in thy sight, 12/ show thy servant [c] the end of the [d] signs which thou didst show me in part on a previous night." [e]

13 He answered and said to me, "Rise [f] to your feet and you will hear a full, resounding voice. 14/ And [g]it will be [g] if the place where you are standing is greatly shaken 15/ while (the voice) [h] is speaking with you, [i] do not be terrified, because the word [j] concerns the end, and the foundations of the earth will understand 16/ that the speech concerns them. [k] They will tremble and be shaken, for they know that their end must be changed." [l]

17 And [m]it came to pass [m] when I heard this, I rose [n] to my feet and listened, and behold, [o] a voice was speaking, and its sound was like the sound of many waters. 18/ And it said, "Behold, the days are coming, and it shall come to pass that

> when I draw [p] near to visit the inhabitants of the earth,

19/ and when I require [q] from the doers of iniquity (the penalty) of their iniquity,

> and when the humiliation of Zion [r] is complete,

20/ and when the seal will be placed upon [s] the age [t] which is about [u] to

Notes

11   a "And I" Lat, Syr, Eth, Georg; "Then I" Ar1, Ar2.

     b Ar1, Ar2 "Lord"; see 7:75 note a.

12   c "Me" Georg, Ar2, Arm.

     d "Thy" Lat; "these" Eth, Georg; Arm varies greatly.

     d–e The text is not as certain as might seem from Violet 2. The translation follows Lat, Syr, Eth, Georg. In Ar1, Ar2 Violet 1's "Zeichen" is in fact an emendation for "days." So what is revealed is "fullness of days" in Ar1 and "the time and the days" in Ar2. For "a previous night," Ar1 has "previous days" and Arm has "end of times." There may, of course, be some Greek readings hidden here, but they are hard to recover and the influence of formulaic phrases should not be excluded.

13   f Eth, Ar1, Arm add "and stand"; cf. similar readings in 6:17. Arm adds, in line with its reformulation of 6:12, "Since you inquire into and investigate the ways of the Most High."

14   g–g Lat, Syr, Georg; Eth, Ar1, Ar2 omit; for this variant, see 5:21; 5:31; 6:17; 6:24; 6:25; 7:1; 7:26; etc. This verse seems to have two Hebraisms, a reflex of infinitive absolute and finite verb ("greatly shaken") and the resumptive pronoun *super eum* and parallels.

15   h Simplified for purposes of translation.

     i Lat omits; Eth has "I speak" for the preceding verb; cf. Arm.

16   j Or "speech."

     k Arm varies.

     l So Lat, cf. Ar1, Ar2; Syr slightly different.

17   m–m Lat, Syr, Georg; Eth, Ar1, Ar2 omit; cf. note g–g above on 6:14.

     n Eth, Ar1 add "and stood."

     o Syr adds "and I heard"; Georg, Ar1 add "and heard"; perhaps secondary.

18   p *Adpropinquare incipio* Lat = Arm, Georg; perhaps going back to Greek μέλλειν (cf. Blake, "Georgian Version," 345). Some versions found difficulty in the first person, wishing to avoid confusing God and the angel. Eth gives a third person here but has inconsistently left a first person in the next verse. Some Eth Mss have "the Most High." Ar1 reads "the Lord" here, "he" in 6:19, but "I" in its unique reading in 6:20.

19   q Lat, Syr, Eth, Georg may here reflect μέλλειν; cf. note p above and note u below. Arm omits 6:19.

     r Ar2 omits; "my servants" Arm.

     s Interpreted by a number of versions (Ar1, Ar2, Arm) as "completed," "fulfilled."

pass away, [v]
then I shall show [w] these signs:
   the books shall be opened before the
    firmament,
   and all shall see it [x] together.

21/ Infants a year old shall speak with
     their voices, [y]
   and women with child shall give birth to
    premature [z] children at three and
    four months,
   and these shall live and dance. [a]

22/ Unsown places shall suddenly appear
    sown, [b]
   and full storehouses [c] shall suddenly
    be found to be empty;

23/ and the trumpet shall sound aloud,
   and when all hear it, they shall sud-
    denly [d] be terrified.

24/ And [e]it will come to pass [e] at that time
   friends shall make war on friends like
    enemies, [f]
   and the earth and those who inhabit it
    shall be terrified,
   and the springs of the fountains shall
    stand still,
   so that for three hours [g] they shall not
    flow.

25/ And [h]it shall come to pass [h] that whoever remains after all that I have foretold to
you shall himself be saved [i] and shall see my
salvation and the end of my [j] world. 26/ And
they [k] shall see the men who were taken
up, [l] who from their birth have not tasted
death; and the heart of the earth's [m] inhabitants shall be changed and converted to a
different spirit.

27/ For evil shall be blotted out,
   and deceit shall be quenched;

28/ faithfulness shall flourish,
   and corruption shall be overcome,
   and the truth shall be revealed,
    which has been so long [n] without
    fruit."

29   And [o]it came to pass [o] while he spoke to me,
behold, [p] little by little the place where I was
standing began to rock to and fro.

t "Life" in Arm; cf. also 4:2; 4:11; 14:16; see
Armenian Text Commentary on 6:20A.

u Reflexes of μέλλειν in Lat, Syr, Eth.

v "Which is coming" Eth, Georg. This was also a
Greek reading. Volkmar suggests διέρχεσθαι for
ἔρχεσθαι.

w Literally, "do." Arm has a long addition here;
cf. 6:24.

x "My judgment" Syr. Our previous view on the
possible Hebrew origin of the variation of the verb
between "see" and "be seen" is no longer acceptable;
see Stone, "Some Remarks," 111–12.

21   y Eth adds "and converse"; "raise up their voices
and talk" Ar1; Ar2 interprets both verbs as relating
to praise of God.

z Eth omits.

a Lat verb is unusual.

22   b Lat is ambiguous. Translation follows the
interpretation of Syr and Eth, Ar1; cf. Ar2. Georg is
idiosyncratic. NEB "Fields that were sown shall
suddenly prove unsown."

c Lat, Syr, Georg; cf. Eth.

23   d Eth, Georg; cf. Ar2. Originality is hard to
determine here.

24   e–e *Et erit* Lat, so also Syr, Ar1, Eth; others omit.
See note m–m above on 6:17.

f Arm has an expanded text here; cf. 6:20.

g "Years" Eth Ms, Ar2; "times" Arm.

25   h–h Lat, Syr, Georg add "it shall be"; cf. note m–
m above on 6:17. RSV chooses to add "it shall be" in
its translation here but in none of the similar cases
above.

i "Be saved" Lat; "live" Syr, Eth, Georg
(σώζω/ζόω); on this terminology, see Violet 2 on
7:60; "will enter eternal life" Ar2.

j So Lat, Eth, Georg.

26   k Lat, Georg; "he" Syr, Eth; "the people" Ar1;
Ar2 incomprehensible; Eth, Georg have "then, at
that time" before the pronoun. Gunkel plausibly
emends the verb to "they will be seen," an inner-
Hebrew corruption. Arm is varied and expanded.

l *In caelum ascendentes* Georg; "those who fly to me
on high" Arm.

m Lat omits, except for Ms L.

28   n Syr "for many years"; Eth "during these times";
Georg "until now"; Ar1 "in those many past years";
Ar2, Arm vary in this part of the verse.

29   o–o Lat, Syr, Georg, Ar1; Eth, Ar2, Arm omit; cf.
note m–m above on 6:17.

p Eth, Georg omit; Arm expands the middle of
this verse.

Form and Structure

This section opens in a form identical with 4:44 and 5:56. This is made up of a vocative address followed by the phrase "if I have found favor in thy sight."[1] Both here and in 5:56 the "if" phrase is followed by a direct request to God: "Show thy servant." A similar vocative address is also followed by the request "Show me" in 4:44.

Indeed, both 4:44 and 5:56 occur toward the end of a "Prediction 1" passage. In both instances unique literary units follow: in 4:44 the literary vision, and in 5:56 the poem on creation and the oracular exegesis "From Abraham to Abraham." In the present context, this address form is followed by the prediction of a portent (6:13–16), the signs of the end foretold (6:17–28), and the realization of the portent (6:29). The reference to "on a previous night" (6:11) relates this Prediction 2 to the corresponding section of Vision 1.

The outline of the subsequent parts of the pericope follows:

A. *Angel's word to Ezra concerning the shaking of the earth (6:13–16).*

B. *Ezra's first person narrative introduction of divine oracle (6:17).*

C. *First person divine prediction in the form of:*
   1. Introduction: "Behold, days are coming, and it shall come to pass that" (6:18).
   2. Two pairs of "when . . . and when . . ." conditional clauses (6:18–20).
   3. Condition fulfillment clause: "Then . . . ," which is the shift to the list of signs.

D. *List of signs falling into several parts:*
   1. Semipoetic list of portents in parallel phrases (6:20–23).
   2. New section opening with "And it shall come to pass" (6:24) also conveying portents, but of a more social and political type.
   3. New section opening with "And it shall come to pass" (6:25) containing a prediction of redemption composed of specific prophecies in prose (6:25–26) and more general oracular ones in poetry (6:27–28). This is the end of the prediction.

E. *Return to the narrative framework, relating that the earth shook (6:29).*

Above, in the analysis in 5:1–13 Form and Structure, p. 107, the structural similarities of the actual prediction segments of 5:1–13 and 6:11–29 were indicated and also the general resemblance between them and 7:26–44. In both Vision 1 and Vision 2 the prediction of portents preceded that of signs. Nonetheless, sections A, B, and E above, as well as the introductory invocation, are unique to Vision 2. The angel's warning about the earthquake (6:13–16 = section A) opens this pericope, which concludes with the narrative of the actual event (6:29 = section E). This sets the prediction within an *inclusio.*

Section B (6:17) is the direct introduction of the portents. It evokes divine speech with the reference to the voice sounding like many waters, and indeed the verses that follow are in the first person and form an elaborate introduction to the actual prediction. This introduction opens in 6:18 with the stock phrase "Behold, the days are coming, and it shall come to pass that" (see for the latter expression 6:24 and 6:25) and concludes in 6:20a. The prediction proper starts with the word "then" in 6:20b.

So, the literary structure is very tightly planned. The whole pericope is linked to the list of signs in Vision 1 by the reference in 6:12 to signs of which part were revealed "on a previous night." This phrase also ties this pericope to the start of the dispute in 5:31, where the same technique of cross-referencing is used, which serves to stress the correspondence of this vision to Vision 1.

This pericope has a more complex internal structure than does the corresponding passage, 5:1–13. It is divided up by a developed series of section openings in 6:18; 6:20; 6:24; and 6:25. Moreover, the last section's opening also signals a change in content from omens of woes to prophecy of redemption. This may be the reason for the rather elaborate introductory segment (6:11–18a), which highlights the solemn fact that it is God who is speaking.

In the preceding pericope a certain fluidity between the angel and God was discerned, with the angel often addressed and speaking as if he were God (e.g., 5:42; 6:6; and see 7:17 Commentary). In Vision 1, moreover, an overall structure of speakers can be noted. Ezra speaks

---

1 See 4:44 Commentary on parallels to and other cases of this. Chapter 6:13–28 is dealt with in detail by Hartman, *Prophecy Interpreted,* 132–37.

alone in the address, the dispute and Prediction 1 are dialogues between Ezra and the angel, while Prediction 2 is all spoken by the angel. A similar structure is also to be observed in Vision 2, except that in it Prediction 2 is predominantly spoken by God himself. This phenomenon is presaged by the fact that already in Prediction 1 of Vision 2, as was just observed, direct divine speech sometimes seems to replace that of the angel. This change of speaker reflects the shift from woe to redemption which is picked up and emphasized by themes and features of the next section, the injunctions. The solemnity of divine speech, the very shaking of the pillars of the earth, and the prophecy of redemption itself all combine to indicate that here the sustained debate and dispute of Visions 1 and 2 have reached a first stage of resolution.

The poetic form of 6:27–28 is worthy of special note.[2] The passage resembles 7:33–35; 7:114; 8:52–53; and 14:18, which passages form a distinctive literary type within the book. They are characterized by short sentences composed of a (predominantly) abstract noun and a verb. The cola are parallel, and bicola predominate in all passages.

6:27–28
For evil shall be blotted out, and deceit shall be quenched;
faithfulness shall flourish,   and corruption shall be
                                                 overcome,
        and the truth shall be revealed,
        which has been so long
        without fruit.

7:33–35
And compassion shall pass away,   mercy shall be made distant,
        and patience shall be
        withdrawn;
But only judgment shall remain,   truth shall stand,
        and faithfulness shall grow
        strong;
And recompense shall follow,   and the reward shall be
                                                 manifested;
righteous deeds shall awake,   and unrighteous deeds shall
                                                 not sleep

7:113–114
corruption has passed away,   sinful indulgence has come to
                                                 an end,

    unbelief has been cut off,
and righteousness has increased,   and truth has appeared.

8:52–53
Paradise is opened,   the tree of life is planted,
the world to come is prepared,   delight is provided,
a city is built,   rest is appointed,
goodness is established and   wisdom perfected beforehand,
the root is sealed up from you,   illness is banished from you,
and death is hidden,   hell has fled,
and corruption has been   sorrows have passed away,
    forgotten;
    and in the end the treasure of immortality is made manifest.

14:18
For truth shall go farther away,   and falsehood shall come near.

The common features of these passages extend beyond literary form alone. First, they are all angelic or divine prophecies; second, the subject of the prophecy is eschatological; third, they are predominantly characterized by five concepts (usually expressed in antithetical pairs):
a. Truth and deceit (6:27–28; 7:34; 7:114; 14:18)
b. Corruption and weakness (6:28; 7:113; 8:53)
c. Faith and faithlessness (6:28; 7:34; 7:114)
d. Good and evil (6:27; 8:52)
e. Justice and injustice (7:34; 7:114).[3]
These striking similarities of form, function, vocabulary, and content are best to be explained by assuming a common, distinct literary form.[4] This form does not seem to have clear biblical antecedents. There are some sentences in the Bible with abstract qualities as subjects and also other sentences resembling individual phrases of our passages. No biblical passage resembles them as a whole.[5] The most sustained biblical passages are in Deutero-Isaiah, for example, 59:14: הסג אחור משפט וצדקה מרחוק תעמד כי כשלה ברחוב אמת (Justice is turned back, and righteousness stands far off, for truth has fallen in the public squares).[6]

---

2   It was first recognized and discussed in Stone, *Features*, 1919–95.

3   Some coincidence in the range of verbs used may also be noted: "pass away" (7:33; 7:114; 8:54); "blotted out" (6:27; 8:53); "flower" or "spring up" (6:28; 7:114; cf. 7:34); "are evident" or "established" (6:28; 7:34; 8:52).

4   Other hypotheses, chiefly of a literary type, can be

excluded by consideration of the poems' felicitous aptness to context and function. So the passages are not parts of one original composition, nor are they secondary forms of such. See further Stone, *Features*, 193.

5   See, e.g., Hos 10:4, יפרח כראש משפט; Ps 85:12, אמת מארץ תצמח.

6   Cf. also Isa 59:9. Similar in structure, but not in

In the pseudepigraphic literature, although there are many poetic descriptions of the eschatological events, the only ones close to our passage in character and function occur in *2 Apocalypse of Baruch*. The two most similar are:

44:9
> For everything will pass away which is corruptible,
>> and everything that dies will go away,
> and all present time will be forgotten,
>> and there will be no remembrance of the present time,
>> which is polluted with evils.

73:1b–3
> Then joy will be revealed,
>> and rest will appear,
> and then health will descend in dew,
>> and illness will vanish,
> and fear and tribulation and lamentation will pass away from among men,
> and joy will encompass the earth,
> and nobody will again die untimely,
>> nor will any adversity take place suddenly.[7]

A similar literary form is to be found in *2 Apoc Bar* 56:6 but in the quite different context of Adam's sin. This is, of course, the opposite of the eschatological benefits.

56:6
> For when he transgressed untimely death came into being,
> grief was named,   and anguish was prepared,
> and pain was created,   and trouble was consummated,
> and disease began to be established   and Sheol kept demanding that it should be renewed in blood,
> and the begetting of children brought about   and the passion of parents was produced,
> and the greatness of humanity was humiliated.   and goodness languished.

Also similar in many respects is the prediction of eschatological woes in *m. Soṭa* 9:15. There some abstract phrases are also to be found:

	חוצפא יסגא
ויוקר יאמיר . . .	חכמת סופרים תסרח
ויראי חטא ימאסו	
והאמת תהא נעדרת	

Insolence shall increase,   and expense shall become oppressive,

the wisdom of scribes shall become vapid,   the sin-fearers shall become contemptible,

and truth shall be absent.[8]

Thus 4 Ezra seems to be presenting a particularly extensive development of a literary form that serves in eschatological contexts. In 4 Ezra nearly all cases are references to redemption or reward. Some of the other sources show similar literary forms used in woes or analogous contexts. The somewhat oracular prophetic and mystifying style is well suited to its use and purpose.

Function and Content

At the heart of the pericope lies the revelation of "the end of the signs" (6:12). This refers back, of course, to the list of signs that is conveyed in Prediction 2 of Vision 1. If this expression is taken seriously, then attempts to relate these two lists with 9:1–13 at the textual level seem superfluous.

In 4:44 Commentary the role of the elaborate introductory formulae such as that here has been noted. They generally mark a major turn in the direction of the inquiry (see also 5:56), and the introductory formula serves to open the renewed prophecy of the signs.

The impression created by this solemn question is further strengthened by the angel's portentous pronouncement that Ezra is to stand, in marked contrast to his prostrate posture during the first four visions (3:1 Commentary). The same effect is reinforced by the "full, resounding voice" (6:13), perhaps a deliberate contrast to Elijah's experience of the "still, small voice" of God (1 Kgs 19:12). In 6:14–16, Ezra is warned not to fear if the earth shakes, for its foundations will tremble before the divine voice which portends their change.

---

content, is Song 7:13. Cf. also Isa 35:10 and 51:1.

7   See also *2 Apoc Bar* 57:2. Poetic eschatological prophecies in different forms may be observed in *Similitudes of Enoch* or in *2 Apoc Bar* 66:7.

8   Other parts of this passage are relevant to the study of the list of signs. Parts of it are paralleled in *b. Sanh.* 97a. On the hiding of truth, see 5:1 Commentary. The expansion of Armenian along the same lines is probably the work of the Armenian editor, perhaps based on a kernel of older material. See *Armenian Text Commentary* on 6:20A–C. A general similarity in style may be observed in *Odes of Solomon* 20–21. A phrase that is quite similar but is spoken of negative qualities is embedded in 7:111; see Commentary there.

A number of themes of biblical theophany here come to the fore. In the preceding paragraph the possible parallel between 6:13 and the theophany in 1 Kgs 19:12 was noted. The shaking of the earth, too, occurs in connection with theophanies,[9] and the cosmic dimension of this event is evident from the fact that the "foundations of the earth" are said to shake. The biblical roots of this language are clear, going back to even more ancient mythological origins.[10] So when the foundations of the earth are to be shaken, "for they know that their end must be changed" (6:16), the context being evoked is quite unmistakable. It is cosmic creation/re-creation, with all that this implies. This is even more striking in view of the language of 6:1–5 (see above). And indeed, the prediction of these verses is fulfilled in 6:29.[11]

In 6:17, Ezra, in obedience to the angel's instructions, rises to his feet and hears a voice characterized as being "like the sound of many waters." This is a transparent proclamation that this voice is divine. The voice or sound like many waters is that of the wings of the beasts of the divine chariot which is "like the voice of the Almighty" (Ezek 1:24).[12]

The next section opens with the prophetic call, "Behold, the days are coming" (6:18; see 5:1 Commentary). The three occurrences of "when" that follow are a general characterization of the period—it will be when the world comes to an end, when the humiliation of Zion is complete, and, above all, when God will come to execute his vengeance. At the time when these things are to take place, God will show forth his signs (6:20).

At this point a dramatic shift takes place and a list of signs, strikingly resembling that in 5:1–11, is given. Above (5:1–13 Function and Content, p. 107), the possible single literary source of these lists was described. The analysis of 6:11–29 presented so far serves to

confirm the observation made there, that even where 4 Ezra uses preexisting literary sources, they are thoroughly integrated into their immediate and broader context.

As has been noted already, this prediction of signs is not uniform, and, from 6:25 on, it is composed not of omens of woe but of assurances of salvation. This shift is marked both by an introduction (6:24) and by the appearance of new literary styles, prose in 6:25–26 and a distinct poetic form in 6:27–28.

The woes of 6:20c–6:23 are in a semipoetic form. It is difficult to discern any particular structure in them beyond the fact that they fall into two groups and a new introduction marks the beginning of the second group. The chief subjects of the prediction in the first group are:

1. Books in the firmament (6:20)
2. Strange births (6:21)
3. Reversal of full and empty (6:22)
4. The frightening sound of the trumpet (6:23)

The second group includes:

1. Reversal of the social order (6:24)
2. Terror (6:24)
3. The springs of the earth stand still for three hours (6:24)

Certain of these are closely paralleled by the signs in chapter 5. The books in the firmament (6:20) and the reversal of full and empty (6:22) are like the "cosmic signs" of 5:4b–5. Furthermore, other themes from 5:1–12 are taken up again in this prediction. In 5:8 monstrous births are predicted, a subject that returns in an altered form in 6:21.[13] This is an element of the confusion of natural order which is the subject of 6:21 and 6:22. The same themes in very similar expressions are to be found in 5:6–8, the context in which the monstrous

---

9 Cf., e.g., 1 Kgs 19:11–12. Different but equally explicit are Judg 5:4; 2 Sam 22:8 = Ps 18:8; Joel 4:16; Nah 1:5; Ps 68:9; 97:4; *1 Enoch* 1:6; 1QH 3:35; et al. It is frequently an eschatological omen; see, e.g., Ezek 38:19. Contrast incidentally *Od Sol* 7:5.

10 Biblical examples are Isa 24:18; Ps 18:8 = 2 Sam 22:8; Ps 82:5; et al.

11 On the passing away of the earth, see 4:26 Commentary. A different experience of shaking is to be observed in *Apoc Abr* 10:3 and 10:5.

12 The clearest other biblical reference is Ezek 43:2. Cf. also Ps 29:3 and 93:4. On the influence of Ezekiel 1

in the Second Temple period, see C. Rowland, "The Vision of God in Apocalyptic Literature," *JSJ* 10 (1979) 137–54.

13 Indeed this is so striking that Box, in his edition, suggests that 6:21–22 is misplaced here. Like Kabisch and Oesterley, he thinks that it belongs after 5:8.

births are predicted in that chapter.[14] The upset of natural order is similarly described.

The sounding of the awe-inspiring trumpet is a final sign (6:23). It is not the eschatological trumpet blast that ushers in the eschaton, however, since it is followed by various other events before the final redemption.[15]

Chapter 6:24 introduces a new section, the final group of signs. Internecine war, already discussed in connection with 5:9, is one of them. The other is the mysterious cessation of the springs of the fountains for three hours (6:24). Whatever the exact significance of this, it is clearly a demarcation between woes and redemption. It is described in terminology most readily related to the associational complex of the messianic kingdom.[16]

Then the prediction of redemption follows in 6:25–28. The changing of the heart is well to be related to other parts of the book. The eschatological poem in 6:27–28 reinforces the impression made by 6:26. The overall impact of 6:26–28 is to change the character of the prediction. The end of the signs has indeed come and with it not just the physical intimations of cosmic change which precede and follow it, for spiritual change, indeed redemption, are what is predicted. This marks the end of the first part of the book. The spiritual struggle of the first two visions has climaxed in the foretelling of redemption.

Commentary

■ **11** "O sovereign Lord" is a form of address found elsewhere; see 3:4 Commentary. "If I have found favor" is discussed in 4:44 Commentary and "servant" in 5:56

Commentary.

■ **12** On the term "signs," see 4:52 Commentary. "On a previous night": the phrase refers to 5:31; see Commentary there and see 6:11–29 Form and Structure, p. 164, and cf. 6:11–29 Function and Content, p. 166. The character and function of night visions are dealt with in 3:1 Commentary.

■ **13** This verse opens the address concerning the shaking of the earth (6:13–16). See also 6:29. Ezra is commanded to stand up,[17] in clear contrast with his recumbent position throughout the visions.[18]

The "full, resounding voice" is to be understood not as a loud, undefined sound (a possible meaning of קול in Hebrew) but as the prophetic pronouncement that is to be made.[19] This has no exact parallel in the Bible. Exodus 19:19 speaks of trumpet sounds accompanying the epiphany; Ezek 1:24 describes the sound of the beasts' wings as "like the sound of many waters, like the thunder of the Almighty, a sound of tumult like the sound of a host"; compare also Ezek 3:12–13[20] and Ezek 43:2; one of the closest parallels is the description of the angelic voice in Dan 10:6 as being like the noise of a multitude.[21] In Function and Content, p. 166, we suggested that this description may be deliberately polar to the "still, quiet voice" of God according to 1 Kgs 19:12.

■ **14** The "if" of this statement does not imply that the earth might or might not shake; it prepares Ezra for his reaction to this shaking. The shaking is of the "foundations of the earth" (6:15), a term clearly hinting at the new creation that will take place.[22] The quaking of

---

14 It is possible, of course, to rearrange the elements of these lists in a more "logical" fashion. See the preceding note. The same scholars cited there also suggest that 6:24 should follow 5:6; this order has not been proved original, however, and we have found no reason to accept the various suggestions made, e.g., by Box and others. If a preexistent literary source was used, the elements might well have been in a different order in it, but this remains conjectural.

15 See on the latter 6:23 Commentary.

16 See Stone, *Features*, 69–71, 135. The language used in 6:25–26 is close to that found in the eagle vision (12:34).

17 Ezra rises to receive a revelation in 4:47 and to praise God in 13:57. Cf. also Isa 32:9. See, for a full discussion, 4:47 Commentary.

18 See 3:1 Commentary. In 4:47 Ezra stands to receive the parabolic revelation. Hartman, *Prophecy Interpreted*, 133, relates this element here to Ezek 2:1; cf. Dan 10:11. The phrases he highlights as referring to biblical texts are commonplace in this section.

19 It is, therefore, not comparable with *Sib Or* 4:175.

20 It seems we should resist the temptation to relate this verse to the earthquake of the coming verses.

21 See also Rev 1:15; 14:2; and 19:6 for similar descriptions of heavenly voices.

22 Perhaps also compare "foundation of the Garden" in 6:2.

the earth on prophetic speech is discussed in Function and Content, pp. 166–67.[23]

■ **15** Here and in the next verse, "end" is used as a technical term. In 4 Ezra it has the primary meaning :"the decisive turning point of events." Just what event that might be is determined in each instance by the context. In the present instance, and in 6:16, it is difficult to discover what precise event "end" denotes.[24]

On the one hand, these verses suggest that the prediction that Ezra is about to hear refers to the end. Following this line of reasoning, the content of that prediction can be examined to determine what the term "the end" refers to. On the other hand, perhaps the answer to our question is already foreshadowed in 6:16—the creation of a new earth, cosmic change, the change of the foundations of the earth. As will be seen below, 6:17–26 most probably refers to the messianic kingdom, yet the prediction of 6:27–28 is most at home in the context of the day of judgment. This context might also be implied by 6:16.[25]

"Word" = "speech," that is the prediction of signs that is to follow. On the "foundations," see 6:14 Commentary.

■ **16** The meaning of the last phrase is presumably "that they will be changed at the end."[26]

■ **17** The return to first person narrative has no parallel in Vision 1, and this difference in style flows from the difference in content. "Like a sound of many waters" is commonly the way a supernatural voice is described.[27] All the elements combine to alert us that God is about to speak.

■ **18** "Behold, the days are coming": see 5:1 Commentary. "And it shall come to pass that" is a phrase that opens a new subsection here, in 6:24 and 6:25.[28] The concept of "to visit" is discussed in 5:56 Commentary. Here the direct divine pronouncement heralds the end of the discussion started in 5:56. The question there was "Through whom will you visit?" In 6:1 and 6:6 the response given in dialogue is that the beginning of the visitation is through a human being and its end through God. In 6:12 the discussion of the "end of the signs" begins, and these will be, God proclaims in a loud, resounding voice (6:18), "when I start (or: am about) to visit." Notably God is the speaker here.[29]

■ **19** "When" is listed three times in 6:19–20a: (1) when I will require punishment of evildoers; (2) when the humiliation of Zion is complete; and (3) when the seal will be placed upon the present age (6:20a). These can be perceived as three dimensions of consummation; the individual in 1; the national in 2; and the cosmic in 3. These three measures must be filled.

The question of the punishment of the evildoers will come to the fore in Vision 3. Here, however, the prophecy can be seen as a response only to the questions asked in 3:28–36. There alone in Visions 1 and 2 are these issues raised specifically. In those same questions the issue of the suffering of Israel is to the forefront. It also dominates the plaint of Vision 2; see particularly 5:35. The completion of the humiliation of Zion seems to imply that it is in a divinely decreed measure.[30]

■ **20** The first part of the verse is the completion of the "when" statements of the previous verse. "Sealing" here

---

23 In *2 Apoc Bar* 32:1 the divine visitation is described as "that time in which the Mighty one is to shake the whole creation"; see also *1 Enoch* 101:2. The trembling of the earth on other such occasions is mentioned in Isa 13:13 and 24:18–19; cf. also Acts 4:31 and 4 Ezra 16:12.

24 In general, see Stone, "Coherence and Inconsistency," and on this passage 234–35; see also Excursus on Natural Order, p. 103.

25 For this paragraph, see "Coherence and Inconsistency," 234.

26 In Dan 8:17, the seer is terrified because he knows that the revelation relates to the end; see 4:26 Commentary.

27 See Function and Content, p. 167; cf. Jer 51:16; 51:55; and rather differently Isa 17:13. See *Apoc Abr* 17:1.

28 See Form and Structure, p. 164.

29 See de Faye, p. 36.

30 The idea is perhaps to be compared with the idea of the filling of the measure of Zion's suffering in Isa 40:2. Cf. also Luke 21:24, where the idea of the fixed measure of Jerusalem's suffering is to be found. A similar sort of predestinatory approach to the suffering of Zion is also to be observed in *2 Apoc Bar* 20:2. To some extent these "when"s are parallel to those of 5:1–3, where perhaps "inhabitants of the earth" is the individual; and "portion of truth" and "land of faith" correspond to Israel. However, this is by no means certain.

presumably indicates the "sealing up" or "finishing" as when a papyrus contract is completed by affixing (a) seal(s) or a wine jar after being filled is sealed with the owner's (maker's) seal. It is intriguing to compare this usage with the nicely ambiguous occurrence in Dan 9:24.[31] This age is about to pass away, a statement that implies a view of two ages. This is discussed in 4:26 Commentary.

The "then" statements mark the start of the omens proper.[32] The most problematic element in this verse is the books that will be opened before the firmament. These are best interpreted as the books associated with divine judgment, in which the deeds of human beings are, presumably, recorded. This idea is clear in Dan 7:10; Rev 20:12; and *2 Apoc Bar* 24:1. Similar books are to be observed in *1 Enoch* 47:3; 81:1–5; and 104:7; cf. 89:61–64; *Asc Isa* 9:22–23; et al.[33] Even if these are the books of the deeds of human beings that figure in judgment, here they are said to be opened before the firmament. This suggests that they appear in the sky as an omen of the coming judgment.[34] Alternative interpretations have been suggested, viz., that it means that the books will be opened before the angelic host in the firmament (Oesterley, Knibb). Certainly books are opened before the heavenly host in judgment contexts in *1 Enoch* 47:3 and Dan 7:10; similar are the books described in *Testament of Abraham* A 12 and B 10.[35]

To accept this interpretation would be to say that this first "sign" is different from all that follow, for all of them are omens or portents that appear to human beings. Indeed, they are being made known to Ezra so that he can observe their progress. Therefore we prefer to see this as an apparition whose meaning and ominous import are drawn from the context of judgment. This interpretation is borne out, of course, by the last phrase of the verse, "and all shall see it together."

■ **21** Various suggestions have been made to relocate 6:21–22 in the book. These seem unnecessary.[36]

The omen is a shortening of life to "absurd" measure. The idea that the devolution of the generations leads to a shortening of life may be extrapolated from the difference between antediluvian and postdiluvian life spans according to Genesis. See also explicitly Gen 6:3. *Jubilees* 23 is structured according to this principle, and of the period just before the end, *Jub* 23:25 says:

> And the heads of the children shall be white with grey hair,
> And a child of three weeks shall appear old like a man of one hundred years,
> And their stature shall be destroyed by tribulation and oppression.[37]

■ **22** In the textual comments on this verse the ambiguity of certain versions was noted. As accepted, the text predicts that unsown shall be sown and full shall be

31 This case differs from 6:5; 8:53; "seal of truth" in 7:104; "seal of glory" in 10:23; again it varies from *2 Apoc Bar* 21:23 and *Prayer of Manasseh* 3, with which cf. perhaps *Od Sol* 23:8–9. See 6:5 Commentary.

32 Violet 2 suggests that all of these phrases that follow are drawn from Jewish Sibylline hexameters that were rendered into Hebrew by the author of 4 Ezra. The basis of this theory remains unclear.

33 Different is Rev 5;1, perhaps magical (Gunkel). The matter of heavenly books is very complex. Many sources are listed by Charles in his commentary on 1 Enoch 47:3 and by Keulers, pp. 69–70. A list of passages dealing with books and an attempt at classification are made by D. G. Meade, *Pseudonymity and Canon* (Grand Rapids: Eerdmans, 1986) 78.

34 The phrase bears some sort of similarity to Gen 1:20.

35 Y. Gutman orally suggested that the books opened before the firmament are in fact the readings of the constellations; cf. also Isa 34:4.

36 See Function and Content, p. 167.

37 The tradition here is not necessarily the same as that of the monstrous births of 5:8. While *Jubilees* and 4

Ezra share the tradition of the shortening of life, in *Jubilees* it is part of a system. This might be taken to indicate that, even though 4 Ezra is later than *Jubilees*, the latter's treatment of this tradition is more developed. Note, however, *Sib Or* 2:155 and Collins's note in *OTP* 1:349. Other parallels are the "Book of Clement" cited by Bousset, *Antichrist*, 268, and the Latin texts in James, *Apocrypha Anecdota*, 153–54. Moreover, this tradition is not the same as that associated in some later texts with the Antichrist, according to which he is sometimes young and sometimes an old man. See *Greek Apoc Esd* 4:33 and Stone's note in *OTP*, ad loc.; cf. also Bousset, *Antichrist*, 150–53.

empty. This is best put into the context of the reversals to be found in 5:8 and 5:9. Moreover, the antithesis of full/empty recurs in 7:25.[38] If this analysis is accepted, then what is predicted here is not famine but the disruption of the natural order.[39]

■ **23** The trumpet blast announced by this verse is not that announcing the eschaton[40] but a fearful omen, the background to which may lie in passages like Amos 3:6.[41] All people will hear it, as in 5:7 they also hear a terrifying voice, and this implies that the sign will be universal. Their reaction is terror, which is a standard part of the divine woes.[42]

■ **24** After a solemn introduction (see Form and Structure, p. 164), here the reversal of social order is described, following the reversal of natural order.[43] The particular sign "friends fighting friends" is also found in 5:9; see also *1 Enoch* 100:1; *Greek Apoc Esd* 3:12–14; and Melito, *Paschal Homily* 51.[44] The terror that strikes the earth was discussed in the previous verse; cf. also 12:3. Then the fountains cease for three hours. This is a reversal of the perennial founts of nature's blessings in *1 Enoch* 69:17 and *Sib Or* 4:15. The same sign also occurs in *Ps Sol* 17:19 (in relationship to the exile of the righteous), *Test Mos* 10:6, and *Test Patr Levi* 4:1. *Signs of the Judgment*, Day 2, states that the sea will dry up.[45]

The omen is the cessation of all the perennial waters for three hours. Gunkel suggests that three real hours

are intended; Oesterly and Kahana are of the view that three periods of time are involved, but the reason for their view is not clear. In fact, there is no ready explanation for the period of "three hours."[46]

■ **25** This verse is the first prophecy of redemption in the predictions in 4 Ezra. It is marked by its own separate introductory phrase and refers back to the woes of the preceding prophecy. It introduces terms and concepts that become increasingly important as the book progresses. The term "whoever remains" refers to those who survive the messianic woes, and it is discussed in detail in 5:41 Commentary. The biblical doctrine of the remnant is well known,[47] and what we have here is the formulation of that notion in an apocalyptic setting.

The survivors are said to "see my salvation and the end of my world." The survivors are said in 7:27 and 13:50 to "see wonders," while salvation is what is seen here, in 9:8 and in 13:48.[48] These parallel contexts suggest that "wonders" and "salvation" are close to synonymous here.[49] "Seeing" seems to refer to the experience of eschatological events; cf. 4:26. In rabbinic literature the expression לראות בנחמה (to see the comfort) is found, as well as ראה לעתיד לבוא (to see the coming future state) (*j. Sanh.* 29b), and a similar usage is to be found in *Ps Sol* 17:44 and 18:6. Psalm 91:16 uses the expression אראהו בישועתי (and I will show him my salvation), which is eschatologically interpreted by CD 20:34.[50] On the

---

38   On antithesis in the author's style, see 6:30–34 Form and Function, p. 173; and 8:19b–36 Function and Content, p. 272.

39   If the text of Latin is followed (text-critically less inviting), then the verse can be regarded as predicting famine: see Keulers, p. 66. The sources for famine as part of the woes are numerous: some are Matt 24:7 and parallels and *2 Apoc Bar* 27:6; 70:8. Other relevant sources might be *1 Enoch* 80:2–3 and *Sib Or* 3:540–542.

40   On "Gabriel's" trumpet, see the discussion by Box; and also Stone, *Signs of the Judgement*, Day 5 and note there (pp. 40, 56).

41   Cf. also *Sib Or* 4:174; the distinction between the different trumpet blasts was drawn clearly by Volz, p. 162.

42   See 5:1 Commentary.

43   On the lists of internecine conflicts, see 5:9 Commentary. On the expanded list of Armenian, see *Armenian Text Commentary* on 5:9.

44   Cf. *2 Apoc Bar* 70:6.

45   Ps 74:15, drawing on mythological concepts,

describes God's creative activity as, *inter alia,* a drying up of the (primordial) streams so that dry land may appear. This may lie in the background of the language here, but the concepts are quite the opposite. Cf. also Rev 21:1.

46   It might be connected with the unclear "third . . ." which must pass before the signs begin, according to 5:4.

47   See, e.g., Gen 45:7; Judg 6:4; Isa 11:11; 17:5–6; 28:5; 30:17; Amos 3:12; 5:3; 5:15; Zeph 2:9; 3:12–13; and 2 Chr 14:12; cf. Isa 17:3.

48   The text in 13:48 is uncertain; see textual note v there.

49   On the terminology of seeing, see 4:26 Commentary and 7:100–115 Function and Content, pp. 248–49.

50   A transitive form is also found in 7:27 and 13:50. Box suggests that the verb means "to enjoy," but that seems to be excluded by the transitive uses observed. Note also Gunkel's emendation in the next verse. On the term "wonders," see 4:26 Commentary.

meaning of end, see the Excursus on Natural Order, pp. 103–4. The context here is of the associational complex we have dubbed "messianic kingdom."[51]

■ **26** As part of the signs, this verse predicts that those who were assumed to heaven without dying will appear and that the hearts of the inhabitants of the earth will be changed to a different spirit. Elsewhere in 4 Ezra the appearance of the assumed together with the Messiah is mentioned (7:28; 13:52), while Ezra is told that he is counted in this company according to 14:9, cf. 8:17.[52] No passage exactly like 6:26 is to be observed, although there are ample references to specific assumed individuals who will appear before the eschaton. The most famous of these is Elijah (Mal 3:23–24).[53] On the other hand, it is clear that the traditions that Enoch and Elijah were "taken up" are deeply rooted and widespread.[54] Moreover, in the apocalypses other individuals are said to be taken up: notably Ezra himself (4 Ezra 14:9; 14:49) and Baruch (2 Apoc Bar 13:3; 43:2; 46:7; 48:30; 76:2; et al).[55] The turn of phrase "did not taste death," used in this connection, is also to be found in the New Testament, so Matt 16:28 and John 8:52, and in rabbinic sources, for example, Gen. R. 3:22 (Theodor-Albeck,

p. 201); compare also Bib Ant 48:1–3 for the reverse expression.

The expectation of change of heart is discussed in the Excursus on Inspiration. It also involves a change of intellectual qualities and is related to 4 Ezra's view that illumination will be part of eschatological redemption. The expectation of a change of heart is also associated in Malachi with the verse expressing the hope for the coming of Elijah.[56]

■ **27** On the poetic form and the terminology of this and the following verses, see Form and Function, pp. 165–66. The opposition of truth and deceit is a commonplace.

■ **28** "Corruption" is a term used in 4 Ezra for things of this world. This is well expressed, for example, in 7:113, and see 4:11 Commentary. For "fruit," see 3:20 Commentary. Truth and faithfulness are both qualities of God as judge according to 7:33–34.

■ **29** See 6:13–16.

---

51 See Stone, *Features*, 105–6.

52 Ezra "and those like him" are also promised eternal life, according to 8:51 and 8:62. The expression, with the seer as a paradigm of the righteous, also occurs in noneschatological contexts in *2 Apoc Bar* 2:1; 21:24; 57:1; 59:1; et al.; cf. also 4 Ezra 4:36. In *2 Apoc Bar* 13:5, however, it is connected with the assumed righteous. Cf. also Arabic1 to 4:10, and see 7:28 Commentary and also Stone, *Features*, 133–34.

53 See, e.g., Sir 48:10–12; Mark 9:4; 9:11–12; and John 1:21. The Elijah tradition is widespread also in rabbinic sources. There are numerous references to the eschatological prophet whose coming will presage the end; some examples are 1QS 9:11; 4QTest 5, and see Deut 18:15; 1 Macc 4:46; 14:41; John 6:14; 7:52; 9:17; *Test Patr Benj* 9:2; and *Test Patr Levi* 8:15. In 4 Ezra the title "prophet" which is integral to this tradition is not found in the relevant contexts. Is the appearance of Moses and Elijah in the transfiguration relevant to this (Matt 17:3 and parallels)?

54 Elijah—2 Kgs 2:9–12; Sir 48:9; et al.; Enoch—Sir 44:16; 49:14; *Jub* 4:23; *1 Enoch* 70:1–3; 89:52; 2

Enoch 36:2; Heb 11:5; etc. Oesterley suggests that Enoch and Elijah are intended here, as did Y. Gutman (orally), referring to *DEZ* 1.

55 Perhaps *1 Enoch* 70:3 refers to assumed or pre-created righteous ones. The assumption of the righteous individual, described in Wisd 4:10–15, sounds suspiciously like that of Enoch, although a specific reference is not so likely there. See also Josephus, *Ant.* 4:326, referring to Moses. In *Yalq. Gen.* 42 a tradition is quoted about those who were taken into paradise, including Enoch, Messiah, Elijah, Eliezer (Abraham's slave), Ebed-Melech the Ethiopian, and Hiram king of Tyre. See further on rabbinic material, Ginzberg, *Legends*, 5:96, who cites yet other sources. See also 14:9 Commentary on Ezra's assumption.

56 On expected presagers of the Messiah, see Bousset-Gressman, pp. 232–33. Armenian refers to the "souls that fly up," evoking the widespread imagery of the soul as a bird; see *Armenian Text Commentary*.

6

30   And he said to me, "I came to show you these things on ᵃ the night which is past. ᵇ 31/ If now ᶜ you will pray again and ᵈ fast again ᵉ for seven days, I will again declare to you greater things than these, 32/ because your voice has surely been heard before the Most High; for the Mighty One has seen your uprightness ᶠ and has ᵍobserved the purity ᵍ which you have maintained from your youth. 33/ Therefore he sent me to show you all these things." And he said to me: ʰ "Believe and do not be afraid! 34/ Do not be quick to think vain thoughts concerning the former times, lest you be hasty ⁱ concerning the last times."

Notes

30   a "As on" Eth, Ar1; Violet 1 suggests Lat *et* ⟨ *ut;* cf. Lat Mss M N in 6:34; Georg omits; is this to be accepted as making sense easily or rejected by rule of *lectio difficilior?*

b Eth, Georg, Ar1 ("days" for "night"); some such verb must also stand behind Lat *venturae nocti;* Syr, Ar2 omit the verb; Arm omits the verse. So this must be a Greek reading. On text-critical principles neither Gunkel's view (supported by, e.g., Schreiner) nor Box's (cf., e.g., Myers) can be accepted, based as they are respectively on unique readings of Syr and Lat, unless a suitable explanation of the textual dynamics emerges.

31   c Uncertain; *ergo* Lat; "new" Syr, Eth; Ar1, Ar2, Arm omit.

c–d Ar2, Arm omit.

e Lat, Eth, cf. Arm; Syr, Georg, Ar1, Ar2 omit.

32   f Ar1, Arm add "of your heart"; perhaps independent cliché expansion.

g–g Lat, Syr, Ar1; Eth, Georg omit; Ar2, Arm quite variant.

33   h Syr, Eth, Georg; "and to say to you" Lat; others omit or differ.

34   i Versions vary; exact sense uncertain.

Form, Function, and Content

These five verses form the conclusion of the second vision. As such they play the same role as 5:13 and 9:23–25, the injunctions at the end of the first and third visions. In general, these three passages differ from the transitions between Vision 4 and Vision 5 and the latter and Vision 6. Indeed, the change is already to be remarked at the end of Vision 3, where, although seven days of prayer are enjoined, no fast is commanded (9:23–24).

There are, moreover, certain unique elements in 6:30–34. In addition to the injunctions proper, the angel submits a message from God that summarizes the seer's experience so far, as well as a second set of injunctions touching on his state of mind. As has been pointed out, by the end of Vision 2 a first turning point in the structure of the book has emerged. This is indicated in the course of Prediction 2 (6:11–29), where a special literary form and special content mark the start of a prophecy of redemption. No such prophecy has been given before. Parallel to it in the injunctions is the special message brought to the seer from God. This includes the

first introduction of the subject of Ezra's acceptability to God. The section then closes with one of the mysterious and antithetical oracular statements with which the author marks important shifts in the revelatory dynamic of the argument.

The passage is composed of the following chief parts:

A. *Angel's first address to Ezra—injunctions and promise*
   1. I came to show you these things this night (6:30=5:13)
   2. Fast seven days and I will show you yet greater things than these (6:31=5:13 //9:23)

B. *Angel's first address to Ezra—message about himself*
   1. Your voice has been heard because of your uprightness (6:32)
   2. Therefore he sent me to show you all these things (6:33)

C. *Angel's second address to Ezra—further injunctions*
   1. Believe and do not fear (6:33—reference back to 6:15)
   2. Do not hasten to think vain thoughts about the former times (6:34)
   3. Lest you be hasty concerning the latter times (6:34)

The command in 6:34 is particularly difficult and has been discussed by a number of scholars (see Commentary). Yet it seems that the "vain thoughts" may well refer to such questions as asked in 4:2; 4:20–21; 5:33; and 5:40. The sense of the passage then is: "Believe because of the signs. Because of them, do not think vain thoughts about the former times and do not be hasty about the latter times."

As a number of scholars have pointed out (see 6:33 Commentary), there is considerable roughness in the second angelic address to Ezra. In fact, a second introductory phrase "and he said to me" (6:33) seems superfluous. It has caused some trouble to the versions.[1] Yet there seems to be no reason to regard it as more than marking the special solemnity of what is about to be said.

Commentary

■ **30** The phrase "the night which is past" has raised considerable difficulties in the versions. The reading accepted here seems quite inevitable on text-critical grounds. See the textual comments. Gressmann *apud* Violet 2 suggests with some plausibility that the phrase means "this night which has just passed," that is, that the end of the dream experiences is taking place toward dawn. Gunkel, however, accepted the reading of Latin here, "that night which is going to come" and also the unique reading of Latin at the end of 6:31. This seems

unacceptable.[2] So then, "these things" must mean the contents of Vision 2.[3]

■ **31** The verse is very close to 5:13 both in function and in its actual wording; see further Form and Content, p. 173. The understanding of the "greater things" depends on the textual decisions made in 6:30. Box suggests that it means the contents of Vision 3. This would also follow from the text accepted here.[4] Ezra is commanded to fast for seven days. Compare *2 Apoc Bar* 43:3: "and afterward fast seven days, and then I will come to thee and speak with thee." On the problem of the seven-day fasts in the book, see 6:35 Commentary.[5]

■ **32** This verse introduces the unique material of the injunctions passage. Together with the beginning of the next verse it forms the start of a topic that recurs repeatedly in 4 Ezra. Ezra is again and again assured by the angel of his worthiness, usually in the context of a promise, either of reward or of revelation. The relationship between worthiness and revelation is clear at a number of points and is graphically illustrated by a comparison of 12:36 and 14:45–46. In the latter passage, it is the wise of the people that are regarded as worthy and therefore receive revelation.[6] No particular virtue is mentioned in a number of instances (see 4:44; 7:44; 7:76–77; 7:104; 10:39; 10:57; 12:36; and 14:7–9; cf. 12:9). In other cases, a particular quality is cited which Ezra is said to have cultivated. Usually these

1   See textual notes.
2   Scholars have made various suggestions about the Greek that might have begotten the versional variants. None of these seems to us to be compelling. Cf. the phrase with 6:12, where Ezra does refer back to the vision received a week earlier in Vision 1 (cf. also 5:31).
3   Thus also Box, who, however, excludes 6:11–29 which he considers to be an interpolation. Gunkel, in line with his textual determination, interprets this expression as referring to Vision 3.
4   Gunkel, who accepted the originality of the words *per diem* at the end of the verse and also of the Vulgate of 6:30, says that "greater things" here means a waking vision, a more weighty experience (see also Keulers, p. 15). Consequently, this refers to Vision 4, a daytime experience, which followed Vision 3, a night vision. So also Schreiner, while Myers presents a mixed view. See also Brandenburger, *Verborgenheit*, 138. Box's suggestion that the words *per diem* belong to the beginning of the next verse must be rejected on the same grounds as those of Gunkel. For the

5   expression "greater things," see 5:13 and 5:32.
    Keulers, p. 21 n. 1, stresses the importance of the symbolism of the number seven in 4 Ezra.
6   Brandenburger has dealt with the theme of the proclamation of Ezra's worthiness (*Verborgenheit*, 121–24). In line with his overall approach, he points to the prominence of this theme in Visions 4–6 (8 occurrences) and its relationship to Ezra's receipt of visions. This leaves the present verse, and indeed Ezra's receipt of revelations in Visions 1–3, in a problematic position, from which Brandenburger's arguments do not extricate him. The difficulty arises because of his idea that the Ezra figure is a literary construct, designed by the author to present views which he desired to refute. Our approach to this differs; see 8:37–62a Function and Content, p. 280, and 13:13b–20a Form and Function, p. 389.

virtues are related to the theme of the context in which they occur. Here "uprightness" and "purity" are mentioned; in Vision 4, grief over Zion (10:39; 10:50);[7] in 8:47–49, humility; and in 13:54–56, devotion to wisdom and to Torah.[8]

God is entitled "Mighty One." This title appears elsewhere in the book, chiefly in parallelism with "Most High" (so 6:32; 10:24; 11:43; 12:47) or as a variant with it (13:23) and once or twice on its own (9:45 and Arabic2 of 7:132).[9]

■ **33** The call not to fear or be afraid occurs in many biblical sources (see, e.g., Deut 1:21; Jos 1:9; 8:1). The chief problem of this verse is the phrase "and he said to me," on which see the textual notes. The implications of our text-critical decision are discussed in Form and Content, p. 174.[10]

■ **34** In 4:34 we read:

He answered me and said, "You do not hasten faster than the Most High, for your haste is for yourself, but

the Highest hastens on behalf of many.
In that verse, the hastening is associated with urgent questioning about the time of the end or, in another mode, about the way divine providence works. Very similar is 5:44, and the sense of hastening in the present verse is presumably the same. In 4 Ezra another *topos* is associated with this idea, the command not to ask questions beyond human ken. This may also be observed in 4:2; 4:21 (cf. 5:32); et al. Compare also *2 Apoc Bar* 23:2.[11]

The exact meaning of the last clause is not completely clear. Critics have proposed that a Hebrew wordplay is at work here. This may well be the case, but the various suggestions are not helpful in resolving the problem.[12]

Box proposes that the general sense is "Do not, by your overcurious question and speculation trifle with your chances of eternal happiness at the last."[13]

---

7 Cf. *2 Apoc Bar* 13:3 citing Ezra's grief over Zion as the reason for his assumption. See further 10:38–54 Function and Content, p. 336.

8 Cf. *2 Apoc Bar* 44:14, which refers to Baruch garnering a heavenly treasure of wisdom. Geoltrain interprets the terms to mean chastity, which he regards as a necessary condition for receipt of revelation. This is not supported by the text or by the ideas of Ezra.

9 See 9:45 Commentary. In 13:23 Latin has *fortissimus* (therefore RSV "Almighty"). The other versions, however, make its differentiation from 6:32 specious. Box and many others suggest, on the basis of LXX usage, that *fortis* ⟨ ἰσχύρος ⟨ האל . Kaminka and Violet 2 suggest, also on the basis of Greek usage, a Hebrew original שדי, while Licht suggests גבור. No decision is possible. Box has rendered the word as

"purity" or "chastity" and sees here an ascetic touch. This seems quite unfounded, and the parallels he cites are not relevant; see 5:13 Commentary on this issue.

10 As a result of the situation outlined there, Violet 2 suggests that the verses are disordered and that the last part of 6:33 should follow 6:30 and be followed in turn by 6:34.

11 8:46 is sometimes interpreted thus; our view differs, and see Commentary there.

12 See Box; Violet 2.

13 On the terminology for "last," see Excursus on Natural Order, pp. 104–5.

6

35 And ᵃit came to pass ᵃ after this I wept ᵇ again and fasted seven days as before, ᶜ in order to complete the three weeks as ᵈI had been told. ᵉ **36/** And ᶠit came to pass ᶠ on the eighth ᵍ night ʰ my heart was troubled ⁱwithin me ⁱ again, and I began to speak in the presence of the Most High. **37/** For my spirit was greatly aroused, and my soul was in distress.

Notes

35   a–a Lat, Syr, Georg, Arm; "then after this" Eth; "after this" Ar1; Ar2 omits; there is much variation throughout the book in this formulaic expression.

        b–c Lat; "and fasted for seven days" Syr, Ar1, Arm; "again as before for seven days and I fasted" Eth; "again as before and I fasted for seven days" Georg; Ar2 reformulated; the readings of the versions reflect generally minor variation, such as the location of καί; a shared Greek reading, however, probably stands behind Eth, Georg.

        c–e Ar2, Arm omit.

        d–e "He had told me" Eth, Georg, Ar1; both readings probably occurred in Greek.

36   f–f Eth, Arm, omit; see note a–a above on 6:35.

        g "That" Eth, Georg; this was a Greek reading and may go back to ταύτῃ for τῇ ᾗ (Volkmar).

        h Arm omits, perhaps because of the omission in c–e.

        i–i Eth, Arm omit; not a conjunctive error.

Form and Function

This introduction is very similar to those preceding Vision 1 (3:1–3) and Vision 2 (5:21–22). The seer's state of mind is discussed, and for analysis of this and his visionary experience, see the Excursus on Inspiration. The mention of three weeks as a given period of mourning indicates here, at the start of the long third vision, that its completion will mark the end of one stage of the book.[1] The length of the third vision is excessive in comparison with the first two visions. No ready explanation of this has emerged, and it is doubly problematic in view of the literary sophistication of the author.[2]

Commentary

■ **35** On Ezra's weeping, see the Excursus on Inspiration. Ezra fasts for seven days. The nature of Ezra's fast, as well as the role of fasting in the book, is discussed in 5:20b–22 Function and Content, pp. 118–19.

A different set of issues is raised by the phrase "in order to complete the three weeks as I had been told." Nowhere is Ezra explicitly commanded to fast for three weeks, and this verse is only the second occasion upon which Ezra is reported to fast for seven days, the previous one being in 5:20. Most scholars regard the three weeks' fast as derived from Dan 10:2–3. Yet this does not solve the literary problem within 4 Ezra.

The solution that nearly all scholars have accepted is that a third fast preceded Vision 1. This would fit the pattern of Visions 2 and 3 (although not that of *2 Apocalypse of Baruch*). There is difference of opinion over the question of whether we must assume some actual literary process (Kabisch, Box) or a certain unevenness, generated by the author's concentration on substance rather than framework (Gunkel, Myers, Box).[3] The author is usually careful about his cross-references, yet if the third fast is assumed to have been lost at the beginning of Vision 1, and that seems most reasonable, then there is no literary sign of it in the text at that point.[4] So what-

---

1   See in detail 9:26–28 Form and Function on the role of seven-day fasts. Cf. also Harnisch, "Prophet," 465–76.

2   Kabisch (p. 62) remarks that the excessive length of the third vision suggests that the hand of R (the mythical "redactor") is to be observed.

3   Licht takes an even more careful view and, while noting the difficulty, is reserved about suggesting any

solution at all. Arabic2 and Armenian omit this whole half-verse, we suggest as part of an exegetical rather than a strictly textual process (*contra* Violet 2).

4   If the Ezra = Salathiel equivalation is considered irrelevant.

ever process is posited, it precedes all the versions and neither proposed resolution is demonstrable.[5]

The number of days' fasting or abstinence is significant, as is discussed in 12:37–39 Function and Content, p. 374.

A further point should be noted. From the table given in 5:20b–22 Form and Structure, p. 119, it emerges that 4 Ezra and *2 Apocalypse of Baruch* have seven-day periods at exactly the same points, that is, between Visions 1 and 2, 2 and 3, 3 and 4, and (skipping 4 and 5) finally between Visions 5 and 6. This is striking, and if

we suggest that 4 Ezra served as a source for *2 Apocalypse of Baruch* or at least is anterior to it, then the pattern as we now have it must be ancient indeed.

■ **36** This verse describes Ezra's distress of soul which regularly precedes inspiration; see the Excursus on Inspiration, p. 121.

■ **37** The actual receipt of inspiration is here described; see the Excursus on Inspiration, p. 121. The expression "my spirit was aroused in me" has been compared with Ps 39:3 and Luke 24:32.

---

5   This does not mean that some process could not have taken place either at a prewritten stage or in the very earliest stage of the written tradition. What it does imply is that that process is lost beyond any reasonable hope of discovery. Brandenburger stresses the view that the influence of Daniel produced not only this literary unevenness but also that in 3:1 (Dan 7:1); see *Verborgenheit*, 107–8.

6

38 I said, "O Lord God, [a] thou didst speak [b] at the beginning of creation, [c] and didst say on the first day, [d] 'Let heaven and earth be made,' and thy word accomplished the work. 39/ And then the Spirit was hovering, [e] and darkness and silence embraced everything, [f] and [g] the sound of man's voice was not yet there. 40/ Then thou didst command that a ray of light be brought forth from thy treasuries, so that thy works might then appear. [h]

41/ "Again, on the second day, thou didst create the spirit of [i] the firmament, and didst command him to separate [j] the waters, [k] that one part might move upward and the other part remain beneath.

42/ "On the third day [l] thou didst command the waters to be gathered together in the seventh part of the earth; six parts thou didst dry up [m] and keep [n] so that some of them might be planted and cultivated and be of service before thee. 43/ For thy word went forth, and at once the [o] work was done. 44/ For immediately fruit came forth in endless abundance and of varied appeal to the taste; and flowers of inimitable color; [p]and innumerable beautiful trees; [p] and inexpressible fragrances. [q] These were made on the third day.

45/ "On the fourth day thou didst command the brightness [r] of the sun, the light [r] of the moon, and the arrangement of the stars to come into being; 46/ [s]and thou didst command them to serve man, who was [t] about to be formed.

47/ "But [u] on the fifth day thou didst command the seventh part, where the water [v]had been gathered together, [v] to bring forth living creatures, birds, and fishes; and [w]so it was done. [w] 48/ The dumb and lifeless water produced living creatures, [x] that therefore the nations [y] might declare thy wondrous works.

Notes

38   a Lat omits, cf. 7:75 note a; Arm varies from here to the end of 6:40, omitting *inter alia* all references to creation through divine speech.

  b A reflex of Hebrew infinitive absolute and finite verb occurs in most versions here.

  c "Judgment" Eth; κρίσεως for κτίσεως (Violet 2); see also Hilgenfeld, pp. xl, xli; Bensly, *MF*, on 7:60; Violet 2 there. "Your creation" Syr, Eth; see 7:33 note c and 7:60 note d.

  d "Night" Georg.

39   e Ar1, Ar2 add "over the waters"; cf. Gen 1:2.

  f Exact sense of the verb is uncertain; Ar1 adds "upon the earth"; Ar2 adds "and the world"; Arm adds "and the earth." It is difficult to determine whether these are reflections of a common Greek or similar exegesis.

  g Lat omits.

40   h Ar1 is reworded and omits 6:40; Arm adds "This (was) on the first day"; cf. 6:44.

41   i Ar2, Arm omit "spirit of," perhaps dogmatic; in the next phrase Ar1 omits "and didst command him"; Arm reads "and you commanded the lower waters." The phrase is quoted by Ambrose, *De spiritu sancto* 2:6 (*PL*, 16:753B).

  j Two verbs in Lat.

  k "Between waters and waters" Syr, Ar1; influence of Gen 1:6.

42   l Arm is shorter and unclear.

  m Ar1 has undergone some fairly far-reaching changes.

  n "To remain" Eth; *posuisti* Georg.

43   o "Thy" Eth Mss, Georg; the whole verse is omitted by Ar2, Arm; see note a above on 6:38.

44   p–p Syr, Eth, Georg, Ar1; Lat omits.

  q Georg, cf. Syr, Eth; Lat "odors of inexpressible fragrance." Arm is quite different for the whole verse.

45   r Verbs in Eth, Georg, Ar1; cf. Arm.

46   s Arm omits this verse.

  t Syr, Ar1, Ar2 "you were."

47   u Eth, Ar1 Ar2 "and."

  v–v "Was" Syr, Georg; Georg adds *quam appellant nageb*, cf. 6:50 a reading perhaps related to Hebrew *qww*, the root used in Gen 1:9–10, where the waters are called מקוה המים. Arm reads the verse as referring to the earth.

  w–w Most versions construe this phrase with the following "and the . . . water became."

48   x Ar2 rewrites the rest of the verse; Arm omits from here to 6:52; Lat adds "as it was commanded."

  y "Generations" Syr, Eth, Ar1; cf. Ar2.

49 **[z]"Then thou didst preserve two living creatures [a]which you created; [a] the name of one thou didst call Behemoth and the name of the other Leviathan. 50/ And thou didst separate one from the other, for the seventh part [b] where the water had been gathered together could not hold them both. 51/ And thou didst give Behemoth one of the parts which had been dried up on the third day, to live in it, where there are a thousand [c] mountains; 52/ but to Leviathan thou didst give the seventh part of [d] the watery part; and thou hast kept them to be eaten by whom thou wilt, [e]and when thou wilt. [e]**

53/ "On the sixth day thou didst command the earth to bring forth [f] before thee [g] cattle, beasts, and creeping things; [h] 54/ and over these thou didst place Adam, as ruler over all the works which thou hadst made previously; [i] and from him we have all come, the people whom thou hast chosen. [j]

55 **"All this I have spoken before thee, O Lord, [k] because thou hast said [l]that it was for us that thou didst create this world. [m] 56/ But as for the other nations which have descended from Adam, thou hast said that they are [n] nothing, and that they are like spittle, and thou hast compared their abundance to a drop from a bucket. 57/ And now, O Lord, behold, these nations, which are reputed as nothing, domineer over us and trample upon [o] us. 58/ But we thy people, whom thou hast called thy firstborn, only-begotten, kin, [p] and dear one, [q] have been given into their hands. 59/ If the world has indeed been created [r] for us, why do we not possess our world as an inheritance? How long will this be so?"**

49 z Ar1 omits to 6:53.
a–a Lat omits; cf. *ex illis creaturis* Georg.
50 b Georg adds *nageb;* cf. 6:47.
51 c "Four" Eth, Georg, this reading existed in Greek; Violet 2 suggests A' = 1000 became Δ = 4.
52 d So Syr, Eth, Georg *(septimam partem maris);* Lat "the seventh part, the watery part"; see Commentary.
e–e Eth, Georg omit; perhaps hmt in Greek.
53 f–g Ar1, Ar2 omit.
g–h So Lat, Syr = Gen 1:24; "birds" replaces "reptiles" in Eth, Georg, and so in their *Vorlage.* Birds were discussed in Gen 1:20 and here in 6:47, where birds are assigned to Day 5; cf. Arm here, which conflates and reads "the quadrupeds, the reptiles and the birds." Volkmar, followed by Box and Violet, suggests ἑρπετά/πτερά.
54 i Lat, Ar1 omit; cf. Arm. Ar1 omits the rest of the verse. Ar2 omits the whole verse. Arm is expanded, and Gry considers this to go back to an Aramaic original.
j Lat, Syr, Eth; Arm varies.
55 k Syr adds "Lord"; see 7:75 note a.
l–m Direct speech in Eth, Georg, Ar1. Arm omits by hmt.
m *Primogenitum saeculum* Lat; "first world" Ar2; "this world" Syr, Georg; "the world" Eth.
56 n "Are" Eth, Ar1, Ar2; "are reckoned" Georg.
57 o Syr, Eth, Ar1; Georg omits; *devorare* Lat.
58 p *Aemulatorem* Lat. Arm has a different interpretation of this and the next verse.
q *Carissumum* Lat.
59 r "You created" Eth, Georg, Ar1, Ar2.

Form and Structure

This passage opens the third vision of the book. It is parallel in general to the addresses or plaints that open the first and second visions (3:4–36 and 5:23–30). A somewhat similar passage also precedes the fourth vision (9:29–37). In the first two visions, as here, the address serves to set the tone for the coming dispute. The function of the address in the fourth vision, however, differs somewhat, just as that vision differs in character from the first three.

As was true of the first two addresses, this one is also divided into two distinct parts (6:38–54 and 6:55–59) which fulfill different roles. The first part, 6:38–54, tells of the works done on the six days of creation. This hexaemeron is not formulated as a simple narrative, however, but as an address to God by the seer. Consequently, it is spoken in the second person. Observe that the first part of the addresses in Visions 1 and 2 is also in a clear and distinctive literary form: in the former a forensic retelling of the mighty acts of God and in the latter a semipoetic praise of election of Israel.[1] In those two visions, the latter part of the address formulated the questions that the seer wished to pose.

Here, the second part of the address sets forth the inferences that can be drawn from the hexaemeron. Indeed, the last verse of the hexaemeron raised the theme that is taken up by this second part of the passage and forms a transition to it (6:54). Moreover, in 6:55–59 that theme is made more explicit and acute by the

1 See Function and Content, p. 180 n. 5, p. 183 on Box's suggestion that it may have had a literary *Vorlage.*

contrast with existential reality. Box remarks, with a measure of justice, that these issues were already raised in the first two plaints, and response to them, we may add, was made in the course of the first two visions, but here they are raised in a definitive form. This is indicated, formally, by the fact that this plaint and address come at the end of the three weeks' fasting that the seer has been commanded to observe.

The Hexaemeron (6:38–54)

This passage opens with an invocation (6:38). It then proceeds with a narrative of the events of creation, basically following the account in Genesis 1. Since it is an address to God, of course, the account is reformulated in the second person, as has been noted.[2] The act of creation is related day by day, and each day is numbered at the start of the section that deals with it. A point of difference from the biblical chapter is that in almost no case is there a concluding formula at the end of a day's creation, and these have apparently been replaced by the opening formulas. Moreover, this account relates only the six days of creation, and the Sabbath is not dealt with in any way. This contrasts with the accounts of creation in Genesis and *Jubilees*.

Again, as Jervell points out, the description of the creation of human beings is notably short in 4 Ezra 6:54; *Jub* 2:14; and *Schatzhöhle* 2–3. This is the result, he suggests, not of an unwillingness to speak of humans as *imago Dei* but of a specific literary tradition.[3] Finally, as in 3:27 and 5:27, so also the statements in 6:54 serve as a bridge between the literarily distinct first part of the address and its second part which poses the questions

that emerge from it.

There has been some discussion of the literary genre of this section. Violet 2 and Harnisch (p. 23) have characterized it as a Midrash on the creation story in Genesis. The passage may well contain certain traditions of Jewish exegesis of Genesis 1, but it is not like a Midrash in any formal way. Indeed, in terms of its relationship to the biblical text, it might be called "rewritten bible." To this extent it resembles *Jubilees* 2.[4]

This recasting of the creation account of Genesis 1 in the second person forms the first part of an address to God that climaxes in the plaint-question of 6:59. We have dubbed it "hexaemeron," which name perhaps does not do justice to the address or prayer aspect of the passage. No other exactly similar use of Genesis 1 is known to us, but that is typical of 4 Ezra's utilization of traditional literary forms in the light of his own very distinct needs and aims. An analogous example is the forensic use of the recital of God's gracious acts in 3:4–26.[5] Very similar to this passage is *2 Apoc Bar* 14:16–19:

16 I shall continue to speak before your presence, O Lord, my Lord. 17 When in the beginning the world did not exist with its inhabitants, you devised and spoke by means of your word, and at the same time the works of your creation stood before you. 18 And you said that you would make man for this world as guardian over your works that it be known that he was not created for the world, but the world for him. 19 And now, I see that the world which was made for us, behold, it abides; but we, for whom it was made, depart.

---

2   On the content, both that shared with Genesis and that varying from it, see below. This passage is analyzed in some detail by O. H. Steck, "Die Aufnahme von Genesis 1 in Jubiläen 2 und 4.Esra 6," *JSJ* 8 (1977) 154–82. His chief conclusions are that (1) 4 Ezra 6 is clearly related to Genesis 1; (2) the particular point of 4 Ezra 6 in contrast to Genesis 1 is the might of God reflected in the acts of creation; and (3) creation was through word, not deed.

3   Jervell, *Imago Dei*, 19–20. He develops his view further there. Suffice it for us to note its existence.

4   See, on the traditional material in this passage, Jervell, *Imago Dei*, 19–20. Harnisch observes the parallel in role between this passage and those in Visions 1 and 2. He characterizes our passage as a "creation Hymn" (p. 20 n. 2). This is a somewhat surprising characterization, for we are not dealing

with a hymn at all but with a prayer or an address. On p. 22 he deals in some detail with the relationship between this passage and the *Klagelieder*, and on this see our comments on 3:4–36 Form and Function, n. 12.

5   See on this Introduction, sec. 4.2.1. Certain scholars have even suggested that the author is reusing a preexistent piece of literature. The evidence for this is weighed below, and the conclusion is not certain; see 4:35–36a. See Function and Content, p. 183. A prayer of exorcism relating the creation is to be found in *Bib Ant* 60:1–3; it is not dependent on Genesis 1 and is not a hexaemeron; see also M. Philonenko, "Remarques sur un hymne essénien de charactère gnostique," *Semitica* 11 (1961), 43–54. Another such recital of creation is *Schatzhöhle*, 2–3.

The Questions (6:55–59)

The integration of 6:55–59 within the address is clear enough. These verses are tied to the preceding passage by 6:54 which forms a transition, as has been noted. They form a complementary part of the address, which focuses the author's problem and sets it up for the ensuing dispute. It should be noted that these verses are not written in a full poetic form and do not show the parallelism so typical of 4 Ezra, which can be observed in the corresponding parts of Vision 1 and Vision 2. Nevertheless, there are some antithetical and balanced phrases that might derive from an underlying poetic style, thought appropriate to divine proclamation. An example is:

> they are nothing
> they are like spittle
> their abundance is like a drop from the bucket. (6:56)

As in the addresses in Visions 1 and 2, however, here too the overall division of the speech into two parts is preserved, 6:55–58 and 6:59.[6] It may be further analyzed as follows:

6:55 creation	→	elect people	
6:56 nations	→	nothing	
6:57 nations	rule	us	
6:58 elect people ruled by them			
6:59 why creation→		election, but not	→ rule

From this outline, it is clear that chiasm invoked by Harnisch (p. 24) is not adequate to explain the intricate structure, which is intimately related to the complex development of thought.

First, the balanced opposition between the two initial verses is clear. Likewise the expanded description of the nations in the first part of 6:56 is also paralleled by the expanded description of Israel in the first part of 6:58. At the same time, by the mention of Adam, the first part of 6:56 is related to the theme of creation that has already arisen in 6:55.

Second, 6:57 and 6:58 really say the same thing, one in the active voice and the other in the passive. Chapter 6:57 describes the character of the nations in 6:56, while 6:58 describes the character of "thy people" in 6:55. These two verses are chiastic in their presentation, but the second element in each of them is represented only by a personal pronoun. Moreover, it should be noted that the mention of creation and election in 6:54 and 6:59 forms a sort of *inclusio*. Within that *inclusio*, however, is a second integrated structure, 6:55 and 6:58 dealing with Israel and 6:56–57 dealing with the Gentiles. Conceptually, the first two verses of the passage set up the implications of the hexaemeron. The second two are the confrontation of these implications drawn from the hexaemeron with the existential situation in which Israel is found. Harnisch (pp. 25–26) points to the words "and now" in 6:57 which mark the move from the inferences drawn from the hexaemeron to the comparison of them with the present situation. The fifth verse (6:59) is the formulation of the questions arising from this confrontation.

It emerges that the literary form and structure of this passage are carefully orchestrated in order to highlight the thought that the author wishes to present. They do not represent any conventional literary form, or even balanced *parallelismus membrorum*. See, however, the structures implied by the preceding paragraph.

Function and Content

The question asked in 6:59 is: "If the world has indeed been created for us, why do we not possess our world as an inheritance? How long will this be so?" This can be taken to express the point of the whole address. Box observes that this question follows from the Esau-Jacob passage (6:7–10), for there Israel has been told that only the future world will be its. To some extent indeed, his observation is a just one, yet there are questions of theodicy lurking in the background of the present pericope that are not accounted for by Box's comment.

The passage 6:38–59 then sets the theme for the coming vision. In Vision 1 the problem is formulated in terms of history moving from creation to exile. In Vision 2 it is put in terms of the election of Israel. The address preceding this third vision combines these two presentations; its chief subject is creation, yet its questions arise from the concept of election.[7]

One might have thought that the prophecy of redemption at the end of Vision 2 would have satisfied the

---

6   Harnisch, p. 20, characterizes this passage as a *Klage*.

7   This dual focus is surely related to the dual typology of redemption, in terms of creation and in terms of

exodus, and the author of this passage is drawing them together. A too rigid set of categories has led Myers to comment that the passage is pervaded by a

author, instead of which he returns, via a back door, to the same basic issues that agitated him in the previous visions: Why is the fate of Israel as it is? How does that sit with divine justice and providence? The emphases are not identical in this address, however, and the gradual illumination of the author's understanding is reflected in the fact that here the destruction of the Temple, the very motive power of the address preceding Vision 1, is not even mentioned.[8]

Something of a mystery surrounds the precise conceptual connection between creation of the world and election of Israel. Chapter 6:55 provides a (bogus?) cross-reference, "Thou hast said that it was for us that thou didst create this world," but in fact that has not been said.[9]

The Hexaemeron (6:38–54)

The function of this part of the address is stated in 6:54. The account of creation is given in order to emphasize the weight attaching to the election of Israel, for whose sake creation was carried out. That this is the point becomes clear only when we see the creation account in the context of the whole address. The latter part of the address makes this explicit; within the hexaemeron, however, it is far from explicit.

The hexaemeron itself is composed of two types of material. The first is a text closely parallel to Genesis 1, which provides the framework for the whole passage.[10] Verses from Genesis 1 are cited throughout the passage, in their biblical order. The second type of material is those passages which contain text different from that of Genesis. Such additional material may, in turn, be divided into two parts: that which, in its context, seems to be related to the function of the address and that which, although sometimes making a particular point, nonetheless is not subordinated to the overall purpose of the address.

The first type of material is exemplified by the series of "so that" statements that give the purpose of specific creative acts. The first, in 6:40, follows the creation of light, "so that thy works might then appear," a general statement about the light created on the first day.[11] Chapter 6:42 states that the dry land was created for cultivation (perhaps cf. Gen 1:11) and to be of service to God. In 6:46 the text states that the purpose of the creation of the luminaries is "to serve man, who was about to be created." Living creatures are created from the waters so "that therefore the nations might declare thy wondrous works" (6:48). Behemoth and Leviathan are preserved "to be eaten by whom thou wilt, and when thou wilt" (6:52). In these statements of purpose we may observe a graduated specificity which leads to the point that creation is for human beings and part of creation is for the eschatological reward.[12]

Consequently, these "purpose" passages make creation subject to human beings and their needs (an idea present already in Gen 1:29–30). This is clearly important to the author, since he continually repeats this message.[13] It is worth observing that these statements do not proclaim that creation is for the sake of Israel, nor do they lead to that conclusion. This is stated baldly at the end of 6:54 but is by no means explicit or even implicit in the passage.

"national" background but it "doubtless received a broader interpretation" (p. 251). See also D. Rössler, *Gesetz und Geschichte: Studien zur Theologie der jüdischen Apokalyptik und der pharisäischen Orthodoxie* (WMANT 3; Neukirchen: Neukirchener, 1960) 76 n. 1.

8   Harnisch observes that even though here the questions are put in terms of election, they are not answered, in the course of the vision, in the same terms. Since he stresses the role of the ensuing answers as authoritative refutations of the questions, Harnisch finds this to be an important indicator of the viewpoint of the circles from which 4 Ezra stemmed (p. 134 note). Our perception is that the book should be regarded as a journal of enlightenment and so the truth is sought precisely in the give-and-take between Ezra and the angel; see further Introduction, sec. 4.

9   The idea itself is commonplace; see below. This does not detract from the fact that within the hexaemeron the election of Israel, or creation for Israel's sake, is nowhere to be found. This apparent hiatus does not prevent the commentators from assuming the relationship. Knibb observes that the problem "is here made more acute by being considered within the wider context of God's original intentions for the nations of this world which he had created" (p. 159). Cf. the comment of Myers (p. 251). We find nothing said or implied about such "original intentions."

10   See Form and Structure, p. 180. The actual verses are cited in the Commentary.

11   On primordial light, see 6:40 Commentary.

12   Above, 6:1–6 deals with the question of the preparation of eschatological things before creation.

In 6:49–53 there is a long passage about the creation of Behemoth and Leviathan. This may also fit the particular purposes of the author in a subsidiary fashion, as we have indicated, because it also serves to emphasize the subordination of creation to divine plan. But, even so, it is a difficult body of material. On the one hand, it is obviously introduced here as an exegesis of the "great sea monsters" of Gen 1:21. On the other, its length is out of all proportion to the amount of text devoted to each of the other elements created. At this point, therefore, the author is incorporating a preexisting tradition that is also to be found in *2 Apocalypse of Baruch* and *1 Enoch* (see 6:49–52 Commentary). This is confirmed by the fact that although these beasts have an eschatological role according to 6:52, they are never mentioned in the descriptions of eschatological events and rewards elsewhere in the book.[14]

A third special theme of the author is that creation is carried out by divine speech. This recurs throughout the hexaemeron: note "thou didst speak at the beginning of creation" (6:38); "thy word accomplished the work" (6:38); "thy word went forth, and at once the work was done" (6:43). Elsewhere in the book, too, he emphasizes the role of God's speech as an agent of creation.[15] It is difficult to see how this fits in with the purpose that emerges from the rest of the author's special material in the pericope, but its occurrence elsewhere in the book shows that it is a response to concerns outside the narrow confines of 6:38–59. So this theme should probably be regarded as belonging to our second subcategory, viz., special material not subordinated to the particular purposes of this passage.[16] One final element peculiar to this author is the "spirit of the firmament" in 6:41.[17]

These observations demand that we consider certain questions of a literary and tradition-historical character arising in this pericope. The first is that the passage dealing with Behemoth and Leviathan draws on a distinctly crystallized preexisting tradition, which has not been integrated into other aspects of the author's eschatology. Beyond this is the broader issue of whether the whole of the hexaemeron is drawn from an external source. This possibility is suggested, but not demanded, by some considerations we have raised. It is a very clearly defined pericope, and, in its broader context, it is integrated with a closely argued passage that is supposed to draw its point from it. Yet, in the hexaemeron itself, that point, viz., that creation was for Israel's sake, is not made integrally; to the contrary, a series of tendentious remarks seem designed to show that creation was for the sake of humankind in general. Even if we take account of views such as that of Harnisch, that mankind often stands for Israel in the book, they serve merely to sharpen our point.[18]

The other chief anomaly in the passage is, as pointed out above, the stress laid on creation through speech, which idea serves no particular function in the context in which it stands. This is ambiguous as evidence, however, since it could well be argued that this idea really fits because it occurs elsewhere in 4 Ezra.[19] We are forced to conclude, however, that the evidence is too ambiguous to support an unequivocal determination.

13   Steck characterizes these statements as "Manifestation der Macht Gottes." See his exposition in "Aufnahme," 176. Our view is somewhat different.

14   Steck, ibid., 178, observes that this material is difficult in context.

15   See 3:4 Commentary.

16   See L. Dürr, *Die Wertung des göttliches Wortes* (Leipzig: Hinrichs, 1938), 40–41. Steck ties this theme to that of the power of God ("Aufnahme," 178); see n. 2 above. The narrative of creation utilizes Genesis 1 as a source to demonstrate the mighty works of the divine word.

17   See 6:41 Commentary.

18   Box reports Charles as suggesting that this passage, *2 Apoc Bar* 14:18, and *2 Apoc Bar* 15:7 probably draw on a preexisting document. An examination of the passages in *2 Apocalypse of Baruch* is not convincing.

Yet his detection of an independent source behind the present passage might be correct. Jervell, *Imago Dei*, 32, deals with this issue, comparing also with *Schatzhöhle*, 1.

19   A similarly distinctive specific point is the idea that the situation before creation was typified by the absence of human speech, 6:39 and cf. 6:48. Yet this idea clearly recurs in 7:30, which refers to "primeval silence." See 6:39 Commentary.

The Questions (6:55–59)

Most of the aspects of the argument of this section were set forth in Form and Structure, p. 181. The argument runs: since the world was created for Israel, and since the nations are accounted as nothing, how is it that Israel is ruled by the nations? When will this situation change? How long will it take? It is interesting that the nothingness of the nations is stressed, using Isa 40:15 which occurs there in the context of creation. Moreover, Israel is designated by a number of epithets transferred from the story of the binding of Isaac. So the election of Israel has been tied not just to creation but to Aqedah, "the Binding of Isaac," perhaps thus hinting in some way at Israel's suffering.

The idea that creation exists for the sake of Israel is widespread and is documented in the verse-by-verse commentary. What should be observed here is that the formulation of this section calls the reliability of the divine word into question. This is really what is at stake in 6:59; the political situation turns God's promise into a mere illusion. Will this be rectified and when?[20] Consequently, the question seems no less revolutionary than the questions asked in the course of the speech preceding the first vision.

Commentary

■ **38** The invocation of God by a doubled name is also found at the start of other addresses in the book; see 3:4 Commentary. The creation on the first day is based on Gen 1:1, cf. *Jub* 2:2, although this latter is much expanded; see also *Schatzhöhle* 3. In some rabbinic sources the question arises whether the verses of Genesis imply the creation of heaven and earth or just (as, e.g., Rashi opines) the creation of light. 4 Ezra is clearly of the view that both were created on the first day; cf. Ps 33:6–7 and *Jub* 2:2.[21]

In 3:4 Commentary and also here in Function and Content, pp. 183–84, the idea of creation through divine word and its position in 4 Ezra is discussed. The concept here is the same as in 3:4. The "word" which accomplished the work is precisely God's speech at the beginning of creation. The emphasis on this idea in the address makes it seem likely that a point is being made vis-à-vis certain other understandings of creation, for example, that it was done by wisdom,[22] but this is not made explicit.

■ **39** This verse is largely based on Gen 1:2.[23] Its most striking feature is the introduction of silence, on which see Function and Content, n. 19. The primordial silence is also mentioned in 7:30, while *Bib Ant* 60:2 is nicely parallel to our passage: *tenebre et silentium erat antequam fieret seculum, et locutum est silentium et apparuerunt tenebre* ("There were darkness and silence before the world was, and the silence spoke, and the darkness became visible").[24] Targum Onqelos translates "breath of life" in Gen 2:7 as רוח ממללא, "speaking spirit." Is this a deliberate contrast to the emphasis on divine creative speech in the previous verse?[25] The occurrence of the expression in *Biblical Antiquities* and its occurrence elsewhere in 4 Ezra suggest that at the time there was an interpretation that viewed speech or its absence as the crucial element in the creation of human beings.

20   See Harnisch, pp. 24–26.
21   See Licht, Kaminka; cf. Urbach, *Sages,* 185.
22   In Wisd 9:1 "word" is parallel to "wisdom."
23   Myers, quoting Speiser on Genesis, wishes to translate "a wind blowing fiercely." It would seem, however, that the Hebrew was interpreted as "spirit" and not "wind" also by *Jub* 2:2. See also in general *Schatzhöhle,* 2–3.
24   See Philonenko, "Remarques," 47–50. In 4 Ezra 7:85 and 7:95 the "profound quiet" of the future state of the righteous is mentioned; see also 7:36 Commentary, and cf. *2 Apoc Bar* 3:7. Wisd 18:14, in a quite different context, has God's active word and also "gentle silence." Jervell, *Imago,* 48, takes the point of silence to be a polemical one—no one was there to help God. Note also 9:18 in this latter connection.
25   Gunkel (p. 367) raises the possibility that this idea is related to Gen 2:19–20, Adam's naming of the animals. It is interesting to observe that in *2 Enoch* 24:1–5 the crucial element is not sound, as here, but vision, and the contrast is of "visible" and "invisible." Arnobius (in his treatise written c. 303–310 C.E.), cited by A.-J. Festugière, *La Révélation d'Hermès Trismégiste* (Paris: Lecoffre, 1953), 3:75, refers to human speech as the characteristic of the creation of people and silence as its opposite. The same idea occurs in *Gospel of the Egyptians* CG III.51:9–13 = IV.30:4–7.

■ **40** See Gen 1:3; cf. also *Jub* 2:2 and *2 Enoch* A 25:1–5. As for the ray of light from the divine treasury: there were thought to be heavenly treasuries or storehouses of natural phenomena; on this see 5:37 Commentary. There was also a good deal of speculation in rabbinic circles about primordial light that was created at the beginning of creation and not subsequent to the luminaries. It is ascribed wondrous qualities and was one of the things that Adam lost when he was expelled from Eden.[26] 4 Ezra omits the division between light and darkness and the naming of day and night which are found in the biblical creation narrative. Instead, it says that the purpose of the creation of light is that God's works might appear (cf. *2 Enoch* A 24:1–5). This idea is also explicit in a dispute in *Gen. R.* 1:3 (Theodor-Albeck, pp. 18–19).

■ **41** See Gen 1:6–8; *Jub* 2:4; *2 Enoch* 28:1; and *Schatzhöhle* 1–3. God creates a "spirit of the firmament" and delivers his commands to this personalized firmament. This concept has analogies elsewhere in the literature of the period, where various forces and phenomena of nature are thought to have guiding spirits; see *1 Enoch* 60:15 and *Jub* 2:2.[27] The textual situation supports "spirit,"[28] yet the reading is strange, for nowhere else in the hexaemeron, or indeed in 4 Ezra, is there personalization of natural forces.[29] This may be another of the anomalies noted in this passage. It is intriguing to ob-

serve *Gen. R.* 4:1, where on Gen 1:7 "and God made the firmament" Ben Zoma protests, "Was it not done by divine speech, as scripture says 'By the word of the Lord the heavens were made' (Ps 33:6)."[30]

■ **42** See Gen 1:9–10; *Jub* 2:5–6; and *2 Enoch* 30:1; cf. Philo, *De opif.* 38–39, and *Schatzhöhle* 1.2. This verse departs from Genesis with respect to the tradition dividing the world into seven parts, into one of which the water was gathered. No exact parallel is known.[31] According to a number of sources, the world is divided into seven κλίματα, over each of which an angel or a star presided.[32] But none of these say that the sea was limited to one of the seven parts. This is another distinctive tradition occurring in the hexaemeron.

The text of the latter part of the verse has been the subject of some discussion. On its function, see Function and Content, p. 182. Gunkel argues that it refers to paradise. That is not certain, although the expression "keep" and the agricultural terms are clearly used in the context of paradise in Gen 2:15. "Keep" here is perhaps related to the idea that the sea has to be held back or it will swamp the land; see 4:17 Commentary.

■ **43** This verse corresponds to the "and it was so" in the middle of the narrative of the creation on the third day in Gen 1:11. There, as here, first there is the command, then this verse, and then the statement that the com-

---

26 On Adam's light, see Ginzberg, *Legends,* 5:8–9, and many sources there. Gunkel, as ever, would ascribe this idea to mythological views about light as part of God's being and only partially revealed in this world. Rowland, *Open Heaven,* 148, follows the same interpretation as we do, viewing this verse as describing "not so much an act of creation as the bestowal on the cosmos . . . of that which already existed with God."

27 See Knibb. Gunkel compares the expression with "spirit of heavens" in *1 Enoch* 15:10. Keulers, p. 26, while listing all the occurrences of angels in the book, notes their minor importance for 4 Ezra.

28 Violet 2 and Kaminka both suggest textual processes that may have turned an original "firmament" into "spirit." Their suggestions are not convincing.

29 See Stone, "Natural Order," 307–8.

30 Box claims that this is a midrash on Gen 1:6, arguing that the address demands an addressee. Yet this "logic" does not work elsewhere in the creation story of Genesis. Armenian has a long addition at the end of the verse which Violet 2 thinks might be original.

31 The number seven is much beloved of the apocalypticists and often occurs in cosmographic contexts; see, e.g., *1 Enoch* 18:6 and 77:5. See Knibb and Keulers, p. 21 note.

32 Pseudo-Clement, *Recognitiones* 9:26; Eusebius, *Praep. ev.* 6.10 (= *PG*, 21:473, attributed to ἀστρονόμοι). Among numerous divisions into seven given in Hippocrates Περὶ Ἑβδομάδων is a division of the earth into seven parts; see W. H. Roscher, *Die Hippokratische Schrift Von der Siebenzahl* (Padeborn: Schöning, 1913), 15–16, and discussion on pp. 156–58; see also pseudo-Galen, ibid., 131. On the seven κλίματα in Greek geographical views, see also Pauly-Wissowa 11.1.841–43. E. Schrader, *Die Keilinschriften und das Alte Testament* (Berlin: Reuther & Reichard, 1902) 617–19, has a long discussion of this matter.

mand was fulfilled. On the idea of the divine creative word, see 3:4 Commentary.

■ **44** It is an old suggestion of Gunkel's that these verses actually refer to the creation of paradise. Box remarks cogently that indeed that may lie in the background, but significantly it is avoided in the verse (cf. Gen 2:9; *1 Enoch* 29–32). Indeed, *Jub* 2:7 sets the creation of paradise on the third day, but that is not the view of 4 Ezra; see 6:2 Commentary.[33] Fragrances are very important in the description of wondrous places and trees, such as paradise or the tree of life, and feature in many poetic descriptions; see, for example, *1 Enoch* 24:3–6; 32:4; *2 Enoch* 8:3; and *2 Apoc Bar* 29:7. See further *Seder Gan Eden* (Jellinek, *BM*, 2:53).

■ **45** See Gen 1:14–19; *Jub* 2:8–10; *2 Enoch* J 30:2–7; and *Schatzhöhle* 1–2. Astronomy was a central subject of the apocalypses. The most extensive treatment is the *Book of the Luminaries* in *1 Enoch* 72–82, which is even longer in the original Aramaic version from Qumran than in the better-known and preserved Ethiopic translation.[34] The courses of the stars are a continuing subject of interest; see Judg 5:20 and Sir 43:9–10; cf. *2 Apoc Bar* 48:9 and *Clem. Recog.* 9:25–26. These were important topics in the ancient world, evidence of the regularity of divine government. In 4 Ezra 5:5 disorder of the stars is one of the upheavals preceding the eschaton.

■ **46** See Gen 1:14. The service of humanity is surely the division of day and night (Knibb). Gunkel suggests appositely that this idea is stressed in opposition to the general view in the ancient world regarding the stars as deities.

■ **47** See Gen 1:20; *Jub* 2:11; *2 Enoch* 30:7; and *Schatzhöhle* 1.2–3.[35] Knibb observes that it is odd that the waters bring forth birds but that this is due to compression of the text of Genesis. Yet it is worth noting that *2 Enoch*

30:7 has the same interpretation and that *Schatzhöhle* 1.2 refers to "Gevögel der Luft und des Wassers" ("winged creatures of the air and of the water").

■ **48** There is no particular biblical passage that praises God for the specific act of creation here specified; Psalm 104 is a sustained praise of God the Creator, and see particularly Ps 104:25 on the seas (cf. also Job 38–39). Other psalms praise God's wondrous works, but they are often historical; see Ps 26:7; 105:2; and 107:24. *Gen. R.* 1:9 (Theodor-Albeck, p. 32) speaks at length in this connection of the waters praising God (quoting Ps 93:4).

■ **49** This verse opens the passage that deals with Behemoth and Leviathan. See in general Function and Content, pp. 182–83. The material is introduced as an exegesis of Gen 1:21. Note that in the corresponding verse in *Jub* 2:11 there is also additional stress on the monsters, a subject already present in Genesis.

Behind the Leviathan and Behemoth there lies old mythological material. They figured in creation myths. Gunkel, Box, and others long ago related them to the sea monsters, such as Tiamat, of the Babylonian creation cycles.[36] However, the discovery of the Ugaritic texts indicates that these monsters may well have Canaanite roots.[37] It has been recognized that there are fragments of a creation myth in parts of the Hebrew Bible, some of which refer to conflicts between God and dragons, sea monsters, or even Leviathan explicitly.[38]

In 4 Ezra the Leviathan and Behemoth are said to be reserved by God for whom and when he wills. This refers to the view that there will be an eschatological banquet of the righteous at which these monsters will be served up. That idea may be found in certain other sources in the Apocrypha and the Pseudepigrapha and extensively in rabbinic literature. Referring to the period when the Messiah will be revealed, *2 Apoc Bar* 29:4 states:

---

33 The verse here mentioning fruit and flowers may perhaps be compared with Gen 1:11, which also mentions fruit and grasses. Steck, "Aufnahme," 177, would also deny the relationship to paradise.

34 See also *2 Enoch* J 30:2–7 and *3 Apocalypse of Baruch* 6–9. See Stone, "Lists," 426–31.

35 Violet 2 suggests that "bring forth" comes from ἐξαγάγετο, which is the LXX rendering of ישרצו (Gen 1:20). Note that the same verb occurs, apparently, in *2 Enoch.* He observes, however, that this only witnesses the influence of the LXX on the translator and not on the author.

36 See Gunkel, *Schöpfung,* 41–69; and Box, ad loc.

37 See particularly M. Pope, *Job* (AB; Garden City, N.Y.: Doubleday, 1964) 268–71, 276–78, and the material adduced by T. H. Gaster, *Thespis* (Garden City, N.Y.: Doubleday, 1961), Index, s.v. A detailed discussion is to be found in M. Delcor, *Etudes bibliques et orientales de religions comparées* (Leiden: Brill, 1979) 228–62.

38 Such are Isa 27:1 (specifically Leviathan); Isa 51:9; Ps 74:13–14 (specifically Leviathan); 89:10–11; Job 7:12; 26:12–13. Job 40–41 is considered to contain descriptions of these monsters.

And Behemoth shall be revealed from his place and Leviathan shall ascend from the sea, those two great monsters which I created on the fifth day of creation, and shall have kept until that time; and then they shall be for food for all that are left.

This statement clearly reflects exactly the same tradition as 4 Ezra; the beasts live in different places, and Leviathan is the sea dweller. They were created on the fifth day; they were preserved; and, *2 Apocalypse of Baruch* adds, they shall be food for the survivors in the messianic kingdom. A slightly different tradition occurs in *1 Enoch* 60:7–10:

7 And on that day two monsters will be separated from one another: a female monster, whose name (is) Leviathan, to dwell in the depths of the sea above the springs of the waters; 8 And the name of the male (is) Behemoth, who occupies with his breast an immense desert, named Dendayn, on the east of the garden where the chosen and righteous dwell, where my great-grandfather was received. . . . 9 And I asked that other angel to show me the power of those monsters, how they were separated on one day and thrown, one into the depths of the sea, and the other on to the dry ground of the desert. 10 And he said to me: "Son of Man, you here wish to know what is secret."

This tradition differs at a number of points from that in 4 Ezra and *2 Apocalypse of Baruch*, but it also shares very significant points with them. The beasts function in an eschatological context. No mention is made of their creation, however, and the tradition about the desert of Dendayn is quite unknown in other sources. These three

are the oldest sources referring to the eschatological function of Leviathan and Behemoth, but their place in the events of the end time in rabbinic literature and subsequent Jewish lore is well established.[39] Our text does not know the sex of the monsters, which figures in *1 Enoch* 60:7,[40] and it clearly regards them both as belonging originally to the class of sea monsters and therefore having been created on the fifth day. Behemoth is obviously a land beast, according to Job 40:15–24.

The term "keep" or "preserve" serves to refer to these two beasts in the sources quoted.

■ **50** The idea that both monsters were originally in one place and that they were subsequently separated is also to be found in *1 Enoch* 60:7.[41] Gunkel and Box make much of the fact that this shows that they were originally sea monsters. This is also implied by *2 Apocalypse of Baruch*, even though it reflects only the situation after they had separated. Their watery origin is witnessed by their creation on the fifth day, and consequently their relationship to Gen 1:21. As for the sea being the seventh part of the world, see 6:42 Commentary.

■ **51** There is no other reference to the Behemoth being assigned one seventh of the dry land to live in. According to *1 Enoch* 60:8, it has its dwelling in the great desert of Dendayn. In *2 Apoc Bar* 29:4 it has "its place," which is clearly not the sea. Job 40:15 and 40:20 relate that it eats grass on mountains. These texts all seem to indicate that it is (or at least becomes) a land dweller. Behemoth may sometimes mean "hippopotamus" and as such would be both a water and a land dweller. The detail of the thousand mountains is due to a common interpretation

39 Targ J Gen 1:21 reads: "and God created the great sea-monsters, Leviathan and its mate, for the Day of Comfort." Wellhausen, *Skizzen*, 6:232, points to Theodotion Ps 74:14: εδωκας (τον δρακοντα) βρωμα τω λαω τω εσχατω ("you gave them [the dragon] as food to the last people"). Rabbinic legends are extensive: see *b. Baba Batra* 74b–75a; *Gen. R.* 1:21 (Theodor-Albeck, pp. 52–54); *Lev. R.* on Lev 11:2; *Num. R.* 21:18; *PRE* 11 and cf. 10; particularly rich traditions are found in *Tanh. Šemini* 7. See further Ginzberg, *Legends*, 5:44–45, and Ch. Albeck, "Agadot im Lichte der Pseudepigraphen," *MGWJ* 83 (1939) 162–65. The Leviathan is also mentioned in *Apoc Abr* 21:4 but with no eschatological reference.

40 *Yalq* on Gen 1:21 says: "Why is 'great fish (i.e. plural)' written? This means Behemoth and Leviathan which have no 'mates.' Resh Lakish said, 'Behemoth has a

mate, but he is without sexual desire.'" In *b. Baba Bathra* 74b, Rabbi Yehuda reports in the name of Rab that God created Leviathan and "the fleeing serpent" (Isa 27:1, but taken as a separate beast) both male and female, but for fear that their union would destroy the world he castrated the male and killed the female and salted away her flesh as food for the righteous. Further legends of Leviathan are reported there, 75a; see also *Midrash Konnen* (BM, 2:26).

41 The translation of *1 Enoch* quoted is that of M. A. Knibb, *The Ethiopic Book of Enoch* (Oxford: Oxford University, 1978). In it the verb is "will be separated." He is certain that this is *Eth here, but comments that "v. 9 appears to demand here a reference to an event in the past."

in ancient Jewish literature of Ps 50:10b. Instead of "the cattle on a thousand hills," it is taken to mean "Behemoth on a thousand hills."[42]

■ **52** The text that is best supported by the versions suggests that the Leviathan lived in one seventh of the one seventh of the world that is water. Latin alone reads "the seventh part, the watery part," a text that is accepted by a number of commentators and translators.[43]

The text is mysterious about who will eat the monsters, but in fact the intention is the righteous at the time of the end. This is a stylistic feature we have already noted in eschatological passages of 4 Ezra.[44] This idea of the messianic banquet made by God for the righteous has biblical roots; see Isa 25:6 and Ps 74:14 (of Leviathan). In rabbinic sources it is often said to be composed of these mythical beasts.[45]

■ **53** See Gen 1:24–25 and *Jub* 2:13; *2 Enoch* puts the creation of beasts on the fifth day (30:7) and the creation of human beings on the sixth (30:8); similarly also *Schatzhöhle* 1.2–3.

■ **54** See Gen 1:26–30; 2:7; *Jub* 2:14; *2 Apoc Bar* 14:18, as well as *2 Enoch* 30:8.[46] The partial non sequitur of the last phrase is discussed in Function and Content, p. 180. Compare the verse with *2 Apoc Bar* 14:18:

> And you said that you would make a man for this world as a guardian over your works that it should be known that he was not created for the world, but the

world for him.

This statement forms a clear contrast with the statement in 4 Ezra about Israel.[47]

It should be noted that the earth is said to have brought forth Adam (7:116) as well as mankind in general (here in 6:54), the human mind (7:62), and cattle (6:53); see 4:40 Commentary.

■ **55** This verse makes quite explicit the idea that this world was created for the sake of Israel. This is also to be found in 6:59 and 7:11 as well as in *Test Mos* 1:12. The world is said to be made for the few or the righteous in 8:1 and 9:13; cf. *2 Apoc Bar* 14:19; 15:7; and 21:24.[48] A third view is that it was created for the sake of mankind, without further specification; this may be observed in 8:44 as well as in *Greek Apoc Esd* 6:19 and *Apoc Sedrach* 3:4. The words "Thou hast said" do not seem to refer to anything preceding, though this view is set in God's mouth in 7:11. It has been suggested that this derives from consideration of Gen 1:26. That passage applies to all mankind, and so its reference would have to have been varied here.[49]

Rabbinic views are somewhat varied. Naturally, the idea of the election of Israel is too central to rabbinic thought to need documenting. That creation was for the sake of Israel is the view found in *Sifre on Deut.* 11:21 (Finkelstein, p. 80); *b. Ber.* 32b; *Gen. R.* 12:2 (Theodor-Albeck, pp. 99–100); *Tanh. (Buber) Berešit* 3 and 10; *Yalq.*

---

42 See, e.g., *Midr. Haggadol* on Gen 1:24.

43 Box, Gunkel, and others are of the view that here two traditions are brought together in our text; according to one, both creatures are sea monsters and according to the other, one is a sea monster and the other a land monster.

44 See Gunkel, p. 368 note; Keulers, p. 19; see 7:26 Commentary and 7:31.

45 The biblical origins are set forth in some detail by S. B. Frost, *Old Testament Apocalyptic* (London: Epworth, 1952) 152–53.

46 Violet 2 suggests that "and over these" probably reflects καὶ ἐπὶ τούτοις; cf. *Jub* 2:14 "and after all this."

47 The possibility raised by Aalen, that "Israel" stands for mankind, which is quoted by Harnisch (pp. 81–82 note), does not help, for here we are forced to say that mankind is taken to be Israel. S. Aalen, *Die Begriffe "Licht" und "Finsternis" im Alten Testament, im Spätjudentum und im Rabbinismus* (Skrift. utg. Norske Videnskaps-Akademii Oslo 2; Hist.-Filos. Klasse 1; Oslo: J. Dybwad, 1951) 207 n. 3 and 209 n. 4.

48 This seems to have been a particularly prominent view in the first century C.E.; see J. J. Collins, "The Date and Provenance of the Testament of Moses," *Studies on the Testament of Moses* (ed. G. W. E. Nickelsburg; SCS 4; Cambridge, Mass.: SBL, 1973) 27. R. H. Charles, *The Apocalypse of Baruch* (London: Black, 1896), in his commentary on *2 Apoc Bar* 14:18, sets up three rigid categories, but the view of Aalen quoted by Harnisch should at least be taken as a warning to avoid such attempts. Jervell, *Imago Dei*, 34 and 37, adduces some sources that seem to reckon Adam in the Israelite line; such are Sir 49:16 and *Jub* 19:24. On this, see 7:1–25 Form and Function, pp. 194–95.

49 Armenian substitutes "man" for "Adam" almost everywhere in 4 Ezra; see *Armenian Text Commentary* on 3:5. On the issue in general, see Jervell, *Imago Dei*, 33–34. The relation of Gen 1:26 is proposed it seems by Rowland, *Open Heaven*, 216.

on Jer, 264; and *Pes. Rab. Ki Tissa* 10 (36a–36b). A more general formulation is to be observed in *Num. R.* 1:4.[50]

■ **56** This verse, which expresses the nothingness of the nations, is largely based on the text of Isa 40:15 and 17:

15 Behold, the nations are like a drop from a bucket, and are accounted as the dust on the scales: behold, he takes up the islands as fine dust [as spittle—LXX].

17 All the nations are as nothing before him, they are accounted by him as less than nothing and emptiness.

Knibb comments, and in this he agrees with earlier authorities, that 4 Ezra "follows the Septuagint version." Now, the comparison with spittle is also to be found in *2 Apoc Bar* 82:5: "They shall be accounted as spittle."[51] This comparison was also used in other contexts; cf. Sir 26:22. Particularly interesting is *Bib Ant* 7:3: *et tamquam stillicidium arbitrabor eos, et in scuto [*emend James *sputo] approximabo eos* ("and I will value them as a drop of water and I will liken them to spittle"). It is thus difficult to avoid the view that all are dependent on a variant form of Isaiah or of the same expression that Isaiah used.

■ **57** The same problem is expressed sharply in 3:28 and 5:28–29; cf. *2 Apoc Bar* 5:1.

■ **58** This collection of titles for Israel is notable. In *Ps Sol*

18:4, Israel is called "firstborn, only-begotten son." Very similar titles are also to be found in Gen 22:2 of Isaac at the time of the binding: "your son, your only one, whom you loved, Isaac," and in Exod 4:22 of Israel.[52]

The parallels to the specific expressions are numerous: "firstborn" occurs in Exod 4:22; Jer 31:8; Ps 89:28; Sir 36:12; and *Jub* 2:20.[53] Israel is termed "only one" in 4 Ezra 5:28; see Jer 6:26; Zech 12:10; and *Ps Sol* 18:4.[54] The term "kin" is difficult on textual grounds, but God's loving relation to Israel is frequently referred to in biblical sources, for example, Isa 5:1; Jer 31:33; and Hos 11:1; cf. here 4:23 and *2 Apoc Bar* 21:21.

■ **59** On the idea that the world was created for Israel, see 6:55 Commentary. Here it is designated as an inheritance, as was the land of Israel in Num 33:54; 34:13; Jos 14:2; etc. Israel is God's inheritance, Deut 32:9. The theme of inheritance is picked up by our author with a variation in 7:9.[55]

The question "How long, O Lord?" is a common one; see here 4:33, and cf. Ps 4:2; 13:2; *2 Apoc Bar* 81:3; etc.

---

50 Cf. also *m. Sanh.* 4:5. Christian sources, such as *Hermas Vis.* 1.1.6 and 2.4.1, speak of the world as created for the church.

51 There is an additional suggestion that דק has been confused with דק, "dust," but it should be recalled that the word in Isa 40:15b is different, viz., שחק. It is difficult to claim the corruption of the two words and at the same time to claim that 4 Ezra is so close to Isaiah as to have definitely used the LXX. The word דק is to be found only in the third phrase of Isa 40:15. 4 Ezra is indeed close to Isa 40:15a, and its second phrase is a combination of Isa 40:15b and 15c. It is not our view that 4 Ezra and *2 Apocalypse of Baruch* were dependent on LXX Isa 40:15 (or its *Vorlage* if it had one). Isa 14:17 is exegeted of the nothingness of the nations in *Tanh. Bamidbar* 23.

52 See 4QDibHam 3:6: "you called Israel 'my son, my

first born'" which utilizes Exod 4:22 (M. Baillet, "Un recueil liturgique de Qumrân, Grotte 4: Les Paroles des Luminaires," *RB* 68 [1961] 195–250). See another series of epithets, but with little in common with our list, in Isa 42:1 and Rom 9:4.

53 Cf. many other places where Israel is designated "son" and God as "father"; e.g., Hos 11:1; Ps 2:7; and Wisd 18:13.

54 This is, of course, a title of Christ; see John 1:18 and Box's comment here.

55 According to *Mek. Bešallah* on Exod 15:16, four things are specifically described as God's possession, even though the whole world is God's: Israel, the land, the temple, and the Torah. On such lists, see also 5:23–30 Form and Function, p. 127.

7

1 And ^ait came to pass ^a when I had ^bfinished speaking ^b these words, the ^c angel who had been sent to me on the former nights ^d was sent to me, 2/ and he said to me, "Rise, Ezra, and listen to the words that I have come to speak to you."

3 I said, ^e "Speak, my lord." And he said to me, "There ^f is a sea set in a wide expanse so that ^g it is broad and vast, 4/ but it has an entrance set in a narrow place, so that it is like a river. 5/ If anyone, then, wishes ^h to reach the sea, to look at it or to rule over ⁱ it, how can he come to the broad part unless he passes through the narrow part? 6/ Another example: There is a city built and set on a plain, and it is full of all good things; 7/ but the entrance to it is narrow and ^jset in a precipitous place, ^j so that ^k there is fire on the right hand and deep water on the left; 8/ and there is only one path lying between them, ^l that is, between the fire and the water, so that ^monly one man can walk upon that path. ^m 9/ If now that city is given to a man for an inheritance, how will the heir receive his inheritance unless he passes through the narrow (place)?" ⁿ

10/ I said, ^o "He cannot, lord." And he ^p said to me, "So also is Israel's portion. 11/ For I made the world for their ^q sake, and when Adam transgressed my statutes, what had been made was judged. ^r 12/ And so the entrances ^s of this world were made narrow and sorrowful and toilsome; they are few and evil, full of dangers and involved in great hardships. 13/ But the entrances of that coming ^t world are broad and safe and yield the fruit of immortality. 14/ Therefore unless the living pass through the difficult and bad ^u experiences, they can never receive those things that have been reserved for them.

15/ But now why are you disturbed,
seeing that you are to perish?
And why are you moved,
seeing that you are mortal? ^v
16/ And why have you not considered ^w in your mind what is to come, rather than what is now present?"

Notes

1   a–a Eth, Ar1, Ar2 omit; see 6:14 note g–g.

b–b Lat, Syr, cf. Ar1; Eth, Georg, Arm "finished"; Ar2 "had spoken"; there were probably two forms of Greek, one with and one without the verb "speaking."

c Eth, Georg, Arm "that."

d Eth "first on that night"; *in prima illa nocte* Georg, Ar2; Ar1 omits; perhaps πρότερον νυκτί for προτέραις νυξί (Violet 2), but "night" is singular in these versions. Lat Ms C has *prioribus* in the margin.

3   e Syr, Eth add "to him."

f Syr, Arm, Georg "if a sea."

g Eth, Georg "and"; see 7:7 note k.

5   h Lat *volens voluerit*, cf. *cogitatione cogitaverit* Georg; reflex of Hebrew infinitive absolute and finite verb, not reflected in the other versions; Georg ⟨ βουλεύομαι for βούλομαι.

i RSV and many other authorities "navigate" from Gunkel's reconstructed corruption; see 7:5 Commentary.

7   j–j Eth, Georg "and is precipitous"; Ar1 "difficult and dangerous"; Arm "thin and rough."

k Eth, Georg "and"; see 7:3 note g.

8   l Syr, Georg "both of them."

m–m RSV; the versions literally mean, with some variation, "that path can hold the footsteps of only one man."

9   n Eth "difficulty" (variant: "narrowness"); Georg *angustum et terribile;* Ar1 "narrow way"; Arm "the narrow (place)"; Lat, Syr "danger set before him" (Violet 2).

10   o Syr, Eth, Ar1 add "to him"; Ar2 omits verse.

p Syr, Arm add "answered and."

11   q Arm "mankind's," and note its expansion of the following phrase. On its tendentious reworking here, see *Armenian Text Commentary.*

r Ar1, Georg "split"; Eth omits; perhaps κρίνω/διακρίνω or, as Violet 2 suggests, κρίνω/σχίζω.

12   s Eth, Ar1 "ways"; Box accepts this on exegetical ground here and in 7:13, supposing ὁδοί/εἴσοδοι. See 7:4 Commentary.

13   t Syr, Georg; Eth "that world"; Ar1 "the coming world"; Lat has *maioris* (with Mss variants) *saeculi;* Eth adds "great" in the next phrase, which may be related to Lat; Volkmar suggests μέλλοντος/μείζονος.

14   u Lat *vana;* some variation in the other versions, perhaps going back to κακά.

15   v The two parts of the verse are transposed in Arm. In Georg the middle of the verse is lost, perhaps by hmt.

16   w Arm "attained" might go back to a mistrans-

17   Then I answered and said, "O sovereign Lord, behold, thou hast ordained ˣ in thy law that the righteous shall inherit these things, but that the ungodly shall perish. 18/ The righteous therefore can endure difficult circumstances while hoping for easier ones; but those who have done wickedly have suffered ʸ the difficult circumstances and will not see the easier ones."

19   And he said to me, "You are not a better judge than God, ᶻ or wiser than the Most High! 20/ Let many perish ᵃwho are now living, ᵇ rather than that the law of God ᶜwhich is set before them ᶜbe disregarded! ᵈ 21/ For God strictly commanded those who came into the world, ᵉwhen they came, ᵉ what they should do to live and what they should observe to avoid punishment. 22/ Nevertheless they were not obedient, and spoke against him;
        they devised for themselves vain ᶠ
          thoughts,
          23/ and proposed to themselves
            wicked frauds;
        they even declared that the Most High
          does not exist,
        and they ignored his ways!
        24/ They scorned his law,
          and denied his covenants; ᵍ
        they have been unfaithful to his statutes,
        and have not performed his works.

25   "Therefore, Ezra, ʰ empty things are for the empty, and full things are for the full.

---

17   lation of καταλαμβάνω.

17   x Eth, Georg "said."

18   y Eth "believed"; Violet suggests πεπόνθασι/-οτες) πεποίθασι/-οτες.

19   z Eth, Georg "the One"; both readings existed in Greek.

20   a–b Eth omits; *huius saeculi* Georg; see next note.

        c–c The phrase is uncertain. In this form it occurs only in Lat; Syr reads "which I have established."

        c–d Syr, Eth "who have disregarded"; Georg "since they have disregarded"; Arm reads "who transgress the commandment of the Lord" for "who are now living," while the next phrase in its text is basically like Lat. It is likely that there were two Greek readings, one with a comparative and one without, but it is not certain whether Arm has a double reading (as it does, e.g., in 6:53, see note g–h).

21   e–e The phrase is omitted by Eth, Arm; *patres illos ante se* Georg.

22   f Eth, Georg "bad."

24   g Georg *mandata;* there is some variation in the nouns of this list in the various versions, but Lat, Syr, and Eth are in general agreement.

25   h Eth, Georg omit.

Form and Structure

The division of the first part of the vision into pericopes is somewhat problematic. Here 7:1–44 is divided into two major sections that appertain to the "Dispute 1" (7:1–25) and to the "Prediction 1" (7:26–44) categories respectively. The reasons for this are clear when these pericopes are compared with those of similar character in Visions 1 and 2. Vision 3 is much longer and much more complex than those two visions, and, as is evident from the outline included in General Structure of the Book above, in the course of it, some literary forms not found in those first two visions are encountered.

Nonetheless, in 7:1–24 we have disputatious dialogue following upon an address (6:38–59), features belonging unmistakably to the dispute form. Moreover, it is followed by a sustained prediction set in the mouth of the angel, in a style typical of Prediction 2 (7:26–44). The latter is preceded by a transitional oracular statement, also typical of this sort of pericope (7:25).[1]

The section 7:1–25 may be analyzed into a number of subdivisions. As always, it is difficult to distinguish completely between those made on purely formal grounds and those made at least partly on grounds of substance, but here the analysis will be based as far as possible on purely formal characteristics.

A. Introductory Sentence and Angelophany (7:1–2)
This passage should be compared with 4:1 and 5:31 which function similarly in almost identical contexts. A new element in our passage is that the seer is commanded to rise. This formal element, which occurs occasionally throughout the book, indicates the partic-

---

1   Many scholars find a break at the end of 7:16. See, e.g., Gunkel, pp. 337–38. This finding is justified as will emerge from our analysis below, but it is to be

regarded as a subdivision within the first pericope. Certainly Brandenburger's division between 7:1–16 and 7:17–44 is not adequate from our point of view.

ular solemnity of what is to ensue.[2] Its occurrence here is perhaps to be connected with the fact that Prediction 1 immediately follows this passage, which leads into it.

B. Two Parables (7:3–9)

These parables are set forth within a question, in this and other features resembling the parable of 4:13–20. Moreover, this pair of parables repeats the same message, a style to be seen in the "literary vision" of 4:48–49, which the text there calls "a parable" (4:47). Doubled parables occur elsewhere in 4 Ezra; see 4:48 Commentary.

C. Implications of the Parables (7:10–14)

The implications of the parables are introduced by the expression "so also" or "so," likewise to be observed in 4:21 and 4:50, following the parables there.

D. Responses to the Address (7:15–16)

From one point of view, the whole of this pericope—indeed one might maintain the whole of Vision 3—is a response to the address. Yet it is in the two verses 7:15–16 that the response is made explicit. The explicit response is composed of two questions, posed by the angel, which are in reality rebukes. Similar questions function thus after the addresses of Vision 1 (4:2) and Vision 2 (5:33). The rebuke-questions, drawn from the parable and responding to the address, initiate the discussion that ensues.

E. Question (7:17–18)

Here a new element of substance should be noted, the formulation of a conflict between revealed scripture, the angelic revelation, and the existential situation.[3] The form of the question itself does not differ from other questions posed in the course of the visions. It is part of the dispute dialogue that constitutes an essential part of the first three visions.

F. Response (7:19–25)

Although the question has been posed to the angel as if he were God (see 7:17 Commentary), the answer is very definitely given by the angel in his own *persona*. It includes a rebuke-question comparing Ezra unfavorably with God (7:19—similar are 4:21 and 5:33), followed by a reference to the Torah as a sort of justification (7:20–21), which is a new element. Then ensues a poetic indictment of the wicked (7:22–24), and the whole is completed by an oracular conclusion which marks the transition to Prediction 2 (7:25, and see Commentary there).

Thus this pericope is clearly marked. It combines forms that are familiar from the preceding dialogue, using them in ways that are also reminiscent of previous contexts. The major new element is one of content, not of form, viz., the reference to scripture. This is not an exact quotation but a clear reference.

Function and Content

The first part of the pericope is 7:1–16. This contains the angelophany, the two parables, their meaning, and the implications drawn from them. Taken in context, this section should be a response to 6:38–59. That passage argued that while creation was for the sake of Israel, in the real world Israel did not inherit that which had been created for its sake: "If the world has indeed been created for us, why do we not possess our world as an inheritance? How long will this be so?" (6:59).

Indeed, some scholars think that 7:1–25 specifically answers the two questions posed in 6:59; viz., Why does Israel not possess its world and how long will this be?[4] Both parables make the point that there is a difficult first stage to be traversed before the spacious future stage is achieved. The difficult first stage is this world, while the spacious future stage is the world to come. If the parables are seen as a response to 6:59, then it follows that not this world but the world to come is Israel's heritage and portion.[5] So the parables imply.

In addition to their general import, however, the second of them uses the imagery of inheritance of a city: "If now that city is given to a man for an inheritance, how will the heir receive his inheritance unless he passes through the narrow (place)?" (7:9).

---

2   On standing up, see 4:47 Commentary.
3   See Function and Content, p. 193.
4   So Harnisch, p. 303. He even suggests that the temporal question ("when") is answered by the parables: it will happen only when all generations will have traversed the world (pp. 304–5).
5   This was already perceived by Box (p. 98), even though he did not regard 7:1–25 primarily as a response to 6:59.

It could be maintained that a city was selected as the figure of the parable because a city is a common way of speaking of the world to come or the heavenly Jerusalem or supernal temple.[6] But even if more cautiously we say that the choice of the image in the parable is purely literary (as probably the choice of the sea is in the previous parable), the heaping up of language of "portion" and "inheritance" is highly significant; in the one single verse we have "inheritance," "heir," and "receive his inheritance." The very next verse (7:10) proclaims, surely not by chance, "So also is Israel's portion"—unless "the living pass through the difficult . . . , they can never receive those things that have been reserved for them" (7:14).

The use of "portion" meaning inheritance is old and well established (see 6:59 Commentary). "The things that are reserved" is a standard term for eschatological rewards (see 7:14 Commentary). These are to be received by Israel, as the heir in 7:9 receives his inheritance. This passage concludes with two sets of questions which say, in other words: "Why are you disturbed at your own mortality?" (7:15). "It should not disturb you," 7:16 implies, "if you considered the future and not the present world. That future world is what Israel will inherit."

The issue raised in 7:17 follows naturally from the angelic injunction in 7:16. As interpreted above, 7:16 tells Ezra not to worry about his mortality but to consider the future world which Israel will inherit.[7] In considering that future world, Ezra becomes concerned about certain apparent injustices and imbalances. One is that, although it seems reasonable to demand of the righteous that they sustain this difficult world, for they will inherit the world to come, the wicked will undergo all the difficulties "and will not see the easier" future world

(7:17–18). Ezra says that he knows of the future state of the righteous and the wicked because it is written in the Law (7:17).[8]

The angel responds by rebuking Ezra for thinking that he knows more about justice than does God (7:19). The many should perish rather than that which is written in the Law be shown untrue (7:20, but see Commentary below). The fate of the righteous and the wicked is written in the Law, but the wicked did not heed its words (7:22). Consequently, the righteous will be rewarded and the wicked punished (7:21–25).

Interpretation of this passage has raised considerable scholarly debate, centered around at least two sets of apparent ambiguities. The first is "world" in 6:59. If it means "this world" in opposition to "the world to come," then what 6:38–59 seems to be complaining of is that Israel, for whom this world was created, does not possess it. This supposition appears to be supported by 7:11, which says that the world was created for Israel's sake and when Adam transgressed, what was made was judged and the ways of this world were made toilsome (7:12), but the text adds, "The ways (or: entrances)[9] of that coming world are broad and safe and yield the fruit of immortality" (7:13). Human beings, 7:14 adds, must traverse the difficult part before "they receive those things that have been reserved for them."

The problem lies precisely here: if this world is that which was created for Israel's sake and that which was judged after Adam's sin, then Israel is indeed never to inherit its world. As the Esau-Jacob passage makes quite clear, Esau is the end of this world and Jacob the beginning of the world to come (6:7–10).[10] One might try to argue that "world" has both a specific sense ("this world"

---

6   See 7:6 Commentary.

7   Note that the injunction at the end of Vision 2 is: "Do not be quick to think vain thoughts concerning the former times, lest you be hasty concerning the last times" (6:34). This prefigures exactly the sort of action for which Ezra is chided here. Violet 2 interprets the second hemistich as adversative, thus reaching the same basic interpretation as we give.

8   It is to be remarked that the themes of these verses recur in a predictive passage later, in 7:96. That is closely tied to the parables here, both by language and by sense. It is, as it were, the realization of the

import of the parables as part of the angelic prediction.

9   See 7:4 Commentary.

10   The word "world" or "age" is ambiguous, as is noted in Excursus on the Term "Age." Keulers, p. 145, here interprets as "this world."

or "the world to come") and a general sense ("the created order") and that it is used sometimes in one sense and sometimes in the other. This would run up against the apparent contradiction of Israel never receiving its world (see above) or of the statements such as 7:11, which says that creation was for Israel and creation was judged for Adam's sin.

Alternatively, one might point out that it is Ezra in his speech in 6:38–59 who pronounces that the world was created for Israel's sake and that what the angel is telling him by means of the parables in 7:3–9 is that he has misunderstood and that which was created for Israel was not this world but the world to come. One could then interpret 7:16 in accordance with this—Ezra has made the mistake of considering the situation of the present world instead of contemplating that which is to come.

The chief difficulty this exegesis encounters is 7:11. That verse should be understood as explaining why this present world is as it is: certainly it cannot be taken logically to mean that everything that was created was blighted by Adam's sin, since, as God says in 6:6, before the creation of all the material world, "then I planned these things [i.e., the eschata], and they were made through me and not through another." Even more explicit is 7:70: "When the Most High made the world and Adam and all who have come from him, he first prepared the judgment and the things that pertain to the judgment." And it is abundantly clear that those eschatological things and the final state which were created, undoubtedly before the creation of this world, are free of all corruptibility.[11] The ambiguity of 7:11 is hidden in

this, and it is not unlike some other ambiguities of 4 Ezra. The author at times denotes different things by the same or very similar terms, sometimes in close contextual proximity.[12]

A further terminological confusion seems to exist in this passage. From all that has been said, it is evident that those who are to inherit the "world" are identified as Israel. This is explicit in 7:10 and flows naturally from 6:38–59, yet it is contradicted by the latter part of the pericope. However, while Israel is very clearly under discussion until 7:10, what is said from that point on refers to righteous and wicked in general, to those coming into the world. This seems to indicate a wider, or a different, frame of reference. Even the allusions to the Law are not unambiguous in this respect. The commandment is said to have been given to "those who came into the world" (7:21). Adam, in 7:11, is said to transgress "my statutes" (plural), a term usually indicating the Torah or divine commandments in general and not the specific command given to him.[13]

Keulers points to the importance of Adam's sin here and elsewhere in 4 Ezra.[14] It is interesting to note that here the discourse shifts from Israel, via Adam's sin, to the general categories of the righteous and the wicked, while in chapter 3 the argument commences from creation of mankind and proceeds, via Adam's sin, to Israel's sin and exile.[15] This matter is discussed further in 6:55 Commentary. It should further be observed that 7:11 refers to Adam's transgression of commandments (plural), and Jervell has pointed out that for a series of texts the commandment given to Adam was understood,

11 See also the discussion of this in Stone, *Features*, 183.

12 The term "end" is a prime example; see Stone, "Coherence and Inconsistency," and Excursus on Natural Order, pp. 103–4; another such mixture is the combination of different types of eschatological language in passages like 4:26–32.

13 Knibb simply says that while 7:11 refers to Israel, 7:14 refers to all humans. Box says that all references are to Israel = the righteous and that the teaching of the passage is that only the Jews will receive the world to come, and cf. his comment on 7:37 and Harnisch, pp. 151–52 and notes. This is also the basic view of Keulers, p. 179. See also 7:37 Commentary and 8:4–19a Form and Function, p. 264. A reverse movement from humanity in general to Israel may be observed between 4:23 and 4:24: see Commentary. In rabbinic sources different state-

ments are made about the Torah having been offered to the Gentiles; see 3:31 Commentary, n. 94.

14 Keulers, p. 160, quoting 3:7, 9, and *Vit Ad* 49–50. See Excursus on Adam's Sin and also 3:7 Commentary.

15 Kabisch and Box claim simply that here "righteous" means "Jews" and that this is an assertion that only Israel will inherit the world to come (Kabisch, pp. 63–64; Box, p. 98). They ignore the importance of 7:17 and 7:21, which emphasize reward and punishment deriving from individual action, and they stress the opposition of Jews and Gentiles as the crucial criterion for eschatological reward. Other scholars have sought compromise formulas, speaking of "primarily Jews" but including all humanity (Oesterley); or follow Aalen (cited by Harnisch, p. 82 note), who suggests that mankind in general actually

"nicht als ein einzelnes Verbot sondern als das mosaische Gesetz in nuce, als Verordnungen, die ein Leben in Heiligkeit und Gerechtigkeit fordern" ("not as one particular injunction but as the Mosaic Law *in nuce,* as prescriptions which demand a life in sanctity and righteousness").[16]

These considerations weaken the claim that because obedience or disobedience to the Law is mentioned, the text must be limited to Israel. In fact, confusions of similar language and ideas occur elsewhere in 4 Ezra and in other works. Jewish writers could use language of this sort to describe faithfulness or unfaithfulness to God, even of Gentiles.[17] A most striking parallel to our passage is *2 Apoc Bar* 14:12–13:

> 12 For the righteous justly hope for the end, and without fear depart from this habitation, because they have with Thee a store of works preserved in treasuries. 13 On this account also these without fear leave this world, and trusting with joy they hope to receive the world which Thou hast promised them.

Harnisch (pp. 148–51) claims to point to a certain disjunction between the general language of this and some similar passages and the overall thrust of Visions 1—3, which attempt to account for the fate of Israel. It should be noted, however, that the concern with the fate of Israel led to a concern with the working of divine providence and divine justice and consequently, perhaps, to perception of anomalies within the fate of mankind. There is no easy reduction of this dual reference either to a progressive shift of meaning or to a terminological unclarity. It seems to us that there is a conceptual ambiguity involved; the issue is divine justice and its apparent miscarriage. Once the response to this has been formulated in terms of this world and that to come, or eternal life and death, the focus cannot very well remain exclusively on the question of whether Israel is subject to Rome. It naturally changes to the issue of whether the lot of mankind is a just one. It is here that the ambiguity enters. It does so, since the author's reference to the righteous and the wicked is unrelated to the historical fate of Israel in specifics, although profoundly connected with it, of course, by Ezra's attempt to understand "the way of the Most High."[18]

It has been stressed above that the preliminaries to Vision 3 serve to emphasize the final and decisive stage or the progressive unveiling of the resolution to Ezra's problems that has here been reached. Kabisch and Box both observed that, in contrast to the first two visions, the first matter discussed in the dialogue is not Ezra's inability to know. They think that this is a result of some literary mishap. It seems more plausible to say that after Ezra has reached the level of revelation of the end of Vision 2, the question of his ability to learn has become a less burning one. Furthermore, the rebuke-question in 7:19 sharply reminds Ezra of his human limitations.

Commentary

■ **1** This verse is parallel to 4:1 and 5:31. Like the latter of these, it mentions the sending of the angel, which is assumed but not stated explicitly by 4:1. Its reference to the preceding nights relates that which follows to the context of the preceding two visions.

■ **2** On the standing, see 4:47 Commentary.

■ **3** An exactly identical expression occurs in 5:33. The origins of the parable of the sea and its entrance are not clear; if they do lie in any more ancient imagery, it is unknown. The teaching of the parable seems clear enough.

■ **4** The conjunction of the images of the sea and the path observed in this pericope[19] may also be seen in *2 Apoc*

---

means Israel.

16 Jervell, *Imago Dei,* 43.

17 See 7:72; 7:127–128; cf. *2 Apoc Bar* 15:5–6, and see also Harnisch, pp. 151–52 note. See 3:32 Commentary, 5:27 Commentary, and 14:20. Note the parallelism of "law," "covenants," "statutes," and "works" in 7:24 and of "iniquity," "commandment," and "law" in 7:72. Cf. the similar text in Isa 24:5. "Covenant" is used in 7:46 in a quite unambiguous context, which is not limited to Israel. See further Harnisch, pp. 30, 31 note, on the terminology, and see Box, note x on 7:24. It is inappropriate to see here a reference to the Noachid commandments or the like, as is perhaps implied by Ginzberg, *Legends,* 6:31.

18 Cf. the comments of Thompson, *Responsibility,* 198–99. He would put the main break between 7:18 and 7:19. Because he is concerned to demonstrate a tension between concern for Israel and a concern for the righteous, he suggests no clear interconnection of these ideas. See Introduction, sec. 3.7.

19 Note the use of the same two parabolic images together, but quite differently applied, in *Test Job* 18:6–7.

Bar 22:3 in a quite different context.[20] Note also *2 Apoc Bar* 85:10, speaking of the closeness of the end:

And the pitcher is near to the cistern,
And the ship to the port,
And the course of the journey to the city,
And life to its consummation.

The word translated "entrances" seems quite unambiguous; contrast 7:7.[21]

■ **5** As observed in the textual notes, many translations accept Gunkel's suggested emendation of "to rule over "to traverse." This is based, not implausibly, on the assumption of a confusion by Greek of Hebrew לרדת, that is, *laredet,* "to travel upon the sea" (cf. Ps. 107:23), and *lirdot,* "to rule over." We refrain from including it in our translation because in the second parable the question of possession or inheritance plays such a large role, which gives oblique support to the reading of the versions.

■ **6** A second parable here follows, leading to a conclusion similar to the first. A similar series of succeeding parables making related points may be observed in Mark 4:26; 4:30; and in Matt 13:24; 13:31 and is also quite a common feature of the Midrashim.[22]

The imagery of the second parable contains a number of interesting elements. Some observations made on apocalyptic symbol structures seem relevant, *mutatis mutandis* to the discussion of it:

The independent meaning of the allegory, if such be present and can be determined, may well be important from other points of view. As far as the author is concerned, he is using this allegory to convey his own ideas and provides an interpretation to make these ideas explicit.[23]

This general observation seems to lead to a disjunction between any intrinsic meaning that symbol structures may convey and the significance given them in context. Nonetheless, it must be remarked that the city full of good things is a highly suggestive image. Jerusalem = Temple is often described as a city, full of every good and rich endowment, and this language is frequently used of the community of the righteous.[24] In somewhat later sources, paradise is also walled like a city and is painted thus.[25] As has also been pointed out, "good things" is frequently a term for eschatological reward.[26] This imagery and language of city may be regarded as highly associative. It is used in a very similar way in *Hermas Sim.* 9.12.5:

For if you wish to enter into a city, and that city has been walled round, and has one gate, can you enter into that city except through the gate which it has, so . . . a man cannot otherwise enter into the kingdom of God except through the name of his Son.

A similar use of this image may be observed in *Test Job* 18:6.

The second group of images in this parable has to do with the ways or entrances (on the term, see 7:7 Commentary). The contrast is between the narrow ways that must be traveled before the city can be inherited (7:9). This is paraphrased in 7:12 as the narrow ways that must be traversed before the spacious and broad can be reached.[27] In this paraphrase, terminology from the first parable ("spacious") is also used.

---

20 *2 Apocalypse of Baruch* 22 also employs a number of other images prevalent in 4 Ezra, such as sowing, fruit, and the womb. This illustrates that they were common in the literature of the age.

21 Cf. the superfluous comment of Philonenko, "L'âme à l'étroit," 122 n. 2. A very long and difficult way and traversing an uncrossable sea are the true path referred to in the Mandean Ginza; see M. Lidzbarski, *Ginza: Der Schatz oder Das grosse Buch der Mandäer* (Göttingen and Leipzig: Vandenhoeck & Hinrichs, 1925) 433, cf. 519.

22 Box suggests that the expression "another example" reflects something like דבר אחר in rabbinic texts, a view rejected by Violet 2.

23 Stone, "Messiah," 304.

24 Typical is the description of jeweled Jerusalem in Revelation.

25 See 6:2 Commentary; in detail see 3:4 Commentary, where paradise is discussed, and 7:6 Commentary, where "city" is analyzed.

26 Particularly in the Armenian version; see Stone, "Some Features," 398.

27 The language of narrow and spacious has eschatological implications; cf. 7:96. Its roots are biblical. In addition to the sources cited in the text below, see *Test Abr* B 7:10.

The idea is widespread that human beings must traverse two ways, or can choose between two ways, one narrow and one broad, one difficult and one easy. There are clear classical parallels.[28] The idea that the narrow and difficult must be traversed, and that the wide leads to destruction, as found in Xenophon citing Prodicus (see n. 28 above), also occurs in Matt 7:13–14. The imagery is richly employed elsewhere. 4 Ezra 7:48 and 8:31 refer to "ways of death" and to "paths of perdition." *Testament of Abraham* A 11, B 8, has Adam sitting between two gateways, one wide leading to hell and the other narrow leading to paradise, and *b. Ber.* 28b // *ARN* A 25 (Schechter, p. 79) speak, in the name of R. Yoḥanan b. Zakkai, of two ways, one to paradise and the other to Gehenna; see 7:36 below. This of course is comparable with Hermas, cited above, and also resembles Luke 13:24 // Matt 7:13–14.

Psalm 66:12 (LXX, Syr, Vulg) is very close to our passage, which may to some extent be dependent on it or on similar formulations:

we went through fire and water;

yet thou hast brought us forth to a spacious place.

The idea of a perilous path that steers its narrow way between fire and water is intriguing. In Sir 15:11 and 15–17 we read:

11 Do not say, "Because of the Lord I left the right way." 15 It was he who created man in the beginning, and he left him in the power of his own inclination. 16 He has placed before you fire and water: stretch out your hand for whichever you wish. 17 Before a man are life and death, and whichever he chooses will be given to him.

Not only is the point of this passage similar in some ways to ours (although omitting Adam's sin) but it also utilizes the same verse from Deuteronomy (30:19; see n. 28). Of great interest is the occurrence of fire and water, although for ben Sira, apparently, the water symbolizes not another form of danger but life.[29] A very similar parable is also to be found in *ARN* A 28 (Schechter, p. 86):

To what may this be likened? To a thoroughfare which lies between two paths, one of flames and the other of snow. If one walks alongside the flames, he will be scorched by the flames; if he walks alongside the snow, he will be frostbitten. What then is he to do? Let him walk between them and take care of himself in

---

28 One form is in Xenophon, *Memorabilia* 2.1.20, and in a form closer to our passage, in which the ways are successive and not opposed, in Hesiod, *Works and Days*, 290–292; cf. on the successive ways, *TDNT*, 5:57. The idea of two ways between which a choice must be made is found in Jer 21:8, probably drawing on Deut 30:19. Although this latter does not mention "ways" explicitly, it is regularly so interpreted by the Sages, e.g., *Yalq.* 2.919. The "way of the righteous" is also commonplace in the Bible and in the Qumran sectarian literature (e.g., Ps 1:6; 2 Sam 22:22; 1QH 4:4; 6:23–24; 7:14). See W. R. Morfill and R. H. Charles, *The Book of the Secrets of Enoch* (Oxford: Oxford University, 1896) 42 note. The idea of two ways, one of wickedness and one of virtue, is to be found in a number of texts between which clear connections have been discerned by scholars, chiefly 1QS 3:13—4:26 and in the *Didache*. See J.-P. Audet, "Affinités littéraires et doctrinales du 'Manuel de Discipline,'" *RB* 59 (1952), esp. 220–22, and idem, 60 (1953) 41–82. The evidence of the Gospel of John has also been introduced in this connection; see F. M. Braun, "L'arrière-fond judaïque du quatrième évangile et la Communauté de l'Alliance," *RB* 62 (1955) 5 n. 4 and 24–26. Somewhat different is the idea of "two ways" in Sir 2:12; see Hengel, *Judaism and Hellenism*, 1:140. Cf.

also *Gen. R.* 21:5 (Theodor-Albeck, p. 200). The idea is given a different and intriguing development in *Exod. R.* 30:16. The concept of narrowness is brought together with that of body in *Test Abr* B 7:10; cf. Philonenko, "L'âme à l'étroit," 424.

29 The imagery of fire and water (including fire that flows like water and "water of life") may be observed in *1 Enoch* 17:4–5. In the Merkabah mystical literature, fire and water are among the perils that characterize the heavenly ascent; see Scholem, *Gnosticism*, 14–16, and idem, *Major Trends*, 50. The pair, fire and water, function differently in 8:8. In somewhat later Iranian eschatology, there is the idea of the bridge which human beings must traverse as part of the process of judgment. If they are wicked, it becomes narrow and they fall to damnation; if they are righteous, it becomes broad and easy to traverse; see J. Duchesne-Guillemin, *La religion de l'Iran ancien* (Paris: Presses Universitaires de France, 1962) 145, 360.

order not to be scorched by the flames and not to be frostbitten. (J. Goldin, trans., *The Fathers According to Rabbi Nathan* [New York: Schocken, 1974] 118; cf. also *j. Hag.* 2.1 [76c])

The expression "city built" or "builded city" is also suggestive of Jerusalem, perhaps under its heavenly aspect. See 5:25 Commentary and particularly the description of Jerusalem in 10:27 and 10:44, where the heavenly city is clearly denoted in this way.

■ 7 See 7:6 Commentary. Kabisch (p. 62) and Box have pointed out that the word translated "entrance" here might also mean "way." It could be a mistranslation into Greek of Hebrew מבוי or מבוא which means in Rabbinic Hebrew "way" or "entrance."[30] Contrast 7:4 Commentary.

■ 8 No commentary.

■ 9 On the language of inheritance used of Israel and the world, see 6:59 Commentary. People are said to inherit the world to come in other sources (see *2 Apoc Bar* 44:13), and it is a common expression in rabbinic literature.[31] In Luke 19:12, as here, there is a parable of a man who travels in order to inherit a kingdom.[32]

■ 10 The two parables are applied to Israel.

■ 11 The meaning of the term "world" here is discussed in Function and Content, p. 193, and the idea that the world was created for Israel's sake in 6:55 Commentary. It is interesting to note that Adam is said to have transgressed divine *statutes*, even though the Bible refers to only one command. The plural usually indicates the Torah given to Israel, but Jervell has pointed out that the language of "Torah" often means the will of God for

living a holy life; cf. Rom 5:12–14.[33]

The idea that the world or creation was judged as a result of Adam's sin is one of a number of views current in Judaism at that time concerning the results of Adam's sin.[34] The term "judgment" is notable, hinting as it does at a legal aspect of the punishment. It is a far-reaching change of all creation for the worse. Above, the varied meanings of this term in 4 Ezra were noted, including rarely the sense found here, that is, the judgment of humans or the world.[35] The idea that Adam's sin had continued results is to be found elsewhere in the book, perhaps most explicitly in 7:117–118 and see 7:118 Commentary.[36]

■ 12 Hardship and difficulty are typical attributes of this world or age (see 4:27; *2 Apoc Bar* 51:16; and many other places). The exact signification of the Latin *saeculum* ("world") and equivalents is not unambiguous. Here it most likely reflects Hebrew עולם, in the sense of "world age" or "age."[37] The terms "this world/age" and "the coming world/age" (7:13) are in deliberate contrast here. They probably reflect the Hebrew terms העולם הזה and העולם הבא, well known in rabbinic sources and also reflected in the New Testament.[38] Therefore this verse clearly reflects a dualism of two world ages—one evil, toilsome, and difficult; the other spacious, easy, and wonderful.[39]

On the term "entrances," see 7:7 Commentary and textual note s to the present verse.

■ 13 On "entrances," see 7:7 Commentary. The fruit of immortality may be understood either figuratively or literally. In either case, the image depends on the idea of

---

30 See Stone, *Features*, 244 n. 53, and textual note t, but if the Hebrew proposed is accepted, then the reading of Ethiopic, Arabic1 must be secondary, either the result of a Greek process (Box) or exegetically engendered; see textual note m on 4:7.

31 Inheritance is used of Christians in a similar context in Gal 4:7.

32 The image of the heir is also used elsewhere; see *Hermas Sim* 5.2.6 in a different parable.

33 See Function and Content, pp. 194–95. Contrast with the meaning of statutes in 7:24 and 9:32.

34 See Excursus on Adam's Sin.

35 See Excursus on the Term "Judgment." Gunkel would perceive in this section a tension between an old, mythological, optimistic view of the world and a later pessimistic one.

36 Harnisch has pointed out that this idea occurs chiefly

in the seer's discourse, not in the angel's response (p. 55 and note). It may somehow form a contrast with the very idea of human choice that is the subject of 7:19–24.

37 See 7:30 Commentary and Stone, *Features*, 179, 274 n. 431.

38 See Excursus on the Two Ages, p. 92, where further examples of this usage are adduced.

39 See also 4:27 Commentary; and Excursus on the Two Ages, pp. 92–93.

a tree yielding a fruit the eating of which gives immortality. This idea is present already in Gen 3:6 and 3:22 and goes back to ancient mythical origins.[40] The same concept recurs in 4 Ezra in 7:123; 8:6; and 8:52 and is found frequently in Jewish literature of the age.[41]

Spaciousness is found as a description of eschatological reward in 7:13 and 7:96. Hence its use here may not be pure chance. The same is true of the next term, "safe," which, while contrasting with the dangers described in the previous verse, also typifies the future state; see 7:121. The removal of corruptibility or immortality is one of the typical signs of the eschatological state; see 4:11 Commentary and the Excursus on Adam's Sin, p. 66.[42]

■ **14** Difficulties must be traversed before the eschatological state can be achieved, an idea very close to the view that troubles will precede the eschaton, and these concepts occur frequently (see n. 42). Stress has been laid by Harnisch on the notion that this verse implies that people must live *through* history in order to achieve the reward that is beyond history.[43] This is perhaps overstated.

The precreation of eschatological things was discussed above in 3:6 Commentary and 6:6 Commentary. The terms "prepared" or "laid up" are typical of the allied concept that the eschatological goods are readied for the righteous and await them.[44]

■ **15** The general interpretation of this and the next verse was set forth in Function and Content, p. 193. The three questions should be contrasted with those in 4:2 and 4:11 and with 5:33 and 5:37. In those verses the questions or

statements serve to rebut Ezra's ability to learn the things about which he has inquired, chiefly in the preceding addresses. Here, however, the final point of the questions is a positive one, the assertion of Ezra's future conquest of his mortality while he is rebuked for not recognizing the true situation.[45]

■ **16** This verse is discussed in some detail in Function and Content, p. 193, and it is interesting to compare it with 6:34, which warns against the sort of speculation for which Ezra is now being chided. The same point, also relating to Ezra's mortality, is made much more specifically in 8:46–54.[46] Some critics consider this verse to be a turning point of the book and that henceforth Ezra is concerned only to inquire about the future and abandons issues of theodicy. There is indeed a break following this verse, for 7:17 starts a new part of Dispute 1. The verse is best taken, however, together with the preceding verse and not seen in such a momentous guise.

■ **17** At many points in the book, in the dialogues, the angel is addressed as God (so 4:38; 5:41; 7:45; 7:58; 7:75; etc.) or talks as if God is speaking (so 5:40; 5:42; 6:6; 8:47; 8:61; 9:18–22). This is also true here.[47]

The reference from scripture is generally assumed to be drawn from Deut 8:1:

All the commandments which I command you this day you shall be careful to do, that you may live and multiply, and go in and possess the land which the Lord swore to give to your fathers.

Kaminka has, with some justification, pointed to Ps 37:9: "For the wicked shall be cut off; but those who wait for the Lord shall possess the land." This also mentions the

---

40   See 3:20 Commentary for a full discussion.

41   Cf. 1QH 5:34; 6:31; and 9:27–28. Cf. also Ps 18:20 and 118:5; see Stone, *Features*, 204. See also discussion of Philonenko, "L'âme à l'étroit," at 4:1–25 Commentary n. 32.

42   The idea that the difficulties must be traversed before eschatological reward is achieved occurs elsewhere: cf. Matt 7:13–14; Acts 14:22; Heb 12:7–12; etc.

43   See 4:27 and Harnisch p. 143.

44   See further 7:70; 7:77; 7:83–84; 8:52; 8:59; 9:18; *Asc Isa* 9:26; Col 1:5; Eph 2:10; *2 Enoch* J 61:2; the Elijah apocryphon quoted at 1 Cor 2:9 (see Stone-Strugnell, *Elijah*, 42–73); *2 Apoc Bar* 84:6; *Apoc Abr* 29:17; 30:2; Targ J Gen 2:8; and other sources. It may also be used of other sorts of eschatological things; cf. 13:18. The term "prepared" is typical of

the Armenian version, where it also occurs in some instances not found in the other versions; see Stone, "Some Remarks," 114; and idem, *Features*, 258–59 n. 246. See especially Arabic1 and Armenian in 7:38 and 7:93; 7:120. In Gen 49:10 "Shiloh" is translated τὰ ἀποκείμενα. Cf. *2 Apoc Bar* 59:6–11.

45   Cf. in general 1 Cor 15:53–54.

46   Contrast 2 Cor 4:18 for a very similar idea expressed in terms of eternal and temporary. The formula is close to Isa 43:18. See 8:46 Commentary.

47   See further 5:33 Commentary and 3:4 Commentary, where the dual title "sovereign Lord" is also discussed.

fate of the wicked which is not so in Deut 8:1. The inheritance of the land was taken eschatologically (see Matt 5:5). Yet since Deuteronomy is cited again in 7:21, we incline to think that the primary reference of 7:17 is Deut 8:1, but that may have been filled out with Ps 37:11.

The overall point of the passage is well paralleled by 7:117–118:

> For what good is it to all that they live in sorrow now and expect punishment after death? O Adam, what have you done? For though it was you who sinned, the fall was not yours alone, but ours also who are your descendants.[48]

■ **18** See 7:117–118, cited in 7:17 Commentary. Indeed, the whole of the passage 7:116–126 is a more detailed working out of the themes raised here. Comparable is also *2 Apoc Bar* 14:12–14. The problem is acute for the author because of the revelation that is made to him.

■ **19** This verse is a rebuke to Ezra delivered by asking him if he aspires to greater justice or wisdom than God. In the preceding two verses Ezra has stated his case, using the citation from the Bible to highlight the problem. Similar rebukes, following such questions, may be found in 4:34 and 5:33 (cf. 4:10–11), although in each case the actual aspect of divine activity mentioned differs. A similar question, probably based ultimately on 4 Ezra, is *Greek Apoc Esd* 2:6. Very similar also is *Apocalypse of Paul* 33.

A basic relationship is seen to exist between justice and wisdom; this is clear in such stories as those of Solomon's wisdom. So in 1 Kgs 3:9, Solomon prays: "Give thy servant therefore an understanding mind to govern thy people, that I may discern between good and evil." The same two features come together in a question resembling ours in Job 21:22.[49] Also among the sages there is a clear relationship between wisdom, knowledge of Torah, and the ability to render just judgment.[50] Here the feature of wisdom may also have been mentioned because Ezra has invoked the Torah and is being told

that he cannot interpret it more wisely and so more justly than God.[51]

■ **20** As set forth in the textual notes on this verse, there seem to have been two forms of the text in Greek. One said, in general, "Let many perish rather than the Torah be disregarded" and the other said, "Let many who disregarded the Torah perish." In both cases, the punishment of the wicked (just like the reward of the righteous) follows from the validity of the Torah. This is demonstrated explicitly in the next verse which quotes the text of the Torah to establish the punishment of the wicked. The same point is also made clearly by *2 Apoc Bar* 19:3:

> But after his [Moses'] death they sinned and transgressed,
> Though they knew that they had the law reproving (them),
> And the light in which nothing could err,
> Also the spheres which testify, and me.

"Perish" is the language of eschatological recompense (Harnisch, p. 139) and is discussed fully in 10:10 Commentary. There is a deliberate contrasting of this term, which signifies eternal punishment, with "those who are now living," that is, in this world. This language relates to Deut 30:15 which is quoted in 7:21. The same reinterpretation of the language of life and death to mean eternal life and death is very typical of Wisdom of Solomon. See particularly chapters 1–3, and note 3:1–4:

> 1a But the souls of the righteous are in the hand of God. . . . 2a In the eyes of the foolish they seemed to have died. . . . 4 For though in the sight of men they were punished, their hope is full of immortality.

The expression "set before" is also drawn from Deut 30:15: "See, I have set before you this day. . . ." The crux in this and the next verse of whether Israel is referred to or mankind in general is discussed in Function and Content, pp. 194–95.

This verse implies the question of the few and the many, on which see 7:47 Commentary.

■ **21** The passage 7:21–24 is the angelic statement of the

---

48 Cf. Mundle, "Religiöse Problem," 225.

49 Questions featuring the aspect of judge, or divine justice, can be seen in Job 4:6–7; 8:3. In the reverse sense, Abraham's rebuke of God may be mentioned, Gen 18:25.

50 See, e.g., *m. Abot* 1:18; 6:1; et al.

51 Violet 2 here has a long note pointing out that the use of the divine name "God" in 7:19–21 contrasts

with the use of many sorts of periphrases in other parts of the book. He considers this either to be the result of the translation of a difficult Greek or Hebrew or to indicate that these verses are drawn from a different source.

sins of the wicked. The present verse refers specifically to God's command, which is clearly that of Deut 30:15, a verse that already influenced the formulation of 7:20: "See, I have set before you this day life and good, death and evil." Exactly the same idea, also apparently based on the passage from Deuteronomy, is to be observed in Sir 15:14–21. Sirach 15:17 says, "Before a man are life and death, and whichever he chooses will be given to him."[52] This passage from Deuteronomy was a particular favorite of our author and is cited again in 7:129.[53]

The passage from Deuteronomy is replete with language of life and death. In addition to denoting physical death, this language was used by 4 Ezra, as by other authors of his age, to signify eternal life and eternal death.[54]

■ 22 It is unclear whether, at the literary level, the first two phrases of this verse are part of the poetic discourse that follows. The theme of speaking against God is part of the more specific indictment taken up in the next verse.[55]

■ 23–24 These verses can be analyzed, together with the last phrase of 7:22, as two tricola followed by a bicolon: 7:22b, 23a, 23b/7:23c, 24a, 24b/7:24c, 24d. These are characterized by parallelism and by a shift in subject matter. The passage moves from sins of attitude and opinions to the actual sinful actions of disobedience.

In general, the wicked are charged not with specific transgressions so much as with overall unfaithfulness in words and actions. This general attitude is to be found elsewhere in 4 Ezra; see 7:79; 7:81; and 8:56. The passage shows clear terminological connections with the passage in Deut 30:16–17 which was also quoted in the preceding verses. However, the Deuteronomic language had become so widespread by the time of 4 Ezra that it is difficult to build very much on these similarities.

The sinners are accused of denying God's existence. This accusation occurs elsewhere in 4 Ezra; see 7:37; 8:55–58; and 9:10, which latter passage is very much like ours here. It has biblical origins of course; thus Ps 14:1 says: "The fool says in his heart, 'There is no God.'"[56] Consequently, other than this sin being a transgression of one of the Noachid commandments, no use can be made of this specific accusation to identify the group possibly referred to.[57]

■ 25 Similar oracular statements occur at transition points between dispute and prediction in the preceding visions. See 4:26 Commentary. In general this sentence may be compared with Jer 2:5 and with *3 Apocalypse of Baruch* 15, where the baskets of prayers are full or empty.[58] It implies that those empty of piety will be empty of reward, and it leads into the next section which describes the fullness of the full.

---

52 On the issue of whether the commandments are given to Israel or to mankind in general, see Function and Content, pp. 194–95.

53 That verse is also quoted by *2 Apoc Bar* 19:1 and has probably also influenced *2 Apoc Bar* 19:3 (quoted in 7:20 Commentary).

54 In 3:20 Commentary the "fruit of immortality" was discussed. See also Excursus on Adam's Sin, pp. 65–66.

55 In may ways, this passage is comparable to Wisdom 2.

56 See also Ps 53:2, almost verbatim; cf. Ps 10:3. There are many similar phrases and expressions; see, e.g.,

Ps 94:11; 95:10; and Job 21:14. This is also the sense of the Greek of Isa 65:2. Cf. 1QS 5:19–20, where the denial of God's existence is not attributed to the wicked; cf. also CD 1:3, etc. This is the obverse of the language of believing or faith, on which see 9:7 Commentary.

57 For the term "covenants" in the plural, see 3:32 Commentary.

58 See also *Hermas Mand.* 11:3, 13, etc. Stylistically cf. Qoh 1:15.

26 | For [a] behold, the time [b] will come, [c] when the signs [d] which I have foretold to you will come, [e]

> that [f]the city which now is not seen [f]
> shall appear,
> and the land [g] which now is hidden
> shall be disclosed.

27/ And everyone who has been delivered from the evils that I have foretold shall see my wonders. [h] 28/ For my [i] Messiah shall be revealed with those who are with him, and he shall make rejoice those who remain [j] for four hundred [k] years, [l] 29/ [m]And after these years my son (or: servant) the Messiah [n] shall die, and all who draw human breath. 30/ And the world shall be turned back to primeval silence for seven days, as it was at the first beginnings; [o] so that no one shall be left.

31/ And [p] after seven days

> the world, which is not yet awake, shall
> be roused,
> and that which is corruptible shall
> perish.

32/ And the earth shall give back [q] those
> who are asleep in it,
> and the dust those who rest [r] in it;
> and the treasuries shall give up the
> souls which have been committed
> to them.

33/ And the Most High shall be revealed
> upon the seat of judgment. [s]
> and compassion shall pass away, [t]
> [u]mercy [v] shall be made distant, [w]
> and patience shall be withdrawn;

34/ but only judgment shall remain,
> truth [x] shall stand,

Notes

26   a Ar, Arm omit; "and" Georg.

   b Syr, Eth "days"; perhaps influence of 5:1 and 6:18; cf. Eth 9:18.

   c Lat adds *et erit;* see 6:14 note g–g.

   d "Sign" Georg, Arm.

   e Lat, Syr, cf. Ar1, Arm; "will be seen" Eth, Georg; "you will see" Ar2. Two Greek readings existed.

   f–f Ar1, Arm. The versions are chaotic. Lat, Syr *apparebit sponsa apparascens civitas;* Eth "and the city which now appears will be hidden"; Georg *et revelabit se ista quae nunc apparet civitas;* Ar2 corrupt. Lat, Syr perhaps originate from νῦν μὴ φαινομένη 〉 νύμφη φαινομένη (Volkmar, Violet, Box); Georg has lost the negative; the *Vorlage* of Eth may have been the same and the negative may have been restored secondarily to the wrong verb. Box compares Eth with *2 Apocalypse of Baruch* 30.

   g Lat, Eth, Ar1; Syr omits; *fovea* Georg, cf. 5:24 note d for a similar reading, and Ar2 here "the deeps"; Arm has for this phrase "and every knee will crawl upon the earth."

27   h Eth, Arm "glory"; Ar1 "son."

28   i See Excursus on the Redeemer Figure, pp. 207–8; the word "son" or "servant" occurred in one Greek tradition (Lat, Syr, Ar1; cf. Ar1 in 7:27) but not in that behind the other versions.

   j Eth "are raised up"; Violet 2 suggests ἀπελείφθησαν/-θεντες 〉 ἀνελήφθεσαν/-θεντες; compare "who does my will" Ar2 with "who persisted in faith and patience" Arm.

   j–l Eth, Arm omit.

   k "Thirty" Syr; "a thousand" Ar2, perhaps Α′ 〉 Λ′ (Violet 2).

29   m Ar1, Ar2 omit this verse; Arm omits to 7:32.

   n Georg *electus unctus meus;* see Excursus on the Redeemer Figure.

30   o Syr singular; "at first" Eth; Ar2 varies and omits from here to the end of 7:31.

31   p Lat, Georg add "and it shall be"; see 6:14 note g–g.

32   q Syr, Ar1 "up."

   r Lat "dwell silently"; Syr "sleep"; others vary.

33   s Eth "which he created" (Violet 2), perhaps κτίσεως for κρίσεως; see 6:38 note c.

   s–t Ar2, Arm vary.

   u–w Lat omits.

   v Eth, Ar1 "grace"; Arm combines 7:32 and 7:33.

   w Ar1, Eth "come"; cf. 6:20.

34   x Eth "his truth"; Georg *veritas apud eum;* apparently these reflect some sort of pronoun in one form of Greek.

and faithfulness shall [y]grow strong.[y]
35/ And recompense [z] shall follow,
and the reward shall be manifested;
righteous deeds shall awake,
and unrighteous deeds shall not sleep.
36/ Then the pit of torment [a] shall appear,
and opposite it shall be the place of rest;
and the furnace of Gehenna [b] shall be disclosed,
and opposite it the paradise of delight.[c]
37/ Then the Most High will say to the nations [d] that have been raised,[e]
'Look and understand
whom you have denied,
whom you have not served,
whose commandments you have despised!
38/ Look opposite you:[f]
here are delight and rest,[g]
and there are fire and torments!'[h]
Thus he will speak to them on the day of judgment.
39/ [i] The day of judgment will be thus:[i]
it has no sun [j] or moon or stars,
40/ or cloud or lightning or thunder,[k]
or wind or water or air,
or darkness or evening or morning,
41/ or summer or spring or harvest,[l]
or heat [m] or frost or cold,
or hail or rain or dew,
42/ or noon or night, or dawn,[n]
or shining or brightness or light,[o]
but only the splendor of the glory [p] of the Most High, by which all shall [q] see what has been determined for them. 43/ For it will last for about a [r]week of years,[r]
44 **This is my [s] judgment and its prescribed order; and to you alone have I shown these things.**

y–y Eth, Georg "grow"; perhaps Greek variant; Ar1, Ar2, Arm vary.

35 z Versions "work"; Wellhausen suggests Greek ἔργον(α) reflecting Hebrew פעל or פעלה, "work" or "reward"; cf. LXX Ps 108 (109):20; Isa 40:10 or πράξις as *2 Apoc Bar* 24:1 (Greek fragment, cited by Violet 2). See further Stone, *Some Features,* 258 n. 234.

36 a Eth, Georg "judgment"; this often alternates with punishment; see 7:38 note h and Stone, *Some Features,* 251 n. 151; Arm, Ar1 vary.

b Lat, Syr, Eth, Georg "Gehenna" ("hell" RSV); "fire" Ar1, Ar2, Arm.

c Arm "true Paradise of delight"; see Stone, "Paradise," 88.

37 d Ar2, Arm "sinners"; perhaps tendentious. Arm is further reworked.

e RSV adds "from the dead"; exegetical.

38 f Lat *contra et in contra;* Box, Violet 1 omit *contra* #1.

g Arm "delight prepared for (you) righteous ones"; Ar2 "grace and joy which I have prepared for my faithful ones." For "prepared," see 7:14 Commentary.

h Eth "judgment"; see 7:36 note a.

39 i–i Lat, Ar1 omit, perhaps by hmt; supplied (probably secondarily) by Lat Ms L.

j Arm adds adjective before nearly every one of the nouns in the following list.

40 k Lat, Ar1, Ar2 "lightning or thunder," but "wind" intervenes in these two versions. The order of elements in this list varies throughout in the versions.

41 l Lat *aestum* has the same meaning as *aestatem* here translated "summer." The other versions are complicated and are translating a polyvalent Greek. The three element list of Lat, Syr, Eth, not the four element list of Ar1, Ar2, Arm, Georg, seems to be original. Box suggests that Hebrew קיץ וחורף are the first two elements. Then the third is probably קציר. If קיץ was translated into Greek θέρος, then קציר might have been something like ἄμητος (LXX for both Hebrew words) or θερισμός with same double sense. Syr remains difficult. See Stone, *Some Features,* 259–60 n. 255.

m Lat "winter"; Eth "neither frost nor cold"; see preceding note and Stone, *Some Features,* 269 n. 256.

42 n Ar1, Arm fragmentary.

o Lat, Georg "light"; Syr, Eth "shining."

p Arm reads: "but only a crown of glory and joy for the just, while for the wicked the undying fire and eternal darkness and unending torment."

q Lat, Syr seem to reflect Greek μέλλειν.

43 r–r Eth, Georg "about seven years"; Georg adds *quod est septem dari;* Ar2 "seventy years."

44 s Syr, Eth "his"; Ar2 omits verse; Arm abbreviated.

Form and Structure

This passage may be characterized as "Prediction 2," since it contains direct angelic prediction. It opens, as do other Prediction 2 passages, with "Behold, days (times) are coming" (7:26; cf. 5:1; 6:18)[1] and concludes with a pronouncement about the special revelation made to Ezra, also typical in this sort of prediction (see 7:44 Commentary). By its mention of signs, 7:26 deliberately relates 7:26–44 to the preceding two Prediction 2 passages and it forms a complement to those passages, continuing the prediction on to the day of judgment. It was not clear whether 6:25–27 referred to the messianic kingdom, to the day of judgment, or to both (see p. 206 below); here, however, the emphasis is clearly on the day of judgment.

Keulers has suggested that the prediction of the city and land at this point (7:26) presages the detail of the coming visions. In Vision 4 the city is predicted, and in Visions 5 and 6 the Messiah.[2] He points to specific elements here, such as "joy" and "survivors," which recur in those visions.

The passage (7:26–44) is structured by the eschatological timetable, going from signs (7:26) to revelation of eschatological Jerusalem (7:26), the Redeemer, and the messianic kingdom (7:28) which concludes with the Messiah's death (7:29) and the reversion of the earth to primordial state (7:30). Next a new creation and resurrection follow (7:31–32) and God is revealed on the throne of judgment (7:33). Four verses of poetic description of the character of judgment now ensue (7:33–36), and their literary form was discussed in 6:11–29 Form and Structure. Paradise and Gehenna are revealed, and God rebukes the wicked (7:37–39). The day of judgment is next described, using a list of characteristics that has roots in biblical literature (7:39–42; see 7:42 Commentary). Finally a prediction of the length of the day of judgment follows (7:43), and the whole concludes with a direct word to Ezra (7:44).

This passage incorporates a number of different literary forms two of which were noted in the preceding paragraph, that is, the poetic material of 7:33–36 and the list of 7:39–42. Notable in addition is the picture of God on the throne of judgment rebuking the wicked by pointing out reward and punishment to them (7:37–38), which doubtless reflects the author's view of a courtroom situation. Its overall literary form, however, is unremarkable, being a simple piece of angelic prediction.

The complex structure of Vision 3 as a whole has been noted (see General Structure of the Book, pp. 50–51), and where in Visions 1 and 2 the Prediction 2 passages were the last major element in the vision, here the Prediction 2 passage is followed by a dispute.

Function and Content

The passage 7:26–44 is a presentation of the whole of the eschatological scheme. It opens with a reminiscence of the signs that were predicted in complementary passages at the end of Visions 1 and 2. There the signs formed a scheme with an overall chronological movement from the messianic woes to the eschatological state that is the subject of 6:25–28. What is particular about 7:26–44 is that it gives a fairly detailed exposition of the eschatological events in a chronological series. The specific events it predicts were outlined in Form and Structure and are discussed in detail in the Commentary.

The passage presents a single, uniform scheme of the order of events. Nearly every element in it is paralleled somewhere else in the book, as is clear from the verse-by-verse Commentary. The overall question that arises is about the relationship between this full rehearsal of events and the other passages that deal with eschatology in the book. The present passage is unique in its broad scope and perspective, but of course there are other passages that discuss one or another event in greater detail.

There have been various scholarly approaches to the eschatology of the book. They are themselves based on general attitudes toward the eschatological material in Jewish texts of the period (see also Volz, pp. 63–66).

a. One approach distinguished different eschatologies in the book. In general, two categories of eschatology have been posited, and this view has been typical of the study of 4 Ezra from the time of Kabisch on. These two eschatologies—one this-worldly, particularist, national and the other otherworldly, universalist, transcendental—were set out in schematic form by Keulers.

---

1   On the structure of these passages, see 5:1–13 Form
     and Structure, p. 107.

2   Keulers, p. 78.

The following is based on his presentation:[3]

National-Earthly	Universal-Transcendental
The nations	Humans
Israel	The pious person
The hostile nations	The evil person
Israel's salvation from its enemies	The pious person's salvation from the troubles of this world
Annihilation of enemies	Damnation of the wicked
Continued existence of the community of salvation	Continued existence of humans after resurrection
Jerusalem, Palestine	New earth, paradise
earth	heaven
Valley of Hinnom	Hell[4]

Kabisch used the two eschatologies, which he regarded as different and contradictory, as criteria for distinguishing supposed source documents. Gunkel, more perceptively, distinguished two major religious problems in 4 Ezra, that of the situation of Israel after the destruction of the Temple and that of the sinfulness of humanity. He regarded the national eschatology as a solution to the former and the universal eschatology as a solution to the latter, while maintaining that the author himself held a more or less integrated view of the two.[5]

As so often, the literary critics drew valuable distinctions, but it remains an open question what it was that they distinguished. It cannot be contested that the eschatological features mentioned by the book can, on the whole, be catalogued in one or another of Keulers' two columns. What is extremely dubious is the assumption that these two columns represent two eschatologies that actually existed as closed, separate, and distinct structures in the author's thought world. There is no single eschatological passage in 4 Ezra where the text as transmitted presents one of these eschatologies as a

"pure," complete scheme.[6]

b. There are other approaches that, while admitting the existence of diverse eschatological elements, claim that there is no need to force them to cohere into a single, united system or even to try to harmonize them. Such a view is indeed implied by Gunkel's approach mentioned in item a above. Thus the many traditional sources (both written and oral) employed by the author may be stressed, and the variety of eschatological elements in the book can be attributed, partly at least, to the complexity of these sources. This attitude has the advantage of keeping in the background assumptions like those of Box and Kabisch that, somehow, quite consistent sources were combined by a rather inconsistent editor.

c. A third approach would admit the existence of different eschatological patterns (while denying them any independent life in the document) and acknowledge complexities engendered by traditional sources. Nonetheless, it would question whether indeed the situation produced by these factors is in fact as chaotic as might at first be thought. Gunkel, in his review of Kabisch's book in 1891, pointed out that many of his so-called "contradictions of views" between source documents were only apparent, and a more precise exegesis would reduce both their number and their severity.[7] At this level of discussion, Gunkel's critique of Kabisch is very telling.[8]

The implications of this approach have been carried farther in an analysis of the term "end" in 4 Ezra which concludes that the supposed contradictions are in fact not such but the result of attributing to terms meanings they do not have.[9]

In such analyses, the preliminary hypothesis should be that the author's thought was coherent. If so, when the examination of a term uncovers prima facie contradictions or inconsistency, it is possible that the meaning

---

3 See Stone, "Coherence and Inconsistency," 235–36, from which this paragraph is adapted.

4 Keulers, p. 143; cf. Kabisch, pp. 67–70, 75, and passim. See further Stone, *Features*, 214.

5 Review of Kabisch in *TLZ* 16.1 (1891), 10–11. For further modifications of this view and later bibliography, see Stone, *Features*, 45.

6 We stress the words "as transmitted," for many textual emendations have been proposed precisely on the basis of the distinction between these two, separate eschatologies. But to argue from such "emended" texts for the separateness of the "two

eschatologies" is completely circular!

7 Gunkel, *TLZ*, 9–10.

8 These views have been echoed since that time, with little variation.

9 Stone, "Coherence and Inconsistency," 214–42, where the argument is set forth in full. It is also presented in Excursus on Natural Order, pp. 103–4.

assigned to it is not exact. Alternatively, there may be an unstated premise, view, or feature, lying outside the explicit statements of the text, that actually provides the author's thinking with coherence. Thus "we should question the criteria by which 'inconsistencies' are described. Has the content of the author's thought been carefully studied? If something seems to be inconsistent, but the ancient author wrote it, what enabled him to do so?"[10]

In study of the eschatology of the book it may be observed that there exist two major groupings of associated eschatological ideas. The one centers around the last generation and the increase of evil until its consummation, which is to be followed by the messianic kingdom. Chief elements of the other are resurrection, judgment, reward, and punishment. These two associational groupings do not occur in 4 Ezra as separate, independent, alternate eschatologies. One indication of this is that they occur together in certain passages such as 6:25–28 and 9:6–12, while in 5:41–56 and 4:26–31 the author moves easily from the one to the other. The present passage, 7:26–44, is the only one in the book in which a detailed eschatological chronology is given, and here the two associational complexes are presented as subsequent to each other.[11]

It is important to distinguish between the existence of associational complexes and the existence of consciously formulated distinct eschatological theories. The existence of groups of associated ideas like those we find in 4 Ezra may arise from their common origin, from a shared focus around a given theme, or from other factors. It in no way implies exclusivity in the thought of the author: the utilization of one group of ideas does not bring with it the rejection of the other. On the other hand, the conscious acceptance of one formulated and express eschatology must necessarily, imply abandonment of other, systematically incompatible eschatological ideas.

Consequently, the notion of two different eschatologies stated in possibility *a* above and implied by possibility *b* does not reflect any ancient reality. These two eschatologies did not exist for the author as independent ideologies which he tried to reconcile in his book. Instead, the various ideas existed in associational groupings that were part of the range of concepts the author brought to bear on the specific problems that faced him.[12]

The author's thought has been described as "non-logical" in that it employs other organizing categories than logical consistency between the meaning of its statements.[13] When the author describes the total eschatological process, as he does in 7:26–44, he does so as a coherent and consecutive structure of events. He is not interested in consistency, however, and feels no need to utilize this same pattern in the same way in all his statements about given aspects of these same events.[14]

This passage (7:26–44), then, is unique in the book, since it sets forth the author's eschatological scheme in a systematic way. It does not take the course of events any farther than the day of judgment itself, which is typical of the author's lack of interest in detailed descriptions of the eschatological state.[15]

There has been some debate regarding which question this prediction responds to.[16] The view of Knibb—that it is a response to, or an illustration of, 7:25, which summarizes the angel's position in 7:1–25—seems to be the most reasonable. Ezra has accepted the basic inevitability of the cosmic process and is now raising questions about its equity and operation. The angel's response to these is that, in the final analysis, God's judgment is just and the wicked will be punished and the righteous recompensed.

---

10   Stone, "Coherence and Inconsistency," 242.

11   The same general sequence of elements is also observed in 6:26–28; 9:6–12; 11:46; and 12:34.

12   At this point we may mention Brandenburger's position that the author needed to use the messianic kingdom eschatology because of the situation of Israel in his time (*Verborgenheit*, 193).

13   Stone, *Features*, 21–22.

14   Such statements frequently mention the eschatological event not with the aim of describing it in detail, but incidentally to some other concern.

15   Rowland, *Open Heaven*, 172, comments that "the interest of the apocalypticist ceases once the triumph of God's representative has been promised."

16   Harnisch claims that it is not a response to "how long" but an answer to "what will be," i.e., it neutralizes apocalyptic urgency (p. 303).

The prediction of 7:26–44 spells out how this will happen.

Excursus on the Redeemer Figure

The figure of the Redeemer or Messiah in 4 Ezra has raised a significant amount of interest. This is due to concerns chiefly outside 4 Ezra itself. Nonetheless, it is worth examining all of the evidence about the Redeemer figure in one excursus. First the title "son of God," given the Messiah in various sources, will be examined and then the presentation of the figure in various contexts and its functions and characteristics.

1. The Messianic title "Son of God"

This title, or rather the terms that have been translated in this way, occurs in a number of places in 4 Ezra. The evidence is best set out in a table (see p. 208).
The chief opinions held about these texts are either that the term that is translated by Latin *filius* was υἱός in Greek and this represented Hebrew בן or that it was Greek παῖς and that this represented Hebrew עבד. The first opinion would make this terminology witness to a Jewish titling of the Messiah as "son of God" toward the end of the first century c.e., while the second would invoke the "servant" language about him.

In general, the arguments for the second alternative seem to be the stronger. They run as follows: Had any Christian translator (and all the translators can be assumed to be Christians) had the word "son" before him, referring to the Messiah or the Christ, it is hard to assume that he would change it for some other word. However, if he had a word before him that could mean "son" but could also mean "child" or "servant," he might have translated it by a word that was unambig-

uously "son" in some cases, while retaining a translation of it as "young man" or "servant" in others. The word παῖς in Greek has precisely this set of meanings, and indeed it may translate Hebrew words that mean "child" or "servant."[17]

The anomalies of the versions adduced to support this view are the following:
a. Versions use words that unambiguously mean "servant" in a number of instances; thus Ethiopic in 7:29 and Arabic2 in 13:52 (as emended) and 14:9.
b. Versions use words meaning "child" that do not occur in the set phrases. So Arabic1 13:32; 13:37; 13:52; and 14:9; Arabic2 in 13:32 and 13:37.
c. Greek had at least two readings in 7:28: one with "son," witnessed by the close group Latin, Syriac, and Arabic1, and one without. It is harder to explain the omission by the other versions or their *Vorlage* than an addition in the *Vorlage* of Latin, Syriac, and Arabic1 by contamination from 7:29.
d. Ethiopic in 13:32 translates "that man"; Armenian omits two instances and translates 13:32 "Most High," 13:52 "secret of the Most High," and 14:9 "me."[18]

The situation is, nonetheless, not unambiguous. First, the readings of the closely related Latin and Syriac versions are completely consistent. Second, Georgian and Sahidic both lack most occurrences by physical lacuna. An additional problem is raised by Georgian which, where it survives in 7:28 and 7:29, reads *electus unctus meus*, introducing the additional element "elect one."[19] After these matters are given their full weight, however, it still seems that *(a)* the reading in 7:28 is very likely secondary and *(b)* that the Greek was probably in all cases παῖς and the Hebrew probably עבד.[20] Knibb remarks, on 7:28:

---

17 In addition to the evidence usually cited, note this equivalation in the *Aramaic Levi* 2:6; see 4QTest Lev[a] 2:10, equivalent to the Greek expansion to 2:3, v 15 in de Jonge's numbering.

18 "Iesus" of Lat in 7:28 is universally regarded as secondary. Armenian, for reasons that remain obscure, translates this word by "Messiah" in only one instance. See Stone, "Some Remarks," 114.

19 S. Gerö, "'My Son the Messiah': A Note on 4 Ezra 7:28–29," *ZNW* 66 (1975) 264–67, would argue that the Georgian goes back to a Greek ἐκλεκτός, a Greek translation of a (late?) Hebrew בר which the other versions rendered as υἱός. Quite apart from the problematic equivalation of this Hebrew with the Greek ἐκλεκτός, which would be forced, this theory would imply that Georgian had access to a second, apparently different, translation into Greek from Hebrew than that available to the other versions.

This is not acceptable because of the close connections between the *Vorlage* of Georgian and that of Ethiopic. Moreover, it would have to be supported by a series of readings to be convincing. The hypothesis that Georgian was translated from a Semitic language, which was mentioned in Introduction, sec. 1.4.2, does not help this argument.

20 This view was already held by J. Drummond, *The Jewish Messiah* (London: Longmans Green, 1877), who has been followed by many scholars; see pp. 285–86. See Stone, *Features*, 71–72, for further remarks.

The Term "Messiah" in the Versions

Verse	Lat	Syr	Eth	Georg	Ar1	Ar2	Arm	Sah
•7:28	filius	bry	masiḥeya	electus†	wldy	'lmsyḥ	unctus	—
	meus	mšyḥ'	—	unctus	'lmsyḥ	dei	—	—
	Iesus	—	—	meus	—	—	—	—
•7:29	filius	bry	qʷel'ēya	electus†	—	—	—	—
	meus	msyḥ'	masiḥeya	unctus	—	—	—	—
	christus	—	—	meus	—	—	—	—
•13:32	filius	bry	we'etu	—	qt'y	qt'y	altiss-	my*
	meus	—	be'si	—	—	—	imus	son
•13:37	filius	bry	waled	—	qt'y	qt'y	—	—
	meus	—	—	—	—	—	—	—
•13:52	filium	bry	lawaled:	—	qt'y	'bdy‡	secretus	—
	meum	—	lawaleda (D	—	—	Ms B:	altiss-	—
	—	—	PR)(la)'egʷala	—	—	qt'y	imi	—
	—	—	'emaḥeyāw (GF)	—	—	—	—	—
•14:9	cum	bry	waledeya	—	qt'y	'bdy	cum	—
	filio	—	for	—	—	—	mihi	—
	meo	—	welūdeya	—	—	—	—	—

* only this instance survives in Sahidic.

† only these two instances survive in Georgian.

‡ emended from 'ndy

> The fact that the Messiah is called 'my son' . . . is
> possibly because of deliberate Christian alteration of
> the text. . . . On the other hand the messianic inter-
> pretation of Ps. 2 . . . , in which God says of the
> anointed king 'You are my son' . . . provides a pos-
> sible Jewish background for the use of this title, and
> it may be wrong to suspect Christian influence.[21]

This was also the view of Box, who suggested that the
reading "son," in chapter 13 in particular, is original.
He sees it, as Knibb does, as based on the messianic
interpretation of Psalm 2. The evidence he brings is

far from convincing, and the one source that might
support a messianic interpretation of Ps 2:7 is much
too late to serve as evidence for 4 Ezra.[22] There is
some evidence for a messianic title "son of God"
current among Jews in the first century c.e. It is also
possible that this might have derived from an
unattested messianic interpretation of Ps 2:7.[23] As far
as 4 Ezra is concerned, however, the textual evidence
seems to be compelling.

2. Occurrences of the Redeemer Figure

The Redeemer figure is definitely referred to in 7:28–
29; 11:37—12:1; 12:31–34; 13:3–13; 13:25–52; and
14:9.[24]

a. 7:28–29

In 7:28–29 he is entitled "my Messiah" or "my servant
the Messiah." He appears after the inception of the
messianic kingdom with his companions and makes the
survivors (i.e., those who survived the messianic woes;
see 5:41 Commentary) rejoice for four hundred years.
Then he dies, together with all the citizens of that
messianic kingdom, and everything reverts to chaos
and is followed by a new creation, resurrection, and
judgment.

b. The Eagle Vision

In the eagle vision (Vision 5), the Messiah plays a significant role. He figures both in the symbolic dream
and in the interpretation of that dream. In the dream
he appears as a lion who indicts and sentences the eagle
(11:37–46), upon which the eagle disappears and the
earth was greatly terrified (12:1–3). In the interpretation he is said to be the Davidid Messiah, reserved for
the end (12:32), who will come, rebuke the last empire,
and destroy it (12:33). He will deliver the rest of the
people in the land of Israel and rejoice with them until
the end and the day of judgment (12:34).

c. The Vision of the Man

The Redeemer figure also plays a large role in the second dream vision, Vision 6 (chap. 13). In the dream,
Ezra sees a man arising from the sea. He flew with the
clouds of heaven, and his glance and voice melted all
who encountered them (13:1–4). He was attacked by

21 See also Stone, *Features*, p. 74. E. Sjöberg, *Der
    Menschensohn im äthiopischen Henochbuch* (Lund:
    Gleerup, 1946), energetically rejects attempts to find
    suffering servant language here (pp. 133–34).

22 The texts that Box adduces to support this view are
    not at all unambiguous. They are *Ps Sol* 17:26; *b.
    Sukka* 52a; and Targ Ps 80:16. Only *b. Sukka* 52a is
    remotely relevant to our concerns. See further
    Stone, *Features*, 75. Other scholars also share Box's
    view.

23 See Stone, *Features*, 75 and 249–50 n. 134. Very
    explicit is *1 Enoch* 105:2. This view is also urged by

Geoltrain on 7:28. J. A. Fitzmyer, "The Contribution
of Qumran Aramaic to the Study of the New
Testament," *NTS* 20 (1974) 391–94, discusses the
Aramaic titles "son of God" and "son of the Most
High" applied to a human being in a pseudo-Danielic
text from Qumran (4Q 243), as yet unpublished.

24 It has also been suggested that the son in Vision 4 is
    the Messiah, but this seems unlikely. See Sjöberg,
    Menschensohn, 134–39, for bibliography and critique.

an innumerable multitude of men, carved out a great mountain for himself and flew upon it (13:5–7). Weaponless, he fought the multitude, and fire from his mouth burned them up (13:8–11). Then a multitude gathered to him, some joyful and some sad (13:12–13). In the interpretation the man from the sea is identified as the one whom God reserved for many ages to deliver the survivors (13:26). His stand against the multitude means that at the end all peoples will unite to fight the Man (13:32–33), who will stand on Mount Zion and reprove them and destroy them by the Law (symbolized by fire) (13:34–38). The peaceable multitude are the ten tribes who will return (13:39–47). Moreover, the survivors in the borders of the holy land will be saved, and he will defend them and show them wonders (13:48–50). In an additional note the hiddenness of the son (or: servant) is stressed (13:52).

d. 14:9

In 14:9 there is an incidental reference to the Messiah in connection with God's promise to Ezra that he would be assumed. He is preserved until the end of times together with the assumed righteous.

3. Functions of the Redeemer

The role of the Messiah or Redeemer differs somewhat in the various visions and should be analyzed first in greater detail as it occurs in them. Only after this can the overall questions be posed.

In 7:28–29 the Messiah's characteristics and role are clear. He is entitled "my Messiah" and "my servant the Messiah." This is a very specific title.[25] He is said to be revealed together with his company which suggests preexistence. After four hundred years he is to die together with all human beings. This specific tradition about his death is almost unparalleled, and only *2 Apoc Bar* 30:1 can be said to be similar to it.[26] He is given no role in the events ushering in the messianic kingdom,

and his appearance seems to be part of the "wonders" that the survivors will see (7:27). He is said merely to make the survivors rejoice for the duration of his kingdom and then to die.

In the eagle vision the situation is much more complex. In the Commentary below, views about the origin of these chapters are discussed and we have been led to maintain the substantial unity of the book on various grounds.[27] The dream and its interpretation cohere, with the interpretation adding some details to those of the dream. The Messiah is presented in the dream as a lion, perhaps suggesting his Judahite descent (cf. Gen 49:9–10, cf. Rev 5:5, *Yalqut Shimoni* 160). The interpretation of the dream identifies the lion as the Davidid Messiah, preserved for the end (12:32). Yet in spite of this, his activity, both in judging and in the subsequent period, is not referred to in royal terminology.[28] Moreover, the text clearly implies that he is preexistent. This feature, which will be discussed further below, clearly intensifies his cosmic role and function.

His activities, which are described in forensic terms, have to do first and foremost with the fate of the Roman Empire. It is interesting that while in the dream he is described as indicting the eagle, in the interpretation it says, "He will first set (the last of the four world empires) up in judgment while they are alive, and it shall be when he will have rebuked them he will destroy them" (12:33). This means not only that his rebuke is spoken of as judgment[29] but he is assigned a series of legal tasks—indictment, pronouncement of judgment, and its execution. The forensic aspects of his activity, already present in the dream symbolism, are further intensified in the interpretation. After this legal activity, he will deliver the rest of the people in the land of Israel and rejoice with

---

25 Knibb gives a conspectus of the history of this title. The literature on it is vast; in general on redeemer figures in Judaism, see Nickelsburg and Stone, *Faith and Piety,* 161–201, and additional references there. Note the strikingly similar phrase with a rather different concept in Targ. Zech. 3:8: "I will bring my servant the Messiah and he will be revealed."

26 This perhaps resembles the idea of the snatching away of the Messiah. One reference to this, *1 Enoch* 70:1, refers to Enoch himself, but he is identified as the Son of man in the next chapter. Still, 4 Ezra's reference to the Messiah's death remains unparalleled.

27 As touches on the present problem, see also Stone, "Messiah," 296–99.

28 The connection is made quite explicit in *Yalq. Shimoni* on Gen 49:9. See also Rev 5:5. The king from the

west in *Apocalypse of Elijah* is also presented as a lion and he takes on other Judahite characteristics as well; see Rosenstiehl, *Elie,* 88. The Prince of the Congregation is called a lion in 1QSb 5:29. The lion appears as a positive symbol, with emphasis on its strength, valor, or majesty in 2 Sam 1:23; 17:10; Prov 28:1; 30:30; etc. Its role as hunter is predominant in Num 23:24; 24:9; etc., while it is a symbol of God in Isa 31:4; Jer 25:30; Hos 5:14; 11:10; 13:8; etc. Here, of course, its Judahite connection is predominant.

29 See Excursus on the Term "Judgment," p. 149, for this usage of the term. The idea that the Messiah will put an end to the wicked is a commonplace.

them until the time of the end and the day of judgment (12:34).

It has been suggested that certain editorial adjustments have been made within this vision, in the verses touching on the Messiah. These are the addition of the phrase "whom the Most High hath kept unto the end of days" in 12:32 and of all of verse 12:34 which is completely secondary. The basis for these suggestions is supposed "contradictions" in the book's ideas about the Messiah. Preexistence supposedly contradicts Davidid descent, while 12:34, referring to the deliverance of the survivors and their joy in the messianic kingdom until the day of judgment, is an addition, for it is "out of harmony" with the allegedly purely political expectations of the vision.

These supposed anomalies are, in fact, far less serious than might be thought. They arise, basically, because modern critics apply to the book categories of logic and consistency that are too rigid.[30] To take just one example: It is illuminating to compare this messianic figure with its supposedly incompatible heavenly origin and Davidid descent, with Melchizedek as presented by *2 Enoch*. There Melchizedek is born before the Flood and assumed to heaven in order to appear later at the appointed time. This is no less strange, indeed perhaps more so, than a Messiah of Davidid descent who is preexistent.

Nonetheless, there is one major difference between what is said about the Messiah in chapters 11–12 and what is said in 7:28–29. There the Messiah appears after the inception of the messianic kingdom, and there is no hint at what is his central task in the eagle vision, that is, the indictment and destruction of the Roman Empire. In the eagle vision, what is more, the Messiah's activity is described in legal terms, reminiscent of the language of God's judicial activity (see, e.g., 7:37).[31] Yet as distinct from the judgment in Daniel 7 or in the *Similitudes of Enoch*, which is unmistakably cosmic in scope, here the elements of universality and resurrection, usually associated by 4 Ezra with final judgment, do not appear, nor do those which serve to typify judgment as cosmic in the other sources mentioned. So, although the Messiah judges in chapters 11–12, his judgment is prior to the end.

The question thus arises of the origin of the form of the Messiah's judicial function found in this vision. Is it to be seen as a modification of the concept of the

Redeemer as cosmic judge? This is to be found in the *Similitudes of Enoch* and may also be seen as a legalization of the eschatological battle, as is already to be observed in Daniel 7. In this connection it is useful to consider *2 Apocalypse of Baruch* 39–40. In spite of the intimate connections between *2 Apocalypse of Baruch* and 4 Ezra, these chapters do not seem to have a literary relationship with 4 Ezra 11–12. *2 Apocalypse of Baruch* 39–40 is a four kingdoms vision (as is 4 Ezra 11–12). The indictment of 4 Ezra 11:38–43 refers to the wicked empire in "antichrist" terminology similar to that used in *2 Apoc Bar* 39:5, both deriving from the characterization of the little horn in Daniel 7. The legal characteristic of judgment of the leader of the last empire (40:1) and also the temporary messianic kingdom (40:3) are also features shared with 4 Ezra. Yet in both visions there is no mention whatsoever of the cosmic, universal aspects of the functions of the judgment by the Redeemer which are to be found in other contexts. In the Excursus on the Term "Judgment," p. 151, we have shown that, in addition to final judgment, there are a number of events that can be regarded as judgment, that is, as the drawing of distinctions between the righteous and the wicked. The Messiah's action here is one of them.

The chief activity that the Messiah performs here, as the man does in the next vision, is the destruction of the Roman Empire. In one way this can be seen as a reflection of the idea of the eschatological conflict between good and evil. This is very much to the fore in the dream in chapter 13. Even though in both 4 Ezra and *2 Apocalypse of Baruch* the Messiah's activity is described in legal terms, yet final judgment is clearly the realm of God alone in both works. So we must assume that behind the situation in 4 Ezra and *2 Apocalypse of Baruch* lies a separation of the eschatological battle from final judgment and a subsequent legalization of the eschatological battle. It will emerge below that this is very typical of the approach of 4 Ezra itself.

To conclude this section it may be stressed once more that the role attributed to the Messiah here differs greatly from that in 7:28–29 precisely in this point. There the Messiah is said to do nothing but "rejoice" the survivors for four hundred years. Here he destroys the wicked kingdom.

In the vision of the man the situation is complex. In

---

30 The views are maintained by Box, xxiii–xxiv; for a detailed discussion and refutation, see Stone, "Messiah," 297. Some very apt comments on the flowing together of purportedly different messianic concepts in 4 Ezra are made by E. Sjöberg, *Der verborgene Menschensohn in den Evangelien* (Acta reg. soc. humanorum litt. Lundensis 51; Lund: Gleerup, 1955) 48 n. 1.

31 Baldensperger pointed out that in Daniel 7 the eschatological battle is given a forensic formulation and that this is relevant to the description in 4 Ezra here (pp. 98–99, cf. 161).

13:20b–55 Function and Content, pp. 398–400, we deal with the question of the literary unity of this vision. The point of view of Box and others who maintained that the whole is drawn from another source and has been adapted by the redactor was found wanting. On the other hand, a series of severe literary problems was observed to exist when the dream is compared with its interpretation and in the interpretation itself.[32] These considerations lead to the conclusion that the author is here writing his own interpretation to a previously existent allegory.[33] Only the attempt to give a new interpretation to a previously extant vision can explain, on the one hand, the contrast between the closely structured allegory and confused interpretation and, on the other hand, the overall contrast between this interpretation and the carefully structured interpretation of the eagle vision.

It was observed above that the Redeemer is called "man" in both the dream and the interpretation, but the title "servant" is to be found only in the interpretation. Chapter 13:32 identifies him as "my servant," and "my servant" continues to be the subject of action in 13:37. The interpretation regards the title "man" as a symbol the meaning of which is "my servant." This is clear from its use in interpretative formulae in 13:25 and 13:51, and an identification is also given in the remaining instance in which it is used (13:32). The

expression "the man" is never used of the subject of action in the interpretation; "the man" is treated by the interpretation as a symbol, just as is the lion in chapter 12.

Box characterized the figure described in the vision as the transcendent "Son of man."[34] The actual form "son of man" is not found in chapter 13, and although this title probably originally meant simply "human being,"[35] the consistent use of the expression "Son of man" in the *Similitudes of Enoch* and the New Testament shows that it early became formulaic. It is important to observe that even if "the man" in the dream was the traditional "Son of man," the figure seems to have needed intepretation for the author or his readers. Moreover, the author of 4 Ezra has shorn this figure of all of its particular characteristics in the interpretation and treated it as a symbol. This would be inconceivable if the "Son of man" concept was readily recognizable to him and his readers.

In the dream, the main feature of the figure is as warrior. This is emphasized here, a situation that contrasts with that in the eagle vision, where, after careful analysis, the warrior characteristics were perhaps discerned in the background of the descriptions of the Messiah's function. The figure is not entitled Messiah, nor is the symbolism of "the man"

---

32 See Stone, "Messiah," 305–6.

33 This view was also adopted by U. B. Müller, *Messias und Menschensohn in jüdischen Apokalypsen und in der Offenbarung Johannes* (SZNT 6; Gütersloh: Mohn, 1972) 108–9. M. Casey, *Son of Man: The Interpretation and Influence of Daniel 7* (London: SPCK, 1979), challenges this analysis. His views are discussed in the course of our treatment of chap. 13. The interpolation theory developed by Box leaves the interpretation with the same literary and structural problems vis-à-vis the vision. Another conceivable hypothesis would regard the interpretation as radically reworked, i.e., that there was an original allegory + interpretation. The allegory was taken over holusbolus, but the interpretation was reworked. In this case, the original interpretation is completely submerged.

34 This title for a redeemer is clearly used in *Similitudes of Enoch* and in the New Testament. It has been the subject of intensive study. A detailed summary is by C. Colpe in *TDNT*, 8: 400–477. Naturally, it is derived immediately from Daniel 7, where this figure appears with God and exercises cosmic functions. It should be noted that in the interpretation in Daniel, as here, the "Son of man" is consistently identified. Box, Volz, and others have suggested, on the basis of the title, that this man is to be identified with the

Urmensch. In his treatment of the much more clearly defined Son of man in *1 Enoch*, Sjöberg concluded that while the figure was influenced by the *Urmensch*, it is not identified with him. The Son of man is identified neither with Adam nor with the *Urmensch.* See Sjöberg, *Menschensohn* 190–98; cf. Volz, pp. 214–16. This view is also opposed by Keulers, pp. 126–29, and energetically by Müller, *Messias*, 114–17. G. Quispel has argued that the expression in *1 Enoch* 46:1 "whose countenance has the appearance of a man" is dependent not just on Dan 7:13 but also on Ezek 1:26, where the Divinity seated upon the chariot throne is described as "a likeness as it were of a human form" (RSV: "Ezekiel 1:26 in Jewish Mysticism and Gnosis," *VC* 34 [1980] 1–2). Beer (*apud* Kautzsch) sees the figure here to have originated in astral religion (p. 278); this view is refuted by Müller, *Messias*, 112–13.

35 See Vermès's ongoing polemic on this, "The Present State of the Son of Man Debate," *JJS* 29 (1978) 123–34. Casey, *Son of Man*, suggests a further distinction. On the basis of Latin and Syriac terminologies, Casey suggests that in the vision (13:3; 13:5; 13:12) terms are used suggesting Greek ἄνθρωπος and Hebrew אדם (בן) and in the interpretation (13:25; 13:32; 13:51) the terminology reflects ἀνήρ and Hebrew איש.

pregnant with hints in that direction, as was the lion in the previous vision.[36] On the other hand, the man is described using symbolic language that is drawn largely from biblical descriptions of God, particularly his epiphanies as warrior. Such epiphanies are regularly preceded by winds,[37] and the clouds come before him or are his chariot.[38] These elements also feature in Daniel 7, which is clearly at play in some way here in 4 Ezra. Fire is also typical of theophanies and is one of God's chief weapons against his enemies.[39] According to Ps 18:9, it issues from his mouth. The melting of enemies like wax before a flame is also appropriate to the divine Warrior.[40]

All of these elements have been freed from the concept of God as warrior before the time of 4 Ezra. It is nonetheless of great significance that none of them is taken up in the interpretation except the fiery elements and these are explicitly interpreted in legal terms.[41]

As has been observed, the cosmic features of the divine Warrior are attracted to the man. Yet in the interpretation they are all excluded or reinterpreted. The forensic aspect is less prominent here than in the eagle vision, but it is treated in the same way. There is rebuke, perhaps sentencing[42] and destruction by the Redeemer's righteous pronouncement.[43] Moreover, the interpretation adds features to the Redeemer figure that were not present in the dream. These include the showing of wonders (13:50), the companions (13:52), and the function of the Redeemer in the destruction of the hostile host (13:26; 13:49–50).

Now, it is those elements which are found in the interpretation and not in the dream that show the greatest connection with the rest of the book. To some extent this may be attributed to the fact that the interpretation is more detailed than the vision. However, when this fact is combined with the unique traits of the Redeemer figure in the vision, the cosmic features and the unadorned military characteristics, which are found nowhere else in 4 Ezra, it becomes evident that it is congruent with our analysis which was made on literary grounds.

As in chapters 11–12 and in opposition to 7:28–29, the activity of the Messiah commences before the beginning of his kingdom and he is active in the overthrow of the wicked nations.

In 14:9 there is the only incidental reference to the Redeemer in the book. Here, in connection with the promise of assumption made to Ezra, the Redeemer is mentioned. He is said to be preserved with the assumed righteous until the end of times. He is called "servant," but no other details are given.

4. The Overall Role of the Messiah or Redeemer in the Book
In general, the following may be observed:
a. All the four texts seem to say that the Messiah is preexistent, although the extent and the nature of this preexistence are not made explicit.[44]
b. Where information is provided, he is expected to take care of the righteous survivors (all sources except 14:9 and the dream of chap. 13).
c. His kingdom is not stated to be eternal, and in two sources it is stated to come to an end (7:29 and 12:34). This point is not discussed in chapter 13 or 14.

---

36   The deep influence of Isa 11:4 on the description of the man's activity in 13:10–11 suggests a confluence of properly "messianic" ideas with those of the cosmic redeemer here; see 13:10 Commentary. This is the central thesis of Müller, *Messias,* 118–22, though he constructs his argument differently. He does not stress the relationship of this figure to the divine Warrior. In the view of the author of 4 Ezra himself, the identification seems complete. Box points out that the mountain might also be related to cosmic war, but it is unambiguously interpreted as Mount Zion. This figure clearly derives from Dan 2:45, as is explicit from 4 Ezra 13:7.

37   See 1 Kgs 19:11–12; Zech 9:14; Job 40:6; etc.; and see 11:2 Commentary. Winds form a chariot in *Ad Ev* 38:4 as they do in a way in 13:2. Cf. also *1 Enoch* 52:1 according to some manuscripts.

38   Preceding theophanies, Exod 19:9; 19:16; Num 12:5; 14:4; 1 Kgs 8:10–11; Ezek 1:4; as his chariot, Exod 19:18; Isa 14:14; 19:1; Nah 1:3; Ps 68:5; 104:3; note *rkb ʿrpt* as title of Baal in Ugaritic texts; see 11:2 Commentary. In an associated text, the

39   clouds summon Enoch to carry him to heaven, *1 Enoch* 14:8.

39   Isa 66:15–16; Ps 97:3–4, cf. 2 Sam 22:9–10 // Ps 18:9–10; 1 Kgs 19:12; Ezek 10:2, cf. Deut 32:22.

40   Thus Mic 1:4; Ps 68:3; 97:5; cf. also Ezek 22:21–22. See Judith 16:15; *1 Enoch* 1:6; 52:6.

41   Box points out that the mountain might also be related to cosmic war, but it is unambiguously interpreted as Mount Zion. This figure clearly derives from Dan 2:45, as is explicit in 4 Ezra 13:7.

42   13:38, the verse is problematic, however, and might refer to future judgment. See also 13:37 Commentary for another possible context implying sentencing. The element of sentencing is not predominant in any case.

43   See Isa 11:4; Wisd 12:9; 18:15f.; *1 Enoch* 62:2; and 2 Thess 2:8; cf. Isa 49:2. Rebuke is also destruction in chap. 11–12; see further 13:10 Commentary. The reinterpretation of the redeemer figure in the interpretation is discussed in 13:20b–55 Function and Content, p. 397. It was recently reasserted by Müller, *Messias,* 127.

d. The term "survivors" is common to all relevant sources except the dream in chapter 13.

e. He is called "Messiah" in 7:26 and 12:32 and "servant" in 7:29; 13:32; 13:37; 13:52; and 14:9.

Thus in these categories, the common features of the Redeemer figure are prominent. Only the dream in chapter 13 is distinguished from the other sources. Certain other features serve to strenghten this overall impression. In spite of the title Messiah, the Judahite descent, and the lion symbol by which he is represented, the Redeemer is nowhere spoken of in the language of kingship. He makes the survivors rejoice (7:28; 12:34), delivers them (12:34; cf. 13:26), and defends (13:49) or directs them (13:26). He never rules over them. Moreover, this view of the Redeemer is strengthened by the fact that nothing is said, except in the most general terms, about what will go on in the messianic kingdom in Visions 5 and 6, for which its advent forms a climax. On the other hand, in 7:28–29 the attention of the author is devoted to the ensuing events, the resurrection and the day of judgment, and the Messiah and his kingdom are mentioned merely as stages on the way to those events.

The differences between presentation of the Redeemer in the vision in chapter 13 and all of the other passages that deal with the Messiah bring us to think that the vision has an independent origin. Moreover, the difference between 7:28–29, in which the Redeemer plays no role in the destruction of the wicked kingdom, and Visions 5 and 6, where his role is central, is significant. We might be tempted to harmonize this by saying that in 7:28–29 the author is not really interested in the Redeemer and his doings, while these form the very point of Vision 6 and play a very major role in Vision 5. However, there are enough unresolved contradictions of this magnitude elsewhere in the book to make this sort of explanation a little suspect, although it is rather neat.

In terms of the overall thought of the book, it must be observed that the Redeemer figure occurs predominantly in those parts of the book which have best claim to be drawing on prior traditions, the two dream visions. In the long first three visions, with their extensive discussion of eschatological matters, he occurs only in the systematic exposition of 7:26–44, where he plays a more or less incidental role. Moreover, even his primary role as destroyer of Rome,

which could have been most appropriately used in the first three visions, is never mentioned there. This could, of course, be attributed to the different sort of material involved in these chapters, but other explanations might also be sought, such as the fact that the dream visions represent the beliefs of the seer after his conversion, when he has taken up, once more, the traditional explanations and they comfort him.

Beyond this, it must be clearly recognized that the Messiah and his kingdom are consistently held to be temporary. Thus they cannot be the final resolution of the writer's problems. But clearly the author is most preoccupied with the Redeemer and with his role in ensuring the passing of Rome and the rule of "the saints of the Most High." In these broad terms the way that the Redeemer is presented responds to the major concern of the first part of the book. There will be a vindication of Israel and a redress of the balance.

Commentary

■ **26** The expression "Behold, the time will come" is very much like the expression with which the two angelic predictions in Vision 1 and Vision 2 are introduced; see 5:1 Commentary. The term "time" is less usual than "days" in this expression but seems to be the best reading; see the textual notes.[45] "Signs" means the messianic woes, those fearsome events presaging the end of the world; see 4:52 Commentary.

The next two phrases are well compared in general tenor with *2 Apoc Bar* 51:8:

For they shall see that world which is now invisible to them,

And they will see a time which is now hidden to them. Here we have the revelation in the end of an unseen world and age to the righteous, and the words "unseen" and "hidden" are in parallelism. However, the exact reference of the terms "city" and "land" in 7:26 is difficult and has raised a plethora of hypotheses.

The phrase "unseen city" is to be taken to refer to the heavenly Jerusalem. This notion occurs elsewhere in 4 Ezra, and particularly in Vision 4 (10:27; 10:42; 10:44; 10:54; etc.), as well as in 8:52 and in 13:36.[46] The idea

44   Hartman, *Prophecy Interpreted,* 37, speaks of the "hiddenness" of the Messiah or the Son of man implied by these verses.

45   It has been suggested that καιρός lies behind this. Does this come from Hebrew קץ which means "delimited period of time" in texts like 1QS 4:16–17 and 1QpHab 7:7, 12? See Stone, *Features,* 53–54, for further discussion of the versions, and cf. also 7:75

and 8:50. "Time" is used similarly in *2 Apoc Bar* 25:4, cf. 44:11, and is discussed in 3:14 Commentary and 9:6 Commentary.

46   Note also Armenian 6:25 for appearance of "my glory."

has roots in the Bible and is widely diffused throughout the literature of the Second Temple age and after.[47] If the "unseen city" is Jerusalem, then that city clearly exists before this event, it is preexistent, an idea also present in Vision 4 and in 13:36, and probably also in 8:52. The city is heavenly inasmuch as it preexists and appears wondrously, and its revelation as part of the eschatological events is predicted here and in 13:36; cf. also 10:53–54. This concept also probably lies in the background of the parable in 7:6 and is discussed in the Commentary there.

The heavenly city is intimately related to paradise in a number of contexts (so in 8:52; *2 Apoc Bar* 4:2–4; *Rev* 22:1–2).[48] The city is referred to simply as "the city" (here; 8:52; 10:27; 10:42; 10:54) and as Zion (10:44; 13:36).[49] Terminology like "unseen" and "hidden" is a standard part of apocalyptic mystification and has been noted elsewhere in the book (see, e.g., 6:52 Commentary). Here the appearance of the city is the first event mentioned following on the messianic woes,[50] and the prediction of its appearance here clearly points ahead to Vision 4, of which it is the chief topic. In all of the texts in 4 Ezra the appearance of the city is specifically related to the events surrounding the messianic kingdom.[51] This is of course particularly to the point in a work that is devoted to resolving problems that arise out of the destruction of the Second Temple and the ensuing exile.

The expression "land which is now hidden" is unparalleled. "Land" alone refers to the land of Israel (5:25; 14:31). "Hidden," like "unseen" in the preceding phrase, seems to imply precreation, but it also reflects the apocalyptic penchant for talking in a mysterious way. The expression might be compared with "the place of faith and the region of hope" which are among the things revealed to Moses in the list in *2 Apoc Bar* 59:10. The land is intimately connected with the survivors and is the locale of the messianic kingdom (9:8; 12:34; 13:48; *2 Apoc Bar* 29:2).[52]

It is possible that this is to be compared with 6:14–16, which speaks of the changing of the foundations of the earth at the eschaton. In another sense this "hidden land" is parallel to the field Ardat, the special place where Ezra must go to see the vision of heavenly Jerusalem, for "no work of man's building could endure in a place where the city of the Most High was to be revealed" (10:54).

47 Bible: Isa 52:1; 54:11–12; 60:10–11; Ezekiel 40–48; Zech 2:5–9; see Y. Kaufmann, *Toledot Ha'emuna HaYisra'elit* (Jerusalem: Mosad Bialik, 1937), 8:236–37. Apocrypha and pseudepigrapha: Tob 13:16–18; 14:5; *Test Patr Dan* 5:12; *1 Enoch* 90:29; *2 Enoch* 55:2; *2 Apoc Bar* 4:2–4; 32:4; 59:4; *Sib Or* 5:420–428; see on this, Stone, "Lists," 446 n. 4. Dead Sea Scrolls: description of New Jerusalem (*DJD*, 3:184–93); rabbinic: *b. Ta'an.* 5a; *b. Baba Batra* 75b; *b. Pesaḥ.* 54a; *j. Ber.* 4.8b–c; *Midr. Teh.* on Ps 90:3; in the last two instances it is one of seven precreated things. Later Jewish apocalypses: *Heavenly Jerusalem* (Even-Shmuel) 20–22, esp. p. 21, lines 25–26. New Testament: Heb 11:10–16; 12:22; Rev 21:2; 21:9–10; Gal 4:26.

48 See also Arm 4 Ezra 6:54a and 6:2 Commentary (on precreation of paradise) and 7:6 Commentary (on paradise as a city).

49 There has been debate between views that maintain that this is a city in heaven (Kabisch and Gunkel) and those taking the view adopted here (Keulers). In detail, see Kabisch, pp. 80–82; Clemen, "Die Zusammensetzung," 240; Gunkel, *TLZ*, 7; M. J. Lagrange, "Notes sur le messianisme au temps de Jésus," *RB* NS 2 (1905) 493–94. Harnisch, p. 111, identifies the city as paradise and as the place of heavenly reward of the righteous (p. 112 n. 1); see

also H. Bietenhard, *Die himmlische Welt im Urchristentum und Spätjudentum* (WUNT 2; Tübingen: Mohr, 1951) 123–24. Paradise was sometimes described as a city; see 7:6 Commentary. Heb 13:14 speaks of "the city which is to come."

50 On the city in the fourth vision, see 10:38–54 Function and Content and 10:21 Commentary. It clearly differs there in some respects from the present context. The descent of the heavenly city is described in *1 Enoch* 90:29; Rev 21:2; *Sefer Eliyyahu* (Jellinek, *BM*, 3:67); and many other sources. Licht would interpret here not of Jerusalem but as a symbol of the world to come. D. Flusser has pointed out that the world to come or paradise is often talked of as heavenly Jerusalem, "Qumran und die Zwölf," *Initiation* (SHR 10; Leiden: Brill, 1965) 134–46. *2 Apoc Bar* 20:2 describes the removal of Zion as a necessary step before the bringing of the eschaton.

51 See Keulers, pp. 104–5, and for some further discussion, see 8:52 Commentary.

52 So also Keulers (p. 79) and Vagany (p. 97); Gunkel and Box, like Baldensperger, p. 162 n. 1, consider "land" here to mean paradise. They point out that paradise and heavenly Jerusalem are referred to side by side in a number of instances; some are cited above, and see also *2 Apoc Bar* 4:6 and Rev 22:2. However, in none of these instances is paradise called

■ **27** "Who has been delivered from the evils that I have foretold" is a phrase that occurs in contexts like this one elsewhere in the book, so also 6:25 and 9:8. The idea of the survivors is discussed in 5:41 Commentary.[53] The survivors are those delivered from the messianic woes (on the latter, see 5:2 Commentary). The expression "See my wonders" means to see eschatological events and particularly rewards; see 4:26 Commentary, where this language is discussed. This language is often used to describe the fate of the survivors in the messianic kingdom.

■ **28** This verse foretells the appearance of the Messiah with his companions and his making the survivors rejoice for four hundred years. The sudden revelation of the Messiah is predicted in many sources. In the Excursus on the Redeemer Figure, p. 209, the evidence that allows us to interpret this phrase here as implying his preexistence is presented. There, also, the title "my Messiah" is examined. A number of texts foresee a messianic kingdom during which God or the Messiah will live in the midst of its citizens (see *Ps Sol* 17:32–36; *1 Enoch* 105:2).

"Those who are with him" seems to refer to some individuals expected to appear together with the Messiah. The idea is also found in 13:52 and 14:9. The concept of the assumed companions of the Messiah is discussed in 6:26 Commentary. The closest parallel to the notion in 4 Ezra here is to be found in 1 Thess 3:13, which refers to the coming of Jesus with his holy ones. The concept as formulated here seems to draw on a well-known tradition, yet comparable passages in other literature do not show any connection with other

assumed people or with the Messiah.[54] What is found in them is the notion that the righteous are associated with the Redeemer in heaven; see *1 Enoch* 39:6–7 and 70:4. Yet these ideas are not presented in a fully systematic way in 4 Ezra.

The view that the messianic kingdom will be limited is found in various sources. In 4 Ezra 12:34 it recurs, although without the number of years being specified. 4 Ezra 6:25–28 is a notoriously difficult passage to interpret from this point of view, but we tend to see in it a combination of language that refers both to the messianic kingdom and to the eternal world to come. Revelation 20:2, 7 refers to the thousand-year kingdom of Christ; see further 7:29 Commentary.[55] It has been suggested that the number 400 is arrived at by a combination of Ps 90:15, "Make us glad as many days as thou hast afflicted us, and as many years as we have seen evil," and Gen 15:13, "and they will be oppressed for four hundred years."[56] This would be another hint setting the messianic kingdom into the context of Exodus; cf. 13:44 Commentary.

It should be noted, and the matter has been discussed in detail in the Excursus on the Redeemer Figure, that here no activity is attributed to the Messiah except rejoicing with the righteous. Contrast, for example, *2 Apoc Bar* 72:2, where he proceeds to preserve the righteous and slay the wicked, as well as many other sources, including 4 Ezra 12:32 et al. No such activity is men-

---

"land"; some support for an eschatological interpretation of "land" is in Matt 5:5 interpreting Ps 37:11.

53 Harnisch points out that the term "preserve" (Latin *servare*), together with *salvare* and their opposite *perire*, is typical of God's action toward the righteous in numerous passages in 4 Ezra (7:20; 7:27; 7:60; 7:85; 7:95; 8:3; 8:41; 8:55; 9:13; 9:15; 13:23 p. 140). On the terminology of preservation and reservation, see the apt comments of Sjöberg, *Der verborgene Menschensohn*, 46–47. See 12:34 Commentary.

54 It may also draw on the angelic host which is to accompany the Messiah; see Gunkel on 13:52. "Holy Ones" is an angelic title; see Yadin, *War*, 229–31, 237. This might apply to 1 Thess 3:13 and 2 Thess 1:7 but does not seem likely for 4 Ezra; see 14:9. Other assumption passages include *1 Enoch* 89:52; *2 Apoc Bar* 13:3; 25:1; 76:2; and *2 Enoch* J 36:1. Cf. in a

different formulation Philipp 1:23–24. A group of eight of whom the Messiah is one is mentioned in *b. Sukka* 52b.

55 A limited messianic kingdom is also mentioned by *2 Apoc Bar* 29:8; 40;3. Something of the sort also seems to be implied by *1 Enoch* 91:13–15, although exact details are unclear. The length of the kingdom is the subject of dispute in a baraitha in *b. Sanh.* 99a. One view there even sets it at 400 years (R. Dosa). The same exegesis is also to be found, attributed to R. Eliezer, in *Pes. Rab.* 1 (Friedmann, p. 4a); see also *b. Sanh.* 97a, 97b.

56 There is some variation in the versions; see textual notes. The relationship with Ps 90:15 was used by the midrash cited in *Yalq.* on Ps 90:15 and *Pes. Rab.* 1 (end; Friedmann, p. 4a). See also the traditions in *Tanhuma 'Eqeb* 7.

tioned by our verse.[57] In 12:34 the same language of rejoicing, in a transitive sense, is used of the Messiah's activity at just this stage of the eschatological process. The language of "joy" is widespread for eschatological reward (see 7:60; 7:95; 7:96; 7:98; 7:131; *2 Apoc Bar* 55:8; 73:1; *Apoc Abr* 29:19; *Midr. Mishle* 16:11; et al.[58]

■ **29** This verse mentions the death of the Messiah and all human beings. This will bring the temporary messianic kingdom to an end, and the events of the new creation and the day of judgment will ensue. The idea of the death of the Messiah seems to have no precise parallels in its explicitness, but according to *2 Apoc Bar* 30:1, at a comparable juncture of events, the Messiah will "return" (apparently to heaven). According to 1 Cor 15:28, after his rule the Son of man will share the state of all human beings.[59]

This text, therefore, makes explicit the idea that the messianic kingdom is of limited duration. A kingdom, ruled by the Messiah, is referred to in three passages in 4 Ezra: 7:29–30; 11:46 with 12:34; and 13:48–49. None of these texts describes the character of this kingdom in any detail (cf., e.g., *2 Apoc Bar* 29:3–8). Chapter 7:29 and 11:44 with 12:34 describe this kingdom as having an end. Chapter 13:48 neither states this nor says that it is eternal; it in noncommittal.

To these explicit references three other passages may be added that seem to refer to the messianic kingdom, even though the Messiah himself is not mentioned. The first is 6:7–10, the Esau-Jacob passage. If our view is accepted and Jacob is taken as the kingdom of Israel, then observe that this is said to be the beginning of the world to come, just as the Roman Empire (Esau) is the end of this world. This seems to imply that the kingdom of Jacob is limited. The second and third passages are parts of prophecies of the signs. In 6:25–28, as shown in

the Commentary, elements occur that are usually associated with the messianic kingdom as well as others that generally typify the day of judgment. In 9:6–12 a similar combination of elements may be found. In both cases, the sequence of elements puts messianic kingdom features before those appertaining to the day of judgment. Although both are very brief and do not set out to present an orderly exposition of eschatology, even in them the elements are, on the whole, in the chronological order implied by our passage, and the movement between them is marked by the word "then."

All of this is relevant, in some measure, to the question that is dealt with in 7:26–44 Function and Content of whether there exists anywhere in 4 Ezra a presentation of eschatology in which what is taught is the eternal messianic kingdom. In the 7:28 Commentary a number of places were cited from Second Temple period literature that speak of a temporary messianic kingdom. This view is particularly prominent in *2 Apocalypse of Baruch*. There are also texts in which the messianic kingdom is proclaimed to be eternal,[60] while others leave the matter unclear.[61]

It has been pointed out that the Rabbis both distinguish between the messianic kingdom and the world to come and tend to confuse them. In a number of texts four versions of the answer to the question about the duration of the messianic kingdom are preserved, all attributed to authorities dating from the early Tannaitic period. None suggests that it is eternal, and one limits it, as does 4 Ezra, to four hundred years.[62]

Consequently, it may be concluded that evidence from within 4 Ezra for a temporary messianic kingdom is overwhelming. Nothing in the book contradicts it, and the idea is consonant with contemporary and later sources. There is no reason to say that at any point 4

---

57 See also the Messiah's activity in *2 Apocalypse of Baruch* 40.

58 Cf. also 13:13. A similar use of the transitive verb, but with God as the subject, serves in Sir 35:19 to describe the rewarding of the righteous. In 7:60 and 7:131 God is said to rejoice over the righteous; see also 7:36 Commentary and Stone, *Features*, 76–77. The term "joy" is discussed in Hartman, *Prophecy Interpreted*, 47–49.

59 A remarkable verbal parallel, with a somewhat different sense, may be observed in Dan 9:26. The expression "those who draw human breath" may be compared with biblical terms in Gen 7:22; Isa 2:22; Ps 150:6; etc.

60 See Dan 7:14; 7:27; *1 Enoch* 10:16–22; 49:1–2; 62:14; 71:15–17; *Jub* 50:5, cf. 23:29–32; *Sib Or* 3:49–60, 767–780; *Test Patr Levi* 18; and *Test Patr Jos* 19:12; cf. also *Test Patr Jud* 22.

61 So, e.g., *Ps Sol* 17:23–46; *1 Enoch* 93:8; and *Sib Or* 5:414–33.

62 Klausner, *Messianic Idea*, 408–413; *b. Sanh* 99a (attributed to Dosa); *Pes. Rab.* 1 end (Friedmann, p. 4a; 400 years, attributed to R. Eliezer) and *Midr. Teh.* on Ps 90:15; see on this W. Bacher, *Die Agada der*

Ezra preaches the idea of an eternal kingdom of Israel ruled by the Redeemer. The fact that the Redeemer figure is not mentioned in 6:25–29 and 9:6, 12, as well as his absence from 6:7–10, reminds us (as was pointed out in the Excursus on the Redeemer Figure) that the author of 4 Ezra felt comfortable speaking of the eschatological events without mentioning him at all. What seems absolutely clear, from the point of view of 4 Ezra, is that, even if we assume with some scholars that the eternal messianic kingdom is an original ideology, adapted to a scheme within 4 Ezra, that independent ideology is not found in 4 Ezra.[63]

■ 30 This verse predicts the reversion of the age to primordial silence for seven days.[64] In 6:39 Commentary the evidence was assembled to show that silence is typical of the state before the creation of human beings. A close parallel to our verse is *2 Apoc Bar* 3:7, "Or shall the world revert to its nature (of aforetime), and the age revert to primeval silence?" This interpretation is strengthened by the last phrase of the verse "so that no one shall be left."

We have translated Latin *saeculum* and equivalents by "world age" here. For the background of this usage, see the Excursus on the Term "Age." It is well known that the Hebrew behind this may mean various things: "world," "age," or "unlimited (past or future) time." It is often difficult or impossible to decide whether in a given passage the meaning "world," or "world age," or "aeon" is intended. The exact equivalation here is complex; we have considered it to mean "world," since the verse deliberately evokes the language and context of creation. However, it should be borne in mind that in verse 32 the earth and dust seem to persist from one "saeculum" to the next. This implies that, although we translate "world," it means something like "world order" or "world age."

The text is well compared with *2 Apoc Bar* 44:9:
For everything will pass away which is corruptible,
and everything that dies will go away,
and all present time will be forgotten.
The reversion to chaos for a week is notable. This is clearly a reference to the seven days of creation. The week of creation, however, ended with a Sabbath, and that Sabbath is very often given an eschatological interpretation. From the point of view of our passage the future age, the world to come, is the eighth day. This intriguingly relates to *Barn.* 15:8: "But that which I have made, in which I will give rest to all things and make a beginning of an eighth day, that is the beginning of another world." It is noteworthy, however, that *Barnabas* is based on a rejection of the acceptability of the Sabbaths of the present order.

■ 31 In *Bib Ant* 3:10 we read:
But when the years of the world shall be fulfilled, then shall the light cease and the darkness be quenched: and I will quicken the dead and raise up from the earth them that sleep: and Hell shall pay his debt and destruction give back that which was committed unto him, that I may render unto every man according to his works and according to the fruit of their imaginations, even until I judge between the soul and the flesh. And the world shall rest, and death shall be quenched, and Hell shall shut his mouth. And the earth shall not be without birth, neither barren for them that dwell therein: and none shall be polluted that hath been justified in me. And there shall be another earth and another heaven, even an everlasting habitation.
This passage echoes many of the themes raised in the pericope we are discussing, from the present verse (7:31) to the end.

Tannaiten (Strassburg: Trübner, 1890) 1:145–46. In general, on rabbinic views, see Finkelstein, *Introduction*, 212–15.

63 Harnisch sees 6:25–28 reflecting traditional material which continues in 7:29–30. It is only with the passing of corruption, he notes, in 7:31 that the true eschatology of the work is presented (p. 128). This observation might be true, if it refers to the blocks with which the edifice of the author's thought is built. If, however, it refers to some literary reality, then problems arise, since the fact of the matter is that it is precisely this sort of eschatology that

predominates in Visions 5 and 6.

64 Cf. *2 Apoc Bar* 31:5. Using quite different language, *Gen. R.* 34:10 (Theodor-Albeck, pp. 321–22) refers to the eventual dissolution of the order of the world, which was guaranteed by the Noachid covenant (Gen 8:21–22).

The seven days of chaos precede the arousal of a world "that is not yet awake" and is well to be compared in its general apocalyptic style with 7:35 and with the "unseen" and "hidden" in 7:26. The actual term is reminiscent of 4:37, where it says "he will not move or arouse" until the end. This language implies that the future age already existed, which of course is what is asserted explicitly in 6:1–6 and in 7:70 (see 6:1 Commentary and 6:6 Commentary). The point has been well taken that this is a renewal of creation rather than a totally new creation and that this is the usual implication of this sort of language in Jewish literature of this age.[65] The term "renew creation" is found in 7:75; see Commentary there, and the concept is also apparently implied by 6:16 and 7:113. In the present pericope the creation story is evoked by the seven days and by the silence.

The passing of the corruptible (the sense is somewhat unclear, is it the "corruptible world" or "corruption" as such?) is the hallmark of the world to come. So *2 Apoc Bar* 40:3 says, speaking of the limited age of the Messiah, "And his principate will stand forever, until the world of corruption is at an end, and until the times aforesaid are fulfilled," and cf. ibid. 44:9, 12. This idea recurs in many other sources, and the corruptible element is, of course, death; cf. 7:15 and *2 Apoc Bar* 21:19, 23, and 42:7 in contrast to life, and see in detail 4:11 Commentary.[66]

Excursus on the Term "Age"

The study of the terminology for "age" is complex.[67] The Latin *saeculum* = Syriac *ʿlm*, and so forth, is equivalent to Hebrew עולם. This word was discussed in some detail as it appears in biblical and extrabiblical sources by E. Jenni. His major conclusions are that in biblical Hebrew, except for Qoh 1:10 and 3:11, it is not used as an independent noun but always adverbially or with a preposition, and further that in all instances in biblical Hebrew, except those two, it means "most distant time" (past or future). In these two latter instances it means "age" or "time."[68]

Jenni also established "most distant time" as the primary meaning of the word in extrabiblical North-West Semitic documents. He traces a development, perhaps under the influence of Greek αἰών, which also translates עלם in Palmyrene bilingual inscriptions, to a meaning of "period of time" or "age," "time," and eventually "world."

The earliest occurrence meaning "world" he discovered in a Palmyrene inscription of 134 c.e. In later Aramaic the absolute form usually means "eternity," "most distant time," while the emphatic form means "world." One of the characteristics of the use of the word in Biblical Hebrew is that it is almost never used as an independent noun but is generally employed in an adverbial sense, most often with a preposition. In the Greek Bible, the only instance of the word in the nominative case is the misreading in Ps 90:8. This indicates that this analysis by Jenni is also reflected by the translators of the Greek Bible. In the Syriac Bible in these instances, ninety had the indefinite form, while only four were definite. When the uses of *ʿlmʾ* in the Syriac of 4 Ezra are examined, the situation is quite different. There are forty-three instances of the definite form, only three of the absolute, and four suffixed forms. The three absolute forms occur with prepositions and clearly mean "most distant time."[69] Armenian reads overwhelmingly

65   Cf. the discussions by Keulers, p. 149, and Jervell, *Imago Dei*, 44, and many references there. See Stone, *Features*, 79, on the concepts involved. The language of renewal of creation is quite widespread; see, e.g., *2 Apoc Bar* 57:2; *1 Enoch* 72:1; *Jub* 1:29; and 4:26. Volz attempts rather schematically to draw various distinctions between different concepts of "renewal of creation" and "new creation" (see pp. 338–40); 4 Ezra, like *2 Apocalypse of Baruch*, seems to expect a renewal of creation. A passage in *Mek. Bešallaḥ* speaks of "the world to come" and "the new world" as two different items in a list of "seven good portions" with which Israel will be blessed if they keep the Sabbath (Horovitz-Rabin, p. 169). The sense of the two terms is not clear.

66   Cf. Isa 25:8. The point is also stressed by Harnisch, p. 128 note, who adduces numerous references. It will, of course, be recalled from Excursus on Adam's Sin that death is what this brought about. Cf. also 1 Cor 15:26. Cf. also Rev 21:4.

67   For detailed statistics and examples, see Stone, *Features*, 149–80.

68   E. Jenni, "Das Wort ʿôlām im Alten Testament," *ZAW* 65 NF 24 (1953) 24; the terminology is also discussed by Harnisch, pp. 90–106.

69   *lʿlm* 8:20 and 9:31; and *mnʿlm* 9:8. But there, Ethiopic and Georgian took the text to mean "from the world."

yawitean in the Bible (98 of 103 instances), while in 4 Ezra, in cases equivalent to *saeculum*, and so forth, *yawitean* occurs only twice, in 8:20 and 9:8, just two of the cases in which Syriac has the sense "most distant time." Armenian lacks 9:31, the third such Syriac reading.

This shared understanding is also borne out by the Latin usage. In Latin, the actual grammatical forms are more ambiguous than in Syriac or Armenian. In two of the three cases that are adverbial in Syriac, Latin also has adverbial usages: 9:8 *a saeculo* and 9:31 *per saeculo*. In 8:20 it takes the word as the object of *inhabitas*, so *qui inhabitas saeculum* alongside Syriac *l'lm* and Armenian *yawitean*. The many uses of *saeculum* in the nominative, accusative, and genitive cases further reflect its role as an independent substantive. Instances of *saeculum* with a preposition but without the adverbial, temporal meaning that the identical form has in the Latin Bible provide a further confirmation of this.[70]

The constructions indicate that 4 Ezra has undergone the major shift of usage from "most ancient time" used in adverbial phrases to a noun meaning something between "time," "age," "world-age," and "world." There is no clear external indicator of which of these meanings may be most appropriate in any given context of 4 Ezra, or even whether they may be truly distinguished. This must be done on contextual grounds.[71] In an examination of the uses in 4 Ezra, the following cases were isolated where the meaning was felt to be unambiguous.

It seemed definitely to mean "age," "world age" in 11:44; 14:10; and 14:11, and also perhaps in 4:36; 7:12–13; and 14:17. It seemed definitely to mean "world" in 5:49; 6:1; 6:59(2x); 7:70; 8:50; 9:20; 11:40; and 13:20.[72]

■ **32** This verse predicts the resurrection of the dead, which will be the first event after the passing of corruption. The idea of the resurrection of the dead is widespread in the Judaism of the age (thus, e.g., Dan 12:2; *1 Enoch* 51:1; and *Sib Or* 4:182).[73] In 7:32 the bodies will arise from the dust (cf. *2 Apoc Bar* 42:8) and the souls from their chambers, and this is the step preceding judgment. The same connection with judgment is found in other passages that deal with resurrection (so 4:33–37 and 14:34–35). In 5:44 and 8:13 nothing is said that contradicts the position of resurrection in the present verse, while the reference in 10:16 is not completely unambiguous.[74] In both 4:33–37 and 14:34–35 resurrection is mentioned as related to, or even the same as, reward of the righteous.

The language of sleep for the dead is found in Dan 12:2; 1 Thess 4:13; 2 Pet 3:4; *Bib Ant* 3:10; 19:12; et al. It is not certain whether it is always connected with the idea of resurrection. The bodies sleep in the earth, and the souls are committed to (see 4:42 Commentary for this expression) their treasuries (on the term "treasuries," see 4:35 Commentary). The reunion of these two elements is resurrection. In 7:75–98 is an extensive passage that deals with the fate of the soul after death, in the intermediate state, preceding resurrection and judgment. There death is described as the separation of the soul from the body (7:78; 7:88; 7:100; cf. 7:75).

After death, the souls of the righteous (not of the wicked) enter treasuries, where they are guarded by angels. This is in exact agreement with 4:35, where only the souls of the righteous in treasuries are mentioned. In

---

70 13:20 *a saeculo,* meaning "from the *saeculum,*" a phrase exactly meaning "of old" in 9:8; cf. Vulg. Gen 6:4; Ps 92(93):2; etc.

71 See 6:7 Commentary for one clear instance. On the concept of two ages, see Excursus on the Two Ages.

72 This is also probably the meaning in 3:34; 4:24; 4:24–27; 5:44; 7:74?; 8:41; 9:5; 9:18(2x); 11:39, and possibly the meaning in 4:11; 7:11; 7:31; 7:112–113; 7:132; 9:2; 14:22. In a number of further instances it is impossible to decide between "world" or "age": 4:2; 6:20; 6:25; 7:47; 7:50; 7:137; 8:1; 8:2; 9:13 (2x); 10:45; 14:20. Expressions like העולם הזה may be observed at 4:2; 4:24; 6:20; 7:13; 7:112; and 8:1; cf. 7:47 probably reflecting העולם הבא. Problematic are the uses in 8:20; 9:8; 9:19; and 9:31. For a detailed analysis of the terminology and its equivalents in 4 Ezra, see Stone, *Features,* 149–80. See further re

Keulers's analysis of the term, ibid., 272–74 n. 429; Harnisch discusses it on p. 105 n. 41.

73 See Oesterley here for many references. In general, see G. W. E. Nickelsburg, *Resurrection, Immortality and Eternal Life in Intertestamental Judaism* (HTS 26; Cambridge: Harvard University, 1972). K. Schubert, "Die Entwicklung der Aufstehungslehre von der nachexilischen bis zur frührabbinischen Zeit," *BZ* NF 6 (1962) 177–214.

74 See 10:16 Commentary.

7:32, however, and 7:101 there is no suggestion of any differentiation between the righteous and the wicked souls at this point of the eschatological process.[75] It is to be questioned whether these are really contradictory views, however, or whether, being convinced that the souls will reside in treasuries, the author speaks of the righteous souls where his discourse is of the righteous (4:35; 7:85; 7:95), while he refers to all souls where his attention is focused more generally (7:32; 7:100).[76] There is no hint in our passage of a dualism that estimated the soul positively while it denigrated the body.

The wonderful divine providence which is evidenced by the process of conception, pregnancy, and birth is extolled in 8:8–13. In 3:5 the body, fashioned from the dust, is said to be the work of God's right hand. The body, the "corruptible vessel" (7:88), returns to the dust from which, as our verse states, it is once again resurrected (cf. also 8:13). Even in 5:50–55, the deterioration of the body is said to be a result of the aging of the earth and not of contact with evil (see 5:52 Commentary). It is important to bear in mind that in the description of the resurrection, there is no suggestion that in the renewal of creation the body or the earth will have lost its material qualities.[77]

■ **33** This verse opens the description of judgment. God alone judges human beings. In the Excursus on the Term "Judgment," p. 151, the other "judgment-like" events are discussed. The divine judgment is a clearly judicial function; the judgment seat is also a legal characteristic. In the Hebrew Bible, the judgment seat is often specifically connected with the king's judicial function.[78]

In Dan 7:9 the divine Judge sits on a throne, and this throne occurs elsewhere in the literature of the Second Temple period.[79] It is this throne which, according to a number of rabbinic sources, is precreated.[80] The enthronement of God as judge marks the beginning of the process of judgment.

The poetic form of this and the following verses, as well as the terminology, is analyzed in 6:11–29 Form and Function. The point made in these verses is that on the day of judgment there will be no role for intercession but only for strict justice. This idea recurs in 4 Ezra and other sources repeatedly. It is related to the notion that judgment is equal for all and is fully revealed at the end.

The absence of intercession does not serve to emphasize the unremitting fate of the sinners (*pace* Gunkel). Their fate is not discussed in any of the relevant passages, nor is any sense of vengeance to be found. The withdrawal of intercession is a function of the full revelation of truth that will characterize final judgment.[81]

■ **34** The verse characterizes judgment and it stresses the intimate relationship between truth and judgment which is witnessed in a number of places in rabbinic thought as well as in 4 Ezra. In *Mek.* on Exod 14:29 (Horovitz-Rabin, p. 112), of the judgment of God, it says הכל באמת והכל בדין ("Every thing is in truth and everything in judgment.")[82] The emphasis on the truth of judgment is related to the withdrawal of mercy at that stage (see 7:33 Commentary). Truth is related to endless glory and eternal peace (1QH 10:27; cf. 1QH 6:12).

■ **35** After judgment, reward and punishment will ensue.

---

75 It is the righteous in *2 Apoc Bar* 30:1, while all types are kept in differentiated chambers in *1 Enoch* 51:1, just to cite one or two parallels; see further 4:35 Commentary.

76 Here no mention is made of any intermediary state of the soul; contrast 7:78–99.

77 It is worth noting in this connection that 7:62 claims that the mind was made of dust.

78 See Isa 16:5; Ps 122:5; Prov 20:8; cf. 1 Kgs 7:7. Ps 9:5 speaks of God's judgment seat; cf. in the New Testament Matt 19:8; 25:31; Luke 22:30; and Rev 3:21; 20:4; 20:11.

79 *1 Enoch* 25:3; 90:20; and of the Son of man in 45:3; 55:4; 61:8; 62:3, 5; and 69:27, 29. The Most High is enthroned, but not as judge, in *Test Patr Levi* 5:1. See also *b. Pesah.* 54a; *b. Ned.* 39b; and *b. Abod. Zar.* 3b.

80 See 3:6 Commentary.

81 The incomplete nature of reward and punishment in this world is stressed in *b. Yeb.* 47a–b. The midrash quoted by Rashi on Gen 1:1 says that "initially God thought to create (the world) with his attribute of judgment. He saw that the world could not survive thus, so he added the attribute of mercy to (the attribute of judgment)." But, we may add, that is clearly less than the ideal situation. Similarly, see the striking passage in *1 Enoch* 50:4–5. See further 7:104 Commentary and also Excursus on the Term "Judgment," p. 150. Hayman, "Pseudonymity," 47–56, deals with the implications of this idea for the concept of God in rabbinic thought.

82 See also *m. Abot* 3:15; and Schechter, *Aspects*, 304–6. See also 1 Esdras 4:38, 40: "Truth endures and is strong forever . . . and there is nothing unrighteous in her judgment." See preceding note for further

The idea is commonplace. The language of our verse is perhaps remotely parented by Isa 40:10: "Behold, the Lord God comes with might, and his arm rules for him; behold, his reward is with him, and his recompense before him." The idea that reward is laid up for the righteous before the Most High occurs in 13:56, and this reward is spoken of in the same sort of way as righteous or wicked deeds.[83] The expression "manifested" reflects, presumably, the concept of the precreation of judgment, on which see 6:6 Commentary; and the terminology "awake, sleep not" is typical of the apocalyptic style of the passage (see 7:31 Commentary).

■ **36** This verse describes the appearance of paradise and Gehenna as a preliminary to the divine address of rebuke that follows in 7:37–38. This description has a number of interesting points in it. The term "appear" may be thought to imply that paradise and Gehenna are already in existence, a concept that has been discussed in 3:6 Commentary.

The two parallel bicola of which the verse is composed give us two terms for the place of reward and two for the place of punishment. The latter is called "pit of torment" and "furnace of Gehenna," while the former is entitled "place of rest" and "paradise of delight." "Torment" is a word often used in 4 Ezra for eschatological punishment or for the intermediate state of the wicked souls.[84] "Pit" is a common term for the underworld in

the Bible (see, e.g., Ezek 31:16 and Ps 28:1); so the expression "pit of torment" indicates the transformation of Sheol to the place of punishment of the wicked. The "furnace of Gehenna" is of course related to the idea that Gehenna will be a fiery place.[85] The place of fire in the punishment of the wicked is preeminent from early times. One verse that had great influence in later times in this connection was Isa 66:24.[86] Fire is also the instrument of the Messiah's action against the wicked nations in Vision 6; see comments in the Excursus on the Redeemer Figure, p. 212.

The place of reward is also described in traditional terms. Opposed to torment is the "place of rest." Rest or quiet is typical in 4 Ezra of the reward of the righteous,[87] corresponding to the profound quiet of the habitations of the righteous in the intermediate state (7:85). Biblical precursors of this are Isa 14:7 and Ps 95:11; in rabbinic texts, compare *b. Sanh.* 110b. "Rest" is thus a technical term of Jewish eschatology. The term "paradise of delight" is probably a literal translation of the rendering of "Garden of Eden" in Greek as παράδεισος τῆς τρυφῆς.[88] This is of course paradise conceived of as the place of eschatological reward.[89] Notable is "true Paradise" of Armenian here and 8:52; see Stone, *Features*, 41, and

references.

83   The presence of the deeds at the time of judgment is mentioned in many sources. It is, of course, a reflection of the basic idea of reward and punishment, which is crucial for eschatological thought. See also 7:77; cf. *2 Apoc Bar* 24:1 and, in a different way, 1 Tim 5:24–25. On the singular/plural variation of "righteousness," see Violet 2.

84   See Stone, *Features*, 77; eschatological punishment here, 7:38; 7:49; 7:67; 7:72; 8:59; 9:9; and 9:12; intermediate state, 7:75; 7:76; 7:80; 7:84; 7:86; and 7:89. Cf. *2 Apoc Bar* 15:6; 30:5; 44:12; 44:15; 51:6; 54:15; 54:21; 55:2; 59:2; 59:11; and 85:9. Different terminology is found in *2 Apoc Bar* 59:10: "the mouth of hell, the standing place of vengeance, the place of faith, the region of hope." Some resemblances of language may be found in *Test Patr Jud* 25:3–6: "fire," "joy," and "sorrow." On "joy," see further 7:28 Commentary. There is a long discussion of Gehenna in *b. Erub.* 19a which, however, does not have particular relationship with our passage.

85   On biblical usage, see *IDB* and *IDBSup* s.v. Latin and

Syriac are to be emended here; see Bensly, *MF*, 55. *1 Enoch* 10:13 describes an "abyss of fire"; cf. 90:24, and a "lake that burns" is described in Rev 19:20 and 21:8.

86   Cf. also Isa 30:33; 31:9; et al. A furnace figures in the parable in 4:48. On fire, see, e.g., *2 Apoc Bar* 44:15; 48:43; 59:11; and *Apocalypse of Peter* (Greek) 22 (James, *Apoc. NT*, 514).

87   See 7:38; 7:75; 7:85; 7:95; and 8:52. See *1 Enoch* 11:2 εἰρήνη. Cf. also Heb 3:18–19; 4:1; 4:9; *Od Sol* 3:5; 8:7; 10:2; 11:3; et al. *2 Apoc Bar* 73:1 predicts that "joy shall then be revealed and rest shall appear."

88   On the terminology of the versions in detail, see Stone, *Features*, 36, 197, and see 7:47. Note the term "paradise" also in 7:123 and 8:52.

89   Observe this picture of Judgment with Paradise and Gehenna standing before the wicked and cf. 7:6 Commentary. On paradise, see further details in 3:6 Commentary.

idem, "Paradise," 88.[90] The same sense is to be found in 7:38; 7:123; and 8:52.[91]

■ **37** Here the divine address to the wicked commences. A rather similar scene of rebuke of wicked nations occurs in *b. Abod. Zar.* 2a–b.[92] The term "nations" here raises the same issue discussed in 7:1–25 Form and Function, n. 31: Is the discussion focused on Israel in contrast to the nations or more generally on the righteous over against the wicked? The terms "nations" and "commandment" might seem to imply the former alternative, but the whole tenor of the description to date seems to point to the latter, with which compare 7:70–74. The denial of God also figures elsewhere in 4 Ezra in such contexts; see 7:23–24; 8:58; and 9:10.[93]

■ **38** The scene described, of the divine judge pointing to the reward and punishment at the start of his address to the raised sinners, bears a resemblance to *Test Abr* B 8:9–11, where the judge sits with the soul before him and there are two gateways, one to paradise and the other to hell. The terminology here closely resembles that in 7:36 and is commented upon in connection with that verse.[94]

■ **39** This verse commences the detailed description of the day of judgment. From here to the end of 7:42a there is a list of divisions of times and seasons that will be abolished at that time. This list is derived from an exegesis of Gen 8:22: "While earth remains, seedtime and harvest, cold and heat, summer and winter, day and night, shall not cease." So, at the end, these divisions will disappear.[95] The eschatological application of this idea in 4 Ezra seems foreshadowed in Zech 14:6–7, describing the day of the Lord's coming:

> On that day there shall be neither cold nor frost. And there shall be continuous day (it is known to the Lord), not day and not night, for at evening time there shall be light.

The same themes are picked up and developed in the third book of the *Sibylline Oracles* (3:88–92):

> There will no longer be twinkling spheres of luminaries, no night, no dawn, no numerous days of care, no spring, no summer, no winter, no autumn. And then indeed the judgment of the great God will come into the midst of the great world.[96]

So the cancellation of these divisions is taken as a characteristic of the day of judgment. Their inception is stated by Gen 1:14 to be part of the process of creation and to be related to the luminaries.[97]

---

90 Even Gen 23:8, usually used by the Rabbis as indicating remote antiquity of paradise, is translated by Targ Y as גינוניתא מטרן לצדיקיא, showing eschatologization. See 3:6 Commentary on this whole issue and see 6:2.

91 On 8:52, which might be thought to have a different sense, see Commentary there. The ideas of paradise are set forth in detail in 3:6 Commentary.

92 See also *Apoc Abr* 29:20 and LXX of Hab 1:5. The expression "Look and understand" seems to have been a cliché; cf. Isa 41:20 and Jer 2:19.

93 See 7:24 Commentary. A similar divine rebuke of the wicked is to be found in *Midr. Mishle* 16:11 (Buber, p. 42a):

> R. Zeira says, "What is the Holy One destined to do to the wicked? He will say to them, 'Wicked, you toiled in vain since you were not busy with the Torah and good deeds, but you were like unwanted, empty vessels in the Holy One's world. Thus he does not want you.' Is it possible that they take their leave and get off free? No! First they will see the joy of the righteous and then they will be condemned to Gehenna."

Here the elements of rebuke and judgment are present, as well as the wicked seeing the reward of the righteous, a theme that recurs in 4 Ezra quite often; see 7:83 Commentary.

94 Armenian and Arabic1 share a special reading "prepared," following "torments"; see textual note q, and see 7:14 Commentary.

95 God rules over day and night and the sun (Ps 74:16) and creates the stars in their orbits and the regular order of nature (Amos 5:8).

96 A different usage, still in an eschatological context, is *Sib Or* 8:425–427. 4 Ezra 7:39 is reused, in a much attenuated form, by *Greek Apoc Esd* 2:29. The cessation of times and seasons in *2 Enoch* 33:2 is attributed by Pines to Zoroastrian ideas. This may be so in the special material relating to time, but the overall framework and conceptions are found in other sources, as indicated above. See S. Pines, "Eschatology and the Concept of Time in the Slavonic Book of Enoch," *Types of Redemption* (ed. R. J. Z. Werblowsky and C. J. Bleeker [Leiden: Brill, 1970] 77–82).

97 Box here would see *Urzeit-Endzeit* patterns at work, but that is not clear.

■ **40, 41** No commentary.

■ **42** In a prophecy of redemption, Isa 60:19–20 reads: The sun shall be no more your light by day, nor for brightness shall the moon give light to you by night; but the Lord will be your everlasting light, and your God will be your glory. Your sun shall no more go down, nor your moon withdraw itself; for the Lord will be your everlasting light, and your days of mourning shall be ended.

Clearly 4 Ezra 7:42b reflects a development and full eschatologization of the ideas of Isaiah.[98] Keulers observed that the term "glory of God" may in fact just be a name for God.[99] Scholem established כבוד (glory) as a theosophic term for him who sits on the throne.[100]

In 4 Ezra, going back to biblical usage, "glory" is connected with the appearance of God on earth. It descends on Sinai (3:19), and the righteous will make God's glory prevail in the world (7:60). It will defend the righteous (7:122). Analogous is the particular eschatological revelation of glory (cf. *2 Apoc Bar* 21:23), which as in our passage is intimately related to judgment. The actual sight of the glory affects judgment (7:87; 7:91), and here in 7:42 a similar case occurs; see also 8:23

Commentary. This is very much like *2 Apoc Bar* 21:25 (of God's majesty); 55:8; and *1 Enoch* 50:4. In 7:112–113 the full revelation of glory removes the possibility of intercessory prayer; that is, glory is not fully revealed except in the world to come.[101]

■ **43** The "week of years," a seven-year period, was often used in apocalyptic reckonings of the times; cf. Dan 9:24; 9:26; *2 Apoc Bar* 28:2; and many other places. Volkmar remarks that the duration of judgment corresponds to the duration of creation (p. 68).

■ **44** This concluding statement is similar to those found at the end of many revelations. It marks the predictive revelatory character of the passage. Note also *2 Apoc Bar* 20:4; 20:6; 4 Ezra 6:33; 8:63; etc. The special character of Ezra is stressed on a number of occasions in the book.[102]

---

98 The word rendered "glory" by Isa is תפארת, while it seems most likely that 4 Ezra goes back to כבוד. This passage is well compared with Rev 21:23, where the glory of God lights the eschatological city. Cf. the description of the state before the cosmogonic acts in Mandean texts: M. Lidzbarski, *Das Johannesbuch der Mandäer* (Giessen: Töpelmann, 1915) 22, lines 1–5. Glory preceded and outshone the luminaries. In 4 Ezra, "glory" may be not only God's but also that of other objects such as paradise or Zion (Violet 2; 7:113; 10:23); cf. on the latter *Pirqe Eliyyahu* (Jellinek, *BM*, 3:69).

99 Keulers, pp. 183–84; cf. 4 Ezra 8:30.

100 See 3:19 Commentary and 7:97 Commentary. The eschatological use of "glory" is discussed in Excursus on the Term "Judgment," p. 150.

101 See Stone, *Features*, 59–61, 206. A similar concept is to be observed in *2 Apoc Bar* 55:8. The withdrawal of God's glory is described in Ezek 11:22–25; cf. Hos 5:6, 15. The glory of Zion is referred to in 10:23 and 10:50; see Commentary. In 10:55, "splendor" describes the brilliance of the heavenly Jerusalem. The Shekinah (the divine presence) is removed for the world according to the Rabbis, for various reasons; see Schechter, *Aspects*, 223 et al. (Box *ad* 7:112).

102 See 6:32 Commentary.

7

45 I answered and said, "O Lord, [a] I said then [b] and I say now: Blessed are those who are alive and keep thy commandments! [c] **46/** But what of those concerning whom I asked? [d] For who among the living [e] is there that has not sinned, or who among men that has not transgressed thy covenant? [f] **47/** And now [g] I see that the world to come will bring [h] delight to few, but torments to many. **48/** For an evil heart [i] has grown up [i] in us, which has alienated us from this, [j] and has brought us into corruption [k] and the ways of death, and has shown us the paths of perdition [l] and removed us far from life—and that not just a few of us but almost [m] all who have been created!"

49 He answered me and said, "Listen to me, Ezra, and I will instruct [n] you, and will admonish you yet again. **50/** For this reason the Most High has made not one world but two. [o] **51/** For whereas you have said that the righteous are [p] not many [q] but few, while the ungodly abound, [r] hear the explanation for

Notes

45 a Lat, Syr add "Lord" which is the basis of RSV; cf. 7:75 note a; Eth Mss omit; Arm omits "O . . . now."

a–b Lat, Syr; other versions omit. Presumably both forms existed in Greek. The proximity of two or three forms of the verb "to speak" in the various versions has engendered the confusion. They are all present only in Syr; Lat omits the first, and the remaining versions omit the second.

c Lat, Syr add "which were established by you."

46 d *Erat oratio mea* Lat, apparently giving rise to RSV "for whom I prayed"; Georg *locvay*1 corresponds to ἐρωτάω in the NT, as well as παρακαλέω, while *locvay*2 corresponds to προσεύχομαι, δέομαι, etc.; the verb is omitted by Eth, Ar1, Ar2, Arm; see Commentary here.

e Syriac 〈 *παρόντες; Latin 〈 *παρόντες (Bensly, MF).

f Lat, Ar1; "commandment" Syr, Eth, Arm; *legem* Georg.

47 g Georg, Ar1, Arm add "as."

h Lat *pertinebit* 〈 *μελήσει for *μελλήσει (Bensly, MF). Uses reflecting μελλεῖν are frequent, some examples being 7:75; 7:88; 7:122; 13:29; 13:46; and others exist.

48 i–i Lat, Eth; "is" Syr; "is set" Georg; other versions vary.

j Syr, Eth; original text uncertain; Lat *ab his;* the other versions vary.

j–l This part of the verse is shortened Ar2, Arm.

j–k Ar1 expands into two hemistichs.

k–l The number of verbs varies. Lat has one verb *ostendit,* which is construed with the first phrase, but the second phrase starts very abruptly with a hiatus. Eth, Georg have a similar verb, but it is construed with the last phrase and the two parts of the verse are linked by "and." Syr links both phrases with "and" and also adds a second verb; its text is more pleasing on a literary plane, but on text-critical grounds we have preferred that of Eth, Georg, which versions also have the indirect support of Lat, Arm.

m Lat, Syr; Eth omits; Ar1, Ar2 vary; Arm omits.

49 n The verb varies somewhat in the versions, but they all reflect the same basic text.

50 o The verse is formulated as a question in Ar1, Ar2.

51 p–q The phrase varies in Eth, Georg.

q–r Lat, Ar1, Ar2, Arm; Syr omits.

q–s "Make yourself a vessel of clay and lead" Eth, Georg. These two versions clearly go back to a

this. 52/ If you have just a few precious stones, [s] will you add to them [t] lead and clay?" [u] 53/ I said, "Lord, how could that be?"

54/ And he said to me, [v]"Not only [w] that, but ask the earth and she will tell you; address [x] her, and she will declare it to you.

55/ Say to her, 'You produce gold and silver and brass, [y] and iron and lead and clay; 56/ [z]but silver is more abundant than gold, and brass than silver, and iron than brass, and lead than iron, and clay than lead,' [a] 57/ Judge therefore which things are precious and desirable, those that are abundant or those that are rare?"

58 I said, "O sovereign [b] Lord, what is plentiful is of less worth, for what is more rare is more precious."

59 He answered me and said, [c]"Weigh within yourself what you have thought, [d] for he who has what is hard to get rejoices more than he who has what is plentiful. 60/ So also will be the judgment [e] which I have promised; [f] for I will rejoice over the few who shall be saved, [g] because it is they who have made my glory to prevail [h] now, and through them my name has now been honored. [i] 61/ And I will not grieve over the multitude of those who perish; for it is they who are now [j]like a mist, and are [j] similar to a flame [k] and smoke—they are set on fire and burn hotly and are extinguished."

62 I replied and said, [l]"O earth, what have you brought forth [m] if the mind is made out of the dust like the other created things! [n] 63/ For it would have been better if the dust itself had not been born, so that the mind might not have been made from it. [o] 64/ But now the mind grows with us, and therefore we are tormented, because we perish and know it.

65/   Let the human race lament,
            but let the beasts of the field be glad;
        let all who have been born lament,
            but let the [p]four-footed beasts and the flocks [p] rejoice!

66/ For it is much better with them than with us; for they do not look for a judgment, nor do they know of any torment or life [q] promised to them after death. 67/ For what does it profit

common Greek in all the variant readings in this lemma. It was shorter than the text behind Lat, Syr. Doubtless the present text of Eth, Georg is the result of a correction after the loss of the preceding material left a torso. Bensly (MF) is of the view that the loss was caused by hmt.

52   s–t Or "will you set alongside them" or "reckon with them"; so Syr, cf. Ar1, Arm. Lat has *plumbum autem et fictile habundat* drawn from 7:58 (Violet 1).
      u Ar2 corrupt; Arm expanded.

54   v–w Ar1, Ar2, Arm omit.
      x Syr, Eth, Georg; "ask," "request" Ar1, Ar2; *adulare* Lat, presumably giving rise to RSV "defer to."

55   y Lat adds *quoque;* so RSV "also."

56   z–a Ar2, Arm start with "clay" or "dust" and conclude with "gold," to which Arm adds "precious stones"; Georg is confused.

58   b Eth, Georg, Ar2 omit "sovereign"; Ar1, Arm omit "sovereign Lord."

59   c–d Ar2, Arm omit.

60   e Lat, Georg *creatura,* i.e., κτίσις for κρίσις (Violet 1); it is not certain that this is a conjunctive error, since the variant is not uncommon (see 6:38 note c).
      f Georg breaks off here and resumes at 7:76.
      g "Live" Syr, Eth; Ar2, Arm vary.
      h Three Greek readings seem to be reflected: (1) κυριεύουσι (Lat as emended); (2) κυροῦσι ⟨ κυρόω (Syr, Ar2); (3) κυροῦσι ⟨ κυρέω (Eth, Georg); Ar1, Arm vary. RSV has followed Lat. See also Gressmann *apud* Violet, ad loc.
      i "Named" Lat, Ar1; Arm seems to have a doublet "who glorified his name . . . and by whom his name is praised."

61   j–j Eth omits, cf. Ar1; Ar2 varies.
      k Ar1, Ar2, Arm all interpret "fire" as "hell fire"; see Commentary.

62   l–n Lat; Box interprets "O earth, what hast thou brought forth, if the mind. . . . It had been better"—so also RSV. Violet 1 gives *O tu terra, quid peperisti! Si sensus . . . melius [enim] erat. . . .* Violet's understanding is also reflected by Syr's longer text, "Oh, what hast thou done, O earth, that these have been born from thee and go into destruction. If, now, the mind . . ."; cf. Arm "O earth! Why did you bear man?" Eth, Ar1, Ar2 vary. The text is uncertain.
      m–n So Lat, Syr; Eth differs, omitting the reference to "mind" or "heart," see, however, 7:63; Ar1, Ar2, Arm omit.

63   o Lat, Syr, cf. Ar2; Ar1, Eth vary; Arm omits.

65   p–p "Herds of cattle" Eth; "quadrupeds" Ar1, Arm.

66   q *Salvationem* Lat; "resurrection" Ar2, Arm; cf. Lat 7:67 *salvati salvibimur.*

us that we shall be preserved alive [r] but cruelly tormented? [s] 68/ For all who have been born are involved in iniquities, and are full of sins and burdened with transgressions. 69/ And if we were not to come into judgment after death, perhaps it would have been better for us."

70 He answered me and said, "When the Most High made [t] the world and [u]Adam and all who have come from him, [v] he first prepared the judgment and [w]the things that pertain to the judgment. [x] 71/ And now understand [y] from your own words, for you have said that the mind grows with us. 72/ For this reason, therefore, those who dwell on earth shall be tormented, because

> though they had understanding
> > they committed iniquity,
> and though they received the commandments
> > they did not keep them,
> and though they obtained the law
> > they [z]dealt unfaithfully [z] with what they received.

73/ What, then, will they have to say in [a] judgment, or how will they answer in the last times? 74/ For how long the time is that the Most High has been patient with those who inhabit the world, and not for their sake, but because of the times which he has foreordained!"

67 r For Lat, see previous notes. Here and in the next verb reflexes of Hebrew infinitive absolute and finite verb are to be found in the various versions.

r–s Eth omits perhaps by hmt.

70 t Lat *faciens faciebat;* cf. Syr.

u–v Lat, Ar1, cf. Arm; Syr, Eth have texts like "the judgment for Adam. . . ."

w–x Eth, Ar1, Arm vary.

71 y Arm omits to the middle of 7:72.

72 z–z Lat; the verb varies in the other versions.

73 a "The day of" Ar1, Ar2, Arm.

Form and Structure

This pericope is complex from the point of view of its form and structure. Leaving aside various suggestions that part or all of it is a secondary addition, suggestions that are both poorly argued and contradictory,[1] the issue of the general characterization and structure of the passage is well raised. In overall terms, we have designated it as a dialogic dispute. Ezra puts questions that urge his point of view over against that of the angel, and this is characteristic of the disputes, in contrast to predictive dialogue (Prediction 1) sections in which the seer's queries are designed to elicit more information on a given point, not to argue a specific position.

The pericope falls into a number of divisions:[2]

A. *Sustained address by Ezra (7:45–48)*

B. *The angel's response, composed of two parts:*
 1. Admonishment of Ezra on the question of two worlds (7:49–50)
 2. Introduction of the parable, in response to the issue of the few and the many (7:51–52)

C. *Ezra's brief prompt (7:53)*

D. *The angel's setting forth of the parable in detail (7:54–57)*

E. *Ezra's stating of the moral of the parable (7:58)*

F. *The angel's drawing out the implications of this, setting them into the context of Ezra's address in section A, above (7:59–61)*

G. *Ezra's lament, harking back to A (7:62–69)*

H. *The angel's detailed, concluding response (7:70–74).*

This response takes up various themes, such as the two worlds and the precreation of judgment from section

1 Hilgenfeld considers 7:45–111 to be a secondary addition, chiefly on the grounds that it rehearses issues a second or third time. Gunkel considers such repetitions, however, to be related to the author's personality (p. 340). See comments on this in Introduction, sec. 3.2.1. De Faye regards various parts of Vision 3 as Christian addition, including 7:45–64, a point of view widely rejected; see already Keulers, p.

43. Kaminka considers 7:45 to resume the genuine text, which had been interrupted by the secondary insertion of 7:26–44.

2 Brandenburger, *Verborgenheit,* would see two different sections where we see only one: 7:45–61 and 7:62–74 (p. 143 n. 167). This division is then adopted by Harnisch.

B; disobedience from section A; and the predetermination and delay of judgment which relate both to the first part of this section and to the material starting in 7:102.

When we look at Vision 3 as a whole we see that the simple pattern of Visions 1 and 2—viz., address, dispute, Prediction 1, and Prediction 2—has been expanded into a number of subcycles. One is composed of the elements of address, dispute, and Prediction 2 and extends from 6:38 to 7:44. Then ensue a dispute and a prediction and a second dispute-like passage covering 7:45–8:3. This is followed by a monologue and a prayer and finally by another dispute (8:4–63). A revelatory prediction passage (9:1–13) concludes the whole vision. The present pericope, therefore, may be seen as opening the second subsection of the vision.[3]

A. Ezra's Speech (7:45–48)

Since this dispute opens a new subsection, it starts with a speech that functions in miniature as do the addresses with which the four first visions commence. Its parts seem to exhibit no notable literary forms, except for the exclamation "Blessed are . . . !" (7:45), which may be comparable with the benedictions of Matthew 5 and *2 Enoch* 52, but see already Ps 1:1; 119:1; and 119:22.[4] The passage is tied to the preceding part of the book by the literary element "For now I see . . ." (7:47) and by the reference to the evil heart in 7:48 (see 3:20).[5] Moreover, although expressions like "ways of death" and "paths of perdition" are not uncommon (see 7:6 Commentary), their use here may specifically point forward to the enumeration, in 7:80–87, of the seven paths the wicked soul must traverse.

B. Angelic Response (7:49–52)

In the formulation of the angel's response the author uses a technique that was already noted by Harnisch (p. 237). He takes Ezra's words in the speech about the two worlds which focus the problem for him in 7:47 and changes their stress and treats them as a solution. Other examples of this technique may be observed in 7:71;

7:112–115; and 8:37. The argumentative style of 7:51, "For whereas . . . ," is also notable. Then the imagery of the parable is introduced (7:52), although the actual usage of the imagery differs from that of the parable that is to follow.

D. The Parable (7:54–57)

This small speech, which commences in 7:54, contains a number of interesting literary elements and techniques. It opens with two stichs in parallelism, giving a solemn and biblical flavor (7:54). Ezra is then told, "Ask the earth . . . ,"[6] with exactly the same rhetorical form and technique used in 4:40 and, *mutatis mutandis,* in 5:51 and 10:9. Moreover, the direct speech to Ezra in 7:57 "Judge therefore . . . ," greatly resembles 4:18, also following a parable: "If now you were a judge between them . . ."; see Commentary there and compare also 4:31. In this passage, then, the parable is presented not just as a didactic exemplar but is set forth in a lively style, using techniques designed to enhance the vivacity of the dialogue.

F. Angelic Response: Implications (7:59–61)

Here the angel uses Ezra's response given in 7:58 to make his point, just as he did in 4:20–21. The similarity between these two passages is notable. The same technique is also employed in 7:71 and 8:37.

G. Ezra's Lament (7:62–69)

This is the most complex of the literary sub-units in this pericope. It is divided into two sections by leading statements and concludes with a third. The first is 7:62, the apostrophe to the earth. The second is 7:65, containing two parallel stichs of lament, while the whole concludes with the statement, "It would have been better. . . ." Following 7:62 and 7:65 ensues an explication of Ezra's reasons for making such provocative proclamations (7:63–64 and 7:66–68). The structure of 7:69 is also interesting, as the verse combines the two elements found throughout the lament, a combative lament statement in its first part and then the cliché "It would

---

3   See General Structure of the book, p. 50.
4   See on this form G. W. E. Nickelsburg, *Jewish Literature Between the Bible and the Mishnah,* 187 and note. A similar form with related contents is *Ps Sol* 18:6: "Blessed shall they be that shall be in those days."
5   It seems in turn to be referred to in 8:37–41.
6   Note that Ezra's speech in 7:62 opens with an address

to the earth. Comparable in technique but not in content are also Job 12:8 and 16:18, while *2 Apoc Bar* 6:8 and 11:6 bear a superficial resemblance to our passage.

have been better . . ." in the second. This latter, of course, picks up a common *topos,* "It would have been better if we were not born" (see 4:12 Commentary).

H. Angelic Response (7:70–74)

This quite sustained response concludes the discussion in the pericope. Chapter 7:71 uses the same technique as 7:59, that is, it turns Ezra's words against his own argument.

Function and Content

The pericope carries the argument yet one stage farther. In 7:1–25 the issues of the suffering of the righteous (?Israel) in this world in contrast with the joy of the world to come and the reason for these sufferings were to the fore. Starting with a discussion of Israel/nations and the relationship between them and suffering of this world, it moves to a discussion of the righteous and the wicked and the world to come. This subject is sustained throughout 7:26–44, where the day of judgment and the situation of the righteous and the wicked in judgment are prominent. The present passage, accepting that the world to come is for the righteous, is concerned with the consequential issue of the few and the many. It makes no reference at all to the contrast of Israel and Gentiles, only of righteous and wicked. In 7:1–25 Function and Content, pp. 194–95, we pointed out that these two pairs are not exclusive, but of course the selection of one rather than another betrays the emphasis of the passage.

Ezra laments the perdition of the many wicked and the tiny number of the saved righteous, only to be told by the angel that this is the way judgment has been predetermined.[7] Ezra bewails the human state, to which the angel responds with a strong assertion of free will and human responsibility.

In 7:45–48, taking his departure from the revelation of the nature of judgment in 7:26–44, Ezra says, "I said then and I say now." In fact, nothing resembling this quotation verbatim is to be found in the book, although the sense of it is present in 7:17–18 and is reasserted by

the angel in 7:25. Indeed, this has often been seen as a reference to 7:17–18.[8] The idea that nearly all humans have sinned because of the evil heart was prominent in Vision 1.[9] Ezra has now accepted the notion of eschatological judgment, of reward for the righteous and punishment of the wicked. At once, as a result, the issue of the few and the many arises. The overall tenor resembles 7:1–25 in many ways, but there the focus is different, for it is on the suffering of the righteous in this world, while here it is on the punishment of the wicked in the world to come. The motivation is not eschatological reward, it is the present quandary which only becomes evident once the revelation about reward has been made and accepted.

"For this reason," the angel says, "the Most High has made not one world but two." This assertion by the angel in 7:50 is not immediately clear. The unclarity stems from the fact that the reason is made explicit only by the following verses. In broad terms the connection is obvious: the promise of eschatological reward implies that God values the righteous highly and so will reward them. To do so, he created the world to come, in which they will be separated from the wicked.

In 7:52 the concepts of precious matter and worthless matter are introduced as an image for the righteous and the wicked. Ezra is asked whether, if he possessed a few precious stones he would add lead and clay to them. His negative answer is a foregone conclusion; so too does God act with respect to the righteous. Taken as it stands, then, this pericope states that there are two worlds so that in the world to come God, the owner of the precious stones, that is the righteous, may keep them separate and unmixed with the lead and clay of the wicked. In the present world, it follows, they are thoroughly mixed.[10]

As many commentators have noted, this implies a rather severe attitude on God's part and a correspondingly pessimistic one on the part of the seer.[11] The angel does not stop with this answer but continues to develop his idea and his parable. He uses the analogy of the

---

7 Brandenburger, *Verborgenheit,* 177–78, points out that usually the angel says "few—many," while Ezra uses a series of expressions designed to highlight the minuscule number of the few.

8 Violet sees a reference to 4:12–13.

9 See Excursus on Adam's Sin.

10 There have been various suggestions as to the secondary nature of the verse; see Hartom and Violet

2. The arguments that would set it at 8:1 are not convincing.

11 See, e.g., 7:46; 8:31; 8:35; 9:14f. Cf. Thompson, *Responsibility,* 210–11. On 212 he proposes in detail, once more, that Ezra's views are nationalistic and Uriel's universal, and that the righteous and the wicked are differently defined by Ezra and by Uriel.

descending order of precious metals and the inverse order of the frequency of their occurrence to point out that the rarer is the more precious (7:54–57). Having received Ezra's assent to this proposition (7:58), he then demonstrates that people rejoice if they gain the rare but are unmoved by the lack of the common dirts. So, he reasons, God acts, rejoicing over the few righteous but taking no account of the many wicked (7:59–61; cf. in general 7:127–131). This parable and its implications are clearly restated in succinct compass in 8:1–3.

The angel's whole argument is no more than a repetition of the point made by Ezra, but with a distinct change of emphasis. There are indeed few righteous and many wicked, and the reward will indeed come after the separation of the righteous from the wicked, but this is *as God desires it.* God rejoices in the righteous and grieves not over the wicked.

Ezra responds to this rather severe reply not by argument but by lament. The lament over the mind, and the radical statements about the futility of creation and of human consciousness, are very striking.[12] No new argument is put forth here, just a repetition of the same problems that had moved him at the start of the pericope. The implications of the angel's statement about the nature of God are taken up subsequently; the seer's immediate response is a cry of distress. He had opened his address at the start of the pericope with the cry, "Blessed are those who are alive and keep thy commandments!" He concludes the body of his argument and lament in 7:69 with the contrasting "And if we were not to come into judgment after death, perhaps it would have been better for us."

The angel concludes the pericope with his carefully argued reply to this, taking up things that were demonstrated earlier in the book. The argument is that *(a)*

judgment is preordained, that is, human action was foreseen and its results provided for in advance. It is to Harnisch that we are indebted for the acute observation that 7:70 is a response to 7:62–63. Ezra should not reproach the earth or creation. Punishment was determined in advance.[13] *(b)* The fact that human beings have a mind means that they exercise free will and consequently bear the results of their action. This might be seen as a response to the tendency evident in 7:46, etc., the view that sin is inevitable. *(c)* This is true also in the case of the Torah, which was given to human beings and which they did not observe. The statement in 7:74 is a little odd. It is as if the angel wishes to forestall a question of Ezra's about the delay of the eschaton. This is not an indication of God's departure from the principles of free will but, as was asserted in Vision 1, a result of the preordained order of times.

Commentary

■ **45** The Latin and Syriac versions read "O Lord, Lord." This is actually an epithet of God, and the angel is often addressed as God in the book.[14] The expression "I said then and I say now" seems to be a reference to something Ezra has said previously. Although certain scholars have suggested 7:17–18 as the place referred to, that does not seem likely.[15] Consequently, either this is a cross-reference with no referent or a general expression meaning something like, "I have often said."

The sentiment that those who are alive and keep the commandments are blessed is a commonplace; see Ps 1:1; 119:1; 119:2; Luke 11:28; and Rev 22:7.[16] This commonplace provides an appropriate point of departure for Ezra, who, in the next verse, proceeds to pose questions that emerge from it. The small number of those who survive is one of the main concepts lying in the back-

---

12   See Excursus on Inspiration, pp. 122–23, on the lament over the mind. There has been a good deal of discussion of the term reflected by Latin *sensus* and parallels. Violet 2 and Harnisch, p. 157, suggest that it was יצר הרע, but this seems to be very difficult to sustain on exegetical and textual grounds. Thus, e.g., 7:64 is a stumbling block for this theory. See also 7:62 Commentary and 7:64 Commentary.

13   Harnisch, pp. 160–62. He sees in this a polemic against dualist views that he perceives to be latent in 7:62–69. But if one does not accept his view that *sensus* = יצר הרע, this view becomes unnecessary.

14   See 3:4 Commentary and 7:17 Commentary.

15   This matter is discussed in Function and Content, p. 228. Note, moreover, that it is a set expression, recurring in 9:15.

16   "Alive" is more literally "those who come" in Latin, and see on this terminology 4:12 Commentary.

ground of the present verse. It is discussed above (5:41 Commentary) and made even more explicit in 7:59–61.[17] Thus, in 7:46, Ezra proceeds to ask, Indeed these survivors are blessed, but what about the rest of mankind? The extreme formulation of this position is to be found in the almost nihilistic lament of 7:62–69 and see also 7:116.[18] This problem is already inherent in the angel's response in 7:20 and is not alleviated by the angelic replies here, culminating in 7:59–61.[19]

■ **46** We have chosen "concerning whom I asked." The textual situation reflected in textual note e is ambiguous at least. The translation "asked" avoids the idea of intercessory prayer, present in alternative renderings of the phrase. Note that there has been no such prayer, but a questioning about this topic may be discerned in 7:17–18.

"For who among the living": see a similar expression in 4:6. This term means human beings,[20] and not just those presently alive, since it is parallel to "men" (Schreiner). We find both terms combined in a single phrase in *Greek Apoc Esd* 5:27: τίς ἄρα ἄνθρωπος γεννηθείς ("Which man having been born").

The broad assertion made by this verse is that all who are born have violated or transgressed the covenant. This has been seen as an expression of the author's pessimism about mankind. The general observation that no human being is without sin is a very ancient one,[21]

and is found repeatedly in scripture; see 1 Kgs 8:46 = 2 Chron 6:36; Prov 20:9; and Qoh 7:20; cf. also *Greek Apoc Esd* 5:26.[22] What is open to question is how exactly it is to be taken. At one level, a consciousness of the universal sinfulness of mankind is inherent in certain modalities of religious understanding. At another, such a consciousness can be transformed into part of a systematic theological outlook. Ezra must twice be assured that he himself is not one of the sinners (7:76; 8:47). In his creation recital he speaks of the universality of the evil heart (3:20–22; 3:26; cf. 4:38), and statements much like that here may also be found in 7:68 and 8:35. These verses seem to indicate that not just a general sense of human sinfulness is at work here but certain more systematic views. At the least, he has embodied such views into his argumentation.[23] The seer, however, often starts his argumentation with rather extreme formulations issuing from his own internal struggles, so we must beware of over-systematization of his thought and interpret it in the light of his rhetorical techniques, *inter alia*. See further 7:67 Commentary on this.

The complex issue of whether the Gentiles were obligated to keep the Torah or commandments has been discussed in detail at 3:32 Commentary and 7:1–25 Function and Content, pp. 194–95.

■ **47** The same idea, that this world is for many but the coming world for few, is found in 8:1–3. It is used

---

17 Cf. a rather similar formulation by Philo in *De migr. Abr.* 61. *Tanh. Buber Berešit* 29 (p. 21) relates that Adam said to the Holy One, in the context of discussion of his sin, "I am not concerned about the wicked who will be, who are going to die, but about the righteous, lest they complain against me."

18 See further in 7:62 Commentary. Note that Armenian here introduces nihilistic phrases from 4:12, which also influenced Armenian of 7:116. On the sentiment so expressed, see *Armenian Text Commentary*.

19 The sentiment is expressed as an accepted statement by the seer in 9:14–16, a graphic illustration of the developmental dynamic of the book.

20 See Harnisch, pp. 102–3.

21 Note the Sumerian text cited by Myers: "Never has a sinless child been born to its mother . . . a sinless workman has not existed from of old," from *ANET Supplementary Texts* (Princeton: Princeton University, 1969) 154.

22 For rabbinic views, see the discussion in Moore, *Judaism*, 1:468–69.

23 Harnisch points out that tension seems to exist between this verse, asserting that all have sinned, and the next verse, referring to the few righteous, i.e., implying that some have not sinned. For this latter concept, see also 7:140; 9:14–15; and 10:10 (pp. 229–30). See 10:10 Commentary for yet another perspective. This shows, Harnisch maintains, that the purpose of the author is to set up the argument so as to show Ezra later abandoning or changing his position. A similar view was already put forth by Brandenburger, *Adam und Christus*, 30, 35. A critique of these views is given by Thompson, *Responsibility*, 303–10, but his position is too extreme, as is pointed out in 10:10 Commentary.

differently here, however, for here Ezra employs it to give point to his disputatious question, while there it is part of the angel's response.[24] The terminology "this world" and "the world to come" is commonplace in Jewish sources.[25] Likewise, the terms "delight" and "torments" are standard for eschatological reward.[26] The issue of the few and the many runs through the rest of this vision; see, for example, 7:59–61; 7:140; 8:1–3; 9:15; and 10:10.[27]

■ **48** Violet regards all of the words from "shown us . . . life" as a secondary doublet, which assumption seems superfluous. The idea of the evil heart is discussed in detail in the Excursus on Adam's Sin, pp. 63–69. In the expression "has estranged us from this" the meaning of "this" is unclear, and there are various speculations about its original.[28] The term "corruption" means "death" and is discussed in 4:11 Commentary and the role of death or perdition in the Excursus on Adam's Sin, pp. 65–66. The two paths or ways, one of life and the other of death, are also found elsewhere in the book (see 7:6 Commentary).[29] Like death, "life" is a technical term for eschatological recompense.[30] The term "almost all" here and in 10:10 (though we do not accept the reading there) is crucial in the arguments put forth by scholars concerning the universality of sin or the contrary. See n. 49 below.

■ **49** This verse has a sapiential character. The phrase "hear . . . instruct" occurs almost verbatim in 5:32; in general, compare also 10:38. The language of wisdom, as well as literary forms drawn from wisdom literature, is to be found throughout the book applied to the angel's

teaching or the secrets revealed to Ezra; compare, for example, 14:18 (and Commentary). The language and the style drawn from the wisdom tradition are found widely in the Jewish literature of the age, designating a variety of different contents.[31]

■ **50** This is one of the clearest statements in the book of the existence of two ages, which is a central concept in the author's thought.[32] The term "age" (Lat: *saeculum* etc.) is analyzed in the Excursus on the Term "Age." The chief exegetical problem of the verse, its relationship to its context, has been discussed in Function and Content, p. 228.

■ **51** Brandenburger observes that this verse is the angel's correction of Ezra's word in 7:47 and, we may add, particularly in 7:46.[33] We have already commented on the technique of one speaker taking up the words of the other and refocusing them.[34] This is part of the author's stock in trade, and he uses it effectively here.

■ **52** Here the parable of the precious and base metals, used to signify the righteous and the wicked, is introduced. Another image used by the author for the righteous and the wicked is that of the droplets and the wave in 9:14.[35] It is the custom of our author to use such parabolic images, drawn from the world of nature, and, indeed, he returns to some of them repeatedly,[36] such as the woman and womb (see 4:40 Commentary), or the fruit, the sowing and reaping (see also 3:20 and 4:28 Commentary).

■ **53** No commentary.

---

24 It also occurs in a parable in 8:41, and see further 7:20; 7:51; 7:60–61; 8:3; 8:55; 9:15; and 9:21. See also the discussion in 8:37–62a Function and Content.

25 See Excursus on the Two Ages, p. 92, and also Stone, *Features*, 76–77.

26 See 7:36 Commentary. Ethiopic renders "torments" as "judgments"; see Excursus on the Term "Judgment," n. 53.

27 See also 8:37–62a Function and Content, pp. 280–81.

28 The most attractive is Violet's "from life"; cf. with the last phrase of the verse, and see also "alienated from the life of God" in Eph 4:18. There is, however, no compelling reason to accept any particular suggestion. The terminology occurs in Ps 58:3; see MT and Greek.

29 Expressions similar to "paths of perdition" occur in Jer 21:8; Prov 14:12; cf. Job 28:22–23.

30 See Excursus on Adam's Sin, p. 66.

31 Nickelsburg and Stone, *Faith and Piety*, 223–30.

32 See the analysis of the verse in Stone, *Features*, 58–59. On the concept and its implication, see Excursus on the Two Ages, pp. 92–93; the term is discussed there. Observe the dictum in *Gen. R.* 53:12 (Theodor-Albeck, p. 569): "Everyone who confesses two worlds (ages) will inherit two worlds (ages)."

33 Brandenburger, *Adam und Christus*, 30–31.

34 See Form and Structure, p. 227.

35 See also Harnisch, p. 231, on this passage.

36 On the use of nature, and particularly on the repetition of images drawn from the natural world, see Excursus on Natural Order, p. 102. A parallel to this use of metals has been found in Tertullian, *De*

■ **54** This verse marks the beginning of the parable that is the chief feature in the next five verses. The angel's somewhat formal address to Ezra marks its opening. Similar openings occur elsewhere in the book.[37]

■ **55** Lead appears in this list, in contrast to that implied by Dan 2:32–33; compare, however, Num 31:22; Ezek 22:18; and 22:20. A somewhat different view of the origins of minerals is implied by *1 Enoch* 65:7–8, which sets the origins of tin and lead in a different way from that of silver.

■ **56, 57** No commentary.

■ **58** The address "sovereign Lord" properly appertains to God; see 3:4 Commentary. However, at numerous points in the book the angel is addressed or referred to as if he were God; see 7:17 Commentary on this.

■ **59** "Weigh within yourself what you have thought" clearly refers not just to the preceding verse but to the implications of that preceding verse. This is obvious when it is set alongside Ezra's strong statement in 7:45. The idea that the righteous survivors are only few in number has occurred before; see 5:41 Commentary. It is also prominent in the next verse.

■ **60** "Name" here is parallel to "glory." They are both rather similar to hypostases, characteristics of God treated as if they were independent entities. For further details on "glory," see 7:42 Commentary and on "name" 4:25 Commentary. The two terms are brought together in *Apoc Abr* 29:17: "in the glory of my name." On language of "grief" and "rejoicing" in 7:60–61, see 7:131 Commentary.[38]

■ **61** The problem of the few and the many is taken up once more, this time from the angel's viewpoint; in general, see 7:45 and 7:46 Commentary. Here the idea is expressed that God sets no store by the wicked, a view already found in earlier sources: Ps 37:28; 37:34–36; 37:38; *1 Enoch* 94:10–11; and 97:2; compare differently Sir 12:14. The wicked are likened to mist or vapor, fire and smoke, all evanescent phenomena. These images are commonplace and may be found in the Hebrew Bible as well as in 4 Ezra and other apocryphal literature.[39]

■ **62** Ezra apostrophizes the earth, which he does elsewhere in diverse contexts throughout the book.[40] The question he poses to the earth, Why was the mind created with mankind? is an adaptation of a common *topos*, the question "Why was I born?" which was raised early in the book and which is also behind the formulation of 7:48.[41] Moreover, he has taken up yet another of his dominant themes when he refers to the earth as a mother or a womb which brings forth the mind (see 4:40 Commentary). Thus this verse opens the lament over the mind, which is discussed in detail in the Excursus on Inspiration, pp. 122–23. In general, the lament here may be compared with 4:12–22, and the overall structure of thought is comparable to 7:116–126.[42]

The crucial issue here exegetically has been the question of the exact denotation of "mind" or "heart" (see Ethiopic: that seems secondary). It is created with human beings and is apparently not the same as the soul. In the Excursus on Inspiration, pp. 122–23, we suggested that it means something like "consciousness." Gunkel thought that Greek νοῦς or the like might have stood behind the Latin *sensus*.[43]

resurrectionis 7. Other parallels exist and it is not at all certain that Tertullian depends on 4 Ezra.

37 See Form and Structure above.

38 See Excursus on Adam's Sin, n. 37.

39 On the smoke or vapor, see 4:48 Commentary. The use of the image to stress the impermanence of humans has biblical origins; so Hos 13:3; Ps 144:4; and Job 7:7. See 4 Ezra 4:48–51 and also Wisd 2:2, 4 and James 4:14. Smoke serves the same end in Ps 37:20, while the burning of fire symbolizes impermanence in Isa 43:17 and Ps 118:12; see the same image in 4 Ezra 4:48–50; cf. also 4QpPs37 2:8. Arabic1, Arabic2, and Armenian seem to construe the fire as hell fire; see textual notes. This is also the view of Volkmar (p. 73).

40 Another apostrophe to the earth is implied by 4:40.

41 See 4:12 Commentary.

42 These laments are analyzed in detail in 7:116—8:3 Form and Structure, pp. 255–56.

43 A contemporary Greek would have been surprised to hear of the νοῦς being created from dust. Brandenburger suggests that the function of the personification of the earth is to sharpen the problem of the material aspect of humans (*Verborgenheit*, 181, 185–86). This does not seem justified. Above we have observed the absence from the book of any hints at identification of the material as bad (see Excursus on Adam's Sin, p. 66; 7:26 Commentary). This connection had already been made by Kabisch, pp. 22–23; de Faye, p. 107. Violet 2 suggests here that the Greek might have been διάνοια ⟨ Hebrew יצר, comparing 7:92. See further discussion of this and of Harnisch's views above, Function and Content, p. 229.

■ **63** This verse is a continuation of the preceding and a further development of the sentiment expressed there.

■ **64** This verse relates eschatological suffering (this is what "torture" denotes) to the possession of mind or understanding. In general, see *Gen. R.* 19:1 (Theodor-Albeck, p. 169).[44] Box, following Gunkel, suggests that the import of the book is that the possession of mind intensifies sufferings because they must be endured with knowledge of their inevitability. There seems to be, however, in the passage, the clear implication that the understanding is related to culpability and does not just enhance the suffering. This is confirmed by the parallelisms of 7:72 as well as by *2 Apoc Bar* 15:6:

> But now, because he trespassed, having understanding, he will be punished because he has understanding.

Or, from a slightly different perspective, *2 Apocalypse of Baruch* speaks of "the great punishment which they have despised, when they knew that they should be punished because of the sins they have committed" (55:2; cf. 48:40). Understanding is not the evil inclination, therefore, but something like consciousness or reason, and it is the possession of that faculty which makes human beings culpable.[45]

■ **65** "As Gunkel remarks the statement expressed in this verse is, from the point of view of the ancients, startling and revolutionary. It represents a phase of doubt which threatened to subvert the whole outlook of the ancient world, which regarded man as lord of creation, and as raised to a pinnacle of superiority over all below him: cf. Gen 1; Ps 8" (Box, p. 137 note b).

Compare also 1QS 3:17–18.

■ **66** The idea that the animals are not judged is found in a few other sources.[46] The general sentiment of the verse is illuminated by comparison with 7:116: "It would have been better if the earth had not produced Adam, or else, when it had produced him, had restrained him from sinning"; compare 7:126.[47] The term "judgment" was dealt with in the Excursus on the Term "Judgment," pp. 149–51.

■ **67** This verse gives a special twist to the idea of the remnant that survives (see 5:41 Commentary). In particular, the language of life, which frequently means salvation (see the Excursus on Adam's Sin, p. 66), here seems to mean something like "survive after death/resurrection," but for punishment, not for reward. The general parallel to 7:116–126, which was noted above, is very marked here; see particularly 7:117 and Commentary. The author, by using the first person, identifies himself with the sinners, as he does elsewhere in the book. "In one mood he does indeed declare all men sinners, but he does not mean this literally."[48] If he did, we might observe in a literalistic way, How could he have a problem of the few and the many? There would be no righteous at all to constitute the "few"![49] These two approaches coexist strikingly in 8:31–36 (see 8:19b–36 Function and Content, p. 272; 8:33 Commentary) and are discussed as well in 7:46 Commentary.

■ **68** This verse again asserts the universality of sin (see 7:46 Commentary) and reflects the author's worldview which is pessimistic in some modalities.

■ **69** The general sentiment here is a repetition of 7:63

---

44 Although similar to the evil heart in some ways (see Excursus on Adam's Sin, p. 65), it is not identical with it. The terminology of "mind" was dealt with in the discussion on the preceding verses.

45 This is also the general direction of the comments of Gry to the present verse.

46 Its comparative rarity should be regarded as an indication not of the prevalence of the opposite view but merely of the fact that the subject is not widely discussed. See, however, *2 Enoch* 58:4 ([J] and [A]); and Ginzberg, *Legends,* 5:189. It is very explicit in the high medieval text cited by Jellinek, *BM,* 1:151.

47 All of these passages, Keulers points out, are concerned more with the immediate fate of human beings after death (p. 145). It is not obvious, however, just why these two ideas should be related.

48 F. C. Porter, *The Messages of the Apocalyptic Writers*

(New York: Scribner's, 1905) 51. See 7:48, and contrast 6:32 (see Commentary there). See also 4:38; 7:75; 7:116–126; and 8:31. See Excursus on Adam's Sin, p. 65.

49 See on this issue also the analysis by Brandenburger, *Adam und Christus,* 29–31, and idem, *Verborgenheit,* 176–79. He argues that statements about universal sin are set in the mouth of Ezra but are repeatedly corrected by the angel (= God = the author's views). See also ibid., 163 n. 56. His approach is overly systematic and, for example, the attempt to integrate statements about Ezra's worthiness into this argument miss their dynamic role in the unfolding of the Ezra character in the book (see ibid., 31: contrast 6:31 Commentary and 8:37–62a Form and Function, p. 282).

(see Commentary), thus concluding the lament on one of its opening themes. The statement has clear affinities with the *topos* discussed at 4:12 Commentary: "better I were not born." That *topos* also occurs at the start of the lament and so brackets it.

■ **70** This verse opens the angel's final address, with which this pericope concludes. It states that "judgment and the things that pertain to judgment" were created by God before he created Adam. A well-known rabbinic dictum, referred to at 3:6 Commentary, enumerates seven things that were created before the creation of the world. These include paradise and Gehenna, that is, things relating to judgment. The same theme has also been discussed in 6:1–6, where creation and judgment are also set into a relationship (see 6:6 Commentary). This implies considerable measure of predestination.[50] In this context the word "prepared" is to be noted as a technical term describing the precreation of the eschatological things; see 7:14 Commentary.

■ **71** This verse cites 7:64, but while there the statement was made in order to raise a question, here it is proclaimed as part of the answer. The technique is discussed in Form and Structure, p. 227.

■ **72** This verse takes up and comments on the second part of 7:64 which has already been the subject of 7:71. The connection between the idea of understanding and that of general accountability is dealt with here explicitly. The accountability of the Gentiles has been discussed in 7:1–25 Function and Content, pp. 194–95, where the view was taken that even language that seems to be specific of Israel, such as "covenant," could be used by

the author in a nonspecific way. The indiscriminate use of this language is highlighted by the expression "obtained the law" here. On the phrase "those who dwell, the inhabitants," see 5:1 Commentary and 7:74 below.

■ **73** Humans in judgment address God in Matt 25:37, 44, just as is implied here. This is apparently part of the process of judgment of which another element is God's rebuke of the righteous and the wicked which is described in 7:36–37 (see 7:37 Commentary and the Excursus on the Term "Judgment," p. 150). The term "times" and its possible Hebrew original was discussed in 3:14 Commentary.

■ **74** The reasons for the apparent delay of the eschaton were already discussed in 4:35–37, and, as in that passage, it is set into a discussion of universal sin (cf. also 4:26–34). What seems like a delay of the eschaton caused by divine long-suffering is in fact only the predetermined order of events. The result of this is to set long-suffering itself within the predetermined divine plan.[51]

The theme introduced here, the relation between judgment and divine mercy, is extensively developed in 7:132–140. The idea that there is no mercy on the day of judgment is widespread in the book; see the Excursus on the Term "Judgment," p. 150.[52]

---

50   See the discussion of some of the implications of the relationship between determinism, Adam's sin, and the state of the world in 7:1–25 Function and Content, pp. 193–95.

51   See Harnisch, pp. 316–18, for an analysis with different emphases.

52   See *2 Apoc Bar* 12:4; contrast 24:2a.

7

75   I answered and said, "If I have found favor in thy sight, O Lord, [a] show this also to thy servant: Whether after death, as soon as every one of us yields up his soul, we shall be kept [b] in rest until those times [c] come when thou wilt [d] renew the creation, [e] or whether we shall be tormented at once?"

76   [f]He answered me and said, "I will show you that also, but do not be associated with those who have shown scorn, nor number yourself among those who are tormented. 77/ For you have a treasure of works [g] laid up with the Most High; but it will not be shown to you until the last times. 78/ Now, concerning death, [h] the teaching [i] is: When the decisive decree has gone forth from the Most High that a man shall die, as the soul [j] leaves the body to return [k] again to him who gave it, first of all it adores [l] the glory of the Most High. 79/ And if it is one of those

> who have shown scorn
>> and have not kept the ways [m] of the Most High,
> and who have despised his law,
>> and who have hated [n] those who fear God—

80/ such souls [o] shall not enter into treasuries, [p] but shall immediately wander [q] about in torments, ever grieving and sad in seven ways. 81/ The first way, because they have scorned the law [r] of the Most High. 82/ The second way, because they cannot now repent and do good [s] that [t] they may live. 83/ The third way, that [u] they shall see the reward laid up for those who have trusted the injunctions [v] of the Most High. 84/ The fourth way, that [w] they shall consider [x] the torment laid up for themselves in

Notes

75   a Eth, Ar1 omit; Syr adds "Lord," cf. 4:38; 6:11; 6:38; 6:55; 7:45, etc., for this variant.

     b Lat, Syr have a reflex of infinitive absolute and finite verb.

     c Eth, Ar1 "time."

     d Lat, Syr seem to reflect $\mu\acute{\epsilon}\lambda\lambda\epsilon\iota\varsigma$.

     d–e "He will carry out his judgment" Eth; "to the day of judgment" Arm; Ar1, Ar2 vary further; the basis of the text is not completely certain.

76   f Georg resumes here.

77   g "Good works" Lat Ms L, Ar1, Arm.

78   h "What you asked me concerning death" Ar2; "concerning which you asked me" Arm. Ambrose, *De bono mortis* 10–11, quotes from here to 7:102 (see Violet 1, pp. 435–36).

     i "Word," "pronouncement" Lat, Syr, Georg, Arm, cf. Eth; Ar1, Ar2 vary.

     j "Spirit" Lat, Syr, Arm; *anima* Georg; "soul" Eth, Ar1, Ar2, cf. 7:80.

     k Lat *dimittatur;* so Syr.

     l Lat perhaps goes back to $\pi\rho\sigma\sigma\kappa\upsilon\nu\epsilon\hat{\iota}\nu$ (Bensly).

79   m Singular Lat; Arm sets the ways of reward before those of punishment, thus placing 7:79–86 after 7:99.

     n "Not accounted" Georg, Eth, cf. Ar1; two Greek readings are probable.

80   o *Inspiratio* Lat; *anima* Georg; Ar2, Arm omit; see 7:78 Commentary.

     p Ar2, Arm vary; Ar2 is greatly expanded.

     q *Vagantes* Lat, so also Eth; "remain" or "be" Syr, Georg; others are unclear; this is probably a Greek variant.

81   r Ar1 replaces this phrase with a more general sentiment. Arm adds "through the Law and the faith"; see for the idea of the corruption of the faith the special material of Arm at 5:11; 6:7; and 7:24, and see *Armenian Text Commentary.*

82   s Syr, Georg, cf. Arm; Lat "make a good repentance"; Eth omits "and do good"; Ar1, Ar2 vary.

     t Arm may come from $\ddot{o}\tau\iota/\ddot{o}\tau\epsilon$ and free translation; see for the variant note w below on 7:84 and note j below on 7:97.

83   u Lat omits.

     v Eth, Ar1; *testamentis* Lat; *repromissis* Georg; Syr omits; Ar1, Arm have "the righteous" for the whole phrase: the word is uncertain.

84   w Lat omits; Georg *quia;* Syr has $\ddot{o}\tau\iota$ (Violet 1); cf. Ar1; see note t above on 7:82.

     x Eth, Georg, Ar1 "see"; perhaps confusion of $\epsilon\hat{\iota}\delta\sigma\nu/\sigma\hat{\iota}\delta\alpha$.

the last times. [y] 85/ The fifty way, that [z] they shall see [a]the treasuries of the other souls [b] guarded by angels in profound quiet. 86/ The sixth way, that [c] they shall see [d]the torments coming upon them from now on. [d] 87/ The seventh way, which surpasses all the ways that have been mentioned, [e] because they shall utterly waste away in confusion [f] and be consumed with shame, [g]and shall wither with fear [h] since they [i] see the glory of the Most High before whom they sinned now [j] while they were alive, and before whom they are to be judged [k]in the last times. [k]

88 "But this is the order [l] of those who have kept the ways of the Most High, [m] when [n] they shall be [o] separated from their mortal vessel. [p] 89/ [q]During the time that they lived in it, [r] they laboriously served the Most High, and withstood danger every hour, that they might keep the law of the Lawgiver perfectly. 90/ [s]Therefore this is the teaching concerning them: 91/ First [t] of all, they shall see with great joy the glory of him who receives them, for they shall have [t]rest in seven orders. [u] 92/ The first order, because they have striven with great effort to overcome the evil thought which was formed with them, that it might not lead them

y Lat *in novissimis;* Syr, Ar1 "in the end"; Eth "in the last time"; Arm, Georg "eternally"; Ar2 "in the other world"; Syriac adds at the end of this verse: wherein the souls of the ungodly shall be reproached, because while they had the time for performance (action) they did not subject themselves to the commandments of the Most High (Box [1917]).

85 z Lat omits.

a–b Lat, Syr; Lat omits "souls"; Eth "the souls of the righteous . . . In their chambers"; Georg "the souls of the others"; Ar2, Arm vary in wording, on the latter see *Armenian Text Commentary.* They do not have "treasuries."

86 c Lat omits.

d–d RSV follows Lat, which is emended both by Bensly and by Violet 1. Arm is quite developed in various directions and in accord with its special tendencies. For "coming upon," Syr has *mtyb lhyn,* "prepared"; this might be corrupt for *mty bhyn,* which would accord with the other versions.

87 e Eth, Georg "predicted"; a world like προλέγω may have both meanings. Ar1, Ar2 are rather different.

f Eth, Georg transpose "confusion" and "shame"; cf. also Arm.

g Lat *honoribus* 〉 τιμαῖς for ἀτιμίας (Violet 1).

g–h Ar1, Ar2, Arm vary.

i Lat "at seeing."

j Lat, Ar1, Arm omit; Ar2 varies.

k–k Lat, cf. Georg *in novissimo illo tempore;* Syr has *bʿḥrytʿ;* Eth omits; the other versions diverge.

88 l Syr, Eth "way"; *renovationem* Georg; Ar1, Ar2 omit; Arm varies.

m Lat omits.

n Syr adds "the day comes that."

o Lat, Eth seem to reflect μελλοῦσιν.

p Lat, Syr, Georg; "body" Eth, Ar1, Ar2, Arm.

89 q Ar1, Ar2, Arm are much abbreviated in this verse.

r Georg *steterunt hoc in mundo* seems to reflect an interpretation of the same text.

90 s Ar1, Ar2, Arm omit this verse, but cf. Arm 7:78.

91 t–t Lacuna in Georg; Arm is much abbreviated in the whole verse.

u The versions predominantly show a word meaning "order," "rank" throughout this section. In some instances a word meaning "way" is found. The reverse was true of the previous section, where almost exclusively a word meaning "way" was to be found. Here Ar2 omits nearly all instances, and Syr, Arm read "way" throughout. Bensly regards *ordo* 〉 τάξις as original and points to Syr's habit elsewhere of "obliterating the distinction between words."

astray from life into death. **ᵛ 93/ The second order, because they see the perplexity ᵂ in which the souls of the ungodly wander, ˣ and the punishment that awaits ʸ them. 94/ The third order, that ᶻ they see ᵃ the witness which he ᵇwho formed them ᵇ bears concerning them, that while they were alive they kept the law which was given them in trust. ᶜ 95/ The fourth order, that ᵈ they understand ᵉ the rest which they now enjoy, being gathered into their treasuries and guarded by angels in profound quiet, and the glory which awaits them in the last days. 96/ The fifth order, that ᶠ they rejoice that they have now escaped what is corruptible, and shall inherit what is to come; ᵍ and besides they see the straits and great ʰtoil from which they have been delivered, ʰ and the spacious liberty which they are to ⁱ receive and enjoy in immortality. 97/ The sixth order, when it is shown to them how ʲ their face is to ᵏ shine like the sun, and how ˡ they are to be ᵐ made like the light of the stars, being incorruptible from then on. 98/ The seventh order, which is greater than all ⁿthat have been mentioned, ⁿ because ᵒ they shall rejoice with boldness, ᵖ and shall be confident without confusion, ᑫ and shall be glad without fear, ʳ for they hasten to behold the face of him whom they served in life and from whom they are to receive their reward when glorified. 99/ ˢThis is the order ˢ of the souls of the righteous, ᵗ as henceforth is announced, and ᵘ the aforesaid are the ways of torment which those who would not give heed shall suffer hereafter."**

92   v Arm is much abbreviated, and Ar1 is much expanded.

93   w Georg *iudicium;* Eth omits; Ar1, Ar2, Arm vary.
w–x Georg omits.
y Ar2, Arm "prepared"; see *Armenian Text Commentary.* Violet 2 suggests that a Greek like ὑπομένουσαν or ἀποκειμένην might account for both readings.

94   z Lat omits.
a Eth omits; *audiunt* Georg, probably secondary.
b–b Ar1 "the Most High"; Ar2 "the Lord"; Arm "God."
c Georg, Ar1 "faith"; perhaps different interpretation of identical Greek.

95   d Lat omits.
e Syr "see and understand"; Eth "see"; Arm "are revealed." The rest of the verse is abbreviated in Ar2, Arm.

96   f Lat omits.
g Ar1 is expanded from here, including a phrase from the same apocryphal statement found in 1 Cor 2:9–10 which is also cited by Arm 5:40, on which see Stone and Strugnell, *Elijah,* 48–49. Ar2, Arm omit the latter parts of the verse.
h–h So Lat (as emended), Syr, and basically Georg. Eth differs.
i Apparently μέλλουσι Lat, Syr. The translation of the end of the verse follows Lat, Syr; the others vary.

97   j Syr, Eth, Ar1 "that."
k Lat, Syr, Eth, Georg(?) reflect μέλλουσι or the like.
l Syr, Eth "that"; Georg omits; Ar2, Arm omit phrase.
m Lat, Syr, Eth, Georg(?) reflect μέλλουσι or the like.

98   n–n Eth, Ar1, Ar2, Arm omit.
o Lat *quoniam;* Georg *quia,* cf. Arm; "that" others.
p Violet 1 suggests appositely that the versions go back to παρρησία.
p–q Ar1 varies; Ar2 omits; this and the next phrase are combined by Eth.
q–r Syr omits.
r Arm omits.

99   s–s "These are the orders" Syr, Georg, Ar1, Arm, cf. Ar2.
t Arm omits from here to end.
u The latter part of the verse has suffered variously in the different versions. Lat has lacunae; Syr is expanded drawing on 7:80.

Form and Structure

This pericope is made up of two chief parts:

1. The seer's question which precipitates the following (7:75).

2. The angel's reply to this question (7:76–99). The angelic response itself, however, is also easily divided into:

a. Introduction on the nature of death (7:76–78)

b. The post-mortem state of the wicked (7:79–87) and the righteous (7:88–98)

c. Conclusion (7:99)

The passage is formulated as prediction. It follows a dispute, a pattern that in broad terms occurs throughout the first three visions (see General Structure of the Book, p. 50). With it, as can be seen clearly from Table 1 on p. 51, the part of Vision 3 that is absolutely parallel to Visions 1 and 2 comes to an end for a time and only resumes in 9:1. However, the basic alternation of dispute and prediction is preserved.

The descriptions of the fate of the righteous and the wicked are closely parallel in their structure.[1] They are sevenfold in character, corresponding, one supposes, to the seven heavens.[2] The originality of this passage in context was questioned by Kabisch, who nonetheless asserts its proper position in his "Salathiel Apocalypse." Moreover, the connections between this pericope and other parts of the vision confirm that it is original to 4 Ezra, as is spelled out in detail in 7:96 Commentary. Furthermore, the intermediate state of the souls is implied at other points in the book, such as 4:33–37, and in the Commentary to the pericope the abundant connections between its terminology and many other places in the book have been chronicled.

These connections do not detract from the very distinct character of the passage 7:79–98. The pericope is introduced by a statement that reads like a title: "Concerning death the teaching is" (7:78). The same terminology is again taken up in 7:90: "Therefore this is the teaching concerning them"; and a final time in the conclusion we also find a formulaic statement: "This is the order of the souls of the righteous, as henceforth is announced, and the aforesaid are the ways of torment." These markers may indicate an adaptation of a prior source, and they result in effect in setting forth ideas in a structured and systematic way, the same outcome also discerned in 7:26–44.

Function and Content

The passage is unique in ancient Jewish literature for its detailed description of the intermediate state of the souls of the righteous and the wicked. The idea that such an intermediate state exists is to be found in other sources (e.g., *Testament of Abraham* A 13–14; *1 Enoch* 22) and elsewhere in 4 Ezra, as was pointed out above. The detailed discussion of the seven ways of the wicked and the seven stages of the righteous, however, is unique here.

Scholars have made much of the relationship between these sevenfold divisions and the ideas of seven heavens (see above) and of seven parts of hell (*b. Sukka* 52a; *Midr. Teh.* 11:6; et al.). In 7:88 Commentary we point out that the difference in terminology for the wicked ("ways") and the righteous souls ("orders, steps, stages") might reflect the idea that while the wicked souls wandered in their punishment, the righteous proceeded through a sort of ascent.[3] Such a picture might be compared, *mutatis mutandis,* with *Test Mos* 10:9–10: "And God shall exalt thee, and he will cause thee to approach to the heaven of the stars . . . and thou shalt look from on high and see the enemies in Gehenna." This, as is pointed out in the Excursus on the Term "Judgment," p. 151, is one of a number of different ways in which 4 Ezra describes the differentiation between the righteous and the wicked, even before or in anticipation of final judgment.

The view put forward by the author of 4 Ezra is very clearly that this intermediate state follows death but is itself succeeded by resurrection and judgment, and indeed the day of judgment is the subject of the next pericope.

Finally, it is to be observed that this prediction as a whole serves to respond to the questions that arise from 7:45–74, a passage concerning the issue of the few saved

---

1   On the symbolism of seven, see Ginzberg, *Legends,* 5:20; and Keulers, p. 21 n. 1. A collection of material relating to rabbinic views of punishment may be found in P. Billerbeck with H. L. Strack, *Kommentar zum Neuen Testament aus Talmud und Midrasch* (Munich: Beck, 1928) 4:1075–83, Box.

2   On the seven heavens and seven stages of ascent, see Lewy, *Chaldean Oracles,* 413–25; and Stone, *Armenian Apocrypha Relating to the Patriarchs and Prophets* (Jerusalem: Israel Academy of Sciences and Humanities, 1982) 101. There are also seven hells according to some traditions; see next note.

3   For further information on seven heavens and seven hells, see Gunkel. Keulers, p. 21, makes much of sevenfold structures, both conceptual and literary, in the book. Geoltrain remarks that Hebrew דרך means often "sorts" or "types." He offers no corresponding explanation of the "steps."

and the many damned. In broad terms, 7:1–25 starts exploring the details of the issues arising once Ezra accepts the idea of reward and punishment. The first response to Ezra's probing is the prediction of 7:26–44. The renewed questioning of 7:45–76 is answered by a second prediction in our pericope. Notably both 7:26–44 and 7:77–99 are "Prediction 2" passages, straight angelic pronouncement with no questioning by the seer except for the initial query.

Commentary

■ **75** This verse opens a new section with a rather elaborate vocative address, "If I have found favor in thy sight . . ." discussed in 4:44 Commentary. The title "Lord" may apply to an angel (7:17 Commentary); it contrasts with the term "servant" or "slave" by which Ezra designates himself (see 5:56 Commentary).

The question that Ezra poses is whether the souls receive some form of reward and punishment immediately after death or (by implication) whether this will happen only at the end. The verse takes the alternatives, rest and torment, and asks, "Shall we be at rest until the eschaton or tormented at once?"[4] The terms "rest" and "torment" often designate eschatological reward and punishment but are used here of the intermediate state of the souls.[5] As was observed above (Excursus on the Term "Judgment," p. 151), there are a number of ways and stages of distinction between the righteous and the wicked, only one of which is eschatological judgment. The use of these eschatological terms for the intermediate state of the souls is indicative, therefore, of this complexity.

This is the reverse of the process of resurrection, which is described in 7:32. Its implications for the relationship of soul to body were discussed in 7:32

Commentary.

The eschaton is called "those times . . . when thou wilt renew the creation." The eschatological age is sometimes described using expressions such as "days" or "times" that are coming; see in further detail 7:26 Commentary. The particular terminology of renewal of creation or of the heavens and earth has its biblical origins in Isa 65:17 and 66:22, and it occurs widely in sources from the second century b.c.e. on, such as the *Apocalypse of Weeks (1 Enoch)* 91:16 and *Jub* 1:29 as well as *Bib Ant* 16:3.[6] In 7:31 Commentary, the general implications of the use of the typology of creation for the description of the eschatological state were discussed as well as possible interpretations of these ideas.[7]

■ **76** This verse recalls the angel's repeated assurance to Ezra elsewhere in the book that he does not belong to the number of the wicked, as he claims, but to that of the righteous. These are well exemplified by 8:47b, "But you have often compared yourself to the unrighteous. Never do that!" (cf. also 8:48–51 and 6:30 Commentary). It is apparently a response to the last phrase of the previous verse (7:75), and in a broader sense it responds to the pericope 7:45–74 which, from Ezra's perspective, is based on the assumption that he is a sinner. The theme of Ezra's righteousness is repeated throughout the following chapters.

■ **77** Ezra is informed of the reason for which he is to be counted, not among the wicked, but among the righteous. His life on earth has garnered a heavenly treasure for him (see also 13:56), but it will be revealed only at the end of days. Elsewhere the virtues of the righteous are described as "treasures" (6:5; 8:36).[8] Ezra's heavenly treasure is described as "of works" here (cf. 8:33). Elsewhere Ezra says that he has no works of righteousness (8:32), no store of good deeds (8:36). The

---

4   This interpretation runs against the view of Gry, who would see here a choice between "la vielle conception des âmes au sheol" and more "modern" views. In the light of the immediately preceding passage, however, it seems to be more reasonable to see the concerns as arising from the discussions of eschatological reward and punishment in the preceding sections (7:26–74).

5   See 7:36 Commentary for this terminology.

6   Note also *2 Apoc Bar* 32:6; 44:12; 57:2; 1QH 11:13 (להתחדש); 1QS 4:25 (עשות חדשה); *Bib Ant* 3:10; 32:17; 2 Pet 3:12–13; Rev 21:1; cf. 2 Cor 5:17; Gal 6:15; *Gen. R.* 1:13 (Theodor-Albeck, p. 12); et al.; cf.

7   for terminology also Ps 104:30.
    See also Stone, *Features*, 78–79, and also Excursus on the Two Ages, p. 92.

8   On the use of the term "treasure house," see 4:35 Commentary. This is presumably also the "treasure of immortality" of 8:54.

eschatological appearance of the deeds of the righteous is mentioned in 7:35. Ezra's particular virtues vary elsewhere in the book, and this theme is discussed in detail in 6:32 Commentary.

Such a heavenly treasure is referred to in a number of other sources, such as Matt 6:20 // Luke 12:33; Matt 19:21 // Mark 10:21; and 1 Tim 6:17–19, which are very similar to *Test Patr Levi* 13:5; see also *Tanh. Ki Tissa* 16 on Exod 33:21, "treasuries of the reward of the righteous," and *2 Enoch* J 51:2. In *2 Apocalypse of Baruch* the heavenly treasury of works of the righteous is mentioned on a number of occasions, such as 14:12; 24:1; cf. 52:7; cf. also 63:3; 85:2. This subject has preoccupied some scholars who are much concerned with the contrast of "works" and "faith," but an expression like 4 Ezra 9:7 serves to remind us that such distinctions were not evident to our author:

And it shall be that every one who will be saved (i.e., from the messianic woes) and will be able to escape on account of his works, or on account of the faith by which he has believed. . . .

(Cf. also 13:23, and contrast Jas 2:18–26.) Indeed, 6:5 refers to "treasures of faith"![9]

This treasure is said to be "laid up" in heaven, an expression that is analogous to Hebrew גנז and perhaps to the Greek θησαυρίζειν. The same usage may be observed in 8:33. There is an analogy of banking or treasure house that is invoked here.[10] The idea of the heavenly store of virtues of a human being is analogous to the equally prominent idea of the eschatological rewards that are prepared in advance, which was dis-

cussed in 7:14 Commentary. In 7:35 people's deeds are said to be present at the time of judgment; here the expression "last days" also clearly refers to the judgment. In 7:83 reward is said to be "laid up."

■ **78** The various understandings of the term "death" are discussed in the Excursus on Adam's Sin, pp. 65–66. Here ordinary physical death is referred to and not, as often, damnation. It is described as the separation of soul from body.

In the Latin version the word translated "soul" is *inspiratio,* which occurs only once more in 4 Ezra, in 7:80. In contexts that contrast soul and body, exactly similar to that here, normally the Latin uses the word *anima.*[11] No ready explanation for this divergence of terminology is to be found, and the concepts are congruent with those elsewhere in the book. The soul and the body have different fates after death; see 7:32 Commentary.

Qohelet 12:7 reads, "And the dust returns to the earth as it was, and the spirit returns to God who gave it." The expression in 7:78, "The soul leaves the body to return again to him who gave it," here seems to be drawn from Qoh 12:7. Gunkel points out, however, that here Qohelet is reinterpreted in the light of 4 Ezra's different view of human beings and his belief in the intermediate state of the soul.[12] In 4 Ezra all of the souls are said first to appear before God and adore his glory. The appearance before the glory apparently initiates the process of immediate reward and punishment.

In 7:33–44 the appearance of the glory of God is part of the process of judgment. That idea is more explicit in

9 See Commentary 6:5. Cf. *b. Abod. Zar.* 5a: "R. Yonatan says, 'Every one who does one good deed in this world is preceded by it to the world to come.'" See also *b. Baba Batra* 11a; cf. Moore, *Judaism,* 2:91–92, for a clear discussion of Tannaitic views. For lack of great distinction, cf. *Test Patr Dan* 6:8–10. Schrader, *Keilinschriften,* 405 note, regards this as a variant of the idea of heavenly bodies which is Babylonian in origin.

10 The verbs are to be found in the passage in *b. Baba Batra* mentioned as well as in the New Testament passages. The banking analogy is to be found very explicitly in *m. Peah* 1:1, and see Moore, *Judaism,* 2:91–92. The expression here should be compared with *Ps Sol* 9:5.

11 See 4:35; 4:41; 7:32; 7:75; 7:93; 7:99; and 7:100. Further uses of *anima* overlap with other words; see

Excursus on Inspiration, p. 121. Bensly, *MF,* 64 n. 80, has a long discussion of *inspiratio* and *anima.*

12 In *Tanh. Wayyiqra'* 8 the verse from Qohelet is interpreted to refer only to the souls of the righteous, who will go directly to God; cf. also *PRE* 34 (trans. Friedlander, p. 257). An expression similar to that here is to be found in Job 34:14f.; see also *Apoc Mos* 31:4. God's giving of the spirit רוח is referred to repeatedly in 1QH (so 12:11; 13:19; etc.). See also the comments in *b. Shabb.* 152b.

the present passage where the sight of the glory of God dismays the wicked souls after death and rejoices the righteous. Glory in these contexts is very close to being a name of God.[13] Earlier we commented on the fact that terms and concepts proper to the eschatological state are applied in the present passage to the intermediate state of the souls.

The term "teaching" seems to imply a didactic context and perhaps hints at the introduction here of a crystallized tradition; cf. also 7:90.

■ **79** This verse is made up of two pairs of parallel hemistichs. Three of the four hemistichs reflect the same language to be found in 9:9–11 ("scorn," "reject ways," "despise law"). In more general terms, this passage resembles 7:22–24 in that both are indictments that are general in character and do not specify certain sins, but they give the semantic range of "sin."[14] The term "scorn" occurs twice more in this section; see 7:76 and 7:81; cf. 8:50. It also occurs in 3:8 and 9:11. "The way of the Most High" here means something like "his commandments"; compare the parallelism in 7:23–24 and 8:56, and cf. 9:9.[15] It is to be distinguished from the meaning of "the way of the Most High" in Vision 1, which means something like "the workings of divine providence."[16] The expression to "despise" his law may perhaps be compared with the verb מאס/ש that occurs in the Dead Sea Scrolls, for example, 1QpHab 1:10; 5:10; 1QS 3:5; CD 8:19; etc. The wicked's hatred of the righteous is to be found again in 5:29; 8:57; 10:23; and 11:42; cf. 2 Chr 19:2.

■ **80** The idea of the treasuries of the souls, as well as the terminology employed by the versions, is discussed in 4:35 Commentary. It has been pointed out that this verse and 7:85; 7:93; and 7:96 seem to imply that the places of the righteous and wicked souls are in sight of one

another, and their close physical proximity has been inferred.[17] This might be the case, but such an explanation may be somewhat too literalistic. No clear parallel to the opposition between the rest of the righteous in treasuries and the wandering of the wicked has been adduced.[18]

■ **81** "Scorned": see 7:79 Commentary, and also for the sentiment; cf. 2 Apoc Bar 51:4. In this book, sometimes the category "law" or "Torah" is applied to individuals in general and not just Israel; see 7:1–25 Function and Content, pp. 194–95; cf. also 7:23 Commentary.

■ **82** Elsewhere in 4 Ezra the idea is propounded that once judgment has commenced, the wicked will no longer be able to repent.[19] In 4 Ezra the point is often made that divine judgment is decisive and final. These characteristics are assigned by our passage also to the "judgment" implied by the intermediate state of the souls. A similar idea is proposed in 1 Enoch 63:5–9; cf. 65:10.

An interesting contrast to the present passage is *Testament of Abraham* A 14. There Abraham witnesses an intermediate judgment of the souls, and his prayer of intercession redeems one soul whose good and evil deeds are equally balanced.[20] The importance of repentance in Judaism of the age is widely documented. One text among many is *Prayer of Manasseh* 7–8.

The language of "life" is used here with clearly eschatological intent. It means future, eternal life. See the Excursus on Adam's Sin, p. 66, and contrast the usage of "death" in 7:75 and 7:78, where physical death is clearly implied.

■ **83** This verse introduces the idea that part of the punishment of the wicked is their seeing the fate of the righteous. This is partly implied already in 7:37 and recurs in the present passage in 7:93. In 1 Enoch 62:12 we read, "And they will become a spectacle to the

---

13 The term is analyzed in greater detail in 3:19 Commentary.

14 See also 1QH 15:18–19. The exact reference of 9:9–12 is somewhat unclear, but it seems to relate to the final judgment (see Stone, *Features*, 137).

15 See further for this usage 7:88 and 14:31, and cf. many places in earlier literature, e.g., 1QS 3:10 and CD 8:41. See also 2 Apoc Bar 14:5.

16 See 3:31 Commentary and also the comments of Harnisch, p. 147 note.

17 Keulers, p. 158. Contrast, however, Luke 16:23 with this view.

18 Matt 12:43 // Luke 11:24, which is sometimes quoted, is not relevant.

19 See Excursus on the Term "Judgment," p. 150, and 7:33 Commentary; cf. 2 Apoc Bar 85:12. There will, equally, be no intercession!

20 Somewhat different are Heb 12:17 and the intent of the words of R. Simeon b. Lakish in *b. Erub.* 19a.

righteous and to his chosen ones; they will rejoice over them." Compare also *Test Mos* 10:10 (as emended by Charles) and *2 Apoc Bar* 30:4. A similar passage is *2 Apoc Bar* 51:5–6, but there the seeing is not part of judgment; instead, it precedes it. See also Ps 118:7. Another variation on this theme is in *Pirqe Eliyyahu* (Jellinek, *BM,* 3:69). The same is absolutely explicit in *Midr. Teh.* 12:5 and *Lev. R.* 32:1, where a statement attributed to R. Judah speaks of the righteous seeing the wicked and one attributed to R. Nehemiah speaks of the wicked seeing the righteous. The theme of vindication is strong there.[21] Other passages speak of the seeing in noneschatological contexts. Indeed, this is clearly the reflection of the profound yearning for vindication that permeates much of the Jewish literature of this age and is still reflected in rabbinic texts. The vindication may be eschatological or noneschatological.[22] This should be distinguished from the seeing by the souls of God's glory which is part of the administration of reward and punishment; see 7:78 and 7:42 Commentary.[23]

On the expression "laid up," see 7:77 Commentary. God's injunctions are here, as often, assumed to be incumbent on all human beings; see 7:1–25 Function and Content, pp. 194–95.[24]

■ **84** This verse describes punishment as the vision of eschatological torment, and 7:86 describes it as vision of the intermediate state of punishment.[25] This is yet another example of the author's freeness in exchanging ideas relating to the future state with those relating to the intermediate state. On "torment," see 7:36 Commentary.

■ **85** This verse is set in contrast with 7:86 and not with the preceding verse. In general, see *Greek Apoc Esd* 1:9: "Woe to the sinners when they see the righteous man (elevated) above angels, and they are for fiery Gehenna";

see also *Midr. Teh.* 12:5 (cited in 7:83 Commentary). Bensly, *MF,* 64 quotes Hippolytus, *Against Plato* (ed. de Lagarde, p. 69), which seems to use the present passage:

They are brought by angel guards to the confines of hell, and those who are so near hear incessantly the agitation and feel the hot smoke. And when that vision is so near, as they see the terrible and excessively glowing spectacle of the fire, they shudder in horror at the expectation of the future judgment (as if they were already) feeling the power of their punishment. And again, where they see the place of the fathers and the righteous, they are in this also punished.[26]

The righteous are said to be guarded by angels also in 7:95. The idea is common, cf. *1 Enoch* 100:5, *2 Apoc Bar* 30:2 and also 23:4.[27]

"Profound quiet" is typically used to refer to eschatological reward; see 7:36 Commentary. It seems to be the same as the "rest" referred to elsewhere in the present pericope.[28]

■ **86** This verse complements 7:84, which referred to the immediate reward of the righteous by talking of the immediate punishment of the wicked. The implications of these ideas were worked out in detail by Hippolytus in the passage succeeding that quoted in the commentary on the preceding verse.[29]

■ **87** This verse relates the final, seventh stage of the wandering of the wicked soul. It beholds the glory of God which has the effect of the execution of judgment.[30] The seeing of the glory and its results are explicitly said to be intermediary, and God will judge the wicked in the last times. The language used of the effect of the seeing of the glory on the souls, "waste away," "be consumed," and so forth, has older roots (cf. Lev 26:39), and numerous parallels have been adduced.[31] Particularly intriguing is the tradition in *Midr. Teh.* 12:5 and *Lev. R.*

21 Similarly also *Midr. Mishle* 16:11: "First they will go and see the joy of the righteous, . . . and afterwards they are punished in Gehenna."

22 Cf. Luke 16:23. In noneschatological contexts, see e.g., Ps 91:8 and Wisd 5:1–8.

23 See further on the seeing of reward, 13:17 Commentary.

24 "Covenants" is the reading of Latin; see textual notes; see also 3:32 Commentary.

25 Despite Gunkel's remarks. This is now clear because of the textual situation.

26 Also quite similar are the words attributed to Simon

Magus in pseudo-Clement, *Recog.* 2.13.7.

27 Harnisch, p. 140, makes much of the language of *servare/salvare* as typical of eschatological reward; cf. 7:27.

28 On primordial silence, see 6:39 Commentary and 7:30 Commentary.

29 See translation *apud* Box.

30 See Excursus on the Term "Judgment," p. 150, and 7:42 Commentary. This seems to be distinct from what is described in 7:78.

31 Thus, e.g., "disgrace of destruction" in 1QS 4:13, while "pine away" is very widely attested, starting like

32:1, where it says of the wicked when they see the righteous in the Garden of Eden, נפשם מתמעכת עליהן, "their souls shrivel up in them."

■ **88** The expression "mortal vessel" means "body."[32] What is described is the soul leaving the body, as in 7:78. In spite of the possible interpretations of "mortal vessel," it is not certain that even here a negative value is given to the body, even though the body and the soul are clearly distinguished. The expression may be compared with "tent" in Wisd 9:15:

for a perishable body weighs down the soul,
and this earthly tent burdens the thoughtful mind.[33]

The fact that the body dies and that death is an extremely negative concept for 4 Ezra still does not result in a negative evaluation of the body. Even in 5:50–55 the deterioration of the body is said to be the result of the aging of the earth and not of contact with evil. See 7:32 Commentary, where the matter is analyzed further.

■ **89** The "labors" and "dangers" are themes that also arise in the parable in 7:3–12. Some would introduce into this passage a discussion about whether 4 Ezra viewed the Torah as fulfillable and compare 3:35–36.[34] It is not certain, however, that this issue is addressed by 4 Ezra in the present verse. Geoltrain would interpret "Lawgiver" of Moses, but the parallelism favors regarding it as a term for God.

■ **90** Many sources speak of seven heavens, but although this idea may lie in the background of the present passage, it is by no means explicit. A later development of this narrative is to be found in the description of the ascent of the righteous soul in *Questions of Ezra* A 19.[35]

■ **91** The term "orders" alternates with "ways" throughout 7:79–87. We may learn from 7:99 that the term "ways" is reserved for the wicked and the term "orders" for the righteous: "This is the order of the souls of the righteous . . . and the aforesaid are the ways of torment." Gunkel opines that *ordines* is equivalent to τάξεις in Greek.[36] It seems likely that the distinction between "ways" and "orders" reflects different ideas of where the righteous and the wicked souls are destined to go. If Gunkel's view of the Greek is accepted, then the word might be translated also "steps," which is the way it was taken in the *Questions of Ezra* A 19. Ascent terminology is involved, and the souls of the righteous ascend to the divine Presence. The term "ways" for the wicked may, in contradistinction to this, be a mode of emphasizing that their souls do not ascend to God. On the meaning of "glory" here, see 3:19 Commentary.

■ **92** The views of the book concerning the evil inclination in human beings are discussed in the Excursus on Adam's Sin, pp. 63–65. Here the idea is emphasized that humans can act righteously only after a great struggle. This is the labor referred to in 7:89, and the same view occurs elsewhere in 4 Ezra, most explicitly in 7:18 and 7:127.[37] In the description of the first way of the wicked souls, reference is made here to their sin (7:81). In the case of the righteous souls too, it is not reward but their deeds that are remarked.

■ **93** This verse discusses that reward of the righteous which is constituted of the vision of the punishment of the wicked. This concept and its reverse, the punishment of the wicked which is constituted of seeing the reward of

---

much of such terminology from Lev 26:39; cf. Ezek 24:23b; *Bib Ant* 16:3; and *2 Apoc Bar* 30:4.

32 Cf. 4:11 for "vessel" which is by clear implication "mortal," and see Commentary there. On the terms "mortal" and "corruptible," see Excursus on Adam's Sin, p. 66.

33 Note that "tent" is σκῆνος and that here Box has suggested that vessel was probably σκεῦος.

34 See Harnisch, pp. 153–55.

35 In *Midr. Teh.* 11:6 there is a long discussion of seven groups of righteous people whose faces will shine like seven different things. See also *Sifre Deut.* 10 (67a) // *Lev. R.* 30:2. *Midr. Mishle* 14:1 (Buber, p. 38a) reports that on Moses' birth the house filled with light. See also n. 46 below. J. H. Charlesworth, *The Old Testament Pseudepigrapha* (New York: Doubleday, 1983) 1:597.

36 Violet 2 adds that this is probably the equivalent of Hebrew דרך. He does not recognize the difference here between the terms used for the righteous and the wicked. Of course, the use of סרך in Qumran literature often resembles τάξις.

37 See also 14:34. Ezra's stress on free will is very great, even when it seems to be in tension with other emphases in the book, such as in 3:20. Arabic1 gives quite a different interpretation of the evil inclination, while Armenian omits mention of it in accordance with its fixed *Tendenz*.

the righteous, has been remarked previously. The same idea also stands behind 7:37 and 7:83 (see 7:83 Commentary). A nice parallel is *Midr. Teh.* 12:5: "R. Judah says, 'When the righteous are in the Garden of Eden and see the wicked being tortured in Gehenna, their soul rejoices. . . . Then the righteous praise and thank the Holy One for the sufferings which he brought upon them in this world.'" This is tied in the Midrash to the idea of vindication. The precreation of punishment is also implied; see 7:95 and in detail 6:6 Commentary.[38] Some scholars would stress the term "wander" as referring to the idea that the wicked souls find no rest. We might well also associate it with the "ways" on which the wicked proceed, compared to the "steps" by which the righteous ascend.

■ **94** The legal language of judgment used in this verse is notable. The fate of the souls in the intermediate state is often referred to in the language used of the final assizes.[39] The verse is quite similar to *Hermas Vis.* 1.3, which may be a reminiscence of it.[40]

■ **95** The reward of the righteous, both in the intermediate state and at the eschaton, is described as "rest" (7:36 Commentary) and "joy" (7:28 Commentary). The righteous souls are gathered into treasuries (4:35 Commentary; 4:41 Commentary). On some occasions, the treasuries are said to be only of the souls of the righteous; on others, of all humans. The souls are guarded (technical term; see 7:28 Commentary, n. 53) by angels, as is also described in 4:35–37 and 7:85. There they will await the end (or "last days") and the eschatological glory which will be bestowed upon them (see the Excursus on

the Term "Judgment," p. 150).

■ **96** The verse refers predominantly to the eschatological state, in contrast with 7:92, which seems to refer to the intermediate state of the souls. Death is seen as an escape from that which is corruptible, the elements that typify life in this world.[41] The contrast of this world and the eschatological state is formulated in language of the narrow and the spacious, terminology that is very prominent in the two parables in 7:3–13. Indeed, the present passage may be described as the realization in angelic prediction of the angelic teaching of the parables in 7:3–18.[42]

■ **97** The faces of the righteous will shine like the sun. They will be henceforth incorruptible, like the light of the stars: so the present verse states. These ideas have a number of ramifications, some of which can be explored here. In 7:125 the faces of the abstinent are said to shine above the stars.[43] This effulgence may be connected with the glory which is said to await the righteous in a number of texts.[44] The shining faces of the righteous, however, form a widespread tradition and may be part of the broader idea of the light of the redeemed.

In both 7:97 and 7:125 the shining face is mentioned specifically.[45] The earliest reference to the shining of the righteous at the end is Dan 12:3: "And those who are wise shall shine like the brightness of the firmament; and those who turn many to righteousness, like the stars forever and ever." The face is not mentioned in Daniel, but a prayer, attributed to R. Ḥanina in *b. Ber.* 17a and using language drawn from Daniel, expresses the wish, "May your face shine like the brightness of the firma-

---

38 Arabic2 and Armenian introduce, as elsewhere, the term "prepared," and see on this 7:15 Commentary.

39 See Excursus on the Term "Judgment," p. 151. The event described here is perhaps analogous to that in 7:37–38.

40 ἐὰν τηρήσωσιν τὰ νόμιμα τοῦ θεοῦ, ἃ παρέλαβον ἐν μεγάλῃ πίστει. This is pointed out by Bensly, *MF*, 68–69, who has a long note on the idea of πίστις here.

41 On this term and its meaning, see 4:11 Commentary.

42 The terminology is discussed in 7:6 Commentary.

43 Armenian here reads "like the sun," Arabic1 "like the luminaries of heaven," and Arabic2 "like lightning." The face of the woman who is Jerusalem flashes like lightning (10:25).

44 See 7:95; 7:98; and 8:49; cf. 9:31. The idea may also be observed in *2 Apoc Bar* 51:5; 54:21; and Rom 8:18. In 8:51 glory may be a term for reward in

general. See on the term "glory" in general 3:19 Commentary, 7:42 Commentary, and Excursus on the Term "Judgment," p. 150. This relationship between the resurrected righteous, glory, and the stars is explicit in 1 Cor 15:39–43.

45 Gunkel suggested that the comparison with the stars hints at the origin of this feature in astral religion; cf. also his comment on 9:31. See also Bousset-Gressmann, pp. 323–25; A. Bertholet, *Das religionsgeschichtliche Problem des Spätjudentums* (Tübingen: Mohr, 1909) 11. Note, however, that the sun figures at least as prominently as the stars in the apocalyptic contexts, as will be explained below.

ment." This is one of a number of rabbinic texts that refer to the future brightness of the faces of the righteous.[46]

In Rev 1:16 the face of the "one like a Son of man" (cf. 1:11) is said to shine like the sun. In *2 Enoch* 1:5 and 19:1 it is the faces of angels that shine like the sun.[47] So the faces both of the angels and of the righteous shine and they are compared primarily with the sun. This is also what 4 Ezra 7:97 says. In 7:125, however, they are said to shine above the stars, and in 7:97b they are as the light of the stars.[48]

An interesting series of passages in rabbinic sources concerns the brightness of Adam's face which was taken from him when he was expelled from Eden.[49] This seems to have been connected with his creation in the image of God.[50] As Ginzberg points out, this originally distinct tradition became combined with the idea of the wondrous light created on the first day and hidden when Adam sinned.[51] In this material there is a clear tradition of the shining faces of the righteous with no connection made with the stars. In other texts the brightness is compared with heavenly bodies, but the faces are not mentioned.

Dan 12:3, "like the brightness of the firmament," has already been mentioned, and its similarity to 4 Ezra 7:97 and 7:125 has been noted. The sun is also found in similar contexts.[52] Another variant on this theme is the passages in which the righteous are said to be like the stars or closely connected with them. Such are 4 Macc 17:5 and *2 Apoc Bar* 51:10.[53] This situation suggests a direct correlation between the righteous and the stars. Indeed, in *2 Apoc Bar* 51:10 the righteous are said to be like angels and equal to stars.

Yet a further series of passages associates the blessed righteous with angels or speaks of their transformation into angels. Thus compare *1 Enoch* 104:2 with 104:6; *2 Apoc Bar* 51:5; and *1 Enoch* 51:4. Both the angels and the righteous have bright faces.[54] The stars as the host of heaven are well documented in the Bible.[55] Most interesting is Job 38:7, where stars are parallel to angels. Elsewhere the stars symbolize angels or the righteous.[56] In the sources cited above, the stars and the angels share their characteristics with the blessed righteous, and this may well be the source of the language in 4 Ezra 7:97.

■ **98** The structure of this verse is very much like that describing the seventh way of the wicked souls in 7:87. The climax is, for the righteous, the vision of the countenance of God. While "the face of God" is a common expression from biblical sources on (cf., e.g., 2 Sam 21:1 and Ps 42:2), it is difficult not to associate 4 Ezra 7:98 with Exod 33:20, which, describing God's epiphany to Moses on Sinai, says, "'But,' he said, 'you cannot see my face; for man shall not see me and live'"; cf. also Exod 33:23. Here, of course, the righteous souls are described

46 *Sifre Deut.* 10 (67a) // *Lev. R.* 30:2; *Midr. Teh.* 11:6 says that in the future the faces of the righteous will be like seven things: the sun, the moon, the firmament, the stars, the lightning, roses, and the Temple candelabrum. Cf. *Midr. Teh.* on Ps 72:5. *Maʿaseh Abraham*, a medieval text, records that on his birth Abraham's face shone like the sun (Jellinek, *BM,* 1:26). See n. 35 above.

47 Cf. Philo, *Vit. Mos.* 2.288, "pure as sunlight"; *2 Enoch* 66:7–8. In *1 Enoch* 71:1 the angel's countenance is like snow.

48 Shining faces with no elements of comparison are found in a number of other sources. Their background lies in such contexts as Qoh 8:1; cf. Ps 4:6 and 31:16; also Num 6:25; Ps 31:16; and 67:1. Such are 1QH 3:3; 4:5; *2 Apoc Bar* 51:3; *1 Enoch* 38:4; cf. 14:21; 89:22; *b. Sanh.* 100a. In *1 Enoch* 51:4–5 the righteous are said to become as angels and their faces lighted up with joy.

49 *Tanh. Buber,* 1:7a–b; *Gen. R.* 12:6 (Theodor-Albeck, p. 102); *Pes. R.* 118a; et al.

50 *Gen. R.* 23:6 (Theodor-Albeck, p. 235).

51 Ginzberg, *Legends,* 5:112–13. *Qoh. R.* 1:1 on v 7 speaks of the eschatological renewal of this light on the faces of the righteous, bringing the two traditions together.

52 See Matt 13:43; *Vit Ad* 20:2; *Sifre Deut.* 6:5, ch. 32 (Friedmann, p. 73b); *b. Sanh.* 101a; 4 Ezra Arm 6:26. Cf. in a different way *Od Sol* 11:11.

53 Isa 14:13 and *Ps Sol* 1:5 describe the overweening pride of the wicked as they attempt to reach the stars. In Isa 14:13, for "stars of God," LXX (and Arm) reads "stars of heaven." More interesting is Targum which reads עמיה דאלהה. In Jer 51:9 the "skies" are mentioned in a similar context.

54 See further Stone, *Features,* 281 n. 533.

55 Jer 19:13; 33:22; Judg 5:20; Ps 148:2–3; Neh 9:6; 2 Kgs 23:5, cf. 21:5; Deut 4:19; cf. also Joseph's dream in Gen 37:9.

56 Angels: *1 Enoch* 86:1, 3; 90:21; etc.; righteous: *1 Enoch* 46:7; 43:1–4; Dan 8:10–11.

after death. In *1 Enoch* 102:8 eschatological reward is described as that which "they will see forever."[57] A striking parallel of exegesis is *PRE* 34: "The soul does not go out of the body until it beholds the Shekhinah, as it is said, 'For a man shall not see me and *live*'" (trans. Friedlander, p. 254).

■ **99** No commentary.

---

57 Cf. also the explicit statements in 1 John 3:2 and Rev 22:4. More general expressions about seeing God are to be found in other sources, such as Matt 5:8.

7

100   I answered and said, "Will time therefore [a] be given to the souls, after they have been separated from the bodies, to see what you have described to me?"

    101/ He answered and [b] said to me, "They shall have freedom for seven days, so that during these seven days they may see the things which have been predicted, [c] and afterward they shall be gathered in their treasuries." [d]

102   I answered and said, "If I have found favor in thy sight, [e] show further to me, thy servant, [f] whether on the day of judgment the righteous will be able to intercede for the ungodly or to entreat the Most High for them, [g] 103/ fathers for sons or sons for fathers, [h] brothers for brothers, [i] relatives for their kinsmen, or friends for friends." [i]

    104/ He answered me and said, "Since you have found favor in my sight, I will show you this also. The day of judgment is decisive [j] and displays to all [k] the seal of truth. Just as now a father does not send his son, or a son his father, or a master his servant, or a friend his dearest friend, [l] to be ill [m] or sleep or eat or be healed in his stead, 105/ so no one shall ever pray for another then, [n] neither shall anyone lay a burden on another; [o] for then everyone shall bear his own righteousness and unrighteousness."

106   I answered and said, "How then do we find that [p] first Abraham prayed for the people of Sodom, and Moses for our [q] fathers who sinned in the desert, 107/ and Joshua [r] after him for Israel in the days of Achan, 108/ and Samuel in the days of Saul, and David for the plague of the people, [s] and Solomon for [t] those in [t] the sanctuary, 109/ and Elijah for those [u] who received [u] the rain, and for the one who was dead, that he might live, 110/ and Hezekiah for the people in the days of Sennacherib, and many others prayed [v] for many? 111/ If therefore the righteous have prayed for the ungodly now, when corruption has increased and unrighteousness has multiplied, why will it not be so then as well?"

112   He answered me and said, [w] "The end of this world (or: age) has not yet come to pass; [w]

Notes

100   a Cited by Ambrose, *De bono mortis* 11; see Violet 1, p. 84, nn. 17–22.

    b Syr, some Eth Mss, Georg; Lat, Ar1, Ar2, Arm omit "answered and"; Arm varies in the rest of the verse.

    c "Which I told you" Eth; "which I foretold to you" Ar1.

    d See 4:36 Commentary; Lat *habitaculum*. Ar1 has an expansion resembling 7:95; Ar2 is also expanded.

102   e–f Ar2, Arm are similar but not identical.

    f–g The translation is based on Lat, Syr, Arm; Eth, Georg have "the righteous will be able to entreat the Most High for the sinners"; Ar1, Ar2 perhaps support Eth, Georg.

103   h All versions but Lat (and Ar2, which omits one phrase) have "fathers" in both clauses. Interestingly, so does Lat Ms L, but it agrees with the other Lat Mss in readings i–i. Georg Ms O has a word meaning "parent." *Greek Apoc Esd* 3:12 and 3:14 seem to indicate a possible γονεῖς, but the matter is uncertain. In a similar list in *Apost. Const.* 2.4 (*apud* Bensly) we find πατέρες.

    i–i All versions but Lat have an identical word in both parts of both clauses. Lat has synonyms; cf. note h above. This is apparently a stylistic feature of Lat.

104   j "Sudden" Eth; Eth, Ar1, Ar2, Arm are all more or less exegetical here.

    k Eth, Georg omit.

    l "Friend" Eth, Ar1; "dear one" Georg.

    m Lat, Ar2 imply forms of νοέω instead of νοσέω (uncial E / Σ; Bensly). The list of verbs is expanded in Ar1, Ar2, and Arm.

105   n Lat and Eth perhaps have οὐδέποτε ⟨ οὐδέτοτε (Violet 2).

    n–o Lat omits, perhaps by hmt.

    o Georg Ms I lacks from here to 7:125.

106   p The Latin *Missing Fragment* ends here.

    q Lat, Syr omit (except Lat Ms L); Georg reads *populo*.

107   r Syr, Georg, Ar2 add "son of Nun." This may be an independent expansion, since this form of the name is most frequent.

108   s Lat, Eth omit "of the people"; "plague" is mistranslated in Lat, Syr.

    t–t Eth, Georg omit.

109   u–u Eth, Georg omit; cf. Ar1.

110   v Lat, Syr omit; the last phrase varies in Ar1, Ar2.

112   w–w Eth, Georg and cf. Lat Ms L, which adds *adhuc non erat;* Lat reads *praesens saeculum non est finis;* Syr has "this world has an end," presumably

the glory of God [x] does not abide [y] in it; therefore those who were strong prayed for the weak. 113/ But the day of judgment will be the end of this world (or: age) and the beginning of the immortal world (or: age) to come,

in which corruption has passed away,
114 sinful indulgence has come to an end,
unbelief has been cut off,
and righteousness has increased
and truth has appeared. [z]
115/ Therefore no one will then be able to have mercy on him who has been condemned in judgment or to harm him who is victorious."

witnessing the same text as Lat with the loss of the negative. The phrase differs in Ar1 and Ar2. "Not yet" may have arisen from οὐκ ἐστι/οὐκέτι.

x So Syr, Eth, Georg; Lat omits. This phrase seems to have been problematic as witnessed by the variety of interpretations in the versions.

y Violet suggests that Syr goes back to συχνῶς μένει, while Ar1 goes back to συνεχῶς μένει; Georg has *aeterna gloria*.

114   z There is no Georg from here to 7:125.

Form and Structure

In broad terms this pericope continues the prediction that started in 7:75. As distinct from 7:75–99, however, here we do not have sustained address by the angel but a series of questions and answers. The chief parts of this pericope are:

A. *Question 1: Transition from Preceding*

7:100 Seer's question

7:101 Angel's answer

B. *Question 2: Intercession*

7:102–103 Seer's question, introducing major new topic

7:104–105 Angel's immediate response

7:106–111 Seer's repetition and expansion of the question

7:112–115 Angel's conclusion and predictive response

The Prediction 2 nature of the dialogue is established by the atmosphere and character of the questions rather than by the structure of the dialogue. The balance between the question and the answer differs from that found in most Prediction 2 passages, with the seer's questions being longer than usual.

Furthermore, one can query whether the question and answer in 7:100–101 should be included in this pericope or in the preceding one. Chapter 7:99 is very clearly the end of the sustained discourse about the fate of the souls after death, while 7:102–115 forms another integrated unit (see below), and 7:100–101 is a transition between the two clearly defined units. This could be reckoned with the preceding or the following pericope. In 7:100–101 are two references to the preceding material: "what you have described to me" (v 100) and "which have been predicted" (v 101).

The discourse opens in 7:102 with a complex pre-

amble, "If I have found favor in thy sight," a form we have noted in 4:44 Commentary to introduce a major new subject. This subject is concluded by the angelic speech in 7:112–115, which is also marked out by two special literary forms. The first is one of those eschatological poems which the author utilizes in connection with predictions. These were analyzed in 6:11–29 Form and Structure, pp. 165–66. The second is a clear statement, using contrasting parallelism, which formulates the conclusion drawn by the angel from the preceding discourse. The passage thus concluded, the author goes on to another related matter in the next verse.

The list of relatives that appears in two different forms in verses 103 and 104 is rather like the lists of those who indulge in internecine strife, which were discussed above in 5:9 Commentary. However, such lists are somewhat of a commonplace, and no implication should be drawn from it. The passage is similar in some respects to *Bib Ant* 33:5 (cited in 7:103 Commentary) and also to material preserved in *Sifre Deut.* on Deut 32:39 (Finkelstein, p. 380).

Function and Content

As is clear from the formal analysis, this passage deals with two chief topics, the first in 7:100–101 and the second in 7:102–115. The question posed in 7:100–101 is not completely clear. In 7:100 the seer asks whether, after the separation from the bodies, time will be given to the souls "to see what you described to me." This last phrase seems to refer to the seven stages of ascent of the righteous souls and the seven ways of torment of the wicked. Is the seer asking about "seeing," which is preliminary to the souls entering on these ways or stages, or does he refer to the experience of the actual stages or

ways themselves? If the latter, then what is the point of
the question, for Ezra has already been told that after
death the soul will enter into this intermediate state?

The angel's response is no clearer. He says that the
souls shall have freedom for seven days to see that which
has been predicted, and then they will be gathered into
their treasuries (7:101). This runs against the idea that
the treasuries are viewed by the souls as part of the stages
of reward and punishment (7:77; 7:95).[1] Yet the seventh
stage of the righteous and wicked souls in the intermediate state is the vision of the presence of God (7:87;
7:98) and not entry into the treasuries. So, if the last
phrase of 7:101 refers to the actual entry of the souls
into the treasuries, then the relationship between this
and the stages of intermediate joy or suffering of the
souls is not made explicit.

Consequently, we may assume that the souls enter the
treasuries only after the experiences described in verses
7:75–95, even though this is not stated explicitly in the
text.[2] If so, the question of 7:100 *seems* to be, Will the
souls have any interval between death and entering the
treasuries? but *in fact* it implies the question, How long
will this intermediate state of visions of reward and
punishment last?

A further point is relevant here. The verses refer to
the souls "seeing the things that have been predicted,"
and the predominance of the language of vision in the
description of the intermediate state is notable. Thus, of
the ways of punishment, five are experienced by verbs of
seeing or understanding (7:83–87), while of the steps of
reward six are described by language drawn from this
realm. It is notable, therefore, that the real emphasis of
the passage is on anticipation of the eschatological. Elsewhere, the role of seeing as actually effecting eschatological punishment according to the book has been

observed (see 6:25 Commentary). In the next section we
shall discuss the role of the revelation of divine glory,
again associated with sight.[3]

As noted in Form and Structure, the formula in 7:102
adverts us to the fact that a major subject is now going to
be broached. Ezra has been informed about the intermediate state in 7:75–99 and now his questioning takes
him on to the day of judgment (or perhaps back to it, for
this had been the subject of the pericope 7:45–74). He
asks about intercession: Will there be intercession on the
day of judgment? The angel's answer is an uncompro-
mising No!

The seer protests that in the past, in an age of imperfection and sin, there has been intercessory prayer, so
why will there be none in the future (7:106–111)? He
strengthens his argument by a series of biblical references (7:106–111). If such prayer has been effective in
this corrupt world, he argues, surely it will be so in the
world to come.[4] The angel's response is that intercession
is an indication of the imperfection of the present world
in which "the glory of God does not abide continually."
In the future, perfect age, there will be no intercession
(7:112–115). In this way he takes up the seer's final point
about the corruption of the world and turns the point
back against its author.[5]

Thus the passage carries the subject matter on from its
previous stage. The seer accepts that in the intermediate
state the souls will undergo the experiences the angel has
enumerated. What will be the situation at the end? Let us
recapitulate the development of this subsection of Vision
3. In 7:45–74 the issue of the few and the many was
raised: Why are many created but only few will be saved?
It ended with a lament on creation: "If we were not to
come into judgment after death, perhaps it would have
been better for us" (7:69). The angel's response is that

1 7:95 might be interpreted to mean that the souls are,
at that point, gathered into treasuries where they
await their eschatological reward, but such a view
conflicts with the ensuing verses, which relate some
further stages of reward.
2 Moreover, 7:78–80 seems to refer to something that
happens immediately after death.
3 See also 6:25 Commentary. A similar sequence of
seeing followed by reward may be observed in *2 Apoc
Bar* 51:6: "for they shall first behold and afterward
depart to be tormented." Seeing of reward and
punishment, or better, of judgment, is the very point

of Abraham's heavenly journey in *Testament of
Abraham*, and in *Greek Apocalypse of Esdras* Ezra sees
the reward and punishment.
4 It has been pointed out that all the examples (except
for Elijah and the widow's child) refer to intercession
on behalf of the whole people and not of individuals.
5 The same technique is discussed in 7:45–74 Form
and Structure, p. 227.

humans have free will and that God's patience in not bringing judgment has been due to the preordination of the times rather than any human virtue.

Then Ezra proceeds to ask about the fate of the soul after death, that is, he seems to have accepted the fact that there are more wicked than righteous or, in any case, to have ceased for the moment to argue about this, and instead he inquires how quickly punishment will come upon the souls after death. (In line with his previous emphasis, in formulating his question, he does not entertain the possibility that people are righteous [7:75].) The angel answers with the predictions about the intermediate state (7:75–99). To these Ezra responds with the question in 7:100, which concludes the previous line of thought. Indeed, 7:100 takes up part of the question asked in 7:75 ("or whether we shall be tormented at once?"). After death the righteous and the wicked souls will experience the intermediate state of reward and punishment. Then they shall enter their treasuries to await the day of judgment. In this overall context, the question about intercession continues the thrust of 7:45–74, focuses on the terrible fate awaiting all mankind at the time of the day of judgment, and seeks some interstices in which some hope or comfort may be found. But he is also denied the comfort of intercessory prayer.

Commentary

■ **100** On the idea of death here, see 7:32 Commentary.

■ **101** See Function and Content, p. 249, on the exact meaning of this verse. The view seems to have been common that the soul remains near the body for seven days after death, and these seven days are those of mourning.[6] This seven-day period has also been compared with the seven days during which the earth will return to chaos before the new creation (7:30–31).[7] On the treasuries, see 4:35 Commentary and 4:41 Commentary.

■ **102** On the term "day of judgment," see the Excursus on the Term "Judgment," p. 149.

■ **103** The passage that this verse opens is strikingly paralleled by *Bib Ant* 33:4–5:

4. And when Debbora spake these words, all the people lifted up their voice together and wept, saying: Behold now, mother, thou diest and forsakest thy sons; and to whom doest thou commit them? Pray thou, therefore, for us, and after thy departure thy soul shall be mindful of us for ever. 5. And Debbora answered and said to the people: While a man yet liveth he can pray for himself and for his sons; but after his death he will not be able to entreat nor to remember any man. (Trans. M. R. James)

This passage deals with precisely the same concern as does 4 Ezra 7:102–115. Moreover, the explicit mention of fathers praying for sons, rather than people for one another or the like, seems to suggest a knowledge of a list like that here; this may well be compared with *Sifre Deut.* 32:39 (Finkelstein, p. 380), which both contains a list and denies the possibility of intercession. Similar too is *Apost. Const.* 2.14.9. Another similar passage in *2 Enoch* 53:1 (J) mentions fathers and sons and denies intercession. In *Biblical Antiquities,* death is the point beyond which no intercession is possible; in 4 Ezra it is related to the day of judgment. On this, see further commentary on the next verse.

■ **104** Bensly cites Hippolytus, *Against Plato* (ed. de Lagarde, p. 71): "No voice of interceding friends shall profit them [viz., the unrighteous] after final judgment and condemnation." This well epitomizes the content of this section. The general point is discussed in the Excursus on the Term "Judgment," p. 150.

Box suggests that this passage is specifically directed against the rabbinic concept of the merits of the fathers which avail the children in judgment.[8] Schechter already pointed out, however, that the relevance of the merit of the fathers to the issue of individual moral responsibility at the time of judgment was negligible, and some rabbinic authorities even held that the merit had ceased to have any effect as from various points in the past.[9]

---

6   See *PRE* 34 (trans. Friedlander, p. 257) for a late parallel. Seven days' mourning is an old idea; see already Sir 22:12 and Judith 16:25. The rabbinic sources are discussed by Ginzberg, *Legends,* 5:78, where he adduces evidence both for a seven-day period of the soul and a three-day one; see Hos 6:2 and contrast *Vit Ad* 43:2 and *Apoc Mos* 13:6. A similar idea relating to a three-day period also occurs in

Mandean sources; see E. S. Drower, *The Secret Adam* (Oxford: Oxford University, 1960) 30. See further Bousset-Gressmann, p. 341. To some extent, similar is *b. Shabb.* 152b, which speaks of a twelve-month period before the soul completely abandons its body.

7   Keulers, p. 155.

8   Page 154. Box quotes *Qoh. R.* on Qoh 4:1.

9   Schechter, *Aspects,* 170–98; Ginzberg, *Legends,*

Nonetheless, many rabbinic dicta refer to an intercessory function of the righteous, often in an eschatological context.[10]

Many sources refer to the absence of intercession on the day of judgment. Such are found elsewhere in the book, as was pointed out in the Excursus on the Term "Judgment," p. 150. In 7:103 Commentary a long passage was cited from *Biblical Antiquities* that clearly makes the same point.[11] Violet, in his comment on 14:4, points out that the word "send" means "commission" and is so used also in 14:4. Observe that this is a specific legal term in rabbinic law meaning "to designate as agent" (cf. *m. Gittin* 4:1), and we suggest that the verb be so understood here as well. Such an interpretation helps to illuminate the force of the present verse.

The expression "the seal of truth" is strikingly paralleled in *b. Shabb.* 55a and *b. Yoma* 69b which comment in a context of judgment: "The seal of the Holy One is truth." Gunkel interprets the phrase here of the judge's seal with which he guarantees the validity of the sentence, a view that is basically in accord with the Talmudic dictum. The relationship between judgment and truth is further explored in 5:1 Commentary and the different views of sealing in 6:20 Commentary.

In broad terms we may say that the problem the author raises about the inequality of the righteous and the wicked, which is the mainspring of this section of the book, is responded to, as elsewhere in 4 Ezra, in terms of "day of judgment" and not of "messianic kingdom."[12]

■ **105** The statement of individual responsibility here may be compared with Deut 24:16; Jer 31:28–29; and Ezek 18:20.

■ **106** The passage 7:106–111 argues from the past. Just as in a series of incidents that are documented in scripture the righteous have prayed for the wicked, and did so

in the present, imperfect world, why will they not be able to intercede in the future, perfect world? Abraham prayed for the people of Sodom, according to Gen 18:23–33. Moses' prayer on behalf of the people is recorded in Exod 32:11–14.

■ **107** The incident referred to is related in Josh 7:6–9.

■ **108** The prayer of Samuel is apparently that on the occasion of the Philistine war (1 Sam 7:8–9); that of David at the time of the plague (2 Sam 24:17–25); and that of Solomon, his great prayer at the time of the dedication of the Temple (1 Kgs 8:22–53).

■ **109** The incident of Elijah and the rain in time of drought is related in 1 Kgs 18:2–6, 36–46, while his revival of the child of the widow of Zarephath is found in 1 Kgs 17:21–23.

■ **110** Hezekiah's prayer at the time of Sennacherib's attack is preserved in 2 Kgs 19:15–19 and Isa 37:16–20.

■ **111** The idea of corruption, which is typical of this world and removed in the future one, is discussed in 4:11 Commentary. The two phrases "corruption has increased and unrighteousness has multiplied" are reminiscent in style of the poetic descriptions of the eschatological age analyzed in 6:11–29 Form and Structure, pp. 165–66. Here, however, the phrases describe the parlous state of this world, not the eschatological condition. The phrase "unrighteousness has multiplied" recurs more or less verbatim in 5:2.

■ **112** The angel replies: intercession has been necessary in this world, for glory does not remain in it continually, but it will be different at the end of this world or age.[13] There will be no intercession of the strong for the weak

---

5:160; and Urbach, *Sages,* 500; for different views, see *Aggadat Bereshit* 10; *m. Abot* 4:1; and *ARN,* p. 69 (trans. Goldin). Cf. also *Qoh. R.* on Qoh 4:1.

10 See Urbach, *Sages,* 494; see *Gen. R.* 33:3 (Theodor-Albeck, p. 308); *b. Sukka* 14a; and specifically of Moses (cf. 7:106 below) see *Exod. R.* 42:1 and *Deut. R.* 3:15.

11 The idea that there will be no repentance after death is connected with this idea; see 9:11 and *2 Apoc Bar* 85:12; cf. *1 Enoch* 5:5. A different point of view, from quite another perspective, may be observed in *Testament of Abraham* 14, particularly vv 10–15.

Another contrast is the passage in *Tanna debe El.* 3:12–14: "The righteous will stand before Him . . . and will dare to say to Him, . . . God will respond, 'If they did indeed do so, go and bring healing to them.' At once the righteous will go and, standing upon the dust to which the wicked had been reduced [by the Holy One], will entreat mercy for them. Then, out of the dust they were reduced to, the Holy One will have the wicked stand up on their feet" (trans. Braude and Kapstein, p. 72). See also previous note.

12 See further Stone, *Features,* 215.

13 On the term "world," see Excursus on the Term

on the day of judgment.[14] The full revelation of divine glory is intimately connected with judgment. Because the end of the world has not yet come and the world is therefore imperfect—that is, divine glory is not revealed in it continually—consequently, judgment is not fully carried out in it and intercession can therefore be effective.[15]

■ **113** The day of judgment here forms a division point between the two worlds or ages,[16] and that decisive turning point is signified by the word "end."[17] The nature of the coming world or age is set forth in a poetic passage that resembles other poetic descriptions of the eschatological state in the book, both in form and in content.[18] The idea of renewal of creation in the future age is implied here, and it may also be observed in 6:16; 7:31; and 7:75. See particularly 7:75 Commentary.

■ **114** As observed in the commentary on the preceding verse, this passage is intimately connected with 6:27–28 and 7:33–35. In them the same literary and content characteristics recur, including the stress on faith/unbelief and the appearance of truth.[19]

■ **115** No commentary.

"Age.", pp. 218–19. The idea of "end" is analyzed in detail in Stone, "Coherence and Inconsistency," and see Excursus on Natural Order, pp. 103–4. Here its primary meaning is "Day of Judgment."

14   See Excursus on the Term "Judgment," p. 150.

15   The meaning of "glory" here has been the object of some discussion. It is now resolved by the textual situation which is decisively in favor of the reading "glory of God" (see textual notes and *contra* e.g. Violet 2 here). On glory in the book, see 3:19 Commentary, 7:42 Commentary, and Excursus on the Term "Judgment," p. 150. See also Stone, *Features,* 206.

16   See Excursus on the Term "Judgment," p. 150, and cf. 12:34; on the two ages, see Excursus on the Two Ages.

17   This is demonstrated in Excursus on Natural Order, pp. 103–4, where the present verse is also analyzed.

18   These are discussed in detail in 6:11–29 Form and Structure, pp. 165–66.

19   *2 Enoch* 53:1 (J). See 6:11–29 Form and Structure.

116 I answered and said, "This is my first and [a]last word, [a] that it would have been better [b] if the earth had not produced Adam, [c] or else, when it had produced him had taught [d] him not to [e] sin. 117/ For what good is it to all [f] that they live in sorrow now [g] and expect punishment after death? 118/ O Adam, what have you done? For though it was you who sinned, the misfortune [h] was not yours alone, but ours [i] also who are your descendants.

119 For what good is it to us, if an immortal age [j]

has been promised to us,
but we have done deeds that bring death? 120/ Or that an everlasting [k] hope
has been predicted to us,
but we are miserably shamed? [l]
121/Or that safe and healthful treasuries have been reserved for us,
but we have erred [m] wickedly?
122/Or that the glory of the Most High will [n] defend those who have led a pure life,
but we have walked in the most wicked ways?
123/Or that a paradise shall be revealed, whose fruit does not spoil [o]
and in which are abundance and healing,
but we shall not enter it,
124/   because we have lived in unseemly places?
125/Or that the faces of [p]those who practiced self-control [p] shall shine [q]more than the stars, [q]
but our faces shall be blacker than darkness?
126/ [r]For while we lived and committed iniquity we did not consider [s] what we should [t] suffer after our death." [u]

127 He answered and said to me, [v] "This is the meaning of the contest [w] which every [x] man who is born on earth wages, 128/ that if he is defeated he shall suffer what you [y] have said, but if he is victorious he shall receive what I have said. 129/ For this is the way of which Moses, while he was alive, spoke to the people, saying, 'Choose for yourself life, that you may live!' 130/ But they did not believe [z] him, or the prophets after him, or even myself who have spoken to them. 131/ Therefore there shall not be grief at their destruction, so much as joy over [a]the life of those who did believe." [a]

Notes

116   a–a Ar2, Arm omit.
    b Eth adds "for us."
    c ἄνθρωπον Greek *Apoc Esd* 1:21; cf. 3:5 note c.
    d Syr, Eth, cf. Ar1; Lat "prevented him from."
    e Eth omits. Violet 1 suggests Greek κατέχειν, "restrain" (= Lat), confused with κατηχεῖν, "instruct" (= Syr, Eth).

117   f Lat, Syr; "us" Eth; Ar1 omits; "men" Ar2; "man" Arm.
    g Syr "here"; Eth omits; Ar1, Arm vary.

118   h Lat, Ar1; *casus* of Lat as emended by Bensly should be translated "misfortune" or the like, and not "fall," thus in accordance with the other versions.
    i Preceded by "all" in Ar1, Arm.

119   j *Tempus* Lat, Syr; "life" Ar1, so also the Arm exegesis "resurrection."

120   k Or "incorruptible"; cf. Syr, Ar1, Ar2.
    l Cf. Syr, Arm.

121   m Syr, Arm "erred"; each other version reads a different text.

122   n μέλλει is implied by the versions.

123   o Lat "remain unspoiled."

125   p–p So Lat, Eth; Syr "the saints"; Arm "the just"; Ar1, Ar2 expand.
    q–q So Lat, Syr; Eth omits; "like the luminaries of heaven" Ar1; "like lightning" Ar2; "like the sun" Arm.

126   r–s Eth "and behold we live"; Georg *et quid prodest vita haec nostra;* perhaps independent developments of a defective *Vorlage.*
    t Greek μέλλειν is implied by Lat, Syr.
    u Lat, Arm omit "our"; Eth omits "after our death," cf. Ar1.

127   v Lat, Arm omit.
    w Lat, Syr; Eth, Georg, Ar1 "this world"; probably going back to ΑΙΩΝΟΣ/ΑΓΩΝΟΣ. Lat, Syr is preferable on contextual grounds. Note stemmatic relations here.
    x Added for sake of clarification.

128   y Lat, Eth, Ar1; Syr could be "I" or "you"; Eth variant has "I," as do Georg, Arm; Ar2 omits.

130   z Two verbs Syr, Ar1.

131   a–a Syr, Eth, Georg; Lat reads *quibus persusa est salus.*

132   I answered and said, "I know, O Lord, that the Most High is now called
         merciful,
             because he has mercy on those who have not yet come
                 into the world; [b] 133/ and
         gracious,
             because he is gracious to those who turn in repentance
                 to his Torah; 134/ and
         patient,
             because he shows patience toward those who have sinned,
                 [c]since they are his own works; [c]
                 135/ and
         bountiful,
             because he would rather give [d]than take away; [d] 136/
             and
         abundant in compassion,
             because he makes his compassions abound more and more to
             those now living and to those who
                 are gone [e] and to those yet to come, [f] 137/ for if he did not make his compassions [g] abound, the world with those who inhabit it would not have life; 138/ and
         giver,
             because if he did not give out of his goodness
                 so that those who have committed iniquities might be relieved of them, not one ten-thousandth of mankind could live; 139/ and
         judge,
             because if he did not pardon those who were created by
                 his word and blot out the multitude of their sins,
140/   there would [h] be left only very few of the innumerable multitude."

8

1   He answered me and said, "The Most High made this world for the sake of many, but the world to come for the sake of few. 2/ But I will explain [i] the parable to you, Ezra. Just as, when you ask the earth, it will tell you that it provides very much clay from which earthenware is made, but only a little dust from which gold comes; so is the course [j] of the present world. 3/ Many have been created, but few shall be saved." [k]

132   b Eth has a variant that Violet suggests goes back to εἰς αἰῶνα (for εἰς τὸν αἰῶνα, we may add, that is implied by the other versions).

134   c–c There is some uncertainty here, our translation being based on a combination of Lat *quasi suis operibus*, Syr "since we are his works," and Eth "as on his children." Something similar also stood behind Georg, Ar1.

135   d–d Lat, Syr; Eth, Georg seem to have had a quite different text, a statement about "their works": Eth "to those who are worthy on account of their works"; Georg *primis illis operibus*, cf. also Ar1. This half-verse should be regarded as doubtful.

136   e Lat, Syr, Ar2; Eth, Georg have words meaning "disobedient"; it is attractive to hypothesize a Greek reading that could have begotten both of these; nothing, however, readily comes to mind.

       f Here once again Eth, Georg have shared reading "give praise" or "be praised"; once more we may speculate that an ambiguous Greek reading is behind this development.

137   g Lat omits.
139   h Lat adds *fortasse*.

8:2   i So Syr, Eth, Georg, Ar1; "I will tell" Lat; "I shall tell you one parable and you respond to me" Arm.

       j Literally, "work" Syr, Eth, Georg.

3   k Syr, Eth "live"; see 9:13 note n, 9:15 note h, and Excursus on Adam's Sin, p. 66.

Form and Structure

Many scholars divide this section into two major parts, 7:116–126 and 7:127—8:3. However, we regard its major parts as:

A. 7:116–126 Ezra's Lament
B. 7:127–131 Angelic Response
C. 7:132–140 Midrash on 13 Middot
D. 8:1–3 Angel's Response and Conclusion

It might be possible to set a major division between 7:131 and 7:132, but the whole seems to hold together, as will become evident below, so that seems unjustified.

Section 8:1–3, which concludes this pericope, also forms the end of the second major division of Vision 3. Vision 3 can be divided into four major parts (see also General Structure of the Book, p. 50). These are the following:

a. 6:38—7:44—Starts from the problems raised by election and concludes with the prediction of the eschaton.

b. 7:45—8:3—Commences and ends with the problems of the few and the many, and contains the prediction of the intermediate state.

c. 8:4–60—Moves from the creation of mankind (a theme set in section a [6:38–60]) to the few and the many (the theme of section b). Section 8:61–63 is transitional.

d. 9:1–22—Prediction of the signs.

A. *Ezra's Lament (7:116–126)*

7:116—"This is my first and last word." An inclusive statement indicating the final nature of what is to follow. Indeed, following this lament and questions, Ezra moves to other sorts of address.[1]

7:117—"For what good is it . . . ?" This literary structure prefigures the extended development of the same in 7:119–126. So, although the formulation of the rest of the declaration differs from the one employed uniformly in that passage, nonetheless this verse may be said to prefigure and in some measure to anticipate that which follows.

7:118—Apostrophe to Adam.

7:119–126—Series of questions, each introduced by "What good is it . . . ?" or "Or . . . ?" Each question asks, "What good is it that X has been prepared for the righteous while they have done Y," where X and Y are carefully contrasted:

> 119 What good is it . . . immortal age . . . deeds that bring death?
>
> 120 Or that . . . everlasting hope . . . miserably shamed?
>
> 121 Or that . . . safe and healthful habitations . . . erred wickedly?
>
> 122 Or that . . . pure life . . . wicked ways?
>
> 123–124 Or that . . . paradise . . . lived in unseemly places?
>
> 125 Or that . . . faces shine . . . faces blacker than darkness?

Ezra's despair is very powerfully communicated by the use of the apostrophe followed by the formulaic repetition of a series of images that culminate in the cry at the loss of paradise and the angelic eschatological state. Structural, literary, and conceptual elements here combine harmoniously to produce a very striking impact.

We have characterized the passage as a lament, even though it is formulated as a series of questions. In the course of the first three visions, four such passages of lament can be isolated. They occur in general at corresponding places in the vision structure and are themselves very similar: 4:12 with 4:22; 5:35; 7:62; and 7:116.

The two verses 4:12 and 4:22 form two parts of a single passage of lament. Chapter 4:12 is the only one of these which is introduced by a statement more complex than a simple "I said" or "I replied and said." It states that the seer prostrated himself before speaking.

Each lament occurs at a point in the discussion at which the seer has despaired of any resolution of his problems being achieved and hence (because of the sorts of questions he is asking) of the very human state itself. The passage 4:12 follows the denial of the possibility of knowledge, as do 4:22 and 5:35. In 7:62, Ezra's questions about the few and the many have been refused any satisfactory reply by God. The denial of the effectiveness of intercessory prayer in the pericope that precedes 7:116 seems to have engendered the same despair and to have triggered the lament that starts in 7:116.

The laments in the first vision, which in fact form two parts of one lament, separated by a question, pose the

---

1   This verse is central to Brandenburger's interpretation of Visions 1–3; see Introduction, sec. 4.2.3.

rhetorical question "Why was I born?" (4:12) and follow it with inquiries "Why . . . ?" (4:22). In 5:35 the lament opens with the same rhetorical question about the purpose of birth and follows it with an inquiry "Why . . . ?" In the third lament, in 7:62 the initial declaration about birth is formulated more obliquely: "O earth, what have you brought forth, . . . ?" while the literary structure following is more complex, including a declarative lament (7:62–68). The section concludes with an inquiry "What does it profit us . . . ?" (v 67). Finally, in 7:116 an opening declaration about the purposiveness of birth and a reference to the earth which brings forth mankind is succeeded by a developed series of "What does it profit us . . . ?"[2]

The laments, therefore, seem to represent a rather fixed form composed of a rhetorical question or a declaration of the pointlessness of birth, followed by the posing of some question arising out of the seer's despair. This question, in at least two of the laments, is put in the form "What does it profit us that . . . ?" The laments serve to express the seer's frustration at the lack of true response to his pleas and to move the argument on to a new stage.

B. The Angel's Response (7:127–131)

The response by the angel to Ezra's outburst concludes this piece of argument. Notable is the use of an explicit biblical quotation to finalize the reply. A very similar structure is to be found in the angel's response to the seer's questioning before the revelation of 7:26–44:

Statement	7:127–128 // 7:19–20
Prooftext	7:129 // 7:21
"They did not obey"	7:130 // 7:22–24
Proverbial conclusion	7:131 // 7:25

This is another instance in the book of the reference to the biblical text for proof of a statement and the only instance of explicit citation.

C. The Midrash on 13 Middot (7:132–140)

It was D. Simonsen, in an article published just as Box's Commentary was also appearing, who set forth the idea that the passage of 7:132–139 was a Midrash on Exod 34:6–7, a passage that was frequently quoted and interpreted, particularly in the context of penitential prayers.[3] The basic outline of the Midrash and its equivalents, as suggested by Simonsen, are set out here in tabular form.

7:132 Most High	=	אל
merciful	=	רחום
7:133 gracious	=	חנון
7:134 patient	=	ארך אפים
7:135 bountiful		
7:136 abundant in compassion	=	רב חסד ואמת
7:137 *expansion*		
7:138 giver	=	נצר חסד?
one ten-thousandth part	=	לאלפים
7:139 judge	=	the rest of the verse, cf. נשא עון

As Simonsen himself comments, there may be differences of opinion about certain of the identifications, but the overall pattern can scarcely be doubted. This sort of extended treatment of a biblical passage is found nowhere else in 4 Ezra, although some cases of implicit

---

2 On this use of "earth," see 7:116 Commentary.
3 D. Simonsen, "Ein Midrasch im 4.Buch Esra," *separatim* from *Festschrift zu Israel Lewy's 70. Geburtstag* (Breslau: Marcus, 1911); Box, p. 165. The formula may be observed in many sources in the Bible and from the Second Temple period; see Joel 2:13 and Jonah 4:2; cf. Ps 103:8; Neh 9:17; Sir 2:11; *Prayer of Manasseh* 7; *Test Patr Zeb* 9:7; and 1QH 11:29–30; cf. *Test Patr Sim* 4:4; *2 Apoc Bar* 77:7; and *Apoc Abr* 17:12. See *Greek Apoc Esd* 1:10–18, where there is a similar midrash on this biblical passage; see also the discussion in Stone, "Apocryphal Notes," 127–29. On its use in rabbinic sources, see Ginzberg, *Legends,* 6:58. Later midrashim on these verses are to be found in *Midr. Teh.* 93:8; *Pes. R. K.* (Buber, p. 161b); et al. D. Boyarin, "Penitential Liturgy in 4 Ezra," *JSJ* 3 (1972) 30–34, maintains that the whole passage from 7:102—8:36 draws heavily on a penitential (*Seliḥot*) liturgy. Most of his parallels are later than 4 Ezra in the particular constellation which they take in the penitential liturgy. His case is intriguing but unproven. See particularly the analysis of 8:19b–36 in Form and Function to that pericope. At present, it is more likely that 4 Ezra and the penitential liturgy depend on common stock.

exegesis have been noted; see General Index s.v. "Bible, exegesis of."

D. The Angel's Second Response (8:1–3)

The angel again answers Ezra. This time his response picks up a group of themes that had already been introduced in 7:45–74. In the analysis above it was shown that 7:45—8:3 forms one of the major subdivisions of Vision 3. Thus the reiteration here of subjects and themes drawn from 7:45–74 marks this angelic response as a conclusion, delimiting this whole segment.[4]

Thus 8:1 refers to the issue of the few and the many which is dealt with in 7:45–74, while 7:50 says "For this reason the Most High has created not one world but two," which statement is explained by 8:1. In 7:54–57 the angel has told the parable of the base and precious metals. This is explicitly referred to by the expression "explain the parable" in 8:2. Both 7:54 and 8:2 use a literary figure: "Ask the earth . . . ," and 8:3 picks up the end of the question that had been posed in 7:48.

Function and Content

As a whole, the passage 7:116—8:3 closes the sustained section of the vision that commenced in 7:45. Note particularly how its themes are raised in 7:17–18. The overall issues of this section are both the assertion of the fates of the few and the many and their inevitability on the day of judgment.

A. Ezra's Lament (7:116–126)

In 7:116–126 a question is posed which sums up the preceding parts of the vision. It may be paraphrased as follows: Given that (1) humans will be judged and punished for their sins (7:45–74); given that (2) punishment will start immediately post-mortem and that the punishment will be immediate and unremitting (7:75–99); and finally given that (3) there will be no alleviation or intercession (7:100–116)—therefore. . . . The actual questions asked are put using two apostrophes. The first is "O earth," (1) why does creation exist when humans sin (v 116) or, in other words, (2) why does present suffering

exist which will be followed by punishment? The second apostrophe is "O Adam, why did you sin?" which resulted (1) in the terrible fate of us all (7:118); and (2) in the situation that the promise of reward is in fact useless, since we are all to be punished anyway (7:119–126).

This whole inquiry which is formulated as a lament (see Form and Structure, pp. 255–56) issues from the angel's answer touching on the few and the many, a problem that was first raised in the present section in 7:45. It is worth noting that 7:119–126, by way of its implications, provides some sort of description of the world to come. Such a description is not found elsewhere in the book in such terms; see 8:52–53 Commentary.

B. The Angelic Response (7:127–131)

The angel's response is along the lines of free will and human responsibility for action. He rejects implicitly the idea of "original sin" or the like, which Ezra seems to have implied, and asserts that mankind has been given freedom of action and the consequent possibility of reward and punishment (7:127–128).[5] Moreover, he adds, you knew that this was the case, since scripture stated it explicitly (7:129–130). Therefore the response to the problem of the few and the many is not some way by which the many can yet be saved from punishment but the reassertion that there will be more joy over the few than there will be grief over the many (7:131; cf. 7:60–61).

C. Ezra's Prayer—Midrash on 13 Middot (7:132–140)

Just as the angel used scripture to make his point, so Ezra too cites scripture in his response. He does not answer the angel on the level of argument but formulates a long prayer, based on Exod 34:6–7, which asserts God's mercy and compassion. The technique is reminiscent, in a different literary genre, of the use by the seer of the list of instances of intercessory prayer that was found in the preceding section (7:106–110). Ezra is demonstrating to the angel, who speaks for God, that God is compassionate because scripture has stated him to be so. Clearly implied is that this compassion must relate to the wicked.

---

4   A series of common themes are shared by the opening and closing pericopes: the contrasts of "life" and "destruction," of joy and grief, the few and the many, and the parable of the rare and common minerals.

5   See further Excursus on Adam's Sin, pp. 64–65. This was, of course, the view of the Rabbis. See also Brandenburger, *Adam und Christus*, 29–36.

The exact relationships between God and humans implied by this passage are complex, but the overall point is very clear, that human beings survive only because of God's mercy.[6]

D. The Angel's Concluding Response (8:1–3)

In the final response, which is also the conclusion to the whole second section of the vision, the angel reiterates the position with which this subdivision opened in 7:45. In a sense, then, the subdivision had gone nowhere. It started and ended with the few and the many, with the inevitability of fate. There is no note of hope here. This contrasts with the situation at the end of the first major part of the vision, which concluded with the eschatological promises of 7:26–44, and the third major division the end of which is the promise of 8:52. Yet it should be recalled that this is the second of three subdivisions of a very complex literary piece, and its overall significance must be analyzed in these broader terms.

Commentary

■ **116** The verse is a lament, and in Form and Structure, pp. 255–56, we have dealt with such laments. It is intriguing that the earth was introduced into the lament in 7:62, while the previous laments in the book formulated this *topos* much more traditionally: "Why was I born . . . ?"[7] Here the earth is said to produce mankind, and in 4:40 Commentary the things that the earth produced are discussed. Interestingly, in 4 Ezra 3:4, as in *2 Apoc Bar* 48:46, God is said to command the dust to produce mankind, while here, in 7:116, the dust is said to produce mankind. In the continuation of the verse the earth is also the one that should have "taught him not to sin," while in 3:8, God is taxed "and thou didst not hinder" (i.e., mankind from sinning). So both of the actions attributed to the earth here in 7:116 are those which (much more naturally) chapter 3 attributes to God. While the earth could be talked of, particularly in a poetic context, as producing mankind, it is very hard to understand what the earth's not preventing mankind

from sinning could mean. Therefore it is possible that some sensitivity about what can be stated of God is at play here.

The implication of the verse is worked out in detail only in 7:118, that is, that Adam's sin brought about a "misfortune" inherited by his descendants. This point of view is implied in our verse by the (secondary) reading of certain witnesses, which is "mankind" for "Adam." The introductory phrase is discussed in Form and Structure, pp. 255–56.

■ **117** The pessimistic thrust of the verse is striking, and it occurs elsewhere in the book (but not exclusively); see 7:67 Commentary. The same basic sense is to be found in *2 Apoc Bar* 14:14, and the formulation is rather like *2 Apoc Bar* 17:2. The expression "What good is it . . . ?" occurs in the latter passage and, of course, occurs throughout the coming verses; see Form and Structure, pp. 255–56. The sentiment expressed here is very much like that in the parallel lament in 7:67–68.

■ **118** This verse, formulated as an apostrophe to Adam, is a restatement of what the author said in 3:20–22, which speaks of the sin of Adam affecting all of his descendants, "the disease" becoming permanent and the "evil root" being in the hearts of humans. It contrasts strikingly with *2 Apoc Bar* 54:19:

Adam is therefore not the cause, except only for himself,

But each of us has become our own Adam.

2 Apoc Bar 54:19, which presents a much more "orthodox" view, reads like a deliberate critique of 4 Ezra.[8] However, in a context similar to here, in *2 Apoc Bar* 48:42 we read:

O Adam, what did you do to all who were born after you?

And what will be said of the first Eve who obeyed the serpent?

The nature of Adam's sin and its results are discussed in detail in the Excursus on Adam's Sin, pp. 64–65, and in 3:22 Commentary. In Latin, the word translated "mis-

---

6 See Thompson, *Responsibility*, 302.

7 This *topos* is dealt with in 4:12 Commentary.

8 The matter is, in fact, complex. 4 Ezra holds both a view of inherited weakness or sin and of free will. This is so striking that Gry postulated that 4 Ezra 7:118 is a Christian interpolation to alleviate the tension; see further 7:67 Commentary and 7:127 Commentary.

fortune" is *casus*, properly "fall," "misfortune." This entered the translations as "Fall" and resulted in a good deal of discussion about the concept of original sin here. This sense is not supported by the other versions, however; see the textual notes to this word.[9]

■ **119** The "immortal age" is the age to come in which "corruption will be overcome" (6:28). The contrast is between the world of eternal life and the deeds that cause death, apparently eternal death.[10]

■ **120** The expression "everlasting hope" may be compared with "living hope" in 1 Pet 1:3, both being expressions of eschatological significance.[11]

■ **121** The term "healthful" to describe the future state of the righteous is uncommon but may be compared with 7:123 and 8:52–54.[12] "Treasuries" (Lat *habitacula*) is a term that occurs elsewhere in the book of the dwelling places of the righteous; see 4:35 Commentary for a full discussion. On the precreation of eschatological rewards, see 3:6 Commentary and 6:6 Commentary.

■ **122** On glory, see 3:19 Commentary. It is possible that the image here is legal, the glory as advocate of the righteous, and so related to the idea of the glory as being the element that executes judgment. Alternatively glory has been regarded as a protection against dangers and compared with Isa 4:4–5 and with the rabbinic idea of the righteous resting beneath the wings of the Shechinah, cf. *b. Shabb.* 31a and Volz, p. 305. Expressions such as "ways of wickedness" are commonplace. It is worth noting that the imagery of the path or way of man is implied already in 7:121, and 7:123 still speaks of entering.[13]

■ **123** The image of paradise is discussed in 3:6 Commentary and its fruit in 7:13 Commentary. Here the fruit is said to be "healing"; compare the ideal state described by Ezek 47:12: "There shall grow all kinds of trees for food.

. . . Their fruit shall be for food and their leaves for healing."[14]

■ **124** No commentary.

■ **125** The idea of the shining of the faces of the righteous above the stars is discussed in 7:97 Commentary. It is interesting to note that in Wisd 3:7 the righteous are said to shine forth at the time of visitation. In *Test Patr Jos* 3:4, Joseph speaks of how well he looked in spite of prolonged fasting, "for those who fast for the sake of God receive graciousness of countenance" (3:4). While ascetic tendencies are present in some Jewish texts, the celebration of ascetic virtue is far less marked than in later Christian circles.[15]

The blackening of the faces of the wicked is the reverse of this brightness. The same idea occurs in *1 Enoch* 62:10; cf. 46:6.[16] Observe the saying in *ARN* (Schechter, p. 79), "If at death one's face is bright, it is a good sign from him; if one's face is overcast [literally, "becomes dark"—M.E.S.], it is a bad sign for him."[17]

■ **126** No commentary.

■ **127** On the idea that humans can achieve righteous action only after a struggle, see 7:92 Commentary. A striking parallel is *Ap John* 26:4–6 (CG 2.1.26, lines 1–8), "For they endure everything and bear up under everything, that they may finish the good fight and inherit eternal life" (*NHL*, p. 113). Behind the phrase here is the view of the conflict between the good and the evil inclinations within the human heart. On this, see the Excursus on Adam's Sin, p. 64. The athletic imagery is here most explicit, cf. 3:21; it is common in Greek literature and was taken over in Jewish texts such as Wisd 4:2 and here.[18] Compare particularly *Apoc Abr* 29:17. This verse

---

9   Moore, *Judaism*, 3:146 n. 198, energetically rejects the translation "fall" here.

10   The latter expression has been compared with Heb 6:1, 9:14 "dead works," but the sense here is different. Cf. Excursus on Adam's Sin, pp. 65–66.

11   Note also the quite similar "hope which will not be cut off" in Prov 23:18 and 24:14.

12   Cf. Volz, p. 390.

13   In 7:124 Violet 1 speculates that Ethiopic may go back to τρόποις ⟨ τόποις; cf. Box. This reading would, of course, sustain the image of the way or path.

14   See 7:122 Commentary above and cf. Rev 22:2. See also the sources cited by Ginzberg, *Legends*, 5:105.

15   See Schechter, *Aspects*, 277–78; there are numerous sources, such as *2 Enoch* 66:6 and others.

16   It does not seem justified to associate this idea with the darkness of Hades or similar ideas, as many scholars do.

17   J. Goldin, trans., *The Fathers According to Rabbi Nathan* (reprint, New York: Schocken, 1974) 105.

18   The same idea is explicit in *2 Apoc Bar* 15:8 and *Od Sol* 9:11.

is then a strong assertion of free will, set in the mouth of the angel. It may be compared in this respect with *2 Apoc Bar* 54:15, and see 7:45–74 Form and Content, p. 229.

■ **128** This verse continues the angelic response to Ezra's lament. The point of the response is almost exactly the same as that of the response to Ezra's outburst in 7:45–48 with which this part of Vision 3 opens. In 7:127–131 a point very similar to 7:59–61 is made: humans can determine their own fate by their own free choice. As for the wicked, there shall not be grief at their destruction so much as joy over the righteous. The language of contest was discussed in the 7:127 Commentary.

■ **129** This is a rare quotation of a proof text, from Deut 30:19. On this use of the biblical verse, see Form and Structure, p. 256.[19] This verse was important in the Second Temple period, as its utilization also in Sir 15:17; *Test Mos* 3:11–12; and *2 Apoc Bar* 19:1 indicates. It was also significant in the development of the ideas and terminology of the "two ways"; see 7:6 Commentary. The rather similar verse Deut 30:15 is used in a very similar, proof-text fashion in 7:21; see Commentary there. As noted, here Syriac conflates Deut 30:19 with Deut 30:15. The point of the citation here is to strengthen the assertion of free will. Its use in *2 Apocalypse of Baruch* is very similar to that here, being in a context of "the few and the many" and free will.

■ **130** There are many texts that speak of rejection of the word of God. The rejection of prophets, too, is an oft-repeated theme; see 2 Chron 36:15–16; Matt 5:17; 23:37; et al. What is notable here is that the angel sets himself in the line of the mediators of the divine word, together with Moses and the prophets.[20]

■ **131** This verse repeats an idea that was already developed at the beginning of this subdivision of Vision 3, in 7:45–74. There we find not only the language of "life" and "destruction" but also (in 7:60–61) the language of "joy" and "grief"; see further Function and Content, p. 257.[21] The same language appears, in a more extreme fashion, in *1 Enoch* 94:10b and c: "And over your fall there will be no mercy, but your creator will rejoice at your destruction"; cf. 97:2.

■ **132** This verse marks the beginning of the Midrash on 13 *Middot* which continues to 7:140. On this, see Form and Structure, pp. 256–57. "Merciful" is drawn from Exod 34:6. The idea is that, although God knows that humans will sin, he is nonetheless compassionate toward them, even before birth. This theme continues in 7:133–135, which refers to God's mercy toward those who are living out their life in the world, while 7:136 speaks of those not yet born, those now living, and those who are dead. It is, nonetheless, notable that throughout the Midrash there is almost no reference to eschatological mercy. The argument is made from the present state of the world; in it, divine compassion may be shown to be at work. "God treats man according to his deserts at each moment."[22] A reference to "those who have not yet" been born is found in the riddle passage in 5:36 and see 4:36 Commentary. Compare also *2 Apoc Bar* 48:8.

■ **133** Compare Exod 34:6. On divine mercy to the repentant, see 2 Chron 30:9 and Targum Exodus 34:7: "forgives those who return to his Torah" (on a different phrase of the same biblical passage). The idea that God is merciful both before humans sin (7:132) and afterward is well expressed in *b. Rosh Hashanah* 17b.

■ **134** Compare Exod 34:6. The attribute "patient" or "long-suffering" is used particularly in a context of forgiveness. The testimonies are numerous; note, for example, 1QH 6:9; 10:13; 11:9; and b. Sanh. 111a–b. Compare *2 Apoc Bar* 24:2. The connection between

---

19 From a text-critical point of view, see Stone, *Features*, 41–42. The text is unremarkable from this perspective. The Syriac fills out the quotation, drawing from Deut 30:15. Cf. also *Gen. R.* 3:8 (Theodor-Albeck, p. 23).

20 Similar ideas are expanded in the Armenian version of 8:62A–62D, but there the various revealers are either humans or God himself. Brandenburger, *Verborgenheit*, 32, thinks that here the author's views, which are expressed, e.g., in Ezra's address in 14:27–35, may have broken through the literary representation. His opinion is based on a different understanding of the dynamic of the dialogue, but the difficulty is well highlighted.

21 On the language of life and death, see Excursus on Adam's Sin, pp. 66–68. On joy and grief, see 7:28 Commentary and 7:36 Commentary; the application in those verses is somewhat different from here.

22 Ginzberg, *Legends*, 5:246.

sinfulness, forgiveness, and humans being created by God is to be observed in Isa 64:7–8.

■ **135** It is not clear to what "bountiful" corresponds in Exod 36:4. Simonsen thinks that it is רב חסד (abounding in steadfast love), which is also reflected in 7:136. The verse has been compared with an interesting passage of *Sed. El. Rab.* that exegetes Deut 28:9 in the light of Exod 34:6 in a way that is often like that of 4 Ezra. In it the bestowing of gifts is an exegesis of חנון (gracious).

> So, as the ways of Heaven are being *merciful and compassionate* toward the wicked and accepting them in repentance, you are *to be compassionate* toward one another. And, as the ways of Heaven are *to be gracious, graciously bestowing gifts* not only upon those who know Him but also upon those who do not know Him, *so you are to bestow gifts* upon one another. And, as the ways of Heaven are *to be long-suffering, long-suffering with the wicked and accepting them in repentance,* so you are *to be long- suffering* [with the wicked] for their good and not impatient to impose punishment upon them. For, as the ways of Heaven are *abundant in loving-kindness,* ever leaning to *loving-kindness,* so are you ever to lean toward *doing kindness* to others rather than lean toward doing them harm. (*Sed. El. Rab.* 135 [trans. Braude and Kapstein, p. 333; the italics are ours]).

■ **136** Compare Exod 34:6.

■ **137** Observe the Midrash on the two divine names in Gen 2:4: "The Holy One said, 'If I create [the world] through the attribute of mercy, its sins will be many; [if I create it] through the attribute of judgment, the world cannot survive. Rather I shall create it through the attribute of mercy and the attribute of judgment (together). Would that it survives.' [This is the meaning of the two divine names] the LORD God" (*Gen. R.* 12:15 [Theodor-Albeck, p. 113]). Simonsen thinks that the

ultimate meaning refers to eternal life. Compare also *2 Apoc Bar* 84:11 and *Ps Sol* 15:13, and see further the Excursus on Adam's Sin, pp. 66–68.[23]

■ **138** Compare Exod 34:7.

■ **139** Compare Exod 34:7. Compare *2 Apoc Bar* 84:11: "For if He judge us not according to the multitude of His mercies, woe unto all us who are born." Compare also *Midrash Tehillim* in the context of the same biblical verses here being quoted. On creation by the word of God, see 3:4 Commentary, and cf. Ps 33:9.

■ **140** The view that there are only very few righteous is to be found often in the book. Closest to the present verse are 7:48 and 9:15–16.

■ **8:1** This verse opens the final conclusion of the second section of the long Vision 3; see Form and Structure, p. 255. It refers back to 7:45–61, and that which is expressed there and in 9:15 in terms of punishment and salvation is expressed here in the terminology of "this world" and "the world to come."[24]

■ **8:2** This verse is, as it were, the answer of the earth that had been called for in 7:55–56: "Say to her [scil., the earth]. . . ." There, the earth's reply was not given. Again, "the course of the present world" here contrasts with and complements "the judgment" of 7:60. The subject of rejoicing is absent here but is prominent in the earlier passage.

■ **8:3** This expression has a proverbial ring. Compare 9:15 and particularly Matt 22:14: "For many are called, but few are chosen." See also 8:41.

---

23   Similar wording with different concepts is to be found in Ps 119:77.

24   On the term "world," see Excursus on the Two Ages and Excursus on the Term "Age."

8

4

I answered and said, "Then take delight in [a] understanding, O my soul, and drink [b] wisdom, O my ears! [c] 5/ [d]For not of your own will did you come [d] (i.e., into the world), and against your will you depart, for you have been given only a short time to live. 6/ O Lord [e], command [f] thy servant [g]that we may pray before thee, [g] and give us [h]seed for our heart and cultivation of our understanding [h] whence fruit may be produced, by which every mortal who bears the likeness [i] of a human being may be able to live. 7/ [j]For thou alone dost exist, [j] and we are a work of thy hands, as thou hast declared. 8/ And because thou dost give life [k] to the body which is now fashioned in the womb, and dost fit together [l] its members, [m]what thou hast created is preserved [m] in fire and water, and for nine months [n]that which thou hast formed bears thy creation [n] which thou created [o] in it. 9/ [p]But that which keeps and that which is kept shall both be kept by thy keeping, [p] And when the womb gives up

Notes

4 a The versions seem to go back to ἀπόλαυε except for Lat, which derives from ἀπόλυε.

b Syr, Eth; *devoret* Lat; *repletae sunt* Georg.

c Lat omits; "heart" Syr; "ears" Eth, Georg, Ar1. The *Vorlage* of Lat, Syr seems to have been corrupt. Violet 2 suggests that all derive from corruptions of φρὴν νοῦν.

5 d–d Violet 1 suggests that Lat, Syr go back to ἧκες γὰρ ἄκουσα. Lat reads ἄκουσα, which actually comes from ἀέκουσα, as if it was an aorist participle of ἀκούω, "to hear," doubtless under the influence of "ears" in the preceding phrase. The same reading, together with expansion, presumably lies behind the variants of Eth ("for the ear has come to hear") and Georg (*O mens advenis ad audiendum*).

6 e Lat adds *super nos;* Syr has *mry' mry*, but all other versions have just "Lord." Could Latin *super nos* derive from *supernus*, with which compare Arm "Most High"?

f So Syr; *pqd* Georg, Ar1, Ar2, cf. Eth.

g–g Eth, Georg omit.

h–h Lat, with which cf. Georg *seminiferum cor et culturam mentis;* the other versions vary more or less; none, however, reading a text necessarily in conflict with that accepted here.

i Lat has *locum;* perhaps τόπος/τύπος (so already Gunkel). Eth has "world," and Violet suggests κόσμος; Georg, however, has "life," which sometimes in Arm is equivalent to "world" deriving from עולם in the other versions, and one might suggest a similar reading in Georg. Along these lines, one might propose εἰκών/αἰών, but then Latin remains unexplained.

7 j–j Lat, Syr, Ar2; there seems to have existed a second Greek reading reflected in "for we are all like" Eth; *qui una in unum* Georg, so also Ar1.

8 k Lat (as emended by Bensly), Syr show a reflex of infinitive absolute and finite verb.

l Syr, Georg; *et praestas membra* Lat; others vary.

m–m Eth, Georg "you preserved it"; two Greek texts are here implied.

n–n Lat, Syr; Eth, Georg apparently go back to "your creation is born" (Eth omits "creation"), cf. Ar2.

o Syr, Eth, Georg, Ar1; "has been created" Lat.

9 p–p Lat, Syr; Georg has short lacunae; Eth "and it will be kept through your own word"; Ar1 "and these created things were kept with you"; Ar2 "and you are he who kept them"; Arm "and it preserves them."

again what ᑫhas been created ᑫ in it, 10/ thou hast commanded that from the members ʳ milk should be supplied which is the fruit of the breasts, 11/ so ˢthat what has been fashioned ˢ may be nourished for a time; and afterward thou wilt guide ᵗ him in thy mercy.

12/ Thou hast nourished him in thy right-
    eousness,
       and instructed him in thy law,
       and taught ᵘ him in thy wisdom. ᵛ

13/ Thou takest ʷ away his life, for he is thy
    creation;
       and thou makest ʷ him live, for he is
       thy work.

14/ ˣIf then thou wilt quickly ʸ destroy him who ᶻwith so great labor ᶻ was fashioned by thy command, to what purpose was he made? ᵃ 15/ And now I will speak out: ᵇ About all mankind thou knowest best; ᶜ but ᵈ(I will speak) ᵈ

       about thy people, for whom I am grieved,
16/   and about thy inheritance, for whom I
       lament,
       ᵉand about Israel, for whom I am sad, ᵉ
       and about the seed of Jacob, for whom
       I am troubled.

17/ Therefore I will ᶠ pray before thee for myself and for them, for I see the failings of us who dwell on the earth, 18/ and I have heard of the ᵍ judgment ʰ that is to come. ⁱ 19a/ Therefore hear my voice, and understand my words, ʲ and I will speak before thee."

10   q–q Lat, cf. Eth; Arm; "is" Syr, Ar1; lacuna Georg; others vary.

10   r Lat adds a gloss: "that is, from the breasts."

11   s–s Eth "your work"; *creationem tuam* Georg.
       t Lat, Syr; cf. Ar2.

12   u "Reproved" Lat.
       v Eth, Georg; *intellectu* Lat; *bskwltnwtk* Syr.

13   w Lat has two futures, giving an eschatological turn to the phrase. This is also the interpretation of the Arabic versions. The present tense is accepted here, since the (secondary) move from a present general statement to a future eschatological one seems more probable.

14   x Many lacunae in Georg.
       y *Facili ordine* Lat, cf. Arm and Syr *b'ql' wqlyl'yt;* other versions omit.
       z–z Eth "in so many days"; Arm has "for so long a time are caused to be born with labor and pains." Does Arm contain a doublet that witnesses indirectly to Eth?
       a Lat, Syr seem to derive from ἐγένετο; Eth, Ar1, Ar2 "did you create him."

15   b Lat, Syr, Eth, Ar1 have a reflex of infinitive absolute and finite verb in Hebrew. Lacuna in Georg.
       c Georg adds *de eo quod imperasti mihi.* The versions are a bit uncertain about the phrase b–c.
       d–d These words are supplied for the sake of the English.

16   e–e Eth, Georg omit.

17   f The versions witness Greek μέλλειν.

18   g Lat adds "swiftness of the."
       h Eth, Georg "law," perhaps κρίσεως ⟩ κτίσεως (Violet 2).
       i Eth "of the future world"; Georg *creationis quod futurum est;* "your creation" Ar1.

19a   j Georg Ar1 add "of my mouth."

Form and Structure

This section introduces the third main subdivision of this very long Vision 3, which concludes at 8:62. Its chief parts are:

A. 8:4–19   *Address—Monologue*
B. 8:20–36   *Prayer*
C. 8:37–62   *Dispute*

The next pericope, a Prediction 2 passage (9:1–13), concludes both this section and the body of the vision. The main themes of this part of Vision 3 are the creation of mankind, the redemption of the righteous, and the few and the many. The creation theme is set in 6:38–59, the address at the start of the first part of Vision 3; the theme of the few and the many and the redemption of

the righteous is introduced in 7:45–74, the dispute with which the second section of the vision opens. Thus the overall, integrated structure of Vision 3 is visible.

This address combines with the following prayer (8:19b–36) to form the introduction to this third subdivision of the vision. It may be that these two pericopes should be treated together, but the shift in the middle of 8:19 is striking, and the literary type of the prayer following this verse is quite different from that of the address preceding it. Moreover, the prayer has had a quite independent history in later transmission that justifies treating it separately.

Together, these two passages form an address set in

the mouth of the seer which is parallel in its structural role to the speeches with which Vision 1, Vision 2, and Vision 3 open (3:4–36; 5:23–30; 6:38–59).[1]

This address, 8:4–19, itself falls into two parts. The first is a presentation of the issues (8:4–14) and the second, the posing of the questions that arise from that presentation (8:15–19). A similar division is to be found in the three preceding addresses in the book, and the turning point in 8:15 is exactly parallel to those in 3:28; 5:28; and 6:55.

The chief parts of this section are:

A. *The Presentation of the Issues*

1. Opening formula and apostrophe to the soul (8:4–5). The formula is a simple one, and the apostrophe to the soul is not unlike apostrophes addressed to the earth (7:62) and to Adam (7:118). The author favors this rhetorical device.
2. Direct address to God starting with "Command thy servant" in 8:6 and concluding with a summary formulation of the seer's argument in 8:13.
3. Concluding question leading into the next part of the speech (8:14).

B. *The Posing of the Questions*

1. Brief phrase introducing the questions, "And now I will speak out" (8:15). Similar phrases may be observed in 3:28 ("Then I said in my heart"); 5:18 ("And now, O Lord"); and 6:55 ("All this I have spoken before thee, O Lord"). In all of these instances, the phrase signals the seer's shift from argument to the questions that are of deepest concern to him.
2. The actual issues are presented only by implication. They are put in 8:15b–16 in the form of four parallel hemistichs that lay the groundwork and then by the introduction of the prayer which in the present instance replaces the formal argument (8:17–19a).

Function and Content

As in the previous addresses, a chief theme is introduced that forms the point of departure for the ensuing dispute. The theme is well summarized by 8:13:

> Thou takest away his life, for he is thy creation, and thou makest him live, for he is thy work.

In other words, the argument put here is that humans have been created by God, they are kept alive by God, and they die according to God's will (8:4–13). Ezra, having laid this groundwork which seems to be universal in application, raises only one specific question: If the creation of humans was such a complex and wondrous procedure, why does God destroy them so quickly?

Having said this, however, he proceeds to formulate his questions in 8:15–19a, saying that he is distressed on account of Israel and is praying on behalf of Israel and himself, for he has seen their failings and future judgment (8:17–18). That is, the issue of the fate of Israel, which has been so predominant in Visions 1 and 2, is again brought to the fore.[2] This last section is a refocusing not merely after the first part of this speech but after the whole second part of Vision 2, in the course of which the issue of the fate of Israel has scarcely been debated. This is a reinterpretation of the issue of the few and the many which was the motif running through that second subdivision of the Vision, though there Israel's fate was not discussed.[3]

On a close reading, 8:4–18 bears a striking resemblance to 3:4–36 in one dominant respect. It is structured, both in content and in style, to reiterate the responsibility borne by God for the creation of mankind. Ezra's apostrophe to his soul in 8:5 sets the tone, gently at first: "For not of your own did you come (into the world), and against your will you depart." In his address to God the theme becomes dominant. "For we are a work

---

1 It is worth observing that the second part of Vision 3 does not open with an address but instead with dispute and lament. Thus, although each part of Vision 3 is a sort of "mini-vision" in structure, this is not carried through completely consistently.

2 Harnisch (p. 81 note) says that Israel here is representative of mankind as a whole, which does not really help to smooth out the roughness of the transmission at this place. For the discussion of another rather similar confusion, see 7:1–25 Function and Content, p. 194. See further the Commentary on 8:18.

3 Harnisch would see this passage as a reflection of the book's negative view of this aeon and the transitoriness of life; see p. 117 note with many references. Such views, expressed with greater or lesser emphasis, certainly are at home in the conceptual world of 4 Ezra, but we would maintain that here the chief motive of the passage is that which we have stressed.

of thy hands, as thou hast declared" (8:7); "and because thou dost give life . . . thou hast created . . . thou hast formed (8:8) . . . kept by thy keeping (8:9) . . . thou hast commanded (8:10) . . . thou wilt guide (8:11) . . . thou hast nourished . . . and instructed (8:12)." This is even more strongly asserted in 8:13 (quoted above), and the point of the argument is made completely explicit in 8:14. God's responsibility for the creation and growth of mortal men and women is thus highlighted, and the literary techniques and effect are very similar to those used in the address before the first vision.

The creation of mankind is treated as a twofold procedure, at least by implication. The author opens with an apostrophe addressed to the soul, in which the explicit reference is not to being born or dying but to "coming into the world" and departing from it, which contrasts with the detailed description of the creation of the body in 8:7–10. This remarkable passage deals with responsibility God bears for conception and birth and shows a deep appreciation of the wondrous nature of this process.

At this point another theme of the passage comes to the fore, the use of language drawn from the wisdom tradition. In the opening apostrophe, the seer calls upon his soul to "take delight in understanding" and to "drink wisdom." These terms derive from the range of sapiential literature, but they are applied in 4 Ezra to the experiences of the soul. Moreover, these words at the start of an address may function as do the descriptions of the onset of inspiration in the other addresses.[4] In 8:6, Ezra asks for "seed of heart and cultivation of understanding" which will give eternal life. Below, in 8:12, God is said to instruct humans in his law and his wisdom. The terminology of wisdom is thus polyvalent here, implying diverse things.[5]

The shift in 8:15 is dramatic. In 8:14 a general issue is posed: given God's responsibility for creation, which has been stressed and restressed in the preceding, if God will destroy so quickly those who are created (cf. the end of the preceding section dealing with the few and the many), what is the purpose of creation? Yet this is not taken up in 8:15. Instead, the problem of the suffering of Israel is raised. Ezra explains his own motivation. He is grieved by the suffering of Israel (8:15–17), which is stressed in fourfold parallelistic repetition. Indeed, on the face of it verse 17 seems to contradict verse 15. In verse 15, Ezra proclaims that he is abandoning concern for mankind in general and that he speaks only for Israel. Yet the general concern apparently returns by the end of 8:17.

The development of ideas is the following. Because of his grief for Israel (8:15–16), Ezra is led to pray on behalf of himself and Israel (8:17a), for he perceives "the failings of us who inhabit the earth" (8:17b). This implies that Israel's suffering derives from Israel's sin and in turn leads him to consider general human sinfulness. He has also accepted the idea of judgment, about which he received revelations previously. Once he has understood both sin and judgment, which together explain Israel's lot, he is moved to pray on behalf of Israel and himself (and by implication on behalf of all humans). Here the interlacing of the "national" and the "universal" themes is complete. The connection of thought in 8:15–17 is allusive and deeply dependent on that which has preceded. Following this, the prayer commences.

Commentary

■ **4** The language of wisdom and understanding is prominent in this verse; see Form and Structure.

■ **5** Quite similar formulations and sentiments to those expressed here are to be found elsewhere; note particularly the following:

For lo! by thy gift do we come into the world,
And we depart not of our own will. (*2 Apoc Bar* 48:15; cf. vv 12–14)

---

4   See Excursus on Inspiration, p. 121. Some of these descriptions also contain wisdom terms.

5   This double meaning of wisdom language, implying both inspiration and divine teaching, is discussed in Excursus on Inspiration, pp. 123–24. The language of 8:19 "hear" and "understand" may be an inversion of the same wisdom language, here applied by Ezra to God.

And:

> For involuntarily you were formed, and involuntarily you were born, and involuntarily you live, and involuntarily you die, and involuntarily you are destined to give account and reckoning before the Supreme King of kings. (*m. Abot* 4:21)[6]

■ **6** Note the shift in the person addressed. Previously it was the soul and now it is God. Moreover, where in other parts of the address the first person singular is used, here and in the next verse the first person plural. The significance of this change is unclear. This elaborate introduction is not quite paralleled elsewhere in the book.

The expression "understanding" is ambiguous in this context, being parallel to "wisdom" in 8:4 and to "heart" here.[7]

The image of seed and sowing is discussed in detail in 4:28 Commentary and 4:30 Commentary. It refers to the working of Torah within human beings. In the background of the present passage is the idea of the tree of life, whose fruit gives immortality.[8] Seed of the heart and its cultivation will produce fruit that will give life, that is, redemption or eternal life.[9] This is connected with the idea, proposed elsewhere in 4 Ezra, that there is a relationship between the mind and eternal reward or punishment.[10] Mind and understanding are of central importance in the book. They will be granted by God and will have an eschatological outcome.

The relationship with the creation stories in Genesis is thus clear, and we may be permitted to speculate (but only that) that the odd expression about mortals who "bear the likeness of man" may go back to an ambiguous Hebrew אדם, which might mean either "Adam" or "human being" and was taken, incorrectly, in the latter sense here. Were this the case, then the association with language like that of 3:20–21 is clear:

> Yet thou didst not take away from them their evil heart, so that thy law might bring forth fruit in them.

> For the first Adam, burdened with an evil heart. . . .

By such an interpretation, our verse is a prayer for reversal of that situation.

■ **7** The first phrase, "Thou alone dost exist," indicates, presumably, the unity of God, his uniqueness as true God, a theme found in the Bible (e.g., Deut 4:35; 6:4; Isa 43:11, and see 43:7, which mentions the idea of creation as well; 44:6; et al.) and in the Pseudepigrapha (e.g., *2 Apoc Bar* 48:24) and, of course, in many other sources. Human beings are asserted to be creations of God's hands elsewhere in 4 Ezra.[11]

It is debatable whether "as thou hast declared" refers to another place in 4 Ezra or to some scriptural source. Oddly, all the instances in 4 Ezra in which humans are asserted to be creations of God's hand are set in the mouth of the seer, not of the angel of God. This might incline us toward a scriptural source.[12] This verse asserts God's sole and direct responsibility for the creation of mankind.

■ **8** This verse starts the description of conception, pregnancy, and birth which continues until 8:11. It is a commonplace for God to be credited with the wonder of conception, and there are differences in the "medical" approach, in sources like Job 10:10–11 and Wisd 7:1–2. No exact parallels have been adduced to the idea that the embryo in the womb is preserved in fire and water.[13] The passage is permeated by an attitude of wonder at the marvels of nature, so revealed; see further the Excursus on Natural Order, p. 102. This should be brought into account when evaluating the negative elements of the author's view of the world and the body.[14] Pregnancy and birth serve the author elsewhere in the book, chiefly as a simile; see 4:40 Commentary.

---

6 Compare *Tanh. Piqqude* 3. See also *2 Apoc Bar* 21:9 for similar ideas and formulation and also 14:11; on shortness of life, see 4:33 and *2 Apocalypse of Baruch* 16. This passage is discussed in Excursus on Inspiration, p. 123.

7 See Excursus on Inspiration, p. 123.

8 See 3:20 Commentary.

9 See Excursus on Adam's Sin, p. 66, on this point. On the ideas of "heart" and its "cultivation," see also ibid., n. 19.

10 The idea is clear in 7:64, and see Commentary there. See discussion in Stone, "Way of the Most High,"

134–38.

11 See 3:5 Commentary. F. M. Cross suggested to me that reference may also be made here to Exod 3:14.

12 In 7:116 the earth is said to have produced mankind. See Commentary there.

13 On these elements, see 7:6 Commentary.

14 Attitudes to the body in general in 4 Ezra are discussed in some detail in 7:32 Commentary and Stone, *Features*, 145–46.

■ **9** Note the use of repetition in this verse. The whole passage has some features in common with *Tanh. Piqqude* 3, particularly the idea of the temporary character of the infant's period in the womb. God's role in the process of conception and birth is stressed also in 1QH 9:29–31.

■ **10** No commentary.

■ **11** The verse carefully stresses God's responsibility not only for conception and birth of the infant but also for its education. This is spelled out further in 8:12.

■ **12** The discussion of the education of the child by God continues. The terminology of instruction and wisdom here is discussed in detail in the Excursus on Inspiration, p. 123.[15] The point of the argument is that this instruction is part of the great trouble that God takes in creation and nurture of human beings. The idea is not developed, as it might have been, in the direction of, "How could you so readily destroy human beings; after all, you educated them, so their actions accord with your teaching," a line of argument that one might imagine the author of 3:1–27 proposing. This situation again illustrates the point that the author of 4 Ezra often adduces arguments by context and focus in spite of the roughnesses or unevennesses they create with other places in the book.[16]

Law or Torah is set parallel to wisdom. This is the end of a process to be observed from the second century B.C.E. in the course of which the idea of wisdom, particularly personified wisdom, is identified with that of Torah. This had very important implications for the idea of Torah, including the accretion to it of clear cosmic aspects.[17] By the time of our work, there is nothing surprising or significant about the free shift between terminology of Torah and wisdom. The use of "Law" of divine commandments incumbent on all humans and not just on Israel was discussed above.[18] It is also apparently present here.

■ **13** This verse concludes the passage on the creation of the infant. That God kills and gives life is a set expression in the Hebrew Bible; see Deut 32:39; 1 Sam 2:6; and 2 Kgs 5:7; cf. also Job 10:8–9. The giving of life here does not seem to refer to resurrection, although that idea is prominent in 4 Ezra.[19]

■ **14** Expressions like phrases of this verse are to be observed in *Greek Apoc Esd* 3:9 and *Apoc Sedr* 3:7. The statement is best taken in the rhetoric of Ezra's address as a sharp formulation of the crux which is not a negation of creation (*pace* Harnisch, p. 298) but the very contradiction perceived in God's action.

■ **15** The question raised in this verse is central to the book and has occurred frequently before; see 3:1–2; 3:28–32; 4:23; et al. Israel's special position as God's heritage is clear from 5:27–28. The idea is old; so already Deut 32:9 and many other places in the Bible. "People" is often found together with "inheritance"; so, for example, Deut 9:26; Joel 2:17; Ps 28:9; 1QH 6:8; and 4 Ezra 8:45.

■ **16** The expression "inheritance" is dealt with in the commentary on the preceding verse. "Seed of Jacob" is a biblical expression; see, for example, Isa 45:19 and Jer 33:26 and cf. 4 Ezra 3:19. Is the implication of the verse the one made explicit in 8:45, that is, that God as creator should have had mercy, and is the limiting of the problem to Israel the author's way of reinforcing his point? This seems likely in view of the continuation of the argument.

■ **17** Instead of "on the earth," RSV reads "in the land," presumably implying in the land of Israel. The Latin could be read this way (but compare Syriac and Ethiopic) and so could the most reasonable putative Hebrew. However, the sense "earth" is predominant in this phrase, which is common in the book. A selection of examples is 3:34; 4:21; 5:1; 5:6; 6:18; 6:24; 11:32; 11:40; 13:30; and there are others.[20]

On exegetical grounds, moreover, the sense "we humans" is what is demanded. The whole point of the disclaimer in 8:15 is that, although the question could be put about all mankind, Ezra is putting it only about Israel in order to strengthen his argument.

---

15 See also 8:4–5 and Commentary.

16 God is said to teach people in such sources as Ps 94:10 and Sir 17:11. In *2 Apoc Bar* 78:3 God's education is said to be a function of his love.

17 Among the earliest instances are Sir 24:8–9 and Bar 3:36—4:1; see Nickelsburg and Stone, *Faith and Piety*, 211–19.

18 See 7:1–25 Form and Function, pp. 194–95.

19 See 7:32 Commentary. On 4 Ezra's idea of death, see Excursus on Adam's Sin, pp. 65–66.

20 Our view is also supported by other translations, such as NEB.

■ **18** On judgment, described as "swift" by Latin alone, see the Excursus on the Term "Judgment." It is, of course, eschatological.

■ **19a** This, the first part of the verse, forms the end of the address proper, and the second part is the title of the prayer.

The Prayer of Ezra

19b [a]The beginning of the words of Ezra's prayer, before he was taken up. He said: [b]

20/ "O Lord who dwellest forever, [c]
whose [d]heavens are exalted [d]
and whose upper chambers are in the air,

21/ whose throne is beyond measure, [e]
and whose glory is beyond comprehension,
before whom the hosts of angels stand trembling

22/ and at whose command they are changed to wind and fire,
whose word is sure
and whose utterances are certain,
whose ordinance is strong
and whose command is terrible,

23/ [f]whose look dries up [g] the depths
and whose threat [h] makes the mountains melt away,
and whose truth is established forever [i]—

Notes

19b a The Latin tradition splits at this point into two distinct texts, published in parallel by Violet and Klijn.

b Syr omits. This title varies greatly in Ar1, Ar2, and Arm.

20 c Lat (some Mss) *qui inhabitas saeculum;* other witnesses "forever, from eternity," etc.; see Stone, "Apocryphal Notes," 130–31. *Greek Apoc Esd* 7:5 ὁ θεὸς ὁ αἰώνιος.

d–d The text is uncertain. Lat φ, Arm have "eyes," and this reading may be related to "see and search out" which Arm, Ar1 read for the verb; this may also be related to Eth "see" and Georg *ik῾cevi = versare* (Blake, and see Molitor, *Gloss. Iber.,* s.v.); the other reading is "heavens," so Lat Ψ, Eth (which reverses "heavens" and "upper chambers"), Georg (*excelsum excelsorum*), Ar2. We are forced to assume two Greek readings, "eyes" and "heavens." The verb is "exalted" Lat Φ, Syr; "are" Lat Ψ, Ar2. Parallelism inclines us toward something like "whose heavens are exalted," although the textual base is uncertain.

21 e Eth, Georg "invincible"; perhaps Greek ἀνίκητος for ἀνείκαστος.

23 f This verse is cited in *Apost. Const.* 8.7, οὗ τὸ βλέμμα ξηραίνει ἄβυσσον καὶ ἡ ἀπείλη τήκει ὄρη καὶ ἡ ἀλήθεια μένει εἰς τὸν αἰῶνα.

g Lat Φ, Ψ "burns up" (different words); so Georg.

h Greek ἀπείλη (cf. Lat Ψ; cf. Ar1, Ar2, Arm) is more precisely "threat," cf. LSJ. "Indignation" is read by the other versions and does not seem to imply a different Greek.

i So *Apost. Const.;* cf. Ar2. The other versions read "is a witness." It is indubitable that in addition to the Greek of *Apost. Const.,* the differing *Vorlage* of the versions (apart from Ar2) also existed in Greek. Violet 2 attempts, not convincingly, to explain the secondary text on the basis of inner-Greek development. The expression עמדת לעד may be observed in Ps 19:10; 111:2; 111:10; and 112:3; cf. לעולם עמדת, Qoh 1:4 and לעולם תעמד, Ps 33:11. Note the predominance of liturgical and psalmodic contexts. Gunkel, followed by Box, Gressmann, and others, suggested two different readings of consonantal Hebrew עמדת לעד. This theory assumes a double contact with the Hebrew text. This would be a rare instance of evidence for such a contact, which might be characterized as glossing. Alternatively, but less persuasively, one might assume "witness" to be original to the Greek, and the text of *Apost. Const.,* Ar2 to be the result of correction at the Greek level under the influence of the biblical expression.

24/ hear, O Lord, the voice ^{j} of thy servant,
and give ear to the petition of thy
creature,
and ^{k} attend to my words.
25/ For as long as I live I will speak,
and as long as I have understanding I
will answer.
26/ ^{l}O look not upon the sins of thy people,
but at ^{m} those who have served thee
in truth.
27/ Regard not ^{n} those who act wickedly,
but those who have kept thy covenants amid afflictions.
28/ Think not on those who have lived
wickedly in thy sight;
but remember those who have
willingly acknowledged that thou
art to be feared.
29/ Let it not be thy will to destroy those
who ^{o}have had the ways of ^{o} cattle;
but regard those who have ^{p}gloriously
taught thy law. ^{p}
30/ Be not angry with those who are deemed
worse than beasts;
but love those who have always put
their trust in thy glory.
31/ For we and ^{q}those who were before us ^{q}
have ^{r}done deeds ^{r} in ways that bring
death,
but thou, because of us sinners, art
called merciful.
32/ For if thou hast desired to have pity on
us, who have no good works, ^{s} then thou wilt
be called merciful. 33/ For the righteous,
who have many ^{t} works laid up with thee,
shall receive their reward ^{u} in consequence
of their own deeds.
34/ But what is man, that thou art angry
with him; ^{v}
or what is a corruptible race, that thou
art so bitter against it?
35/ For in truth there is no one among those
who have been born who has not
acted wickedly,
^{w}and among those who have existed
there is no one who has not
transgressed. ^{w}
36/ For in this, O Lord, thy goodness ^{x} will be
declared, when thou art merciful to those
who have no store ^{y} of good works."

24   j *Orationem* Lat Φ; Ar2 omits; "voice" is the
unanimous reading of the other versions.
k Lat Φ omits.
26   l Arm has a substantial addition here, which
accords in its basic ideas with what ensues in all the
versions.
m The awkwardness of the parallelism has led
Eth, Georg to expand, each differently, here.
27   n So Eth, Georg, Ar1, Arm; Lat Φ *studia;* Syr
"foolishness."
29   o–o "Become like" Syr, Eth, Ar2; the word "ways"
here has the support of both Latin texts and Arm.
p–p "Glory" is an attribute of "Law" in Syr, Lat Ψ,
Ar1.
31   q–q Lat Φ *patres.*
r–r Syr, Eth, Arm; Lat Φ *mortalibus moribus egimus,*
Lat Ψ *corruptum locum egimus* deriving from
τόπος/τρόπος.
32   s So Lat Φ, Eth, Ar1, Ar2, Arm; "works" Syr,
Georg; "works of justice" Lat Φ. Conceivably the
original was "works," which was treated differently
in the various versions.
33   t Syr, Georg, Ar1 omit; "good" Eth.
u Lat Φ, Lat Ψ (Ms L), Georg, cf. Arm; Lat Ψ, Syr
omit; others vary; perhaps some Greek texts did not
have this word.
34   v Ar1, Arm add "in truth" or "justice."
35   w–w Eth, Georg, Arm omit.
36   x Lat Φ *iusticia tua et bonitas tua;* "your mercy and
righteousness" Ar2.
y Syr, Georg "power"; Eth omits.

Form and Structure

These verses form a prayer pronounced by Ezra as the
second part of his introductory speech. The prayer is in
the second person, directed toward God. It is characterized by parallelism, which is predominantly synonymous, and is not unlike biblical poetry. Its formal
characteristics are best seen in the context of Jewish
prayers.

The prayer falls into a number of distinct parts:
A. Title (8:19). This varies between the versions and,

although it clearly existed at a Greek level, makes the
impression of being secondary.
B. Opening Doxology (8:20–23)
C. Call for Attention and Statement of Purpose (8:24–25)
D. Body of the Prayer Itself (8:26–35)
    1. Intercessory petition for amnesty (8:26–30; cf. 2
    Sam 19:20)
    2. Confession (8:31)
    3. The motivation or grounds for granting the petition
    (8:32–35)

E. Concluding Doxology (8:36). Prediction of future proclamation of divine righteousness

The prayer contains the same elements of doxology, confession, and petition that occur in other earlier prayers, strikingly in Ezra 9; Nehemiah 9; and Daniel 9.[1] The prayer here would be categorized by J. Heinemann as a confessional prayer, belonging to the broader class of Petitionary Prayer offered at a time of distress.[2] From a formal viewpoint, the combination of confession and intercession is unusual, but compare Ezra 9. Moreover, the long doxology is not common in this type of prayer but is comparable with *2 Apoc Bar* 48:2–10. The prayer is connected with other parts of 4 Ezra by its contents and themes (see Commentary passim, but particularly on 8:25 and 8:29–31).

Function and Content

The broader context of this prayer is, once again, the issue of the punishment of the most part of mankind and the salvation of only very few. This problem has been central to the discussion since 7:45 and was already raised before. So, in the immediately preceding address Ezra has praised God for the wondrous creation of mankind and reproached him for destroying so readily what he had, with such great trouble, created. The thrust of this prayer is a call for divine mercy—all humans have sinned; please, God, be merciful to the wicked. Notably, the reference to Israel, which was so prominent in the preceding address, here disappears.

The *doxology* in 8:20–23 stresses the awesome aspect of God's rule: his supernal habitation, the terror of the angels before him, the drying up of the depths and the melting of the mountains (themes coming from theophany language). Finally, in 8:23, God is said to be the one "whose truth is established forever." The seer then moves to the *call for divine attention,* for he intends to speak: "Hear . . . give ear . . . attend" (8:24). Note the descent within the prayer, from the heavens, to the throne, to the hosts, to the active divine word which is

significantly related to the use of theophany language in 8:23.

The body of the prayer ensues, presented in a contrasting form that is analogous both in content and in structure to 7:119–126. All the verses from 8:26–36 are fomulated antithetically, but there does not seem to be a specific, explicit lien between the characteristics highlighted in the two parts of the verse.[3] First, God is urged: Regard not those who have sinned but those who have lived righteously. This is followed by a confession, "We and our fathers have sinned" (8:31), and a call for mercy, "but thou art called Merciful" (referring back to the Midrash on the 13 *Middot*, particularly 7:132–139). The whole concludes with a short doxology.

There is a certain problem as to the coherence of this part of the prayer. In 8:26–30, God is asked, "Look not at the sins of thy people but at *those who served thee,*" which presumably meant "those among thy people who served thee." This may also be the sense of each of the statements of 8:26–30. If so, the group referred to in the two parts of each of the series of antithetical statements is the same. Furthermore, 8:31 makes sense in this light; compare 3:36 as well as the end of the prayer. In general, the thrust of the present passage resembles that of *2 Apoc Bar* 14:2, while Knibb points out the analogy of Gen 18:22–23. However, in 8:31–36 there is a development of the theme of God's mercy. The tone is set in 8:31: "Thou, because of us sinners, wilt be called merciful." This marks the beginning of an *inclusio* that concludes with 8:36: "For in this, O Lord, thy goodness will be declared, when thou art merciful to those who have no store of good works." The structure of the intervening verses supports this:

a. If you desire to pity us sinners, you will be called merciful (8:32).

b. The righteous do not need mercy (8:33).

c. The stature of humankind is not such as to justify God's anger (8:34).

d. In truth all have sinned (8:35).

---

1   The prayer in Ezra 8 is most similar typologically to the present passage, both being confessional and intercessory, but there are also many striking parallels with Daniel 9 and Nehemiah 9. The petition at time of distress serves as a prototype for the confessional prayer and often incorporates a confession, as do Daniel 9 and Nehemiah 9.

2   J. Heinemann, *Prayer in the Talmud* (Studia Judaica 9;

Berlin and New York: de Gruyter, 1977) 124. Cf. also M. Greenberg, *Biblical Prose Prayer: A Window to the Popular Religion of Ancient Israel* (Taubman Lectures in Jewish Studies, Sixth Series; Berkeley and Los Angeles: University of California, 1983) 9–18.

3   An isolated similar statement is *2 Apoc Bar* 84:10. The subject there is also divine mercy.

The first group of verses, 8:26–30, implies a residual righteousness of Israel and petitions for mercy on that basis. The second group (8:31–36) takes a quite different tack, proclaiming the general sinfulness of human beings as of its very nature requiring divine mercy. The point of the prayer, that is, the petition for mercy, is quite clear and ordinary. The actual arguments are contradictory, as, for example, the comparison of 8:33 and 8:35 makes explicit. Of course, the tension between the assumption of universal sinfulness and that of the few righteous has been found repeatedly in the book, and the use of both ideas in support of the central thrust of the prayer, the appeal for divine mercy, serves as yet another warning against oversystematization of the author's thought. See further 7:67 Commentary.

Taken as a whole, then, this address accepts the conclusions of section 2 of the vision (8:1–3): "Many have been created but few shall be saved." Yet, the claim is, this does not jibe with the care of the creation. The prayer artfully changes the pace of the dialogue. The seer appeals to the mighty and powerful God, terrible Lord of the forces of heaven and earth, to be merciful to sinful humans, since he is called "Merciful One." Moreover, at least implicitly, this prayer relates as much to Israel as to mankind in general. It thus picks up Ezra's special pleading for Israel at the end of the preceding address.[4]

Commentary

■ **19b** This is the title of the Prayer of Ezra. On literary grounds it appears to be a gloss, while the textual evidence shows that the gloss must have entered at the Greek level. Ezra's assumption is mentioned elsewhere (see 14:9 and 14:49); the assumed righteous also figure as the company of the Messiah in 6:26; 7:28; and 13:52. The idea of the assumption of human beings was widespread (see 6:26 Commentary).

■ **20** The background of this verse may lie in mythological conceptions of the heavenly palace of the deity. Expressions similar to "dwellest forever" are to be found in the Bible (see Ps 9:8; 102:13; cf. Isa 57:15).[5] The "upper chambers" are mentioned in more ancient sources as well, in similar contexts, referring to the dwelling of the deity (see Ps 104:3 and cf. Amos 9:6).[6] This verse then opens the doxology of the prayer by describing God as the one who lives in the heavenly realm.[7]

■ **21** Continuing the doxology, this verse mentions three aspects of the awesome presence of God: his throne, his glory, and the angelic hosts which stand before him. The picture is one of God, seated on his glorious and fiery throne, surrounded by the ministering hosts. This is found in 1 Kgs 22:19; Isaiah 6; Daniel 7; and many other later sources, such as *1 Enoch* 14; *2 Apoc Bar* 21:6; and 48:10–11.[8]

The term "glory" is intimately related to God. The

---

4   There are some quite striking parallels in later Jewish prayers, showing how the structures of these petitions persisted. Such are the *Taḥanun* prayer in the *Siddur of R. ʿAmram Gaʾon*, secs. 65, 109–10, and the Confession for the Day of Atonement in the same source (sec. 118; ed. D. Goldschmidt, *Maḥazor LaYamim ha-Noraʾim* [Jerusalem: Koren, 1970], 2:160–62); and the Prayer of Maimonides in the Oxford manuscript, also published by D. Goldschmidt, "Maimonides' Order of Prayer According to the Oxford Manuscript," *Bulletin of the Institute for the Study of Hebrew Poetry in Jerusalem* 7 (1958) 200–201 (in Hebrew). E. Chazon most graciously read this section and provided me with invaluable information. She has noted: "These prayers, like the prayer in 4 Ezra 8, are Confessionals and contain the elements: *Doxology* (especially the *Taḥanun* of R. ʿAmram Gaʾon), *Petition* (for amnesty, mercy, attention, and acceptance of prayer), *Confession*, *Motivation* (negation of self-worth, inability to justify oneself)."

5   On the term "forever," see Excursus on the Term

"Age," pp. 218–19.

6   God is often said to inhabit the heavens; see Job 11:8; 22:12; and Isa 14:14. Such ideas as these are also implied by the expression "Father in Heaven" (e.g., Matt 6:9; *m. Abot* 5:24). The variant reading "eyes" of the preceding phrase (see textual note d) finds a nice parallel in Tertullian, *De praescr. Haer.* 3, who cites a reading of Jer 32:19.

7   The doxology is in some ways comparable to the words cited in *Hermas Vis.* 1.3.4, which also catalogues God's power over creation and his mighty word.

8   On the throne, see further, e.g., *Test Mos* 4:2 and *Test Patr Levi* 5:1; in *PRE* 4 the throne is described in detail.

parallelism here of "throne" and "glory" is notable, particularly in view of the fact that "Throne of Glory" becomes a technical term for God's throne, and even for the presence of the Godhead, in rabbinic and Merkabah texts. See further 3:19 Commentary.

This verse combines with the previous one to convey a powerful impression of the apocalyptic picture of the heavenly presence of God. It is notable that, though elsewhere 4 Ezra systematically denies the possibility of knowledge of such heavenly realities, nonetheless the present poetic context is permeated by this type of description. It is, however, part of a doxology, not of a revelation.

■ 22 The first phrase of this verse is parallel to the last phrase of the preceding. It expresses the idea that the angelic hosts, at God's command, are transformed into fire and water. The idea that angels are made of fire and flame is quite widespread; so, for example, 2 Apoc Bar 21:6; 48:8; and Gen. R. 78:1 (Theodor-Albeck, p. 917). The combination of wind and fire here, however, is rather unusual, and it has been related directly to Ps 104:4, which could be translated:

who makest thy angels of winds,
    thy ministers of fire and flame.

This is strikingly taken up in the later PRE 4:

(As for) the angels created on the second day, when they are sent (as messengers) by His word they are changed into winds, and when they minister before Him they are changed into fire, as it is said, "who maketh his angels winds; his ministers a flaming fire." (Ps 104:4)[9]

This seems very likely also to lie behind the text here.

The rest of this verse describes the divine word or command that was often spoken of as having various powers and qualities of its own. A similar listing of attributes of the word occurs, as Box pointed out, in the first paragraph of the *Ge'ulla* prayer following the *Shema'* in the Jewish daily liturgy, which is old and perhaps pre-Jamnian. "True and firm, established and enduring, right and faithful, beloved and precious, desirable and pleasant, revered and mighty, well-ordered and acceptable, good and beautiful is this thy word unto us for ever and ever."[10]

There is then a hierarchical descent in the doxology, from the divine dwelling, to the court, to his angels, and then to his active word.[11]

■ 23 The language recalls that used in the Bible to describe God's awesome epiphany. The drying up of the depths is similar to what we find, for example, in Isa 50:2; 51:10; and Ps 74:15. This is a weakened reflection of old mythical themes of the conflict between the deity and the waters or depths. Similarly, the mountains melting is also one of the signs of the theophany (see Mic 1:4; Ps 97:5; *1 Enoch* 1:6; cf. 52:6).[12] It should be noted that there are considerable similarities to the effects of the appearance of the human figure in the vision in chapter 13. There all tremble at his glance (13:3); his active word kills his enemies or effects judgment (13:4, 37; see 8:22 Commentary); and the theme of melting occurs (13:4). It is worth observing that these are prominent themes in the vision part of the experience there but are missing from the interpretation or much reduced in it. Indeed, these cosmic elements are eliminated deliberately by the interpretation (see the Excursus on the Redeemer Figure, pp. 211–12). Their antique roots are borne out by their affinities with the description of God's powers here.

A final observation is that the language of seeing occurs here in 8:23a, inserted in a series of terms relating to word or speech. This relates to the idea of the glory of

---

9   Trans. Friedlander, pp. 21–22. Note also *Jub* 2:2, which relates, next to one another, the creation of "the angels of spirit of fire" and "the angels of spirit of winds."

10   J. H. Hertz, *The Authorized Daily Prayer Book* (London: Shapiro and Valentine, 1947) 127. On the active word of God, see also Isa 11:4; Wisd 12:9; 18:15–16; *1 Enoch* 62:2; and 2 Thess 2:8; cf. Isa 49:2. See Stone, "Question of the Messiah," n. 22. This is discussed in detail in 13:10 Commentary. The divine word is active particularly in judgment; see Ps 46:6. See also the use of the classical biblical texts, applied to the Prince of the Congregation in 1QSb (1Q28:6) 5:24–25. A different view of the active divine word is *Od Sol* 29:9–10.

11   The idea of creation through the divine word may be found in 3:4 Commentary and 6:38–59 Function and Content, p. 183.

12   General parallels illustrating the effect of God's epiphany on nature are even more numerous; see, e.g., Ps 18:7; 104:32; 4 Ezra 3:9; and *Test Mos* 10:4. See also for theophany language Sir 16:18–19. Other reflexes of mythological themes are discussed in 4:15 Commentary.

the divine countenance, that his very look effects results, just as his speech does.[13]

■ **24** The use of verbs of hearing in parallelism in invocations such as this is quite common; see 5:32 Commentary. Ezra refers to himself as "servant," as found elsewhere in the book. In 5:56 Commentary it was noted that nearly always when the term "servant" appears, the designation "Lord" is also found. Moreover, "servant" seems to be parallel to "creature" only here. The verse is the beginning of the petition following on the completion of the doxology. Ezra has praised God's power, and concludes with the assertion of the eternity of God's truth.

■ **25** This verse expresses Ezra's resolution to speak his word of petition before God regardless of consequences. It is most closely paralleled by *Greek Apoc Esd* 2:7; 4:1; 4:4; and 6:20. Various biblical parallels have been adduced, but they are not exact and do not really illuminate the verse. "Answer" is used, as often in biblical Hebrew, to mean "begin to speak."

■ **26** As has been noted in Form and Structure, 8:26 marks the turning to intercession, and in this and the ensuing verses Ezra prays on behalf of the people. The detail of the argument has been outlined, and its overall thrust is "Regard not the wicked of the people, but those who have served you." The expression "in truth" may be compared with Ps 145:18 et al.[14] Some scholars would regard the expansion of Armenian here as a form of some original text, but it is the frequent habit of this version to expand using the patterns of the surrounding verses.[15] The reference to the people opens the intercession and closes it in 8:31 (for this is surely the reference of the "we" there).

■ **27** The expression "kept thy covenants amid afflictions" seems to be paralleled only in 7:89. The keeping of

God's covenants (or not doing so) is a common subject in the book; so 3:32; 3:35; et al.[16]

■ **28** The virtue of the "fear of God" is mentioned often in the Hebrew Bible (see Prov 2:5; Qoh 12:13; et al.).

■ **29** In this and in the next verse (8:30) the author compares the conduct of the wicked to animals, here to domestic creatures and there to wild creatures. The comparison to domestic animals is already to be found in Ps 49:13; 49:15; 49:21; 73:22; Job 18:3; etc. In 4 Ezra 7:65–66 we find the same mention of both domestic and wild animals. There they are contrasted with humans, as lacking understanding (and therefore accountability). This also seems to be the point of the comment in Ps 73:22. It is, perhaps, by no chance that the antithesis is "those who have gloriously taught thy law." The association of glory with this function is to be found in Dan 12:3, and cf. also Prov 6:23. Study of the Torah is one of Ezra's virtues, according to 13:54. This relationship between the antithetical parts of the sentence should not be pushed too hard, however, since it is scarcely explicit in the next verse.

■ **30** This verse is the continuation of the previous one. On the idea of glory, see 3:19 Commentary.

■ **31** This verse, as has been noted in Form and Structure, p. 270, marks the beginning of the confession part of the prayer and is the opening of a sustained passage that concludes in 8:36. It combines confession and petition, using turns of phrase that are known from biblical and other literature. Daniel 9:4–6 is particularly close to this verse both in phraseology and import.[17] The expression "done deeds in ways that bring death" seems like a combination of 7:119, "deeds that bring death," and 7:122, "wicked ways."[18]

The argument is opened, and will be pursued in the following, that God's mercy must exist for the sinners.

---

13 See discussion in 7:42 Commentary and the further comments of Jervell, *Imago Dei*, 45.

14 Truth is, of course, intimately associated with divine judgment; see Excursus on Judgment, p. 150.

15 See Gry, basing himself on Violet 2.

16 It is open to question whether this language is suggestive of a context of persecution for the observance of Torah, such as we find in the literature of the Maccabean revolt or the Hadrianic persecutions. It would seem to us that were the language forged in such a context, it would be more prominent in 4 Ezra than it is. There are ample passages in

the book in which such a reference would be appropriate.

17 Even closer in language is Ps 106:6, but differences subsist.

18 On "death" here, see Excursus on Adam's Sin, p. 66.

This idea will be discussed in 8:33 Commentary. The reference of "art called" is most likely 7:132, which reflects Exod 34:6 ("The 13 *Middot*").

■ **32** Oesterly comments, quoting Rom 3:19–26, "This is, in effect, the teaching of justification without works."

■ **33** This verse, asserting that the righteous are rewarded in view of their actions, implies that the sinners, not the righteous, are in need of mercy. The same idea is developed in other texts with respect to repentance, in Prayer of Manasseh 8 and 13–14; similar but less explicit is *Ps Sol* 9:6. The view of reward as "treasure" which is "laid up" in heaven is discussed in 7:77 Commentary. Both ideas, that of reward for works and that of the heavenly storehouse, are of wide diffusion.[19] This verse stands, obviously, in tension with 8:35. The author wishes to argue that, on the one hand, mercy should be extended to the wicked, while, on the other, all humans have sinned, making the question of mercy the more acute. This is a fine example of just what Porter stressed, the self-contradictory views of the author on this issue; see 7:67 Commentary.

■ **34** The sentiment of the nothingness of human beings opposed to the might of God is to be found in particular in the context of prayers. See, for example, Ps 8:4 and Job 7:17. The same theme in a similar literary form may also be observed in *2 Apoc Bar* 48:14 and 48:17.[20] In general, such attitudes are balanced by assertions of the goodness of God, and so forth, as is discussed in 4:24 Commentary. The idea of "corruptibility" is discussed in 4:11 Commentary.

■ **35** This verse asserts that all human beings have sinned. The idea is in apparent contrast with 3:33. This variation of ideas between asserting that all have sinned and asserting that there are only a few righteous (who have not sinned) is chiefly attibutable to context and style rather than to conceptual incoherence. Exactly the same may be observed by comparing 7:46 with the ensuing verses. This has been termed a difference of mood.[21]

The sentiment is to be found in other, earlier sources; see, for example, Prov 20:9 and Qoh 7:20. 4 Ezra 7:46 is similar not just in content but in its interrogative form.[22] The verse here seems to have provided the basis for *Greek Apoc Esd* 5:27: καὶ τίς ἄρα ἄνθρωπος γεννηθεὶς οὐχ ἥμαρτε; ("Which of men, having been born, did not sin?").

■ **36** This verse takes up and concludes the idea that is expressed in 8:31b. It expresses the seer's petition with which the prayer concludes. He has here abandoned any basis for appeal to God other than the appeal to God's own nature as revealed in his epithets.[23]

---

19 Scholars have been exercised by the relationship between works and reward, chiefly in view of passages such as Rom 3:19–26. This concern is, however, extraneous to 4 Ezra.

20 See also *Greek Apoc Esd* 1:17.

21 For a discussion, see 7:46 Commentary and 7:67 Commentary.

22 A similar form also occurs in other places, e.g., 4

Ezra 4:6; *2 Apoc Bar* 14:9; 75:5.

23 A not dissimilar view is expressed among others in *Midr. Teh.* 62:13. *Midr. Teh.* 30:4 presents the idea of a balance and of God's tipping the pan in favor of humans: contrast 3:34, and see Commentary there.

8

37 He answered me and said, ᵃ"Some things ᵃ
you have spoken rightly, and it will come to
pass according to your words. 38/ For indeed
I will not concern myself about the fashioning ᵇ of those who have sinned, or about
their death, their judgment, or their destruction; 39/ but I will rejoice over ᶜthe creation
of the righteous, over their pilgrimage also, ᶜ
and their life, ᵈ and their receiving their
reward. ᵉ 40/ As I ᶠ have spoken, therefore,
so it shall be.

41 "For just as the farmer sows many seeds ᵍ and
plants a multitude of seedlings, and yet not
all that have been sown will live ʰ in due
season, and not all the plants will take root;
so also those who have been sown in the
world will not all live." ⁱ

42 I answered and said, "If I have found favor
before thee, let me speak. ʲ 43/ For if the
farmer's seed does not come up, ᵏbecause it
has not received thy ˡ rain in due season, ᵐ or
if it has been ruined by too much rain, it
perishes. ⁿ 44/ But man, who has been
formed by thy hands and resembles ᵒ thy own
image ᵖ, and for whose sake thou hast
formed all things— ᑫhast thou also made him
like the farmer's seed?
45/ No, O Lord ʳwho art over us! ʳ
But spare thy people
and have mercy on thy inheritance,
for thou hast mercy on thy own creation."

46 ˢHe answered me and said, "Things that are
present ᵗ are for those who live now, ᵘ and

Notes

37   a–a Lat, Syr; "all" Georg; Eth, Ar1, Ar2 omit.

38   b Syr *gbylthwn;* Georg *operum;* these readings seem
to derive from a text like the *Vorlage* of Lat; cf.
8:39. Box and Violet suggest a possible derivation
from יצר, but both the putative Hebrew form and
the sense weigh against this.

39   c–c Syr *m'tyt' dgbylthwn dzdyq'* apparently goes
back to a mistranslation of a genitive chain in Greek
which meant the same as Lat (*contra* Violet). Georg
also supports this text; Eth omits.
   c–e Lat, Ar1, cf. Syr; Eth and Georg seem to
witness a text without "over their pilgrimage also."
   d Syr, Eth ("how they live"), Georg (*resurrectio
illorum*), Ar1; Lat *salvatio,* cf. 8:41.

40   f Lat, Syr; Eth, Georg "you"; observe that Syr *mllt*
could be first or second person; see Commentary.

41   g Lat, Ar1 add *super terram,* cf. Ar2; this is
probably an expansion.
   h Syr, Eth, cf. Ar1; Lat *salvabuntur;* Georg *crescit;*
we have translated "live" because of the end of the
verse.
   i Lat, Georg *salvabuntur.*

42   j Syr, Eth add "to you"; probably independent
stylistic variation.

43   k–m So Lat, Georg, cf. Eth; Syr formulates as a
question; the other versions vary in formulation.
   l Lat, Syr; the other versions omit.
   m–n This phrase appears only in Lat, Syr with the
possible support of Ar2, see Violet 2, p. 355; moreover, in Lat "it perishes" is corrupt.

44   o Lat *nominatus.*
   p Lat, Eth, Ar1 all have an additional phrase here,
but it is not identical, although its general tenor is
like Lat "because he is made like thee." Both
readings, that with this phrase in whatever form and
that without, existed in Greek. The additional
phrase may well have developed out of a doublet of
the preceding.
   q Eth, Georg "Why hast . . . ?"

45   r–r Uncertain; the translation is from Lat, but the
other versions vary wildly from it. Syr has *l' b'y 'n'
mnk mr' mry,* "no, I beseech you, Lord my Lord";
Eth "be this far from you, O Lord"; Georg *ne
destruxeris domine;* Ar1 "no, O Lord"; Ar2 "Lord";
Arm "therefore, Lord." The original is beyond
recovery.

46   s The verse is variously corrupt in Georg Ms O
(Ms I is defective) and Ar2; Arm omits from here to
the end of 8:49; Ar1 omits from here to 9:1.
   t Eth, Georg "in this world."
   u Eth, Ar1 "this world"; Georg omits t–v by hmt.

things that are future ^{v} are for those who will live hereafter. ^{w} 47/ For you come far short of being able to love my creation more than I love it. But you have often compared yourself to the unrighteous. Never do so! ^{x} 48/ But even ^{y} in this respect you will be praiseworthy before the Most High, 49/ because you have humbled yourself, as is becoming for you, and have not deemed yourself to be among the righteous, so that ^{z} you will receive greater ^{a} glory. 50/ For many miseries will affect those who inhabit the world in the last times, ^{b} because they have walked in great pride.
51/ But think of your own case,
 and inquire concerning the glory of
  those who are like yourself,
52/ because it is for you ^{c} that
 paradise is opened, ^{d}
  the tree of life is planted,
 the world ^{e} to come is prepared,
  delight ^{f} is provided,
 a city ^{g} is built,
  rest is appointed,
 goodness is established and
  wisdom ^{h} perfected beforehand.
53/ The root [i.e., of evil] ^{i} is sealed up from you,
 illness is banished from you,
 and death is hidden;
 hell has fled,
 and corruption has been forgotten;
54/ sorrows have passed away,
 and ^{j}in the end ^{j} the treasure of immortality is made manifest.
55/ Therefore do not ask any more questions about the multitude of those who perish. ^{k}
56/ For they also received freedom,
 but they despised the Most High,
 and were contemptuous of his law,
 and forsook ^{l} his ways.
57/ Moreover they have even trampled upon his righteous ones, 58/ and said in their hearts that there is no God— ^{m}though knowing full well that they must die. ^{n} 59/ For just as the things ^{o} which have been predicted ^{p} await you, so the thirst and torment which are prepared (await them). ^{q}

v Eth "in that world."

w Eth, Georg "that world"; Ar1 "the coming world." The readings of Eth, Georg in t-w seem to have existed in Greek.

47   x Syr, Georg "Let it not be so!"; Eth, Ar1 "although you are no sinner." These are probably two interpretations of similar or identical Greek. Violet 2 suggests μὴ οὕτως, but that would not account for Eth, Ar1. Ar2 "set yourself not in such a place" probably goes back to the same as Syr, Georg.

48   y Eth, Ar1, Ar2 omit.

49   z Lat could also be construed to mean (as RSV translates) "in order to receive," but cf. Syr, etc. Greek was probably ambiguous and the decision is exegetical.

   a Lat *plurimum.*

50   b Lat *in novissimis;* Syr "in the end"; Eth "in the last days"; Arm "the future time" may reflect the same phrase.

52   c "You" is plural except in Arm. Ar2 omits from the start of 8:52 to 9:1.

   d *Apoc Sedrach* 1:19 (22) ὁ παράδεισος ἠνέῳκται.

   e Syr, Eth; Lat *tempus;* Georg *veniens regnum;* Arm "that (future) life"; in Arm "life" sometimes reflects *saeculum* etc., see textual note on 6:20.

   f Syr, Eth, Arm; Georg *felicitas;* Lat *habundantia.*

   g Eth, Georg omit this word.

   h Eth, Georg "root of wisdom" deriving "root" from the first phrase of the next verse, from which these versions omit it. From the start of 8:53 the subjects may be taken to precede the predicates. This is so in Lat, Syr; but Eth, Georg, cf. Arm, take the phrases the other way. If construed thus, there should be a superfluous verb in the last phrase of the next verse. This is in fact the situation in Georg, while a different verb has been omitted by each of Eth, Arm. See J. Dupont, *Rev. Bén.* 57 (1947) 4–7.

53   i "Of evil" is added for the sake of clarity; see preceding note. The phrases in Eth, Georg, Arm vary accordingly.

54   j–j Eth, Arm omit; Georg *completum* surely goes back to the same text as Lat, Syr.

55   k Arm omits from here to 8:59.

56   l Syr *bṭlw;* Violet 1 suggests κατέλυον for κατέλιπον.

58   m–n Georg interprets as *propter hoc et sciunt mortem suam.*

   n Syr *dmmt mytyn* with infinitive absolute and finite verb.

59   o Eth, Georg "good things," which reading probably existed in Greek; Eth has apparently lost the rest of the verse and reads by correction "thus now that destruction for them."

   p Arm "I stated before"; RSV has "I have predicted," with no sound textual base.

   q Added in the translation for stylistic reasons.

   q–r Note here the paraphrase of Arm (in Arm

For the Most High did not intend that men should be destroyed; [r] 60/ but they themselves who were created

    have defiled the name of him who made them,

    and have been ungrateful to him who [s] prepared life [t] for them.

61/ Therefore my judgment is now drawing near; 62a/ [u]I have not shown this to [v] all men, but only to you and a few like you."

8:60): "And I made man that he might observe my commandments and avoid eternal death." This again stresses the question of individual responsibility in terms of law and commandments, and cf. the addition of Arm to 8:62 below. See *Armenian Text Commentary*.

60   s Lat adds "now."

    t Lat, Syr; apparently lost in the *Vorlage* of Eth, Georg: Eth omits, while Georg reads *bonum*.

62a   u Arm has an extensive addition which probably contains old elements, although not original to 4 Ezra. Cf. Stone, "Some Features of the Armenian Version," 395–400. Because of its interest we quote it in full:

8:62A I replied, I spoke with the Lord and I said, "I beseech you, speak with this wretched people, that they may hear from you and believe, that they may fear and repent and not perish, but be saved. 8:62B For if someone else should speak perhaps they would not have faith and this is a human being."

8:62C And the Lord answered and said, "I myself always revealed myself to my servants who were pleasing to me; I spoke with those who were worthy of me, but to the others I made myself known through men. 8:62D I am the Lord who tests the heart and the reins and I know man and what is in him before he comes from the womb. I know (that) if I should speak with them face to face, they will not obey, but will be even more strongly disobedient."

8:62E I answered the Lord and I said, "I ask of you, Most High, why was there not given to us a heart such that we should know only the good, and we should do it alone and we should desire it alone, and it should be sweet for us to know it alone? 8:62F Accordingly, since we received the knowledge of evil, why do we desire that which you hate? 8:62G Why indeed did you create it at all, that we should have it and through it we might sin?"

8:62H The Lord answered and said, "I made man, not that he might perish, but that he might live this life with honor and inherit that (future) life. 8:62I And, like to my angels, I gave him wisdom to know what is good and what is evil. 8:62J And I honored him and gave him the authority to do whatever he desired and I made subject to him all things which are under heavens that he might rule over them. 8:62K And I gave the Law and commandments how he might be able to live and how he might obtain immortal goods. 8:62L And he received these great goods and authority from me. That which was created well, he did not use well and he sinned. Not that I created anything evil, but everything which I created was very good: each thing which existed, existed for its own purpose, just as iron existed, not that it might kill, but that it might work the ground and fulfill the needs of all men. 8:62M But men did not remain in that same state in which they were created, but they undertook that which was not made for good. Thus also in other things, that which had come into being for good, they changed to evil. 8:62N The cause was then not he who creates things well, but he who did not use them well; he offended their Creator. Therefore torments await them. 8:62O For all should be guided by those things which have come into being through me so that they might know me. He too, who does not enjoy them, has known me. Cease, therefore, and care nothing concerning them."

Observe that in 8:62H there is text drawn from 8:59 for which Arm has supplied another form, as noted above.

v Georg *propter*.

Form and Structure

This pericope is composed of two speeches by the angel, between which is a short address by the seer. It presents, properly speaking, a mixture of disputatious and predictive discourse. Although the seer's inquiry in 8:42–45 is of argumentative character and forms a strong response to the angel's immediately preceding address (8:36–41), the reply to the seer's inquiry contains dominant elements of prediction (8:46–62). The pericope bears the mark of ending the long discussion of Vision 3. The definiteness of the angel's comment in 8:40 ("As I have spoken, therefore, so it shall be") contributes to this, as does the whole tenor of 8:61–62.[1] Indeed, we observed above that with this passage the third subdivision of Vision 3 comes to an end.[2]

A. *Angelic Address (8:37–41)*
1. Response to the preceding and reiteration of position (8:37–40)
2. Parable (8:41)

B. *Seer's Response (8:42–45)*
1. Argumentative question about interpretation of the parable (8:42–44)
2. Petition for mercy (8:45)

C. *Angel's Predictive Discourse (8:46–62)*
1. Oracular statement (8:46)
2. Rebuke (8:47a)
3. Pronouncement of Ezra's virtue (8:47b–49)

4. Eschatological prediction (8:50–55)
   a. The fate of the wicked (8:50)
   b. The fate of the righteous (8:51–55)
5. Admonition and concluding argument (8:55–60)
   a. Admonition—do not ask (8:55)
   b. Reasons (8:56–60)
6. Concluding prediction (8:61)
7. Authentication statement (8:62)

It will be readily observed that the angel's predictive discourse is particularly complex from a structural point of view, being composed of many elements.

At a number of points throughout, this pericope is deliberately linked with what precedes. Thus 8:37 utilizes a technique we have observed elsewhere and turns the seer's words in the preceding pericope against him. What Ezra has posed as a question, because it concerned him, the angel presents as a strong predictive statement.[3] This very obviously ties the section to the preceding. In the seer's response, perhaps the reference to creation of mankind by God's hand refers back to 3:5, while the statement that creation was for the sake of humankind takes us back to the question in 6:59 with which Vision 3 began: "If the world has indeed been created for us, why do we not possess our world as an inheritance?" Furthermore, the petition in 8:45 clearly links us back into the Prayer of Ezra in which mercy is a leitmotif (8:26–36), and even farther back into 7:119.

---

1 On 8:40, however, see Commentary.
2 See General Structure of the Book, pp. 50–51.
3 See 7:45–74 Form and Structure, pp. 227–28, on this technique.

This evocative character of the section continues in the ensuing address. Chapter 8:46 sounds very much like 4:21; the admonition in 8:47 is close indeed both in formulation and ideas to 5:33. The themes of creation and love here tie into deeply ingrained ideas of the book. Creation is particularly prominent in the opening address of this vision (6:38–59) and in 8:4–19a, and love in Vision 2 (5:23–30; and see Form and Function, p. 127). In 8:55 also the reference to "any more questions" clearly directs the reader back into what preceded.

It is noteworthy, therefore, that both by direct cross-reference and by deliberate literary reminiscence this pericope is intimately tied to all preceding parts of the book.

In terms of the smaller literary units, three are notable. The parable in 8:41 contains both the parable and its interpretation.[4] The list of eschatological things in 8:52–54 is one of the poetic lists of eschatological things that were described in 6:11–29 Form and Structure, p. 165. Volkmar, Violet, and others have pointed out that 8:52–54 is composed of fourteen phrases, just as is 6:1–6.[5] Finally, the oracular, balanced statement of 8:46 is of a type that we find elsewhere. It serves as an answer to questions and often introduces predictive passages; it is discussed in detail in 4:26 Commentary.

The rather elaborate introduction to the question of Ezra in 8:42 is to be noted. Elaborate formulae like this usually serve to introduce major new matters, but here it seems designed to stress the importance of what ensues, even though it is not new.[6]

Indeed, as has been observed above, 8:52–54 is one of a number of eschatological poems in the book that are marked out by distinctive formal characteristics and function.[7] Above, the "oracular" nature of such angelic predictions, typified by parallelism and a "mysterious" style, was analyzed. This is particularly true of 8:52–54.[8]

Function and Content

At the broadest level it is important to see the message of this pericope in relation to the overall development of the vision as a whole. The first thing that is notable is that the position of the angel = God has not changed throughout. The most part of humans have sinned, they bear the responsibility for their sin, and they will be punished. God will rejoice over the few who are saved; that is what is significant rather than the multitude that will perish. The question arises immediately, therefore, what this pericope adds that is special. After all, Ezra has gone through the remarkable passages of the address on creation (8:4–19a) and the prayer for mercy (8:19b–36) in the immediately preceding section. How is the angel's answer here responsive to that, and what is the seer's response to the whole section?

The special element here is one that was first raised earlier in the vision, that Ezra and those who are like him, that is, the righteous, will receive reward. The theme of Ezra's individual righteousness is raised and repeated in a most striking fashion in 8:37–62. This is the point of the passage, as is indicated by Ezra's docile acceptance of it and his turning, in 8:63, to detailed questions about the signs. Admittedly, Ezra reiterates the problem of the few and the many in 9:14, and the angelic response there seems to go a stage farther than here; nonetheless, it appears that a new stage has been reached here in Ezra's understanding. Therefore he is willing and eager to receive the revelation of further details about the signs.

It is worthwhile, in this perspective, to review the overall development of Vision 3. In the opening address (6:35–59) the stress is on creation of the world and the question is, "If the world has been created for us, why do we not inherit it?" In response to this, in 7:1–25 there are the two parables of the broad and the narrow, which indicated that the world that is referred to in the previous section may be the world to come. In the course of this pericope, the referent changes, and from the preoccupation explicitly with Israel the author moves to preoccupation with the righteous and the wicked. The pericope 7:1–25 concludes by stressing that the wicked disobeyed God's commandments and therefore "Empty things are for the empty, and full things are for the full" (7:25).

No questions ensue; nothing intervenes between this and the prophecy of the eschatological events (7:26–44). This passage complements the previous predictions of the signs, which have concluded in a brief eschatological

---

4   On its form, see 4:18 Commentary.
5   See 5:41—6:10 Form and Structure, p. 144.
6   See 4:44 Commentary on these complex preambles.
7   See 6:11–29 Form and Structure, pp. 165–66.
8   See 5:1–13 Form and Structure, p. 107.

prophecy. It tells of the sequence of events from the end of the signs to the end of the day of judgment. The stress is on the fate of the righteous and the wicked, and the prophecy of 7:26–44 as a whole serves to explain what is meant by the reward and punishment to which the end of 7:1–25 referred.

This prophecy takes the discourse a step farther. Ezra accepts that this fate will await the righteous and the wicked and does not question either divine justice or the course of events. But the acceptance of the idea of reward and punishment raises the issue that is to dominate the rest of the vision, that of the few and the many. This problem is raised in 7:45–61. Few will be saved but many perish, Ezra is told, and God rejoices over the precious few and does not grieve over the many sinners who perish. Ezra responds not by a question but by his lament over the mind. What a terrible fate this is! No note of argument is to be found here, no questioning of God's justice is explicit, just distress at the pronouncement. The angel responds by asserting, once more, that the wicked bear the responsibility for their own fate (therefore, he implies, what is Ezra fussing about?).

A new question is raised, perhaps seeking some respite from the predicted fate (7:75–95): After death, what will be the intermediate state of the righteous and the wicked? The angel replies by a prediction teaching that they will straightway enter into punishment and reward. No respite is granted here. Again Ezra tries to find a basis for softening this severe decree: Will there be intercessory prayer? This possible way out is also closed to him (7:100–115). Again he responds by an extended lament in which he asks what is the purpose of reward when "we" have sinned (7:116–126). Once more the angel asserts, humans have the choice, so the wicked bear the responsibility for their own fate.

The seer, still distressed by this issue, takes another tack. Instead of argument or questions, he resorts to petition and prayer. This is done in three stages. The first is the "Midrash on 13 *Middot*" in 7:132–140: God is called merciful because he is merciful; this is established on the basis of exegesis of scripture, responding perhaps to the quotation of scripture by the angel in the preceding passage to prove the severity of judgment. Again the angel responds, "Many have been created, but few shall be saved" (8:3). In his address in 8:4–19a, Ezra argues from creation: God is responsible for the creation

of human beings, their wondrous complexity and their education and training. If he will destroy mankind, why did he create mankind? Humans have sinned, and the judgment is inexorable. Only in this address does the truly reproachful tone toward God arise once more.

Having set the problem up thus, Ezra then offers a prayer, in which he combines praise of God's might, confession of sins, and an impassioned appeal for divine mercy (8:19b–36). It is to this prayer that the angel is responding in our present pericope. What is very notable in all of this development is that Ezra, in spite of his questioning and argument, does not raise basic issues of the conduct of the world, of "the way of the Most High," until the address and the prayer in 8:4–36. Even there the reproach is much milder than in the previous visions. So it comes about that Ezra has assented to the basic teachings of the angel, although he finds the fate of human beings extremely difficult to accept. It seems to him pointless and out of tune both with God's character as merciful one and with the actual work of creation as he perceives it.

The role of the present passage within the overall framework is thus clear. The angel stresses and restresses the fact that God rejoices over the reward of the righteous and does not grieve over the fate of the sinners. This is the point of his address in 8:37–41. He rejects Ezra's argument from creation, posed in 8:4–19, with the words "I will not concern myself about the fashioning of those who have sinned . . . but I will rejoice over the creation of the righteous" (8:38–39), and he illustrates this with the parable of the farmer. Ezra responds to the parable by stressing God's responsibility for the rain which determines the fate of the seeds. God formed humans with his own hands, will he treat them the same way (8:42–45)? The argument of 8:4–19a is repeated here in the context of the parable. Ezra offers no reason for God to change his action, he simply appeals for such a change: "But spare thy people" (8:42–45). The implication of Ezra's response to the parable is that as God is responsible for the rain which determines the fate of the seeds, so he is responsible for the conditions that determine the fate of mankind. The point is very much like that emerging from the address in chapter 3, but it is made far more mildly. Indeed, this inference is not even drawn explicitly, Ezra simply implies it: "Hast thou also made him [i.e., man] like the farmer's seed?" (8:45).

The angel's response in 8:46 makes skillful use of the two senses of "live," to live in the conventional sense and to live eternally. It sets the theme for what follows. The conditions of this world are irrelevant for those who will inherit the world to come. This is what is told to Ezra, and he is one of those. The angel continues: Although you, Ezra, express love for humankind by your concern, you love them much less than God. God's love is expressed precisely in his rejoicing over the righteous and his rewarding them (8:46–47).[9] Ezra's concern for the wicked is misplaced; he should instead rejoice in his own reward and that of the other righteous people, and that reward is spelled out in a list of the elements of eschatological goods (8:51–54). This is the true expression of God's philanthropy. The angel repeats his argument: the wicked have determined their own fate; not only did they act wickedly, they despised and denied the Most High and they persecuted the righteous (8:57). They did this, knowing that they must die, not a physical death but an eternal one. So this death of the wicked in 8:58 corresponds to the future life of those for whom the eschatological goods were prepared (8:46). The heart of the passage is bracketed between these two poles. That is made explicit in the next verse: "For just as the things which I have predicted await you, so the thirst and torment which are prepared await them" (8:59).

At the conclusion, the angel hints at another aspect of the problem of predetermination. God did not create mankind to perish, but by their sins humans determined their own fate, "and have been ungrateful to him who prepared life for them" (8:60). The point is clear then, and it complements the author's views throughout the book. In the final analysis, the judgment is true, without compassion, severe. Until the judgment, the complementary qualities of mercy and repentance are active and available. In judgment they are withdrawn. In judgment, humans bear the responsibility for their own sins, and in judgment God does not grieve for their fate. Nor should Ezra; he should rejoice in the reward of the righteous.

Two classical apocalyptic themes conclude the pericope: the end is near and to Ezra alone and the few righteous has this all been revealed. These themes often occur at the end of apocalyptic revelations.

It is worth observing that to the question of 6:59, When will we inherit our world that was created for us?—for clearly we do not do so here and now—God responds that the world was created for Israel, for the righteous in the world to come. This corresponds to the answer to the question here: Why did he labor so at the creation of humans (8:4–19b)? The response is that he labored at the perfection of the righteous (9:22). This too is the context of the stress on creation in 8:39.[10]

The stress on Ezra's righteousness is notable. In 7:76, Ezra is told not to reckon himself among the wicked. This is a change from earlier in the book, where his including himself among the wicked is not contested. The prophecy about Ezra's own future is in a way a response to the question that was not answered in 4:52. There the angel says that he was not sent to tell Ezra about his life. Here the focus has changed. Ezra's position as a paradigmatic righteous one (the righteous are those who are like him) is to the fore. His own fate, his eternal life, is predicted to him. The problem of the few and the many is resolved—the many perish not as God's responsibility but on their own. The few will be rewarded, and Ezra is one of them.

The author uses the contrast of the "pride" of the wicked (8:50) and Ezra's humility (8:49). These terms do not occur for the virtues of Ezra or for the vices of the wicked elsewhere.[11]

Observe that the overall structure we have described relates Ezra's intellectual knowledge of the angelic message but his emotional inability to accept it. He does not ever deny the conclusion that few will live and many die. However, he cannot be at peace with it. He tries all the means at his disposal to change the divine view: argument, lament, proof from scripture, prayer, and petition. His state of mind appears to become more

---

9   See also 9:22 Commentary.

10   Harnisch makes the same point from a different perspective when he contrasts the use of creation as the basis of Ezra's petition for intercession in 8:42–45 with the angel's invoking it as the basis for the fate of the wicked in 8:59–61 (p. 175 n. 4).

11   The pride of the eagle in 11:43 is the closest.

distressed as the intractability of this problem grows in his eyes. It even forces him, in 8:4–19a, back to the sort of questioning of the underpinnings of his world view by which he had been afflicted at the start of Vision 1 and from which he had been partially released as a result of spiritual development in the course of the preceding visions. The profundity of his distress is signaled by this recurrence of axiomatic uncertainty. It is still evident in the last pericope of the vision.

Commentary

■ **37** Ezra's words that are mentioned are those which he has spoken in the preceding pericope. The angel, as elsewhere in the book, uses this rhetorical technique to make his point.[12]

■ **38** The terms "death," "judgment," and "destruction" all refer to eternal perdition. They have been discussed in detail above.[13] The point of this passage with its stress on creation as well as on divine judgment is clear.[14] God rejoices over the righteous and does not grieve over the wicked. Some scholars have tried to interpret "fashioning" as deriving from Greek πλάσμα, which arises in turn from Hebrew יצר, that is, "inclination." This is philologically doubtful; moreover, the theme of creation is exceptionally important here. Not only did the whole of Vision 3 commence with this idea (6:38–56) but it is also dominant in 8:4–19a and recurs again in 9:22. Naturally, the four central terms used in this verse, that is, "fashioning" and the three synonyms for eternal death, have their exact parallels in the following verse.

■ **39** This verse describes the reward of the righteous in terms corresponding to those for the punishment of the wicked in 8:38. "Life," Latin *salvatio,* means "eternal life."[15] The main difficulty of the verse is the word "pilgrimage" which correponds to "death" of 8:38. Elsewhere the book uses similes for reward, such as "harvest" in 4:35. The literary figure here may derive from the idea that the soul travels, or ascends, to its eternal abode. This idea is inherent in the ascent terminology that is applied to the righteous soul in 7:77–99. At the end of this vision, too, Ezra is commanded to "go in" to the heavenly Jerusalem (10:55).[16] This language also suggests the idea of "the spirit returns to God" (Qoh 12:7). Oesterley's formulation is apt: "What is the death to the wicked is but a 'pilgrimage' to the better land for the righteous" (p. 106).[17] *Apoc Mos* 13:6 speaks of the "fearful upward journey" of Adam's soul; cf. ibid., 37:3–5. Compare also *2 Apoc Bar* 14:13.

■ **40** In Form and Structure, p. 283, we gave an exegesis based on the reading "I have spoken" witnessed by Latin and Syriac. The other chief witnesses, Ethiopic and Georgian, show "you have spoken"; see textual note f. Were that reading accepted, then this verse would form a summarizing conclusion to the preceding three verses. The passage is clearly delimited by the references to speaking in 8:37 and 8:40.

■ **41** In this verse a parable is presented complete with its interpretation. Its opening phrase may have formed the basis of *Greek Apoc Esd* 5:12: ὥσπερ γεωργὸς καταβάλλει τὸν σπόρον τοῦ σίτου ἐν τῇ γῇ ("Just as a farmer casts down the seed of corn into the earth"). The imagery of seed and sowing is quite widespread in the book.[18] It

---

12   See Form and Structure, p. 279. This point is true whether we accept the reading given here or whether, with Ethiopic and Georgian, we read "all things. . . ." Harnisch, p. 237 n. 6, speaks of irony, where we prefer to speak of rhetorical technique.

13   See Excursus on Adam's Sin, pp. 64–67. On the equivalation of "life" and "salvation," see ibid., nn. 38–39.

14   See Function and Content, p. 281.

15   See Excursus on Adam's Sin, p. 66, and Violet 2, here.

16   This is not the idea or the metaphor of "way" meaning "conduct" that is discussed in the Commentary on 7:6, and see also 7:129.

17   Oesterley, p. 106.

18   It is discussed in detail in 4:28 Commentary and in the Excursus on Natural Order, p. 102. It is used in *2*

Apoc Bar 22:5 in a fashion close to the present context. A similar parable is Mark 4:1–9 and 14–20. On the agricultural aspects of this, see E. Linnemann, *Parables of Jesus: Introduction and Exposition* (London: SPCK, 1966) 115–19. See also A. Feldman, *The Parables and Similes of the Rabbis: Agricultural and Pastoral* (Cambridge: Cambridge University, 1927), esp. chap. 1. Observe his comments on p. 54 concerning sprouting as a simile of resurrection.

serves to highlight once more the idea of the few redeemed righteous and the many damned wicked which dominates this whole part of the third vision.[19]

Some aspects of the terminology used in this verse should be noted. Latin uses *salvare* for "live" of the other versions, a term typical of God's action toward the righteous in 4 Ezra.[20] The textual note here deals with this term, and the play on the meanings of "life" here and in 8:39 is interesting (cf. also Function and Content, p. 280). Second, the polyvalent word *saeculum* and parallels here seem to designate "world" rather than "age."[21] Finally, the expression "in due season" is particularly typical of agricultural contexts; see Ps 1:3; Luke 20:10; *2 Apoc Bar* 22:5; et al. Even though not taken up in the interpretation of the parable, it clearly implies predetermination, the fixed course of events.[22]

■ **42** The verse opens with the phrase "If I have found favor before thee," which in 4 Ezra often introduces a major new matter. Here, however, this is not the case.[23]

■ **43** On the expression "in due season," see 8:41 Commentary. In Function and Content, p. 281, we discussed the implications of the formulation "thy rain" which points to God's responsibility for the success of the crop and by inference therefore for the fate of human beings.

■ **44** In a number of ways this verse stresses the significance of the creation of humans and the importance that God attributed to it. This makes the final question, "Hast thou also made him like the farmer's seed?" the more telling. The idea that mankind was created by God's hands occurs in 3:5 and is discussed in the commentary on that verse. The book presents differing views, both that the world was created for the sake of Israel and that it was created for the sake of mankind in general.[24] This is the only occasion in the book where the biblical idea that Adam was created in the image of God is to be found, but it is in no way exceptional and serves the point of this passage admirably.[25]

■ **45** This verse is an appeal for mercy, one of a number of such passages found throughout this part of the book, such as 7:132–139 and 8:32–36. "People" is often found parallel to "inheritance,"[26] and here these terms clearly designate the people of Israel. The argument of the last phrase, "for thou hast mercy," could be interpreted to mean "since mankind is thy creation, and Israel too, thou hast mercy." Alternatively, it might be thought to argue, as in 7:132–139: It is known (e.g., from scripture) that God has mercy on his creation, so let him have mercy on Israel. Phrases from 8:44 and 8:45 seem to be reflected in *Greek Apoc Esd* 2:23: ἐλέησον τὴν σὴν πλάσιν· οἰκτίρησον τὰ ἔργα σου ("Pity, your own molding and have mercy upon your works"), and *Apoc Sedrach* 13:2–3: ἐλέσον κύριε, τὴν εἰκόνα σου, καὶ σπλαγχνίσθητι ("Have mercy, lord, upon your image and be compassionate").[27]

■ **46** This formulation is partly based on the idea of two ages, which is discussed above.[28] Its antithetical form resembles that of 4:21 and even more closely that of 7:25. The point seems to be here the recompense meted out to the righteous and the wicked, and the key concept, the idea of "life," was noted in 8:41 Commentary to be central to the whole passage. Those who will live eternally will be rewarded in the world to come, while those who live *only* now will receive the things of this world.[29] In other words, following Violet 2, we interpret the verse in the light of 7:25 and particularly of 7:16. Through this, the mercy Ezra asks for will be found.[30]

■ **47** This verse makes two main points. The first is contained in the reproach to Ezra, that he cannot love creation more than God.[31] Exactly the same reproach is to be found in 5:33, where it forms part of the angel's reply to Ezra's address on election; here it is in his

---

19 Function and Content, p. 280, and 7:47 Commentary.
20 See Excursus on Adam's Sin, p. 66.
21 See 7:30 Commentary and Excursus on the Term "Age," pp. 218–19.
22 See also 3:9 and Commentary there.
23 On this phrase, see 4:44 Commentary.
24 For a discussion, see 6:55 Commentary.
25 See Gen 1:26–27; Sir 17:3–4; et al.
26 See 8:15 Commentary.
27 It seems that here *Greek Apocalypse of Esdras* and *Apocalypse of Sedrach* draw from slightly different parts of 4 Ezra, a fact significant for illustrating the relationship between them. See Himmelfarb, *Tours of Hell*, 24–26.
28 See Excursus on the Two Ages, pp. 92–93.
29 In Stone, *Features*, 62–63, the verse was interpreted in line with 4:21, the things of this world can be understood only by those who live in this world, etc. This would make it much less responsive to context than the view proposed in the present commentary.
30 Cf. also, from a different viewpoint, *2 Apoc Bar* 24:3. The lack of coherency, noted by Kaminka, is thus only apparent and his emendations are superfluous.

response to the petition for pity. It implies that "since God, the Creator, truly loves his creation and since he has determined the relationship between human action and recompense, for Ezra to ask for pity is presumption —Ezra cannot love the creation more than God."[32] This is like the argument forwarded above that God's true love and rejoicing are over the righteous and their fate (8:39 and see Commentary). The angel speaks as if he were God, a phenomenon that has been noticed before.[33]

Ezra is assured, once more, that he is not a sinner. This theme is first found in 7:76, and it recurs in the latter part of the book. The reasons given for his righteousness vary. Here it is his very humility in reckoning himself with the sinners. This presages the major changes in the attitude toward Ezra that occur in the latter part of the book and, of course, is related to the assertion of Ezra's reward that is prominent in the rest of the present pericope.[34]

■ **48** No commentary.

■ **49** The reasons for which Ezra is considered righteous are discussed above,[35] but this is the only occasion on which his humility is mentioned in this context. The sentiment is a common one; see, for example, Matt 23:12 (// Luke 14:11). We have preferred to translate the last phrase "so that you will receive . . . ," a meaning the putative Greek or Hebrew could bear. After all, the point is surely that Ezra's glorification was the result of his self-humiliation but not its purpose, as would be implied by a translation "in order to receive" (RSV). "Glory" is a common concept used in various ways, including the glory of God,[36] and the idea of the eschatological glory of the righteous, here promised to Ezra, occurs elsewhere in the book.

■ **50** This verse opens a short prediction, which is struc-

tured not chronologically but by subject. The fate of the wicked at the end is contrasted with that of the righteous. The "many miseries" that are foretold as coming upon them are those terrible events called elsewhere the "messianic birth-pangs."[37] They are described as punishment for sinfulness. It is unclear whether what is implied is that human sin will cause the disruption of the order of the world, which will lead to the woes, or whether, since the woes are destined to come as part of the course of history, those who sin are those who will suffer through them.[38]

The use of "times" is somewhat unusual. It also occurs in 7:26 above (see Commentary) in a similar context. The ambiguous term lying behind Latin *saeculum* and equivalents seems to mean "world" here.[39]

The pride of the sinners is stressed. This is, of course, a commonly mentioned sin. It has particular eschatological connections, however, in the context of the *hybris* of the last ruler or kingdom. This is clear from 11:43 and compare Dan 4:37 and many other texts. The present usage, however, sets it in contrast with Ezra's humility, which was stressed in the last verse.[40]

■ **51** The sentiment expressed here should be compared with 9:13, while in *2 Apoc Bar* 48:48, Baruch is told, "But now let us dismiss the wicked and inquire about the righteous." Notably, attention is focused in this verse on Ezra himself, which is one of the particular emphases of the whole passage, as has been observed above. "Glory," which Ezra is destined to receive, plays many roles in the book; compare its use in 8:49 with that here.[41] Ezra's paradigmatic position among the righteous is also stressed,[42] and they are designated by the expression

---

31   4:34 is formulated in a rather similar fashion.
32   The same relation to God as Creator is highlighted by the word "Maker" in 5:33.
33   See 7:17 Commentary on this.
34   See 7:76 and 7:77 and Commentary to those verses. It is worth recalling that the same author elsewhere asserts the universal sinfulness of humans; the seeming contradiction is inherent to his thinking which is not truly systematic. See discussion in 7:46 Commentary and 7:67 Commentary. A somewhat similar situation with a rather different attitude toward the seer's righteousness is to be observed in

Hermas Vis. 3.1.9.
35   See 6:32 Commentary in detail.
36   On eschatological glory, see Excursus on the Term "Judgment," p. 150, and Commentary on 7:97; glory in general is discussed in Commentary on 3:19.
37   These woes are discussed in 4:52 Commentary.
38   See Stone, "Natural Order," 299 n. 4.
39   See Excursus on the Term "Age," p. 218.
40   See the comments of Volz, p. 89, on pride in the eschatological context.
41   See further Commentary there.
42   See also Function and Content, p. 282.

"those who are like you," both here and in 8:62.[43] These two specific usages again highlight the extent to which Ezra's personal virtue is brought to the fore. The angel repeatedly assures Ezra of his own righteousness (see in detail 6:32 Commentary).

■ **52** In general, 8:52 lists features that will form part of the world to come, while 8:53–54 records phenomena that will be absent. There has been considerable discussion among scholars about whether these various eschatological elements are to be understood materially or as having undergone a process of spiritualization. Was paradise, for example, an earthly garden or a way of referring to a heavenly, spiritual state? This issue will be examined more closely below, but it should be recalled that for authors of the age of 4 Ezra, heavenly objects were no less real than earthly ones, so that opposed categories "material" and "spiritual" seem irrelevant.[44]

This passage is a list that, at least in 8:52, is not arranged in chronological sequence. It also contains some parallels with 7:117–126, a passage which also presents eschatological elements in a nonchronological order:

8:51	glory	7:125	faces . . . shall shine
8:52	paradise is opened	7:123	paradise shall be revealed
	tree of life planted	7:123	whose fruit does not spoil
	world to come is prepared	7:119	an immortal age has been promised
	delight is provided	7:123	in which are abundance and healing
	a city is built	7:121	safe . . . treasuries
	rest is appointed		
	goodness is established		
	wisdom is perfected beforehand		
8:53	root of evil is sealed up	7:118	(*Adam's sin led to inherited misfortune*)
	illness is banished	7:121	healthful habitations
8:54	sorrows have passed away	7:117	live in sorrow now

These striking parallels indicate that this is a range of terminology which evokes the eschatological state, for there does not appear to be direct dependence between the two passages. This is, then, not a chronological description of the advent of the eschaton but a list of evocative features.

The same coincidence of "rest," "paradise," and "fruit" is also found in *Test Patr Levi* 18:9–10. It is an obvious and a traditional combination of elements. Note that "you" is plural and here indicates "Ezra and those like him," while in the previous part of the speech it was singular, referring to Ezra alone.

The expression "paradise is opened" also occurs in *Apoc Sedrach* 12:2: ὁ παράδεισός σοι ἠνοίγη. The term "paradise" has various senses in 4 Ezra, and here, as in 7:123, it means the place of eschatological reward of the righteous.[45]

The idea of the tree of life, implied by the fruit motif, may be found in 7:13; 7:123; 8:6; and 8:52. It is the tree whose fruit gives immortality, of which the righteous will partake in the eschaton.[46]

The phrase "the world to come is prepared" reflects two notions: that there are two worlds or ages and that the world to come was created by God in advance. These ideas are to be found elsewhere in the book, and the precreation of other eschatological elements in the present list is also implied.[47]

The term "delight" probably derives from "Eden," which in Hebrew may be taken to mean "delight" and so it should be associated with the other features related to paradise.[48]

The concept of "city" is much more complex. In the first place, of course, it is related to the idea of the pre-existent, heavenly Jerusalem. Here, as in 7:26; 10:27; 10:44; and 10:54, it is referred to merely as "city," and

---

43 See 6:26 Commentary n. 51. As was observed above, a similar expression designates the companions of the Messiah; see 7:28 Commentary.

44 Keulers maintains inappropriately but energetically that all these terms are spiritualized; see 3:6 Commentary and Stone, *Features*, 197–202.

45 See 3:6 Commentary on paradise as place of eschatological reward; see also Schieffer, 30–31. Here it may be identified with heavenly Jerusalem (Keulers, pp. 181–88); this is discussed further below.

46 See 3:20 Commentary and 7:13 Commentary for a discussion of the various aspects of this idea.

47 On the idea of the two ages and on their character, see Excursus on the Two Ages. Precreation is discussed in 3:6 Commentary and 6:6 Commentary and the term "prepared" in 7:14 Commentary.

48 See 7:36 Commentary.

the appearance of the heavenly city is the chief topic of Vision 4.[49] In 4 Ezra, we should observe, heavenly Jerusalem is usually related to the "messianic kingdom" complex of ideas, and this is not readily to be reconciled with its connection with paradise in a number of contexts.

The term "rest" indicates eschatological reward. In *2 Apoc Bar* 73:1 we read "rest will appear," which is very much like the phrase "rest is appointed" in 4 Ezra 8:52. The passage in *2 Apocalypse of Baruch* is also drawn from an eschatological poem like 4 Ezra 8:52–54.[50] "Goodness" is another technical term for eschatologicial reward, and it is one of the characteristic ideas of the eschatological poems.

Wisdom, according to many texts, was created before the creation of the world.[51] That this concept is common explains the striking parallel in 1 Cor 2:7, which speaks of the wisdom that "God decreed before the ages." This precreated wisdom will be granted to the righteous at the eschaton, as is stated not only here but in many apocalypses.[52] Wisdom is regarded by the book as a very central virtue. The converse of the prediction here is that the hiding of wisdom is part of the woes that will precede the eschaton.[53]

■ **53** A number of the elements of this verse are found in reverse, as it were, in a list of the things introduced into the world by the sin of Adam, according to *2 Apoc Bar* 56:6. This list is formulated similarly to the eschatological poems of which the present context is one:

untimely death came into being,
mourning was mentioned,

affliction was prepared,
illness was created,
labor accomplished,
pride came into existence,
the realm of death began to ask to be renewed with
blood . . .
And goodness vanished.

Box justly noted the progression of thought in 8:53–54, from the eradication of evil to the removal of consequences of sin and from that to the manifestation of the treasures of immortality. It may be added that what is described is a reversal of the situation created by Adam's sin, which is related in chapter 3.[54]

The term "evil root" is quite old and occurs elsewhere in 4 Ezra.[55] It seems to refer to the evil heart which causes death. The eschatological removal of the evil root or inclination is a widespread expectation in Jewish sources of this age.[56] Note the call to let Sheol be sealed in *2 Apoc Bar* 21:23 and compare also *Prayer of Manasseh* 3, which has the "sealing up of the deep."[57]

Illness is one of the chief afflictions of this world, and its disappearance will be typical of the future age; see *2 Apoc Bar* 73:2: "Health will descend in dew and illness will vanish."[58] Not only illness but death too will be removed at the end, and death plays a role in all the eschatological poems. "Mortal" and "corruptible" are virtual synonyms.[59] The overcoming of death is prominent in 1 Cor 15:25, 55. The synonymous parallelism of death and Hades is common; see, for example, Isa 28:15; Prov 5:5; Rev 1:18; and 6:8.

49   See 7:26 Commentary.
50   See 6:11–29 Form and Structure, p. 166, and 7:36 Commentary.
51   See Nickelsburg and Stone, *Faith and Piety*, 209–15.
52   It is discussed in Excursus on Inspiration, pp. 123–24.
53   See also ibid.
54   See Excursus on Adam's Sin, pp. 63–67.
55   See 3:22 Commentary.
56   See Excursus on Adam's Sin, n. 21. J. Dupont suggests a textual corruption and an original reading:

est préparée   la racine de la sagesse,
est scellée   la maladie
("there is prepared   the root of wisdom
there is sealed   illness.")

("La sagesse préparée pour les élus: Etude sur le texte de 4 Esdras 8,52–54," *Revue Bénédictine* 57 [1947] 3–

11.) He then adduces texts dealing with the root of wisdom, on which see our Commentary on 3:22. On the textual issue, see textual note h. Both "evil root" (cf. 3:22; etc.) and "root of wisdom" could occur in the book. The evidence for eschatological granting of wisdom is marshaled in the preceding paragraph.

57   The sealing of death in Wisd 2:5 employs a different sense of the word, the signing and sealing of a decree. The various uses of "sealing" are discussed in 6:5 Commentary and 6:20 Commentary.

58   This is also one of the eschatological poems. See 6:11–29 Form and Function, p. 166. Cf. also 7:121 "safe and healthful habitations" and Commentary there. A direct contrast is to be found in *2 Apoc Bar* 56:6 (6:11–29 Form and Function, p. 166).

59   On attitudes toward death and its abolition in the eschatological state, see Excursus on Adam's Sin, pp.

"Hell" here clearly means death.[60] We may question whether, as, for example, in some Christian texts, Hades is personified, and in the background of the text here lies a more mythical idea that Hades is overcome in a battle at the eschaton. This was a beloved theme of early Christian art.[61] A common point is shared throughout this part of the prediction but formulated in different terms.

■ **54** The toils or troubles of this world are one of the results of Adam's sin and will be removed at the eschaton. Many other places in 4 Ezra also characterize this world as toilsome.[62] The process of the reversal of the results of Adam's sins reaches its climax with the restoration of immortality.[63] The heavenly treasure laid up by the righteous was a common theme.[64] Box comments justly that "in the end" means after the things described in the preceding two verses.

■ **55** The injunction not to ask questions, given in a somewhat oracular form, may also be observed in 6:10 and 9:13. Indeed, this and the following verses resemble 9:9–13 in many respects. Here there is a repetition of the dismissal of the theme of the few and the many; on this, see 7:47 Commentary.

■ **56–58** Verse 56 and the following two verses contain a listing of transgressions which is shared with many other places in the book; see particularly 5:29; 7:22–24; 7:37; 7:79; 7:81; and 9:9–13. We deal with the three verses together here.

"Freedom" is related to the idea of free will which is strongly stressed by the angel, and this is, of course, the point of the following verses 8:59–60; note the very similar phrase in 9:11 and such passages as 7:20; 7:72;

and 7:127–130. The idea is widespread in Jewish literature of this age.[65] The implication of this idea of free will in the present context is, as Harnisch pointed out, that humans cause their own ruin (p. 174).

The accusation of despising the Most High is frequently repeated in one form or another; see 7:23–24 and 9:10 ("did not acknowledge me in their life").[66] This is what is described in 7:37 and 7:81. The denial of God mentioned in the next verse also occurs in 7:23, and it is a specific form of this general accusation.[67] The expressions "were contemptuous of his law and forsook his ways" take up a theme that is central to almost all indictments of sinners in the book. Thus it may be observed in 7:20; 7:24; 7:37; 7:79; 7:81; et al. In 5:29 the wicked are "those who opposed thy promises," and in 9:11 they are those who "scorned my law." The contempt of the law is a charge also leveled at Gentiles; indeed, it seems to be a general term for disobedience to God (cf. 7:23–24 and Commentary; 7:79; 7:81). The expression "though knowing full well that they must die" highlights the idea of the responsibility of the wicked for their own sin.[68]

The final element of this list of sins is the accusation that the wicked trampled or oppressed the righteous. This occurs in the same passages that have been mentioned, that is, 5:29 and 6:57–58.[69] Thus this short indictment gives the quintessence of the divine accusation of the sinners and sets it in the context of free will and therefore of their culpability.

■ **59** The expression "just as" serves to highlight the idea of punishment as parallel and corresponding to reward which is dominant in the formulation of other passages in

---

65–67. On the role of death or corruption in the eschatological poems, see 6:11–29 Form and Structure, pp. 155–56. On "corruption," see 4:11 Commentary.

60 On the idea of the underworld, see 4:41 Commentary. Reference to many texts dealing with the underworld without the association of hell as an infernal place are gathered by Volz, pp. 328–29.

61 See liturgical and iconographical material in F. Cabrol and H. Leclercq, *Dictionnaire de archéologie chrétienne et de liturgie* (Paris: Letouzey et Ané, 1920), vol. 4.1, pp. 682–96; J. Siebert, *Lexikon der christlicher Kunst* (Fribourg: Herder, 1980) 146–48; L. Reau, *Iconographie de l'art chrétien, 2.2 Nouveau Testament* (Paris: Presses Universitaires de France, 1957) 727–57. On views in *2 Apoc Bar,* see Commentary 4:41.

62 See Excursus on Adam's Sin, p. 65, and 7:12

Commentary.

63 Note the use of verbs similar to "manifest" in the other eschatological poems; see 6:11–29 Form and Structure, n. 3.

64 See 7:77 Commentary.

65 On free will, see Excursus on Adam's Sin, p. 65.

66 See 7:23–24 Commentary; on its reversal as faith, see 9:7 Commentary.

67 See 5:29 Commentary and 7:23–24 Commentary, p. 201.

68 Cf. *2 Apoc Bar* 55:2. As explained above, we take "die" to mean something like "eternal punishment." Oesterley takes it in the sense of physical death, and the verse to mean *carpe diem;* cf. Isa 22:13; Wisd 2:5–20; and 1 Cor 15:32.

69 See 7:79 Commentary. For the expression "trampled," see 5:29.

the book, such as 7:36; 7:38; and 7:81–98.[70] The "things which I have predicted" are eschatological reward,[71] while thirst and torment signify eschatological punishment.[72] These are "prepared," a term pregnant with meaning and serving to stress the precreated or predetermined nature of the various elements of the eschatological things.[73] The final phrase has been remarked upon above (Form and Function, p. 282). With it compare also such statements as Ezek 33:11 and 2 Pet 3:9. The basic idea, again repeated here, that humans are responsible for their own fate was discussed in 7:116—8:3 Function and Content, p. 257.

■ **60** At the start of this verse the angel emphasizes the idea of creation. The seer had drawn extensively on this in the preceding material (8:4–19; 8:42–45), but in the angel's discourse it is used differently. While Ezra had stressed God's responsibility to humans as their creator, the angel stresses the human's responsibility toward God as a creature; compare Isa 45:9–13. "The defiling of God's name" occurs often in the Bible. Here and in a number of other instances it means acting publicly in such a way as to disgrace or ignore God; see Lev 18:21; Ezek 36:23; 43:8; and *1 Enoch* 45:2 ("deny name").[74]

Some have taken the word "life" to mean "salvation" in the last phrase of the verse (as it often does).[75] This view should be abandoned and the intepretation should be based on the parallelism with "him who made them." The ungratefulness of the sinners is stressed by *2 Apoc Bar* 13:12 and 48:29, and in the context of eschatology, in 55:2. Harnisch (p. 176n) has observed the importance of acknowledgment of God already in biblical sources;

see Isa 45:9; Rom 1:20–21; etc.

■ **61** This remark signals the transition to prediction. In earlier parts of the book, such transitional remarks were usually of oracular character. That is missing from the present context. Perhaps this is the first of the clear series of markers differentiating the conclusion of Vision 3 from the conclusions of the preceding visions.[76]

This verse deals with the idea of judgment. It is close. The same aspect is stressed in 5:51.[77] The sense of haste and urgency that besets Ezra is an ongoing theme of the book and also may be observed in, for example, 4:33 and 4:38–39; compare *2 Apoc Bar* 48:2. This is, of course, one central aspect of apocalyptic eschatology.[78]

In this verse the angel speaks of "my judgment," taking on the *persona* of God, a phenomenon we have observed elsewhere in the book.[79]

■ **62a** This verse brings the angelic address toward its conclusion. Similar ideas about revelations only for the few righteous, chiefly centered on Ezra, are to be found in 7:47; 12:36–38; 13:53–56; 14:26; and 14:46–47. This feature often occurs in the conclusion of apocalypses or in contexts related to the views of apocalyptic esoteric transmission of writings.[80] "You and those like you" is a phrase found also in 8:51.[81] It designates the righteous but is clearly focused on Ezra, as is appropriate to the *Tendenz* of this part of the vision.

---

70 Cf. also *2 Apoc Bar* 42:2.

71 See 4:27 Commentary.

72 The element of thirst is rarely mentioned. One instance seems to be Luke 16:24; cf. as a possible source Isa 5:13. "Torment," however, is widely attested, and see further 7:36 Commentary.

73 See 7:14 Commentary.

74 "Him who made them" occurs quite often in *2 Apoc Bar;* see 78:3; 79:2; and 82:2. In the specific context of sin, see *2 Apoc Bar* 60:2 and 79:2.

75 See, e.g., Stone, *Features,* 187; cf. Myers, who compares with John 14:2b.

76 This issue is dealt with further below. On the role of this and similar verses, see *Visions* 2.

77 The terminology of judgment is discussed in Excursus on the Term "Judgment," p. 149. On the sense of proximity, cf. also 14:18. This idea also characterizes the "Day of the Lord" in the Hebrew Bible; cf. Joel 3:14; Obadiah 15; et al.

78 See 5:41—6:10 Function and Content, p. 146.

79 See 7:17 Commentary.

80 See Stone, "Apocalyptic Literature," 431–33.

81 See Commentary there.

8

62b Then I answered and said, 63/ "Behold, O Lord, [a] thou hast now shown me a multitude of the signs which thou wilt [b] do in the last times, but thou hast not shown me [c]when thou wilt do them." [c]

9

1 He answered me and said, "Measure carefully [d] in your mind, and [e] when you will see that a certain part [f] of the predicted signs [g] are past, 2/ then you will know that it is the very time when the Most High is about to [h] visit the world which he has made. 3/ So when there shall appear in the world
    quaking of places, [i]
    tumult of peoples, intrigues of nations,
    wavering [j] of leaders, [k]confusion of princes, [k]
4/ then you will know that it was of these that the Most High spoke [l] from [m] the days that were of old. [n] 5/ For [o] just as with everything that has occurred in the world, the beginning is evident [p], and the end manifest; 6/ so also are the times [q] of the Most High: the beginnings are manifest [r] in wonders and mighty works, and the end in deeds [s] and in signs. 7/ And it shall be that everyone who will be saved and will be able to escape on account of his works, or on account of the faith by which he has believed, 8/ will survive the dangers that have been predicted, and will see my salvation [t] in my land and within my borders, [u] which I have sanctified for myself [v]from the beginning. [v]
    9/ Then those who have now abandoned [w] my ways
      shall be amazed
    and those who have [x]rejected them [y] with contempt [z]
      shall dwell in torments.
10/ For as many as did not acknowledge me in their lifetime, although they received my benefits, 11/ and as many as scorned my law while they still had freedom, [a] and did not understand but despised it while an

Notes

8:63 a Arm adds "who do not bear resentment, my soul does not have temerity to question you. Listen to your servant concerning that."

b $\mu\acute{\epsilon}\lambda\lambda\epsilon\iota\varsigma$ is implied by Lat, Syr, Eth.

c–c Literally, "at what time"; Georg adds *erit;* Arm adds "when it will be"; these readings are probably independent.

9:1 d All versions seem to have reflexes of Hebrew infinitive absolute and finite verb here.

e Lat, Arm add "and it shall be"; Ar2 resumes here.

f "A few" Eth, Ar2; "sign" Georg.

g Ar1 resumes here.

2 h $\mu\acute{\epsilon}\lambda\lambda\epsilon\iota$ implied by Lat, Syr, Eth; lacuna in Georg.

3 i Two words in all versions, contrast RSV "earthquakes"; the ensuing list is rephrased in Ar1; Georg, Ar2, Arm omit one of the next two phrases.

j Lat, Syr, Georg, Arm; others vary.

k–k Arm has an expansion.

4 l–n Syr "previously"; Eth "before their time"; Lat, Ar2 alone add *ab initio.*

m Georg, Ar1 "in."

5 o Eth, Georg omit; so also Lat Ms A; Georg is fragmentary in the rest of the verse.

p Corrupt in Lat; Eth "in the word"; Hilgenfeld and Volkmar suggest $\dot{\epsilon}\nu \phi\omega\nu\hat{\eta} \langle \dot{\epsilon}\mu\phi\alpha\nu\hat{\eta}.$

6 q Eth "world."

r Eth "in the word"; see 9:5 note p.

s So Lat, Eth, Georg, Ar1; Syr reads *bnys' wb'twt' wbhyl'.* Georg is fragmentary from here to the end of 9:15. RSV is based on the unsupported reading of Syr. The next word is repetitively *wb'twt'* in Syr, and the corruption of these two words indicates that the whole phrase was corrupted in this version.

8 t Ar2 omits to 9:13.

u Ar1 "mountain" $\ddot{o}\rho o\varsigma \langle \ddot{o}\rho\iota o\nu$ (Volkmar).

v–v Eth and apparently Georg read "from this world," and perhaps all versions go back to $\dot{\alpha}\pi\dot{o} \tauo\hat{\upsilon} \alpha\dot{\iota}\hat{\omega}\nuo\varsigma.$ For possible Greek originals of this and similar expressions, see Stone, *Some Features,* 156–71.

9 w Lat *abusi sunt;* Hilgenfeld suggests that the versions may all be explained by $\pi\alpha\rho\alpha\chi\rho\hat{\eta}\sigma\theta\alpha\iota$ which might have both meanings. Violet 2 has further suggestions.

x–y Two verbs in Syr, Eth.

z Eth ("best MSS," *sic* Violet!) "my commands"; Eth (*reliqui*) "fear"; Ar1 "my fear."

11 a Arm is quite different in the first part of the verse and also omits from here up to 9:13; cf. Ar1, and see note t above on 9:8.

opportunity of [b] repentance was still open to them, 12/ these must in torment acknowledge (me) [c] after death. 13/ Therefore, do not continue to be curious as to how the ungodly will be punished; but inquire how the righteous will live, [d] those to whom the age belongs [e] and for whose sake the age was made."

14 I answered and said, 15/ [f]"I said before, [f] and I say now, [g]and will say it again: [g] there are more who perish than those who will live, [h] 16/ as a wave [i] is greater than a drop of water."

17 He answered me and said, [j]
"As is the field, so is the seed;
[k]and as are the flowers, so are the colors; [k]
and as is the work, so is the judgment; [l]
and as is the farmer, so is the threshing floor.

18/ For there was a time in this age [m] when I was preparing for those who now exist, before [n]they came into being, the world [n] was made for them to dwell in, and no one opposed me then, for no one existed; 19/ but now those who have been created in this world which is supplied both with an unfailing table and an inexhaustible pasture, [o] have become corrupt in their ways. 20/ So I considered my [p] world, and behold, it was lost, and my earth, [q] and behold, it was in peril [r] because of the devices [s] of those who had come into it. 21/ And I saw and spared some with great difficulty, and saved for myself one grape out of a cluster, and one plant out of a great forest. [t] 22/ So let the multitude perish which has been born in vain, but let my grape and my plant be saved, because with much labor I have perfected them. [u]

b Literally, "place" Lat, Syr, Eth.

12 c Eth "me," cf. Ar1; in fact, RSV "it" (i.e., "my law") is also possible, since the object is not stated explicitly in Lat, Syr, and the object in Eth, Ar1 seems to be secondary. Our translation, however, chooses to follow the ancient exegesis of these two versions.

13 d Lat, Ar1 *salvabuntur;* see 8:3 note k; cf. Excursus on Adam's Sin, p. 66. Ar2 and Arm both resume at the start of this verse.

d–e Eth, Ar1 both make explicit, each in its own way, that reference is being made to the world to come.

15 f–f Syr omits.

g–g Eth omits.

h Lat *salvabuntur,* and cf. Ar1; see note d above on 9:13.

16 i Eth, Ar1 "flood, torrent."

17 j Arm has an expansion. The last part may be a paraphrase of the text found in the other versions. Arm subsequently omits up to 9:22.

k–k Lat, Syr; Eth omits; Ar1, Ar2 rephrase.

l Or "reward," from Greek κρίσις; versions are complex: "judgment" occurs in Eth, Georg, Ar1; "reward" in Arm, cf. Ar2; Latin "creation," ⟨ κτίσις ⟨ κρίσις (Volkmar); Syr *rhn'* probably derives from *dyn',* which in turn again reflects κρίσις.

18 m Eth "days"; see 7:26 note b.

n–n Lat *eis his qui nunc, antequam fieret illis, saeculum.* Violet persuasively suggests that Lat, Syr, Eth, Georg can be explained as deriving from πρὶν ἢ γενέσθαι and that the subject of this phrase is properly the inhabitants. The last phrase of the verse supports this.

19 o "Law" in versions from νόμος for νομός "pasture" (so Volkmar, widely adopted).

20 p Lat, Syr; "the" Eth; "this" Ar1; Ar2 is periphrastic.

q See Commentary.

r Georg Ms I breaks off here.

s Word uncertain; Lat *cogitationes;* Syr *hwpkyhwn* "perverseness"; Eth, Ar1 "deeds."

21 t Lat *tribu* derives from φύλης for ἀφ ὕλης (Volkmar).

22 u Syr "are created"; Eth "increased"; Ar1 "prepared"; the verb is active in Lat, Ar1 and passive in Syr, Eth. Arm resumes in this verse. It is periphrastic in the latter part and contains a long addition.

Form and Structure

This pericope may be divided into four sections: two major addresses by the angel, each of which is introduced by a question posed by the seer. At the end of Visions 1 and 2 we observed two complementary revelations of such signs (5:1–13 and 6:11–28) which might even have been two parts of a single document. The heart of the present pericope is also the revelation relating to the signs of the end. With this passage, therefore, the close structural parallel to Visions 1–2 is resumed.[1]

The two earlier revelations particularly stressed the messianic woes, and the end of the second one contained predictions of the messianic kingdom and the day of judgment. Thus they combined to form a complete eschatological revelation. The present passage fulfills the corresponding role for Vision 3. However, as 9:1 makes explicit, it assumes the two preceding passages but is not intended to add to their list of signs.[2]

We observed two earlier passages of predictive prophecy in this third vision (7:26–44 and 7:75–99). These are almost essays on specific aspects of eschatology. Although 7:26–44 is not as closely linked to the two preceding revelations as they are to one another, it complements them. It spells out the eschatological details to which 6:11–28 merely alludes. Furthermore, it is put into relation to the signs. The passage 7:75–99 also fills in a gap in previous predictions, but the gap is not a sequential one. The present passage, clearly felt to be important in context on formal and structural grounds, is also not true prediction of future signs. It is introduced by a question, the seer's request for knowledge, and is followed by a further question and answer. It is significant to note that in the rest of the book we do not find similar substantial questions and answers following the predictions. This is unique to the present passage.[3]

A. Seer's Request Relating to the Signs (8:62b–63)
This request refers back to the earlier revelations of the signs in 5:1–13 and 6:11–28 and structurally is not dissimilar to the requests with which the signs are introduced in Visions 1 and 2.

B. Prediction of Signs in the Mouth of the Angel (9:1–13)
This predictive discourse set in the angel's mouth generally resembles those in Visions 1 and 2. It too opens in 9:1–2 with the establishment of the time of the events predicted, equivalent to the "Behold, days are coming" (9:2). Note that the structure of this opening passage does not resemble 5:1, "Now concerning the signs," but it is similar in structure to the start of the signs in Vision 2, with a speech directed at Ezra, followed by a prediction (6:13–17).[4] The first part of the address (9:1–6) is the answer to the seer's questions, while in 9:7–12 the angel moves to prediction concerning the fate of the righteous and the wicked. This prediction is followed, in 9:13, by an admonition. Just as the seer's concluding comment (see below) refers back to the section starting with 7:45, so the angel's remarks here contain many elements parallel to the opening part of the whole vision, particularly 7:1–25. The chief parallels are 9:10 // 7:23; 9:11 // 7:21; 9:12 // 7:2; 9:13 // 7:25 and particularly to the point of 6:59—7:16.

The prediction is almost completely in prose, broken in 9:17 by some rhythmic pronouncements of an oracular character. In 9:5 there is what might be characterized as a statement of gnomic character.

C. Seer's Concluding Comment (9:14–16)
In this responsive comment Ezra returns to the problem that has been exercising him since 7:45, that of the few and the many.

D. Angel's Concluding Address (9:17–25)
This section (9:17–25) contains the concluding remarks by the angel (9:17–22).

This final pericope of the vision, then, by its deliberate references back to the beginning, serves to bracket the whole vision and give a sense of coherence to this long and complex composition.

Function and Content
The seer's opening request, as we have noted, refers back to the revelation of the signs with which the two previous visions concluded. It is no longer a request to learn about the signs but instead focuses on the issue of when the signs will take place. This was, after all, the first question asked after the oracular revelation in Vision 1 (4:33).[5] Moreover, the sense of haste and urgency and the questions to which it gives rise had occupied Vision 1 (4:34) and Vision 2 (5:43–55). Another prediction of the closeness of the last times is to be found in 5:4.[6]

---

1 See 7:75–99 Form and Structure, p. 238, on this.

2 On the structure, see General Structure of the Book, pp. 50–51, and 7:116—8:3 Form and Structure, p. 248.

3 For a possible source analysis of this passage, see discussion and critique in 5:1–13 Function and Content, p. 108.

4 Cf. also 7:76–77. See also 5:1–13 Form and Structure, p. 107, on the literary character of this introduction.

5 See also Commentary there for further instances of this question; see 8:63 Commentary.

6 See Commentary there.

The angel's response in 9:1–13 contains the following points. In 9:1–2 the angel tells Ezra to examine the situation in the world, and when he observes that the signs that have been predicted are starting to happen, he will know that the end is coming. This important passage highlights why the knowledge of the signs was significant: it enabled people to know when the end was approaching. A similar concern for "diagnostic" signs may be seen in *b. Sanh.* 98a–b. This is interestingly compared with the comment in the *Greek Apocalypse of Esdras* where Ezra asks for the revelation of the description of the antichrist: "Make known to me what sort of appearance he has and I will inform the race of men lest they believe in him" (4:28). In the ensuing verses 3–4 some of these signs are mentioned in greater detail, in particular the feature of internecine warfare which had only been hinted at in 5:9.

The next two verses quote a gnomic expression about the things of the world: their beginnings are evident and their ends manifest, likewise the beginnings of the times are manifest in wonders and mighty works, the ends in requital and signs (9:5–6). The exact meaning of this saying is not quite clear, but we suggest that the beginnings that are "wonders and mighty works" refer to the mighty deeds of creation, while the ends, the "requital and signs," are the *eschata.* This is explicated in 9:7–8, which seems to refer to the messianic kingdom. The land was sanctified *from the beginning,* a deliberate development of 9:5–6, and will be the site of the beginning of the reward. The relationship between the address at the start of the second vision, which is devoted to the problems arising from election, and that at the start of the third vision, which is devoted to the creation, is notable. Observe also the use of "beginning" and "end" about the eschaton in 6:1: "The beginning is through man and the end is through myself." The idea of the precreation of the eschatological goods is present in many places in the book. This sentence, therefore, introduces the idea of the purposiveness of creation, of the divine intent that is expressed in the eschatological reward.

If the "two eschatologies" model discussed above is invoked,[7] it will be noted that 9:6–8 mentions various elements appropriate to the "messianic kingdom" complex of ideas. The torment after death discussed in 9:9–12 is strange to this complex of ideas, however, and probably refers either to torment at judgment or in the intermediate state of souls. A similar combination of eschatological elements was observed in 6:25–29, and it must be concluded that 9:6–12 does not present an integrated "messianic kingdom" eschatology but a superficial and evocative description of the eschatological events.[8] Nonetheless, as has been noted above, in both 6:25–29 and 9:6–12 the sequence of elements puts "messianic kingdom" features before those appertaining to the "day of judgment."[9] So, even in these brief passages, on the whole the chronological sequence implied by 7:26–44 is sustained.[10]

It is to be observed that in general in 4 Ezra the signs precede the messianic kingdom. This is true in 7:28, but note that there the term "wonders" refers to eschatological events, not to primordial ones. In 9:10–11 the idea is expressed, found earlier in the book, that in this world order repentance is possible only until death. Humans die for their own sins; in particular, the theme of the scorning of the Law, which was already raised in 7:20, is prominent. It is the reason for the punishment of the wicked. Ezra, however, is urged to inquire about the righteous for whom the age was made. The relationship between this present passage and 7:1–25 was noted above. This is particularly striking when we remember that 7:1–25 is also a response to a question "When?" asked in 6:59: "How long will this be so?"

The seer has moved from questioning to acceptance, albeit grudgingly, of the inevitability of the punishment of most humans and the salvation of only a few. It has been his struggle against accepting this that we have followed throughout the vision. When this assertion was made, for example, in 7:59–61, having no argument left, he burst out into lament (7:62–69).[11] Here, however, he simply reasserts his position emphatically. The formulation of this statement is like 7:116, in a similar context. There is no argument with God now, nor any reproach of him.

The angel's final address accepts Ezra's answer and recapitulates high points of the discussion so far. Using images mostly drawn from earlier parts of the book, the

---

7   See 7:26–44 Function and Content, pp. 204–6.
8   See Stone, *Features,* 136–38; cf. 79–80 and 218.
9   See 7:29 Commentary.
10 This passage does not mention the Messiah, on which see ibid.
11 See 7:45–75 Form and Structure, pp. 227–28.

angel strongly asserts in 9:17 the relationship between deed and reward. He then goes on, speaking for God in the first person. Before the world was created, while he was preparing it, none disobeyed him, for none existed. (These creative acts are most likely the wonders and mighty works referred to in 9:6.) But mankind sinned and thus condemned the good creation (9:19–20). God here does not accept the responsibility for the destruction of the good creation, so these verses are the final refutation of the point made in 3:4–27, where Ezra argued for God's ultimate responsibility for the destruction of Zion. In contrast, God does take as his responsibility the redemption of the righteous and their perfection. This takes up an issue raised by Ezra in his address in 8:4–19a, where he argued from the labor God invested in the creation of mankind to plead for mercy. That labor, our verse implies, is in the perfection and reward of the righteous (9:21–22). The angel's concluding remarks reiterate God's responsibility for creation; they return to the corruption of the world and to God's gracious redemption of the "one grape out of a cluster."[12]

Commentary

■ **8:62b** No commentary.

■ **8:63** The verse refers back to the revelation of signs in 5:1–13 and 6:18–28.[13] "Signs" is a technical term used to denote those events elsewhere called the messianic woes, a term found elsewhere in 4 Ezra and in other contemporary works. The chief passages that deal with the signs were discussed in connection with their enumeration in 5:1–13 and 6:18–28.[14] The question here, as noted in Function and Content, p. 293, is not about the signs themselves but about the apocalyptic timetable. This question "When?" has recurred throughout the

book, starting from 4:33, but is here asked and answered in the most explicit way.[15] Observe that the angel is addressed as if he were God, as is often the case in 4 Ezra.

■ **9:1** As we observed in Function and Content, p. 293, the enumeration of the signs given earlier in the book here serves as a sort of diagnostic basis for finding out the eschatological timetable. On the basis of the lists of signs already revealed, Ezra is told to calculate which of them have passed. Behind this command is the idea of the fixed measure of the times and the set timetable of eschatological events; see 4:36–37 and 14:11–12.[16] This is a widespread idea in the apocalypses. A number of sources speak of a division of the actual woes into a number of parts or stages. This is a further extension of the same idea.[17] The expression "predicted signs" is a deliberate cross-reference to 5:1–13 and 6:18–28.

■ **2** The term "visit" means "penal visitation" in 4 Ezra[18] and is therefore a term associated with the idea of judgment.[19] The divine visitation is discussed in 5:56—6:6. Myers points out correctly that the knowledge of the meaning of the signs is part of the revelation mediated to the seer, and above we noted the function of this revelation of the signs. A striking parallel is *2 Apoc Bar* 28:1, and compare particularly 27:15: "so that those may not understand who are upon the earth in those days that this is the consummation of the times. Nevertheless, whosoever understandeth shall be wise."[20]

■ **3** This verse mentions certain signs whose passing will be a clear indicator of the approaching end. The first is earthquake, and this is followed by disorder among the peoples of earth and their leaders, related in two bicola.

The earthquake here mentioned is not to be identified with that phenomenon which is part of the shaking of the whole of nature on the epiphany of God.[21] In descrip-

---

12 The selection of the two images, grapes and trees, is not mere chance; see Commentary on these verses.

13 The statement is equivalent to 6:12, and cf. also 13:32.

14 The term is discussed in 4:52 Commentary; central passages are listed in 5:2 Commentary n. 79.

15 See 4:33 Commentary; see also Mark 13:4, which is close to the present question in character.

16 See 14:11 Commentary.

17 See *2 Apocalypse of Baruch* 27; the matter is discussed in detail with a number of examples in Stone, *Signs of the Judgment*, 15–16.

18 See 5:56 Commentary.

19 See Excursus on the Term "Judgment," n. 50.

20 So Myers; he also compares, less relevantly, Dan 12:10 and some other sources.

21 On this, see 6:11–29 Form and Function, p. 167.

tions of the messianic woes, earthquakes are often found; instances are *2 Apoc Bar* 27:7; Mark 13:8; and *Signs of the Judgment* 8.[22] The woes are discussed above,[23] and conflicts of various sorts are one of the characteristics of them.[24] Although tumult of the peoples is found elsewhere (e.g., 5:5, and see Commentary; *2 Apoc Bar* 70:2), the other elements of these two bicola do not occur in the lists of woes prior to 4 Ezra. The passage bears a certain similarity to Ps 2:1–2:

Why do the nations conspire,
and the peoples plot in vain?
The kings of the earth have set themselves,
and the rulers take counsel together.[25]

The confusions and waverings of the leaders are also reflected, it seems, at some points in the description of the little wings in the eagle vision (see particularly 12:30).

It is intriguing to speculate whether these signs are influenced in some way by the political situation in the author's days, just as the eagle vision was. They are to some extent exceptional in the lists of signs.[26]

■ **4** Gunkel interprets this verse to be a reference to older apocalypses, particularly those associated with the names of figures from the primordial history, such as Adam, Noah, and Enoch. The expressions "days that were of old" and "beginning" seem to point to creation, and it seems to be more likely that what is meant is that the course of eschatological events, including the signs, was created in advance and formed by God in the primordial time, an idea found elsewhere in the book.[27] The word "spoke" then might point to the idea of God's creative word,[28] but it might well also refer to the revelation of eschatological things made to Abraham and Moses; see in further detail 14:3–18 Function and Content, pp. 416–17.

■ **5** In 9:5–6, a point is made about the things of the end time, that they are manifested in deed and in signs. This refers clearly to the signs that have just been mentioned and the visitation that God is about to carry out. These will make the end known; through them the end will be perceived by those that know them.

Two levels of analogy are introduced. The first is in 6:6: just as the beginnings are manifested in wonders and mighty deeds, that is, just as creation is evident through God's works, so also the end will be manifest through the signs. Here there is at play the idea of the symmetry of creation and eschaton that is expressed in other terms in 5:42 and 6:1–6. This is not an identification of the former and latter things but a pattern of balanced relationship. The second analogy is presented earlier in the pericope, in 9:5. It is broader, relating to the whole idea of 9:6. It argues from the ordinary world: just as in it the beginnings of events and things are evident and the ends manifest, so it will be with the times. The accuracy of this statement might be doubted on empirical grounds, but its import in context is quite clear. So the point is made that just as God's power is manifest in the acts of creation, so it will be in the events of the eschaton, and the eschaton itself will be revealed in and through those events.

■ **6** Often the term "wonders" usually refers to eschatological acts or the revelation of them. If so, then in this verse it would support the view that "the times of the Most High" are equivalent to the eschatological events. However, since "wonder" is used in 6:48 of creation, our exegesis that "the times of the Most High" are the times of the world is not without parallel.[29] Moreover, the use of "times" to indicate the total course of the world is to be found in other parts of 4 Ezra.[30] The eschatological events mentioned in the ensuing passage are discussed in

---

22 See Stone, *Signs of the Judgment*, 37, for further parallels.
23 See n. 14 above.
24 See 5:9 Commentary.
25 The passage should also be compared in general to *2 Apoc Bar* 27:2–3.
26 The Armenian version in its expansions here reflects a reference to religious sectarianism.
27 See 6:1; 6:6; 7:70; cf. 12:32 and 13:26. The matter is discussed in 6:6 Commentary.
28 See 3:4 Commentary.
29 See Stone, *Features*, 105; see in further detail 4:26 Commentary, esp. n. 12.
30 See 4:37; 7:74; 11:39; 11:44; and 12:9; cf. also the use of "former" and "latter" times in 6:34. The term "times" is discussed in 3:14 Commentary, 4:37 Commentary, and 7:26 Commentary.

their relation to larger eschatological schemes in Function and Content, p. 293.[31]

■ **7** The idea of the survivors, and even more specifically those who will escape the terrible events of the messianic woes, is to be found elsewhere in the book. It is discussed in detail in 5:41 Commentary. The woes, then, serve as one of the means by which the righteous are differentiated from the wicked.[32] Here the survivors are said to escape from the upheavals of the end time by virtue either of their works or of their faith. It is notable that these two terms are used almost indiscriminately in the book. Those actions which righteous humans do are clearly the subject of discussion in 7:21; 7:24; 7:77; 8:33; 8:36; et al. Moreover, Ezra is told in 7:76 not to associate himself with those who have shown scorn, for he is said to have treasuries of works in heaven in 7:77, while according to 6:5 the righteous have treasuries of faith. Indeed, the sin in 7:76 is lack of faith, while 7:77 asserts treasuries of works. The idea of faith is the obverse of the common indictment of scorning or denying the Most High.[33] While not asserting that these two concepts, faith and works, are identical, we may say that they were not very clearly differentiated and are used interchangeably. This, of course, contrasts strongly with the New Testament usage, such as is found in Rom 3:27 et al. In any case, the stress is on individual responsibility for action, as throughout the book.[34] The present verse, as has been discussed above, relates to the ideas associated with the messianic age (Function and Content, p. 293.

■ **8** The verse describes events connected with the messianic kingdom which regularly follows descriptions of the woes; see 6:15 and 12:34. The woes are never said, in this book, to be followed directly by the day of judgment.

The expression "survivors" is a technical term, particularly when related to the predicted dangers. It indicates those left alive after the terrible events of the messianic woes.[35] In 12:34; 13:26; 13:48–49, cf. *2 Apoc Bar* 29:1–2; 32:1; 40:2; and 71:1, the survivors are specifically those dwelling in the land, which may also be implied here.[36]

The expression "predicted evils" or "dangers" is a fixed, technical term, also found in 6:25 and 7:27; cf. also 14:16. It refers to the messianic woes.[37]

These survivors are said "to see my salvation." The expression comes from Ps 91:16, which is given an eschatological interpretation in CD (Ms B) 20:34. The same term is used in 6:25, and it is analogous to "see wonders" used in similar contexts in 7:27 and 13:50. "Seeing" in this book often means seeing the eschatological events.[38] The location of these events is "within my borders," that is, in the land of Israel; see 12:34; 13:48; and *2 Apoc Bar* 29:2. The idea that only those within the land will survive the messianic woes is found elsewhere in the book (see above).[39]

The land is said to have been sanctified from the beginning. In 5:24 the idea of the election of the land of Israel is stated very explicitly, and that election implies its sanctification. In the Hebrew Bible the categories of "sanctification" and "pollution" are often applied to the land.[40] The expression "from the beginning" also clearly

---

31 Note the importance of the knowledge or revelation of beginnings and ends of events in Isa 41:23 and 42:9.

32 See Excursus on the Term "Judgment," p. 151.

33 The treasuries are discussed in 7:77 Commentary; on denial of God, see 8:56–58 Commentary. Note in general the prominence of language of believing or trusting: 3:32; 5:1; 5:29; 6:33; 7:94; 7:114; 7:130; and 8:30.

34 See Excursus on Adam's Sin, pp. 63–64. See also Mundle, "Religiöse Problem," 229–31.

35 On the idea of the survivors, see 5:41 Commentary.

36 See 5:41 Commentary. The term "survivors" or "those who remain" is sometimes of broader application, referring to the righteous who will survive, see ibid.

37 Thus particularly 13:19 and 23–24, and see 14:16

Commentary on "dangers."

38 See 6:25 Commentary.

39 See also 12:34 Commentary. On the land in general, see 7:26 Commentary. The role played by the land of Israel in Jewish thought, from the Hebrew Bible on, scarcely needs documenting here. It is related to redemption in biblical prophecies; see e.g., Ezek 36:24–28. Many other references could be adduced.

40 See, by way of example, Jer 2:7 and 16:18; see also Wisd 12:3 and Sir 39:22.

implies the preparation of the land in advance or its precreation. This is also clearly the case in 7:26.[41]

■ **9** This verse opens a passage that lists the sins of the wicked. It is very similar to 7:79 and 8:56–58, both of which passages share terms and phrases with 9:9–11.[42]

It is notable that the idea of torment after death is not part of the complex of ideas associated with the messianic kingdom, which is to the fore in the preceding passage. As has been noted, 9:9 is parallel to 6:26 in that they represent a movement to "day of judgment" ideas. Both occur in passages that mention eschatological events but do not set forth a strict timetable. Nonetheless, the events mentioned in these passages follow the overall sequence of messianic kingdom and then day of judgment. In both instances, the transition from the messianic kingdom ideas is marked by the word "then" (6:26; 9:9).[43]

The terminology of "ways" is widespread, being found both in the book and outside it to indicate action in accordance with God's will.[44] Likewise, "torments" is a technical term for eschatological punishment.[45]

■ **10** The general point of this and the following verses is that those who have not acknowledged God and his commandments during their lives will do so through punishment, after their death. This idea, as well as the expression "while they were alive," recurs concerning the post-mortem state of the souls in 7:87 and 7:98: "since they see the glory of the Most High before whom they sinned while they were alive, and before whom they are to be judged in the last times." This reflects the idea that after death there is no change in human situation.

Judgment will be decisive and final. The particular offense of not acknowledging or denying God has been remarked upon above.[46] Note particularly 7:37; 7:81; and 8:58–59. In a striking image in Isa 1:3, Israel is accused of not recognizing God, who had done them benefits.[47]

■ **11** The two parts of this verse repeat, in other words, the ideas that were expressed in 9:10. The accusation of scorning the Law is often found together with that of denying God.[48] The stress is on not acting righteously while alive, for after death it will be impossible to repent of sins.[49] Moreover, the verse clearly implies that human beings have the freedom of choice and bear the responsibility for their actions. Again we encounter ideas that the author has repeated many times.[50]

The expression "opportunity of repentance" is literally "place of repentance"; see textual note b. The translation is confirmed by *2 Apoc Bar* 85:12, where "place of repentance" has the same meaning as here.[51] The wicked, therefore, have not taken advantage of God's long-suffering; cf. *2 Apoc Bar* 48:29 and Hermas *Vis.* 3.5.5. The Rabbis, of course, make frequent reference to God's desire to accept repentance.[52]

■ **12** "Torments" is a term for the ultimate fate of the wicked or their suffering in the intermediate state.[53] On the idea that the wicked, after death, will be forced to acknowledge God, see in a different mood the description in *1 Enoch* 63:1–2, where the punishment of earthly monarchs and their consequent confession of God are described in mythological terms. The verse implies what is also clear from 8:38 and 14:35, that punishment and

---

41 See 3:6 Commentary on precreation in general and 7:26 Commentary on precreation of the land. On the expression *a saeculo*, see Excursus on the Term "Age," p. 219.

42 See in detail 8:56–58 Commentary.

43 See further Stone, *Features*, 137.

44 See 7:79 Commentary for further discussion.

45 See 7:36 Commentary.

46 See 8:56–58 Commentary, and in 9:7 Commentary the obverse of this idea, the concept of "faith," is discussed.

47 Similar expression, but with different emphasis, is Matt 10:32–33 and 1Q 27 1:34.

48 See 8:56–58 Commentary.

49 See in detail Excursus on the Term "Judgment," pp. 149–51.

50 See on this Excursus on Adam's Sin, p. 65, and

51 7:116—8:3 Function and Content, p. 249.
    See also the similar expressions in Heb 12:17 and Wisd 12:10, 20. The expression is discussed in detail by B. F. Westcott, *The Epistle to the Hebrews* (London: Macmillan, 1889) 408–9. He cites yet further occurrences of the expression.

52 Note also the famous saying in *m. Abot* 2:10: "Repent one day before your death"; cf. also *b. Sanh.* 97r. In *b. Shabb.* 153a the Talmud comments that a human being does not know when he will die, "perhaps today, perhaps tomorrow, so let all his days be passed in repentance." This implies the view found in 4 Ezra that humans can repent only before they die. See further the extensive discussion in *b. Yoma* 86b, and see *b. Taʿan.* 16a.

53 See 7:36 Commentary.

reward are expected after death.

■ **13** The angel instructs Ezra not to inquire about the punishment of the wicked but to ask about the reward of the righteous, for whose sake the world was created. It is instructive to observe that throughout the book, Ezra is interested not in *how* the ungodly will be punished but *why* they are punished. The angel's comment here, therefore, as in other places, seems to be slightly beside the point. However, behind it lies the clear change of perspective about the righteous and the wicked, and about Ezra's own self. Moreover, although Ezra had not inquired about the mode of punishment of the wicked, at the end of chapter 8 the angel at some length informed him about how the righteous will be rewarded. It is possible, therefore, that the angel's command refers to Ezra's question about the signs in 8:63. That might have been taken as equivalent to an inquiry about the fate of the sinners.

Such commands to cease asking questions occur in a few other places in the book; see particularly 6:10 and 8:55.[54] The present passage has a number of similarities to 8:51–55, and 8:51 says, "But think of your own case, and inquire concerning the glory of those who are like yourself."

"Live" means "be saved," as has been pointed out before, and "saved" is the reading of two versions here.[55] The contrast here is live—be punished; elsewhere we find joy or delight—torture; reward—punishment.[56] It is impossible to determine whether the sense of the Hebrew word behind the translation "age" is properly "age" or "world."[57] What is clear is that it refers to the future world or age. That world is said to have been created for the righteous (so also 8:1). Other views present in the book speak of the world being created for the sake of Israel or of all mankind.[58]

■ **14** No commentary.

■ **15** In 9:14–15, Ezra asserts that the many will perish and only few survive. He has accepted this idea and uses it to summarize his argument against the angel. In very similar language in 7:47–48 he has posed the question, "Will the many perish and only few survive?" From the contrast of these two verses we may clearly see the development that has taken place in Ezra's position during the latter part of the third vision.[59] In the angelic address that follows, since Ezra has accepted the idea of the few and the many, a little more of the divine purpose is revealed, as is explained below.[60]

The change of perspective is emphasized also by the fixed expression "I said before and I say now," which occurs in a similar, emphatic position in 7:45.[61] This verse forms the first half of a statement with a proverbial ring, the second half of which occurs in the next verse.[62]

■ **16** A very similar image occurs in 4:50. The proverbial character of this expression was mentioned above.

■ **17** This verse expresses the idea of the relationship between action and result and does so by a series of proverbs. Other proverbial forms have been observed in the book; see, for example, 5:42. Particularly close is the expression in *j. Sanh.* 2 (20d) "as is the generation so is the leader, as is the leader so is the generation, . . . as is the garden so is the gardener."[63] The seed and harvest imagery is used often in the book. A particular concentration of it is in 4:28–30, where also the word "threshing floor" in the sense of harvest occurs.[64] The language of harvest is particularly related to judgment, as has been demonstrated above (4:28 Commentary). The word "judgment" is somewhat difficult in context and seems to mean "punishment."[65]

■ **18** The verse raises a number of interesting issues. Its basic import is that in this age, at the time when God was

54   This command is, wrongly in our view, compared with Sir 3:22, which is a general warning to refrain from questions about the unknowable. Here the fate of the wicked and the recompense of the righteous both belong beyond the normal realm of human knowledge, and the point of the warning is different.
55   See Excursus on Adam's Sin, p. 66, and n. 38, and 7:21 Commentary on the terminology.
56   See 7:36 and Commentary.
57   See Excursus on the Term "Age," p. 218.
58   See 6:55 Commentary.
59   The overall development of this subject in the book is discussed in 8:37–62a Form and Function.
60   See also 8:37–62a Function and Structure, p. 280.
61   The turn of phrase and weight of 8:25 is different. In a general way, cf. Jonah 4:2.
62   Somewhat similar in style and point is 8:3.
63   See also *Gen. R.*, chap. 80 (Theodor-Albeck, p. 952).
64   See 4:28 Commentary and 4:30 Commentary.
65   See textual note l on this word.

preparing the world for humans to live in but had not yet created it, no one opposed him, since no one existed. The word translated "age" has been discussed above, and it can have various meanings. Here it seems to mean something like "aeon" or "world age," but its exact sense remains unclear.[66] The idea that the world or various other created beings were planned in the mind of God has been observed above. It recurs in rather numerous sources in the Pseudepigrapha and in rabbinic literature.[67] "Prepared" is a technical term for the precreation of created things and is found frequently in the book.[68]

So God is saying that in that part of the world age when he was "preparing" for the creation of humans and the world, no opposition was expressed to him, since no one existed. This implies, first and foremost, that opposition to God is the work of humans. When the complex myths about angelic opposition to the creation of human beings are borne in mind, on the one hand, and the numerous traditions associating other beings with God in the creation of the world, on the other (cf. exegeses of Gen 1:26), then the present pronouncement receives a very distinct point.[69] If the idea of opposition to the creation of mankind is only implied here, the stress on God's action alone as creator is repeated throughout the book.[70] This means that before human beings were created, there was no corruption in the world. Finally, we may perhaps compare certain of the ideas expressed here with *Bib Ant* 28:4: "Yet will I remember the time which was before the ages, even in the time when there was not a man, and therein was no iniquity, when I said that a world should be."[71] As often, in our verse God adduces creation and its purpose as a response to questions about the eschaton (cf. 6:1–6). This response is comprehensible only in view of a well-developed idea of predetermination.

■ **19** This idealized description of the plenitude of the earth uses images already found frequently in the Hebrew Bible, and the terms "pasture" and "table" come strikingly together in Ps 23:1 and 23:5.[72] The corruption of humans and their ways is mentioned in this connection in chapter 3 of the book. The particular use of corruption not for the earth but for the ways of mankind may be observed in 8:31 (cf. 7:119, although the exact terminology differs).[73] The sinful character of mankind is a frequent theme in the book (see 7:46; 8:17; and 8:20–30).

■ **20** This verse conveys a tone of regret. The world lost, the earth is in peril, because of human actions;[74] the fate of God's world is made the direct result of the actions of human beings. Indeed, the idea that the fate of the world or its state stands in mutual relationship with the righteousness or unrighteousness of humans is not new, but the simple formulation we have just given hides some of the complexities involved.

With the idea of predetermination of the times is connected that of the deterioration or senescence of the earth. This is said, in 14:17, to be responsible for the troubles of the end time. According to 5:50–55, the old age of the earth causes the lesser stature of human beings. This concept flows from that of the fixed measure of the times, found elsewhere in the book.[75]

---

66 This is discussed in some detail in Excursus on the Term "Age," n. 72. The term here is not קצי עולמים (1QS 4:16), and other suggestions are not more convincing.

67 See 6:6 and Commentary there.

68 See 7:14 Commentary.

69 For the myths of opposition to God at creation, see *Vit Ad*, chaps. 12–16, and also the rabbinic materials assembled in Ginzberg, *Legends*, 5:69.

70 See the discussion of primordial silence in 6:39 Commentary; cf. also 7:30. Jervell, *Imago Dei*, 48, points out the polemical character of this stress.

71 The time before humans were created is also highlighted as a sort of category in Ps 90:2 and John 17:5.

72 Cf. also Ps 78:19. Many other instances could be adduced. The whole language of shepherding and pasture describes God's care of Israel often in the Bible. The images, like those in 9:21, are drawn from agriculture. Box and Oesterley both would see here a reference by implication at least to the eschatological banquet, but that does not seem plausible.

73 The term "corruption" is discussed in 4:11 Commentary. The corruption of the earth is clear already in Gen 6:11–12.

74 Cf. rabbinic statements about the wicked who "destroy the world," e.g., *Gen. R.* 10:9 (Theodor-Albeck, p. 86).

75 4:36–37; 5:49; 6:5; 7:74; 11:44; 13:58; 14:9; see 5:50 Commentary, where the idea of the senescence of the earth is discussed in detail.

Keulers thinks that the passing away of the world is to be seen in a systematic way as a direct result of the sins of mankind.[76] He points to 7:11–12, which associates the toils and distresses of life in this world with the transgression of Adam. This raises the complicated ideas involved in the sin of Adam and its effects.[77] Thus, in 7:11–12 the troubles of this world are linked to Adam's sins and they are also said to be removed at the end. Equally, 9:19–20 states that the corruption of mankind has brought troubles to the world. Adam's transgression is, in 7:118, considered responsible for the toils of human existence. All of these verses occur in quite different contexts from those which deal with the troubles stemming from the senescence of the earth. In 8:50 the messianic woes are said to come as punishment for human sinfulness. Thus this verse also attributes troubles to human action, and not to the age of the earth.

Either the deterioration of the earth or human action may be seen as the cause of troubles, depending on the purpose and context of the particular passage. Nonetheless, it does seem that Keulers goes too far when he says: *Wenn Esra es auch nicht ausdrücklich ausspricht, der Weltuntergang am Ende der Zeiten . . . ist für ihn die Folge der Sünden der Menschen* (Even if Ezra does not express it explicitly, the destruction of the world at the end of times. . .is for him the result of the sins of men") (p. 145). This may be implied by 9:20; yet the predestinarian view of the times, the precreation of eschatological things in general (6:6) and of judgment in particular (7:70), weighs against this, for judgment, we are told, was made before Adam and before the world. Ezra can even suggest, in 4:39, that the end is being delayed by human sins.

Thus there is tension and unclarity on this point. Both

the almost mechanistic view of the deterioration of the earth, and that view giving human action as the cause of the troubles of this age, seem to be held.[78] It is illuminating to bear in mind the text of Gen 6:12: "And God saw the earth, and behold, it was corrupt; for all flesh had corrupted their way upon the earth."

The word *saeculum* and parallels definitely have the sense "world" here and are parallel to "my earth."[79] The use of "peril" may perhaps be compared with its use in 13:20 (see Commentary). It expresses here, however, not so much the idea of the difficult character of this earth as of the threat hanging over it because of the deeds of mankind. "Devices" or plots are a characteristic of the wicked in many texts.[80]

■ **21** This verse uses two similes to express the idea that only very few will be saved out of the many wicked. These similes are drawn from the agricultural realm which, also in the Hebrew Bible, has provided figures for this idea; see, for example, Isa 17:6 and Amos 3:12. The rescue of the few righteous also resembles the description of Noah and his generation in 4 Ezra; see 3:11, which in turn draws on Gen 7:23 and 8:18. The two particular images chosen, however, also serve as ways of denoting Israel. One of them, the grapevine, is already to be found in the catalogue of images in 5:23.[81] The "root of planting" is also drawn from biblical sources; see Isa 60:21 and 61:3. This image was richly developed by the Qumran sect; see, for example, 1QH 6:15.[82] At the most, however, this sort of background may have determined the selection of the figures of speech.[83] Here the language that originally described Israel is probably used to refer to the eschatological survivors, an idea found repeatedly in 4 Ezra.[84]

■ **22** This verse sustains the imagery of the grape and the plant that was introduced in 9:21. It again draws from

---

76 Keulers, p. 145; see also Harnisch, who seems to be making a similar argument (p. 118).

77 See Excursus on Adam's Sin, p. 64.

78 See Excursus on Adam's Sin, p. 65.

79 On terminology, see Excursus on the Term "Age," esp. n. 72, and Stone, *Features*, 274–75 n. 432.

80 E.g., 1QpHab 3:5; 1QH 6:22; et al.

81 See 5:23 Commentary, where also the biblical background of the image is adduced.

82 Israel is described as "root" above, 5:28. Note that in *Bib Ant* 28:4 the language of plantation and that of the grapevine are combined. This imagery is described in some detail in J. Maier, *Die Texte vom*

Toten Meer (Munich and Basel: Reinhardt, 1960), 2:89–91.

83 On other images used for the few and the many, see 5:23–30 Function and Content, p. 127.

84 See 5:41 Commentary and also Harnisch, p. 140 n. 1.

the problem of the few and the many the conclusion that what is significant for God is the few righteous. Here the themes of creation and judgment are brought together, as they are in the same context earlier in the book; see 8:4–19a and 8:38–39. Previously it had been stressed that the wicked determined their own fate and God's concern is for the righteous.[85] Here the same

point is subtly made by the formulation of the verbs of creation. While the multitude that perishes is said to have "been born," employing a passive verb, of those who are saved God says, "*I* have perfected them."[86]

---

85 See 8:37–62a Function and Content, p. 282.

86 This is also perhaps to be related to the same motive as the author's reserve about stating outright that God created the evil heart; see Excursus on Adam's Sin, p. 63.

9

23   "But if you will let seven days more pass— ªdo
      not fast during them, ª however; 24/ but go
      into a field of flowers ᵇ where no house has
      been built, and eat only of the flowers of the
      field, and taste no meat and drink no wine,
      but eat only flowers, 25/ and pray to the
      Most High continually—then I will come and
      talk with you."

Notes

23   a–a Eth, Ar1 "and fast"; Arm omits. Eth, Ar1 may
      be under the influence of 5:13 and 6:31.

24   b Eth, Arm omit. Eth has "fruit of the field" in the
      next phrase and "fruit" at the end of the verse.
      Presumably the eating of flowers, attested by Lat,
      Syr, Arm, seemed too bizarre. Note that below he
      "sits among the flowers and eats plants" (9:26).

Form and Function

The final injunction of Vision 3 is found in 9:23–25.
This passage is parallel in position and function to 5:14–
20 and 6:30–34.

The injunctions include a seven-day period, no fast,
and going into a field and eating flowers. There is no
promise of revelation of "yet greater things than these"
(5:13; 6:31), just "I will come and talk with you."

When these commands are contrasted with the structures following Visions 1 and 2, it is clear that a turning
point has been reached. The signs of mourning, and
particularly the fasting, are modified. This is no longer a
complete fast but an abstention from meat and wine and
the ingestion only of the flowers of the field. Moreover,
Ezra's weeping is not mentioned here (contrast the end
of Vision 2).[1] Furthermore, the action no longer takes
place in Ezra's bedroom but in the field of Ardat, outside
the city. These are all clear signs of the major shift that
will take place in the fourth vision, and immediately they
indicate a diminution of Ezra's mourning.

Commentary

■ **23** This concluding injunction again bears on a seven-
day period; however, it is not a period of fasting but of
abstention and dwelling in a field. Similar seven-day
periods are mentioned above in 5:20; 6:31; and 6:35.
Significantly Ezra is not told to lament and pray.[2]

■ **24** This verse goes beyond the prohibition of 9:23 and
contains a number of positive injunctions. Ezra is to go
into a field where no house has been built, and he is to
eat only "flowers" and to refrain from meat and wine.
The injunction about the field is explained at one level
later on by the angel's comment "For no work of man's
building could endure in a place where the city of the
Most High was to be revealed" (10:54).[3] At a broader
level, however, the same shift we have been observing in
other ways is also signaled by this. At the start of Vision
1, Ezra is in his house, indeed on his bed, in Babylon.
Now he is told to go out of this house and into an untouched field. Something new is clearly about to happen.

Above we discussed the command to eat plants in
contrast with the fasting.[4] In fact, what is enjoined is the
eating of vegetable food, not an exclusive diet of flowers
(9:26 and 12:51). Why flowers alone are mentioned here
is an interesting question.[5] The eating of plants alone is
the situation that prevailed between Adam's expulsion

---

1   On the whole issue of these injunctions and their
     gradation, see 5:20b–22 Form and Function, p. 118.
     The importance of the narrative structure for
     understanding the book was greatly stressed by
     Brandenburger, *Verborgenheit*, 94–124. It is discussed
     from the perspective of the present commentary in
     Introduction, sec. 4.2.4.

2   See Form and Function, on this page.

3   This is perhaps to be compared with the use of "field"
     in 4:29, where a new field is required for the growth
     of the eschatological good. Note also the field and
     flowers that play a role in 9:17.

4   See Form and Function, on this page.

5   Kabisch, pp. 78–80, and again pp. 135–43, develops
     a complicated theory according to which this
     injunction is a form of asceticism based on a strong
     body/spirit dualism which is paralleled by an

earthly/heavenly one symbolized by the terminology
of light and darkness. The purpose of fasting is
purification of the body, and, that achieved, the
eating of flowers means the ingestion of "Lichtstoff"
derived from the heavenly world which is the
supernal σόφια. This view is ingenious but has no
basis in the book which does not exhibit the views
about body and matter that Kabisch claims and which
shows nothing of the "Light Theology" Kabisch sets
forth.

from the garden and the Flood, according to P (see Gen 1:29 and 9:3–4). This attitude found considerable echoes in the Second Temple period and later. One striking example is the *Life of Adam and Eve*, particularly in the form of text preserved in Armenian and Georgian.[6] Adam's search for food outside Eden is a major theme of the first part of that book and the revelation of vegetable food one of its high points. Perhaps this theme is present here, and Ezra, for the revelation of visions, is set on the same level as Adam as far as alimentation is concerned. However, it is important to recall that in Vision 7, Ezra is presented as a second Moses. Just as Moses neither ate nor drank at the time of receiving the Torah, similar injunctions are laid upon Ezra in Vision 7. We have pointed out above that it is difficult to regard this fasting and abstention as due to ascetic ideas about the need to purify the body.[7] It is possible that it is to be set into the context of technical preparation for vision experience, but the evidence for this is also thin.[8]

The fasting, weeping, and lament found in the first three visions seem to us most plausibly associated with mourning. The evidence for this has been developed above.[9] Particularly explicit is Dan 10:2–3: "I, Daniel, was mourning for three weeks. I ate no delicacies, no meat or wine entered my mouth, nor did I anoint myself at all, for the full three weeks." This being the case, as Breech pointed out, the shift from complete fast to vegetable food becomes symbolic for the movement from lament on the way to consolation. Conceived of in this light, the shift to vegetable food is to be related to the absence of any command to mourn or pray and to the shift of venue. The author uses all of these elements to signal the change in Ezra's position that has taken place. The expression "where no house has been built" is reminiscent of expressions found on a number of occasions throughout the book about "built cities." This language is reminiscent of Jerusalem.[10]

■ **25** No commentary.

---

6   See M. E. Stone, *The Penitence of Adam* (CSCO 429–30; Scriptores Armenieci 13–14; Louvain: Peeters, 1981), chaps. 1–6; J.-P. Mahé, "Le Livre d'Adam géorgien," *Studies in Gnosticism and Hellenistic Religions: Quispel FS* (ed. R. van den Broek and M. J. Vermaseren; Leiden: Brill, 1981) 227–60 (esp. chaps. 1–6).

7   See 5:20–22 Form and Function, p. 118.

8   See Stone, "Vision or Hallucination?" 55–56.

9   See 5:20–22 Form and Function, p. 118. Box too would associate Ezra's regimen here with the sort of half-fasting observed by Jews in the period of mourning preceding the Ninth of Ab, the fast commemorating the destruction of the Temple or, we may add, in the period between Rosh Hashanah and Yom Kippur.

10   See discussion of this matter in 5:25 Commentary. Volkmar already saw the field as the *Vorbild* of the Holy Land (p. 129).

9

26 So I went, as he directed me, into the field which is called Ardat; [a] and there I sat among the flowers and ate of the plants of the field, and the nourishment they afforded satisfied me. 27/ And [b]it came to pass[b] after seven days, as I lay on the grass, my heart [c] was troubled again as it was before. 28/ [d]And my mouth was opened,[d] and I began to speak before the Most High, and said,

Notes

26 a "Arpad" Syr, Eth; "Araab" Ar1; "Ardab/p" Arm; Latin Mss also offer "Ardad" (A), "Ardas" (C V), "Ardaf" (M), "Ardaph" (L), et al. The original form is uncertain, but the third and fifth consonants seem to have metathesized. Many speculations have been offered; see Violet 2, Box, etc. None is convincing.

27 b–b Lat, Syr, Eth, Arm.
  c "My heart began to be troubled" Syr; "I began to feel in my heart" Ar2.

28 d–d Lat, Syr, Ar2, Arm; Eth, Ar1 "I opened my mouth."

Form and Function

This small pericope is the introduction to the fourth vision.[1] In the introductions to the previous visions there is nothing corresponding to 9:26, which highlights the special nature of the eating of flowers and plants. This is a new departure, but in what follows familiar themes recur: in 9:27 we find the setting and time of the new vision, in 9:27b the seer's distress is described, in 9:28a the onset of inspiration, and in 9:28b the beginning of speech under the influence of the inspiration.[2]

The combination of familiar and new elements in this introduction serves to highlight the pivotal role of Vision 4. On the one hand, the structure of the introduction and the onset of inspiration and of speech are described in the same way as in the previous three visions. On the other, a new physical setting is given—no longer is Ezra in his Babylonian bedroom, he is in a field outside the city. This same physical setting is sustained through Visions 5, 6, and 7. Its importance is highlighted by the special explanation of it given below in 10:51–56. In *2 Apocalypse of Baruch* 47, as here, a new setting is given, although it does not have the symbolic importance of the field here.

Similarly, Ezra's abstention from meat and wine here, and his partaking of the flowers and plants of the field, lie in a middle position between the full fasting of the first three visions and the absence of any dietary discipline at all in the fifth and sixth. Breech has suggested that this represents in a physical form the shift from mourning to consolation.[3] This appears to be only one function of fasting in the book. The eating of vegetable food is parallel to Adam's eating of vegetable food (see 9:24 Commentary), while in the final vision Ezra, like Moses before him, fasts for forty days.

The stress on Ezra's well-being resulting from the consumption of the grass or flowers is parallel to the description of Joseph's fast in *Test Patr Jos* 3:4 and also to Dan 1:8–15. This is a common theme, although in the above instances it is expressed in terms of external appearance rather than subjective satiety.

In a more limited context, this introduction carefully ties this vision to those which precede yet indicates a measure of disjunction. Thus the literary tags "as he had commanded me" (9:26) and "as it was before" (9:27) deliberately establish connections with the preceding. The seven-day abstention that is laid upon him strongly recalls the seven-day fasts that were mandatory (apparently) before the first vision and (definitely) before the second and third ones. Yet this seven-day abstention is not included in the three-week fasting that is mentioned in 6:35, another indication of its similar yet different role.[4] This three-week period, mentioned in 6:35, is an indication of the deliberate structure of the book, since, already at the start of the third vision, it

---

1 The structure of all these introductions has been discussed in detail in 5:20–22 Form and Function, p. 118.

2 The inspired experience of speech is dealt with in Excursus on Inspiration, p. 121.

3 Form and Function, on this page. On the nature of the fasting in the book as a sign of mourning rather than an ascetic discipline, see 5:20–22 Function and Content, p. 118, and 9:24 Commentary. D. Merkur, "Visionary Practice," differs from our view.

4 See Commentary there.

foreshadows the deep change that will take place at its end. A pattern of seven days is maintained in 9:26–28, yet they are not days of fasting but of vegetarian food.

Commentary

■ **26** The chief problem in this verse is the name of the field. It is somewhat uncertain (see textual note a), and the form that we have accepted seems to have the soundest textual base. The field is the site of this and the following two visions, being mentioned incidentally on a number of occasions (e.g., 10:58 and 12:51). Its meaning and significance are discussed in 10:51–54, where it is described as a place where no human building has been set and thus suitable for the epiphany of the heavenly Jerusalem. This special discussion serves to demonstrate how important the physical context of the field was to the author.

The form of the name has given rise to various speculations. None of them is more convincing than the others, for none of them accounts for the actual form of the name.[5]

■ **27** In this verse Ezra is said to be lying on the grass when inspiration comes upon him. In the preceding verse (9:26) he was sitting, so the lying down here is significant and should be set into a relationship with his prostrate position in 3:1. It is unclear whether he is seen as continuing to lie throughout the extensive vision experience of 9:38—10:29, but he is certainly lying down (and perhaps unconscious or semiconscious) when the angel sets him up on his feet in 10:30. Although Visions 1–3 and Visions 5–6 took place at night, it is not certain that this is true of the present vision as well.[6] The stage of the visionary experience here undergone is discussed in detail in the Excursus on Inspiration.[7]

■ **28** This verse describes the onset of the seer's inspiration and the beginning of his speech.[8]

5 Gunkel suggests that it is an eschatological secret word. Other explanations are recorded or repeated by the various commentators; see Violet 2, Gry, Oesterley, Kaminka, J. Schreiner, *Das 4.Buch Esra* (ed. W. G. Kümmel et al.; JSHRZ 5.4; Gütersloh: Mohn, 1981); et al. E. Preuschen, on the basis of material preserved about Montanists by Eusebius, *Hist. eccl.* 5.16.7, thinks that this name, in the form "Ardab," was taken up by the Montanists: E. Preuschen, "Ardaf, IV.Esra 9,26 und der Montanismus," *ZNW* 1 (1900) 265–66. *Hermas Sim.* 9.1.4 gives an apparently meaningless name of a mountain where the seer is taken to receive a vision.

6 See further 3:1 Commentary.

7 See Excursus on Inspiration, pp. 121–22.

8 See Excursus on Inspiration, p. 121.

9

29   "O Lord, thou didst indeed ᵃ show thyself ᵇ to
      our fathers in the wilderness when they
      came out from Egypt and ᶜwhen they came ᶜ
      into the wilderness ᵈ which is ᵉ untrodden
      and unfruitful; ᶠ 30/ and thou didst say, ᵍ
          'Hear me, O Israel,
              and give heed to my words, O ʰseed of
              Jacob. ʰ
      31/ For behold, I sow my law in you, and it
      shall bring forth fruit in you, and you shall be
      glorified through it forever.' 32/ But though
      our fathers received the law, they did not
      keep it, ⁱ and did not observe the statutes;
      yet the fruit of the law did not perish—for it
      could not perish, ʲ because it was thine. 33/
      Yet those who received it perished because
      they did not keep ᵏwhat had been sown in
      them. ᵏ 34/ And behold, ˡ it is the rule that,
      when the ground has received seed, or the
      sea a ship, or any dish food or drink, ᵐ and
      when it happens that ⁿwhat was sown, or
      what was launched, or what was put in ⁿ is
      destroyed, ᵒ 35/ but the things that held
      them remain; yet ᵖwith us ᵖ it has not been
      so. 36/ ᵍFor we who have received the
      law and sinned will perish, as well as our
      heart which received it; 37/ the ʳ law,
      however, does not perish but remains in its
      glory."

Notes

29   a Lat, Syr, Eth, Ar1, Arm show reflexes of
Hebrew infinitive absolute and finite verb.
      b Lat adds *in nobis;* cf. 8:6 and 8:45.
      c–c Eth omits; Syr, Arm "transversed."
      d The word "land" occurs in different places in a
number of versions of this verse.
      d–e Arm omits.
      e–f So basically Lat and perhaps the *Vorlage* of
Eth; Syr reverses the elements. Ar1, Arm "waterless
and unfruitful."

30   g Lat *dicens dicisti,* cf. Ar1; Syr, Ar2, Arm add "to
them"; no determination can be made in such
formulaic expressions.
      h–h Eth omits.

32   i Arm omits from here to 9:36, having merely
"because of that they perished." It thus lacks the
whole of the following comparison. Ar2 omits from
here to the end of the verse and replaces with some
expansionary material from 9:5.
      j Lat omits except for Lat Ms L, which has *perire.*

33   k–k Ar1, Ar2 omit.

34   l Syr, Eth omit.
      m Syr and some Eth Mss omit; Syr, Eth add
"placed it in"; Ar2 adds a verb with each of the
three phrases.
      n–n Syr has two verbs, omitting "what was sown";
Eth has two verbs, omitting "what was launched";
Ar1 retains only the first verb, and Ar2 differs.
      o Eth omits from here to the end of 9:37. Lat
adds *exterminentur.*

35   p–p Syr omits.

36   q The translation follows Lat, Syr, Ar1; Eth
omits; Arm edits to fit its preceding omission; Ar2 is
expanded.

37   r Syr, Arm "your."

Form and Structure

This passage is an address directed by the seer toward
God. It is the opening of this vision, exactly parallel to
the addresses with which the three preceding visions
began (3:4–27; 5:23–30; and 6:38–59). The subject of
the address is the Torah, which was mentioned in 9:11–
12 but has not been a major topic of the book so far.

   This address turns to God and poses a question to him,
basing the question on a historical recital. In this general
pattern it is not unlike the addresses at the beginning of
the first and third visions. It is peculiar to the present

vision that not only does the seer use historical recital to
make his point but he also quotes God's own words to
him. The use of quotations has been observed in one or
two other places in the book (see 7:21; 7:129 and Commentary). What is intriguing about this instance (9:30–
31), however, is that the quotation is not to be found in
the Bible.[1] Instead, it is based on 4 Ezra itself, on 3:19–
20. A similar "false" quotation is to be found in 14:6.

   The quotation opens with a call for attention, similar
to that in the seer's address in 14:28 but also characterized by parallelism. The quotation forms the basis for

---

1   See Function and Content for a detailed discussion of
     this.

the ensuing argument which is presented first in a direct fashion (9:32–33). The passage introduced by 14:28 is very similar. Following it a use of analogy is to be found, a feature that was also noted in the previous section. Moreover, this analogy is used in an inverted fashion (9:34–35). In other words, the author uses the analogy to point out how unusual the phenomenon is to which he is directing attention. The address concludes with a restatement of the issues (9:36).

There are two aspects of the structure of the address, and more particularly of its structural relationship to the rest of the book, that are worthy of attention. The first is the most striking. The ensuing part of Vision 4 does not respond either directly or indirectly to the address. In a work as carefully crafted as 4 Ezra this is a real and significant problem. The solution to it must be sought, however, at an exegetical rather than a structural level.

The other observation to be made is that this address is closely linked to the rest of the book. Its focus on Torah ties in to 9:11–12; its putative quotation of divine speech is based on 3:19–20; and it uses an invocation form that is picked up again in 14:28. Yet, in spite of its links to the rest of the book, it is isolated within the vision.

Function and Content

The address focuses on Torah, a subject that had been raised, in a minor key, in the previous part of the book. The scorn of the Torah had been condemned in 7:24 and again in 9:11.[2] Here some problems arising out of the concept of Torah are raised. The address is formulated as an exhortation, partly patterned on biblical expressions. "Hear, O Israel" is a typical deuteronomistic expression; see, for example, Deut 5:1; 6:4; 9:1; and 20:3.[3] In none of these instances in Deuteronomy,

however, is it parallel to "descendants" or "seed of Jacob," which expression does not occur very often at all, but compare 3:19 and 8:16.[4] It is to be found in Isa 45:19 but in a context different from ours and with no parallel. Indeed, the invocation here is very close to *2 Apoc Bar* 31:3: "And you, O seed of Jacob, pay attention, and I shall teach you." There the expression "seed of Jacob" recurs parallel to Israel.

This opening gives a very solemn and biblical feeling to the passage. The address in 14:28–36 opens also with the reference to the giving of the Torah and Israel's disobedience. That passage is much briefer than the present one, since here the Torah is the very point of the address.

As has already been stated, the quotation itself is not biblical. It does, however, strongly resemble 4 Ezra 3:19–20, which is quoted here with the closest parallels italicized:

And thy *glory* passed through four gates of fire and earthquake and wind and ice, *to give the Torah to the descendants of Jacob*, and thy commandment to the posterity *of Israel*. Yet thou didst not take away from them their evil heart, *so that thy Torah might bring forth fruit in them*.

These expressions are typical of 4 Ezra, and particularly the association of the imagery of sowing and giving fruit with the Torah.[5]

The theme raised by this quotation is further developed in 9:32–36. Torah was given but not observed. This has affected the vessel that contains the Torah (the human heart) or mankind in general, but not the Torah itself, nor its fruit, which is eternal life. The Torah, given by divine glory (3:19) to glorify humankind (9:31), remains in its glory even if the humans perish (9:37).[6]

In the background of this address is a developed

---

2 Some of the ambiguities inherent in this idea are dealt with in 7:1–25 Function and Content, p. 193.

3 Cf. also Ps 50:7.

4 "Seed of Jacob" parallel to Israel is associated with Moses in the giving of the Torah in *2 Apoc Bar* 17:4 in a narrative literary form. "Seed of Israel" is also found, but not in hortatory contexts; cf. 1 Chron 16:13; CD 12:22; et al.

5 See 3:20 Commentary and 4:28 Commentary. Cf. also 8:6.

6 On the idea of glory in the book, see 3:19 Commentary. A much later text, *Midrash Hekalot*, in J. M.

Eisenstein, *Otzar HaMidrashim* (New York: Eisenstein, 1915) 1:121, has a long passage on the glory of Torah: Torah will only be given with its glory in the ecshatological Temple.

concept of the cosmic role or function of Torah. Though not very explicit in 4 Ezra, this exaltation of the idea of Torah, the attribution of cosmic functions to it, is a prominent idea in Judaism of the period.[7]

In this context, then, and taken as it is presented, this address refocuses Ezra's concern. He is no longer occupied with the anomalies flowing from the divine governance of the world. So the issues of the few and the many, or those of theodicy, are left behind. This is an indication of the further development of his thinking. He has accepted in basic terms the position that the angel has presented in the previous visions. Yet, it seems, his mind is not completely at ease. He raises a series of anomalies inherent in the concept of Torah.

Torah is a divine gift; it has a heavenly being, yet it is disobeyed, because of which humans will perish.[8] God gave Torah, yet left the evil inclination in the heart of the people, so that the Torah was unable to produce its fruit of eternal life. These ideas had been sharply formulated in 3:19–22. They have not been addressed so far in the course of the book and here are raised again in a sharp fashion. The anomalies inherent in the concept of Torah are set forth strikingly by the use of the analogy of 9:35. The eternal life-giving Torah survives the vessel that contains it.

Yet the vision that ensues does not form a response to this address and to the real issues in the author's thought that this address raises. That is a point to which we shall return, but it is enough here to observe that this development is inexplicable simply in terms of literary composition. After all, the author was very capable indeed in his literary craftsmanship. Yet here he raises an issue without resolving it, or even without showing the partial acceptance by the seer of a divine solution. Indeed, he does not even tell us what the divine solution is.

One explanation may be that this sudden shift reflects a shift in the author's vision experience. The resolution is no longer found at the level of discussion and argument: the particular problem is not resolved. Instead, there is a basic reorientation of the author's perception of the world, in the course of which his attitude toward these issues is changed and they cease to concern him.

Commentary

■ **29** The self-revelation of God mentioned refers to the events of Sinai, which are also central for the author in 3:17–19 and 14:4–5. A similar expression occurs in 14:3, but there it is the burning bush that is under discussion.

In this connection, the mention of the wilderness wanderings is both natural and important to the author (cf. 7:106). This theme is developed here in terms that seem dependent largely on Jer 2:6. There, God's leading Israel "in a land that none passes through, where no man dwells" is mentioned. Here the desert is described as pathless and unfruitful. "Pathless" means untrodden if it is dependent on Jer 2:6. It is a term used elsewhere in 4 Ezra to imply desolate (see 5:3 with 5:11). The physical aspect of the wilderness in which the passage of humans and beasts leaves clearly discernible tracks obviously lies behind this adjective. As in Jeremiah, so here, the point is precisely that God met Israel in the pathless desert. The selection of the adjective "pathless" highlights the special nature of the encounter with God in a place where there are no humans.[9]

A similar literary dynamic controls the description of the desert as "unfruitful." This is surely pointing directly to the idea, found in 9:31, that the Torah, received by Israel in the unfruitful desert, produces fruit in humans.[10]

---

7   See Nickelsburg and Stone, *Faith and Piety,* chap. 6, on the development of this idea (p. 210). Gunkel points to the Torah's divine and heavenly origin and eternal glory, comparing Rom 7:14 and 2 Cor 3:7–9. Its eternity is stressed also by Wisd 18:4; *Bib Ant* 11:2; cf. 11:5; *2 Apoc Bar* 59:2 (all referring to "eternal law"). Many further references could be adduced.

8   Harnisch, pp. 170–75, would contrast the general assertion of disobedience here, in 7:129–131 and in 14:28–30, with such passages as talk of some who obeyed the covenants in 3:32–36; 5:29; 7:37; 7:45–46. But the point and contents of the arguments in the two types of passages are very different.

9   The expression "trackless waste" also occurs, e.g., in Ps 107:40, but there "waste" is Hebrew תהו, which term is not usually associated with Israel's desert wandering. Violet 2 points out that in Jer 2:6 the Hebrew צלמות is rendered by the Greek ἀκάρπῳ, although it is hard to see that this indicates more than that 4 Ezra was using the same vocabulary to describe the desert, since it is unlikely that its text was influenced by the LXX of Jeremiah.

10   The nostalgia for the time of the wilderness

A further point may be that the uninhabited desert is suitable for the self-revelation of God, to some measure parallel to Ezra's field where there is no human building (9:24). In such places, untouched by human hand, revelations of a heavenly nature occur, "for no work of man's building could endure in a place where the city of the Most High was to be revealed" (10:54).

■ **30** This verse is discussed in detail in 9:29–37 Function and Content, p. 307.

■ **31** The figure of sowing the Torah like seed in the human heart and its bringing forth fruit there, which is eternal life, has been observed before, and closest to our context is 3:20: "that thy law might bring forth fruit in them."[11] The heart, as Harnisch comments, is sometimes used in 4 Ezra as the term for the place where the Torah or the evil inclination is planted. This is one of a number of meanings that "heart" has in this book and in contemporary literature.[12] The fruit of the Torah is eternal glorification. "Glory" is a term for eschatological reward, and the eschatological glorification of the righteous is often mentioned.[13] The translation "forever" or "for most distant time" indicates the adverbial use of the word עולם, a word that was changing meaning at this period.[14]

■ **32** The point of this verse relates not to the question of human obedience as such to the Torah (contrast, e.g., 7:72) but to the tension between human disobedience, on the one hand, and the eternity of the Torah, on the other.[15] The parallelism of "statutes" and "law, Torah" may also be seen in 7:24, but "statutes" seems also to occur in a less specific sense (see 7:11 Commentary). The different possible senses of the word "keep" meaning

"observe" (9:32; 9:33; 14:30; et al.) and "keep" meaning "guard," "preserve" (in, e.g., 8:9) should be noted.

■ **33** No commentary.

■ **34** This verse employs a triple inverted analogy, the structure of which was discussed in Form and Structure, p. 307.

■ **35** No commentary.

■ **36** This verse and the following draw the conclusions from the analogy. Its role and the structure of its two contrasting parts are very much like that of *2 Apoc Bar* 14:19 in the passage 14:18–19:

> And now I see that as for the world which was made on account of us, lo! it abides, but we, on account of whom it was made, depart.

The style and content are very much like *2 Apoc Bar* 77:15: "And though we depart, yet the law abideth." The idea of "heart" is discussed in 9:31 Commentary.[16] The whole point of the assertion here is not the universal wickedness of humans who sin universally against the Torah (therefore to draw a parallel to Rom 3:20, as some would do, is to miss the point). At its heart lie instead the eternity of the Torah (cf. Bar 4:1; Wisd 18:4; and *1 Enoch* 99:2) and the contrast between this eternity and the actual conduct of humans observing it.

■ **37** No commentary.

---

wanderings to be seen in Jer 2:2 is not to be observed here, although the same literary instrument is used. The desert is called "a land not sown," while Israel is "the firstfruits of his harvest."

11 See 3:20 Commentary and 4:28 Commentary for detailed discussion of this. This idea is not to be related directly to the imagery of the community as a righteous planting found in the Qumran literature. The expression "planted in our midst," applied to the Torah, is to be found in the Jewish morning liturgy; see Hertz, *Authorized Daily Prayer Book*, 191.

12 See in detail 4:30 Commentary. Some scholars seem much exercised to demonstrate the veneration with which God's gift of Torah was regarded by Judaism, which related it to "life" or "salvation," e.g., Bousset-Gressmann, p. 142; Knibb here.

13 A detailed analysis is given in 7:97 Commentary and

Excursus on the Term "Judgment," p. 150.

14 See Excursus on the Term "Age," n. 72, and Stone, *Features*, 176f.

15 Note, e.g., the use of "perish" here applied negatively to Torah, while in 9:20 the same human disobedience leads to the fact that the world does perish. See also the somewhat similar contrast of divine, spiritual law and human action, of course in a completely different application, in Rom 7:9 and 12–14. On *perire*, etc., see Harnisch, p. 143 n. 3.

16 See also Excursus on Inspiration, pp. 120–21.

9

38 When I said these things in my heart, [a] I lifted up my eyes and saw a woman on my right, and [b] she was mourning and weeping with a loud voice, and was deeply grieved at heart, and her clothes were rent, [c] and there were ashes on her head. 39/ Then I dismissed the thoughts with which I had been engaged, and turned to her 40/ and said to her, "Why are you weeping, and why are you grieved at heart?"

41 And she [d] said to me, "Let me alone, my lord, that I may weep for myself and continue to mourn, for I am greatly embittered in spirit and deeply afflicted."

42/ And I said to her, "What has happened to you? [e] Tell me."

43 And she said to me, "Your servant was barren and had no child, though I lived [f] with my husband thirty years. 44/ And so [g] every [h]day and every hour [h] during those thirty years I besought [i] the Most High, [j] night and day. [k] 45/ And [l]it came to pass [l] after thirty years,

God heard your [m] handmaid,
and looked upon my affliction, [n]
and considered my distress,
and gave me a son.

And I rejoiced greatly over him, I and my husband and all my townsfolk; [o] and we gave great glory to the Mighty One. [p] 46/ And I brought him up with much care. 47/ So [q] when he grew up and I came [r] to take a wife for him, I set a day for the marriage feast.

10

1 "But it happened that when my son entered his [s] wedding chamber, he fell down and died. 2/ Then we [t] put out the [u] lamps, [v] and my townsfolk [w] attempted to console [x] me; and I remained quiet until evening of the second day. 3/ But [y] when [z]they all had stopped consoling [z] me, that I might be quiet, I got up in the night and fled, and came to this field, as you see. 4/ And now I intend not to return to the [a] city, but to stay here, and I will neither eat nor drink, but without ceasing mourn and fast until I die."

Notes

9:38   a Hebraism; cf. 3:29.

b Lat adds "behold."

c Active Ar2, Arm.

41   d Syr, Arm add "answered and"; formulaic.

42   e Lat *passa es.*

43   f Lat *habens;* Syr, Eth "was"; Ar1, Arm "having lived with."

44   g Ar1, Ar2, Arm omit.

h–h Lat *per singulas horas et per singulos dies;* in Syr, Eth, Ar1, Arm "days" precedes "hours"; Ar2 is periphrastic.

i Syr, Ar1 have two verbs, but they are not identical; probably independent expansions.

j Lat, Syr, Eth, Arm "Most High"; Ar1 "God"; Ar2 "the Lord"; see Commentary.

j–k Ar1 "that he send fruit to my body"; Ar2 "since no child was vouchsafed me"; independent expansions motivated by a similar exegetical urge.

45   l–l Lat, Syr, Arm; Eth, Ar1, Ar2 omit; no determination is possible on textual grounds, since this is a fixed formula.

m Eth, Ar1 "his"; Ar2 "me."

n So Eth, Ar1, Arm; see 9:41; Lat *humilitatem;* Syr *mwkk'.*

o Lat, Arm *cives;* Syr, Eth, Ar1, Arm "townsfolk."

p Eth, Arm "God"; Ar1 "God the Mighty One"; see 9:44 Commentary.

47   q Lat Φ = Arm "and it came to pass"; formulaic.

r Arm "we wished"; oddly note Lat Mss M N *voluissem,* probably coincidental; Eth, Ar1 omit.

10:1   s Ar1 adds "secret," "hidden" for unknown reasons.

2   t Lat adds *omnes.*

u Eth, Ar1, Ar2 "our"; Ar1 has misunderstood and is exegetical.

v Explanatory expansions are found here in Eth, Ar1, Ar2, Arm. They are each different and were generated by the exegetical problem of the meaning of "put out the lamps."

w See 9:45 note o.

w–x Lat, Ar *surrexerunt;* Eth, Ar1 "began to"; probably reflect similar Greek.

3   y Lat, Arm "and it came to pass"; formulaic.

z–z Text uncertain; we give the reading of Lat, Arm; Syr has "they all fell asleep and believed that I too had fallen asleep." The verb "believe" recurs in Ar2, which has "those who were with me believed that I no ⟨more⟩ thought of them and fell asleep"; Ar1 is rewritten.

4   a Ar1, Ar2 "my."

Form and Structure

This section continues the first person narrative from the previous section. From this point on, the overall structure of Vision 4 is more in accord with the traditional apocalypses than the previous part of the book has been. There is a vision experience (9:38—10:28), followed by an angelophany (10:29–37), an interpretation (10:38–54), and concluding injunctions (10:55–59). Some points of difference are, of course, to be found. One is the very character of the vision—it is presented as a waking encounter with a weeping woman. Another is the address with which it opens.

We have chosen to divide the very long description of Ezra's encounter with the woman into two parts, the first (9:38—10:4) presenting the initial encounter and the woman's tale, and the second (10:5–27) being Ezra's response to the tale. The ensuing events are related in the transformation and angelophany (10:25–28 and 10:29–37).[1]

Gunkel suggested that the actual tale the woman tells was a preexistent unit that the author incorporated into his work. It contains folklore motifs like that of the bride whose groom dies, which also occurs in Tobit. The theme of the barren woman who eventually bore child is already to be found in the Samuel story (1 Samuel 1–2). Indeed, Oesterley thinks that the Book of Samuel might be the point of origin of our story. Either view may well be true, or elements of two different narrative sources may be at play here. However, if the author has used a tale he found before him in the tradition, he has not transmitted it completely, for the story on its own has no resolution or ending. It is, indeed, very much subordinated to the dynamic and specific demands of 4 Ezra.

A number of considerations might indicate the originally independent character of this tale. First, there is the peculiar character of the names of God used in it (see 9:45 Commentary). Second, there exist some parallel stories in rabbinic literature, admittedly without the detail of our text (see 10:7 Commentary). The image of

Zion as desolate and mourning is common. The story of the woman here, however, seems rather to have been adapted to this theme than created to express it.

The chief parts of the pericope are then the background and context (9:38–39); the dialogue with the woman (9:40–42); and the woman's first person narrative (9:43—10:4).

Function and Content

In 9:38 we are presented with Ezra in the field. He sees a woman weeping, with rent clothing and with ashes on her head, all the traditional signs of mourning. "Then I dismissed the thoughts with which I had been engaged, and turned to her" (9:39). In this revealing verse, the author apparently tries to account for the problem discussed above (9:29–37), that is, that the address makes a serious point which is never the object of a response in the book. The same phrase is repeated in 10:5, as, for a second time, Ezra turns his mind to dialogue with the woman.

This suggestion does not serve as a conceptually satisfying explanation of the gap which, as we have suggested above, may reflect something in the author's actual experience. But it does indicate the author's sensitivity to the problem which is in accord with his usual expert literary skills. Moreover, this repeated assertion may have a second level of significance, according to which, what is abandoned is not only the train of thought expressed in the address but the whole set of questions that have preoccupied the seer from the start of the book.[2]

It is thus the culmination of a series of indications that, since the end of the third vision, have shown that something new is happening. Thus Ezra is not enjoined to weep; his fast is modified; and the location changes from his bedroom to the field. However, the author continues to cultivate the connection and resemblance to the first three visions, with the description of the onset of inspira-

---

1   See further 10:29–37 Commentary.
2   This point is also made energetically by Brandenburger, *Verborgenheit,* 76–77, following on the observations of Harnisch, "Prophet," 479–80. He does not admit the first, obvious meaning as well. The repetition also established a literary relationship between these two scenes.

tion (9:27–28) and the address. The pericope thus partakes both of the preceding and that which will follow. Moreover, it is perhaps of some significance that the verbs in it are active throughout 9:26–27. Ezra's action is voluntary and decisive.

The dialogue in 9:40–42 is designed to elicit from the woman the cause of her grief, and then in 9:43—10:4 we have the actual narrative of the events. The woman explains to Ezra that she is grieving sorely and she rejects his interest in her plight. When he persists in asking her, however, she tells her tale—barren for thirty years, she prayed to God, who eventually granted her a son. She, her husband, and neighbors rejoiced greatly, raised him with care. But on the joyous evening of his nuptials, he entered the bridal chamber and fell down dead. She then mourned, with her neighbors trying to comfort her, and was quiet until the second evening, when they left her to rest. So she fled to the field, resolved to fast there, and to mourn until her death.

The narrative is clear enough. There are a few obscure points, of course, which will be elucidated in the Commentary. One or two features, however, are worth remarking upon here. One is the rather mystifying role of the "neighbors" or "fellow citizens" who rejoice with her joy and mourn with her grief. They play no further role in the narrative, nor are they mentioned in the interpretation. This might be construed as support for Gunkel's view, mentioned above, that the tale was originally independent. We observed that, if this is true, it is only rather partially preserved, and it is more than possible that these neighbors had a role to play in its original ending. The original ending may also have included the revival of the child; cf. 10:16 and 2 Kings 4:18–37. See 10:16 Commentary.

The following elements are prominent in the narrative and play no role in the explanation: (1) the ceaseless prayer (9:44); (2) the neighbors (9:45; 10:2);[3] (3) the significance of the death on the wedding night (10:1); (4) the significance of the extinguishing of the lamps (10:2);[4]

and (5) the significance of the mourning until the second night (10:3).[5]

There is, moreover, a certain lack of balance between 10:18, presumably the end of the folk tale, and that which ensues, i.e. Ezra's proffered "comfort" and the woman's transformation (10:19–24 and 10:25–28). The same unevenness is evident in the interpretation (10:49–50) where the woman's proclamation of 10:18 is ignored.

The parallels between the woman and Ezra are also worthy of comment. The date of thirty years is suggestive of the thirty years of the captivity mentioned in 3:1, for the redemption is promised to Ezra after thirty years, just as the woman receives the grace of a child after the same period of time (9:45). Moreover, her conduct in fasting, mourning, and weeping over her loss is exactly like Ezra's conduct described in the narratives between Vision 1 and 2 and between Visions 2 and 3. Indeed, it may be significant that this conduct is attributed to the woman at a point in the narrative in which Ezra has moved beyond such conduct. Are the neighbors, in some way, then like Paltiel (5:16–18), who tries to comfort Ezra, or like the angel, who in a different way attempts to respond to Ezra's distress?

But this series of associations is just that, in this part of the vision, and takes on deeper significance only when we consider the role reversals between Ezra and the angel, between the woman and Ezra, that become explicit in what follows.

The vision is presented as a real, waking experience in which the visionary plays a major active role. This contrasts with the preceding three visions and the following two, but it is true also of the seventh vision. This character is highlighted by 10:36, particularly when it is contrasted with the two ensuing dream visions. In them Ezra knows clearly that he is dreaming. Note also in the angelophany the expression "I saw and still see" (10:32), that is, as he talks with the angel the city is still standing there. Compare also 10:55.

---

3 Note, however, that in Luke 1:58 the neighbors and kinsfolk rejoice in Elizabeth's giving birth; cf. also the role of the neighbors in Luke 15:6, 9. Their function may be simply to highlight the public character of the events in order to add a dramatic dimension, but they might also have played a more active role in the original story.

4 As observed in 10:2 Commentary, this was a

mourning custom, and so to search for special significance may be beyond what is implicit in the text.

5 The comment made in the previous note also applies here.

Commentary

■ **38** The expression "said in my heart" has been characterized as a Hebraism. This is also true of "I lifted up my eyes and saw." The woman whom Ezra saw was on his right-hand side. This is generally a position of strength or dexterity (cf. 3:6), but 4:47, where Ezra is told to stand on the angel's right-hand side to receive a vision, is particularly close to our passage.[6] The expression "lifted up . . . eyes . . . and saw" seems to imply suddenness of perception. Ezra saw the woman, quite unexpectedly.[7] The woman whom he saw is not explicitly or implicitly more than that in the present pericope. As will be pointed out in the Commentary on the following pericope, the symbol is pregnant with meaning, implying of course Jerusalem bereft of her children.[8] The absence of any particularly suggestive language here seems to hint at the possible independent literary origin of this part of the narrative, as was discussed above in Form and Structure. The rending of clothes and the putting of ashes on the head are traditional signs of mourning.

■ **39** This important verse indicates the change in Ezra's own position, as is discussed in Function and Content, pp. 311–12. Compare also 10:5.

■ **40** No commentary.

■ **41** The language of this verse is very similar to that used by Hannah according to 1 Sam 1:10, a story that has probably influenced the present tale; see Form and Structure, p. 311. From a literary point of view, the woman's statement that she is weeping for herself sets the stage for Ezra's emphasis on the common, national mourning over the destruction in the next chapter where he talks of "our mourning" and "Zion, mother of us all" (10:6–7).

■ **42** No commentary.

■ **43** The style of this verse is deliberately biblicizing. The combination of a third person self-address "maidservant" followed by first person speech is commonly to be found; compare also 12:8 and 13:14. The most striking parallel is 1 Sam 1:16, perhaps partly a source of this passage.[9] A second biblical phrase is "barren and had no child"; cf. Gen 11:30; Jud 13:2; et al. This phrase is not found in 1 Samuel 1. The theme of the barren woman, eventually blessed with child, is common in biblical sources and beyond.[10]

The number of years of barrenness is, of course, explained in the interpretation of the vision as the three thousand years from creation to the construction of the Temple. There are, however, some problems of fit between the tale and its interpretation, as we have noted. This may also be a deliberate reference to the period of thirty years in 3:1, which is the amount of time that elapsed after the exile, before Ezra received the revelation of redemption.[11] Another possible explanation is that this period of time belongs to the old level of the tale and is meant to indicate how acute the problem of the woman's infertility was and how wondrous her conception and birth.

■ **44** The phrases "every hour and every day" and "night and day" combine to present a hyperbolic expression of the sustained nature of the woman's prayer. The central role of Hannah's prayer in 1 Sam 1:9–11 is a general parallel.[12]

---

6   For a fuller discussion, see 4:47 Commentary.

7   Gunkel notes a parallel in Mark 16:5 where an angel appears on the right-hand side. Brandenburger, *Verborgenheit,* 75, stresses the mysterious or wondrous aspect of this. The expression is nicely paralleled in Gen 22:4. Abraham travels for three days, suddenly he lifts up his eyes and sees the designated place. In Gen 22:13 he lifts up his eyes and unexpectedly sees the ram caught in the thicket. Brandenburger perhaps overstresses the mysterious atmosphere thus evoked.

8   See 10:7 Commentary in detail.

9   The observation in 5:56 Commentary on "servant" and "Lord" does not seem to apply here, perhaps because the protagonists differ.

10   See Gen 21:1–7; 30:22–24; 1 Samuel 1; and Luke 1. Further sources are plentiful.

11   Some traditions also set the birth of Cain and Abel three years after the expulsion; see *Apoc Mos* Ms B, start.

12   It seems to be open to question whether the reading of most witnesses "night and day" refers specifically to one way of dividing up the day and night— starting in the evening, rather than another— starting in the morning. This was certainly a point of difference of opinion in the Second Temple period, e.g., between the Qumran sect and other groups; see S. Talmon, "The Calendar Reckoning of the Sect from the Judaean Desert," *Scripta Hierosolymitana* 4 (1958) 162–99. The Rabbis, of course, reckoned the day from the evening.

■ **45** Gunkel aptly observes that one of the functions of the emphasis on the praise of God here is to obviate any possibility that the coming misfortune was deserved by ingratitude. As to the role of the neighbors, see Function and Content, p. 312.

Violet observed that, while the divine title Most High is prevalent in 4 Ezra, here we find "God," and in 9:45 we find "Strong One" in Latin, Syriac, and Arabic1, "God" in Ethiopic, Arabic1, and Armenian, and "Most High" in Arabic2. He further noted that in 9:44, where most versions have "Most High," Arabic1 has "God" and Arabic2 has "the Lord." This situation arises, in his view, from the fact that the original literary unit of the tale used the name "God," which 4 Ezra tends to avoid. It certainly is striking that "God" occurs in only half a dozen places outside the present passage: 7:19; 7:20; 7:21 (these three bunched together); 7:79; 8:58; and 10:16. In two of these instances, 7:19 and 7:79, "God" is in parallelism with "Most High." Latin *fortis* and parallels occur also in 6:32; 10:24; 11:43; and 12:47.[13] "God" is not found in any version in those instances.

The view that "God" was original in 9:44 seems difficult to sustain on text-critical grounds, although one might maintain that since "Most High" is so dominant in the book, the very occurrence of the variants in the Arabic versions shows that it is secondary here. The situation in 9:45 is not so simple, and there the variants of the versions seem to indicate that "God" might have been an original reading, replaced in part of the Greek tradition by a divine name drawn from elsewhere in the book. The reading "God" is not secure enough, in our view, to replace *fortis* in the translation. This group of readings, therefore, may provide some oblique support to the idea that the usage of divine names in this passage differs from the rest of the book, and that difference is evidence for a separate literary origin.

■ **46** No commentary.

■ **47** In Gen 21:21 the mother is said to take a wife for her son, as here. *M. Kidd.* 2:1; 3:7–9; etc. speaks of a father taking a spouse for his daughter.[14] The marriage feast was a standard part of wedding celebrations (see Matt 25:1–10; *Apocryphon of Ezekiel apud* Epiphanius, *Against Heresies* 1:2; et al.) and is used in many instances in parables in the New Testament and rabbinic literature.

■ **10:1** The death of the bridegroom on entry into the nuptial chamber is also a central factor in the story in Tobit; see Tob 7:11 and 8:10.

■ **2** The night of the second day was the end of a first period of mourning according to a later Jewish mourning custom.[15] The turning over or extinguishing of the light, although not required, was also customary, as Lieberman points out: "How do men mourn? . . . The mourner rends his garments . . . the mourner sits by himself and shows his face . . . the mourner turns over his bed . . . the mourner extinguishes the lamps."[16] Not only is the extinguishing of lamps in our text a mourning custom but also the sitting in silence, which is implied by the expression "sits by himself."[17] Gunkel had remarked on the contrast between the woman's quiet or silence and the usual expressions of maternal grief. The passage receives a much more significant point, however, when we realize that each of the three elements that the woman enumerates were part of Palestinian, Jewish mourning customs. Thus the point is: after my son's death I observed the required mourning customs.

■ **3** No commentary.

■ **4** This verse, according to Gunkel, concludes the folk tale that has been included in the book.

---

13   On the name "Mighty One," see 6:32 Commentary.
14   Both father and mother are involved in Judg 14:1–5.
15   So S. Lieberman, *Hellenism in Jewish Palestine* (New York: Jewish Theological Seminary, 1950) 104, quoting *Semaḥot* 6:2–7, 11 (Higger, p. 134).
16   *Eka Zuṭa* vers. i (ed. Buber, p. 66); parallels occur also in *Pes. R. K.* 15:3 and *Eka Rabbati* 1:1.
17   See Lieberman's note to this place (p. 166).

10

5 **Then I broke off the reflections [a] with which I was still engaged, and answered her [b]in anger [b] and said, 6/ [c]"You most foolish of women, do you not see our mourning, and what has happened to us? 7/ [d]For Zion, the mother of us all, is in [e]deep grief and great affliction. [e] 8/ [f]It is most appropriate to mourn now, because we are all mourning, and to be sorrowful, because we are all sorrowing; you, however, are sorrowing for one son. [g] 9/ Now ask the earth, and she will tell you that it is she who ought to mourn over so many who have [h]come into being [h] upon her. 10/ And [i]from the beginning [j] all have been born [k] of her, and others will come; and behold, [l] all go to perdition, and a multitude of them are destined for destruction. 11/ Who then ought to mourn the more, she who lost so great [m] a multitude, or you who are grieving for one? [n] 12/ But if you say to me, [o] 'My lamentation is not like the earth's**

Notes

5 a Lat, Arm *sermones.* Box suggests λόγους for λογισμούς.

b–b Eth, Ar2 omit.

6 c Ambrose, *De exec. sat.* 1.2, quotes 10:6–11 (Bensly, p. xxxiv).

7 d The text of Lat, Syr, cf. Arm is accepted here; Ar1 and Ar2 also seem to witness the same but are expanded; in Eth the last phrase of the verse refers to "us," not to "Zion."

e–e In both cases, Lat has what might reflect Hebrew infinitive absolute and finite verb, as does the first verb in Arm and the second verb in Syr.

8 f–g The text of the verse is corrupt in the various versions. The translation follows Lat from "It is" to "one son." Syr has omitted "and to be sorrowful—sorrowing," presumably by hmt. Eth has omitted "because we are all mourning," presumably by an analogous textual process. Ar1, Ar2, Arm are all paraphrases.

g Syr adds, most appropriately, "but we, the whole world, for our mother." This is accepted by RSV, but its textual basis is inadequate.

9 h–h Lat *germinatium;* Syr *dhwwn;* Eth (*are born*); cf. Ar1. Probably some corruption of γίνομαι - γεννάω is at play here. See also 4:12 note v, and see note j-k below on 10:10.

10 i–j Corrupt in most Lat witnesses, Violet reconstructs *ex ipso initio;* "from of old" Eth.

j–k Lat reads a principal clause and the next phrase is in parataxis. Syr reads "all who have been and the others who will come." This syntactic structure with some textual variations recurs in Eth, but the basic interpretation of Lat is supported by Ar1 and Ar2. There is, in the verb "born" of Syr, Ar1 a variant engendered by the same confusion of γίνομαι/γεννάω referred to in note h-h above, and cf. Ar1, Ar2 for the next verb, which is, however, "to come" in Lat, Syr, Eth.

l Lat adds *paene,* "almost," perhaps exegetical and based on the next phrase where Greek πλῆθος αὐτῶν might have been taken inexactly as a partitive, cf. Ar1, Arm. Thompson (*Responsibility,* 303–10) draws textual conclusions on exegetical grounds, a doubtful procedure.

11 m So Lat, Arm, cf. Eth "so many"; Syr "this great," cf. Ar1.

n Lat Ms M, Arm add "son"; Ar1 adds "only son."

12 o Lat, Syr "to me"; not found in Eth, Ar1, Ar2, Arm but clearly in Greek from the *Vorlage* of Lat, Syr. It is difficult to know whether the omission reflects a different *Vorlage* and if so, how that is to be evaluated.

sadness, p for I have lost the fruit of my womb, which I brought forth in pain and q in sorrow; 13/ but it is with the earth r according to the way of the earth r—the multitude s that is now in it goes as it came'; 14/ then t I say to you, 'As you brought forth in sorrow, u so the earth also has from the beginning given her fruit, that is, man, to him who made her.' v 15/ Now, therefore, keep your sorrow to yourself, w and bear bravely the troubles x that have come upon you. 16/ For if you acknowledge the decree y of God to be just, you will receive your son back in due time, and will be praised among women. 17/ Therefore go into the city to your husband."

18 She said to me, "I will not do so nor will I go into the city, but I will die here."

19 So I spoke again to her, and said, 20/ "Do not do that thing, z but let yourself be persuaded because of the troubles of Zion, and be consoled because of the sorrow of Jerusalem. 21/ For you see that

our sanctuary a has been laid waste,
    our b altar thrown down,
    cour temple d destroyed; e
22/ our harp f has been laid low,
    our song has been silenced,
    and our rejoicing has been ended;
    the light of our lampstand has been put out,
    the ark of our covenant has been plundered,
    our holy things g have been polluted,
    and the name hby which we are called h has been profaned;
    iour free men have suffered abuse,
    our priests have been burned to death, j
    our Levites have gone into captivity; k
    our virgins have been defiled,
    and our wives have been ravished;
    our righteous men have been carried off,

p Lat, Syr omit.

q Lat adds *genui;* Syr adds *rbyt.* The *Vorlage* is uncertain, though Lat, Syr probably go back to a common reading.

13 r–r Lat, Syr, cf. Arm; Eth omits; Ar1, Ar2 vary.

s Arm has *sukʿ,* "grief," probably reflecting a confusion of ΠΕΝΘΟΣ – ΠΛΗΘΟΣ.

14 t Lat, Arm "and."

u Ar1, Ar2 have two words.

v Lat Ms A*, Syr, Ar1 read "him"; Arm has the reflexive, presumably referring back to "earth" (*pace* Violet 2). Chapter 10:15–16 is cited by Ambrose, *De exec. sat.* 1.2 (Bensly, p. xxxiv).

15 w There is some variation in Eth, Ar1, Ar2, but they do not seem to witness a different *Vorlage.* Arm has "place," clearly corrupt.

x Eth, Ar1 add "and judgment." Eth tends to favor the word "judgment"; see Excursus on the Term "Judgment," p. 151. Eth, as Violet 1 remarks, may have taken the word from 10:16, where it omits it.

16 y Eth omits; see preceding note x.

20 z Ar2 omits; Arm has *ban,* which can be translated "word" or "thing," but goes back to the same *Vorlage* as the other versions, probably Greek ῥῆμα 〈 דבר in Hebrew meaning "word" or "thing." We may assume that the Greek translator took it in the former sense, while the latter sense would have been more appropriate. Therefore, all versions have a verb meaning "do." This is translated, without comment, by "say" in RSV, perhaps a possible meaning of the Latin phrase but not of the other versions. We translate accordingly "thing," presuming the Greek to be a mistranslation; see also Violet 2. Ambrose quotes 10:19–24 in *De exec. sat.* 1.2.

21 a–d Eth omits, apparently by hmt, having a word for "temple" in both places.

b The versions have "and" preceding each of these phrases. It has been omitted from the translation in most instances and also is omitted in some instances by some Latin manuscripts.

c–e Ar1 and Arm omit.

22 f The sense of the word in Syr, Eth is "psalm." In Ar1, Ar2, Arm the first two phrases of this verse are represented by a single phrase.

g Singular in Eth, Ar1, Ar2. Perles ("Notes," 185) suggests a Hebrew variant to explain this form, but it is unconvincing.

h–h Lat "which has been named over us."

i–j Ar1 and Ar2 are rather reworked here.

j Perles ("Notes") suggests that Arm derives from Greek ΚΛΑΙΟΝΤΕΣ, while the other versions come from ΚΑΙΟΝΤΕΣ; the form κλαίοντες is impossible in context, but some other form may have intervened.

k Arm retains only one phrase between here and "and our strong men."

ᴵour little ones have been cast out,
our young men have been enslaved, ᴵ
and our strong men made powerless.
23/ And, what is more than all, ᵐthe seal of
Zion—for she has now ⁿ lost the seal of her
glory, and has ᵒ been given over into ᵖ the
hands of those that hate us. 24/ Therefore
shake off your great sadness and lay aside
your many sorrows, so that the Mighty One
may be merciful to you, ᑫ and the Most High
may give you rest ʳ from your troubles."

l–l The two phrases are transposed in Eth and
Ar1.

23   m–p Eth "Zion is sealed and her glory has withdrawn from her"; Ar1 "the seal, which was in Zion,
has been trampled and it has been made inglorious";
Ar2 "the dissolution of the glory of Zion"; Arm
"Zion was rejected like a worthless vessel and her
glory was taken away." These are all probably
exegeses of a text like Lat, Syr, and no two of them
agree exactly.

n Lat, Syr; other versions omit. Clearly existed at
least in the *Vorlage* of Lat, Syr.

o–p Eth, Arm "We have been given over."

24   q Lat has *repropietur*, giving "be merciful . . .
again" in RSV. In spite of the translations of it, Arm
does not have the idea of "again" in the text, nor do
any of the other versions.

r Lat adds "a relief."

Form and Structure

This pericope forms the second segment of Ezra's vision.
It may be divided into four chief parts. Chapter 10:5
provides narrative continuity with the preceding, while
in 10:6–17 we have Ezra's speech of comfort directed to
the mourning woman. This is followed by the woman's
brief response (10:18) and Ezra's concluding address
(10:19–24). It should be noted that while in the first part
of the vision the speech by the woman dominated, here
her role is reduced to making small comments, to which
Ezra responds with long addresses. The same pattern was
observed above in the analysis of the dialogue between
Ezra and the angel in Visions 1 and 2.

In Ezra's speech of comfort (10:6–17) a number of
themes from earlier and later in the book are taken up
and used. These are detailed in the next section (Function and Content). They serve to show how deeply this
pericope is rooted in the book. A very deliberate pointer
to the latter part of Vision 4 is the expression "Zion,
mother of us all." This is the use of a dramatic figure in
which the reader knows the continuation of the story,
but Ezra himself does not; see further on this 10:9
Commentary.

The form of the apostrophe in 10:9 "Ask the earth" is
notable. This seems to be a quotation from 7:54, and the
rhetorical form is the same.[1] The same literary figure
and content are also to be noted in 4:40, where the earth

is treated as a womb. In 10:12–14 we find an "if" statement that summarizes the preceding discussion. It is very
similar to what we find in 5:51–55 in a similar context.[2]
Ezra's injunctions and promise, given in 10:15–17,
greatly resemble the injunctions with which the first
three visions conclude (5:13; 6:30–34; and 9:23–25).

The poetic forms that are to the fore in 10:19–24 are
notable. Chapter 10:20 is made up of two rather long,
parallel stichs. More remarkable is the lament in 10:21–
22, which is a fine piece of poetic composition. Here we
note a structure of tricola, broken by a single colon,
leading to the climactic verse 10:23. Set out schematically we have:

10:21	A	B	C
10:22	A	B	C
	A	B	C
	D		
	A	B	C
	A	B	C
	A	B	C
10:23	climax		

Our literary analysis differs at some points from that of
Violet, who stresses the sevenfold form of the lament.[3]
The lament is characterized by simple phrases, noun and
verb, in parallelism. Somewhat similar structures may be

---

1   See 7:45–74 Form and Structure, p. 227.

2   See 5:41—6:10 Form and Structure, p. 144, where
this is discussed.

3   Violet compares also with 5:36–37d; 6:1d–5c; and
7:132–139. Much is made of the same point by
Keulers, p. 21 n. 1.

seen, for example, in Lam 1:4–5.[4] Note also the laments in 1 Macc 1:36–40 and 2:7–13. Indeed, 1Macc 2:7–9 is in many ways close to our text:

7/ Alas! Why was I born to see this,
   the ruin of my people, the ruin of the holy city,
and to dwell there when it was given over to the
   enemy,
   the sanctuary given over to aliens?
8/ Her temple has become like a man without honor,
   9/ her glorious vessels have been carried into
captivity,
Her babes have been killed in her streets,
   her youths by the sword of the foe.[5]

These passages are similar enough to the present one to suggest the existence of a shared body of traditional lament material, already evident in 2 Chron 36:19. This same traditional material has probably determined the stress on the things relating to the Temple in this lament. In the preceding part of the book, although the Temple is mentioned from time to time in the context of destruction, it is Zion or Israel that holds pride of place. In this lament, however, the majority of the things bewailed are specifically related to the Temple.[6]

It is worth remarking on the close parallel between 10:8 and 10:11.[7] Once the text of 10:8 is clarified, the last phrase concludes the verse exactly as the similar phrase concludes 10:11.[8] The verse 10:8 concludes the reference to Zion's sorrow, just as 10:11 concludes the first part of the discussion of the earth's sorrow.

Function and Content

This section is of great interest for the development of the thought of Vision 4. In the discussion of the previous pericope, we noted the disjunction between the address with which the vision opened and the ensuing vision and that the author attempted to soften this by stating that Ezra "dismissed the thoughts" with which he had been occupied. This is repeated here in 10:5[9] and serves to reemphasize the change in the seer's orientation. It is extremely important to note the reversal of roles in this section. Brandenburger observed acutely that in this vision Ezra changes from the one comforted to the giver of comfort.[10]

From the discussion of the preceding pericope, it emerged that in her address the woman took on many of the characteristics that Ezra had exhibited during the first three visions. In the present pericope, where Ezra's action is to the fore and not the woman's, the complementary reversal of roles between Ezra and the angel is very prominent.

In 10:6, Ezra reproaches the woman. He says, in effect, "Do you think you can mourn more than we do?" just as the angel had said to him, "Do you think you can do X more than God?" (4:2; 5:33; et al.). The angel had

---

4   The poetics of Lamentations 1 are dealt with by F. M. Cross, "Studies in the Structure of Hebrew Verse: The Prosody of Lamentations 1:1–22," *The Word of the Lord Shall Go Forth: D. N. Freedman FS* (ed. C. L. Meyers and M. O'Connor; Winona Lake, Ind.: Eisenbrauns, 1983) 129–55. Other more or less contemporary laments are *2 Apoc Bar* 10:6–19 and 35:2–4, but their literary form is quite different. Bogaert discusses the laments in *2 Apocalyspe of Baruch* at some length; see *Baruch,* 1:129–33.

5   On these passages of 1 Maccabees, see H. A. Attridge, "Historiography," *Jewish Writings of the Second Temple Period* (CRINT 2.2; Assen and Philadelphia: van Gorcum and Fortress, 1984) 171–76. Perhaps an echo of these laments may be discerned in Josephus, *Ant.* 3:18–19.

6   Contrast the centrality of the concept of sacrificial service in Matthew, highlighted by B. Gerhardsson, "Sacrificial Service and Atonement in the Gospel of Matthew," *Reconciliation and Hope: L. L. Morris FS* (ed. R. J. Banks; Exeter: Paternoster, 1974), esp. 26–29. Two qualifications should be added to this remark.

First, the name Zion was, of course, originally deeply tied to the idea of the sanctuary. Second, the matter of sacrifices is important, at least by implication, to the author of the interpretation of 10:45 (see Commentary there).

7   The structural parallelism between the speech in 10:5–17 and earlier parts of the book is discussed below in Function and Content.

8   In textual note g on 10:8 the basis for the rejection of the reading of Syriac (followed by RSV) is given.

9   Brandenburger also notes the technique of repetition of central themes in other places in this pericope; cf. 10:15–16 and 10:24, etc. (*Verborgenheit,* 81 and n. 55).

10 Brandenburger, *Verborgenheit,* 81.

indicated not that Ezra's mourning was unbased but that Ezra did not see the broader implications of the situation, just as here Ezra's reproach of the woman does much the same. Moreover, in the course of his discussion with the woman in 10:9, Ezra used the same literary means that the angel had earlier employed in his discussion with Ezra (7:54). This is the most striking in a series of instances in which there is a clear parallel between the rhetorical technique used previously by the angel in reproving and instructing Ezra and that employed here by Ezra in addressing the woman. Such cases are 10:12–14 // 5:51–53; 10:15–17 // 5:54–55; 6:30–34; and 9:23–25.

This reversal of roles is possible, since Ezra has now accepted the implications of what the angel has said to him in the previous visions. We observed that, even at the very end of Vision 3, Ezra had difficulty in unquestioningly assenting to the clear results of the teachings he received. In 10:10, however, he states as part of his comfort offered to the woman that "almost all go to perdition and a multitude of them are destined for destruction." This statement is extended to the woman by way of comfort of sorts—since this is the fate of most humans, and since Zion is mourning her children, how can she concentrate such grief on the loss of a single child? But what is striking is that this teaching, offered to the woman by Ezra, is precisely that which he rebels at accepting at the end of the previous vision, that is, the teaching of the few saved and the many damned. That was the point of the whole discussion that dominated Vision 3.

However, Ezra's acceptance here of the consolation the angel had offered him earlier is even more radical than this. At the beginning of Vision 3 he had even questioned the righteousness and justice of God. Bearing that in mind, observe what Ezra says here, in 10:16: "For if you acknowledge the decree of God to be just, you will receive your son back in due time." The first part of this statement serves precisely to focus Ezra's own prior concerns. He had great difficulty in accepting the justice of God's action; it is now that very justice that he holds out to the woman, by way of a *principium consolationis*. Her recognition of God's justice, he tells her, will bring her son back "in due time."

It may be remarked further that there is a broad structural parallelism between the first three visions and Ezra's speech of comfort in 10:5–17. The book opened with the problem of the destruction of Zion, just as the speech opens with Zion's mourning (10:6–8). The book then laid great stress on the problem of the few and the many, just as the speech bewails the fate of the many in 10:9–15. The eschatological passages in Visions 1–3 offer the message of redemption and conclude with Ezra's own personal reward; the speech concludes, in 10:16: "You will receive your son back in due time, and will be praised among women." Thus, in the speech Ezra rehearses *as comfort* those problems which had disturbed him throughout the first three visions. Moreover, he offers the same promise that had been offered him.

The implications of Ezra's statement in 10:16 are interesting. In 9:38—10:4 Function and Content, p. 312, we inferred from the present verse that the end of the story was probably the restoration of the dead son. Now the structure of Ezra's speech parallels the angel's comfort of Ezra earlier in the book, and, in the light of this, Ezra's promise of restoration corresponds to the angel's predictions of future redemption. Moreover, the phrase "in due time" is worthy of special note. It occurred in 8:43 and even more intriguingly in 3:9. In both instances it reflected ideas of predestination. The time of redemption, of the resurrection of the dead child, is fixed in advance. So Ezra urges the woman to accept the chief teachings of the first visions: God's ways are inscrutable, but they are just. In due time he will reward the righteous and give them their proper recompense.

Ezra comforts the woman, then, by stressing to her exactly those ideas and concepts which he himself has struggled to accept since the beginning of the book. He does this without any sense of conflict or contradiction, without bringing up his own doubts, without referring in any way to his own inner conflicts. He offers wholeheartedly the comfort that he was himself unable to accept fully when it was extended to him. This is a clear sign of how profoundly he has changed since the beginning of his quest. From another perspective, here a deep irony may be discerned.

The author here, then, is clearly marking for us the shift that has taken place in Ezra's own understanding and spiritual state. As was true of the injunctions at the end of Vision 3 and the introduction to this vision, here too this change is highlighted by literary means. There a series of signs indicated that Ezra had reached a different perception of things; this different perception also reigns here. Yet, in spite of this, or perhaps because of it, his mourning for Zion becomes particularly poignant. In 8:48–49 the angel highlighted Ezra's humility as a great virtue, but in the present vision (10:39) it is Ezra's sorrowing for Zion that is especially noted. Once he had accepted all that he was taught, the issue of the few and the many withdrew to the background and the mourning for Zion reasserted itself. We are indebted to Westermann for the observation that the lament for Zion in this chapter is the last lament in the book.[11] Again the shift in Ezra's attitude is clear.

Vision 3 had opened with this very lament, the destruction of Zion and the abundance of Babylon (3:2), and of course the same theme is completely dominant in this fourth vision. It is the meaning of the woman's tale, it is the mainspring of Ezra's comfort afterward. Why then, we may ask, did this vision open with a discussion of Torah, a discussion that was abandoned after Ezra's address and never resumed? This address on Torah raised real issues and was related to the way the argument was developed in the first three visions. This disjunction, we have suggested, may reflect the writer's real experience. It remains to add that the access of the woman's grief and the human need to comfort her seem to have channeled Ezra's deep emotions about the destruction of Zion. His worldview is starting on a process of new integration in the light of his experiences. This new integration, involving internalization of the conclusions the angel has offered him, was perhaps catalyzed (and represented, for, after all, the woman was a projection) by the need to comfort another person. There is deep psychological insight in this representation.

One further element should be brought into account

here. In 10:5, Ezra is said to respond to the woman's tale of grief "in anger" and he berates her: "You most foolish of women" (10:6). This attitude contasts sharply with that which he himself encountered from the angel, who showed him endless patience. At one level this may be compared with *Test Abr* 10:13–14 in which writing Abraham's human wrath against sinners is dramatically contrasted with God's mercy.[12] At another level, however, which becomes evident when we recall the role reversal in this vision, Ezra's anger is directed against himself, against his own resurgent grief—how transparent is "Do you not see our mourning?"!

Here too there may lie the key to another difficult part of this vision. In 10:19–24, Ezra offers a lament over Zion which, he claims, should comfort the woman. We should all mourn over Zion. "Therefore, shake off your great sadness," he says, so that the Mighty One "may be merciful to you again" (10:24). Just why his beautiful lament over Zion and the Temple should comfort the woman mourning over her son is not clear at the level of argument. But, of course, here his own yearning for comfort is being described. He pains for Zion, but because he has come to accept the ideas of predeterminism, of the justice of God's action, and of the coming reward, his mourning now contains the dynamic of comfort.[13]

Indeed, the situation that has been created is now very complex. On the one hand, Ezra has accepted (or reaffirmed) the very axiomatic position he had questioned at the start of Vision 1. No longer does he question the justice of God, the ways of providence, the issue of the few and the many. Indeed, he has heard the message of redemption and that in the most personal way. Yet his distress and grief are not thereby resolved, so he is seized again by speech; but this time the response is not an

---

11 "Klage," 78–79.
12 Brandenburger makes much of Ezra's implicit, prophetic role here. The anger is prophetic wrath! He derives the prophetic role here from 5:16–19, where, however, we observe language related to leadership rather than to prophecy (*Verborgenheit*, 76, 78).
13 Note that this analysis also accounts for the apparent tension between 10:20 and 10:8. Box points to the moving lament as evidence that the work was composed when the pain of the destruction of the Temple was still fresh. This is not certain, and if

medieval Jewish laments over the Temple are any criterion, then truly moving laments could be written many generations after the event. The lament genre is found in the Hebrew Bible, of course, a prime example being the Book of Lamentations.

angelophany but the meeting with the woman who is in fact his own grief, both the pain and its cause. With great insight the author describes as anger Ezra's reaction to her cry of grief. On the face of it, it is anger over her lack of a sense of proportion, of her exaggeration of personal mourning when all of Zion mourned. Below the surface, the anger surely reflects his own desperate struggle, in spite of all, to handle his own distress and mourning.

Commentary

■ **5** See 9:39; this significant expression is discussed in Function and Content, p. 318, and in 9:38—10:4 Function and Content, p. 311.

■ **6** This is a specific reference to the destruction of the Temple and Zion, which is discussed in detail in the commentary on the next verse.

■ **7** The dramatic structure of this verse, using a sort of double entendre, is discussed in Form and Structure, p. 317. The mourning mother is Zion, as emerges later in the chapter. 4 Ezra often uses the image of a mother elsewhere in the book, predominantly referring to the earth.[14] The motivation of this verse, indeed of the whole vision, is the mourning over the destruction of Zion. This is a dominant theme elsewhere in the book. Thus note the "humiliation of Zion" in 6:19.[15] Zion or Jerusalem as a mother is a figure that has clear biblical roots and also appears in the New Testament.[16] It is found in the apocryphal literature as well; see *2 Apoc Bar* 3:1 and 10:16 (both in the context of the desolation of Zion). Particularly striking is the parallel passage in *Pes. Rab.* 26 (Friedmann, p. 131b). Ginzberg says of this:

> The prophet [i.e., Jeremiah] met a woman in mourning, who informed him that she was mourning and weeping for her husband who "went far away from her," and for her seven sons, who in the absence of

their father, were killed by a house falling upon them. . . . Jeremiah attempted to console her, saying to her: "Thou art not better than my mother Zion, and yet she became pasture for the beasts of the field." The woman answered: "I am thy mother Zion, I am the mother who lost her seven children" (comp. Jer. 15:9). Jeremiah then consoled her, pointing out that her fate was similar to that of Job, and like him she would at the end be compensated for all her suffering. He closed his consoling address with the message of God: "A mortal of flesh and blood built thee, a mortal of flesh and blood laid thee waste; but in the future I shall build thee."[17]

This is strikingly similar to the present vision, first in the basic motif and second in a number of specific details, including the message of comfort, the heavenly city built by God.[18]

Some stylistic similarities are also to be noted. Thus in *Pesiqta Rabbati* Jeremiah relates his whole experience in the first person, rather like our text. Ginzberg commented: "A similar vision is also found in 4 Ezra 9:38—10:28; yet it is inconceivable that there is direct dependence of the Midrash upon Ezra."[19]

It should be remarked, however, that this section of *Pesiqta Rabbati* is unique on literary and structural grounds. Moreover, the story of the mourning woman, found in section 26 (Friedmann, p. 131b), is tied in with Jeremiah's rebuke of his mother (=Zion) as if she were a *soṭa* (a faithless wife) and his comforting Zion (not her children).[20] Again, it is precisely this section of *Pesiqta Rabbati* that is dependent (directly or indirectly) upon *2 Apocalypse of Baruch*.[21] So one might suspect that this section of *Pesiqta Rabbati* draws somehow on the earlier sources, despite Ginzberg's view.[22]

The image of Zion as a bereft mother also is expressed

14   See 4:40 Commentary, 5:48 Commentary, 10:9 and 10:14.

15   This subject also occurs prominently in other post-destruction works, most notably *2 Apoc Bar* 10:16.

16   See Isa 50:1; Jer 50:12; Hos 2:4; 4:5; and Gal 4:26; cf. Bar 4:16; 4:19–23; 4:36–37; and 5:5–6.

17   Ginzberg, *Legends*, 6:403.

18   On the heavenly Jerusalem, see 7:26 Commentary and Stone, *Features*, 101–2.

19   Ginzberg, *Legends*, 6:403.

20   See Heinemann, "A Homily," 33 and 38. The text of this *pisqa* was reedited from the preferable Parma Ms

by W. G. Braude, "The *Piska* Concerning the Sheep Which Rebelled," *PAAJR* 30 (1962) 1–35.

21   See Bogaert, *Baruch*, 1:222–41.

22   Heinemann remarked that only in this section of the *Pisqa* does the midrashist create the words set in Jeremiah's mouth, while otherwise he uses biblical quotations (ibid., 35). Heinemann (p. 28) seems to imply that this is an earlier piece incorporated into *Pesiqta Rabbati*. A similar tradition is found in *Echa Rabbati* on Lam 1:2.

in the special addition to the *Amida* for the Ninth of Ab: "Comfort, O Lord our God, . . . the city that is in mourning, laid waste, despised and desolate; in mourning—for that she is childless; laid waste—in her dwellings; despised—on the downfall of her glory; and desolate—through the loss of her inhabitants: she sitteth with her head covered like a barren woman who hath not borne."[23] Significant here is not only the image of the bereft and barren mother but also the references to loss of glory, a theme also arising in 4 Ezra.[24]

The similarity with another source, the beginning of *Hermas, Vision* 3, has also been remarked.[25]

■ **8** The structure of this verse is just like 10:20, made up of two parallel stichs composed of a main clause and a second clause opening with "because." A somewhat similar structure may be observed in 9:20. The additional phrase of Syriac breaks the tight sequence, and 10:9 in fact contrasts with the last clause of 10:8.[26]

■ **9** The earth is said to beget humans (5:48; 6:53) and other beings; see 4:40 Commentary and 5:48 Commentary. As a corollary, earth is said to mourn her children (10:9 and 10:12).[27] The argument in this part of the chapter is a little complex, for Ezra responds to the woman in a double-barreled way. He says to the woman, Why do you mourn? For *(a)* we are all mourning because of Zion (10:8); and *(b)* the earth should mourn the many that come forth upon it (10:9–11). The argument that

opened in 10:7 about Zion is not continued, however, and above we indicated that this formulation might be a literary artifice to signal to the reader that the woman is in fact Zion.[28]

■ **10** "Destruction" here may go back to Greek ἀπωλεία and Hebrew אבדון, a technical term for the underworld, parallel to "Sheol" and "Mawet" in the Hebrew Bible.[29] Note, therefore, the parallelism of "corruption"/"ways of death"/"paths of perdition" in 7:48. Consequently, the term "perdition" does not necessarily imply annihilation but death, which is regarded in 4 Ezra either negatively or neutrally.[30] The point here is not the universal damnation of all humans but the comparison between the death of all Mother Earth's offspring and the sudden death of the mourning woman's only child.

■ **11** No commentary.

■ **12** The imagery of the earth giving birth was discussed in 10:9 Commentary. The expression "pain and sorrow" apparently refers to Gen 3:16, perhaps the implication being that the earth is not touched by the curse laid upon Eve.[31]

■ **13** The exact sense of "according to the way of the earth" seems to be "in its own way," in comparison with the way human women bear, which was mentioned in the preceding verse.[32]

■ **14** The creation of mankind is discussed in 3:5 Commentary, and the idea of the earth as a woman or womb

---

23 Cited from Singer, *Authorized Daily Prayer Book,* 49. Hertz observes that the present form of this prayer goes back to the time of Sa'adya Gaon, at least, but this is far later than 4 Ezra and probably than *Pesiqta Rabbati* (*Authorized Daily Prayer Book,* 285).

24 Ginzberg observes (loc cit.) that Kalir's dirge אז במלאת for the Ninth of Ab is based on the same passage of *Pesiqta Rabbati.* The idea of Zion as a bereaved mother whose children are restored in the future is also to be found in another form in *Pes. R. K.* 20:1. There is something of a debate between Kabisch (pp. 85–91) and Box, who interpret the woman as being the heavenly Jerusalem, and those who disagree, regarding her as the destroyed earthly city (so Keulers, p. 103). See further 10:9 Commentary.

25 So already D. Völter, *Die Visionen des Hermas, die Sibylle und Clemens von Rom* (Berlin: Schwetschke, 1900) 46–48.

26 See textual note g.

27 The expression "those that come forth upon it" should be compared with 5:48; see 5:44; 7:21; 9:20;

and also 7:116.

28 See Form and Structure, p. 317. Kaminka suggests that "those come forth upon it" here means "Israel" ("Beiträge zur Erklärung der Esra-Apokalypse und zur Rekonstruktion ihrer hebräischen Urtextes," *MGWJ* 76 NF 40 [1932] 606).

29 See Job 26:6; 28:22; 31:12; Prov 15:11, cf. 27:20; and Ps 88:11. Cf. also Rev 9;11; 1QH 3:16, 19.

30 See Excursus on Adam's Sin, pp. 65–66. Harnisch's discussion, therefore, about whether here the reference is to all mankind or only to nearly all mankind is a little beside the point. See pp. 229–30; see also 7:46 Commentary and 7:67 Commentary. The verse has been regarded as a crux for the question of universal sin versus the righteous remnant; see, e.g., Thompson, *Responsibility,* 303–10, who criticizes Harnisch's views on this. This is surely to overexegete the passage in the light of concerns quite exterior to this passage.

31 See, also, for similar language, Armenian of 4:42 (Violet).

32 Violet suggests comparing with Gen 19:31 and *2*

is discussed in 10:9 Commentary. The verse says that the earth's bringing forth humans *is* comparable to the woman's travail, that is, it too is a sort of travail.[33] The expression "from the beginning" is a reference to primordial things; compare "at the beginning" in 3:4 and also the interpretations of מקדם in Gen 2:8.[34]

■ **15** Some scholars have compared "the troubles that have come upon you" with 3:10. It is not certain, however, that if the present verse is taken in the context of the story, these two verses are really comparable.

■ **16** The general import of this verse as reflecting the reversal of Ezra's role was discussed above.[35] The acknowledgment of the justice of God is a theme often raised in connection with destructions of the Temple (so *Ps Sol* 8:7; cf. *Ps Sol* 3:3 and 4:8. This is also clear in *2 Apoc Bar* 78:5.[36]

The promise that the woman will receive her son back has raised a good many difficulties of interpretation. It might be thought to refer to the resurrection of the dead, an idea often found in 4 Ezra.[37] Alternatively, a miracle like that of the Shunamite woman and Elisha might be intended: a supposition strengthened by the elements in this story which indicate, as Gunkel proposed many years ago, that it arose from some folk tale.[38]

The difficulty of this narrative element here, as he noted, is apparent when the interpretation is examined. There the birth of the son is the institution of sacrifices, his death the destruction of the city, and so, implicitly (for it is not stated explicitly), his resurrection or restoration, the promise of the heavenly city which Ezra has seen. There is an apparent difficulty here in that the symbol "son" does not have a specific role in the symbol structure. This may be complementary to the literary difficulty noted above (10:9 Commentary), where in Ezra's response, the analogy of Zion is abandoned very quickly for the analogy of the earth.

Yet Zion as a mother seems to call for Israel as children, and these themes, not clearly brought out in 4 Ezra, are specifically related to resurrection and restoration in 2 Esdr (5 Ezra) 2:15–17:

Mother, embrace your sons; bring them up with gladness, as does the dove; establish their seed, because I have chosen you, says the Lord. And I will raise up the dead from their places, and will bring them out from their tombs, because I recognize my name in them. Do not fear, mother of sons, for I have chosen you, says the Lord.[39]

The expression "in due time" usually implies some idea of predestination; see 3:9 Commentary. The fact that a woman is renowned among other women for giving birth or other maternal feats seems to have been a commonplace in ancient Israelite society; see Gen 30:13; Ruth 4:14; and *2 Apoc Bar* 54:10. A reversal of this praise is to be seen in Sarah's comment in Gen 21:6.

■ **17** The secondary role of the husband, previously mentioned only in 9:43, is noteworthy throughout this story.

■ **18** Two different actions appear to be involved, but in fact this is a case of hendiadys used for emphasis.[40]

■ **19** Violet compares "again" here with the angelic promises to tell Ezra "more" in such instances as 5:32 et al. Observe, however, that the "again" refers to Ezra's second speech, following upon that which began in 10:5.

■ **20** This verse is composed of two parallel stichs, which rhythmically mark the shift of the ensuing lament to the poetic form. The difficulty of Ezra's assertion that the woman should somehow find comfort for her personal pain in the mourning for or of Zion, and the psychological dynamic behind it that rings true, are discussed in Form and Function, pp. 319–21.

---

33 *Apoc Bar* 44:12, but in both those places the similar expression means "as is usually done (by humans)." This seems to be the very opposite of what is expected here.

Violet sees the point of comparison as lying in the earth's "sacrifice" or "devotion," exhibited in the bringing forth of humans. Interestingly, in a similar context R. Tanḥuma cites Gen 3:17, thus suggesting as a possible exegesis here that the earth was cursed just as Eve was and, in the background, the idea that the earth's very curse came about because of Eve (*Gen. R.* 1:2 [Theodor-Albeck, p. 15]).

34 See 3:6 Commentary.
35 See 9:38—10:4 Function and Content, p. 312, and Function and Content, pp. 318–19.
36 See Stone, "Reactions," 197.
37 See 7:32 Commentary.
38 See Stone, *Features*, 269 n. 385.
39 See further, 10:38–54 Function and Content, p. 335, on the symbols of the vision.
40 Violet points to the Hebrew of Gen 31:26 and 41:34 where similar constructions may be observed.

■ 21 This verse opens the lament that continues in 10:22–23. The verse is composed of three parallel stichs dealing with the desecration of the Temple.[41] The desecration of the Temple was central to the tradition of laments, as is clear from Lam 1:10 and 2:7. Compare in particular 1 Macc 1:37: "They even defiled the Temple." By far the largest part of the whole lament deals with various Temple-related subjects, which is a proportion quite different from the rest of 4 Ezra, which scarcely mentions the Temple. This is another indication of the traditional nature of the Temple/Zion laments, discussed above (Form and Structure, pp. 317–18).

It should also be recalled that the desecration or destruction of the Temple formed a central theme for much of the literature of the Second Temple period. It was a focus for many of the issues of theodicy that 4 Ezra took up later, in a rather different way.[42] 4 Ezra, however, does not describe the Temple in Jerusalem as *axis mundi*, an idea lying behind, for example, *2 Apocalypse of Baruch* 4, even though he talks of a future or heavenly city.[43]

■ 22 The first three hemistichs here refer to the cessation of the Temple service, in which music played a considerable role. This is also reflected in the iconography of certain Bar Cochba coins, which show a harp, symbolizing the Temple or its service.[44] Explicit references to the Temple vessels are common in the laments (see 1

Macc 2:9; 4:49; *2 Apoc Bar* 6:7), and they formed a central concern in Ezra 1:6–11; Daniel 5; and other sources.[45] Among the Temple vessels, the lampstand held a particularly important place; this is reflected in 1 Macc 4:49–50; cf. also *2 Apoc Bar* 10:12. The whole Hannuka legend turns around the role of the lampstand in the rededication of the Temple.[46] The "ark of the covenant" is also a biblical expression.[47] The ark was not found in the Second Temple, having disappeared with the destruction by Nebuchadnezzar. Thus its mention here is surely part of the pseudepigraphic context in which the author is working.[48] Another traditional element is that Israel is called by God's name, an idea that is discussed in detail above.[49]

After the mention of the various Temple-related items, a number of groups of the populace are mentioned. Among these the priests and Levites are associated with the Temple, but they are likely mentioned here simply as a part of the social structure. Such afflictions of the civilian population were (and remain) part of the effects of war. Consequently, it is difficult to know whether there is any significance in such parallels as Judith 4:12, and compare also Josephus, *War* 6.271 in the description of the destruction by Titus. The priests are especially mentioned in a similar list in 1 Macc 1:46 and descriptions of burning in Josephus, *War* 6.280.

Among these various groups, perhaps only "the

---

41 On the literary form, see Form and Structure, p. 317.

42 See Stone, "Reactions," 195–200.

43 See R. Goldenberg, "The Broken Axis: Rabbinic Judaism and the Fall of Jerusalem," *JAAR* 45.3 Suppl (1977) 871–73; see 7:26 Commentary. S. D. Cohen, "The Destruction," 24, remarks, speaking of Lamentations and *Lamentations Rabbati,* that "although both works lament the destruction of Jerusalem and the loss of the temple, neither is bothered by the cessation of the sacrificial cult." The same is true of the lament in 4 Ezra, though the institution of the sacrificial cult is stressed in 3:24 and 10:45–46. Vaganay, p. 98, already pointed out that the restoration of the Temple cult is not mentioned in 4 Ezra's eschatological predictions.

44 So also Box. Music is also said to cease as part of the eschatological turmoil in Isa 24:8, but here clearly it is specifically the Temple and not just the end of general joyousness that is indicated.

45 See the material assembled by Ginzberg, *Legends,* 6:410.

46 Harnisch ties the light of the lampstand to the light

of the Law and ideas of illumination in the book (p. 204). This is an interesting suggestion, but the context of 10:22 seems quite unambiguous. Other places in the book do refer to the destruction of the Torah, e.g., 4:23, but that is not even mentioned here. This may be because of the traditional nature of the lament focusing on the Temple and its furnishings.

47 On the term "covenant," see 3:32 Commentary. On the ark, see the summary in *IDB* s.v.

48 This observation was already made by Oesterley.

49 See 4:25 Commentary.

---

righteous" is a bit exceptional]. In 8:57 we found the affliction of "the righteous ones" by the wicked. *2 Apoc Bar* 85:1 reckons "righteous ones" along with the prophets as part of the ancient constitution of Israel.[50] The "little ones" may be compared with Nah 3:10 and the "young men" with 1 Macc 2:9, cf. Lam 2:21.

■ **23** "The seal of Zion, for now she has lost her glory" is a difficult expression. At the syntactic level, these words are some sort of parenthesis. In the substance, here we should isolate two elements. There is much emphasis on the loss of glory caused by the destruction of the Temple (so see 1 Macc 1:40; 2:8–9; see already 1 Sam 4:21). Sealing is an idea that occurs elsewhere in the book with a number of possible meanings.[51] It seems most likely that this is a way of speaking about the evident glory of the city with the Temple and the glory of God in its midst. Perhaps the idea of the Shechinah is here involved.[52] The expression about handing over the city is very similar to 3:27.

■ **24** The word "again" implies "as he was in the gift of the son" (9:45). Note that "Mighty One" is picked up here again, significantly as is explained in 9:45 Commentary.[53]

---

50 Cf. also the older title "Hasideans" (i.e., "pious ones") discussed, *inter alia*, in Nickelsburg and Stone, *Faith and Piety,* 19–24.

51 See the Commentary on 6:5; 6:20; and 8:53.

52 Gunkel suggests that it is the seal of state; cf. Esther 3:10; 8:2; and 1 Macc 6:15. A similar interpretation is seal, meaning coinage, the loss of which is a result of the loss of independence (so Box and Oesterley).

53 See also 6:32 Commentary.

10

25 ᵃAnd it came to pass, ᵃ while I was talking to her, behold, her face suddenly ᵇ shone exceedingly, and her countenance flashed like lightning, ᶜ so that I was too frightened to approach her, ᵈand my heart was terrified. ᵈ While I was wondering what this meant, 26/ behold, ᵉ she suddenly uttered a loud and fearful cry, so that the earth shook at her ᶠ voice. 27/ And I looked, and behold, the woman was no longer visible to me, but there was an established city, and a place of huge foundations showed itself. ᵍ Then I was afraid, and cried with a loud voice and said, 28/ "Where is the angel Uriel, who came to me at first? ʰ For it was he who brought me into this overpowering bewilderment; ⁱ

my end ʲ has become corruption,
and my prayer a reproach."

Notes

25 a–a Lat, Syr, Arm, cf. Eth; Ar1, Ar2 omit.
b Syr, Arm omit.
c Arm adds "and her form so fearsome."
d–d Lat omits.

26 e Lat, Ar1; Arm "and"; Ar2 "then"; Syr, Eth omit.
f Lat, Ar1 omit. Because we have accepted the possessive, we must translate the next word "voice" rather than "sound" (RSV).

27 g Lat, Syr; Eth "I saw"; Ar1, Ar2, Arm omit.

28 h Syr, Arm "on the first (former) day."
i Eth "investigations," perhaps ⟨ ἐξέτασις for ἔκστασις (Violet 1); Arm, Ar1 add "place."
j Box, Violet 2 suggest Hebrew תכליתי/תפלתי; Gressmann demurs.

Form and Structure

This pericope, which describes the transformation of the woman into a city, has no true parallel in the book, nor in fact is anything quite like it known from the other Jewish apocalypses. Four stages of the transformation are described:

A. *Illumination of the Woman's Countenance*
Ezra responds with terror (10:25).
B. *Her Cry and the Shaking of the Earth (10:26)*
C. *Her Transformation into a City*
Ezra responds with fear and a cry (10:27).
D. *The Contents of Ezra's Cry (10:28)*
Observe that the call to Uriel is a deliberate tie to the preceding part of the book.

Function and Content

The most striking thing about this passage is the description of the woman's transformation. There had been nothing that we can perceive in the narrative of the encounter with the woman that hinted in the direction of her being other than what she seemed, except for some instances of double entendre. Then, suddenly (10:27) she is transformed before the seer's very eyes into a city with huge foundations. This remarkable event is described in some detail as well as the seer's response to it.

In the first place, Ezra's visual sense is assaulted. The woman's countenance becomes bright and shining, and flashes like lightning. Next he hears her utter a loud cry, which is an event affecting his sense of hearing. Finally

the earth shakes, indicating a major disturbance of his perception of the physical world. This description is unlike anything elsewhere in the apocalypses, and for that reason it is the more striking. Below, we shall consider the possible traditional sources of these elements and their exegetical significance. For the moment, however, it is important to concentrate on the description of the event itself.

Ezra's response to this vision which is mentioned in the two stages of the experience is characterized by fear and terror. He is badly frightened by what he has experienced, so much so that he loses consciousness (see 10:30, which describes him as lying "like a corpse"). Before he lost consciousness fully, he shouted out his call for his angelic guide in words that express fear and, we suggest, the sensation of fainting (10:28). This is indicated by the words "My end has become corruption and my prayer a reproach." Corruption is death; his prayer for illumination, so he thinks, has brought about his death.

Clearly, then, a very powerful experience is being described by the author. The seer's reactions to the revelations in the first three visions do not resemble this. Nor do those which follow upon the dreams in Visions 5 and 6. We suggest that the experience being described here was absolutely crucial for the whole development of the book. It is analogous to the major sort of reorientation of personality that is usually associated with religious conversion.[1] However, the term "conversion" is not really appropriate, since this is not an adherence to a new deity or faith. Sometimes the term "intensification" is used to describe a type of powerful emotional experience that results in the restructuring of the personality in the light of the beliefs that were previously assented to but that did not affect the believer's perception of the world in the same way.

Here the event complements the intensity of unrelieved stress that is evident in the first part of the vision, as we have explained above. The stress precipitated an intense experience that resulted in the reorientation of the seer's worldview. It is unparalleled in the apoca-lypses, which indicates, we venture to suggest, that behind it may well lie a personal experience of the author.

The transformation of the woman bears a striking similarity to 6:13–16. There Ezra is told that the earth will shake on the sound of a loud voice. Indeed, the voice is heard, it is the divine voice predicting the signs of the end, and after it has spoken, the earth does shake. The elements of voice and shaking of the earth, then, seem to be present, but typologically that which we have found in 10:25–28 is more primitive, for the sound of the voice has no cognitive content. Indeed, it seems likely that the basic pattern behind the elements of lightning, loud sound, and shaking of earth is the thunderstorm.

The various singular elements of the transformation do have parallels. The shining of the countenance (but not the lightning) is paralleled in 7:125, and see particularly the analysis of this element in 7:97 Commentary. In Dan 10:6 the face of the angel flashed like lightning; in Ezek 1:13 something like lightning is in the midst of the creatures. In general, as is evident from the similarity to the thunderstorm, the language of theophanies of God in the Bible often reflects lightning, thunder, and the shaking of the earth.[2]

The city that Ezra sees, of course, is the heavenly Jerusalem, as will be explained in the ensuing angelic interpretation.[3]

Commentary

■ **25** In the course of the transformation the woman's face shines like lightning. The shining faces of heavenly and exalted persons are a common theme; see the places cited in 7:99 Commentary. A similar thing is stated of the angel in Dan 10:6.[4]

■ **26** The earth quakes at fearsome and portentous events. The revelation at Sinai is associated with earthquake (3:18); the prophecy of the end in 6:15–16 causes the earth to shake. Loud cries accompany such events; see 6:13–14; and see also 5:5; 5:7; and 6:23, although there the contexts differ.

■ **27** This verse describes the transformation of the woman into a city. Elsewhere in the book we have reference to Zion or a city that will be manifested at the end. This we find in 7:26 (and see Commentary), 8:52 (and see Commentary), and 13:36. The city is pre-existent and wondrous. It is described as a city that is built or "established." The same expression occurs in other mentions of cities in the book (see 5:25; 7:6), and the term is discussed in 5:25 Commentary and 13:36. The special mention of the foundations may also be found in Rev 21:14 and 21:19, and they also figure in Heb 11:10. Note in Ezra 3:10–11 the importance of the laying of the foundations of the Temple.

The verse also describes Ezra's physical and mental state after the powerful emotional experience.[5] Much has been made by the commentators of whether the woman is the symbol of the heavenly Jerusalem, and particularly of how the symbol structure functions in the interpretation. We will discuss this in detail in 10:38–54

---

1 See the preliminary comments in Stone, "Reactions," 203, and see Introduction, sec. 4.4.3, where the phenomenon is discussed in further detail.

2 See 3:19 Commentary on some of these elements. The similarity is not total, however, and even texts like 1 Kgs 19:11–12 are not identical with our text.

3 On the meaning of the woman and son and their interpretation by the author, see 10:7 Commentary, 10:16 Commentary, and 10:38–54 Form and Function, pp. 333–35.

4 See also here 13:3. Extensive traditions relate to the shining of Adam's face before the Fall; see *Death of*

Adam 14 and commentary there. See also *1 Enoch* 38:4. In 7:99 Arabic2 reads "lightning" and not "sun." A heavenly woman is described in Rev 12:1. In *2 Apoc Bar* 53:8–12 "lightning" is the symbol of the Messiah, which shows its general associations.

5 See Function and Content, p. 336, and 5:14–15 Form and Structure, p. 115. The matter is discussed in detail in Excursus on Inspiration, p. 122.

Form and Function, pp. 333–35. It is not really relevant to the exegesis of the present verse as it stands.

■ **28** Uriel is the regular *angelus interpres* in this book.[6] Ezra's reproachful cry is unlike the rather humble petitions that come at this position in 12:3–9 and 13:13b–20. In Dan 7:15–16 and 8:15–17, the seer's bewilderment is noted and the angel is said to appear, with no prayer involved. The term for bewilderment here has been discussed above.[7]

---

6 See 4:1 Commentary.
7 See Excursus on Inspiration, p. 122, and 5:33 Commentary n. 13.

10

29 As I was speaking ªthese words,ª behold, ᵇ the angel who had come to me at first came to me, and he looked upon me **30/** as ᶜ I lay there like a corpse and I was deprived of my understanding. Then he grasped my right hand and strengthened me and set me on my feet, and said to me, **31/** "What is the matter with you? And why are you troubled? And why are your understanding and the thoughts of your mind troubled?"

32 I said to him, ᵈ "Because you have forsaken ᵉ me! For I did as you directed, ᶠ and, behold! ᵍ I saw, ʰand still see, ʰ what I am unable to explain."

33 He said to me, "Stand up ⁱlike a man, ⁱ and I will instruct you."

34 I said, "Speak, my lord; only do not forsake me, lest I die before my time. **35/** For I have seen what I did not know, ʲ and I have heard what I do not understand. **36/** Or is my mind deceived, ᵏ and my soul dreaming? ˡ **37/** Now therefore I entreat you to give your servant an explanation of this." ᵐ

Notes

29   a–a Lat *haec;* Syr *hlyn;* Eth, Ar1, Ar2 "thus"; Arm omits.

b The position of this word is uncertain; Lat Φ and Eth have it; other extant versions omit. See next note.

20   c Lat, Arm add "behold" here; cf. note b above.

32   d Lat Ms L, Syr, Georg, Ar1; Lat, Ar2, Arm omit; such instances are difficult to decide, but the weight of readings seems to bespeak accepting "to him."

e Lat, Eth, Ar1 seem to preserve reflexes of Hebrew infinitive absolute with finite verb.

f Lat, Ar1, Arm "according to your words" ("word" Arm); Ar2 omits.

g Ar1, Ar2 omit.

h–h Lat Mss C M N V, Eth, Ar1, Ar2 omit. It was certainly in the *Vorlage* of Lat, Syr; what is unclear is whether it was absent from some other Greek text (or Greek texts).

33   i–i Syr omits; Ar2 paraphrases.

35   j Eth, Ar1, Arm "seen"; perhaps Greek οἶδα/εἶδον.

36   k–l Ar1, Ar2 omit.

l Arm "astounded."

37   m Uncertain; Lat *excesso;* Syr *ḥzw' hn' dḥyl';* some Eth Mss "all"; Ar1 "this hidden speech"; Arm "these wonders." Probably all expansions, the translation follows Eth, Ar2.

Form and Structure

In 10:29 the appearance of the angel is described using a form very much like that in 5:31 and 7:1.[1] The angelic action here is different from those instances, however, for there the angelophany follows an address and precedes the ensuing dialogue. In the structure of the present vision, however, the encounter with the weeping woman intervenes between the speech and the angelophany, and the angel comes to explain the vision and its symbols, a much more traditional role.[2]

Ezra's emotional and physical state is set forth in 10:30. The angel strengthens him, and once again the language employed to describe this is like that in 5:14 (at the end of Vision 1). It is interesting to observe that this element occurs only in these two instances in the book, perhaps because the vision experience in both of these cases marks a sort of new beginning. Vision 1 starts the dialogues; the present vision marks the change from dialogue to something new. After this encounter, in 10:31–32 a short dialogue sequence ensues culminating in a request for enlightenment.

The appearance of the angel here, then, is like that in other apocalyptic visions, and in the remainder of Vision 4 he plays the conventional role of *angelus interpres.*[3]

Function and Content

This passage fulfills a number of functions both in its broader and in its narrower context. First, it introduces the same angel who had appeared before, thus supplying a link between this different vision experience and the

1   See in detail on angelophanies in 4 Ezra 4:1–25 Form and Structure, p. 80.

2   The overall structure is discussed in 9:38—10:4

Form and Structure, p. 311.

3   Collins, "Introduction," *Semeia* 14 (1979) 6, 24, et al.

first part of the book. Second, it conveys a very strong sense of Ezra's turmoil, which is evident from the description of him prostrate in a faint as well as from those things which he says in the course of the dialogue in 10:31–32. This aspect of the description is so much stronger than that which is found anywhere else in 4 Ezra that it must be regarded, at the very least, as a most sophisticated literary instrument. It is, however, much more probable that it is a faithful reflection of a particular experience of the author. The element of fear in reaction to the powerful vision experience is particularly notable (see below).

It is of considerable interest to contrast the question posed in 10:31 with that raised by 4:2. In both, the angel directs inquiries to the seer. In 4:2 he states: "Your understanding is confounded," and he inquires, "Why do you seek to comprehend the way of the Most High?"[4] Here, however, the angel simply asks, "Why is your understanding confounded?" A different perspective is reflected at this point. The angel makes his appearance in response not to an excited address but to a cry of despair rising from the powerful emotional experience the author has undergone. At issue is the seer's confusion of mind, the experience he has had, and not his attempt to understand something.[5]

In 10:33, Ezra is instructed to stand up. This element has occured before, in 4:47; 6:13; and 7:2. In all instances it is an angelic command. It might seem that here it is simply a natural result of the angel's comforting him, for he has fainted. However, the examination of the two earlier contexts shows that this is a sign that the revelation that is to follow is particularly solemn. It occurs again in the book, in 14:2, where Ezra rises, at God's command, to hear his direct summons.[6]

Chapter 10:35 is related to the end of the vision where the angel, in his concluding injunctions, says, "Go in and see . . . as far as it is possible for your eyes to see it, and afterward you will hear as much as your ears can hear" (10:55–56). In both instances, the sense of *tremendum*

surrounding the experience is clearly reflected, and the tension created here is released in 10:55–56. These verses are infused with a vivid sense of the limited ability of humans to comprehend such visions.

As is pointed out in 10:32 Commentary, the object of the vision is regarded with a deep sense of the ineffable. Ezra is to see and hear that which lies beyond the normal human perception. That the basis of this is real experience is confirmed by 10:34. There the seer expresses his fear of dying as a result of such an experience. The element of danger, which is known to accompany many trance experiences, is here clearly present, even though it is not common in the apocalypses.[7]

In broad terms, then, a progression may be observed. In 10:25, on the transformation of the woman, Ezra is frightened and "wondering what this meant." After the appearance of the city and the angel's encouragement in 10:35–36 he is more explicit: "I have seen what I did not know, and I have heard what I do not understand." He has come to realize that this fear-inspiring event is a revelation, but one beyond his capabilities to comprehend. The angel has explained the meaning of the vision to Ezra. In his command he negates both of Ezra's fears. In 10:25 Ezra said, "I was too frightened to approach her." In 10:55 the angel tells him not to fear but to enter the city. In 10:35 he has spoken of the inability of his eyes and ears to comprehend the vision. In 10:55–56 he is told to see as much and to hear as much as he can. The progression is clearly marked and very striking.

Commentary

■ **29** This verse opens the angelophany which forms the major subject of this section. The angel is Uriel, who has been Ezra's interlocutor in all the previous visions.[8]

■ **30** This verse describes the seer's reactions to the vision and the angel's deeds. The seer seems to have fainted, and in 5:14 too it says that he fell on his face after a vision. What is described here is not prostration which occasionally precedes the posing of a question,[9] while the

4 Similar but even milder is 5:33, which opens with "I will instruct you" (5:32).

5 Cf. the seer's confusion of mind and perplexity in 12:4–6. This was the result of the dream vision of the eagle, itself triggered, we are told (12:4), by Ezra's desire to understand the way of the Most High. See further 12:3b–9 Function and Content, pp. 354–55.

6 See 4:47 Commentary and 10:33 Commentary.

7 See further 10:34 Commentary.

8 On the role of angelophanies in the book, see 4:1–25 Form and Structure, p. 80, and Form and Structure, p. 329. On Uriel, see 4:1 Commentary.

9 On the prostration, see 4:11 Commentary. On the fainting and other reactions to visionary experiences, see 5:14–15 Form and Structure, p. 115, and Excursus on Inspiration, p. 122, where such expe-

setting on his feet resembles Ezek 2:1–2. The theme is also found elsewhere.[10] In all of these instances the angel's action is clearly indicated. The author describes the event as the departure of Ezra's understanding. Here "understanding," which has a number of meanings in the book, clearly denotes something like "consciousness."[11]

■ **31** The terms describing the seer's bewilderment of mind resulting from his experience resemble those describing Ezra's emotional and mental state before each of the first three visions.[12] Note also their similarity to the terms for the mental confusion that will form part of the messianic woes according to 5:9. Here the angel asks Ezra a question very similar to the one Ezra himself had posed to the woman in 9:42: "What has happened to you? Tell me!"

■ **32** The expression "and still see" should be noted. This implies that the builded city has not disappeared, that the vision was not a passing experience. The expression "what I am not able to understand" has been compared with 2 Cor 12:4, but in fact it differs. Indeed, there a vision experience is described, but the terminology points not to the incomprehensible nature of the vision but to the ineffable and inexpressible nature of what the visionary saw. That context is much more like 10:56, which makes the same point. Here, however, the inexplicability of the vision is under discussion.

■ **33** Ezra is commanded to stand on his feet. On the one

hand, this must be seen in the context of his prostrate position discussed in the previous pericope. On the other, as was pointed out in the discussion of 10:30, Ezra is repeatedly commanded to stand when some particularly momentous announcement or event is going to take place.[13]

■ **34** The most important point in this verse is the need Ezra feels for the angel's presence because of the danger that surrounds him in the course of his experience. This theme of the danger was prominent later in the Merkabah literature, where it accompanies the visionary in the course of his heavenly ascent.[14]

■ **35** On this verse, see Function and Content, p. 330.

■ **36** Here a dream is mentioned as something originating in confusion or sowing confusion. This attitude toward dreams should be contrasted with Visions 5 and 6, which are presented as dreams of the highest significance.[15] In the present context, Ezra's uncertainty, lack of understanding, and confusion are highlighted; deception of mind and dream are parallel to each other. The view that most dreams are deception of mind and only a few are divinely ordained is well set forth in ben Sira 34:1–8.

■ **37** The self-designation as "servant" and the corresponding use of "lord" for the angel are discussed in 5:56 Commentary.

---

riences elsewhere in the book are discussed.

10 See Function and Content, p. 330. In Dan 8:17–18 the seer's fainting and the angel's setting him on his feet are described. In Dan 10:8–10 the seer is set on his knees from a similar faint. The faint, with no raising up, is described in Rev 1:17. On Ezra's posture throughout the vision, see 9:27 Commentary. In *1 Enoch* 71:3–4, Enoch falls on his face when he sees heaven, and again in 71:11 when he sees God; cf. *2 Enoch* 22. One might wonder, at another level, whether some aspects of this scene might derive from court etiquette; cf., e.g.,

Esth 8:3–4.

11 See Excursus on Inspiration, p. 112.

12 See Excursus on Inspiration, p. 122. Cf. also the formulation of *2 Apoc Bar* 55:4, where the seer's state of mental confusion is described using very similar language.

13 See the discussion in 4:47 Commentary.

14 Cf. Exod 33:18–23. The danger in the Merkabah ascent is discussed by Scholem, *Major Trends*, 50; and idem, *Gnosticism*, 14–19.

15 See 11:1 Commentary, pp. 347–48.

10

38 He answered me and said, "Listen to me and I will [a]inform you, and tell you[a] about the things which you fear, for the Most High has revealed many secrets[b] to you. 39/ For he has seen your righteous conduct, that you have sorrowed greatly[c] for your people, and mourned greatly over Zion. 40/ This therefore is the word.[d] 41/ The woman who appeared to you a little while ago, [e]whom you saw[f] mourning and began to console— 42/ but you do not now see the form of a woman, but an established city [g]has appeared to you[g]— 43/ and as for her telling you about the misfortune of her son, [h]this is the interpretation:[h] 44/ This[i] woman whom you saw, whom you now behold as an established city, is Zion. 45/ And as for her telling you [j]that she was[j] barren for thirty years, (it is)[k] because there were[l] three thousand[m] years in the world before any offering was offered in it. 46/ And[n] after three thousand[o] years Solomon built the city,[p] and offered offerings;[q] then it was

Notes

38 a–a Lat, Syr, Ar1, Ar2 have two verbs; Eth, Arm have only a verb "to teach." Ar2 has moved the verb "to inform" to the end of the phrase. The two verbs in Ar1 are in the reverse order to Lat, Syr.

b Eth "a hidden secret"; Ar1 "a mighty secret"; Ar2 omits the adjective. Wellhausen suggests Hebrew רב taken wrongly as "many" rather than "great."

39 c Lat *sine intermissione;* similarly Arm. The other versions have simply "greatly."

40 d So Lat Mss V L (*sermo*), Syr, Eth, Arm (plural in Arm); only Lat Ψ C M N have *intellectus visionis,* which is probably an explanatory gloss. "Word" probably derived from λόγος and implies something like "meaning," "explanation," cf. Ar1: so also Violet 2.

41 e–f Lat, Ar1; the other versions omit; original is uncertain.

f Ar2 omits from this word to the end of 10:43.

42 g–g In Syr, Eth the woman is the subject of the verb.

43 h–h Eth, Arm omit; Violet 2 considers this a gloss in Greek.

44 i Ar2 resumes here, but its text of 10:44 seems to be a secondary invention to fill a lacuna.

45 j–j Eth, Ar1, Arm "I was"; original cannot be determined, see note r-r below on 10:47.

k So Lat, accepted in translation here only for stylistic reasons.

l The variation of the verbs in the versions probably goes back to something like a dative of possession and a verb "to be" in Greek.

m Most Lat Mss omit; the others have various editorial supplements of which A** succeeds in restoring *tria milia.* The *Vorlage* of Arm may have had the same omission, since Arm reads "many years"; see note o below on 10:46. Probably goes back to γ' for ,γ. (Box).

46 n Lat, Syr add: "it came to pass"; the variant is not uncommon.

o Lat omits; see 10:45 note m above. The whole numeral "three thousand" is omitted by Ar2, Arm.

p Lat Ms L adds *civitatis murum iherusalem et templum domino in eo construxit;* Ar1, Arm add "and the temple"; Ar2 reads "an altar" for "the city"; these are all probably exegetical; cf. Stone, "Manuscripts and Readings," 51–52, and 3:24 Commentary.

q Syr, Ar1, Arm add "in it"; Ar2 adds "to the Most High"; probably expansions.

that the barren woman bore a son. 47/ And as for her telling you [r]that she brought him up with much care, [r] that was the (period of) residence in Jerusalem. 48/ And as for her saying to you, 'When my son entered his wedding chamber he died,' [s]and that misfortune had overtaken her, [t] that was the destruction which befell Jerusalem. 49/ And behold, [u] you saw her likeness, how she mourned for her son, [v] and you began to console her for what had happened. [w] 50/ For now the Most High, seeing that you are sincerely [x] grieved and profoundly [y] distressed for her, has shown you the brilliance of her glory, and the loveliness of her beauty. 51/ Therefore I told you to remain in the field where no house had been built, 52/ for I knew that the Most High would [z] reveal all [a] these things to you. 53/ Therefore I told you to go into the place [b] where there was no foundation of any building, 54/ for no work of man's building could endure in a place where the city of the Most High was to be [c] revealed.

47   r–r Direct speech in Eth, Ar1; cf. note j–j above on 10:45; Arm omits verse.

48   s–t Syr omits.
      t Lat *ei;* Eth "me"; Ar1 first person; Ar2 "her"; Arm omits.

49   u Syr, Ar2, Arm omit.
      v Syr, Eth "sons."
      w Lat adds *haec erant tibi apparienda;* Ar2 adds "and all this God showed and revealed to you"; there is a lacuna in Syr.

50   x Literally, "with all [Ar1, Lat omit 'all'] your soul" Lat, Syr, Eth, Ar1.
      y Literally, "with all [Ar1 omits 'all'] your heart" Lat, Syr, Eth, Ar1, Arm.

52   z The versions seem to imply Greek μέλλειν here.
      a Lat omits.

53   b Lat "field"; Eth "thither"; Violet 2 suggests Greek τόπος to explain all readings.
      c The versions seem to imply Greek μέλλειν here.

Form and Structure

This pericope contains the angel's interpretation of the vision that Ezra saw. It is all in the form of an address by the *angelus interpres,* with no intervening questions by the seer.

A. 10:38–39 Introduction
This establishes the special nature of what is to follow. The passage opens in 10:38a, as similar predictions often do, with a call for attention. Such a call is to be found most fully developed in 5:32, where it is composed of two synonymously parallel stichs: "Listen to me, and I will instruct you; pay attention to me, and I will tell you more." Here it is as if the first verb of the second hemistich has been lost, and exactly the same structure may be observed in 7:49. This call is followed by the pronouncement about the nature of the prediction to follow in the expression "the Most High has revealed many secrets to you"(10:38b).[1]

B. 10:40–49 Detailed Interpretation of the Vision
1. 10:40 Formal heading of the interpretation, "This therefore is the word (i.e., meaning)." General titles of interpretations occur also in 12:10, "This is the interpretation of this vision which you have seen," and in 13:25, "This is the interpretation of the vision." Note also the title and conclusion of the segment in 7:78–99. In 10:41–43 we find a sort of preliminary summary, comparable perhaps to 13:21–24 and 12:11–12. The inter-

pretation proper follows. At the start of the interpretations of Vision 5 and Vision 6, we find "Behold, days are coming" (12:13 and 13:29), which is not found here. This formal difference also reflects a difference of content. The phrase "Behold, days (times) are coming" usually marks eschatological prophecy in the book (see 5:1 Commentary). The eschatological character of the predictions in those two visions is already marked in 10:59, where they are called "what the Most High will do to those who dwell on earth in the last days." Vision 4, however, is not marked as eschatological in the same sense.

2. 10:41–43 Summary of the contents of the vision, again ending with the phrase "This is the interpretation."
3. 10:44–48 Detailed interpretation of elements of the vision a number of which have already been listed in 10:41–43: 10:44—the woman, who is Zion (repeating 10:42); 10:45—her thirty years' barrenness, which is three thousand years before offerings were made in Zion (repeating 10:43); 10:46—Solomon built the city and made offerings, which is the birth of the woman's son (not mentioned in 10:41–43); 10:47—she nurtured him with care, which is the period of residence of Israel in Jerusalem (not mentioned in 10:41–43); 10:48—the death of the son is the destruction of Zion (not mentioned in 10:41–43).

In 9:38—10:4 Function and Content, p. 312, those

1   Such calls for attention are found, of course, in prophecy and wisdom texts such as Prov 1:8; Ps 34:11; and Isa 1:10 and 48:12.

elements found in the vision which are not discussed at all in the interpretation are considered.

A final point about this part of the exegesis is that while in 10:44; 10:45; and 10:47–48 the symbol is given first, and then its interpretation, in 10:46 the interpretation precedes the symbol. This variation contrasts with the regularity with which, overwhelmingly throughout the interpretation of the following visions, the symbol precedes the explanation in the formula "As for your seeing . . . this is . . ." or "This is the interpretation."[2]

10:49–54 Explanation This part of the pericope explains Ezra's experience to him, and not the symbolism of the vision. Verse 49 holds a transitional position, being an explanation of the symbolism but formulated in terms of Ezra's subjective experience.

1. 10:49–50 explains the reason for Ezra's experience of the woman.

2. 10:51–54 explains by way of summary and conclusion the very first element in Vision 4, the field.

Function and Content

This pericope is the interpretation of the vision. As such it shares with other interpretations of visions certain elements of structure and overall patterns which were described in the preceding section. The content of this passage is of very considerable interest.

The angel in his address is solicitous first to allay the seer's fear. This he does in 10:38–39, and at the same time he introduces the theme of the revelation of secrets to Ezra. Indeed, the passage is bracketed by references to the revelation of secrets, for they recur in 10:55–56, thus forming a sort of *inclusio*. Above we pointed to the fact that 10:35 tells us of the seer's confusion and 10:56 of its reversal. This dynamic also enhances the point made by the references to the revelation of secrets. After all, in 10:55–56 he is told to enter the city and see and hear as much as his capabilities allow. This becomes possible because the angel succeeds in allaying his terror.

A change takes place, therefore, in the view of what is revealed to Ezra. It is described as "great secrets" (see textual note b), and the term "secret" is otherwise applied only to the esoteric revelations to Abraham (3:14) and to Moses (14:5–6), to the eschatological revelation of the eagle vision (12:36), as well as by implication to the esoteric books revealed to Ezra in 14:46.

Certain predictions earlier in the book were said to be specially revealed to Ezra alone (see 7:44 and 8:62),[3] and these are obvious references to eschatological predictions.[4] After the present point in the book, Ezra receives more and deeper revelations of secrets and eventually takes on a full prophetic role.[5] This apparently contradicts Ezra's being without wisdom, as stated clearly in Visions 1 and 2, where his knowledge of cosmological and similar secrets is denied. Here, in contrast, the revelation to him of eschatological secrets forms a climax of the book, and this is not a new view, for in chapter 3 it is already stated of Abraham.[6]

The whole passage makes three chief points: in 10:38–39 Ezra is told that the vision is the revelation of secrets; in 10:40–50 he is given the actual meaning of the vision; and in 10:51–54 he is told that he is in a particular place in which such a special secret will be revealed to him.

A further observation should be made about the content of the vision and its interpretation. In his vision Ezra sees both the woman and her transformation into the builded city. Both elements are parts of the vision, but they differ. The woman whom Ezra saw symbolizes Zion, while the city he saw, her true nature, does not symbolize Zion, it is Zion.[7] Both elements, however, are seen in the vision, and both are explained in the interpretation. What is more interesting is that there is no suggestion that the city disappears or that Ezra awakes from a "dream." Indeed, the city is clearly very much present in the next pericope, for Ezra is told to enter it! So this is no passing dream.

The restoration of Zion is the actual message of the vision and its interpretation. This is the central part of the consolation which Ezra has been seeking. After all, at

2   Cf. 12:10–36 Form and Structure, p. 360, and 13:20b–55 Form and Structure, pp. 394–95.

3   See also 13:53; cf. 12:36 and 13:14.

4   See also *2 Apoc Bar* 20:3–4 and Stone, *Features*, 27.

5   See further 12:37–39 Function and Content, p. 373; 12:40–51 Function and Content, p. 376.

6   See, e.g., 5:39; see 5:31–40 Function and Content, p. 135, and 5:36 Commentary, where the limits of knowledge in 4 Ezra are discussed. The apparent contradiction is analyzed in 14:3–18 Function and Content, p. 417.

7   On Zion as mother, see 10:16 Commentary.

the beginning of chapter 3 the problem which precipitates the whole of the first three visions is the problem of the destruction of Jerusalem. Another part of the consolation offered is the promise of Ezra's personal reward. This had been made at the end of Vision 3. The various psychological and emotional events that have deeply affected the seer were dealt with in the discussion of 10:29–37 Function and Content, p. 330.

From the above, it follows that we have taken a position on the vexed question of the exact meaning of the city and the son. As stated, 10:44 identifies the city as Zion. In 10:46–48 the usual order of interpretative statements (i.e., symbol followed by interpretation) is reversed. The interpretation is given first, followed by the symbols. We set out the interpretations and symbols offered in this passage in tabular form. The letters A and B indicate the actual order of the elements in the text.

	Symbol		Interpretation
44	the woman who becomes a city (A)	=	Zion (B)
45	the thirty years' barrenness (A)	=	3,000 years of no offering (B)
46	the woman bore a son (B)	=	Solomon built the city and offered sacrifice (A)
47	the woman nurtured him (A)	=	period of residence (B)
48	when the son entered his nuptial chamber he died (A)	=	destruction (B)

This is the plain meaning of the symbolism offered by the text. In it one can observe no explanation or interpretation of the son; indeed, he is merely a cardboard player. The center stage is held by the woman and city; the things that happen to her are interpreted in terms of the city. Among them are the birth, nurture, and death of the son. The birth is a new, happy beginning; the nurture a period of peace; and the death the tragedy of destruction. The son as such plays a completely passive role.[8]

The revelation of the city is not tied by the author to an eschatological or heavenly context. The city is seen as real (see 10:32 Commentary); Ezra is commanded to enter it and experience it (10:55–57). Questions as to whether the city is the heavenly Jerusalem or an eschatological one should probably be answered with an ambiguous "Yes!"

This ambiguity may be seen when we consider the following. In 10:46, Solomon is said to have built the city (so too was David in 3:24). At the same time, 9:24 and particularly 10:54 stress greatly that no human building could stand where the city of the Most High was to be revealed. The conflict between the assertions about the city is very clear.

To judge from what is said elsewhere in the book, the author expected the revelation of a city at the eschaton (see 7:26) and also included it in the lists of the rewards of the righteous (8:52).[9]

The point is that Ezra here is singled out particularly for the revelation of secrets previously given only to

---

8 Consequently, it follows that the views of Kabisch (followed by Box), according to which the woman is the heavenly Jerusalem and the son the earthly Jerusalem, have no basis in the text. See Kabisch, pp. 85–91; and Box, pp. 232–33. This view is also followed by Thompson, *Responsibility*, 221. The "buttressing" of these interpretations by opinions as to what the author of the supposed S document could, or could not, have said or thought serves only further to weaken an already rickety edifice. Therefore, most of the scholarly debate has been about a pseudo-issue. See further 10:16 Commentary. The attempt recently reasserted by Geoltrain in his comment to 10:45, to see the son's death as referring to the death of the Messiah, had already rightly been rejected by Sjöberg, *Menschensohn*, 135–37. Sjöberg's outline of the symbolism on p. 137 resembles ours, though he has not pursued his analysis to its conclusion. Cf. also the somewhat similar analysis by Brandenburger, *Verborgenheit*, 82.

9 The dual nature of the city is discussed in detail in 7:26 Commentary. See Sjöberg, *Menschensohn*, 135–37, who discussed clearly, but briefly, the ambiguities in the concept of the woman/city. See also 10:21 Commentary.

Abraham and Moses (3:14 and 14:5–6) because he has grieved over Zion (10:39).[10] This grief, of course, has been the motive force of the book from the start of Vision 1. At the same time, Ezra's understanding has sufficiently developed for him to take on the prophetic and angelic role of comforting and learning secrets. This change has been signaled since the end of Vision 3 and has reached its peak in the transformation and conversion experiences (10:25–37).[11] Once he can offer comfort, once he has accepted the righteousness of God, he is given comfort himself. The revelation of the future or heavenly city and the experience of it are the true comfort for his grief over Zion's fall. From this point in the book Ezra ceases to mourn and becomes the recipient of eschatological revelations.

Commentary

■ **38** This verse is discussed in Form and Structure, p. 333. Note also that "many secrets" perhaps ought to be "great secrets," as is explained in textual note b. The word "secrets" is rare in the book and is an indication of rather special material to follow.[12]

■ **39** This verse explains why Ezra was considered worthy to receive the great revelation of this vision and interpretation. Similar assertions are found on a number of occasions in the book, and reasons are usually offered.[13] The reason given is often related to the context of the statement, and here, as in 10:50, it is said to be his grief over Zion. A similar sentiment is found in the dictum attributed to R. Papa: "Everyone who mourns over Jerusalem will have the privilege of seeing her joy" (b. Baba Batra 60b).[14]

■ **40** This is the general start of the interpretation. A similar expression occurs in 4:47 and particularly preceding the interpretations of the symbolic dreams in Visions 5 and 6.[15] On the meaning of "word" here, see textual note d.

■ **41** This verse, which forms part of a summary of the preceding events, refers to the matters related in 9:38—

10:4. Ezra continues to console the woman throughout the address and dialogue in 10:5–24. The rebukeful nature of this consolation is not brought up!

■ **42** The events referred to are related in 10:27.

■ **43** This verse is the end of the long summary of the vision that started in 10:41. The expression "This is the interpretation" marks the shift from relating the symbol to offering its explanation.[16] The events are narrated in 10:1; compare 10:15, and perhaps 10:20 is also reminiscent of the same language of misfortune.

■ **44** Mourning for the city or Zion has been, of course, the central motive of the book so far; that mourning finds its consolation in the present chapter. The use of "city" in the context of consolation is significantly dominant; see 3:1; 3:27; et al. Eschatological reward includes a city (see 7:6 Commentary); heavenly Jerusalem will appear as part of the eschatological events (7:26 Commentary). Jerusalem as mourning mother and glorious city is the chief subject of the present vision (see 10:7 Commentary). Moreover, 4 Ezra particularly likes to call cities "established" or "built" (see 5:25 Commentary).

■ **45** The events referred to are related in 9:43–44. For "thirty," Latin reads "three," which number is accepted by Gunkel but is secondary, as has been pointed out in the textual notes. The idea of barrenness is used metaphorically in 4 Ezra on a number of occasions; see particularly 5:1 and 6:28, both of which are related to the eschatological events. The woman's thirty-year barrenness is interpreted as three thousand years in which no offerings were made in Zion. The centrality of the offerings in the Temple goes back, of course, to ancient ideas of the world-sustaining function of Temple cult. In 3:24, which also deals with the building of the Temple, the making of offerings is highlighted. Offerings form part of the subject matter of special revelations made to apocalyptic seers in 2 Apoc Bar 59:9 and Bib Ant 19:10. The latter sets *mensuram sanctuarii et numerum oblationum* ("the measure of the sanctuary and the

---

10   On Ezra's special virtues, see 6:32 Commentary.

11   See Function and Content, p. 334.

12   See Function and Content, p. 334, on this term and its full implications.

13   See 6:32 Commentary for a detailed discussion.

14   At that point, the Talmud has a detailed discussion of the extreme mourning customs attributed to certain groups, devoted to mourning over the destruction of

the Temple.

15   The detailed discussion of the structure of the interpretation may be found in Form and Structure, pp. 333–34.

16   See also Form and Structure, p. 333, on the relationship of these elements.

number of the offerings") among the things revealed to Moses.[17]

It may be asked what was the significance of the figure 3,000. Did it actually relate to some era of creation according to which the building of the Temple was *anno mundi* 3,000? Some such reckonings are known from later than 4 Ezra and they set the building of the Temple early in the fifth millennium.[18] Some sort of millennial reckoning is also at play in the fragmentary verses at the start of the *Testament of Moses* (1:2), where a date of 2,500 is given, apparently *anno mundi*, and seemingly related to the life of Moses. If these assumptions are correct, this reckoning, in general, might be like that in 4 Ezra here.

A reckoning like the conventional one mentioned above is much more likely to be reflected in the date given in 14:48, which sets Ezra's assumption at five thousand years, three months, and twenty-two days. According to this, however, the building of the Temple could not have been in the year 3,000. The date of the building of the Temple may have been reached schematically. If by the time of 4 Ezra the idea of the world age of 6,000 years had developed, to be followed by a seventh, sabbatical, millennium, then 3,000 would be the middle point of the world age. On the other hand, it can be maintained that such an idea is probably later than the end of the first century c.e.; moreover, its implications are in conflict with 4 Ezra's sense of the impending end. Further, it might be added that if the division of the world age into twelve parts in 14:11–12 is taken seriously, and each of these parts is 500 years, that would support the idea of there being a world age of $12 \times 500 = 6,000$ years. Ezra would then be living in the period from 4,500 to 5,000, which would, once more, conflict with all of the above schemes.[19]

However, considering 4 Ezra's reserve about exactly this sort of special information, the two and a half parts remaining according to 14:11–12 might well be typological and dependent on Daniel "two times and half a time" (Dan 12:7). Daniel is referred to explicitly in that

pericope. It may be that the author used all sorts of symbolic and typological dating schemes to make his point about the imminence of the end, or of Ezra's assumption, or of the centrality of the building of the Temple, without ever working them together into a single, coherent scheme.

The word *saeculum* and equivalents reflect an ambiguous Hebrew, and this is one of a number of instances in which it is impossible to determine whether its precise connotation is "age" or "world."

■ **46** Jerusalem is typically "the City of David" (see 3:24 Commentary) and in 3:24 has David as builder of the city and he who offered sacrifices in it (see Commentary there). Scholars have made much of the fact that here these deeds are attributed to Solomon, and many scholars have suggested emending Solomon to David (e.g., Box and Kabisch). In the Armenian version and Latin Ms L of 3:24, Solomon's role is mentioned, but that is probably secondary.[20] Knibb points out that "neither David nor Solomon actually built Jerusalem, but both made additions to it" (referring to 2 Sam 5:9; 11:1; and 1 Kings 6–7, to which further citations could be added). It has already been observed that the characterization "built city" is most central of Jerusalem in this book, indeed of cities in general as mentioned by the book.[21] The emphasis on "built" might explain the difficulty raised by Knibb: David and Solomon both might have been said to *build* the city, even though that was not precise, because of the importance of "built cities" for 4 Ezra. Furthermore, the very point being made by 4 Ezra arises from the destruction of the city, which is of course the opposite of its being built. Above all, however, this is a stereotypical history, and in such a stereotype the building after barrenness is what makes the point.[22] A clear distinction was not always made between city and temple and consequently the indiscriminate confusion of the names of David and Solomon is not surprising.

■ **47** The events referred to by this verse are related in 9:45–46. It is to be noted that the marriage of the son

---

17   See 10:5–24 Form and Function, n. 6, on this matter.

18   See Stone, *Patriarchs and Prophets*, 82–83.

19   See further 14:11 Commentary. A world age of 4,000 years seems to be implied in *Bib Ant* 28:8.

20   See further 3:24 Commentary.

21   See 5:25 Commentary.

22   In *2 Apoc Bar* 61:2 the time of David and Solomon is characterized at that of the building of the city and the dedication of the altar.

(9:47) is not given any interpretation by the angel. Those scholars like Box and Kabisch who insisted that the woman is the heavenly Jerusalem were faced with the problem of explaining the "dwelling" mentioned here. They generally talked of the Shechinah dwelling in Jerusalem until the destruction of the Temple. In our view, however, this is unnecessarily complicated and the "dwelling" means the dwelling of Israel in Jerusalem which was ended by the destruction.[23] The "care" is probably God's sending of the prophets and judges to lead and reprove Israel.

■ 48 This verse refers to the events related in 10:1–2. The destruction of Jerusalem is a central theme of 4 Ezra, as we have remarked.

■ 49 The events referred to in this verse are related in 9:38–40 and 10:6–24. Ezra's consolation, it is implied, is effective in a remarkable way, while that of the townsfolk is not (10:2). The chief exegetical problem of the verse is the word "likeness," Latin *similitudo* and Syriac *dmwt'*. The Latin word occurs on a number of occasions in the book, but there it means something like "parable."[24] Here it simply means "appearance," that is, "You saw her appearance, how she mourned."[25] The imagery and language used of Zion underlies the passage, of course, as is clear from the linguistic similarity with *2 Apoc Bar* 10:7: "Because we see the afflictions of Zion, and what has befallen Jerusalem."[26]

■ 50 On first examination, this verse seems to refer to the events related in 10:21–23, Ezra's expression of grief for Zion which forms part of his comfort offered to the woman. Ezra's grief for Zion is a theme often repeated in the book; see 5:21; 5:34; 8:15; and 10:39. In this chapter his mourning for Zion is the qualification for his receiving the revelation of the heavenly city.[27] Of course, such comfort corresponds well to the cause of the grief. Ezra's

grief is described as "sincere" and "profound," and these terms actually translate "with all your heart" and "with all your soul," reminiscent of the *Shema'* in Deut 6:5, which is also taken up in the New Testament (Mark 12:30 and parallels).

What is intriguing here is that apparently "for her" is already shifting to mean "Zion." Admittedly, the literal context seems to say that because Ezra is sincerely grieving for the woman, therefore God showed him the heavenly Zion. That does not make much sense, however, and the technique of double entendre noted above is here employed again (cf. 10:5–7 and Commentary there). Here is another twist on the changing of roles that was noted above to be typical of this vision. The woman's grief has elicited Ezra's expression of mourning for Zion, and that is described here as his concern for the woman, who is indeed Zion, though that is not yet explicit in the interpretation. The psychological dynamic is quite clear.

The idea of glory in 4 Ezra has been discussed in detail above in 3:19 Commentary and 7:42 Commentary. Here we need just remark that Zion's glory is related to God's. Just as God's abandonment of Zion is the removal of his glory (see already Ezek 10:18–19 and 4 Ezra 10:23), so the restoration of Zion will involve a renewal of her glory and of God's indwelling; see *2 Apoc Bar* 32:4; Bar 5:1; and *Sib Or* 5:420–428; and cf. Ps 50:2.[28]

■ 51 The events referred to in this verse are related in 9:24. Box is of the opinion that 10:51–52 is a secondary doublet of 10:53–54. What is certain is that 10:51 and 10:53 are particularly close. The verse highlights the importance of the physical setting of the vision, which has been discussed above.[29] The observation certainly adds to the sense of realism that the author builds around the appearance of heavenly Jerusalem.

---

23 It might be commented that the idea of the Shechinah ceasing to dwell in heavenly Jerusalem is also an odd one. The contortions required by the imposition of the wrong conceptual structure are considerable.

24 See 4:3; 4:47; and 8:2. See 4:3 Commentary.

25 Therefore it should not be related, as Violet and Box do, to the "pattern" of the heavenly city; cf. Exod 25:9; 25:40; *2 Apoc Bar* 59:4–5; Heb 8:5; etc. Clearly, Ezra did not see the heavenly prototype of the city or the heavenly city until the transformation took place, and that is not related until 10:50.

26 Cf. similar expressions in *2 Apoc Bar* 77:8.

27 See 6:32 Commentary for a full discussion of this.

28 "Glory" is associated with brightness; see 10:25. And the promise of the eschatological city is a well-known one in the book; see 7:26 Commentary. Cf. the expression with *Ps Sol* 2:5 referring to the Temple.

29 See 9:26–28 Form and Function, pp. 304–5.

■ **52** No commentary.

■ **53** The events referred to are, once again, those in 9:24. Note, however, that the foundations are not mentioned there. They play a special role, as has been noted above in 10:26 Commentary.

■ **54** The heavenly city has been discussed above. See on it, and on the terminology "city" or "Zion," 7:26 Com-

mentary. On the appropriateness of the field, see 9:24 Commentary and particularly 9:29 Commentary.

10

55 "Therefore do not be afraid, and do not let your heart be terrified; but go in and see the splendor and vastness of the building, [a] as far as it is possible for your eyes to see it, 56/ and afterward you will hear as much as your ears can hear. 57/ For you are more blessed than many, and you have been named [b] before the Most High, as but few have been. 58/ But tomorrow night you shall remain here. 59/ and the Most High will show you in those [c]dream visions[c] what the Most High will do to those who dwell on earth in the last days."

60 So I slept [d] that night and the following one, as he had commanded me.

Notes

55   a Eth "walls"; Ar1 adds "of that city."

57   b Syr, Eth, Ar1, Ar2; Lat *vocatus;* Arm "are pleasing."

59   c–c Lat, Eth, Arm (singular Arm); Syr has *ḥzw' dglyn',* similar to Ar1 "revelation of the vision"; Ar2 "the other visions."

60   d Lat, Eth; Syr, Ar1, Ar2 add "there"; it seems difficult to determine originality here and either Lat, Eth or Syr, Ar1, Ar2 might be accepted. Arm has "fell asleep" in Mss H W, while *Y* has the graphically similar "entered the house." However, Arm contradicts its own text in 10:58. Consequently, it may be regarded as glossed here, and its underlying text presumably did not have "here" or else the gloss would have been superfluous.

Form and Structure

This pericope forms the conclusion and the injunctions of the fourth vision. In general terms, it occurs at the point where similar passages occur in the first three visions. Its verses can be characterized as follows.

A. *Encouragement (10:55)*—cf. 10:38

B. *Injunctions (10:55b–56)*

C. *Explanation (10:57)*

D. *Concluding Injunctions (10:58–59)*

Function and Content

Although the structure of this pericope resembles that of the injunctions at the end of the preceding visions, its actual contents differ. In the words of encouragement in 10:55, Ezra is told not to fear because the Most High has chosen to reveal wonders to him. The phrasing is interestingly parallel to 6:33: "Believe and do not be afraid." In 6:33 the word "believe" comes at the start of the revelation of redemption, for in all the preceding signs, only woes have been foretold. Here, however, the word "believe" is not found, since Ezra already believes; indeed, it is his belief that has precipitated the fear. Similarly, the whole of 8:46–62 forms a parallel to this, for it too is a revelation of redemption. This is also indicated by 8:62, which states that the revelation has been made only to Ezra and the few like him, a standard element of special revelations.

In 10:55b, Ezra is told to go in and see the building. As has been noted above, this clearly implies that the building is still there, a point already stressed in 10:32: "I saw, and still see." What is not clear is whether "and afterward" in 10:56 implies "after you have entered the building" or "in the coming revelations." We tend to prefer the former explanation, particularly in view of 10:35, but the latter is certainly possible. If the reference is to what Ezra sees in the building, then that is never discussed further in the book, although there were narratives of the appearance of the heavenly city, its details, and even its measurements in other apocalypses.[1] This is the case, in whichever way the seeing and hearing are taken. Moreover, the interpretation that 10:56 means "after you have entered the building" receives direct support from the fact that the promise of the next revelation is actually given three verses later, in 10:59.

The expression "as much as" is worthy of note. It is related to 4 Ezra's reserved views about revelations of special knowledge. Thus, although there is no parallel to a command like this in the rest of the book, it may contain a hint at the full revelation of consolation which will in fact resolve the issue raised at the start of Vision 1. This resolution of the issue, however, is not made explicit verbally but remains at an experiential level and was regarded, at least, as esoteric. The expression "eye cannot see, ear cannot hear," which lies behind the text

---

1   At the most formal we may observe the parallel in Ezekiel 40–48 and the *Description of the New Jerusalem* from Qumran.

here, is a *topos* indicating eschatological revelation.[2]

In 10:57, Ezra is proclaimed to be elected. For this, the expression "named" is employed, which does not occur earlier in the book. Ezra is similarly regarded earlier in the book. So, for example, 8:62 says that the revelation is made only to Ezra and a few like him. Nothing like this is said, however, at the end of the preceding visions. Once again, as in 10:55–56, this verse seems to refer to some revelation transcending that which the book says was granted to Ezra and which stretched the author's view of special knowledge to its limits. This might be the entry into the city, but then the city would be the heavenly palace of God, an idea not in itself strange but certainly out of tune with the main *Tendenz* of 4 Ezra. Alternatively, the verse might refer to Ezra's assumption, which is related in chapter 14 (see especially 14:9).

In 10:58–59 we find the concluding injunctions. These include three elements: *(a)* Remain here two nights; *(b)* you will experience dream visions; and *(c)* the visions will concern "what he will do to those on earth at the end of days," that is, a particular part of eschatology.

The structure of these injunctions may be compared instructively with the end of Vision 3. There Ezra was to remain for seven nights, to observe a partial fast, and to pray, and he would, as a result, receive a waking vision (9:23–25). Here two nights, no fast, and the dream vision are mentioned. In addition, the venue is stressed. Moreover, it is significant that sleep is mentioned here, something that does not occur in Visions 1–3 or 5–6. Ezra is promised the revelations of "whatever it pleases the Most High to show you."[3]

Commentary

■ **55** The actual terms referring to the revelation to Ezra

and the nature of what was revealed have been discussed in Function and Content, p. 340. The expression "splendor" is also used of the revelation of the eschatological glory of God in 7:42. As has been pointed out, this verse and the next seem to preserve a reminiscence of the citation of the Elijah apocryphon also quoted in 1 Cor 2:9.

■ **56** No commentary.

■ **57** The verse speaks of Ezra's election or special role. That he is like only few, particularly in the contexts of revelation and reward, is an idea that occurs elsewhere in the book (3:14 [Abraham]; 8:62 Commentary). The idea of being named by God has various connotations; indeed, it is deeply related to the idea of name in general. "In biblical thought a name is not a mere label of identification; it is an expression of the essential nature of its bearer. A man's name reveals his character. Adam was able to give names to beasts and birds (Gen 2:20) because, as Milton says, he understood their nature (*Paradise Lost*, bk. VIII, ll.352–3)."[4]

According to 5:26, Israel is the dove that God has named for himself and God has named Israel by special names (6:58) or by his own name (4:25 and Commentary there). This idea is well expressed in Isa 45:4 (referring to Cyrus): "For the sake of my servant Jacob, and Israel my chosen, I call you by your name, I surname you, though you do not know me." Therefore, although there is no precise parallel to this expression elsewhere in the book, it clearly refers to the election of Ezra by God. Chapter 14:35 reflects the same concept of name.

■ **58** No commentary.

■ **59** The verse refers to a future dream vision that is going to be revealed to Ezra. This introduces a new sort of vision into the book, for, although the previous visions had been night visions, they were apparently regarded as

---

2   See Stone and Strugnell, *Elijah*, 41–47. Add to the texts given there Hippolytus, *Refut.* 5.24.1 (GCS 26, p. 51), and cf. the textual form there with that in Stone-Strugnell, III c. Cf. also Hippolytus, *Refut.* 5.26.16 (GCS 26, p. 129); 5.27.2 (GCS 26, p. 133); and 6.24.4 (GCS 26, p. 151). See the article of P. Prigent, "'Ce que l'oeil n'a pas vu,' 1 Cor 2,9," *TZ* 14 (1958) 416–29. E. von Nordheim, "Das Zitat des Paulus in 1.Kor. 2,9 und seine Beziehung zum koptischen Testamentum Jacobs," *ZNW* 65 (1974) 112–20, claims that it is a citation from the *Testament of Jacob,* which is denied by H. D. F. Sparks, "1 Kor.

2.9, A Quotation from the Coptic Testament of Jacob?" *ZNW* 76 (1976) 269–76. This discussion was continued in *NTS* 26 (1978) 270–83 in an article by K. Berger, "Zur Discussion über die Herkunft von 1 Kor 2.9," who adds a number of further citations. This debate arose in the literature while the book by Stone-Strugnell, *Elijah*, was in the printer's hands.

3   On similar promises, see 5:32 Commentary.

4   *IDB*, s.v. "Name."

waking visions.[5] The dream vision is, of course, quite common in the apocalypses. The vision is of that which will befall "those who dwell upon the earth." As has been pointed out, in 4 Ezra this expression occurs predominantly in eschatological contexts.[6]

Indeed, this verse is full of terminology that is regularly used in 4 Ezra for eschatological events. This includes the expression "last days," which, together with "last times," regularly refers either to the messianic woes or to the events of judgment.[7] Here the revelation of the events of the last generation including the destruction of Rome is intended. 4 Ezra mentions these last events, in one form or another, rather frequently.[8] Here for the first time, in a conclusion and injunctions section, the coming vision is said to be of these terrible events.

---

5   See 3:1 Commentary.
6   See 5:1 Commentary.
7   See 6:34; 7:73; 7:77; 7:84; 7:87; 7:95; 8:50; and 8:63. The terminology is discussed, together with its possible Hebrew original, in Stone, *Features*, 53. Similar terms also occur in 1QpHab 9:6; 1QSa 1:1; et al., and in other Qumran writings.
8   On the references in 4 Ezra, see 4:52 Commentary.

11

1 aAnd it came to pass a on the second night b I
had a dream, c and behold, d there came up
from the sea an eagle that had twelve e
wings and three heads.

2 And I looked, and behold, he spread f his
wings over all the earth, and all the winds of
heaven blew upon him, g and the clouds
were gathered about him. h 3/ And I looked,
and out of his wings there grew opposing
wings; and i they became little, puny wings.
4/ But his heads were at rest; the middle
head was larger than jthe other heads, j but
it also was at rest with them.

5 And I looked, and behold, the eagle flew k with
his wings, to reign over the earth and over
those who dwell in it. 6/ And I saw how all
things under heaven were subjected to him,
and no one spoke against him, not even one
of the creatures that was on the earth.

7 And I looked, and behold, the eagle rose upon
his talons, and uttered a cry to his wings,
saying, 8/ "Do not all watch at the same
time; let each sleep in his own place, and
watch in his turn; 9/ but let the heads be
reserved for the last."

10 And I looked, and behold, l the voice did not
come from his heads, but from the midst of
his body. 11/ And I counted his opposing
wings, and m there were eight of them.

12 And I looked, nand behold, n on the right side
one wing arose, and it reigned over all the
earth. 13/ oAnd while o it was reigning, its
end came to it and it disappeared, so that its
place was not seen. Then the next wing arose
and reigned, and pit continued to reign p a
long time. 14/ qAnd while q it was reigning r
its end came also, so that it disappeared like
the first. 15/ And behold, a voice sounded,
saying to it, 16/ "Hear me, you who have
ruled the earth sall this time; s I announce
this to you before you disappear. 17/ After
you no one shall rule tas long as you, t or even
half as long." 18/ Then the third wing raised
itself up, and uheld the rule u like the former
ones, and it also disappeared. 19/ And so it
went with all the wings; they wielded power
one after another and then vwere never
seen v again. w

20 And I looked, and behold, in due course the
wings that followed also rose up on x the
right side, in order to rule. There were some
of them that ruled, yyet disappeared suddenly; y 21/ and others of them rose up, but
did not hold the rule.

22 And after this I looked, and behold, the twelve
wings and the two little wings disappeared;
23/ and nothing remained on the eagle's

Notes

11:1 a–a Eth, Ar2 omit; RSV omits, perhaps for
stylistic reasons.
b–c Ar2, Arm omit.
c Syr, Ar1 "vision."
d Lat, Syr, Arm; Eth, Ar1, Ar2 omit.
e Lat adds *pennarum* against all the other versions.

2 f Lat, Syr, Ar1; Eth, Ar2 "flew"; Arm has the
doublet "raised its wings and flew," indicating that
both readings existed in Greek; cf. note k below.
g Masculine in Lat Φ, Violet suggests because of
underlying Greek referring to ὁ ἀετός.
g–h Lat, Arm have lost these words probably by
homoeoteleuton.

3 i RSV gives "but" against the evidence of all the
versions and implying an exegesis that is not
required.

4 j–j Syr "these others"; Eth "its two other heads";
Ar1 "all the heads"; Ar2, Arm "the others"; text
uncertain.

5 k Syr *pqd*; Hilgenfeld suggests ἔφη ⟩ ἔπτη; Ar2
"spread out"; Arm "raised up"; cf. note f above on
11:2.

10 l Lat, Arm; other versions omit. There is variation
with this expression, and originality is difficult to
determine.

11 m Lat adds "behold."

12 n–n Eth, Ar2, Arm omit.

13 o–o Lat "and it came to pass, while it was
reigning" and cf. Ar1 as emended and Arm "and
while this took place"; Syr "and I saw"; Eth "and as
the time"; Ar2 abbreviated. The text is very
uncertain and we follow RSV *faut de mieux*.
p–p Lat, Eth, Arm have two verbs. The other
versions omit the second verb.

14 q–q Lat, Syr "and it came to pass while."
q–r Eth, Ar1, Ar2 omit.

16 s–s Eth "so long a time"; Ar1 "this long time"; Ar2
"a long time."

17 t–t Lat *tempus tuum;* Syr *'yk hn' kl' zbn',* cf. Arm;
Eth, Ar1, Ar2 all vary to a greater or lesser extent.

18 u–u Syr, Eth "and ruled."

19 v–v So Lat, Ar2; literally, "and disappeared" Syr,
Eth, Arm.
w Syr, Ar1 omit.

20 x Lat *ad;* Syr, Eth, Arm "from"; missing from
Ar1, Ar2.
y–y Eth omits; Ar2 varies.

body except the three heads that were at rest ᶻand six little wings. ᶻ

24 ᵃAnd I looked, and behold, ᵃ two little wings separated from the six ᵇ and remained under the head that was on the right side; ᶜ but four remained in their place. 25/ ᵈAnd I looked, and behold, ᵈ these four ᵉ little wings planned to set themselves up and hold the rule. 26/ ᶠAnd I looked, and behold, ᶠ one was set up, but suddenly disappeared; 27/ ᵍa second also, and this disappeared more quickly than the first.

28 ʰAnd I looked, ⁱ and behold, ʲ the two that remained were planning between themselves to reign ᵏ; 29/ and while they were planning, behold, ˡ one of the heads that were at rest (the one which was in the middle) awoke; for it was greater than the other two heads. 30/ ᵐAnd I saw how it allied the two heads with itself, 31/ and ⁿ the head turned with ᵒ those that were with it and it devoured the two little wings which were planning to reign. 32/ Moreover this head gained control of the whole earth, and with much oppression dominated ᵖ its inhabitants; and it had greater power over the world than all the wings that had gone before.

33 And after this I looked, and behold, the middle head also suddenly ᑫ disappeared, just as the wings had done. 34/ But the two ʳ heads remained, which also ruled over the ˢ earth and ᵗ its inhabitants. 35/ And I looked, and behold, the head on the right side devoured the one on the left.

36 Then I heard a voice saying to me, "Look before you and consider what you see." 37/ And I looked, and behold, ᵘa creature like ᵘ a lion was aroused out of the forest, roaring; ᵛ and I heard how he uttered a man's voice to the eagle, and spoke, saying, ʷ

38 "Listen and I will speak to you. The Most High says to you, 39/ 'Are you not the one that remains of the four beasts which I had made ˣto reign ˣ in my ʸ world, so that the end of the ᶻ times might come through them? 40/ You, the fourth that has come, have conquered all the beasts that have gone before; and you have held sway over the world with much terror, and ᵃover all the earth with grievous ᵇ oppression; ᶜ and for so long you have dwelt on the earth with deceit. 41/ And you have judged the earth, but not with truth; 42/ for you have afflicted the meek and injured the peaceable; you have hated those who tell the truth, and have loved liars; you have destroyed the fortifications ᵈ of

---

23   z–z Ar2, Arm omit.

24   a–a Eth, Ar2 omit.
      b Syr, Ar1 omit.
      b–c Ar2 varies.

25   d–d Lat, Syr; Eth, Ar1, Ar2 omit, but see Violet 1 note re Ar2; Arm "and I saw."
      e Lat, Ar1 omit.

26   f–f Lat, Syr, Arm; "and I saw" Ar1; Eth omits; lacuna Ar2.

27   g Arm, Ar2 omit this verse.

28   h–j Eth omits.
      i–j Lat, Syr, Arm; Ar1, Ar2 omit.
      k RSV adds "together," apparently reflecting Lat *et ipsae*, but that reading finds no support in the other versions.

29   l Ar2, Arm omit.

30   m The first part of the verse is missing from Syr, perhaps by hmt. The whole verse is omitted by Ar2. The words "and I saw" survive only in Lat, Ar1; Eth, Arm have "then."

31   n Lat adds *ecce;* Ar2 adds "then."
      o Syr, Ar1, Ar2 add (with some variation of formulation) "both of." This is probably a contamination from the preceding phrase.

32   p Syr, Eth "humiliated."

33   q Lat, Syr; other versions omit. This is a standard apocalyptic formula.

34   r Ar1, Ar2 add "other."
      s Syr, Ar1 add "whole"; secondary.
      t Ar1, Ar2 add "all"; secondary.

37   u–u Literally, "something like"; omitted by Eth, Ar2 (unemended); standard apocalyptic formula.
      v Syr, Arm "crying and roaring"; perhaps independent expansions.
      w Lat Mss S A*, Syr; most Lat Mss and the other versions omit; probably existed in one Greek text-type, but such formulae are very difficult to evaluate. Violet 2 assumes a Hebrism אמר לאמר. Syr, Ar1 add "to him."

39   x–x Ar1 has "from the beginning"; the variant may go back to a confusion of forms of ἄρχειν/ἀρχή.
      y Lat, Syr, Arm; the other versions omit.
      z Lat alone (followed by RSV) has "my."

40   a–b Eth, Ar1 omit.
      a–c Lat, Syr; Arm omits; Ar2 is rewritten.

42   d Lat alone has *habitationes* (followed by RSV); Box supposes that the variants go back to different Greek and different Hebrew: dubious.

those who brought forth fruit, [e]
and have laid low the walls of those who
did you no harm.
43/ And so your insolence has come up
before the Most High,
and your pride to the Mighty One.
44/ And the Most High has looked upon his
times, and behold, they are ended, and his
ages are completed!

45 Therefore you will surely [f] disappear, you
eagle, and your terrifying wings, and your
most evil little wings, and your malicious
heads, and your most evil talons, and your
whole unjust [g] body, 46/ so that the whole
earth, freed from your violence, may be
refreshed and relieved, and may hope for the
judgment and mercy of him who made it.'"

e Lat; Syr *d'ylyn dkhynyn;* Eth "righteous"; Arm
"mighty." Clearly, Greek was problematic, and Box
and Violet 2 suggest εὐθυνόντων/εὐθηνούντων.

45 f The versions have a reflex of Hebrew infinitive
absolute and finite verb.

g Lat *vanum;* Violet 2 supposes ἄχρηστος, which
he claims would account for all the versions.

12:1 h Eth "Merciful One"; ἐλεῶν/λέων (Hilgenfeld,
Volkmar).

2 i Syr adds "suddenly"; a formulaic apocalyptic
element.

j–j Eth omits; we follow Lat, Syr, Arm; Ar1, Ar2
vary but might witness the same text.

3a k–k Eth, Ar2, Arm omit.

12

1 While the lion [h] was saying these words to the
eagle, I looked, 2/ and behold, the remaining
head disappeared. [i] And the two wings that
had gone over to it arose and set themselves
up to reign, [j]and their reign was brief and
full of tumult. [j] 3a/ And [k]I looked, and
behold, [k] they also disappeared, and the
whole body of the eagle was burned, and the
earth was exceedingly terrified.

Form and Structure

This long pericope is the narration of the content of a
complex symbolic dream that the seer experiences.
Unlike Visions 1–4, it is not preceded by a description of
his psychological state, nor of the onset of inspiration. All
we are told is that it is a dream vision. The description of
the dream is very detailed, but in general it resembles
descriptions of such dreams in other apocalypses. It is
implicitly related to prior apocalyptic tradition by the
observations that the beast is the fourth of those the Most
High appointed (11:40), even though the four are
mentioned nowhere else in the vision.[1] This hint is
transformed into an explicit reference to Daniel 7 in
12:11 but is, in any case, absolutely clear. The detailed
dependence on Daniel will emerge in the course of the
Commentary, and it suffices to explain certain elements
of the vision that play no role in the interpretation.

The interpretation of this vision is crucial for the
dating of the book, as will be explained in 12:10–36
Function and Content.

In the present introductory comments, however, we
shall try first of all to clarify the internal structure and
content of this vision. Second, the differences between

the dream vision and the previous waking experiences
will be stressed. Moreover, finally, as we shall demonstrate, the overall character of the vision is much more
traditional than were the first four visions, when seen
from the perspective of apocalyptic visions in general.[2]

The vision may be divided into three main parts: the
part that is almost exclusively the description of the eagle
(11:1–35), the judgment scene (11:36–46), and the
execution of the judgment (12:1–3). These parts are not
balanced in length but instead are in a descending order:
35 verses, 10 verses, and 3 verses. This being the narrative, supposedly, of a dream experience, the vision
contains no identifiable structure that can be discerned,
no balance and no particular form. Its only notable
structural feature is the repetition of phrases such as
"And after this I looked, and behold."

The actual description of the eagle may be divided
into a series of "scenes" or "stages," each featuring a new
element. The start of the description of each new element is signaled by the phrase "And I looked, and
behold" (11:2; 11:5; 11:7; 11:10; 11:12; 11:20; 11:22;
11:24; 11:25; 11:26; 11:28; 11:33; 11:35; 11:37;[3] 12:1–
2; 12:3). Variants of this long formula are "Then I

1 On the four empires, see 12:10–36 Function and
Content, p. 361.
2 Some such general characteristics are set forth in

many sources; see, e.g., Russell, *Method and Message,*
118–27; and Collins, *Genre,* 1–19, esp. 14.
3 An alternative slightly different analysis might also be

counted . . . , and behold" (11:11) and "Then I heard a voice saying to me, 'Look before you and consider what you see.' And I looked" (11:36–37). Within the sections thus marked, lesser developments are signaled by shorter formulae: "And I looked" or "saw" (11:3; 11:6; 11:15; 11:30), "and behold" (11:31), "and I heard" (11:37).

The repetition of these expressions is a very notable characteristic of the style and presentation of this dream. That it is a dream is clear from 11:1, and compare 12:3b: "Then I awoke."

Violet is of the view that 11:40–44 yields seven poetic hemistichs, and he is at pains to reconstruct them. Clearly 11:40–43 is in rhythmic parallelistic prose, verging on poetry. This provides a solemn atmosphere for the indictment of the eagle. Violet's reconstruction is, however, uncertain.

Function and Content
The content of this pericope is the symbol structure of the vision. The dream is seen and described in very great detail. It involves primarily visual experience, but auditory aspects also play a role in it. None of the other senses are involved. Using the introductory phrases noted above as demarkers, one may describe the dream experience as having fifteen stages. These are here enumerated, together with their content.

Stage 1: General Description
    Ezra sees an eagle with twelve feathered wings and
        three heads (11:1).

Stage 2: Initial Stance of the Eagle
    The eagle opened his wings over the whole earth:
        All the winds blew upon him (11:2).
        Clouds were gathered about him (11:2).
        Out of his wings grew puny, opposing wings (11:3).
        The heads, including the middle, larger head, were
        at rest (11:4).

Stage 3: Extension of the Eagle's Rule Over the Whole Earth
    He flew with his wings to reign over the earth and its
        inhabitants (11:5):

        All things were subject to him (11:6).
        No single creature on earth spoke against him
        (11:6).

Stage 4: Preparation for Sequence of Rule
    He rose on his talons and spoke to the wings (11:7).
        Do not all watch at the same time but seriatim
        (11:8).
        Let the heads be reserved for the end (11:9).

Stage 5: Summary and Observations So Far
    The voice came from the middle of the eagle (11:10).
    There were eight opposing wings (11:11).

Stage 6: Rule of the Wings on the Right-hand Side
    One wing on the right arose, reigned, and disappeared
        (11:12):
            While it was reigning, it came to an end and dis-
            appeared (11:3).
    The next wing arose and reigned for a long time
        (11:13–14):
            A voice said, "None shall rule even for half as
            long as you" (11:15–17).
    The third wing arose, reigned, and disappeared
        (11:18).
    So the remaining (i.e. right-hand) wings arose,
        reigned, and disappeared (11:19).

Stage 7: Rule of the Left-hand Wings
    The remaining wings arose upon the right side:
        Some ruled and disappeared (11:20).
        Some rose up and did not rule (11:21).

Stage 8: Summary to This Point
    The twelve wings and two of the little wings had
        disappeared (11:22).
    The three heads and six of the little wings remain
        (11:23).

Stage 9: Rule of Four Little Wings
    Two little wings separated from the six on the right-
        hand side and stayed under the head, while four
        remained (11:24).
        These four planned to set themselves up and rule
        (11:25).

---

    proposed:
        11:35 New section: "And I looked and behold"
        (discounting the expression "Then I heard a voice,
        etc." in 11:36).
        11:37 New section: "And I looked and behold."

One was set up but suddenly disappeared (11:26).
The second disappeared even more quickly (11:27).
Stage 10: The Fate of the Next Two Little Wings
These planned to reign together (11:28).
The middle head awoke (11:29) and allied the other two with it (11:30).
The middle head devoured the little wings (11:31).
The middle head gained control of the earth, dominated its inhabitants, and held more power than all that had preceded it (11:32).
Stage 11: The Fate of the Heads[4]
The middle head disappeared, as did the wings (11:33).
Two heads remained (11:34).
The right-hand one devoured the left-hand one (11:35).
Stage 12: The Appearance of the Lion
Ezra is summoned by a voice (11:36).
The lion issues from the forest roaring (11:37):
He spoke to the eagle with human voice (11:38).
Stage 13: The Indictment of the Eagle
Invocation (11:38).
Background: God established you as last of the beasts so that the end might come through you (11:39).
Offenses: You conquered all preceding beasts and held sway with oppression and deceit (11:40).
You judged the earth untruthfully (11:41).
You afflicted the meek and loved the wicked (11:42).
You laid low the walls of those who harmed you not (11:42).
Summary: Your insolence and pride have come up to the Most High (11:43).
Stage 14: Sentencing of the Eagle
He saw that the times are ended (11:44):
Therefore you and all your parts will disappear (11:45).
And the earth refreshed will await him (11: 46).
Stage 15: Execution of the Sentence
While he said this:
The head disappeared (12:2).
The two wings set themselves up and ruled tumultuously (12:2).

They disappeared, the body of the eagle was burned, and the whole earth was terrified (12:3).
It is worth noting that the speech (stage 13) and the subsequent two stages represent a legal process very clearly. Although the lion speaks for him, it is the Most High himself who judges. The stages of general indictment, laying of the specific charges, sentencing, and execution of the sentence are very clear in this section of the vision.

It is also worth observing that there is a certain inconsistency in the extension of the imagery. Indeed, the fearsome eagle and all its parts represent an empire and its rulers. The various vicissitudes of the parts of the eagle similarly represent the varying fates of its rulers. The lion is (to anticipate the next major pericope) the Messiah. Yet, unlike the situation in *1 Enoch* 89:14–76, God himself is here referred to simply as the Most High. *1 Enoch* gives him a special name, in order to integrate him into the symbolism. A further possible shift from the symbolic into the real world may be the expression in 11:42: "You have laid low the walls of those who harmed you not," which might well be a reference to the Roman destruction of Jerusalem.

A further sign of the mixture of categories typical of dreams is the (albeit limited) self-involvment of the dreamer in the dream, which may be observed in 11:36, where Ezra is addressed. There is, beyond this, no hint of an angelic guide in the vision, nor of the seer's attributing some action to himself. His subjective feelings are not mentioned as part of the dream experience.

Commentary

■ **11:1** The fifth and sixth visions take place at night, as did the first three, but they are dreams. They are introduced by a simple statement of the onset of the experience which contrasts with the complex descriptions of Visions 1–4.[5] Dreams have been previously mentioned in the book only in a quite different context in 10:36. Attitudes toward dreams were complex, but at least some dreams were regarded as sent by God to reveal things to the dreamer. Thus ben Sira 34:1–6 (note particularly v 6):

---

4   See preceding note.
5   See Excursus on Inspiration, p. 121.

1 A man of no understanding has vain and false
  hopes, and dreams give wings to fools.
2 As one who catches at a shadow and pursues the
  wind, so is he who gives heed to dreams.
3 The vision of dreams is this against that, the likeness
  of a face confronting a face.
4 From an unclean thing what will be made clean?
  And from something false what will be true?
5 Divinations and omens and dreams are folly, and
  like a woman in travail the mind has fancies.
6 Unless they are sent from the Most High as a visitation, do not give your mind to them.

Dreams were considered to tell of the future; cf., for
example, Genesis 37; 41; Daniel 2; *2 Apoc Bar* 36:1.

The expression "on the second night" implies that two
days elapsed between the end of the fourth vision and
the start of this one. This turn of language occurs twice
elsewhere in the book, in 5:16 and 10:2.

The general inspiration of this vision is drawn, of
course, from Daniel 7, and at a number of points it shows
specific dependence on Daniel; see also 12:11 Commentary.[6] In Dan 7:3 the four beasts are said to come up
from the sea. In the apocalyptic symbolism used here, the
sea appears to be the deep, the primordial abyss. This is
also true of Rev 11:7 and 13:1, but that text too is
dependent on Dan 7:2. Montgomery, in his commentary
on Daniel, points out that "sea" is often used of agitated
peoples in the Bible.[7] Observe that the man comes up
with the winds from the sea in Vision 6 (13:2). It is likely
that the sea, which is explained neither in Vision 5 nor in
Vision 6, has become a stock element of the setting of
such visions, quite freed from its original mythological
context.[8]

In Dan 7:4–8 the beasts are described, but Daniel did
not state the appearance of the fourth beast.[9] The first
beast, indeed, was said to have eagle's wings (see below),
but the striking, symbolic multiplication of members
which signify kings or kingdoms is to be found particularly on the fourth Danielic beast. Another case of an
omen with three heads, interpreted as three pretenders,
is to be found in Philostratus, *Vita Apollonii:* "Now when
they reached Syracuse a woman of a leading family was
brought to bed of such a monster as never any woman
was delivered before; for her child had three heads, and
each head had a neck of its own, but below them was a
single body." Apollonius interprets it as follows: "It
signifies three emperors of Rome; . . . and not one of
them shall enjoy complete dominion, but two of them
shall perish after holding sway in Rome, and the third
doing so in the countries bordering upon Rome" (*Vita
Apollonii* 5:13).[10] The text goes on to tell how the prophecy was fulfilled in the lives of Galba, Vitellius, and Otho.

The selection of the eagle to represent Rome is
probably determined by the symbol found on the standards of the Roman legions.[11] Perhaps the eagle is the
enemies of Israel in *Test Mos* 10:8, and it is the symbol of
a wicked king in *Sib Or* 3:611.[12] Its use here is facilitated,
however, by the general attitudes to eagles familiar to
the author. Thus, repeatedly here the eagle spreads its
wings, a chief characteristic of the eagle in the Bible (see,
e.g., Exod 19:4; Deut 32:11; Jer 48:40; 49:22; Ezek
17:3; 17:7; and Prov 23:5). Its destructiveness is stressed
in Hos 8:1; Job 9:26; cf. Prov 30:19 on its flight; and Jer
49:22.[13]

Harnisch characterizes the eagle vision as representing
a certain way of seeing history, stressing not the acts of
God but the events of the eschaton. It is this stress which
leads to the delimitation of the scope of the vision to the
last of Daniel's beasts.[14]

■ **2** The spreading of wings is one of the actions of the

6   This is analyzed in some detail by Casey, *Son of Man,*
     122–24.
7   J. A. Montgomery, *A Critical and Exegetical Commen-
     tary on the Book of Daniel* (Edinburgh: T. & T. Clark,
     1927) 285. See Isa 17:12–13; Jer 46:7–8; and Rev
     17:15; see further also Keulers, p. 129.
8   Basic Israelite attitudes toward the hostile ocean are
     summarized well in P. Reymond, *L'eau, sa vie, et sa
     signification dans l'A.T.* (VTSup 6; Leiden: Brill,
     1958) 181–86. Three warriors come up from the sea
     in *Sefer Eliyyahu* (Even-Shmuel, 4 line 15) as well as
     other figures of the eschatological combat.
9   On the four beasts, see 12:10–36 Function and

     Content, pp. 361–65.
10   *Philostratus, The Life of Apollonius of Tyana* (trans. F. C.
     Conybeare; LCL; London and New York: Heine-
     mann and Macmillan, 1912) 1:491.
11   See also 12:11 Commentary; this was remarked by R.
     Loewe, "A Jewish Counterpart to the Acts of the
     Alexandrians," *JJS* 12–14 (1961) 119–20. Cf. also
     the use of the eagle in 1QpHab 3:11–12 (Geoltrain).
12   G. von Kuhn, "Zur *Assumptio Mosis,*" *ZAW* 43 (1925)
     127–28, would find the same image in *Test Mos* 7:2,
     but the text is very poor there and his case is not
     persuasive.
13   Other features stressed in the Bible are its swiftness

eagle that is most typically stressed in biblical descriptions of this bird.[15] The idea is that the eagle casts the shadow of its rule over the whole earth. The fact that the whole earth is involved is to be noted, and the earth is mentioned repeatedly as the arena of action throughout this chapter.[16] Isaiah 14 has an overall theme similar to this vision, and the stress on the whole earth is also to be observed there in 14:26. The point is, of course, that the wicked kingdom reaches the zenith of evil and extends its rule over the whole of the earth, and similarly that redemption also relates to the whole earth.

The remaining elements in this verse are part of the setting of the stage and not discussed in the interpretation. The general scene is derived from Daniel 7. The particular element of the winds may be found in Dan 7:2, and they are used in a way not dissimilar to the present context in 4 Ezra 13:2. The four winds are an element of divine destruction in Daniel 7 as well as in Zech 6:5; cf. Zech 6:1. More problematic are the clouds. They are usually an element of the divine epiphany; cf. Ezek 10:4, and in another form in Exod 19:9; 19:16; Ps 97:2; et al.[17] It should also be observed that, albeit in a different sense, the clouds also appear in the opening of Vision 6 (13:3). The difficulty is that the clouds do not usually appear as an element of destruction or chaos. Knibb comments appropriately that "in the Old Testament clouds regularly accompany the self-revelation of God (e.g. Exod 19:9, 16), but also symbolize the gloom of God's day of judgment (e.g. Joel 2:1–2); neither idea suits the present passage. It is just possible that the motif has been inappropriately taken from Dan 7:13 'and I saw one like a man coming with the clouds of heaven.'"[18] Clouds in the more traditional sense serve as the man's vehicle in 13:3.

■ 3 The vision describes the proliferation of various limbs

of the eagle, which, it turns out, have a clear and immediate significance.

■ 4 In Rev 13:3 the heads of a symbolic beast also play a distinct role.

■ 5 The special role of the eagle's wings is discussed in 11:2 Commentary, while the expression "those who dwell on the earth," particularly favored in eschatological contexts, is discussed in 5:1 Commentary.

■ 6 Perhaps "creatures" signifies simply "human beings," a meaning also found in Rabbinic Hebrew, which occurs elsewhere in the book; see 5:45; 8:24; cf. 9:19.

■ 7 The emphasis on the feet or claws of the fourth beast is to be found in Dan 7:7 and 7:19. The rising up contrasts with the previously quiescent pose of the beast. It is not to be related, it seems, to the rising to one's feet to receive a particularly solemn revelation, an idea found elsewhere in the book.[19] The exact meaning of the eagle's giving voice is not clear, unless it is a dramatic means of conveying information and giving a sense of portentousness. Giving voice is part of the woes (5:5; 5:7), but the relationship of that sign to the present passage is unclear.

■ 8 The word translated "watch" presumably means "wake up" or "be awake." The general idea of the fixed order of creation is very prominent in the book.[20] The specific concept of the fixed length of reigns of rulers may also be found in *1 Enoch* 90:1 et al.

■ 9 The term "the last" is discussed in the Excursus on Natural Order, pp. 104–5, and is a technical term for the eschatological events.

■ 10 Knibb comments justly that the sound came from the middle of the body and not the heads: "because the Roman Empire itself is speaking, and not one of the emperors."

■ 11 Chapter 11:10–11 has frequently been the object of

(Deut 28:49; 2 Sam 1:23; Jer 4:13; Hab 1:8; Lam 4:19; cf. Exod 19:4) and the height of its flight (Isa 40:31; Jer 49:16; Prov 30:19). It serves as a positive symbol, particularly in Ezekiel 1 and *Test Patr Jud* 25:5, and as a negative symbol in *1 Enoch* 89:10 and 90:2, 16. More could be added on the eagle, and see also *IDB*, s.v. "Eagle."

14 Harnisch, pp. 254–55.

15 See Commentary on previous verse.

16 See 11:2; 1:5; 11:12; 11:16; 11:32; 11:34; 11:40; 11:41; and 12:23.

17 Cf. also 1 Kgs 8:10–11 for this sort of language; see also Excursus on the Redeemer Figure, p. 212.

18 Knibb, p. 239.

19 *Pace* Box. See 4:47 Commentary. It is certainly not comparable to the angel's strengthening of a fainted seer (e.g., 5:15).

20 See 4:37 Commentary and Excursus on Natural Order, p. 102.

the suspicion of scholars who would discern various levels of reworking in this vision. Below we have discussed these theories.[21]

■ **12** Box considers the mention of the right side to be secondary, or else, he comments, we would expect a mention of the left side later on. However, note 11:20; perhaps all the wings were considered as being on the right side. In any case, throughout the vision, the right side is both dominant and favorable. The rule over the whole earth was discussed in 11:2 Commentary.

■ **13** The wing that ruled long receives especially detailed treatment because, as will be evident below, it plays a particularly important role in the historical interpretation; see 12:10–36 Function and Content, p. 364. The stress on "its place was not seen" means that it completely disappeared.[22]

■ **14, 15, 16** No commentary.

■ **17** This verse concludes the discussion of the second wing, which had commenced in 11:13.

■ **18** Often in this vision the periphrasis "held rule" is preferred.[23]

■ **19** From this verse it is evident that the wings ruled singly and not in pairs, in spite of certain theories that have been formulated.

■ **20** The verse is problematic. Verse 19 seems to mark the end of the treatment of the main wings. Verses 22–23 clearly mark the beginning of the treatment of the little wings. The summary in 11:20–21, however, is so lacking in specific detail that it might be taken either to summarize the preceding large wings and their fate or to present an overall view of the destiny of the small wings which are dealt with in the following. In Function and Content, p. 346, we have taken these verses as completing the description of the twelve large wings. The chief objection to this view is that 11:20–21 seems pleonastic when compared with 11:19, which deals with the fate of the wings. However, it is possible that 11:18–19 deals with the fate of the right-hand wings and 11:20–21 with that of those on the left-hand side (if there were

such). This would be supported by the beginning of the treatment of the small wings in the next verse. In either case, 11:20–21 adds no new details to the information presented so far in the vision.[24] On the role of the right-hand side, see 4:47 Commentary.

■ **21, 22, 23** No commentary.

■ **24** This verse and the three following definitely preclude the possibility raised by some scholars that the little wings should be taken in pairs.

■ **25** It seems that the reading "four" of most versions should be accepted. In any case, this verse refers to the group of four little wings, whose fate is the subject of the passage down to 11:32.

■ **26** This and the next verse describe two little wings that achieved rule, one after the other, but whose rule was ephemeral.

■ **27** No commmentary.

■ **28** These, the third and fourth of the little wings described in 11:25, are said to plan to rule and be devoured by the heads (11:31). This seems to mean that they did not even achieve rule, however briefly, but were destroyed by the heads before that.

■ **29** The history of the heads, the last major limbs of the eagle, starts here.

■ **30** No commentary.

■ **31** "Those that were with it" are, apparently, the other two heads.

■ **32** Reference is made to the oppression of the middle head and its universal power. It impressed the author even more than the second wing. The expression "inhabitants of the earth" is particularly favored in eschatological contexts; see 5:1 Commentary.

■ **33** No commentary.

■ **34** On "inhabitants of the earth," see 5:1 Commentary.

■ **35** In 1QpHab 3:11 reference is made to the Kittim which devour like an insatiable eagle. Devouring was also the work of the eagle in 11:31.

■ **36** Here Ezra becomes involved himself in the dream. The terms "look" and "consider" are standard parallels

---

21 See 12:10–36 Function and Content, p. 363. The various views are represented by Wellhausen (*Skizzen*, 6:243–44), Violet, Keulers (p. 121), etc. They include the completely secondary nature of these verses or the view that an original number 6 has been changed into 8. We find them all unpersuasive.

22 For a similar expression in a quite different context, see Ps 103:16.

23 Box would compare κρατεῖν τῆς ἀρχῆς in 1 Macc 10:52 and 2 Macc 4:10.

24 Box, following Drummond, *The Jewish Messiah*, 102–3, takes the verses as referring to the following little wings.

(cf. 9:45). It is not likely that "consider" has the sense "contemplate" as sometimes elsewhere in the book.[25] The verse calls attention to a major change in the narrative, which we have identified above as the beginning of a new section.

■ **11:37** The lion is a positive symbol and, as becomes explicit in 12:31–34, represents the Messiah.[26] The uttering of a voice as a sign or portent is well known in the book; see 5:5; 6:13; 6:17; and 10:26.[27] The special role of the human voice as representing created order is highlighted in 6:39 (and see Commentary there). The context here differs, however, and the voice is a clear sign distinguishing the lion from the preceding beast. It is an element of humanity.[28]

■ **11:38** This verse is a call for attention. It opens the lion's address to the eagle. That address is full of legal elements, and the summons may be part of them.[29] As will be evident from the following, this speech is parallel to *2 Apoc Bar* 36:7–11 in many ways, but there is no summons at the start of that speech.

■ **11:39** This verse establishes the identification of the eagle. It is exactly parallel to the same element in the speech of the vine to the cedar in *2 Apoc Bar* 39:7: "Art thou not that cedar which was left of the forest of wickedness, and by whose means wickedness persisted, and was wrought all those years, and goodness never?" It seems most reasonable to view these structural parallels as rooted in the legal context of these speeches. Dominion of kings, of course, is seen as deriving from God. This is a biblical concept and also occurs in postbiblical texts (see, e.g., Wisd 6:3; *Test Mos* 8:1). Here it is com-

bined with the political theory of the four empires destined to hold sway in the world.[30] God not only appoints kings in general but has ordained that there be four empires in the world, "so that the end of my times might come through them." In other words, the empires are part of the foreordained progress of world history. The order of the created world is fixed and so is the end of this age.[31] Here the idea of preordination which is prominent in 4 Ezra is once again to the fore.

The end is called the "end of times." The expression recurs in 3:14, and similar are 11:44 and 12:9.[32] Here is a revelation of the "end of times" to Ezra. Compare the revelation of the end of times to Abraham (3:14) and to Moses (14:5). Ezra is conscious of the importance of what is revealed to him, as is explicit from 12:9.

We find both the term "world" (translating *saeculum* and parallels)[33] and the term "times," which seems to indicate the total course of world history.[34]

God gave the eagle dominion in this world so that the end of the world age might thereby be brought about. Since the eagle is clearly the zenith of evil, its rule is part of the "messianic woes" which must precede the eschaton, for evil must come to its climax before the good can follow. These ideas are implied by "so that the end of times might come through them."

■ **11:40** This verse is the main part of the actual indictment of the eagle, which continues into 11:43. It is exactly parallel in structure to *2 Apoc Bar* 39:8. The legal context is thus sustained. The sins of which the eagle is accused are considerably influenced by the idea of the evil king of the end, the "antichrist" figure.[35] In addition

25 See 5:54 and 7:16; in 7:37 "look" is parallel to "understand."

26 See in detail on the symbolism Excursus on the Redeemer Figure, p. 209.

27 See particularly 10:26 Commentary.

28 In the *Animal Apocalypse* in *1 Enoch*, animal forms contrast with the human. In Dan 7:4 the first beast arising from the sea is granted a "human mind." This is probably a reflex of a positive attitude toward Nebuchadnezzar underlying the four empires there; on that attitude in Daniel 2, see Collins, *Daniel*, 8.

29 See Form and Function, p. 347, and Excursus on the Redeemer Figure, p. 209.

30 See in detail 12:10–36 Function and Content, p. 361.

31 Discussed fully in Excursus on the Two Ages, p. 93.

32 See 3:14 Commentary for full discussion. On "end," see Excursus on Natural Order, pp. 103–4.

33 See Excursus on the Term "Age," pp. 218–19.

34 See 9:6 Commentary. The terminology is discussed in 7:26 Commentary and the concept in 3:9 Commentary and 4:37 Commentary. See also 11:44 Commentary.

35 See in detail on the antichrist 5:6 Commentary.

to the antichrist figure, other aspects of the woes cycle have also been crucial formative elements here. Thus the description evokes the fearsome events of the end of history. This evocation is strengthened by the mention of "terror." In 4 Ezra, terror almost exclusively accompanies fearful events and portents; see 5:1; 6:15; 6:23; 6:24; 10:25; and 12:3. Thus the use of the term here evokes the "supernatural" dimension of the wicked kingdom's deeds.

The "deceit" contrasts with truth in the next verse; compare 6:27–28, which discusses the role of deceit and truth in the woes. These two terms are also opposed in a similar context in *2 Apoc Bar* 56:2.[36] The perversion of social ethics and the perversion of judgment are among the chief sins of the eagle emphasized here.

■ **41** No commentary.

■ **42** The terms "meek" and "humble" are very rare in 4 Ezra. In 8:49, Ezra's own humility is praised. The use here, however, is much more like that in Matt 5:3 and 5:5 and may even have some sociological overtones.[37] Truth is hidden as part of the woes preceding the end and will be fully manifested at the end; see 5:1; 6:28; 7:34; 7:104; and 7:114. Lie and deceit are typical of the antichrist.[38]

■ **43** The pride of sinners recurs in the book in an eschatological context; see 8:50 and Commentary. This is particularly a characteristic of the eschatological wicked ruler or kingdom. The *loci classici* in the Hebrew Bible include Isa 14:13 and Dan 7:8; 7:11; 7:25; and 11:36.[39] There are very numerous instances of the pride of the wicked kingdom of the end.[40] This may be related to the terms "meek" and "peaceable" in the preceding verse, as was 8:50 in its context. The term "come up before the Most High" recalls, on the one hand, the actual ascent of Lucifer in Isa 14:13–14 and the ascent before the Most

High of the plaint resulting from the arrogant action of the Watchers in *1 Enoch* 9:1–2.

■ **44** The construction of the sentence here is almost identical to that in 9:20. This verse says that God examined "his times" and observed that they had come to an end. "Times" means something like "the course of history" (cf. 9:6 Commentary). In this statment are found a number of ideas that occur elsewhere in the book. First, there is the idea that God controls and determines the length of the world age. This is fixed and can be known or revealed.[41] In accordance with this, *saeculum* and equivalents are here translated "ages."[42] These times and this age will reach an end; indeed, that end is approaching.[43] The possessive "his" serves to emphasize God's control of the historical process.

■ **45** This verse and the following form the pronouncement of sentence upon the eagle.

■ **46** Here there is a rather allusive description of what will happen after the destruction of the eagle. The earth will be freed from the eagle's violence.[44] The expression "refreshed and relieved" describes the relief from the oppression of the eagle. It also recalls the terminology "rest and quiet" used for reward (7:36 Commentary). This is apparently a hint at a messianic kingdom which will precede the day of judgment.[45] Judgment and mercy are a standard pair, attributes of God. In 4 Ezra very often mercy is said to be withdrawn on the day of judgment, and strict justice alone to prevail.[46] The situation in the present verse, however, seems to contrast with that view and speaks of divine judgment and mercy that will be exhibited in final judgment. The way this will happen is perhaps prefigured by the use of judgment referring to the eagle and of mercy referring to the inhabitants of the earth in the description of the eagle's destruction in 12:33–34: "For first he will set them living before his

---

36   Of course, truth and falsehood are an operative opposed pair in Qumran thinking.

37   Cf. *TDNT*, s.v. πραΰτης.

38   See, e.g., *Greek Apoc Esd* 4:26–35 and commentary *apud* Charlesworth, *OTP*.

39   See also same language in Isa 37:29; Job 20:6; et al.

40   Many such are cited by Volz, p. 89.

41   The idea of fixed or predetermined times is discussed above in 3:9 Commentary and 4:37 Commentary; cf. also Gal 4:4; see n. 33 above.

42   See further Excursus on the Term "Age," pp. 218–19.

43   On the idea of "end," see Excursus on Natural Order, pp. 103–4; on "end of times," see 3:14 Commentary.

44   The language of freedom is usually used in the book in a different context, that of human freedom of action in this life and before death; cf. 7:101; 8:56; and 9:11.

45   See 7:29 Commentary.

46   See Excursus on the Term "Judgment," p. 150.

judgment seat. . . . But he will deliver in *mercy*. . . ."

■ **12:1** This verse opens the description of the execution of judgment that continues to 12:3. Box and others regard this passage as a later adaptation of the "original" vision to changed circumstances.

■ **2** This verse describes the disappearance first of the head and then of the remaining two little wings. Their exact meaning and the reason for their inclusion here remain unclear.

■ **3a** In the destruction of the eagle two elements are invoked that point clearly to the context of great cosmic events. Fire is a standard element by which God destroys his enemies[47] and which is part of eschatological judgment. Terror usually accompanies such cosmic events, and it is discussed in 11:40 Commentary. It is the earth that is terrified, just as it has been the earth that is the arena of action throughout this vision.[48] The destruction of Rome was foretold already in 5:3, and, as has been remarked, this is true of much of eschatological prophecy in the book.

---

47 See Mal 3:19; 5:8 Commentary; Excursus on the Redeemer Figure, p. 212; and Volz, 319, who adduces many more references.

48 See 11:40 Commentary. The earthly creation shudders and shakes and generally gives an impression of a certain precarious existence. See, e.g., 3:18; 6:16; and 10:26.

12

3b **Then I awoke in great perplexity of mind and great fear, and I said to my spirit, 4/ "Behold, you have brought this upon me, because you search out the ways of the Most High. 5/ Behold, I am still weary in mind and am ᵃ very weak in my spirit, and ᵇnot even a little ᵇ strength is left in me, because of the great fear with which I have been terrified this night. 6/ Therefore I will now beseech the Most High that he may strengthen me to the end."**

7 **And I said, "O sovereign Lord, if I have found favor in thy sight and if I ᶜhave been favored ᶜ before thee beyond many others, and if my prayer has indeed ᵈ come up before thy face, 8/ strengthen me and show ᵉthy servant ᵉ the interpretation and meaning of this terrifying ᶠ vision, that thou mayest fully comfort my soul. 9/ For thou hast judged ᵍ me worthy to be shown the end of the times ʰ and the last events of the times."**

Notes

5 a First person in Lat, Arm; the "spirit" is the subject in the other versions.

b–b Lat, Syr; "no" in other versions.

7 c–c This seems to be the general sense of the versions except for Lat *iustificatus sum*.

d Lat, Syr, Arm; Eth, Ar1 omit; Ar2 omits verse.

8 e–e Ar1, Ar2 omit.

f Syr omits; Syr, Arm add "which I saw"; Violet suggests that the reading of Syr may be due to an inner-Syriac corruption, but this is not likely. Probably a Greek gloss.

9 g Literally, "held" Lat, Syr, Ar2; Eth, Ar1, Arm have "made."

h Eth has "days" in both instances; Arm has "years" here.

Form and Structure

This passage is parallel in function, and largely also in structure, to 10:5–24; cf. 10:29–37 and 13:13b–20. These three pericopae describe the seer's reaction to symbolic dreams or visions and present his prayer for enlightenment and interpretation. In all three passages certain common elements recur, in the same order: *(a)* fear—10:25; 12:3; 13:13; *(b)* wonderment in his own mind—10:25 (cf. 10:28); 12:4–6; cf. 13:14 ("wonder"); and *(c)* prayer—10:28 (but there a cry for help); 12:7–9; 13:14–20. At the literary level, the passage carries the reader from the vision to the interpretation. In contrast to the first four visions, no angelophany is mentioned explicitly here; it is, however, implicit, since it is clear in both Vision 4 and Vision 6.

The passage, like others in 4 Ezra, contains deliberate reminiscences of material found elsewhere in the book and cross-references to it. The expression "to search out the way of the Most High" clearly evokes an idea that is of central importance in the first vision. This evocation is strengthened by the reference to bewilderment of mind which occurs there often in the context of the search for the way of the Most High. Similarly, Ezra's reference to

being counted among the righteous refers to the point about his personal righteousness made repeatedly in the preceding chapters (8:48–49; 10:39; 10:57).

The passage may be divided into three parts:

A. *Introduction* presenting the seer's state of mind (12:3)

B. *Apostrophe* directed to the mind (12:4–6)

The author uses the apostrophe elsewhere in the book; one of the most impressive instances is 7:62.[1]

C. *Prayer* to God (12:7–9)

Particularly notable from a formal viewpoint is the complex introduction to the prayer (12:7) which is composed of three "if" clauses. The only other similarly elaborate introduction is to be found in 4:44. Such elaborate formulae mark the start of an important new matter, here the interpretation of the dream. The introduction is followed by a petition (12:8), and the whole concludes with the justification of the petition (12:9).

Function and Content

In the introduction Ezra's perplexity of mind and great fear are highlighted. As a result of these, he turns in an apostrophe to his own mind and upbraids it for bringing

---

1 See Commentary there.

him to this state: "You have brought this upon me, because you search out the ways of the Most High." He is wearied, he continues, as a result of all this searching and therefore will beseech the Most High for help. It is notable that in 7:62, he also uses the literary form of apostrophe to express his distress or anger at the nature of the mind. Finally, in the prayer itself, Ezra cites God's grace extended to him in the past to plead for revelation of the interpretation of the vision.

The speech directed to his mind recalls the laments over the mind elsewhere in the book. The almost independent function of mind, which is addressed as if it were an autonomous being, is discussed above.[2] It is in the light of this attitude that Ezra reproaches his mind, which by its searching, a motive force from the very start of the book, has precipitated the whole exhausting and terrifying series of experiences of which the dream he has just experienced is the most recent. This reproach forms a nice contrast with 4:2, where the angel says to Ezra: "Your understanding is quite confounded regarding this world, and do you wish to comprehend the way of the Most High?" Here, Ezra's understanding is confounded precisely by his desire to comprehend the way of the Most High. In this pericope, the reference to his perplexity of mind together with "the way of the Most High" evokes the first vision.[3] We have pointed out above that there is some parallelism between Vision 1 and Vision 5, each of which starts a new section of the book. Ezra's perplexity is noted in both instances as a response to a new kind of vision experience.

The formulation here stands in an interesting contrast with those discussed in 10:29–37 Function and Content, p. 330. There the perplexity caused by the search for understanding (Vision 1) is contrasted with the perplexity caused by the vision experience itself (Vision 4). Here the search for understanding is said to have brought about the dream experience and that, in turn, to have caused the perplexity of mind. These differences of emphasis form yet another index for evaluating the seer's spiritual progress.

Physical weakness is a response to the vision, and the seer prays to be strengthened or is granted strength. These elements also recur in 5:14; 10:25; 10:28; 10:30–31; and 13:13b (fear).[4]

The nature of these experiences is discussed in detail in the Excursus on Inspiration, p. 122. Among the specific, significant points is a striking example of the observation made by Bensly that usually where the seer addresses God as "Lord" he also refers to himself as "servant." So we find "Lord" in 12:7 and "servant" in 12:8.[5] Yet this language is formulaic and Ezra no longer deprecates his own worthiness, as he had done previously, but, having accepted it, he uses it as a basis for his petition directed toward God. This shows how fully he has accepted the angel's point about his own righteousness made repeatedly from the very end of Vision 3 and through Vision 4.

Commentary

■ **3b** The second part of this verse introduces the pericope that describes the seer's reaction to his vision experience. The experience is understood by the author to be a dream, as is clear from 11:1 and from the present verse. In general, it resembles similar passages elsewhere in the book.[6] The term "perplexity of mind" is also used elsewhere to describe the seer's mental state; see 5:33 Commentary n. 13. This state of mind is elsewhere also connected with the "searching for the way of the Most High."

■ **4** Ezra blames his spirit for causing his fear by searching out the way of the Most High, as a result of which he has undergone the frightening experience of the dream. The dream caused the distress he was currently experiencing. The role here of "search out the ways of the Most High," a term typical of Vision 1, is discussed in Form and Structure, p. 354. The meaning of this terminology has also been dealt with in detail above.[7]

■ **5** Compare the seer's reactions to the vision described

---

2   See Excursus on Inspiration, pp. 122–23.
3   Concerning the terminology, see Excursus on Inspiration, p. 122.
4   See 5:14–15 Form and Structure, p. 115; 10:25–28 Function and Content, p. 326; 10:29–37 Function and Content, p. 330.
5   See 5:56 Commentary.
6   See Function and Content, on this page.

7   See 3:31 Commentary; Excursus on Inspiration, pp. 119–24; and Stone, "Way of the Most High," 134.

here with the reactions described in Dan 7:15 following a four empires vision. Note the use of "mind" parallel to "spirit" as a reference to Ezra's own consciousness and emotional state.[8]

■ **6** The sense of "to the end" is unclear. Does it mean "completely" or "to the end of the current dream experience" or "to the end of the age"? Perhaps it should be compared with the equally problematic use of "in the end" in 8:54.[9]

■ **7** Here the object of Ezra's address changes. In the first verse of the present pericope he had apostrophied his spirit. Now he turns to God, calling him "sovereign Lord" (cf. 3:4 Commentary). His address to God is a petition and commences, as do many petitions in the book, with the phrase, "If I have found favor in thy sight." The feeling that the petition is urgent is enhanced by means of the repetition of "if" statements in three parallel clauses. This literary technique is used only on one other occasion in the book, in 4:44.[10] Intriguingly, these three statments assume that Ezra is accounted righteous and that his prayer is accepted by God. This may refer back to angelic assurances given to him that he is righteous, and particularly to 10:57: "For you are more blessed than many, and you have been called before the Most High, as few have been." In the pericope 8:37–62a we discerned the start of a change in attitude toward Ezra, both on the part of the angel and on his own part. This changed attitude was the constituent of Ezra's preparation for the vision of conversion (Vision 4). Following this vision, he is promised great, eschatological revelations, and the present passage seems to reflect his realization that he has indeed received such. The verse 10:57 just cited is actually part of that angelic promise of eschatological revelations.

■ **8** This verse starts to give the general meaning of the petition. Ezra asks for the interpretation of the terrifying vision. It is worth comparing the term "interpretation" with that employed in Dan 2:26 and 5:26, and of older texts, with Gen 40:12 and 40:18.[11] Such requests were not uncommon in apocalypses; compare, for example, *2 Apoc Bar* 54:6: "Thou hast shown thy servant the vision, Reveal to me also its interpretation." In *2 Apocalypse of Baruch* and here the seer uses "servant" as self-designation. This is common in 4 Ezra and is discussed above.[12] The "comfort of soul" Ezra prays for is to be explained by his words to himself in 12:6. There he says he will ask to be strengthened "to the end"; in his actual petition he asks (in the present verse) to be strengthened and shown the interpretation of the vision, so that his distress, described in 12:3–6, may be fully alleviated.

■ **9** Here Ezra clearly recognizes the special nature of what has been revealed to him. The expression "the end of the times" designates the special revelations made to Abraham (3:14) and to Moses (14:5). In Vision 5 this is what is said to be revealed (11:39; 11:44).[13] So when Ezra uses this terminology, he not only talks about the content of his vision but he also is signaling that what has been revealed to him sets him directly into the tradition of special and secret revelation going back to most antique times.

The expression "end of the times" is discussed above.[14] Here, it probably means something like "the beginning of the messianic age."[15] The terminology rendered here "last events" (Latin *novissimis*, etc.) has also been dealt with previously.[16] Behind this statement, of course, lie presuppositions about the fixed nature of the times and predetermination which make the future course of history something that can be known by God and revealed to humans. This idea, of course, permeates the book and is one of its central concepts.[17]

---

8   Cf. Excursus on Inspiration, pp. 122–23.
9   See 12:8 Commentary. It may be that the expression was something like עד תמם in Deut 31:24; 31:30; and Josh 10:20 (Box). On the technical eschatological term "end," see Excursus on Natural Order, pp. 103–4.
10   See 4:44 Commentary for a full discussion.
11   Violet 2 deals at some length with aspects of the terminology of this verse, particularly with the word translated "meaning" and with the term "vision." He suggests that this might reflect Greek and Hebrew words meaning "secret" or "mystery," but that seems superfluous.
12   See 5:56 Commentary.
13   See in further detail 3:14 Commentary.
14   See 3:14 Commentary; cf. also 4:37 Commentary.
15   See Excursus on Natural Order, p. 103.
16   See Excursus on Natural Order, p. 104.
17   See Excursus on Natural Order, pp. 102–3.

Ezra's righteousness, therefore, has qualified him for this revelation. It signifies the change in his position which has been becoming evident throughout this vision. This new role of Ezra's follows upon the particular experience of the fourth vision and the change which that has wrought in him.

12

10   a*He said to me, a* "This is the interpretation of this *b* vision which you have seen: 11/ The eagle *c*which you saw *c* coming up from the sea is the fourth kingdom *d*which appeared in a vision to your brother Daniel. *d* 12/ But it was not explained to him as I now explain *e* it to you. 13/ Behold, the days are coming when a kingdom shall arise on earth, and it shall be more terrifying than all the kingdoms that have been before it. 14/ And twelve kings shall reign *f* in it, one after another. 15/ But the second that is to reign shall *g*hold sway *g* for a longer time than (any other of) *h* the twelve. 16/ This is the interpretation of the twelve wings which you saw. 17/ As for your seeing *i* a voice that spoke, coming not from the eagle's heads but from the midst of his body, this is the pronouncement: *j* 18/ In the midst of *k* the time of that kingdom not a few *l* struggles shall arise, and it shall be in danger of falling; nevertheless it shall not fall then, *m* but shall regain *n*its former power. *n* 19/ As for your seeing eight little wings arising from *o* his wings, this is the pronouncement: *p* 20/ Eight kings shall arise in it, *q* whose times *r*shall be short and their years *r* swift;

Notes

10   a–a Lat, Eth, Arm; Syr prefixes "he answered and"; Ar1, Ar2 prefix "he appeared to me and"; the origin of the reading of the Arabic versions may lie in a Greek corruption of forms of φαίνομαι/φῆμι.

    b Syr "the"; Eth "this your"; Ar2 omits the whole phrase a-b.

11   c–c Eth, Ar2, Arm omit; this may be a doublet of the phrase from the end of the preceding verse. In Lat, the preceding word, *aquilam*, is accusative, explained by Volkmar as a Graecism, an accusative of respect.

    d–d Ar1 "which your brother Daniel, the prophet, saw"; Ar2 "which your brother Daniel saw."

12   e Lat, Syr add "or have explained," cf. Ar2; this is probably a gloss in their *Vorlage*, according to Violet, whose view can be accepted on exegetical grounds.

14   f Ar1, Ar2 "arise."

15   g–g Literally, "hold."

    h Supplied in translation; literally, "than the twelve." The sense seems clear, nonetheless.

17   i Lat, Arm "hearing"; these two readings are best understood as independent corrections. "Seeing" often refers to auditory phenomena.

    j Syr, Eth, Arm have "word," "pronouncement"; Lat has *interpretatio;* Ar1 has "voice"; cf. note p below on 12:19, note v below on 12:22, note d below on 12:30, 13:22 note d, and 13:28 note n.

18   k Lat has *post;* Violet suggests μέτα ⟨ μεταξύ; Ar1, Ar2, Arm have simply "in."

    l Lat *non modicae,* so also Ar1, Arm; Syr, Eth "many"; the reading of Syr, Eth can be seen as arising from Lat, Ar1, Arm. The reverse process is difficult to posit.

    m Eth, Ar1 "in that time"; Ar2, Arm omit.

    n–n Lat, Syr "in its beginning"; Violet suggests ἐν ἀρχῇ ⟨ εἰς ἀρχήν.

19   o Lat *coherentes;* all the other versions have "arising from," "springing from," or the like. RSV "clinging to" follows Lat.

    p Syr, Eth, Arm have "word," "pronouncement"; Lat has *interpretatio;* Ar1 has "voice"; cf. note j above on 12:17.

20   q "It" is masculine and refers to "time" in Lat; it refers to the kingdom in Syr, Eth, to the wings in Ar2, while Arm is ambiguous. Ar2, Arm have "from" instead of "in."

    r–r There is variation in the versions' rendering of "times" and "years." The text given here is the reading of Lat alone. "Times" is shared with Syr, Ar1, Arm; Ar2 varies. "Years" occurs only in Lat, but the other versions also differ from one another

21/ and two of them shall perish ^swhen the middle of ^s its time draws near; and four shall be kept for the time ^twhen the end of (its ?) time approaches; ^t but two shall be kept until the end. 22/ As for your seeing three heads at rest on it, ^u this is the pronouncement: ^v 23/ In its last days ^w the Most High will raise up three kings, ^x and they shall renew many things in it, and shall oppress ^y the earth 24/ and its inhabitants more oppressively than all who were before them. For this reason they are called the heads of the eagle, 25/ since it is they who shall ^zbe the heads of ^z his wickedness and perform his last actions. 26/ As for your seeing that the large ^a head disappeared, one of the (kings) ^b shall die in his bed, but in agonies. 27/ But as for the two who remained, the sword shall devour them. 28/ For ^cthe sword of one shall devour him who was with him; ^c but he also shall fall by the sword in the last days. 29/ As for your seeing two little wings passing over to the head which was on the right side, 30/ this is the pronouncement: ^d It is these whom the Most High has kept for its ^e end; this was the reign ^f which was brief ^g and full of tumult, as you have seen.

as well as from Lat. Perhaps a word designating "periods of time" existed in the *Vorlage* and was variously interpreted by the different versions. E.g., Eth has "days," cf. Ar1 which, however, has transposed the two words; Arm has "hours," "periods."

21   s–s Lat, Syr, cf. Arm. This text also stood behind Eth; Ar1, Ar2 vary.

t–t Lat has *cum incipiet adpropinquare tempus eius ut finiatur;* it is best compared with Arm "when the consummation of the time will desire to approach them." The Syr *dkd ymṭ zbnˀ dnšlm* is somewhat difficult when compared with Lat, but behind these three versions must lie a common (and wordy) Greek which has been "simplified" by the remaining versions, each in a slightly different way. Although μέλλει often lies behind Lat *incipiet,* here Syr and Arm ("will desire") do not support it. The Arabic versions have shortened the text.

22   u Lat, Ar1 omit; Ar2 abbreviates.

v Lat, Ar1 *interpretatio;* Syr, Eth, Arm "word," "pronouncement"; see note j above on 12:17.

23   w Literally, "at its consummation" or "end" in Lat, Ar1, Arm; Syr "at the end of times"; Ar2 "at the conclusion of time."

x Latin *regna* goes back to a confusion βασιλείας/βασιλεῖς (Volkmar).

y Lat *dominabunt.*

25   z–z Lat has *recapitulabunt,* translated by RSV "sum up." Volkmar proposes that this reading derives from ἔσονται οἱ ἀνακεφαλαιώσαντες, reflecting a Greek wordplay. The other versions have texts like that given here, presumably deriving from some form of κεφαλή (except Syr, Ar2, which vary). Lat might have derived from a text like the other versions, and if their text is accepted, then also the sentence division of vv 24–25 is implied. The paronomasia is that the *heads* are *heads* of evil and *ends* of the kingdom.

26   a Lat *maius;* cf. Eth.

b Literally, "them."

28   c–c Eth, Ar1 omit, but Eth preserves the first two words; Arm also omits most of this phrase.

30   d Syr, Eth, Arm "word," "pronouncement"; Lat *interpretatio,* cf. Ar1; Ar2 rephrased; cf. note j above on 12:17.

e Lat *suam;* Syr, Arm "its"; Eth, Ar1 "the." Lat *suam,* being a reflexive, properly should be translated "His"; Syr *lšwlmh* is ambiguous; Arm refers to the eagle. That seems better on contextual grounds, and the variation in Greek would be minor. The alternative translation could also be supported.

f Eth, Ar1, Ar2 have taken ἀρχή as "beginning," not "rule," and their texts variously developed from this misunderstanding.

g The word is uncertain. Lat has *exile;* Syr "has an end"; Eth may have originated in a text like this;

"And as for the lion whom you saw rousing up out of the forest and roaring and speaking to the eagle and reproving him for his unrighteousness, and as for all his words that you have heard, 32/ this is the Messiah [h] whom the Most High has kept until the end of days, who will arise from the posterity of David, and will come and speak to them; [i] he will denounce them for their ungodliness and for their wickedness, and will cast up before them their contemptuous dealings. 33/ For first he will set them living in judgment, [j] and when he has reproved them, then he will destroy them. 34/ But he will deliver in mercy the remnant of my [k] people, those who [l]have been saved[l] throughout my [m] borders, [n] and he will make them joyful until [o]the end comes, the day of judgment,[o] of which I spoke to you at the beginning. 35/ This is the dream that you saw, and this is its interpretation. 36/ And you alone were worthy to learn [p]this secret[p] of the Most High.

Ar2, Arm have both transposed the two adjectives; Arm has "worthless"; Ar2 "whose disappearance (is at hand)."

32 h Lat, Syr, Arm; Eth, Ar1 have "he"; Ar2 "the king"; most likely Ar2 is a gloss on a text like Eth, Ar1. Two Greek readings seem most likely to have existed, but though it is possible that that behind Lat, Syr, Arm is in turn derived from a glossed Greek, no decisive determination can be made.

i Arm "him"; secondary and so throughout vv 32–35.

33 j Syr "their judgment"; Ar1, Arm "his judgment"; RSV translates "before his judgment seat" misleadingly.

34 k Eth, Ar1 omit; Arm "his," cf. note m below.
l–l Syr, Arm "remain."
m Arm "his," cf. note k above.
n Ar2 "mountains" confusion ὄρος/ὅριον. (Hilgenfeld, Volkmar).
o–o Thus Lat; Syr "the end of the judgment"; Eth "the day of judgment"; Ar1 "the fullness of the judgment"; Ar2 "the end of the aeon"; Arm "the end of judgment"; no version is certain here, except that Ar2 is definitely secondary.

36 p–p Lat, Eth; Syr "the secret"; Ar1, Ar2 "the secrets"; Arm is ambiguous and could be translated "the secrets" or "this secret."

Form and Structure

This passage presents the angel's interpretation of the dream that the seer has experienced.

12:10 Introduction

The form of the superscription may be compared with 10:40 and 13:22. This verse is taken up again in the conclusion of this pericope in 12:35–36. Such clear shifts from vision to interpretation are typical of the apocalypses; see Dan 2:36.

12:11–34 Interpretation

General 12:11–12. The eagle is identified in general with the fourth kingdom, Daniel is referred to, and the superiority of Ezra's revelation is asserted, a theme taken up again in 12:36.[1]

First Stage 12:13–16. This passage opens with the set phrase, "Behold, days are coming when." This form recurs in 5:1; 6:18; and 7:26, all strictly predictive passages.[2] The introduction is followed by predictions about the kingdoms, in 12:13–15, while in 12:16 this is asserted to be the interpretation of the wings. Structurally, therefore, this first stage has an inversion of the usual interpretative formula which first states the symbol and then its meaning. Together with the introductory sentence, this inversion adds particular weight and solemnity to the revelation made to Ezra.

Second Stage 12:17–18. Here the conventional order of symbol, formula, and interpretation is maintained. So 12:17: "As for your seeing . . . , this is the pronouncement." In Dan 2:41; 2:43; et al. we find "As for your seeing" but without the words "this is the interpretation" or "pronouncement."[3] The same formulaic structure occurs throughout the interpretation in the next vision.

Third Stage 12:19–21. Again the formula of interpretation is adhered to strictly. This is true of the following stages, except where noted specifically.

Fourth Stage 12:22–25.

Fifth Stage 12:26–28. The formula differs slightly here.

1 See also 12:9 and Commentary there.
2 On its use, see further 5:1 Commentary.
3 Note Dan 5:25–26, in a slightly different context.

Sixth Stage 12:29–30.

Seventh Stage 12:31–34. As in the vision, the interpretation of the section that deals with the lion is marked by shifts in structure and is much longer than the preceding stages of the interpretation.

12:35–36 Conclusion

This is composed of a general conclusion to the whole interpretation, well compared with Dan 7:28. The author also returns to the assertion of Ezra's worthiness. It is to be noted how much more complex this interpretation is, including its formulaic structure, than Daniel 7, the vision on which 4 Ezra is based.

Function and Content

In general, this pericope presents the interpretation of the complex dream of the eagle which precedes it. This interpretation is carefully related to the Book of Daniel, setting the vision in the context of the continuing apocalyptic tradition. The expression "fourth kingdom" refers to a widespread theory in the Jewish apocalypses that there will be four great empires, followed by a fifth, messianic kingdom. This theory is already to be found in Daniel 2 and 7 and recurs in later works.[4] In Daniel 7 the fourth kingdom is clearly the Greeks, but here it is Rome.[5]

There is a theory current among scholars that the scheme of four empires followed by a fifth was of Persian origin and, mediated through the Greeks, became part of the anti-Greek propaganda of the subject Oriental peoples.[6] This theory has been the object of some debate, but whatever its origins, the four empires conception holds a prominent position in Jewish apocalyptic historiography from the time of Daniel on, and 4 Ezra is consciously reinterpreting Daniel's traditions. This is a fairly rare instance of explicit reference by an apocalypse

to prior apocalyptic writings. Moreover, both the vision and its content are of a much more traditional type than those of the first part of the book. This surely is no mere chance.

In detail, the interpretation can be divided into seven parts. We shall enumerate them, also taking note of those elements in the dream which are not mentioned in the interpretation, while also recording those elements brought into the interpretation which have no symbolic counterpart in the dream. The seven parts of the interpretation are preceded by a general statement, identifying the eagle as the fourth kingdom (12:11//11:1). The material enumerated in stage 2 of the dream description is not explicated. This includes the opening of the eagle's wings, the blowing of the winds, and the initial description of the little wings and heads (11:1–4). Likewise, the content of stage 4 of the vision is not explained (11:7–9).

First Stage of Interpretation: Chapter 12:12 is an introduction; in 12:13, explaining 11:5–6, the rise of a kingdom more terrifying than all of its predecessors is predicted, but the interpretation gives little detail, contrasting with that given in the dream description. Chapter 11:12–19 and 11:20–21 are then explained as being a prophecy of the rise of twelve kings (12:14). No reason is offered for the differentiation between the right-hand wings and the left-hand wings in the dream. Then, in 12:15 the interpretation of 11:13–17 is offered. The second king is to reign longer than any of the others. The reference to his rule being twice as long as any other, made in the vision, is not explained or mentioned. Thus, set out schematically so far:

11:1	//	12:11
1:1–4		not interpreted
		12:12

---

4   See *2 Apocalypse of Baruch* 39 for another example. Many references are adduced by Volz, p. 311.

5   So also Josephus, *Ant.* 10:276 and many rabbinic sources, e.g., *Mek.* on Exod 20:18 (Horovitz-Rabin, p. 236); *Gen. R.* 42:2 (Theodor-Albeck, p. 399); Targ J Gen 15:12–14; *Pes. Rab.* 4 (Friedmann, p. 13a); and *Midr. Teh.* on Ps 90:17 (Buber, p. 197a).

6   See J. W. Swain, "The Theory of Four Monarchies," *Classical Philology* 35 (1940) 1–21. D. Flusser develops this view and finds the same ideas in the Fourth Sibylline Oracle: D. Flusser, "The Four Empires in the Fourth Sibyl and in the Book of

Daniel," *IOS* 2 (1972) 148–75. See further Momigliano, "Universal History." H. G. Kippenberg, "Dann Wird der Orient Herrschen und der Okzident Dienen," *Spiegel und Gleichnis: Jacob Taubes FS* (ed. N. W. Bolz and W. Hübner; Würzburg: Königshausen & Neumann, 1983) 40–48, casts further light on aspects of this propaganda.

11:5–6	//	12:13
11:7–9		not interpreted
11:12–19		12:14
11:20–21		12:14
11:13–17		12:15

Thus, on the whole, in the initial interpretation of the eagle and its wings, the two texts run side by side, but the interpretation is less detailed than is the dream itself.

Second Stage of Interpretation: The voice that came from the middle of the eagle (11:10) is said to indicate that in the middle time of the kingdom there will be struggles (12:17–18).

Third Stage of Interpretation: This passage, 12:19–21, deals in general with the little wings and has been found by some scholars (e.g., Box) to be out of concordance with the content of the dream, showing the hand of a redactor at work. In 12:19 is a general mention of the eight little wings which are, in 12:20, identified as eight kings who will rule for a short time. Of them, 12:21 says, two will perish toward the middle time of the kingdom, an idea that is perhaps implicit in 11:22 but not stated outright there. Then four will perish close to its end, as is indicated by 11:24–31. The comment in the dream that "they planned to rule together" (11:28) is not explained. Finally, two are reserved for the end, an interpretation of 12:2.

Fourth Stage of Interpretation: This passage, 12:22–25, deals with the rule of the three heads. In 12:22 they are stated to be three in number, and their meaning is that they will renew many things (12:23) and that their rule is to be very oppressive. For this reason, the text says, they were called heads. This is not stated in detail about all three heads in the dream, but it is implied by the image of a head and is stated explicitly about the middle head in 11:32. The comment in the interpretation about renewing many things does not follow naturally from any of the dream's symbolism.

Fifth Stage of Interpretation: The disappearance of the large head is said, for no reason that is obvious, to mean that one of these three kings will die on his bed in agonies (12:26). All that 11:33 states is that the large head disappeared. This therefore, like the details about the death of the next two heads, is the importation of information known to the author into the interpretation. Since this is the reverse of the general tendency throughout this interpretation, which is to be briefer than the dream itself, it is a clear indication of the contemporary relevance of these facts for the author. So, in 12:27–28 the one head is said to devour the other, which means that one will kill the other (the fact that they are left and right according to the dream is not interpreted, just as it was not interpreted above with respect to the wings; see First Stage of Interpretation). However, an important additional fact added by the interpretation is that the killer will himself be killed by the sword.[7] These points, as will emerge below, are important for the chronological interpretation of Vision 5.

Sixth Stage of Interpretation: In these verses (12:29–30), 11:24 is interpreted. Its subject is the little wings which in 12:30 are said to be kept for the end and whose reign will be brief and full of tumult. The basis for the latter statement in the dream is not clear.

Seventh Stage of Interpretation: This passage (12:31–34) deals with the lion. No explanation is offered of the summoning of the seer in 11:36, indicating perhaps that it serves chiefly to add solemnity to the events related in the dream. In 12:31 is a summary of the lion's activity corresponding to 11:39–43. The only notable element lacking here is the explanation of the lion's "human voice" in 11:38. Then in 12:32 the lion is identified as the Davidid Messiah who will denounce the wicked kings, and in the next verse he is said to set them up in judgment, reprove them, and destroy them. This is implicitly (but not explicitly) an interpretation of 11:45—12:3. The final verse (12:34) is additional and not related to the vision symbolism.

From the above analysis it clearly appears that the vision and its interpretation cohere closely. In general, the description of the vision is more detailed than of the interpretation, but still the correspondence is very close.

The whole of the eagle vision is, as it were, a close-up view of a particular part of the eschatological process. This is the last time of the world empire and its destruc-

---

7   Cf. the saying of Hillel in *m. Abot* 2:6: "He who drowned you will be drowned."

tion. The climax is clearly the expected appearance of the Messiah and the inception of his kingdom. In 12:34 it is equally clearly indicated that the messianic kingdom expected is a temporary one, to be followed eventually by the day of judgment (cf. also 11:46 in the recital of the dream).[8] In a way, therefore, it is similar to the vision of the heavenly Jerusalem, on the one hand, and to the vision of the man on the other. Each of these does not present a complete eschatological scheme but focuses on a particular element of redemption.

A number of scholars, on the basis of the supposedly exclusively "national" eschatology of this vision, have supposed that those parts of the interpretation which exhibit "universalist" features are interpolated.[9] This theory falls together with those views which use supposed "inconsistencies" of eschatological ideas to identify interpolations and sources. They have been discussed above.[10]

A particular importance adheres to the eagle vision, however, from the point of view of the criticism of the book. It belongs to the genre of historical and political visions.[11] Such historical surveys are particularly typical of the period of the Second Temple and are a function of the understanding of history and divine action at that time.[12] History is seen as a whole, schematic process, and the author's interest is not merely to present such a scheme abstractly as an academic endeavor in historiography. Instead, he wishes to know exactly where he stands in the course of that process. This is a question which was asked in another way at the end of the third vision: "Behold, O Lord, thou hast now shown me a multitude of the signs which thou wilt do in the last times, but thou hast not shown me when thou wilt do them" (8:63). Here in the eagle vision the response is rather specific. Because he is hiding both behind his

pseudepigraphic role and behind the symbolism of the vision itself, the author speaks in a veiled, yet explicit way of his own days. It is to be presumed that the author had knowledge of events past and contemporary but not future. So the point at which he abandons the actual course of events to predict future happenings is the point of time in which he lived. This point in the historical recital is also clearly indicated in most similar visions by the fact that it is preceded by an increasingly detailed account of the events in the immediate past. In other words, the identification of the wings, the small wings, and the heads with actual historical figures will yield an indication of the actual time of the author. This technique, well known in the study of the historical visions of the apocalypses, has been used extensively in the past in the study of 4 Ezra.

In 1900, E. Schürer made an excellent analysis of all scholarly writing on this matter down to his day,[13] and his major conclusions seem to us to remain valid, since no innovation has been made in the exegesis of the chapters since then that would invalidate them.[14] The central point in any study of the symbolism and its interpretation is the identification of the three heads. It is clear from our analysis above that the end is expected to come during the days of the third head, and if the identifiable events of history also cease at that moment, then indeed it is the author's own time so presented. Three main identifications have been suggested for these heads, resulting in three major dates either for the book as a whole or at least for the document containing the eagle vision. The first is that proposed by Laurence, Lücke (2d ed.), van der Vlis, Hilgenfeld, and most recently Geoltrain (pp. 1469–70), all of whom see the heads as Pompey, Sulla, and Caesar, thus dating the book, with some variations, in the last third of the last century

---

8 See Excursus on the Redeemer Figure, pp. 209–10; and Stone, "Question of the Messiah," 210, for demonstration of the inherent role of these verses in the vision.

9 So, e.g., Box, 274–75; cf. Kabisch, 93–101, particularly relating to 12:34 and parts of 12:32; see critique cited in n. 8 above.

10 See 7:26–44 Function and Content, pp. 204–7, for a detailed critique.

11 On this, see Collins, *Genre,* 1–20; and Russell, *Method and Message,* 193–94.

12 See Stone, "Apocalyptic Literature," 388, 436–37;

and idem, "Three Transformations," 224.

13 Schürer, 3:236–39.

14 See the modern views cited in the following note which predominantly echo older analyses.

B.C.E.[15] Schürer has marshaled convincingly the main arguments against this view from within the chapter, to which may be added the observation that the obvious origin of 4 Ezra in the period subsequent to the destruction of the Temple precludes it.

The other extreme is that view which would date the book to 218 C.E. This interpretation of chapters 11–12 was first proposed by Gutschmid in 1860. He maintained, however, that the eagle vision was a later interpolation into a book written in the last decades B.C.E.[16] The same terminal date was also reached by Le Hir.[17] These two treatments differ to some extent in their identifications of the wings and the little wings, and these variations and omissions highlight the fact that the crucial point for this theory is that the heads are identified as Septimus Severus, Geta, and Caracalla. The second wing, which ruled more than twice as long as any other, is Augustus (11:13; 11:16–17; 12:15). The identifications between these two extremes then vary.

Similar views were held by Barry and Völter.[18]

There are a number of serious objections to this analysis. First, the book was used by Clement of Alexandria in the last part of the second century, and so it must have been written before that time. Second, although there is some unevenness, the vision as a whole fits in its present position and cannot be excised without destroying the overall structure of the book.[19] Moreover, the basic unity of the text witnessed by the versions mitigates against any major tampering with it at this late date. Third, 12:18 and 12:21 state that after the first two little wings rule, shortly before the middle of the kingdom, there will be an interregnum which will be a time of distresses and confusions. This does not fit the time of Titus and Nerva, who are, according to this theory, the first two little wings. Fourth, the identifications ignore the position of Galba, Otho, and Vitellius. Fifth, the position of Commodus is problematic.[20]

The third major theory identifies the heads with

---

15 Laurence, *Versio Aethiopica,* "General Remarks," 312–15. On p. 319 he definitely proposes a pre-Christian dating. Thus also van der Vlis, *Disputatio Critica,* 167–89; Lücke, pp. 205–6. Nearly all of these scholars identify the little wings and the wings with rulers of monarchical and republican Rome. Geoltrain regards the wings as twelve successors of Alexander and the little wings as eight Hasmonean rulers (pp. 1468–69). Hilgenfeld's earlier views, as expressed in *Apokalyptik,* 218–21, identify the wings with the Ptolemies and the heads with Caesar, Anthony, and Octavian, thus placing 4 Ezra and the end of Jewish apocalyptic before the beginning of Christianity. His later view put in "Die jüdische Apokalyptik und ihrer neuster Forschungen," *ZfWT* 3 (1860) 335–58, retains this terminal dating and identification of the heads but identifies the wings and little wings with the Seleucids. Kuhn, "Zur *Assumptio Mosis,*" 127–28, identifies the heads with Octavian, Anthony, and Lepidus. Attestations of three heads as three kings have been gathered by E. Fehr, *Studia in Oracula Sibyllina* (Uppsala: Almqvist & Wiksell, 1893) 61.

16 Gutschmid, "Apokalypse des Esra," 68.

17 A. M. Le Hir, "Du IVe livre d'Esdras," *Etudes bibliques par M. l'abbé Le Hir* (Paris: Albanel, 1869), 1:139–250. The vision is treated on pp. 167–92.

18 Thus Gutschmid reckons Commodus as the third little wing, while Le Hir is not sure whether to combine him with M. Aurelius or omit one of the preceding emperors and make him an independent twelfth wing. Le Hir introduces Clodius Albinus as

the sixth little wing, while he is given no place in Gutschmid's scheme. Neither of them includes Galba, Otho, and Vitellius, while major figures like Titus and Nerva are the two first little wings. This is also the view of P. Barry, "The Apocalypse of Ezra," *JBL* 32 (1913) 261–72. He would, with hesitancy, speak of a "lost Hadrianic apocalypse," embedded in 4 Ezra (p. 270). A more recent presentation of the same view is J. Schwartz, "Sur la date de IV Esdras," *Mélanges André Neher* (Paris: Adrien et Maisonneuve, 1975) 191–96. He would speak of an original twelve-emperor vision dated at the time of Hadrian, reworked in 217 C.E. Völter's theory is similar, but he dates the "original" vision to the period between September 97 and January 98 C.E. D. Völter, "Die Gesichte vom Adler und vom Menschensohn im 4.Esra nebst Bemerkungen über die Menschensohn-Stellen in 1. Henoch," *NTT* 8 (1919) 241–73.

19 This is clear from the structural analysis in General Structure of the Book.

20 Some of these difficulties are avoided by Vagany, who regards the vision as an original piece of the time of Domitian reworked in 218 C.E. (pp. 21–23). On this theory, all references to the little wings are secondary. The interpolator added 11:3; 11:10–11; 11:22–30; 12:1–3; 12:17–21; and 12:29–31a. He also retouched 12:14 (but forgot to fix 11:21) and 12:27–28. For similar views, see A. Dillmann, "Über das Adlergesicht in der Apokalypse des Esra," *Sitzungsberichte der Berliner Akademie* 8 (1888) 215–37; Clemen, "Die Zusammensetzung," 242; and Gry, 1:xcviii-c.

Vespasian, Titus, and Domitian. Since the second wing is Augustus, there are more wings and little wings than there are known kings and usurpers (eighteen or twenty in all). This difficulty is solved in various ways by different scholars. The wings and the little wings, or just the wings, were taken in pairs, each pair signifying one ruler.[21] This nicely reduced the number of rulers to a reasonable figure. But, as Box points out, 11:24–28 precludes the possibility of taking the little wings in pairs. It should be noted further that 12:14–16 states specifically that the twelve wings are twelve kings (cf. 11:12–14), and 12:20 is equally explicit about the little wings. Thus it seems that the theory of pairs is inadequate as an explanation.[22]

Those who suggest that twenty rulers are indicated are fairly unanimous on the identification of the twelve wings. They are Caesar, Augustus, Tiberius, Caligula, Claudius, Nero, Galba, Otho, Vitellius, and the usurpers Vindex, Nymphidius, and Piso.[23] This theory encounters difficulties, however, in the identification of the little wings, and they have been interpreted in two main ways, either as non-Roman rulers[24] or later generals and pretenders.[25]

The heads seem indeed to be the Flavians, for the details given in the text admirably suit the contemporary rumors about and knowledge of the Flavians.[26] Furthermore, it has been seen above that the arguments for taking the wings in pairs are inconclusive. Thus there are too many wings, and it must be admitted that no simple solution to this problem has been found. Consequently, we are forced to accept some theory such as that of Schürer and Gunkel and to ascribe to the author more detailed knowledge of this period than is available today.[27] Therefore, the three heads should be regarded as the three Flavian emperors, Vespasian, Titus, and Domitian, and the date of the composition of the vision in the time of Domitian (81–96 c.e.) and probably in the latter part of his reign, when the cruelty and oppression of his rule reached a peak. Thus the composition of this vision is probably best placed in the early part of the 90s.[28]

Commentary

■ **10** This verse is the title and introduction to the interpretation; similar titles occur in 10:40 and 13:25. Note that in it there is no explicit mention of the appearance

---

21 This is desiderated by the view that would take the wings as "originally" in pairs, which view is clearly contradicted by 11:12 and 11:14–16; cf. 11:1; 11:13; and 11:18.

22 Thus Volkmar, 2:157–58 and note; Dillmann, "Adlergesicht," 215–37; and Wellhausen, *Skizzen*, 6:241–42. Wellhausen also considers that the last pair of little wings is an addition after the time of Domitian. C. Sigwalt, "Die Chronologie des 4.Buches Esdras," *BZ* 9 (1911) 147, accepts all wings and little wings as original but takes them in pairs. Box, p. 265, also accepts this hypothesis for his "original form" of the vision as far as the wings are concerned, but in the light of 11:24–28 he is forced to take the little wings singly and not in pairs. The only reason that he can adduce for this differentiation is the greater importance of the wings. The reworking, c. 120 c.e., by R, he says, was made on the basis of one wing = one emperor. Thus R is responsible for phrases in 11:12; 11:19; 11:20; 11:32; and particularly in 12:14.

23 Völter suggests substantial excisions from the text and as a result dates the vision between September 97 and January 98 c.e.

24 Thus A. Gfrörer, "Das Jahrhundert des Heils," Part 1 of *Geschichte des Urchristentums* (Stuttgart: Schweizerbart, 1838) 82–84; A. Dillmann, art. "Pseudepigrapha," *Real-Encyklopädie für protestantische*

Theologie und Kirche (ed. J. J. Herzog; 1st ed.; Gotha: Besser, 1860), 12:312; K. Wieseler, "Das vierte Buch Esra nach Inhalt und Alter untersucht," *TSK* 43 (1870) 270–71; Gunkel, p. 345; idem, *Der Prophet Esra*, xxv-xxvi; and Schürer, 3:242–43.

25 Gfrörer, "Jahrhundert," 88–89; and Wieseler, "Das vierte Buch Esra," 272–73, take them as Herodians; Kabisch, p. 163, takes them as various rulers of Palestine but thinks that in any case they are probably interpolated; similarly also Oesterley, pp. 144–47.

26 Dillmann, "Pseudepigrapha," 12:312, suggests that they may be generals or pretenders but thinks that they are interpolated. The former view is supported by Gunkel, p. 345; idem, *Der Prophet Esra*, 22, xxvi, who thinks that the two little wings which fell with Vespasian were Mucianus and Tiberius Alexander, the rulers of Syria and Palestine. He suggests that in the case of the little wings the author is drawing on information not preserved in the surviving sources. This is also the view of Schürer, 3:243.

27 See Schürer, 3:241–42, where the major arguments are summarized. Nothing of substance has since been added to them; see also Commentary on 12:27 and 12:28.

28 Myers (pp. 300–301) would include the Flavians in the twelve wings and considers the heads and little

of the angel. He is simply assumed to come in answer to the prayer. This is even briefer than the abrupt introduction of the angel in 4:1.

■ 11 The eagle is here given a general interpretation. In this important verse, three points are made. The eagle is the fourth beast, a reference to the theory of four kingdoms of which it represents the last.[29] This is the basic principle according to which the interpretation is made. The angel adds "which was revealed to your brother Daniel." This marks the present vision and intepretation as developments of Daniel 7 (cf. also Daniel 2). Specifically the eagle is identified with the fourth beast mentioned in Dan 7:7 and 7:23. This sets 4 Ezra into the tradition of apocalyptic writing also shared by Daniel. Such explicit statements are virtually unknown elsewhere, and this one is extremely important for the hint it gives us about the author's view of his own role.[30] He sees himself as part of a tradition of apocalyptic teaching, has contemplated and developed prior writing (Daniel), and views his own role as like that of Daniel, whom he terms "brother."

The final significant point in this verse is the clearly implied identification of the eagle with Rome. The appropriateness of the eagle as a symbol because of the associations with it in biblical literature is clear.[31] Various symbolic identifications were used for Rome in this book, clearly showing how central the Roman Empire was for our author.[32] Thus this verse sets up the triple equivalation of eagle/fourth empire/Rome.[33] This was widely accepted, and since the fourth empire is the last one, the identification concords with Ezra's preceding statement that "the end of the times" has been revealed to him.

■ 12 This verse implies that the author of 4 Ezra viewed himself as part of an apocalyptic tradition that went back to Daniel, and even farther, as is explained above. It also implies that he was the recipient of a specially inspired interpretation of this tradition that went beyond that which Daniel had known. The comment in 12:12 is very reminiscent of 11QpHab 7:3–6, where the author of the Commentary says that there were revealed to him things in the words of the prophet that the prophet himself did not know.[34]

At one level this can be seen merely as a justification of the reinterpretation of Daniel that is here being discussed. At another, however, if the words of the book about the tradition of secret teaching are taken into account as well as Ezra's personal position as it is presented here, as the one to whom "the end of the times" is revealed, then the assertion takes on a new perspective. It is a claim to possess an inner meaning of scripture, for the Book of Daniel by this time was surely regarded as sacred scripture. This may well provide a hint also at the nature of the tradition of which the author of 4 Ezra partakes, and it enables us to assume that it included, at least, contemplation of the visions of prior apocalypticists. Moreover, it also offers an insight into the self-consciousness of the apocalypticists. Here there is no claim, comparable to that the Habakkuk Commentary, to exegete the text of Daniel in a new way. Instead, it is the revelation of the same things as were revealed to Daniel, but in a new way. Thus, although the Book of Daniel was probably regarded as scriptural by the author of 4 Ezra, his attitude toward it was not exegetical. Indeed, he claims that his vision here supersedes Daniel's.

■ 13 Here the particular terror of the last beast, the fourth kingdom, is emphasized, as it was in Dan 7:7; 7:19; 7:23; and 2 Apoc Bar 39:5–6. The same idea is expressed in different terms in 1 Enoch 90:2. It is clearly

wings to be "rulers who lived in the author's time." The particular knowledge of the heads and the stress laid upon them by the vision, as noted above, make it most likely, however, that major rulers are designated. The agreement of the traditions about them with the knowledge and rumors about the Flavian emperors in the East was pointed out by Schürer, 3:241–42, and cannot just be dismissed.

29   See in detail Function and Content, pp. 361–65.
30   See Function and Content, p. 363; see discussion in 14:23–26 Function and Content, p. 431.
31   See 11:1 Commentary. In a rather different context,

the eagle is one of a series of birds representing wicked peoples in 1 Enoch 89:10 and 90:2.
32   Esau is identified as Rome in 6:8–10; see Commentary there. Babylon represents Rome throughout the book, and see in detail 3:1 Commentary. The present identification with an eagle is discussed in 11:1 Commentary.
33   See ibid.
34   See Stone, "Apocalyptic Literature," 390–91; and Dimant, "Qumran Sectarian Writings," 505–6.

connected with the notion that the last king of this most dreadful kingdom will be particularly horrible. This is clear below in 12:23–24; compare *Test Mos* 8:1, "king of kings of the earth."[35]

■ **14** This verse makes it explicit that the twelve wings are twelve kings, which tells against scholars' theories of interpolation.

■ **15** This verse is interpreting 11:13; compare 11:16. The king who reigns more than twice as long as the others is usually taken to be Augustus.

■ **16** This verse concludes the first section of the intepretation.

■ **17** Here 11:10 is interpreted; it is not certain, however, whether the voice mentioned here is also the voice of 11:15. In any case, that verse is not explicitly discussed in the intepretation. On the interpretative formula, see Form and Structure, p. 360. Note the same expression also in 12:19 and 12:22; in these three instances, as in 6:16 and 10:40, not the word "interpretation" but a word meaning "word," "pronouncement" is to be found.[36]

■ **18** This verse is interpreting 11:10. The expression "in danger of falling" might be compared with 9:20, but the sense is quite different.[37]

■ **19** This verse is interpreting 11:3; cf. 11:11.

■ **20** This verse continues the interpretation of 11:11.

■ **21** This verse interprets material presented in the vision, in 11:24–31 and 12:2. "The end of time" could be a technical eschatological term, but in context it might also be nontechnical. The translation "its" reflects this exegetical uncertainty; cf. also 12:28.[38] It refers to the end of the time of the eagle, and to make this clearer, we have added "its."

■ **22** This verse interprets 11:23; cf. 11:29. It is formulated in a standard way, as often happens in the interpre-

tations of apocalyptic visions.[39]

■ **23** This verse is to be compared with 11:29–33. The expression "last days" is discussed above.[40] The idea is that, with the accession to rule of the three heads, the evil of the fourth kingdom will peak. That was a common expectation and is found elsewhere in the book.[41] Most evil rulers will come before the end; cf. also *2 Apoc Bar* 36:7. The expression "inhabitants of the earth" is predominantly used in context of woes in 4 Ezra.[42]

■ **24** Here the interpretation of the heads is continued. The wordplay that is completed in 12:25 starts in the last phrase of this verse.

■ **25** The term "last" is discussed in the Excursus on Natural Order. The whole verse turns on a pun in which the "head" is the beginning. This is very natural in Hebrew, as Violet pointed out.[43] A similar idea is the exegesis of "hand" and "heel" in 6:10, but there the terminology is determined by the biblical verses discussed.[44]

In the description of the heads in this interpretation, the antichrist associations may be less powerful than in the vision. Thus, notably, the pride of the head, so stressed in 11:43 and typical of the antichrist ideas, is absent from the interpretation. Equally, note also the plural "them" in the punishment section 12:32–33. That plural may be used, since the trial and the indictment are not just of one head, or of three heads, but of the whole eagle. The plural then would refer, presumably, to the Roman emperors in general.

■ **26** This verse interprets 11:29 and 11:33. It has been noted above that a number of details in the interpretation of the heads are not to be found in the vision. Since, on the whole, the interpretation is briefer than the vision, this added material is a clear indication that the author here interleaves details relating to his own time.

---

35 The arrogance of the Roman Empire was also a particularly prominent associated theme; cf. *Ps Sol* 2:1 and 17:6.

36 Cf. also *2 Apoc Bar* 68:1.

37 The element of danger has other meanings in the book; cf. 7:12; 7:89; and 9:8 Commentary.

38 On "end" as a technical term, see Excursus on Natural Order, pp. 103–4. On the nontechnical meaning of end here, see Stone, *Features*, 255 n. 202.

39 See Form and Structure, p. 360.

40 See Excursus on the Natural Order.

41 See 5:2 Commentary on the woes and their peaking

at the end.

42 See 5:1 Commentary. Three wicked rulers of Rome are also expected to be part of the events preceding the end in *Sib Or* 3:52. These are, however, identified by Collins, *apud* Charlesworth, *OTP*, as the second triumvirate.

43 See Violet 2, ad loc.

44 See 6:8–10 Commentary.

The head is apparently Vespasian, who did die in his bed, an exception, perhaps, in those stormy days. However, the agonies find no ready interpretation.[45]

■ **27** This verse is commenting on 11:35; cf. 12:1. As observed in the commentary on the preceding verse, here too, many details are added beyond those implied by the vision. Following the view that these two heads are the next two Flavian emperors, they can be identified as Titus and Domitian. See further next verse.

■ **28** This exegetes 11:35. The term "last days" is not taken eschatologically. This seems likely, but it is not a necessary exegesis.[46] This view in turn might reflect on the meaning of "end" in 12:21. All of the details given here about the sword are not found in the vision in chapter 11.

In fact, Titus was not killed by Domitian, but as Schürer pointed out, this was popularly believed to be the case.[47]

■ **29** "Its" refers to the eagle's. Alternatively, one might find support in the versions for "the"; see textual note e. The exegetical problem is similar to that encountered in the previous verse.[48]

■ **30** The brief reign of the two little wings is mentioned in 12:2. Schürer suggests that there is no need to seek identifications for them since they appertain to the end time. The term "end" is used in 12:30–34 with a number of different meanings: in 12:30 in the context of the eagle; in 12:32 in that of the Messiah, where it seems to mean the messianic kingdom; and in 12:34 from the perspective of that kingdom, where it means "day of judgment." This variability of referent is mentioned in the commentary on the previous verse and is discussed in detail above.[49] It is at one with the way the term is used in the book.

One might compare the confusion here said to ensue upon the end of the three heads with the confusion after the "third" (where the noun qualified is lost) in 5:4. In the Commentary there (in note 19), a number of other instances are assembled of confusions following upon series of three terrible events in the end time.

■ **31** This verse restates 11:37–43, which passage is actually interpreted in 12:32–33. The whole passage is very closely parallel to *2 Apoc Bar* 39:8—40:3:

39:8 And as touching that which thou hast seen, the lofty cedar, which was left of that forest, and the fact, that the vine spoke those words with it which thou didst hear, this is the word.

40:1 The last leader of that time will be left alive, when the multitude of his host will be put to the sword, and he will be bound, and they will take him up to Mount Zion, and My Messiah will convict him of all his impieties, and will gather and set before him all the works of his hosts. 40:2 And afterwards he will put him to death, and protect the rest of My people which shall be found in the place which I have chosen. And his principate will stand for ever, until the world of corruption is at an end, and until the times aforesaid are fulfilled. This is thy vision, and this is its interpretation.

The lion is the Messiah, and this identification as well as the chief features of the messianic figure is discussed in the Excursus on the Redeemer Figure, pp. 209–10. The lion symbolism arouses Judahite associations; the Davidid descent is here claimed most clearly in the book. The idea is found here that the Messiah is kept or prepared in advance for the end. This involves the conception of the precreation of eschatological things, and in some sources "the name of the Messiah" is said to have been created before the creation of the world.[50] Our author finds no conflict between predetermination and the Davidid

---

45   Box would view them as Vespasian's remorse, but the tradition is too specific. Perhaps some tradition known in the East is behind this, as it was behind the idea (not historical) that Titus was killed by Domitian; see 12:28 Commentary.

46   See Excursus on Natural Order.

47   See Schürer, 3:241; he quotes Dio Cassius 66.26; Suetonius, *Domitian* 2; *Sib Or* 12:120–123 on Domitian's conduct that led to this view; and Aurelius Victor, *Caes.* 10, 11, who states it as a fact.

48   It should be observed that, in view of the analysis offered of the term "end," being the decisive point in

the eschatological process, with the exact referent determined by context and association (see Excursus on Natural Order, pp. 103–4), the determination between these two possibilities makes little substantial difference to the understanding of the chapter or of the eschatology of the book in general.

49   See Excursus on Natural Order, pp. 103–4. This is exhaustively analyzed in Stone, "Coherence and Inconsistency," 232, 236, 239–40.

50   On precreation of the eschatological things, see 7:14 Commentary. On the precreation in more general terms, and as relates to the Messiah, see 3:6 Com-

descent. The final point, already discussed above, is the forensic aspect of the Messiah's function, which is much stressed here. This is so, although other aspects of his activity might have been expected to be brought up by the highlighting of his royal, Davidic origin. This forensic aspect is even more striking here in the interpretation than it was in the vision.[51] This dimension of the Messiah's activity is also prominent in the passage from *2 Apocalypse of Baruch* quoted above.

■ **32** The relationship between this verse of the interpretation and the vision was discussed in the commentary on the preceding verse. Likewise, most of the aspects of the presentation of the figure of the Messiah were discussed there. It is worth noting that the title "Messiah" occurs only here and in 7:28.[52] In any case, this title and its implications do not play a central role in the expectations of the book. Above, in the commentary on 12:25, we suggested that the plural "them" seems to refer either to all the heads or to the whole eagle. It softens the antichrist associations of the great head. The function of the Messiah here is similar to that of the Messiah in 13:37, in indictment and legal action. It also much resembles that in *2 Apoc Bar* 40:1 (cited in full in 12:31 Commentary).

■ **33** This verse describes the execution of judgment by the Messiah. In many respects it may be compared with *2 Apoc Bar* 40:2. In 12:3, in the vision, the destruction of the eagle is spoken of impersonally and not attributed to the Messiah. Here, however, it is said to be the work of the Messiah. The means by which he carries out this destruction are not mentioned. In a quite similar passage in 13:37–38 it is said to be the Messiah's very pronouncement that destroys.[53] The kings, or the eagle, are said to be set up "living" and destroyed. This might be taken to refer to a revivification of those that had perished, but the point being made rather seems to be that the judg-

ment is carried out at the end of the present world order.

It was pointed out that in 11:46 the "judgment and mercy" of God is awaited by those in the messianic kingdom. That is not mentioned here explicitly, but the term "judgment" in this verse and "mercy" in the next evoke that prediction. Of course, the eschatological time referred to differs; there it is the day of judgment, while here it is the inception of the messianic kingdom. Both elements, however, seem to belong to this sort of association.

■ **34** This verse has been considered central to the criticism of the book. Box regards the eagle vision as a separate source on the grounds of the supposed incompatibility of its eschatology with that of Visions 1–4. Within that separate source, he discerns in 12:34 an addition by the redactor designed to harmonize its views with those of the rest of the book. This point has been refuted above, and the general views of Box are also discussed in the Introduction.[54] The verse is a description of the messianic kingdom which resembles 9:8 and 13:48, both in broad lines and in many details. In general, in the book the messianic kingdom is considered to follow the woes (6:25–28; 7:27–28; and 9:8). In no instance is it said to be followed directly by the day of judgment.

Nearly all of the specific ideas in 12:34 have already been discussed in detail. The Messiah will deliver the remnant of the people who have been saved in mercy. "The remnant of my people" means those who survive the terrible events of the pre-messianic generation, specifically here the rule of the heads and the period of tumult. The expression and ideas particularly resemble those in 6:25; 7:27; 9:8; and 13:19–20.[55] In particular,

mentary; 13:26; 13:52; 14:9; et al. Cf. also *1 Enoch* 48:2–3, 6; 62:7 of the Son of man and the implications of *2 Apoc Bar* 29:3 and 30:1. Baruch is said to be preserved to the end in *2 Apoc Bar* 13:3; 25:1; and 76:3; cf. also Acts 3:21 of Christ. On the terminology of preservation and reservation, see 7:27 Commentary n. 53.

51 See in particular Excursus on the Redeemer Figure, pp. 209–12.

52 See Excursus on the Redeemer Figure, p. 208. On the precreation of the Messiah, see 12:31 Commentary.

53 See further 13:10 Commentary there. The Messiah's function in the destruction of the eagle may be compared with that of the "king from the sun" in *Sib Or* 3:652–656.

54 See Excursus on the Redeemer Figure, pp. 210–11, and in further detail Stone, *Features*, 29 and 111–12.

55 See the full discussion in 5:41 Commentary; the similarities with 9:8 are particularly striking, and see Commentary there.

the term "whoever remains" raises the idea of the righteous remnant, already found in biblical prophecy and here applied to the righteous of the last generation.[56] The idea of the surviving righteous of the last generation is bound up with the view of the messianic woes as one of the events that distinguishes the righteous from the wicked.[57]

Here and in 13:48 the idea is found that, in that last tumultuous generation, only those in the Holy Land will be saved. This idea is found also on a number of occasions in *2 Apocalypse of Baruch* (see 29:1–2; 32:1; 40:2; and 71:1). The connection between the land, the messianic kingdom, and the survivors occurs elsewhere in the book, although not in the same terms as here, except in 13:48.[58] The hidden land appears at the beginning of the Messianic kingdom according to 7:26.

The Messiah's rule is described as "making the survivors rejoice." His rule is described in exactly this terminology in 7:28. It has already been pointed out that an important difference between the view of the Messiah here and in 7:28 is that here he takes a most active role in the inception of his kingdom, while in 7:28 he appears only after the destruction of the wicked rule and world order. The term "joy," however, is shared by both texts and is also a broadly occurring term for the eschatological reward.[59] The term "mercy" typifies the Messiah's rule.[60] It is intriguing to note that neither this vision nor the next, both of which are chiefly concerned with the beginning of the messianic kingdom, tells us anything detailed about that kingdom but speaks of it only in general terms.[61] It is discussed further in 7:29 Commentary.

The messianic kingdom will come to an end; it is not eternal. Admittedly, not every occurrence of this idea in the book makes explicit that it has an end, but none of them says that it will be eternal. A number of instances, however, do say explicitly that it is going to come to an end and will be followed by the day of judgment.[62] The identification of the end as the day of judgment is noteworthy and should be put into relationship with the idea discussed immediately above about the exact meaning of the term "end" in 4 Ezra.[63] The day of judgment is the division point between the two ages, and that idea is also to be found clearly in 7:113 (and see Commentary there).

"At the beginning" means "formerly" and refers to the earlier eschatological prophecies in the book; cf. also 13:14.

■ **35** This is the concluding sentence of the actual interpretation. It is interestingly similar to the concluding sentence of Daniel 2: "The dream is certain and its interpretation sure" (Dan 2:45). In 13:53 at the conclusion of Vision 6, the angel mentions only the interpretation. In Daniel 2 the mention of both dream and interpretation is appropriate, since Daniel has revealed both to the king. Here, however, Ezra saw the dream and the angel has revealed only the interpretation, yet both are mentioned by the angel. Consequently, it is very likely that the direct influence of Daniel 2 is to be discerned here. After all, it too is a four-kingdoms vision.

■ **36** This verse forms the conclusion of the interpretation and the transition to the injunctions that follow. As in certain of the preceding visions, at the end the importance of what has been revealed is stressed. Statements of Ezra's worthiness appear throughout the book and have been analyzed above.[64] Here the angel stresses not just his worthiness but the special secret status of what has been revealed to him. This takes up the theme of 10:38–39, where the revelation of secrets to Ezra is clearly possible only after the experience of conversion in the

---

56 See in particular 5:41 Commentary.
57 Discussed in Excursus on the Term "Judgment," p. 151.
58 See 7:26 Commentary and 9:8 Commentary. The special role of the land of Israel in connection with resurrection is highlighted in *b. Ketubot* 111a and *j. Kilayim* 30c; see also S. Schechter, "Geniza Fragments," *JQR* 16 (1904) 447 n. 1. In *Midr. Tann.* 58 (ed. Hoffmann) the idea is found that the dead in the land of Israel will be resurrected first, while *Midr. Mishle* 17:2–7 makes a series of partly hyperbolic statements about the saving power of the habitation of the land of Israel. See also *Alfa-Beta de R. Aqiba* (Jellinek, *BM*, 3:31).
59 See 7:28 Commentary.
60 See 12:33 Commentary and Excursus on the Term "Judgment," p. 150.
61 See Excursus on the Redeemer Figure, p. 213.
62 See Excursus on Natural Order, p. 103, and 7:28 Commentary.
63 See Excursus on Natural Order, pp. 103–4.
64 See 6:32 Commentary.

fourth vision. In general, in 4 Ezra, secrets that are
revealed are eschatological in character. The eagle
vision, however, is the first of the new sort of revelation
given to Ezra after the change in his role.[65] The same
special character of the revelation of the eschatological
secrets in the eagle vision may be found in the following
pericope. See also 13:14.

65　See in detail 10:38–54 Function and Content, p. 336.

37   **Therefore write all these things that you have seen in a book, and put it in a hidden place; 38/ and you shall teach them to the wise among your people, whose hearts you know are able to comprehend and keep these secrets. 39/ But wait here seven days more, so that you may be shown whatever it pleases the Most High to show you." Then he left me.**

Form and Structure

This passage is part of the conclusion of the vision. In many respects it follows the conclusions of the preceding visions in structure.[1] On the one hand, they provide a conclusion for the vision that has just passed; on the other, they bridge the transition to the next vision.

By analogy with the earlier passages, the present conclusion and injunctions properly also include 12:51. This verse provides the information about the fulfillment of the commands and the transition to the next vision. However, in this case, as in the passage representing the transition from Vision 1 to Vision 2, a piece of narrative comes between the two parts of this pericope. As there, the narrative has to do with the reassurance of the people because of Ezra's prolonged absence.

In 12:37–39 a number of features deliberately refer back to what has preceded, while others point forward and link with or anticipate that which is to follow. So the word "here" in 12:39 indicates the field mentioned already in 9:26 and 10:32. This field is the location of the whole latter part of the book. The reference to seven days' time passed in the field also ties in with the seven days' fasting and limited food enjoined at the end of most previous visions.[2] The commands to write down the content of the vision and to transmit it secretly to the wise of the people both foreshadow themes that are extensively developed in chapter 14 and are discussed below in the next section.

Function and Content

The move into the injunctions is marked by the word "therefore" (12:37), and we may compare the use of the same word in the same context in 10:55. A completely new element, as far as 4 Ezra is concerned, is the command to write the content of the vision in a book, to put it in a hidden place, and to teach and transmit it only to the truly wise of the people.

This element is to be found at the end of a number of other apocalyptic visions. A prominent instance is Dan 12:4; compare Dan 12:9. There are a number of others.[3] Much has been written both on the function of pseudepigraphy in general and, in particular, on the function of such commands that seem to supply an explanation for the transmission of the pseudepigraphic books.[4] Here, suffice it to say that at the very least the function of such material is authenticating but that these ideas may also arise from the nature of the tradition in which the author is immersed.

What is quite striking is that this is the first occasion on which such a command is given in the book and that it is also not given at the end of the sixth vision. However, the theme of the writing down of the revelation in books and its transmission to the wise is central to the whole of chapter 14. Since this is a traditional element, it is also most significant to note that this eagle vision as a whole is particularly deeply rooted in apocalyptic tradition. Its subject, the four empires, recurs elsewhere; its form—the interpreted dream vision of historical events—is commonplace; indeed, in 12:11 we find the striking statement that the whole dream is a further explanation of the vision of Daniel 7. In other words, not only does the author use traditional material and forms, he

---

1   These basic structures are analyzed in 6:30–34 Form, Function and Content, pp. 173–74.

2   These relationships in structure and pattern are further reinforced by 12:51.

3   See, e.g., *1 Enoch* 81:6; 82:1; et al.; *2 Enoch* 47:1 and 48:6–7. See Stone, "Apocalyptic Literature," 431–32.

4   These themes are extremely important in chap. 14.

explicitly informs us of his place in an ongoing stream of apocalyptic interpretation and reinterpretation.

It is by no chance that all of these elements come together here. On the one hand, the first three visions were very unconventional when viewed from the perspective of the other Jewish apocalypses, embodying a sort of dialogic revelation which, as we have noted, is rather rare. Moreover, the fourth vision was shown to be pivotal, partaking of elements of the first three visions but also representing a major shift in Ezra's self-consciousness. If in the first three visions, Ezra as the challenger and questioner of God (Shealtiel, see 3:1 Commentary) plays a role that is very unusual, in the fourth vision the role is reversed. Ezra, who had been the challenger of God comforted by the angel, becomes himself the comforter of the mourning woman and then receives the great vision of the heavenly Jerusalem.

Both in form and in content this vision marks a change in Ezra's position. In the first three visions Ezra underwent a gradual change, in the course of which he accepted certain basic premises about God's conduct of the world and eschatology. Only with the powerful experience of the fourth vision, however, did a kaleidoscopic rearrangement of the elements of his worldview, and consequently of his own role, take place. The experience described there is not presented as a symbolic dream but as a waking experience of the same sort described in the first three visions. But its impact was staggering.

The change of Ezra's role from challenger to comforter was made possible by his acceptance of the basic way that the world is conducted. In his new role he functions, in Visions 5 and 6, just as do the apocalyptic seers in the other visions. He is more receptive, asks no questions of principle, and receives revelations. Once he has reached this position, so the command to write the books and transmit them teaches us, he becomes the recipient of specific visions about what the Most High will do at the end of days (see 10:59). Now Ezra has

experienced visions basically like those of other apocalyptic seers, and he must therefore transmit them as secret knowledge.

Two further observations should be made in this connection. Above, in our discussion of the first two visions, we made much of the rejection by Ezra and by the angel of the idea of special knowledge and revelation. This apparently lies in contradiction with the idea that Ezra receives esoteric knowledge that he is to transmit to the wise of the people. Yet some distinctions are to be drawn.[5]

In 4:5–9 and 5:36–37 it is not all types of revealed information that are rejected. It was observed there that immediately after this rejection, Ezra proceeds to ask about eschatological secrets.[6] What is rejected is cosmological and uranographical speculation, mystical ascent and theosophical speculations. To the contrary, starting from the revelation to Abraham of eschatological secrets in 3:14, and continuing with the description of the revelation of eschatological secrets to Moses on Sinai as part of the giving of the Torah in 14:5, and concluding with the giving anew of the Torah (twenty-four public books and seventy secret ones) to Ezra, the new Moses and giver of the Torah in chapter 14, the book has a consistent view about eschatological secrets. These are a proper subject of revelation. Thus when Ezra, now playing the traditional role of the apocalyptic seer, receives specific revelations about these, he is told to record the revelations and transmit them secretly.[7]

One more element is worthy of note here and relates to the same idea but is expressed structurally. Ezra is commanded to remain in the field for seven days. If all the days of fasting, partial abstention, and remaining in the field, from Vision 1 to Vision 6, are counted, they make a total of forty. This total is arrived at by taking the "three weeks" referred to in 6:35 as meaning not just the two seven-day periods mentioned between Vision 1 and Vision 2, and between Vision 2 and Vision 3, but also assuming a seven-day period, not mentioned explicitly in

---

5   This matter is discussed in detail in 10:38–54 Function and Content, p. 334, and 14:3–18 Function and Content, pp. 416–17. The broad issue of special knowledge in the apocalypses is broached in Stone, "Lists"; and idem, "Way of the Most High."

6   See Stone, "Way of the Most High," 134–37.

7   This idea of secret transmission has been discussed

above and will be dealt with further below in connection with chap. 14.

the text, preceding Vision 1. To these twenty-one days, we add the seven days between Vision 3 and Vision 4 (9:23; 9:27), the two days between Vision 4 and Vision 5 (10:58; 11:1), the week of the present passage, and the three days between Vision 6 and Vision 7 (13:58). This makes a total of forty.

Now, while Breech has suggested with great plausibility that a correlation exists between Ezra's fasting and his eating of vegetarian food (as did mankind before Noah),[8] and his shift from mourning to consolation, but which we might describe a little differently, no explanation has ever been found of the variation of the length of the periods of abstinence and separation between the visions. If, as we have hinted, the revelation of the times is the peak of what is to be revealed according to Ezra, and if Ezra is a second Moses, then not only does the story of his receiving of the Torah involve a forty-day fast (14:23) but also the whole of the previous six visions which are summed up, from another focus, in that giving of the Torah, are also the revelation of the same secrets and so involve the same overall period of fasting. This important hint at the function of chapter 14 is also borne out by the very command to write the material and transmit it secretly that is also set here. Ezra's new role, the consummation of all that has preceded, now comes into clear focus. This structure will be shown to have been developed in enormous detail in the last vision and is central to understanding it.[9]

Ezra is not commanded to pray, nor to fast, merely to remain in the field. He eats only plants and flowers, according to 12:51, even though this is not mentioned in the injunctions themselves. His alimentation is likewise not mentioned explicitly between Vision 4 and Vision 5 or between Vision 6 and Vision 7. He will be shown what it pleases the Most High to show him.

Commentary

■ **37** In the Function and Content section above, the main issues of this verse have been discussed. It is intriguing to note the force of "therefore": because Ezra was so worthy and learned the secrets, therefore he is to write them in the books and secrete them. This reinforces the point that the type of revelation made to him changes as a result of his different role. The command to write apocalyptic revelations in books and a concern for their transmission is found in many works of the day.[10]

■ **38** This verse introduces a new element. Ezra is not only to record his visions but to teach them to the wise secretly. This adds a further dimension of esotericism to the command[11] and has not been referred to previously in the book. In 8:62 the limited nature of revelations is stressed: "I have not shown this to all men, but only to you and a few like you," but this is still not the idea of an esoteric or limited tradition of transmission.[12]

■ **39** Ezra is told to remain in the field. Although seven days are mentioned, as in previous visions, nothing is said about fasting, praying, or any of the other activities upon which he engages in those prior instances. The angelic promise of further revelations is standard in such contexts.[13] The verb "show" is most regularly used of revelation in the books; see 4:3–4; 4:45; 4:47–48; 5:56; et al. In promises like the present one it occurs, for example, in 6:30–33 and 10:59, in the latter of a dream vision. Note also the usage in 12:9–10, where Ezra refers to the eagle vision.

---

8   See Breech, "These Fragments," 272; on the primordial diet, see Gen 1:29 and cf. with Gen 9:3–4. See also the Adam literature, and particularly the comments in Stone, *Penitence of Adam*, xiii-xiv.

9   Brandenburger, *Verborgenheit*, 139, also pointed out the parallelism of the number of days but saw its significance predominantly as a demonstration of the literary link between Visions 1–6 and Vision 7 (p. 139).

10   See, e.g., Dan 8:26; 12:4; 12:9; *1 Enoch* 82:1; *2 Enoch* 35:2; 40:1–2; Rev 22:10; *Jub* 1:5; *Sib Or* Prologue; 11:170–171; and *Test Mos* 1:16–17. On revelation in

secret, see *1 Enoch* 107:3.

11   See Stone, "Apocalyptic Literature," 431–32.

12   Box stresses the supposed contradiction between the command to Ezra to write this vision and the command to the five scribes to write the vision in chap. 14. We fail to perceive the difficulty.

13   See 5:32 Commentary.

12

40 When all the people heard that the seven days were past and I had not returned ᵃ to the city, they all gathered together, from the least to the greatest, and came to me and spoke to me, saying, ᵇ 41/ "How have we offended you, and what harm have we done you, that you have forsaken us and sit in this place? 42/ For of all the prophets you alone are left to us, like a cluster of grapes from the vintage, and like a lamp in a dark place, and like a haven for a ship saved ᶜfrom a storm. ᶜ 43/ Are not the evils which have befallen us sufficient, ᵈthat you also forsake us? ᵈ 44/ Therefore if you also ᵉ forsake us, how much better it would have been for us if we ᶠ had been consumed in the burning of Zion! 45/ For we are no better than those who died there." And they ᵍ wept with a loud voice.

Then I answered them and said,

46/ "Take courage, O Israel;
and do not be sorrowful, O house of Jacob;

47/ for the Most High has you in remembrance,
and the Mighty One has not forgotten you ʰforever. ʰ

48/ As for me, ⁱI have neither forsaken you ʲnor withdrawn from you; ᵏ but I have come to this place to pray on account of the desolation of Zion, and to seek mercy on account of the humiliation of our sanctuary. ˡ 49/ Now go, every one of you to his house, and after these days I will come to you." 50/ So the people went into the city, as I told them to do. 51/ But I sat in the field seven days, as he [i.e., the angel] ᵐ had commanded me; and I ate only of the flowers of the field, and my food was of plants during those days.

Notes

40 a Syr, Eth Mss, Ar1 "come."

b This word, a stylistic Hebraism, is found only in Lat, Syr.

42 c–c The versions vary in this phrase.

43 d–d Lat, Eth, Ar1, Arm omit. Probably the similarity of this and the next phrase is responsible for the omission.

44 e Lat, Syr omit; see next note.

f Lat, Syr add "also"; see preceding note.

45 g Syr, Ar1 "I," deriving from ambiguous Greek ἔκλαιον (Mussies, p. 108).

47 h–h So Syr, Arm; Lat *in contentione*, cf. Ar1; Violet 1 suggests εἰς ἀγῶνα ⟨ εἰς αἰῶνα; Eth, Ar2 omit. Perles ("Notes," 185) suggests לנצח ⟨ εἰς νῖκος (but understood as "forever" by Syr [?Arm] on the basis of biblical usage), while Lat, Ar1 derive from εἰς νεῖκος. This is accepted by Violet 2 but does not seem compelling to us unless other similar instances can be proved to exist in 4 Ezra. See further Stone, *Features,* 39, and "Some Features of the Armenian Version" against possible double translations from Hebrew.

48 i–k Ar1 omits.

j–k Arm omits.

l Eth "happiness" might derive from ἀγαλλίασμα ⟨ ἁγίασμα (Hilgenfeld). Arm omits.

51 m Lat Ms L and Arm W Y add *angelus domini;* Arm H has just *angelus;* cf. Stone, "Manuscripts and Readings," 51–54.

Form and Structure

This passage is a narrative interlude inserted into the conclusions and injunctions. Indeed, properly speaking, 12:51 belongs with the injunctions discussed above. The only other similar narrative in the book follows Vision 1, in 5:16–18. It is notable that each of these passages occurs after the first vision in a distinct section of the book; Vision 1 is the first of the three dialogic visions and Vision 5 is the first dream vision. It is also significant that both passages use a series of similes in the people's description of Ezra (cf. also 12:42 and note there), and there are other resemblances between them that will be discussed below.

The cross-references implied by this passage also tie it

to that which precedes. The reference to the desolation of Zion immediately recalls the opening phrases of the book (see 3:2), while the language about the humiliation of the sanctuary evokes the lament over the destruction in 10:21–22. This narrative may be divided into the following parts:

A. Introduction (12:40)

The introduction uses a familiar Hebrew figure of speech, "from the least to the greatest," to indicate the whole people, a characteristic biblical merism.

B. People's Address to Ezra (12:41–45)

This address is composed of a question, "How have we offended you that you have forsaken us?" (12:41), followed by an expression of concern: "You alone remain" (12:42), which is strengthened in 12:42 by three similes. The first is a grape from the vintage, which seems to be a deliberate reference back to 9:20–22. The second and third, the lamp in the dark place and the haven in the storm, do not occur elsewhere in 4 Ezra, but the lamp may be compared with *2 Apoc Bar* 59:2. The final part of the address is the exclamation "Better that we die with Zion than you abandon us!" (12:43–45). This exclamation takes up and reapplies a *topos* about humans that Ezra has already used extensively; see 4:12 Commentary.

C. Ezra's Response (12:46–49)

This is composed of the following elements. First, words of response are spoken in a rhetorical form (12:46). This saying uses both synonymous and contrasting parallelism, standard features of Hebrew poetic composition. Next follows an assurance of divine comfort: "God remembers you" (12:47)—God, Ezra tells the people, has not forsaken you. Then follows the pronouncement of Ezra's prophetic help: "I have not forsaken you." Indeed, Ezra says, the purpose of my absence is to intercede on your behalf (12:48). As a result, he instructs the people to go home (12:49).

D. Narrative Conclusion (12:50)

E. Conclusion of the Injunctions Pericope (12:51)

The narrative has been inserted into the middle of an injunctions pericope, like those found at the end of the other visions. We have called this Injunctions and Conclusion, and it started in 12:37–39, while in fact 12:51 is its true conclusion.

Function and Content

A key to the understanding of this passage is the reapplication of the *topos* "better my death than my life" in 12:44 as "Better that we die with Zion than that you abandon us!" This cry had been Ezra's, and piercingly so, in 4:12. Now it is put into the mouth of the people. In chapter 4, speaking for God, the angel responds to Ezra's cry, while here Ezra, speaking in God's name (12:47),

offers comfort to the grieving people. Thus, here Ezra is playing the role played by the angel, while the people function as Ezra himself did.

A similar reversal of function was already observed to have taken place in the fourth vision where, unconsciously as it seems, Ezra turns to comfort the weeping woman, just as he himself had been addressed and comforted earlier in the book. Here, however, the change of Ezra's role is made much more explicit. We suggested in Form and Structure that the image of the grape is dependent on the same type of views as expressed in 9:20–22; compare also the poetic statement in 5:23 (pp. 127–28). Consequently, this image is deeply tied to the idea of election. Now all the similes applied to Ezra by the people express primarily the idea that Ezra alone remains, but the particular use of the language of grape and vine adds the dimension of election to this. The idea of election, previously related to Israel, is here applied to Ezra, who alone remains. This strengthens the implications of the role reversal.

A further new element arises in the presentation of the figure of Ezra here. The people say, "For of all the prophets you alone are left to us" (12:42).[1] Here, for the first time in the book, Ezra is referred to as a prophet. His speaking for God may be understood in accordance with this. As pointed out, now he comforts the people just as God's other spokesman, the angel, had comforted him. Ezra's self-consciousness and the way he is presented in the book have changed. This is the consummation of a process we have traced from the end of the third vision. In the discussion of the Function and Content of the preceding pericope we pointed out that this vision is marked as being the expression of Ezra's full entry into the role of apocalyptic seer (p. 373). The implications and results of his conversion in the fourth vision have come to fruition. He has received a vision of the true secret tradition of eschatological mysteries. Now, in this narrative passage he is designated "prophet," and his changed role is made completely explicit.

---

1   Intriguingly, in the last chapter of the book, Ezra's prophetic role is reconfirmed, since he is assimilated there to Moses, the greatest of the prophets. See 14:23–26 Function and Content, p. 428 and n. 6. Both Breech ("These Fragments," *passim*) and Brandenburger (*Verborgenheit*, 75–76, 119, et al.) make much of Ezra's prophetic role earlier in the book. This is nowhere explicit, and both scholars are led to it by their overall interpretations of the book rather than by the text. Meade, *Pseudonymity and Canon*, 75, has overlooked the significance of Ezra's being called "prophet" when he writes: "The heroes [i.e., of the apocalypses] are never called prophets or called to prophesy."

Ezra had been instructed by the angel to transmit the book in which he writes the secrets, that is, the contents of the eagle vision, to the wise and the worthy of the people (12:38). It is intriguing, however, that in this narrative passage, when he has to explain to the people what he had been doing during his long absence, he makes no reference to the revelation of secrets. Instead, he refers to his activity as "praying on account of Zion." This is to be understood in the light of the attitudes expressed in 12:38 about exoteric and esoteric revelation (see also 14:46). There Ezra is instructed not to reveal the content of the revelations in public. Consequently, here he simply refers to his activity as "praying on account of Zion." Here he carries out the implications of the angelic command of 12:38: "And you shall teach them to the wise among your people, whose hearts you know are able to comprehend and keep these secrets."

The fact that his activity is called prayer on behalf of the people, however, is also related to the role he has been given and accepted, that of prophet. It indicates that in some way his activity is mediating (as was that of Moses, who received the Torah on behalf of the people). This is quite appropriate for one designated "prophet," as it is for one who, as will be clear from chapter 14, is described according to the type of Moses. It is worth stressing, therefore, that Ezra does not reject the role of prophet but implicitly accepts it.

The position in the book of the only two narrative passages, that in 5:16–20 and the present one, should be considered further. The first one occurs at the end of the first vision of the first part of the book. The second one, presently under discussion, occurs at the end of the first vision of the second part of the book. The first part of the book is dialogue; the second part of it (Visions 5 and 6) is dreams. This structure also highlights the particular role that is played by the fourth vision. It is pivotal and crucial and signifies the changing of role, of atmosphere, and of the seer's consciousness, and these changes are also expressed by the change in the type of religious experience and the corresponding change in literary forms. The fourth vision does not form the start of the second part of the book, however, but partakes of both parts and is pivotal between them. The second part of the book commences with the revelation of eschatological secrets, promised at the end of Vision 4. From what has been said, it is abundantly clear, then, that this elaborate structure conveys a clear message.

The comparison of the contexts of these two narrative passages is also instructive. In the present one Ezra is approached by the whole people, but in 5:16 only by Paltiel. There Paltiel came on the second night; here the people come after seven nights.[2] There Ezra offers no explanation of his activities and offers no words of comfort. He merely says, "I will tell you the matter" (5:19)—surely cold comfort. Here he gives a long explanation of his absence and offers detailed words of consolation. This reflects the change that had taken place in Ezra's person.[3]

The language in which the people's concern is expressed in the first passage differs from here. In 5:18 they are concerned that his fasting may lead to his death, while here they are concerned that he might abandon them. The central concern is the same, but of course here Ezra is no longer fasting. It is also interesting that in both instances there are narrative pointers that are not taken up. Chapter 5:19 says, "Depart from me and do not come near me for seven days, and then you may come to me and I will tell you the matter." Yet Paltiel is not said to come to him after the next seven-day period, nor does he tell them "the matter." Similarly in the present passage, "and I will come to you" (12:49) is not fulfilled immediately or explicitly, though it might be taken to refer to 14:27–36.

As far as designations of the seer are concerned, while he is called prophet here, the implication of the simile of the "shepherd" in 5:18 is clearly in the realm of kingship and leadership. Paltiel, too, is called "a chief of the people."[4]

---

2   Brandenburger raises an exegetical difficulty at this point, setting 12:40 "the seven days were past" over against 12:51 "But I sat in the field for seven days." The second mention of "seven days" contradicts the first one. Brandenburger explains this as an unevenness caused by the deliberate patterning of this passage after 5:15–18 (*Verborgenheit*, 111–12).

3   See ibid., 118.

4   Ezra's designations are discussed in detail by Kraft, "'Ezra' Materials," 124–30, esp. pp. 128–29.

In this passage, then, it is Ezra who responds to the people's plaint over destruction, and his response is that the Most High had not abandoned Israel. What a dramatic contrast with Visions 1–3!

A most important point arises from this incident with the people. It provides, admittedly still in the "artificial" pseudepigraphic framework, a social context. In this social context, and by it, Ezra's position is confirmed. The people here form an audience for Ezra's speech. They clearly have certain expectations of Ezra as a leader. They have recognized, from Ezra's actions, that he has special roles first as a leader (in chapter 5) and then as a prophet (in the present passage). This implies that he is functioning in a way that is expected and recognized by his audience. His conduct is in accordance with their expectations of the holder of the role or position of prophet.

Once Ezra has been so identified by the people, he responds both positively and negatively. On the negative side, he does not deny the prophetic identification. On the positive side, he acts as a mediator by praying for the people but also acts, as is proper for a recipient of special revelation, by withholding the secret knowledge available to him.

All of these implications are to be found in the narrative which is part of the pseudepigraphic framework. The possibility must be raised that such expectations and views of Ezra, here presented pseudepigraphically, are in fact direct reflections of expectations of the social group in which the author operated. Perhaps the author transferred to Ezra something from the actual social context

in which he lived. We should stress, a social context in this sense need not be the society as a whole, it may be a limited group or circle within the larger society. Roles such as that of prophet or seer received their definition not just from the actual action of their bearer but also from the expectation of his group or audience. Indeed, those expectations often contributed to the definition of the action of the seer.[5]

Commentary

■ **40** The seven days mentioned here correspond to the seven days found between many of the preceding visions. The exact nature of the abstention between each vision is discussed above.[6] The significance of the numbers is discussed in 12:37–39 Function and Content, pp. 372–74. The people are said here to come to him after seven days, that is, at the end of his period of waiting. In the corresponding text in 5:16 they come to him "on the second night" and he instructs them to go away for seven days.[7] "The city" referred to is presumably Babylon.[8] This is part of the pseudepigraphic background of the book. The people are said to assemble "from the least to the greatest," a cliché in biblical language stressing that all of them assembled.[9] The introduction of the people in both narrative passages sets Ezra's vision experience into a social context, as has been spelled out in detail in Function and Content. This is not a private, personal experience but a public one, recognized by a community and, as we shall see, clearly identified by them.

■ **41** There are a number of biblical examples adduced by commentators that are parallel to the individual phrases

---

5 This passage goes beyond, say, *2 Apocalypse of Baruch* 44, Baruch's address to the people, for here the people recognize Ezra's role and he acts in accordance with their recognition.

6 See 5:20b–22 Form and Function, p. 118. Brandenburger, *Verborgenheit,* 112, following Müller, *Messias,* thinks that here only one or two days are past. This view is partly based in the parallel narrative in Vision 1. In fact, the problem does not exist. It is created by 12:51, which is actually the conclusion of 12:37–39. By the insertion of the narrative pericope the author has, not quite felicitously, given the impression that 12:51 is narrating another group of seven days, additional to that mentioned in 12:40. Once the formal character of the conclusion and injunctions pericope is recognized, the reason for the introduction of the seven days in 12:51 is obvious and

Brandenburger's difficulty disappears.

7 See Brandenburger, *Verborgenheit,* 112. There is an apparent problem in the text of 5:19. Ezra is commanded to fast for seven days (5:13). Paltiel came "on the second night" (5:16) and is said to go away to return after seven days. Ezra's command to this effect has been seen as creating a contradiction and a total of nine days. However, as observed already, this is a loose end in the narrative, and Paltiel is not said, in any case, to return.

8 See 3:1 Commentary.

9 See Gen 19:11; Jer 6:12, and many other places. In reverse formulation in a similar context, see *2 Apoc Bar* 77:1.

of this verse. The whole verse is very similar to *2 Apoc Bar* 32:8 and 33:3. The people here have not comprehended the reason for Ezra's absence and think him to be offended. This is different from 5:16–18, where the concern expressed is not that Ezra has absented himself and thus abandoned them but that he has not eaten.

■ **42** The function of the images was analyzed above.[10] It should be added that the image of the lamp as a leader is most clearly paralleled in *2 Apoc Bar* 77:13.[11] The shining of a lamp in darkness is an obvious image and occurs often (see, e.g., Isa 9:1 [Heb]; 58:10; 2 Pet 1:19). The image of the ship is rare in the Bible, perhaps reflecting the objective reality that the Israelites were not great seafarers, in contrast with prevalent nautical images in Greek literature; cf. also 4 Ezra 9:34. Note, however, *2 Apoc Bar* 85:10. Of note is the people's identification of Ezra as a prophet, which he does not deny. They have not related his absence to his prophetic function; on the contrary, they fear that his absence is for other reasons and will affect his prophetic activities.

■ **43** No commentary.

■ **44** On the underlying *topos*, see the discussion in Function and Content, p. 376. The idea that mourning for the loss of a leader may even lead to a wish to die is found elsewhere in the sources, for example, *Test Mos* 11:4 and *2 Apoc Bar* 33:3.

■ **45** This is a statement of despair. One might claim that it implies a view according to which those who died in the burning of Zion were more deserving of death than those who survived in the exile. The point would then be that Ezra's abandoning the people would imply that they were as wicked as those who had already died. But it is perhaps simpler to view the verse as meaning: "We are *no better off* than those who died, if Ezra abandons us." No hint at the former view is to be found anywhere else in the book.

■ **46** This verse opens Ezra's encouragement of the people. It uses biblical clichés common to the literature dealing with the exile, for example, Bar 4:5. The parallelism of Israel and Jacob, or seed of Jacob, predominantly in that order, is common. The expression "house of Jacob" does not occur elsewhere in the book.[12] Here Ezra's role as a consoler comes to the fore; he consoles

Israel. Earlier in the book, in 10:5–24, he had consoled Zion. Baruch is given the same function in *2 Apoc Bar* 78:7.

■ **47** The assertion that God's relationship to his people is, in the final analysis, inalienable is deeply rooted in biblical thought. Knibb would see in this assertion a reflection of the change of attitude that took place after the end of the third vision. Yet observe that here Ezra is consoling the people of Israel; previously, too, when the angel consoled Ezra, he consistently urged God's ultimate concern for Israel and the redemption. The message of comfort of Israel here is the exoteric expression of the meaning of the secret revelation of the eagle vision.

A rather similar reassurance of the righteous can be observed in *1 Enoch* 103:1–4. That text, however, makes it completely explicit that special revelation is the basis for the assurance—Enoch has read it on the heavenly tablets. This contrast nicely shows up 4 Ezra's use of a common theme and his particular application of it.

It is significant, therefore, that one point at which the interpretation of the man vision differs from the dream is in the prophecy of the restoration of the ten tribes. This is a spelling out of the promise of restoration made here. The divine title "Mighty One" is discussed in 6:32 Commentary.

■ **48** Ezra's assurance that he will neither forsake nor abandon the people corresponds to and answers their fears expressed in 12:41–45. He describes his activity in the field as prayer for mercy on Zion. This is accurate only in the most general way; even in his long prayer in 8:20–36 the point is mercy on all mankind, not just on Zion. Instead, the expression is best understood as referring to Vision 4 in particular, which, though not strictly a prayer for Zion, is in fact a call for mercy and restoration of the city. The reference to the sanctuary, evoking as it does 10:22–23, tells in favor of this interpretation.

■ **49** Scholars holding a source theory maintain that "these days" refers to the days mentioned in 12:39 and that the redactor erred and forgot that he had not pictured Ezra

---

10   The expression is somewhat formulaic in *Mek.* 1 (Horovitz-Rabin, p. 6), where Baruch's position is also described by use of similar images.

11   See 2 Pet 1:19.

12   See 3:19; 3:32; 5:35; 8:16; and 9:30; cf. also *2 Apoc Bar* 31:3.

communicating them to the people.[13] Two comments appear to be relevant. The first is that there is no reason for such an error to be typical of a redactor rather than an author. The second is that, according to 12:40, those days mentioned in 12:39 had already passed. We would propose that "these days" are part of Ezra's "misleading" of the people and, in fact, mean the days in which he is praying on behalf of the people.

■ **50** No commentary.

■ **51** The importance of the eating of the flowers and the significance are discussed in 9:24 Commentary and 9:26 Commentary.

---

13   So Box, Kabisch.

13

1 After [a] seven days I dreamed a dream [b] in the night; 2/ and [c] behold, a great [d] wind arose from the sea [e]so that it [e] stirred up all its waves. 3/ [f]And I looked, and behold, [g] this wind made [h]something like the figure of [h] a man come up out of [i]the heart of [i] the sea. [j]And I looked, and behold, [j] that man flew with the clouds of heaven; and wherever he turned his face to look, everything under his gaze trembled, 4/ and wherever the voice [k]of his mouth [k] issued forth, all who heard his voice melted as wax melts when it feels the fire.

5 After this I looked, and behold, [l] an innumerable multitude of men were gathered together from the four winds of heaven to make war against the man who came up out of the sea. 6/ And I looked, and behold, he carved out [m] for himself [n] a great mountain, and flew [o] upon it. 7/ And I tried to see [p] the region or place [q] from which the mountain was carved, [r] but I could not.

8 After this I looked, and behold, [s] all who had gathered together [t]against him, [t] to wage war with him, were much afraid, [u] yet dared to fight. [v] 9/ And [w] when he saw the onrush of the approaching multitude, he neither lifted his hand nor held a sword [x] or any weapon of war; 10/ but I saw only how he sent forth from his mouth [y]as it were [y] a stream of fire, and from his lips a flaming breath, and from his tongue he shot forth a storm of fiery coals. [z] 11/ All these were mingled together, the stream of fire and the flaming breath and the great storm, and fell on the onrushing multitude which was prepared to fight, and burned them all up, so that suddenly nothing was seen [a] of the innumerable multitude [b] but only the dust of

Notes

1   a Lat, Syr "And it came to pass"; this phrase is omitted by the other versions. Both texts probably occurred in Greek.

b Ar1, Ar2 omit.

2   c Lat Ψ adds *et vidi;* Arm also adds this word and omits "behold"; Ar1, Ar2 omit "behold" and have "I saw" in the previous verse. Probably a Greek doublet is here involved: ἰδοῦ/εἶδον. Originality is difficult to determine and we follow RSV without particular conviction. The influence of the beginning of the next verse weighs against the Latin Ms reading; cf. note f-g below on 13:3.

d Lat, Ar2 omit.

e-e Eth, Ar2 "and"; Arm abbreviated.

3   f-g Lat, Syr; Eth, Ar1, Ar2 "and I saw"; Arm omits; cf. note c above on 13:2.

f-j Lat omits by homoeoarchton; Lat Ms L *virum ascendebat de corde maris et* which Violet 1 regards as secondary.

h-h Eth, Arm "something like a man"; Ar2 "the figure of a man."

i-i Eth, Ar2 omit.

j-j Syr, Lat as reconstructed; others omit; cf. note l below on 13:5 and note s below on 13:8.

4   k-k Lat, Syr, Arm; Syr, Arm have "of his mouth"; Lat has "from his mouth."

5   l Lat, Syr; others omit; cf. note j above on 13:4.

6   m Eth "built"; Ar1 "made"; see note r below on 13:7.

n Lat, Syr, Arm; others omit.

o Syr "flew and set himself on"; Ar1 "mounted"; Arm "entered into"; perhaps two Greek texts lie behind the readings here.

7   p Eth "to know"; Arm "to find"; Eth may go back to a confusion of Greek forms εἰδέναι/ἰδεῖν.

p-q Eth "where"; Ar1, Ar2 "the place."

r Eth "built"; Arm "made"; see note m above on 13:6.

8   s Lat, Syr; Arm "this also"; Ar1 "this"; Ar2 omits; there were probably two Greek readings; see note j-j above on 13:3.

t-t Lat, Arm; other versions omit.

u Lat, Syr, Arm; Eth, Ar1, Ar2 add "of him."

v Lat, Syr, Arm; Eth, Ar1, Ar2 "against him."

9   w Lat adds "behold."

x Lat *frameam.*

10   y-y Eth, Arm omit.

z Syr, Eth; Lat *scintillas;* Ar1, Ar2 omit the word; Arm omits the whole phrase.

11   a Eth, Ar1 "remained."

a-b Eth, Ar1 "them."

ashes and the smell of smoke. When I saw it, I was amazed. c

After this I saw the same man come down from the d **mountain and call to him another multitude which was peaceable. 13a/ Then the forms of** e **many people came to him, some of whom were joyful and some sorrowful; some of them were bound,** f **and some were bringing others as offerings.** f

12

13a

c Eth, Ar2 "awoke."

d Syr, Eth "that"; in this and the previous phrase "that man" Arm has "a certain"; the origin is uncertain but it provides some indirect support for Syr, Eth here.

e Syr, Ar1 with indirect support of Lat *vultus;* probably something like this also lies behind Arm; Eth, Ar1 omit.

f–f Lat, Syr; Eth, Ar2, Arm omit; Ar1 varies.

Form and Function

This passage forms the first part of the sixth vision of the book. It is composed of two segments: an introduction (13:1) and the narration of the actual dream (13:2–13a). However, the narration also falls into a number of different episodes.

A. Introduction (13:1)

B. The Dream (13:2–13a)

Episode 1: The Appearance of the Man (13:2–4)
Introduction ending with "and behold" (13:2). Vision (13:3–4), marked into parts by "And I looked, and behold" in 13:3a and 13:3b

Episode 2: Preparations for Attack and Defense (13:5–7)
This opens in 13:5 with "After this I looked, and behold" and has one subsection in 13:6 "And I looked, and behold."

Episode 3: The Battle (13:8–11)
This opens with "After this I looked, and behold" and concludes with the remark, "When I saw it, I was amazed" (13:11).[1]

Episode 4: The Redemption (13:12–13a)
This also opens with a distinct phrase "After this I saw the same. . . ."

Thus the beginning of each of the four episodes into which the action of the dream is divided is clearly marked by distinct phrases. The first one is set off by the introductory sentence and the other three by the formula "After this I looked" or "saw." Within each episode, the various events are also introduced by a particular formula "And I looked, and behold."

The same technique of providing clear signals at the beginning of new subsections was observed in the structure of the previous vision. However, it is notable that the expression "After this I looked" does not occur at all in that fifth vision, where "And I looked, and behold," which in the present vision only marks a secondary stage, formed the marker for the major divisions of the narration of the dream.

This dream narrative is set within a very simple narrative framework, composed of two phrases, one in 13:1 and the other in 13:13b. The simplicity of the narrative framework is paralleled by the simplicity of the actual symbolic structure. Here the story can be followed with ease—the appearance of the man, the attack of the enemies, the victory in battle, and the ingathering of the multitude are clear and uncomplicated. This contrasts strongly with the complex and intricate set of symbols and events in the previous vision. It is very different from the convoluted wings, little wings, and heads and all their doings.

As distinct from the previous dream vision, the present one contains no cross-references to other places in the book apart from the seven days of the framework (13:1). Another small stylistic note is the brief introduction of the author's *persona* in 13:11.

Function and Content

This vision has attracted a good deal of attention because of the redeemer figure in it who is symbolized by a human form in the vision, thus reminiscent of the Son of man of Daniel 7, of *1 Enoch* 37–71, and of the New Testament. This aspect of the vision has been discussed elsewhere.[2] Here we shall restrict our comments, for the moment, to the exegesis of the dream as a whole.

Above it was noted that it is divided into an introduction which is followed by a narrative of the actual dream divided by clear formal signals into four parts. It is worthwhile reviewing the content of the vision in some detail.

---

1   Müller, *Messias,* 109, regards 13:5–11 as one unit, but 13:8–11 as a subunit within 13:5–11.

2   See Excursus on the Redeemer Figure and further references there.

A. Introduction (13:1)

After seven days, Ezra tells us, he dreamed a dream in the night. These seven days are referred to in the conclusion and injunctions section of the last vision (12:51) and set this vision into the framework of the book. The experience that is narrated is called a "dream in the night." This is a different type of experience from those related in the first three visions of the book.[3] The contrast between Visions 1–3 and 5–6 is very clear. The present verse may be compared also with 11:1 which makes very explicit that Vision 5 is also a dream experienced at night. The reference to seven days points back to 12:51 and therefore to the physical location of the vision. From the point of view of framework, this is a continuation of the type of experience related in the preceding section.

B. The Dream: Episode 1 (13:2–4)—The Appearance of the Man.

The appearance of the man is introduced by the statement that a wind arose from the sea and stirred the waves (13:2). This is reminiscent of Dan 7:2: "I saw in my vision by night, and behold, the four winds of heaven were stirring up the great sea." In Daniel the monstrous beasts arise from the sea, and Daniel there seems to draw on mythological patterns according to which the sea is the origin of forces of evil. Here, however, "something like the figure of a man" came up out of "the heart of the sea," certainly not an evil force! He flew with the clouds (as did the human figure in Dan 7:13 and as God does in Isa 19:1 and Ps 104:3). This element is close to or derived from Dan 7:13, which has clearly also influenced Matt 24:30 and Mark 13:26.[4] Wherever he turned his face, all trembled, and wherever his voice issued, all who heard it melted. The melting of enemies is one of the major characteristics of God as the divine warrior in the Hebrew Bible.[5] Generally the biblical passages do not speak of melting at the voice of the divinity but simply at his appearance. Nonetheless, the connection with biblical passages is very clear because they use the image, also

prominent here, "as wax melts before the fire."

Thus in the description of the appearance of this figure a number of themes combine to suggest a superhuman role or aspect of the figure. The stirring of the waves, the flying on the clouds, and melting like wax all together evoke a very specific set of associations.

C. The Dream: Episode 2 (13:5–7)—Preparations for Battle

Three different events are related in this episode. The first is that an innumerable multitude assembled from all directions to make war upon the man (13:5). He, in response, carved out a great mountain and flew upon it (13:6). To these two actions a comment by the dreamer is added: "I tried to see the region . . . from which the mountain was carved, but I could not." So, the forces are drawn up, the innumerable host on the one hand and the man flying upon the mountain on the other. He has changed his vehicle, for when he came up from the sea he flew upon the clouds.

D. The Dream: Episode 3 (13:8–11)—The Battle

The assembled hostile multitude is affrighted, yet it attacked the man (13:8). He saw the charge but held no weapons of war (13:9); instead, he sent forth a stream of fire, flaming breath, and a storm of burning coals from his mouth, lips, and tongue (13:10). These were mingled together and consumed the onrushing multitude, so that all that was seen was dust of ashes and the smell of smoke (13:11). Then, as at the end of Episode 2, a first person comment intervenes: "I saw it and I was amazed" (13:11b).

What seems to be very notable in this passage is the stress laid upon the weaponlessness of the man and his destruction of the enemies by means of his fiery breath. Again we have an association with the biblical presentation of God who is surrounded by fire and for whom fire is one of the chief instruments of destruction of his enemies.[6] Moreover, the idea of the active divine word, God's speech which is effective, is also to be found in biblical literature.[7] So, once again, the nature of the man's activity recalls that of the divine warrior.

---

3   See Excursus on Inspiration, n. 14.

4   R. B. Y. Scott, "Behold, He Cometh with Clouds," *NTS* 5 (1958/59) 127–32, has claimed that the clouds in Daniel are not a vehicle of flight but "introductory to the whole scene" (p. 130). In this case, however, 4 Ezra, like a number of other sources, has interpreted them as the man's vehicle. Casey, *Son of Man*, 124–26, has discussed the

terminology for "man" in 4 Ezra in some detail. Cf. also the article by J. A. Emerton, "The Origin of the Son of Man Imagery," *JTS* NS 9 (1958) 225–42.

5   See Ps 97:5 and Mic 1:4; cf. Judith 16:15 and *1 Enoch* 1:6.

6   See Ps 97:3; cf. 1 Kgs 19:12; 2 Sam 22:9 // Ps 18:9.

7   See 13:10 Commentary for a detailed discussion of this.

E. The Dream: Episode 4 (13:12–13a)—The Redemption

The man descends from the mountain and summons a peaceful multitude (13:12). This multitude came, some joyous and some sad, some bound and some bringing others as offerings (13:13). The meaning of these elements is not clear, but what is obvious is that here a picture is being drawn that deliberately contrasts with the attacking host of the earlier part of the vision.

In general, then, and as distinct from the previous vision, this is not a complex symbol structure of no apparent meaning. The meaning of the dream symbols of the sixth vision is not completely patent, but it is obvious enough that a clear story is being told of a wondrous man who annihilates a hostile attacking host and who gathers and summons a peaceful and joyous multitude.

Commentary

■ **1** This verse is the introduction to the vision. At night, apparently in a prostrate posture (cf. 13:57), Ezra sees a dream, just as he did in Vision 5 (11:1; 12:35).[8] The function of the seven days' interval is discussed above, and, as in 12:51, Ezra also is said to eat grasses or flowers. There is no more complete fasting in the book.[9]

■ **2** Here the narrative of the dream commences and it continues up to 13:13a. A wind arose from the sea and stirred up all its waves, signaling that something momentous was about to happen. In general, the human figure that came from the sea (13:3) is described with cosmic characteristics that highlight his superhuman nature. These are analyzed in detail above.[10] The sea is not explained in the interpretation of the eagle vision but is offered some sort of explanation in the present instance (see 13:51–52). The winds and the clouds are not discussed in the interpretation at all. The winds, sea, and clouds that feature in 13:2–3 also figure in 11:1–2, the setting of the stage for the eagle vision. Both descriptions are indebted to Daniel, particularly to Dan 7:2.[11]

■ **3** The role of the wind is discussed above.[12] The wind brings up from the sea "something like the figure of a man." This, it eventuates, is a reference to the redeemer. Throughout this vision the figure is called "man" or "that man" (13:3; 13:5; 13:12; 13:25; 13:51). Only here do we find the expression "something like" (cf. also 13:32). In this figure (as we have discussed in the Excursus on the Redeemer Figure, p. 211), Box rightly discerns a transcendent redeemer, a Son of man figure.[13] Clearly the figure here is dependent on Daniel; see particularly chapter 7.[14] Keulers observes that the very expression "one like" here is a reminiscence of Daniel; cf. Dan 10:18.[15] The history and the significance of this figure are discussed in detail above.[16] This figure arises from the heart of the sea, an expression that also occurs in 4:7 and throughout the present vision. It has a biblical ring; cf. Jonah 2:4.[17] It is true that in the previous vision and in earlier sources the sea is either malevolent or the source of malevolent beings (see, e.g., Rev 13:1). Here however, it is the redeemer who arises from the sea, a situation perhaps comparable to *Sib Or* 3:72–73.[18] The man flew with the clouds, an image drawn from Dan 7:13, which is discussed above (Function and Content, p. 383). This is a combination of originally independent

8   See 3:1 Commentary; and 11:1—12:3a Form and Structure, pp. 345–46.

9   See 5:20b–22 Function and Content, pp. 118–19; cf. 12:51.

10   See Function and Content and also Excursus on the Redeemer Figure passim.

11   See further in 11:2 Commentary.

12   See Excursus on the Redeemer Figure, p. 212.

13   Müller sees the Man in this vision but observes that he has absorbed elements of the Messiah figure. It is not clear whether Müller distinguishes clearly the figure here in the dream from that in the interpretation (see *Messias*, 121).

14   See Keulers, pp. 125–27.

15   See also Ezek 1:5 and *1 Enoch* 46:1. Keulers also observes that the dropping of "one like" here, compared with Daniel, shows that Daniel's symbol has here become a real figure. The significance of this observation is not clear. On the terminology, see also Excursus on the Redeemer Figure, n. 20.

16   See Excursus on the Redeemer Figure, pp. 211–12.

17   Violet 2 would distinguish the use here from that in 4:7 which, in his view, is equivalent to "abyss." This distinction seems superfluous. Müller, *Messias*, 122, relates the expression to Dan 7:3, but the content does not favor that. El's abode is in the "midst" or "heart" of the sea.

18   See further also Keulers, p. 129.

descriptions (cf. also Müller, *Messias*, 113).

At the man's gaze all trembled. There is a clear parallel between the descriptions of God's power in 8:23 and the effects of the appearance of the man here.[19] Trembling, like terror, is an obvious reaction to numinous persons and events; here, perhaps, the use of the language is even stronger and is drawn from descriptions of theophanies; compare also the descriptions of the epiphany of the man in 13:8 and see 6:16 and 8:21.

The trembling is produced by the face of the man. Heavenly persons have shining faces; see 7:99 Commentary. A similar description is used for God in Ps 104:32: "the Lord . . . , who looks on the earth and it trembles, who touches the mountains and they smoke!"; cf. Hab 3:6.[20]

■ **4** Not only is the man's gaze effective but also his voice. It is to be observed that, in the interpretation, the voice is explained only in the secondary prophecy of woes in 13:29–36 and not in the main body of the interpretation. The man's voice produced a result—those who heard it melted as wax. In 13:10 Commentary, we shall examine further the idea of the active divine word, that speech whose very issuing forth is effective. It is notable in a different context in 8:22, and the parallels between the characteristics of the man here and those attributed to God in the prayer in 8:19–36 have already been noted.[21] The melting as wax is discussed in the context of this human figure in the Excursus on the Redeemer Figure, p. 212. It is a standard element of epiphany language in the Bible and in postbiblical texts and its transfer here to the human figure is significant.[22]

■ **5** The idea that the forces of evil will mount a great attack on Jerusalem as one of the expressions of the peaking of evil just before redemption is well known. Its biblical roots include notably Deut 28:49; Joel 2:1–10; Ps 2:1–2; and Zech 14:2, but the biblical text that has most influenced this concept is Ezekiel 38–39, the prophecies of Gog and Magog. Although originally referring to the Scythians, these prophecies early took on an eschatological dimension, and in rabbinic literature and other sources the eschatological battle is called the "War of Gog and Magog." The idea is found in texts of the Second Temple period as well as in the New Testament, not to speak of other Jewish texts and early Christian literature.[23] The expression "the four winds of heaven" is found in biblical Hebrew and means "the four points of the compass."

■ **6** This verse relates how the man carved out a great mountain for himself and flew upon it. The verse is clearly dependent on Dan 2:34 and 2:45, where a stone is referred to that is cut out "without hands" and becomes a great mountain.[24] The stone has a redemptive function in Daniel. In the present verse, the human figure is said to cut out the mountain, which differs from Daniel. Here, the mountain is also the vehicle of the human figure; in 13:3 the clouds had been his vehicle.[25] There is nothing really like this verse, other than Daniel. It could be pointed out that God is said to destroy his enemies standing on a mountain (e.g., Joel 4:16–17; Zech 14:4). More similar is perhaps the Lamb standing on Mount Zion in Rev 14:1. But such texts do not really resemble ours.

■ **7** Violet 2 points out that a feeling of seeking and not being able to find is congruent with dream experience.

■ **8** The attack of the hostile host is discussed in 13:5 Commentary. It is intriguing that the host is said to tremble (cf. 13:3), a feature that is not mentioned in the interpretation.[26] In spite of the numinous terror, they dare to attack. There is an overlapping of characteristics of the antichrist and the hostile host or wicked empire,

---

19 Analyzed in 8:23 Commentary.

20 See 8:23 also for the active divine look. Often trembling is the response to the divine epiphany; cf., e.g., Isa 64:1 and Sir 16:18–19.

21 See also *2 Enoch* 1:5, where the angels' mouth is said to be fire and in *2 Enoch* 39:3 God's mouth is said to be fire.

22 Keulers raises a pseudo-problem: if everyone has melted here, who makes up the host of 13:5!

23 See, e.g., *Sib. Or.* 3:663–665; *Test Patr Jos* 19:8 (in a Christian passage); Rev 16:12–14 and particularly 20:7–10; the LXX of Num 24:7 reads Γωγ for

"Aggag." See also Targ J on Num 27:17. Further rabbinic references are numerous. Cf. also *1 Enoch* 65:5–7. A graphic later description of these events is in *Sefer Eliyyahu* (ed. Even-Shmuel, Midreshei Ge'ula, 46, lines 70–74).

24 Violet 2 has a discussion of the possible original of the verb.

25 On divine vehicles, see Excursus on the Redeemer Figure, p. 212.

26 F. Fallon, in an unpublished paper, suggested that this reflects the double attack by Gog, one in Ezekiel 38 and the other in Ezekiel 39; his view was influ-

and, as was quite evident from 11:43, pride or *hybris* is a prominent characteristic of the king of the wicked empire. Perhaps this characteristic is also implied by "dared" here.

■ **9** The fact that the man held no weapons is stressed. As will be evident from the commentary on the next verse, this is related to various terminology about the modes by which he will achieve his victory. Similarly, the Messiah in *Ps Sol* 17:33–34 carries no weapons of war. Perhaps to some extent behind this lie the Holy War ideas that God has the power to confound and defeat his enemies and that he does not depend on the number or quality of human military. This comes out, for example, in the story of Gideon in Judges 7.[27]

■ **10** This verse describes how fire and flames issued from the man's mouth. In the next verse we are told that they destroyed the wicked, while in the interpretation of the dream, in 13:37–38 these fiery emissions are described as the reproof, reproach, and destruction of the wicked. At the present point, therefore, it will be helpful to discuss the complex of ideas about effective divine breath or speech, on the one hand, and fire as the instrument of divine punishment, on the other.

In some texts, God's word is regarded as ipso facto effective: "So shall my word be that goes forth from my mouth; it shall not return to me empty, but it shall accomplish that which I purpose" (Isa 55:11), and compare also 8:22.[28]

The particular connection we seek is that between God's, or the redeemer's, word or fire and judgment. Here two biblical passages, which were understood eschatologically in the Second Temple period, are particularly important. Speaking of the judging function of the "stump of Jesse," Isa 11:4 states: "and he shall smite the earth with the rod of his mouth, and with the

breath of his lips he shall slay the wicked."[29] The other verse is in Psalm 2, which does not refer to the word but which pronounces to the king, "You shall break them with a rod of iron, and dash them into pieces like a potter's vessel" (v 9).

It is the overlap of the rod or staff, as well as the later messianic interpretation of both passages, that makes possible the combination of ideas to be found in *Ps Sol* 17:23–24: "to smash the arrogance of sinners like a potter's jar; to shatter all their substance with an iron rod; to destroy the unlawful nations with the word of his mouth." Later in the same *Psalm of Solomon* we read, "He will strike the earth with the word of his mouth forever" (17:35), which makes the combination of these two verses explicit. This is the Psalm of Solomon that deals extensively with the Davidid Messiah.[30] These intriguing passages dealing with the redeemer's word involve the application to him of an idea of the effective word that is of divine origin. See also Hos 6:5. This idea is very prominent in Wisdom of Solomon. Wisdom 11:20 speaks of God's breath that kills the wicked.[31] God's word is said to kill the wicked in Wisd 12:9, and the matter is completely explicit in Wisd 18:15, referring to the slaying of the firstborn in Egypt:

thy all-powerful word leaped from heaven, from the
    royal throne,
into the midst of the land that was doomed,
    a stern warrior carrying the sharp sword of thy
      authentic command,
and stood and filled all things with death,
    and touched heaven while standing on the earth.

Clearly connected is the idea in 2 Thess 2:8 that Christ will kill the antichrist by his breath.

In 4 Ezra 11:38—12:3 the lion's speech brought about the destruction of the eagle (although the interpretation

---

      enced by L. Hartman, *Prophecy Interpreted*, 85 n. 61.

27   See L. E. Toombs, art. "War, Ideas of," *IDB* 4, particularly p. 797b.

28   See 8:22 Commentary and also, for a similar idea, Heb 1:3. Our presentation of the biblical sources is not historical or developmental. An author in the Second Temple age would have viewed the biblical materials synchronically. The idea of the active divine word was closely related to contemporary concepts of *logos* and wisdom, the full exploration of which would take us far abroad. Consequently, our treatment will be subordinated to the exegetical task

laid upon us. The active divine word was already discussed by Baldensperger, p. 110.

29   It is perhaps significant that the words "mouth," "lips," and "breath" all occur both here and in Isa 11:4 (F. Fallon, *4 Ezra 13: Old Testament Motifs* [Harvard NT Seminar, Fall 1971]).

30   These ideas were also combined, though in a different way, in Rev 19:15. See also *1 Enoch* 62:2 for a similar concept.

31   So does that of the Messiah kill Armilos, according to *Sefer Zerubbabel*.

of Vision 5, in 12:33, changes this).

In the present chapter, the ideas discussed so far are relevant chiefly to the interpretation, in 13:37–38. Even though we have argued that the interpretation offers a tendentious reformulation of this matter, that reformulation is based on a clear set of ideas. If the word or breath that comes forth from God's (or the redeemer's) mouth destroys the wicked by its judgmental power, so does fire. It might be maintained that the fiery stream in the dream description is, as it were, a materialization of the divine word or breath.

The parallel nature of these two emissions is very clear from *1 Enoch* 102:1: "And in those days if he brings a fierce fire upon you, whither will you flee, and where will you be safe? And when he utters his voice against you, will you not be terrified and afraid?" The context in *1 Enoch* is eschatological, and the text sets the breath and the fire in parallel as two instruments, or as the same instrument, of destruction.

Fire, of course, is God's standard instrument of destruction. It issues forth from him or he sends it to burn up the wicked or his enemies; see Deut 32:22 and Ezek 22:21. In Dan 7:11 the fourth beast is burned up with fire. A different view is in *Test Patr Levi* 3:2; this is also implied by 4 Ezra 8:23. In Isa 30:27–28 and Ps 18:9//2 Sam 22:9, fire specifically issues from God's mouth for these purposes.[32]

It is quite interesting that the passages referring to breath or word are applied both to God and to the redeemer, but, other than our present passage, the passages in which fire is specifically mentioned all refer to God. Therefore, the present passage is unique in this respect and serves to emphasize the cosmic role of the human figure, which in any case many other elements of the text highlight. But the explanation in the interpretation that the fiery breath of the dream which destroys the wicked is a judicial word is not far-fetched. It is implicit in the traditions that the author has at hand, as we have shown.

The reading "coals," accepted on textual grounds in the last phrase of the verse, is supported by Ps 18:9//2 Sam 22:9: "and devouring fire from his mouth; glowing coals flamed forth from him."

■ **11** Most of the points in this verse are dealt with in 13:10 Commentary. Note the similar expressions about smoke and ashes also in 4 Ezra 4:48 and 7:61. A multitude is that which is often said to perish in the book; so 7:61; 9:22; and 10:11.

■ **12** This verse prophesies the gathering of a peaceful multitude and its coming to the human figure. It is structurally symmetrical with the hostile host and indicates, apparently, the ingathering of the exiles of Israel or the coming of the Gentiles bringing the exiles, as is explicit in the interpretation. Such an ingathering was an old part of the hope for restoration; see Isa 11:12; Hos 11:10–11; et al.[33] It is described as being peaceful also in Ep Jer 2. Another description of the same idea is *1 Enoch* 57.

■ **13a** The general opinion of the commentators is that this verse describes the ingathering of the converted Gentiles who bring with them the dispersed of Israel. The idea of the survivors who outlasted the messianic woes is to be found discussed in detail in 5:41 Commentary. Here the language typical of that idea is not to be found. The joyous are interpreted as the Israelites, and the sorrowful as the Gentiles. The verse is most indebted to Isa 66:20: "And they shall bring all your brethren from all the nations as an offering to the Lord, upon horses, and in chariots, and in litters, and upon mules, and upon dromedaries, to my holy mountain Jerusalem, says the Lord." The idea in general as well as the detail of bringing as offerings is clearly drawn from Isaiah.[34] The verse from Isaiah was taken up in a context similar to ours in *Ps Sol* 17:31. The detail of those bound is perhaps related to Isa 45:14.[35]

---

32   In another way angels, God's instrument of destruction in many texts, are made of fire; cf. 8:22; *2 Apoc Bar* 21:6; and particularly Ps 104:4. Note how the effective word is set forth by God, according to Wisd 18:15 cited above. The idea in *Sib Or* 3:72–74 is different. A bizarre parallel is the story of the fire-breather told in Diodorus Siculus 34.2.6–7. Jerome applies this imagery differently in *Contra Rufinum*

3.31 (*PL*, 23:502).

33   See also *1 Enoch* 90:33.

34   It also resembles Isa 49:22; 60:4; and 60:9. On the bringing of gifts, see also Tob 13:11.

35   Joy is an eschatological term (see 7:28 Commentary), though it is not certain that that usage is involved here.

13

13b   Then from great fear ^a I awoke; and I besought the Most High, and said, 14/ ^b"From the beginning thou hast shown thy servant these ^c wonders, and hast deemed me worthy to have my prayer heard by thee; 15/ now show me also the interpretation of this dream. 16/ ^dFor as I consider it in my mind, alas for those who will be left in those days! And still more, alas for those who are not left! 17/ For those who are not left will be sad, 18/ because they understand ^e what is reserved for the last days, but cannot attain it. 19/ ^fBut alas for those also who are left, and for that very reason! ^f For they shall see great dangers ^g and much distress, as these dreams ^h show. 20a/ ⁱYet it is better to come into these things, though incurring peril, ⁱ than to pass from the world like a cloud, and not to see ^j what shall happen in the last days."

Notes

13b   a Literally, "multitude of" Lat, Syr, Arm; Ar2 omits.

14   b Ar1, Arm add "lord"; note "servant" also in this phrase, and cf. 5:56 Commentary. Violet 2 thinks this may be to soften the abrupt opening of the prayer.
   c Eth, Arm "your."

16   d Ar2 omits this verse; Arm omits from here to the end of 13:18; Eth corrupt.

18   e Eth, Ar1 add "not"; this is secondary, as is clear from the fact that each of these two versions solves the exegetical problem thus created in a different way. Eth adds a phrase at the end of the verse and Ar1 omits the last phrase of it.

19   f–f Lat, Syr, cf. Eth; Ar1, Ar2 are shortened; Arm omits.
   g Lat, Syr; "troubles, etc." Eth, Ar1, Arm; Ar2 omits the whole latter part of the verse.
   h Singular Eth, Ar1, Arm.

20a   i–i Lat, Syr, cf. Eth; Ar1, Ar2 vary but apparently derive from the same text; Arm omits "though incurring peril."
   j Eth "know," perhaps ἰδεῖν/εἰδέναι (Volkmar).

Form and Structure

This passage functions similarly to the parallel passage in the previous vision, that is, 12:3–9. It succeeds the narrative of the dream and precedes the interpretation, serving to link the two. The corresponding passage in the fourth vision also bears a certain similarity to these two but differs from them, since it mediates not between a dream and its interpretation but between the powerful experience of Vision 4 and the interpretation.[1]

Here the seer's experience on awakening from his dream is described. His fear is mentioned and his prayer (13:13b), but the "perplexity of mind" noted by 12:3 is not discussed. Indeed, this omission is significant, as will become evident below.

The phrase "in the beginning" refers back to earlier experience. In Vision 5, when Ezra awoke from his dream he spoke of the fatigue and confusion of mind that resulted from it, and then he turned to God, saying, "O sovereign Lord, if I have found favor in thy sight, and

if I have been accounted righteous before thee beyond many others, and if my prayer has indeed come up before thy face, . . . show me, thy servant, the interpretation and meaning of this terrifying vision, . . . for thou hast judged me worthy to be shown the end of the times and the last events of the times" (12:7–9). The theme of the seer's worthiness had been raised already in a very explicit way in the pericope 8:46–62, which repeatedly declared Ezra's virtue, but the assertion there is set in the mouth of the angel. The same idea, still placed in the angel's mouth, also occurs in 10:39 and 10:57.

The change here, of course, is that it is Ezra who asserts his own worthiness, thus taking up and developing a theme that has been prominent and changing in a dynamic fashion in this whole latter part of the book. This serves as an integrating factor in this part of 4 Ezra.

The reference to the revelation of "wonders" may refer to the preceding visions, but it is likely that it points to the totality of the eschatological signs revealed in the

---

1   Detailed parallels in structure between the two are analyzed in 12:3b–9 Form and Structure, p. 354.

book.[2] In any case, this term clearly ties the present context into the series of revelations that have been made so far.

The seer then continues with two "woe" or "alas" cries. The first bewails the fate of those who are left, and even more the fate of those who have already died and will not see these signs. Those who will have died by then, he continues, will be sad "because they understand and cannot attain," while those who are left will experience the tribulations of the last generation. This clear literary form, the "woe" call, often associated with eschatological prophecies,[3] is enhanced by the special literary structure, a : b followed by b : a, producing the effect called chiasm.

The passage concludes with an aphorism, an adaption of a sentence, and an idea found a number of times in 4 Ezra and in much other contemporary literature.

Function and Content

It is instructive to observe both the similarities and the differences that exist between this passage and the parallel one in 12:3–9. The main point of difference is in the seer's new attitude toward himself and his role. In the previous vision the seer had talked of his own fear and disorientation on receiving the vision. Here he accepts his worthiness and immediately asks for the interpretation of it. Above in Form and Structure we pointed to the theme of the seer's worthiness. The change in attitude toward the seer has already started at the end of Vision 3. There the angel asserted energetically to Ezra that he is not to reckon himself among the sinners (8:46–62). There, too, the revelation is tied to his worthiness. The assertion there is set into the angel's mouth and Ezra neither assents nor disagrees. The subject of his virtue is taken up once more by the angel in 10:39 (see Commentary) and particularly in 10:50–59:

10:57 For you are more blessed than many . . . 10:59 and the Most High will show you in those dream visions what the Most High will do to those who dwell on earth in the last days.

This theme of Ezra's worthiness recurs in his own mouth in 12:7, as we have observed. His condition ("if I have found favor in thy sight, and if I have been accounted righteous before thee") is fulfilled, for he receives the revelation of the interpretation of the dream that he has been requesting. So he is worthy in God's sight. This conclusion is strengthened by the angelic assertion, once again repeated at the end of the interpretation pericope of Vision 5: "and you alone were worthy to learn this secret of the Most High." By the time of the present vision, Ezra himself asserts his own worthiness. This change, which we have traced, is dramatic when his self-deprecation earlier in the book is borne in mind.[4]

Not only does he speak of his own worthiness, he goes farther and draws conclusions from his own interpretation of the dream vision: "for as I consider it in my mind" (13:16), and the following verses draw the implications from this understanding. Indeed, the two cries of "Alas!" follow from his own understanding.

It is of interest to observe that Ezra does not draw from his two "Alas!" statements the implication of the closeness of the end. They are neutral when examined from that perspective: a sense of urgency is neither encouraged nor denied. This pattern of neutrality is, in fact, observed throughout Visions 5 and 6; nowhere do they imply the proximity of the eschaton.

In 13:20 a sort of reversal of the *topos* "it were better not to have been born, or having been born to die," which is to be found throughout the book (see 4:12 Commentary), is to be observed. Here 13:20 says that those who are alive are more fortunate (or less unfor-

---

2   See 4:26 Commentary.
3   See Luke 6:24–26; *1 Enoch* 94:6–8; 95:4–7; 96:4–8; et al.; and *2 Enoch* 52.
4   Brandenburger, *Verborgenheit*, makes much of the assertions of Ezra's worthiness, intending to show that Ezra is regarded (1) as a prophet (e.g., pp. 76–80) and (2) as a sage, knower of eschatological secrets (pp. 157–59, 187). He wishes to read Ezra's sapiential character back into Vision 4, where this language does not occur (p. 81). At the same time, he tries to correlate the intensity of the assertions of righteousness with the types of revelation to Ezra (p. 91).

Nonetheless, he has to speak of exceptions to this pattern (p. 119). Ezra and the author, Brandenburger maintains, are part of the group of the elect wise, a circle traced back to Moses (pp. 157–59, 187). See also 6:32 Commentary.

tunate) than those who are dead.[5] In his new role as prophet, in his new self-consciousness, in his new eschatological hope, Ezra no longer despairs of this world and of life in it. Again, the contrast with his attitude earlier in the book is noteworthy.

The issue that Ezra raises in his question, the comparative fate of those who will live in the last generation and those who will not, is answered in the next section. As he presents it, those who will not be alive at that time will be the worse off because they understand what will happen but cannot attain it. This problem is discussed in the commentary to the text here.

Commentary

■ **14** "From the beginning" means, it seems, "formerly"; compare the similar use in 12:34. There it refers to previous eschatological prophecies. Ezra refers to himself in the third person, "servant," followed by the first person, a common feature of formal style.[6]

"Wonders" is a term used in this book primarily for eschatological acts or revelations, as had been discussed above. The reference here is to previous eschatological prophecies.[7] Ezra's rather confident attitude toward himself here, mixed with humility, expressed here contrasts with his reproachful cry to Uriel in the context of the different experience of the fourth vision (10:28). The prayer here is well contrasted with 12:7–9, which may be the previous occasion referred to.[8]

■ **15** No commentary.

■ **16** The verse is in the form of a woe pronouncement, not unusual in eschatological contexts.[9] "Those who will be left" is a fixed term used to describe those who will survive the messianic woes. It also occurs elsewhere in 4 Ezra.[10] The background of the verse is the idea of the messianic woes, the fearsome events that will precede the

eschaton. They figure in greater detail in the interpretation of the dream, in 13:29–31.[11] In 4:51 the expression "in those days" serves, as it does here, to refer to the times preceding the end when the messianic woes will take place.

■ **17** No commentary.

■ **18** In 4 Ezra the idea of seeing either one's own recompense or that of others is part of the eschatological events and is applied to a variety of points on the eschatological timetable. Thus it may be observed in 7:66; 7:83; 7:84; 7:93; and 7:96. In another sense this dynamic underlies the lament in 7:119–125, which refers to things that will not be seen by the wicked. It is even more dramatically presented in 7:37–38.[12] The terms "reserved" or "preserved" are technical and refer to predestination or precreation, particularly of eschatological things.[13]

The terminology relating to "last days" or "times" is dealt with in detail above.[14] The actual eschatological reward in the messianic kingdom is described briefly in a number of passages in the book; see 6:25; 7:27–28; 11:46; and 12:34.

■ **19** The idea and the term the "survivors" have been mentioned in 13:16 and are discussed in detail in 5:41 Commentary. The "perils" or "dangers" here mentioned are the messianic woes, from which the survivors will escape; on this term, see 9:8 Commentary.[15]

■ **20a** This verse is based, as the preceding verses are, on the idea that the age or the world is going to come to an end.[16] The expression "pass from the world" is a standard idiom for dying; cf. also 4:24 and 2 Apoc Bar 14:2. This latter is in a very similar context. In 4:24, Ezra has used the similes of "locusts" and "mist," both of which had solid biblical basis. The present simile, cloud, is not so strongly based in biblical usage, but see Job 7:9, cf. 13:15. It is found in the same sense as here in 2 Apoc Bar

---

5   A similar form of exclamation may be observed in 2 Apoc Bar 28:3. The reverse sentiment is found at 2 Apoc Bar 48:41. The context there is comparable, but the content differs.

6   See, on this, 9:43 and Commentary.

7   See 12:36 and Commentary; on "wonders," see 4:26 Commentary.

8   Of course, predictions were often revealed to Ezra; see, e.g., 7:44; 8:62; and 12:36.

9   See Form and Structure, p. 389.

10 The idea and the terminology are discussed in detail in 5:41 Commentary.

11 See for a detailed discussion 5:1–13 Function and Content, pp. 107–8, particularly 5:2 Commentary.

12 On that address, see further 7:38 Commentary.

13 See further 7:27 Commentary n. 53.

14 See Excursus on Natural Order, pp. 103–4.

15 See also 9:8 Commentary and on the woes in general the discussion in 5:2 Commentary. These terms also refer to the troubles or dangers of this world in 7:12 and 7:89. The use in 9:20 is problematic, and see Commentary there.

16 See in more detail Excursus on Natural Order, pp. 103–4. On meaning of "world," see Excursus on

82:9. The point is that it is better to live and incur the perils of the terrible events of the messianic woes than to die and not to see the eschatological events. The focus here is clearly on the last generation, and the whole issue has been discussed above.[17]

---

the Term "Age."
17   5:41 Commentary.

20b He answered me and said, 21/ "Both ª will I tell you the interpretation of the ᵇ vision, and I will also explain to you the things which you have mentioned. 22/ As for what you said about those who are left ᶜand about those who are not left, ᶜ this is the pronouncement: ᵈ 23/ He who brings ᵉ the peril at ᶠ that time ᶠ will himself protect those who fall into peril, who have works and have faith in the Almighty. ᵍ 24/ Understand ʰ therefore that those who are left are more blessed than those who have died. 25/ This is the interpretation of the vision: As for your seeing a man come up from ⁱthe heart ⁱ of the sea, 26/ this is he whom the Most High has been keeping for many ages, through whom he will deliver his creation; ʲ and he will direct those who are left. 27/ And as for your seeing fiery breath ᵏ and a storm coming out of his mouth, 28/ and as for his not holding a spear ˡ or weapon of war, yet destroying the onrushing ᵐ multitude which came to conquer him, this is the pronouncement: ⁿ 29/ Behold, the days are coming when the Most High will ᵒ deliver those who are on the earth. ᵖ 30/ And bewilderment of mind shall come over those who dwell on the earth. ᑫ 31/ And they shall plan to make war against one another, ʳcity against city, ˢplace against place, ᵗ people against people, and kingdom against kingdom. ᵘ 32/ And when these things come to pass and the signs occur which I showed you before, then my servant ᵛ will be revealed, whom you

Notes

21   a Lat, Syr, Arm; Eth, Ar1, Ar2 omit.
   b Lat, Ar1; "your" Syr; "this your" Eth; "this" Arm; Ar2 has "what you have seen" for this phrase and also paraphrases the next clause.

22   c–c Lat omits; Ar2 omits the whole verse; Arm varies.
   d Lat *interpretatio;* Ar1 omits the phrase; see 12:17 note j.

23   e Lat; Violet suggests that Syr derives from ὑποίσων/ἐποίσων; Eth "will see" perhaps derives from ὁρῶσιν or ὄψονται (Violet 2); Ar1 "will be," cf. Arm.
   f–f Eth, Arm "those days."
   g Lat Ψ, Ar1; Lat Φ, Ar2 "Most High"; Syr, Eth "Most High and Almighty"; Arm omits; the original reading cannot be determined.

24   h Syr "know," perhaps ἰδεῖν/εἰδέναι.

25   i–i Eth, Ar2, Arm omit.

26   j This is the sense of most versions; Lat has translated the Greek differently: *qui per semetipsum liberabit . . . ;* cf. Violet 1, n. 2, to Syr; Wellhausen, *Skizzen,* 6:236 n. 1, suggests δι' αὑτοῦ ⟩ δι' αὐτοῦ (Box says δι οὗ); RSV has "who will himself deliver his creation."

27   k Syr, Ar1, Arm; Lat *spiritum et ignem;* for the whole phrase, Eth has "fire and flame and coals as a storm"; Ar2 "the fire and the wind"; Arm omits "and storm."

28   l Lat *frameam;* Arm "weapon."
   m Lat, Syr, Arm; other versions omit; there may have been two different Greek texts.
   n Lat *interpretatio;* Ar1 "meaning"; see 12:17 note j.

29   o Lat Φ, Syr, Eth, and Arm seem to have reflexes of Greek μέλλει.

30   p–q Eth omits by hmt; the Sahidic fragment commences with the last phrase of 13:30.
   q–t Sah omits.

31   r–t Ar2 omits. Arm has a different order of elements in this list.
   s–t Eth "land with land"; Ar1 "house with house."
   u Arm adds "leaders with leaders, priests with priests: the faith of worship shall be split into various sides," and see on this Stone, "Some Remarks," 114. With this reading is associated the expansion of Arm in 13:34; see note a below on 13:34; see also 5:9 Commentary.

32   v Lat, Syr "son"; Eth, Arm "that man"; Ar1 "my youth"; Ar2 "my servant"; Sah "my son the man"; on this reading, see Excursus on the Redeemer Figure, p. 207.

saw as a man coming up ʷfrom the sea. ˣ 33/ And when ʸ all the nations hear his voice, every man shall leave his own land ᶻ and the warfare that they have against one another; 34/ and an innumerable multitude shall be gathered together, ᵃ as you saw, desiring to come and conquer him. 35/ But he shall stand on the top of Mount Zion. ᵇ 36/ And Zion will come and be made manifest to everybody, prepared and built, as you saw the mountain carved out without hands. 37/ And he, my servant, ᶜ will reprove the assembled nations for their ungodliness ᵈ(this was symbolized by the storm), ᵈ 38/ and will reproach them to their face with their evil deeds ᵉ and the torments with which they are to be ᶠ tortured (which were symbolized by the flames), and will destroy them without effort ᵍby the law ᵍ (which was symbolized by the fire). 39/ And as for your seeing him gather ʰ to himself another multitude that was peaceable, ⁱ 40/ these are the nine and one half ʲ tribes which were led away from their own land into captivity in the days of King ᵏ Hoshea, whom Shalmaneser the king of the Assyrians led captive; he took them across the river, and they were taken into another land. 41/ But they formed this plan for themselves, that they would leave the multitude of the nations and go to a more distant region, where no human race had ever lived, 42/ that there at least they might keep their statutes ˡ which they had not kept in their own land. 43/ And they went in by the narrow passages of the Euphrates river. 44/ For at that time the Most High performed wonders for them, and stopped the springs ᵐ of the river until they had passed over. 45/ To ⁿ that region there was a long way to go, a journey of a year and a half; and that country is called Arzareth. ᵒ

w–x Omitted by Lat (except for Ms L) and Syr.

x Arm adds "and some of the heathen will destroy the images of their abomination"; see on this Stone, "Some Remarks," 109–10.

33   y Lat, Sah "and it shall come to pass when."

z Sah breaks off, except for isolated letters, and resumes in 13:40.

34   a Arm adds here "of all the inhabitants of the earth, to serve the Lord faithfully, and at the approach of the end they will be separated from one another. This is the multitude"; on this reading, see note u above on 13:31.

35   b Ar2 has "Golgotha in Zion," reflecting a confused identification of Golgotha with Mount Zion.

37   c Lat, Syr "son"; Eth "child"; Ar1, Ar2 "youth"; others omit or have lacuna; on the reading, see Excursus on the Redeemer Figure, p. 207.

d–d Lat, Syr, cf. Eth; Ar1, Ar2 vary; Arm omits.

38   e Lat *cogitamenta*, whence RSV "thoughts"; Ar1, Ar2 are quite different for the whole first part of the verse.

f The versions reflect Greek μέλλουσιν.

g–g The text is uncertain; this is the reading of Syr; Lat reads *et legem;* Eth has "with sin," and Violet proposes δι' ἀνομίαν/διὰ νόμον and thinks the former to be original (Violet 2); Ar1, Ar2, Arm omit the phrase.

39   h Syr, Ar1; Ar2 has "summon and gather."

i There are variants in each version of this verse.

40   j Lat (most Mss) "ten"; Lat A* C V L "nine"; Eth "nine" (two Mss "nine and a half"); Ar2 "remainder of the nine"; Arm greatly changes the whole section down to 13:49. This is probably related to the special reading of Arm in 13:21; 13:22; and 13:24. The omission by Arm might be caused by anablepsis to "peaceful multitude."

k Sah breaks off from here until the middle of 13:41.

42   l Lat *legitima*, plural also in Ar1; singular "law" in Syr, Eth; Ar2 "service of God"; Sah breaks off until the end of 13:43.

44   m So most versions; Lat *venas*, cf. 4:7 and below, and note r below on 13:47.

45   n Lat "through"; Syr, Sah omit "to that region"; Ar2 is paraphrastic.

o So most Lat Mss; Syr 'rzp; Eth 'azaf; Ar1 corrupted; Ar2 'arsaf (Ms B 'arwan); Sah illegible. We have accepted the reading of RSV which is the majority reading of Lat. However, a case could be made on textual grounds for there having existed an (additional?) Greek ΑΡΣΑΦ/ΑΡΣΑΡΘ. If so, those two readings would derive from a corruption between final Φ/Θ (cf. Volkmar, who proposed the same graphic confusion but different forms).

46 "Then [p] they dwelt there until the last time; and now, when they are about to [q] come again, 47/ the Most High will stop the springs [r] of the river again, [s] so that they may be able to pass over. Therefore you saw the [t] multitude gathered together in peace. 48/ But those who are left of your people, who are found within my holy borders, [u] shall be saved. [v] 49/ [w]And it will be [w] when he destroys [x] the multitude of the nations that are gathered together, he will defend the people who remain. [y] 50/ And then he will show them very many wonders."

51 I said, "O sovereign Lord, explain this to me: Why did I see the man coming up from the heart of the sea?"

52 He said to me, "Just as no one can [z]explore or know [z] what is in the depths of the sea, so no one on earth can see my servant [a] or those who are with him, except in the time of his day. 53/ This is the interpretation of the dream which you saw. And you alone have been enlightened about this, 54/ because you have forsaken your own ways [b] and have applied yourself to mine, and have searched out my law; 55/ for you have devoted your life to wisdom, and called understanding your mother.

46 p End of Sahidic fragment.

q Most versions have a reflex of μέλλουσιν. Lat in such cases usually has a form of *incipio*, but here it reads *coeperunt*.

47 r So most versions; Lat *venas*, cf. note m above on 13:44; Lat, Eth add "again."

s Lat, Eth; Syr, Ar1, Ar2 omit.

t Arm resumes here.

48 u Ar1, Ar2 "mountain," reflecting confusion ὁρίον/ὄρος, cf. 12:34 note n (Volkmar).

v Syr alone reads "shall be saved"; Lat omits; Eth omits "But those . . . people"; Eth and Ar2, in different ways, combine this with the preceding. The situation of the versions seems to witness an incomplete sentence in Greek. It is impossible, in fact, to determine whether Syr alone preserves the original reading or is a rather successful restoration. Latin Ms L also restores, but differently: *per opera bona fidesque habuerit salvabitur*. The basic sense, distinguishing this group of redeemed from the preceding (*contra* Eth, Ar2), seems assured on exegetical grounds.

49 w–w Lat, Syr; Lat adds *ergo*, "therefore," with the support of no other version.

x Lat has *incipiet perdidere*, but μέλλει is not reflected in the other versions.

y Arm is both rewritten to include 13:50 and expanded.

52 z–z Lat; Syr, Ar1 have "investigate and find or to know"; Eth "to know" (perhaps εἰδέναι/ἰδεῖν – Volkmar); Ar2 "investigate"; Arm "see or investigate or know."

a Ar1, Ar2; Lat, Syr, Eth "son"; Eth Mss "the Son of man"; Arm "the mysteries of the Most High"; see Excursus on the Redeemer Figure, p. 207.

54 b Literally, "your own affairs"; Arm is somewhat paraphrastic at the end.

Form and Structure

This passage is the interpretation of the dream offered by the angel. In general, it is discourse set in the angel's mouth, interrupted only once, in 13:51, by the seer. It is made up of a number of discrete and unequal parts:

A. Angelic Address (13:20b–21)—Introduction

The angel will reveal *(a)* the interpretation of the vision, referring back to 13:1–13a, and *(b)* the things he asked, referring back to 13:13b–20a. These two revelations follow.

B. Explanation of the Seer's Question (13:22–24)

This explanation is composed of three parts: *(a)* an introduction (13:22); *(b)* a prophetic statement (13:23); and *(c)* a concluding aphorism (13:24). This concluding

statement is the summary of the response to Ezra's question.

C. Interpretation of the Vision (13:25–55)

This is clearly marked off by an introduction (13:25) and a conclusion (13:53). Between these occur a number of interpretative segments of varied literary type. In order to clarify the literary character of this vision, it is important to analyze them clearly.

1. An intepretation of the man coming up from the sea which is presented by "As for your seeing . . . , this is he . . ." (13:25–26).

2. An interpretation formulated as interpretation of the attack and the battle. This opens with "As for . . ." (13:27–28), but instead of continuing with the usual

formula, "this is he . . . ," there is a prediction. In form the prediction opens like the other revelatory predictions in the book with "Behold, the days are coming when . . ." and deals with signs. This is a standard term in this book for the messianic woes (13:29–31).[1]
These formal features resemble those of the Prediction 2 texts found throughout the first three visions (e.g., 5:1–13; 6:11–29; 9:1–22; and cf. 7:26–44). The continuation of this prediction, however, is specific to the present vision, being the interpretation of the dream. This "predictive interpretation" deals with a number of elements, marking each with "whom" or "as you saw." What is unusual is that these references follow the interpretation, while predominantly in the apocalypses such references precede the interpretation. The elements of the dream dealt with are (a) the appearance of the man (13:32), (b) the attack (13:33–34), (c) the mountain (13:35–36) and, finally, (d) the man's destruction of his enemies (13:37–38).
3. A new section of dream interpretation starts in 13:39. Its subject is the peaceable multitude. It opens, as do the elements in section 1 above, "And as for your seeing . . . , these are" (13:39–40). However, the passage following the words "these are" is a long discourse on the ten lost tribes (13:40–47a). This passage concludes with a resumption of the initial statement: "Therefore you saw the multitude gathered together in peace."
4. This is followed by a prediction, not tied to anything in the dream, which deals with the fate of the "remnant within my holy borders" who will be saved (13:48–50).

D. Seer's Question about the Man (13:51)
E. Angelic Response (13:52)
In this response the formula "Just as . . . , so no one . . ." is used, which is found nowhere else in the vision.
F. Conclusion (13:53) and Final Remarks on Ezra's Worthiness (13:54–55)
A considerable measure of unclarity and repetitiveness is immediately evident from this outline of the structure. The chief example of this is the triple interpretation of the meaning of the arising of the man from the sea (13:25–26; 13:32; and 13:51–52). The fairly strict formal structure of interpretation, found, for example, in Visions 4 and 5, is here broken. This departure from strict structures is reflected both in the treatment of the sequence of elements of the dream by the interpretation and also in the actual formulae of interpretation used. The interpretation commences from the beginning of the dream (13:25–26) and advances to a certain point. It then moves back to the beginning and pursues events through the destruction of the hostile host (13:32–38). Finally, with the seer's new question (13:51), it returns once more to the meaning of the man.[2]

---

1   See 4:52 Commentary.
2   Müller, *Messias,* 124, suggests that the interpretation falls into two sections, 13:27–38 and 13:39–50, the one culminating in the judgment by the Messiah and the other in his rule over Israel. This overall division, however, obscures the complex and disorderly character of the pericope. Casey, *Son of Man,* 126–29, argues against our contention in Stone, "Messiah" which is repeated here, that the interpretation is written by the author of 4 Ezra to a preexistent vision. Casey explains the disjunction of 13:25 and 13:51 by saying that the author was most concerned about the appearance of the Messiah and so put it last to give it emphasis (p. 126). Yet he takes no account of the overall structural difficulties of the interpretation, nor of the fact that, as Vision 5 shows, the author was quite capable of writing a structured interpretation. Moreover, he adduces no other instances of the coherence of an interpretation being violated in order to set emphasized matters at the end.
          Second, on p. 127 he denies that the voice interpreted in 13:33 is the same voice mentioned in 13:4. Yet, in rereading the text we remain convinced of our former position. The exact context of events is the same, the Messiah's voice preceding the gathering of the host. The dream does not make the relationship between the voice and the gathering of the host explicit, yet the sequence of events in the dream has, in the interpretation, led to this view.
          Casey's assertion is that the ten tribes material makes "perfect sense" as interpretation of 13:12–13. It is clear from our analysis of the structure above that it does not. However, the original independence of this material is in fact a matter of indifference to the subject under present discussion (whether 13:1–13 comes from a prior source).
          Fourth, Casey attempts to soften the introduction of the companions of the Messiah into the interpretation, though they do not occur in the vision (pp. 127–28). Yet this is just one of a number of instances in which the interpretation has features that are in common with the rest of 4 Ezra and that do not occur in the vision. These we point out in detail in

Not only are the formulae and techniques of interpretation mixed but a variety of literary forms are embedded within this passage. There are formulaic interpretations, "As for your seeing x, this is y." There is predictive prophecy: "Behold, days are coming when. . . ." Narrative is found in the passage dealing with the ten tribes. Ezra's question and the angel's answer introduce yet another style of interpretation that is not found in the other interpretations of symbol structures in the book.

Function and Content

In general, of course, this section is the interpretation of the dream vision that the seer has experienced and that is related in the first part of the chapter. It understands the dream to refer to the Messiah, the attack on him by a host of hostile nations, his victory over them and annihilation of them, and finally the ingathering and redemption of the multitude of the exiles.

When this interpretation is compared in general terms with the dream vision, we may note the following overall points. In Visions 4 and 5 there is a rather tight correlation between the content and sequence of the dreams or visions and the interpretations of them. This tight correlation is missing here. So the overall situation contrasts with the type of relationship between symbol structure and interpretation found in the preceding comparable parts of the book. Furthermore, however, there is a strong contrast between the tight, coherent dream in this very vision, Vision 6, which is divided into four clear, sequential and fast-moving episodes, and the interpretation of this dream in the same vision. The interpretation is complicated, diffuse, and somewhat incoherent. In order to evaluate the particular points being made by the author, it is interesting to inquire which elements of the dream are not interpreted at all and which elements of the interpretation are not based on elements in the dream. It will be recalled that a similar examination of the preceding eagle vision turned up rather minor points of difference.

The only feature of Episode 1 of the dream (13:1–4) that is taken up in the interpretation, and it is repeated thrice, is that of the man coming up from the sea. The winds that stirred up the sea, the flying on the clouds, and the effect of the man's gaze and his voice on those things which encountered them are not brought up, even though they form a separate subsection of the dream, introduced by "And I looked, and behold" (13:3).

In the summary of the preparations, the attack, and the battle (13:26–28), no mention is made of the mountain. This is brought up only in 13:36, at the end of this passage of interpretation. The next episode is interpreted as part of the same passage (13:30–38). The words "were much afraid, yet dared to fight" (13:8) are not interpreted. The mingling together of the stream of fire, the flaming breath, and the great storm (i.e., of sparks) which is made much of in 13:10 is not only ignored by the interpretation but each of these three elements is interpreted independently (13:37–38). Indeed, the interpretation also ignores the latter part of 13:11 "so that nothing was seen of the innumerable multitude but only the dust of ashes and the smell of smoke."

Although, as we shall see directly, the interpretation of Episode 4 is enormously longer than the dream (13:40–50), some elements of the dream's two verses that are here being interpreted are ignored, or at best interpreted very obscurely, particularly the words "Some of them were joyful and some sorrowful; some of them were bound, and some were bringing others as offerings" (13:13a).

There are, therefore, a number of elements of the dream that are not interpreted by the angel, and in view of the brevity of the dream and the expansiveness of the interpretation this should be regarded as of potentially great significance. The reverse situation is also true, and there are numerous elements in the interpretation that seem to have no basis, or at least very little basis, in the dream.

---

the present section. It is naive to regard the human figure of the vision as a simple symbol with no independent meaning. Casey's own proof that it depends on Daniel 7 shows that. Indeed, Casey's underlying agenda is clearly set forth on p. 126 (the italics are mine):

> Stone's argument [i.e., that 13:1–13 is an older piece] *requires* refutation, *for it implies that the exegesis* of Dan. 7 in this vision *was found in an earlier source* and the *son of man aspect of the problem becomes much more complex* if a definite written source is presupposed.

The usual reason for refuting a scholarly view is that it is mistaken, not that it compounds the complexity of one's own theory.

The most striking of these is to be found in the interpretation of the fourth episode of the dream. The description of the gathering of a multitude to the man after his victory is a very brief one in the dream. In the interpretation it serves as a very slight basis for the introduction of the long and complex tradition about the ten tribes (13:40–47). This detailed tradition, however, does not explain or even relate to one of the mere two verses that deal with the peaceable multitude in the dream (13:13). Moreover, this tradition is not adequate for the author to express his views, and as a result, having concluded the interpretation of the peaceable multitude (which is, for him, the ten tribes), he proceeds in 13:48–49 to append a new prediction about "those who are left of your people" and this is weakly tied to the preceding by the "Therefore" clause in 13:49. It refers to an event, the Messiah's defense of the remnant, that is not mentioned at all in the vision.

It should also be observed that the "nonspecific" prophecy in 13:29–32, which refers back to woes prophecies earlier in the book, has no basis in the dream symbolism, although it is integrated into the Prediction 2 type of material that has been introduced into the text at this point.

It is clear, therefore, from this examination of the contents and from the discussion of the form and structure of the pericope above, that a considerable number of issues remain to be resolved at the literary level relating to this vision. These will be better evaluated, however, once the overall contents of the chapter have been evaluated.

In the first part of the interpretation, that responding to Ezra's question, the angel reasserts that those who are left are more blessed than those who have died. This refers, of course, to those who are alive in the last generation. This question is one that has arisen, in other terms, elsewhere in the book. The most striking instance is 5:41, where, with no particular preceding prompt, the seer interprets the eschatological promises as relevant for the last generation.[3] Thus the relevance of one set of eschatological predictions or promises for those alive at the time of the last generation is an idea that is well known within the book. The assertion here is that, in

spite of Ezra's (correct) inference about the terrible events of the last generation, it is still preferable to be one of the remnant or survivors.

Indeed, to survive in that generation is a boon granted only to the righteous, those who "have works and have faith in the Almighty." This last expression also takes ideas that are found elsewhere in the book. The righteous are described often as those who have works, or those who have faith, and the two terms occur together in 9:7. Indeed, 9:7–8 contains a number of terms and expressions that are close to our passage:

> 9:7 And it shall be that everyone who will be saved and will be able to escape on account of his works, or on account of the faith by which he has believed, 9:8 will survive the dangers that have been predicted, and will see my salvation in my land and within my borders, which I have sanctified for myself from the beginning.[4]

Not only do the works and faith occur in this passage but also the idea of the dangers or perils, also found in 13:23. That verse asserts that God, who has brought about the messianic woes, can also save people from them. The angel's response in the present passage of the interpretation, therefore, reaffirms Ezra's position expressed in 13:16–20 in the dialogue with the angel or God.

The man is interpreted as the Messiah, precreated and prepared in advance by God, who will deliver creation and direct those who are left. The role of the Messiah with the survivors also occurs elsewhere in the book. He is described in 12:32 as created in advance for the end, and in general the eschatological things are considered to have been precreated. This may be noted, for example, at the end of 9:8 in the quotation given in the preceding paragraph, and the matter is discussed in 3:6 Commentary and 9:18 Commentary.[5]

In the following prediction, which explains the Messiah's weaponlessness and destruction of enemies, many themes are raised that are familiar from elsewhere in the book. The background is laid, that of the messianic woes. Through the language and terminology employed, once again reminiscent of the Prediction 2 passage in chapter 9 and particularly of 9:3, the preliminary stages are

---

3　The same problem with variations arises in 1 Thess 4:13–17. See also 5:41—6:10 Form and Function, p. 145.

4　See also "treasures of faith," 6:5 and Commentary; "treasures of works," 7:77 and Commentary.

5　See also 3:6 Commentary. The Messiah is also

established. There will be chaos and confusion. Interestingly, here the coming time is described as the time at which the Most High will approach to deliver those upon the earth, while in both 6:11–29 and 9:1–13 it is described as a time of punitive visitation.[6] This is perhaps because here the focus of the whole is on the redeemer figure and his activity. The internecine strife is a frequent feature of the description of the messianic woes. It is ended, according to the present prediction, by the uniting of all of the wicked to attack the Messiah. Observe that these standard "woes" elements, including the internecine strife, are not hinted at in the dream symbolism.

The "mountain carved out" (13:7) is said in 13:6 to have been carved out by the man. The image is most likely drawn from Daniel 2. There, in the description of the king's dream, reference is made to "a stone . . . cut out by no human hand" (Dan 2:34) which "became a great mountain and filled the whole earth" (2:35). In the interpretation of Dan 2:45 this is said to be "a stone was cut from a mountain by no human hand." In the dream of 4 Ezra the "mountain which was carved" from an unseen place is clearly dependent on Daniel. The man rides upon it and destroys the enemies, a variation of the idea that the stone itself destroyed the idol (= the enemy empires) in Daniel 2.

What is quite extraordinary in 4 Ezra is that in the interpretation the man's mounting the mountain and flying are completely ignored, but the element "carved out *without hands*" is added, in direct contradiction to the dream, in which the man is explicitly said to carve out the mountain (13:6). The mountain is interpreted as Zion, and Zion's appearance as a builded city is said to be the meaning of its being carved without hands. This view about Zion is, of course, found elsewhere in the book *in extenso,* notably in Vision 4. The term "builded city" is particularly characteristic of 4 Ezra's description of the future city.[7]

The man, on Zion, will destroy the multitude by his reproof. This is how the interpretation understands his fiery breath, and so forth. It has already been observed that a great part of the emissions from his mouth have been omitted; the rest are reinterpreted as judgmental, not warrior, in function.[8] The scene of the judgment or reproof of the enemies bringing about their destruction, and a rather similar set of terms, may be observed, for example, in 7:84 of the intermediate state. The same idea with rather different but analogous terminology is to be seen in the scene of eschatological judgment in 7:36–38, but there it is God who is the actor.[9]

The details of the passage on the ten tribes will be dealt with in the Commentary. It is one of the earliest forms of this tradition known and a very singular one. Clearly this tradition has been introduced here holus-bolus and bears only a very superficial relationship with its context or with the dream symbolism, although it is significant, of course, as part of the author's eschatological expectation.

With the additional prophecy in 13:48–50 we return to the familiar language of the survivors and their redemption. This is very much like the material cited above from 9:7–8, and the details will be discussed in the Commentary. The overall notion is that the Messiah, after his victory over the enemy, will rule peacefully over the survivors within the Holy Land until the eschaton.

The central critical issue that must be addressed therefore in this section is thus evident. It is the question of the literary unity and authorship of this vision. Views on this have differed. As typical of the source-analysis approach, we shall examine the views of Box. He maintains that Vision 6 is an independent source that was incorporated into 4 Ezra by the redactor, who also took certain steps in order to integrate its views with those he was promoting. Specifically, Box maintains that the redactor is responsible for 13:13b–24, the middle phrase of 13:26, all of 13:29–32, 13:36, 13:48, and the reference to the companions of the Messiah in 13:52.[10] The arguments he adduces to show that Vision 6 is an inde-

---

discussed in detail in Excursus on the Redeemer Figure.

6   In 5:56 Commentary, we showed that "visitation" in 4 Ezra is always punitive.

7   See also 5:25 and Commentary.

8   See Excursus on the Redeemer Figure, pp. 211–12.

9   This theme is discussed in detail in 13:10 Commentary.

10   See Box, pp. 286 and 300 note. See Stone, *Features,* 122–25. This point is taken up again by Müller, *Messias,* 127.

pendent source resemble those he has used relating to other parts of the book, that is, that its eschatological ideas, first and foremost, differ from those of the redactor. He points to the following distinctive features of this source: the fact that all of the heathen powers and not just the Roman Empire are involved; the fact that the redeemer is the transcendental Son of man and not the Davidic Messiah; and the tradition about the ten tribes, which, he maintains, must have come from before the exile of Judea.

Of these three considerations, we may immediately question the first and the third. Concerning the author's supposed reference to the heathen powers in general, and not just the Roman Empire, it should be remembered that while Vision 5 appertains to the very distinct type and tradition of the "Four Empires," the present vision belongs to an equally distinct tradition about the assault of all the heathens as part of the eschatological woes. There is no reason for one author not to have used both traditions.[11] As to the third point, that the ten tribes tradition must imply a date prior to the destruction of the Second Temple, this is true only if the total prophecy of redemption presented by the author is composed just of that tradition. However, that is not the case, and the ten tribes tradition is followed by what is, as we pointed out above, a structurally unjustified section dealing with the survivors in the land. Box has excised 13:48. Having done this, he has the ten tribes tradition as an isolated one. But to use its consequent isolation to prove something about the composition of the vision is surely circular. Box's comments relating to the presentation of the messianic figure will be discussed further below. On the basis of these comments, however, it is clear that the argument that Vision 6 as a whole derives from another source must fall by the way.

What is not taken into account by these theories of Box is that there are severe differences between the description of the vision and that of the interpretation. These have been pointed out above. The structure of the dream itself is clear.[12] The problems arising in the interpretation are very severe, both in regard to its internal coherence and structure and with respect to its relationship to the vision.[13] The author is clearly a very capable literary craftsman indeed. When that is borne in mind and at the same time the situation of this vision and interpretation is also considered, we are led to the conclusion that the author produced such a botched job because he was writing an interpretation to a strongly crystallized preexistent vision. It is possible, as we have suggested before, that this preexistent vision came to our author in a literary form, but other possibilities might also be entertained. Only the attempt to give a new interpretation to a vision that the author had before him can explain, on the one hand, the contrast between the closely structured allegory and the confused interpretation and, on the other, the general contrast between this interpretation and the clearly formulated interpretation of the eagle vision.

Gunkel, in his treatment of Visions 4–6, pointed out the need to distinguish between material deliberately composed by an apocalypticist as allegories (we might wish to say symbolic structures) and materials that existed previously, often in mythical form, and that are subsequently employed by the apocalyptic writer as allegories. The former, he maintained, have no independent meaning, while the latter do. He is not certain into which category the present vision falls.[14] Adapting Gunkel's second category, in certain instances we may speak of original stories, allegories, or even reports of dreams, used by a later writer with a new interpretation. It is important, in the present context, to bear in mind that this dream vision may well originally have expressed very different ideas from those which are expressed by

---

11 One might even wish to question whether, for an author of the first century c.e. there was a great distinction between the Roman Empire and all the heathen world.

12 Some seeming anomalies within the vision itself have been pointed out by scholars, but these are not more severe than those found in other apocalypses. See, e.g., Box, p. 282; Keulers, p. 123; and others.

Keulers, e.g., raises two problems. The man both rises from the sea and flies on the clouds, and if in 13:4 everybody has melted, who makes up the innumerable host of 13:5?

13 This is expounded in detail in the preceding part of this section. A first analysis of this problematic was published in Stone, *Features,* 123–24.

14 Gunkel, pp. 346–47.

the interpretation. Those of the interpretation will be the ones the author is interested in promoting.[15]

In the Excursus on the Redeemer Figure, pp. 210–11, we dealt with the question of the differences between the presentation of the redeemer figure in the dream part of the vision and in the interpretation. *In nuce* the point that emerged there is that the interpretation is congruent with the view of the Messiah presented elsewhere in the book, while that of the dream vision is very different, seeming to draw on a tradition of a cosmic redeemer with important analogies elsewhere in Jewish literature of the Second Temple period but quite isolated in 4 Ezra. This situation emerging from the material analysis of the chapter fits with our literary hypothesis.

The final part of the interpretation is the conclusion: "This is the interpretation of the dream which you saw" (13:53a). That is followed, as is the corresponding statement in the previous vision, by an assertion of Ezra's worthiness to receive this revelation.[16] What is intriguing is that the change of perspective about Ezra is again accentuated in this passage. Previously Ezra was praised for his virtue or humility (e.g., at the end of Vision 3, 8:46–51). At the end of Vision 4 (perhaps because of the nature of that vision) it is his grief for Zion and his general righteous conduct that are cited (10:39 and 10:50). Here he is praised for his devotion to God's ways. That is an interesting twist on the theme of the search for the way of the Most High that had been so dominant in Vision 1 and that came up once more in Ezra's address to his own soul in 12:4, in reaction to the experience of the dream about the eagle. But not only his devotion to God's ways but also his searching out of the Law, and then his love of wisdom and understanding, are here cited (13:54–55). The implications of this wisdom are followed through in the next, small pericope of conclusion and injunctions.

It should be noted that in the third, repetitive explanation of the appearance of the servant from the sea (13:52–53) the fixed time of his revelation is stressed:

"No one on earth can see my Son or those who are with him, except in the time of his day" (13:52).

Commentary

■ **20b** No commentary.

■ **21** This verse promises two prophecies to Ezra. The first is the interpretation of the vision and the second the explanation of the "things which you have mentioned." The vision is, of course, the dream of 13:1–13a, and its explanation takes up the major part of that which follows. The things of which Ezra has talked are the questions and observations he has made in 13:13b–20, and these are the subject of the angel's discourse in 13:22–24.

Violet 2 has observed that, as distinct from the preceding chapter, here no angelophany is mentioned. Indeed, in the prayer in 13:13b–20a Ezra does not ask for an angel, and the simple interpretation of the context is that it is God who is speaking with Ezra and not an angel at all. This might find some support from the fact that no departure of the angel is mentioned either. It is certainly the case that in chapter 14, God alone speaks with Ezra, with no angel present, but here, though not mentioned, the analogy with the preceding visions and with similar visions elsewhere seems to imply an angelic interpreter. The special introduction to Vision 7 (chap. 14) with its theophany seems to imply the new departure there, with God alone talking to Ezra and no angel interposed.[17]

■ **22** The explanation of Ezra's words is introduced with the same formula that is used in the course of these two visions for the elements of the dream interpretation. The two parts of the interpretation noted above may be compared with the two parts of the vision interpretation in 10:38–43 and, more exactly, with 4:51, where a similar distinction is drawn between Ezra's questioning and the prophecy of the signs.

■ **23** The point is that he who brought the peril can also protect people from the danger. The angel confirms

---

15   This point, made by the writer in "Messiah," 303–10, is taken up and developed by Müller, *Messias,* 109. An analogous argument is proposed about Revelation 17 by Rowland, *Open Heaven,* 237–39.

16   The setting of the end of this pericope in 13:55 is somewhat arbitrary. The considerations governing it are set forth in 13:56–58 Form and Structure.

17   A case could be made, nonetheless, that this, the final vision of the six of which the major revelatory part of the book is composed, reaches the same level of direct revelation as the seventh vision which is the peak of the revelation in the book. See further discussion in 14:1–2 Function and Content, p. 411.

Ezra's surmise, expressed in 13:19–20, and does not differ from Ezra's own views. The idea of the peril is discussed in 9:8 Commentary and refers to the messianic woes. The same reference is implied by the term "at that time," which is well compared with "in those days" in 13:16 (and see Commentary). On the works and faith, see in detail the discussion in Function and Content, p. 397.[18]

■ **24** This verse is the conclusion of the first part of the interpretation. The idea of those who are left and the terminology are discussed above.[19] This is a reversal of the common sentiment, expressed, for example, in 4:12, that it is better to die than to live. This is a central motif in the preceding pericope.[20]

■ **25** This second stage of the interpretation opens with an expression very much like the first stage. It forms the superscription of the whole dream interpretation and as such can be compared with 12:10.[21] The verse introduces the treatment of the Messiah and is best seen as a direct response to 13:3. This verse is the repetition of the dream symbol the explanation of which is to be found in 13:26. In the dream in 13:3 the Redeemer is referred to as "something like the figure of a man," but only there. In all subsequent parts of the vision, including the present verse, he is simply called "the man" or "that man." Throughout the interpretation the man is taken as a symbol of the Messiah, and so again in 13:51. In 13:51 a question is posed similar to that answered here.

■ **26** This verse offers the meaning of the man arising from the sea: he is the Messiah whom the Most High has kept for many ages. Here the idea of the precreation of the Messiah again comes through in a very explicit way (cf. also 12:32). Indeed, not just the Messiah but many eschatological things are said to be precreated.[22] The fact that the Messiah has been kept for many ages in preparation is, perhaps, a reflection of the feeling that the ages to pass until redemption are very long; cf. 6:28 and 11:40. Such an idea could be transmuted into the perception of the delay of redemption, but that is not explicit in 4 Ezra.

The Messiah will deliver creation, quite a regular function of the Messiah; cf. also 13:29.[23] Less usual is the remark that he will "direct" those who are left. The vision contains no hint of this function, found also in 13:49. It is not described in royal terms or military language, a significant difference from the view put forward in the vision.[24] The idea of the survivors, those left after the messianic woes, is discussed in 13:16 Commentary and in 5:41 Commentary. This general view of the Messiah's function with the survivors is also to be found elsewhere, for example, *2 Apoc Bar* 40:2.[25]

■ **27** Here 13:10–11 is restated, preparatory to its interpretation, but it is are not interpreted here. Instead, a body of other material intervenes and its interpretation only occurs in 13:36–38. This odd structure has been discussed in Form and Structure, pp. 394–95.[26] The significance of the fiery breath is discussed in 13:10 Commentary.

■ **28** This verse continues the restatement of the dream symbol and concludes it with a formula for its interpretation. Curiously, the weaponlessness of the man, made much of in this verse and in the dream (13:9), is not

18 The term "Almighty" is discussed in 6:32 Commentary. "Protect" or "preserve" is typical of God's action toward the righteous; see 7:27 Commentary n. 53. Cf. also God's action in *Vit Ad* 29:10–11 (manuscript groups II-IV there).

19 See 13:16 Commentary.

20 13:13b–20a Function and Content, pp. 389–90.

21 On these formulae, see 10:38–54 Form and Structure, p. 334.

22 On the Messiah, see 12:31 Commentary and also 3:6 Commentary. In some rabbinic sources the "name of the Messiah" is said to have existed before creation.

23 This is the subject of detailed discussion in Müller, *Messias*, 129–34. A detailed treatment of the Messiah is given in Excursus on the Redeemer Figure.

24 See on this in detail Excursus on the Redeemer Figure.

25 A detailed description of the Messiah's kingdom is to be found in *2 Apocalypse of Baruch* 73–74. This verse of 4 Ezra, particularly the middle phrase of it, has been attributed by the source critics to the "Redactor." This view and a critique of it are set forth in detail in Function and Content, pp. 398–99.

26 The significance of the fiery breath is discussed in 13:10 Commentary.

given any interpretation at all, even in 13:36–38. This is another of the structural difficulties to be observed in this interpretation.

■ **29** This opens the interpretation of what has been restated in the previous two verses. The expression "Behold, the days are coming" is also to be found in the interpretation of Vision 5, at its start (12:13). Here, as usually in the book, it marks the beginning of a predictive passage.[27] The days are those when the Most High is about to deliver the earth. Two features are particularly notable in this expression. Redemption is assigned to the Most High, even though in fact the point of the whole interpretation is that the Messiah will execute it. This serves to remind us that the Messiah is seen only as God's instrument.

The second point is that in fact, as is evident from the following, this verse forms the immediate introduction of a prophecy of woes.[28] A certain apparent non sequitur is thus to be observed. In general terms, of course, this could be taken to be the introduction to the whole prediction that follows, and that surely is, in the long run, a prophecy of redemption, not of woes. Here the balance changes from the earlier woes predictions, which are described as visitations, always punitive in 4 Ezra (see 6:18 and 9:2) even though some of them contain explicit prophecies of redemption. Yet, of course, this is a matter of perspective, and from another point of view, because the eschatological scheme is fixed, a prophecy of woes is implicitly a prophecy of redemption. Such earlier predictions are 5:1–13 and 6:11–28. In the vision here, the woes are not even hinted at.[29]

■ **30** This is the first element of the woes that is prophesied to Ezra in this vision. It may be compared with a similar sign in *2 Apoc Bar* 25:3 and 70:2.[30] As has been noted, the expression "inhabitants of the earth" occurs

primarily in eschatological contexts, although it is not certain that this is a significant conjunction.[31]

■ **31** As in the texts cited from *2 Apocalypse of Baruch* above, the bewilderment of mind leads to internecine strife. This is an old traditional element describing the onset of chaos and particularly used of the turmoil of the messianic woes. It has already occurred, in a fixed literary form, in 4 Ezra 5:9; 6:24; and 9:3–4 and has been analyzed in detail above.[32] This is the most extensive list of participants in such conflict in 4 Ezra.[33] Because of the traditional character of this element, attempts to interpret it in the light of contemporary, political conflicts must be resisted.[34]

■ **32** This verse should be compared with 9:1–2. There are problems about the order of events. Are the signs mentioned here additional to those already revealed to Ezra, for example, in 9:1–13? In 9:1–3, Ezra is instructed to use the signs to determine whether the end is close. There, as here, when part of the signs is past, the time of visitation will be at hand. This might suggest to us that the signs mentioned here are regarded as additional to those already mentioned.

The man is here identified with God's "servant," and the servant remains the subject of action down through 13:38. This title is found, in Vision 6, exclusively in the interpretation.[35]

■ **33** This verse is an interpretation of 13:4. Note, once again, that the order of events in the interpretation varies from that in the dream. The voice of the Messiah here can be compared with the human voice of the lion, raised in indictment, in 11:37. Behind this is the idea of the active word of the Messiah or God; see 13:10 Commentary. In general, the voice plays a special role in eschatological and other great numinous events.[36]

The question of the eschatological battle will be

---

27   See in detail 5:1 Commentary.

28   Lists of woes are discussed in 4:52 Commentary.

29   The source critics assign 13:29–33 to the Redactor (Box, p. 286), and see critique of this solution in Function and Content, pp. 398–99.

30   It is probably to be distinguished from the bewilderment to be observed in 5:1 and similar contexts (see Commentary there).

31   See 5:1 Commentary.

32   See 5:9 Commentary.

33   The Armenian is expanded here and also in the list in 5:9. See textual note y. The possible motives for

this are discussed in 5:9 Commentary.

34   See, e.g., the older views of Hilgenfeld, rebutted in Introduction, sec. 2.1.

35   On the title in detail, see Excursus on the Redeemer Figure, p. 211.

36   See 10:26 Commentary. Note the voice of the unknown eschatological figure in 5:7. The voice in creation in 6:39 is quite different; see Commentary there.

discussed in the commentary on the next verse. It contrasts with the friendly multitude that assembles according to 13:39–49.

■ **34** This verse follows the order of the vision and recapitulates the events of 13:5 prior to their being explained in the following verses. The gathering of the nations is for the eschatological battle which is described in numerous sources. A final assault of the forces of evil on Zion will be repulsed by the Messiah, and all the nations will assemble and execute this attack.[37] This was not the only possible order of events. Thus, for example, in *2 Apoc Bar* 29:3 the revelation of the Messiah is followed by the institution of his kingdom, as happened also in the preceding Vision 5. It seems likely that the author of 4 Ezra did not work these differing views into a unified single pattern and was content to talk of a fourth empire being destroyed in the context of a traditional political apocalypse (Vision 5) and of an assault by the heathen nations in general in the different sort of context found here.

■ **35** This verse is the beginning of the interpretation of 13:6–7. It is worth noting that here the interpretation is the reverse of the usual order, first giving the meaning of the symbol and then stating what the symbol is. That is done in the latter part of 13:36. The man's standing on the mountain is perhaps drawn from biblical patterns, since in the vision he is said to fly upon the mountain. Standing is not mentioned in the vision, nor is the flying mentioned in the interpretation.

A most interesting parallel is to be seen in Ps 2:6, a text often given a messianic interpretation in the Second Temple period. There in the context of the attack made upon the king by the nations it states, "I have set my king on Zion, my holy hill." This is followed by his destruction of his enemies. Note also Isa 31:4b: "The Lord of Hosts will come down to fight upon Mount Zion and upon its hill." The exchange of such ideas between the divine warrior and the Messiah is a common feature.[38] Thus, the standing of the Messiah upon Mount Zion is easily

put into the context of his function as a warrior and destroyer of enemies.[39]

■ **36** The mountain carved out without hands[40] is identified as Zion which is manifested as "built." The manifestation of Zion at the end of days is a common idea in the book and in general in Jewish and Christian literature of this age. The city appears in 7:26, and the revelation of the city is also the main topic of Vision 4; see particularly 10:25–27 and 10:54.[41] The adjective "built" is particularly used of Zion and sometimes of other cities,[42] and the "built city" is referred to in 8:52; 10:25–27; and 10:44. This language implies the preexistence of Zion, an idea also found elsewhere in the book.[43] There are very numerous texts in the Hebrew Bible that speak of Zion as a mountain. Compare, for example, Isa 2:2. The heavenly city is named Zion only here and in 10:54. Here it may be the mountain that provides the connection.[44]

■ **37** On the title "servant" in this vision, see 13:32 Commentary. This verse is the first part of the interpretation of the man's exhalations, detailed in 13:10–11. The mixture of language of fire and of judgment is strikingly to be found in a passage like Isa 66:15–16: "For behold, the Lord will come in fire, and his chariots like storm-wind, to render his anger in fury, and his rebuke with flames of fire. For by fire will the Lord execute judgment." In general, the presentation of this aspect of the Messiah's activities resembles that in the interpretation of Vision 5; see particularly 12:32. However, the legal features are less prominent here. At one level, the reproach may be compared with God's reproach of the arisen humans in 7:37–38. Since the reproach is fire, and both reproach and fire are instruments of divine destruction, in the present interpretation it is possible to say that the reproach itself destroys the wicked. A similar use is to be found in 1QpHab 5:4–5.[45]

---

37   See 13:5 Commentary.
38   See also Zech 14:4 for a graphic description of this. The idea of the deity residing upon a holy mountain, of course, goes back to pre-Israelite antiquity. See, e.g., Anat 3:27–28.
39   In *2 Apoc Bar* 40:1–2 the role of Mount Zion in the punishment of the eschatological wicked ruler is notable, though the context is different from here.
40   On this detail, see Function and Content, p. 398.
41   See 7:26 Commentary for full discussion with examples.
42   See 5:25 Commentary.
43   See 7:26 Commentary.
44   The source critics have attributed this verse to the Redactor, a view that has been critiqued above.
45   B. Nitzan, *The Habbakuk Commentary Scroll* (Jeru-

No other instruments are mentioned by which God carries out his judgment.[46] Fire as God's instrument of destruction of the wicked has often been discussed before. The idea is well established.[47]

■ **38** This verse interprets 13:10b–11. The general notion of the Messiah's judgmental word has been discussed above (see 13:10 Commentary). The function attributed to the Messiah in 12:32–33 is very similar to that here.[48]

■ **39** This verse recapitulates 13:12–13 prior to its interpretation which runs from 13:40 to 13:47. The peaceable multitude is the exiled nine and one half tribes. Directly following this passage is a discussion of those who remained in the land, and real problems arise of the coherence of these two predictions. Certainly, the second one, which commences in 13:48, is not hinted at in the vision which ends with 13:13.

■ **40** Behind the traditions in this section lies the general picture of the restoration of the full community of Israel in their land as part of the future hope. This is, of course, known already from biblical sources such as Isa 11:11–13 and Jer 30:3. The community of ideal Israel in many sources of our period was considered to be that of twelve tribes; see, for example, Aristeas 47–50; 1QS 8:1, et al.; James 1:1; Rev 7:4–8; and many other sources. As to the exiles, the northern kingdom was held to be of ten tribes from early times; cf. 1 Kings 11:31; 11:35; et al. Many sources of the Second Temple period reckon the exiles of the north to be ten tribes and those of the south (exiled or not) as two. Some of these sources are *Test Mos* 3:4–6; 4:8–9; Josephus, *Ant.* 11.133; and rabbinic texts such as *Gen. R.* 73:6 (Theodor-Albeck, p. 850); cf. also *Sib Or* 2:171–173.

The textual witnesses to 4 Ezra here offer three readings: "ten" (most Latin); "nine and a half" Syriac, Arabic1, and two Ethiopic manuscripts; and "nine"

Ethiopic, cf. Arabic2, and Latin manuscripts A* C L V. Box, like most others, accepts the reading "ten," commenting that the "nine and a half" is surely derived from a confusion with the tribes who remained in trans-Jordan (Josh 22:7–10). Yet the very uncommon reading of "nine and a half" or "nine" inclines us to the view that Latin represents a correction in the direction of the widely held understanding. This view finds corroboration in *2 Apocalypse of Baruch* in which work the figure of 9½ is found repeatedly (77:17; 77:19; 78:1). The same figure of 9½ is to be found in the Greek and fragmentary Latin of the later Christian works, *Asc Isa* 3:2 and Commodian.[49] Intriguingly, there the Ethiopic has "nine," just as most Ethiopic manuscripts of 4 Ezra do here. This evidence suggests that Box's easy assumption of the secondary nature of 9½ must be reconsidered. It is possible that half of the tribe of Manasseh was being considered, but it is equally possible that the half was considered to be the Levites, for half of the tribe of Levi went into captivity with the north, while half remained.[50]

It is notable that this is the oldest developed tradition about the tribes, their withdrawal to a farther land, and their eventual return. The tradition of their special fate is known, for example, to Josephus, but he is just about contemporary with 4 Ezra. Its relative rarity in the period of the Second Temple is notable.

This block of independent, semilegendary tradition is comparable to 6:49–52.

■ **41** This tradition deals with the withdrawal of the tribes to a remote region in trans-Euphrates, where they reformed their ways and lived in accordance with God's precepts. In Josephus, *Ant.* 11.133, we find a similar legendary tradition of innumerable folk of the ten tribes living in the region of trans-Euphrates.[51]

■ **42** The word translated "statutes" is singular in some

---

salem: Mosad Bialik, 1986) 165, has remarked that there the word ובתוכחתם means both the pronouncement of judgment and its execution and that both meanings of this root are already to be found in biblical Hebrew.

46   See 13:10 Commentary for a detailed discussion of the interrelationship between various elements of divine judgment.

47   See Excursus on the Redeemer Figure, p. 212, and 13:10 Commentary.

48   See also *2 Apoc Bar* 72:2. A similar series of events may be observed also in Isa 66:15–23, which was the

paradigm of many later concepts of redemption: punishment, ingathering, restoration of the cosmos.

49   *Carmen de duobus populis* 943–946; see *apud* Bogaert, *Baruch*, 1:345.

50   Bogaert, *Baruch*, 1:339–52, discusses the matter in some detail and also raises this possibility, following Origen (p. 349).

51   Cf. Commodian, *Carmen apologeticum* 941–946. Indications for later rabbinic, medieval Jewish, and Moslem developments are given by Ginzberg, *Legends*, 6:408. A. Neubauer, "Where Are the Ten Tribes?" *JQR* 1 (1888–89) 14–28, 95–114, 185–201,

versions, giving the translation "Law," "Torah."[52] In *2 Apoc Bar* 1:2–3 a certain tendency to find the sins of the ten tribes less grave than those of the remaining two may be found. A somewhat analogous tradition of repentance of all tribes may be found in *Testament of Moses* 3.

■ **43** The exact sense of "narrow passages" here is unclear. It might refer to a narrow passage opened by God in the waters of the river, or it might refer to its narrow headwaters or tributaries.[53]

■ **44** This is, of course, based on the miracle of the splitting of the Red Sea (Exod 14:21–31). That formed a paradigm for later miracles of redemption and, of course, one of the great patterns of redemption in 4 Ezra. The same structure is perhaps also operative in 7:28, where four hundred years of the messianic kingdom balance the four hundred years of servitude in Egypt. A particularly interesting parallel is to be found in the *Life of Ezekiel,* which refers to the withdrawal of the Israelites in Babylonian exile to the far side of a river, perhaps the Chebar, which was dried up miraculously by God. This is, perhaps, dependent on the same underlying tradition as 4 Ezra and Josephus. Knibb observed that this miracle served to stress the inaccessibility of the trans-Euphrates abode of the ten tribes.[54]

■ **45** This name, Azareth, is perhaps derived from Hebrew ארץ אחרת.[55] In *m. Sanh.* 10:3 a difference of views is found concerning the return of the ten tribes. R.

Aqiba denies that they will return, while R. Meir asserts it. In this context the land in which they dwell is also designated by this expression from Deuteronomy.[56]

■ **46** The term "last times" implies the proximity of the eschatological events. "Times" is not an obvious expression in Hebrew (cf. 3:14 Commentary). On "last," see also the discussion in the Excursus on Natural Order, p. 104.

■ **47** The eschatological redemption associated with the inception of the messianic kingdom is equivalent to the exodus. See further 13:44 Commentary.

■ **48** This verse is closely connected in ideas and terminology with 9:8 and 12:34. This verse and the next discuss the inception and nature of the Messiah's rule. The various specific ideas in it are discussed in detail elsewhere in this commentary, and that discussion will not be repeated here.[57] Note that, in spite of a measure of textual uncertainty,[58] the group of survivors in the land about whom this verse prophesies are quite distinct from the ingathered exiles of the nine and one half tribes discussed in the preceding verses.

■ **49** The function of the Messiah in this verse is to defend or protect those survivors who will live in his kingdom. This particular function is of some interest and can be compared with *1 Enoch* 100:5. There God is said to establish angelic guards to protect the righteous in the terrible events of the end time. It is also noteworthy that,

---

408–23, gathers many medieval traditions about the ten tribes.

52 Harnisch, p. 152 note, points to the great variations of terminology in this respect. Such variety should serve as a warning not to take such scholarly constructs as "apocalyptic understanding of the Law" too seriously.

53 Cf. the narrow ways or entrances in 7:4 and 7:7.

54 This material developed into the later Jewish legends about the river Sambatyon and the ten tribes; see on this, Ginzberg, *Legends,* 6:407–9, and further references there. The typology exodus/redemption also lies behind *m. Ber.* 1:5; *Mek. Bo* (Horovitz-Rabin, p. 60); and *b. Sanh.* 99a.

55 Schiller-Szinessy cited by W. A. Wright, "Note on the 'Arzareth' of 4 Esdr. 13.45," *Journal of Philology* 3 (1871) 114; this view has been followed by many scholars. The transcription thus implied, however, would differ from that customary in the Greek Bible.

56 See also *t. Sanh.* 13:12; *b. Sanh.* 110b; *j. Sanh.* 29b; and *ARN* A 36 (Schechter, p. 108). This view is rejected by F. Perles, "Notes sur les apocryphes et les

pseudépigraphes," *REJ* 73 (1921) 185, on grounds that are not totally clear. On the text of the versions here, see textual note o. Violet 2 suggests that behind the versions may lie ארץ אחרם on the basis of 2 Kgs 19:37 and Isa 37:38. He also raises some other suggestions, none of which is more persuasive. Note 9:26, where the name of the field Ardat is equally enigmatic.

57 The survivors in the land are mentioned explicitly in 9:8 and 12:34, and see Commentary on those verses; on the idea of the holy land in general in the book, see 5:24 Commentary. The concept of the survivors is discussed in detail in 5:41 Commentary, while the messianic kingdom is discussed in 7:29 Commentary.

58 See textual note v.

although the Messiah is the son of David, his action is not referred to in monarchical terms.[59] In 7:28 and 12:34 he makes them rejoice, and in 12:34 and 13:26 he delivers them. This is not hinted in the vision.

■ **50** The expression "show wonders" is frequently used of the activity of the Messiah in his kingdom; cf. 4:26; 7:27; 13:14; 13:57; and 14:5. It refers to the eschatological goods.[60] The exact meaning of the phrase has been discussed and some scholars have suggested that "to see" means "to enjoy." This is not certain.[61] The activity of the Messiah after the inception of his kingdom, including the elements mentioned in this verse, is not inherent in the dream.

■ **51** The question asked by the seer here about the meaning of the man rising from the heart of the sea returns, in a somewhat repetitive fashion, to a point made at the beginning of the interpretation.[62] Violet 2 points out that questions about details of apocalyptic or symbolic visions or dreams are quite common. He cites a number of sources; among them are Rev 7:12; *1 Enoch* 23:3; 24:5; and 27:1; *2 Enoch* 7:2 and 10:4; *3 Apocalypse of Baruch* 1; 2; and 3; and *Hermas Vis.* 3.3.5 and 3.4.1. These passages all reinforce the theory proposed here, for in all of them the question about the detail comes at the appropriate point in the sequence of development of the interpretation. It is not repetitive or out of order.

The double divine name at the opening of this question is of a type found in such contexts elsewhere in the book.[63]

■ **52** This verse supplies another explanation of the meaning of the man arising from the sea. The unknowability of the heart of the sea was proverbial and had served already as a prime example in the riddle questions in 4:7.[64] The unknowability of the depths of the sea symbolizes the hiddenness of the Messiah. The notion of the future revelation of presently hidden things is found on a number of occasions in the book, such as 7:26–28 and 7:31. The expression here should also be compared with 13:26, where the Messiah is said to be the one whom the Most High has been keeping for many ages.[65] Together with him, his companions are mentioned, a concept found also in 6:25; 7:28; 13:52; and 14:9. The companions are, on the basis of those other passages, to be interpreted as those humans who were taken alive to heaven, such as Enoch or Elijah. Such righteous were expected to appear together with the Messiah.[66] The companions are yet one more element that was not mentioned in the dream. "The time of his day" means the predetermined time of his appearance.[67] Sjöberg would stress the hiddenness of the man here and in 13:3, viewing it as part of the Jewish background of the concept of the hiddenness of the Messiah in earliest Christianity.[68] Luck, on the other hand, stresses its opposition to the concept of the Son of man in *1 Enoch* 37–71, where the preknowledge of the man is exactly the subject of the revelation to Enoch.[69]

■ **53** This verse initiates the conclusion of the vision. The structure of such conclusions is conventional; cf. 8:61–62; 12:35–36; and *2 Apoc Bar* 71:2. The angelic response in 10:38–40 is also similarly structured, but the revelation of interpretation is promised for the future, which is understandable in context. The expression "you alone" is particularly notable; cf. *2 Apoc Bar* 71:2.[70]

■ **54** This verse starts to explore the reasons for Ezra's worthiness. This subject is repeated throughout the book. Here, notably, it is his wisdom that is praised, and his investigation of the Torah (see in detail 13:55 Commentary).[71] The parallel between Torah and wisdom is common; cf. Ps 119:34 and *2 Apoc Bar* 38:1–4, particularly 38:4: "For Thou knowest that my soul hath

59   See further Excursus on the Redeemer Figure, p. 209.
60   See the detailed analysis in 4:26 Commentary.
61   Discussed in 6:25 Commentary.
62   See Function and Content, p. 396.
63   See 3:4 Commentary.
64   See on these questions 4:1–25 Form and Structure, pp. 80–81.
65   Cf. the statement about the Messiah in *Sefer Zerubbabel:* "This is the Messiah son of David and his name is Menahem son of Amiel. He was born at the time of David, king of Israel, and the spirit lifted him

up and hid him in this place until the end time" (trans. M. Himmelfarb). This is a much more specific expression of the same idea.
66   See in detail 6:26 Commentary.
67   See on predetermination 3:9 Commentary.
68   Sjöberg, *Der verborgene Menschensohn*, 46–47.
69   Luck, "Weltverständnis," 298. It seems to us doubtful that this opposition is deliberate. The differences in perspective are probably due to a deeper difference between the two works in respect to the revelation of heavenly secrets.
70   On the nature of Ezra's virtue and the exclusive

always walked in Thy law, and from my (earliest) days, I departed not from Thy wisdom"; cf. also *2 Apoc Bar* 51:3.

■ **55** It is difficult to know whether this is a general sentiment relating to Ezra's virtues or a reference to the search for the way of the Most High.[72] The eschatological role of wisdom has been encountered earlier in the book. In 5:9, as part of the woes, it is said to hide itself.[73] Ezra says that he is without wisdom in the riddle questions in 5:38, he calls on his heart to drink wisdom (8:4), and God is said to teach humans wisdom (8:12). The concept of wisdom is complex and not every instance is to be identified as a "technical" use. Undoubtedly technical is the fact that wisdom typifies the tradition of eschatological teaching and the inspiration that comes upon Ezra in 14:40 and 14:47. Chapter 14 is a

response to Ezra's search for wisdom.[74]

The expression "called . . . your mother" is frequent in such cases or in catalogues of vices; see Prov 7:4 ("your sister") and contrast Jer 2:27 and Job 17:14.

Certain scholars have made very much of the role of sapiential ideas in the book.[75] The point is well taken that in 4 Ezra this terminology denotes those to whom eschatological secrets can be made known, perhaps a distinct social group.[76] Even then, the significance of the use of this terminology must be assessed carefully in view of its wide spread in the Second Temple period.[77]

---

revelation to him, see Function and Content, p. 400.

71   See on Ezra's virtues the discussion at 6:32 Commentary.

72   Note that the word "ways" is not to be taken into account here, since it is a stylistic addition in the translation.

73   See further on the eschatological hiding and finding of wisdom 5:9 Commentary.

74   On 14:40 in particular, see Excursus on Inspiration, p. 121.

75   See the views of Brandenburger, *Verborgenheit*, discussed in Introduction, sec. 3.3, and of Knibb and

Luck (ibid.).

76   See Knibb, "Apocalyptic and Wisdom," 63–65. He highlights other "wisdom features" in the book (pp. 65–69).

77   Meade, *Pseudonymity and Canon,* observes, "The learned character of apocalyptic, however, should not be exaggerated. The chief value of recognizing it lies in the light it sheds on the form of the literature more than its content" (p. 75).

13

56	Therefore I have shown you this, ^afor there is a reward laid up with the Most High. ^a And ^b after three ^c days I will tell you other things, and explain ^d wondrous matters to you."
57	Then I arose and walked in the field, giving great ^e glory and praise to the Most High because of his wonders, which he did from time to time, 58/ and because he governs the times and whatever things come to pass in their seasons. And I stayed there three days.

Notes

56   a–a Ar2, Arm omit; Ar2 has supplied some text from another source.

     b Lat Ms L has an expansion here: *tibi reposita tributio multa gracia. Tu autem adhuc reside in hunc campum orans dominum et gratias illi agens super omnibus his que nota sunt tibi. Et iterum (ergo . . .).*

     c Lat, Ar2, Arm; the reading is uncertain; Arm omits "other things" in the next phrase.

     d The versions vary here. Lat *gravia et mirabilia* (whence RSV "weighty and wondrous"); Syr, Ar1 "the last wonders"; Eth, Arm "wonders"; Ar2 omits the phrase.

57   e Eth, Ar2, Arm omit.

Form and Structure

This pericope contains the injunctions and the conclusion of the second dream vision. It represents a continuation of the angel's speech and could be regarded as part of the preceding pericope. The interpretation of the dream actually ends with the conclusion in 13:53a. But that is followed, like that in Vision 5, by an assertion of Ezra's worthiness which has here been set at the end of the interpretation. The present section and the corresponding part of the preceding vision both open with a "Therefore."[1]

The major parts of this small pericope are the angelic assurance, followed by the injunction to wait three more days. The promise of future revelation ensues, and then, in 13:57–58, is a small narrative piece. The pericope concludes with the fulfillment by Ezra in 13:58 of the injunction laid upon him in 13:56.

This passage thus also forms the end of the dream visions and of the major revelatory strand of the book.

Function and Content

The function of this passage is clear from its structural role, but that function is effected not just by the structural and formal considerations but by its content. At the end of the preceding pericope Ezra had been praised by the angel for his wisdom and understanding. As a result of this, he is told that "reward is laid up with the Most High."[2] Moreover, because of his love of wisdom, the angel promises him, "I will tell you other things and explain weighty and wondrous matters to you." So the clear import is that Ezra has advanced his understanding very significantly and now, having reached the position where his adherence to God's way, his knowledge of the Torah, and his wisdom and understanding are his chief virtues, he will be told yet weightier and more wondrous matters.

He is enjoined to fast yet another three days. Above we showed that these three days will complete forty days' fast, abstention, or separation that Ezra has observed in the book so far.[3] Another difference in the content of the narrative passage marks it off from similar ones elsewhere in the book. Ezra is said to arise (he did this previously only to receive predictions, e.g., 4:47; 6:13; and 6:17, and see Commentary there), and, on his feet, he remains walking in the field and praising God.

In order to assess the full import of this seemingly

---

1   In Vision 4 the situation is even more complex and the break between the pericopae could be put at 10:50 or at 10:55. We chose 10:50, but that choice is more a matter of convenience than one of principle.

2   In the closely corresponding positions in Visions 4 and 5, Ezra's virtue, but not his reward, is referred to.

3   See 12:37–39 Function and Content on the 40 days (pp. 373–74).

simple statement, one must view it in the context of the overall structure of the book. This conclusion of the sixth vision stands in deliberate, deeply significant contrast to the opening of the first one. The book had opened with Ezra's lying on his bed in Babylon, at night, weeping and bewailing the state of Zion and accusing God, whose conduct of the world has brought this state of affairs to pass. As the end of six vision experiences, Ezra is standing, walking in the field and praising God "because he governs the times and whatever things come to pass in their seasons" (13:58).

These contrasts are too systematic and thorough to be pure chance. Indeed, they are deliberate and can be understood only in the light of the overall development of the book. As was shown above, the major shift that takes place during the first visions is the recognition that God determines and controls the course of events. This is the first stage in the shift from accusation with which he opens to the unreserved praise here. Next Ezra accepts the basic justice of God's control of events. These changes are internalized in the fourth vision, and in the light of them Ezra undergoes a profound conversion.

It is only in the fifth and sixth visions, however, that the implications of this are realized and Ezra reaches the fuller understanding that the determination of times involves the promise of redemption, of the destruction of Rome (Vision 5), or of evil in general (Vision 6). At the end of Vision 5 much was made, in our discussion, of the secret tradition of transmission of knowledge of the times.[4] On the one hand, it is a logical but graphic implication of Ezra's new role. On the other, it opens the way to Vision 7, which profoundly differs from the six preceding ones.

The point of the seemingly superfluous third interpretation of the man coming up from the sea is that the time of redemption is fixed. This is properly to be understood, as it is by Ezra in his prophetic state, as a promise of redemption and an assurance of salvation.

Consequently, this pericope is a clear indication of the final move in Ezra's understanding. It marks most tellingly the progression of his thought and development.

Commentary

■ **56** The expression "wonders" has occurred a number of times in this part of the chapter. It is discussed in detail in 4:26 Commentary, and its primary meaning is eschatological. The angel promises to reveal other things and explain "weighty and wondrous matters." Similar promises occur at the end of the preceding visions (see 5:13; 6:31; 10:59; and 12:39), but the expression "weighty and wondrous matters" has no parallel in the book. The idea that Ezra's reward is laid up in heaven is in line with many points in the book. The precreation of reward is found in 8:52–53; 8:59; et al., while the term "laid up" is used often of the heavenly treasure of good deeds and faith. The reward corresponds to this heavenly treasure.[5] The three days are required in order to complete the forty days of fasting and abstinence of the first six visions.

■ **57** This verse and the next one form a transitional section to Vision 7, like 5:16–20; 6:30–34; 9:26–27; 10:55–6; 12:40–51; and 13:57–58. "From time to time" expresses the idea of the fixed time and order of events and is well compared with 5:46; 5:48; and 11:8.[6]

The "wonders" here are perhaps both past and future. Ezra, unlike in the preceding instances, is elated by the revelation and arises and sings God's praise.[7] "Give glory" means "praise," "glorify." It is also used of the woman's expression of thanks to God in 9:45.

■ **58** This verse again stresses the predestinarian ideas with the expression "in their seasons."[8] The term "times" is common in the book, although it raises some philological problems. The idea presented here is well compared with 2 Apoc Bar 48:2–3 and 54:1, both of which are prayers in the course of which Baruch celebrates God's control of the times and seasons. On Ezra's time spent in the field and his conduct there, see the discussion in 12:39 Commentary. Here he fulfills the angel's commands.

---

4 See 12:37–39 Function and Content, pp. 373–74.
5 See particularly 7:77 Commentary.
6 See 3:9 Commentary.

7 See Function and Content, pp. 408–9.
8 See 3:9 Commentary, 4:37 Commentary, and Excursus on Natural Order, p. 102.

14

1   **ᵃAnd it came to pass, ᵃ on ᵇ the third day, while I was sitting under an oak, ᶜ behold, a voice came out of a bush opposite me and said, "Ezra, Ezra." 2/ And I said, "Here I am, Lord," ᵈ and I rose to my feet.**

Notes

1   a–a Lat, Syr, Arm; the other versions omit; this is a common variant.

      b Lat, Eth, Arm Ms H; Syr, Ar2, Arm Mss W *Y* "after."

      c Eth, Ar1 "tree."

2   d Lat, Ar2, Eth Mss; the other versions omit. A corresponding word does not occur in Exod 3:4; cf. Gen 22:1 and 1 Sam 3:4, 8.

Form and Structure

This passage is the introduction to the seventh vision. It is composed of a narrative introduction, which sets the vision in context and location. The form of the ensuing is a call. Ezra is called directly, with a double repetition of his name, just as Moses, Abraham, and Samuel were.[1] He responds to the call in the same formulaic way that the biblical figures did, with the answer, "Here I am, Lord."

Function and Content

By its reference to the third day, this passage ties this vision into that which precedes. The context it establishes differs from the preceding visions in some significant ways. Ezra, admittedly, is still in the field, but on this occasion he is not lying on the grass but is sitting under an oak tree. This reminds us of the "oak trees of Mamre," associated with Abraham (Gen 18:1), and of Deborah, who is said to be sitting under a tree when she is summoned to be judge of Israel (Judg 4:5).[2] Much more similar to our passage are *2 Apoc Bar* 6:1 and 77:18; cf. 55:1. In these instances Baruch also sits under an oak tree. This detail is so specific to the two works that a direct connection between them seems likely.[3]

It is uncertain whether a tree was mentioned here because it was connected in some way with the idea of a sacred tree or because in a hot climate normally someone in a field would sit under a tree. Compare *Para Jer* 5:1: "But Abimelech carried the figs in the heat (of the day), and coming upon a tree, he sat under its shade to rest a little."[4] More pointed is the fact that Ezra is sitting. In all previous visions he has been prostrate either in his bed or in the field. In 13:57 he walks around, but here he is sitting (not lying) under the tree. The difference in posture points to a new stage in the process of revelation.

Even more striking is the next element. Ezra is sitting opposite a bush from which the divine voice issues. There is no doubt that this is a deliberate reference to the burning bush from which Moses received his call (Exod 3:2), and this reference is reinforced by the explicit recalling of this event in 14:3: "I revealed myself in a bush and spoke to Moses."[5]

The association with Moses is very clear. Ezra receives his call in a situation similar to that of Moses and in an identical fashion. The language of the call, the double repetition of the name, and the response, although often found in call scenes (see above), take on great specificity

---

1   See Exod 3:4; Gen 22:11; and 1 Sam 3:10.

2   A further instance of a specific oak is that mentioned in connection with the burial of another Deborah under an oak called Alon Bekuth (Gen 35:8). Cf. also Susanna 58 and Hos 4:13. Yet another oak tree is mentioned in connection with Isaiah's burial in *Vitae Prophetarum, Isaias*.

3   Hartom makes the literalistic observation that Ezra's tree was in Babylon, while Baruch's was near Jerusalem.

4   Cf. also John 1:50. A similar incident of secret teaching transmitted under an olive tree is that of

Rabbi Joḥanan ben Zakkai and Rabbi Eliezer ben Arach, who discussed *Maaseh Merkabah* under an olive tree (*b. Ḥag.* 14b). The same ambiguity about the function of the tree exists there.

5   The same point is again highlighted by Ezra's forty-day fast; see 14:23 Commentary. The figure of Ezra as presented in this vision was considered central to the whole book by P. G. de Villiers, "The Ezra-Legend in 4 Ezra 14:1–48" (paper circulated for 1981 Pseudepigrapha Seminar of the SBL).

of reference because of the deliberate association with Moses.

The idea that Ezra was worthy to receive the Torah in the same measure as Moses is to be found in a number of places in rabbinic literature. In *t. Sanh.* 4:7 we read:

R. Yose said, "Ezra was worthy that the Torah be given through him, but Moses anticipated him. Of Moses, the term 'ascent' is used and of Ezra, the term 'ascent' is used. Of Moses, as it said "And Moses ascended to God" (Exod 19:3); of Ezra—"He, Ezra, came up [i.e., ascended (M.E.S.)] from Babylon" (Ezra 7:6).[6]

The text continues to prove that both Moses and Ezra taught Torah to Israel. Moreover, Ezra's writing of the Torah in Aramaic is compared with Moses' writing of the Torah. The text then deals with the square Aramaic script, attributed to Ezra and connected with his "giving of Torah." Another important text in this connection is *b. Sanh.* 21b:

Mar Zutra said, Mar ʿUqba said, "Originally the Torah was given to Israel in Hebrew script and the holy tongue. It was given to them again in the time of Ezra in the square script and Aramaic tongue. Israel selected the square script and the holy tongue and left for simple folk the Hebrew script and the Aramaic tongue."

Then in the Talmudic text the same dictum "Ezra was worthy . . ." is adduced.[7] This tradition is doubtless connected with the "characters which they did not know" in which Ezra's scribes recorded his revelation, according to 14:42 (see Commentary there).

In the rabbinic sources the Torah is said almost to have been forgotten or lost in Ezra's time, but Ezra is not said to give it anew but to have given it in a new way. Thus see *Sifre Deut.* 48 (Finkelstein, p. 112) and similarly in *b. Sukka* 20a.[8] The Christian tradition was far more daring in this respect, and many Patristic and Byzantine sources speak of a complete loss of scripture in the destruction of the Temple and of Ezra's restoration of it.[9] That very notion is a witness to the strength of the tradition of Ezra as giver of Torah, which is a basic motif of our chapter.[10]

It is most significant that Ezra is addressed directly from the bush by God. In this case no angel is mentioned, and indeed, the *angelus interpres* has completely disappeared from this chapter. Ezra's interlocutor is now God alone, and so he remains throughout the chapter.[11]

Brandenburger has argued that the role of the angel diminishes throughout the last three visions. He changes from Ezra's interlocutor and the chief agent of revelation in Visions 1–3 to the *angelus interpres*, a far more limited role, and then finally disappears in Vision 7.[12] This change corresponds, of course, to Ezra's transformation.

Ezra is called and declares himself ready and responsive. He rises to his feet. This is an unusual position, as we noted at the end of the last chapter.[13] On the one hand, it may be drawn from Exodus, where Moses is standing up on his feet as he is addressed by God from the bush (Exod 3:5). On the other, it is the pattern throughout 4 Ezra for the seer to rise on occasions of particular solemnity and importance.[14] In 6:13–15 he

---

6   Cf. *b. Sanh.* 21b–22a.

7   A further form of this complex of material is in *j. Meg.* 71b–c. Jerome, *Prologus Galeatus* (start) and *Prologus in Libro Regum* (start), reports that Ezra invented the square Aramaic script.

8   See Ginzberg, *Legends*, 6:445–46.

9   The sources are assembled by Kraft, "'Ezra' Materials," 125–27. This is asserted in the most explicit way by Tertullian, *De cultu feminarum* 1:3, in a passage also dealing with the transmission of the *Book of Enoch*.

10 Contrast this with the different idea of the eternity of the Torah which is central to 9:29–37.

11 This is not just the phenomenon of occasional speech of the angel in God's name we have observed above; see 7:17 Commentary.

12 Brandenburger, *Verborgenheit*, 68, 101–3. His point is

well taken, though it is not quite clear that uncertainties about whether God or the angel is speaking are part of the same, deliberate phenomenon, as he would claim (see ibid.). The range of instances cited in 7:17 Commentary, running clear through the first three visions, weighs heavily against this view. So perhaps we should speak of the change in the angel's role rather than of a process of diminution. In that case, his disappearance from Vision 7 becomes even more striking. Above, in 13:21 Commentary, the role of the angel in Vision 6 was discussed.

13 See 13:56–58 Function and Content, p. 408; see in general 4:47 Commentary.

14 See 6:13 Commentary, and cf. 6:17.

stands to receive predictions about the end, given in a divine voice.

Thus the introduction uses a number of means to mark off this vision from the preceding ones and to endow it with a particular solemnity. First, this revelation to Ezra is deliberately patterned after that to Moses. Second, Ezra is in an unusual physical context and stands on his feet. Third, he is summoned by a divine call to which he responds, and his interlocutor is God himself.

In addition to these points, it should be noted that the mental and emotional state that precedes this vision is not mourning or distress as before the first visions, nor the neutrality which typified, for example, Vision 6, but rather the joyful exultation and assurance of illumination which permeated his prayer and activities in the concluding pericope of the last vision. No new comments are made in this introduction about Ezra's mental or emotional state, nor about any inspiration coming upon him. He is in the field, giving great glory to God, and is summoned. Clearly the types of experience engendered by anguish and despair are all behind him. Something new and different is going to happen.

There has been a good deal of discussion about the function of this vision. Thus Kabisch declares that it is not designed to legitimate the book but is just a "historical appendix."[15] Box would view the vision differently, as designed to guarantee the "officially recognized" place of apocalyptic literature. This theme of legitimation is taken up by others but applied to the legitimation not of apocalyptic literature in general but of the preceding six visions.

As has been observed above, one major hint at the function of the vision is given by the figure of forty days' revelation and fasting which is shared both by Ezra and by Moses in this vision but which is also the sum of all the days' fasting and abstinence in the preceding six visions.[16] This provides the hint that this vision must be viewed not only in terms of the typology of Sinai but in relationship to the carefully designed structure of revelation that has preceded.

The vision is a narrative about revelation, but the content of the revelation is discussed only in the most general terms. This revelation has two aspects, one private and the other public. In that respect it is like the revelation to Moses (14:5). However, initially, Ezra is told in 14:7–8 that what he has received so far, that is, the preceding visions, is secret (cf. 12:37–38). He is to keep this secret. In 14:19–22, Ezra, in his prayer, asks for the public part of Moses' revelation, and the rest of the chapter relates how that prayer was granted.

The revelation that Ezra receives is central for redemption. On the one hand, this is true of the public revelation (14:22) and, on the other, of the secret one (14:47). It is in this connection that the forty days are to be viewed. In the first part of the book, the preceding six visions, we learn how Ezra gains prophetic status or the status of a true seer. In these visions he receives revelation of the secret teaching (12:37–39), and he ends this whole process with rejoicing and praise of God. This is the result of the activity of the first forty days. The development here forms a deliberate contrast with Visions 1–3. The rejoicing and the praise of God for his way with the world are obvious instances of this. Ezra's second forty days' fast and revelation is in a sense supplementary to the first forty days (cf. 14:36). Nonetheless, this is a full, complete revelation given to him. It is a narrative telling about the full implications of the first six visions. This full revelation is what happens to a prophet, and Ezra's call is one of a number of signs of his status. Note that the additional things revealed here are the *public* books, since the heart of the apocalyptic tradition, the "secrets of the times," has already been revealed to him. That special knowledge is embodied in the seventy secret books.

The indications provided here show that what is involved in this vision is not merely a "legitimation" or a historical context of the book. This vision completes and complements the process of revelation that is one of the chief motifs of the book.

Commentary

■ **1** This verse refers to the incident related in Exod 3:2—4:17 of the divine revelation to Moses in the burning bush. The third day is the third of those enjoined upon Ezra in 13:58. Perhaps the three days correspond to the three days' preparation of the people to receive the

---

15   Kabisch, pp. 117ff.
16   See 12:37–39 Function and Content, pp. 373–74.

Torah according to Exod 19:10–11. Note that in 13:56, Ezra's interlocutor has promised "I will come" and it is God and not the angel who appears.

■ **2** The significance of Ezra's standing up is discussed in Function and Content, p. 411.

14

3 Then he said to me, "I revealed ª myself in a bush ᵇ and spoke to Moses, when my people were in bondage in Egypt; 4/ and I sent him and led ᶜ my people out of Egypt; and I led him ᵈ up to Mount Sinai. And I kept him ᵉ with me many days; 5/ and I told ᶠ him many wondrous things, and showed him the secrets of the times and ᵍdeclared to him ᵍ the end of the times. Then I commanded him, saying, 6/ 'These words you shall publish openly, and these ʰ you shall keep secret.' 7/ And now I say ⁱ to you; 8/ Lay up in your heart the signs that I have shown you, ʲ the dreams that you have seen, and the interpretation ᵏ that you have heard; 9/ for you shall be taken up from among men, and henceforth ˡ you shall be ᵐ with my servant ⁿ and with those who are like you, until the times ᵒ are ended. 10/ ᵖFor the age has lost its youth, and the times begin to grow old. 11/ For the age is divided into twelve ᑫ parts, ʳand nine ˢ of its parts have already passed, ᵗ as well as half of the tenth part; ᵘ 12/ so ᵛ two of its parts ʷ remain, ˣ besides ʸ half of the tenth part. ᶻ 13/ ªNow therefore, ª set your house in order, ᵇand reprove your people; ᵇ comfort the lowly among them, ᶜand instruct those that are wise. ᶜ And now renounce the life that is corruptible, 14/ and put away ᵈfrom you ᵈ mortal thoughts; cast away from you the burdens of man, and divest yourself now of your weak nature, 15/ and lay ᵉto one side ᵉ the thoughts that are most grievous to you, and hasten to escape

Notes

3 a The versions other than Ar1 and Ar2 all reflect Hebrew infinitive absolute and finite verb.

b Ar2 "mount Sinai"; Gunkel suggests סני/סנה; this is not likely, see Violet 2 and Stone, "Some Remarks," 111. Violet 1 observes that Ar2 lacks "thornbush" in the previous verse as well.

4 c Syr, Ar1 "and he led"; Ar2 "to lead."

d Lat *eum* is ambiguous, though the next clause makes it likely that it refers to Moses (cf. RSV "him"). The other versions all refer to the people here. However, from context it is clear that Greek misconstrued αὐτόν (referring to Moses) to refer to the people. Here we follow the evident sense of the text, despite the versions. The readings noted in e below bear this out.

e Lat, Syr; "it" (the people) Eth, Ar1; "them" Arm; "Moses" Ar2.

5 f Syr "explained"; Ar1 "revealed."

g–g Lat omits.

6 h Syr "the others"; Ar1, Ar2 "and which," cf. Arm.

7 i Ar1, Ar2 "teach."

8 j Syr, Arm add "previously."

k Lat *interpretationes*.

9 l Lat *residuum*, perhaps reflecting Greek τὸ λιοπόν (Volkmar).

m Lat *converteris;* Eth "remain"; Ar1 "your life will be": see Violet 2.

n Ar1 "young man"; Ar2 "servant"; Arm "with me": see Excursus on the Redeemer Figure, p. 207.

o Eth, Ar2 "world"; Ar1 "times of the world."

10 p Arm omits 14:10–12.

11 q Lat, Ar2; Eth "10"; other versions omit. The text throughout this section is based on very few witnesses: Syr, Arm omit 14:11–12; Ar1 omits 14:11 and changes 14:12; Ar2 omits 14:12. Violet 2 considers Ethiopic "10½–½" to be original.

r–t Eth "and has come to the tenth."

s Lat Mss S A C V, Ar2 "ten"; Lat Mss M N L *undecime.*

t–u Lat; Ar2 "and half a part"; the other versions omit. Syr, Arm omit the whole verse.

12 t–y "And there remains" *tantum* Eth.

v–w Lat literally *eius duae;* other versions omit.

x–z Ar2 omits; Ar1 "and only a little remains."

13 a–a Ar1 "And now"; Ar2, Arm "so."

b–b Lat, Eth omit.

c–c Lat omits.

14 d–d Eth, Ar2 omit.

15 e–e Lat, Syr, Ar1; Eth, Ar2 omit; Arm "from yourself."

from ᶠthese times. ᶠ 16/ For evils worse than those which you have now seen happen shall be done hereafter ᵍ 17/ For the weaker the world becomes ʰthrough old age, ʰ the more shall evils be multiplied among its inhabitants. 18/ For truth shall go farther away, and falsehood shall come near. For the eagle which you saw in ⁱthe vision ⁱ is already hastening to come."

16

17

18

f–f Lat, Syr; Eth, Ar1 "this world"; Ar2 "the time"; Arm "this earth."

g Ar1 and Ar2 are rather free but do not seem to reflect a different text.

h–h Ar2, Arm omit.

i–i Eth, Ar2 omit.

Form and Structure

This is God's ante-mortem address to Ezra, giving him instructions for his conduct. It may be divided into three parts.

A. Historical (14:3–6)

This section may be described as the history of the revelation to Moses. It opens with God's self-identification (14:3). This is followed by a long sentence that encapsulates the biblical history: I called Moses and I sent him to bring the people out of Egypt, I led him to Sinai, I kept him with me, I told him, I commanded him. The reference to God's command to Moses concludes this section.

This historical recital forms a most significant contrast with that with which Vision 1 opens. That recital, which is set in the seer's mouth, is typified by "Thou" which stresses over and over again the seer's indictment of God for creating the world the way it is. Here the repeated "I," God's own, first person speech, is God's celebration of his own action on behalf of Israel in making the revelation. These stylistic and substantial differences strikingly encapuslate the change that has taken place in the course of the book.

The divine command referred to in 14:6, "These words you shall publish openly, and these you shall keep secret," is apocryphal and does not occur in the Hebrew Bible. A similar phenomenon was encountered in 9:29–31, where a similar apocryphal citation turned out to be drawn from 4 Ezra itself. Here, also, the point and much of the language of the supposed citation are to be found in 14:45. Admittedly, the two instances are not quite parallel, since 9:28 referred back to cite verses from chapter 3, while 14:6 refers forward to the end of the present chapter. Furthermore, in 9:30–31 reference is made to God's words which are spoken to Moses, accord-

ing to 4 Ezra. In 14:6, God's words to Moses are explicitly mentioned, but these words were actually spoken to Ezra in 14:45. Nonetheless, the parallel is clear enough, and we can characterize this as an integral part of the author's technique. It may also be that this attribution is not merely technical or formal. Perhaps the author really gave this type of authority to his words. Such an attitude would not be out of step with his view of his own activity in the present chapter.

B. Predictive (14:7–12)

This segment of the address opens with the words "And now" (14:7). The call for attention is imperative (14:8) and is followed by a prediction about Ezra's personal fate (14:9) and a prophecy about the future of the age (14:10–12). Both of these latter predictions are presented as "for" clauses, that is, Ezra is told, "Pay attention to the signs because of (a) and because of (b)." Indeed, 14:10–12 is composed itself of two "for" clauses. The first, in 14:10, sets forth the general point, and the second, in 14:11, comes to substantiate it.[1] Both of the reasons imply the imminence of his passing and so give the passage the character of an announcement of his death.

C. Final Injunctions (14:13–18)

This third part of the divine address opens "Now, therefore." On the one hand, it is tied to the preceding by the causality of "therefore" and, on the other, clearly forms a new departure, marked by the "Now" which is parallel to the "Now" with which the previous segment opened. Structurally the passage is made up of two parts, each typified by *parallelismus membrorum*. The first part deals with Ezra vis-à-vis the people and is composed of two bicola: 14:13a//14:13b::14:13c//14:13d. The second part deals with Ezra himself and is made up of three bicola: 14:13e//14:14a::14:14b//14:14c::14:15a//

---

1   In Stone, *Features*, 95, it was suggested that the last phase of 14:9 provided the basis of which 14:10–12, otherwise not connected with the thought of the passage, was introduced. The analysis here has uncovered a more complex structure.

14:15b. The last hemistich seems at the formal level to be far too long for the parallelistic structure but must be seen as part of it because of the clear parallel in meaning. The formulation in the Semitic original might have been more evenly balanced.

The last part of this address (14:16–18) is a recapitulation of the reasons offered for thinking that the end of the world is at hand. Some more signs are mentioned, and in particular reference is made to the eagle of Vision 5. This serves to tie the visions together. It is preceded by a short piece of eschatological woes-prediction poetry (14:18), which carries the reader back to the predictions following the first two visions (5:1–13 and 6:17–18).[2] Thus, from a structural point of view, in this address many themes are raised that serve to focus attention on the idea of revelation and imminence. The end is at hand, and Ezra's own death is at hand. The climax and the summary of the book are approaching.

Function and Content

The overall function of this pericope at an overall level is to introduce a number of ideas and themes that reinforce the sense of the crucial nature of the revelation that is to be granted. This special character of the revelation is already signaled by the introduction (14:1–2). This vision opens with an address, like the first four, but here, instead of the seer, the speaker is God. God addresses Ezra, and not Ezra God.[3] The following two pericopes then continue this conversation.

This passage uses literary means to lead toward the conclusion of the book as a whole and so discusses in some detail Ezra's end and that of the world. The pericope contains a double prediction of imminent end, the end of Ezra and the end of the world (14:9–12; 14:16–17), which heightens the sense of solemnity and impending doom.

The theme of secret revelation is introduced here into the vision, and it forms one of its leitmotifs. This is the peak of the historical narrative with which the pericope opens (see below). It was already hinted at in 3:14 but in a context that had no direct application to Ezra and his doings.[4] In a specific revelation context it was raised for Ezra himself in 12:36–38. It is destined to be prominent once more at the end of this chapter in a particularly important context (14:45–46).[5] It is highly significant to observe that Sinai is discussed in some detail in 3:17–22, and that passage is cited once more in 9:30–31. In neither of those contexts, however, is secret knowledge said to have been revealed to Moses. Here, however, Moses is said, explicitly, to have received both open and secret revelations (14:5), while Ezra is commanded to keep the revelation to him secret (14:8), just as he had been instructed in 12:37–38. The point of that command is sharper because it follows directly upon the instruction to Moses to publish certain material and to hide other. Ezra, at this point, has only the esoteric knowledge.[6] We have pointed out that the stress on the secret revelation to Ezra here, in contrast with Moses' double one, is a reflection of the author's understanding of the preceding revelations and particularly the eschatological prophecies. Moreover, this structure is a literary or rhetorical device which reaches resolution in the passage commencing in 14:22.[7]

It should further be noted that in 14:13, Ezra is instructed, "Reprove your people; comfort the lowly among them, and instruct those that are wise." This command is carried out partly in 14:27–35, which passage contains the reproof and the comfort but not the instruction of the wise. Moreover, the same themes are implicit in the prayer in 14:19–22. Here Ezra, to whom only an esoteric revelation has been made, asks for the exoteric one. When, in 14:25–26, he is told he will receive both exoteric and esoteric revelations, his role becomes equated with that of Moses.

Ezra's secret revelation referred to in 14:7 is part of the tradition that goes back to Moses and Abraham. The link showing identity of content is provided by 12:36–37 and particularly 12:9. The content of that dream and

---

2 On the form of these eschatological poems, see 6:11–29 Form and Structure, pp. 165–66. In "Prophet," 484–85, Harnisch analyzes the main part of Vision 7 into two episodes, 14:1–17 and 14:18–36. This analysis stems from his view that Visions 5 and 6 are secondary, a view that cannot be maintained (see Introduction, sec. 3.2).

3 See 14:1–2 Function and Content, pp. 410–11.

4 In 3:14 Commentary, the double nature of that revelation and examples of its content are to be found.

5 This theme is explored in 14:5 Commentary.

6 See on this 14:1–2 Function and Content, p. 412.

7 See further 14:7–8 Commentary.

interpretation is clearly eschatological. So 4 Ezra has a view of a transmitted secret revelation of eschatological character, made to Abraham and to Moses, revealed to Ezra and taught by him to the wise (12:38; 14:26; 14:46). Therefore, "lay up in your heart" in 14:8 apparently means "keep secret." Ezra does not ask for esoteric revelation in 14:9–22, because he already has it. He asks for exoteric revelation, and his request is granted. Thus he truly becomes like Moses, who received both revelations.[8]

Chapter 14:3–18 is, therefore, a divine speech. The first part of it is a historical recital that goes only down to Sinai and that is followed by some instructions that God issues to Ezra. These are introduced by "and now I say to you." He is to lay up in his heart "the signs that I have shown you, the dreams that you have seen, and the interpretations that you have heard" (14:8). This appears to be a deliberate reference to the chief eschatological prophecies of the book. The "signs" were the theme of the Prediction 2 passages throughout. The "dreams" that were seen and the "intepretations" that were heard seem to be deliberate references to the preceding two dream visions. These are given special weight by phrases such as 10:59: "The Most High will show you in those dream visions what the Most High will do to those who dwell on earth in the last days." In 12:36, referring to the "dream" and its "interpretation" (12:35), we read "and you alone were worthy to learn this secret of the Most High." In our passage he moves, not by chance, directly from Sinai to these revelations of signs, dreams, and interpretations. That is to say that the revelation to Moses is set right alongside the revelation to Ezra. The signs are set into the context of the Abrahamic and Mosaic revelations, at least by implication, in 9:4, where they are described as events "of which the Most High spoke from the days that were of old."

Chapter 14:9 is a prophecy of Ezra's translation. In the prediction in 6:26 the translation of select righteous is mentioned.[9] They are referred to as "the men who were taken up, who from their birth have not tasted death." Ezra is here told, it seems, that he is to be one of that number. This appears to be a deliberate reference back to 13:52, which says, "No one on earth can see my Son or those who are with him, except in the time of his day."[10] Ezra is to consider the eschatological revelations made to him because his translation is close. The reason for this, moreover, is that the times have grown old. The idea of the senescence of the earth is found elsewhere in the book and recurs here in 14:17.[11]

Thus the prophecy of Ezra's translation is followed by one of the imminent end of the earth. This, he is told in 14:17–18, will bring about all sorts of troubles, and he is to be spared them.

The aging of the earth is epitomized by the calculation in 14:10–12. The world age is divided into twelve parts, ten and one half of which have passed. This is the only instance of an eschatological timetable in the book. The idea that the world age is divided into a fixed number of parts and that the number that have passed can be revealed to a seer is a widespread one. But in 4 Ezra this is the only hint at such a view, and it is rather obscure in itself. This idea is introduced here in order to stress the approaching end, the closeness of the consummation. Perhaps, too, such calculations are considered part of the secret eschatological lore and are here imparted to Ezra by God.

Following this dual prophecy, God proceeds to instruct Ezra as to the actions that he must undertake before his assumption. Two basic concepts are prominent here: on the one hand, Ezra is to instruct the people by comforting the humble and instructing the wise. On the other, he is to set aside his mortal thoughts and prepare himself to "escape these times" (14:15). Ezra's leaving of his body is, thus, spoken of here as if it is volitional; at least he is to put himself in the correct mental state for leaving his body. The verb "hasten" in 14:15 raises the association of urgency which is strengthened by 14:16–17 and reaches its climax in 14:18: "For

---

8   Perhaps, in a quite different dimension, Ezra's reference to his eagle vision as a development of that of Daniel also witnesses the author's sense of belonging to a tradition of eschatological learning; see 12:11 Commentary.

9   See 14:9 Commentary and also 6:26 Commentary, where this subject is fully discussed.

10 See also 8:51 Commentary on the expression "those that are like you."

11 See 4:27 Commentary.

the eagle which you saw in the vision is already hastening to come."

The prophecy that there will be great evils before the eschaton takes up a much belabored theme. Moreover, this prophecy in 14:18 is formulated in the style of the special eschatological poems that were isolated and analyzed above.[12]

The reference to the eagle is particularly troubling. On the one hand, it is a clear and deliberate reference to the eagle vision. Yet the whole preceding context is not that the Roman Empire, with all its kings and usurpers, is about to start its rule but that the end of the empire is on the doorstep. In that case, the phrase about the eagle should mean that "the end of the eagle" is about to come; or perhaps, the events that are overtaking the eagle and that you saw in your vision are about to come to pass.

It is extremely interesting to observe that in 9:1–13, when Ezra asked about the timetable of events, he was told by the angel to observe the signs, the events that were happening in the world, and when he saw the prophecies starting to be fulfilled, he would know that the end was close. Here, he is told explicitly by God that the woes are coming, that the greater part of the world age has passed, that the eagle is about to receive its due (if that is what is meant), and that he himself is to be translated. He is told, therefore, a goodly portion of the very events he earlier was instructed to search out. This is yet another indication of the fashion in which this vision complements those which preceded it.

It is still unclear, however, whether the author of 4 Ezra saw himself to be living at the end of the world age. Ezra is told that there are still two and one half parts to come; he is told that the earth had grown old and that the woes will start. Therefore he is being translated, as a sign of grace, in order to escape the suffering. The ambiguity about the eagle may also be a pointer in the same direction. Moreover, the pseudepigraphic issues may be at play here. The author is obviously deeply distressed by the destruction and yearns for vindication and redemption. On the other hand, although living at the end of the first century, he attributes his book to a hero half a millennium earlier. Sometimes, as in 9:1–4, the discourse suggests that the end is at hand. The

author's self and his presentation of his own concerns through the instrumentality of the *persona* of Ezra predominate in such instances. This same sense is conveyed also by 14:16–18, in particular, in the present pericope. Yet we may speculate that the imperatives of the pseudepigraphic framework may have tempered the author's sense of urgency, or at least its explicit enunciation. After all, Ezra had lived long ago and the destroyed Temple had not yet been restored in the heavenly city. The position of 4 Ezra, with the personal involvement of the seer even in eschatological prophecies, consequently differs from that, say, of Enoch in *1 Enoch*. These events will be fulfilled in the future (i.e., the future from the fictional perspective of Enoch). In 4 Ezra, however, the ambiguity on this point is very notable.[13]

On the basis of this passage, therefore, what seems to be immediately expected is Ezra's translation, with the great upheavals of the messianic woes and the end of the world somewhat farther off.

Commentary

■ **3** Chapter 14:3–4a is a summary of Exod 3:2–12. The implicit correspondence between Ezra and Moses is very meaningful in this verse. The bondage in Egypt is exactly parallel to the Babylonian exile, just as Ezra's role here is parallel to Moses'. This implies that just as God redeemed the people from Egypt, so he will redeem them from Babylon, though it is by no means certain that this implication is being clearly drawn here.

■ **4** The incident is like those described in Exod 24:15–18 and Exodus 34. Note that the description of the revelation of the Torah in 3:17–19, in accordance with the author's different rhetorical purpose there, stresses God's descent onto the mountain rather than Moses' ascent. In accord with that purpose, Moses' part in the exodus is not mentioned in 3:17 but is stressed here. The term "sent" probably reflects שלח, which means "to commission."[14]

■ **5** This verse describes the revelation to Moses on Mount Sinai. This is characterized as being of "many wondrous things," of "secrets of the times," and of "end of the times." In a number of sources the idea is found that the revelation to Moses on Sinai included a secret revelation,

12   See 6:11–29 Form and Structure, pp. 165–66.
13   It was also discussed in some detail in 4:26 Commentary.
14   See 7:104 Commentary.

additional to that of the Torah; see *2 Apoc Bar* 59:4; *Lev. R.* 26:7; and *Num. R.* on Num 34:2. The *Book of Jubilees* presents itself as having been revealed in this way, as does the *Apocalypse of Moses.*[15] Other traditions set additional revelations to Moses into different contexts; see *Bib Ant* 19:10.[16] The revelation of "wondrous things" means the revelation of eschatological things, for "wonders" has a very specific eschatological denotation in 4 Ezra.[17]

The secrets of the times are also what was revealed to Abraham in the Covenant Between the Pieces; see 3:14.[18] These eschatological secrets were also revealed to Ezra at the end of the process of personal development described in the preceding six visions of the book; see 12:36–39.[19] Compare also 12:9.[20] The revelation of the terminus of the times, of course, implies the idea of predeterminism; cf. also 3:14 and 12:9 (see 3:9 Commentary).[21]

■ **6** The words "these . . . these" refer to two groups of revealed tradition, one exoteric and the other esoteric. On the analogy of 4 Ezra 14:45–46 we may conclude that the exoteric is the Torah (or the Bible). The esoteric tradition is described, as we have noted, in terminology used of eschatological revelation and, in chapter 12, of the eschatological revelations to Ezra. Consequently, as will also be shown below, it is not far-fetched to identify it with apocalyptic, eschatological traditions.[22] The command that God gives Ezra is presented as a quotation, but it is not a quotation of the Bible but seems to be drawn loosely from 4 Ezra 14:45. The practice of using such "false" quotations is part of 4 Ezra's style and has been discussed above.[23]

One of the functions of this command is to authenticate and to provide a basis for current apocalyptic tradition. In a more technical way this is also done by *Test Mos* 1:16–17.[24] Analogous commands are to be found in Rev 10:4; *Jub* 1:5–7; and 1:26; cf. Dan 12:4, 9–10, as well as, of course, 4 Ezra 12:37.

Kaminka observes that this verse may be correlated with Deut 29:28: "The secret things belong to the Lord our God; but the things that are revealed belong to us and to our children forever, that we may do all the words of this law." The meaning of the words in the context of Deuteronomy is different from that in 4 Ezra, but the idea of two sets of meaning, one secret and one revealed, and their connection with Moses, is suggestive.

■ **7–8** Gry notes the contrast between the revelation to Ezra and that to Moses. Moses' revelation was said to contain both esoteric and exoteric aspects, while Ezra is commanded to keep the revelation made to him secret. Gry does not observe the important development of structure within the vision, for it is only in the first stage of the vision that Ezra is instructed to keep all that is revealed to him secret. The point of the whole section from 14:19 on is precisely that Ezra is subsequently put fully into the position of Moses and receives both esoteric and exoteric books. It is the revelation of the first six visions that is esoteric, as is already clear from 12:36–37. It seems that this is one of the underlying structures of the chapter: at first, though the figure of Moses is evoked, Ezra is differentiated from Moses in that the revelation to him, which has culminated in Visions 5 and

15 The matter is discussed in some detail in Stone, "Lists," 444 n. 1.

16 See Stone, "Lists," 417–18.

17 See 4:26 Commentary.

18 On the term "secret," see 10:38–54 Function and Content, p. 334.

19 The matter is discussed in detail in 3:14 Commentary and 12:37–39 Function and Content, p. 373. On the term "end," see Excursus on Natural Order, pp. 103–5, while "times" is discussed in Excursus on the Two Ages, p. 92.

20 A double revelation to Moses, with a divine statement that part is special, is to be found in *Pes. R. K.* (Friedmann, p. 64a). Cf. also the sources cited by Ginzberg, *Legends,* 6:446, on Mishnah as "secret," given to Israel alone, while Torah was revealed to all mankind. So also *Tanh. Ki Tissa* 34. The revelation in

Hermas is to be written down in two parts, *Vis.* 5.5.

21 The expression "end of times" or "of the age" may be found in 6:7; 6:9; 7:112; 7:113; 12:21; and 12:32.

22 In 12:37–39 Function and Content, p. 373, we discussed Ezra's rejection of all types of speculative secret knowledge except the eschatological. The views expressed in chap. 14 about secret knowledge accord with that.

23 See Form and Structure, p. 415.

24 See on this Stone, "Apocalyptic Literature," 383.

6, is all eschatological and all secret. Later in chapter 14 things change.

The expressions "signs," "dreams," and "interpretations," as has been pointed out in Function and Content, p. 417, refer to the specific eschatological revelations made to Ezra earlier in the book: the "signs" are those passages of eschatological revelation with which the first three visions conclude, our Prediction 2 passages. The "dreams" and "interpretations" we take as specific reference to Visions 5 and 6.[25]

It is interesting to note that here attention is focused on Ezra himself, not on the people. This concentration on Ezra and his fate is also true particularly of the end of Vision 3, and it also occurs in the various texts that celebrate Ezra's virtues, such as 6:32; 7:76–77; et al.[26] While God speaks, the concentration is on Ezra; but in the continuation of the chapter, precisely at the point at which Ezra himself poses a question, the focus shifts (14:19–22). At that point too, the similarity to Moses, already implied by the first verses of the chapter, becomes more prominent. Simultaneously, the character of the revelation to Ezra changes from just esoteric to both esoteric and exoteric, as we have pointed out in the preceding paragraphs. It is as if here he is bringing fully into the play his designation as "prophet" given by the people in the narrative passage in the fifth vision, which he himself accepted.

■ 9 This verse foretells Ezra's assumption alive to heaven; see also 14:48. There he will be preserved with the Messiah ("my servant": see the Excursus on the Redeemer Figure, pp. 212–13) and the righteous until the end of times. In 4 Ezra there are a number of references to humans who were taken up to heaven alive, an idea that is related in 4 Ezra to an overall evaluation of life and death.[27] The references to assumption are discussed in detail in 6:26 Commentary, where the origins and development of this idea are analyzed. Ginzberg points out that, although the idea of the assumed righteous is to be found in a number of later rabbinic sources, nowhere in rabbinic literature are they associated with the Messiah.[28] The idea is to be found in 4 Ezra, however, that there are "companions" associated with the Messiah. This is very explicit in 7:28 and 13:52.[29] It is nowhere clear in 4 Ezra whether the companions of the Messiah are all assumed. They are denoted often by the turn of phrase "you and those like you."[30]

Ezra is to remain there "until the times are ended." The idea that time is coming to an end is often found in the book. It implies predetermination and is sometimes associated with a sense of haste and urgency. The structure of history is thereby clearly seen.[31] In 10:55–60 Function and Content, p. 341, we discussed the possibility that Ezra's entry into the heavenly Jerusalem might be an oblique reference to his assumption. That view is neither strengthened nor weakened by the present context.[32]

■ 10 The term *saeculum* and equivalents mean here "age," "world age."[33] The view expressed here refers only to this world age, not to the future, eschatological one.[34] Behind the concept is, of course, the idea that there are two world ages and that one of them will come to an end. These world ages may also be referred to, as in the

---

25 Violet 2 would take the word we translated "interpretation" as *Beiträge* and thinks that it denotes chap. 14 itself. The terminology of the texts, however, concords with that used in Visions 5 and 6 to denote the angelic interpretations.

26 See in further detail 6:32 Commentary.

27 See Excursus on Adam's Sin, pp. 65–66.

28 See Ginzberg, *Legends,* 5:96. The function of the Messiah here is incidental and is discussed in Excursus on the Redeemer Figure, p. 209.

29 See the detailed discussion in 7:28 Commentary. In 13:52 the Messiah is said to be preserved until the end.

30 On the other hand, the assumed are often said to appear as part of the events surrounding the messianic kingdom. See discussion of this idea, as well as of the terminology, in 6:26 Commentary.

31 This matter is discussed in Excursus on Natural Order, p. 102. "Times" means "this world" or "this age" here; see Excursus on the Two Ages, p. 92.

32 RSV differs in verse numbering from Box, starting a new verse here.

33 See Excursus on the Term "Age" for an analysis of this term. More detailed argument may be found in Stone, *Features,* 181. Keulers opines that here it means "world" (p. 179).

34 See Excursus on the Two Ages, passim.

present passage, as "times."[35] The order of the times is seen as fixed.[36]

This world age, then, Ezra is told is now old. The idea of the senescence of this age occurs elsewhere in the book, most notably in 5:50–55. The terminology is applied, indifferently, to "world age" or "world" or "times." In this context, "world" is parallel to "creation."[37] In 5:55 the idea is presented that this degeneration is the cause of the "fact" that those born in the earth's old age are of lesser stature than those were whom she bore in her youth. A similar expression of this idea is found in the subsequent verse 14:17: "For the weaker the world becomes through old age, the more shall evils be multiplied among its inhabitants."

The image of senescence, as used here, expresses the view that the major part of time is past. The idea is found often in 4 Ezra; see 4:45–50.

■ **11** In this verse, *saeculum* and equivalents unambiguously mean "age."[38] The general idea that the world is hastening to pass away may be found earlier in the book and is part of the author's worldview.[39] The unique feature of this verse in 4 Ezra is the actual reckoning. On text-critical grounds, it is not completely clear whether the division is 9 ½—2½ or 9½—½, as is discussed in the textual notes q through u. In general, the schematic division of history into fixed periods is found in a number of apocalyptic sources from the period of the Second Temple.[40] Tenfold and twelvefold divisions are known beyond the present source; see *Sib Or* 4:47–48 and *Apocalypse of Weeks* (*1 Enoch* 91–93; both tenfold); and *2 Apocalypse of Baruch* 53 and *Apoc Abr* 29:2 (twelvefold).[41]

Behind these divisions, of course, lies a search for precision as to the eschatological timetable. Compare Ezra's request in 4:33 with Moses' prayer in *Bib Ant* 19:14: "And shew me what measure of time hath passed by and what remaineth." In his comments on 4:25, Knibb suggests that the reason the author of 4 Ezra on the whole avoids such reckonings is the dangers that attended Israel from this type of speculation and the national disasters that such hopes brought in their wake.[42] It is perhaps preferable, however, to relate it to the book's attitudes toward special knowledge. The implications of the idea of the calculation of the times have been explored above and, it may be remarked, that conceptually the idea of using the messianic woes as a sort of diagnostic tool for reckoning the eschatological timetable is quite similar to the present passage.[43]

Behind all of these views lies the belief in predetermination which stands, as has been noted earlier, in tension with the seer's sense of urgency.[44]

The actual reckoning has been related to Daniel's "a time, two times and half a time" as well as to the mysterious "the third . . ." in 5:4.[45] Licht suggests that the 2½ here are half of the Persian realm, the Greeks, and the Romans, accounting for the period from historical Ezra to the time of the author. In fact, the actual basis of the reckoning is unclear, and it is most likely a typological one.[46]

■ **12** No commentary.

■ **13** Violet 2 thinks that 14:13–17 was originally seven poetic stichs. This is not certain, but the verses are written in a rhythmic, parallelistic semipoetic style typical

35   See Excursus on the Two Ages, p. 92.
36   See 4:37 Commentary.
37   See 5:41—6:10 Function and Content, pp. 145–49, 5:50 Commentary, and 5:52 Commentary.
38   See Excursus on the Term "Age."
39   See 4:26; 6:20; and Excursus on Natural Order, pp. 102–5.
40   See, e.g., *Sib Or* 4:47–48; *Apocalypse of Weeks* in *1 Enoch* 91 + 93; see the comments in Stone, *Signs of the Judgment*, 16, and some further sources cited there. A particularly interesting discussion of the matter is to be found in the article of J. S. Licht, "Time and Eschatology in Qumran," *JJS* 16 (1965) 177–82.
41   See for a further type *2 Apocalypse of Baruch* 27. Such schemes also occur in rabbinic writings; see *b. Abod. Zar.* 9a and *b. Sanh.* 97a–b, 99a.
42   See *b. Sanh.* 97a.

43   The notion is discussed in Excursus on Natural Order, pp. 102–3, while the diagnostic use of signs, found in 9:1–3, is discussed in 9:1 Commentary.
44   See 5:50 Commentary.
45   See 5:4 Commentary.
46   In 10:45 Commentary we discussed the possibility that the parts are each of 500 years, which would put Ezra between 4,500 and 5,000 *anno mundi*. That would accord with certain later reckonings of the era of creation but would fit neither with the time of Ezra's assumption according to the last verse of the book nor that of the building of Jerusalem if 10:45 is taken to mean 3,000 years of an era of creation.

of other places in 4 Ezra. The command "Set your house in order" has been interpreted using the idea that "house" means "house of Israel" (Volkmar). It is more likely that this is an element drawn from the ante-mortem context of this incident. It is thus rather similar to *Test Abr* 1:4; moreover, the description of Abraham's impending death there in 1:7 is not dissimilar to the present context.[47] *2 Apoc Bar* 43:2–3 is rather like this passage, and the latter part of the present verse, with its command to instruct the people, resembles *2 Apoc Bar* 76:5.

Ezra is instructed to reprove and comfort the lowly among people and to instruct the wise. This command is permeated by wisdom terminology; cf., e.g., Prov 9:8–9 and 19:25. In such a context, however, the term "comfort" is unusual. Knibb has aptly pointed out that here a distinction is being drawn between two groups.[48] From a number of parallels it is clear that it means "comfort in present distress by the revelation of eschatological benefits yet to come"; see 12:8, and cf. *2 Apoc Bar* 22:1 and strikingly *2 Apoc Bar* 54:4: " You are the one who reveals to those who fear that which is prepared for them so that you may comfort them." This combination of elements of wisdom language, regularly used in 4 Ezra of the revelation of eschatological secrets, and the termi-nology of comfort form an instruction to Ezra to share with the people his acquired hope and faith in the future restoration and vindication.

The end of the verse discusses Ezra's assumption to heaven. The "corruptible," as elsewhere in 4 Ezra, indicates that which perishes, just as "corruption" indi-cates physical death.[49] The parallels in the next verse make this evident. Typically in 4 Ezra the language of death means physical death rather than eternal death or damnation.[50]

■ **14** The first phrase is in fact the stich parallel to the last stich of 14:13. The sentiment is similar in language and content to 1 Cor 15:53–54. By the expression "burdens of man," doubtless, in part the corruptible body is

denoted.[51] Corruptibility is described as a burden; see 4:11 and 7:88 Commentary. In *2 Apoc Bar* 43:2, we read: "For thou shalt depart from this place, . . . and thou shalt forget whatever is corruptible, and shalt not again recall those things that happen among mortals." This statement is made in the context of a prophecy of Baruch's assump-tion.

In general, the setting aside of death is an integral part of future hope, from which one may infer, in dialectical fashion, certain of the negative features of this life.[52] Harnisch, in consonance with his overall views, much stresses the negative view taken by the author of exis-tence in this world. In 5:52 Commentary the possibility was discussed that the material nature of this world was that which brought about its degeneration and evil. This view was rejected, but the unsatisfactory nature of this world or age remains a prominent idea.[53] Human life in this world or age is equally characterized by the author as toil and suffering; see 4:24; 4:33; 7:12; and 7:96.[54] Yet these two elements are not combined by the author into a thoroughgoing dualism of good spirit and evil matter, of good soul and evil body. Indeed, this world is regarded as that from which release should be sought, an attitude that formed a basis for many of the aspects of redemption mentioned by the author. In the present context, however, the reference seems to be more simple. Ezra's coming translation to the heavenly realm is being described. This is said to be an act of God's grace, since otherwise he would suffer the pangs of the growing degeneration of the world. In this context the language about mortality and corruptibility is naturally intro-duced.

■ **15** Notably, in 4:34 and 6:34, Ezra is admonished for hastening, for his deep sense of urgency. There, how-ever, "hastening" means "hastening the world order," and Ezra's intense desire to see redemption already coming permeates 4:26–52. This desire is in large measure slaked by Ezra's acceptance of the predeter-mined and fixed character of the progression of the

47   Isaiah also instructs Hezekiah to set his house in
     order in a similar context in 2 Kgs 20:1 = Isa 38:1.
     The role of admonishment in guaranteeing eternal
     reward is evident in *Hermas Vis.* 1.3.1–2.
48   Knibb, "Apocalyptic and Wisdom," 62.
49   See 4:11 Commentary.
50   See Excursus on Adam's Sin, pp. 65–66.
51   See Excursus on Adam's Sin, pp. 64–65.

52   See Excursus on Adam's Sin, p. 66.
53   See the discussion in Excursus on the Two Ages, pp.
     92–93.
54   Cf. also *2 Apoc Bar* 21:13–14; 44:9; and 85:5.

times which is a main result of Vision 1.[55] The idea
behind this verse, as becomes evident in the next, is of
Ezra's translation which will protect him from the toilsomeness of this age. The expression "leave the world" or
"age" should be compared with *2 Apoc Bar* 14:13 and
John 13:1.[56]

■ **16** The idea of the senescence of the earth is again to the
fore here. It will produce the woes, the terrible events
that presage the eschaton.[57] These events will produce
peril or danger for Ezra. Danger is an element commonly
found in this connection. The Messiah is said, for example, to preserve the righteous remnant from danger
(12:34 and 13:23).[58] It is to be noted that elsewhere
danger is applied to the people, or the righteous remnant, while here it is applied in a personal way to Ezra.
This is a repetition of the pattern noted above about
haste, where similarly God applied to Ezra personally an
idea that previously had been applied to the whole world.
The new focus of this vision is hereby illuminated.

The events "that now happen" refer, presumably, at
the surface level to the destruction of the First Temple
but in fact to the destruction of the Second Temple. The
author lived with the sense that the events even now
happening foreboded the upheavals of the last time; see
9:1–8.

■ **17** This verse expresses the idea that the increase of evils
is a result of the senescence of the earth. This is related,
as becomes explicit in the next verse, to the idea of the
increase of evils that will occur just before the end time,
and the terminology "increase" or "multiply" is often
found in this kind of context; see, for example, 7:111.
These "messianic woes" have been described above, the
major passages being 5:1–13; 6:18–28; and 9:1–4.[59]
The idea of the increasing age of the earth is continued
from 14:10, and it has already occurred earlier in the

book. The word *saeculum* and equivalents here surely
mean "material world" rather than "world age,"[60] while
the expression "inhabitants of the world" may be a
technical eschatological term. It certainly occurs predominantly in eschatological contexts.[61]

■ **18** The first two hemistichs of this verse are in poetic
form. Above we analyzed the passages in which this form
is to be found, and they all are eschatological in content.
In contrast with the earlier passages, which deal with
eschatological weal, here it is the woes that are to the
fore.[62] The hiding of truth is a standard part of the woes
and was mentioned in the very first woes prophecy in the
book.[63] The concept of haste was discussed above, in
14:15. Here the world is said to be hastening to its end.
Again, this idea was encountered in the first vision;
see 4:26.[64] The feeling imparted by this verse is that of
the swift degeneration of the earth. This is also conveyed
by the statement that the eagle was hastening to come.
The eagle is, of course, that referred to in Vision 5. Logically, of course, from the perspective of the historical
Ezra, the eagle was still in the future, so its hastening to
come would imply that the start of Roman rule was close.
That would still have been several hundred years before
the destruction of the Second Temple. It would also
form a historical anomaly with Ezra, unless one of the
chronologies was at play that shortened the Persian
period.[65] This is not satisfactory, either, just as the two
and one half times in 14:10–11 are not satisfactory. It
runs against the manifest message of the verse that the
crisis and the end are imminent, that the woes are even
now coming on the world, and that Ezra is, by the grace
of God, assumed to heaven in order to avoid them.

What is happening, of course, is the expression of a
tension that we have also seen elsewhere in the book,
between the personal position and convictions of the

---

55 The tension between haste and predetermination is
    explored in 5:50 Commentary.

56 In *Bib Ant* 50:7 it means "to die." The overall attitude
    of the book toward death is discussed above, and it is
    notable that Ezra's departure is not formulated in
    terms of soul and body.

57 On the old age of the earth, see 14:10 Commentary;
    the woes will be discussed in the Commentary on the
    next verse.

58 The idea of danger is discussed in 9:8 Commentary.
    It is also discussed in Stone, *Features*, 69, and note
    119.

59 The woes are discussed and parallels adduced in the
    Commentary on those passages. See detailed analysis
    in 4:52 Commentary and 5:2 Commentary.

60 See Excursus on the Term "Age."

61 See 5:1 Commentary.

62 See in full 6:11–29 Form and Structure, pp. 165–66.

63 It is fully discussed in 5:1 Commentary.

64 See Commentary; see also 4:43, and contrast the
    haste of the dead souls to receive reward in 7:98.

65 On this problem, see 3:1 Commentary.

author within his own particular context and the pseud-epigraphic framework of Ezra at the time of the Restoration. Therefore he writes that the eagle is hastening to come, but his message is that the eagle is hastening to its destruction.[66]

---

66 The sense of the imminence of the end may also be found in *2 Apoc Bar* 20:6 and 48:39.

14

19 Then I answered and said, "Let me speak in thy presence, Lord. ª 20/ For behold, I will go, as thou hast commanded me, and I will reprove the people ᵇwho are now living; ᵇ but who will warn ᶜthose who will be born hereafter? ᶜ For the world lies in darkness, and its inhabitants are without light. 21/ For thy law has been burned, and so ᵈ no one knows the things which have been done or ᵉwill be done ᵉ by thee. 22/ If then I have found favor before thee, send the holy spirit [or: spirit of holiness] into me, and I will write everything that has happened in the world from the beginning, ᶠ the things which were written in thy law, that men may be able to find the path, ᵍ and that those who wish to live ʰ in the last days ⁱ may live." ʲ

Notes

19   a Eth, Ar2 omit; Eth adds "Lord" in the next phrase; Georg resumes with this verse.

20   b–b Ar1 and Ar2 paraphrase.

c–c Ar1 and Ar2 paraphrase.

21   d Lat *propter quod;* Georg *propter hoc;* Arm "after this"; other versions omit. Ar2 had a lacuna in 14:20–25 which it has filled in with some secondary text.

e–e Lat has lost the main verb; Lat, Syr, Eth seem to reflect μέλλεις; for the whole phrase Arm has "nor the commandments which you commanded."

22   f Syr, Eth add "all."

g Eth adds "of life"; Arm *Y* adds "of salvation"; Eth, Ar1 "thy path."

h Eth omits from here to end of verse.

h–i Lat, Syr; Georg *aeternum;* Ar1 paraphrases the whole expression "wish ⟨to have⟩ the other life."

i–j This phrase is doubtful; Lat has simply *vivat,* whence RSV "may live," and this might have some support from Arm "to live in purity of way"; we could also have translated, on the basis of Syriac, "might know the way" and Georg *exquaerant vias tuas.* Again, Arm may give this some oblique support. *Non liquet.*

Form and Function

This passage continues the dialogue between Ezra and God and is Ezra's response to the preceding divine address. It should be observed that this dialogue differs from the dialogues in the first three visions: it is neither disputatious nor predictive. Ezra's response, as often in speech addressed to God, opens with a formula expressing his humility and lowly position. The two parallel stichs with which 14:20 ends are notable. In 14:22 the phrase "If I have found favor before thee," a standard opening of petitions, is to be found.[1]

Function and Content

In this passage, the first point made is that Ezra accepts the commands that God has laid upon him. In particular he accepts his own imminent translation. This is intriguing in view of the fact that his opposition to his own death becomes a dominant theme in a later Ezra composition such as the *Apocalypse of Sedrach* (10:4).[2]

He says that he will "reprove the people who are now living." This is a fulfillment of part of the command given in 14:13, but here he makes no reference to its second element, that of teaching or instructing the wise (14:13). Elsewhere, the angel or God "teaches" or "instructs" Ezra (4:4; 5:32; 7:49; 7:90; 10:33; cf. 8:12). The subject of such teaching or instruction is generally eschatological secrets. God or the angel also commands Ezra to teach or instruct the wise in 12:38. Ezra, however, never talks of himself as teaching secrets to the wise. One might ask whether this is a deliberate limit laid upon Ezra or a rhetorical device designed to prepare the way for that which follows. It is, of course, intriguing to assess how far the present book, with its revelation of

---

1   See 4:44 Commentary.
2   See article by E. Glickler Chazon, "Moses' Struggle for His Soul: A Prototype for the *Testament of*   *Abraham,* the *Greek Apocalypse of Ezra,* and the *Apocalypse of Sedrach," Second Century* 5 (1985–86) 151–64.

eschatological secrets, is considered to be part of such secret revelations.[3]

In 14:20, however, true to character, Ezra has a question to pose to God. His reproof will be received by those now alive, he asserts, but what about those who have not yet been born? This question is rather like that in 5:41 which concerns the applicability of the eschatological prophecies that Ezra has received to those who are not yet born.[4] Ezra's question here also seems to imply that he does not expect that the end will come in his own generation but that there will be time for those who live to die and for a new generation to arise. This might be related to the ambiguity already noted to exist concerning Ezra's expectation of the end.[5] It is possible, however, that it is a rhetorical device designed to introduce the next question.

Ezra follows this formulation of the difficulty with a request. He asks for the holy spirit to be sent into him and for him to write down "everything that has happened in the world from the beginning, the things which were written in thy law." This request is completely unparalleled elsewhere in the book. On no previous occasion did Ezra ask for inspiration, and when it came upon him, it was involuntary.[6]

Here he asks for it, and with the specific purpose of writing the Torah down once more. The view that the Torah was lost or burned was expressed in 14:21, but it is also found earlier in the book, in 4:23.[7] This is part of the tradition used by our author in structuring his views about Ezra, Moses, and the new giving of the Torah upon which, as has been noted, the present chapter is based.[8]

The purpose for which mankind must have the Torah is in order to live. It has often been pointed out that "life" means "eternal life."[9]

The term "last days" means, presumably, the eschatological era, so the purpose of the renewed giving of the Torah is so that people can gain eternal life. This is regularly said to be the purpose of Torah (cf., e.g., 9:31). Ezra is asking to be granted the privilege of transmitting the Torah, lost in the fire of exile, once more to future generations, to assure their eternal life.

Commentary

■ **19** This verse is unique in the book in its formulation.
■ **20** The issue about the salvation of future generations is similar to that raised by 5:41 and has been discussed above.[10] The imagery of light and darkness already occurred in 12:42 in a specific way referring to prophets (see Commentary there). In more general terms, this imagery is widespread from the Hebrew Bible on; cf. Isa 9:2; 60:1–2; 1QM passim; et al. In Ps 36:10 light is brought into close connection with life: "For with thee is the fountain of life; in thy light do we live." In more specific terms, God's commandment or Torah is said to be light, so in a number of instances in the Hebrew Bible (Prov 6:23; Ps 119:105; et al.) as well as in the Apocrypha and the Pseudepigrapha (e.g., *2 Apoc Bar* 17:4; 19:3; 46:2–3; 59:2; *Test Patr Levi* 19:1).[11]

As pointed out above, "world" means "material world," while "inhabitants of the world" is used predominantly in eschatological contexts.[12] In this verse, therefore, Torah is applied to the "inhabitants of the world" as a whole, an idea encountered above; see 7:1–25 Function and Content, pp. 193–94.
■ **21** The idea that the Torah was burned or lost in the course of the destruction of the Temple may also be found in 4:23.[13] It underlies this chapter. By implication the contents of the Torah is what God has done or will do. That resembles what was revealed to Moses accord-

---

3   See further 14:37–40 Function and Content, p. 439.
4   The problem is not unique to 4 Ezra; it is discussed in some detail in 5:41 Commentary.
5   See 14:18 Commentary and 14:3–18 Function and Content, p. 418.
6   In Excursus on Inspiration, Ezra's theory of inspiration is discussed.
7   See 14:1–2 Function and Content, p. 411.
8   See 14:1–2 Function and Content, pp. 410–12.
9   See Excursus on Adam's Sin, p. 66.
10   See Form and Function, on this page, and 5:41 Commentary.
11   Cf. also 2 Cor 4:4 "light of the Gospel." Torah enlightens, e.g., Ps 19:8. In Eph 6:12 this age or world is called "this present darkness"; cf. also 1 John 2:11. See the comments of M. Desjardins, "Law in 2 Baruch and 4 Ezra," *Studies in Religion / Sciences Religieuses* 14 (1985) 30, and the discussion by G. Vermès, "The Torah Is a Light," *VT* 8 (1958) 436–38. Cf. also *Exod. R.* 36:3, where this theme is extensively developed.
12   On "world," see Excursus on the Term "Age"; on "inhabitants," see 5:1 Commentary.

ing to *Jub* 1:29.[14] Here, in any case, the term "Torah" implies the whole of sacred scripture.[15]

■ **22** The expression "If I have found favor" opens many petitions in the book.[16] Ezra asks for the holy spirit to be sent into him. The expression "holy spirit" is to be found in the Hebrew Bible (e.g., Isa 63:10; Ps 51:13); in the Apocrypha and the Pseudepigrapha (e.g., Susanna [Th] 45–46; Wisd 1:5; *Ps Sol* 17:37; *Jub* 1:21; *Asc Isa* 5:14); in the Dead Sea Scrolls (e.g., CD 2:12; 1QH 7:7; 9:32; and often); in rabbinic literature and in the New Testament.[17]

The meaning here is clearly in the sense of "spirit of inspiration" or "prophecy"; see also Wisd 9:17; 1QS 8:16; 1QH 12:12, cf. 14:13; Targ J Gen 43:14. In all of these instances the adjective "holy" is an attribute of the spirit of prophecy. Similar in 4 Ezra is "spirit of understanding" in 5:22. Other such expressions are "spirit" (*1 Enoch* 91:1); "spirit of truth" (*Jub* 25:14); and "spirit of understanding" (*Test Patr Levi* 2:3).[18] Ezra's prayer is

answered in 14:40–41.

The scriptures contained everything from creation to eschaton, as was already remarked in the previous verse. The expression "from the beginning" means "creation" also in 9:8 and 10:14.[19] "Live" denotes "eternal life."[20] A very similar turn of phrase is *2 Apoc Bar* 76:4–5, where Baruch is told of his impending assumption:

Now this shall befall after forty days. Go now therefore during these days and instruct the people so far as thou art able, that they may learn so as not to die at the last time, but may learn in order that they may live at the last times.

The Torah enables humans to achieve eternal life.[21]

---

13 See 14:1–2 Form and Function, p. 411. Violet 2 thinks that this might have been inspired by the burning of Torah Scrolls in the course of the destruction of the Second Temple.

14 See the emendation of Stone, "Apocryphal Notes," 125–26.

15 See 4:23 Commentary.

16 See 4:44 Commentary.

17 It has received a disproportionate amount of attention in the commentaries because of its particular importance in the New Testament. See for a summary *IDB*, 2:626–39. Detailed listing of sources of many types is to be found in *TDNT*, 6:332–451.

18 On the latter expression, see the detailed notes of Hollander and de Jonge, *Commentary*, 133.

19 The concept of "world" here is discussed in Excursus on the Term "Age."

20 This is discussed in detail in Excursus on Adam's Sin, p. 66.

21 See 3:19 Commentary.

14

23 He answered me and said, "Go and gather the [a] people, and tell them not to seek you for forty days. 24/ But prepare for yourself many writing tablets, [b] and take with you Sarea, Dabria, Selemia, [c]Elkana, and Asiel [c]—these five, because they are trained to write rapidly; [d] 25/ and you shall come here, and I will light in your heart the lamp of understanding, which shall not be put out until you finish [e] what you are about to [f] write. 26/ And when you have finished, some things you shall make public, and some you shall [g]deliver in secret [g] to the wise; tomorrow [h] at this hour you shall begin to write."

Notes

23 a Syr, Eth Ms "your."

b Georg breaks off here and resumes at the end of 14:26.

c–c These two names are present in the versions in various forms. The first is "Elkana" according to Syr, Eth, Arm. It is "Ethen" in Lat, while the second name, which is "Asiel" or variants thereof in most versions, is "Ethen" in Arm. Thus it seems clear that "Elkana" and "Asiel" are well based in the versions; however, the common reading of Lat, Arm "Ethen" indicates that this name too must go back to Greek. The original text is impossible to restore.

d Arm omits.

25 e Lat *finiantur,* hence RSV "is finished"; Arm "the completion."

f Lat, Syr, Eth have clear reflexes of μέλλεις (cf. Volkmar).

26 g–g Syr, Eth, Ar1 "hide and deliver."

h Georg resumes here.

Form and Structure

This pericope is God's answer to Ezra's prayer. It does not say that the prayer was granted but issues instructions to Ezra that are based on the assumption that this is indeed the case. The passage also is concerned to fix a deliberate setting in time and place "at this hour" (14:26), a phenomenon with no parallels in the book. In the meanwhile the location remains fixed.

Function and Content

Ezra is told to gather the people and instruct them not to seek him for forty days. The number forty immediately strengthens the evocation of Moses, which has already been observed in the earlier part of the chapter. Ezra, to whom the scriptures are to be revealed, is to go away for forty days, the same period of time that Moses was on Sinai. Above, moreover, we demonstrated that this figure is the total number of days in which the first six visions took place. After these six visions, Ezra had reached a new stage of revelation. Thus the first forty days are parallel to the second forty days. They complement and balance them, providing a climax of revelation before Ezra's assumption to heaven.

Previously the people sought Ezra, both in 5:16–19 and in 12:40–45. In those instances he commanded them not to seek him for seven days. Here God commands them (at least indirectly) for a period of forty days.

Next, Ezra is instructed to prepare writing tablets and to take five skilled scribes with him. These two elements, the material upon which to write and the persons who are to write, serve to remove from the story of the revelation to Ezra certain of the wondrous elements of the Mosaic revelation. They explain in "naturalistic" terms how the revelation was recorded and also distinguish Ezra from Moses in spite of the similarities between them. Moreover, perhaps these elements gave a measure of verisimilitude to the story of Ezra. After all, the production of ninety-four books in forty days without scribes would have demanded a very great miracle. So this incident reads as if it were an answer to rationalist objections to the Sinai story. Admittedly, even in 4 Ezra, the writing had miraculous elements to it, but its basic mechanism was explained and comprehensible.

Ezra is told that his prayer for inspiration to renew the scriptures will be granted. This is the third element in this divine response.[1]

---

1   In Excursus on Inspiration we have dealt at length with the understanding of inspiration in this chapter.

The final element is one that is becoming increasingly prominent in this chapter. The revelation that will be made to Ezra will be partly for public distribution and partly secret. The subject was discussed above in connection with 14:3–18. Once more the special, dual nature of revelation of both revealed and secret books is made clear.

There are some further features of the incident of the revelation of scriptures to Ezra that should be discussed here. The interchange with the people and the appointment of the five scribes have a special function. In all of the previous visions Ezra's receipt of revelation was private. Here the people are present, and he announces to them that he is going to experience a revelation. This provides an audience for him. In previous visions, when other people were present (in the final incidents of Visions 1 and 5) they were there on their own initiative. Here Ezra summons them on divine command and by the nature of his address makes them part of the dynamic of revelation. Moreover, this audience is set over against not merely Ezra himself but Ezra together with a group of five scribes. This social context is reinforced by certain other elements that hint at the presentation of a specially staged event—the noting of the exact time at which the revelation will occur and that it occurred in a particular place. A threefold set of relationships is thus established between the people (the audience), the witnesses (the five scribes), and the seer himself. These are anchored in time and place.

With this we may compare the incident when Baruch took a group of five men with him, together with "all the honorable men of the people," and narrated his revelation to them (2 Apoc Bar 5:5). This again presents us with three groups of actors.[2]

The nature of the revelatory event that Ezra expe-rienced was analyzed above in the Excursus on Inspiration, pp. 119–20. The chief points should be rehearsed, however, since they are pivotal for the understanding of the rest of this vision. The fulfillment of the promise by God in 14:25 to "light the lamp of understanding" in Ezra's heart is described in 14:39–41. He drinks a goblet full of the holy spirit as the result of which his "heart poured forth understanding" and his spirit retained its memory, that is, the wisdom and understanding that resulted from the inspiration.[3] In other words, these verses describe the onset of inspiration, the feeling of enlightenment, the retention of the contents of the inspiration, and the inspired ability to articulate this.

To Hans Lewy we owe the important comparison of this passage with the prologue to the Sibylline Oracles (lines 87–88). That passage takes up a standard theme found also in other sources that, on the one hand, the Sibyl's memory did not retain the content of the revelation after the revelation ceased, while, on the other, the scribes were often not swift enough to record the gush-ing prophetic speech.[4]

At a literary level, the passage in 4 Ezra seems to be a deliberate response to this topos. Chapter 14:26 stresses that the inspiration will continue "until what you are about to write is finished." The same point is emphasized again by 14:40, which states that his "spirit retained its memory." Thus not only was the content of Ezra's revelation true (like that of the Sibyl), but, unlike the Sibyl, he remembered its content until it was written down.

4 Ezra goes even farther. In the Sibylline text, the scribes are said to be ignorant and to be the cause of errors, while in 4 Ezra, the scribes are said to be inspired as well as the seer. They wrote with some sort of auto-matic writing "in characters which they did not know."[5]

---

2 Considering also the oak tree mentioned in 2 Apoc Bar 6:1, we may be tempted to posit a literary relationship between 2 Apocalypse of Baruch and 4 Ezra 14 at this point. Isaiah is surrounded by his disciples as he makes his ascent, according to Asc Isa 6:10–17, and this is similar to the situation described in Hekaloth Rabbati 18; see Rowland, Open Heaven, 230.

3 See Excursus on Inspiration, pp. 119–20, for a detailed analysis.

4 See Lewy, Sobria Ebrietas, 95 n. 2. In the Sibylline context too a threefold cast is present: the Sibyl, the scribes, and the audience. The presence of the scribes in both the Sibylline Oracles and 4 Ezra is particularly notable. The Greek scribes are called ταχυγραφοι while Ezra's are "trained to write swiftly."

5 Below we will discuss the possible historical reminis-cences in this phrase. Whatever they be, its function in context is left unimpaired.

The Most High is said to give them too "understanding" (14:42). Thus 4 Ezra seems deliberately to be besting the type of claims made for pagan prophecy. Not only did the seer speak the inspired truth; he remembered it and he dictated it to the scribes who were themselves, though to a lesser extent, inspired.[6]

Behind this claim may be discerned the attitude of our author to inspired scripture. If the Sibylline writer wished to account for possible instances in which the prophecies were not fulfilled, 4 Ezra desired to obviate any possible basis for claiming that there was any human error in revealed scripture. He uses a common *topos* of his age to do so, adapting it to his own needs.[7]

In the *Epistle of Thessalos,* which describes the religious experience of a pagan of the Hellenistic period, certain of these themes recur. Thessalos receives his vision at a time fixed in advance; it takes place in a special location, and Thessalos sneaks in pen and paper in order to note down whatever is appropriate (CCAG, 8:136).[8] The last theme, the surreptitious introduction of writing implements, also occurs elsewhere in Hellenistic pagan literature.[9] This is surely related to Ezra's preparation of tablets. Intriguingly, the *Epistle of Thessalos* does not relate what Thessalos did with the writing implements. In 4 Ezra, in contrast, they are prepared at divine behest and the mode of their employment is particularly stressed.

The same themes are at play in chapter 23 of *2 Enoch.* In chapter 22, Enoch has been transformed into the likeness of an angel. Then we read:

And the Lord summoned one of his archangels, Vrevoil by name, who was swifter in wisdom than the other archangels, and who records all the Lord's deeds. And the Lord said to Vrevoil, "Bring out the books from my storehouses, and fetch a pen for speed-writing, and give it to Enoch and read him the books." (22:10b–11a)

Enoch hears all of Vrevoil's instruction, and "Vrevoil instructed me for 30 days and 30 nights, and his mouth never stopped speaking. And, as for me, I did not rest" (A 23:3). Vrevoil again instructed Enoch for thirty days and thirty nights "and I wrote 360 books" (A 23:6).[10] Note here Enoch's inspiration (this is after his trans-figuration), the preparation of pens and tablets, the angel's unceasing dictation "for 30 days and 30 nights" and Enoch's unceasing writing. The relation to the type

---

6 In 12:40–51 Function and Content, p. 376, Ezra's prophetic role is discussed. Since it is assimilated to Moses', the final confirmation of his prophecy is that he is given the privilege of writing the books. Note the change in perspective from the prophets of ancient Israel, of whom A. N. Wilder aptly said, "In Israel's tradition God's servants the prophets did not write unless they were ordered to, however it might be with the scribes" (*Early Christian Rhetoric: The Language of the Gospel* [London: SCM, 1964] 21).

7 In general, the great role of memory in rabbinic school practice is often reflected in dicta in the literature. This is a result of the actual practice of the academies in which a major stress is laid upon memorization. P. Schäfer has argued that Merkabah mystical invocations of "Prince of Torah" who would give wondrous knowledge of Torah show the extent to which this issue preoccupied writers in ancient Judaism. See P. Schäfer, *Gershom Scholem Reconsidered: The Aim and Purpose of Early Jewish Mysticism* (The Twelfth Sacks Lecture; Oxford: Oxford Centre for Postgraduate Hebrew Studies, 1986). The issues are a little different, however, from those of the retention of vision experience.

8 Text in P. Boudreaux, *Catalogus Codicum Astrologorum Graecorum* (Brussels: Lamertin, 1898–1953), vol. 8.3, (1912) p. 133 (attributed to Haprocrates,

which attribution was corrected in vol. 8.4 of the same work, pp. 253–54); translation and commentary in A.-J. Festugière, "L'expérience religieuse du médecin Thessalos," *Revue Biblique* 48 (1939) 45–77. The passage referred to occurs on pp. 55–57.

9 See Festugière, "Expérience religieuse," 62 n. 23, for further references.

10 A curious, related tradition is to be found in the apocryphal (Bogomil?) *Book of St. John the Evangelist.*
And I asked the Lord and said: What shall be in that time? And he said to me: From the time when the devil fell from the glory of the Father and (lost) his own glory, he sat upon the clouds, and sent his ministers, even angels flaming with fire, unto men from Adam even unto Henoch his servant. And he raised up Henoch upon the firmament and showed him his godhead, and commanded pen and ink to be given him: and he sat down and wrote three score and seven books. And he commanded that he should take them and deliver them unto his sons. (James, *Apoc. N.T.,* 190)

of tradition reflected in 4 Ezra is indubitable. It is intriguing that the stylus is called "a pen for *speed-writing*" (J 22:11), the same term found in the Greek Sibyl of the scribes. This obviously reflects something like 4 Ezra but is typologically secondary to it, for the description in 4 Ezra is much closer to the possible *Sitz im Leben* of this material.[11]

When the insight gained into the Hellenistic context of these traditions is combined with the observations made above about the nature of the sociological framework of 4 Ezra implied by this chapter, there emerge important implications which can be explored.[12]

It is unclear whether the Greek oracular cases reflect aspects of actual practice. Inspired oracular persons were not usually accompanied by scribes who wrote down their words. In the texts we have cited, however, the presence of the scribes, who witnessed the inspired speech, served as a verification of the event. This may provide some hint at possible practice of seers of the type of the author of 4 Ezra.

Certain other passages in the book, when combined with the present one, serve to raise the following issue. Clearly, what is described in the narrative passage 12:40–50 is the dynamic by which Ezra's new, inner recognition of his prophetic role is transformed, indeed in part precipitated by his interaction with his audience, the people. They recognize his role and this brings him to act as a prophet.[13]

The question must be raised, therefore, whether here we have more than merely a literary attempt to assert the infallibility of Ezra's revelation. The striking function of

the five scribes and the audience as verification and confirmation of Ezra's role and self-understanding should be borne in mind. This rings true and may reflect something of the social realities behind apocalyptic vision experience.

A further aspect of this social context may be hinted at by the passages that distinguish "the wise" from the rest of the people. This is clear in 12:38; 14:13; and 14:46; cf. 14:6. These wise were to receive, preserve, and transmit the secret revelation. Ezra does not reveal the actual vision experience of Vision 5 to the people (12:47–48), although he has been commanded to teach it to the wise (12:38). The group so designated may have been a distinct social circle. Knibb utilizes this idea to describe 4 Ezra as a work not for *hoi polloi* but as "a product of learned study intended for a learned audience."[14] That 4 Ezra stood in a distinct speculative tradition has been discussed in 12:11 Commentary. It is still not certain in our mind that 4 Ezra must be seen as predominantly a sort of learned or interpretative writing, as Knibb claims.[15]

Commentary

■ **23** This verse takes up the theme of forty days' fast and revelation from the Sinai incident; see Exod 24:18; 34:28; Deut 9:9; and 9:18. The same elements with similar wording are taken up in two further apocalyptic revelation contexts, *2 Apoc Bar* 76:2–4 and *Apoc Abr* 12:1–3. The pattern was clearly influential, but neither of these sources deals with the revelation of scripture.[16]

■ **24** In *2 Apoc Bar* 5:5, Baruch took a group of five men

---

11   Wilder has commented on the preference for oral rather than written discourse in this period, adducing both rabbinic and Christian parallels (*Early Christian Rhetoric*, 48–62, particularly 49). This serves to highlight Ezra's particular concern with written scripture and to provide insight into Ezra's use of the Greek context.

12   In a recent article, C. Forbes marshals much of the evidence and many of the references to pagan Greek oracular practice ("Early Christian Inspired Speech and Hellenistic Popular Religion," *NT* 28 [1986] 257–68). The closest analogies to the situation implied by 4 Ezra and by the data from the *Sibylline Oracles* are Hellenistic traditions about personages who mediated oracles, putting them into verse (pp. 262–64). Neither in the data Dr. Forbes considers in that article nor (as he informs me in personal

communication) in the extensive other sources he has examined has he encountered a recognized office of "tachygrafoi," nor even the term.

13   See 12:40–51 Function and Content, p. 376.

14   Knibb, "Apocalyptic and Wisdom," 72. A different interpretation of the same ideas is that of Brandenburger, *Verborgenheit*, 197. The significance of the term "wise" here, though circumscribed by Knibb, is perhaps even less than he would claim.

15   Knibb, "Apocalyptic and Wisdom," 73.

16   Cf. also Jesus' 40 days' withdrawal in Matt 4:2; Mark 1:14; and Luke 4:2.

with him to narrate his revelation to them. It may be that five was a traditional number for a group of disciples. In *Masseket Kelim* 48, Ezra is associated with five companions: Haggai, Zechariah, Malachi, Shimur the Levite, and Hezekiah, who wrote the Mishnah.[17] Some have also compared this group with the five famous disciples of R. Yoḥanan b. Zakkai at Jabne (see *m. Abot* 2:8).[18]

As pointed out in the textual note c-c, there is some uncertainty about the names. But all six names offered by the manuscript tradition, the five given in the translation and Ethen, have clear biblical precedents, mostly of postexilic times. Thus we note Saria (Ezra 7:1; Neh 10:3; et al.); Dabria (if = Dibri, Lev 24:11); Selemia (Ezra 10:39; Neh 3:30; 13:13); Elkana (1 Sam 1:1; 1 Chron 9:16; 12:7; 15:23); Asiel (not clear what name, but cf. 1 Chron 4:3); Ethen (1 Chron 2:6; 15:17).

■ **25** This verse relates the divine response to Ezra's prayer in 14:22. It describes the process of inspiration that is called, using an image still current today, enlight-

enment. The language of light has been observed in various senses above, and two of these are also evident in a similar verse in *Biblical Antiquities*: "I the Lord will kindle for him my lamp to dwell in him, and will . . . shine for him a perpetual light."[19] It has been observed that "to write" here means "to dictate."[20]

■ **26** This verse describes the disposition of the things revealed to Ezra and written down. They are divided into two groups, one exoteric and the other esoteric. The idea of a tradition of secret knowledge already came up in 3:14, while the notion of a dual revelation may be observed in 14:5 and 14:45–46. That the secret revelation is to be transmitted only to the wise is also a familiar idea; see 12:37; 14:46; and cf. 8:62.[21] It is noteworthy that so far in this vision, that revelation which Ezra received has not been called "books."

---

17 The reference to *Masseket Kelim* is drawn from Ginzberg, *Legends,* 6:51.

18 Gry has pointed out a possible relationship between the five scribes and the five books of the Torah, though it should be recalled that 24 or 94 books were revealed to Ezra.

19 See Excursus on Inspiration, pp. 119–20; on the imagery of the lamp, see 12:42 Commentary and in

yet a different sense in 14:20 Commentary.

20 So Licht, p. 82.

21 See Commentary on these various verses for detailed analysis.

14

27   Then I went as he [a] commanded me, and I gathered all the people together, and said [b]to them,[b] 28/ "Hear these words, O Israel. 29/ At first [c] our fathers dwelt [d] as aliens in [e] Egypt, and they were delivered from there, 30/ and received the law of life, which they did not keep, which you also have transgressed after them. 31/ Then land [f]was given[f] to you for a possession in [g] the land of Zion; but you and your fathers committed iniquity and did not keep the ways which [h]the Most High[h] commanded you. 32/ And because he [i] is a righteous judge, he took from you what he had given [j]in due time.[j] 33/ And now you are here, and your brethren are farther in the interior. [k] 34/ If you, then, will rule over your minds and discipline your hearts, you shall be kept alive, [l]and after death you shall obtain mercy.[l] 35/ For after death the judgment will come, when we shall live again; and then the names of the righteous will become manifest, and the deeds of the ungodly will be disclosed. 36/ But let no one come to me for forty days."

Notes

27   a Georg, Arm "the Lord."

      b–b Lat, Georg omit.

29   c Ar1, Ar2 omit.

      d Lat, Eth, Georg, Arm preserve a reflex of Hebrew infinitive absolute and finite verb.

      e Syr, Eth, Ar1, Ar2 add "the land of."

31   f–f Eth, Georg, cf. Ar1 "he gave."

      g Eth omits; Georg, Ar1 vary; the Greek probably had the difficulty reflected by Lat, Syr, Arm.

      h–h Syr "Moses the servant of the Lord"; Georg, Ar1 "he"; Ar2 "the Lord."

32   i Syr, Georg, Ar1, Ar2 "the Most High," cf. note h–h above on 14:31.

      j–j Syr, Eth, Georg, Arm; follows "righteous judge" Lat; Ar1, Ar2 omit.

33   k Eth, Syr, Ar1, Arm add "than you"; this reading might have existed in Greek; Syr paraphrased the whole verse.

34   l–l The phrase is lost in Eth, Arm.

Form and Structure

This is Ezra's speech directed to the people delivered in response to the divine command in 14:23. It is composed of four parts, which are preceded by a brief narrative introduction (14:27). The first part is the call for attention (14:28). Next comes an account of the historical sins of Israel which serves to explain the present situation (14:29–33). This is actually made up of a historical recital (14:29–31) and the drawing of implications from it (14:32–33). Third, there follows an exhortation of the people and a promise made to them (14:34–35), and finally, the whole ends with a concluding injunction (14:36).

The passage uses a number of obvious literary forms. It opens with a call for attention, followed by a historical recital of sins, implications, injunction, and promises. The call "Hear these words, O Israel" (14:28) draws on familiar Deuteronomic formulae reminiscent of Moses' addresses in that book. Similar expressions have been discussed previously here.[1] The historical recital, too, is a form with which our author is intimately familiar, and it dominates the address at the start of chapter 3, just to mention the most prominent example in the book.

The historical recital is counterpointed with an indictment of Israel for its sins. Such a contrasting of Israel's sins and God's merciful deeds is found in many psalms and prayers. They are found in Nehemiah 9, but there the two subjects are given in separate blocks of text, not interwoven. They are more integrated in Ps 106:7–15. Less specific listings of God's mercies may be found in 4Q504, cols 6–7, and in Daniel 9.

All of this forms a farewell speech (*Abschiedungsrede*), which is a widely found literary form. Those elements of exhortation to faithfulness and mention of rewards and punishments are standard in such contexts.[2]

Function and Content

In the historical recital, each stage is set forth as God's grace and Israel's unfaithfulness. The story starts from Egypt. The exodus and the giving of the Torah are next mentioned, and in immediate counterpoint Israel's transgression in the past and present (14:29–30). Next the gift of the land is celebrated, but again "you and your fathers committed iniquity" (14:31). This recital is then summarized: you sinned and because God is judge he took your land and now you are in exile (14:32–33).

---

1   See 9:29–37 Function and Content, p. 307.

2   J. Munck, "Le discours d'adieu dans le Nouveau Testament et dans la littérature biblique," *Mélanges*

M. Goguel (Neuchatel: Delachaux et Niestlé, 1950), particularly pp. 159 and 168 on the constitutive elements of such discourses.

Note that, with its stress on the events leading up to Sinai, this historical review is parallel to the story of the Mosaic revelation in 14:3–6. There God is the speaker, while here it is Ezra. The recital is then followed by an exhortation, the message of which is "There is still hope!" If you are good, the people are told, you will be rewarded, for after death there is judgment and recompense.

The language of life has been a basic theme in this chapter. It means "eternal life" or "redemption."[3] So Ezra is told, in 14:9, "You shall live with my servant and those who are like you, until the times are ended." Again, Ezra in 14:22 refers to "those who wish to live in the last days." In 14:30 the Torah is called "the law of life," and the whole is made explicit in our present passage, "for after death the judgment will come, when we shall live again." The way that judgment is described in this passage much resembles the description in 7:26–44.

The message here does not take up the subject of the destruction of Zion and its restoration which bore the major import of the first six visions. The concern here is almost solely with the Torah and its function. This brings to mind the question raised in the address at the beginning of the fourth vision where the eternal and cosmic nature of the Torah was contrasted with the imperfect human vessel that received it (9:29–37). Here the attitude seems to be different. On the one hand, Ezra speaks of the Torah having been burned; of mankind no longer possessing its redeeming knowledge. On the other, it is called a "law of life" and in its renewal human beings will find the way to life. Although the precise issues of the address of the fourth vision are not discussed, the problem of Torah does lie at the heart of his concern here as well.

We have indicated that the first six visions with their forty days are parallel to the seventh vision with its forty days. The first six visions brought Ezra to the role of prophet. They did this by resolving the issues of the destruction of Zion through the idea of its determined redemption and by explaining the suffering of the righteous through the concept of their eschatological redemption. The present chapter takes the author's thought farther; here the renewal of "the law of life" is recounted. This revelation transcends and complements those of the preceding dream visions. As has been pointed out, there are many literary and formal signals that indicate to us the crucial nature of this final vision. It is not an authentication of the book, as has often been claimed, but it is a completion.

Knibb observes: "The speech consists of a summary of the main events of Israel's history from the time in Egypt to the exile, and as such it seems intended to provide a deliberate contrast to the summary given in the prayer with which 2 Esdras 3–14 begins. In ch. 3 Ezra blamed God for the situation in which Israel found herself, but here the exile is accepted as being the fully merited punishment for Israel's sin, and God is called a 'just judge' (verses 29–33). Furthermore, whereas ch. 3 ended on a note of despair, this speech ends on a note of hope (verses 34–5)" (p. 279).

As has been remarked above, this speech is also parallel to 14:3–6, but from a different perspective. Note also the overall resemblance to Deuteronomy 27–30, Moses' farewell address. Deuteronomy 30 also concludes with a conditional promise of "life." Nonetheless, in many respects 9:29–30 is closest to the present passage, as will be evident from our comments on the specific verses. Not only does it share rhetorical structures with the present passage but it also starts with the exodus.[4]

Commentary

■ **27** In this verse Ezra calls the people together and prepares to address them. This contrasts with 5:16 where Paltiel, the leader of the people, came to Ezra on his own initiative, as "the people" did in 12:40. In *2 Apoc Bar* 31:1–2 and 77:1, Baruch assembles the people and addresses them. He opens his address with formulae like that found in 14:28.[5] Ezra's task here, admonishing the

---

3   See in general Excursus on Adam's Sin, p. 66.
4   Brandenburger has made much of the congruence of Ezra's views here with those of the angel in Visions 1–3. This he claims shows the basic purpose and intent of the author (pp. 50–52). Our view of the import of this fact differs greatly in perspective; see Introduction, secs. 4.4.1 and 4.5.7.
5   See Commentary on that verse.

people, is a prophetic one. In most of the preceding part of the book, Ezra has addressed God on the people's behalf or presented their point of view (4:23–24; 5:23–30; 8:15–36; and cf. 12:48). Only in the speech starting in 12:46 does he address the people to comfort them, and that is after the recognition of his prophetic role.

■ **28** This is a call for attention, as is 9:30, but there in words attributed to God. There too it is followed in 9:30–33 by a passage like that here. This invocation ties in with its earlier use, also God's speech to Israel over the giving of the Torah. The formula is Deuteronomistic.[6] A similar invocation also opens the addresses in *2 Apoc Bar* 31:3 and 77:2.

■ **29** The historical recital, like that in 9:29–30, commences from the exodus. So does that in 14:3–5 but from a different perspective. Not only were such historical recitals common but 4 Ezra features the exodus in the preceding three instances, in 3:17; 9:29; and 14:4.

■ **30** Here the giving of the Torah is mentioned (cf. 3:17–22; 5:27; 9:30–31). The Torah is called "Torah of life" in Sir 17:11 and 45:5, and it is closely associated with "life" in *2 Apoc Bar* 38:2. This close association is also clearly implied in 9:30–32, and "life" is clearly a term denoting "eternal life."[7] The reproach of disobedience to the Torah is commonplace and the term "keep" means "observe."[8]

■ **31** This verse sets in counterpoint the gift of the land and the sins of Israel. The term "ways" means here something like "commandments" or "Torah."[9] "Land" here means the land of Israel. Violet 2 has pointed out that the expression "land of Zion" is unique and thinks that it may go back to a corruption for the "land of Canaan." This is quite unverifiable, but the language of the verse bears some resemblance to Ps 105:11: "To you I will give the land of Canaan as your portion for an inheritance" (see 1 Chron 16:18).

■ **32** This verse draws the general conclusion from the preceding recital of history. The idea that exile or destruction is the result of sin is commonplace from the

Pentateuch on. What is striking here is the contrast with the address of the first vision where not the righteousness but the injustice of God's actions to Israel are set forth.[10] The terms "judge" and "judgment" sometimes refer to God's historical actions toward humans,[11] and the term "righteous judge" highlights the contrast with Vision 1.[12] "In due time" conveys the idea of determinism or of the regularity of the structure of natural events or history.[13] This is one of the determinative ideas in the book.

■ **33** The expression here can be compared with *2 Apoc Bar* 77:5, "But behold! ye are here with me." The reference is to the nine and one half tribes that are exiled in a "further land"; see 13:40–41.[14] This is another tradition tying this vision to the preceding.

■ **34** This is an exhortation to the people to act in a way that will ensure their well-being and eventual bliss. It is formulated as an "if" clause.[15] Behind this statement lie assumptions about the nature of humans, of the evil inclination, and of human abilities to overcome it. These ideas have been discussed in detail above and may be seen clearly in, for example, 7:92 and 7:127–128.[16] More specific is the idea that the rule over the intellectual faculties helps salvation. This idea is also found elsewhere in the book in a variety of formulations.[17] The expression "discipline your hearts" is comparable with Ps 16:7.

If humans succeed in this mission, then they will receive a double boon: they will be kept alive and will receive mercy after death. It seems that "alive" here does not mean eternal life but refers to life in this world, since the phrase is contrasted with "mercy after death." If so, then is it an oblique reference to the dangers of the eschatological times, those woes to avoid which Ezra has been told that he will be assumed?

Mercy after death is unclear. From the next verse, it appears that the intent is resurrection, but as it stands, this might also be a reference to the intermediate, post-mortem state of souls. Observe the richness of the concept of mercy in 4 Ezra. It has been the object of

6   See 9:29–37 Function and Content, p. 307.
7   See Excursus on Adam's Sin, p. 66.
8   See 9:32 Commentary.
9   See 7:79 Commentary.
10   See 3:4–36 Function and Content, pp. 61–63.
11   See Excursus on the Term "Judgment," p. 150, for further instances.
12   A similar expression in Ps 7:12.

13   See 3:9; 8:41; 8:43; 10:16; and 11:20.
14   See Commentary on those two verses.
15   A similar sentiment in similar language is to be found in *2 Apoc Bar* 85:4.
16   See Excursus on Adam's Sin, p. 65.
17   See Excursus on Inspiration, pp. 123–24.

major petitionary prayers offered by Ezra (7:132; 8:32–36) in which he appeals to God to show mercy in judgment. In 7:33 and 7:115, in contrast, mercy is said to be withdrawn in final judgment.[18] Here he uses the term to indicate a post-mortem or eschatological reward, in a way that is comparable with 10:24. Both of these passages have the implication of resurrection.[19]

■ **35** The expression "live again" denotes resurrection; cf. 5:45. This undoubtedly reflects Hebrew use of the pi'el of חיה with this meaning. The verse relates resurrection to judgment.[20] This refers to resurrection that will come at the eschaton, though the expression mentioning only resurrection after death, is somewhat unclear.[21] Resurrection is discussed in detail in 7:32 Commentary.

In 7:104 we find the idea that there will be a full disclosure on the day of judgment. This is usually said to be disclosure of reward and punishment, but here it refers to disclosure of the true nature of human actions. On the idea of the naming of the righteous in heaven, see

10:57.[22] This is a recognition of their position, just as is the disclosure of the deeds of the wicked, with which compare Wisd 4:20 and *1 Enoch* 89:63.

This passage has, naturally, related reward and punishment to judgment and therefore to human conduct. This is, in basic terms, comparable to dominant biblical ideas. Similarities and differences are highlighted by a verse like Deut 5:33: "You shall walk in all the way which the Lord your God has commanded you, that you may live, and that it may go well with you." Differences are in the nature of the historical perspective—4 Ezra's is eschatological, while that of Deuteronomy is explicit in the end of this verse "and that you may live long in the land which you shall possess."

■ **36** No commentary.

---

18 For other dimensions of this concept, see 4:24 and 12:34.
19 For a similar list of rewards not structured chronologically, see 8:53.
20 On the concept of judgment, see Excursus on the Term "Judgment."
21 There are a number of analogous expressions in the book; see Excursus on the Term "Judgment," p. 151.

22 See further 10:57 Commentary.

14

37 So I took [a] the five men, as he commanded me, and we proceeded to the field, and remained there. [b] 38/ And [c]it came to pass, [c] on the next day, behold, a voice called me, saying, [d] "Ezra, [e] open your mouth and drink what I give you to drink." 39/ Then I opened my mouth, and behold, [f] a full cup was offered [g] to me; it was full of [h]something like [h] water, but its color was like fire. 40/ And I took it and drank; [i]and when I had drunk it, [j] my heart poured forth understanding, and wisdom increased in my breast, and [k] my spirit retained its memory; 41/ and my mouth was opened, and was no longer closed. 42/ And the Most High gave understanding to those [l] five men, and by turns they wrote what was dictated, in characters which they did not know. [m]They sat [m] forty days, and wrote during the daytime, and ate their bread at night. 43/ As for me, I spoke in the daytime and was not silent at night. 44/ [n]So during the forty days ninety-four books were written. 45/ And when the forty days were ended, the Most High spoke to me, saying, [o] "Make public the twenty-four [p] books that you wrote first and let the worthy and the unworthy read them; 46/ but keep the seventy [q] that were written last, [q] in order to give them to the wise among your [r] people. 47/ For in them are the springs [s] of understanding, the fountains [t] of wisdom and the river [u] of knowledge." 48/ And I did so. [v] 49/ In the [w]seventh year of the sixth week, [w] five

Notes

37   a Ar1, Ar2 add "with me."
      b Syr adds "as he had said to me"; Ar2 adds "as the Most High had commanded me."

38   c–c Eth, Ar2 omit; Lat *factus sum.*
      d Eth, Georg add "to me."
      e Syr, Eth Mss, Ar1, Ar2, Arm repeat the name.

39   f Syro-Arabic fragment commences with this verse. Syr, Syro-Arabic "behold," corruption ἰδου/εἰδον. Ceriani suggests inner-Syriac *wh'* lost by anablepsis before *hw'.*
      g Eth, Georg, Ar2 "he offered."
      h–h Eth, Georg omit, cf. Ar2.

40   i–j Eth, Georg omit, perhaps by hmt.
      j Syr, Syro-Arabic add "behold"; in Lat a senseless *in eo* precedes "when," which might be corrupt for *ecce.*
      k Lat *nam,* whence RSV "for."

42   l Ar1, Ar2 "the"; Lat also does not read "those."
      m–m Lat, cf. Eth "they remained"; Syr, Syro-Arabic, Arm "I sat"; Georg, Ar1 "I was"; Ar2 "we remained"; the text is uncertain, chiefly as to whether there was a first person singular or a third person plural. One is tempted to think of a variant perhaps engendered by the Greek imperfect.

44   n Ar2 "And they wrote what I dictated." The text of this version ends here.

45   o Syr, Syro-Arabic, Eth add "to me."
      p Lat, Eth, Arm omit.

46   q–q Syr, Syro-Arabic, Eth, Georg omit.
      r Syr, Arm omit.

47   s Lat "spring"; Eth, Georg "lamp," "fire"; Ar1 "leaven"; Arm "proverbs." Clearly the Greek was problematic; we follow Syr, Syro-Arabic with the support of Latin; Eth and Georg go back to a common Greek reading.
      t Lat, Georg, cf. Arm "fountain"; Ar1 omits.
      u Syr, Syro-Arabic "light"; Ceriani suggests *nwhr',* going back to *nhr'.*

48   v Lat stops here. Eth, Arm "I did so." Eth and Georg derive from different *Vorlagern* in 14:48–50.

49   w–w There is no doubt that the versions surviving preserve a common text which has become corrupt, especially in its numerals. The translation is based on Syr, Syro-Arabic; "seventh" is also supported by Georg and perhaps obliquely by "seventy-six" of Ar1; Eth, Arm have a common text for the end of 14:48 and for this date, which is corrupt and must have been so at the Greek level, viz.: "I did so in the fourth year of the week(s [Eth]) of years after"; Georg has *in anno illo septimo in quinto anno ille* which is corrupt; Ar1 has "seventy-six years."

thousand years ^x and three months and twenty-two ^y days after creation. 50/ At that time Ezra was caught up, and taken to the ^z place of those ^z who are like him, ^a after he had written all these things. And he was called the Scribe of the knowledge of the Most High ^b forever. ^c

x So all except Georg "5020" and Ar1 "5025."

x–y The text accords with Syro-Arabic, Eth, Ar1; Syr has corrupted "twenty-two" to "twelve"; Georg *in quinto mense die tertio;* Arm "after two months of days."

50

z–z Georg "kingdom with those"; Ar1 "lands of the living"; Arm "company of those."

a Georg ends here.

b Ar1 adds "to whom is the fame and the power"; Arm *Y* adds "to whom is the glory"; Arm H ends here.

c Syr adds "The first discourse of Ezra is ended"; Arm W adds "this book of Ezra is ended"; Georg adds "glory to God"; Ar1 adds "end of the first writing of the books of Ezra, scribe of the Law; and the second follows it."

Form and Structure

This passage deals with the revelation of the secret and public books to Ezra. In form it is a narrative in the first person and it represents the last part of the story of how Ezra carried out the injunctions that God laid upon him according to 14:23–26. Thus:

14:23 is carried out in 14:27, 14:36;
14:24 is carried out in 14:37;
14:25 is carried out in 14:38–44;
14:26 is carried out in 14:45–48.

It includes a few particular literary forms, beyond the divine addresses to Ezra with which it is punctuated. Thus there is rhythmic, parallelistic prose in 14:40–41 and in 14:47. Even more interesting is that the passage narrates a waking experience of Ezra's, the drinking of the cup of the holy spirit (14:38–39). This is in some ways comparable with the visionary parables in chapter 4, though here Ezra's personal involvement in the experience is direct and profound and there is no hint of its bearing an allegorical character.

The position of this passage in the chapter is confirmed by the interrelations laid out in the first paragraph of this section. The setting of the passage is the field. According to 14:27 "Then I went . . . ," Ezra had gone presumably from the field to the place where the people were situated. Now Ezra and the five men return to the field. This variation of venue and of Ezra's position (sitting, lying, standing) is very different from his fixed venue and position in all that precedes. The rest of the passage is a continuous and coherent narrative. Its heart is the revelation of the secret books. This ties it deeply into the rest of the book, which is so structured that this revelation forms a climax.

The position of the last sentence about Ezra's translation has in the past been considered indefinite on text-critical grounds. That is not our view, and it is definitely part of the book as we have indicated in the textual notes. Moreover, on literary grounds, if it were not original, then the end of the book would be Ezra's words "And I did so," that is, he transmitted the secret books to the wise of the people. From a structural point of view, however, the mention of the translation seems to be required. Ezra has been told to take all these steps and had also requested the special revelation because of his impending assumption to heaven (14:14–15). The specification of the assumption thus forms a satisfactory conclusion to the book.

Function and Content

The passage opens with Ezra's recounting that he took the five men, as he had been commanded, and went and stayed in the field (14:37). The next day he had a waking experience: first in an audition he heard a voice saying "Take this and drink!" (14:38) and then in a vision, he saw a cup and took it and drank its clear, fiery contents (14:39). Upon drinking this, he felt himself to be inspired. The actual onset of the inspiration is described in language that resembles that used earlier in the book in some respects, but is much more explicit.[1] Moreover, in all the previous instances the speech that came upon him was a bitter or argumentative one. Here it is the revelation of scripture.

1 The inspiration experience is analyzed in Excursus on Inspiration, pp. 119–20.

It is interesting to consider the actual nature of this experience. At one level it is perhaps symbolic. Drinking and drunkenness were terms used for the experience of inspiration.[2] Consequently, at least the symbolism of the experience is derived from a common terminology and metaphor. But the text makes no hint at anything other than that Ezra actually saw a goblet and drank its contents. The result of this was complex, as has been pointed out, and among other things "his spirit retained its memory," that is, his mind retained the wisdom that resulted from his drinking of the cup of the spirit.

In other terms, what is described is (1) the onset of the inspiration, (2) the feeling of enlightenment, (3) the retention of the content of the enlightenment, and (4) the ability to articulate or dictate this retained content. A similar set of terms to denote what is revealed is to be found in 14:47, where it is used to describe the secret revelation.

The function of this description of inspiration is not just to authenticate Ezra's vision. It serves, in part, to add plausibility to the dictation of ninety-four books; moreover, perhaps it reflects the actual reality of the author's experience.

The next element of the plot is the actual writing down of the words and books that Ezra dictated in his inspired state. The five copyists are also said to be inspired, although clearly their experience is not comparable to Ezra's. One sign of their inspiration is the odd comment that they wrote in "characters they knew not." This is perhaps a reference to the same tradition known to the rabbinic Sages that the square Hebrew script (i.e. the Aramaic characters) was brought back by Ezra from Babylon.[3] At the same time, this wondrous writing serves to validate yet another aspect of the creation or transmission of the scriptures.[4] So Ezra dictated, and the scribes wrote, ninety-four books in the stipulated forty days.

God then instructed Ezra what to do with those books. He is to publish twenty-four of them. This is clearly a reference to the twenty-four books of the Hebrew Bible. Twenty-four is one of the traditional Jewish numbers for biblical books, and this is its first occurrence.[5] He is to hide the seventy, for they are the books that contain true knowledge and wisdom and are to be transmitted only to the wise among the people.

There are a number of points of great interest in this passage. The first is that these books, the esoteric ones, are also those which contain saving knowledge. A distinct attitude both to written scriptures and to esoteric scriptures is reflected here. Just what the seventy books were is unknown. One hint that they might include 4 Ezra itself, and perhaps other eschatological or apocalyptic writings, is to be found in 12:36–38. In that passage Ezra is commanded about the secret transmission of the teaching of the eagle vision. The language used to denote the vision and its transmission is exactly the same as the language used by chapter 14 to describe the transmission of the secret writings. Another, somewhat formal consideration might well be that, if 14:47–50 is taken seriously, it would also explain the transmission of 4 Ezra itself.[6]

In any case, it is clear that in this incident is described an event of very great importance to the author. It is central to the structure of the chapter, which turns about the issue of the revealed writings. It is also central to the whole book. The revelation being described in this section is what Ezra receives once he has achieved the status of prophet. It is of the scriptures given so that "those who wish to live in the last days may live" (14:22). It is of the tradition and corpus of esoteric and exoteric writings.

This vision is in some way, then, also about the revelation of 4 Ezra itself. The key is given by the forty days. The present narrative, at one level, tells of the revelation of the ninety-four books. At another it tells of the revelation of the esoteric knowledge that Ezra himself has become worthy to receive.

The final two verses give the date, perhaps hinting at

---

2   See Excursus on Inspiration, p. 120.

3   See 14:1–2 Function and Content, p. 411, where the sources are adduced. In fact, a historical memory of the introduction of the Aramaic script is retained by this tradition.

4   See 14:19–22 Function and Content, p. 426.

5   The alternative tradition of 22 books, according to the letters of the Hebrew alphabet, first occurs in

Josephus, *Contra Apionem* 1.38.

6   Meade, *Pseudonymity and Canon*, 97, just states baldly that this refers to Ezra's own work. As put by him, that is not exact.

the proximity of the end, and provide details of Ezra's fate and his special title, received as a result of the experiences that he has undergone as related in this book.

Commentary

■ **37** The description of Ezra's inspiration found in this and the succeeding verses has already been discussed in detail.[7] Ezra returns to the field where he has received the major visions of the last part of the book and which he had left, it seems, in order to address the people. The vision is marked by repeated changes of venue.

■ **38** He receives the command to drink the goblet of fiery liquid. Drunkenness was a standard way of speaking of inspiration in the Hellenistic world.[8] It is used here in this way, but as in the "visionary parables" above, the literary figure is transmuted into an experience of the visionary. The mode of God's address to him is standard and may be found in various descriptions of revelations.[9]

■ **39** Lewy pointed to the similar drink of the Gnostic Markos, which is mentioned by Irenaeus and which was colored red and purple.[10] The fiery appearance of the water brings to mind the linking of baptism with fire and the Holy Spirit in Matt 3:11.[11]

■ **40** This verse describes how Ezra received inspiration.[12] Comparable in a number of ways is the description of the powerful access of religious feeling in *Od Sol* 36:7:

and my mouth was opened like a cloud of dew
and my heart gushed forth like a garden of righteousness.

The content of Ezra's inspiration is described in wisdom language which intersects with that used to describe the nature of the esoteric revelation in 14:47.[13] Observe that Ezra is often said to have "understanding" (4:22; 8:25). Earlier in the book his understanding is said to be deficient (4:2), to seek wisdom (13:55), and is set parallel to wisdom (8:4). This terminology of "understanding" shows, as we have demonstrated above, two meanings, one something like "mind" and the other the content of his knowledge.

■ **41** Note the passive expression here. In 9:28 too, the passive "my mouth was opened" describes the onset of inspiration. Such expressions are also common in the Bible.[14]

■ **42** The inspiration of the five men is described. The writing in unknown characters serves not merely to intensify the sense of the miraculous, as Licht suggests, but also to highlight their inspiration and to guarantee the accuracy of that which they wrote.[15] This is also related to the traditions that set the introduction of the square Aramaic script into the period of Ezra. This is known to the Rabbis and to Jerome and perhaps preserves actual historical memory.[16] The writing for forty days is the fulfillment of the command given in 14:23 and is designed to evoke the Mosaic revelation.[17] As distinct from Ezra, the scribes abstain from food only during the day, but they eat at night.[18]

■ **43** The stress on Ezra's unceasing flow of speech is similar to that on Enoch's unceasing writing in *2 Enoch* 23:3. In addition to the relationship between the forty days' fast and that of Moses, it may be significant that Ezra did not eat anything more after drinking the

---

7 See Excursus on Inspiration, pp. 119–20.
8 See Excursus on Inspiration, p. 120.
9 See 14:1–2 Form and Structure, p. 410.
10 Lewy, *Sobria Ebrietas*, 96–97; and Irenaeus, 1.13.2 (*PG*, 7:580).
11 Other instances of the Holy Spirit being like fire exist; see Acts 2:3–4 and *Test Patr Benj* 9:3. Water and fire often form a pair, usually opposed, so 4 Ezra 7:7 and Sir 15:16. The very anomaly of their combination is a sign of the superhuman nature of the drink. Cf. also *b. Ḥag.* 14b, where heavenly fire surrounds R. Eleazar as he expounds the *Maʿaseh Merkabah*.
12 See Excursus on Inspiration, pp. 121–22; 5:22 Commentary; and 14:19–22 Function and Content, pp. 425–26.
13 See Excursus on Inspiration, p. 120.
14 See Excursus on Inspiration, p. 121.
15 See in detail on this theme 14:23–36 Function and Content, pp. 428–29.
16 The sources are cited in 14:1–2 Function and Content, p. 411.
17 See 14:23 Commentary. This phrase is alluded to explicitly by Priscillian, *De fide et apocryphis;* see Violet 1, p. 438.
18 This is also the pattern for public fasts, a less rigorous form of abstention; see *m. Taʿan.* 1:5.

wondrous, heavenly contents of the goblet.

■ **44** The question of the ninety-four books has raised some debate. All seem agreed that the twenty-four books are the books of the Bible. This figure is the traditional Jewish number, and occurs here for the first time. The next references are in rather later rabbinic sources.[19] The alternative figure of twenty-two, in accordance with the letters of the Hebrew alphabet, is first found in Josephus, *Contra Apionem* 1.38, and recurs in a series of later Patristic sources. Of particular interest here is the tradition found in Epiphanius, *De mensuris et ponderibus* 10. There the story of the translation of the LXX is told, and the Jewish elders are said to have sent to Ptolemy, from Jerusalem, "the twenty-two of the (Old) Testament and the seventy-two that are apocryphal."[20] It is at least possible that Epiphanius knew the tradition of ninety-four books that 4 Ezra knew, was familiar with the idea that they were the biblical books and the apocryphal ones, but used the figure of twenty-two for the biblical books, in accordance with his own views elsewhere in *De mensuris*. This tradition bears the closest known resemblance to 4 Ezra.

More debate has surrounded the issue of the identification of the secret books. The regnant view is that the seventy books are apocalyptic works like 4 Ezra.[21] The arguments for this are chiefly based on the similarity between these commands and those in 12:36–37, as well as the identification of this esoteric tradition with the esoteric revelations to Abraham (3:14) and Moses (14:5–6).[22]

■ **45** This command, of course, is prefigured in 14:26. These two groups of books, the esoteric and the exoteric, have been discussed above in 14:5 Commentary and 14:6 Commentary.

■ **46** Unlike Dan 8:26; 12:4; *2 Apoc Bar* 20:3 and other places, this is not a command to seal up the apocalyptic revelation to the end but to transmit it to the wise of the people. As has been pointed out, 4 Ezra has a very strong sense of the tradition of apocalyptic teaching and this command partakes of it.

■ **47** The imagery of this verse has many resonances in contemporary and earlier literature. The series of wisdom terms is nicely paralleled in *2 Apoc Bar* 59:7, where, in the list of things revealed to Moses on Sinai, are "the root of wisdom, and the riches of understanding, and the fount of knowledge."[23] Ezra is said to have received both understanding and wisdom as a result of his inspiration in 14:40, so it is natural that the books be full of them. The imagery of fountains or streams is also common in this connection. For example, "springs of wisdom" are mentioned in Prov 18:4 and in *1 Enoch* 48:1. The image of the stream is richly developed in a wisdom context in Sir 24:30, and, once again, many parallels could be cited.

---

19   Cf. *b. Ta'an.* 8a. In the passage in *b. Baba Batra* 14b that deals with the order and authorship of the biblical books, the number is not included. In *Num. R.* 13:15–16 there is a discussion of 24 books of the written Torah and 80 books of the oral Torah.

20   So the Syriac; see J. E. Dean, *Epiphanius' Treatise on Weights and Measures: The Syriac Version* (Studies in Ancient Oriental Civilization 11; Chicago: University of Chicago, 1935) 26; cf. also "the twenty-two and the seventy-two that are apocryphal" (5, p. 20). The Greek version of this work, which is secondary, omits this second reference. The same reading also occurs in the Georgian version (ed. M. van Esbroek, *CSCO*, vols. 460–461) and in the unpublished Armenian versions; see M. E. Stone, "Concerning the Seventy-two Translators: Armenian Fragments of Epiphanius' *De mensuris et ponderibus*," *HTR* 73 (1980) 331–36.

21   See Function and Content, p. 439, on this.

22   The esoteric and exoteric revelations are discussed in 3:14 Commentary. Kaminka suggests that this is the Oral Law, and cites some texts that he claims reckon the Oral Law as seventy books. Ginzberg discusses material referring to the Mishnah as "secret" in comparison with the Bible as he identifies the Oral Law as the seventy books. However, he does not try to reach a reckoning of seventy; see Ginzberg, *Legends*, 6:446; cf. *Tanh. Wayera'* 5; *Tanh. Ki Tissa* 34, where the Mishnah is called the מסטורין which God gave to Israel additional to the written Torah; and *Exod. R.* 47:1: cf. the text from *Num. R.* discussed in n. 19 above. Box would see the issue here in terms of canonicity and the attempt to assert for the apocalyptic tradition a claim to an "officially recognized place" in Jewish tradition (p. 305). This is based on a view of the structure of Jewish canonical authority that is outdated; see A. C. Sundberg, *The Old Testament of the Early Church* (HTS 20; Cambridge: Harvard University, 1964) 113–28.

23   Note also *2 Apoc Bar* 44:14. The language is common, and many parallels could be found.

It is striking that this verse claims the superiority of the esoteric revelation. It is the secret books that are denoted by all of these wisdom terms, for the esoteric knowledge that they contain has redemptive qualities. Such a view as this is not common in Jewish sources.

■ **48** No commentary.

■ **49** In our opinion, the textual evidence is adequate to show that the conclusion of the chapter is part of the original text. It would never have been doubted, had it not been lost from the Latin version. We have divided it into two verses, since it is too long easily to treat as one.

The date is a calculation by millennia. This is discussed in some detail in 10:45 Commentary. Such dates are (*pace* Artom) in existence from the time of *Jubilees* at least. In *b. Sanh.* 97a we find a number of calculations of the end by dates *anno mundi*. The first is based on the idea of a week of millennia: the world will exist for six thousand years, then will come the end, a sabbatical millennium. The second calculation reckons the end as

coming after 85 jubilees (4,250 years). An additional tradition is quoted which, drawn from a scroll in square Hebrew letters seen by the tradent, sets the end at 4290 and then speaks of the renewal of creation after 7,000 years. Both this last tradition and the first one are based on the idea of a world week. 4 Ezra here may also be dating Ezra sometime in the fifth millennium, though it is far from certain that it knew this 6,000 + 1,000 scheme.[24]

■ **50** Ezra's assumption has already been prophesied in 14:9, and in the Commentary to that verse the idea of assumption is discussed. He is to be with those who are like him, a standard part of such prophecies.[25] The title "Scribe of the Knowledge of the Most High" is most probably an adaption of Ezra's title in the Bible. In Ezra 7:6 he is called "scribe skilled in the Law of Moses" and in 7:21 "scribe of the Law of the God of Heaven." Since now he had received a revelation of much more than the Law of Moses, his title was adapted accordingly.[26]

---

24 The verse is discussed in detail by Strack-Billerbeck, vol. 4.2, p. 995. Oddly, there it is remarked *Die 5000 Jahre bedeuten die Dauer der gegenwärtigen Weltzeit;* cf. 10:45 Commentary on this. Strack-Billerbeck suggest (ibid., 996) that the rest of the date, "three months and twelve days," is a development from Daniel's "time, two times and half a time" (12:7), interpreted as three and one half months. Their attempts in this respect are not convincing.

25 On assumption in broader terms, see 6:25 Commentary.

26 In *1 Enoch* 12:4 and 15:1, Enoch is called "Scribe of Righteousness."

Bibliography
Indices

Aalen, S.
Die *Begriffe "Licht" und "Finsternis" im Alten Testament, im Spätjudentum und in Rabbinismus* (Skrift utg. Norske Videnskaps-Akademie i Oslo 2; Hist.-Filos. Klasse 1; Oslo: J. Dybwad, 1951).

Adler, N. and Davis, J., eds.
The Service of the Synagogue: Day of Atonement, part 2 (14th ed.; London: Routledge & Kegan Paul, 1949).

Adler, N., and Davis, J., eds.
The Service of the Synagogue: Passover (14th ed.; London: Routledge & Kegan Paul, 1949).

Agourides, S.
"Apocalypse of Sedrach," *OTP,* 1:605–13.

Albeck, Ch.
"Agadot im Lichte der Pseudepigraphen," *MGWJ* 83 (1939) 162–69.

Andrae, W.
"Der kultische Garten," *Die Welt des Orients,* vol. 1 (Wupperthal: Putty, 1947).

Aptowitzer, V.
"Heavenly Temple According to the Aggadah," *Tarbiz* 2 (1931) 137–53, 257–87. In Hebrew.

Ararat, N.
"Ezra and His Activity in the Biblical and Post-Biblical Sources," *Beit Mikra* 17 (1972) 451–92.

Artom, A. S.
Hasefarim HaHiṣonim: Ḥezyonot, part 2 (Tel Aviv: Yavneh, 1969).

Attridge, H. A.
"Historiography," *Jewish Writings of the Second Temple Period* (CRINT 2.2; Assen and Philadelphia: van Gorcum and Fortress, 1984) 157–84.

Audet, J.-P.
"Affinités littéraires et doctrinales du 'Manuel de Discipline,'" *RB* 59 (1952) 219–38; 60 (1953) 41–82.

Bacher, W.
Die Agada der Tannaiten (Strassburg: Trübner, 1890).

Baethgen, F.
"Beschreibung der syrischen Handschrift 'Sachau 131' auf der königlichen Bibliothek zu Berlin," *ZAW* 6 (1886) 193–211.

Bailey, J. W.
"The Temporary Messianic Kingdom in the Literature of Early Judaism," *JBL* 53 (1934) 170–87.

Baillet, M.
"Un recueil liturgique de Qumrân, Grotte 4: Les Paroles des Luminaires," *RB* 68 (1961) 195–250.

Baldensperger, W.
Das Selbstbewusstsein Jesu im Licht der messianischen Hoffnungen seiner Zeit. I. Die messianisch-apokalyptischen Hoffnungen des Judentums (3d ed. rev.; Strassburg: Heitz & Mündle, 1903).

Ball, C. J.
The Ecclesiastical or Deuterocanonical Books of the Old Testament (Variorum Reference Edition) (London: Eyre & Spottiswoode, 1892).

Baltzer, K.
"The Meaning of the Temple in the Lukan Writings," *HTR* 58 (1965) 253–76.

Barry, P.
"The Apocalypse of Ezra," *JBL* 32 (1913) 261–72.

Basset, R.
Les apocryphes éthiopiens, no. 9 (Paris: Bibliothèque de la haute science, 1899).

Batey, R. A.
New Testament Nuptial Imagery (Leiden: Brill, 1971).

Beale, G. K.
"The Problem of the Man from the Sea in 4 Ezra 13 and Its Relation to the Messianic Concept of John's Apocalypse," *NT* 25 (1983) 182–88.

Bensly, R. L.
The Fourth Book of Ezra with Introduction by M. R. James (Texts and Studies 3.2; Cambridge: Cambridge University, 1895).

Bensly, R. L.
The Missing Fragment of the Latin Translation of the Fourth Book of Ezra (Cambridge: Cambridge University, 1875).

Berger, K.
"Zur Discussion über die Herkunft von 1. Kor. 2.9," *NTS* 26 (1978) 270–83.

Bergren, T. A.
"The 'People Coming from the East' in 5 Ezra 1:38," *JBL* 108 (1989) 657–83.

Bertholet, A.
Das religionsgeschichtliche Problem des Spätjudentums (Tübingen: Mohr, 1909).

Betz, H. D.
"The Problem of Apocalyptic Genre in Greek and Hellenistic Literature: The Case of the Oracle of Trophonius," *Apocalypticism in the Near East and the Mediterranean World* (ed. D. Hellholm; Tübingen: Mohr, 1983) 577–97.

Bezold, C.
Die Schatzhöhle (2 vols.; Leipzig: Hinrichs, 1883).

Bialer, Y. L.
Min Hagenazim: Description of Manuscripts and Historical Documents (Jerusalem: Hechal Shlomo, 1969). In Hebrew.

Bidawid, R. J., ed.
"4 Esdras," *The Old Testament in Syriac According to the Peshiṭta Version,* part 4, fasc. 3 (Leiden: Brill, 1973).

Bietenhard, H.
Die himmlische Welt im Urchristentum und Spätjudentum (WUNT 2; Tübingen: Mohr, 1951).

Biggs, R.

"More Babylonian 'Prophecies,'" *Iraq* 29 (1967) 117–32.

Billerbeck, P., with Strack, H. L.

Kommentar zum Neuen Testament aus Talmud und Midrasch (Munich: Beck, 1928).

Blake, R. P.

"The Georgian Text of Fourth Esdras from the Athos Manuscript," *HTR* 22 (1929) 57–105.

Blake, R. P.

"The Georgian Version of Fourth Esdras from the Jerusalem Manuscript," *HTR* 19 (1926) 299–375.

Bloch, J.

"The Ezra-Apocalypse: Was It Written in Hebrew, Greek or Aramaic?" *JQR* NS 48 (1957–58) 279–94.

Bloch, J.

"Some Christological Interpolations in the Ezra-Apocalypse," *HTR* 51 (1958) 87–94.

Bloch, J.

"Was There a Greek Version of the Apocalypse of Ezra?" *JQR* NS 46 (1956) 309–20.

Böhmer, E.

"Zur Lehre von Antichrist, nach Schnacken-burger," *Jahrbücher für deutsche Theologie* 4 (1859) 405–67.

Böklen, E.

Die Verwandtschaft der jüdisch-christlichen mit der parsischen Eschatologie (Göttingen: Vandenhoeck & Ruprecht, 1902).

Bogaert, P. M.

L'Apocalypse syriaque de Baruch (Sources chrétiennes 144–145; 2 vols.; Paris: Cerf, 1969).

Bogaert, P. M.

"Une Version longue inédite de la 'Visio Beati Esdrae,' dans le Légendier de Teano (Barberini Lat. 2318)," *Revue Bénédictine* 94 (1984) 50–70.

Bornkamm, G.

"Sohnschaft und Lieden," *Judentum, Urchristentum, Kirche: J. Jeremias FS* (ed. W. Eltester; BZNW 26; Berlin: Töpelmann, 1960) 188–98.

Boudreaux, P.

Catalogus Codicum Astrologorum Graecorum (Brussels: Lamertin, 1912-).

Bousset, W.

The Antichrist Legend (trans. A. H. Keane; London: Hutchinson, 1896).

Bousset, W.

Die Religion des Judentums im späthellenistischen Zeitalter (Handbuch zum NT 21; 3d ed. rev. H. Gressmann; Tübingen: Mohr, 1926).

Box, G. H.

The Apocalypse of Ezra (London: SPCK, 1917).

Box, G. H.

The Ezra-Apocalypse (London: Pitman, 1912).

Box, G. H.

"4 Ezra," *Apocrypha and Pseudepigrapha of the Old Testament* (ed. R. H. Charles; Oxford: Clarendon, 1913) 2:542–624.

Boyarin, D.

"Penitential Liturgy in 4 Ezra," *JSJ* 3 (1972) 30–34.

Brandenburger, E.

Adam und Christus: Exegetisch-Religionsgeschichtliche Untersuchung zu Röm 5:12–21 (1. Kor. 15) (WMANT 7; Neukirchen: Neukirchener, 1962).

Brandenburger, E.

"Die Auferstehung der Glaubenden als histo-risches und theologisches Problem," *Wort und Dienst* 6 (1967) 16–33.

Brandenburger, E.

Die Verborgenheit Gottes im Weltgeschehen (ATANT 68; Zurich: Theologischer Verlag, 1981).

Braude, W. G.

"The *Piska* Concerning the Sheep Which Rebelled," *PAAJR* 30 (1962) 1–35.

Braude, W. G., and Kapstein, I. J.

Tanna Debe Eliyyahu: The Lore of the School of Elijah (Philadelphia: JPS, 1981).

Braun, F. M.

"L'arrière-fond judaïque du quartrième évangile et la Commaunaté de l'Alliance," *RB* 62 (1955) 5–44.

Breech, E.

"These Fragments I Have Shored Against My Ruins: The Form and Function of 4 Ezra," *JBL* 92 (1973) 267–74.

Brock, S. P.

Review of Charlesworth, *JJS* 35 (1984) 200–209.

Bruyne, D. de

"Fragments d'une apocalypse perdue," *Revue Bénédictine* 33 (1921) 97–109.

Bruyne, D. de

"Une lecture liturgique empruntée au IVe livre d'Esdras," *Revue Bénédictine* 25 (1908) 358–60.

Bruyne, D. de

"Un manuscrit complet du IVe livre d'Esdras," *Revue Bénédictine* 24 (1907) 254–57.

Bruyne, D. de

"Quelques nouveaux documents pour la critique textuelle de l'Apocalypse d'Esdras," *Revue Bénédictine* 32 (1920) 43–47.

Bruyne, D. de

Review of Violet, vol. 1 (GCS 18), *Revue Bénédictine* 28 (1911) 104–8.

Burkitt, F. C.

Jewish and Christian Apocalypses (Schweich Lectures for 1913; London: Oxford University, 1913).

Cabrol F., and Leclercq, H.

Dictionnaire d'archéologie chrétienne et de liturgie (Paris: Letouzey et Ané, 1920).

Caquot, A., and Philonenko, M.

"Introduction générale," *La Bible: Ecrits inter-testamentaires* (Pairs: Gaillimard, 1987) i–cxlix.

Casey, M.

Son of Man: The Interpretation and Influence of Daniel 7 (London: SPCK, 1979).

Ceriani, A. M.

Monumenta Sacra e Profana e codicibus praesertim

Bibliothecae Ambrosianae (Milan: Ambrosian
Library, 1861).

Ceriani, A. M.
*Translatio Syra Pescitto Veteris Testamenti ex codice
Ambrosiano sec. fere VI photolithographice edita* (Milan:
Pogliani, 1876–79).

Charles, R. H.
The Apocalypse of Baruch (London: Black, 1896).

Charlesworth, J. H.
*The Pseudepigrapha and Modern Research with a
Supplement* (2d ed., SBLSCS 7S; Chico, Calif.:
Scholars, 1981).

Charlesworth, J. H., ed.
The Old Testament Pseudepigrapha (2 vols.; Garden
City, N.Y.: Doubleday, 1983, 1985).

Charlesworth, J. H., ed. and trans.
The Odes of Solomon (Oxford: Oxford University,
1977).

Chazon, E. Glickler
"Moses' Struggle for His Soul: A Prototype for the
Testament of Abraham, the *Greek Apocalypse of Ezra,*
and the *Apocalypse of Sedrach,*" *Second Century* 5
(1985–86) 151–64.

Clemen, C.
"Die Zusammensetzung des Buches Henoch, der
Apokalypse des Baruch und des vierten Buches
Esra," *TSK* 71 (1898) 211–46.

Cohen, G.
"Esau as Symbol in Early Medieval Thought,"
Jewish Medieval and Renaissance Studies (ed. A.
Altmann; Lown Institute Studies and Texts 4;
Cambridge: Harvard University, 1967) 19–48.

Cohen, S. D.
"The Destruction: From Scripture to Midrash,"
Prooftexts 2 (1892) 18–39.

Collins, J. J.
Apocalypse: The Morphology of a Genre (*Semeia* 14;
Missoula, Mont.: Scholars, 1979).

Collins, J. J.
The Apocalyptic Imagination (New York: Crossroad,
1984).

Collins, J. J.
The Apocalyptic Vision of the Book of Daniel (HSM 16;
Missoula, Mont.: Scholars, 1977).

Collins, J. J.
"The Date and Provenance of the Testament of
Moses," *Studies on the Testament of Moses* (ed. G. W.
E. Nickelsburg; SCS 4; Cambridge, Mass.: SBL,
1973) 15–32.

Collins, J. J.
"Introduction," *Apocalypse: The Morphology of a
Genre* (*Semeia* 14; Missoula, Mont.: Scholars, 1979)
1–19.

Colpe, C.
"ὁ υἱὸς τοῦ ἀνθρώπου," *TDNT*, 8:400–477.

Conn, W. E.
*Conversion: Perspectives on Personal and Social
Transformation* (New York: Alba House, 1978).

Conybeare, F. C.
Philostratus, The Life of Apollonius of Tyana (LCL;
London and New York: Heinemann and Mac-
millan, 1912).

Cowley, A. E.
Aramaic Papyri of the Fifth Century B.C. (Oxford:
Clarendon, 1923).

Cross, F. M.
"Studies in the Structure of Hebrew Verse: The
Prosody of Lamentation 1:1–22," *The Word of the
Lord Shall Go Forth: D. N. Freedman FS* (ed. C. L.
Meyers and M. O'Connor; Winona Lake, Ind.:
Eisenbrauns, 1983) 129–55.

Crum, W. E.
"The Literary Material," *The Metropolitan Museum
of Art Egyptian Expedition: The Monastery of Epiphanius at Thebes,* by H. E. Winlock, vol. 1 (New
York, 1923; reprint, Milan: Ristampe Anastatica,
1977).

Dahl, N. A.
"Christ, Creation and the Church," *The Background
of the New Testament and Its Eschatology* (ed. W. D.
Davies and D. Daube; Cambridge: Cambridge
University, 1956) 422–43.

Dashian, J.
*Katalog der armenischen Handschriften in der
Mechitaristen Bibliothek zu Wien* (Vienna: Mechi-
tarists, 1895). In Armenian.

Dautzenberg, G.
"Das Bild der Prophetie im 4. Esra und im
SyrBar," *Urchristliche Prophetie* (BWANT 6.4;
Stuttgart: Kohlhammer, 1975) 90–98.

Davies, W. D.
*The Gospel and the Land: Early Christianity and Jewish
Territorial Doctrine* (Berkeley and Los Angeles:
University of California, 1974).

Dean, J. E.
*Epiphanius' Treatise on Weights and Measures: The
Syriac Version* (Studies in Ancient Oriental Civi-
lization 11; Chicago: University of Chicago, 1935).

Delcor, M.
Etudes bibliques et orientales de religions comparées
(Leiden: Brill, 1979).

Denis, A.-M.
*Introduction aux pseudépigraphes grecs d'Ancien
Testament* (SVTP 1; Leiden: Brill, 1970).

Denis, A.-M., ed.
*Fragmenta pseudepigraphorum quae supersunt graeca
una cum Historicorum et auctorum Judaeorum
Hellenistarum Fragmentis* (PVTG 3; Leiden: Brill,
1970).

Dentan, R. C.
"The Second Book of Esdras," *The Interpreters One-
Volume Commentary on the Bible* (ed. C. M. Laymon;
London and Glasgow: Collins, 1971).

Desjardins, M.
"Law in 2 Baruch and 4 Ezra," *Studies in Religion /
Sciences Religieuses* 14 (1985) 25–37.

Diamant, D.
"Qumran and Sectarian Literature," *Jewish Writings of the Second Temple Period* (CRINT 2.2; Assen and Philadelphia: van Gorcum and Fortress, 1984) 483–550.

Dillmann, A.
"Pseudepigrapha," *Real-Encyklopädie für protestantische Theologie und Kirche* (ed. J. J. Herzog; vol. 12, 1st ed.; Gotha: Besser, 1860) 312.

Dillmann, A.
"Über das Adlergesicht in der Apokalypse des Esra," *Sitzungsberichte der Berliner Akademie* 8 (1888) 215–37.

Dillmann, A., ed.
Biblia Veteris Testamenti Aethiopica, vol. 5: *Libri Apocryphi* (Berlin: Asher, 1894).

Dinzelbacher, P.
"Die Vision Albrichs und die Esdras-Apokryphe," *Studien und Mitteilungen zur Geschichte des Benediktiner-Ordens* 87 (1976) 435–42.

Drower, E. S.
The Secret Adam (Oxford: Oxford University, 1960).

Drummond, J.
The Jewish Messiah (London: Longmans Green, 1877).

Duchesne-Guillemin, J.
La religion de l'Iran ancien (Paris: Presses Universitaires de France, 1962).

Dürr, L.
Die Wertung des göttliches Wortes (Leipzig: Hinrichs, 1938).

Dupont, J.
"La sagesse préparée pour les élus: Etude sur le texte de 4 Esdras 8,52–54," *Revue Bénédictine* 57 (1947) 3–11.

Ebied, R. Y.
"Some Syriac Manuscripts from the Collection of Sir E. A. Wallis Budge," *Orientalia Christiana Analecta* 197 (1974) 509–39.

Eisenstein, J. M.
Otzar HaMidrashim (New York: Eisenstein, 1915).

Eissfeldt, O.
The Old Testament: An Introduction (trans. P. R. Ackroyd; Oxford: Blackwell, 1965) 624–27.

Emerton, J. A.
"The Origin of the Son of Man Imagery," *JTS* NS 9 (1958) 225–42.

Even-Shmuel, Y.
Midrĕšei Ge'ula (Tel Aviv: Mosad Bialik, 1943).

Ewald, H. G. A.
Report on Armenian 4 Ezra in *Nachrichten von der Gesellschaft der Wissenschaften zu Göttingen* (1865) 504–16. *Non vidi.*

Ewald, H. G. A.
Das vierte Ezrabuch: Nach seinem Zeitalter, seinen arabischen Übersetzungen und einer neuen Wiederherstellung (AKGWG 11; Göttingen: Dieterichs, 1863).

Fallon, F.
4 Ezra 13: Old Testament Motifs (Harvard NT Seminar, Fall 1971).

Faye, E. de
Les apocalypses juives (Paris: Fischbacher, 1892).

Fehr, E.
Studia in Oracula Sibyllina (Uppsala: Almqvist & Wiksell, 1893).

Feldman, A.
The Parables and Similes of the Rabbis: Agricultural and Pastoral (Cambridge: Cambridge University, 1927).

Ferch, A. J.
"The Two Aeons and the Messiah in Pseudo-Philo, 4 Ezra, and 2 Baruch," *Andrews University Seminary Studies* 15 (1977) 135–51.

Festugière, A.-J.
"L'expérience religieuse du médecin Thessalos," *RB* 48 (1939) 45–54.

Festugière, A.-J.
L'hermétisme et la gnostique païenne (Paris: Aubier-Montaigne, 1967).

Festugière, A.-J.
La révélation d'Hermès Trismégiste, vol. 3 (Paris: Lecoffre, 1953).

Fiensy, D. A.
"The Revelation of Ezra," *OTP*, 1:601–3.

Finkelstein, L.
Introduction to the Treatises Abot and Abot de R. Nathan (New York: Jewish Theological Seminary, 1950). In Hebrew.

Fitzmyer, J. A.
"The Contribution of Qumran Aramaic to the Study of the New Testament," *NTS* 20 (1974) 382–407.

Fitzmyer, J. A.
The Dead Sea Scrolls: Major Publications and Tools for Study (Sources for Biblical Study 8; Missoula, Mont.: SBL and Scholars, 1977).

Flusser, D.
"The Four Empires in the Fourth Sibyl and in the Book of Daniel," *IOS* 2 (1972) 148–75.

Flusser, D.
"Qumran und die Zwölf," *Initiation* (SHR 10; Leiden: Brill, 1965) 134–46.

Fohrer, G.
"Die Struktur des alttestamentlichen Eschatologie," *TLZ* 85 (1960) 401–20.

Forbes, C.
"Early Christian Inspired Speech and Hellenistic Popular Religion," *NT* 28 (1986) 257–68.

Freidhof, G.
Vergleichende sprachliche Studien zur Gennadius-Bibel (1499) und Ostroger-Bibel (1580/81) (Frankfurter Abhandlungen zur Slavistik 21; Frankfurt-am-Main: Athenäum, 1972).

Frey, J. B.
"Le 4e livre d'Esdras ou l'Apocalypse d'Esdras,"

Dictionnaire de la Bible Supplement 1 (Paris: Letouzey et Ané, 1928) 411–18.

Friedlander, G.
Pirkê de Rabbi Eliezer (London: Kegan Paul Trench Trubner, 1916).

Firtzsche, O. F.
Libri apocryphi Veteris Testamenti (Leipzig: Brockhaus, 1871).

Frost, S. B.
Old Testament Apocalyptic (London: Epworth, 1952).

Fuchs, H.
Der geistige Widerstand gegen Rom (Berlin: de Gruyter, 1964).

Gardiner, A. H.
"New Literary Works from Ancient Egypt," *Journal of Egyptian Archaeology* 1 (1914) 100–106.

Gaster, T. H.
Myth, Legend and Custom in the Old Testament (New York and Evanston: Harper & Row, 1969).

Gaster, T. H.
Thespis (Garden City, N.Y.: Doubleday, 1961).

Geoltrain, P.
"Quatrième Livre d'Esdras," *La Bible: Ecrits Intertestamentaires* (ed. A. Dupont-Sommer and M. Philonenko; Paris: Gallimard, 1987) 1400–1470.

Gerhardsson, B.
"Sacrificial Service and Atonement in the Gospel of Matthew," *Reconciliation and Hope: L. L. Morris FS* (ed. R. J. Banks; Exeter: Paternoster, 1974) 25–35.

Gerö, S.
"'My Son the Messiah': A Note on 4 Ezra 7:28–29," *ZNW* 66 (1975) 264–67.

Gfrörer, A.
"Das Jahrhundert des Heils," *Geschichte des Urchristentums,* vol. 1 (Stuttgart: Schweitzerbart, 1838).

Gildemeister, I.
Esdrae liber quartus Arabice e codice Vaticano (Bonn: Adolphus Marcus, 1877).

Ginzberg, L.
Die Haggada bei den Kirchenvätern und in der apokryphischen Literatur (Berlin 1900).

Ginzberg, L.
The Legends of the Jews (6 vols.; Philadelphia: JPS, 1928).

Glatzer, N. N.
"After the Fall of Jerusalem," *The Judaic Tradition* (Boston: Beacon, 1969) 159–72.

Glatzer, N. N.
Untersuchungen zur Geschichtslehre der Tannaiten (Berlin: Schocken, 1933) 15–26.

Goeij, M. de
Psalmen van Salomo, 4 Ezra, Martyrium van Jesaja (de Pseudepigrafen; Kampen: Kok, 1980) 43–96.

Goldenberg, R.
"The Broken Axis: Rabbinic Judaism and the Fall of Jerusalem," *JAAR* 45.3 Supplement (1977) 870–81.

Goldenberg, R.
"Early Rabbinic Explanations of the Destruction of Jerusalem," *JJS* 33 (1982) 517–25.

Goldin, J.
The Song at the Sea (New Haven: Yale University, 1971).

Goldin, J., trans.
The Fathers According to Rabbi Nathan (reprint, New York: Schocken, 1974).

Goldschmidt, D.
Maḥazor laYamim ha-Nora'im (Jerusalem: Koren, 1970).

Goldschmidt, D.
"Maimonides' Order of Prayer According to the Oxford Manuscript," *Bulletin of the Institute for the Study of Hebrew Poetry in Jerusalem* 7 (1958) 185–213. In Hebrew.

Grabbe, L. L.
"Chronography in 4 Ezra and 2 Baruch," *SBL 1981 Seminar Papers* (ed. K. H. Richards; Chico, Calif.: Scholars, 1981) 49–63.

Gray, M. L.
"Towards the Reconstruction of 4 Esdras and the Establishment of Its Contemporary Context (B.Litt. thesis, Oxford University, 1976).

Greenberg, M.
Biblical Prose Prayer: A Window to the Popular Religion of Ancient Israel (Taubman Lectures in Jewish Studies, Sixth Series; Berkeley and Los Angeles: University of California, 1983).

Greenfield, J. C., and Stone, M. E.
"The Enochic Pentateuch and the Date of the Similitudes," *HTR* 70 (1977) 51–65.

Greenfield, J. C., and Stone, M. E.
"Remarks on the Aramaic Testament of Levi," *RB* 86 (1979) 214–30.

Gry, L.
Les dires prophétiques d'Esdras (2 vols.; Paris: Geuthner, 1930).

Gry, L.
"Essai sur le plus ancien teneur et la fortune du catalogue des signes de la fin: IV Esdras V 1–14, VI 18–29, VII 26–31," *RSPT* 29 (1940) 264–77.

Gry, L.
"La 'mort du Messias' en 4 Esdres 7:29," *Memorial Lagrange* (Paris: Gabalda, 1940) 133–39.

Gunkel, H.
Der Prophet Esra (Tübingen: Mohr, 1900).

Gunkel, H.
Review of Kabisch (q.v.), *Theologische Literaturzeitung* 16, no. 1 (1891) 5–11.

Gunkel, H.
Schöpfung und Chaos in Urzeit und Endzeit (Göttingen: Vandenhoeck & Ruprecht, 1895).

Gunkel, H.
"Das vierte Buch Esra," *Die Apokryphen und Pseudepigraphen des alten Testaments* (ed. E. Kautzsch; Tübingen: Mohr, 1900) 2:331–402.

Gunkel, H., and Begrich, J.
Einleitung in die Psalmen (Göttingener Hand-kommentar zum AT; Göttingen: Vandenhoeck & Ruprecht, 1933).

Gutschmid, A. von
"Die Apokalypse des Esra und ihre spätern Bear-beitungen," *ZfWT* 3 (1860) 1–81.

Harnisch, W.
"Das Geschichtverständnis der Apokalyptik," *Bibel und Kirche* 29 (1974) 121–25.

Harnisch, W.
"Die Ironie der Offenbarung: Exegetische Erwägungen zur Zionvision im 4.Buch Esra," *ZAW* 95 (1983) 74–95. Also: *SBL 1981 Seminar Papers,* 79–104.

Harnisch, W.
"Die Metapher als heuristisches Prinzip: Neuer-scheinungen zur Hermeneutik des Gleichnisreden Jesu," *Verkündigung und Forschung* 24 (1979) 53–89.

Harnisch, W.
"Der Prophet als Widerpart und Zeuge der Offenbarung: Erwägungen zur Interdependenz von Form und Sache im 4.Buch Esra," *Apoca-lypticism in the Mediterranean World and the Near East* (ed. D. Hellholm; Tübingen: Mohr, 1983) 461–93.

Harnisch, W.
Verhängnis und Verheißung der Geschichte: Unter-suchungen zum Zeit- und Geschichtsverständnis im 4.Buch Esra und in der syr. Baruch-apokalypse (FRLANT 97; Göttingen: Vandenhoeck & Ruprecht, 1969).

Hartman, L.
Asking for a Meaning (Coniectanea Biblica, N.T. Series 12; Uppsala: Almqvist & Wiksell, 1979).

Hartman, L.
Prophecy Interpreted (Coniectanea Biblica, N.T. Series 1; Lund: Gleerup, 1966).

Hartom, A. S.
Hasefarim Haḥiṣonim: Ḥezyonot, part 2 (Tel Aviv: Yavneh, 1969).

Harvey, J.
"Le 'Rîb-Pattern,' réquisitoire prophétique sur la rupture de l'alliance," *Biblica* 43 (1962) 172–96.

Hayman, A. P.
"The Problem of Pseudonymity in the Ezra Apocalypse," *JSJ* 6 (1975) 47–56.

Hayman, A. P.
"Rabbinic Judaism and the Problem of Evil," *Scottish Journal of Theology* 29 (1976) 461–76.

Heinemann, J.
Agadot veToldotehen: Iyyunim beHishtalshelutan shel Masorot (Jerusalem: Keter, 1974).

Heinemann, J.
"A Homily on Jeremiah and the Fall of Jerusalem," *The Biblical Mosaic: Changing Perspectives* (ed. R. Polzin and E. Rothman; SBLSS; Philadelphia: Fortress and Scholars, 1982) 27–41.

Heinemann, J.
Prayer in the Talmud (Studia Judaica 9; Berlin and New York: de Gruyter, 1977).

Hengel, M.
Judaism and Hellenism: Studies in Their Encounter in Palestine During the Early Hellenistic Period (trans. J. Bowden; Philadelphia: Fortress, 1974).

Herford, R. T.
Talmud and Apocrypha (London: Soncino, 1933).

Hertz, J. H.
The Authorized Daily Prayer Book (London: Shapiro and Valentine, 1947).

Hilgenfeld, A.
Die jüdische Apokalyptik in ihrer geschichtlichen Entwickelung (Jenna: Mauke, 1857).

Hilgenfeld, A.
"Die jüdische Apokalyptik und ihrer neuster Forschungen," *ZfWT* 3 (1860) 300–362.

Hilgenfeld, A.
Messias Judaeorum (Leipzig: Reisland, 1869).

Hilgenfeld, A.
Die Propheten Esra und Daniel und ihre neusten Bearbeitungen (Halle: Pfeffer, 1863).

Himmelfarb, M.
"Sefer Zerubbabel," *Rabbinic Fantasies: Imaginative Narratives from Classical and Medieval Hebrew Literature* (ed. M. Mirsky and D. Stern; Phila-delphia: JPS, 1990).

Himmelfarb, M.
Tours of Hell: An Apocalyptic Form in Jewish and Christian Literature (Philadelphia: University of Pennsylvania, 1983).

Hollander, H. W., and Jonge, M. de
The Testaments of the Twelve Patriarchs: A Com-mentary (SPVT 8; Leiden: Brill, 1985).

Hunt, A. S., ed.
The Oxyrhynchus Papyri (London: Egyptian Exploration Fund, 1910) 7:1–15.

Issaverdens, J., trans.
The Uncanonical Writings of the Old Testament Found in the Armenian Mss. of the Library of St. Lazarus (Venice: Monastery of St. Lazarus, 1901; 2d ed., 1934).

Jacobs, I.
"Elements of Near Eastern Mythology in Rabbinic Aggadah," *JJS* 38 (1977) 1–11.

James, M. R.
Apocrypha Anecdota (Texts and Studies 2.3; Cambridge: Cambridge University, 1893).

James, M. R.
Apocrypha Anecdota (second series) (Texts and Studies 5.1; Cambridge: Cambridge University, 1897).

James, M. R.
The Apocryphal New Testament (Oxford: Clarendon, 1963).

James, M. R.
The Biblical Antiquities of Philo (London: SPCK, 1917; reprint with Prolegomenon by L. H. Feldman, New York: Ktav, 1971).

James, M. R.
"Ego Salathiel qui et Ezras," *JTS* 18 (1917) 167–69.

James, M. R.
"Inventiones Nominum," *JTS* 4 (1902/03) 218–44.

James, M. R.
The Lost Apocrypha of the Old Testament (London: SPCK, 1920).

James, M. R.
"Salathiel qui et Esdras," *JTS* 19 (1918) 347–49.

James, M. R.
The Testament of Abraham (Texts and Studies 2.2; Cambridge: Cambridge University, 1892).

Jellinek, A.
Bet ha-Midrasch (reprint, Jerusalem: Bamberger and Wahrmann, 1938; 6 vols. in 2).

Jenni, E.
"Das Wort ʿôlām im Alten Testament," *ZAW* 64 (1952) 177–246; 65 (1953) 1–35.

Jervell, J.
Imago Dei (Göttingen: Vandenhoeck & Ruprecht, 1960).

Jonge, M. de, et al.
The Testaments of the Twelve Patriarchs (PSVTG 1.2; Leiden: Brill, 1978).

Jülicher, A.
Die Gleichnisreden Jesu (Tübingen: Mohr, 1899).

Kabisch, R.
Das vierte Buch Esra auf seine Quellen untersucht (Göttingen: Vandenhoeck & Ruprecht, 1889).

Kahana, A.
HaSefarim HaHitsonim (Tel Aviv: Masada, 1959). In Hebrew.

Kaminka, A.
"Beiträge zur Erklärung der Esra-Apokalypse und zur Rekonstruktion ihres hebräischen Urtextes," *MGWJ* 76 NF 40 (1932) 121–38, 206–12, 494–511, 604–7; 77 NF 41 (1933) 339–55. Also *separatim* Breslau: Marcus, 1934.

Kaminka, A.
Sefer Ḥazonot ʾAssir Sheʾaltiʾel (Tel Aviv: Dvir, 1936). In Hebrew.

Kaufmann, Y.
Toledot Haʾemuna HaYisraʾelit (Jerusalem: Mosad Bialik, 1937).

Kee, H. C.
"'The Man' in 4 Ezra: Growth of a Tradition," *SBL 1981 Seminar Papers* (ed. K. H. Richards; Chico, Calif.: Scholars, 1981) 199–208.

Keulers, J.
"Die eschatologische Lehre des vierten Esrabuches," *Biblische Studien* 20, nos. 2–3 (1922) 1–240. Also *separatim* Freiburg i. Br.: Herder, 1922.

Kippenberg, H. G.
"Dann wird der Orient Herrschen und der Okzident Dienen," *Spiegel und Gleichnis: Festschrift für Jacob Taubes* (ed. N. W. Bolz and W. Hübner; Würzburg: Königshausen & Neumann, 1983) 40–48.

Klausner, J.
The Messianic Idea in Israel (trans. W. F. Stinespring; London: Allen & Unwin, 1956).

Klijn, A. F. J.
"Textual Criticism of 4 Ezra: State of Affairs and Possibilities," *SBL 1981 Seminar Papers* (ed. K. H. Richards; Chico, Calif.: Scholars, 1981) 217–27.

Klijn, A. F. J., ed.
Der lateinische Text der Apokalypse des Esra (TU 131; Berlin: Akademie, 1983).

Kneucker, J. J.
Das Buch Baruch (Leipzig: Brockhaus, 1879).

Knibb, M. A.
"Apocalyptic and Wisdom in 4 Ezra," *JSJ* 13 (1983) 56–74.

Knibb, M. A.
The Ethiopic Book of Enoch (Oxford: Oxford University, 1978).

Knibb, M. A., and Coggins, R. J.
The First and Second Books of Esdras (Cambridge Bible Commentary; Cambridge: Cambridge University, 1979).

Koch, K.
"Esras erste Vision: Weltzeiten und Weg des Höchsten," *BZ* NF 22 (1978) 46–75.

Koch, K.
The Rediscovery of Apocalyptic (Naperville, Ill.: Allenson, 1972).

Koch, K.
"Der Schatz im Himmel," *Leben angesichts des Todes: H. Thieleke FS* (Tübingen: Mohr, 1969) 47–60.

Kraft, R. A.
"'Ezra' Materials in Judaism and Christianity," *Aufstieg und Niedergang der römischen Welt* (Band 19.1; ed. H. Temporini and W. Haase; Berlin: de Gruyter, 1979) 119–36.

Kuhn, G. von
"Zur *Assumptio Mosis*," *ZAW* 43 (1925) 124–29.

Kʿurcʿikidze, Cʿ., ed.
Dzveli Agʿtʿkʿmis Apokʿripʿebis Versiebi (2 vols.; Tbilisi: Mecʿniereba, 1970, 1973).

Lacocque, A.
"The Vision of the Eagle in 4 Esdras: A Rereading of Daniel 7 in the First Century C.E.," *SBL 1981 Seminar Papers* (ed. K. H. Richards; Chico, Calif.: Scholars, 1981) 237–58.

Lagrange, M. J.
"Notes sur le messianisme au temps de Jésus," *RB* NS 2 (1905) 481–514.

Lagrange, M. J.
Review of Vagany (q.v.), *RB* NS 4 (1907) 614–16.

Lambert, W. G.
Babylonian Wisdom Literature (Oxford: Oxford University, 1960).

Laurence, R.
Primi Ezrae Libri Versio Aethiopica (Oxford: Oxford University, 1820).

Lazarus-Yaffe, H.
"Ezra-ʿUseir: History of a Pre-Islamic Polemical Motif Through Islam to the Beginning of Biblical Criticism," *Tarbiz* 55 (1986) 359–79. In Hebrew.

Leclercq, H.
Dictionnaire de archéologie chrétienne et de liturgie (Paris: Letouzey et Ané, 1920).

Le Hir, A. M.
"Du IVe livre d'Esdras," *Etudes bibliques par M. l'abbé Le Hir* (Paris: Albanel, 1869) 1:139–250.

Lee, F.
An Epistolary Discourse Concerning the Books of Ezra, Genuine and Spurious (London: "by a Friend," 1722).

Leipoldt, J.
"Ein säidisches Bruchstück des vierten Esra-buches," *ZfÄS* 41 (1904) 138–40.

Leslau, W.
A Falasha Anthology: The Black Jews of Ethiopia (1951; reprint, New York: Schocken, 1969).

Lewy, H.
The Chaldean Oracles and Theurgy (Recherches d'archéologie, de philologie et d'histoire 13; Cairo: Inst. Franc. d'arch. orien., 1956).

Lewy, H.
Sobria Ebrietas: Untersuchungen zur Geschichte der antiken Mystik (BZNW 9; Gießen: Töpelmann, 1929).

Licht, J. S.
The Rule Scroll (Jerusalem: Bialik Institute, 1965). In Hebrew.

Licht, J. S.
Sefer Ḥazon ʿEzra (Sifriyat Dorot 6; Jerusalem: Bialik Institute, 1968). In Hebrew.

Licht, J. S.
"Taxo or the Apocalyptic Doctrine of Vengeance," *JJS* 12 (1961) 95–103.

Licht, J. S.
"Time and Eschatology in Qumran," *JJS* 16 (1965) 177–82.

Lidzbarski, M.
Ginza: Der Schatz oder Das grosse Buch der Mandäer (Göttingen and Leipzig: Vandenhoeck & Hinrichs, 1925).

Lidzbarski, M.
Das Johannesbuch der Mandäer (Gießen: Töpelmann, 1915).

Lieberman, S.
Hellenism in Jewish Palestine (New York: Jewish Theological Seminary, 1950).

Lieberman, S.
"Roman Legal Institutions in Early Rabbinics and in the *Acta Martyrum*," *JQR* 35 (1944/45) 1–57.

Linnemann, E.
Parables of Jesus: Introduction and Exposition (London: SPCK, 1966).

Loewe, R.
"A Jewish Counterpart of the Acts of the Alexandrians," *JJS* 12–14 (1961) 105–22.

Loewenstamm, S.
"The Death of Moses," *Studies on the Testament of Abraham* (ed. G. W. E. Nickelsburg; SCS 6; Missoula, Mont.: Scholars, 1976) 198–201.

Luck, U.
"Das Weltverständnis in der jüdischen Apokalyptik dargestellt am äthiopischen Henoch und am 4. Esra," *ZfTK* 73 (1976) 283–305.

Lücke, F.
Versuch einer vollständingen Einleitung in die Offenbarung des Johannes und in die apokalyptische Literatur überhaupt (2d ed.; Bonn: Weber, 1852).

Mahé, J.-P.
"Le Livre d'Adam géorgien," *Studies in Gnosticism and Hellenistic Religions: Quispel FS* (ed. R. van den Broek and M. J. Vermaseren; Leiden: Brill, 1981) 227–60.

Maier, J.
Die Texte vom Toten Meer (2 vols.; Munich and Basel: Reinhardt, 1960).

Martini, R.
Pugio Fidei adversus Mauros et Judaeos cum observationibus (ed. J. de Voisin; reprint, Farnborough: Gregg Press, 1967).

Matter, E. A.
"The 'Revelatio Esdrae' in Latin and English Traditions," *Revue Bénédictine* 92 (1982) 376–92.

McNamara, M.
The Apocrypha in the Irish Church (Dublin: Institute for Advanced Studies, 1975).

Meade, D. G.
Pseudonymity and Canon (Grand Rapids: Wm. B. Eerdmans, 1986).

Mercati, G. S.
"The Apocalypse of Sedrach," *JTS* 11 (1910) 572–73.

Mercati, G. S.
Note di Letteratura Biblica e Cristiana Antica (Studi e Testi 5; Rome: Vatican, 1901).

Merkur, D.
"The Visionary Practice of Jewish Apocalyptists." Forthcoming.

Messel, N.
Die Einheitlichkeit der jüdischen Eschatologie (BZAW 30; Giessen: Töpelmann, 1915).

Metzger, B. M.
"The Fourth Book of Ezra," *OTP*, 1:516–59.

Metzger, B. M.
"The 'Lost' Section of II Esdres (= IV Ezra)," *JBL* 76 (1957) 153–65.

Molitor, J.
Glossarium Ibericum in quattuor evangelia et actus apostolorum antiquioris versionis etiam textu Chanmeti et Haemeti complectens (CSCO 228, Subsidia 20; 2 vols.; Louvain: CSCO, 1962).

Momigliano, A.
"The Origins of Universal History," *Annali della Scuola Normale Superiore di Pisa*, ser. 3, 12.2 (1982) 533–60.

Montgomery, J. A.
Daniel: A Critical and Exegetical Commentary (Edinburgh: T. & T. Clark, 1927).

Moore, G. F.
"Intermediaries in Jewish Theology—Memra, Shekinah, Metatron," *HTR* 15 (1922) 41–85.

Moore, G. F.
Judaism in the First Centuries of the Christian Era (3 vols.; Cambridge: Harvard University, 1962).

Morfill, W. R., and Charles, R. H.
The Book of the Secrets of Enoch (Oxford: Oxford University, 1896).

Mueller, J. R., and Robbins, G. A.
"Vision of Ezra," *OTP*, 1:581–90.

Müller, U. B.
Die griechische Ezra-Apokalypse (JSHRZ 5; Gütersloh: Mohn, 1976).

Müller, U. B.
Messias und Menschensohn in jüdischen Apokalypsen und in der Offenbarung Johannes (SZNT 6; Gütersloh: Mohn, 1972).

Munck, J.
"Le discours d'adieu dans le Nouveau Testament et dans la littérature biblique," *Mélanges M. Goguel* (Neuchâtel: Delachaux et Niestlé, 1950) 155–70.

Mundle, W.
"Das religiöse Problem des IV.Esrabuches," *ZAW* NF 6 (1929) 222–49.

Mussafia, A.
"Sulla Visione di Tundalo," *Sitzungsber. d. Kaiserl. Ak., Phil.-Hist. Klasse* (Vienna: 1871) 157–206. *Non vidi.*

Mussies, G.
"When Do Graecisms Prove that a Latin Text Is a Translation?" *Vruchten van de Uithof: H. A. Brongers FS* (Utrecht: Theologisch Institut, 1984) 100–119.

Myers, J. M.
1 and 2 Esdras (AB 42; Garden City, N.Y.: Doubleday, 1974).

Nau, F.
"Analyse de deux opuscules astrologiques attribués au prophète Esdras," *ROC* 12 (1907) 14–15.

Nestle, E.
Review of Violet 1, *ThLB* (1910) 507–8.

Neubauer, A.
"Where Are the Ten Tribes?" *JQR* 1 (1888–89) 14–28, 95–114, 185–201, 408–23.

Nickelsburg, G. W. E.
"Apocalyptic and Myth in 1 Enoch 6–11," *JBL* 96 (1977) 383–405.

Nickelsburg, G. W. E.
"The Bible Rewritten and Expanded," *Jewish Writings of the Second Temple Period* (ed. M. E. Stone; CRINT 2.2; Assen and Philadelphia: van Gorcum and Fortress, 1984) 89–156.

Nickelsburg, G. W. E.
Jewish Literature Between the Bible and the Mishnah (Philadelphia: Fortress, 1981).

Nickelsburg, G. W. E.
Resurrection, Immortality, and Eternal Life in Intertestamental Judaism (HTS 26; Cambridge: Harvard University, 1972).

Nickelsburg, G. W. E., and Stone, M. E.
Faith and Piety in Early Judaism (Philadelphia: Fortress, 1983).

Nitzan, B.
The Habbakuk Commentary Scroll (Jerusalem: Mosad Bialik, 1986). In Hebrew.

Nötscher, F.
Gotteswege und Menschenwege in der Bible und in Qumran (BBB 15; Bonn: Hanstein, 1958).

Nötscher, F.
Zur theologischen Terminologie der Qumran-Texte (BBB 10; Bonn: Hanstein, 1956).

Nordheim, E. von
"Die Zitat des Paulus in 1. Kor. 2,9 und seine Beziehung zum koptischen Testamentum Jacobs," *ZNW* 65 (1974) 112–20.

Oesterley, W. O. E.
2 Esdras (The Ezra Apocalypse) (Westminster Commentaries; London: Methuen, 1933).

Oesterley, W. O. E., and Box, G. H.
The Religion and Worship of the Synagogue (London: Pitman, 1907).

Outtier, B.
Review of Kʿurcʿikidze in *Bedi Kartlisa* 33 (1975) 380–83.

Perles, F.
"Notes sur les apocryphes et les pseudépigraphes," *REJ* 73 (1921) 173–85.

Philonenko, M.
"L'âme à l'étroit," *Hommages à André Dupont-Sommer* (ed. A. Caquot and M. Philonenko; Paris: Adrien-Maisonneuve, 1971) 421–28.

Philonenko, M.
"Remarques sur un hymne essénien de charactère gnostique," *Semitica* 11 (1961) 43–54.

Philonenko, M.
"La sixième vision de 4 Esdras et les 'Oracles d'Hystaspe,'" *L'apocalyptique* (ed. M. Philonenko; Etudes d'histoire des religions 3; Paris: Geuthner, 1977) 127–35.

Philonenko, M., Picard, J. P., Rosenstiehl, J.-M., and Schmidt, F.
Pseudépigraphes de l'Ancien Testament et Manuscrits de la Mer Morte 1 (Cahiers de la Revue d'Histoire et de Philosophie Religieuses 41; Paris: Presses Universitaires de France, 1967).

Pines, S.
"Eschatology and the Concept of Time in the Slavonic Book of Enoch," *Types of Redemption* (ed. R. J. Z. Werblowsky and C. J. Bleeker; Leiden: Brill, 1970) 77–82.

Polotsky, H. J.
"Suriel der Trompeter," *Le Muséon* 49 (1937) 231–43.

Pope, M.
Job (AB; Garden City, N.Y.: Doubleday, 1963).

Pope, M.
Song of Songs (AB; Garden City, N.Y.: Doubleday, 1964).

Porter, F. C.
The Messages of the Apocalyptical Writers (New York: Scribner's, 1905).

Porter, F. C.
"The Yeçer Hara," *Biblical and Semitic Studies: Yale Bicentennial Publications* (New York: Scribner's, 1902) 93–156.

Preuschen, E.
"Ardaf, IV.Esra 9,26 und der Montanismus," *ZNW* 1 (1900) 265–66.

Preuschen, E.
Review of Violet (q.v.), *Berliner Philologischer Wochenschrift* 18 (1913) 547–51.

Prigent, P.
"'Ce que l'oeil n'a pas vu,' 1 Cor 2,9," *TZ* 14 (1958) 416–29.

Prigent, P.
L'Epître de Barnabé i-xvi et ses sources (Etudes Bibliques; Paris: Lecoffre, 1961).

Pritchard, J.
Ancient Near Eastern Texts (Princeton: Princeton University, 1954).

Quispel, G.
"Ezekiel 1:26 in Jewish Mysticism and Gnosis," *VC* 34 (1980) 1–13.

Rad, G. von
Der heilige Krieg im alten Israel (Zurich: Zwingli, 1951).

Rad, G. von
"Hiob xxxviii und die altägyptische Weisheit," *Gesammelte Studien zum Alten Testament* (Munich: Theologische Bücherei, 1958) 252–71.

Rad, G. von
Wisdom in Israel (trans. J. D. Martin; Nashville and New York: Abingdon, 1978).

Rambo, L. R.
"Conversion," *Encyclopedia of Religions*, 4:73–79.

Rambo, L. R.
"Current Research on Religious Conversion," *RSR* 8.2 (1982) 146–59.

Reau, L.
Iconographie de l'art chrétien, 2.2 Nouveau Testament (Paris: Presses Universitaires de France, 1957).

Reese, J. M.
Hellenistic Influence on the Book of Wisdom and Its Consequences (Rome: Biblical Institute, 1970).

Reymond, P.
L'eau, sa vie, et sa signification dans l'A.T. (VTSup 6; Leiden: Brill, 1958).

Riessler, P.
Altjüdisches Schrifttum ausserhalb der Bibel (Heidelberg: Kerle, 1928).

Rigaux, P. B.
L'antéchrist et l'opposition au royaume messianique dans l'ancien et le nouveau Testament (Paris: Gabalda, 1932).

Robinson, J. M.
The Nag Hammadi Library (New York: Doubleday, 1977).

Rössler, D.
Gesetz und Geschichte: Studien zur Theologie der jüdischen Apokalyptik und der pharisäischen Orthodoxie (WMANT 3; Neukirchen: Neukirchener, 1960).

Roscher, W. H.
Die Hippokratische Schrift von der Siebenzahl (Paderborn: Schöningh, 1913).

Rosenstiehl, J.-M.
L'Apocalypse d'Elie (Textes et Etudes pour servir à l'histoire du Judaism intertestamentaire 1; Paris: Geuthner, 1972).

Rosenthal, F.
Vier apokryphische Bücher aus der Zeit und Schule R. Akiba's (Leipzig: Schulze, 1885).

Rouse, W. H. D., trans.
Lucretius, de rerum natura (rev. by M. F. Smith; Loeb Classical Library; Cambridge, Mass., and London: Harvard University and Heinemann, 1982).

Rowland, C.
The Open Heaven (New York: Crossroad, 1982).

Rowland, C.
"The Vision of God in Apocalyptic Literature," *JSJ* 10 (1979) 137–54.

Rubinkiewicz, R.
"Un fragment grec du IVe Livre d'Esdras (Chapitres XI et XII)," *Le Muséon* 89 (1976) 75–87.

Russell, D. S.
The Method and Message of Jewish Apocalyptic (OTL; Philadelphia: Westminster, 1964).

Rutherford, A.
"The Apocalypse of Sedrach," *Ante-Nicene Fathers* (5th ed.; Edinburgh: T. & T. Clark; Grand Rapids: Wm. B. Eerdmans, 1986) 10:175–80.

Ryle, H. E., and James, M. R.
Psalms of the Pharisees commonly called The Psalms of Solomon (Cambridge: Cambridge University, 1891).

Sanders, E. P.
Paul and Palestinian Judaism (Philadelphia: Fortress, 1977).

Sanders, J. A.
The Psalms Scroll of Qumrân Cave 11 (Discoveries in the Judean Desert of Jordan 4; Oxford: Oxford University, 1965).

Sargant, W. W.
Battle for the Mind: A Physiology of Conversion and Brainwashing (New York: Doubleday, 1957).

Sarghissian, B.
Studies on the Apocryphal Books of the Old Testament (Venice: Monastery of St. Lazarus, 1898). In Armenian.

Sayler, G. B.
Have the Promises Failed: A Literary Analysis of 2 Baruch (SBLDS 72; Chico, Calif.: Scholars, 1984).

Schäfer, P.
Gershom Scholem Reconsidered: The Aim and Purpose of Early Jewish Mysticism (The Twelfth Sacks Lecture; Oxford: Oxford Centre for Postgraduate Hebrew Studies, 1986).

Schäfer, P.
"Die Lehre von den zwei Welten im 4.Buch Esra und in der tannaitischen Literatur," *Studien zur Geschichte und Theologie des rabbinischen Judentums* (AGAJU 15; Leiden: Brill, 1978) 244–91.

Schäfer, P.
"Der Termin der Erlösung im 4.Buch Esra und in der tannaitischen Literatur," *ZDMG Suppl.* 4 (1980) 134–36.

Schechter, S.
"Geniza Fragments," *JQR* 16 (1904) 425–52.

Schechter, S.
Some Aspects of Rabbinic Theology (London: Black, 1909).

Schieffer, F. W.
Die religiösen und ethischen Anschauungen des 4. Ezrabuches (Leipzig: Dörffling & Franke, 1901).

Schmidt, F.
"L'autorité du 'Quatrième Livre d'Esdras' dans la discussion sur la parenté des Juifs et des Indiens d'Amérique (1540–1661)," *La littérature inter-testamentaire, Colloque de Strassbourg (17–19 Octobre, 1983)* (ed. A. Caquot; Paris: Presses Universitaires de France, 1985) 203–20.

Schmidt, F.
"Azareth en Amérique: L'autorité du Quatrième Livre d'Esdras dans la discussion sur la parenté des Juifs et des Indiens d'Amérique," *Moïse géographe: Recherches sur les représentations juives et chrétiennes de l'espace (1530–1729)* (ed. F. Desreumaux and F. Schmidt; Paris: Vrin, 1988) 155–201.

Schmidt, F.
"Histoire du judaïsme à l'époque héllénistique et romaine," *An. Ec. Prat. Htes Et. 91 5e Sect. Sc. Rel.* (1982/83) 289–90.

Schmidt, F.
"Le Testament d'Abraham" (diss., Strassbourg, 1971).

Schmidt, F.
"The Two Recensions of the Testament of Abraham," *Studies on the Testament of Abraham* (ed. G. W. E. Nickelsburg; SCS 6; Missoula, Mont.: Scholars, 1976) 65–84.

Scholem, G. G.
Jewish Gnosticism, Merkabah Mysticism and Talmudic Tradition (New York: Jewish Theological Seminary, 1960).

Scholem, G. G.
Major Trends in Jewish Mysticism (New York: Schocken, 1941).

Schrader, E.
Die Keilinschriften und das Alte Testament (Berlin: Reuther & Reichard, 1902).

Schreiner, J.
Das 4.Buch Esra (ed. W. G. Kümmel et al.; JSHRZ 5.4; Gütersloh: Mohn, 1981).

Schubert, K.
"Die Entwickelung der Aufstehungslehre von der nachexilischen bis zu frührabbinischen Zeit," *BZ* NF 6 (1962) 177–214.

Schürer, E.
Geschichte des jüdischen Volkes im Zeitalter Jesu Christi (3 vols.; 4th ed.; Leipzig: Hinrichs, 1909).

Schürer, E.
The History of the Jewish People in the Age of Jesus Christ (rev. and ed. G. Vermès and F. Millar; 3 vols.; Edinburgh: T. & T. Clark, 1973, 1979, 1986).

Schütz, R.
Die Offenbarung des Johannes und Kaiser Domitian (FRLANT 50; Göttingen: Vandenhoeck & Ruprecht, 1933).

Schuller, E.
Non-Canonical Psalms from Qumran: A Pseud-epigraphic Collection (HSS 28; Atlanta: Scholars, 1986).

Schwartz, J.
"Sur la date de IV Esdras," *Mélanges André Neher* (Paris: Adrien-Maisonneuve, 1975) 191–96.

Scott, R. B. Y.
"Behold, He Cometh with Clouds," *NTS* 5 (1958–59) 127–32.

Shutt, R. J. H.
"The Apocalypse of Sedrach," *The Apocryphal Old Testament* (ed. H. D. F. Sparks; Oxford: Oxford University, 1984) 953–66.

Shutt, R. J. H.
"The Greek Apocalypse of Esdras," *The Apocryphal Old Testament* (ed. H. D. F. Sparks; Oxford: Oxford University, 1984) 927–41.

Shutt, R. J. H.
"The Vision of Esdras," *The Apocryphal Old Testament* (ed. H. D. F. Sparks; Oxford: Oxford University, 1984) 943–51.

Siebert, J.
Lexikon der christlicher Kunst (Fribourg: Herder, 1980).

Sigwalt, C.
"Die Chronologie des 4. Buches Esdras," *BZ* 9 (1911) 146–48.

Simonsen, D.
"Ein Midrasch im 4.Buch Esra," *Festschrift zum Israel Lewy's 70. Geburtstag* (Breslau: Marcus, 1911) 270–78 and *separatim*.

Singer, S., trans.
The Authorized Daily Prayer Book (London: Eyre & Spottiswoode, 1900).

455

Sjöberg, E.

Der Menschensohn im äthiopischen Henochbuch (Lund: Gleerup, 1946).

Sjöberg, E.

Der verborgene Menschensohn in den Evangelien (Acta reg. soc. humanorum litt. Lundensis 51; Lund: Gleerup, 1955).

Smith, J. Z.

"The Prayer of Joseph," *Religions in Antiquity: E. R. Goodenough Memorial* (ed. J. Neusner; SHR 14; Leiden: Brill, 1968) 253–94.

Smith, M.

"Pseudepigraphy in the Israelite Literary Tradition,' *Pseudepigraphai* (Entretiens sur l'antiquité classique 18; Vandoeuvres-Geneva: Fondation Hardt, 1972) 191–227.

Smith, M.

Tannaitic Parallels to the Gospels (JBLMS 6; Philadelphia: SBL, 1961).

Soden, W. von

"Zum akkadischen Wörterbuch. 88–96," *Orientalia* 26 (1957) 127–28.

Sparks, H. D. F.

The Apocryphal Old Testament (Oxford: Oxford University, 1984).

Sparks, H. D. F.

"1 Kor. 2.9, A Quotation from the Coptic Testament of Jacob?" *ZNW* 76 (1976) 269–76.

Speyer, W.

Bücherfunde in der Glaubenswerbung der Antike (Göttingen: Vandenhoeck & Ruprecht, 1970).

Speyer, W.

Die literarische Fälschung im heidnischen und christlichen Altertum (HAW 1,2; Munich: Beck, 1971).

Steck, O. H.

"Die Aufnahme von Genesis 1 in Jubiläen 2 und 4.Esra 6," *JSJ* 8 (1977) 154–82.

Stone, M. E.

"Apocalyptic Literature," *Jewish Writings of the Second Temple Period* (ed. M. E. Stone; CRINT 2.2; Assen and Philadelphia: van Gorcum and Fortress, 1984) 383–441.

Stone, M. E.

"Apocalyptic: Vision or Hallucination?" *Milla wa-Milla* 14 (1974) 47–56.

Stone, M. E.

"The Apocryphal Literature in the Armenian Tradition," *Proceedings of the Israel Academy of Sciences and Humanities* 4 (1969) 59–77.

Stone, M. E.

"Apocryphal Notes and Readings. 7. Saeculum as 'Heaven' in 4 Ezra," *IOS* 1 (1971) 129–31.

Stone, M. E.

Armenian Apocrypha Relating to the Patriarchs and Prophets (Jerusalem: Israel Academy of Sciences and Humanities, 1982).

Stone, M. E., "Coherence and Inconsistency in the Apocalypses: The Case of 'the End' in 4 Ezra," *JBL* 102 (1983) 229–43.

Stone, M. E.

"The Concept of the Messiah in 4 Ezra," *Religions in Antiquity: E. R. Goodenough Memorial* (ed. J. Neusner; SHR 14; Leiden: Brill, 1968) 295–312.

Stone, M. E.

"Concerning the Seventy-two Translators: Armenian Fragments of Epiphanius' *De mensuris et ponderibus*," *HTR* 73 (1980) 331–36.

Stone, M. E.

"Ezra, Apocalypse of," *Encyclopedia Judaica*, 6:1108–9.

Stone, M. E.

Features of the Eschatology of IV Ezra (Harvard dissertation, Cambridge: Harvard University, 1965; HSM, Atlanta: Scholars, 1989).

Stone, M. E.

"Greek Apocalypse of Ezra," *OTP*, 1:561–79.

Stone, M. E.

"Lists of Revealed Things in the Apocalyptic Literature," *Magnalia Dei (G. E. Wright Memorial)* (ed. F. M. Cross, W. E. Lemke, and P. D. Miller; Garden City, N.Y.: Doubleday, 1976) 414–54.

Stone, M. E.

"Manuscripts and Readings of Armenian 4 Ezra," *Textus* 6 (1968) 48–61.

Stone, M. E.

"The Metamorphosis of Ezra: Jewish Apocalypse and Medieval Vision," *JTS* NS 33 (1982) 1–18.

Stone, M. E.

"A New Manuscript of the Syro-Arabic Version of the Fourth Book of Ezra," *JSJ* 8 (1977) 183–84.

Stone, M. E.

"The Parabolic Use of Natural Order in Judaism of the Second Temple Age," *Gilgul: Werblowsky FS* (ed. S. Shaked, D. Shulman, and G. Stroumsa; Numen Supplement 50; Leiden, Copenhagen, and New York: Brill, 1987) 298–308.

Stone, M. E.

"Paradise in 4 Ezra iv.8 and vii.36, viii.52," *JJS* 17 (1966) 85–88.

Stone, M. E.

The Penitence of Adam (CSCO 429–430; Scriptores Armeniaci 13–14; Louvain: Peeters, 1981).

Stone, M. E.

"Pseudepigraphy and Reflexivity." Forthcoming.

Stone, M. E.

"The Question of the Messiah in 4 Ezra," *Judaisms and Their Messiahs at the Turn of the Christian Era* (ed. J. Neusner, W. S. Green, and E. S. Frerichs; New York: Cambridge University, 1987) 209–24.

Stone, M. E.

"Questions of Ezra," *OTP*, 1:591–99.

Stone, M. E.

"Reactions to Destructions of the Second Temple," *JSJ* 12 (1982) 195–204.

Stone, M. E.

Scriptures, Sects and Visions: A Profile of Judaism from Ezra to the Jewish Revolts (Philadelphia: Fortress, 1980).

Stone, M. E.

Signs of the Judgement, Onomastica Sacra and The Generations from Adam (University of Pennsylvania Armenian Texts and Studies 3; Chico, Calif.: Scholars, 1981).

Stone, M. E.

"Some Features of the Armenian Version of 4 Ezra," *Le Muséon* 79 (1966) 387–400.

Stone, M. E.

"Some Remarks on the Textual Criticism of 4 Ezra," *HTR* 60 (1967) 107–15.

Stone, M. E.

"Three Transformations in Judaism: Scripture, History, and Redemption," *Numen* 32 (1985) 218–35.

Stone, M. E.

"II Esdras," *The Books of the Bible* (ed. B. W. Anderson; New York: Scribner's). Forthcoming.

Stone, M. E.

"Two New Discoveries Touching on the Non-canonical Ezra Books," *Sion* 52 (1978) 45–50. In Armenian.

Stone, M. E.

"The Way of the Most High and the Injustice of God," *Knowledge of God Between Alexander and Constantine* (ed. R. van den Broek, T. Baarda, and J. Mansfeld; Leiden: Brill, 1989) 132–42.

Stone, M. E., ed.

The Armenian Version of IV Ezra (University of Pennsylvania Armenian Texts and Studies 1; Missoula, Mont: Scholars, 1979).

Stone, M. E., and Strugnell, J.

The Books of Elijah: Parts 1–2 (SBLTT 18, PS 8; Missoula, Mont.: Scholars, 1979).

Ströbel, A.

"Die Allegorie von der Ferse Esaus," *Untersuchungen zur eschatologischen Verzögerungsproblem* (Leiden and Cologne: Brill, 1961) 37–41.

Sundberg, A. C.

The Old Testament of the Early Church (HTS 20; Cambridge: Harvard University, 1964).

Swain, J. W.

"The Theory of Four Monarchies," *Classical Philology* 35 (1940) 1–21.

Talmon, S.

"The Calendar Reckoning of the Sect from the Judean Desert," *Scripta Hierosolymitana* 4 (1958) 162–99.

Tarchnisvili, M.

Geschichte der kirchlichen georgischen Literatur (Studi e Testi 185; Rome: Vatican, 1955).

Theisohn, J.

Der auserwählte Richter (Göttingen: Vandenhoeck & Ruprecht, 1975).

Thoma, C.

"Jüdische Apokalyptik am Ende des ersten nach-christlichen Jahrhunderts: Religionsgeschichtliche

Bemerkungen zur syrischen Baruchapokalypse und zum vierten Esrabuch," *Kairos* 11 (1969) 134–44.

Thompson, A. L.

Responsibility for Evil in the Theodicy of IV Ezra (SBLDS 29; Missoula, Mont.: Scholars, 1977).

Tischendorf, C. von

Apocalypses Apocryphae Mosis, Esdrae, Pauli, Iohannis (Leipzig: Mendelssohn, 1866).

Toombs, L. E.

"War, Ideas of," *IDB*, 4:796–801.

Torrey, C. C.

The Apocryphal Literature: A Brief Introduction (New Haven: Yale University, 1945).

Torrey, C. C.

"The Messiah Son of Ephraim," *JBL* 66 (1947) 253–77.

Torrey, C. C.

"A Twice-buried Apocalypse," *Munera Studiosa* (ed. M. H. Shepherd and S. E. Johnson; Cambridge, Mass.: Episcopal Theological School, 1946) 23–39.

Tundeanu, E.

"Dieu créa l'homme de huit elements et tira son nom des quatre coins du monde," *Revue des Etudes Roumaines* 13.4 (1974) 163–94.

Turner, N.

"Esdras, Books of," *IDB*, 2:142.

Unnik, C. J. van

"Die 'Zahl der vollkommenen Seelen' in der Pistis Sophia," *Abraham unser Vater: O. Michel FS* (ed. O. Betz, M. Hengel, and P. Schmidt; Leiden: Brill, 1963) 467–77.

Urbach, E. E.

The Sages: Their Concepts and Beliefs (Cambridge: Harvard University, 1987).

Vagany, L.

Le problème eschatologique dans le IVe livre d'Esdras (Paris: Picard, 1906).

Vassiliev, A.

Anecdota Graeco-Byzantina (vol. 1; Moscow: Imperial University, 1893).

Vermès, G.

"The Present State of the Son of Man Debate," *JJS* 29 (1978) 123–34.

Vermès, G.

"The Torah Is a Light," *VT* 8 (1958) 436–38.

Villiers, P. G. de

"The Ezra Legend in 4 Ezra 14:1–48" (paper circulated for the 1981 Pseudepigrapha Seminar of the SBL).

Villiers, P. G. de

"Understanding the Way of God: Form, Function and Message of the Historical Review in 4 Ezra 3:4–27," *SBL 1981 Seminar Papers* (ed. K. H. Richards; Chico, Calif.: Scholars, 1981) 357–78.

Violet, B.

Die Apokalypsen des Esra und des Baruch in deutscher Gestalt (GCS 32; Leipzig: Hinrichs, 1924).

Violet, B.
  Die Esra-Apokalypse (IV Esra), vol. 1: *Die Über-
  lieferung* (GCS 18; Leipzig: Hinrichs, 1910).
Vlis, C. J. van der
  *Disputatio Critica de Ezrae Libro Apocrypho Vulgo
  Quarto Dicto* (Amsterdam: Müller, 1839).
Völter, D.
  "Die Gesichte vom Adler und vom Menschensohn
  im 4.Esra nebst Bemerkungen über die Menschen-
  sohn-Stellen in 1.Henoch," *NTT* 8 (1919) 241–73.
Völter, D.
  *Die Visionen des Hermas, die Sibylle und Clemens von
  Rom* (Berlin: Schwetschke, 1900).
Volkmar, G.
  *Das vierte Buch Esrae ("Esdra Propheta") Handbuch
  der Einleitung in die Apokryphen*, vol. 2 (Tübingen:
  Fues, 1863).
Volz, P.
  Die Eschatologie der jüdischen Gemeinde (2d ed.;
  Tübingen: Mohr, 1934).
Wahl, O.
  *Apocalypsis Esdrae, Apocalypsis Sedrach, Visio Beati
  Esdrae* (PVTG 4; Leiden: Brill, 1977).
Weber, R., ed.
  "Liber Ezrae IIII," *Biblia Sacra Iuxta Vulgatam
  Versionem* (3d ed.; Stuttgart: Deutsche Bibelgesell-
  schaft, 1969) 2:1931–74.
Wellhausen, J.
  "Zur apokalyptischen Literatur," *Skizzen und
  Vorarbeiten* (Berlin: Reimer, 1899) 6:215–49.
Westcott, B. F.
  The Epistle to the Hebrews (London: Macmillan,
  1889).
Westermann, C.
  "Struktur und Geschichte der Klage im Alten
  Testament," *ZAW* 66 (1954) 44–80.
Whiston, W.
  *Primitive Christianity Reviv'd: Vol. IV An Account of
  the Faith of the Two First Centuries* (London: The
  Author, 1711).
Wieseler, K.
  "Das vierte Buch Esra nach Inhalt und Alter
  untersucht," *TSK* 43 (1870) 263–304.
Wilder, A. N.
  Early Christian Rhetoric: The Language of the Gospel
  (London: SCM, 1964).
Wilson, R. McL.
  "The Early History of the Exegesis of Gen 1,26,"
  Studia Patristica 1.1 (TU 63; Berlin: Akademie,
  1957).
Winston, D.
  "Freedom and Determinism in Greek Philosophy
  and Jewish Hellenistic Wisdom," *Studia Philonica* 2
  (1974) 40–50.
Wood, J. S.
  "The Missing Fragment of the Fourth Book of
  Esdras," *Journal of Philology* 7 (1877) 264–78.
Wright, G. E.
  "The Lawsuit of God: A Form-Critical Study of

Deuteronomy 32," *Israel's Prophetic Heritage: Essays
  in Honour of James Muilenberg* (ed. B. W. Anderson
  and W. Harrelson; London: SCM, 1962) 26–67.
Wright, W. A.
  "Note on the 'Azareth' of 4 Esdr. 13.45," *Journal of
  Philology* 3 (1871) 113–14.
Yadin, Y.
  *The Scroll of the War of the Sons of Light Against the
  Sons of Darkness* (Oxford: Oxford University,
  1962).
Yovsēp῾ian῾, S.
  Ankanon Girk῾ Hin Ktakaranac῾ (Venice: Monastery
  of St. Lazarus, 1896). In Armenian.
Zimmerli, W.
  Die Weltlichkeit des Alten Testaments (Göttingen:
  Vandenhoeck & Ruprecht, 1971).
Zimmermann, F.
  "Underlying Documents of 4 Ezra," *JQR* 51
  (1960/61) 107–34.
Zohrabian, J.
  The Scriptures of the Old and New Testaments (Venice:
  Monastery of St. Lazarus, 1805). In Armenian.

c / The Apocrypha (Deuterocanonical Books) and the Pseudepigrapha

These books are arranged in alphabetical order by title. References to 4 Ezra are only included for the Introduction and not for the Commentary.

3 Apocalypse of Baruch (Greek)

d.3 Rabbinic and Other Jewish Sources

This section is divided into two parts, the first listing Halachic writings and the second containing Midrashic, Aggadic and other works

d.3.1 Halachic Writings

d.3.2 Other Later Jewish Writings

3. Subjects

This index contains selected references to chief topics.